THE ROUGH GUIDE TO

The Pacific Northwest

There are more than two hundred Rough Guide titles
covering destinations from Alaska to Zimbabwe
and subjects from Acoustic Guitar to Travel Health

Forthcoming travel guides include

Devon & Cornwall • Ibiza • Iceland • Malta
Tenerife • Vancouver

Forthcoming reference guides include

Cuban Music • 100 Essential Latin CDs • Personal Computers
Pregnancy & Birth • Trumpet & Trombone

Rough Guides Online

www.roughguides.com

ROUGH GUIDE CREDITS

Text editor: Stephen Timblin
Series editor: Mark Ellingham
Editorial: Martin Dunford, Jonathan Buckley, Jo Mead, Kate Berens, Amanda Tomlin, Ann-Marie Shaw, Paul Gray, Helena Smith, Judith Bamber, Orla Duane, Olivia Eccleshall, Ruth Blackmore, Geoff Howard, Claire Saunders, Gavin Thomas, Alexander Mark Rogers, Polly Thomas, Joe Staines, Lisa Nellis, Andrew Tomičić, Richard Lim, Duncan Clark, Peter Buckley, Sam Thorne, Lucy Ratcliffe, Clifton Wilkinson, David Glen (UK); Andrew Rosenberg, Mary Beth Maioli, Yuki Takagaki (US)
Production: Susanne Hillen, Andy Hilliard, Link Hall, Helen Ostick, Julia Bovis, Michelle Draycott, Katie Pringle, Robert Evers,

Mike Hancock, Robert McKinlay, Zoë Nobes
Cartography: Melissa Baker, Maxine Repath, Ed Wright, Katie Lloyd-Jones
Picture research: Louise Boulton, Sharon Martins
Online: Kelly Cross, Anja Mutić-Blessing, Jennifer Gold, Audra Epstein (US)
Finance: John Fisher, Gary Singh, Edward Downey, Mark Hall, Tim Bill
Marketing & Publicity: Richard Trillo, Niki Smith, David Wearn, Chloë Roberts, Birgit Hartmann (UK); Simon Carloss, David Wechsler, Kathleen Rushforth (US)
Administration: Tania Hummel, Demelza Dallow, Julie Sanderson

ACKNOWLEDGEMENTS

Phil: A special thanks to the tourist departments of Washington State and Oregon, without whose splendid assistance I would have been struggling. Particular thanks are also due to Billie Rathbun-Moser; Dawn Tryon; Carrie Wilkinson-Tuma; and Joanne Holland-Bak. It was great to meet Myra Plant and Janet Dodson, who provided oodles of information, as well as Lynne Sterling who plied me with champagne.

Tim: A special thanks to James and Vicky Ballantyne, Jane Wigham at Air Canada, Ruth Roberts at Tourism British Columbia (London),

Amanda Newby at Travel Alberta (in the UK) and Greyhound (UK).

The editor would like to thank all those who contributed to this edition: Don Bapst for his invaluable editing assistance, Julia Bovis, Mike Hancock and Michelle Draycott for smooth production, Russell Walton for proofreading, Sharon Martins for her photo research, Maxine Repath and Melissa Flack for putting together such useful maps, Narrell Leffman and Kate Davis for Basics research, and Andrew Rosenberg for overall guidance.

PUBLISHING INFORMATION

This third edition published February 2001 by Rough Guides Ltd, 62–70 Shorts Gardens, London WC2H 9AH.
Distributed by the Penguin Group:
Penguin Books Ltd, 27 Wrights Lane, London W8 5TZ
Penguin Putnam, Inc. 375 Hudson Street, NY 10014, USA
Penguin Books Australia Ltd, 487 Maroondah Highway, PO Box 257, Ringwood, Victoria 3134, Australia
Penguin Books Canada Ltd, 10 Alcorn Avenue, Toronto, Ontario, Canada M4V 1E4
Penguin Books (NZ) Ltd, 182–190 Wairau Road, Auckland 10, New Zealand
Typeset in Linotron Univers and Century Old Style to an original design by Andrew Oliver.
Printed in England by Clays Ltd, St Ives Plc.
Illustrations in Part One and Part Three by Edward Briant.

THE ROUGH GUIDE TO

The Pacific Northwest

written and researched by

Tim Jepson and Phil Lee

With additional contributions by

Tania Smith and Richie Unterberger

ROUGH GUIDES

TRAVEL GUIDES • PHRASEBOOKS • MUSIC AND REFERENCE GUIDES

 We set out to do something different when the first Rough Guide was published in 1982. Mark Ellingham, just out of university, was traveling in Greece. He brought along the popular guides of the day, but found they were all lacking in some way. They were either strong on ruins and museums but went on for pages without mentioning a beach or taverna. Or they were so conscious of the need to save money that they lost sight of Greece's cultural and historical significance. Also, none of the books told him anything about Greece's contemporary life – its politics, its culture, its people, and how they lived.

So with no job in prospect, Mark decided to write his own guidebook, one which aimed to provide practical information that was second to none, detailing the best beaches and the hottest clubs and restaurants, while also giving hard-hitting accounts of every sight, both famous and obscure, and providing up-to-the-minute information on contemporary culture. It was a guide that encouraged independent travelers to find the best of Greece, and was a great success, getting shortlisted for the Thomas Cook travel guide award, and encouraging Mark, along with three friends, to expand the series.

The Rough Guide list grew rapidly and the letters flooded in, indicating a much broader readership than had been anticipated, but one which uniformly appreciated the Rough Guide mix of practical detail and humor, irreverence and enthusiasm. Things haven't changed. The same four friends who began the series are still the caretakers of the Rough Guide mission today: to provide the most reliable, up-to-date and entertaining information to independent-minded travelers of all ages, on all budgets.

We now publish more than 200 titles and have offices in London and New York. The travel guides are written and researched by a dedicated team of more than 100 authors, based in Britain, Europe, the USA and Australia. We have also created a unique series of phrasebooks to accompany the travel series, along with an acclaimed series of music guides, and a best-selling pocket guide to the Internet and World Wide Web. We also publish comprehensive travel information on our Web site:

www.roughguides.com

THE AUTHORS

Phil Lee first experienced the States as a bartender in Boston. Subsequent contacts have been less anarchic and have given him an abiding interest in the country. Phil has worked as a freelance author with Rough Guides for more than ten years. Previous titles include *Mallorca & Menorca, Norway, Belgium & Luxembourg, Canada* and *Toronto*. He lives in Nottingham, where he was born and raised.

Tim Jepson's career began with street busking and work in a slaughterhouse. Having acquired fluent Italian, he went on to better things as a Rome-based journalist and a leader of walking tours in Umbria. He is also author of Rough Guides to *Canada, Tuscany & Umbria* and *Vancouver*.

READERS' LETTERS

Many thanks go to the readers who have taken the time to contact us with comments and suggestions. These include:

Rachel Allen, Brenda Bickerton, Kathy Boyden, Angela Bryant, Lucia Calland, Armando Combati, Adam Cornish, Marcus Dale, Richard and Charlotte Dawson, Lino N. Dee, Anna Douglas, Jim Dress, David Lee Ellwood, Larry Gellar, Matthew Gorman, T.M. Grubis, Nicola Harris, Nicholas Hunt, Mike Johnson, Marissa Koster, Jennifer LaRoche, Bill Littlewood, Eugene McConville, Martin O'Connell, Hazel Orchard, Carol Pardy, Charles Paxton, Diane Penttila, Stephen and Kathi Quinn, Dorota Rygiel, Terence Sakamoto, Tia and Stephen Sedley, Rachel Shephard, Peter Skeggs, Ann-Marie Smith, Sara Thompson, Anton Visser, Susan Wassermann, Jeff Wilson, Robert Young and the many folks who contacted us via email but preferred to remain anonymous.

CONTENTS

Introduction x

PART THREE CONTEXTS 618

BACKGROUND BOXES

LIST OF MAPS

MAP SYMBOLS

▭	Interstate	– – –	Chapter division boundary	♟	Museum
⬡	US highway	◆	Point of interest	⚹	Ski area
⬡	Province/state highway	◉	Accommodation	⛳	Golf course
🍁	Trans-Canada highway	Ⱥ	Campsite	Ⓗ	Hospital
– – – – –	Path/track	▣	Restaurant/pub	ⓘ	Tourist office
▬▬	Railway	🏕	Picnic area	✉	Post office
Ⓜ	MAX route	⌇	Mountains	▪	Building
★	Bus stop	▲	Peak	✚	Church
✈	Airport	☀	Viewpoint	▒	Park
– –	Ferry route	ℓ	Waterfall	▦	National park
▨▨	Waterway	◠	Cave	▨	Forest
▬▬▬	International borders	♜	Castle/fort	⋮	Glacier
▬▬ ▪	Province / Territory borders	⛾	Lighthouse		

INTRODUCTION

F ew areas of North America owe so little to national and provincial boundaries as the **Pacific Northwest**. A loosely defined region cutting across the western redoubts of both the United States and Canada, it's geographically isolated from the rest of the continent and looks out across the Pacific almost as much as it refers back east to the older, federal centres of power in Ottawa and Washington DC. Extending from Oregon and Washington in the south, then hopscotching through British Columbia and the Canadian Rockies to the Yukon in the north, it encompasses – most impressively of all – richly varied and awe-inspiring landscapes. Mountains, lakes and pristine wilderness are the finest features, with abundant wildlife offering the chance to see creatures – from whales to wolves – in their natural habitats. But it is also a region of high historical adventure, the stuff of a thousand cowboy movies, and home to intriguing Native-American and Inuit cultures, superb cuisine (seafood in particular), state-of-the-art museums and some of the most urbane and civilized cities in North America.

Leading the way in this last respect are **Vancouver** and **Seattle**, both dynamic, cosmopolitan and instantly likeable – and destined to be pivotal points of any trip. Vancouver is preceded by a well-deserved reputation as one of the world's most beautiful cities, cradled in a mountain and seafront setting that provides its laid-back citizens with all manner of hedonistic possibilities from hiking, skiing and sailing to world-class theatre and the more simple West Coast pleasures of bar-hopping and beach-bumming. Seattle, though somewhat grittier, also benefits from a dramatic setting: its hilly suburbs bump around the deep blue of the Pacific Ocean, while its busy, bristling centre is alive with great restaurants and some of the finest live-music nightspots around.

Of the smaller cities, genteel **Portland** is perhaps the most agreeable, its downtown peopled by latte-drinking urbanites and graced with whimsical street sculptures. But not far behind comes **Victoria**, on Vancouver Island, which offers an ersatz taste of old England as well as one of the continent's finest museums. **Calgary** comes alive during its famous Stampede, and also boasts a glittering oil-funded downtown, an appealing base for trips to the Rockies and the fine sights of southern Alberta. Similarly well-placed is Oregon's **Bend**, a relaxed and energetic resort just a few minutes' drive from the mountains and a medley of fascinating volcanic remains.

Indeed, many visitors regard the cities of the Pacific Northwest as little more than a preamble to the region's **land and seascapes**, and it's certainly true that these attract inordinate amounts of purple prose – with every justification. Put baldly, this is one of the world's most beautiful places, embracing majestic peaks, icy glaciers, thundering rivers, swaths of Arctic tundra, smoking volcanoes, dramatic sea cliffs, long driftwood-covered beaches and endless forests. There are some scenic surprises too amongst the less familiar terrain of the Pacific Northwest, ranging from the sun-scorched, sage-brush plateau of eastern Oregon and to wetlands, house-sized sand dunes, brightly coloured fossil beds, temperate rainforests and benignly rippling grasslands. Much of this remains as wilderness, wild and empty and barely touched by the twentieth century, yet at the same time rendered accessible by a network of superbly run national, state and provincial **parks**.

Almost any part of this giant-sized wilderness will provide enough jaw-dropping scenery, hiking trails and outdoor pursuits to last a long vacation. There are, however, several obvious highlights beginning in the south with the magnificent sand- and rock-strewn Oregon coastline and, just inland, the southern reaches of the **Cascade Mountains**, which shelter elegiac **Crater Lake** and the geological oddities – cinder

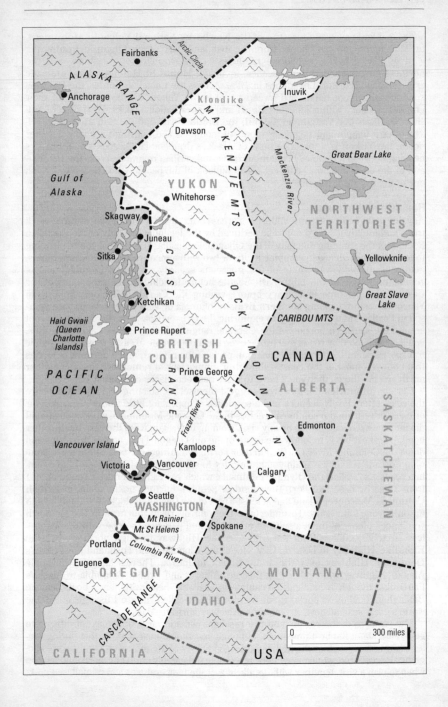

cones and lava caves and forests – of the **Newberry National Volcanic Monument**. In Washington you can choose from the lush landscape of the **Olympic Peninsula**, with its glacial peaks, temperate rainforests, and storm-tossed seashore, and the northern continuation of the Cascades, including **Mount St Helens**, whose dramatic eruption captured world headlines in 1980. Across the Canadian border, the **Rockies** continue in a huge northward sweep towards the Yukon, displaying some of their grandest scenery within Alberta's **Banff** and **Jasper** national parks. West of here, off-shore enclaves like **Vancouver Island**, the **Haida Gwaii** and the **San Juan** archipelago offer a unique and beguiling blend of mountain and maritime scenery. Further north, the **Yukon** is a foretaste both of Alaska's dramatic landscapes – vast glaciers nestling between ferociously cold mountains, and caribou roaming across the tundra – and of the often individual-cum-eccentric outlook of the people who choose to live on one of the world's last frontiers.

Routes and itineraries

Any one of the region's many wilderness areas could easily occupy a two- or three-week trip – and frankly it's hard not to be seduced by the legendary beauty of the Canadian Rockies or the stunning diversity of the Olympic Peninsula. That said, if you're planning to **tour**, the best idea is to combine a city or two with a mixture of land and sea routes, getting acquainted with some of the gorgeous scenery en route. Permutations, of course, are endless: you might visit Seattle before heading to the mountains of the Cascades; spend time in Calgary before visiting the Canadian Rockies; hole up in Vancouver before tackling southern British Columbia or Vancouver Island; base yourself in Portland as a preliminary to exploring the Oregon Coast; or stay in Bend to root around the southern portion of the Cascade range including Crater Lake. In all this, you'll be facilitated by roads that probe even the most remote areas, a reasonable public transport system (better in the Canadian parts of the region), and a network of ferries that cobwebs most of the coast – though it's important to remember that the further north you go, the further you'll have to drive between places of interest.

Certain **itineraries** do, however, suggest themselves, starting with **Oregon** where the coast offers lovely scenery and a sequence of appealing little towns – just an hour or two's drive from the southern reaches of the Cascade Mountains, which you should dip into at least once or twice on any visit. Coming to Oregon from the east, on the other hand, your best bet is to follow the route of the old Oregon Trail, across the plains and down the Columbia River Gorge. Further north, **Washington State** offers more stunning Cascade scenery – again you should try to sample at least a couple of the mountain roads – as well as the Olympic Peninsula, which you can either drive round or visit from a nearby base like Port Townsend or Sequim. Further north again, in **British Columbia**, Vancouver Island and at least a part of the Canadian Rockies should be high up on anyone's itinerary. To undertake the long overland journeys in the far north you'll need plenty of time, a spirit of adventure and patience to cope with the feature-less stretches: choose from the wild **Cassiar Highway** through northern BC; the **Klondike Highway** to Dawson City, site of the Klondike gold rush; and the **Yukon**'s **Dempster Highway** over the arctic tundra to Inuvik. There's also the 1500-mile **Alaska Highway** which slices up through Alberta and British Columbia to Alaska's Fairbanks, though a nautical alternative is available here with ferry boats leaving Bellingham (and other ports) to sail up along the so-called **Inside Passage**, one of the world's great sea journeys stretching all the way north to Alaska.

The vastness of the region, and the resultant climatic variations, make it difficult to generalize about the best time to go, although you should bear in mind that during winter many areas – such as the higher peaks and passes of the mountain ranges – are altogether inaccessible, while many more are simply unbearably cold. For more guidance on when to plan a visit, together with details of average temperatures and rainfall, see p.74.

PART ONE

THE

BASICS

GETTING THERE FROM BRITAIN

Three major cities in the Pacific Northwest are accessible by nonstop flights from the United Kingdom – Calgary, Vancouver and Seattle. Your choice of carrier is more limited than to some other North American destinations, though you're sure to find an appropriate option if you're prepared to take into account direct flights (which may land once or twice en route, but keep the same flight number throughout their journey), as well as flights via such "gateway cities" as San Francisco, Chicago and Toronto.

Nonstop flights take between nine and eleven hours. Following winds ensure that return flights are always around an hour shorter than outward journeys. Because of the time difference between Europe and the Northwest, the most convenient flights leave Britain around noon, which means you land in mid-afternoon, local time; flights back from Calgary tend to arrive in Britain early in the morning, and from Seattle in time for lunch. Most nonstop flights are from London Heathrow, though you can also reach Calgary, Vancouver and Seattle via nonstop flights to Toronto, and US hub airports from Manchester, Birmingham and Glasgow.

FARES AND AIRLINES

Britain remains one of the best places in Europe to obtain flight bargains, though **fares** vary widely according to season, availability and the current level of inter-airline competition. As a general indication, prices with scheduled airlines to Seattle start at around £400 return in high season; fares to Calgary vary between £500 and £660 return. Lower

---

NONSTOP FLIGHTS FROM THE UK TO THE NORTHWEST

Air Canada, Gresham Chambers, 45 West Nile St, Glasgow (☎0870/524 7226); c/o Star Alliance Ticket Office, 7/8 Conduit St, London W1R 9TG. For reservations and enquiries (☎0990/247226, *www.aircanada.ca*). From Heathrow to Calgary (daily) and Vancouver (twice daily).

British Airways (☎0345/222111, *www.british-airways.com*). From Heathrow to Vancouver (one or two daily) and Seattle (one or two daily).

Canada 3000 (☎01293/571700, *www.canada3000.com*). From Gatwick to Vancouver (1 weekly in winter, 3 weekly in summer) and Calgary (2 weekly). Also nonstop and direct flights (1 weekly in summer) from Glasgow and Manchester to Calgary and Vancouver. Flights from all these UK destinations, and Birmingham, to Toronto.

DIRECT AND CONNECTING FLIGHTS ON US AIRLINES

Contact the following airlines for details of direct or connecting flights via main US hub airports such as New York and Chicago and on to Seattle, Vancouver and Calgary.

American Airlines (☎0345/789789, *www.aa.com*)

Continental (☎0800/776464, *www.continental.com*)

Delta (☎0800/414767, *www.delta-air.com*)

Northwest (☎0990/561000, *www.nwa.com*)

TWA (☎020/8814 0707, *www.twa.com*)

United Airlines (☎0845/844 4777, *www.ual.com*)

FLIGHT AGENTS IN THE UK

Dial-a-Flight (☎0870/333 4488, www .dialaflight.com). Telephone sales of scheduled flights, with a Web site useful for tracking down bargains.

Expedia UK (expedia.co.uk). Microsoft's venture into the Internet travel market, with a "flight wizard" listing many (but not all) airline options, its own "special fares" and an online booking service.

Flightline (☎01702/715151, www.flightline.co.uk). Another telephone-based outfit offering online searches for cheap charter and scheduled flights.

Lastminute.com (www.lastminute.com).Vast Web site selling everything from holidays to mobile phones, but with a good section on cheap travel.

North-South Travel, Moulsham Mill Centre, Parkway, Chelmsford, Essex CM2 7PX (☎01245/608291). Friendly, competitive travel agency, offering discount fares worldwide – profits are used to support projects in the developing world, especially the promotion of sustainable tourism.

STA Travel, 86 Old Brompton Rd, London SW7 3LQ; 117 Euston Rd, London NW1 2SX; 38 Store St, London WC1 (all: Europe ☎6161, worldwide ☎020/7361 6262, www.statravel.co.uk); 38 North St, Brighton (☎01273/728282); 25 Queens Rd, Bristol BS8 1QE (☎0117/929 4399); 38 Sidney St, Cambridge CB2 3HX (☎01223/366966); 75 Deansgate, Manchester M3 2BW (☎0161/834 0668); 78 Bold St, Liverpool L1 4HR (☎0151/707 1123); 88 Vicar Lane, Leeds LS1 7JH (☎0113/244 9212); 9 St Mary's Place, Newcastle-upon-Tyne NE1 7PG (☎0191/233 2111); 36 George St, Oxford OX1 2OJ (☎01865/792800); 27 Forrest Rd, Edinburgh (☎0131/226 7747); 184 Byres Rd, Glasgow G1 1JH (☎0141/338 6000); 30 Upper Kirkgate, Aberdeen (☎0122/465 8222); and branches on university campuses in London, Birmingham, Bristol, Canterbury, Cardiff, Coventry, Durham, Glasgow, Leeds, Loughborough, Nottingham, Sheffield and Warwick. Worldwide specialists in low-cost

flights and tours for students and under-26s, though other customers welcome.

Trailfinders, 1 Threadneedle St, London EC2R 8JX (all destinations ☎020/7628 7628); 42–50 Earls Court Rd, London W8 6FT (long-haul ☎020/7938 3366); 194 Kensington High St, London W8 7RG (long-haul ☎020/7938 3939); 215 Kensington High St, London W8 6BD (transatlantic and European ☎020/7937 5400); 58 Deansgate, Manchester M3 2FF (☎0161/839 6969); 254–284 Sauchiehall St, Glasgow G2 3EH (☎0141/353 2224); 22–24 The Priory Queensway, Birmingham B4 6BS (☎0121/236 1234); 48 Corn St, Bristol BS1 1HQ (☎0117/929 9000); 7–9 Ridley Place, Newcastle NE1 8JQ (☎0191/261 2345); (all: www.trailfinder.com). One of the best informed and most efficient agents for independent travellers; their Web site offers "best buy" information and provides a brochure ordering service.

The Travel Bug, 125 Gloucester Rd, London SW7 4SF (☎020/7835 2000); 597 Cheetham Hill Rd, Manchester M8 5EJ (☎0161/721 4000); (all: www.travel-bug.co.uk). Large range of discounted tickets; the Web site offers a flight price "wizard" as well as a brochure request service.

Travel CUTS, 295a Regent St, London W1R 7YA (☎020/7255 1944); 33 Prince's Square, London W2 4NG (☎020/7792 3770); (all: www.travelcuts.co.uk). British branch of Canada's main youth and student travel specialist.

UsitCAMPUS, 52 Grosvenor Gardens, London SW1W 0AG (☎020/7730 3402); 541 Bristol Rd, Selly Oak, Birmingham B29 6AU (☎0121/414 1848); 61 Ditchling Rd, Brighton BN1 4SD (☎01273/570226); 39 Queen's Rd, Clifton, Bristol BS8 1QE (☎0117/929 2494); 5 Emmanuel St, Cambridge CB1 1NE (☎01223/324283); 53 Forrest Rd, Edinburgh EH1 2QP (☎0131/668 3308); 105–106 St Aldates, Oxford OX1 1BU (☎01865/484730); (all: www.usitcampus.co.uk). Student/youth travel specialists, with branches also in YHA shops and on university campuses all over Britain.

fares may be picked up by flying with one of the ever-increasing number of charter companies such as Canada 3000, which has flights to Calgary and Vancouver from London and Manchester from £330 return between May and October. Remember to add £25–35 to these fares to take account of UK

airport taxes, and departure taxes are levied in airports such as Vancouver.

Special offers are often advertised in many newspapers' weekend travel supplements, or, if you can afford to travel at short notice, **Ceefax** hosts a large number of travel agents touting lastminute discounted tickets. Better still, all major airlines have Web sites on the **Internet**, giving up-to-the-minute information about timetables, fares and online booking; there are also a growing number of flight agents' Web sites offering instant access to the best deals. Some of these are listed opposite, others can be found through Cheapflights (*www.cheapflights.co.uk*), which will signpost you to the booking agent or airline offering the lowest prices. Bear in mind, though, that if you're a **student or under 26** it's always worth checking out the student specialist flight agents, like STA or UsitCAMPUS as well.

Once in North America, an airpass can be a good idea if you want to do a lot of travelling. These are only available to non-US and Canadian residents, and must be bought before reaching North America (see p.39).

PACKAGES

Packages – fly-drive offers, accommodation packages and guided tours (or a combination of all three) – can work out cheaper than arranging the same trip yourself, especially for a short-term stay. For example, there are packages to Vancouver including the flight, car hire and a week's accommodation for as little as £500. Drawbacks include the loss of flexibility and the fact that you'll probably be made to stay in chain hotels in the mid-range to expensive bracket, even though less expensive accommodation is almost always readily available.

TOUR OPERATORS

Air Canada Vacations, 525 High Rd, Wembley, London HA0 2DH (☎0990/747100, *www.aircanadavacations.com*). Packages and tours in the Canadian west at reasonable rates.

All Canada Travel & Holidays, Sunway House, Raglan Rd, Lowestoft, Suffolk NR32 2LW (☎01502/585825, *www.all-canada.com*). Offers heli-hiking (which flies you to and from the hike's start and end), fly-drive, escorted coach and rail tours in BC and Alberta.

British Airways Holidays, Astral Towers, Betts Way, London Rd, Crawley, West Sussex RH10 2XA (☎01293/722727). Bargain packages and tours of most descriptions.

Canadian Connections, 10 York Way, Lancaster Road, High Wycombe, Buckinghamshire HP12 3PY (☎01494/473173). Canada-wide. Everything from booking a single hotel to organizing trekking, whale-watching or other tours.

Canadian Travel Service, 16 Bathurst Rd, Folkestone, Kent CT20 2NT (☎01303/249000). Organised tours and group travel in western Canada.

Contiki Services, Wells House, 15 Elmfield Rd, Bromley, Kent BR1 1LS (☎020/8290 6777, *travel@contiki.co.uk*). Specialist in holidays for the 18–35 age range offering a Rockies trip.

Experience Canada, 1st Floor, 14a Terminus Rd, Eastbourne, East Sussex BN21 3LP (☎01323/416699). Tours and tailor-made holidays.

Flydrive USA, PO Box 45, Bexhill-on-Sea, East Sussex TN40 1PY (☎01424/224400, *www.flydriveusa.co.uk*). Offers some of the best fly-drive deals.

Kuoni Travel Ltd, Kuoni House, Deepdene Ave, Dorking, Surrey RH5 4AZ (☎01306/747000, *www.kuoni.co.uk*). Tailor-made and guided tours to Alberta and BC and city breaks.

Leisurail, PO Box 5, 12 Coningsby Rd, Peterborough PE3 8XP (☎0870/750 0222). UK agents for VIA Rail, Rocky Mountaineer rail tours (through the Rockies) and Brewsters coach tours.

North America Travel Service, Kennedy Building, 48 Victoria Rd, Leeds LS11 5AF (☎0113/246 1466, *northamericatravelservice.co.uk*). Efficient tour operator offering tailor-made tours in all parts of North America. Everything from motorbikes through to RV tours. They cater to the top end of the market, but their sister Key to America (same details) focus on the bargain end of the market.

Travelbag, 3-5 High St, Alton, Hampshire GU34 1TL (☎0870/737 7864); 373–375 Strand, London WC2R 0JE (☎0870/737 7806); 52 Regents St, London W1B 5DX (☎0870/737 7880); 26–28 Drury Lane, Solihull B91 3BG (☎0870/736 7336); 28 Princess St, Knutsford, Cheshire WA16 6BU (☎0870/730 3231); (all: *www.travelbag.co.uk*). Tailor-made trips, car hire, flights and itineraries to suit all budgets. Canada- and US-wide.

Vacation Canada, 8 Cambridge St, Glasgow G2 3DZ (☎0141/332 1511). Skiing, city tours, guided coach tours, rail journeys, etc in western Canada.

High-Street travel agents have plenty of brochures and information about the various combinations available. Most charter deals from agents include accommodation along with the flight. Prices are based on two or more people travelling together; and this can be such a bargain that even if you do end up paying for a hotel room, which, of course, you don't have to use, it may still be cheaper than the standard fare. Flight-only deals do turn up at the last minute to fill unused seats; scan High-Street travel agents for the latest offers.

FLY-DRIVE

Fly-drive deals, which give cut-rate car rental when buying a transatlantic ticket from an airline or tour operator, are always cheaper than renting on the spot and give great value if you intend to do a lot of driving. On the other hand, you'll probably have to pay more for the flight than if you booked it through a discount agent. Competition

between airlines and tour operators means that it's well worth phoning to check on current special promotions.

Northwest Flydrive, PO Box 45, Bexhill-on-Sea, East Sussex TN40 1PY (☎01424/224400, *www.flydriveusa.co.uk*), offers excellent deals for not much more than an ordinary Apex fare. Several of the companies listed in the box on p.5 offer similar packages.

For complete car-rental and driveaway details, see "Getting Around" (p.43).

FLIGHT AND ACCOMMODATION DEALS

There are oodles of **flight and accommodation packages** to the Pacific Northwest – see the box, overleaf, for a few ideas as to where to start. Many offer very good deals and, indeed, although you can do things more cheaply if you stay independent, you will pay more to do the same things. However, note that pre-booked accommodation schemes, under which you buy vouchers for use in

---

ADVENTURE AND SPECIAL INTEREST HOLIDAYS

AmeriCan Adventures, 64 Mount Pleasant Ave, Tunbridge Wells, Kent TN1 1QY (☎01892/512700, *www.americanadventures.com*). Adventure camping and a broad range of nerve-testing activities.

Discover the World, 29 Nork Way, Banstead, Surrey SM7 1PB (☎01737/218800, *www.arctic-discover.co.uk*). Various Orca-watching and kayaking trips around Vancouver Island from £900.

Exodus Travels, 9 Weir Rd, London SW12 0LT (☎020/8675 5550, *www.exodus.co.uk*). Fifteen-day walking holidays exploring the Rockies and Vancouver Island from around £1300.

Explore Worldwide, 1 Frederick St, Aldershot, Hants GU11 1LQ (☎01252/760000, brochure line 01252/760100, *www.explore.co.uk*). Tours and treks in the Rockies.

Go Fishing Worldwide, 2 Oxford House, 24 Oxford Rd North, London W4 4DH (☎020/8742 1556, *www.go-fishing-worldwide.com*). Freshwater fishing trips to Canada and the US.

Great Rail Journeys, Saviour House, 9 St Saviourgate, York YO18 8NL (☎01904/521930 or 521900). Well-conceived Canadian and US rail journeys.

Limosa Holidays, Suffield House, Northrepps, Norfolk NR27 0LZ (☎01263/578143). Fourteen-

day bird-watching trips in the Rockies, with hotel accommodation for around £2400.

Ramblers Holidays Ltd, Box 43, Welwyn Garden City, Herts AL8 6PQ (☎01707/331133, *www.ramblersholidays.co.uk*). Walking tours in the Rockies arranged by the Ramblers Association's holiday company.

Saddle Skedaddle, 21 Longmoor Rd, Long Eaton, Notts NG10 4FQ (☎0115/972 1123, *www.skedaddle.co.uk*). Sixteen-day cycling, hiking and camping tours of the Rockies from £1100.

Trek America, 4 Waterperry Court, Middleton Rd, Banbury, Oxon OX16 8QG (☎01295/256777, *www.trekamerica.com*). Wide range of small group, largely US "active camping" trips, starting at around £550 excluding flight.

Waymark Holidays, 44 Windsor Rd, Slough SL1 2EJ (☎01753/516477). Fourteen-night walking holidays in the Rockies for £1725 with lodge/inn accommodation. The holidays are graded according to the strenuousness of the routes.

Wildlife Worldwide, 170 Selsdon Rd, South Croydon, Surrey CR2 6PJ (☎020/8667 9158, *www.wildlifeworld.com*). Offers a number of trips seeking out whales and bears. Offers self-drive holidays and hotel/lodge accommodation. Tours start from around £1600.

a specific group of hotels, are not normally good value – see p.52.

TOURING AND ADVENTURE PACKAGES

A simple and exciting way to see a chunk of the Northwest's Great Outdoors, without being bothered by too many practical considerations, is to take a specialist touring and adventure package, which includes transport, accommodation, food and a guide. Some of the more adventurous carry small groups around on minibuses and use a combination of budget hotels and camping (equipment, except sleeping bag, is almost always provided). Most also have a food kitty of perhaps £25 per week, with many meals cooked and eaten communally, although there's plenty of time to leave the group and do your own thing. In all cases, check that the holiday cost includes the flight.

A selection of the operators offering a range of Northwest adventure holidays are listed in the box opposite; details of local US/Canadian specialists are given in the appropriate sections of the *Guide*.

CRUISES

For some, the main reason to come to the Northwest is to enjoy a **cruise** along the spectacular Pacific coast. Possibilities range from short trips from Seattle to the islands of the Puget Sound with Washington State Ferries (see p.214); cruises to the Gulf Islands from Vancouver or Vancouver Island (see pp.345–349); expeditions up the magnificent Inside Passage and Discovery Coast and the trip to the Haida Gwaii (Queen Charlotte Islands) aboard BC Ferries (see p.382 and p.576); and the three-day voyage on the Alaska Marine Highway from Bellingham or Washington to ports in Alaska (see p.229 and p.574).

Such trips can in theory be arranged on the spot, but you won't save significant amounts of money by doing so, and in any case almost any excursion longer than a half-day ferry ride is likely to be booked up months ahead if you're taking a car – most of them as block bookings by major tour operators. If you plan to take a long (half-day plus) cruise, it definitely makes sense to arrange it as far in advance as possible, either directly with the ferry or cruise companies or through one of the many companies whose brochures litter the offices of High-Street travel agents (some of which are listed in the box on p.5).

GETTING THERE FROM IRELAND

There are no nonstop direct flights from Ireland to Seattle and Portland, but two airlines do operate nonstop scheduled services to other parts of the US. From both Dublin and Shannon airports, Aer Lingus flies to New York, Chicago, Los Angeles and Boston, while Delta flies to New York and Atlanta. Both can arrange onward flights to Seattle and Portland, and often offer good-value special deals. Otherwise, the cheapest flights to North America – if you are under 26 or a student – are available from UsitNOW. In addition, other airlines – primarily British Airways and Air Canada – can quote you through-fares from Dublin to Seattle and Portland via major gateway cities.

All flights from Dublin to the Pacific Northwest's **Canadian destinations** are via London. Return flights to Vancouver via London for around IR£700. From Belfast with Air Canada a return flight to Vancouver via London costs upwards of £500 return. Again, Usit often offer the cheapest deals if you are under 26 or a student.

AIRLINES

Aer Lingus, 40/41 Upper O'Connell St, Dublin 1 (☎01/705 3333 reservations); 46/48 Castle St, Belfast BT1 1HB (☎0845/973 7747); 2 Academy St, Cork (☎021/327155); 136 O'Connell St, Limerick (Shannon) (☎061/474239); (all: *www.aerlingus.ie*). Dublin and Shannon to New York, Chicago, Los Angeles and Boston. Also Dublin, Cork and Shannon to London Heathrow and Dublin to London Stansted and Manchester.

Air Canada, c/o 7 Herbert St, Dublin 2 (☎01/679 3958, *www.aircanada.ca*). Routings to the Pacific Northwest via London.

British Airways, in the Republic: c/o Aer Lingus (address above; reservations ☎1800/626747); in Northern Ireland at 1 Fountain Centre, Fountain St, Belfast BT1 6ET (reservations ☎0345/222111); (all: *www.british-airways.com*). Dublin and Cork to London Gatwick and Heathrow, and Shannon to London Heathrow.

British Midland, Nutley, Merrion Rd, Dublin 4 (☎01/283 8833); Suite 2, Fountain Centre, College St, Belfast 1 (☎0870/607 0555); (all: *www.britishmidland.com*). Belfast and Dublin to London Heathrow.

Delta (☎1800/768080, *www.delta-air.com*). Dublin and Shannon airports to New York and Atlanta.

Ryanair (☎01/609 7800, *www.ryanair.ie*). From Dublin, Cork, Knock and Kerry to London Stansted.

TRAVEL AND FLIGHT AGENTS

American Holidays, 9 Lombard St, Belfast BT1 1BH (☎028/9023 8762); 39 Pearse St, Dublin 2 (☎01/679 8800). General package agent offering good deals.

Aran Travel, Granary Hall, 58 Dominick St, Galway (☎091/562595, *arantvl@iol.ie*). Well-informed and competitive holiday agent, but with flight-only bargains.

Dial-a-Flight Ireland, 11/12 Warrington Place, Dublin 2 (☎01/662 9933). Scheduled flight specialists.

Fahy Travel, 3 Bridge St, Galway (☎091/563055, *fahytrav@iol.ie*). Has a good selection of last-minute bargains.

Joe Walsh Ltd, 8–11 Baggot St, Dublin 2 (☎01/676 3053); 117 St Patrick St, Cork (☎021/277959). General budget fares and package tour agent.

Thomas Cook, 11 Donegall Place, Belfast BT1 5AJ (☎028/9024 0833); 118 Grafton St, Dublin (☎01/677 1360); (all: *www.thomascook.com*). Package holiday and flight agent, with occasional discount offers.

Trailfinders, 4–5 Dawson St, Dublin 2 (☎01/677 7888). Flight agent.

Twohigs Travel, 8 Burgh Quay, Dublin (☎01/677 2666); 13 Duke St, Dublin (☎01/670 9750). Packages and flight agent.

UsitNOW, O'Connell Bridge, 19–21 Aston Quay, Dublin 2 (☎01/602 1600); Fountain Centre, Belfast BT1 6ET (☎028/9032 4073); 66 Oliver Plunkett St, Cork (☎021/270900); 33 Ferryquay St, Derry (☎028/7137 1888); Victoria Place, Eyre Sq, Galway (☎091/565177); Central Buildings, O'Connell St, Limerick (☎061/415064); 36–37 Georges St, Waterford (☎051/872601); (all: *www.usitnow.com*). Ireland's main student and youth travel specialists.

It's often possible to save money by flying independently from Dublin to London – where there's a much wider choice of flights (see p.3) – on a domestic carrier such as Ryanair which runs regular flights daily from Dublin to London Gatwick with return ticket costing IR£50 or less.

GETTING THERE FROM NORTH AMERICA

Travelling to the Northwest from anywhere else in North America is straightforward, but any means of transportation other than flying is likely to be inordinately time-consuming without necessarily saving significant amounts of money. Vancouver and Seattle are very much the major points of access.

BY AIR

The principal airports in the Northwest are those at Seattle, Portland, Vancouver and Calgary. Major US air carriers such as American, Delta, United, Continental and Northwest regularly fly to most of these cities from other cities in the US, though services to Seattle and Portland tend to be both more direct and more frequent. Air Canada should be your first choice for frequent service from major cities in Canada.

See "Getting Around", p.34, for details of transportation within the Pacific Northwest.

With the major carriers involved in continuing price wars, it's always worth checking the Sunday newspapers for limited special offers, as well as getting in touch with such discount travel agents as STA Travel or Council Travel (see box, overleaf). The best value ticket to buy is the **APEX** (Advanced Purchase Excursion Fare), which has to be purchased between 7 and 21 days ahead of your departure date and requires a Saturday night stay-over.

Note that the approximate return fares quoted below are the lowest currently available from the major carriers. They are exclusive of taxes and subject to availability and change.

FROM EASTERN AND CENTRAL US

From New York: to Seattle or Portland $533; to Calgary $620; to Vancouver $560. From Chicago: to Seattle or Portland $310; to Calgary $520; to Vancouver $480.

FROM THE WEST COAST

From LA: to Seattle or Portland $260; to Calgary $320; to Vancouver $250.

FROM CANADA

Flights on Air Canada leave Toronto daily for Vancouver. Their lowest round-trip APEX fares are approximately Can$446/575. (Internal Canadian fares, unlike those in the US, are seasonal, which

---

AIRLINES IN THE US AND CANADA

Air Canada ☎1-888/247-2262, *www.aircanada.ca*
America West ☎1-800/235-9292, *www.americawest.com*
American Airlines ☎1-800/433-7300, *www.aa.com*
Continental ☎1-800/231-0856, *www.flycontinental.com*
Delta ☎1-800/221-1212, *www.delta-air.com*
Horizon Air ☎1-800/547-9308, *www.horizonair.com*

Kenmore Air ☎1-800/543-9595, *www.kenmoreair.com*
Northwest ☎1-800/225-2525, *www.nwa.com*
Reno Airlines ☎1-800/433-7300, *www.aa.com*
United Airlines ☎1-800/241-6522, *www.ual.com*
United Express ☎1-800/241-6522, *www.ual.com*
US Air ☎1-800/428-4322, *www.usairways.com*

accounts for the variation.) At the time of writing, they also offer a low-season fare, on overnight flights, of Can$399. Fares start at around Can$613 to Seattle and Can$873 to Portland. Rates from Montréal are about Can$50 extra.

BY TRAIN

The only reason to consider travelling to the Pacific Northwest **by train** from the other side of the North American continent is if you think of the rail journey as an enjoyable part of your vacation in itself. Services are not as frequent as they used to be, and not necessarily any less expensive than a flight.

ACROSS THE USA

For travellers who wish to cross the **USA** by rail, **Amtrak** has a daily service aboard the Empire Builder, which takes a northern route from Chicago to Seattle; the Pioneer travels from Chicago to Seattle or Portland. With even more time, the Californian Zephyr runs west from Chicago and to Denver and Oakland (for San Francisco). From San Francisco you can pick up the Coast Starlight, which begins in Los Angeles and makes stops throughout western Oregon and Washington en route to Seattle and Vancouver.

Fares are generally more expensive than Greyhound buses over the same routes – and sometimes also pricier than air travel. Single fares don't vary according to season – a single cross-country trip costs around $350 – but return journeys can be much cheaper between September and May (excluding the Christmas period). **Discounts** are available at any period to senior citizens (15 percent); travellers with disabilities (25 percent); and children from 2 to 15 accompanied by an adult (half-fare): children under 2 travel free. You can also cut costs dramatically with Amtrak's **Explore America** fares, which allow three stopovers and a maximum trip duration of 45 days. These divide the US into three regions, Eastern, Central, and Western, with the latter covering Washington and Oregon. The fare within any one region is $279 (off-peak)/ $299 (peak), rising to $359/$399 if you travel within and between two regions, and $429/$499 among three. You must plan your itinerary beforehand, as well as your exact dates. The route may not be changed once travel has begun, though specific times and dates can be altered, for a fee of $30 (adults) or $15 (children), later on in the trip. Details can be found on p.34.

For all **Amtrak** information, call ☎1-800/USA-RAIL, www.amtrak.com

For all **VIA Rail** information, call ☎1-800/561-7860 in Canada, or ☎1-800/561-3949 in the US, www.viarail.ca

Amtrak also offers a North America **Railpass**, good for unlimited travel for 30 days in Canada and the USA. Trip must include travel in both Canada and the USA, and costs $459 (off-peak)/$656 (peak), with a 10 percent discount for senior citizens, children 2 to 18 and students.

Always **reserve** as far in advance as possible; Amtrak recommends two to three months in advance for summer travel. All passengers must have seats, and some trains, especially between major cities, are booked solid. Supplements are also payable for **sleeping compartments** (which cost around $100 per night for one or two people, including three full meals). However, even standard Amtrak carriages are surprisingly spacious, and there are additional dining cars and lounge cars (with full bars and sometimes glass-domed 360° viewing compartments).

ACROSS CANADA

The railroad may have created modern **Canada**, but passenger services are now few and far between – at the beginning of 1990 over half the services of **VIA Rail Canada** were eliminated at a stroke, and fares increased dramatically. Like Amtrak, trains are notoriously slow and delays common as passenger services give way to freight; however, rail travel can still be highly rewarding, especially on trains with special "dome cars" that allow an uninterrupted rooftop view of the countryside.

One of the saddest losses of the VIA cutbacks was the legendary **Canadian** train that followed the Canadian Pacific lines across the country daily from Montréal to Vancouver via Calgary and Banff in Alberta. Today's Canadian now departs three times weekly from Toronto, and though it still crosses the Northwest, its route follows the more northerly Canadian National lines. These take it to Edmonton and Jasper in Alberta, and then on to Vancouver via Kamloops North in BC, passing en route – like its predecessor – through some of the grandest scenery in the Canadian Rockies. The cheapest one-way ticket from Toronto to Vancouver costs Can$615 between mid-June and mid-September.

For further details of VIA Rail services within western Canada and for information concerning the **Canrailpass** see p.37.

BY BUS

Options for long-distance **bus travel** to the Pacific Northwest are basically limited to **Greyhound** (☎1-800/231-2222, www.greyhound.com) and the funkier **Green Tortoise** (see box below). Ordinarily, the 2-day, 20-hour coast-to-coast Greyhound trip from New York to Seattle costs $143 (single) or $218 (return). Booked 7 days in advance, it's $109/$195. Apart from budget considerations, the only other reason to go Greyhound is if you want to visit other places en route. Greyhound's AmeriPass, valid for unlimited travel within a certain time, rates are 7 days ($209), 15 days ($319), 30 days ($429) or 60 days ($599) (see p.37 for details of bus travel within the Northwest).

GREEN TORTOISE

One alternative to Long-Distance Bus Hell is the slightly countercultural Green Tortoise, whose buses, furnished with foam cushions, bunks, fridges and rock music, run between Los Angeles, San Francisco and Seattle (including a new "commuter" line from Seattle to Los Angeles, where you can board at any point). In summer, they also cross the US from New York and Boston, transcontinental trips which amount to mini-tours of the country. They take either 10 ($349) or 14 days ($399) (plus $111/$121 toward the food fund), and allow plenty of stops for hiking, river-rafting, and hot springs. Other orga-nized Green Tortoise excursions include a 30-day trip from San Francisco north to Alaska, the latter with a ferry ride along the Inside Passage and side-trips into the Canadian Rockies ($1500, plus $250 for food). To be sure of a place on any ride, book one or two months in advance, though services often have space at departure. A deposit of $500 is required for the Alaska trip ($100 for most of the smaller excursions).

Green Tortoise Adventure Travel, 494 Broadway, San Francisco, CA 94133; ☎1-800/867-8647 or 415/956-7500, www.greentortoise.com

TOUR OPERATORS IN NORTH AMERICA

All prices quoted below exclude taxes and are subject to change. Where applicable, return flights are from New York and accommodation is based on single person/double occupancy.

American Airlines Vacations (☎1-800/321-2121, *www.aavacations.com*). Five-night Vancouver city packages from $1100 (airfare, hotel, car and tax included); 6-night Seattle packages from $900 (airfare, hotel and tax included).

American Express Vacations, 110 East Browad Blvd, Fort Lauderdale, FL 33301 (☎1-800/241-1700). Airfare and hotel packages.

Amtrak Vacations (☎1-800/321-8684, *www.amtrakvacations.com*). Rail/hotel customised packages.

Backroads, 801 Cedar St, Berkeley, CA 94710-9862 (☎1-800/GO-ACTIVE or 462-2848, *www.backroads.com*). Over a dozen cycling/walking and hiking/multisport packages. Heli-hike and bike in Banff and Yoho National Parks while staying in luxury accommodation, starting at $2098 (land only).

Contiki Holidays, 300 Plaza Alicante, Suite 900, Garden Grove, CA 92840 (☎1-800/CONTIKI or 714/740-0808, *www.contiki.com*). Specialists in travel for 18–35s. "Canada and the Rockies" 10 days including coach, hotels/chalets, and some meals $955 (land only).

Cosmos/Globus Gateway, 150 S Los Robles Ave, Suite 860, Pasadena, CA (☎1-800/556-5454, *www.globusandcosmos.com*). Coach tours bookable only through a travel agent.

Elderhostel, 75 Federal St, Boston, MA 02110 (☎617/426-8056; *elderhostel.org*). Specialists in educational and activity programmes, cruises and homestays for senior travellers (companions may be younger). A wide range of programmes on offer including a 5-day "Mountains and Millenniums: Natural and Human History in the Majestic Rockies" $588 (land only).

Gray Line of Seattle, 4500 W Marginal Way SW, Seattle, WA 98106 (☎1-800/426-7505, *www.graylineofseattle.com*). Extensive range of day-tours, overnight packages and longer trips.

Their 7-day "North West Triangle" covers Seattle, Victoria, Vancouver and just about everything in between. From $575 (land only).

Holland America Line Westours, 300 Elliott Ave W, Seattle, WA 98199 (☎1-800/426-0327, *www.hollandamerica.com*). Cruises and land tours in the Canadian Rockies.

International Gay Travel Association, 4331 N Federal Hwy, Suite 304, Ft Lauderdale, FL 33308 (☎1-800/448-8550, *www.iglta.com*).Trade group that will provide lists of gay-owned or gay-friendly travel agents, accommodation and other travel businesses.

Maupintour, 1515 St Andrews Drive, Lawrence, KS 66046 (☎1-800/255-4266 or 913/843-1211, *www.maupintour.com*). Nine-day "Seattle, Vancouver and Victoria" tour starting at $1845, (land only).

Questers Worldwide Nature Tours, 381 Park Ave S, New York, NY 10016 (☎1-800/468-8668, *www.questers.com*). Specialists in natural history tours.

Saga Holidays, 222 Berkeley St, Boston, MA 02116 (☎1-800/343-0273 or 617/262-2262, *www.sagaholidays.com*). Travel for the over 50s. Fourteen-day tour of the Northwest national parks. Coach, hotel/lodge accommodation $1979 (land only).

Suntrek Tours America, 77 W 3rd St, Santa Rosa, CA 95401 (☎1-800/292-9696, SUNTREK or 707/523-1800, *www.suntrek.com*). Wide range of camping tours with optional extras like gold-panning, horse-back and sled-dog riding, river rafting and helicopter flying.

Trek America, PO Box 189, Rockaway, NJ 07866 (☎1-800/221-0596, *www.trekamerica.com*). Multi-activity camping/adventure tours. The 21-day hiking, biking, rafting "Canadian Parks West" starts at $1537 (land only).

In Canada, Greyhound Canada offers regular intercity bus routes along the Trans-Canada Highway from Toronto and Montréal to Vancouver and Calgary. Toronto to Vancouver takes 2 days and 21 hours and costs approximately Can$312; Toronto to Calgary takes 2 days 2 hours and costs around Can$269 (the return fare is just double the single fare). They also offer a range of passes. All have to be booked 7 days in advance, and are good for travel on Greyhound Canada, Grey Goose and Vancouver Island Coachlines. Rates are approximately 7 days (Can$249), 15 days (Can$379), 30 days (Can$449) and 60 days (Can$599). Seats can be reserved in advance and tickets purchased by mail.

BY CAR

Driving your own **car** (or renting one) may maximize your freedom and flexibility, but, once again, if you're travelling cross-country you'll need to allow plenty of time. If you do use your own car, make sure your insurance is up to date and that you are completely covered. In Canada and the US, automobile insurance is mandatory. General advice and help with route planning can be had from either the **American Automobile Association** (AAA), which has offices in most US cities (☎AAA-HELP or 1-800/222-4357 for road-side help; ☎212/757-2000 for general information or *www.aaa.com*), or **the Canadian Automobile Association** (CAA) at Suite 200, 1145 Hunt Club Rd, Ottawa, ON KIV 0Y3 ☎1-800/267-8713, *www.caa.ca*).

If you don't have a car, or you're not sure whether the car you do have will make the distance, consider working with an **automobile transit company**, who match drivers with car owners who need their cars moved from one city to another. The only expenses are gas, food, tools and lodging, and the company's insurance covers any breakdowns or damages. You must be at least 21, have a valid driver's licence and agree to drive about 400 miles per day on a fairly direct route. For more information, contact Auto Driveaway, 310 S Michigan Ave, Chicago, IL 60604, plus offices throughout the US and Canada (☎1-800/346-2277, *www.autodriveaway.com*). Provided you're prepared either to give plenty of advance notice, or to wait, you should get the route you want.

American citizens planning to drive their own cars into Canada should be certain to carry proper owner registration and proof of insurance coverage. The Canadian Non-Resident Inter-Provincial Motor Vehicle Liability Insurance Card, available from any US insurance company, is accepted as evidence of financial responsibility in Canada.

Toll-free numbers for **car rental** companies are listed on p.44.

PACKAGE TOURS

If you're happy to have everything planned for you, including transportation, a **package tour** can make your vacation much easier; if you don't yet know what you want to do, they're worth checking out for ideas. Free-spirited, adventuresome types may appreciate the convenience of the "independent packages" put together by the airlines tour departments. For details of the wide range of **cruises** that explore the magnificent Pacific coast, see p.7, or contact the tour operators listed in the box opposite.

GETTING THERE FROM AUSTRALIA AND NEW ZEALAND

Other than seasonal bargains and all-in packages which may be on offer from high street travel agents, the cheapest flights from Australasia to the US and Canada are available from the discount travel agents listed in the box overleaf.

From **Australasia** most flights to Pacific Northwest destinations either land in Vancouver or are routed through LA, with regular direct services, starting at A$1599/NZ$1899 in the low season, on Qantas and Air New Zealand to Vancouver or LA, while United Airlines fly direct to LA and San Francisco with connections to Seattle or Vancouver for A$1699/NZ$1999. You can expect to pay around A$300/NZ$350 on top of the usual fare to Calgary. However, if you intend to do a fair amount of flying around, you'd be better off taking advantage of some of the **coupon deals** that can be bought with your international ticket and cost US$100–300 each depending on the distance involved. A number of

AIRLINES

☎0-800 and 1-800 numbers are toll-free, but only apply if dialled outside the city in the address. The prefix ☎13 is charged at the local rate nationwide.

Air Canada (Australia ☎1-300/656 232 or 02/9232 5222; New Zealand ☎09/377 8833); Coupons for extended travel in Canada and the US.

Air New Zealand (Australia ☎13 2476; New Zealand ☎09/357 3000, *www.airnz.com*). Daily flights to Vancouver from major Australasian cities via Auckland, and either Honolulu or LA.

Cathay Pacific (Australia ☎13 1747 or 02/9931 5500; New Zealand ☎09/379 0861, *www.cathaypacific.com*). Several times a week to Vancouver and LA from major Australasian cities via a transfer or stopover in Hong Kong.

JAL Japan Airlines (Australia ☎02/9272 1111; New Zealand ☎09/379 9906, *www.japanair.com*). Several flights a week to Vancouver via either a transfer or overnight's stopover in Tokyo or Osaka included in the fare.

Qantas (Australia ☎13 1313; New Zealand ☎09/357 8900 or 0-800/808 767, *www.qantas .com.au*). Daily to Vancouver and LA from major Australasian cities either nonstop or via Honolulu with onward connection to other destinations.

Singapore Airlines (Australia ☎13 1011 or 02/9350 0262; New Zealand ☎09/303 2129 or 0-800/808 909, *www.singaporeair.com*). Three flights a week to Vancouver via Singapore from major Australian cities and once a week from Auckland; several times a week to LA via Singapore from major Australian cities.

United Airlines (Australia ☎13 1777; New Zealand ☎09/379 3800, *www.ual.com*). Daily to Vancouver, Seattle and Calgary via a transfer in LA from Sydney, Melbourne and Auckland, with onward connections to PNW destinations.

DISCOUNT TRAVEL AGENTS

All the agents listed below offer competitive discounts on airfares as well as a good selection of packaged holidays and tours, and can also arrange car rental and bus and rail passes.

Anywhere Travel, 345 Anzac Parade, Kingsford, Sydney (☎02/9663 0411, *anywhere@ozemail.com.au*).

Budget Travel, 16 Fort St, Auckland, plus branches around the city (☎09/366 0061 or 0-800/808 040, *www.budgettravel.co.nz*).

Destinations Unlimited, 220 Queen St, Auckland (☎09/373 4033).

Flight Centres, Australia: 82 Elizabeth St, Sydney (☎02/9235 3522), plus branches nationwide (for the nearest branch call ☎13 1600). New Zealand: 350 Queen St, Auckland (☎09/358 4310 or 0-800/354 448), plus branches nationwide; (all: *www.flightcentre.com*).

Northern Gateway, 22 Cavenagh St, Darwin (☎08/8941 1394, *oztravel@norgate.com.au*).

STA Travel, Australia: 855 George St, Sydney; 256 Flinders St, Melbourne; other offices in state capitals and major universities (for nearest branch call ☎13 1776); telesales (☎1-300/360 960). New Zealand: 10 High St, Auckland (☎09/309 0458); other offices in major cities and university campuses (for nearest branch call ☎0-800/874 773); telesales (☎09/366 6673); (all:

www.statravel.com). Fare discounts for students and those under 26, as well as visas, student cards and travel insurance.

Student Uni Travel, 92 Pitt St, Sydney (☎02/9232 8444, *sydney@backpackers.net*), plus branches in Brisbane, Cairns, Darwin, Melbourne and Perth. Student/youth discounts and travel advice.

Thomas Cook, Australia: 175 Pitt St, Sydney (☎02/9231 2877); 257 Collins St, Melbourne (☎03/9282 0222); plus branches in other state capitals (for nearest branch call ☎13 1771); telesales (☎1-800/801 002). New Zealand: 191 Queen St, Auckland (☎09/379 3920); (all: *www.thomascook.com.au*).

Trailfinders, 8 Spring St, Sydney (☎02/9247 7666); 91 Elizabeth St, Brisbane (☎07/3229 0887); Hides Corner, Shield St, Cairns (☎07/4041 1199); (all: *www.travel.com.au*).

Usit Beyond, Shortland St and Jean Batten Place, Auckland (☎09/379 4224 or 0-800/788 336, *www.usitbeyond.co.nz*); plus branches in major cities. Student/youth travel specialists.

flights go via Honolulu, where you can usually stop off for no extra charge. A slightly more roundabout route that can sometimes work out a little cheaper is via Asia, with the best fares to Vancouver on JAL from A$1500/NZ$1850, including a night's accommodation either in Tokyo or Osaka. Add around NZ$150 for Christchurch and Wellington departures. However, if you don't want to spend the night, Cathay Pacific and Singapore Airlines can get you there from Australia from A$1799 via a transfer in the home cities of Hong Kong and Singapore.

Tickets purchased direct from the airlines are usually at published rates, which are often more expensive than a **round-the-world** fare. Travel agents offer better deals on fares and have the latest information on limited special offers, such as free stopovers and fly-drive-accommodation packages. Flight Centres and STA (which offer fare reductions for ISIC card holders and under 26s) generally offer the lowest fares. You might also want to have a look on the Internet, *www.travel.com.au* offers discounted fares online, as does *www.sydneytravel.com*.

Seat availability on most international flights out of Australia and New Zealand is often limited, so it's best to **book several weeks ahead**.

Airfares vary throughout the year, with seasonal differences generally working out between A$/NZ$200–300. For most airlines low season is from mid-January to the end of February and

SPECIALIST AGENTS AND OPERATORS

If you're interested in skiing, cruising or adventure holidays and prefer to have all the arrangements made for you before you leave, then the specialist agents below can help you plan your trip. Unfortunately there are few pre-packaged tours that include airfares from Australasia, however, most specialist agents will also be able to assist with flight arrangements. In turn many of the tours below can also be arranged through your local travel agent.

Adventure Specialists, 69 Liverpool St, Sydney (☎02/9261 2927). A good selection of adventure treks and tours.

Adventure World, 73 Walker St, North Sydney (☎02/9956 7766 or 1-300/363 055), plus branches in Adelaide, Brisbane, Melbourne and Perth; 101 Great South Rd, Remuera, Auckland (☎09/524 5118); (all: *www.adventureworld .com.au*). Individual and small group exploratory tours and treks in British Columbia and Alberta; rail tours and cruises.

American Express Travel, 344 Queen St, Brisbane (☎07/3220 0878). US and Canadian travel arrangements.

Creative Tours (bookings through travel agents only). Escorted bus tours, airpasses and accommodation packages.

Insight Vacations (bookings through travel agents only). First class accommodation packages, car rental and bus tours.

IT Adventures, Level 4, 46–48 York St, Sydney (☎1-800/804 277); Agents for Exodus' extended small group camping trips tracing the gold rush days through the Rockies and Yukon.

Peregrine Adventures, 258 Lonsdale St, Melbourne (☎03/9663 8611), plus offices in Brisbane, Sydney, Adelaide and Perth. Offer a variety of active holidays from short camping, walking and sea-kayaking trips in the Pacific Northwest to longer overland Rocky Mountain adventures.

The Ski & Snowboard Travel Company, 343 Pacific Highway, Crows Nest, NSW (☎02/9955 3759 or 1-800/251 934, *skitrav@ozemail.com.au*). Individual, group and family ski holidays in British Columbia, Alberta and northwest US.

Swingaway Holidays, International, 1141 Toorak Rd, Camberwell, Melbourne (☎03/9809 2699 or 1-800/623 266). Agents for a host of ski and snowboarding holidays in the Pacific Northwest. Including Summit Ski's 15 nights fully guided ski and snowboard tours.

Sydney International Travel Centre, 8/75 King St, Sydney (☎02/9299 8000, *www .sydneytravel.com.au*). All US and Canadian travel arrangements, including accommodation, ski packages, bus and rail tours.

Travel Plan, 118 Edinburgh Rd, Castlecrag, Sydney (☎02/9958 1888 or 1-300/130 754). Heli-skiing and ski holiday packages in the Pacific Northwest.

Wiltrans/Maupintour, 10/189 Kent St, Sydney (☎02/9255 0899). Five- and six-star all-inclusive escorted tours and cruises taking in the delights of the Pacific Northwest.

October to the end of November; high season is mid-May to the end of August and December to mid-January; shoulder seasons cover the rest of the year.

FROM AUSTRALIA

From **Australia** fares to Vancouver, LA and Seattle from eastern capitals cost much the same, with Ansett and Qantas providing a shuttle service to the point of international departure; whereas from Perth they're about A$400 more.

Qantas offer the most direct through-service to destinations **via Vancouver** – for example you'll pay around A$1899 low season and A$2699 high season to Calgary, while United Airlines fares start at A$1950 to Portland and A$1999 to Calgary. The lowest fares via the Pacific are Air New Zealand's at A$1599 via Auckland and Honolulu.

FROM NEW ZEALAND

The choices are much the same as with Australia, with Air New Zealand either via Honolulu or direct to Vancouver, or Qantas via either Sydney or Honolulu and United Airlines via LA to Vancouver all from NZ$1899 low season to NZ$2500 high season; providing daily connections to Calgary

from NZ$2150 as well as other destinations in the Northwest. Via Asia Cathay Pacific and Singapore Airlines fly via a transfer or stopover in their home cities also from NZ$1899.

ROUND-THE-WORLD

If you intend to take in the Northwest as part of a world trip, then **round-the-world** tickets and circle fares offer the best value for money, often working out just a little more than an all-in ticket. There are numerous airline combinations to choose from; for example, a ticket from Sydney or Auckland to Honolulu, then Vancouver, London, Paris, Bangkok, Singapore and back home, starts at A$2099/NZ$2399. There are also more comprehensive and flexible routes are offered by "One World" and "Star Alliance" allowing you to take in destinations in the USA and Canada, Europe, Asia as well as South America and Africa; prices are mileage-based from A$/NZ$2700, for a max of 29,000 miles up to A$/NZ$3700 for 39,000 miles. Another option that enables you to visit some of the Pacific Islands on your way to and from Vancouver is Air New Zealand's "Circle Pacific Fare" starting at A$1899/NZ$2299 low season which allows stopovers in Auckland, Apia, Nadi, Rarotonga, Honolulu, Papeete and LA.

ENTRY REQUIREMENTS FOR FOREIGN VISITORS

For EU, Australian and New Zealand tourists planning short stays of up to ninety days in the Pacific Northwest, the only documenta-

tion required is a full, valid passport. Visas are, however, required in all cases for entry into the United States for stays of ninety days or more, and the same usually applies – though there is a little more flexibility – to Canada. Visas are also required for entry into both countries for those planning to work or study there. Slightly different again is the situation regarding US and Canadian nationals crossing into each other's countries – see box opposite.

UNITED STATES

The **United States** has speeded up its immigration procedures in the last few years by using the **Visa Waiver Scheme**. Visitors from 29 countries, including Britain, Ireland, Australia, New Zealand and most European countries, carrying a valid passport do not need a visa for stays in the

US AND CANADIAN TRAVELLERS

United States and Canadian citizens have previously enjoyed the freedom of crossing the border without a passport, as long as they are carrying some form of official ID. This still applies to car drivers, but most if not all airlines and the major bus companies will now insist on both photo identification and proof of citizenship before accepting you as a passenger. In all cases, it's certainly recommended to take your passport and, if you plan to stay for more than ninety days, you'll need it along with a visa.

Bear in mind that if you cross the border in your car, boot (trunk) and passenger compartments are subject to spot searches by the customs personnel of both countries. Officers at the more obscure entry points on the border – and there are several in the Northwest – can be real sticklers, so you may be delayed. Remember, too, that both nationalities are legally barred from seeking gainful employment in each other's country.

United States of up to ninety days as long as the trips are for tourism or business. This excludes you from working or studying. You will need to complete a **visa waiver form**, which is handed out on incoming planes, on ferries and at border crossing points (with Canada and Mexico). The completed forms are processed during immigration control at your initial point of arrival on US soil. The form requires details of where you are staying on your first night and the date you intend to leave the US. If you give the name and address of a friend as your initial night's stay, don't be surprised if immigration check. You should be able to prove that you have enough money (a credit card or about $300 cash per week should suffice) to support yourself while in the US. You may experience difficulties if you admit to being HIV positive or having AIDS or TB. A part of the form will be attached to your passport, where it must stay till you leave.

Citizens of all other countries should contact their local US embassy or consulate for details of current entry requirements as they are often required to have both a valid passport and a **non-immigrant visitor's visa**. To obtain a visa, fill in the application form available at most travel agents, as well as at dozens of sites on the Internet, and send it with the appropriate fee, currently US$45, two photographs and a passport – valid for at least 6 months from the end of your planned stay – to the nearest US embassy or consulate. Visas are not issued to convicted criminals and anybody who owns up to being a war criminal or drug dealer.

CANADA

British citizens, as well as citizens of the European Union (EU), Scandinavia and most British Commonwealth countries do not need an entry visa to visit **Canada**: all that is required is a full valid passport. In addition, all visitors to Canada have to complete a **customs/registration form**, which is handed out on incoming planes, on ferries and at border crossing points (with the US). The completed forms are processed during immigration control at your initial point of arrival on Canadian soil. The form requires details of where you are staying on your first night and the date you intend to leave Canada. Admission is normally granted for a period of up to ninety days and you may be asked to demonstrate that you have enough money to pay for your stay – Can$400 per week in cash or a credit card should be sufficient. If you plan a longer trip, Canadian immigration officials may permit stays of up to a maximum of six months: check with the Canadian High Commission for details before you leave.

CUSTOMS

Customs officers in both Canada and the US will relieve you of your **customs declaration form** which you receive with your waiver form when it is handed out on incoming planes, on ferries and at border crossing points. It asks if you're carrying any fresh foods and if you've visited a farm in the last month: if you have, you could well lose your shoes.

As well as foods and anything agricultural, in the US it's prohibited to carry into the country any articles from such places as North Korea, Cambodia, Iraq, Libya or Cuba, while both countries draw the line at things like obscene publications, lottery tickets, protected wildlife species or pre-Columbian artefacts. Anyone caught bringing drugs into either country will not only face

US EMBASSIES AND CONSULATES ABROAD

AUSTRALIA
Embassy
21 Moonah Place, Canberra, ACT 2600
(☎02/6214 5600, *usaemb@cs.net.au*).

Consulates
553 St Kilda Rd, PO Box 6722, Melbourne, VIC
3004 (☎03/9625 1583, *usgcmelb*
@labyrinth.net.au).

19–29 Martin Place, Sydney, NSW 2000
(☎02/9373 9200, *usconsyd@ozemail.com.au*).

13th Floor, 16 St George's Terrace, Perth, WA 6000
(☎08/9231-9400, *usgperth@starwon.com.au*).

CANADA
Embassy
100 Wellington St, Ottawa, ON K1P 5T1
(☎613/238-5335).

Consulates
Suite 1050, 615 Macleod Trail, SE Calgary, AB
T2G 4T8 (☎403/266-8962).

Suite 910, Cogswell Tower, Scotia Square,
Halifax, NS B3J 3K1 (☎902/429-2480).

PO Box 65, Postal Station Desjardins, South
Tower, Montréal, PQ H5B 1G1 (☎514/398-9695).

2 Place Terrasse Dufferin, Québec City, PQ G1R
4T9 (☎418/692-2095).

360 University Ave, Toronto, ON M5G 1S4
(☎416/595-1700).

1095 W Pender St, Vancouver, BC V6E 2M6
(☎604/685-4311).

IRELAND
42 Elgin Rd, Ballsbridge, Dublin 4 (☎01/668
8777, *aedublin@indigo.ie*).

NEW ZEALAND
Embassy
29 Fitzherbert Terrace, Thorndon, Wellington
6001 (☎04/472-2068).

Consulate
29 Shortland St (corner of O'Connell St),
Auckland 1001 (☎09/303 2724, *amcongen*
@ihug.co.nz). Address for visa applications: Non-
Immigrant Visas, Private Bag 92022, Auckland 1.

UK
24/31 Grosvenor Square, London W1A 1AE
(☎020/7499 9000: visa hotline ☎0891/200290).

3 Regent Terrace, Edinburgh EH7 5BW
(☎0131/556 8315).

Queens House, 14 Queen St, Belfast BT1 6EQ
(☎028/9032 8239).

FOREIGN EMBASSIES AND CONSULATES IN THE US

AUSTRALIA
Embassy
1601 Massachusetts Ave NW, Washington, DC
20036 (☎202/797-3000, *www.austemb.org*).

Consulates
150 42nd St, 34th Floor, New York, NY 10017
(☎212/408-8400).

Century Plaza Towers, 2049 Century Pk., E., 19th,
Los Angeles, CA 90067 (☎310/229-4800).

1 Bush St, 7th Floor, San Francisco, CA 94104
(☎415/362-6160).

CANADA
501 Pennsylvania Ave NW, Washington, DC
20001 (☎202/682-1740, *wshdc*
@dfait-maeci.gc.ca).

IRELAND
2234 Massachusetts Ave NW, Washington, DC
20008 (☎202/462-3939).

NEW ZEALAND
37 Observatory Circle NW, Washington DC,
20008 (☎202/328-4800, *www.nzemb.org*).

UK
Embassy
3100 Massachusetts Ave NW, Washington, DC
20008 (☎202/462-1340, *www.britainusa.com*).

Consulates
The Wrigley Building, 400 N Michigan Ave,
Chicago, IL 60611 (☎312/346-1810).

11766 Wilshire Blvd, #400, Los Angeles, CA
90025 (☎310/477-3322).

1001 Brickell Bay Drive, #2800, Miami, FL 33131
(☎305/374-1522).

845 Third Ave, New York, NY 10022 (☎212/745-
0200).

1 Sansome St, #850, San Francisco, CA 94104
(☎415/981-3030).

**For details of foreign consulates in the USA's Pacific Northwest, see the
relevant city accounts for Seattle and Portland.**

CANADIAN EMBASSIES AND CONSULATES ABROAD

AUSTRALIA

Commonwealth Ave, Canberra, ACT 2600
(☎02/6270 4000).

Level 5, Quay West Building, 111 Harrington St,
Sydney, NSW 2000 (☎02/9364 3000).

Consulates in Perth and Melbourne also.

IRELAND

65 St Stephen's Green, Dublin 2 (☎01/478 1988).

NEW ZEALAND

9th Floor, Jetset Centre, 44–48 Emily Place,
Auckland 1 (☎09/309 8516).

UK

Macdonald House, 1 Grosvenor Square, London
W1X 0AB (☎020/7258 6600).

UNITED STATES

Suite 2400, 2 Prudential Plaza, 180 N Stetson
Ave, Chicago, IL 60601 (☎312/616-1860).

9th Floor, 550 S Hope St, Los Angeles, CA 90071-
2627 (☎213/346-2700).

16th Floor, Exxon Building, 1251 Avenue of the
Americas, New York, NY 10020-1175 (☎212/596-
1628).

501 Pennsylvania Ave NW, Washington, DC
20001 (☎202/682-1740).

**There are also consulates in Atlanta,
Boston, Buffalo, Dallas, Detroit, Miami,
Minneapolis, San Francisco, San Jose and
Seattle. Check the phonebook for details.**

FOREIGN EMBASSIES AND CONSULATES IN CANADA

AUSTRALIA

50 O'Connor St, Ottawa, ON (☎613/236-0841).

IRELAND

130 Albert St, Ottawa, ON (☎613/233-6281).

NEW ZEALAND

99 Bank St, Ottawa, ON (☎613/238-5991).

UK

80 Elgin St, Ottawa, ON (☎613/237-1530).

US

Embassy

100 Wellington St, Ottawa, ON (☎613/238-
5335).

Consulates

Suite 1050, 615 Macleod Trail, SE Calgary, AB
T2G 4T8 (☎403/266-8962).

Suite 910, Cogswell Tower, Scotia Square,
Halifax, NS B3J 3K1 (☎902/429-2480).

PO Box 65, Postal Station Desjardins, South
Tower, Montréal, PQ H5B 1G1 (☎514/398-9695).

2 Place Terrasse Dufferin, Québec City, PQ G1R
4T9 (☎418/692-2095).

360 University Ave, Toronto, ON M5G 1S4
(☎416/595-1700).

1095 W Pender St, Vancouver, BC V6E 2M6
(☎604/685-4311).

**For details of foreign consulates in
Canada's Pacific Northwest, see the rele-
vant city accounts for Vancouver and
Calgary.**

prosecution but be entered in the records as an undesirable and probably denied entry for all time. The **duty-free allowance** in the **US** if you're over 17 is 200 cigarettes and 100 cigars (not Cuban) and, if you're over 21, a litre of spirits. The duty-free allowance if you're over 19 in **Canada** (18 in Alberta) is 200 cigarettes and 50 cigars, plus 1.1 litres of liquor or 24 x 355ml-sized bottles of beer. For more information regarding customs in the US call ☎202/354-1000 or visit

their Web site at *www.customs.gov*, for Canada call ☎1-800/461-9999, *www.ccra-adrc.gc.ca*.

EXTENSIONS

On entry into the **US**, the date stamped on your immigration form is the latest you're legally allowed to stay. Leaving a few days later may not matter, especially if you're heading home, but more than a week or so can result in a protracted, rather unpleasant, interrogation from officials which may cause you to miss your flight. Overstaying may also cause you to be turned away next time you try to enter the US. To get an extension before your time is up, apply in the United States to the nearest **US Immigration and Naturalization Service** (INS) office; their address will be under the Federal Government Offices listings in the front of local phone books.

At every **Canadian** point of entry, the immigration officer decides the length of stay permitted up to a maximum of six months, but not usually more than three. For visits of more than possibly three and definitely six months, study trips and stints of temporary employment, contact the nearest Canadian embassy, consulate or high commission for authorization prior to departure (see box, overleaf). Inside Canada, if an extension of stay is desired, written application must be made to the nearest **Canada Immigration Centre** well before the expiry of the authorized visit.

In both countries officials will usually assume that you're working illegally if you apply for an extension and it's up to you to convince them otherwise. Do this by providing evidence of ample finances, and, if you can, bring along an upstanding American or Canadian citizen to vouch for you. You'll also have to explain why you didn't plan for the extra time initially.

WORK AND STUDY

Anyone planning an extended stay in the United States or Canada should apply for a special **working visa** at any Canadian or American embassy/high commission before setting off.

Different types of visas are issued, depending on your skills and length of stay, but unless you've got relatives (parents or children over 21) or a prospective employer to sponsor you, your chances are at best slim.

Illegal work is nothing like as easy to find as it used to be, especially in the States now that the government has introduced fines of up to $10,000 for companies caught employing anyone without the legal right to work in the US. Even in traditionally more casual establishments such as restaurants, bars and fish canneries, things have really tightened up, and if you do find work it's likely to be of the less visible, poorly paid kind – washer-up instead of waiter.

Students have the best chance of prolonging their stay in either country. One way is to get on to an Exchange Visitor Program in the US, for which participants are given a J-1 visa that entitles them to take paid summer employment and apply for a social security number. However, you should note that most of these visas are issued for jobs in American **summer camps**, which aren't everybody's idea of a good time; they fly you over, and after a summer's work you end up with around $500 and a month to blow it in. If you live in Britain and are interested, contact BUNAC (16 Bowling Green Lane, London EC1R 0BD; ☎020/7251 3472), or Camp America (37 Queens' Gate, London SW7 5HR; ☎020/7581 7373). If you want to **study** at an American or Canadian university, apply to that institution directly; if they accept you, you're more or less entitled to unlimited visas so long as you remain enrolled in full-time education.

INSURANCE, HEALTH AND SAFETY

It's absolutely essential when visiting the Pacific Northwest to have travel insurance to cover loss of possessions and money as well as the cost of all medical and dental treatment. The US has no national health system, and you will probably pay heavily for even minor medical treatment; Canada has an excellent national health service, but non-residents have to pay anything up to $2000 a day and more to use it. There is no free treatment, and in some Canadian provinces doctors and hospitals actually add a surcharge to treatment meted out to foreigners.

Many bank and charge accounts include some form of travel cover, and some level of medical or other insurance is sometimes offered if you pay for your trip with a credit card (notably American Express). In all cases, you must make sure you keep all **medical bills** to support a claim for subsequent reimbursement and, if you have anything stolen, get a copy of the **crime report number** when you report the incident – otherwise you won't be able to claim. Remember also that time limits may apply when making claims after the fact, so promptness in contacting your insurer is highly advisable.

Remember that certain activities, like scuba diving, mountain climbing and other **risky sports**, are unlikely to be covered by most policies, although by paying an extra premium you can usually get the additional cover required. Also note that few insurers will arrange **on-the-spot payments** in the event of a major expense or loss; you will usually be reimbursed only after going home – though most credit card and travellers' cheque companies will reimburse or replace pretty much immediately.

HEALTH ADVICE FOR FOREIGN TRAVELLERS

If you have a serious accident while in the US or Canada, emergency medical services will get to you quickly and charge you later. For emergencies or ambulances in both countries, dial ☎911 (or whatever variant may be on the information plate of the pay phone). Note, though, that in parts of rural Canada you may still have to call ☎0 for the operator instead.

Should you need to see a **doctor**, lists can be found in the *Yellow Pages* under "Clinics" or

---

ROUGH GUIDES TRAVEL INSURANCE

Rough Guides now offer their own **travel insurance**, customized for our readers by a leading UK broker and backed by a Lloyds underwriter. It's available for anyone, of any nationality, travelling anywhere in the world, and we are convinced that this is the best-value scheme you'll find.

There are two main Rough Guide insurance plans: **Essential**, for effective, no-frills cover, starting at £11.75 for 2 weeks; and **Premier** – more expensive but with more generous and extensive benefits. Each offer European or Worldwide cover, and can be supplemented with a "Hazardous Activities Premium" if you plan to

indulge in sports considered dangerous, such as skiing or scuba diving. Unlike many policies, the Rough Guides schemes are calculated by the day, so if you're travelling for 27 days rather than a month, that's all you pay for. You can alternatively take out annual **multi-trip insurance**, which covers you for all your travel throughout the year (with a maximum of 60 days for any one trip). For a **policy quote**, call the Rough Guides Insurance Line on UK freefone ☎**0800/015 0906**, or, if you're calling from outside Britain on **(+44) 1243 621 046**. Alternatively, get an online quote at *www.roughguides.com/insurance*.

See p.60 for advice on the specific **health issues** entailed by travelling in the great outdoors of the Pacific Northwest.

"Physicians and Surgeons". A basic consultation fee is around $50–75, payable in advance. Medications aren't cheap either – keep all your receipts for later claims on your insurance policy.

Many **minor ailments** can be remedied using the fabulous array of potions and lotions available in **drugstores**. Foreign visitors should bear in mind that many pills available over the counter at home need a prescription in the US and Canada – most codeine-based painkillers, for example – and that local brand names can be confusing; ask for advice at the pharmacy in any drugstore.

Travellers from Europe do not require **inoculations** to enter the US or Canada.

CRIME AND PERSONAL SAFETY

No one could pretend that the Pacific Northwest is trouble-free but it is a much safer region than other more urban parts of North America, and in its Canadian component in particular, **crime** is unusual. Away from the urban centres, crime is low-key – except for the odd bar brawl in a rough-and-ready small town. Even the lawless reputation of larger American cities tends to be exaggerated, and most parts of these cities, by day at least, are fairly safe; at night, though, a few areas should be off-limits. By being careful, planning ahead and taking good care of your possessions, you should, generally speaking, have few real problems.

Foreign visitors tend to report that the police are helpful and obliging when things go wrong, although they'll be less sympathetic if they think you brought the trouble on yourself through carelessness.

MUGGING

Remember that although theft is rare, especially in Canada, it's still a good idea to be aware of the potential threat of **mugging**. It's impossible to give hard and fast rules about what to do if you're confronted by a mugger. Whether to run, scream or fight depends on the situation – but most local people would just hand over their money. Of course, the best thing would be simply to avoid being mugged, and there are a few basic rules worth remembering: don't flash your money around; don't peer at your map (or this book) at

every street corner, thereby announcing that you're a lost stranger; and even if you're terrified or drunk (or both), don't appear so. Also, try to avoid dark streets, especially ones you can't see the end of, and in the early hours stick to the roadside edge of the pavement so it's easier to run into the road to attract attention. If you have to ask for directions, choose your target carefully. Another idea is to carry a wad of cash, perhaps $50 or so, separate from the bulk of your holdings so that if you do get confronted, you can hand over something of value without it costing you everything.

If the worst happens and your assailant is toting a gun or (more likely) a knife, try to stay calm: remember that he (for this is generally a male pursuit) is probably scared, too. Keep still, don't make any sudden movements, and hand over your money. When he's gone, you should, despite your shock, try to find a phone and dial ☎911 (the emergency number in both Canada and the US), or hail a cab and ask the driver to take you to the nearest police station. Here, report the theft and get the **reference number** of the report to claim insurance and travellers' cheque refunds. If you're in a big city, ring the local helpline or Travelers Aid (their numbers are listed in the phone book) for sympathy and practical advice. For specific advice for women, in case of mugging or attack, see p.49.

Another potential source of trouble is having your hotel room **burgled**. Always store valuables in the hotel safe when you go out; when inside keep your door locked and don't open it to anyone you are suspicious of; if they claim to be hotel staff and you don't believe them, call reception on the room phone to check.

THEFT AND LOSS

Needless to say, having bags snatched that contain travel documents can be a big headache, none more so for foreign travellers than **losing your passport**. If the worst happens, go to the nearest embassy or consulate and get them to issue you a temporary passport, basically a sheet of paper saying you've reported the loss, which will get you out of Canada or America and back home. If you were planning to travel on from Canada or the US, however, you'll need a new passport – a time-consuming and expensive process.

Another possible problem is **lost airline tickets**. On scheduled and most charter flights, the

EMERGENCY NUMBERS FOR STOLEN TRAVELLERS' CHEQUES AND CREDIT CARDS

American Express cards ☎1-800/528-4800
American Express cheques ☎1-800/221-7282
Citicorp ☎1-800/645-6556
Diners Club ☎1-800/234-6377
MasterCard ☎1-800/826-2181
Thomas Cook/MasterCard ☎1-800/223-9920
Visa cards ☎1-800/336-8472
Visa cheques ☎1-800/227-6811

airline will usually honour their commitment on the lost ticket – especially if they can contact the issuing agent – but sorting a replacement ticket can take several hours, if not longer, and you can expect to pay an administration fee of around $50. Even worse, you may have to pay for a new ticket and wait a period (often as long as six months) for reimbursement. This is much more likely if you can't produce the lost ticket's number. In addition, bargain-basement tickets are not usually honoured by the airlines, who will often make you pay for the flight again, though you may be able to evade the rap if you can produce the lost ticket's number. Similarly if **you lose your travel insurance policy document**, you won't be able to make a claim unless you quote its number. To avert these calamities, keep a copy of the numbers or documents at home. For **lost travellers' cheques**, if you've followed the issuer's suggestion and kept a record of the cheque numbers separate from the actual cheques, all you have to do is ring the issuing company on their given toll-free

number to report the loss. They'll ask you for the cheque numbers, the place you bought them, when and how you lost them and whether it's been reported to the police. All being well, the missing cheques should be reissued within a couple of days – and you may get an emergency advance to tide you over.

CAR CRIME

Crimes committed against tourists driving **rented cars** in a few parts of North America – especially Florida and California – may have garnered headlines around the world in recent years, but they remain rare in the Pacific Northwest. In major urbanized areas, any car you rent should have nothing on it – such as a particular licence plate – that makes it easy to spot as a rental car. When driving, under no circumstances stop in any unlit or seemingly deserted urban area – and especially not if someone is waving you down and suggesting that there is something wrong with your car. Similarly, if you are "accidentally" rammed by the driver behind, do not stop immediately but drive on to the nearest well-lit, busy area and phone the emergency number (☎911) for assistance. Keep your doors locked and windows never more than slightly open. Do not open your door or window if someone approaches your car on the pretext of asking directions. Hide any valuables out of sight, preferably locked in the boot or in the glove compartment (any valuables you don't need for your journey should be left in your hotel safe).

In the rougher areas of Seattle, several motorists have been gunned down in recent years for sounding their car horns at (young male) drivers who have blocked traffic by halting their vehicles in the middle of the road in order to talk to friends.

COST, MONEY AND BANKS

To help with planning your vacation, this book contains detailed price information for lodging throughout the Pacific Northwest. Prices are given in either US or Canadian dollars as appropriate, with a label – US$ or Can$ – where confusion may arise. The two currencies do not have a one-for-one exchange rate, though Canadian shops and hotels are often prepared to accept US dollars, but not vice versa.

Unless otherwise stated, the hotel price codes (explained on p.51) are for the cheapest double room in high season, exclusive of any local taxes and special deals. For museums and similar attractions, the prices we quote are for adults; children and seniors usually get in half-price or free.

COSTS

Even when the exchange rate is at its least advantageous most Western European visitors find virtually everything – accommodation, food, petrol, cameras, clothes and more – to be better value in the US, and to a lesser extent Canada, than it is at home. You should also be prepared for regional variances; most prices in tourist areas, or in the far north, for example, tend to be above those in the rest of the region.

Generally, if you're sticking to a very tight budget – camping and buying food from shops – you could squeeze through on £17–25/US$20–35 per person a day. You're not going to last long living like this, though, and a more comfortable average daily budget, covering a motel room, bus travel, a museum or two

and a restaurant meal would work out at around £40–45/US$65–75. Naturally, once you upgrade your accommodation, eat out two or three times a day, and take in the city nightlife, this figure can easily double.

Accommodation is likely to be your biggest single expense. Few hotel or motel rooms in the cities of either country cost under US$40/Can$45 – it would be more usual to pay something like US$55/Can$65 – though rates in some rural areas are a little cheaper. Hostels offering dorm beds – usually for US$10–15 – are something of a rarity, and in any case they save little money for two or more people travelling together. Camping, of course, is cheap, ranging from free to perhaps US$20/Can$27 per night, but while an excellent prospect in the Pacific Northwest's great out-doors, it's rarely practical in or around the big cities. Accommodation prices may often be higher from June to early September, and throughout the more remote areas of the north, particularly the Yukon and parts of the NWT.

As for **food**, around US$15 a day is enough to get an adequate life-support diet, while for a daily total of around US$35 you can dine pretty well.

Travelling around using buses and trains is reasonably economic too – in cash terms if not in time, whilst a group of two or more, renting a car, at around US$150 a week, can be a very good investment, not least because it will enable you to stay in the ubiquitous budget motels along the interstates instead of expensive city-centre hotels. As an example of bus fares, the 12-hour journey from Vancouver to Calgary costs about Can$102. Trains cost a good deal more – Can$175 for the 18-hour trip from Vancouver to Jasper in Jasper National Park – but usually much less than internal flights, though charter companies like Canada 3000 are bringing prices of these flights down: Vancouver to Calgary, an hour's flight, will cost around Can$120 (excluding tax) on an early morning or late-evening charter while Seattle to Portland can cost from about US$130 (see "Getting Around" for more details).

TAXES

In almost every state and province, **sales tax**, at varying rates up to fifteen percent in Canada and

MONEY: A NOTE FOR FOREIGN TRAVELLERS

US and Canadian currency comes in bills worth $1, $5, $10, $20, $50 and $100, plus various larger (and rarer) denominations. In the United States, confusingly, all are the same size and same green colour, making it necessary to check each bill carefully. In Canada the notes all have different colours and designs, whilst the country's $1 bill has been replaced by a gold-coloured coin known as a **"loonie"** (after the bird on one face). No one's really come up with a decent name for the $2 coin, though "twoonie" has been tried.

The dollar in both Canada and the US is made up of 100 cents in coins with the same names in both countries: 1 cent (known as a **penny**), 5 cents (a **nickel**), 10 cents (a **dime**) and 25 cents (a **quarter**). In the US, look out for the **new "state" quarter** designs being introduced one month at a time, and also the new golden **"Sacagawea" dollar coin**, named after the Native American women who assisted Lewis and Clark on their expeditions through the uncharted West. Very occasionally in the US, you might come across the **JFK half-dollars** (50¢), **Susan B. Anthony dollar coins**, or a **two-dollar bill**. Change (quarters are the most useful) is needed for buses, vending machines and telephones, so always carry plenty.

---

ten percent in the US, is added to virtually everything you buy in shops, but it isn't usually part of the marked price, so be prepared for everything to be more expensive than a first glance at the price tag suggests. The shock is strongest when it comes to hotel bills, where certain regions levy a **hotel rooms tax** on top of provincial and federal sales taxes. Alberta, with its big oil revenues, has no local sales tax, nor does the Yukon, but both Alberta and British Columbia levy a room tax (usually between five and ten percent).

All of Canada, though, levies the national seven percent **Goods and Services Tax (GST)**. However, note that a GST rebate is available to visitors for certain goods and **accommodation expenditure** over Can$200 during a maximum period of one month. This can add up to a significant amount, so take the trouble to pick up claim forms, available from many shops, hotels or from any Canadian embassy. Return them, with **all receipts**, to Visitor Rebate Program, Canada Customs and Revenue Agency, Summerside Tax Centre, 275 Pope Rd, Suite 104, Summerside, PE C1N 6C6. For more information call ☎902/432-5608 (outside Canada) or ☎1-800/668-4748 *www.ccra-adrc.gc.ca/visitors*.

TRAVELLERS' CHEQUES

US or Canadian dollar **travellers' cheques** are the best way to carry money, for both North American and foreign visitors; they offer the great security of knowing that lost or stolen cheques will be replaced. In most cases they can also be widely used as "cash" if they're made out in the currency in which you're spending them. Only if you're restricting your travels to Canada alone is it worth opting specifically for Canadian dollar cheques. In neither country are you likely to have any problems using cheques in shops, restaurants and petrol stations, but it's definitely worth investing in one or other of the two best-known types of cheque – American Express or Visa. Be sure to have plenty of the $10 and $20 denominations for everyday transactions.

Banks in both countries are generally open from 10am until 4pm Monday to Thursday, and 10am to 6pm on Friday, although the trend is towards longer hours and Saturday morning opening. Travellers' cheques can be cashed at most banks, though the commission charged (which usually incorporates both a flat fee and a percentage levy) varies substantially. In general, you do better to change large amounts occasionally than small amounts frequently. Cheques made out in Canadian dollars can often be used as cash for many transactions. For converting **foreign currency** in either country, exchange bureaux such as Thomas Cook or American Express, always found at airports, tend to charge less commission. Rarely, if ever, do hotels change foreign currency.

PLASTIC, MONEY AND CASH MACHINES

If you don't already have a **credit card**, you should think seriously about getting one before you set off. For many services, it's simply taken for granted that you'll be paying with plastic. When renting a car (or even a bike) or checking into a hotel, you may well be asked to show a credit card to establish your creditworthiness – even if you intend to settle the bill in cash. **Visa**, **MasterCard** (previously known in the UK as Access), **Diners Club**, **Discover** and **American Express** are the most widely used.

With MasterCard or Visa it is also possible to **withdraw cash** at any bank displaying relevant stickers, or from appropriate automatic teller machines (**ATMs**) – Diners Club cards can be used to cash personal cheques at Citibank branches. American Express cards can only get cash, or buy travellers' cheques, at American Express offices (check the *Yellow Pages*) or from the travellers' cheque dispensers at most major airports. Most **Canadian** credit cards issued by hometown banks will be honoured in the US and vice versa.

North American holders of ATM cards are likely to discover that their cards work in the machines of certain banks in other states and provinces (check with your bank before you leave home).

Most cash-dispensing cards issued by **foreign banks** are accepted in the US and Canada, as long as they are linked to international networks such as Cirrus and Plus – once again, check before you set off, as otherwise the machine may simply gobble up your plastic friend. Overseas visitors should also bear in mind that fluctuating exchange rates may result in spending more (or less) than expected when the item eventually shows up on a statement.

EMERGENCIES

If you run out of money abroad, or there is some kind of emergency, the quickest way to get money sent out is to contact your bank at home and have them wire the cash to the nearest bank. You can do the same thing through Thomas Cook or American Express (free to cardholders) if there is a branch nearby, and can also have cash sent out through Western Union (☎1-800/235-0000 or 361-1872 in Canada; ☎0800/833833 in UK; ☎1-800/325-6000 or 752-6777 in US; ☎1-800/649 565 in Australia; ☎0800/270 000 in New Zealand) to a bank, post office or local agent – a process which takes just minutes but will be expensive (reckon on the deduction of ten percent commission).

It's a bit less expensive to get a bank to transfer cash by cable, while if you have a few days' leeway, sending a postal money order through the mail, which is exchangeable at any post office, is cheaper still. The equivalent for foreign travellers is the **international money order**, for which you need to allow up to seven days in the international air mail before arrival. An ordinary cheque sent from overseas takes two to three weeks to clear.

Foreigners in difficulties have the final option of throwing themselves on the mercy of their nearest national **consulate** (see p.18–19), who will – in worst cases only – repatriate you, but will never, under any circumstances, lend you money.

TELEPHONES, MAIL AND EMAIL

Visitors from overseas tend to be impressed by the speed and efficiency of communications in North America – with the exception of the US mail. The break-up of the old Bell System monopoly has left a plethora of competing telephone companies, and though they may prioritize local and domestic calls over international links, keeping in touch with home is generally easy.

TELEPHONES

Public telephones in the US and Canada invariably work, and in cities at any rate can be found everywhere – on street corners, in railway and bus stations, hotel lobbies, bars and restaurants.

TELEPHONE AREA CODES WITHIN THE PACIFIC NORTHWEST

Oregon (OR) excluding Portland, Salem, Astoria	☎541
Portland, Astoria, Salem	☎503
Western Washington excluding Seattle (WA)	☎360
Seattle	☎206
Eastern Washington (WA)	☎509
British Columbia (BC) (excluding Vancouver)	☎250
Vancouver	☎604
Southern Alberta (AB)	☎403
Yukon (YT)	☎867

They take 25¢, 10¢ and 5¢ coins. The cost of a **local call** from a public phone (within a limited radius, rather than the entire area covered by any one code) is 25–35¢.

Some numbers covered by the same area code are considered so far apart that calls between them count as **non-local** (zone calls). These cost much more and usually require you to dial 1 before the seven-digit number. Pricier still are **long-distance calls** (to a different area code), for which you'll need a stack of change. Non-local calls and long-distance calls are much less expensive if made between 6pm and 8am (the cheapest rates of all are 11pm–8am), and calls from **private phones** are always much cheaper than those from public phones. Calls from **hotel phones** are usually the most expensive of all but some hotels offer free local calls from rooms – ask when you check in. Detailed rates are listed at the front of the telephone directory (the *White* or *Yellow Pages*, a copious source of information on many matters).

An increasing number of phones accept **credit cards**, while anyone who holds a credit card issued by a major North American bank can obtain an **AT&T** (or similar) **charge card**, sometimes known as an **affinity card**.

Many government agencies, car rental firms, hotels and so on have **toll-free numbers**, which usually have the prefix ☎1-800, or more rarely ☎1-888 or ☎1-877. Generally these can be dialled from anywhere in mainland North America, but in the Northwest you may find the line is toll-free only within either the US or Canada, but not both. Other numbers may only be toll-free in a single state or province. Phone numbers with the prefix ☎1-900 are pay-per-call lines, generally quite expensive and almost always involving either sports or phone sex.

States and provinces within the Northwest have different **area codes** – three-digit numbers which must precede the seven-figure number if you're calling from abroad or from a region with a different code. In this book, we've highlighted the local area codes at appropriate moments in the text, and they're also listed in the box. On any specific number we give, we've only included the area code if it's not clear from the text which one you should use, or if a given phone number lies outside the region currently being described.

INTERNATIONAL CALLS

In Britain, it's possible to obtain a free BT chargecard (☎0800/345144), with which all calls from overseas can be charged to your quarterly domestic account. To use these cards in the US, or to make a **collect call** (to "reverse the charges") using a BT operator, contact the carrier: AT&T ☎1-800/445-5667; MCI ☎1-800/444-2162; or Sprint ☎1-800/800-0008. To avoid the international operator fee, BT credit-card calls can be made directly using an automated system: AT&T ☎1-800/445-5688; MCI ☎1-800/854-4826; or Sprint ☎1-800/825-4904.

British visitors who are going to be making a number of calls to the US or Canada, and who want to be able to call ☎1-800 numbers, otherwise inaccessible from outside the country, should take advantage of the Swiftcall telephone club (☎0800/769 0800). You need a touch-tone phone. Once you've paid, by credit card, for however many units you want, you are given a PIN. Any time you want to get an international line, simply dial ☎0800/769 8000, punch in your PIN, and then dial as you would were you in the US, putting a 1 before the area code, followed by the number. Calls to the US and Canada – including ☎1-800 calls – can save up to 50 percent.

In the **US** you can get telephone calling/bank credit cards from the companies listed below, who can also supply long-distance phonecards and "prepaid" debit phonecards: AT&T ☎1-800/451-4341 or Sprint ☎1-800/746-3767.

Telephone cards such as **Australia's** Telstra Telecard or Optus Calling Card and **New Zealand's** Telecom's Calling Card can be used to make calls abroad, which are charged back to a domestic account or credit card. Apply to Telstra ☎1-800/038 000, Optus ☎1300/300 300, or NZ Telecom ☎123.

CALLING THE NORTHWEST FROM ABROAD

Calling US/Canada from the UK, dial 001 + province code + subscriber number.

Calling Canada from the US, dial province code + subscriber number.

Calling US from Canada, dial area code + subscriber name.

Calling US/Canada from Australia dial 0011 + country code.

Calling US/Canada from New Zealand dial 00 + country code.

MAIL SERVICES

Post offices in the US and Canada are usually open Monday to Friday from 9am until 5pm, and Saturday from 9am to noon. **Stamps** can also be bought from automatic vending machines, the lobbies of larger hotels, airports, train stations, bus terminals and many retail outlets and newsstands. Mailboxes are blue in the US, red in Canada. Ordinary mail are around a dollar (US and Canadian) for letters abroad, about half that for postcards, aerogrammes and letters weighing up to half an ounce (a single thin sheet). **Air mail** between the US and Europe generally takes about a week. There is no separate air mail rate in Canada for mail sent abroad: **aerogrammes** can only be mailed to destinations within Canada.

The last line of the address is made up of an abbreviation denoting the state or province (Washington is "WA", the Yukon is "YT", for example, though you can spell it in full if you're unsure; see the list in the phone codes box, overleaf) and a multi-digit number – the **zip code** (US) or **postal code** (Canada) – denoting the local post office (codes in Canada have a mix of numbers and letters). Addresses must include the zip, or postal code, as well as the sender's address on the envelope. Letters which don't carry a code are liable to get lost or at least delayed; if you don't know it, phone books carry a list for their service area, and post offices – even in Europe – have directories.

Letters can be sent c/o **General Delivery** in both the US and Canada (what's known elsewhere as **poste restante**) to the one relevant post office in each town or city (we list these in the *Guide* for larger cities), but must include the zip code and will usually only be held for thirty days (fifteen days in Canada) before being returned to sender – so make sure there's a return address on the envelope. If you're receiving mail at someone else's address, it should include "c/o" and the regular occupant's name otherwise it, too, is likely to be returned. Letters will also be held at **hotels** – mark such mail "Guest Mail, Hold For Arrival" but ensure you place a date for collection. If you hold an **American Express** card or travellers' cheques you can have mail sent to Amex offices throughout the Northwest (label such mail "client letter service", and confirm arrangements in advance). Others can pick up mail from Amex for a small fee (we give addresses of Amex offices in the larger cities).

EMAIL AND INTERNET ACCESS

Email is often the cheapest and most convenient way to keep in touch. **Cybercafés** can still be found in most towns of any size, though their hey-day has largely passed and many travellers resort to the **free Internet access** provided by almost all public libraries. Generally you just reserve a half-hour slot and away you go, but high demand has forced some libraries either to charge for using email or ban it altogether. If neither of these options fit the bill, or you just need a fast machine with assorted peripherals, then find a commercial photocopying and printing shop (look under "Copying" in the *Yellow Pages*). They'll charge around 20¢ a minute for use of their computers, but you're guaranteed fast access. Most upscale hotels also offer email and Internet access – though again at a price.

By far the easiest way to collect and send email on the road is to sign up with one of the advertisement-funded **free email accounts**. Any of the major search engines will take you straight to one – *www.hotmail.com*, *www.excite.com*, and *www.yahoo.com* to name just a few – and all can be accessed from any Net-linked computer. To sign up with one, all you need to do is pick a site and fill out a few forms. When you want to send or check your email, just go to the Webpage and enter your name and password. Emails are kept indefinitely, but you are typically limited to a total of 2Mb of disk space and if you fail to use the account for three or six months (depending on the service supplier) you'll be closed down.

TELEGRAMS AND FAXES

To send a **telegram** (sometimes called a wire), don't go to a post office but to a Western Union office in the US, or a CN/CP Public Message Centre in Canada (listed in the *Yellow Pages*). Credit-card holders can dictate messages over the phone. In Canada you can also phone in **telepost** messages, a guaranteed next-day or sooner service to anywhere in Canada or the US. **International telegrams** cost slightly less than the cheapest international phone call: one sent in the morning from North America should arrive at its overseas destination the following day. For domestic telegrams ask for a **mailgram**, which will be delivered to any address in the country the next morning.

Public **fax** machines, which may require your credit card to be "swiped" through an attached device, are found in the Pacific Northwest at pho-tocopy centres and, occasionally, bookstores and libraries.

INFORMATION AND MAPS

maps, leaflets and brochures distributed by national tourist offices in the UK, US or elsewhere, and each of the various state and provincial tourist offices, all of which are listed in the box overleaf. Write well in advance of your departure, and be as speci-fic as possible about your interests – or just print the stuff off from their Web sites.

LOCAL INFORMATION

There are various **state and provincial tourist offices** in the Pacific Northwest (see box over-leaf for contact details). These offer a vast range of free brochures and other material. They are particularly helpful if you're able to specify a par-ticular interest – fishing in BC, for example – in which case they'll be able to save you huge amounts of time and trouble by sending you the

The most useful source of information on the Northwest is the enormous range of free

STATE AND PROVINCIAL TOURIST OFFICES

Alberta Travel Alberta, 10155 102nd St NW, Edmonton, AB T5J 4G8 (☎780/427-4321, toll-free within Canada and mainland US ☎1-800/661-8888, fax 780/427-0867, *www.discoveralberta.com*).

British Columbia Tourism British Columbia, Parliament Buildings, Victoria, BC V8V 1X4 (☎604/603-6000, toll-free within Canada and mainland US ☎1-800/663-6000, *www.tbc.gov.bc.ca/tourism/information.html* or *www.hellobc.com*)

Northwest Territories Northwest Territories Arctic Tourism, PO Box 610, Yellowknife, NT X1A 2N5 (☎867/873-7200, toll-free within Canada and mainland US ☎1-800/661-0733, fax 867/873-4059, *www.nwttravel.nt.ca*).

Oregon Oregon Tourism Commission, 775 Summer St NE, Salem, OR 97310 (toll-free within Canada and mainland US ☎1-800/547-7842, *www.traveloregon.com*).

Washington Washington State Tourism Development Division, 101 General Administration Building, PO Box 42500, Olympia, WA 98504-2500 (toll-free within Canada and mainland US ☎1-800/544-1800, *www.experiencewashington.com*).

Yukon Territory Tourism Yukon, PO Box 2703, Whitehorse, YT Y1A 2C6 (☎867/667-5340, toll-free within Canada and mainland US ☎1-800/661-0788, fax 867/667-3546, *www.touryukon.com*).

TOURIST OFFICES IN THE UK

Canada Visit Canada Centre, 62–65 Trafalgar Square, London WC2N 5DT. Open weekdays 9am–5.30pm. (☎0891/715000. Call for brochures and general information. Premium-rated line).

British Columbia British Columbia House, 1 Regent St, London SW1Y 4NS (☎020/7930 6857).

USTTA The United States Travel and Tourism Administration – USTTA – has offices all over the world, usually in US embassies and consulates (see box on p.18). In the UK, they have a premium-rated number for ordering brochures and obtaining general information (☎0906/550 8972).

latest rules, regulations, equipment rental shops, tour operators and so forth regarding your request.

Visitor centres go under a variety of names throughout the Northwest – in BC, for example, they're called infocentres – but they all provide detailed information about the local area. Typically they're open Mon–Fri 9am–5pm, Sat 9am–1pm, except in summer, when in more popular areas they're often open seven days a week from 8am or 9am until 6pm or later. In smaller towns many offices will close for the winter from about mid-September to mid-May. In the US, visitor centres are often known as the "Convention and Visitors Bureau" (CVB), while in smaller towns in both Canada and the US many operate under the auspices of the **Chamber of Commerce**, who promote local business interests. Most large communities also have **free newspapers** carrying entertainment listings. You'll also find small visitor centres in the arrival halls of the region's airports and there's usually a free phone system connecting to leading local hotels too.

Park visitor centres (again, the name varies) should invariably be your first port-of-call in any national, state or provincial park. Staff are usually outdoors experts, and can offer invaluable advice on trails, current conditions and the full range of outfitting or adventure possibilities. These are also the places to go to obtain national park permits and, where applicable, permits for fishing or backcountry camping (see "Outdoor Pursuits", p.58).

MAPS

The **free maps** issued by each state, provincial or local tourist office are usually fine for general driving and route planning and can be used in conjunction with the maps provided in this guide. To get hold of tourist office maps, either write to the office directly (see box above) or stop by any visitor centre.

As for larger **road maps**, Rand McNally produces good commercial maps of the US and Canada, bound together in their *Rand McNally Road Atlas*, or printed separately for individual states and provinces. They also run 24 stores

USEFUL PACIFIC NORTHWEST WEB SITES

TRAVEL
City of Seattle
www.cityofseattle.net The official tourist guide to Seattle is loaded with information on everything from local politics to road conditions. Head for the Visiting Seattle section for entertainment and sightseeing guides.

Rough Guides
www.roughguides.com Post any of your pre-trip questions – or post-trip suggestions – in Travel Talk, our online forum for travellers.

Tourism Vancouver
www.tourismvancouver.com Comprehensive city guide offering accommodation options and an events guide that's updated daily.

Where Rocky Mountains Online
www.whererockymountains.com Comprehensive online tourism magazine covering the Canadian Rockies, complete with entertainment guides, restaurant and accommodation tips and various feature stories. There's a similar in-depth site for Calgary (*www.wherecalgary.com*).

DAILY NEWSPAPERS
For information on both local and national news, weather updates, sports scores and entertainment happenings, check the following sites:

Calgary Herald
www.calgaryherald.com

Portland Oregonian
www.oregonian.com

Seattle Post-Intelligencer
http://seattlep-i.nwsource.com

Vancouver Province
www.vancouverprovince.com

OUTDOOR PURSUITS
Backcountry Resource Center
www.jps.net/prichins/backcountry_resource_center.htm Superb non-commercial site laden with valuable information on backcountry skiing, climbing and general outdoor interests. Be sure to check the links pages, which can send you directly to hundreds of more specific sites.

Environment Canada Weather
http://weather.ec.gc.ca/index_e.shtml Useful when visiting the great outdoors, this is the official Canadian government weather site.

Great Outdoor Recreation Page
www.gorp.com Highly recommended site covering outdoor pursuits throughout the world, but best on North America. Before planning an excursion, check the Community section for personal recommendations and warnings on your destination. Particularly strong on hiking advice and locations.

Ski Maps
www.skimaps.com The latest snowfall reports, plus the snow-base depth and trail maps for all the major skiing and snowboarding resorts in the region, as well as the rest of the world.

MISCELLANEOUS
Bumbershoot
www.bumbershoot.org Well-presented site, outlining the Seattle arts festival and offering online ticket sales.

Calgary Stampede
www.calgary-stampede.com Everything you want to know about the rodeo, and ticket sales for this festival's events.

Directory listings
www.infospace.com Comprehensive yellow and white pages listings. If you want to find a vet in Moosejaw or a body piercer in Madras, this will have it.

Vancouver Aquarium
www.vanaqua.org An amazingly detailed collection of online exhibits and worthy features on various aspects of marine biology. The Orca ("Killer Whale") pages contain helpful advice on whale-watching in the area.

---

across the US; call ☎1-800/333-0136 (ext 2111) or visit *www.randmcnally.com* for their locations, or for direct-mail maps. The American Automobile Association (AAA; toll-free ☎1-800/222-4357, *www.aaa.com*), based at 4100 E Arkansas Drive, Denver, CO 80222, provides free maps and assistance to its members, and to British members of foreign motoring organisations.

The well-equipped bookstores that you'll find in Seattle, Vancouver, Calgary, Portland and all large towns, as well as camping shops, and park ranger or warden stations in national parks, state and provincial parks and wilderness areas, will all sell good-quality local **hiking maps** for a few dollars. Among the best of the many small companies producing such maps, at the necessary 1:50,000 level

MAP OUTLETS IN THE UK

Glasgow
John Smith and Sons, 57–61 St Vincent St, Glasgow G2 5TB (☎0141/221 7472).

London
Daunt Books, 83 Marylebone High St, London W1M 3DE (☎020/7224 2295).

National Map Centre, 22–24 Caxton St, London SW1H 0QU (☎020/7222 2466, *www.mapsworld.com*).

Stanfords, 12–14 Long Acre, London WC2E 9LP (☎020/7836 1321); 52 Grosvenor Gardens, London SW1W 0AG; 156 Regent St, London W1R 5TA (☎020/7434 4744). Maps by mail or phone order also available: ☎020/7836 1321.

The Travel Bookshop, 13–15 Blenheim Crescent, London W11 2EE (☎020/7229 5260).

IRELAND
Dublin
Easons Bookshop, 80 Middle Abbey St, Dublin 1 (☎01/873 3811).

Fred Hanna's Bookshop, 27–29 Nassau St, Dublin 2 (☎01/677 1255).

Hodges Figgis Bookshop, 56–58 Dawson St, Dublin 2 (☎01/677 4754).

Belfast
Waterstone's, Queens Building, 8 Royal Ave, Belfast BT1 1DA (☎028/9024 7355).

MAP OUTLETS IN NORTH AMERICA

Chicago
Rand McNally, 444 N Michigan Ave, Chicago, IL 60611 (☎312/321-1751, *www.randmcnally.com*).

Montréal
Ulysses Travel Bookshop, 4176 St-Denis, Montréal, PQ H2W 2M5 (☎514/843-9447, *www.ulyssesguides.com*).

New York
The Complete Traveller Bookstore, 199 Madison Ave, New York, NY 10016 (☎212/685-9007).

Rand McNally, 150 E 52nd St, New York, NY 10022 (☎212/758-7488, *www.randmcnally.com*).

Traveler'sChoice Bookstore, 2 Wooster St, New York, NY 10013 (☎212/941-1535, *tvlchoice@aol.com*).

Palo Alto
Phileas Fogg's Books & Maps, #87 Stanford Shopping Center, Palo Alto, CA 94304 (☎1-800/533-FOGG, *www.foggs.com*).

of detail, is Earthwalk Press, 5432 La Jolla Hermosa Ave, La Jolla, CA 92037 (☎1-800/828-MAPS). Also check the "Listings" and "Practicalities" sections of individual town and city entries in the *Guide* for details of local map shops.

If you want to be absolutely sure of getting the maps you need for independent wilderness travel in Canada, contact the **Canada Map Office**, 130 Bentley Ave, Ottawa, ON K1A 0E9 (☎613/952-7000). It supplies map indexes, which will identify the map you need; it also produces two useful brochures entitled *How to Use a Map* and *Maps and Wilderness Canoeing*, and publishes two main series of maps, 1:250,000 and 1:50,000.

Britain's best source of maps is Stanfords (see above), who have a mail-order service.

Portland

Powell's Travel Store, 701 W 6th St, Pioneer Courthouse Square, Portland OR (☎503/228-1108, *www.powells.com*).

San Francisco

The Complete Traveller Bookstore, 3207 Fillmore St, San Francisco, CA 94123 (☎415/923-1511).

Rand McNally, 595 Market St, San Francisco, CA 94105 (☎415/777-3131, *www.randmcnally.com*).

Santa Barbara

Map Link Inc., 30 S La Patera Lane, Unit 5, Santa Barbara, CA 93117 (☎805/692-6777, *www.maplink.com*).

Seattle

Elliott Bay Book Company, 101 S Main St, Seattle, WA 98104 (☎206/624-6600, *www.elliottbaybook.com*).

Toronto

Open Air Books and Maps, 25 Toronto St, Toronto, ON M5R 2C1 (☎416/363-0719).

Vancouver

International Travel Maps and Books, 552 Seymour St, Vancouver, BC V6B 3J5 (☎604/687-3320, *www.itmb.com*).

Washington DC

ADC Map and Travel Center, 1636 I St NW, Washington, DC 20006 (☎202/628-2608).

Rand McNally, 1201 Connecticut Ave NW, Washington, DC 20036 (☎202/223-6751, *www.randmcnally.com*).

Travel Books & Language Center, 4437 Wisconsin Ave, Washington, DC 20016 (☎1-800/220-2665).

MAP OUTLETS IN AUSTRALASIA

Adelaide

The Map Shop, 6 Peel St Adelaide (☎08/8231 2033).

Auckland

Specialty Maps, 46 Albert St Auckland (☎09/307 2217).

Brisbane

Worldwide Maps and Guides, 187 George St Brisbane (☎07/3221 4330).

Christchurch

Mapworld, 173 Gloucester St, Christchurch (☎03/374 5399, fax: 5633, *www.mapworld.co.nz*).

Melbourne

Mapland, 372 Little Bourke St Melbourne (☎03/9670 4383).

Perth

Perth Map Centre, 1/884 Hay St Perth (☎08/9322 5733).

Sydney

Travel Bookshop, Shop 3, 175 Liverpool St Sydney (☎02/9261 8200).

GETTING AROUND

With distances of anything up to one hundred miles between settlements, it's essential to plan carefully how you'll get around. Your choice of transport will have a crucial impact on your trip. The days when you could explore the region by train are long gone and nowadays Amtrak in the US and VIA Rail in Canada only provide a skeletal service, though they do link the major cities and have several particularly scenic routes. In both the US and Canada, Greyhound buses provide a more extensive network of services, reaching all the big cities and most of the larger towns. Local bus companies supplement Greyhound's coverage, but more so in Canada than the US. Along the coast, the boats of BC Ferries and Washington State Ferries are frequent, fast and efficient. Flying is a key way – sometimes the only way – of reaching some destinations in the Northwest, but it is more expensive, though competition in the skies can lead to some decent bargains.

On most forms of public transport there are **discounted fares** for children under 12, for youths between 13 and 21, and over-60s. It has to be said, however, that things are always easier if you have a **car**. Many of the most spectacular and memorable destinations in the Pacific Northwest are way out in the sticks, far removed from the cities and obstinately aloof of public transport. Even if a bus or train can take you to the general vicinity of a national park, for example, it can prove impossible to explore the interior without your own vehicle.

BY TRAIN

Travelling by **rail** is not a terribly viable way of getting around the Northwest, though if you have the time it can be a pleasant and relaxing experi-

ence. Neither the American Amtrak, nor the Canadian VIA Rail networks serve many centres these days, and services are generally restricted to one or two trains a day, sometimes on only a few days each week. That said, the train is by far the most comfortable – and often the most scenic – way to go, and long-distance rides especially can be a great opportunity to meet people.

AMTRAK

Details of the two Amtrak routes that connect the states of **Washington** and **Oregon** with the rest of the United States, together with information on Amtrak's transcontinental pricing and reservation policies, can be found on p.10. Within the Pacific Northwest, the most appealing of the rail routes is the **Coast Starlight**, which picks its daily way up the coast from Los Angeles and California's Oakland (for bus connections from San Francisco) to cross the Oregon border near Klamath Falls. From here, the train pulls across the Cascade Mountains for Eugene, Salem and Portland, travelling on to Seattle. The Coast Starlight terminates here, connecting with buses travelling on to Vancouver, in Canada, or you can wait overnight in Seattle for the train connection. There's one other major regional train, the daily **Empire Builder**. This originates in Chicago and runs to Spokane, in eastern Washington, from where it rattles across the Cascade Mountains to either Portland or Seattle.

Always **reserve** as far in advance as possible; all passengers must have seats, and some trains, especially between major cities, are booked solid. Supplements are also payable for **sleeping compartments** (which cost around $100 per night for one or two people, including three full meals). However, even standard Amtrak carriages are surprisingly spacious, and there are additional dining cars and lounge cars (with full bars and sometimes glass-domed 360° viewing compartments).

For any one specific journey, the train can be more expensive than taking a Greyhound or even a plane, though **special deals**, especially in the off-peak season (Sept–May), bring the costs down considerably. In addition to these, Amtrak divides the US into three zones – with the Northwest included in the western zone – to apply its **All Aboard America** fares, which

DRIVING DISTANCES THROUGHOUT THE PACIFIC NORTHWEST

Driving distances in kilometres and miles
(Kilometres shown first then miles)

Spokane to Whitehorse is via Calgary/Edmonton
Victoria: assumes journey via Vancouver/ferry connections

	Calgary	Edmonton	Eugene	Portland	San Francisco	Seattle	Spokane	Vancouver	Victoria	Whitehorse
Calgary	–									
Edmonton	299/185	–								
Eugene	1341/833	1640/1018	–							
Portland	1199/745	1498/930	142/88	–						
San Francisco	2236/1383	2535/1568	885/550	1027/638	–					
Seattle	907/570	1206/755	416/258	274/170	1313/816	–				
Spokane	689/428	988/613	652/405	510/317	1537/955	425/264	–			
Vancouver	977/606	1164/722	644/400	504/313	1541/958	228/142	653/406	–		
Victoria	1067/661	1244/771	732/455	592/368	1629/1013	316/197	741/461	88/55	–	
Whitehorse	2385/1479	2086/1293	3341/2072	3201/1985	4236/2630	2935/1824	3074/1906	2697/1672	2785/1727	–

allow three stopovers within 45 days for the cost of one inclusive fare.

Visitors can reduce costs by buying an Amtrak **rail pass**: the **North America Rail Pass** is issued in conjunction with VIA Rail (see below) and is valid for 30 consecutive days of travel up to one year from the date of purchase and you may travel up to four times, one way, over any given route segment. The pass is valid for coach (second-class) travel, but can be upgraded to Amtrak's Custom Class, Club Class or Metroliner, or VIA 1 or Sleeper class for an additional charge. Many trains fill quickly, so it's worth making reservations.

For more **information** or **to purchase passes**, call ☎1-800/USA-RAIL in the US or ☎1-888/842-7245 in Canada, *www.amtrak.com/promotions* or *www.viarail.ca*. Passes can also be purchased either before departure or at any staffed Amtrak station in the US, Via Rail stations, some travel agents and general sales agents outside Canada and the US. The **price** of the passes depends on when you wish to travel: during peak times (June 1–Oct 15) the price is US$656/Can$965; off-peak (Jan 1–May 31 & Oct 16–Dec 31) the cost is US$459/Can$675. A ten percent discount on all these prices is available for seniors, children and young people under 18, and students with an ISIC card in Canada or Student Advantage Card in the US. Note that if any portion of your trip falls within the peak period, then the peak rate applies for your entire pass. In the UK and Ireland, you can buy them from Leisurail (0870/750 0222); in Australia, Thomas Cook World Rail (☎1300/361 941); and in New Zealand, Walshes World (☎09/379 3708).

VIA RAIL, ROCKY MOUNTAINEER AND BC RAIL

Details of VIA Rail services from the rest of Canada to the Northwest – insofar as they still exist – and of the company's transcontinental pricing and reservation policies are covered on p.11. Within the Northwest, the **hub** of the VIA Rail operation is Jasper, from where you can travel either northwest to Prince George and Prince Rupert, southwest to Kamloops and Vancouver, or east to Edmonton. Both routes thread through some spectacular Rockies scenery. At Prince Rupert you connect with BC Ferries over to Port Hardy on Vancouver Island or the Haida Gwaii (Queen Charlotte Islands) and the Alaska Marine Highway, which heads north to

TOLL-FREE RAIL INFORMATION
USA
For all information on Amtrak fares and schedules, and to make reservations, call ☎1-800/USA-RAIL. Alternatively, check out the Amtrak Web site, *www.amtrak.com*. Do not phone individual stations.

CANADA
Within Canada's Pacific Northwest, including the Yukon and NWT, VIA Rail's toll-free information line is ☎1-800/561-8630 or 1-888/842-7245. Their Web site is *www.viarail.ca*.

Alaska and south to Bellingham, in Washington. From Vancouver, you can travel south to Seattle by both Amtrak train and bus. The final VIA Rail service in British Columbia links Victoria with Nanaimo and Courtenay on Vancouver Island.

Elsewhere, various private companies operate passenger trains which reach parts of the Canadian Northwest VIA Rail have abandoned. Most spectacular is the **Rocky Mountaineer** from Vancouver to Banff and then on to Calgary, or to Jasper, which is best experienced through a package – there are around six different options – from Rocky Mountaineer Railtours (☎1-800/665-7245, *www.rockymountaineer.com*). These tours, which are swiftly booked out, mostly run from May to September, but there are some winter departures. Prices mean they are for a select few only, however – the trips' costs vary according to the precise itinerary, duration and side excursions, but start upwards of Can$500. To book in the UK and Ireland, contact Leisurail (☎0870/750 0222); in Australia call Asia Pacific Travel (☎02/9319 6624); and in New Zealand call Greyhound World Travel (☎09/479 6555).

Another Northwest option is the provincially administered **BC Rail** (within BC call ☎604/984-5246, rest of Canada and US ☎1-800/663-8238, *www.bcrail.com*) service from Vancouver to Prince George via Lillooet. Stations are not shared with VIA Rail in Prince George, but there is generally a shuttle bus between the train stations.

Single **fares** from Jasper to Vancouver give an idea of the cost of VIA Rail travel, which averages out as being a little less expensive than Amtrak. Note that there are no reductions for return fares: they simply cost twice the single fare. Some reductions are available outside the summer (June to mid-Oct) if you purchase tickets more than seven days in advance. These are limited in number, so in practice you need to book well ahead of the seven-day deadline. **Coach** class from Jasper to Vancouver, the Canadian equivalent of second class, with reclining seats, costs Can\$176 in high season, while **sleeper** class comes in three categories: **double berths**, with large seats that become curtained bunks at night; **roomettes**, private single rooms with a toilet and a bed that folds out from the wall; and **bedrooms**, which are spacious cabins with two armchairs, large windows, a table, toilet, wardrobe and bunk bed. Meals are included in the price of all three sleeper-class categories. Ten percent **reductions** are available for the over-60s, and 2- to 15-year-olds pay half fare. A 25 percent (and sometimes even 40 percent) reduction applies on "Coach" travel from November to mid-December and early January to late April; a week's advance purchase is necessary. Passengers with certain types of disability and their companions are charged a single fare.

Non-North American visitors can cut fares by buying a **Canrailpass** (Can\$399; Can\$639 peak season – June to mid-Oct), which allows unlimited "Coach" class travel for 12 days within a 30-day period. There are discounts on passes for the under-25s, students with ISIC or similar card and the over-60s. You can add up to three days' extra travel for Can\$54 a day (Can\$32 off-peak), either in advance or at any time during the 30-day validity period. You should try to book places on trains once you have the pass, as places for those with passes are generally limited. For further details, VIA can be reached on the Internet (*www.viarail.ca*) and they also have an international network of ticket agents: in the UK and Ireland, contact Leisurail, PO Box 113, Peterborough PE3 8HY (☎0870/750 0222); in Australia, Thomas Cook World Rail (☎1300/361 941); and in New Zealand, Walshes World (☎09/379 3708). Canrail passes can also be purchased in Canada from any VIA Rail station.

BY BUS

If you're travelling on your own, and making a lot of stops, **buses** are by far the least expensive way to get around. The main long-distance service is **Greyhound** in both the US and Canada (though separate companies run the two national schedules). Greyhound buses link all major cities and many smaller towns in the Northwest, with Greyhound's BC and Alberta coverage being particularly extensive. The main exception is in the Yukon, where the Greyhound network stops at Whitehorse. More particularly in Canada, Greyhound services are supplemented by various smaller companies, nowhere more so than in the far north – see box overleaf. Shoestring and vaguely alternative buses are also a feature of the Yukon and Canadian Rockies national parks. Here, also, several enterprising companies provide inexpensive connections to trailheads, to hostels and between main towns. Check hostel infoboards or visitor centres for details, as such companies inevitably go in and out of business fairly quickly.

Out in the **countryside** and amongst the smaller towns, buses are fairly scarce, sometimes appearing only once a day, and here you'll need to plot your route with care. But along the **main highways**, buses run around the clock to a fairly full timetable, stopping only for meal breaks (almost always fast-food dives) and driver changeovers. Nearly all Greyhounds are non-smoking, have toilets and are less uncomfortable than you might expect – except perhaps in northern BC and the Yukon, where Greyhounds have only about a dozen seats, the rest of the bus being given over to freight. It's feasible to save on a night's accommodation by travelling overnight and sleeping on the bus – though you may not feel up to much the next day. To avoid possible hassle, lone female travellers in particular should take care to sit as near to the driver as possible, and to arrive during daylight hours, since bus stations are often in fairly dodgy areas.

It used to be that any sizeable community would have a **Greyhound station**, but these days many have had their bus depot closed, and the best you'll do is a shop or petrol station doubling as the bus stop and maybe ticket office. Neither can you expect the bus stop to be anywhere near the town centre. Furthermore, in some remoter settlements buses do not make scheduled stops at all, only halting at specified **flag stops** if there is anyone waiting; you must be sure of the correct location, as drivers are not obliged to stop anywhere else. Seats can be **reserved** – either in person at a bus station or on the toll-free number – but this is rarely necessary and only recommended on the busy, medium-haul inter-city services like the one between Seattle and Portland or Vancouver to Calgary. Even if you arrive to find a bus full, another bus will also be put on to take overflow passengers.

THE NORTHWEST'S PRINCIPAL BUS COMPANIES

Alaskan Express-Gray Line Yukon
(☎867/668-3225, *www.yukon.net/westours*).
Skagway, Whitehorse, Fairbanks and other
Alaskan destinations.

Brewster Transportation (☎403/762-6767 or
1-800/661-1152, *www.brewster.ca*). Services
Calgary, Calgary airport, Banff Lake Louise and
Jasper.

Clallam Transit (☎360/452-4511, *www
.clallamtransit.com*). Services around
Washington's Olympic Peninsula.

Dawson City Courier (☎867/993-6688).
Services from Whitehorse, Yukon and Dawson
City to Inuvik, NWT.

Greyhound America (☎1-800/231-2222,
www.greyhound.com). Services throughout
Washington and Oregon.

Greyhound Canada (☎403/265-9111
or 1-800/661-8747, *www.greyhound.ca*).

Long-distance buses across western
Canada.

Jefferson Transit (☎360/385-4777,
jeffersontransit.com). Services around
Washington's Olympic Peninsula.

Laidlaw (☎250/385-4411 or 1-800/318-0818,
www.victoriatours.com). Services on Vancouver
Island.

Pacific Coach Lines (☎604/662-8074 or
250/385-4411, *www.pacificcoach.com*). Services
in and around Vancouver, Vancouver Island and
on the Sunshine Coast.

Perimeter (☎604/261-2299, *www.perimeterbus
.com*).Services from Vancouver and Vancouver
airport to Squamish and Whistler.

Quick Shuttle (☎604/940-4428 or 1-800/665-
2122, *www.quickcoach.com*). Connections
between Sea-Tac Airport, Seattle, Bellingham,
Vancouver and Vancouver airport.

Greyhound fares are relatively inexpensive, but over long distances soon add up – for example, it costs around US$25 from Portland to Seattle, and Can$100 from Vancouver to Calgary. For long-trip travel riding the bus costs a little less than the train in both countries, though considering the time involved on some journeys – and the preponderance of discount airfares – it's not always that much cheaper than flying. However, the bus is the best deal if you plan to visit a lot of places: in the US, the domestic **Ameripass** (☎1-800/231-2222, *www.greyhound.com/ampass*) is good for unlimited travel nationwide for 7 days ($209), 10 days ($259), 15 days ($319), 30 days ($429), 45 days ($469) and 60 days ($599); discounts are available for children under 12, seniors over 62 and students enrolled in a college or university. To buy online, you must purchase your pass no fewer than 14 days prior to the start of travel. Otherwise you can purchase a pass at any participating Greyhound terminal or agency. The **reduced rates** for **passes for non-US citizens** only purchased abroad are shown below. Note that Greyhound's Ameripass is not valid for travel in Canada except for the **Seattle to Vancouver** route.

Greyhound's **Canada Pass** works in a similar way, allowing unlimited travel within a fixed time limit on almost all Greyhound Canada lines. Rates are 7 days (Can$220), 14 days (Can$295), 30 days

(Can$400) and 60 days (Can$510); the rates for passes purchased abroad are shown below. No daily extensions are available on either pass.

The free *Official Canadian Bus Guide*, containing all Canadian bus **timetables**, is produced bi-monthly but is not made readily available to travellers. It is pretty hefty anyway, so you are better off picking up free individual timetables from major bus stations. The US equivalent is the *Greyhound System Timetable*, but again this is hard to come by – you actually stand more chance of getting one from a Greyhound agent abroad than one in the US. Always double-check routes and times by phoning the local Greyhound terminal (we've included telephone numbers for most cities), or use their toll-free number – see the box above, which also gives the details of the region's smaller bus companies.

BUS PASSES BOUGHT ABROAD

Travellers intending to explore the Northwest by bus can save a lot of money by purchasing a **bus pass** before they reach North America. The **Greyhound International Canada Pass** allows unlimited travel within a fixed time limit on almost all Greyhound Canada lines, including Toronto–Vancouver on the Trans-Canada, and services in Alberta and mainland British Columbia. **Rates in Canadian dollars** exclusive of 7 percent GST tax are: 7 days within a 10-day period ($249); 15 days within a 20-day period ($379); 30 days within a 40-day period ($449); and 60 days within an 80-day period ($599). The following **rates in sterling** include two prices, the first the **discounted rate** available to students with ISIC cards, the second the normal **full cost** of the pass: 7 days (£98/109), 15 days (£149/165), 30 days (£176/195) and 60 days (£233/259).

In the US, the international **Greyhound Ameripass** for non-US citizens works in similar fashion, offering visitors bound for Oregon and Washington (and the rest of the US) unlimited travel within a set time limit. **Rates** in US dollars for online booking (*www.greyhound.com/ampass*) are: 7 days ($179), 10 days ($229), 15 days ($269), 30 days ($369), 45 days ($399) or 60 days ($499). Sterling rates for student discount and full-price passes are 4 days (£68/75), 5 days (£80/89), 7 days (£86/95), 10 days (£113/125), 15 days (£131/145), 30 days (£179/199), 45 days (£194/215) and 60 days (£242/269). If you wish to purchase online, then you must buy the pass no fewer than 21 days prior to the start of travel. International Ameripasses are not available from Greyhound terminals, but international passengers can purchase the domestic pass (see opposite) once they're in the US at the standard domestic rates. No daily extensions are available on either the Canadian or US pass.

Most travel agents can oblige with either or both passes, or in the UK you can apply to Greyhound (☎020/8939 5413, *www.greyhound .com*) and – good for student discounts – Usit CAMPUS (☎0870/240 1010, *www.campustravel .co.uk*). For agents in Ireland, contact SAYIT (☎021/279188); in Australia call CATS (☎02/9922 4600); and in New Zealand contact Greyhound International (☎09/479 6555).

BY PLANE

Clearly, taking a **plane** is much the quickest way to get about the Pacific Northwest. Several of the larger towns and, of course, the cities have airports and across the region the big international airlines – principally **Northwest Airlines** in Oregon and Washington and **Canadian** in Canada – compete with a plethora of smaller, regional companies. The busiest routes are Vancouver–Seattle–Portland and Vancouver–Calgary. Perhaps the most useful links for the visitor are those like Vancouver–Calgary – flights from the coast into the interior (or vice versa), sav-

ing hours if not days on the bus or in the car. Furthermore, if you plan ahead, flying can be reasonably economic when compared with the train or the bus – especially if you take into account how much you save not having to pay for food and drink while you're on the move. Air travel can also – as in the case of certain places in the Yukon – be the only way of getting where you want.

Most airlines offer comparable one-way and return fares, but any good travel agent, especially student and youth-oriented ones, can usually get you a much better deal. Phone the airlines to find out routes, schedules and fares, then buy your ticket using the **Fare Assurance Program**, which processes all the ticket options to find the cheapest fare, taking into account the requirements of individual travellers. Few stand-by fares are available, and the best discounts are usually offered on tickets booked and paid for at least two weeks in advance, which are almost always non-refundable and hard to change.

If you're planning to zip around the Northwest by plane, then you might consider purchasing an **airpass**. All the main US and Canadian airlines (and British Airways in conjunction with various carriers) offer airpasses. Conditions vary from airline to airline, but all share the same basic principles, notably that passes must be bought before you travel and with the proviso that you cross the Atlantic with the relevant airline. All the deals are broadly similar whether you are flying with US or Canadian carriers, and involve the purchase of between a minimum of three and maximum of ten flight **coupons**. **Air Canada**, for example, offers between three and eight coupons, and offers best rates on the pass if you cross the Atlantic with Air Canada or United. Rates are higher for other trans-Atlantic carriers, but these carriers can only be a non-North American airline such as British Airways. Three coupons bought in the UK would **cost** Can$519 in low season and Can$569 in high season (July–Aug); eight coupons would cost Can$869 or Can$994. Although tickets are purchased outside Canada (or the US), prices are always quoted in Canadian or US dollars and converted into the current sterling exchange. Coupons can be used for any routing, but **conditions** apply. These are similar across most airlines: in the case of Air Canada you must specify a routing (but not necessarily precise dates and flights) for all coupons at the time of purchase. The first routing cannot be changed, but subsequent routings may be altered for a fee.

See p.9 for a list of **toll-free airline numbers** in the US and Canada.

BY FERRY

Ferries play an important role in transportation in the Pacific Northwest – indeed, some of the islands that dot the region's long and fretted coastline can only be reached by boat. Around Seattle and Vancouver ferries transport thousands of commuters a day to and from work, but for visitors, they're a novelty: an exhilarating way to experience the sheer scenic splendour of the area. Ferry travel can be expensive, however, when you bring a car along.

The main ferry companies are **Washington State Ferries**, who operate a virtual monopoly on shorter crossings in and around the Puget Sound, and also connect with Sidney, on Canada's Vancouver Island; and **BC Ferries**, whose principal services link Prince Rupert with the Haida Gwaii (Queen Charlotte Islands), run between the Canadian mainland and Vancouver Island, and cover a section of the so-called **Inside Passage**, one of the most scenic waterways in the world. The American-run **Alaska Marine Highway** runs a long-distance voyage up the coast from Bellingham in Washington and Prince Rupert in BC to Skagway, in Alaska, along all of the Inside Passage; this is one of the finest cruises in the world. Foot passengers using any of these companies should have few problems boarding boats, but if you're taking a car and hope to grab a cabin on longer journeys with BC Ferries and the Alaska Marine Highway, you'll have to have booked places on summer sailings many months in advance. The same caution applies to any cross-border service offered by Washington State Ferries, but they do not operate a reservation system on any of their domestic routes. Contact the ferry companies directly for booking information (see box).

BC FERRIES

BC Ferries, also known as the "Friendship Fleet", operate some forty ships to serve more than forty ports of call along the coast of British Columbia, from tiny two-minute lake crossings in the interior to the endless shuttles that ply back and forth across the Georgia Strait between Vancouver and Vancouver Island. Its most popular sailing, however, is the *Queen of the North* boat, which operates year-round along a portion of the Inside Passage, taking around ten hours to connect Port Hardy on the northern tip of Vancouver Island (see box p.382) with Prince Rupert, where passengers can join Alaskan ferries heading north or VIA Rail trains setting off east through the Rockies. The ferry leaves four times weekly in summer, when reservations are strongly recommended, and once weekly in winter.

The company's other long-haul routes are the almost equally scenic Discovery Passage (see box p.383) and the seven-hour MV *Queen of Prince Rupert* ferry from Prince Rupert to the **Haida Gwaii** (Queen Charlotte Islands) (see box p.576), with daily sailings in summer. It also runs several boats from Vancouver to **Vancouver Island**: the most heavily used are the Tsawwassen to Swartz Bay (for Victoria), and Horseshoe Bay to Nanaimo crossings (see "Getting to Vancouver Island", p.328). Numerous smaller boats crisscross between the **Gulf Islands** that lie scattered between Vancouver Island and the BC mainland.

WASHINGTON STATE FERRIES AND OTHER FERRIES

Easily the largest of the other Northwest ferry companies is **Washington State Ferries**, whose commuter-oriented fleet of some twenty-five ferries handles more than 23 million passen-

---

NORTHWEST FERRY COMPANIES

Alaska Marine Highway From outside North America ☎907/465-3941, 250/627-1744 or 627-1745; from the US and Canada ☎1-800/642-0066.

BC Ferries In Victoria ☎604/386-3431; in Vancouver ☎1-888/223-3779; from outside BC ☎604/444-2890, www.bcferries.com.

Black Ball Transport In Port Angeles ☎360/457-4491; in Victoria ☎250/386-2202 or 1-800/633-1589, www.northolympic.com/coho.

Victoria Clipper In Victoria ☎250/382-8100; in Seattle ☎206/448-5000 or 1-800/888-2535 toll free outside Seattle and BC, www.victoria-clipper.com.

Victoria Express In Port Angeles ☎360/452-8088 or 1-800/633-1589 (May to Oct only).

Washington State Ferries In Seattle ☎206/464-6400; in Victoria ☎250/381-1551; in Sidney ☎250/656-1531.

gers per year. They run between Anacortes, Washington and Sidney, BC (for Victoria and Vancouver Island); from Anacortes to the San Juan Islands; from Port Townsend to Keystone on Whidbey Island; and between Seattle and points on the Kitsap Peninsula. Reservations are not accepted – except on cross-border services – and you should try to avoid peak commuter travel times.

Black Ball Transport runs from Port Angeles, Washington, to Victoria, with a crossing time of ninety minutes and no reservations, a crossing also made – in an hour – by **Victoria Express**. **Victoria Clipper** operates passenger-only jet catamarans between Seattle and Victoria daily. Two increasingly popular boats provide unforgettable trips off Vancouver Island: the MV *Lady Rose* from Port Alberni, which runs through the gorgeous seascapes of the Pacific Rim National Park (see p.362), and the *Uchuck III*, a World War II minesweeper-turned-ferry, which patrols the villages of the island's northwest coast (see p.379).

BY CAR

Although the weather may not always be ideal and parking in Seattle and Vancouver can be a pain, travelling by **car** is easily the best way to see the Pacific Northwest. Apart from anything else, a car makes it possible to choose your own itinerary and to explore the wide-open landscapes that may well provide your most enduring memories of the region.

The Northwest holds some of the continent's greatest highways, from the Rockies' awe-inspiring **Icefields Parkway** to frontier, wilderness routes like the **Cassiar Highway** through northern BC and the **Dempster** across the Arctic Circle. Further south, Washington boasts the **North Cascades Loop**, which enables travellers to penetrate the glaciated heart of the spectacular Cascade Mountains, while Oregon offers the dramatic bluffs and waterfalls of the **Historic Columbia River Highway** and the diverse beauty of the **Oregon Coastal Highway**. Even in the **cities**, a car remains by far the most convenient way to negotiate your way around – give or take the occasional parking problem – especially as public transport is generally scarce, though the big cities are on-the-up in this regard. Many Northwestern towns sprawl for so many miles in all directions that your hotel may be miles from the sights you came to see, or perhaps simply on the other side of a freeway which there's no way

See p.23 for advice on **car crime**.

of crossing on foot. Even in smaller places the motels may be six miles or more out along the highway, and the restaurants in a brand-new shopping mall on the far side of town.

In both Canada and the US, most vehicles – and almost every rental car – run on unleaded petrol, which is sold by the litre in Canada and by the gallon in the US; prices vary, but are generally around Can70–80¢ per litre, US$1.50 per gallon. **Fuel** is readily available – there are literally hundreds of petrol stations, though they thin out markedly in the more remote regions where you should exercise some caution by checking locally about the distance to the next one, and its opening hours.

The main **border crossing** between the US and Canada, by car, is on Interstate 5 (I-5) at Blaine, Washington, 30 miles south of Vancouver; immigration procedures are usually quick and simple, with the crossing open 24 hours a day. At other, more obscure entry points – and sometimes at this one – the duty officers can be real sticklers, so don't be amazed if you're delayed. For more on this see p.16.

BACKCOUNTRY DRIVING

The Northwest possesses an extraordinarily extensive and well-maintained network of **roads**, especially considering that the mountains which backbone the region experience the fiercest of winters. Every major and almost all minor towns and villages are reachable on a paved road, but for some of the scenic highlights you're likely to have to use rougher **forest roads** – usually paved, but sometimes not – and even gravel and dirt roads. These gravel-topped roads are often in poor condition and can be treacherously greasy when wet. Dust and flying stones represent major **hazards** too, as does subsidence caused by ice (**frost heaves**) and the thundering heavy lorries that use such routes with little regard for automobiles. **Weather** is another potential danger, with severe snow falls possible in some areas even in August, and dense fog plaguing the coast of Washington and Oregon. If you're planning to do a significant amount of driving along these **gravel and dirt roads**, then radiators and headlights should be protected from stones and insects with a wire screen and headlight covers.

Always carry a spare tire and fan belt, petrol can (preferably full), fill up at every opportunity, and check where the next petrol station is available (on the Cassiar or Dempster it could be literally hundreds of miles away). It goes without saying your car should be in excellent shape: it's also a good idea to carry flares, jack and a good set of tools and wrenches. These precautions may sound over the top, but after you've travelled a few wilderness roads, and seen the desolation to either side, they'll make more sense – and they might also save your life. Indeed, if you're planning a lot of dirt-road driving, you'd be well-advised to rent a four-wheel-drive or perhaps a pick-up. For information on car rental and back-country driving see opposite.

ROADS, RULES AND REGULATIONS

The best **roads** for covering long distances quickly are the straight and fast multi-lane highways which radiate out from major population centres. These are a maximum of six lanes divided by a central causeway and are marked on maps with thick lines and shields that contain the highway or US interstate number. Outside populated areas and off the principal arteries, highways go down to one lane each way and, though paved, the hard shoulder consists of gravel – which you must on all accounts avoid hitting at speed as this will throw you into a spin, a potentially lethal experience. Up in the north and off-the-beaten-track, forest roads and other byways may be gravel-topped – and broken windscreens are an occupational hazard (see "Backcountry Driving" overleaf). In Canada, the **Trans-Canada Highway** (TCH), which travels from coast to coast, is marked by maple-leaf signs at regular intervals along its length. Different sections of the TCH do, however, carry different highway numbers and in some places the TCH forks to offer more than one possible routing. In Washington and Oregon, the principal highways are the **interstates**. Across the region, lesser roads go by a variety of names – county roads, provincial routes, rural roads or forest roads – but for the most part we've used the general "highway" designation in the *Guide* unless a road's rough condition or other special feature prompts otherwise.

Americans and Canadians drive on the **right-hand** side of the road. In most **urban areas** streets are arranged on a grid system, often with octagonal "Stop" signs at all four corners of junctions: **priority** is given to the first car to arrive,

and to the car on the right if two or more cars arrive at the same time. Traffic in both directions must stop if a yellow school bus is stationary with its flashing lights on, as this means children are getting on or off.

Out of town, exits on multi-lane highways are numbered by the kilometre distance from the beginning of the highway, as opposed to sequentially – thus exit 55 is 10km after exit 45. This system works fine, but gets a little confusing when junctions are close together and carry the same number supplemented by "A" or "B" etc. Rural **road hazards** include bears, moose and other large animals lumbering onto the road – particularly in the summer, and at dawn and dusk, when the beasts crash through the undergrowth onto the highway to escape the flies, and in spring, when they are attracted to the salt on the roads. Warning signs are posted in the more hazardous areas. Headlights can dazzle wild animals and render them temporarily immobile.

The uniform **maximum speed limit** on major highways is 100kph in Canada or 65mph in the USA – though there has been some provincial/state tinkering with the maximum limit, experiments which may result in permanent change. Americans and Canadians have a justifiable paranoia about speed traps and the traffic-control planes that hover over major highways to catch offenders – if you see one, slow down. On-the-spot fines are standard for speeding violations, for failing to carry your **licence** with you, and for having anyone on board who isn't wearing a **seat belt**. Needless to say, **drunk driving** is punished severely – you'd be well-advised to keep any alcohol you're carrying in the boot of the car. On the road, spot checks are frequently carried out, and the police do not need an excuse to stop you. If you are over the limit your keys and licence will be taken away, and you may end up in jail for a few days.

In cities **parking meters** are commonplace. Car parks charge up to Can$35, US$25 a day. If you park in the wrong place (such as within five metres of a fire hydrant) your car will be towed away – if this happens, the police will tell you where your car is impounded and then charge you upwards of Can$150/US$100 to hand it back. A minor parking offence will set you back around Can$25/US$20; clamps are also routinely used in major cities.

If you're using your own vehicle – or borrowing a friend's – get the appropriate insurance and make sure you're covered for free **breakdown service**. Your home motoring organization – in the UK the RAC and AA – will issue an appropriate insurance and breakdown policy with all the appropriate documentation. The Canadian Automobile Association (☎613/820-1890 or 1-800/267-8713, www.caa.ca), is the biggest recovery and repair company in Canada, and has offices in most major cities. The US equivalent is the AAA (☎1-800/AAA-HELP or 1-800/222-4357, www.aaa.com), again with offices in most major cities.

CAR RENTAL

Conditions for **renting a car** – including the names of the rental companies – are virtually identical in both Canada and the US. Any US, Canadian and UK national over 21 with a full driving licence is allowed to drive in the Northwest, though rental companies may refuse to rent to a driver who has held a full licence for less than one year, and under-25s will get lumbered with a higher insurance premium. Car rental companies will also expect you to have a credit card; if you don't have one they may let you leave a hefty **deposit** (at least $300), but don't count on it. The driving licences of other countries are recognised throughout the Pacific Northwest too – check with your home motoring organization. It is vital to note, also, that the majority of car rental companies are going to be extremely reluctant to rent cars if they know you're intending to travel on gravel roads (don't think they won't notice if you do – the dents in the paintwork will be a dead giveaway). Ask what arrangements they might be able to make, and if they refuse, rent a car from a backcountry-based outlet: they tend to be more understanding and their cars are probably both more robust and more battered into the bargain. Pick-ups and four-wheel-drives are worth considering too. Incidentally, note that standard rental cars have **automatic transmissions** and that if you're renting a car in winter, you should check where and if chains and other tackle are required or advised.

Often the least expensive way to rent a car is either to take a fly-drive package (see p.5) or book in advance with a major rental company like Avis, Budget, Hertz or Thrifty. Specialist agents can also offer economical deals – in the UK, Holiday Autos (☎0990/300428) are particularly good. Bear in mind also that at the height of the season, in the more popular tourist areas, it's by no means uncommon to find that you can't locate an available vehicle for love nor money – another reason to book ahead. Amongst the big car rental companies, competition is fierce and, as you might expect, special deals are more commonplace in the shoulder- and low-season when there are scores of vehicles lying idle, though note that rates are consistently higher on the islands and in the wilderness north than they are in the city. It's always worth ringing round to check rates – Alamo and Budget usually have competitive tariffs: reckon on a ballpark figure of Can$200/US$150 a week for their **cheapest vehicles** with unlimited mileage. Finally, if you take a transatlantic flight, check to see if your airline offers discounted car rental for its passengers.

In the Pacific Northwest itself, expect to pay from around Can$200/US$150 a week for a two-door economy saloon in low season to Can$350/US$250 for a four-door medium car in high season, though throughout the year special promotions are offered by the major companies, which can get rates down to as low as Can$150/US$110 per week. **Taxes** are extra, but the biggest **hidden surcharge** is often the **drop-off charge**, levied when you intend to leave your car in a different place from where you picked it up. This is usually equivalent to a full week's or more rental, and can go as high as Can$500/US$350. Also be sure to check if **unlimited mileage** is offered, an important consideration in a region where towns are so widely dispersed: the usual free quota is 150–200km/100–150miles per day – woefully inadequate if you're contemplating some serious touring – after which an extra charge of around Can20¢/US15¢ per kilometre is fairly standard.

You should also check the policy for the excess applied to claims and ensure that, in general terms, it provides adequate levels of financial cover. Additionally, the **Loss Damage Waiver** (LDW) – sometimes called the Collision Damage Waiver (CDW) – is a form of insurance which isn't included in the initial rental charge, but is well worth the expense. At around Can$16/US$12 a day, it can add substantially to the total cost, but without it you're liable for every scratch to the car – even if it wasn't your fault.

For **breakdown** problems, there'll be an emergency number attached to the dashboard or stored in the glove compartment. If you're stranded on a main road, you could do as well to sit tight

MAJOR CAR RENTAL COMPANIES

NORTH AMERICA

Alamo domestic ☎1-800/354-2322, international ☎1-800/522-9696, *www.goalamo.com*

Avis domestic ☎1-800/331-1212, international ☎1-800/331-1084, *www.avis.com*

Budget ☎1-800/527-0700, *www .budgetrentacar.com*

Dollar ☎1-800/800-4000, *www.dollar.com*

Hertz domestic ☎1-800/654-3131, international ☎1-800/654-3001, *www.hertz.com*

National ☎1-800/CAR-RENT, *www .nationalcar.com*

Rent-A-Wreck ☎1-800/535-1391, *www.rent/a /wreck.com*

Thrifty ☎1-800/367-2277, *www.thrifty.com*

US Rent-a-Car ☎1-800/777-9377, *www .us-rentacar.com*

UK

Avis ☎0990/900500
Budget ☎0800/181181
Hertz ☎0990/996699
Holiday Autos ☎0990/300400

National ☎01895/233300
Thrifty ☎0990/168238

IRELAND

Avis Northern Ireland ☎0990/900500, Republic ☎01/605 7500

Budget Rent-A-Car Northern Ireland ☎0800/181181, Republic ☎0800/973159

Hertz Northern Ireland ☎0990/996699, Republic ☎01/676 7476

Holiday Autos Northern Ireland ☎0990/300400, Republic ☎01/872 9366

AUSTRALIA

Avis ☎13 6333
Budget ☎1300/362 848
Hertz ☎1800/550 067

NEW ZEALAND

Avis ☎09/526 5231 or 0800/655 111
Budget ☎0800/652 227
Hertz ☎09/309 0989 or 0800/655 955

and wait for the police who cruise by fairly regularly. An extra safety option is to rent a **mobile telephone** from the car rental agency – you often only have to pay a nominal amount unless you actually use it. Having a mobile can be reassuring at least, and a potential life-saver for trips into the wilderness. Speaking of life-savers, **air conditioning** can turn a hot, sweaty journey across, say, the sagebrush desert of eastern Oregon into an enjoyable, if long-winded, drive.

Finally, if you take a rental car **across the US–Canada border**, be sure to keep a copy of the contract with you. It should bear an endorsement stating that the vehicle is permitted entry into the States or Canada.

DRIVEAWAYS

A variation on car rental is a **driveaway**, whereby you drive a car from one place to another on behalf of the owner. The same rules as for renting apply, but you should look the car over before taking it as you'll be lumbered with any repair costs and a large fuel bill if the vehicle's a big drinker.

Most driveaway companies will want you to give a personal reference as well as a deposit in the Can$200–400/US$150–300 region. In Canada, the most common route to the Northwest is along the Trans-Canada Highway to Vancouver, whilst in the US there's often call for people to drive vehicles from one of the big eastern cities to Seattle. That said, there's a fair chance you'll find something that needs shifting more or less to where you want to go. You needn't drive flat out, although not a lot of leeway is given – around eight days is the allocation for driving from Toronto to Vancouver. Driveaway companies are included in some city listings, or check under "Automobile Driveaways" or "Automobile Transporters" in the *Yellow Pages*; phone around for current offers. In the US, Auto Driveaway, based at 310 S Michigan Ave, Chicago, IL 60604 (☎312/341-1900), has over sixty branches.

RENTING AN RV

Recreational vehicles (RVs) can be rented through most travel agents who specialize in US and Canadian holidays. It's best to arrange rental before getting to the Pacific Northwest, as RV rental outlets are not too common there (most people who drive them, own them), and foreign

HITCHHIKING

The usual advice given to **hitchhikers** is that they should use their common sense, in fact, of course, common sense should tell anyone that hitchhiking in the United States or Canada is a bad idea. We do not recommend it under any circumstances.

travel agents will often give cheap rates if you book a flight through them as well. You can rent a huge variety of RVs right up to giant mobile homes with two bedrooms, showers and fully-fitted kitchens. A price of around US$900/Can$1200 in low and US$1400/Can$1900 in high season for a five-berth van for one week is fairly typical, and on top of that you have to take into account the cost of fuel (some RVs do less than fifteen miles to the litre/twelve miles to the gallon), drop-off charges, and the cost of spending the night at designated trailer parks, which is what you're expected to do. Regulations for dumping and overnighting are especially strict in all national, state and provincial parks. Canada and the US also have strict but different regulations on the size of vehicle allowed: if you're planning to venture into both countries, check the regulations with your travel agent. The best UK-based rental company is Hemmingways Ltd, 56 Middle St, Brockham, Surrey RH3 7HW (☎01737/842735), with various packages and pick-up points.

BY BIKE

As a rule, **cycling** is an affordable and healthy method to get around the Pacific Northwest, whether it's in the parks – you'll find that most have rental outlets and designated mountain-bike trails – or in the big **cities**, all three of which have (at least some) cycle lanes. In **country areas**, roads are usually well maintained and many have wide shoulders. For casual riding, bikes can be **rented** by the hour, half-day, full day or, sometimes, by the week. Rates vary considerably depending on the type of bike you rent: reckon on US$15 to US$35 per day. Outlets are usually found close to beaches, parks, university campuses, or simply in areas that are good for cycling. Local visitor centres should have the details. If you're taking a bike round with you, Greyhound will take bikes (so long as they're in a box), and VIA Rail and Amtrak make small charges for their transportation. Carriage charges on ferries are reasonable too, but the terms of transportation and costs do vary considerably – check with individual companies (see "By Ferry", p.40). A number of companies across the region organise multi-day cycle tours, either camping out or staying in country inns, we've mentioned local firms where appropriate. Oregon, in particular, excels itself with its cycling routes, and boasts the outstandingly scenic and well-maintained **Oregon Coast Bike Route**, which runs right along the state's 360-mile shoreline, a detailed brochure is available from the Oregon tourist office. All the region's state and provincial tourist offices provide general cycling information – their addresses are on p.30.

Before setting out on a **long-distance cycling** trip, you'll need a good-quality, multi-speed bike, panniers, tools and spares, maps, padded shorts, a **helmet** (not a legal obligation but a very good idea), and a route avoiding major highways and interstates (on which cycling is unpleasant and usually illegal). Of **problems** you'll encounter, the main one is traffic – RVs driven by people who can't judge their width, and huge eighteen-wheelers (especially logging trucks) which scream past and create intense back-draughts capable of pulling you out into the middle of the road.

TRAVELLERS WITH DISABILITIES

The US and Canada are extremely accommodating for travellers with mobility problems or other physical disabilities. All public buildings have to be wheelchair accessible and provide suitable toilet facilities, almost all street corners have dropped kerbs, public telephones are specially equipped for hearing-aid users, and most public transport systems have such facilities as subways with elevators, and buses that "kneel" to let people board.

INFORMATION

Most states and provinces provide information for disabled travellers – contact the tourism departments on p.30. In **Canada** the Canadian Paraplegic Association can provide a wealth of information on travelling in specific provinces, and most of its regional offices produce a free guide on the most easily accessed sights. Provincial tourist offices are also excellent sources of information on accessible hotels, motels and sights: some also supply special free guides. You may also want to get in touch with Kéroul in Montréal (see box opposite), an organisation which specializes in travel for mobility-impaired people, and publishes the bilingual guide *Accès Tourisme* (Can$15 plus $3 postage). Twin Peaks Press, PO Box 129, Vancouver WA 98666 (☎360/694-2462), also publishes useful guides: the *Directory of Travel Agencies for the Disabled* (Can$19.95) which lists more than 370 agencies worldwide, *Travel for the Disabled* (Can$19.95) and the *Directory of Accessible Van Rentals* and *Wheelchair Vagabond* (Can$14.95), all of which are loaded with handy tips.

Among national organisations in the **United States** are SATH, the Society for the Advancement of Travel for the Handicapped (347 Fifth Ave, Suite 610, New York, NY 10016, ☎212/447-7284), a non-profit travel-industry grouping that includes travel agents, tour operators, hotel and airline management, and people with disabilities. They will pass on any enquiry to the appropriate member, allow plenty of time for a response. Mobility International USA (PO Box 10767, Eugene, OR 97440, ☎541/343-1284) offers travel tips to members ($25 a year) and operates an exchange programme for disabled people.

The Golden Access Passport, issued free to US citizens with permanent disabilities, gives free lifetime admission to all **national parks**. *Easy Access to National Parks*, by Wendy Roth and Michael Tompane (Sierra Club, $15), explores every national park from the point of view of people with disabilities, senior citizens and families with children. *Disabled Outdoors* is a quarterly magazine specialising in facilities for disabled travellers who wish to get into the countryside, its office serves as a clearing house for all related information.

Larger **hotels**, including most Holiday Inns, have at least one or two suites designed specifically for their disabled guests, and the entire Red Roof, Best Western, Embassy Suites, Radisson and Journey's End chains are fully accessible to travellers with disabilities. Motel 6 is a budget chain with access at most of its locations.

GETTING AROUND

In order to obtain a Canadian **parking privilege permit**, drivers with disabilities must complete the appropriate form from the province in question. Contact addresses and organisations vary from province to province, though the permit, once obtained from one province, is valid across Canada. Contact provincial tourist offices for details. In British Columbia you should contact the Social Planning and Research Council of British Columbia, 106-2182 W 12th Ave, Vancouver, BC V6K 2N4 (☎604/718-7733 or 718-7744). Their conditions are typical: enclose a letter with name, address, phone number and date of birth, the medical name of the disabling condition, a letter from a doctor with original signature (not a photocopy) stating the disability that makes it difficult for a person to walk more than 100m and whether the prognosis is temporary or permanent. You should also include date of arrival and departure in Canada, a contact address if known, a mailing address for the permit to be sent to, date and signature, and a cheque or money order (call for latest charge) to cover processing.

The larger **car rental** companies, like Hertz and Avis, can provide cars with hand controls at no extra charge, though these are only available on their most expensive models, book one as far in advance as you can – Hertz insists on the

CONTACTS FOR TRAVELLERS WITH DISABILITIES

AUSTRALIA AND NEW ZEALAND

ACROD (Australian Council for Rehabilitation of the Disabled), PO Box 60, Curtin, ACT 2605, (☎02/6282 4333); 24 Cabarita Rd, Cabarita, NSW 2137 (☎02/9743 2699). Provides lists of travel agencies and tour operators for people with disabilities.

Barrier Free Travel, 36 Wheatley St, North Bellingen, NSW 2454 (☎02/6655 1733). Independent consultant – draws up individual itineraries for people with disabilities for a fee.

Disabled Persons Assembly, 4/173–175 Victoria St, Wellington (☎04/801 9100). Resource centre with lists of travel agencies and tour operators for people with disabilities.

BRITAIN

Holiday Care Service, 2nd Floor, Imperial Buildings, Victoria Rd, Horley, Surrey RH6 7PZ (☎01293/774535, fax 784647). Information on all aspects of travel.

RADAR, Unit 12, City Forum, 250 City Rd, London EC1V 8AF (☎020/7250 3222). A good source of advice on holidays and travel abroad.

Tripscope, The Courtyard, Evelyn Rd, London W4 5JH (☎020/8580 7021). Offers advice and information on travel for sick, elderly and disabled people.

CANADA

BC Coalition of People with Disabilities, 204–456 W Broadway, Vancouver, BC (☎604/875-0188). Offers advice and assistance for travellers in BC.

Canadian Paraplegic Association, main office is at Suite 320, 1101 Prince of Wales Drive, Ottawa, ON, K2C 3W7 (☎613/723-1033, fax 723-1060, and there are offices in every province; 520 Sutherland Drive, Toronto, ON M4G 3V9 (☎416/422-5644); 780 SW Marine Drive, Vancouver, BC V6P 5YT (☎604/342-3611); 825 Sherbrook St, Winnipeg, MB (☎204/786-4753).

Jewish Rehabilitation Hospital, 3205 Place Alton Goldbloom, Chomedy Laval, PQ H7V 1R2 (☎450/688-9550 ext 226). Guidebooks and travel information.

Kéroul, 4545 Pierre-de-Courbetin, CP 1000, Montréal (☎514/252-3104, *www.keroul.qc.ca*).

VIA Rail, Information and reservations for the speech and/or hearing impaired are available on ☎416/368-6406 from Toronto, ☎1-800/268-9503 from elsewhere.

Western Institute for the Deaf, 2125 W Seventh Ave, Vancouver, BC V6K 1X9 (☎604/736-7391 or 736-2527). Gives advice for the hearing-impaired.

USA

Access First Travel, 239 Commercial St, Malden, MA 02148 (☎1-800/557 2047). Current information for disabled travellers.

Directions Unlimited, 123 Green Lane, Bedford Hills, NY 10507 (☎1-800/533-5343). Tour operator specialising in custom tours for people with disabilities.

Mobility International USA, PO Box 10767, Eugene, OR 97440 (☎541/343-1284 voice and TDD, *www.miusa.com*). Information and referral services, access guides, tours and exchange programmes. Annual membership $25 (includes quarterly newsletter).

Society for the Advancement of Travel for the Handicapped (SATH), 347 Fifth Ave, Suite 610, New York, NY 10016 (☎212/447-7284, *www.sath.org*). Non-profit-making travel industry referral service that passes queries on to its members as appropriate.

Travel Information Service (☎215/456-9600). Telephone only information and referral service for disabled travellers.

Wheels Up!, PO Box 5197, Plant City, FL 33564-5197 (☎1-888/389-4335, *www.wheelsup.com*). Provides discounted airfare, tour and cruise prices for disabled travellers, also publishes a free monthly newsletter and has a comprehensive Web site.

---

request being made five days before the car is needed and supplies are limited. A wheelchair-accessible coach with hydraulic lift and on-board accessible toilet can be rented from National Motor Coach Systems, Box 3220, Station B, Calgary, AB T2M 4L7 (☎403/240-1992). The American Automobile Association produces the *Handicapped Driver's Mobility Guide* for disabled drivers (available from Quantum-Precision Inc, 225 Broadway, Suite 3404, New York, NY 10007).

Most **airlines**, transatlantic and domestic, do whatever they can to ease your journey, and will usually let attendants of more seriously disabled people accompany them at no extra charge. (Air Canada is the best-equipped Canadian carrier.)

Almost every **Amtrak train** includes one or more coaches with accommodation for handicapped passengers. **VIA Rail** offer a particularly outstanding service: apart from considerable support and help, all trains can accommodate wheelchairs that are no larger than 81cm by 182cm and weigh no more than 114kg without notice. Guide dogs travel free and may accompany blind passengers in the carriage. Try to give 24-hours' notice. Hearing or speech-impaired passengers can get information from Amtrak on ☎1-800/523-6590, and from VIA Rail on ☎ 1-800/268-9503.

Greyhound, however, is not to be recommended. Buses are not equipped with lifts for wheelchairs, though staff will assist with boarding (intercity carriers are required by law to do this), and the "Helping Hand" scheme offers two-for-the-price-of-one tickets to passengers unable to travel alone (carry a doctor's certificate). Greyhound in Canada allow free travel for companions of blind passengers. The American Public Transit Association, 1201 New York Ave, Suite 400, Washington, DC 20005 (☎202/898-4000), provides information about the accessibility of public transportation in cities.

Both BC Ferries and the Alaska Marine Highway offer discount cards to disabled travellers on their **ferries**, for a few dollars the latter also offers a two-year pass good for free stand-by travel on all boats from October to April, and on some boats from May to September. BC Ferries allow a companion to travel free unless the disabled passenger is taking a car onto the ferry. For full details contact the companies directly (see p.40).

TRAVELLING WITH CHILDREN

Travelling with kids in the more populated parts of the Pacific Northwest is relatively problem-free, children are readily accepted – indeed welcomed – in public places across the region, hotels and motels are well used to them, most state and national parks organise children's activities, and virtually every town or city has clean and safe playgrounds.

Restaurants often try hard to lure parents in with their kids. Most of the national chains offer high chairs and a special menu, packed with huge, excellent-value (if not necessarily healthy) meals – cheeseburger and fries for 99¢, and so on. Virtually all **museums** and tourist attractions offer reduced rates for kids. Most large cities have natural history museums or aquariums, and quite a few have hands-on children's museums. State, city or provincial **tourist offices** can provide specific information and ideas on activities or sights that are likely to appeal to children. A huge range of books and guides are also now available on the subject.

GETTING AROUND

Children under 2 **fly free** on domestic routes, and usually for 10 percent of the adult fare on inter-national flights – though that doesn't mean they necessarily get a seat. When aged from 2 to 12 they are usually entitled to half-price tickets.

Travelling **by bus** may be the cheapest way to go, but it's also the most uncomfortable for kids. Under-2s travel (on your lap) for free, ages 2 to 4 are usually charged 10 percent of the adult fare, as are any toddlers who take up a seat. Children under 12 are charged half the standard fare.

Even if you discount the romance of rail travel, **taking the train** is by far the best option for long journeys – not only does everyone get to enjoy the scenery, but you can get up and walk around, relieving pent-up energy. Most cross-country trains have sleeping compartments, which may be quite expensive but are a great adventure. Children's discounts are much the same as for bus or plane travel.

Most families choose to travel **by car**, but if you're hoping to enjoy a driving holiday with your kids, it's essential to plan ahead. Don't set yourself unrealistic targets, pack plenty of sensible snacks and drinks, plan to stop (don't make your kids make you stop) every couple of hours, arrive at your destination well before sunset, and avoid travelling through big cities during rush hour. Also, it can be a good idea to give an older child some responsibility for route-finding – having someone "play navigator" is good fun, educational and often a real help to the driver. If you're doing a fly-drive vacation, note that when **renting a car** the company is legally obliged to provide free car seats for kids.

Recreational Vehicles (RVs) are also a good option for family travel, successfully combining the convenience of built-in kitchens and bedrooms with the freedom of the road (see "Getting Around" on p.44).

WOMEN TRAVELLERS

Women's support centres, bookstores, bars and organisations across the Northwest provide testimony to the continuing, and widespread commitment to female emancipation in the US and Canada.

Practically speaking, a woman **travelling alone** in the Northwest, especially in cities such as Seattle and Vancouver, is not usually made to feel conspicuous, or liable to attract unwelcome attention. But as with anywhere, particular care has to be taken at night: walking through unlit, empty streets is never a good idea, and if there's no bus service, take cabs.

In the major urban centres, provided you listen to advice and stick to the better parts of town, going into **bars** and **clubs** alone should pose few problems: there's generally a pretty healthy attitude towards women who do so and your privacy will be respected. Gay and lesbian bars are usually a trouble-free and welcoming alternative.

However, **small towns** and mining and lumber centres in the north and interior are not blessed with the same liberal or indifferent attitudes toward lone women travellers. People seem to

jump immediately to the conclusion that your car has broken down, or that you've suffered some terrible tragedy, in fact, you may get fed up with well-meant offers of help. If your **vehicle breaks down** in a country area, walk to the nearest house or town for help, on interstate highways or heavily travelled roads, wait in the car for a police or highway patrol car to arrive. One increasingly available option is to rent a portable telephone with your car, for a small additional charge – a potential lifesaver.

As in the rest of the US **rape** is a very real danger and it goes without saying that you should **never hitch** alone – this is widely interpreted as an invitation for trouble, and there's no shortage of weirdos prepared to provide it. Similarly, if you have a car, be careful who you pick up: just because you're in the driving seat doesn't mean you're safe. Avoid travelling alone at night by public transport – deserted bus stations, if not actually threatening, will do little to make you feel secure – and wherever possible you should team up with a fellow traveller. There really is security in numbers. On Greyhound buses, follow the example of other lone women and sit as near

WOMEN'S TRAVEL SPECIALISTS IN THE US

Call of the Wild, 2519 Cedar St, Berkeley, CA 94708 (☎510/849-9292). Tour operator offering hiking adventures for women of all ages and abilities. Trips include visits to aboriginal peoples' ruins, backpacking in Californian national parks, cross-country skiing, dog-sledding and some jaunts to Hawaii.

Womanship, The Boathouse, 410 Severn Ave, Annapolis, MD 21403 (☎410/267-6661). Live-aboard, learn-to-sail cruises for women of all ages. Destinations include the Pacific Northwest and elsewhere. Choice of 3- 5- or 7-day trips.

to the front – and the driver – as possible (new booking schemes make it possible to select seats in such positions in advance, see "By Bus" p.37). Should disaster strike, all big cities and the larger towns have some kind of rape counselling service, if not, the local RCMP or sheriff's office should arrange for you to get help and counselling, and, if necessary, get you home.

In the States a central group protests women's issues, lobbying by the **National Organization for Women** (featuring Gloria Steinem and Betty Friedan) has done much to effect positive legislation. NOW branches, listed in local phone directories, can provide referrals for specific concerns such as rape crisis centres and counselling services, feminist bookstores and lesbian bars.

Further material can be found in Ferrari Guides' *Women's Travel in Your Pocket* (US$14, Ferrari Publications, PO Box 37887, Phoenix, AZ 85069, ☎602/863-2408), an annual guide for women travelling in the US, Canada, the Caribbean and Mexico.

GAY AND LESBIAN TRAVELLERS

The big cities of the Pacific Northwest have healthy and conspicuous gay scenes – gay life in Seattle centres on Capitol Hill, in Vancouver it's based around Denham and Davie, and Portland too has a number of gay and lesbian bars and clubs. In many backwoods Northwest towns, though, old prejudices die hard.

For all its high profile in the cities, the gay community tends to be more of a forceful pressure group rather than the major power-player it is, say, in San Francisco. Gay politicians, and even police officers, are however more than a novelty, and representation at most levels is a reality.

Things change as quickly in the gay and lesbian scene as they do everywhere else, but we've tried to give an overview of local **resources**, **bars** and **clubs** in each of the major cities. But head into the backwoods in both countries and life more than looks like the Fifties – away from large cities homosexuals are still oppressed and commonly reviled, and gay travellers would regrettably be well advised to watch their step to avoid hassles and possible aggression.

Publications to look out for, most of which are available from any good bookstore, include the range of guides produced by The Damron Company (☎1-800/462-6654 or 415/255-0404, *www.damron.com*). These include the *Address Book* (US$15.95), a pocket-sized yearbook full of listings of hotels, bars, clubs and resources for gay men; and the *Women's Traveler*, which provides similar listings for lesbians (US$12.95). Other works to check out are the travel books published by **Ferrari** (☎602/863-2408, *www.q-net.com*). Also, keep a look out for the free *Columbia Fun Maps* – available at bars, clubs and bookstores – that highlight gay-friendly establishments in the larger cities.

The Advocate (US$3.95; *www.advocate.com*) is a bimonthly national gay news magazine, with features, general info and classified ads (not to be confused with *Advocate Men*, which is a soft-porn magazine). The nation's most widely circulated gay and lesbian publication, *Out* (US$4.95), is more progressive, though since it has recently been purchased by *The Advocate*, it remains to be seen how editorial content will be affected. *Instinct* (*www.instinctmag.com*) and *Genre* (*www.genremag.com*) are two more popular (if somewhat fluffy) nationals for gay men. For women, *Curve* (*www.curve.com*) is the leader, with *Girlfriends* (*www.girlfriends.com*) running not far behind. Another useful lesbian publication is *Gaia's Guide* (132 W 24th St, New York, NY 10014; $6.95), a yearly international directory with a lot of US information.

ACCOMMODATION

Accommodation costs will form a significant proportion of the expenses for any traveller exploring the Northwest. Depending on your priorities, you may choose to economise by concentrating on the wide range of budget accommodation detailed in this book, but we've also tried to highlight as many as we can of the truly memorable hotels and B&Bs that are scattered throughout the region.

At the bottom of the accommodation pile, price-wise, are campsites and hostel dormitory beds, though be warned that both are heavily used in the Northwest's major cities and resorts. **Campsite** rates range from free to around $30 in both countries: beds in a **hostel** in the US or Canada usually cost between US$10 and US$25. However, with basic room prices away from the major cities starting at around US$30 per night, groups of two or more will find it little more

expensive to stay in the far more abundant motels and hotels. Many places will set up a third single bed for around US$10 on top of the regular price, reducing costs for three people sharing. On the other hand, the lone traveller will have a hard time of it: "singles" are usually double rooms at an only slightly reduced rate.

Since inexpensive beds in tourist areas tend to be taken up quickly, **always reserve in advance**, especially in cities and in and around the region's national parks. Also look out for local events and festivals such as the Calgary Stampede, when beds will be even harder to find at such times. If you get stuck try **visitor centres**: most offer free advice and will either book accommodation for you or perhaps provide a "courtesy phone" to call round after vacancies. Big resorts, like Banff and Lake Louise in the Rockies, often have privately run central reservations agencies which will (for a fee) find you a room in your chosen price range.

Reservations can be made over the phone by credit card (see box on p.53 for UK contact numbers of North American chains). Wherever possible take advantage of toll-free numbers, but note that almost all are accessible only in restricted areas, typically a single province or state across Canada, within mainland US or in North America only; if you call them from abroad you'll either pay international call rates or find the number is unobtainable. Reservations are only held until 5pm or 6pm unless you've told the hotel you'll be

---

ACCOMMODATION PRICE CODES

Throughout this book, accommodation prices have been graded with the symbols below, according to the cost of the least expensive double room.

However, with the exception of the budget motels and lowliest hotels, there's rarely such a thing as a set rate for a room. A basic motel in a seaside or mountain resort may double its prices according to the season, while a big-city hotel in Seattle or Vancouver which charges $200 per room during the week will often slash its tariff at the weekend when all the business types have gone home. As the high and low seasons for tourists vary widely across the region – as a rule prices are higher the further north you go – astute planning can save a lot of money. Remember, too, that a third person in a double room usually costs only a few dollars more.

Only where we explicitly say so do these room rates include local taxes.

① up to US$30	up to Can$40	⑤ US$80–100	Can$100–125
② US$30–45	Can$40–60	⑥ US$100–130	Can$125–175
③ US$45–60	Can$60–80	⑦ US$130–180	Can$175–240
④ US$60–80	Can$80–100	⑧ US$180+	Can$240+

DISCOUNT VOUCHERS

For the benefit of overseas travellers, many of the higher-rung hotel chains offer **prepaid discount vouchers**, which in theory save you money if you're prepared to pay in advance. To take advantage of such schemes, British travellers must purchase the vouchers in the UK, at a usual cost of between £30 and £60 per night for a minimum of two people sharing. However, the money you may save is counterbalanced by a loss in flexibility and the dullness in staying with the same hotel chain wherever you go. Good-value accommodation is not difficult to find in the Northwest.

Chains currently running voucher schemes include Best Western ("North American Guestcheque"), Ramada ("Freedom Hotel Pass"), Days Inn ("Go as You Please Hotelpass") and the linked Howard Johnson, Ramada and Super 8 "Liberty Pass". For details of UK contact numbers, for information or to purchase vouchers see the box opposite.

arriving late – be sure to stress the fact if you know you're going to be late.

It can also be worth confirming check-in/check-out times, particularly in busy areas, where your room may not be available until late afternoon. Check-out times are generally between 11am and 1pm. Be certain to **cancel any bookings** you can't make, otherwise the hotel or motel is within its right to deduct a night's fee using your credit card details. Most places have a 24-hour notice cancellation policy, but in places like Banff it can be as much as three days.

Wherever you stay, you'll be expected to **pay in advance**, at least for the first night and perhaps for further nights too, particularly if it's high season and the hotel's expecting to be busy. Payment can be in cash or in travellers' cheques, though it's more common to give a credit-card imprint and sign for everything when you leave. Virtually every state and province has a sales or **room tax**: all go under different names, but all have the effect of adding a few dollars to the advertised price of a room.

HOTELS

Hotels in both Canada and the United States tend to fall into three categories: high-class five-star establishments in big cities and major resort areas, mid-range, often chain-owned establishments, and grim downtown places, often above a bar.

Top-of-the range hotels can be very grand indeed, catering to rich tourists in the resorts and business travellers in the cities. Rooms in high season cost anywhere between US$150 and US$500, though US$250 would get you a first-class double anywhere in the Northwest. It's always worth enquiring about midweek reductions and out-of-season discounts, as these can reduce rates to as low as $100 a night. If you are going to treat yourself, consider whether you want the sort of old-style comfort and building offered by traditional hotels or the high-tech polish provided by the new breed of luxury hotel: most cities and some resorts have both types.

Mid-range Canadian and American hotels usually belong to one of the big chains, and offer standard-issue modern facilities, often in a downtown location. In most cases, though, mid-range hotels are thin on the ground, their role often being filled by motels. You should be able to find a high-season double in this price bracket for around US$80/Can$80–150.

Bottom-bracket hotels – those costing around US$25 to US$40 – are mostly hangovers from the days when liquor laws made it difficult to run a bar without an adjoining restaurant or hotel. Found in many medium- and small-sized towns, they have the advantage of being extremely central – often they've been there since the town first sprang to life – but the disadvantage is that the money-generating bars come first, with the rooms usually an afterthought. Many have live music likely to pound until the small hours, and few pay much attention to their guests, many of whom are long-stay clients as seedy as the hotel itself. Rooms are mostly battered but clean, and probably won't have much in the way of facilities beyond a wash basin and TV. Basic meals are often on hand in the bar, though you'd usually do better to eat in a nearby café or restaurant.

MOTELS

It is consistently easy to find a basic **motel** room in most of the Northwest. Drivers approaching any significant town are confronted by lines of motels along the highway, with prominent neon

HOTEL, HOSTEL AND MOTEL CHAINS

Many of the hotel and lodging chains listed below are found all over the Northwest, and publish handy free directories (with maps and illustrations) of their properties. If you stay one night in one of their properties, many offer discounts on subsequent overnight stops in their establishments elsewhere. Although we've indicated typical room rates (using the codes explained on p.51), bear in mind that the location of a particular hotel or motel has a huge impact on the price: as a general rule, the further from downtown, the cheaper the room.

The toll-free 1-800 numbers usually only apply in North America: from Britain, Ireland and elsewhere you pay normal international rates. However, some of the chains have UK contact numbers which can be used to book hotels in the US and Canada. Where applicable we've listed these UK contact numbers (prefixed 0800, 020, 01483 or 0845) and the toll-free numbers in the US and Canada (1-800). Note that *www.hotelchoice.com* will access a large number of North American chain hotels.

Baymont Inns & Suites (③) ☎1-800/428-3438, *www.baymontinns.com*

Best Western (③–⑥) ☎0800/393130, ☎1-800/528-1234, *www.bestwestern.com*

Canadian Pacific-Fairmont Hotels (⑦–⑧) ☎020/7389 1126, ☎1-800/441-1414, *www.cphotels.ca*

Choice Hotels International Booking agents in the UK for the Clarion, Comfort, Quality, Sleep Inns, Econolodge and Rodeway chains. ☎0800/444444

Clarion (④–⑤) ☎1-800/252-7466, *www.hotelchoice.com*

Comfort Inns (④–⑤) ☎1-800/228-5150, *www.hotelchoice.com*

Courtyard by Marriott (⑤–⑥) ☎0800/221222, ☎1-800/321-2211, *www.courtyard.com*

Days Inn (④–⑤) ☎01483/440740, ☎1-800/329-7466, *www.daysinn.com*

Econolodge (②–④) ☎1-800/553-2666, *www.econolodge.com*

Embassy Hotels (⑥) ☎1-800/362-2779, *www.hampton-suites.com*

Fairfield Inns (③) ☎1-800/228-2800

Friendship Inns (③) ☎1-800/424-4777, *www.friendshipinns.com*

Hampton Inns (④–⑤) ☎1-800/426-7866, *www.hampton-inns.com*

Hilton Hotels (⑤–⑧) ☎0845/758 1595, ☎1-800/445-8667, *www.hilton.com*

Holiday Inns/Crowne Plaza (⑤–⑧) ☎0800/897121, ☎1-800/HOLIDAY, *www.holiday-inn.com*

Hostelling International American Youth Hostels (①) ☎1-800/444-6111,

Hostelling Canadian Youth Hostels (①) ☎1-800/663-5777, *www.hostellingintl.ca*

Howard Johnson (②–④) ☎01483/440470, ☎1-800/446-4656

Hyatt Hotels & Resorts (⑥–⑧) ☎0845/758 1666, ☎1-800/233-1234

Intercontinental (⑥–⑧) ☎0845/758 1444, ☎1-800/327-0200, *www.interconti.com*

La Quinta Inns (④) ☎1-800/531-5900, *www.laquinta.com*

Marriott Hotels (⑥–⑧) Also booking agents for Courtyard, Fairfield Inns and Ramada Inns. ☎0800/221222, ☎1-800/228-9290, *www.marriotthotels.com*

Quality Inn (③–④) ☎1-800/228-5151, *www.qualityinn.com*

Ramada Inns (④–⑧) ☎01483/440470, ☎1-800/272-6232

Red Carpet Inns (②) ☎1-800/251-1962, *www.reserveahost.com*

Renaissance Hotels (⑤–⑧) ☎0800/181737, ☎1-800/468-3571, *www.renaissancehotels.com*

Rodeway (②–④) ☎1-800/228-2000, *www.rodeway.com*

Sandman (③–⑤) ☎1-800/762-3626, *www.sandman.ca*

Scottish Inns (②) ☎1-800/251-1962, *www.reserveahost.com*

Select Inns (②) ☎1-800/641-1000, *www.selectinn.com*

Sheraton (⑤–⑧) ☎0800/353535, ☎1-800/325-3535, *www.sheraton.com*

Sleep Inns (③) ☎1-800/753-3746, *www.sleepinn.com*

Sonesta (⑤–⑧) ☎1-800/766-3782, *www.sonesta.com*

Super 8 (②–④) ☎1-800/800-8000, *www.super8.com*

Susse Chalet (②–③) ☎1-800/524-2538, *www.sussechalet.com*

Travelodge (②) ☎1-800/578-7878, *www.travelodge.com*

signs flashing their rates. Along the major routes the choice is phenomenal. Only in the far north, in the wilds of BC and in southeast Oregon are places thinner on the ground. In these areas don't assume that because a place is prominent on the map it's going to have rooms: check first.

In most towns mentioned in this book we've recommended particular establishments, but you can also assume that there are a whole lot more we haven't got the space to list. Only where there is a genuine shortage of accommodation have we explicitly said so.

The very cheapest properties tend to be family-run, independent motels, but there's a lot to be said for paying a few dollars more to stay in motels belonging to the **national chains**. After a few days on the road, if you find that a particular chain consistently suits your requirements, you can use its central reservation number, listed in the box overleaf, to book ahead, and possibly obtain discounts as a regular guest. Visitors from the UK and Ireland can book rooms before they go using UK and Irish contact numbers for many of the chains: discount **voucher schemes** can also be booked before travelling (see box p.52).

Motels may be called inns, lodges or motor hotels, but most amount to much the same thing, reliable and reasonably priced places on the main highways just outside towns or cities. There are few differences between Canadian and American versions, many chains being common to both countries, though prices across the board are generally a few dollars higher in Canada. The **budget** ones are pretty basic affairs, but in general there's a uniform standard of comfort everywhere – double rooms with bathroom, TV and phone – and you don't get a much better deal by paying, say, US$50 instead of $35. Over about US$50 or Can$60, the room and its fittings simply get bigger and better, and there'll probably be a swimming pool or other frills which guests can use for free. Paying over US$100 or Can$125 will probably bring you into the decadent realms of the en-suite jacuzzi. Not many budget hotels or motels bother to compete with the ubiquitous diners and offer **breakfast**, although there's a trend towards providing free self-service coffee and sticky buns. Ritzier spots may have a restaurant, but generally you can expect nothing in the way of food and drink beyond a drinks machine.

During **off-peak periods** (usually Oct–April) many motels and hotels struggle to fill their rooms, and it's worth **haggling** to get a few dollars off the asking price. Staying in the same place for more than one night usually brings further reductions. Some places have cheap triple- or quadruple-berth rooms, and most are fairly relaxed about introducing an extra bed into a "double" room. Many places also offer a Family Plan, whereby youngsters sharing their parents' room stay free. Additionally, pick up the many **discount coupons** which fill tourist information offices. Read the small print, though: what appears to be a tantalizingly cheap room rate sometimes turns out to be a per person charge for two people sharing and limited to midweek. As a rule of thumb, prices drop in the larger towns and cities the further you move from downtown. In the Northwest's more remote areas, or in hiking or resort towns, remember that many places are likely to close off-season.

BED AND BREAKFAST

Over the last decade or so, **bed and breakfast** has become a popular option in both Canada and the United States, as a comfortable and usually less expensive alternative to conventional hotels. Sometimes B&Bs – also known as **guesthouses** and **inns** – are just a couple of furnished rooms in someone's home, and even the larger establishments tend to have no more than ten rooms, often laden with flowers, stuffed cushions and an almost over-contrived homely atmosphere. In many parts of the Northwest, you may find yourself in a "heritage home" of great charm, or in some stunning mountain location.

The **price** you pay for a B&B – which can vary from $40 to over $100 in both Canada and the US – may include a huge and wholesome breakfast that'll set you up for the day, though the trend is increasingly to provide only a "continental" breakfast (toast, coffee and perhaps cereal). The other crucial determining factor on price is whether or not each room has an en-suite bathroom, those that do tend to average between $60 and $100 per night for a double, more in busy resorts such as Banff. Check what's on offer when making a booking.

Another factor to look out for is (at least if you're staying for several nights or more) whether they have a **private guest entrance**, useful if you're likely to be staggering in late or simply don't want to mix with your hosts.

B&B establishments tend to open and close with greater rapidity than hotels, but those that last are often **reserved** well in advance. To find one it's often best to visit tourist offices, some of which have bulging catalogues and photographs of what's available, or in the big cities contact one of the many private agencies who can line you up with something suitable. Take careful note of an establishment's **location**: in cities and larger towns they're often out in the suburbs and inconvenient for transport and downtown sights, though some hosts will pick you up from the airport or bus station on your arrival.

YOUTH HOSTELS

Although **hostel**-type accommodation is not as plentiful in the US and Canada as it is in Europe and elsewhere, provision for backpackers and low-budget travellers is good in the hiking and outdoors areas of the Canadian northwest. Unless you're travelling alone, however, most hostels work out little cheaper than motels, so there's only any real point using them if you prefer their youthful ambience and sociability. Note also that many are not accessible on public transport, or particularly convenient for sightseeing in the towns and cities, let alone in rural areas.

Most of the region's hostels are affiliated to either the **Hostelling International Canada** (HIC) network or the **American Youth Hostel** (AYH) network, these organisations are, in turn, affiliated to **Hostelling International**. There are also privately-run hostels in the Northwest and in the US, and some of these are members of the **"Rucksackers Hostel"** network. Additionally

there are **YMCA/YWCA** establishments (often known as "Ys"), that sometimes offer dormitory mixed-sex or, in a few cases, women-only accommodation, but which increasingly have rooms, facilities and reservations procedures to match those of mid-range hotels.

To stay in a hostel in either country, you're supposed, in theory, to be a **HI member** but in practice you can join the HI on the spot, or rely on most hostels making a slightly higher charge for non-members. Be warned that members are usually given priority when it comes to booking which is an important consideration in some of the more popular locations. Most places offer communal recreational and cooking facilities, plus pillows and blankets, though in simpler places you're expected to provide your own sleeping bag and towels. Especially in high season, it's advisable to **reserve ahead**, in writing, or by credit card over the phone, either to the relevant hostel or via a central reservation number. Some hostels will allow you to use a **sleeping bag**, though officially AYH affiliates should insist on a **sheet sleeping bag**.

For overseas travellers details of HI-affiliated Canadian and US hostels are available from their respective national organisations as is the invaluable *International Handbook* covering the Americas, Africa and the Pacific – see box above. The *Hostelling Handbook for the USA and Canada* produced each May, lists over 400 HI and private hostels and is available for $3 (send a money order for $6 from outside the US) from Jim Williams, Sugar Hill House International House Hostel, 722 Saint Nicholas Ave, New York, NY 10031 (☎212/926-7030).

CANADIAN HOSTELS

Almost half of the **HI's** 80 or so hostels are in Alberta and British Columbia, and frequently offer the only accommodation in more remote areas of these provinces. Additionally there are a growing number of unaffiliated hostels which may feature in HIC literature and are often aspiring to full hostel status.

HI hostels are graded in four categories (basic, simple, standard and superior), and accommodation is mostly in single-sex dorms which cost about $10–25 for members ($12–28 for non-members), depending on category and location, though family and private double rooms are becoming more prevalent. Most hostels offer communal recreation areas and all have cooking facilities, plus pillows and blankets, though you're expected to provide, or rent, your own sheet sleeping bag and towels – normal sleeping bags are generally not allowed.

Most hostels are open from 8–9am to 8–9pm (or 24 hours) and lockouts during the day are now rare. Curfews, or "quiet times" (typically 11pm–7am) are, however, usually imposed and so is a three-day limit on stays. Many hostels have been renovated in the past few years and often have cafeterias and recreation areas.

A computerised **booking scheme**, means you can book into most hostels in BC and Alberta (including Calgary, Vancouver, Banff and Edmonton), up to six months ahead. These major hostels accept credit card and fax bookings, although you still might have to send a deposit for the first night's stay. You may also use a HI Advance Booking Voucher, available from any HI office or specialist travel agents – though check that the hostel you're after accepts them. The larger hostels also act as booking agents for a number of smaller hostels around the region (see entries in the main text for details). Details of private hostels are included in the *Guide*.

US HOSTELS

In **Washington** and **Oregon**, hostels are fewer and further between than in Canada, with most located either in cities or in coastal towns, though a smattering can be found in good hiking country. In both states, hostels may still observe the old

hostelling niceties – a limited check-in time (usually 5–8pm) and strict daytime lockouts (9.30am–5pm). **Rates** range between about $10 and $25 per night depending on grade and location, non-HI members pay a few dollars extra.

YMCAS AND YWCAS

Both the YMCA and YWCA – often known as "Ys" – have establishments in most of the Pacific Northwest's big cities. In many cases the quality of accommodation is excellent, matching that of the cheaper hotels, and invariably exceeding that of most other hostel-type lodgings. Often the premises have cheap cafeterias open to all, and sports facilities, gymnasium and swimming pools for the use of guests. Prices, however, reflect the comforts, and though you can sometimes find bunks in shared dorms from about $20, the trend is increasingly for single, double and family units (with or without private bathrooms), ranging between $30 and $70 depending on private or shared bathroom. This still reflects excellent value, especially in cities, where Ys are usually in central downtown locations. In places such as Banff and Vancouver they can offer the best-value rooms around.

As Ys become more like hotels, so you need to treat them as such, with credit-card reservations in advance virtually essential to secure private singles and doubles in high summer. Most places keep a number of rooms and dorm bunks available each day for walk-in customers, though in places like Banff it's not unknown for queues for these to develop around the block first thing in the morning. The old demarcation of the sexes is also breaking down, though many YWCAs will only accept men if they're in a mixed-sex couple. Some YWCAs accept women with children, others only in emergencies.

CAMPING

Few areas of North America offer as much scope for **camping** as the Pacific Northwest. Most urban areas have a campsite, and all national parks and a large proportion of state and provincial parks have outstanding government-run sites. Most state and provincial tourist literature covers campsites in some detail. In many wilderness areas and in the vast domain of Canada's Crown Lands and the United States' public land you can camp pretty much anywhere you want (ask permission or get a permit wherever necessary).

We've covered this **wilderness camping** in more detail below and on p.59.

If you're travelling with a tent it's vital to check a campsite's details for the number of unserviced (tent) sites, as many places cater chiefly for **recreational vehicles** (RVs), providing them with full or partial hook-ups for water and electricity (or "serviced sites"). Anywhere described as an "RV Park" ought to be avoided completely unless, of course, you're travelling with an RV. If you want peace and quiet, it might also be worth checking the number of tent sites available: there's a lot of difference between a cosy 20-pitch site and a 500-site tent village. Province- and state-wide campsite details are available from the major tourist offices and the tourist boards listed in the box on p.30.

As well as plenty of campsites, there are plenty of people intending to use them: take special care plotting your route if you're camping during public holidays or the high season (July and Aug), or hoping to stay at some of the big campsites near lake or river resorts, or in any of the national parks (this applies both to main and backcountry campsites). Either aim to arrive early in the morning or book ahead — we've given phone numbers wherever this is possible. Reservations can be made at private campsites and at many national and provincial/state parks, though in the parks, most sites are available on a first-come, first-served basis. US national forest sites are almost entirely non-reservable.

Oregon and Washington state parks share the same campsite reservation line, Reservations Northwest (☎1-800/452-5687). See p.390 for details of the booking system in British Columbia. Finally, check that your chosen site is open — many campsites only open seasonally, usually from May to October.

CAMPSITE TYPES

At the bottom of the pile are **municipal camp-sites**, usually basic affairs with few facilities, which are either free or cost only a few dollars — typically $5 per tent, $10 per RV, though many often have tent places only. **Private campsites** run the gamut: some are as basic as their municipal cousins, others are like huge outdoor pleasure domes with shops, restaurants, laundries, swimming pools, tennis courts, even saunas and jacuzzis. Best-known among the latter is the family-oriented Kampgrounds of America (KOA) network, with campsites across the Northwest; the company publishes an annual directory of its campsites in both countries (Kampgrounds of America, Billings, MT 59114-0558, ☎406/248-7444). Lone or budget travellers may appreciate their facilities but not their commercial atmosphere.

As for **price**, private campsites have several ways of charging. Some charge by the vehicle, others per couple, comparatively few on a tent or per person basis. Two people sharing a tent might pay anything between $2.50 and $25 each, though an average price would be nearer $7–11. Where we've given a price it's invariably for two people sharing a tent. You can book places in private campsites but there's often no need outside busy areas as most are obliged to keep a certain number of pitches available on a first-come, first-served basis.

National park campsites are generally run by Parks Canada and the National Park Service in the US: individual provincial and state parks are run by state and provincial governments. All are immaculately turned out and most, in theory, are open only between May and September. In practice most are available year-round, though key facilities are offered and fees collected only in the advertised period: off-season you may be expected to leave fees in an "honesty box". You'll usually find at least one site serviced for winter camping in the bigger national parks, particularly in the Rockies. Prices vary from about $8.50 to $19 per tent depending on location, services and the time of year — prices may be higher during July and August. See overleaf for more details.

Sites in the major national parks, especially close to towns, usually offer a full range of **amenities** for both tents and RVs, and often have separate sites for each. As a rule, though, provincial sites and more remote national park campsites tend to favour tents and offer only water, stores of firewood (usually there's an additional charge for wood) and pit toilets. Hot showers, in particular, are rare. But both national park and provincial sites, of course, invariably score highly on their scenic locations.

OUTDOOR PURSUITS

The Pacific Northwest is scattered with fabulous backcountry and wilderness areas, swathed in dense forests, scoured by mighty white-water rivers, and capped by majestic mountains and vast glaciers. Opportunities for outdoor pursuits are almost limitless, and the facilities to indulge them some of the best on the continent.

We've concentrated on the most popular activities – hiking, skiing and rafting – and on the region's superlative national parks. Other popular activities such as whale-watching, horseback riding, fishing and rafting are covered in some detail in the main text, but whatever activity interests you, be sure to send off to the various state and provincial tourist offices for information before you go (see box on p.30 for contact details). Once you're in the Northwest you can rely on finding outfitters, equipment rental, charters, tours and guides to help you in most areas: tourist offices invariably carry full details or contact numbers. Also make a point of visiting local bookstores – most have a separate outdoor pursuits section with a wide variety of specialist guides.

THE PARKS SYSTEM

Protected backcountry areas in both Canada and the United States fall into a number of potentially confusing categories. **National parks** in both countries are large federally controlled areas of great natural beauty or historical significance. **Provincial parks** in Canada and **state parks** in the US are other areas of outstanding natural beauty – often barely indistinguishable from national parks in terms of size or splendour – run by local state and provincial governments.

Lesser protected areas include **national monuments** in the States and **national historic sites** in Canada and the US, usually outstanding geological or historical features covering much smaller areas than national parks and not having quite the same facilities or broad tourist appeal. National seashores, lakeshores and so on are self-explanatory, while the tracts of **national forest** that often surround national parks are also federally administered, but are much less protected, and usually allow some limited logging and other land-based industries – ski resorts and mining the most common.

National parks are usually supervised locally by a ranger (US) or warden (Canada) based at a park office or a **park information centre** – the terminology may vary from park to park. These are usually smart and excellently run affairs. In parks in both countries they should be your first port-of-call, as they provide the lowdown on hiking and other activities: park centres are also the places to visit if you intend to fish, camp or climb in the backcountry, pursuits which in both countries usually require a **permit** (see below). Most offer information and audiovisual displays on flora, fauna and outdoor activities, and virtually all employ highly experienced staff who can provide firsthand advice on your chosen trail or pursuit. Many also offer free campfire talks or guided walks.

Regulations common to all parks include a total ban on firearms, hunting, snowmobiles or off-road vehicles, the feeding of wildlife, and the removal or damaging of any natural objects or features. Most national park regulations relating to the care of the environment and campsite behaviour are usually applicable to **state** (US) and **provincial** (Canada) parks. It's unusual for state and provincial parks to have dedicated visitor centres, though local tourist offices or Chambers of Commerce usually carry relevant background material.

PARK FACILITIES

While any of the above areas will have at least basic facilities for **camping** (see opposite), many national and smaller parks offer extremely limited **supplies and services**. In general, the better known a place is, the more likely it will be to have some semblance of the comforts of home, with shops, petrol stations and lodges – all of which are handy but can detract from the natural splen-

For up-to-the-minute information on the **national park system** in the US, access the official park-service Web site at *www.nps.gov /parklists/nm.html*. It features full details of the main attractions of the national parks, plus opening hours, the best times to visit, admission fees, hiking trails and visitor facilities. In Canada the equivalent Parks Canada Web site can be found at *http://parkscanada.pch .gc.ca/parks/main_e.htm*.

dour. Elsewhere, particularly in the Yukon's protected areas, southeast Oregon and Canada's Banff and Jasper parks, it's as well to be aware that food, fuel and shelter can be literally tens, if not hundreds of miles away.

The parks' superb back-up – in the shape of maps, brochures and visitor centres – can also often obscure the fact that these are wild places. Some planning is essential, even if it's just making sure you have enough fuel in the tank to get you to the next known petrol station. Weather can also turn, even in summer: it's not been unknown, for example, for people to have become trapped by snow and died in their cars on the famous Banff to Jasper Icefields Parkway, a heavily travelled route that nonetheless reaches heights of almost 8000 feet and has just one service stop in over 150 miles.

ENTRANCE FEES

In **Canada** all individuals and motor vehicles, including motorbikes, must have a **Park Permit**, obtainable from park visitor centres, certain stores, automated machines (in a few cases) or a roadside booth at the point where the road crosses the park boundary. Permits cost around $5 per day, $35 annual, and are valid for all parks. Once people entering on foot, bicycle, boat or horseback were exempt – not any more, though in practice collecting fees is difficult from individuals who've hiked into a park or come in by bus. There are exemptions for vehicles passing straight through certain parks without stopping overnight. Annual and group permits are also available. See p.486 for precise details of national park permits in western Canada. Provincial parks are usually free.

Comparable arrangements exist in the **United States**, though here fees range from around $5 to $20, which covers a vehicle and all its occupants. Fees are always collected at roadside entrance kiosks. If you plan to visit more than a couple of national parks, buy a **Golden Eagle passport** ($50), which gives unlimited access to a named driver and all passengers in the same vehicle to (almost) any national park or national monument. Special discounts or free passes are available for travellers with disabilities – see p.46. Most US state parks are free.

CAMPING IN THE PARKS

If your time and money are limited, but you want to get a feel for the wilderness, one of the best options is to backpack or tour around by car, **camping** out at night and cooking your own meals on a camp stove (if local regulations allow). If you don't fancy roughing it all the way, there is usually also a wide selection of public and commercially run **campsites** in or very near areas of great beauty, together with special federally run campsites in national parks. Every state or province produces comprehensive lists of the campsites in its parks: we've mentioned the most useful or most scenic in the *Guide*.

Park and wilderness campsites usually range from **primitive** (a flat piece of ground that may or may not have a water tap, and may charge nothing at all) to **semi-primitive**, which usually provide wood, water and pit toilets, and where "self-registration" is the norm and a small fee (around $5–15) is left in the box provided. In bigger park campsites like Banff and Lake Louise, the facilities match and often exceed those of big commercial campsites, with shops, restaurants and washing facilities, and nightly rates in both countries of around $12–25. Additional fees of around $4 may sometimes be charged if you want to use specially provided firewood.

Campsites in national parks are bound by special rules, and in both Canada and the US are always federally run concerns administered by dedicated national park bodies: there are no private sites. Some are for tents, some for RVs only, and most parks have at least one site which remains open for basic **winter camping** (check all opening times carefully: most park sites open only from around mid-May to mid-Sept). Fees depend on facilities, and currently run from around US$5 (Can$7) per tent (semi-primitive) to around US$10 (Can$25) for those with electricity, sewage, water and showers. Most campsites are operated on a first-come, first-served basis but advance reservations are accepted at an increasing number of parks.

PRIMITIVE CAMPING

Official permission and registration is required in both countries' parks for **backcountry camping**, whether you're rough camping or using designated primitive or semi-primitive sites. This enables the authorities to keep a check on people's whereabouts and to regulate the numbers. Bucking the system is unfair as well as dangerous – someone should always know your itinerary and planned return time when you're headed off to the backcountry. It also goes without saying that you should be properly equipped and prepared for any wilderness ventures.

To camp in the backcountry in Canadian parks you must obtain an **overnight or wilderness permit** from a park centre or the park office. These are either free or cost a few dollars, in addition to any campsite fees you may also have to pay. Increasingly, quota systems are in operation, and you may need to book campsites and/or the trails required to reach them: details are given under individual park entries.

Note, however, that while registration and permits are obligatory, other regulations for rough camping vary enormously. Some parks, like Jasper in the Canadian Rockies, for example, allow backcountry camping only in tightly defined sites; others, like nearby Banff, have a special **primitive wildland** zone where you can pitch tent within a designated distance of the nearest road or trailhead. Throughout the US and Canadian national parks, though, a quota system operates in the more popular backpacking areas: no more permits will be issued once a set number have been allocated for a particular trail or backcountry campsite.

When **camping rough**, check that fires are permitted before you start one (often they're not on the Arctic tundra of the Yukon or areas where the fire risk is high), even if they are, try to use a campstove in preference to local materials – in some places firewood is scarce, although you may be allowed to use deadwood. In wilderness areas, try to camp on previously used sites. Where there are no toilets, **bury human waste** at least eight inches into the ground and two hundred feet from the nearest water supply and campsite. It'll be hard to do, but also try to avoid using toilet paper if possible (leaves, stones and acceptable bio-safe soaps are alternatives). Never wash directly into rivers and lakes – use a container at least 50 feet from either, and try to use a biodegradable soap. It is *not* acceptable to burn any rubbish: the preferred practice is to **pack out**, or carry away all rubbish, the ideal being to leave no trace whatsoever of your presence.

HEALTH OUTDOORS

Camping or hiking at **lower elevations** should present few problems, though the thick swarms of **insects** you're likely to encounter near any body of water, particularly in the Yukon, can drive you crazy. April to June is the **blackfly** season,

and the **mosquitoes** are out in force from July until about October: DEET and Avon Skin-so-soft hand-cream are two fairly reliable repellents. Before you go, it could be worth taking three times the recommended dosage of Vitamin B, and continuing with the recommended dosage while you're in the region – it's been shown to cut bites by 75 percent. Burning coils or candles containing allethrin or citronella can help if you're camping or picnicking. Once bitten, an antihistamine cream like phenergan is the best antidote. On no account go anywhere near an area posted as a blackfly mating ground – people have died from bites sustained when the monsters are on heat.

If you develop a large rash and flu-like symptoms in the backcountry, you may have been bitten by a **tick** carrying **lyme borreliosis** (or "lyme tick disease"). This is a problem spreading with alarming speed through North America, and it's particularly prevalent in wooded country. Check with the local park authority. The condition is easily curable, however, so see a doctor, but if left can lead to nasty complications. Ticks – tiny beetles that plunge their heads into your skin and swell up – can sometimes leave their heads inside, causing blood clots or infections, so get advice from a park ranger or warden if you've been bitten. If the prospect of tick encounter fills you with horror, invest in a strong tick repellent and wear long socks, trousers and sleeved shirts when walking.

One very serious backcountry problem you must confront camping is **Giardia** (or "Beaver Fever"), a water-borne bacteria causing an intestinal disease, of which the symptoms are chronic diarrhoea, abdominal cramps, fatigue and loss of weight. Treatment at that stage is essential, much better to avoid catching it in the first place. **Never drink** from rivers, streams or glaciers, however clear and inviting they may look (you never know what unspeakable acts people – or animals – further upstream have performed in them), water that doesn't come from a tap should be boiled for at least ten minutes, or cleansed with an iodine-based purifier (such as Potable Aqua) or a Giardia-rated filter, available from any camping or sports store. Neither ordinary filters nor standard water-purification tablets will remove the bacteria.

Beware, too, of **poison oak**, an allergenic shrub that grows all over the Pacific Northwest, usually among oak trees. Its leaves come in groups of three and are distinguished by prominent veins and shiny surfaces (waxy green in spring, rich red and orange in autumn). It causes open blisters and lumpy sores up to ten days after contact. If you come into contact with it, wash your skin (with soap and cold water) and clothes as soon as possible – and don't scratch: the only way to ease the itching is to smother yourself in calamine lotion or to take regular dips in the sea. In serious cases, hospital emergency rooms can give antihistamine or adrenaline jabs.

There's also a danger of being bitten or stung by various **poisonous creatures**. You'll soon know if this happens. Current medical thinking rejects the concept of cutting yourself open and attempting to suck out venom; whether snake, scorpion or spider is responsible, you should apply a cold compress to the wound, constrict the area with a tourniquet to prevent the spread of venom, drink lots of water and bring your temperature down by resting in a shady area. Stay as calm as possible and seek medical help immediately.

Hiking at **higher elevations** you need to take special care: late snows are common, even into July, and in spring there's a real danger of avalanches, not to mention meltwaters making otherwise simple stream crossings hazardous. Altitude sickness, brought on by the depletion of oxygen in the atmosphere, can affect even the fittest of athletes. Take it easy for the first few days you go above seven thousand feet, drink lots of water, avoid alcohol, eat plenty of carbohydrates, and protect yourself from the increased power of the sun. Watch out for signs of **exposure** – mild delirium, exhaustion, inability to get warm – and on snow or in high country during the summer take a good **sun block**.

HIKING

The Pacific Northwest boasts some of North America's finest hiking, and whatever your abilities or ambitions you'll find a walk to suit you almost anywhere in the region: you don't need wilderness training or huge amounts of hiking experience to tackle most trails. All the national and provincial or state parks have well-marked and remarkably well-maintained trails, and a visit to any park centre or local tourist office will furnish you with adequate **maps** of local paths. Park trails are usually sufficiently well marked and well worn not to need more detailed maps for short walks and day-hikes. If you're entering into the backcountry, though, try to obtain the appropriate maps (see p.32–33). For key hiking areas

we've given a brief summary of the best hikes in the appropriate parts of the *Guide*, though with over 1500km of paths in Canada's Banff National Park alone, recommendations can only scratch the surface. Be sure to consult park staff on other good walks, or to pick up the **trail guides** that are widely available in local bookshops for most of the region's prime walking areas.

Wherever you're hiking, and at whatever altitude, it goes without saying that you should be **properly prepared and equipped** and treat all terrain – not just the mountains – with the respect it deserves. Good boots, waterproof jacket, warm clothing and spare food and drink to cover emergencies are all essential. On longer walks be sure to tell the park centre of your intentions, so if something goes wrong there's a chance someone will come and find you. Be prepared for sudden changes of weather – check with park centres before you set off. Also be ready for encounters with wildlife, especially **bears**, which are present throughout much of the Canadian Rockies (see p.250), and for the sort of health considerations now sadly a fact of life in the North American backcountry (see opposite). Outdoor clothing can be bought easily in most towns, and in most mountain areas there's a good chance of being able to **rent** tents and specialized cold-weather gear.

MAIN HIKING AREAS

In picking out the Northwest's prime walking areas we've chosen the parks which are accessible by road (occasionally by boat), where maps and guides are available, where the trail system is developed, and where you can turn up without too much planning or special wilderness training.

Some of the best-known and most developed of these are the national parks of the **Canadian Rockies** in Alberta and British Columbia. Thousands of well-kept and well-tramped trails crisscross the "big four parks" – Banff, Jasper, Yoho and Kootenay – as well as the smaller but no less spectacular or approachable Glacier, Revelstoke and Waterton Lakes national parks. Scope for hiking of all descriptions is almost limitless, as it is in the national parks of Washington, most dramatically among the glacial peaks of the **North Cascades** and around the highest Cascade mountain of them all, **Mount Rainier**.

Smaller areas dotted all over the region boast walking possibilities out of all proportion to their size. In Oregon, pint-sized **Crater Lake National**

Park presents some of the Pacific Northwest's most stunning scenery, while Washington's **Mount St Helens Volcanic Monument** bears remarkable charred and dusty testimony to the force of the eruption that blew the mountain to pieces in 1980. In British Columbia, which has some of the best smaller protected areas, all the following provincial parks offer day-hikes, short strolls and longer trails that could keep you happy for a week or more: **Wells Gray**, north of Kamloops, **Kokanee Glacier**, near Nelson, **Manning**, east of Vancouver, **Garibaldi**, north of Vancouver, and **Strathcona**, on Vancouver Island.

LONG-DISTANCE FOOTPATHS

In areas with highly developed trail networks, seasoned backpackers can blaze their own **long-distance footpaths** by stringing together several longer trails. Recognised long-haul trails, however, are relatively rare, though more are being designated yearly. One of the best is the **Chilkoot Trail** from Dyea in Alaska to Bennett in British Columbia, a 53-kilometre hike that closely follows the path of prospectors en route to the Yukon during the 1898 gold rush (see p.592). Another very popular path is the **West Coast Trail**, which runs for 80km along the edge of Vancouver Island's Pacific Rim National Park (see p.373), a southern equivalent is the **Oregon Coast Trail**, hugging the 360 miles of coastline from the Columbia River to the Californian border. The **Pacific Crest Trail**, a 2620-mile path from Mexico to the Canadian border, offers manageable one- or two-week stretches in Oregon and Washington (with a network of cabins if you're not camping). Another long trail across Canada from west to east was completed in 2000, but mapping is still patchy. The 150-mile **Oregon Desert Trail**, across the southeast portion of the state, is still under construction, and will eventually form part of a putative long-distance desert trail from Canada to Mexico. Most trails have a growing body of guides to help you with practicalities and route-finding.

SKIING

Wherever there's hiking in the Northwest, there's also usually **skiing**. Washington has sixteen ski areas, mostly in the **Cascades**, and many within easy striking distance of Seattle. Oregon boasts **Mount Batchelor**, offering some of North America's finest skiing, and **Mount Hood**, where

you can ski throughout the summer. For details of all these areas contact the Pacific Northwest Ski Areas Association, PO Box 2325, Seattle, WA 98111-2325 (☎206/623-3777). Increasingly, however, it is the big resorts in the Canadian Rockies and British Columbia's Coast Ranges that are grabbing the headlines. Resorts such as **Whistler** (see p.395) north of Vancouver – with North America's longest vertical run – and **Lake Louise** (see p.514) in Banff National Park, are widely acknowledged to offer some of the finest skiing anywhere in the world. See the special features throughout the *Guide* for more information on these resorts. Furthermore, both these areas, together with countless others in the Rockies, are less than 90 minutes from major cities, making them readily and cheaply accessible.

Despite the expense involved, **heli-skiing** is also taking off, a sport that involves a helicopter drop deep into the backcountry (or to the actual summits of mountains) followed by some of the wildest and most exhilarating off-piste skiing you're ever likely to experience. The main centres, again, are mostly in the Rockies and Coast Mountains, though it's one of the fastest growing adventure sports in the region, contact visitor centres for details of packages and outfitters.

US and Canadian **ski packages** are available from most foreign travel agents, while companies and hotels in many Northwest cities organise their own mini-packages to nearby resorts. It is, however, perfectly feasible to organise your own trips, but be sure to book well ahead if you're hoping to stay in some of the better-known resorts. In the first instance, contact state or provincial tourist offices in the Northwest, or their offices abroad (see p.30); most publish regional ski and winter sports directories. On the spot, visitor centres in ski areas open up in the winter to help with practicalities, and most towns have ski shops to buy or rent equipment. **Costs** for food, accommodation and ski passes, in Canada at least, are still fairly modest by US and European standards (see the box, opposite, for some cost-cutting tips). Generally you can rent equipment from about Can$15 per day, and expect to pay perhaps another Can$40 per day for lift tickets. A cheaper option is **cross-country skiing**, or ski-touring. Backcountry ski lodges dot mountainous areas, offering rustic accommodation, equipment rental and lessons, from as little as Can$10 a day for skis, boots and poles, up to about $100 for an all-inclusive weekend tour.

SKIING – HOW TO SAVE MONEY

The Northwest features some of the best ski terrain in the world, but without careful planning a ski vacation can be horribly expensive. In addition to the tips listed below, phone (toll-free) or write in advance to resorts for brochures, and when you get there, scan local newspapers for money-saving offers.

- Visit during early or late season to take advantage of lower accommodation and lift ticket rates.

- The more people in your party, the more money you save on lodgings. For groups of four to six, a condo unit costs much less than a standard motel.

- Before setting a date, ask the resort about package deals including flights, rooms and lift tickets. This is the no-fuss and often highly economical way to book a ski vacation.

- Shop around for the best boot and ski rentals – prices often vary significantly.

- If you have to buy lift tickets at the resort, save money by purchasing multiday tickets.

- If you're an absolute beginner, look out for resorts that offer free "never-ever" lessons with the purchase of a lift ticket.

- Finish your day's skiing in time to take advantage of happy hours and dining specials, which usually last from 4pm until 7pm.

FISHING

The Pacific Northwest is **fishing** nirvana. While each area has its dream catches, from the arctic char of the Yukon to the Pacific salmon of Washington and British Columbia, excellent fishing can be found in most of the region's superabundant lakes, rivers and coastal waters. Most towns have a fishing shop for equipment, and any spot with fishing possibilities is likely to have companies running boats and charters. As with every other type of outdoor activity, states and provinces publish detailed booklets on outfitters and everything that swims within the area of their jurisdiction.

Fishing in Canada and the US is governed by a medley of **regulations** that vary from state to state, and province to province. These are baffling at first glance, but usually boil down to the need for a non-resident permit for freshwater fishing, and another for saltwater. These are obtainable from most local fishing or sports shops for about US$45 (Can$30) and are valid for a year. Short-term (one- or six-day) licences are also available in some areas. In a few places you may have to pay for extra licences to go after particular fish, and in Canadian national parks you need a special additional permit. There may also be quotas or a closed season on certain fish. Shops and visitor centres always have the most current regulations, which you should check before you set out.

ADVENTURE TRAVEL

The opportunities for active travelling in the Northwest are all but endless, from white-water rafting down the Rogue, Kenai and Fraser rivers, to mountain biking in the volcanic Cascades, polar-bear watching in Inuvik, horse riding in the Cariboo, and ice-climbing on the glacial monoliths of the Columbia Icefields. While an exhaustive listing of the possibilities could fill another volume of this book, certain places have an especially high concentration of adventure opportunities, notably the Rockies' parks, the Yukon and the Cascades. We occasionally recommend guides, outfitters and local adventure-tour operators, but a quick visit to any local visitor or park centre should provide you with reams of material on just about any outdoor activity you care to name.

SPORTS

Few occasions provide better opportunities for meeting the locals than catching a baseball game on a summer afternoon or joining in with the screaming throngs at a football or ice-hockey game. Professional sports almost always put on the most spectacular shows, but big games between college rivals, minor league baseball games – even Friday-night high-school football – provide an easy and enjoyable way to get on intimate terms with a place.

BASEBALL

Baseball, because the teams play so many games – around 162 in total, usually five or so a week throughout the summer – is probably the easiest sport to catch when travelling in the United States, and it's also among the cheapest sports to watch (at around $10 a seat), with tickets usually easy to come by. The **Seattle Mariners** (☎206/628-3555), who play in the American League, are the Northwest's big deal, but watch out for minor league or so-called "Farm teams" such as the Portland Beavers, Calgary Cannons and Vancouver Canadians.

THE RULES OF BASEBALL

To the uninitiated baseball is as arcane – and almost as slow and soporific – as cricket. To the aficionado it's an essential part of the American (and to a lesser extent Canadian) landscape. Steeped in history, it's a game full of names that have entered American folklore, as well as one occasionally ravaged by controversy and commercial greed.

The basic setup looks like the English game of rounders, to which it must owe its origins, with four **bases** set at the corners of a 90-foot-square **diamond**. The base at the bottom corner is called home plate. Play begins when the **pitcher**, standing on a low pitcher's mound in the middle of the

diamond, throws a ball towards the catcher, who crouches behind home plate, seven other defensive players take up positions, one at each base and the others spread out around the field of play.

A **batter** from the opposing team stands beside home plate and tries to hit the ball. If the batter swings and misses, or if the pitched ball crosses the plate above the batter's knees and below his chest, it counts as a **strike**, if he doesn't swing and the ball passes outside of this strike zone, it counts as a **ball**. An umpire (referee) behind the catcher adjudicates, indicating strike or ball with a hand signal or shout. If the batter gets three strikes against him he is out, four balls and he gets a free walk, and takes his place as a runner on first base. Pitchers do more than simply "throw" the ball, however: not only are they launching it at speeds of around a hundred miles an hour, they're also spinning and curving it almost at will in a variety of ways to try to bamboozle the batter.

If the batter succeeds in hitting the pitched ball into a legitimate area of the field – namely the wedge between the first and third bases – the batter runs towards first base, if the opposing players catch the ball before it hits the ground, the batter is out. Otherwise they field the ball and attempt to throw it to first base before the batter gets there, if they do he is out, if they don't the batter is safe – and stays there, being moved along by subsequent batters until he makes a complete circuit of the bases and scores a run. The most exciting moment in baseball is the home run, when a batter hits the ball over the outfield fences, a boundary 400ft away from home plate, he and any runners on base when he hits the ball each score a run. If there are runners on all three bases it's called a grand slam, and earns four runs.

The nine players per side bat in rotation, each side gets three outs per inning, and there are nine innings per game. Games normally last two to three hours, and are never tied, if the scores are level after nine innings, extra innings are played until one side pulls ahead and wins.

FOOTBALL

Pro football is quite the opposite of baseball – tickets are expensive and difficult to get, particu-

---

SPORTING SEASONS

Baseball	April–Oct
Basketball	Nov–June
Football	Sept–Jan
Ice Hockey	Oct–June

larly if the team is successful. Of the teams in the Northwest, only the Seattle Seahawks have made the big time, their nearest Canadian rivals being second division outfits in the Canadian Football League (the British Columbia Lions, Calgary Stampeders and Edmonton Eskimos). **College football** is a passionate affair too, with Seattle's University of Washington Huskies, one of the best in their class, being enthusiastically supported.

AMERICAN FOOTBALL

American football may look like a disorganised all-male orgy to outsiders, but in truth the game is highly structured, the rules straightforward and the basic aim pretty simple. When it all works, as in most sports, the end result can be spell-binding. There are two teams of eleven men. The field is 100 yards long by 40 yards wide, while each end of the field has a pair of 'H'-shaped posts and an area known as the **endzone**. The game begins with a kickoff, after which the team catching the ball from the kickoff – the team in possession – tries to move the ball downfield in a series of moves to score a **touchdown**, achieved by taking the ball into the opposing side's endzone. The opposing team does everything legally possible to stop them.

The attacking team has four chances to move the ball forward ten yards and gain a **first down**. Failure to do so, or if the ball is legally intercepted by the opposing team, means they forfeit possession to the opposition. After the kickoff the quarterback, the leader of the attack, has several ways to move the ball forward: he can pass the ball to a running back (who then takes off at speed towards the endzone until tackled), throw the ball through the air downfield to a receiver (who also sets off at speed towards the endzone), or run with the ball himself (usually a last resort). If more than ten yards is gained through any of these ploys, so much the better. For most spectators a tackle breaking run or a long pass are a game's highlights – few things are as exhilarating as seeing a ball rifled a huge distance through the air and dropping in a graceful arc directly into the hands of a receiver running at full tilt.

All manner of complicated moves, or **plays**, are devised to open up gaps on the field for backs and receivers to run at or through, as well as to shield the quarterback and give him enough time to pick and complete an option. Above all he must be protected from the opposition – being caught in possession of the ball by the opposition, a

sack, is considered about as low as a quarterback can sink. Play ends when the man with the ball is tackled to the ground, or if the pass attempt falls **incomplete** (touches the ground without being caught by a fellow team member). Once a first down is achieved, the process starts again, enabling a team to encroach gradually closer to the opposing side's endzone.

A touchdown, worth six points, is made when a player crosses into the defending team's endzone carrying the ball, a field goal, worth three points, is scored when the placekicker – usually the smallest man on the team – kicks the ball through the goalposts that stand in the endzone. If the attacking team has failed to move the ball within scoring range, and seems unlikely to gain the required ten yards for another first down, they can elect to punt the ball, kicking it to the other team.

A change of possession can also occur if the opposition players manage to intercept an attempted pass. This, to say the least, is something to celebrate for an opposing team, and like many moments in football (a sack being one of the best) is the occasion for much backslapping, high fives and extravagant celebration.

CANADIAN FOOTBALL

Professional Canadian football, played under the aegis of the Canadian Football League (CFL), is largely overshadowed by the National Football League in the US, chiefly because the best home-grown talent moves south in search of better money while NFL cast-offs move north to fill the ranks. The two countries' football games vary slightly but what differences do exist tend to make the Canadian version more exciting. In Canada the playing field is larger and there are twelve rather than eleven players on each team. There is also one fewer down in a game – ie after kickoff the attacking team has three, rather than four, chances to move the ball forward ten yards and score a first down en route to a touchdown. Different rules about the movement of players and the limited time allowed between plays

---

NORTHWEST FOOTBALL TEAMS

BC Lions	(☎604/930-5466)
Calgary Stampeders	(☎403/289-0258)
Seattle Seahawks	(☎206/515-4791)

results in a faster-paced and higher-scoring sport, in which ties are often decided in overtime or in a dramatic final-minute surge.

Despite the sport's potential, the CFL has suffered a blight of media and fan indifference which has caused immense financial problems, though recently the crisis seems to be easing, with high-profile celebrity investment. The CFL tried to expand into the US several years ago, but all the expansion teams folded at the end of the '95–'96 season. The season, played by two divisions of eight teams, lasts from June to November, each team playing a match a week. At the end of the season are the play-offs, which culminate with the hotly contested Grey Cup – which the Toronto Argonauts have won some twenty times. Tickets are fairly easy to come by, except for important games, and vary in cost from around $10 to a Grey Cup final price of over $100.

ICE HOCKEY

Ice hockey ignites the passions of virtually all Canadians – and many Americans as well. Two of the best of the National Hockey League's teams are from the Northwest, the Calgary Flames, and Vancouver Canucks (see box).

Portland's Winter Hawks and Seattle's Thunderbirds play in the lesser Western Hockey League.

With players hurtling around at 50kph, and the puck clocking speeds of 160kph, it's a tremendous

ICE HOCKEY TEAMS

For information on ice hockey teams (Calgary Flames and Vancouver Canucks), venues, tickets and games, contact Ticketmaster outlets in individual cities (see "Listings" or "Entertainment" sections) or ☎403/777-0000 (in Calgary) and ☎604/280-4400 (Vancouver).

sport to watch live, the adrenalin rush increased by the relaxed attitude to physical contact on the rink – "I went to see a fight and an ice-hockey game broke out" is how the old adage runs. Teams play around ninety games over a season that runs from October to May. Tickets for all but the biggest games are usually available, though it's always an idea to try and obtain seats in advance: prices start at around $10–15.

BASKETBALL

Basketball, on both the college and pro level, also focuses local attention and emotions. The major Northwest teams with a following and showing in the National Basketball Association include the Portland Trailblazers (☎503/234-9291), who play at the Memorial Coliseum, the Seattle Supersonics (☎206/281-5800), based at the Coliseum in the Seattle Center, and the Vancouver Grizzlies (☎604/899-4667), who hoop it up in the General Motors Place Arena.

FOOD AND DRINK

The sheer number of restaurants, bars, cafés and fast-food joints in the Northwest is staggering, but for the most part there's little to distinguish the mainstream urban cuisines of the region's towns and cities: in both Canada and the US, shopping malls, main streets and highways are lined with pan-American food chains, each trying to outdo the other with their bargains and special offers. However, this overall uniformity is leavened in the bigger cities by a plethora of ethnic restaurants, and places that specialize in Pacific Northwestern seafood dishes. Even out in the country – the domain of often grim family-run diners – you'll find the odd ethnic or seafood restaurant to save the day.

BREAKFAST

Breakfast is taken very seriously all over the Pacific Northwest, and with prices averaging between US$5 and US$8 (Can$6–11) it can be very good value. Whether you go to a café, coffee shop or hotel snack bar, the breakfast menu, on offer until around 11am, is a fairly standard fry. **Eggs** are the staple ingredient: "sunny side up" is fried on one side leaving a runny yolk; "over" is slipped over in the pan to stiffen the yolk; and "over easy" is flipped for a few seconds to give a hint of solidity. Scrambled, poached eggs and omelettes are popular too. The usual meat is **ham or bacon**, streaky and fried to a crisp, or skinless and bland **sausages**. Whatever you order, you nearly always seem to receive a dollop of fried potatoes, called **hashbrowns** or sometimes

home fries. Other favourite breakfast options include **English muffins** or, in posher places, **bran muffins**, a glutinous fruitcake made with bran and sugar, and **waffles or pancakes**, swamped in butter with lashings of maple syrup.

Whatever you eat, you can wash it down with as much **coffee** as you can stomach: for the price of the first cup, the waiters will keep providing free refills until you beg them to stop. The coffee is either **regular** or **decaf** and is nearly always freshly ground, though some of the cheaper places dilute it until it tastes like dishwater. As a matter of course, coffee comes with cream or **half-and-half** (half cream, half milk) – if you ask for skimmed milk, you're often met with looks of disbelief. **Tea**, with either lemon or milk, is also drunk at breakfast, and the swisher places emphasise the English connection by using imported brands – or at least brands which sound English.

LUNCH AND SNACKS

Between around 11.30am and 2.30pm many big-city restaurants offer **specials** that are generally excellent value. In Chinese and Vietnamese establishments, for example, you'll frequently find rice and noodles, or dim sum feasts for US$5 to US$8, and many **Japanese** restaurants give you a chance to eat sushi for under $10, far cheaper than usual. **Pizza** is also widely available, from larger chains like Pizza Hut to family-owned restaurants and pavement stalls. Favourites with white-collar workers are **café-restaurants** featuring whole- and vegetarian foods, though few are nutritionally dogmatic, serving traditional seafood and meat dishes and sandwiches too; most have an excellent selection of daily lunch specials for around US$8.

For quick **snacks** many **delis** do ready-cooked meals from US$4, as well as a range of sandwiches and filled bagels. Alternatively, shopping malls sometimes have **ethnic fast-food stalls**, a healthier option than the inevitable **burger chains**, whose homogenized products have colonized every main street in the land. Regional snacks are all things nautical – from salmon and halibut to clams and shrimps. The Northwest's cities are also crowded with specialist **coffeehouses**, breezily informal places where a mind-boggling range of coffees are

COPING AS A VEGETARIAN

In the big cities of the Northwest, being a **vegetarian** presents few problems. Cholesterol-fearing North Americans are turning to health-foods in a big way, and most towns of any size boast a wholefood or vegetarian café, while America's Mexican restaurants tend to include at least one vegetarian item on their menus. However, don't be too surprised in rural areas if you find yourself restricted to a diet of eggs, cheese sandwiches (you might have to ask them to leave the ham out), salads and pizza. If you eat fish, the Northwest's ubiquitous salmon may well become a staple, though some apparently "safe" foods such as baked beans, and the nutritious-sounding red beans and rice, often contain bits of diced pork. Amongst the chains, the Mexicanesque Taco Bell, which boasts outlets as far north as Alaska, sells meatless tostadas and burritos.

served up alongside cakes and/or light snacks. Many of them specialise in **espressos**, though **latté**, made with milk and served in a tall glass, is also a favourite. At present, the trend hasn't spread far beyond the big cities, but it's hard to imagine they won't colonise the country towns too. Many urban **diners** have latched on to the coffee and ethnic-food fashions, adding a bit of variety to the American standbys that they prepare so well.

Some city **bars** are used as much by diners as drinkers, who turn up in droves to gorge themselves on the free **hors d'oeuvres** laid out between 5pm and 7pm from Monday to Friday in an attempt to grab commuters. For the price of a drink you can stuff yourself with pasta and chilli. That apart, the old-style urban drinkers' bar is on the defensive hereabouts – as in other parts of North America – replaced by the **café-bar**, many of which serve up a wide range of bistro-style food influenced by Italian and French cuisine.

MAIN MEALS AND SPECIALITIES

While the predictable burgers, piles of ribs or half a chicken, served up with salads, cooked vegetables and bread, are found everywhere, you should aim to explore the diverse regional cuisines of the Pacific Northwest when it comes to the main meal of the day. **Beef** is especially prominent in Alberta, while **fish and seafood** – anything from salmon and lobster to king crab, oysters and shrimp – dominate the menus of just about all the coastal areas. **Salmon**, especially, is predominant, either served straight or stuffed, or sometimes in unlikely mixes with pasta. **Shellfish** are also popular, notably **clams**, Washington's highly rated **Dungeness crab** – smoother and creamier than the average crab – and, most strikingly, Puget Sound **geoduck** (pronounced "gooey-duck"), huge molluscs of intensely phallic appearance that are often served coyly chopped up. In the northern regions you may well come across some of the most exotic offerings – things like **arctic char** and **caribou** steak.

Ethnic variations are endless, especially in the big cities of Seattle, Portland and Vancouver. Chinese food is everywhere, and can be among the cheapest available. Japanese is not far behind, at least in Vancouver and Seattle, and is not quite as expensive – or fashionable – as it once was. As Pacific Rim immigration gathers pace, other Far Eastern imports are currently making headway, especially Thai, Indonesian and Vietnamese cuisines. Italian food is popular, and can still be cheap in the "Little Italy" of Vancouver. Away from simple pastas, however, it can become expensive, particularly if you venture into the world of exotic pizza toppings and specialist Italian cooking, which is catching on fast in major cities. French food, too, is available, though always pricey, and the favoured cuisine of the urban rich. Be on the lookout also for Native American restaurants, where you enjoy the likes of venison, buffalo and black-husked wild rice, though they are few and far between.

More generally, **Californian cuisine** has made its presence felt throughout the region. Geared towards health and aesthetics, it's basically a development of French **nouvelle cuisine**, utilising the wide mix of fresh, locally available

TIPPING

Almost everywhere you eat or drink, the service will be fast and friendly – thanks to the institution of **tipping**. Waiters and bartenders depend on tips for the bulk of their earnings and, unless the service is dreadful, you should top up your bill by at least fifteen percent. A refusal to tip is considered rude and mean in equal measure. If you're paying by credit card, there's a space on the payment slip where you can add the appropriate tip.

ingredients. The theory is to eat only what you need, and what your body can process. Vegetables are harvested before maturity and steamed to preserve both vitamins and flavour. Seafood comes from oyster farms and the catches of small-time fishers, and what little meat there is tends to be from animals reared on organic farms. One result has been the creation of a clutch of expensive – very expensive – restaurants in the big cities, another has been to stimulate the development in Washington and Oregon of **Northwest cuisine**, with its emphasis on fish. Similar attitudes – and influences – to food and nutrition also underpin the scores of vaguely countercultural restaurants that dot the Pacific Northwest, often owned by former Sixties' "Love Children".

Mexican food has gained a foothold in the big-city restaurants of the Northwest, but is much more prominent in the small, agricultural towns dotting the eastern foothills of Washington's Cascade Mountains, where Mexican farm labour has helped pick the crops since the 1940s. This is one of the cheapest types of food to eat, and even a full dinner with a few drinks will rarely be over $10. As a general rule, Mexican food in the US is different from that in Mexico, making more use of fresh meats and vegetables, although the essentials are the same: rice and pinto beans, often served refried (ie boiled, mashed and fried), with variations on the tortilla, a very thin corn or flour pancake that is wrapped around the food which is then eaten by hand (a burrito); folded, fried and filled (a taco); rolled, filled and baked in sauce (an enchilada); or fried flat and topped with a stack of food (a tostada). Meals are usually served with complimentary nachos (chips) and a hot salsa dip. The chile relleno is a good vegetarian option – a green pepper stuffed with cheese, dipped in egg batter and fried.

DRINKING

Canadian and American **bars** are mostly long and dimly lit counters with a few punters perched on stools gawping at the bartender, and the rest of the clientele occupying the surrounding tables and booths. Yet, despite the similarity of layout, bars vary enormously, from the male-dominated, rough-edged drinking holes concentrated in the blue-collar parts of the cities and the resource towns of the north, to the far more fashionable city establishments which provide food, live entertainment and an inspiring range of cocktails.

Indeed, it's often impossible to separate cafés from bars.

BUYING AND CONSUMING

To buy and consume alcohol in the US, you must be 21, and you may be asked for ID even if you look older. In Alberta the legal drinking age is 18, and 19 in BC and the Yukon. In Canada it's rare to be asked for ID, except at government-run liquor shops, which hold a virtual monopoly on the sale of alcoholic beverages direct to the public. Buying is easier in Washington and Oregon, where laws are more relaxed, and wine and beer are sold by most supermarkets and groceries. Hard liquor, however, attracts tighter regulation, and in both Washington and Oregon it can only be purchased from a state liquor store. Across the Pacific Northwest, bars usually stay open until 1.30am.

BEER

American **beer** tends to be limited to fizzy and tasteless national brands like Budweiser, Miller and Coors; Canada has two national brands, Molson and Labatts, each marketing remarkably similar products under a variety of names – Labatts Blue, Molson Canadian, Molson Export, drinks that inspire, for reasons that elude most foreigners, intense loyalty. Fortunately there are alternatives. Of especial interest to travellers, **microbreweries** and **brewpubs** have sprung up all over the Northwest, and in these establishments you can drink excellent beers, brewed on the premises and often not available anywhere else. They are usually friendly and welcoming places too, and almost all serve a wide range of good-value, hearty **food** to help soak up the drink. Brands to look out for in particular include Henry Weinhard's, one of the best and most widely available; ESB and Red Hook Ale in Seattle; Grants in Yakima; and Deschutes Black Butte Porter in Bend, Oregon – though the list of tangy brews is potentially endless.

Drinking bottled beer in a bar works out a good deal more expensive than the draught, which is usually served by the 170ml glass; even cheaper is a **pitcher**, which contains six to seven glasses.

WINE AND SPIRITS

Both Washington and Oregon produce large quantities of **wine** and have done since the 1960s. In Washington, the main wine-producing area is along the Yakima Valley (see p.277), though there are also vineyards on Puget Sound and around Walla Walla; in Oregon, the vineyards are concentrated along the Willamette Valley south of Portland, with others pocketed in the vicinity of Roseburg and Ashland. Both states have their own appellations and the quality of production is closely regulated. Largely as a result, the general standard is high, with the finest vintages (especially from the Yakima Valley) receiving international plaudits. In Canada, parts of BC's Okanagan produce acceptable wines, though most of the time you'll find yourself drinking the stuff more for the novelty than its intrinsic merits.

Northwest wines are readily available amongst the region's cafés, restaurants and bars, and it's well worth experimenting. Wines are sold by grape-type as much as by vineyard, and as well as delicious reds and whites there's also blush wine, a crisp and faintly fizzy variation on rosé first pioneered in California in the 1980s. The finest wines are generally reckoned to come from Washington and bear the **Columbia** trademark (see p.277). Columbia wines are widely distributed in Washington and Oregon, and the Columbia Winery has its own retail outlets at

Grandview in the Yakima Valley (see p.277 and at Woodinville, not far from Seattle (see p.215).

The industry takes itself very seriously and free **tours and tastings** of the region's **wineries** (and sometimes vineyards) are commonplace. Every local visitor centre can provide opening times and directions. For an overview – and a glossy brochure – contact the **Washington Wine Commission**, PO Box 61217, Seattle, WA 98121 (☎206/441-3130); or the Oregon Wine Advisory Board, 1200 NW Naito Parkway, Suite 400, Portland, OR 97209 (☎1-800/242-2363).

Wine may have made some inroads, but Northwest bars really excel with their **spirits**. Even in run-of-the-mill places there are startling arrays of gins, rums and vodkas, as well as a good selection of whiskeys featuring both imported and domestic brands. Both Canadian Club and VO rye whiskey are made in Canada and are well worth trying. In the smarter bars, you can experiment with all sorts of **cocktails**, anything from dry martinis and creamy brandy Alexanders through to sweet Singapore slings.

ENTERTAINMENT AND MEDIA

In terms of entertainment and media, visitors touring the Pacific Northwest will find themselves travelling through a fairly homogenised cultural landscape: American-style images and icons predominate, a hegemony that's only shattered at the edges by the region's many minorities – who are, at least, given some degree of influence in Canada's state-subsidised TV stations and film productions.

MUSIC

All the major cities and some of the larger towns of the Northwest have good **live music** scenes – with differences of emphasis arising from the comparative local popularity of C&W, R&B, rock, and jazz. Seattle possesses the Pacific Northwest's real claim to musical fame for – setting aside local lad Jimi Hendrix – this is where **grunge** music really hit the big time through local bands like Nirvana, Soundgarden and Pearl Jam. The suicide of Kurt Cobain and the whims of pop fashion mean that

grunge's day has now long gone, but the grunge scene is still more than a fond memory as it was instrumental in making the city one of North America's more fashionable metropolises.

FILM AND THEATRE

Travellers who want to be ahead of the crowds back home should take in a film or two while in the Northwest, Hollywood **movies** are generally on show three to six months before they would reach back home. Most cities have good movie theatres downtown – the biggest, especially Vancouver and Seattle, have some excellent alternative cinemas, too – though in smaller places you often have to make your way out to the multiscreen venues in the malls on the edge of town. Sadly, you don't come across many drive-ins these days. Vancouver has also hit the big time in terms of film and TV production, ranking third in North America behind LA and New York: *The X Files* is the best-known of the shows to have been produced in and around the city.

Theatre is very hit and miss in the big cities, though Vancouver, Portland and Seattle have a well-deserved reputation for the quality of their repertory and independent theatre groups. The larger college towns tend to feature well-funded performances of Shakespeare and the usual canon, while throughout the region – even in the most backwoods areas – local companies provide their own stimulating alternatives. Oregon's tiny Ashland also hosts one of the country's premier Shakespearian festivals (see p.148).

Most major cities have at least one **comedy club**. Standards vary enormously, in some, sexist xenophobes pander to the basest of prejudices, in others the material is fresh, incisive and above all funny. We've listed some of the best venues, though as ever you should consult the local entertainment weeklies.

NEWSPAPERS

In the US, no national **newspapers**, with the exception of the business-oriented *Wall Street Journal* and the lesser *USA Today*, possess much clout. As a consequence, local city papers such as Seattle's *Post-Intelligencer* or Portland's *Oregonian* can be very good indeed. Canada, by contrast, has the *National Post* and more staid and longer-established *Globe and Mail*, an Ontario broadsheet also published in a western edition and available more or less everywhere in BC, Alberta and the Yukon. National news magazines are also available, principally *Maclean's* in Canada, and *Time* and *Newsweek* in the United States.

Most Canadians and Americans still prefer their newspapers grainy, inky and local. Every large town, state or province has at least one morning and/or evening paper, generally excellent at covering its own area but relying on agencies for foreign – and even national – reports. Bigger cities such as Vancouver and Calgary usually have at least two main city papers – one of which is invariably a trashy tabloid.

One good thing most newspapers share is their low cost – normally US35¢ (Can50¢) to US50¢ (Can75¢), with the enormous Sunday editions selling for around US$2 (Can$2.50). Newspapers are sold from vending machines on street corners, outside big cities, newsagents are very rare.

Every community of any size has at least one **free newspaper**, found in street distribution bins or in shops and cafés. Like town, city and provincial papers these can be handy sources for bar, restaurant, nightlife and other listings information, and we've mentioned the most useful titles in the relevant cities.

TV

For low-budget travellers, watching cable **television** in an anonymous motel room may well be the predominant form of entertainment. Bar local stations, the Canadian Broadcasting Corporation (CBC) and one or two public broadcasting channels in Canada, the TV of the Pacific Northwest is effectively the TV of mainstream America.

American, and by implication Canadian TV, can be quite insanely addictive, it certainly comes in quantity, and the quality of the best of it can keep you watching indefinitely. With perhaps thirty-odd channels to choose from, there's always something to grab your attention. The schedules are packed with sycophantic chat shows, outrageous quizzes and banal sitcoms, persistently interrupted by commercials. As for **news** coverage, local reports are comprehensive: a couple of hours each night, sometimes more but world events which don't directly affect the US barely get a look-in.

Cable TV is widely found in motels and hotels, although sometimes you have to pay a couple of dollars to watch it. Most cable stations are worse than the major networks (ABC, CBS and NBC), though some of the more specialised channels are consistently interesting. CNN (Cable Network News) offers round-the-clock news, HBO (Home Box Office) shows recent big-bucks movies, AMC (American Movie Company) shows old black-and-white films, and ESPN exclusively covers sport. Finally, there's MTV (Music Television), which, with the exception of its occasional slots on rap, electronica and the like, is wearingly mainstream and mostly inane.

RADIO

Radio stations are even more abundant than TV channels, and the majority, again, stick to a bland commercial format. Except for news and chat, stations on the **AM** band are best avoided in favour of **FM**, in particular the nationally funded public and college stations, found between 88 and 92 FM. These provide diverse and listenable programming, be it bizarre underground rock or obscure theatre, and they're also good sources for local nightlife news.

Though the large cities boast good specialist **music** stations, for most of the time you'll probably have to resort to skipping up and down the frequencies, between rerun Eagles tracks, Country and Western tunes, fire-and-brimstone Bible thumpers and crazed phone-ins. Driving through rural areas can be frustrating, for hundreds of miles you might only be able to receive one or two (very dull) stations. It's not usual for car rental firms to equip their vehicles with cassette players.

FESTIVALS AND PUBLIC HOLIDAYS

Someone, somewhere is always celebrating something in the USA or Canada, although apart from national holidays, few festivities are shared throughout the respective countries. Instead, there is a disparate multitude of local events: art and craft shows, county fairs, ethnic celebrations, music festivals, rodeos, sandcastle building competitions, and many others of every hue and shade.

PUBLIC HOLIDAYS

The biggest and most all-American of the US **national festivals and holidays** is **Independence Day**, on the Fourth of July. **Canada Day** three days earlier is similar, but is accompanied by slightly less nationalistic fervour. **Halloween** (October 31) lacks patriotic overtones, and is not a public holiday despite being one of the most popular yearly flings. More sedate is **Thanksgiving Day**, on the last Thursday in November in the US, the second Monday in October in Canada.

On the national **public holidays** listed below, shops, offices, banks and government buildings are liable to be closed all day. Many states and provinces also have their own additional holidays, and in some places Good Friday is a half-day holiday. Such holidays are moveable feasts, their

---

NATIONAL HOLIDAYS IN THE NORTHWEST

IN THE US
New Year's Day
Martin Luther King's Birthday (third Mon in Jan)
President's Day (third Mon in Feb)
Easter Monday
Memorial Day (last Mon in May)
Independence Day (July 4)
Labor Day (first Mon in Sept)
Columbus Day (second Mon in Oct)
Veterans' Day (Nov 11)
Thanksgiving Day (fourth Thurs in Nov)
Christmas Day

IN CANADA
New Year's Day
Good Friday
Easter Monday
Victoria Day (Mon before May 25)
Canada Day (July 1)
Labour Day (first Mon in Sept)
Thanksgiving (second Mon in Oct)
Remembrance Day (Nov 11)
Christmas Day
Boxing Day (Dec 26)

MAJOR NORTHWEST EVENTS AND FESTIVALS

For further details of the selected festivals and events listed below see the relevant page of the guide, or contact the local tourist authorities direct. The provincial state tourist boards listed on p.30 can provide free calendars for each area.

JANUARY
Polar Bear Swim, Vancouver, BC. A New Year's Day swim in the freezing waters of English Bay Beach – said to bring good luck for the year.

FEBRUARY
Oregon Shakespeare Festival, Ashland, OR. Premier Bard fest from mid-Feb to Oct in a cute smalltown location.

MARCH
Pacific Rim Whale Festival, Vancouver Island, BC. Celebrating the spring migration of grey whales with lots of whale-spotting expeditions as well as music and dance events.

APRIL
TerrifVic Jazz Party, Victoria, BC. Dixieland, and other jazz bands, from around the globe.

MAY
Northwest Folklife Festival, Seattle, WA. Well-regarded folk fest with US-wide and international artists. Memorial Day weekend.

Maifest, Leavenworth, WA. Community knees-up with parades and marching bands, and the odd drink here and there.

JUNE
Banff Festival of the Arts, AB. Young artist showcase – music, opera, dance, drama, comedy and visual arts.

Portland Rose Festival, Portland, OR. Parades and displays on and of roses. Early to mid-June.

JULY
Calgary Stampede, Calgary, AB. One of the biggest rodeos in the world, all the usual cowboy trappings, plus hot-air balloon races, chuckwagon rides, craft exhibitions, native dancing and a host of other happenings. Billed as the Greatest Outdoor Show on Earth.

Canada Day, throughout Canada. Fireworks, parades and a day off for patriotic shenanigans. July 1.

Festival of American Fiddlers, Port Townsend, WA. Second weekend in July. Big and prestigious folk music do.

Klondike Days, Edmonton, AB. Pioneer era in Edmonton revisited with gold panning, raft races, pancake breakfasts and gambling.

Independence Day. The entire United States grinds to a standstill on July 4 as people get drunk, salute the flag and partake of firework displays, marches, beauty pageants and more, all in commemoration of the signing of the Declaration of Independence in 1776.

Oregon Country Fair, Veneta, OR. 1st weekend after 4th July. Huge fair and live music shindig.

Pow-wows. Traditional aboriginal Canadian celebrations that take place on reserves across the country in July and Aug.

AUGUST
Squamish Days Loggers Sports Festival, BC. A lumberjack's convention with impressive logging competitions.

Bumbershoot, Seattle, WA. Massive art, music and lit fest that will "saturate your soul", apparently. Labor Day weekend.

SEPTEMBER
Pendleton Roundup, Pendleton, OR. Mid-Sept rodeo: one of the biggest, meanest and wildest in the West.

OCTOBER
Vancouver International Film Festival, BC. Another of Canada's highly rated film fests.

Halloween (October 31). One of the year's most popular flings. Traditionally, kids bang on doors demanding "trick or treat", and are given pieces of candy. These days that sort of activity is mostly confined to rural and suburban areas.

NOVEMBER
Thanksgiving Day. Fourth Thursday in Nov for US (second Mon in Oct in Canada). Essentially a domestic affair, when relatives return to the family home to eat roast turkey, a carry-on that recalls the first harvest of the Pilgrims in Massachusetts – though Thanksgiving was a national holiday long before anyone thought to make that connection.

DECEMBER
Coral Ships, Vancouver, BC. Coral singers sail around Vancouver Harbour in sparkly boats.

dates changing slightly from year to year. The traditional season for tourism runs from Memorial Day in the US, Victoria Day in Canada to Labor Day (around Sept 5 in both countries), and some tourist attractions, information centres, motels and campsites are only open during that period.

CLIMATE AND WHEN TO GO

Despite a reputation for rain and damp, the climate of the Pacific Northwest is characterised by wide variations, not just from region to region and season to season, but also day to day and even hour to hour. Most weather patterns are produced by westerly winds sweeping in from the Pacific, but the region's mountain ranges and the extreme northerly latitudes of the Yukon produce climates and microclimates that can range from the near desert conditions of parts of southern BC and eastern Oregon to the arctic onslaught frequently experienced in the far north.

Certain generalisations can be made. Temperatures tend to rise the further south you go, and to fall the higher you climb, while the climate along the coast is milder and more equable than inland. Mountains, throughout the region, are powerful influences on climate.

Oregon and **Washington** display mixtures of weather, with gentle blue-skied summers, but often dismally grey and wet periods, particularly on the west side of the Cascade Mountains between October and June. Winters here, while soggy, are rarely cold, temperatures hovering above freezing point. The drizzle stops east of the mountains, and the temperatures become more extreme – pleasant in spring, less so in summer, and with colder winters. The coastal peaks of Washington's Olympic Peninsula ensure that this is the wettest area of either state – wet enough to foster temperate rainforests.

The prairies of **Alberta**, some of the region's most benign-looking landscapes, ironically experience some of the continent's wildest climatic extremes, suffering the longest, harshest winters, but also some of the finest, clearest summers. Extremes are also more marked between the south and north of the region, with far lower tem-

		Jan	Feb	March	April	May	June	July	Aug	Sept	Oct	Nov	Dec
AVERAGE TEMPERATURES (°F) AND RAINFALL													
Edmonton	av. max temp	15	22	34	52	64	70	74	72	62	52	34	21
	av. min temp	-4	1	12	28	38	45	49	47	38	30	16	5
	days of rain	12	9	10	8	12	15	14	12	9	9	11	12
Portland	av. max temp	44	48	54	61	66	72	77	77	71	62	53	46
	av. min temp	34	36	39	43	47	53	56	56	52	47	41	37
	days of rain	19	17	17	14	13	10	3	4	8	12	17	19
Seattle	av. max temp	45	48	52	58	64	69	72	73	67	59	51	47
	av. min temp	36	37	39	43	47	52	54	55	52	47	41	38
	days of rain	18	16	16	13	12	9	4	5	8	13	17	19
Vancouver	av. max temp	41	44	50	58	64	69	74	73	65	57	48	43
	av. min temp	32	34	37	40	46	52	54	54	49	44	39	35
	days of rain	20	17	17	14	12	11	7	8	9	16	19	22

To convert °F to °C, subtract 32 and multiply by 5/9

peratures in winter in the north. Winter skiing brings lots of people to the **Rockies**, where weather is related closely to altitude and position: colder higher up, drier on the more easterly slopes (see p.450 for details of Chinooks, the curious warm winds associated with the eastern Rockies). Summer is still the busiest time in these mountains, however, especially July and August, the months that offer the best hiking conditions (though snow can linger even on popular low-lying trails as late as June). Lower-slope hiking can be better in spring and early summer, when there are less insects too.

Much of **British Columbia** – western Vancouver Island and the Haida Gwaii (Queen Charlotte Islands) in particular – bear the brunt of Pacific depressions, making them some of the region's damper areas, though southwestern parts of the province enjoy remarkably benign weather: the fruit- and wine-producing Okanagan valley has a Californian climate of long hot summers and mild winters, while the area to the north around Kamloops experiences near desert conditions.

Winters across the **Yukon** are bitterly cold, with temperatures rarely rising above freezing for months on end (-10°F is an average, -70°F a pos-

sibility), but precipitation year-round is among the region's lowest, making the "dry" cold slightly more bearable. Summers, by contrast, are short but surprisingly warm, and spring – though late – can produce outstanding displays of wild flowers across the tundra. In the extreme north, for example, the sun doesn't set for 82 days from late May to early August, producing inland temperatures in the 90s°F. At the same time, summers can also throw up dreadfully cold and wet days. Another problem in the warmer months are the voracious swarms of mosquito and blackfly that can blight trips into the backcountry.

For detailed daily **weather forecasts in the US**, tune in to TV's 24-hour Weather Channel. Many smaller stations offer similar services, especially in popular hiking and skiing areas such as the Canadian Rockies. Such areas usually also offer special phone lines for up-to-the-minute forecasts. Be sure to check weather before setting off on longer hikes: conditions can change quickly and dramatically in mountain regions. In more remote mountain areas it also pays to check weather conditions before driving – several people a year are trapped and freeze to death in their cars.

DIRECTORY

ADDRESSES Generally speaking, roads in built-up areas in both Canada and the United States are laid out on a grid system, creating "blocks" of buildings. The first one or two digits of a specific address refer to the block, which will be num-

bered in sequence from a central point, usually downtown, for example, 620 S Cedar Avenue will be six blocks south of downtown. It is crucial, therefore, to take note of components such as "NW" or "SE" in addresses, 3620 SW Washington Blvd will be a very long way indeed from 3620 NE Washington Blvd.

AIRPORT TAX This is invariably included in the price of your ticket, though certain departure taxes may not be. At Vancouver an "Airport Improvement" tax (see p.290) is levied on all departing passengers taking both internal and international flights. Pay with cash or credit card.

CIGARETTES AND SMOKING Many agencies in the US and Canada are strongly concerned about smoking's detrimental effects on health, with smoking now severely frowned upon in the vast majority of public places. Most cinemas are non-smoking, restaurants are usually divided into non-smoking and smoking sections, and smoking is universally forbidden on public transport – including almost all domestic airline flights. Work places, too, tend to be smoke-free zones, so employees are reduced to smoking on the street outside.

DATES In the North American style, the date 1.8.00 means not August 1 but January 8.

ELECTRICITY 110V AC in both the US and Canada. All plugs are two-pronged and rather insubstantial. Some European-made travel plug adapters don't fit American sockets.

FLOORS The first floor in the US and Canada is what would be the ground floor in Britain, the second floor would be the first floor, and so on.

ID Should be carried at all times. Two pieces should suffice, one of which should have a photo: a passport and credit card(s) are your best bets.

MEASUREMENTS AND SIZES The US has not gone metric, so measurements are in inches, feet, yards and miles, weight in ounces, pounds and tons. American pints and gallons are about four-fifths of imperial ones. Clothing sizes are always two figures less what they would be in Britain – a British women's size 12 is a US size 10 – while British shoe sizes are 1 1/2 below American ones. Canada, by contrast, officially uses the metric system (though many people still use the old imperial system): distances are in kilometres, temperatures in degrees Celsius, and food, fuel and drink are sold in grams, kilograms and litres.

TAX Be warned that federal and/or state and provincial sales or services taxes are added to virtually every goods or service purchased in both the US and Canada, but isn't generally part of the marked price. The actual rate varies from place to place, though Alberta has no local sales tax. Hotel tax will add 5 to 15 percent to most bills. See also p.24.

TEMPERATURES Given in Fahrenheit in the US, in Celsius in Canada.

TIME ZONES The Northwest spreads over two different time zones, the Mountain zone covers Alberta and is two hours behind the East Coast, seven behind the UK, the Pacific Standard zone includes Oregon, Washington, BC, Yukon and is three hours behind New York, eight hours behind the UK.

TIPPING Many first-time visitors to North America think of tipping as a potential source of huge embarrassment. It's nothing of the sort, tipping is universally expected, and you quickly learn to tip without a second thought. You really shouldn't depart a bar or restaurant without leaving a tip of at least 15 percent (unless the service is utterly dismal). About the same amount should be added to taxi fares – and round them up to the nearest 50¢ or dollar. A hotel porter who has lugged your suitcases up several flights of stairs should get $3 to $5. When paying by credit or charge card, you can add the tip to the total bill before filling in the amount and signing.

VIDEOS The standard format of video cassettes in North America is different from that in Britain. You cannot buy videos in the US or Canada compatible with a video camera bought in Britain.

PART TWO

THE

GUIDE

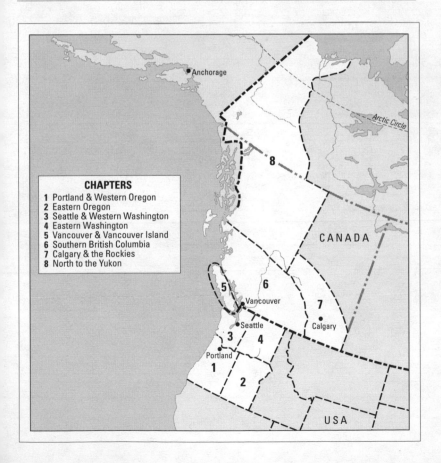

CHAPTERS
1 Portland & Western Oregon
2 Eastern Oregon
3 Seattle & Western Washington
4 Eastern Washington
5 Vancouver & Vancouver Island
6 Southern British Columbia
7 Calgary & the Rockies
8 North to the Yukon

CHAPTER ONE

PORTLAND AND WESTERN OREGON

or nineteenth-century pioneers, driving in their covered wagons across the mountains and deserts of the Oregon Trail, the green **Willamette Valley**, running for just over a hundred miles parallel to and just inland from the Pacific coast, was the promised land. Rich and fertile, it became the home of Oregon's first settlements and towns, and the valley is still at the heart of the state's social, political and cultural existence. Most of Oregon's population is concentrated here, either in the cities strung along the Willamette River or in the hinterland of rural villages, and many remain dependent on agriculture and forestry – the twin pillars of what has always been a resource-based economy.

In early days, the produce of Oregon's farms and forests spawned a handful of trading centres, bustling townships such as Oregon City, Salem, Eugene and, most successful of all, Portland, from where ships left for Europe and the East Coast laden with raw materials. It was the lack of safe anchorages along the storm-battered coast that inspired the success of Portland and it was through its burgeoning docks that the other Willamette Valley towns gained access to the Pacific via the Columbia River, now the boundary between Oregon and Washington. Even today, Coos Bay is Oregon's only major coastal port.

It was, however, a different sort of natural resource that boosted the pioneer economy sky-high. In 1852, **gold** was unearthed on the Rogue River, in the south of the state, and during the subsequent gold rush the prospectors' colony of Jacksonville was even touted as the state capital. However, the gold gave out in the 1880s, and Oregon, albeit fuelled by the injection of cash, resumed its more pedestrian agricultural progress. Only in the recent past have tourism, electronics and hydroelectricity provided some diversification, and those pockets of industrialization that do exist remain quite small.

A sense of **pastoral** continuity, rare in the Pacific Northwest, underpins the slight (semi-humorous) disdain expressed by many well-established Oregonians for their Californian neighbours. This hauteur is demonstrated by frequent reference to an apocryphal signpost on the Oregon Trail: the route to California was marked by a cairn of

---

ACCOMMODATION PRICE CODES

All the accommodation prices in this book have been coded using the symbols below, corresponding to US dollar prices in the US chapters and equivalent Canadian dollar rates in the Canadian chapters. Prices are for the least expensive double room in high season, excluding special offers. For a full explanation see p.51 in Basics.

① up to US$30   ③ US$45–60   ⑤ US$80–100   ⑦ US$130–180
② US$30–45   ④ US$60–80   ⑥ US$100–130   ⑧ US$180+

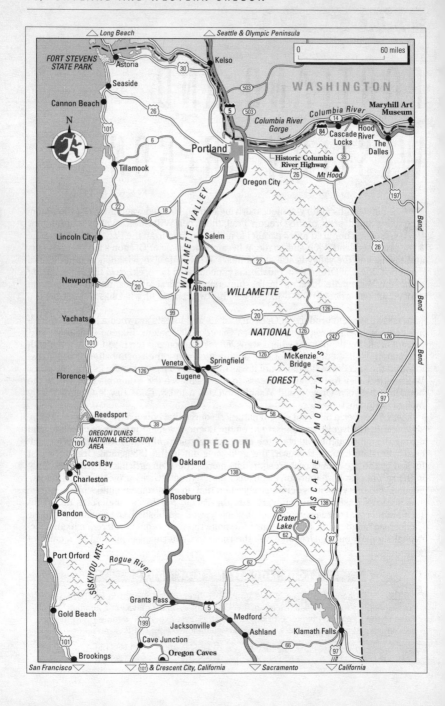

shimmering quartz, the other by a marker with the legend "To Oregon". The pioneers who could read (and were therefore, so the assumption goes, respectable and hard-working) came to Oregon; the rabble went south. In the manner of such folklore, this self-image doesn't bear too much historical scrutiny – the farmers of the Willamette rushed off to the Rogue River gold fields as fast as anyone – but, together with the allure of the Pacific coast, it has, in the last thirty years, attracted thousands of Americans disenchanted with mainstream culture. Most visibly, these new arrivals have combined with a string of reformist governors to stave off the worst excesses of urban development, keeping the downtowns of the two largest cities, **Portland** and **Eugene**, to manageable proportions, friendly to pedestrians, joggers and cyclists alike. Each of these cities, at either end of the Willamette Valley, merits a two- or three-day stay, though Portland is particularly agreeable. A relaxed and easy-going place, it offers an appealing assortment of fine old buildings, the occasional art gallery and museum as well as good restaurants and coffeehouses, and an amiable nightlife.

Both Portland and Eugene are also within easy striking distance of the **Cascade Mountains**, once the final barrier to incoming pioneers, but now a major recreation area, where the forested slopes and severe peaks feature a superbly rugged terrain, crisscrossed by trails and liberally strewn with campgrounds and mountain lodges. In particular, Portland is less than an hour's drive from the fine scenery of the 22-mile **Historic Columbia River Highway**, the most popular tourist route hereabouts, as well as **Hood River**, the region's premier windsurfing centre. Pushing on, the city is also a little less than two hours' drive from the art collection of the eccentric tycoon Sam Hill, displayed in the singular **Maryhill Museum**, over on the Washington side of the Columbia River, whilst mighty **Mount Hood**, where skiing is a big wintertime deal, is just sixty miles from the city. By comparison, Eugene is rather less well-appointed and although it's near the edge of the Willamette National Forest, it's best regarded as a staging post on the way to Bend (see p.168), the most convenient and enjoyable base for exploring this segment of the Cascades.

From the Willamette Valley, it's west across a slender line of scenic hills and forests to the northern section of the 350-mile **Oregon Coast**, a magnificent preamble (if you're heading on into Washington) to the stunning land- and seascapes of the Olympic Peninsula (see pp.237–251). The Oregon shoreline weather-beaten headlands, great strips of sandy beach, Sahara-like sand dunes and mysterious-looking sea stacks. On a sunny day (of which there are many) the trip along the coast is wonderfully exhilarating, though some claim stormy days are even better. This superb scenery is often best appreciated from the string of state parks – and their campgrounds – that monopolize much of the seashore, though several of the coast's towns are appealing too, with highlights being the offbeat charms of **Newport**, the grand old mansions of **Astoria** and the prettiness of both **Bandon** and **Cannon Beach**. Each of these makes for a lovely one- or two-night stay, and all four have evaded the crass development that has engulfed small sections of the Oregon Coast, the worst example being at **Lincoln City**.

Back inland, beyond the Willamette Valley, the southern reaches of the Oregon Cascades hold **Crater Lake**, an extraordinarily beautiful volcanic crater protected as a national park. It's one of the state's finest attractions and is within easy reach of both Bend and the towns of the Rogue River and its tributaries, amongst which **Ashland**, home of the first-class Oregon Shakespeare Festival, is the most diverting. Ashland is just a few kilometres from the Californian border – either a quick but unexciting zip

TOLL-FREE INFORMATION NUMBER AND WEB SITE

Oregon Tourism ☎1-800/547-7842, *www.traveloregon.com*

THE OREGON TRAIL

Perhaps more than any other American leader of his day, **Thomas Jefferson** realized the opportunities presented by the vast lands west of the Mississippi, and after he became President in 1801 he was in a position to act upon his expansionist vision. He had, however, to be cautious. The French held the **Louisiana Territory** between the Mississippi and the Rockies, and the British claimed the land from the Rockies to the Pacific – a vast wilderness known as the **Oregon Country**, buffered by Russian Alaska and Spanish California. Consequently, when Jefferson began organizing an American overland expedition to the Pacific he was careful to define its purpose purely in terms of trade and commerce. It was a diplomatically difficult enterprise, but luck was on his side. The European powers were embroiled in the Napoleonic Wars and the French were keen to raise cash. Obligingly, Napoleon sold the Louisiana Territory to the Americans in 1803, thereby halving Jefferson's international problems at a stroke. And so, when the **Lewis and Clark expedition** left St Louis for the Pacific in 1804, it was as much to do with taking stock of the Americans' new possessions as the long-term strategy of contesting British influence. In the event, Anglo-American territorial rivalry dragged on until 1846, but by this time the British claim to the region south of the 49th Parallel (present-day Washington and Oregon) had become academic. It had been swept away by the rising tide of overland immigration launched by pioneer farmers, the majority of whom came from the Midwest, just east of the Mississippi.

The detailed reports emanating from the Lewis and Clark expedition laid the foundations for the migration west, but the migrants – or **movers**, as they're often called – were much more inspired by the missionaries who went west to Christianize the "Indians" in the 1830s. After all, Lewis and Clark had travelled by canoe, but the missionaries had headed out in simple covered wagons encumbered by farming equipment and livestock – precisely as the pioneers had to do. The missionaries also sent back glowing and widely circulated reports of the Oregon Country's mild climate, fertile soil and absence of malaria, and confirmed that the lands of the West Coast were well forested. This was crucial: mid-nineteenth-century American farmers judged the fertility of land by the size of the trees it supported. This was, of course, quite wrong, but it explains why they ignored

down Interstate 5, or a delightful if time-consuming haul west and then south along highways 99 and 199. The latter leads through the dark forests, deep ravines and wild coastal mountains that span this part of the Oregon–California border.

Finding a **place to stay** is rarely a problem in the towns of the Willamette Valley, with Portland having the widest range of choices, notably a cluster of delightfully refurbished, old downtown hotels. Elsewhere, the coast has a huge supply of hotels and motels and many B&Bs too, but it's still advisable to ring ahead in summer particularly if you're keen to stay by the seashore. Tourist offices will advise on availability and often have detailed descriptions of local B&Bs. Oregon State Parks operate a central reservation system for many of their **campgrounds** (☎1-800/452-5687, *www.prd.state.or.us*), taking bookings for no less than two days and no more than eleven months ahead. Most of their campgrounds are open all year, unlike those of the US Forest Service, whose national forest sites usually operate from Memorial Day to the Labor Day weekend. Most US Forest services campgrounds operate on a first-come, first-served basis, but a small percentage can be reserved in advance (☎1-800/280-2267).

Getting around

With **Greyhound** (☎1-800/231-2222, *www.greyhound.com*) and, to a lesser extent, Amtrak (☎1-800/872-7245, *www.amtrak.com*) linking major towns, and local bus services extending the network, **getting around** on public transport is a feasible proposi-

the treeless prairie that barred their route just beyond the Mississippi, commonly calling it the "Great American Desert" – and leaving it to a later generation of farmers.

The expectations of prospective migrants were further raised by the Senate when, in 1842, it considered legislation giving generous land grants to Oregon Country settlers. As it turned out, the legislation was not passed, but it was clear that the US would – sooner rather than later – incorporate the region and parcel out the land. This was quite enough for many would-be migrants and, in the spring of 1843, one thousand of them gathered at Independence and Westport on the banks of the Missouri, to prepare for what is now known as the **Great Migration**. The pioneers were a remarkably homogeneous bunch, nearly all experienced farmers, travelling in family groups in ordinary ox-pulled farm wagons with flimsy canvas roofs. Only too aware of the difficulties of the journey, the movers voted in wagon-train leaders after the first hundred miles – nobody wanted to be saddled with a charlatan – and established camp rules to govern everything from the grazing of livestock to the collection of fuel (usually buffalo dung).

Traversing almost two thousand miles of modern-day Kansas, Nebraska, Wyoming and Idaho, they cajoled their wagons across rivers, struggled over mountain passes, endured the burning heat of the plains, chopped their way through forests, and paused at the occasional frontier fort or missionary station to recuperate. Finally, after six months on the trail, they built rafts which, with the assistance of local Native-Americans, they steered from The Dalles down the treacherous lower reaches of the Columbia River. Despite orders to the contrary from his employer, **John McLoughlin**, head of the British-owned Hudson's Bay Company's Fort Vancouver, helped the newcomers to recover from their ordeals. Their arrival doubled Oregon's American population, and pushed the US government into the creation of the **Oregon Territory** just five years later.

Over the next thirty years, further waves of settlers followed the Oregon Trail, whittling away at the time it took by pioneering short cuts. Overall, they swelled the population of the Willamette Valley by some 53,000 and only with the coming of the railroad – in the 1880s – did the trail fall into disuse. Precious little survives today to remember the pioneers by, but out in eastern Oregon one or two hillsides still show the ruts made by the wheels of their wagons and there are several interpretive centres, the pick of which is outside Baker City (see p.165).

tion if you're content to stay in the larger settlements. However, once you leave the main towns, bus and train services soon fade away and smaller places are rarely able to muster more than one or two buses a day. Furthermore, if you're venturing into the great outdoors you'll be lucky to find any buses at all and having your own vehicle is pretty much essential. Portland is as easy a place to get to as anywhere in Oregon: it's well-connected by train and bus with California to the south and Seattle and Vancouver in the north, and has a first-rate municipal transit system. Portland is also the hub of **Oregon's bus** and **train** routes with Amtrak running south to Salem, Eugene and Klamath Falls, and east along the Washington side of the Columbia River to Spokane and ultimately Chicago. Greyhound buses follow the line of I-84 to Pendleton, La Grande and Baker City before proceeding on into Idaho, whilst other Greyhound buses link Portland with Salem, Eugene, Bend, Ashland and Grants Pass. Greyhound also run from Portland to Lincoln City and points south along the coast, though for the Astoria/Cannon Beach area you're reliant on local buses.

More energetically, the popular **Oregon Coast Bike Route** relies for the most part on reasonably wide, cyclist-only shoulder lanes on either side of Hwy 101, though small sections do travel quiet country roads. From May to October, the prevailing winds blow from the Northwest, so you're advised to cycle from north to south – Oregon Tourism produce a detailed brochure. Most **hikers** are more than satisfied with the hundreds of walking trails that crisscross the state's wilderness areas and national forests – anything from short afternoon strolls to full-scale expeditions. However, western Oregon also has two long-distance hiking routes, the **Oregon Coast Trail** (the OCT), which weaves through some of Oregon's finest coastal scenery, and a portion of the 2600-mile **Pacific Crest Trail** (the PCT; *www.pcta.org*), a tumultuous route running from Mexico to Canada across Oregon's Cascades (see p.62). Information on the OCT is available from Oregon State Parks, 1115 Commercial St NE, Salem, OR 97301-1002 (☎503/378-4168, *www.prd.state.or.us*).

PORTLAND

Portland is a city for civilized living. It's not the most obvious tourist destination – there are no major sights – but it's got an appealing air of quirky whimsicality and enough galleries, outdoor markets, fine old architecture, coffeehouses and bars to keep most people going for a few days. Add the fact that it's an excellent base for touring the surrounding coast and mountains, and take away the hassles of the larger West Coast cities, and you've got a place that deserves to be on any Northwest itinerary.

The city was named after Portland, Maine, following a coin toss between its two East Coast founders in 1845 ("Boston" was the other option). It was then no more than a clearing in the woods, but its location on a deep part of the Willamette River, near the Columbia River just eighty-odd miles from the Pacific, and surrounded by fertile valleys, made it a perfect trading port. It grew rapidly, supplying lumber to San Francisco and the Californian gold fields, and as the money poured in, Portland's elite built themselves elegant mansions and a suitably opulent business district, replacing the initial clapboard buildings with impressive Gothic, Florentine and Second Empire edifices. An entrepreneurial spirit dominated the emergent city, but not everyone was convinced: John Reed, the founder of the Communist Party of the USA and author of *Ten Days That Shook the World* – an eyewitness account of Russia's Bolshevik Revolution – was born here in 1887.

Neither did everyone benefit from the boom. Away from the richer parts of town lurked the seamier side of Portland – the "North End" (along the waterfront north of Burnside St), a violent, bawdy district, notorious for gambling, liquor, prostitution and opium dens. At its peak, towards the end of the nineteenth century, the North End's vice industry was so well-entrenched, and the police so heavily bribed, that its ringleaders were even able to run a large-scale shanghaiing operation (see box, p.92), with scores of unwitting men drugged, drunk or beaten unconscious to wake up as members of a ship's crew out on the Pacific. Things are much calmer today, but the North End is where you'll still find the city's poor and dispossessed.

In the 1920s, when the new ports of Puget Sound – principally Seattle – gained regional ascendancy, Portland declined (and the North End emptied), leaving behind huge swaths of derelict riverside warehouses and rail yards. As a consequence, city planners in the 1970s faced a downtown in tatters, its historic buildings decayed or sacrificed to parking lots and expressways. Portland scrupulously salvaged what was left of its past while risking the odd splash of postmodernist architectural colour, and undertook much assiduous gap-filling, even to the extent of grassing over a riverside highway to convert it into the Tom McCall Park. Meanwhile, a levy on new construction funded all manner of public art – most obviously in the life-size statues that now decorate downtown streets. Pockets of seediness remain, but nowadays much of the downtown area bears the stamp of these renewal projects, with redbrick replacing concrete, cycle routes and extensive public transit taking the place of cars. Progress is still to be made but, overlooked by extensive parkland on the green West Hills, ecology-conscious, arts-conscious Portland is an attractive and very liveable city.

The Portland area telephone code is ☎503

Arrival

Portland International Airport (PDX) is located about twelve miles northeast of downtown, beside the Columbia River. From the terminal building, **MAX trains** shuttle passengers downtown, travelling along SW 1st Avenue and SW Morrison Street – or at least they will do when the line is completed in late 2001. The journey time is expected to be around forty minutes; for more details of MAX, see "City transport" below. Bus services from the airport to downtown may well change after the new MAX line is completed, but in the meantime Gray Line operates an **airport express shuttle bus** (every 45min from 5am to midnight; $15 one way), which drops off at sixteen downtown hotels. Alternatively, the local **Tri-Met bus #12** (2–5 hourly, 7am–11.30pm; $1.45) runs downtown to the 5th Avenue transit mall in about 45 minutes. Both bus services leave from outside the terminal building. A **taxi** from the airport into town costs in the region of $25–30.

In downtown Portland, the Greyhound **bus station** is at 550 NW 6th Ave and Glisan (☎243-2357 or 1-800/231-2222). The Amtrak **train station** is a few metres away, at 800 NW 6th Ave (☎273-4865 or 1-800/872-7245). From here, it's about ten-minutes' walk south to the city centre (at Pioneer Courthouse Square), but if you arrive at either terminal at night take a taxi – this part of town is not safe after dark. Arriving by **car**, I-5 will bring you into the city from the north or south: heading south, take the City Center/Morrison Bridge exit 300B; northbound use the Naito Parkway/Front Avenue exit 299B. Approaching from the east, I-84 joins I-5 just north of downtown – and exit 300B. The city centre is fairly easy to navigate with Broadway serving as the north–south axis and West Burnside Street channelling traffic along its northern edge.

Information

Portland's **visitor centre** is located downtown, on the ground floor of the glassy World Trade Center, by the Willamette River at 26 SW Salmon St and Front Avenue (May–Oct daily 9am–5pm; Nov–April Mon–Fri 9am–5pm & Sat 10am–2pm; ☎275-9750 or 1-877/678-5263, *www.travelportland.com*). They issue free city maps, bus timetables and a glossy city brochure, which includes accommodation listings. They also have plenty of information on the rest of the state, with details on everything from state parks, cycle routes and bus services to lists of forthcoming events. Usefully, **Ticket Central**, who sell tickets for a wide range of events, share the same premises. This is a walk-in service, but there is a day-of-show information line (☎275-8358).

Orientation

The Willamette River divides Portland in half – east from west – and works in tandem with Burnside Street, which spans the river, to divide the city into quadrants. Avenues run north–south, are numbered and are prefixed by the relevant quadrant, as are streets, which are named and run east–west: thus SE 11th Avenue is a long way from NW 11th Avenue. **Downtown Portland**, where you'll probably spend most time, is on the west bank, mostly falling within the southwest quadrant, while the eastern part of the city – the northeast and southeast quadrants – is largely residential. The downtown area is fairly compact and you can see much of it on **foot**, but, if only to get to where you're staying, you may need to use the city's excellent public transit network.

City transport and cruises

The **Tri-Met bus system** is based at the downtown transit malls along 5th Avenue (southbound) and 6th Avenue (northbound). Each bus shelter is labelled with a symbol

– brown beaver, purple rain, blue snowflake, etc – which serves as a code for a route in a particular area of the city. Though designed for simplicity, the system can still be pretty confusing: visit the **Tri-Met Customer Assistance Office** on Pioneer Courthouse Square (Mon–Fri 8am–5pm; ☎238-7433; for disabled customers ☎962-2455, *www.tri-met.org*) to get a free transit map and route-planning advice. Buses (and MAX, see below) are free in the downtown zone – **"Fareless Square"** – edged by I-405 to the south and west and the Willamette River to the north and east, but including the east bank's Rose Garden arena and Lloyd Center. Outside of this zone, fares are between $1.15 and $1.45 – pay the bus driver (exact change only) or, at some stops, use the automatic ticket machine. Tickets are valid for 1hr 45min and can be used as transfers for onward travel within the same zone (there are 3 fare zones altogether). The Tri-Met office also sells day tickets (all zones) for $3.60 and books of ten tickets at a discount – $13.50 (all zones).

Also operated by Tri-Met, **MAX** (Metropolitan Area Express), Portland's light railway, shunts passengers around downtown, travelling east along SW Yamhill Street and west along SW Morrison Street, between SW 18th and SW 1st avenues. On SW 1st Avenue, MAX travels in both directions, passing through the Old Town on its way to the Steel Bridge over to the northeast quadrant and (from late 2001) the airport. West from SW 18th Avenue, MAX tunnels under Washington Park (and the zoo) bound for the Hillsboro suburb. The MAX tariff is the same as the bus, but tickets must be purchased before you start your journey. There are ticket machines at every stop and these both issue new tickets and validate unused ones purchased ahead of time. Further extensions to the transit system are planned, principally a streetcar link between downtown and the Nob Hill district

Vintage trolley cars, aimed at the tourist trade, also use the more central of the Max lines, heading along SW Morrison Street, SW Yamhill Street and SW 1st Avenue as far as Burnside Street (every 30min; March–April Sat & Sun 10am–6pm; May–Dec Mon–Fri 10am–3pm, Sat & Sun 10am–6pm; free). Note also that Portland's **taxis** rarely stop in the street and to catch one you either have to go to a hotel, where they line up outside the main entrance, or telephone; try Broadway Cabs ☎227-1234 or Portland Taxi ☎256-5400.

Finally, few would claim Portland's slice of the Willamette River is much to look at, but Portland Spirit River Cruises gamely offers dinner cruises ($52 per person) and **two-hour sightseeing boat trips** (April–Oct 1–2 daily; $15; ☎224-3900 or 1-800/224-3901), departing from the jetty at the foot of Salmon Street. A replica stern-wheeler, the *Columbia Gorge* (☎223-3928), offers a similar service with two-hour sightseeing trips (Oct–June Sat & Sun 2 daily) costing $12.95, and three-hour dinner cruises running $37.95 (Oct–June 1 weekly). Departures are from the Tom McCall waterfront Park, just north of the Morrison Bridge at the foot of Stark Street. Much more enticing, if you have the time and money, are the **week-long boat trips** along the Columbia and Snake rivers operated by Cruise West of Seattle (☎1-800/426-7702, *www.cruisewest.com*). These cruises, which begin and end in Portland, head east up the Columbia River Gorge (see p.102), passing through a series of locks and stopping at points of interest on the way – Multnomah Falls (see p.103), the Maryhill Museum (see p.106) and the northern tip of Hells Canyon (see p.163) to name but three. There are between three and five cruises weekly from mid-March to April and from mid-September to late October. Prices vary considerably, depending on the date and category of cabin, For example, a cruise in the least expensive cabin in March might cost just $700 per person, whilst a deluxe cabin in September runs $3295.

Accommodation

Dozens of inexpensive motels line the main roads into Portland – Sandy Boulevard to the northeast of the city centre being a case in point – but for a few dollars more you're far better staying downtown, where you'll be able to savour the city's laid-back, amiable atmosphere. Downtown options include the occasional modern **motel** along with **hotels** to suit most budgets, from the modest and mundane through to the chic and smart, the pick of which occupy grand and beautifully restored old buildings. The city also has two reputable **hostels** – one each in the southeast and northwest quadrants, and both a quick bus ride from downtown. Finally, be aware that Portland has its share of downtown flophouses on and around West Burnside Street near Burnside Bridge.

Hotels, motels and B&Bs

Benson Hotel, 309 SW Broadway at Oak St (☎228-2000 or 1-888/523-6766, fax 226-4603). Classy hotel with a superb walnut-panelled lobby dating from 1912. Extremely comfortable bedrooms with plush and tastefully arranged modern furnishings. Facilities include a health club and two restaurants. ⑧.

Best Western Imperial Hotel, 400 SW Broadway at Stark St (☎228-7221 or 1-800/452-2323, fax 223-4551). Plain, modern but perfectly comfortable rooms in a handsome, c.1900 high-rise. Some of the restoration work has, however, been cack-handed – try not to look at the modern, ill considered window frames. ⑥.

Days Inn City Center, 1414 SW 6th Ave at Clay St (☎221-1611 or 1-800/899-0248, fax 226-0447). Great downtown location and good value with well-tended motel-style rooms. ④.

Four Points Downtown Sheraton, 50 SW Morrison St at Front Ave (☎221-0711 or 1-800/899-0247, fax 274-0312, *www.fourpointsportland.com*). This modern hotel has a great location near the Old Town district and across (busy) Front Ave from the Willamette River. The rooms at the front overlook the river, but they don't have balconies, whereas those at the side do. The rooms themselves are largish and comfortable with modern furnishings and fittings. The lounge bar is classic 1960s design, all clean lines and regular angles. ⑥.

General Hooker's B&B, 125 SW Hooker St (☎222-4435 or 1-800/745-4135, fax 295-6410, *www.generalhookers.com*). Each of the four guestrooms in this attractive late nineteenth-century home are pleasantly decorated and air-conditioned. Located about twenty-minutes' walk south of Market St along SW 1st Ave, or take brown-coded bus #17 from the downtown transit mall. ④.

Governor Hotel, 611 SW 10th Ave at Alder St (☎224-3400 or 1-800/554-3456, fax 241-2122, *www.govhotel.com*). Luxurious downtown hotel mostly housed in an imaginatively styled Italian Renaissance office building of 1923. The lobby holds a striking sepia-toned mural inspired by the Lewis and Clark expedition. The rooms are furnished in crisp modern style but original features – particularly the carved woodwork – have been preserved wherever possible. ⑦.

Heathman Hotel, 1001 SW Broadway at Salmon St (☎241-4100 or 1-800/551-0011, fax 790-7111, *www.heathmanhotel.com*). Many regard this as Portland's top hotel. The *Heathman* occupies a finely restored building with an elegant, teak-panelled interior and generous amounts of marble and brass, especially in the high-style wainscoted lobby bar. First-rate and splendidly commodious rooms make this hotel a real treat. Substantial discounts are frequently offered on the weekend. ⑦.

Mallory Hotel, 729 SW 15th Ave at Yamhill St (☎223-6311 or 1-800/228-8657, fax 223-0522, *www.malloryhotel.com*). In an old, slightly careworn neighbourhood on the edge of downtown, this attractive hotel has a handsome facade of sandy-coloured brick decorated with geometric and herringbone patterns. The lobby is similarly stylish, with grand wooden fittings, chandeliers and a coffered ceiling, but the rooms beyond are much plainer. The hotel is footsteps from the MAX light railway into town. ⑤.

Mark Spencer Hotel, 409 SW 11th Ave at Stark St (☎224-3293 or 1-800/548-3934, fax 223-7848, *www.markspencer.com*). Large, modern and fairly comfortable rooms with kitchenettes, but located in a loud, relatively dodgy downtown location. ⑤.

Paramount Hotel, 808 SW Taylor at Park Ave (☎223-9900 or 1-800/426-0670, fax 223-7900, *www.portlandparamount.com*). Extravagantly refurbished Art Deco high-rise in a great, central location. There are more than a hundred and fifty rooms, each tastefully decorated in modern style. The hotel has a fitness centre and some rooms have balconies. Not nearly as expensive as you might expect. ⑥.

Silver Cloud Inn, 2426 NW Vaughan St at NW 25th Ave (☎242-2400 or 1-800/205-6939). Smart, well-kept motel with eighty rooms on the edge of the Nob Hill district. ④.

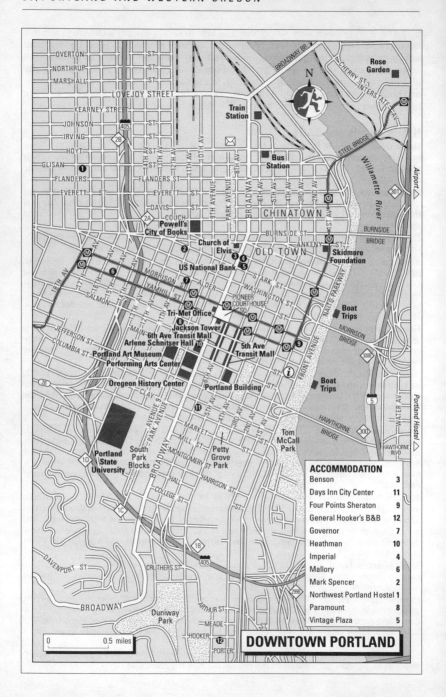

DOWNTOWN PORTLAND

ACCOMMODATION

Benson	3
Days Inn City Center	11
Four Points Sheraton	9
General Hooker's B&B	12
Governor	7
Heathman	10
Imperial	4
Mallory	6
Mark Spencer	2
Northwest Portland Hostel	1
Paramount	8
Vintage Plaza	5

Vintage Plaza, 422 SW Broadway at Washington (☎228-1212 or 1-800/243-0555, fax 228-3598, *www.vintageplaza.com*). Luxury downtown hotel in a handsome old building complete with imaginative settings and decor. Well-appointed doubles and even split-level suites at twice the regular rate given here. ⑦.

Hostels

Northwest Portland HI International Hostel, 1818 NW Glisan St (☎241-2783, fax 525-5910, *hinwp@transport.com*). This newly opened HI hostel has self-catering facilities, a laundry room and café. Dorm beds cost $15 per person per member and there are also family rooms ($45). Reservations are recommended. Bus #17, colour-coded salmon red, from the 6th Ave transit mall.

Portland International HI Hostel, 3031 Hawthorne Blvd SE (☎236-3380, fax 236-7940). HI hostel with good facilities squeezed into a cheery old Victorian house in a lively neighbourhood on the east side of the Willamette. Separate dorms for men and women, plus family rooms ($35). Dorm beds cost $13 for HI members, and there's a modest surcharge for non-members. Reservations recommended. Take bus #14, coded "brown beaver", from the transit mall on SW 5th Ave.

The City

When the sun shines, life in **downtown Portland** converges on **Pioneer Courthouse Square** to mill around in true West Coast style, sipping lattes and listening to street musicians. Within a few blocks are the city's leading department stores, theatres and museums, notably the **Portland Art Museum**, whose enjoyable permanent collection is enhanced by a first-rate programme of temporary exhibitions. Engagingly laid-back, the city centre also boasts a harmonious mix of old and new architectural styles, where fading plasterwork and terracotta reliefs face concrete and glass, all punctuated by small grassy parks and whimsical street sculptures. The centre really is quite delightful and as it stretches north it fades seamlessly into **Old Town**, between the Morrison and Burnside bridges. This was where the first merchants and loggers set up shop and where today restored nineteenth-century buildings are occupied by busy restaurants and bars – in unhappy contrast to the dejected street people crowded around the Salvation Army mission at SW Ankeny and 2nd Avenue. It only takes a few hours to explore downtown Portland, and afterwards the pick of the outlying attractions are amongst the wooded hills to the west of the city centre – the **West Hills** – notably the ornate **Pittock Mansion** and the leafy trails and formal gardens of sprawling **Washington Park**.

Restaurants, coffeehouses and café-bars cluster downtown, but there are other lively districts to eat and drink in too, especially the fashionable **Nob Hill** area, off Burnside Street a mile or so northwest of downtown.

Pioneer Courthouse Square and around

Red-bricked, with powered waterfalls and curving shelves of steps, **Pioneer Courthouse Square** is the modern centrepiece of downtown's new look (it used to be a parking lot), its character cheerily encapsulated by a folksy life-size bronze of a man with an open umbrella – *Allow Me* by Seward Johnson. The square brightly upstages the **Pioneer Courthouse** behind, the first major federal building in the Pacific Northwest, completed in a stolid version of the Italian Renaissance style in 1868. Across the square, at the corner of Yamhill Street, is a second building of note, the **Jackson Tower**, a splendid concoction faced with white-glazed terracotta panels and dating to 1912.

Leading off Pioneer Courthouse Square is **SW Broadway**, which more than any other street pulls together Portland's combination of old grandeur and modern style.

The buildings at the SW Broadway and Main Street intersection epitomise this mix, with the 1927 **Arlene Schnitzer Concert Hall**, a flamboyant ex-vaudeville theatre refurbished to house the Oregon Symphony Orchestra, standing cheek-to-cheek with the modernistic **Portland Center for the Performing Arts**. The latter is a flashy construction of brick and dark glass, whose cherry wood-panelled lobby is topped with a spectral light dome that changes colour with the light of the sky.

Behind the Center for the Performing Arts are the **South Park Blocks**, consisting of a narrow strip of elm-shaded lawn, where students from the nearby campus of Portland State University come to relax. On the lawn are several statues, notably two bronzes from the 1920s, the first of which features a gloomy-looking Abraham Lincoln – so gloomy, in fact, that the city almost sent it back to the sculptor. A few yards away is the second, a militaristic bronze of Theodore Roosevelt, shown as a "Rough Rider" from his days as a cavalry man in the Spanish-American War of 1898.

Close by, on the south side of the blocks, rises the top-heavy tower of the **First Congregational Church**, an ungainly structure allegedly in the Venetian Gothic style and dating to 1890. The interior is mildly interesting for its stucco work and stained glass. The adjacent **Oregon History Center** (Tues–Sat 10am–5pm, Sun noon–5pm; $6) is primarily a research facility, but it does have some modest exhibitions exploring different facets of the state's history. The centre has a huge archive of old photographs, so be sure to check out any photographic exhibitions being put on.

Portland Art Museum

On the far side of the South Park Blocks lies the long, low, understated facade of 1930s architect Pietro Belluschi's **Portland Art Museum** (Tues–Sat 10am–5pm, Sun noon–5pm, open until 8pm the first Thurs of the month; $7.50; *www.pam.org*), next door to which – and in use by the museum's curators – is the ponderous pile of the old Masonic Temple. The museum prides itself on its temporary exhibitions, but it also possesses a large permanent collection – too large, in fact, to show at any one time, which means that exhibits are regularly rotated. The collection is spread over three floors, with the ground floor featuring two main sections. One is devoted to contemporary, mostly American artists and the other, the Asian Art Galleries, has one room each for Korean, Japanese and Chinese pieces. The basement holds prints and a modest sample of African applied art – masks, figurines and so forth.

Rather more interesting – and on the top floor – are the European Galleries, which trace the evolution of European fine art, beginning with medieval painted wooden panels and Italian Renaissance paintings and running through to modernism. The strongest feature here is the **Impressionists**, with examples of the work of Cézanne, Monet, Pissarro, Renoir and Degas. On the same floor, there is a room of finely crafted English silverware and a separate section for the museum's Native-American collection, with the emphasis on the Pacific Northwest. Moving on, the Hirsch Wing focuses on American painters from the eighteenth century to modern times. Amongst the early works, look out for a couple of routine portraits by Gilbert Stuart (1755–1828), the artist responsible for the portrait of George Washington that appears on every one-dollar bill. Stuart painted his first "George Washington" in 1796 and it proved so popular that he went on to produce no less than seventy copies. The Hirsch Wing also contains a good sample of nineteenth-century landscape painters who frequently visited or moved to the Pacific Northwest. The works of these painters are often more interesting for their historical content than any artistic value, but there are exceptions. In particular look out for **Cleveland Rockwell** (1836–1907), a New Yorker who came to Oregon in 1868 to survey the coast for the US government and painted soft and warmly-hued land- and seascapes in his spare time. Of the later artists on display, two of the more impressive are the Fauvist-influenced **Milton Avery** (1877–1965) and **Julian**

Alden Weir (1852–1919), a local painter whose tense realism is well illustrated by his *Ice Cutters* of 1898.

The Portland Building

A couple of minutes' walk away, at the junction of Madison and 5th, is Portland's one sight of national, if not world, renown – architect Michael Graves's **Portland Building**, a squarely sat concoction of concrete and glass, adorned with dark-red and blue-green tiling with pale bluish-green rosettes to match. It's quite possible to walk straight past without realising this is anything special, but on closer examination it's certainly an eclectic structure, an uninhibited (some say flippant) reworking of classical and other motifs that was one of the most talked-about US buildings of the 1980s. Portland positively relished the controversy, and, in a burst of civic zeal, hoisted the colossal copper figure of *Portlandia* (a sort of Portlandian *Liberty*) on to the porch above the main entrance – where she kneels, one hand clutching a trident, the other reaching down towards 5th Avenue. The avenue was also a keystone of the city's rejuvenation: both here and on 6th Avenue stretches of street are lined with bus shelters, twin **transit malls** whose smoked-glass bus stops, complete benches and TV information screens are a study in user-friendliness.

Close by, at Main Street and 3rd Avenue, is a pleasant little park in which the **Soldiers' Monument** commemorates those Oregon volunteers who died in the Spanish-American War of 1898. Also here, in the middle of Main Street, is a bronze **elk**, which was one of the city's earliest street sculptures, plonked on top of the granite horse trough that still rests beneath it in 1900. It's not a very successful piece – the poor animal looks strangely lopsided – but it did prompt a major municipal row when plans were announced to move it to speed traffic. In the event, the planners caved in and Main Street now loops round it.

North along Broadway to West Burnside Street and Nob Hill

Back at Pioneer Courthouse Square, a brief stroll north along Broadway takes you past a sequence of handsome office blocks, hotels and banks, the pick of which date from the first decades of the twentieth century. Particularly fine buildings include the exuberantly Neoclassical **US National Bank** building at Broadway and Stark Street, and just opposite the imposing red-brick-and-stone symmetries of the **Benson Hotel**. Close to the Benson, and entirely different, is the peculiar **24-Hour Church of Elvis**, off Broadway at 720 SW Ankeny St (usually noon–5pm, but also open by request – call ☎226-3671; donation). The chaotic creation of local artist Stephanie G. Pierce, the "church" is no more than a couple of rooms full of junk, where the point of a visit is the quick-fire commentary (harangue) given by Pierce herself. As part of the performance, Pierce urges visitors to look at – or sit on – bits of her accumulated junk, but in truth she is a Not-So-Merry Prankster and the mood can quickly turn sour if you don't show the responses she wants.

From the Church of Elvis, it's a short walk west to **Powell's City of Books**, W Burnside Street and 10th Avenue (daily 9am–11pm), which claims to be the largest bookstore in America. The bookshop occupies an entire city block and issues free maps so customers can find their way around. It's particularly gratifying to find a wide selection of used, out-of-print and discounted titles here and there's a coffee shop where you can browse before you buy.

West Burnside Street between 8th Avenue and the riverfront is itself a seedy thoroughfare that marks the southern limit of the poorest – and most unsafe – part of Portland. This sleazy district has long been the haunt of drug dealers, addicts, and prostitutes and although the city council have made attempts to revamp the area, closing

SHANGHAIING

Until the end of the nineteenth century, international trade depended on wooden sailing ships and these required large **crews**. The problem for the ship-owners was that when their vessels reached their outward port, a ready cargo was hard to find as patterns of supply and distribution were still too rudimentary, and besides sailing times varied enormously depending on the weather. The result was that ships could lie empty in harbour for weeks, if not months. To keep costs down, captains habitually dismissed most of the ship's crew when they reached their destination, but this created difficulties when they were ready to leave – low wages and poor conditions never attracted enough volunteers. Into the breach stepped dozens of waterfront hoodlums, or **crimps**, who were hired to supply the crews with no questions asked. **Shanghaiing**, as it became known in the US (as this was the principal destination), was big business, nowhere more so than in Portland where hardmen like Joseph "Bunco" Kelly and Jim Turk – who contemporaries described as "220 pounds of florid-faced, beef-fed muscle" – worked the scam, owning boarding-houses from whose residents they could select their victims with all the violent aplomb of a press gang. And if this failed, they simply roamed the waterfront brothels and bars.

By and large, shanghaiing was immune to scandal, but there was a bit of a stink in 1893 following Kelly's work "recruiting" for a British ship, the *Flying Prince*. On a dark and stormy night, Kelly stumbled across a large party of revellers who had forced open a sidewalk trap door to enter the cellar below. They thought the cellar held supplies for a nearby bar, but actually it belonged to an undertakers and they compounded their mistake by drinking embalming fluid as if it was liquor. They were all either dead or dying when Kelly found them, but undeterred he still rushed them onto the British ship and, as crimps often delivered unconscious men, the captain didn't bat an eyelid – until the following day. Kelly was never charged. It was the steamship rather than the law that polished off Portland's crimps.

down flophouses, moving the poor and extending the iron grip of respectability, their efforts have yielded only partial success. Tucked away in this area are the bus and train stations as well as the scant remains of **Chinatown**, whose only noticeable feature is the ornate, even tacky, oriental gateway at Burnside Street and NW 4th Avenue. In the middle of the nineteenth century, Portland had the second-largest Chinese community in the US, but white unemployment in the 1880s led, as elsewhere, to racist attacks. The Chinese were threatened, their homes dynamited or burned, and most were forced to ship out.

From the Chinatown gateway, it's a short walk east along Burnside to Old Town (see below), or a quick bus ride (#20; every 15–30min) west to the **Nob Hill** district, which stretches north from Burnside Street focused on a dozen blocks of NW 21st and NW 23rd avenues. The name was borrowed from San Francisco, imported by a grocer who hoped the area would become as fashionable as the Nob Hill back home. It did, almost, and a few multicoloured wooden mansions add a San Franciscan tinge – though the main interest up here is the neighbourhood cafés and restaurants, which are among the city's best.

Old Town and the Tom McCall Waterfront Park

Old Town, beside the river between the Morrison and Burnside bridges, was where Portland was founded in 1843, and as early as the 1850s wealthy Portlanders were edging the streets with grand cast-iron frame buildings for their businesses. At the time, cast-iron was the latest thing, both structurally and decoratively. Cast-iron buildings were less expensive and faster to build than their stone and brick predecessors and had the added advantage of extra strength – supporting piers could be much narrower than before which, in turn, let in more light. The popularity of the material was, however, short-lived. In 1889, almost at a stroke, it was replaced by steel, mostly with terracotta embellishments, a fashion which lasted until the 1930s. But long before then Old Town had fallen into decline: the area tended to flood, and when the railroad came in 1883 the town centre started to shift away from the river, a gradual process which eventually pushed Old Town right down the social scale. "Improvement" schemes in the 1950s almost finished the district off, and gaps still show where buildings were pulled down to make way for parking lots. Recent attempts at **rejuvenation** have been more tactful, and the area now holds an attractive patchwork of restored old buildings, many of which house bistros and boutiques. That said, Old Town is a chancy area after dark: the poverty of Burnside Street is too close for comfort and, particularly around the Salvation Army mission at Ankeny Street and SW 2nd Avenue, the well-heeled and the down-and-out eye each other dubiously in a division that is – for Oregon at least – uncomfortably sharp.

The best time to visit Old Town is on the weekend, when the **Saturday Market** (March–Dec Sat 10am–5pm, Sun 11am–4.30pm) packs the area under the west end of the Burnside Bridge with arts and crafts stalls, street musicians, spicy foods and lively crowds. In the middle of this, at 1st Avenue and Ankeny Street, stands the **Skidmore Fountain**, a bronze basin raised by caryatids above a granite pool, designed to provide European elegance for the citizens – and water for hard-worked nineteenth-century "men, dogs and horses" as the opening ceremony had it. The fountain was opened to the cheers of a large and enthusiastic crowd, though many of them might not have been so appreciative if they had known that the city fathers had previously declined a local brewer's offer to pipe free beer through the fountain on its first day. Across the MAX tracks from the fountain is the restored **New Market Theater**, whose interior, with its Venetian-style arcaded galleries and cast-iron trimmings, dates from 1872. Built by Alexander Ankeny, who made a fortune in the California gold fields, it was designed to house a vegetable market downstairs and a theatre upstairs – and, after years of neglect, it has been returned to its original layout.

Old Town's other architectural highlights begin with the 1889 **Rodney Glisan Building**, 112 SW 2nd Ave at Ash Street, which cleverly incorporates several styles, its cast-iron columns, Gothic pediment and Neoclassical entrance presently home to *Kells Irish Pub*. Just along 2nd Avenue at Oak Street is the old **Portland Police Headquarters**, a heavyweight American Renaissance edifice of 1912 which served as police headquarters until the 1980s. It was here that George Baker, the big and loud-mouthed Mayor of Portland from 1917 to 1924, installed a special police detail, the "red squad", to hunt down every socialist and labour activist in sight. Skilfully exploiting the primitive patriotism stirred up by World War I, Baker kick-started one of the most reactionary periods in Oregon's history. He even worked hand-in-glove with the Ku Klux Klan, who set up office here in 1921 and promptly set about intimidating their favourite targets – Catholics, Jews, Asians and, most viciously of all, the Wobblies (see p.627).

Further along 2nd Avenue, you'll see the 1891 **Concord Building**, no. 208 at the corner of Stark Street, whose elegant brick and sandstone-trimmed lines mark an early departure from the more ornate buildings that went before. Opposite, and in striking contrast, is the Gothic Revival **Bishop's House**, a brick, cast-iron and stucco structure built in 1879 for the city's Catholic archbishop and subsequently used as a Prohibition speakeasy and now a restaurant, *Al-Amir*. Round the corner, at 3rd Avenue and Washington, are two of the city's finest buildings, the **Postal Building** of 1900, whose American Renaissance orderliness is adorned by frilly terracotta panels and a delightfully intricate cornice, and opposite the slightly earlier **Dekum Building**, constructed for the confectioner Frank Dekum in 1892. Here, the red-brick and terracotta upper levels perch on roughly cut sandstone in an outstanding example of the American Romanesque style, which represented an influential departure from the daintier preoccupations of the 1880s.

A short walk to the east lies the **riverfront**, which has been rescued from over a century of burial beneath wharves, warehouses, and, more recently, an express highway. Now the mile-long grassy strip, rechristened the **Tom McCall Waterfront Park**, accommodates a popular walking and cycling path, which offers views along the river, with its clutter of old bridges. In the distance you can spy the triangular, snow-capped hump of Mount Hood. The park is named after Governor McCall, a key figure in the late 1960s and 1970s movement to improve the city and the prime mover behind dozens of environmental measures. A larger-than-life figure, McCall famously declared "We want you to visit our state…often…But, for heaven's sake, don't move here to live", though he was not, as is commonly thought, the originator of the celebrated phrase "Don't Californicate Oregon", meaning to overdevelop it. The McCall Park runs south from Burnside Bridge to the marina at the foot of Clay Street. On the way, opposite Salmon Street, you'll find the Portland Spirit River Cruises jetty (see p.86 for cruise details) and the playful, gushing fountains of the **Salmon Street Springs**, in the lee of the modern, grey and glassy **World Trade Center** (home of the visitor centre).

A couple of blocks north of Salmon Street, the tiny **Yamhill Historic District** is dotted with nineteenth century buildings, though the district's focal point, the **Yamhill Marketplace**, at 1st Avenue and Yamhill Street, is a reproduction, dating from 1982. From here, it is a brief stroll west along Yamhill back to Pioneer Courthouse Square.

The West Hills

The long line of wooded bluffs that make up the **West Hills** has long restricted Portland's capacity to expand westward and although a good slice now accommodates the homes of the wealthy, there remain large chunks of dark and dense forest, webbed by hiking trails. This is the most scenic part of Portland and an excellent place to begin a visit is the **Pittock Mansion** (daily noon–4pm, closed most Jan; $4.50), a luxurious country home located off – and up in the hills from – West Burnside Street, a couple of miles from town at 3229 NW Pittock Drive. Perched on a ridge with great views of the city, the mansion was built for Henry Pittock, who came to Portland in 1853 as a sixteen-year-old printer's helper. Eight years later he founded *The Oregonian*, still the state's most influential newspaper, and his publication rapidly became the flagship of the political Right under the formidable editorship of the long-serving, walrus-moustached Harvey W. Scott. Scott was a brow-beating conservative who took few prisoners – he labelled the editor of a rival rag a "pimp generalissimo of a small, cheap paper" – but he wasn't the only member of his family to master the biting phrase. When Harvey's editorials declared against women's suffrage in 1900, his sister Abigail wrote "My Dear Brother . . . the most charitable construction the many loyal women of your acquaintance can put upon your conduct towards . . . (women's suffrage) . . . is that the cheap male sycophants who suck their sustenance from your editorial seats have flattered you until you are insane on the sex question."

Completed in 1914, it took five years to build Pittock Mansion, a broadly French Renaissance-style structure whose twenty-two rooms are a perfect illustration of the energetic virtuosity of the American tycoon. The house is stuffed with antique furnishings and fittings and there's a mind-boggling mix of styles: the library is of English Jacobean design, the smoking room Turkish and the drawing room French Renaissance. Neither did the tycoon neglect the latest mod cons, installing a room-to-room telephone system, showers with multiple showerheads and an ambitious central vacuum-cleaning system. It's a delightful spot and when you've finished looking round, you can stroll the carefully manicured gardens. For a longer hike, the wooded hills of the elongated **Forest Park** extend from the parking lot at the back of the house and offer a variety of hiking trails – maps and advice are available at the house.

To get to Pittock Mansion by **bus** from downtown, take orange-coded elk bus #20 west along W Burnside Street and you'll be dropped at the start of the steep, signed, half-mile side road that winds up to the entrance.

Washington Park

Cutting through the West Hills from the south side of downtown Portland (take Clay St), Hwy 26 serves as the main approach road to **Washington Park**, a green and hilly expanse where the most popular attraction is **Oregon Zoo** (daily: April–Sept 9am–6pm; Oct–March 9am–4pm; $6.50; *www.oregonzoo.org*), on the park's southern perimeter. The zoo's star turn is its Asian elephants, now a sizeable breeding herd that, in 1962, produced the first birth of an Asian elephant in the western hemisphere. But, although there's no doubt that the zoo has played a major role in conserving the Asian elephant, seeing the animals in confinement – no matter how spacious their lodgings – stirs mixed feelings. The zoo puts on a programme of live music throughout the summer and shows are free with the price of admission: ring ☎226-1561 or ask at the city visitor centre for details.

Back at the zoo entrance, it's a couple of minutes' walk over to the smart **World Forestry Center** (daily 9/10am–5pm; $4.50; *www.worldforest.org*), which explains the ins and outs of forest management using lots of interactive exhibits. Among several displays, the push-button reconstruction of the "Tillamook Burn", a fire that ravaged a vast stretch of Oregon's coastal forests in the 1930s, is the most diverting.

A miniature train connects the zoo and the forestry centre with two formal gardens further north in the park. The **Washington Park International Rose Test Garden** (daily 7am–9pm; free) is at its best between May and August, when eight thousand rose bushes cover layered terraces with a gaudy range of blooms. It earns its name by testing new varieties of rose sent here by growers. The new roses are tested for two years and are judged on their colour, fragrance and form. The garden goes some way to justifying Portland's claim to be the "City of Roses", as does the crowded and colourful **Rose Festival** held each June, when thousands flock to Burnside Bridge to watch a massive parade. On the hill above the roses, the **Japanese Garden** (daily: April–Sept 10am–7pm; Oct–March 10am–4pm; $6) is more subtle in its appeal, with cool, green shrubs reflected in pools, and an abstract sand-and-stone garden making minimal use of colour.

In terms of access, side roads weave through Washington Park connecting all of its (clearly signposted) attractions. To reach the zoo by **public transport**, take MAX west from downtown to the Washington Park station; to go straight to the Japanese Gardens or the International Rose Test Garden from downtown, take the orange coded elk bus #63 (hourly) from the 6th Avenue transit mall at Main.

East of the Willamette River

While the west side of the Willamette River provided a deep port, the **east side** was too shallow for shipping and the area remained undeveloped for the first fifty years of Portland's life. The Hawthorne Bridge crept across the river in 1910 and the Steel and Broadway bridges followed shortly afterwards, and residential neighbourhoods have rapidly spread east since, stretching out towards the forested foothills that prefigure Mount Hood (see p.107). These extensive suburbs now accommodate most of Greater Portland's population of around 1.8 million. Specific attractions hereabouts are thin on the ground, the main exception being the lavish and large **Oregon Museum of Science and Industry** or OMSI for short, on the east bank of the Willamette at 1945

SE Water and Clay (mid-June to early Sept daily 9.30am–7pm; early Sept to mid-June Tues–Sun 9.30am–5.30pm; $6.50, $4.50 for seniors and; children 3–13 years old, *www.omsi.edu*). OMSI specializes in interactive exhibits and these are distributed amongst a series of themed halls. In the Space Science hall, for example, you can check your weight on Mars and clamber into a space capsule. In addition, there's an OMNI-MAX theatre (an extra $6.50, $4.50 for seniors and children 3–13 years old), a planetarium ($3 extra) and a USS submarine ($3 extra) docked in the Willamette River, though the sight of children admiring military hardware – and stroking torpedoes in particular – is not to everyone's liking. To save costs, OMSI does a full museum package covering all its attractions for $15 ($11.50 for seniors and children 3–13 years old). Bus #63 (hourly) serves the site from the downtown transit mall at 5th Avenue and Salmon Street.

Eating and drinking

Friendly and unpretentious, Portland is a great place to **eat** and **drink**, especially as intense competition almost invariably keeps prices down to reasonable levels. There is, of course, the inevitable slew of fast-food joints, but these are easily avoided in favour of more distinctive places, the best of which are – for the most part – concentrated downtown and in the Nob Hill district, off W Burnside Street along the first few blocks of NW 21st Avenue and NW 23rd Avenue. Portland can't really claim to have a distinctive cuisine, but it has picked up on the gastronomic trends common along the seaboard of the Pacific Northwest. In these dishes, lighter, healthier sauces are preferred to creamy, heavy ones and there is an emphasis on local ingredients. **Seafood** features prominently, with salmon a particular favourite, either grilled, seared or broiled, or used in more elaborate dishes including pastas and stews.

The city has an excellent range of **restaurants**, with some of the best focusing on modern renditions of American dishes and others adopting the classic French style – and everywhere you're likely to encounter a New Age flourish or two. Many also have bars where you can eat and/or drink as the mood takes you. There's a reasonably wide range of ethnic restaurants too, amongst which Italian places are the most common. Portland's **cafés** are another good bet, often serving up food similar to their restaurant rivals but at cheaper prices. These range from bistro-style neighbourhood joints with a New Age bent to slicker, smarter places catering for the business trade; many make little distinction between drinking and eating. Where cafés tail off, the city's **microbreweries** take over, proof of the resurgence of the Northwest's proud brewing traditions. These establishments brew their beers and ales on the premises and almost always offer bar food, sometimes to a very high standard. Finally, coffee has become a big deal in Portland, as it has in other American cities. This has given rise to the specialist **coffeehouse**, which mostly takes the form of a takeaway bar with a few stools where a bewildering variety of coffees are on offer together with cakes and snacks. It is, however, a trend the more streetwise cafés have picked up on, and these tend to have the edge in terms of atmosphere.

Restaurants

Basta's Pasta, 410 NW 21st Ave (☎274-1572). Informal Italian restaurant in the Nob Hill district that's one of the best of its type in the city. An imaginative menu ranging from the basics of pizzas and pastas to more original dishes, that still manages to keep its rural, North Italian heart; the home-made bread is known right across the city.

The Portland area telephone code is ☎503

Brasserie Montmartre, 626 SW Park Ave at Alder St (☎224-5552). Smart, bistro-style restaurant with elegant decor – lots of wood panelling – and free live jazz on most evenings. Delicious French and Italian dishes, with freshly made pasta. Main courses around $15.

Fernando's Hideaway, 824 SW 1st Ave at Yamhill St (☎248-4709). Popular Spanish place in a handsome old building with a restaurant and bar serving wonderful and authentic tapas. Sunday is paella day. Reasonably priced.

Heathman, 1009 SW Broadway at Salmon St (☎241-4100). One of the ritziest restaurants in town, the *Heathman* offers outstanding PNW cuisine at dinner time and extravagant teas in the afternoon. In the evening, main courses average around $22 – very reasonable considering the quality. Their seared salmon is especially delicious.

Higgins, 1239 SW Broadway at Jefferson St (☎222-9070). Mouthwatering PNW cuisine featuring the freshest of local ingredients; the shellfish in particular is worth a taste. By Portland standards, it's a formal kind of place – but reasonably priced with main courses around $18.

Hunan, Morgan's Alley, 515 SW Broadway at Washington St (☎224-8063). Well-established Chinese restaurant on the mezzanine level of Morgan's Alley, a tiny shopping precinct leading off Broadway. Courteous service with all the frills. The dim sum is highly recommended.

India House, 1038 SW Morrison at 11th Ave (☎274-1017). This reliable East Asian restaurant serves all the classics plus a few more at inexpensive prices. The premises are modern and plain, but the food more than compensates. The curries and the khormas are tops.

Jake's Famous Crawfish, 401 SW 12th Ave (☎226-1419). For nearly 100 years this polished-wood oyster bar has been Portland's prime spot for fresh seafood, though at weekends it's packed and veers toward singles bar territory. The food, especially the daily fish specials, is excellent and not exorbitantly priced, but be sure to save room for dessert.

Jake's Grill, 611 SW 10th Ave at Alder St (☎220-1850). This superb restaurant – arguably Portland's best and sister to *Jake's Famous Crawfish* – occupies a tastefully converted 1910s building, complete with mosaic floors, dinky glass domes and yards of thick wooden panelling. The unpretentious menu is strong on meat and seafood with dishes finely presented; desserts are gorgeous too. For two people, each eating two courses, plus a bottle of house wine, reckon on paying about $100. Busy bar section as well.

McCormick and Schmick's, 235 SW 1st Ave at Oak St (☎224-7522). Good fish restaurant, with a variety of fresh nightly specials, and a lively oyster bar. Located in a down-at-heel part of Old Town. At its most enjoyable during the city's Saturday Market (see p.93). Main courses around $15.

Persian House, 1026 SW Morrison St at 11th Ave (☎243-1430). Cosy and low-key Persian restaurant serving tasty, traditional dishes at inexpensive prices. Main courses average about $10.

Ruth's Chris Steak House, 309 SW 3rd Ave at Oak St (☎221-4518). Downtown restaurant – one of a chain – providing juicy steaks in a cheerful pastel-painted atmosphere. A quality range of Northwest wines and microbrews are also on offer. Moderately expensive.

South Park Seafood Grill, 901 SW Salmon St at 9th Ave (☎326-1300). This brisk bistro-style restaurant specializes in seafood, of which it offers a wide variety, washed down by a good range of beers and wines. It's a popular spot, but some of the fancier dishes are over-elaborate – stick to the more straightforward offerings. Main courses around $18.

Wildwood, 1221 NW 21st Ave and Overton St (☎248-9663). Young, hip and upmarket Nob Hill restaurant. The menu features lots of seafood cooked the Northwest way and there's a good list of Oregon wines too.

Café

Besaw's Café, 2301 NW Savier St at 23rd Ave (☎228-2619). Old-fashioned, NY-style bar and grill. Lots of dark-wood panelling, good-sized burgers, steaks and sandwiches, plus onion rings to kill for.

Bijou Café, 132 SW 3rd Ave (☎222-3187). This laid-back, well-established downtown café uses local, organic ingredients (wherever possible) in its wide-ranging menu. Lunches are especially good with meat and fish dishes as well as vegetarian-friendly offerings like quesadillas and tofu.

Bread and Ink Café, 3610 SE Hawthorne Blvd (☎239-4756). This busy, spacious café, on the east side of the Willamette, puts together a varied menu of bagels, burritos and Mediterranean food; come on Sunday for the special Jewish brunch.

Great Harvest Bread Company, 810 SW 2nd Ave at Yamhill St. Really a bakery rather than a café, *Great Harvest* sells a wonderful range of breads with different types featured every day, including a free taster. Elephantine cinnamon buns and the city's best muffins too. Sandwiches Monday through Friday till 3pm only. Opening hours: Mon–Fri 7am–6pm & Sat 8am–5pm.

Hawthorne Café, 1310 NW 23rd Ave (☎232-4982). The original *Hawthorne Café* is on the east side of the Willamette, but this Nob Hill location is rather more convenient. A fashionable, popular spot offering a wide-ranging menu with a Mediterranean slant – the home-made hummus is first rate.

Kornblatt's Delicatessen and Bagel Bakery, 628 NW 23rd Ave (☎242-0055). Portland's most authentic East Coast deli – mouthwatering bagels and lots of smoked meats.

Maya's Taqueria, 1000 SW Washington at 10th Ave (☎226-1946). Bright and breezy Mexican café with all the favourites – enchiladas, burritos and so forth – at inexpensive prices. Sit-in or takeaway.

Papa Haydn, 701 NW 23rd Ave (☎228-7317). Chic, upscale café serving first-class bistro-style meals with various types of salad as house specialities. Fabulous desserts, including a world-beating chocolate mousse.

Virginia Café, 725 SW Park Ave at Yamhill St. The wooden booths get crowded in this popular downtown café as it serves up choice budget food all day. New Age clientele mixed up with just about everyone else.

Bars and microbreweries

Atwater's, 111 SW 5th Ave, in the US Bancorp Tower (☎205-9400). Skip this restaurant's pricey meals and head straight for happy hour at its primo cocktail bar, which not only offers tasty beers, wines and martinis, but also one of the best views of the city, from the 30th floor of Portland's tallest building.

BridgePort Brewery and Pub, 1313 NW Marshall St. Huge Victorian warehouse that's home to Oregon's oldest microbrewery (1984) and one of the city's largest and liveliest beer bars, pouring pints of home-brewed BridgePort Ale. Tasty pizzas and bar food as ballast.

Goose Hollow Inn and Tavern, 1927 SW Broadway (☎228-7010). Besides offering a solid assortment of imports and microbrews, also serves up the city's best Reuben sandwich and is owned by colourful former mayor Bud Clark.

Huber's, 411 SW 3rd Ave (☎228-5686). Hands-down the most historic bar in town, an 1879 marvel with a stained-glass skylight, classic brass fixtures, terrazzo flooring, and mahogany panelling throughout. Also famed for its Spanish coffee – hot or iced – and a fine array of beers, wines and cocktails.

Kells Irish Restaurant and Pub, 112 SW 2nd Ave (☎227-4057). Munch on shepherd's pie and soda bread while sampling a wide range of Irish and Scotch whiskies at this Portland institution, which also offers a nice selection of microbrews and imported beers.

Portland Brewing Brew House Taproom and Grill, 2730 NW 31st Ave. The various beers and ales on tap have made this one of the city's more renowned microbreweries. The menu features Northwest and traditional German food, either indoors or on the outdoor patio.

Produce Row, 204 SE Oak St (☎232-8355). Stuck in a low-rent Eastside industrial district and offering crude, no-frills decor, this is an unexpected paradise for beer lovers, with nearly thirty taps and countless bottled brews, and a colourful clientele of hard-bitten regulars and even a few newbies.

Rock Bottom Brewery, 206 SW Morrison and 2nd Ave. Brewpub with five different beers, ranging from the light and crispy Cryin' Coyote to the full-bodied, head-banging Black Seal Stout. The bar food here is filling and tasty – but it's probably best to stick to the more straightforward dishes. Burger and fries cost just $8. The brewpub is housed in an attractive old building with lots of space, and there's also a small outside area on the sidewalk.

Coffeehouses

Anne Hughes Coffee Room, inside Powell's City of Books, West Burnside St and 10th Ave. Not too big on atmosphere, but an easy-going place to spend some time over a book.

Coffee People, 506 SW Washington. A splendid range of coffees that is arguably the best in town. Mostly takeaway, but there are a few stools to relax on. Also at 817 NW 23rd Ave and Hoyt St.

Peet's Coffee & Tea, cnr SW Broadway and SW Washington St. Cheerfully decorated coffeehouse with teas as an added bonus. Rather smarter than many of its rivals. Sit-in or takeout.

Seattle's Best Coffee, 1001 SW 5th Ave at Main St. Although primarily a takeaway, this café serves a rich range of coffees that are much better than the cakes on offer. Opposite the Portland Building. Also at 930 SW 4th Ave at Salmon.

Nightlife and entertainment

Many of Portland's cafés and all its microbreweries (see opposite) heave and hum till one or two in the morning, and so do a goodly number of restaurant bars. Together they form the fulcrum of the city's nightlife, sometimes chipping in with live sounds once or twice weekly. In addition, there is a reasonable range of more specialist **live music venues**, featuring the full gamut of folk, rock, jazz and blues, as well as **clubs** featuring a revolving cast of DJs and musical styles. Except for big-name bands, cover charges – where they exist at all – are minimal.

Portland's performing arts scene revolves, logically enough, around the Portland Center for the Performing Arts (PCPA) complex on Broadway and Main – though confusingly the term 'PCPA' often includes the Portland Civic Auditorium on SW 2nd Avenue and Clay Street too. Broadway's PCPA is where you'll find much of the city's best **theatre**, though several good-quality companies perform elsewhere. The complex also incorporates the Arlene Schnitzer Concert Hall, the place to go for **classical music** and home to the prestigious Oregon Symphony Orchestra. Portland also lays on an enticing crop of summertime **free concerts** – both classical and rock/pop – the pick of which are held outdoors on Pioneer Courthouse Square and the Tom McCall Waterfront Park. Portland is sprinkled with **cinemas**, mostly the big chains, though the Northwest Film Theater breaks the pattern – and is one of the region's most adventurous art-house cinemas. All the mainstream cinemas share the same programme information line (☎225-5555), with each of them having their own extension.

The comprehensive *Willamette Week* (*www.wweek.com*) and the slimmer *ourtown* (*www.ourtownmag.com*) carry up-to-the-minute weekly **listings** and reviews of what's on and where. They are available free in the self-service stands on many street corners and at leading bookshops. The Friday edition of *The Oregonian*, the main local newspaper, has a useful listings section too. **Tickets** can be purchased either direct or from **Ticket Central**, inside Portland visitor centre, at 26 SW Salmon St and Front Avenue (May–Oct daily 9am–5pm; Nov–April Mon–Fri 9am–5pm & Sat 10am–2pm; ☎224-4400). This is a walk-in service, but there is a day-of-show information line (☎275-8358).

Music venues and clubs

Ash Street Saloon, 225 SW Ash St (☎226-0430). Popular Old Town club featuring a wide range of bands, many of which are very good. A place to spot up-and-coming local talent of the rock variety. Microbrews on tap.

Benson Hotel, 309 SW Broadway (☎228-2000). Live jazz in one of the city's smartest downtown hotels. Mostly local acts, but occasional touring stars too.

Brasserie Montmartre, 626 SW Park Ave (☎224-5552). Live jazz for the price of a dinner or a drink (see "Restaurants", p.97 for more).

Cobalt Lounge, 32 NW 3rd Ave (☎225-1003). One of Portland's better clubs, featuring anything from drum 'n' bass to deep house, depending on the night.

Crystal Ballroom, 1332 W Burnside St at SW 14th Ave (☎778-5625). This three-storey place contains a *McMenamins* microbrewery (one of the larger brewing companies in the area) and a dance club with nightly live music – everything from the obscure and oddball through to some big international names. The place oozes history – Glenn Miller played here and so did the likes of Marvin Gaye, Tina Turner and James Brown.

The Green Room, 2280 NW Thurman at 23rd Ave (☎228-6178). An unassuming, tiny club out on the northern edge of Nob Hill which offers what many locals consider the best folk, blues and soul acts in town.

Jazz de Opus, 33 NW 2nd Ave (☎222-6077). Live jazz is the mainstay here, but other types of music, from Cajun through to blues, are showcased too. The place has a well-deserved reputation for pulling in some top acts. Good grilled food.

Ohm, 31 NW 1st Ave (☎223-9919). Located under the Burnside Bridge, this is one of Portland's most popular dance clubs. Visiting and home-based DJs take turns, with techno and breakbeats leading the musical charge.

Rose Garden Arena, 1401 N Wheeler Ave (☎224-4400). This is where the big touring rock acts appear. On the east side of the Willamette River, just north of downtown, the arena seats 21,000 and is part of a larger shopping complex.

Satyricon, 125 NW 6th Ave (☎243-2380). Regionally renowned post-punk club in a down-at-heel neighbourhood. Attracts some quality acts covering a wide range of music from indie to country.

Theatre, ballet, opera and classical music venues and companies

Artists Repertory Theater, 1516 SW Alder St (☎241-1278, *www.artistsrep.org*). The emphasis here is on modern plays, with imaginative scripts and strong acting.

Back Door Theater, 4319 SE Hawthorne Blvd (☎938-1482). A good spot to catch modern plays – both avant-garde and modern classics – performed by some of the city's most talented theatre groups.

Oregon Ballet Theater, 1120 SW 10th Ave (☎222-5538, *www.obt.org*). Oregon's premier ballet company has a core repertoire of the classics, but they do modern pieces too. The company is housed in the Portland Civic Auditorium, but some performances are at the Broadway PCPA.

Oregon Symphony Orchestra, 921 SW Washington St, Suite 200 (☎228-1353 or 1-800/228-7343, *www.orsymphony.org*). This first-rate orchestra performs at the opulent Arlene Schnitzer Concert Hall, part of the Broadway PCPA complex, between September and May. The orchestra's programme is beefed up with special events and guest performers.

Portland Center for the Performing Arts (PCPA), 1111 SW Broadway at Main (☎248-4335, *www.pcpa.com*). The PCPA on Broadway offers a varied programme of performing arts from theatre through chamber music, opera and ballet. The Broadway complex comprises the Arlene Schnitzer Concert Hall and the New Theatre Building, which is itself divided into the Dolores Winningstad Theatre and the Newmark Theatre.

Portland Center Stage, at the Portland Center for the Performing Arts, 1111 SW Broadway at Main (☎248-6309, *www.pcs.org*). Portland's premier professional theatre troupe offers contemporary and classical works. The speciality is Shakespeare and the troupe has links with Ashland's Shakespeare Festival (see p.148).

Portland Civic Auditorium, SW 2nd Ave and Clay St (☎274-6560). Large venue for one-off concerts, operas, musicals and big theatrical productions.

Portland Opera, 1515 SW Morrison St (☎241-1407, *www.portlandopera.org*). At the top of its game, Portland Opera puts on five annual productions, mixing the operatic canon with more modern stuff. Their season runs from September to July and performances are at the Portland Civic Auditorium (see above).

Cinemas

Broadway Metroplex, 1000 SW Broadway at Main (☎225-5555 ext 4607). Blockbuster new releases on tap nightly.

Lloyd Cinemas, 1510 NE Multnomah St at 15th Ave (☎225-5555 ext 4600). Mainstream films in this large, ten-screen cinema on the east side of the Willamette River, close to the Lloyd Center MAX stop.

Northwest Film Center, at the Portland Art Museum, 1219 SW Park Ave and Madison (☎221-1156, *www.nwfilm.org*). Art-house, foreign-language and classic movies are all shown here. The selection is adventurous and often obscure, and be sure to look out for the themed evenings and events ranging from Film Noir to Chaplin.

Sundance Cinemas, Pioneer Place Mall, 888 SW 5th Ave (☎228-5800). Seven-screen complex with the emphasis on independent and speciality films. Part of Robert Redford's chain.

Listings

Airlines Air Canada (☎1-800/776-3000); American Airlines (☎1-800/433-3700); Continental (☎domestic 1-800/523-3273; international 1-800/231-0856); Delta (domestic ☎1-800/221-1212; international (☎1-800/241-4141); Lufthansa (☎1-800/645-3880); Northwest Airlines (domestic ☎1-800/225-2525; international (☎1-800/447-4747); Qantas (☎1-800/227-4500); United Airlines (domestic ☎1-800/241-6522; international ☎1-800/538-2929).

Airport Portland International Airport (PDX), 7000 NE Airport Way; general enquiries (☎1-877/739-4636).

American Express Travel service with **poste restante**, 1100 SW 6th St (☎226-2961).

Banks A number of banks have downtown branches including Bank of America, 1001 SW 5th Ave at Main, and US Bank, 1200 SW Morrison at 12th Ave and 1340 SW 2nd Ave at Columbia. ATMs at the airport and across town.

Bike rental Downtown, 732 SW 1st Ave at Yamhill (☎227-4439); Bike Gallery, 1001 SW Salmon St (☎222-3821).

Bookshops Powell's City of Books, 1005 W Burnside St (daily 9am–11pm; ☎228-4651, *www.powells .com*), is a huge labyrinth of new and secondhand books. There's a branch, Powell's Travel Store (Mon–Sat 9am–7pm, Sun 10am–5pm; ☎228-1108), on Pioneer Courthouse Square, where you can buy travel guides and maps. The excellent Borders bookshop, 708 SW 3rd St and Taylor (☎220-5911), has a particularly well-selected section devoted to contemporary PNW writers.

Car rental Avis, 330 SW Washington St (☎227-0220) and at the airport (☎249-4950; toll-free ☎1-800/831-2847); Budget, 2033 SW 4th Ave and at the airport (☎249-6500; toll-free ☎1-800/527-0700); Dollar, 132 NW Broadway at Davis (☎228-3540) and at the airport (☎249-4792; toll-free ☎1-800/800-4000); Hertz, 330 SW Pine St (☎249-5727) and at the airport (☎249-8216; toll-free ☎1 800/654-3131); Thrifty, 632 SW Pine St (☎227-6587) and at the airport (☎254-6563).

Consulates Belgium, 1235 SW Myrtle Ct (☎228-0465); Germany, 200 SW Market (☎222-0490); Norway, 5441 SW Macadam (☎228-8828). The British consulate (☎227-5669) seems to exist only as an answerphone, redirecting you to Seattle or Los Angeles.

Emergencies Police and medical emergencies ☎911.

Gay and lesbian *Just Out* (*www.justout.com*), a twice monthly free newsheet, has interesting articles and reviews on gay issues and also provides listings of particular interest to the gay community. The best place to pick it up is at Powell's City of Books, 1005 W Burnside St. There's a gay and lesbian Counselling Center at 620 SW 5th Ave, Suite 710 (☎223-8299).

Hospital The Legacy Good Samaritan Hospital and Medical Center, 1015 NW 22nd Ave and Lovejoy, in Nob Hill (information ☎413-7711); medical emergencies ☎911.

Internet access Downtown at Kinko's (24hr), 221 SW Alder St at 2nd Ave (☎224-6550).

Police Central Precinct, 1111 SW 2nd Ave (☎823-0097).

Post office There is a post office on Pioneer Courthouse Square (Mon–Fri 8am–5.30pm). For other locations and their opening hours, plus zip codes and mailing rates, call ☎1-800/275-8777 (24hr).

Road conditions ☎222-6721.

State parks Oregon State Parks' office is south of downtown near the Marquam Bridge at Suite 100, 2501 SW 1st Ave and Arthur (Mon–Fri 8am–5pm; ☎731-3293 or 1-800/551-6949). They have separate brochures on almost all of Oregon's parks and run a Web site (*www.prd.state.or.us*). Camping reservations for many Oregon and Washington state parks can be made on ☎1-800/452-5687.

Taxi Broadway Cabs (☎227-1234) or Portland Taxi (☎256-5400).

Tours Gray Line, PO Box 17306 (☎285-9845 or 1-800/422-7042), operate a range of summer bus tours visiting spots throughout Oregon. Examples are tours of Mount Hood/Columbia Gorge (April–Oct; 9hr; $45; 3 weekly) and the North Oregon coast (mid-May to mid-Oct; 9hr; $45; 3 weekly).

Weather ☎291-6030 ext 2215.

Wine tours South of Portland, to the west of the Willamette River, are clustered over thirty vineyards. Most of them offer free tastings and tours and the Portland visitor centre carries leaflets detailing locations and opening hours. One of the most prestigious wineries is Willamette Valley Vineyards, 8800 Enchanted Way SE (☎503/588-9463, *www.wvv.com*; tours and tastings daily 11am–6pm). It is located south of Salem and to the east of the river. From I-5 (Exit 248), take Delaney Rd east to Turner and watch for the Enchanted Way turning on the right.

Wines Oregon Wines, 515 SW Broadway at Washington (Tues–Sat noon–8pm; ☎228-4655) has a wide selection of the state's wines and regular tasting sessions.

Women's Crisis and Rape Hotline ☎235-5333.

WESTERN OREGON

Portland is just a few miles from the mighty **Columbia River**, which rises in Canada's Rocky Mountains and traverses Washington before the last leg of its journey to the Pacific. Although a sequence of dams now regulates its flow, turning what was once, when the rains came, a raging torrent into a comparatively docile river, its width still impresses. As it was for the pioneers and the Native-Americans before them, the last portion of the **Columbia River Valley** is the quickest and most obvious route between the wet, wooded valleys of west Oregon and the arid plains of the east. Nowadays, the journey is easily done on I-84, which runs along the river's south bank from Portland to Boardman, near Pendleton (see p.157). The most scenic part of the valley is the eighty-mile **Columbia River Gorge**, which begins just beyond Portland's eastern suburbs and is where the river has cut a deep canyon in the Cascade Mountains beneath the imposing slopes of **Mount Hood**.

Alternatively, visitors heading south from Portland have the choice of two main parallel routes, each of which, in their different ways, possesses spectacular scenery and passes through some delightful towns. It is easy enough to switch between these routes, sampling a little of each, or to complete a long loop, but we have described the two routes in separate sections in the pages that follow. The slower, more popular route is the 350-mile journey along the **Oregon coast**, which – though rarely warm enough for sun and sea bathing – offers some of Oregon's most exquisite and diverse scenery. Several highways link Portland with the seashore, weaving through the intervening mountain forests, but the coastal towns and resorts to head for are **Astoria** and **Cannon Beach** in the north, **Newport** in the centre, and **Bandon** to the south. Nevertheless, the scenery is often best appreciated from the string of state parks – and their campgrounds – that stretch along much of the shoreline. The second, faster route is inland, where I-5 shoots south from Portland, thumping down the 120-mile-long **Willamette Valley**. En route, I-5 passes a string of towns amongst which the most diverting are **Salem**, the state capital, and **Eugene**, a laid-back, amenable kind of place within easy striking distance of the **McKenzie River Valley**, part of the forested Cascade Mountain range. Further south still, only a couple of hours' drive east of I-5, **Crater Lake National Park** sits on the crest of the Cascades, vaunting a pristine lake held within the shell of a burnt-out volcano – a stunningly beautiful foretaste of the volcanic landscapes around Bend (see p.171). Back on I-5, the pick of the towns near the California border is good-looking **Ashland**, whose pride and joy is its summer-long Shakespeare Festival.

The Columbia River Gorge and Mount Hood

Carved by the Columbia River as it powered through volcanic layers to the sea, the **Columbia River Gorge**, stretching 80 miles from Corbett – 22 miles east of Portland – to Maryhill, was scoured deep and narrow by huge glaciers and rocks during the Ice Age. Now its western reaches are covered with green fir and maple trees, which turn fabulous shades of gold and red in the fall, while narrow white waterfalls cascade down its sides over mossy fern-covered rocks – fine scenery that's at its best along the delightful 22-mile **Historic Columbia River Highway**. Further east, roughly halfway along the gorge, pocket-sized **Hood River** is a lively little town, a popular windsurfing centre with several good places to stay. It's easily the most appealing settlement hereabouts and is also an important crossroads: it's south for the forested slopes of **Mount Hood** (see p.107) and ultimately either Bend (see p.168) or Portland via the Mount Hood Loop Highway; or it's a further forty miles east, with the forests left behind for the bare, sweeping steppes of the interior, to the **Maryhill Museum of Art**, home to one of the Northwest's most enjoyable art collections.

The best way to see the gorge is by **car** – there's no public transportation along the Historic Columbia River Highway, though Greyhound **buses** do stop at Hood River and Biggs, near Maryhill, as they whizz along I-84 to and from Portland. Another alternative is Gray Line (☎503/285-9845 or 1-800/422-7042), who operate day-long **tours** (April–Oct; 9hr; 3 weekly) of the gorge from Portland during the summer for $45, but they don't really allow you time to do the scenery justice, and it's frustrating not to have time to take a hike. Indeed, it's only when you get out on one of the many short **hiking trails** dotted along the Historic Columbia River Highway that the real charm of this lushly forested ravine becomes apparent – which means it's a good idea to spend the night locally, preferably at Hood River.

The Historic Columbia River Highway

A tired Lewis and Clark were the first whites to pass through the **Columbia River Gorge**, floating down it on the last stage of their 28-month (1804–1806) trek across the continent. Just forty years later it had become the perilous final leg of the Oregon Trail (see p.82), negotiated by pioneer families on precarious rafts. Thereafter, when gold was discovered in eastern Oregon, the river turned into a lifeline for pioneering miners and farmers, and a prime target for a lucrative transportation monopoly. A Portland-based company saw the opportunity, put steamboats on the river and was soon raking in the profits from the dependent (and bitter) residents of the arid east. By the 1880s, the steamboats were already carrying tourists, too.

The advent of car-borne tourism prompted the construction of what is known today as the **Historic Columbia River Highway** in 1915 – and it's this 22-mile stretch of road, now bypassed by I-84, which offers the area's prettiest views. It's also the most popular day out from Portland and so can be very busy, especially at the weekend, but even then it doesn't take much effort to escape the crowds that congregate round the parking lots beneath the several waterfalls. Most people come from Portland via I-84, getting off at Corbett (Exit 22), but there are several other access points, including one at Multnomah Falls (Exit 31), where there's a visitor centre (see below).

Leaving I-84 at Exit 22, it's a short drive to **Crown Point Vista House**, an Art Deco belvedere with a few incidental historical displays and panoramic views out over the gorge. Moving on, the road winds through dense forests and weaves past cascading waterfalls before it reaches the 242-foot **Wahkeena Falls**, the starting point for a number of hiking trails into the backcountry of the Mount Hood National Forest. In particular, the two-mile **Perdition Trail** is a stiff hike that takes you high above Wahkeena through thick groves of cottonwood and maple. At the end of Perdition Trail is the junction with Larch Mountain Trail, which you can follow for the mile-long descent to the tallest and most famous of the gorge's waterfalls, the two-tier **Multnomah Falls**. This plummets 542 feet down a mossy rockface, collects in a pool, then tumbles another 70 feet to the ground. Folklore has it that when a sickness threatened the Multnomah tribe, the chief's daughter threw herself over the falls to appease the Great Spirit. You're supposed to be able to see her face in the mist – the quaint Benson Bridge, spanning the rocks above the lower waterfall, was partly built with this in mind. At the foot of the falls, the appealing rustic stone and timber *Multnomah Falls Lodge* **restaurant** has been catering for tourists since 1925. The food is inexpensive, but pretty standard tourist fare – stick to the home-made bread and soups. The **visitor centre** (June–Sept daily 10am–6pm; ☎503/695-2376) next door issues free maps of the Historic Highway's hiking routes – though for the longer routes you'll need to buy one of their more detailed maps.

Multnomah Falls can get jam-packed, but within easy striking distance to the east is the much less visited and equally impressive **Horsetail Falls**, a powerful torrent that comes crashing down close to the road. From here, the Horsetail Falls Trail climbs the short distance to the quieter **Ponytail Falls** before pushing on to the **Oneonta Falls**, just over a mile from the trailhead. It's a lovely hike and rather than returning the way you came, you can scramble back to the road just west of Horsetail Falls beside the **Oneonta Gorge**, following a shallow stream along the bottom of the sheerest of the gorge's many side-canyons.

Rejoining I-84 at the east end of the Historic Highway, it's a few minutes' drive to the **Bonneville Dam**, the first of the chain of WPA dams which made the Columbia River the biggest producer of hydroelectric power in the world (for more on the Columbia dams see p.282). Four miles on, at **CASCADE LOCKS**, a 1920s toll bridge marks the site of the Native-Americans' **Bridge of the Gods**. Legend has it that a natural stone bridge once crossed the water here, but the sons of the Great Spirit, who had been sent to earth as snow mountains, quarrelled and belched out so much fire, ash and stone that the sun was hidden and the bridge was destroyed. There's some truth in the story: about a thousand years ago, a gigantic landslide blocked the river here, creating an inland sea which eventually tunnelled right through the barrier leaving a natural stone bridge suspended above. Cascade Locks gets its present name from the locks that were built here in the nineteenth century to protect river traffic from dangerous rapids, though the backwaters of the Bonneville Dam covered these long ago.

Hood River

Some twenty miles further east, the next bridge across the Columbia River abuts the town of **HOOD RIVER**, one of the most popular **mountain biking** and **windsurfing** centres in the Pacific Northwest. The steep slopes of neighbouring Mount Hood satisfy the bikers, while windsurfers benefit from an unusual but relatively reliable phenomenon: in summertime the heat of the eastern steppes draws cooler air in from the west at a rate that is too great to be smoothly absorbed within the narrows of the Columbia Gorge. By around noon, the pressure has built up to such an extent that it has to be released – in great gusts of air that rip along the gorge, with the windsurfers ready and waiting to "catch the blow".

Since they appeared on the scene in the early 1980s, the windsurfers have effectively reinvented Hood River, whose compact centre (take I-84, Exit 63) now comes complete with laid-back cafés and restaurants and all manner of outdoor sports equipment stores. The end result isn't especially pretty – the **town centre** is just a few modern blocks sandwiched between the I-84 to the north and Hood River to the east – but it's certainly lively. Furthermore, there's aesthetic compensation in the old and handsome timber houses that stretch out along Oak and Cascade streets just to the west of the centre in full view of the gorge.

The town's premier mountain **bike rental** company, Discover Bicycles (☎541/386-4820) is handily located downtown at 205 Oak St and 2nd. They have a good range of mountain bikes to choose from and will give advice as to which of the many nearby cycle trails will be most to your taste. Windsurfers, on the other hand, gather down beside the Columbia River Bridge, just below and a little to the east of the town centre – take I-84, Exit 64. Here, the well-established Rhonda Smith Windsurfing Center (daily: mid-May to early Sept; ☎541/386-9463 or 1-800/241-2430) rents out water-sports equipment and gives windsurfing lessons. Otherwise, the **Mount Hood Railroad** (☎541/386-3556 or 1-800/872-4661, *www.mthoodrr.com*) offers a 20-mile sightseeing trip down along the Hood River Valley to the south of town. The railroad was originally built in 1906 to service the valley's agricultural communities, but today it's just a tourist junket – and the antique trains are a good deal more interesting than the scenery. Trains depart from the old railway station at the east end of the town centre, just off 2nd Street (April–Oct 2–4 weekly; $23 return; departures at 10am and/or 3pm; 4hr 15min). There are (more expensive) brunch and dinner trips too.

Practicalities

Long-distance Greyhound **buses** from Portland in the west and points east pull in at Port Marina Park, near I-84's Exit 64. From here, it's a five- to ten-minute walk southwest to the town centre, on the other side of the interstate. There are no Amtrak trains. The **Chamber of Commerce** (☎541/386-2000 or 1-800/366-3530, *www.hoodriver.org*) is located down by the river off I-84 (Exit 63), directly below – but a good ten-minute walk from – the town centre. The chamber has free town maps, comprehensive accommodation listings and details of recommended sports outfitters.

The town has a reasonable supply of motels, hotels and B&Bs, but finding a **place to stay** can still get a little difficult in the summer, when advance reservations are advised. Amongst a handful of medium-priced **B&Bs** to the west of the town centre, one of the more central is the *Hackett House*, 922 State St at 9th Street (☎541/386-1014; ③), an attractive Dutch Colonial villa with four comfortable bedrooms. As for **hotels**, the pleasantly renovated *Hood River Hotel*, downtown at 102 Oak St (☎541/386-1900 or 1-800/386-1859, *www.hoodriverhotel.com*; ③), offers a wide range of rooms and suites with kitchenettes, running from the basic and functional to the plush with river views. However, easily the best hotel is the outstanding *Columbia Gorge Hotel,* 4000 Westcliff Drive (☎541/386-5566 or 1-800/345-1921, *www.columbiagorgehotel.com*; ⑦), whose exquisite gardens and hacienda-style buildings, created for the lumber king Simon Benson in 1921, perch on a clifftop right above the gorge. The hotel gardens even have their own waterfalls and the rooms are lavish and relaxing with modern furnishings of antique appearance. The hotel is situated about a mile west of the town centre, just off – and signposted from – I-84 (Exit 62).

Good places to **eat** in the town centre include the easy-going and very popular *Holstein's Coffee Company Café*, 12 Oak St at 1st (daily 6am–9pm), which serves up tasty light meals, great coffees and sandwiches, and the rather more traditional *Bette's Place*, at the Oak Mall, 416 Oak St and 5th(closes 4pm). Alternatively, the *6th Street Bistro & Loft* (☎541/386-5737), at the corner of Cascade and 6th Street, offers burgers and pasta dishes as well as full dinners, all at affordable prices. The busiest bar in town is the *Full Sail Brewing Co. & Pub*, 506 Columbia St and 4th (daily noon–8pm), though the *Big Horse Brewpub*, 115 State and 2nd Street, is a close rival – and it stays open a bit later, till 9pm Sunday through Thursday, 10pm on Friday and Saturday. To cool down, *Mike's Ice Cream*, 504 Oak St at 5th, sells a great range of ice creams.

The Dalles

Ignoring, for the moment, the lure of neighbouring Mount Hood (see p.107), it's twenty miles east from Hood River on I-84 to the ugly industrial township of **THE DALLES**, an old military outpost and halting point on the Oregon Trail. It was here that many of the pioneers transferred to rafts and bateaux for the perilous journey down the last stretch of the Columbia River. Before then, this spot had been a meeting place for French-speaking Canadian trappers, who named it after the basaltic rocks that lined this stretch of the river, looking – so they thought – like flagstones (*les dalles*). Just a mile or two upstream, but now flooded by **The Dalles Dam**, the Columbia once tumbled over a series of rocky shelves called **Celilo Falls**, long used by Native-Americans as fishing grounds and the source of much folklore – "the great fishing place of the Columbia" echoed Washington Irving. The dam was completed in 1957, in typical disregard of local Native-American traditions, and the town is resolutely unenticing – not a patch on Hood River (see opposite). That said, local history, along with displays on the formation of the Columbia Gorge, is well explained at the lavish **Columbia Gorge Discovery Center** (daily 10am–6pm; $6.50), on the riverbank at the western edge of The Dalles at 5000 Discovery Drive; the centre is clearly signposted from I-84 (Exit 82).

Maryhill Museum of Art

East of The Dalles, along the Columbia River Gorge, the trees thin out and then fade away to be replaced by the barren gulches and escarpments that herald the sagebrush plateaux of eastern Oregon. It's an austere, often majestic landscape and here, forty miles from Hood River, just across the Columbia on Hwy 97 (I-84, Exit 104), is Washington State's extraordinary **Maryhill Museum of Art** (mid-March to mid-Nov daily 9am–5pm; $6.50). The museum was the singular creation of an idiosyncratic tycoon by the name of **Samuel Hill**, who was born into a Quaker family in North Carolina in 1857. Nothing if not ambitious, Hill moved to Seattle in the early 1900s and married the daughter of a railroad owner before skilfully amassing a fortune by manipulating the stock market. With money matters out of the way, he set about all manner of projects – some, like his championing of road construction, eminently sensible, others downright daft.

In the latter category came his plan for "Maryhill" – named after his wife and daughter – which he declared a "Garden of Eden" and where in 1907 he planned to establish a Quaker farmers' colony. But the Quakers he brought over took one look at the parched slopes of the Columbia Gorge and opted out, and he concentrated on the house instead, building a three-storey poured concrete and steel extravagance in what can only be described as a sort of penitentiary style. Not content with this, Hill got the concrete out again and built a miniature copy of **Stonehenge** (daily 7am–10pm; free) on a hill overlooking the Columbia four miles upstream from his Maryhill mansion. It still stands, a pacifist's tribute to those who died in World War I, for Hill believed Stonehenge to be a sacrificial site, its faithful reproduction appropriate as "humanity is still being sacrificed to the god of war".

Despite Hill's best endeavours, however, no one, and least of all his family, showed the slightest interest in living at Maryhill and the house stood neglected for years. Then, in the 1920s – in another strange twist – two of Hill's European chums, **Queen Marie of Romania** and the well-connected Folies-Bergere dancer and Rodin model **Loie Fuller**, saved the whole enterprise. First they persuaded Hill to turn the house into an art museum and then helped by donating a generous sample of fine and applied art. Their gifts remain the kernel of the collection, which is displayed over the mansion's three floors. On the entry level are the assorted baubles and trinkets given by Queen Marie, including a small but delightful collection of Russian icons, Marie's Fabergé coronation crown and an imposing corner throne carved in Byzantine style in 1908. Marie was something of a romantic, surrounding herself with furnishings and fittings of medieval design – though this served other purposes too: until 1862, Romania had been part of the Ottoman Empire and its royals, who took over the running of the country thereafter, were desperate to create a sense of historical legitimacy. Marie managed to carry all this off, but her dynasty was short-lived. Her son, Carol, polished off the Romanian throne by his dalliance with Hitler. Also on this floor is a small selection of late 1940s French mannequins kitted out by some of the leading fashion houses of the day. There was a desperate shortage of fabric in postwar Europe and these were an ingenious way around the problem of how to advertise new designs.

Downstairs, there's a fine sample of the sculptures of Auguste Rodin, the gift of Loie Fuller, and a bizarre collection of chess sets – including a *Nixon v McGovern* edition. There's also a Native-American gallery and this is at its best in the sections devoted to

From the Maryhill Museum of Art, it's around 100 miles east along I-84 to the enjoyable cowboy-town of Pendleton (see p.157).

the bands of the Columbia River Valley and its environs – with everything from small totemic figures and arrow straighteners through to petroglyphs and pile drivers. There's a **café** on this floor too (10am–4.30pm), while the uppermost floor is largely given over to temporary exhibitions.

Mount Hood

Back at Hood River, Hwy 35 heads south towards the snow-capped mass of **Mount Hood**, which is, at 11,235 feet, the tallest of the Oregon Cascades. The road begins by running through the Hood River Valley (fruit-growing country, whose speciality is red Anjou pears), before climbing to skirt the mountain's heavily forested southern flank. Eventually, after about forty miles, the road reaches its highest point, **Barlow Pass**, named after Samuel Barlow, a wagon train leader who blazed a new last leg to the Oregon Trail. The Columbia River Gorge was impassable by wagon and when the early pioneers reached The Dalles, they were forced to change their means of transport, floating down the river on rafts. Knowing how much the pioneers dreaded the river trip, Barlow led a party off to blaze a new trail around the south side of Mount Hood in 1845. They were trapped by snow while chopping their way through thick forests, and had to leave their wagons behind in the struggle to reach the Willamette Valley before they starved or froze. But Barlow returned a year later, and this time he completed the **Barlow Road** (the upper reaches of which are still followed by highways 35 and 26), and many migrants chose to brave its steep ridges, where wagons frequently skidded out of control, rather than face the Columbia. To the irritation of many pioneers, Barlow grew rich on his endeavours, charging them a crunching $5 a wagon to use his road, while his partner completed the rip-off at the end of the trail by opening the one and only general store.

Beyond Barlow Pass, Hwy 35 meets Hwy 26, which leads either west to Portland or southeast to Madras and Bend (see p.168). Travelling towards Portland, it's about a mile from the crossroads to the signposted, six-mile-long turning that weaves up the mountainside to **Timberline Lodge** (☎503/622-7979 or 1-800/547-1406, fax 503/622-0710, *www.timberlinelodge.com*; ⑦, chalet bunkrooms with shared baths ④), one of Oregon's most celebrated hotels. Raised in the 1930s as part of a New Deal job-creation scheme, the hotel is a handsome affair, solidly built in rough-hewn stone and timber with an interior that oozes Arts and Crafts-style wooden furniture and fittings. Highlights include the main staircase, which is decorated with finely carved animals, rooms with wooden bedframes and panelled walls and an expansive atrium with wooden galleries and a huge, stone fireplace. But, appealing though all this may be, the hotel is much too popular for its own good and the assembled hordes rob it of any atmosphere – the main bar being a particular case in point. Incidentally, the lodge was used as the location for Stanley Kubrick's *The Shining*.

At 6000 feet, *Timberline* is also at the centre of a busy, **all-year ski and snow-boarding resort** – one of three (and undoubtedly the best) on the mountain – with 6 chair lifts and 32 runs to suit all abilities, though the majority are for the experienced. The highest chair lift climbs to an elevation of 8540 feet and the average snowfall is 350 inches per year. Ski passes ($34 per day) are available at *Timberline* and the adjacent (and amazingly ugly) Wy'east Day Lodge. Wy'east is also the place to **rent ski equipment** (skis, boots and poles $21 per day; snowboards and boots $33) and is the location of a ski school (☎503/231-5402). To check snow conditions, call ☎503/222-2211 or 1-877/754-6734; also check if tire-chains are required for the last leg of the journey up to the lodge – they are often necessary until well into summer. From *Timberline Lodge*, it's 55 miles to Portland.

The Oregon Coast

Although the **Oregon coast** is as beautiful as any stretch of America's Pacific seaboard, the Californian sun draws off the tan-seeking masses (summer temperatures here stay in the sixties and low seventies), leaving Oregonians and their visitors to wander the elongated shoreline with barely a crowd in sight. It's a wonderfully diverse coast too, incorporating dramatic headlands, mountainous sand dunes and interminable sandy beaches, and much of it has long been protected as public land with a string of state parks (and their scenic campgrounds) lining up along the seashore. Here also, extensive and sometimes isolated beaches offer a multitude of free activities, from beach-combing to shell-fishing, whale-watching or, in winter, storm-watching – but rarely swimming: the currents are too strong and floating logs too common a hazard to make this practicable. However, the Oregon coast has not escaped commercialism – far from it – but rather it's proved long enough to absorb the development that has occurred without too much difficulty. Indeed, the coast sports a series of resorts, the pick of which are **Cannon Beach** and **Bandon**, pretty little places of wooden houses and fashionable cafés – in sharp contrast to the dullness of retirement **Brookings** and the downmarket tackiness of sprawling **Lincoln City**. **Seaside** is another busy resort, tacky perhaps but somehow rather cheerful and not too big to be too off-putting. Interrupting this series of resorts are several small fishing villages that have, with the decline of the fishing industry, been obliged to reinvent themselves as tourist destinations – with great success at laid-back **Newport** and less so at over-commercialized **Florence**. Different again is **Astoria**, once an important nineteenth-century port at the mouth of the Columbia River, and now an agreeable place with a couple of good museums and a bevy of first-class B&Bs occupying its grand old mansions.

Right along the coast, the offshore islands, rocks and reefs are incorporated in the **Oregon Islands National Wildlife Refuge**, where in the summer you can expect to see elephant seals, harbor seals and steller sea lions as well as herons, cormorants, oystercatchers, puffins and many other sorts of seabird. There's considerable variety in the flora too, with hemlock, sitka spruce, cedar and Douglas fir common in the north, madrones, redwoods, ash and myrtles more frequent in the south – though these are but a few of the many trees to be found along the coast.

It's a lucky traveller who finds anything but the most spartan **accommodation** without booking ahead in July and August, though fortunately one- or two-days' advance notice will normally suffice for all but the most popular hotels, inns and motels. You will also find that prices can rise steeply at peak times, when some places also insist on a minimum of two-night's stay. In addition, about one-third of the sixty-odd state parks that dot the coast have **campgrounds** (the others are day-use only) and fourteen offer novel accommodation in the form of **yurts**. The latter are domed circular tents with wooden floors, electricity and lockable doors; yurts come equipped with bunk beds, sleep up to eight people and cost in the region of $25 a night. Yurts and many campgrounds can be reserved on the **State Park Campground Reservation Line** (☎1-800/452-5687) no less than 48 hours before arrival. Oregon State Parks Web site is *www.prd.state.or.us*.

One of Greyhound's Portland–San Francisco **bus** services is routed along the Oregon coast between Lincoln City and Brookings, but north of Lincoln City you're reliant on spasmodic local buses, the most significant of which is the Pacific Trails service linking Portland, Astoria and Seaside. Neither can you expect Greyhound to drop you in the middle of town – you're just as likely to be left beside the main road, a long

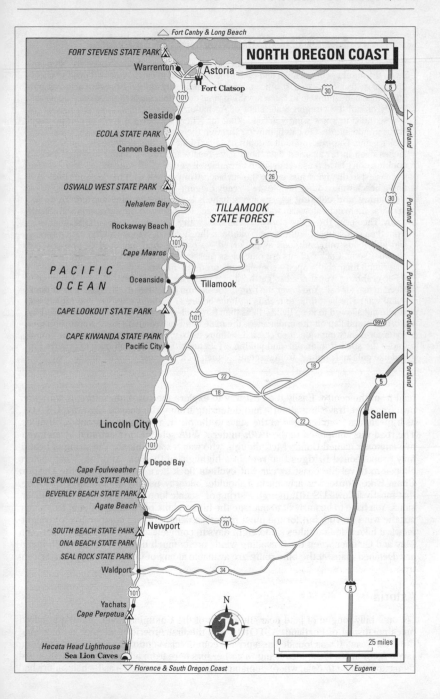

△ Fort Canby & Long Beach

FORT STEVENS STATE PARK

NORTH OREGON COAST

Warrenton
Astoria
Fort Clatsop
30
5

101

Seaside

ECOLA STATE PARK

Cannon Beach
26

OSWALD WEST STATE PARK

Nehalem Bay
TILLAMOOK
STATE FOREST

Rockaway Beach
101
6

Cape Mearos

PACIFIC
OCEAN

Oceanside
Tillamook

CAPE LOOKOUT STATE PARK
101

CAPE KIWANDA STATE PARK
Pacific City
99W

22
18

Lincoln City
101
18
22
Salem

Depoe Bay

Cape Foulweather
DEVIL'S PUNCH BOWL STATE PARK
BEVERLEY BEACH STATE PARK
Agate Beach

SOUTH BEACH STATE PARK
Newport
20

ONA BEACH STATE PARK
SEAL ROCK STATE PARK
Waldport
34

101

Yachats
Cape Perpetua

Heceta Head Lighthouse
Sea Lion Caves

N

0   25 miles

▽ Florence & South Oregon Coast
▽ Eugene

△ Portland
▷ Portland
▷ Portland
▷ Portland
▷ Portland
▷ Portland

FOOD FORAGING ALONG THE COAST

With patience, the region's beaches can yield a **hearty meal**, though there are often limits on the numbers of shellfish and crabs you're allowed to catch, so you'll need to check for local restrictions – tourist offices, for one, can usually oblige. Be aware also that pollution has made it unsafe to catch anything at all on certain parts of the coast – again ask locally or call the Oregon State Dept of Agriculture (☎503/986-4720). And you do, of course, need to know what you're looking for. There are several sorts of **clams**: razor clams are the hardest to catch, moving through the sand remarkably quickly; others are easier game. **Gapers**, found at a depth of 14 to 16 inches, and **softshells**, found 8 to 14 inches deep in firmer mud flats, both have meaty and rather phallic-looking "necks"; **cockles** don't have these (a decided advantage if you're at all squeamish) and are also the easiest to dig, lying just below the surface. Arm yourself with bucket and spade and find a beach where other people are already digging – obviously a likely spot.

Cleaning and cooking gapers and softshells is not for the faint-hearted. To do so, immerse them in fresh warm water until the neck lengthens so the outer skin will slip off easily. Then prize the entire clam out of its shell with a sharp knife, peel off the outer skin from the neck, and slit lengthwise. Split open the stomach, remove all the cark material and gelatinous rod, and cook as preferred – steamed, fried, battered or in a chunky chowder soup. Cockle clams are much less messy; you just steam them in fresh or salt water until their shells open – some people prefer them almost raw.

For **crabbing**, you'll need to get hold of a crab ring (often rentable) and scrounge a piece of fish for bait. You lower the ring to the bottom of the bay from a boat, pier or dock – and wait. The best time to crab is an hour before or an hour after low and high tides; you're not allowed to keep babies (less than 5.75 inches across) or females (identified by a broad round flap on the underside – the male flap is narrow). To cook a crab, boil it in water for twenty minutes, then crack it, holding its base in one hand, putting your thumb under the shell at midpoint, and pulling off its back. Turn the crab over to remove the leaf-like gills and "butter" from its centre – then pick the meat from its limbs.

haul from the centre. Easily the best way to explore the coast, therefore, is with your own transport, travelling along – and detouring from – the coastal highway, **US-101**, as it meanders from one end of the state to the other, a distance of around 350 miles. The road was completed in the 1930s under a WPA scheme orchestrated by an inventive engineer named Conde McCullough, who was responsible for the string of beautifully proportioned **bridges** that remain a highlight of the coastal drive. Most visitors choose to travel the coast by car, but **cyclists** flock here as well to use the **Oregon Coast Bike Route**, a clearly marked shoulder bikeway, usually around three feet wide, that mostly follows US-101, though a string of "scenic loop" roads provide lovely diversions. You have to be fairly fit to manage the hills and the occasional logging truck may put the wind up you, but for the most part it's a delightful and comparatively straightforward bike ride that takes six to eight days to complete. It's best attempted between May and October when the prevailing winds pretty much dictate a north–south itinerary. Detailed maps of the bike route are available at any of Oregon's major visitor centres.

Astoria

Set on a hilly tongue of land near the mouth of the Columbia River, about a hundred miles northwest of Portland, **ASTORIA** was the first American attempt at colonizing the West Coast. It was founded as a private commercial venture by the millionaire John Jacob Astor in 1811, the idea being to gather furs here from all over the Northwest and then export them to Asia, where demand verged on the feverish – as British sailors had

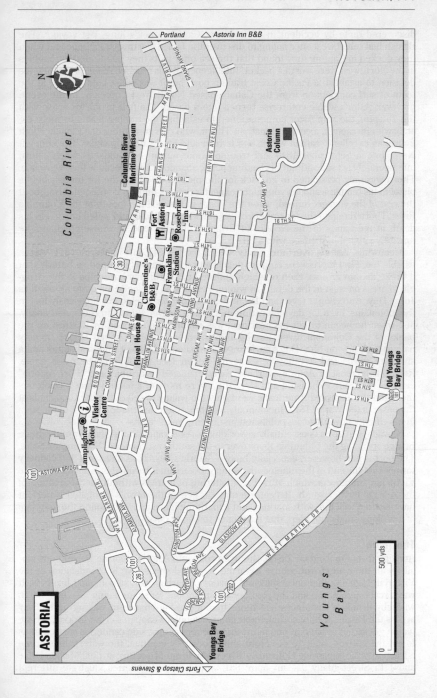

△ Portland   △ Astoria Inn B&B

N

Columbia River

Columbia River Maritime Museum

Astoria Column

Fort Astoria

Rosebriar Inn

Franklin St. Station

Clementine's B&B

Flavel House

Visitor Centre

Lamplighter Motel

ASTORIA BRIDGE

MARINE DRIVE

GRAND AVENUE

MARINE DRIVE

EXCHANGE STREET

IRVING AVENUE

COXCOMB DR

16TH ST

20TH ST

18TH ST

17TH ST

16TH ST

15TH ST

14TH ST

12TH ST

11TH ST

10TH ST

9TH ST

8TH ST

7TH ST

5TH ST

4TH ST

8TH ST

7TH ST

5TH ST

4TH ST

GRAND AVE

HARRISON AVE

IRVING AVENUE

JEROME AVE

KENSINGTON AVENUE

LEXINGTON AVENUE

LEXINGTON AVENUE

DUANE ST

FRANKLIN AVENUE

BOND STREET

COMMERCIAL STREET

GRAND AVE

WEST IRVING AVE

LEXINGTON AVE

JACKSON AVE

WEST MARINE DR

AGATE AVE

GLASGOW AVE

FLORENCE AVE

WEST MARINE DR

Old Youngs Bay Bridge

Youngs Bay Bridge

Youngs Bay

ASTORIA

500 yds

0

△ Forts Clatsop & Stevens

discovered quite by accident in 1779 during Captain Cook's long, last voyage. The British had sailed west after failing to discover the fabled Northwest Passage and when they docked in Canton, they found that the sea otter pelts they had traded for baubles in the Northwest were worth a packet. Intelligence of this reached Astor, prompting his decision to establish a Pacific Coast trading post, but it was still a bold gamble in the teeth of stiff competition from the Canada-based North West Company. In the event, however, Astor's whole enterprise turned into a fiasco. The first problems arose with the *Tonquin*, the ship Astor commissioned to establish the trading post – or more exactly with its captain, a certain Jonathan Thorn, who cuts something of a Captain Bligh figure: an excellent seaman with a bad temper and few leadership skills. The ship left New York in September 1810 and trouble broke out in the Falklands when Thorn intemperately set sail without his landing party, abandoned just because they were late. Thorn was only persuaded to go back for the men when one of the fur traders held a pistol to his temple – and, as you might expect, relations remained strained throughout the rest of the voyage. Indeed, when the *Tonquin* reached the mouth of the Columbia River, Thorn dumped the fur traders off as quickly as possible and sailed north – to his death at the hands of the Nootka of British Columbia, one of whose chieftains he unwisely rubbed in the face with a fur.

Meanwhile, Astor's **overland party**, which had left St Louis in March 1811, was in trouble too. First there were endless delays and then the party argued so bitterly that it broke up into groups, each of which endured extraordinary hardships in the struggle to press on west in the depths of winter. Perhaps no one endured quite as much as **John Day**, who caught fever and lay at death's door for weeks; got hopelessly lost in the mountains; lived for days by eating moccasins, beaver skins and roots; and finally, just when he began to get his bearings, was robbed and stripped by hostiles on the banks of the Columbia River, forcing him to wander around naked before friendly natives took pity on him. Day's sufferings soon acquired almost mythical status and a string of towns and a valley in eastern Oregon (see p.172) now bear his name. Remarkably, most of Astor's overland party managed to dribble into "Fort Astoria" early in 1812, but, exhausted and sick, they were more of a liability than a reinforcement and the dispirited Americans were only too willing to sell out to the Canadians at the onset of the War of 1812. Incidentally, Washington Irving made the best of the saga in his chunky novel *Astoria*, published just twenty years later.

Nowadays, Astoria is essentially a working port operating in the shadow of the huge **bridge** spanning the Columbia River over to the southwest corner of Washington State. The port is not, however, especially busy – Astoria's heyday as a seaport and cannery town was at the end of the nineteenth century, boom times recalled by a string of ornate **Victorian mansions** which attract a smattering of tourists without the razzmatazz of the resorts further south. Recent attempts to gee-up the town's elongated waterfont have worked well too, with marinas and a maritime museum interrupting the long line of low-slung sheds and piers that hark back to busier days.

The Town

Arriving from Portland on US-30, the main road into Astoria (Marine Drive) runs parallel with the **waterfront**, whose assorted piers and sheds give little indication of the Victorian high-jinx that once spawned dozens of harbourside saloons and brothels. It was a real rough house and the port became notorious for shanghaiing (see box, p.92), whereby drunken customers had more than a passing chance of waking up halfway across the Pacific, sold to complement an unscrupulous captain's crew. Indeed, the situation got so out of hand at one point that workers at quayside canneries carried guns to get themselves safely to the night shift. Today, by contrast, the waterfront's prime attraction is the expansive **Columbia River Maritime Museum**, at 1792 Marine Drive and 17th Street (daily 9.30am–5pm; $5), whose several galleries illustrate different facets of the region's nautical history, beginning with a large main hall containing models and mock-ups of old boats. Of the galleries that follow, one of the more interesting is the "Sailing Vessels" section, with its melodramatic ships' figureheads and fancy ship's sideboard, retrieved from the wreck of a British barque, the *Peter Iredale* (see overleaf). Elsewhere, the "Fishing, Tanneries and Whaling" section holds a fascinating collection of old Astoria photographs, as well as several walrus tusk Inuit sculptures – notably scrimshaws and a cribbage board – sold as souvenirs to visiting sailors. "Navigation and Marine Safety" focuses on the treacherous sand bar that broke the back of many a ship as it pushed into the Columbia River from the Pacific. With its combination of strong currents, shifting sand bars, breakers, frequent fog and stormy weather, the mouth of the Columbia was extraordinarily difficult to negotiate and around two-thousand ships are known to have sunk there. Dredgers, automated buoys and a pair of gigantic moles have made navigation much easier today, but ships still require the services of Astoria's pilots, whose powerful little boats are often to be seen bobbing about the river. The buoys were installed in 1979, replacing the red-hulled *Columbia* lightship, which is now part of – and moored outside – the museum.

From Marine Drive, numbered streets climb towards the uptown area, where the wealthy of the late nineteenth century built their elegant **mansions**, well away from the noise of the port. Prettily restored, with contrasting pastel shades picking up the delicacy of the carving, these appealing timber homes are distinguished by their fanciful verandas, attractive bay windows and high gables – and some of the most enjoyable are concentrated on Exchange, Franklin and Grand avenues between 11th and 17th streets. Here also, at 15th Street and Exchange, is a replica timber **bastion of Fort Astor**, a modest tribute to the travails of this unhappy group.

The most impressive of Astoria's mansions is, however, the 1880s **Flavel House**, downtown at 441 8th St and Duane (daily 10am–5pm; $5). Restored and refurnished in the manner of its first owner, Captain George Flavel (1823–1893), the house's cresting balconies, shingles, angular tower, wrapround verandas and hipped roofs are a fine example of the Queen Anne style. Flavel began by piloting ships across the Columbia River bar, but he grew rich as a ship owner, a razor-sharp entrepreneur who trained a beady eye on his property from the telescope he placed in his mansion's tower.

Beyond the fancy Victorian mansions of the uptown area, on top of Coxcomb Hill (follow the signs up 16th St and then Coxcomb Drive), stands the **Astoria Column**, painted with a mural depicting the town's early history and offering – from the observation platform at the top – superb views over the Columbia River and its surroundings. In particular, look out for the twin moles that protect the mouth of the river and the shifting sandbanks in between. On top of the hill also is a concrete replica of a Native-American **burial canoe**, which serves as a memorial to Chief Comcomly of the Chinook. He was on good terms with the first white settlers, one of whom married his daughter, until he caught his son-in-law hoeing potatoes (women's work in the chief's opinion). Comcomly's son, on the other hand, is said to have proposed to **Jane Barnes**, a barmaid from Portsmouth who arrived on an English ship in 1814 to become, Astorians claim, the first white woman in the Northwest. Jane turned him down, which wrought havoc with local race relations. There's nothing inside today's concrete canoe, but the original would have been crammed with tools and weapons to help the body in the afterlife. The Chinook always placed their burial canoes above ground to keep them out of the reach of predators, putting them either in the branches of trees or on isolated rocks in the river – much to the disgust of the whites.

Fort Clatsop National Memorial and Fort Stevens State Park

Having finally arrived at the mouth of the Columbia River in November 1805, the explorers Lewis and Clark needed a winter base before the long trudge back east. They built **Fort Clatsop** (daily: mid-June to Aug 8am–6pm; Sept to mid-June 8am–5pm; $2) beside a tributary river – which now carries their names – a few miles south of today's Astoria and had a thoroughly miserable time there. It rained on all but 12 of their 106 days, and most of the party were infested with fleas. Morale must also have been deflated by the leaders' insistence that the men keep away from native women – no matter how Lewis dressed it up in his *Journals*: "(A group of Chinook women) have formed a camp near the fort and seem determined to lay close siege to us, but I believe, notwithstanding every effort of their winning graces, the men have preserved their constancy to their vow of celibacy."

Lewis and Clark's winter fort, a straightforward log stockade, has been reconstructed here as a national memorial and although it's hardly impressive, the setting is delightful – deep in the forest by the water's edge – and the **visitor centre** nearby has an outstanding display on the explorers' expedition, explaining its historical background as well as providing details of the journey itself. Fort Clatsop is located south of Astoria and is most easily reached via US-101: from downtown Astoria just follow the highway over the Youngs Bay bridge and watch for the signs. The fort is about three miles east of US-101.

Ten miles west of Astoria, and also signposted from US-101 beyond Youngs Bay Bridge, is **Fort Stevens State Park**, a large recreational area, which occupies the tapering sandspit that nudges into the mouth of the Columbia River. Hundreds come here to wander the bike and hiking trails, go freshwater lake swimming, and stroll miles of beach before **camping** (☎503/861-1671; pitch $17–20, yurt $27 for up to five people) down for the night. There's also some historical interest a mile to the west of the campground in the beached and rusting **wreck of the Peter Iredale**, a British schooner which got caught out by high winds in 1906, and in the "Historical Area" to the north of the campground where a hotchpotch of **military ruins** spreads out over the park. Fortifications were first constructed here to guard against Confederate raiders during the Civil War and the army continued to use the site until the end of World War II. Fort Stevens was shelled one night by a passing Japanese submarine, which makes it, incredibly, the only military installation on the mainland US to have been fired on by a foreign power since 1812. You can wander the ruins to your heart's content – and a self-guided walking tour leaflet is available from the tiny **Military Museum** – but frankly it's not frightfully interesting unless you're into scrabbling around old gun batteries.

Practicalities

Pacific Trails (☎503/692-4437) operates a once-daily **bus** from Portland to downtown Astoria, a service that continues south along the Oregon coast as far as Seaside. Astoria's clearly signposted and well-stocked **visitor center**, 111 W Marine Drive (June–Aug daily 8am–6pm; Sept–May Mon–Fri 9am–5pm, Sat & Sun 10am–2pm; ☎503/325-6311 or 1-800/875-6807), is located near the base of the whopping US-101 bridge over the Columbia River. They issue a free and extremely detailed brochure on the town and its surroundings and also sell a detailed *Walking Tour* leaflet ($3) guiding visitors round the town's historic homes. If walking doesn't appeal, an antique **trolley** rattles its way along the waterfront, but it all seems rather forlorn.

As for **accommodation**, Astoria prides itself on its **B&Bs**, mostly housed in the splendid old mansions uptown. Among several options, the comfortable *Franklin St Station*, 1140 Franklin Ave at 11th Street (☎503/325-4314 or 1-800/448-1098; ⑤), built by a local shipbuilder for his son at the end of the nineteenth century, has a handful of en-suite rooms and a potpourri of period furnishings. The five-bedroom *Clementine's B&B*, in the town centre at 847 Exchange St (☎503/325-2005 or 1-800/521-6801; ④), occupies a handsome villa of 1888, and provides delicious breakfasts and again has period decor. Other possibilities include the larger and less personal *Rosebriar Hotel,* in another old mansion at 636 14th St (☎503/325-7427 or 1-800/487-0224; ③), and the *Astoria Inn B&B*, 3391

Irving Ave (☎503/325-8153 or 1-800/718-8153; ④), an 1890s farmhouse offering sweeping views across the Columbia from its location high up on the bluff a mile or so east of the town centre. Amongst the town's **motels**, one particularly good option is the *Crest*, 5366 Leif Erickson Drive (☎ & fax 503/325-3141 or 1-800/421-3141, *www.crest-motel.com*; ④), an immaculately maintained, two-storey motel perched on a wooded ridge two and a half miles east of the town centre along US-30. The rooms here are large and pleasantly decorated in modern style with kitchenettes, microwaves and balconies that provide fine views over the river. If you're on a tighter budget, there are a number of more routine modern motels on Marine Drive – with the *Lamplighter*, yards from the visitor centre at 131 W Marine Drive (☎503/325-4051 or 1-800/845-8847; ②), being a reasonable bet. There's a large campground – and yurts – at Fort Stevens State Park (see opposite).

Good places to **eat** are thin on the ground, but the small and unassuming *Columbian Café*, 1114 Marine Drive at 11th Street (usually 8am–2pm & 5–9pm), has tasty vegetarian and seafood as well as daily specials, often Mexican, which are always good value. There is also the modern *Pig 'n Pancake*, footsteps from the visitor centre at 146 W Bond St, which is popular with locals who congregate here for the big and hearty breakfasts. If you're looking for a larger meal, head for the *Pacific Rim Brewery*, 144 11th St and Marine, for tasty bar food, microbrews and live music.

Seaside

Seventeen miles down the coast from Astoria, **SEASIDE** is an endearingly tacky family resort, with a long sandy **beach** paralleled by a 1920s concrete walkway known as "The Prom". It was here that every member of the Lewis and Clark expedition had to take a tedious turn boiling down seawater to make salt, vital to preserve meat for the return journey. The reconstructed salt works – a few boulders and pans – are located towards the south end of The Prom and there's a commemorative statue of Lewis and Clark halfway along The Prom at the Turnaround traffic circle.

Seaside has lots of **hotels** and **motels**, and the **visitor centre**, at the junction of Hwy 101 – here Roosevelt Drive – and Broadway (☎503/738-6391 or 1-800/444-6740, *www.seasideor.com*), has the complete list. The most expensive are those overlooking the sea, and amongst them is the glitzily modern *Shilo Inn Oceanfront*, a chain hotel at 30 N Prom (☎503/738-9571 or 1-800/222-2244, fax 503/738-0674; ④). At the other end of the market, the HI *Seaside Hostel*, 930 N Holladay Drive (☎503/738-7911; $13), is located a few blocks north of Broadway and a stone's throw from the Necanicum River, which runs parallel to – and a few blocks from – the beach. Pacific Trails (☎503/692-4437) operates a once-daily **bus** from Portland to downtown Astoria and Seaside. In addition, Sunset Empire Transit (☎503/325-0563) links Astoria with Seaside and Cannon Beach.

Cannon Beach

Nine miles south of Seaside, **CANNON BEACH** is a more upmarket resort. The town, which takes its name from several cannon washed on to the beach from the wreck of a USS warship, the *Shark*, in 1846, sees itself as a refined and cultured place, and has building regulations to match – neon signs are banished and there are certainly no concrete high-rises. Painters sell their work from weathered cedar galleries and Portlanders wander from bookshop to bistro, reinforcing the tiny town centre's sedate and moneyed air. But locals do let their hair down at the annual **Sandcastle Competition**, a one-day event held late May or early June and starting when the tide permits. What Hollywood is to film, Cannon Beach is to sandcastle-building, and past themes have included dinosaurs, sphinxes, Elvis, and even the Crucifixion.

The **beaches** of Cannon Beach are some of the most beautiful on the Oregon coast, beginning with the wide strip of sand which backs onto the town centre at the mouth of Ecola Creek. They continue – about half a mile to the south – with a narrower strand that's dominated by the 240ft **Haystack Rock**, a craggy and imposing monolith with nesting seagulls on top and starfish, mussels and other shellfish in the rock pools at the bottom. More remote and less visited beaches are within a few miles of Cannon Beach too – the pick being in **Ecola State Park**, a couple of miles north of town, where dense conifer forests decorate the basaltic cliffs of Tillamook Head with seastack-studded beaches down below. A hiking trail runs through the forest along the nine miles of coast within the park and there's a primitive, hikers only campground about halfway along the trail – the park's only facilities.

Practicalities

Sunset Empire Transit (☎503/325-0563) operates a limited daily **bus** service from Astoria and Seaside to Cannon Beach, and the bus stop is right in the centre of town a few metres from the **visitor centre** (☎503/436-2623, *www.cannonbeach.org*) at 2nd and Spruce streets. The best way to see Cannon Beach is on **foot**, but if you're after exploring the local coastline it's a good idea to rent a **bike** from Mike's Bike Shop, downtown at 248 N Spruce St (☎503/436-1266).

There's a wide range of **accommodation** to choose from, but things still get very tight over the summer and impossible during the sandcastle competition. Furthermore, the inns, motels and hotels that trail along the coast south of the centre tend to lack charm and you're much better off paying a little more to stay downtown. Excellent oceanfront options here include the modern, cedar-shingled *Schooners Cove Inn*, 188 N Larch St (☎503/436-2300 or 1-800/843-0128, fax 503/436-2156, *www.schoonerscove.com*; ⑥), a smart and well-equipped establishment where most of the rooms have sea-facing balconies; the *Waves Motel,* 188 W 2nd St (☎503/436-2205 or 1-800/822-2468, fax 503/436-1490, *www.thewavesmotel.com*; ⑤), another dapper, modern place right on the oceanfront; and the marginally more modest, but equally well sited *Webb's Scenic Surf Motel*, 255 N Larch St (☎503/436-2706 or 1-800/374-9322, fax 503/436-1229; ⑦). If your budget is more constrained, there are less pricey alternatives south of the centre near the Haystack Rock – try the *Cannon Beach Hotel*, 1116 S Hemlock St at Gower Street (☎503/436-1392 or 1-800/238-4107, fax 503/436-1396; ③), which has a pleasant boarding-house atmosphere that's a big improvement on many of its motel-style rivals.

For **food**, the town centre is the best bet with a string of appetizing places dotted along the main drag, N Hemlock Street. Among them, the informal *Lazy Susan Café*, next to the Coaster Theater at no. 126, does excellent health food and breakfasts; *Osburn's Deli*, at no. 240, has a good deli selection and sidewalk benches; and the *Bistro*, at no. 263 (☎503/436-2661), has tasty seafood and an intimate bar. *Bill's Tavern & Brewhouse*, at Hemlock and 2nd, is the town's busiest bar, offering bar food along with their handcrafted brews.

South to Oswald West State Park

South of Cannon Beach, Hwy 101 threads through the wooded hills that overlook the ocean before looping through **Oswald West State Park**, a rugged and densely forested chunk of seashore that incorporates two headlands. The first is **Cape Falcon**, the second the 1660-foot **Neah-Kah-Nie Mountain**, meaning "place of fire" after the local Tillamook's habit of burning the mountain forest to provide better grazing for the deer and elk they relied upon. Less prosaically, Neah-Kah-Nie has also been linked with buried treasure ever since white settlers first heard a Tillamook tale of an enormous canoe – presumed to be a Spanish galleon – swept onto the shore with its great white wings flapping in the wind. The Spaniards, so the story continued, stashed their valuables in a hole in the mountainside and rounded off the enterprise by slitting the throat of a black crew member before burying his body on top of the treasure – which, if nothing else, should have given the Tillamook a clue as to the treatment they might expect from Europeans. Some support has been given to the legend by the discovery hereabouts of a handful of Spanish artefacts and several tons of beeswax – a favourite Spanish trade item – but the treasure has never been discovered, though lots of people have had a bash at digging it up.

In between the two headlands at the mouth of Short Sand Creek, the park possesses a beach, which is good for surfing, a picnic area and a small and simple **campground** (mid-March to Oct; $10) with tables, fireplaces, drinking water and flush toilets. It is a wonderful spot, popular with young surfers, and it's only accessible on foot, a quick third-of-a-mile hike down the hillside from US-101, where one of the parking lots is for campers only, with plastic wheelbarrows provided to help lug in equipment; it is clearly signed – the other parking lots are for day-users. From the campground, there's a choice of two short **hikes**: either the stiff, four-mile climb south to a vantage point near the top of Neah-Kah-Nie Mountain, or the easier two-and-a-half-mile hike north to the tip of Cape Falcon, weaving through patches of old-growth sitka spruce before reaching some superb coastal views.

South to Tillamook

Continuing south, there are magnificent vistas out along the coast as US-101 twists round the southern flanks of Neah-Kah-Nie before the road steers down to the sandspit-sheltered waters of **Nehalem Bay**. Inland the **Tillamook State Forest** stretches vast and green, having recovered from the forest fires of 1933 and 1945 which devoured over five hundred square miles of premium logging land. In the first fire, a week-long blaze started when a wire rope in a remote lumber camp sawed across – and set fire to – a dead tree. The scorched area, known as the Tillamook Burn, meant hard times for local logging communities, but it was the second fire, possibly started by a Japanese balloon bomb (see p.144), which really threatened the area's economy: seed sources will survive one conflagration, but not two. To stave off ruin, the timber companies and the state authorities combined to replant the Tillamook forest in a colossal undertaking that took thirty years to complete – the genesis of Oregon's state-managed forestry.

Pressing on, the dreary sprawl of the resort town of **ROCKAWAY BEACH**, about twenty miles south of Cannon Beach, mars the beauty of the adjacent strand, whose white and windswept sands extend for over seven miles. Beyond the resort, the highway veers east to swing round **Tillamook Bay**, once called "Murderer's Harbor" after natives killed a sailor from Gray's expedition here in 1788, and then cuts inland to cross the wide, green valley that announces **TILLAMOOK**. This plain dairy town holds two cheese-making factories, which are – oddly enough – among the region's most popular tourist attractions. In a bright and cheerful building on the north side of town beside US-101 is **Tillamook Cheese** (daily: June–Sept 8am–8pm; Oct–May 8am–6pm; free), where the self-guided factory tour provides glimpses of hair-netted workers beside conveyor belts and bent over large, milky vats. But the factory plays second fiddle to the gift shop, which sells every type of bovine souvenir imaginable. It also offers free samples of cheese, though you have to be fiendishly skilful with a cocktail stick to spear a sizeable portion – and the cheese is pretty bland anyway. The company's tasty ice cream (which you pay for) is much better. The other factory, the **Blue Heron French Cheese Company** (daily: June–Sept 8am–8pm; Oct–May 9am–5pm; free), signposted off US-101 a couple of minutes' drive to the south, specializes in locally produced French-style cheeses (like Brie) and has a cheese- and Oregon wine-tasting area.

South to Lincoln City

Heading south from Tillamook on US-101, it's a humdrum forty-five-mile trip along a series of inland valleys to Lincoln City (see below) – but there's a much more enjoyable (and time-consuming) coastal alternative in the clearly signposted **Three Capes Scenic Loop**, named after capes Meares, Lookout and Kiwanda. This 38-mile detour begins (or ends) in Tillamook. From here you travel west along the edge of Tillamook Bay and then south over a heavily forested headland to reach the short turning for the **Cape Meares lighthouse** (May–Sept daily 11am–4pm; free). A late nineteenth-century structure of sheet iron lined with brick, the lighthouse boasts gorgeous views out along the rough and rocky shoreline. While you're here, take a look also at the so-called "octopus tree", an oddly-shaped sitka spruce a couple of hundred yards from the parking lot.

Two and a half miles further on, **OCEANSIDE** is an agreeable little resort that spreads along the seashore and up the steep, wooded hill behind. There are fine views of the offshore **Three Arch Rocks**, a favourite with nesting seabirds, especially the tufted puffin, and a long sandy beach. There are also a couple of places **to stay**. Down near the seashore is the simple, small and modern motel-style *Oceanside Inn* (☎503/842-2961 or 1-800/347-2972; ③) and up above, high on the hill with great views, is the rather more appealing *House on the Hill Motel*, 1816 Maxwell Mountain Rd (☎503/842-6030, *www.houseonthehillmotel.com*; ⑤), a timber, pastel-painted modern place where the sea-facing rooms have balconies.

Pushing on down the coast from Oceanside, the shallows of **Netarts Bay** are almost entirely enclosed by a sandspit that protrudes from the bay's south shore. At the base of the sandspit, behind the beach, is the picnic area, **campground** and **yurts** (☎503/842-4981; pitch $16–20, yurts $27 for up to five people) of **Cape Lookout State Park**, which is named after – and also incorporates – the forested headland immediately to the south. From the campground area, you can stroll out onto the spit and go clamming and crabbing in the sheltered waters of the bay. Alternatively, it's a brief drive – or a stiff two-and-a-half-mile walk up – from the campground to the trailhead and parking lot ($3) of the Cape Trail. This is a mildly strenuous and very popular two-and-a-half-mile jaunt out to the tip of **Cape Lookout** as it pokes a precipitous finger out into the Pacific.

The third and final cape on the scenic loop is **Cape Kiwanda**, a sandstone promontory that's trimmed by sand dunes and partly protected by a monolithic seastack, Haystack Rock. The headland is near the tiny town of **PACIFIC CITY**, a desultory sort of place hidden away near the mouth of the Nestucca River and sheltered from the sea by another sandspit. The fishermen here are known for their ability to launch their fishing dories straight from the seashore into the oncoming surf – a real skill even though outboard motors long ago replaced oars.

From Pacific City, it's about four miles back to US-101 and then around twenty miles south to what is perhaps the ugliest resort on the Oregon coast, **LINCOLN CITY**, actually the merged version of five small beach towns, run together in 1965. The resort rattles along the highway for seven congested, motel-lined miles with precious little to entice you to stop. If you're marooned, there's plenty of inexpensive accommodation to choose from – the **visitor center**, 801 SW US-101 (☎541/994-8378 or 1-800/452-2151) has the complete list. One of Greyhound's Portland–San Francisco **bus** routes reaches the Oregon coast at Lincoln City, shooting through here as it heads south on US-101; drop-off details on ☎1-800/231-2222.

South to Cape Foulweather and Beverly Beach

Beyond Lincoln City, US-101 skirts Siletz Bay before slicing down to **DEPOE BAY**, an unassuming coastal settlement straddling the tiniest of harbours. South of here the highway climbs up towards the forested mass of **Cape Foulweather**, discovered and named by a jaded Captain Cook, whose historic expedition up the Pacific Coast had nearly been dispatched to a watery grave by a sudden Northwest storm – the winds hereabouts can gust at 100mph. A short and narrow sideroad leads off US-101 to the cape's lookout from where there are stirring coastal views – but be prepared to negotiate some hair-raising switchbacks on the way.

Returning to US-101, it's just a couple of miles further south to an easier turning that makes the brief trip down to the **Devil's Punchbowl**, a sandstone cave whose roof has fallen in. The sea foams and churns cauldron-like at high tide – and at low tide the waters recede to reveal a lattice of rock pools. It only takes a few minutes to look around and soon you'll be back on the highway, passing the elongated sands of **Beverly Beach**, part of which is designated a state park with picnic facilities, yurts and a large and well-equipped **campground** (☎541/265-9278; pitch $16–20, yurts $27 for up to five people).

From the Beverly Beach campground, it's seven miles south to Newport, past Yaquina Head and Agate Beach – for more on which see below.

Newport

With a population of just nine thousand, **NEWPORT** occupies the humpy seashore at the mouth of Yaquina Bay, about 25 miles south of Lincoln City. It's one of several Oregonian fishing ports labouring to turn itself into a resort – and here it works really well, with the bits and pieces of the old fishing port decorated by the occasional mural and imaginatively set against more recent development. This lively, often ad hoc mixture is at its most diverting on the north side of the bay down by the **harbour** where restaurants, bars and fish plants jostle along a short stretch of **SW Bay Boulevard**. Neither is this the only interesting part of town. Away from the docks, Newport reveals another side of its character amongst the old and peeling timber houses that ramble along the oceanfront north of Yaquina Bay. From 2nd Street to around 10th Street, immediately behind the long and uncrowded sands of **Nye Beach**, the hippies of yesteryear have bequeathed an arty atmosphere, manifest in a pair of **arts centres** – one for Performing Arts, at 777 W Olive St and SW Coast Street (☎541/265-9231), the other for Visual Arts, at 839 NW Beach Drive (☎541/265-6540).

South of SW 2nd Street – but still north of Yaquina Bay – the Nye Beach district gives way to the shiny oceanfront hotels of SW Elizabeth Street and the commercial centre of town, an uninspiring modern sprawl along US-101, which doubles as the main drag. More promisingly, the **Yaquina Bay Lighthouse** (daily 11am–5pm; donation) stands amidst the manicured greenery of the tiny state park at the foot of Elizabeth Street – and near the handsome 1930s bridge over Yaquina Bay. It's one of the coast's more interesting late nineteenth-century lighthouses, the forty-foot tower attached to the old keeper's house, a pleasant timber building constructed in the Cape Cod style and complete with period furnishings. Actually, it's surprising the lighthouse has survived: it was only in operation for three years during the 1870s while a much larger – and now fully automated – edition was built on a basalt headland three miles north of town. This, the **Yaquina Head Lighthouse** (daily noon–4pm), has been incorporated into the **Yaquina Head Outstanding Natural Area** (daily dawn to dusk; $5), whose visitor centre (daily: June–Sept 10am–6pm; rest of year 10am–4pm) has displays on local flora and fauna. More inspiringly, the lighthouse and the adjacent headland offer unsurpassed views of the coast and of the local wildlife, such as seals and seabirds gathered on the offshore rocks; if you're lucky you may even glimpse a passing whale. Down below, Quarry Cove is easily accessible too, and is noted for its **tide pools** inhabited by purple urchins, starfish, hermit crabs and anemones.

Returning towards Newport, in between Yaquina Head and Nye Beach, lies the wide sweep of **Agate Beach**, where winter storms toss up agates from gravelly beds under

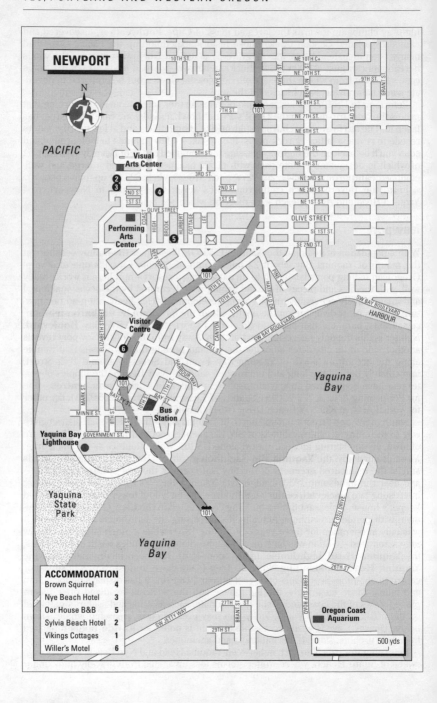

NEWPORT

N

PACIFIC

Visual Arts Center

Performing Arts Center

Visitor Centre

Yaquina Bay Lighthouse

Yaquina State Park

Yaquina Bay

Yaquina Bay

Bus Station

Yaquina Bay

HARBOUR

Oregon Coast Aquarium

ACCOMMODATION

Brown Squirrel	4
Nye Beach Hotel	3
Oar House B&B	5
Sylvia Beach Hotel	2
Vikings Cottages	1
Willer's Motel	6

0   500 yds

the sea – though many locals prefer to rock hound at Seal Rock State Park, ten miles south of Newport on US-101. If you walk along either beach towards the sun on an out-going tide, the agates (after a winter storm, at least) sparkle up at you: moonstone agates are clear, carnelians are bright red and transparent, and ribbon agates have coloured layers. Newport visitor centre (see below) provides further information.

Back in Newport, there are a couple of attractions over the bridge on the south side of Yaquina Bay – principally the large and impressive **Oregon Coast Aquarium** (daily: summer 9am–6pm; rest of year 10am–5pm; $9.25), signposted off US-101 at 2820 SE Ferry Slip Rd. This is home to marine mammals like the sea otter and seal, seabirds like the tufted puffin and a whopping octopus in a glass-framed sea grotto. There are also mock-ups of rocky and sandy shores, wetlands and coastal waters where the jelly-fish steal the show. It's all very professionally done and attracts tourists in their droves.

Practicalities

Newport's Greyhound **bus depot** is just north of the Yaquina Bay bridge, off the main drag (US-101) on SW Bayley Street (☎1-800/231-2222). The **visitor centre** is nearby on US-101, at 555 SW Coast Hwy (Mon–Fri 8.30am–5pm; ☎541/265-8801 or 1-800/262-7844, *www.newportnet.com*). They issue maps and brochures on the town and its environs, can advise about agate hunting and have complete motel and campground listings. There are no buses within the town limits, which can be a bit of a pain if you don't have a vehicle – the visitor centre is a good mile from both the harbourfront to the south and Nye Beach to the north. Newport is a good place to try your hand at **deep-sea fishing**: Newport Tradewinds, down by the harbour at 653 SW Bay Blvd (☎541/265-2101 or 1-800/676-7819) offers a variety of trips from year-round halibut and sea-bottom fishing – for sea bass, rock cod, sea trout, etc – to seasonal salmon and tuna fishing. A five-hour excursion costs $60 per person, $150 for twelve hours. From March to October, **whale-watching** excursions are possible here too with – among several operators – Marine Discovery Tours, 345 SW Bay Blvd (☎541/265-6200 or 1-800/903-2628, *www.marinediscovery.com*).

Newport offers a wide range of **accommodation**, but easily the most appealing place is the *Sylvia Beach Hotel*, 267 NW Cliff St (☎541/265-5428 or 1-888/795-8422, *www.sylviabeachhotel.com*), which occupies an attractive timber and cedar-shingle building overlooking Nye Beach from the foot of NW 3rd Street. The three-storey hotel is named after the owner of the Shakespeare & Co bookstore in the Paris of the Twenties and Thirties and each of the twenty rooms bears the name of a famous writer. The rooms are divided into three categories, two of which, the "Classics" (⑦) and the "Best Sellers" (⑤), have ocean views, unlike the "Novels" (④). Breakfasts here are fabulous too, with a buffet-style selection of home-made fruit and cake bars, granolas and juices in addition to a hot dish; non-residents are charged just $7 for breakfast – a real snip. Next door to – but just inland from – the hotel is the *Sea Cliff Bed & Breakfast*, 749 NW 3rd St (☎541/265-6664 or 1-888/858-6660; ⑤), a dinky little place with just two neat bedrooms. Close by again is the *Oar House B&B*, 520 SW 2nd St (☎541/265-9571 or 1-800/252-2538, *www.newportnet.com/oarhouse*; ⑤), which has five plush, en-suite rooms in a handsome old house that comes complete with a lovely garden and a tower offering sea views; the gourmet breakfasts here are first rate too. Another Nye Beach option is the pleasingly old-fashioned *Vikings Cottages*, 729 NW Coast St (☎541/265-2477 or 1-800/480-2477, *www.vikingsoregoncoast.com*; ⑤) – and condominiums (⑥). Amongst Newport's other less distinctive lodgings are the run-of-the-mill **motels** dotted along US-101, where it's less the roar of the sea than the roar of the motor car, and the flashy, modern places on the bluff above the beach on Elizabeth Street. Amongst the latter, the *Elizabeth Street Inn*, at no. 232 (☎541/265-9400 or 1-877/265-9400, fax 541/265-9551, *www.elizabethstreetinn.com*; ⑥), is particularly large and modern, and its spacious rooms have kitchenettes and sea-facing balconies. There's also a popular **campground** (and yurts) in Beverly Beach State Park seven miles north of town, and another – not as well-appointed – in **South Beach State Park** (☎541/867-4715; pitches $16–20), a mile or so south of the Yaquina Bay bridge.

Cafés and **restaurants** line up along the harbourfront's SW Bay Boulevard. Easily the best place here is the *Whale's Tale*, at no. 452 (☎541/265-8660), which offers delicious seafood at affordable prices in cosy, vaguely nautical surroundings. Nearby, just up from the harbourfront, is a second good place, the pleasant, pink-painted *Canyon Way Restaurant and Bookstore*, 1216 SW Canyon Way (☎541/265-8319), where, amongst a wide range of seafood, Dungeness crabs are a speciality ($14), though it's hard to beat their seafood bouillabaisse ($22). At Nye Beach, the best bet is the eclectic menu of the restaurant in the *Sylvia Beach Hotel*, 267 NW Cliff St (see overleaf). For a **drink**, the *Rogue Ales Public House*, 748 SW Bay Blvd, serves up the best microbrews in town, everything from light ales like Oregon Golden to the dark and tangy oatmeal Shakespeare Stout.

South to Yachats, Cape Perpetua and Heceta Head

South of Newport, US-101 sticks close to the seashore, bobbing past a series of state park beaches amongst which **Ona Beach**, seven miles beyond the bridge, lies at the mouth of a pretty little creek and has places to swim and fish. A couple of miles further, **Seal Rock State Park** is an attractive spot too, with dramatic basalt and sandstone seastacks framing a sandy beach. Western gulls, black oystercatchers and guillemots are among the many types of seabird that gather here, there are tide pools to ferret around in, and it's a good spot for digging for clams.

From Seal Rock, it's five miles south to the unexciting little port of **WALDPORT**, which straddles the mouth of Alsea Bay. Beyond, the green flanks of the Siuslaw National Forest close in around the highway as it zips down to **YACHATS**, a low-key resort whose ribbon of cottages and motels is at its prettiest round the mouth of the Yachats River. There's nothing exciting about Yachats, but the next few miles of coast are startlingly beautiful and staying here is handy if you're keen to explore its nooks and crannies. One of the more enticing places to **overnight** is the pretty, well-tended but rather spartan *Rock Park Cottages*, at 431 W 2nd St (☎541/547-3214; ③). Another good choice, the *Shamrock Lodgettes*, just to the south of town at 105 US-101 (☎541/547-3312 or 1-800/845-5028; ④), offers comfortable and pleasantly old-fashioned cabins. For food, *La Serre Restaurant* (☎541/547-3420), down by the river, serves delicious steaks and seafood.

Heading out of Yachats, US-101 winds its way up the densely forested edge of **Cape Perpetua**, formed by volcanic action and, at eight hundred feet, one of the most scenic peaks on the coast. The cape is latticed by hiking trails and the first place to head for is the tiny **interpretive centre** (☎541/547-3289), two and a half miles from Yachats, where you can pick up a map with trail descriptions; if the centre is closed these are available from the rack outside. Of the ten **hikes** to choose from, perhaps the most impressive is the strenuous three-mile return trip along the **St Perpetua Trail** running from the interpretive centre to the viewpoint at the cape's summit. From here, the views over the coast are simply fabulous – and you can drive up the mountain too: take US-101 north from the interpretive centre, turn down Forest Road 55 and then take Forest Road 5553. This climbs up to the parking lot and from here it's a straightforward, ten-minute stroll – on the **Whispering Spruce Trail** – to the viewpoint. Other short but steep trails beginning at the interpretive centre snake down to the seashore – either to tide pools, the beach, or the **Devil's Churn**, where the ocean pounds up a narrow gash in the basalt seashore. The US Forest Service operates a small **campground** (May to mid-Sept; $12) beside a creek in the shadow of the cape: it's signposted from US-101 just north of the interpretive centre, down Forest Road 55. Note also that in the summertime the cape's parking lots fill up fast, so try to arrive early.

Beyond Cape Perpetua, the drive along US-101 is incredibly scenic, with dense forests climbing above and the anything-but-pacific surf crashing against the rocks below. After eleven miles, you reach the idyllic **Heceta Head Lighthouse State Park** (day-use only; parking $3), where the slender arc of Devil's Elbow beach lies at the back of a charming cove. From the beach, it's a short and easy walk to the old light-house keeper's **Heceta House** (guided tours June–Aug Thurs–Sun 11am–3pm; free), an 1893 Queen Anne-style structure you can spot on the headland before you, and another short stroll round to the **lighthouse** beyond (same details).

A mile further on, the much-publicized and privately-owned **Sea Lion Caves** (daily 9am–dusk; ☎541/547-3111; $6.50) possesses an elevator, which shoots down through the sea-cliffs to a winding path that leads down the cliffside to an observation point into a dark, cavernous sea cave. So far so good, but the Steller sea lions – when they are there – are too far away to be impressive and anyway seem to spend a fair bit of time fast asleep. All in all, it's much better to catch sight of them along the seashore than holed up here.

Beyond the caves, US-101 cuts inland on its eleven-mile journey to Florence.

Florence – and the Oregon Dunes National Recreation Area

Sitting on the north bank of the Siuslaw River, **FLORENCE** was founded in the 1850s as a timber port, but it was never more than a minor player in the lumber business and would probably be struggling today were it not for its proximity to the Oregon Dunes National Recreation Area (see overleaf). It was tourism that saddled the town's main drag (US-101) with its string of routine motels, but the developers did much better down by the river in the **Old Town**, a pint-sized affair whose sturdy early twentieth-century architecture has been revamped to accommodate (a few too many) cafés and gift shops. With the exception of its striking 1930s Art Deco **bridge**, Florence has no sights as such, but the Old Town does have an amiable, cheerful air – despite its excessive popularity on sunny, summer weekends.

As for practicalities, Greyhound **buses** zip through Florence on US-101 – call ☎1-800/231-2222 for drop-off details. The **visitor centre**, just north of the bridge on US-101

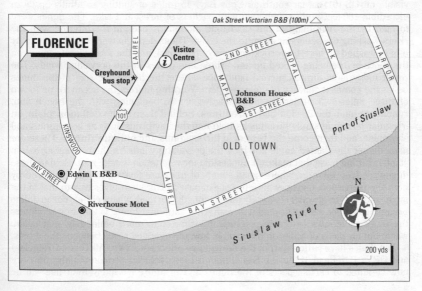

(☎541/997-3128), has information on the town, including a long list of accommodation. It also carries bits and pieces on the Oregon Dunes National Recreation Area (see below).

If you decide to **stay the night** in Florence, it's worth paying a few dollars more to stay in the Old Town in preference to the motels on US-101. Good Old Town options include the smart, seven-room *Edwin K Bed & Breakfast*, 1155 Bay St (☎541/997-8360 or 1-800/833-9465, *www.edwink.com*; ⑤), which occupies an attractive two-storey timber house at the foot of the riverside bluff; the *Johnson House B&B*, in a simple but well-kept little house one block from the river at 216 Maple St and 1st Street (☎541/997-8000; ④); and the comfortable and cottage-like *Oak St Victorian B&B*, 394 Oak St (☎541/997-4000 or 1-800/853-4005), tucked away beside a wooded bluff at the end of Oak and with a pretty veranda and garden. The last has four guestrooms – two with private bathrooms (⑤) and two without (④). Alternatively, the *Riverhouse Motel*, 1202 Bay St (☎541/997-3933 or 1-877/997-3933; ④), has an appealing setting right down by the river underneath the bridge – and from here you can see a huge sand dune piled up against the opposite river bank. There are several **campgrounds** in the vicinity of Florence, both to the north back along US-101 and in the national recreation area to the south. With over two hundred tent sites and a handful of yurts, the **Jessie M. Honeyman Memorial State Park** (☎541/997-3641; pitch $16–20, yurts $27 for up to five people) three miles south on US-101, has a freshwater lake on one side, the dunes on the other.

The Old Town's **cafés** and **restaurants** are geared up for the day-trippers, with the emphasis on speed rather than quality. Two of the better places are the *Bridgewater Restaurant*, at 1297 Bay St (☎541/997-9405), which specializes in seafood, and the workaday *Traveler's Cove*, 1362 Bay St, a café with a riverside patio offering snacks and light meals. Away from the Old Town, the *Windward Inn*, 3757 US-101 (☎541/997-8243), is in a different league, offering tasty steaks and seafood at reasonable prices.

The Oregon Dunes National Recreation Area

Beginning at Florence, it's **the dunes** that dominate the coast (though they are rarely visible on US-101) as far south as Coos Bay: 45 miles of shifting sandhills up to an incredible 180-feet high, punctuated with pockets of forest and lake. The dunes were formed by the crumbling of the sandstone mountains back in the interior, with the rivers washing the sediment down to the coast. These deposits were supplemented by others washed up here from rockier parts of the coast, and the whole lot dried out on the shore before being picked up and drifted into dunes by the prevailing winds. The result today is an almost surreal landscape where the house-like size of the dunes belies the complex delicacy of the ecosystem. Working in from the ocean for up to two or three miles is a succession of distinctive zones, beginning with the **beach** and, running behind, the 20–30ft high **foredunes**. Behind them is the **deflation plain**, an irregular terrain of sandy hummocks held together by plants such as beachgrass and shorepine, and then come the largest of the sandhills, the **oblique dunes**. These are named after the slanted angle at which the prevailing winds hit them, creating a constantly shifting mass that makes it impossible for vegetation to take root. Behind these dunes are **tree islands**, where small stands of trees are floating in sand, followed by both the **transition forest**, where the ocean-based ecosystem gives way to that of the land, and the freshwater **coastal lakes**, mostly formed when either ocean inlets became cut off or sand dammed a stream. One cautionary note is that in wet winters the water table rises to create patches of swamp and, more ominously, quicksand: watch out for pools of water on the sand in low, unvegetated areas between the dunes.

The dunes have suffered from the destructive effects of ATVs (All-Terrain Vehicles) and ORVs (Off-Road Vehicles). But although these vehicles remain popular they are now confined to certain parts of the dunes and in future it's likely their use will be

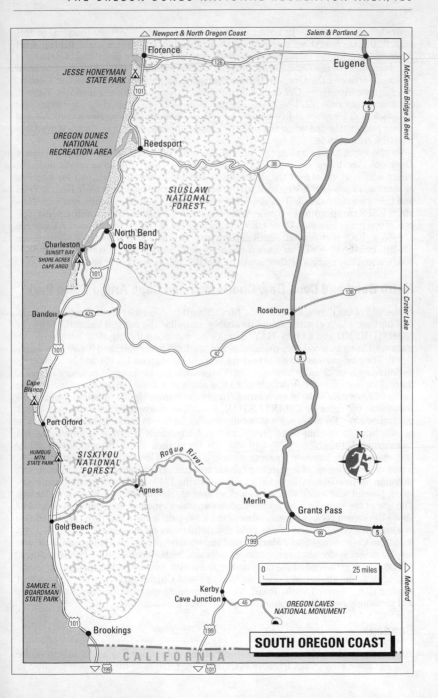

Florence

126

Eugene

5

McKenzie Bridge & Bend

JESSE HONEYMAN
STATE PARK

101

OREGON DUNES
NATIONAL
RECREATION AREA

Reedsport

38

SIUSLAW
NATIONAL
FOREST

138

North Bend

Coos Bay

Charleston
SUNSET BAY
SHORE ACRES
CAPE ARGO

101

Roseburg

Creter Lake

Bandon

425

101

42

5

Cape
Blanco

Port Orford

Rogue River

SISKIYOU
NATIONAL
FOREST

HUMBUG
MTN.
STATE PARK

Agness

Merlin

Grants Pass

99

5

Medford

Gold Beach

199

0   25 miles

SAMUEL H.
BOARDMAN
STATE PARK

Kerby

46

Cave Junction

OREGON CAVES
NATIONAL MONUMENT

N

101

Brookings

199

SOUTH OREGON COAST

CALIFORNIA

199   101

restricted even further – in favour of more environmentally-friendly tourism. In this regard, the US Forest Service, who manage the dunes, maintain eight **hiking trail** areas that are, for the most part, motor vehicle free. These are described in detail in a free booklet – *Hiking Trails in the Oregon Dunes* – which is available from some local visitor centres and the **Oregon Dunes National Recreation Area Visitor Center**, 855 Highway Ave (June–Oct daily 8.30am–4.30pm; Nov–May Mon–Fri 8am–4.30pm & Sat 10am–4pm; ☎541/271-3611), at the junction of US-101 and Hwy 38, twenty-one miles south of Florence in Reedsport. Indeed, the visitor centre carries a veritable raft of free information and when the office is closed, the most useful leaflets are available from the rack outside.

Of the eight hiking trail areas, one of the most enjoyable is the **Oregon Dunes Overlook**, ten miles south of Florence on US-101. Here, the observation platform offers smashing views over the dunes to the sea and acts as the trailhead for a couple of short and fairly easy hiking trails to the beach – the one-mile **Overlook Beach Trail** and the two-and-a-half-mile **Tahkenitch Creek Loop**. There are slightly longer trails – and a USFS **campground** – a mile to the south on US-101 at **Tahkenitch Creek**. You can, if you must, hire an ATV or ORV from a long list of rental companies. Charges are $30–35 an hour plus deposit. Sandland Adventures, about a mile south of Florence on US-101 (☎541/997-8087, *www.sandland.com*), and Sand Dunes Frontier (☎541/997-5363), about three miles further south on US-101, are as good as anyone.

North Bend and Coos Bay, Charleston and Cape Arago State Park

At the end of the dunes, a fine Conde McCullough bridge spans **Coos Bay**, a deep natural harbour which groups around its shabby shoreline the merged industrial towns of **NORTH BEND** and **COOS BAY**. There's no mistaking the big deal here, with the main road lined by wood-chip mountains and stacks of cut timber, and it's all very unenticing. The obvious thing to do is to drive straight through on US-101 and head directly to Bandon, about 25 miles to the south. That said, if you've a couple of hours to spare, there is an enjoyable detour which takes you southwest along the coast to a trio of state parks within a mile or so of each other. To get there from US-101 in North Bend/Coos Bay, follow the signs for **CHARLESTON**, a small, workaday sports-fishing town about nine miles away. From here, it's about three miles further to **Sunset Bay State Park**, a popular spot on account of its pretty sheltered bay, sandy beach, safe swimming and **campground** (☎541/888-8867; $16–20). The next park along, **Shore Acres** (daily 8am–dusk; $3), is, however, far more diverting and much less crowded. Green and lush, it was once the estate of a shipping tycoon and lumber man, one Louis Simpson, and although his palatial mansion was demolished in the 1940s the formal gardens have survived, planted with exotic species as well as azaleas, rhododendrons, roses and dahlias. The site of the mansion now accommodates an observation shelter, perched on a bluff above the jagged rocks of the seashore, and a footpath leads down through the woods to a secluded cove. It's one of the most delightful parks on the coast and it's also just a mile from **Cape Arago State Park**, a wild and windswept headland where you'll usually be able to spy Steller sea lions, elephant seals and harbor seals on the offshore rocks.

The cape is at the end of the road and on the return journey, rather than going all the way back to the US-101 in Coos Bay, you can – in Charleston – take the sign-posted turning along **Seven Devils Road**. This is a meandering country road which slowly and pleasingly twists its way south to US-101 near Bandon.

Bandon

Further south along the seashore, some 25 miles from Coos Bay at the mouth of the Coquille River, easy-going, likeable **BANDON** (or Bandon-by-the-Sea, as it's known in

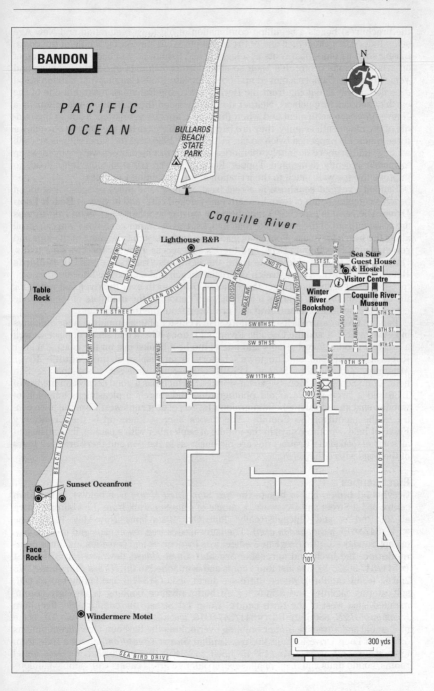

BANDON

PACIFIC OCEAN

BULLARDS BEACH STATE PARK

PARK ROAD

Coquille River

Lighthouse B&B

Table Rock

JETTY ROAD

MADISON AVENUE

LINCOLN AVENUE

OCEAN DRIVE

2ND ST

1ST ST.

CHICAGO AVE.

Sea Star Guest House & Hostel

Visitor Centre

EDISON AVE.

DOUGLAS AVE.

BANDON AVE.

OREGON AVENUE

Winter River Bookshop

Coquille River Museum

7TH STREET

8TH STREET

NEWPORT AVENUE

JACKSON AVENUE

HARRISON

SW 8TH ST.

SW 9TH ST.

SW 11TH ST.

CHICAGO AVE.

DELAWARE AVE.

ELMIRA AVE.

5TH ST.

6TH ST.

9TH ST.

BALTIMORE ST.

ALABAMA AVE.

101

10TH ST.

BEACH LOOP DRIVE

Sunset Oceanfront

FILLMORE AVENUE

Face Rock

101

Windermere Motel

SEA BIRD DRIVE

0   300 yds

the brochures) boasts a beguiling combination of old town restoration and New Age style. Indeed, it's altogether one of the nicest places to stay on the whole of the coast, having shed its blue-collar roots as a logging and fishing port to become something of an arts and crafts centre. It's been so since former habitués of Haight Ashbury and Venice Beach in California moved up here in the late 1960s claiming that Bandon stood directly on a ley-line going from the Bering Sea to the Bahamas, making it one of the earth's "acupuncture points". Neither do the vibes end there: Bandon was originally a Native-American settlement and when the local Coquille were swept aside in the middle of the nineteenth century, they are supposed to have cursed the town to burn down three times; it's happened twice so far, in 1914 and 1936, and the superstitious are still waiting. Rather more definitely, memories of these troubled times were stirred when townsfolk recently dynamited Tupper Rock, a sacred tribal site on Jetty Road, to improve the sea wall, much to the irritation of the remaining Coquilles.

Bandon's rugged **seashore** is a real treat, with several miles of seastack-studded beach stretching south of town beneath pine-pricked cliffs and in view of **Beach Loop Drive**. The coast is especially magnificent in stormy weather, when giant tree stumps are tossed up out of the ocean like matchsticks, and in calmer conditions you can stroll along the beach for hours. Footpaths lead down to the beach from most of the inns and resorts lining Beach Loop Drive and there's also access from several tiny state parks. On the other (north) side of the river, the lighthouse marks the start of **Bullards Beach State Park**, a long stretch of pristine beach and sand dune knee-deep in contorted piles of driftwood. To get there, take US-101 north over the river and watch for the turning on the left. And, as if all that wasn't enough, the mud-flats of the Coquille estuary are perfect for **clamming** and **crabbing** from the town's jetties.

Bandon **town centre** is itself no more than a cluster of unassuming timber buildings in between US-101 and the Coquille River, but it does have a real sense of place as well as several good café-restaurants and one of the best bookshops on the coast – Winter River, at 170 SE 2nd St. The town's history is on display at the **Coquille River Museum**, 270 Fillmore St and US-101 (June–Aug Mon–Sat 10am–4pm & Sun noon–3pm; Sept–May Mon–Sat 10am–4pm; $1), which has a good section on the fire of 1936 and a large sample of old photographs, and there's a pleasing hotchpotch of wooden shacks and fishing buildings along 1st Street as it runs west from the town centre to the mouth of the Coquille. The town's biggest knees-up is the **Cranberry Festival** held over three days in the middle of September with a parade, live music and all sorts of food stalls. Cranberries are big business in Bandon and there are even tours of the bogs where they grow.

Practicalities

Greyhound **buses** pull in beside the *Sea Star Guest House* (see below), in the town centre at 1st Street and Delaware, a couple of minutes' walk from the **visitor centre** at 300 2nd St and Chicago (daily: June–Oct 10am–5pm; Nov–May 10am–4pm; ☎541/347-9616, *www.bandon.com*). The latter issues free town maps and their daily – except Sunday – *Coffee Break* newssheet lists local news and activities. As for **accommodation**, the lively and agreeable *Sea Star Guest House*, downtown at 370 1st St (☎541/347-9632; ③), has just four rooms and is attached to the *HI Sea Star Hostel*, 375 2nd St (same number), where there are dorm beds ($13–16) and family rooms (①), self-catering facilities and a laundry. At both, advance booking is strongly recommended. Just west of the town centre, along 1st Street, the comfortable, five-room *Lighthouse B&B*, 650 Jetty Rd (☎541/347-9316, *www.lighthouselodging.com*; ⑥), occupies an old and attractive timber building overlooking the harbour. Oceanfront options on Beach Loop Drive include the outstanding *Sunset Oceanfront*, about a mile from town at no. 1775 (☎541/347-2453 or 1-800/842-2407; ③–⑦), which comprises motel rooms, condo units and, best of all, several older seafront cabins with simply fabulous views along the coast – it's well worth paying the extra. Another mile or so out of town is the rather more modest *Windermere Motel*, at no. 3250 (☎541/347-3710; ④), which has dinky chalet-huts. If rooms are tight – as they often are in the summer – try the routine modern motels dotted south of the centre along US-101, which runs inland from – and parallel to – Beach Loop Drive. Finally, north of the centre, across the river, there's a sheltered **campground** and a handful of yurts in the woods behind the beach in **Bullards Beach State Park** (☎541/347-2209; pitch $16–20, yurts $27 for up to five people).

Amongst Bandon's supply of **cafés** and **restaurants**, the *Sea Star Bistro*, in the hostel, does an excellent range of meals from just $10. Not far away, *The Station Restaurant*, 635 2nd St (US-101) at Fillmore, is a family-style place that's a popular spot for an all-American breakfast. More upmarket options include two restaurants noted for their seafood, the *Bandon Boatworks* (☎541/347-2111), west of the town centre by the river at the end of Jetty Road, and the smart *Lord Bennett's*, about a mile south of the centre at 1695 Beach Loop Drive (☎541/347-3663).

South to Cape Blanco and Port Orford

Towns become fewer and further between as you travel south from Bandon with US-101 staying a few miles inland to rattle through the forested hills. After about 23 miles, the highway reaches the turning for **Cape Blanco State Park**, which fills out a bumpy, triangular headland between the Sixes River and a Victorian **lighthouse** (April–Oct Thurs–Mon 10am–3.30pm; donation), perched high on the clifftop some five miles from US-101. Signs of the early homesteaders who colonized the coast are rare, but here in the park, in a lovely tranquil spot overlooking the river, is the solitary, shingle-clad **Hughes House** (May–Sept Thurs–Mon 10am–3.30pm; donation), a sturdy two-storey structure built in the 1890s and now refurnished in period style. The surrounding farmland has been left pretty much untouched too, and nearby are the scant remnants of a pioneer cemetery. Amongst several **hikes**, one short trail leads to the coast from the boat ramp near the house; the **campground** (☎541/332-6774) is in the woods behind the seashore.

Back on US-101, it's four miles more to **PORT ORFORD**, a desultory little fishing-port-cum-resort. Its only attraction is **Battle Rock**, a much-trampled-over outcrop, which was the site of an early struggle between white settlers, in the form of the crew of the steamship *Sea Gull*, and a band of local Rogue natives in 1851. The Rogues lived on the seashore and they tried to resist the landing of the whites – with the usual disastrous consequences. The rock pokes up above the seashore beside US-101 on the south side of town, next door to the seasonal **visitor centre** (☎541/332-8055). Greyhound **buses** shoot through Port Orford on US-101 – call ☎1-800/231-2222 for drop-off details. If you break your journey here, you can choose from four run-of-the-mill **motels** (③) and a more appealing **B&B**, the cosy *Home by the Sea*, 444 Jackson at 5th Street (☎541/332-2855, *www.homebythesea.com*; ⑤), which offers pleasant views over the coast and has just three guestrooms.

Gold Beach and the Rogue River

Five miles south of Port Orford, US-101 loops round **Humbug Mountain State Park**, comprising a mighty coastal headland whose 1756-foot summit is reached from the highway along a three-mile switchback hiking trail. The park **campground** (☎541/332-6774; $16–20) is down by the river, beside the main road beneath the mountain. Beyond the park, US-101 sticks close to the coastline in the shadow of forested mountains which sweep smoothly down to the sea. These mountains mark the western limit of the **Siskiyou National Forest**, a vast slab of remote wilderness that is most easily explored by boat along the turbulent Rogue River from **GOLD BEACH**, at the river mouth 23 miles from Humbug Mountain. Gold Beach has always been dependent on the Rogue: in the 1850s the town prospered from the gold the river had washed into its dark sands and later the Rogue fed its salmon canneries. Nowadays, the town is largely devoted to packing visitors off on **jet boats**, up canyons and through the Rogue's roaring rapids – which, to be frank, is just as well: the town, a long ribbon of modern development strung along US-101, is unexciting with the exception of the handsome 1930s bridge. Among several Rogue River boat operators, the pick are Mail Boat Hydro-Jets (☎541/247-7033 or 1-800/458-3511, *www.mailboat.com*), whose wharf is on the north side of the river, and Jerry's Rogue Jets (☎541/247-4571 or 1-800/451-3645, *www.roguejets.com*), who are on the south bank. There are daily jet-boat trips from May to October and charges begin at about $30 per person for six hours through to $75 for an eight-hour excursion. There's a two-hour break for lunch at a riverside lodge, but food isn't included in the price; reservations are strongly advised.

Exciting though jet boating is, it's easier to concentrate on the scenery around the Rogue River on foot. The forty-mile **Rogue River National Recreation Trail** (also see p.146) begins at Grave Creek, thirty-odd miles to the northwest of Grants Pass and – as it's much better to negotiate the trail heading downriver and downhill – your best bet is to travel upriver by boat and then hike down. None of the Gold Beach boats get anywhere near Grave Creek, but they do travel far enough upriver to provide a good long hike on the journey back. There are regular first-come, first-served campgrounds ($10–20) along the trail as well as a series of strategically placed lodges on its lower half – each a day's hike from the other. For detailed advice, go to Gold Beach's **Siskiyou National Forest Ranger Station**, just south of the Rogue River on US-101 at 29279 Ellensburg Ave (Mon–Fri 8am–5pm; ☎541/247-4909). The adjacent **visitor centre** (☎541/247-7526 or 1-800/525-2334, *www.goldbeach.org*) has details of all the local jet-boat operators and will know where Greyhound **buses** currently drop and pick up – or call ☎1-800/231-2222. There are lots of modern **motels** south of the river along US-101. One of the more appealing is the simple and well-kept *Ireland's Rustic Lodges*, 29330 Ellensburg Ave at 11th Street (☎541/247-7718, fax 547/247-0225; ③), which has a number of quaint wooden chalets.

Brookings

Down towards the California border is Oregon's "banana belt" – of which **BROOKINGS**, 29 miles south of Gold Beach, is the capital. Warmed by drifting thermal troughs from the Californian coast, this area is unusually sunny (often over 60°F in January) making it popular with retirees, and the local industry is, appropriately enough, the genteel art of flower growing. Most of North America's Easter lilies are grown here, and some of the local azaleas are over twenty feet high and three hundred years old, inspiring the annual **Azalea Festival** on Memorial Day weekend at the end of May. Greyhound **buses** pass through town and there's a **visitor centre** (Mon–Fri 9am–5pm; ☎541/469-3181) down by the harbour, but the town is much too glum to keep you from the rugged seashore a few miles to the north. Here, the **Samuel Boardman State Park** is a ten-mile coastal strip whose various viewpoints, picnic areas and footpaths – from the bluffs down to the beach – are accessed via US-101: **Whalehead Cove** – eight miles north of town – is as scenic a spot as any.

There isn't anything to detain you between Brookings and California, but just over the border the mighty redwoods of the **Jedediah Smith Redwoods State Park** (see p.150) shade US-199 near its junction with US-101. You have to take US-199 over California's Siskiyou Mountains to make the loop to the Oregon Caves and Grants Pass (see p.146).

The Willamette Valley

South of Portland, I-5 slices through the placid scenery of the **Willamette Valley**, zipping past its principal towns where industry has, for the most part, supplanted agriculture as the economic mainstay. Easily the most diverting of the valley towns are the state capital, **Salem**, which has a neat and appealing centre, and burgeoning **Eugene**, Oregon's second largest city, a buoyant, lively kind of place with a New Age feel. Just 110 miles from Portland, Eugene is also within easy striking distance of the **Willamette National Forest**, whose rugged landscapes and turbulent rivers lie on the western slopes of the Cascades – though Bend (see p.168), 130 miles east across the mountains, or possibly Crater Lake (see p.140) are somewhat better bases for exploring the most magnificent mountain scenery. Back in the Willamette Valley, a third town to visit is **Oregon City**, on the periphery of Portland and of historic interest both as the settlement at the end of the Oregon Trail and as the first state capital, although frankly there's precious little to actually see.

Public transportation along the Willamette Valley is excellent with regular Greyhound **buses** running between Portland, Salem, Eugene, Ashland, Klamath Falls and points south in California; Amtrak operates a comparable **train** service. Portland's transit system, Tri-Met, covers Oregon City.

Oregon City

Set beside the confluence of the Willamette and Clackamas rivers, about thirteen miles south of downtown Portland, **OREGON CITY** is, in a sense, where the state began. This was the end of the Oregon Trail and the first capital of the Oregon Territory – though, ironically enough, it was actually founded by the British-owned Hudson's Bay Company: its local factor, John McLoughlin, built a lumber mill here in 1829, when American settlement of the Northwest was little more than a twinkle in President Andrew Jackson's eye. Today, the split-level town consists of an unappetizing modern section, down by the river, and – up above – an uptown area of old wooden houses set on a bluff, that's ascended by both steep streets and steps.

Located on this compact, gridiron upper level, amongst a series of nineteenth-century clapboard houses, is the restored **McLoughlin House**, at 713 Center St and 7th Street (Tues–Sat 10am–4pm & Sun 1–4pm, closed Jan; $3.50), which was moved up from the riverfront c.1900. It was once the home of John McLoughlin, who ignored both political antagonisms and the instructions of his employers in providing the Americans who survived the Oregon Trail with food, seed and periodic rescue from hostile Indians. His main base was north of here in Vancouver on the Columbia River, but he retired to Oregon City in 1846 confident that his cordial relationship with – and generosity to – the American pioneers would stand him in good stead. He was wrong. He underestimated the nationalistic prejudices of his American neighbours and the local administration stripped him of his Oregon City landholdings, leaving McLoughlin an embittered man. His two-storey house has been refurnished in period style, with a good scattering of McLoughlin's own possessions; he and his wife are buried in the grounds. Of lesser interest, the **Ermatinger House**, 619 6th St, dating from the 1840s, was where the name of "Portland" was chosen on the flip of a coin; and, just down the street at no. 603, is the **Stevens Crawford Museum** (Feb–Dec Tues–Fri 10am–4pm; $3.50), a historic 1908 home, restored to something of its original appearance.

Down below the bluff, on the northern edge of the lower town, lies Oregon City's most publicized attraction, the **End of The Oregon Trail Interpretive Center**, at 1726 Washington St (Mon–Sat 9am–5pm & Sun 11am–5pm; $5.50), a gallant attempt to give the flavour of the pioneer's difficult and dangerous trek. It's housed in a trio of giant, imitation covered-wagon canvases, which certainly makes it distinctive, and although artefacts are thin on the ground, the costumed staff give the lowdown with great gusto.

Tri-Met **buses** #32 and #33, colour-coded green, run from Portland's downtown transit malls to various points in Oregon City, including the upper town.

Salem

The build-up of motels and fast-food chains that ushers you into **SALEM**, some fifty miles south of Portland, is deceptive, for this is, in fact, a small and rather staid little town, content to dutifully point visitors around its quota of attractions – principally the Capitol building and the Mission Mill Village – but not particularly expecting them to linger. It was founded by the Methodist missionary Jason Lee, who set up Oregon's first US mission a few miles north of Salem in 1834. Lee originally intended to convert the Native-Americans, but his sermons went down better with the white fur-traders who had retired to farm in the area, and Lee, deciding white settlement was the best way to further the cause, requested more recruits. The Methodist Missionary Board sent a shipload of pioneers, and, usefully, the machinery for a grist mill and a sawmill, which

Lee set up by a dam in Salem, building himself a house nearby and thus laying the cornerstone for the present town. His ideal of a self-sufficient Willamette farming community was advanced further when an enterprising pioneer managed to herd a flock of high-grade sheep over the Oregon Trail in 1848 – no mean feat in itself. The woollen mills that resulted, worked mostly by local women, sprang the rural valley into the industrial age – and Salem became established as a workaday mill town, leavened only by the presence of the state legislature.

The Town

Downtown Salem has a compact collection of nineteenth-century low-slung red-brick, the showpiece of which is the 1869 **Reed Opera House**, at Court Street and Liberty, once the centre of local cultural activity and now a trim, little shopping mall. Opera houses sprang up all over the Northwest in the second half of the nineteenth century – "opera" in the broadest sense as these boisterous establishments showed pretty much anything that was touring, from Shakespeare to dancing dogs. Oscar Wilde, for one, did a reading and speaking tour of the west, going down a storm with the miners of Colorado in 1883 and famously observing a sign above the piano which read "Please do not shoot the pianist. He is doing his best". From Salem's downtown core, it's a short walk east along Court Street to the town's real centrepiece, the tall, white, Vermont-marble **State Capitol Building** (Mon–Fri 7.30am–5.30pm, Sat 9am–4pm & Sun noon–4pm; free), finished in 1938 and topped with a gold-leaf pioneer, axe in hand, eyes towards the west. At the entrance, there's a marble carving of explorers Lewis and Clark processing regally towards (presumably) the Willamette Valley, its caption – "Westward the Star of Empire Takes its Way" – an odd sort of motto, considering the amount of blood and effort expended getting rid of the British only a few years before Lewis and Clark set off. Inside are murals celebrating the state's beginnings and on the floor, under the wings of a bald eagle, there's a large bronze version of the state seal, in which wheat, a covered wagon and trading ships symbolize the Oregon state as accepted into the union in 1859. Throughout the summer, there are regular **guided tours** (June–Aug 9am–4pm, hourly on the hour except noon; free) round the Capitol, beginning at the information desk inside the rotunda. Back outside, manicured gardens surround the building, with statues of Jason Lee and John McLoughlin on the east side.

Next to the Capitol, leafy **Willamette University** is the oldest university in the West, originally a mission school set up by Jason Lee and more recently an institution that has churned out local politicians by the score. Just to the east of the campus is the **Mission Mill Museum**, off 12th Street at 1313 Mill St SE (Tues–Sat 10am–3pm; $5), which groups a nineteenth-century woollen mill, a small museum and the old frame houses of several early pioneers with a café and a few shops. It's all rather well done and gives an insight (albeit prettified) into Salem's early history; the town's main visitor centre (see overleaf) is here too. Around the back, the modest **Marion County Historical Society Museum** (Tues–Sat 10am–4.30pm; $1) has an exhibit on the Kalapuyan, who lived in the Willamette Valley until a combination of white settlers, the Klickitat and disease drove them out. As much as ninety percent of the native population were killed by a nineteenth-century malaria epidemic. The museum's pride and joy is a rickety and rare 125-year-old canoe, hollowed out, in the traditional manner, by hot coals.

Practicalities

Only an hour from Portland, and easy to reach along the main I-5 corridor, Salem can be visited on a day-trip from Portland or, better, on the way south towards Eugene and Ashland. The Greyhound **bus** station is convenient for downtown at 450 Church St NE and Center, and so is the Amtrak **train** station, at 13th Street SE and Bellevue. The **vis-**

COVERED BRIDGES

Homesteaders in the **Willamette Valley** put roofs over their bridges to protect the wooden trusses from the Oregon rain, lengthening the bridge's life-span from ten to thirty years or more – a tradition which continued until fairly recently. The privacy they afforded earned them the nickname of "kissing bridges". There are no less than thirteen covered bridges in the vicinity of **Eugene** and although it's unlikely you'll want to see them all, three old ones, dating from the 1930s and 1940s, are clustered together around tiny **Dexter**, roughly twelve miles southeast of town along Hwy 58, off I-5. A special brochure details the exact location of all the Willamette Valley's covered bridges; it's available from any major visitor centre hereabouts.

itor centre is part of the Mission Mill Museum, off 12th Street at 1313 Mill St SE (☎503/581-4325 or 1-800/874-7012, *www.scva.org*).

Salem has its share of modern, budget **motels**, but most of the more enticing places are a little way out from the centre. Amongst them, one good option is the comfortable *Phoenix Inn – South Salem*, south of downtown at 4370 Commercial St SE (☎503/588-9220 or 1-800/445-4498, fax 503/585-3616; ④), which has ninety-odd trim and spacious modern rooms, a pool and jacuzzi. More central is the *Ramada Inn*, a modern hotel on the south side of downtown at 200 Commercial St SE and Trade (☎503/363-4123 or 1-800/272-6232, fax 503/363-8993; ④). If you're **camping**, head for **Silver Falls State Park** (☎503/873-8681; $16–20), a large park 26 miles east of Salem via highways 22 and 214, where hiking trails nudge through the lush fir and hemlock forests of a sinuous canyon.

For **food**, the area around the university is not the busy scene you might expect, and you're better off downtown. Here you'll find the *Dairy Lunch Café*, 347 Court St near Liberty, a classic 1960s diner offering meals and snacks that are both tasty and inexpensive. In the evening, the *Arbor Café*, 380 High St NE at Chemeketa (closed Sun), sells an imaginative range of sandwiches and coffees, salads and pastas, whilst the *Da Vinci Restaurant*, 180 High St SE (☎503/399-1413), offers authentic Italian cuisine and pizzas fired in a wood-burning oven.

Eugene

Some 65 miles south of Salem on I-5, **EUGENE** dominates the lower end of the Willamette Valley. Unlike its industrial annexe Springfield, just across the Willamette River, it's a lively social mix of students, professionals, hippies and blue-collar workers. The city's role as a cultural focus began with the travelling theatre groups that stopped here on their way between Portland and San Francisco in the late nineteenth century. The city takes its name from one **Eugene Skinner**, the first person to build a homestead in the area in 1846, his success based on the abundant supply of timber rather than the ferry service he ran for local farmers – sunken logs and gravel bars were a constant hazard. Other settlers followed Skinner's tree-cutting example and thereafter, Eugene developed as a supply centre for the local agricultural communities and boomed from the 1870s when the California–Eugene–Portland railroad was completed. More recently, this is where Ken Kesey and some of the Merry Pranksters came to live in the woods after tiring of the California scene; it's where the famous Nike running shoe was first tried and tested by University of Oregon athletes; and it's where much of *Animal House* was filmed.

Eugene's biggest annual event is the **Oregon Country Fair**, a big hippie-flavoured festival of music, arts, food and dancing held during the second weekend in July in **Noti**, just west of Veneta, itself ten miles west of Eugene on US-126. Traffic is heavy,

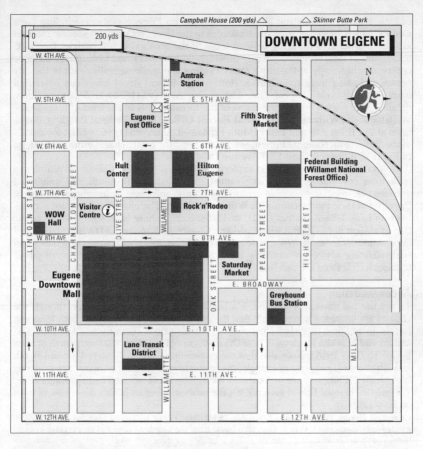

Campbell House (200 yds) △   △ Skinner Butte Park

DOWNTOWN EUGENE

0   200 yds

W. 4TH AVE.

W. 5TH AVE.   E. 5TH AVE.

Amtrak Station

WILLAMETTE

Eugene Post Office

Fifth Street Market

W. 6TH AVE.   E. 6TH AVE.

Hult Center   **Hilton Eugene**   **Federal Building (Willamet National Forest Office)**

W. 7TH AVE.   E. 7TH AVE.

Visitor Centre (i)   **Rock'n'Rodeo**

WOW Hall

CHARNELTON STREET   OLIVE STREET   WILLAMETTE   PEARL STREET   HIGH STREET

LINCOLN STREET

W. 8TH AVE.   E. 8TH AVE.

Eugene Downtown Mall   **Saturday Market**

OAK STREET   E. BROADWAY

Greyhound Bus Station

W. 10TH AVE.   E. 10TH AVE.

Lane Transit District   MILL

WILLAMETTE

W. 11TH AVE.   E. 11TH AVE.

W. 12TH AVE.   E. 12TH AVE.

N

so even if you have a car it's easier to travel there by local shuttle bus – there's a special service and it is free. Note that fair tickets must be purchased before you get there – call ☎541/343-4298 for details. There's another big summer festival at **Cottage Grove**, twenty miles south of Eugene on I-5. This, the **Bohemia Mining Days**, in the third week of July, recalls the nineteenth-century gold strike of one James Bohemia Johnson.

Arrival, information and getting around

Eugene is easy to get to by public transit: Greyhound **buses** link the city with Klamath Falls to the southeast, Portland and the towns of the Willamette Valley to the north and with Ashland and California to the south. Amtrak's Pacific coast **train**, running from Los Angeles to Seattle and Canada's Vancouver, passes through Eugene too. In Eugene, the train and bus **terminals** are both handily located downtown with Greyhound pulling in at Pearl Street and E 10th Avenue, Amtrak at 5th Avenue and Willamette Street. For information, there's a useful **visitor centre** downtown at 115 W 8th Ave at Olive (Mon–Fri 8.30am–5pm & Sat 10am–4pm; also June–Sept Sun 10am–4pm; ☎541/484-5307 or 1-800/547-5445). They have a full list of local accommodation and all sorts of leaflets on Eugene and surrounding Lane County, which stretches from the Cascades to the Oregon Coast. Of specific interest are those brochures detailing driving tours of the area's covered bridges (see box, p.134) and of local wineries – many of which do free tours and tastings. The visitor centre also has maps of the city's many **cycling** and **walking** trails, both in the city centre and along leafy river banks. Both mountain and street bikes can be rented from Paul's Bicycle Way of Life, 152 W 5th Ave (☎541/344-4105). In addition, detailed information and hiking maps of the forested hills to the east of Eugene are available at the **Willamette National Forest Office**, in the Federal Building, down-town at 211 E 7th Ave and Pearl (Mon–Fri 8am–4.30pm; ☎541/465-6521); for details of the Willamette National Forest, see p.138. For 24hr Internet and **email** access, go to Kinko's, Willamette and 13th Avenue (☎541/344-3555).

Downtown Eugene is itself best explored on **foot** – it only takes about ten minutes to walk from one side to the other. Named streets run north–south and numbered avenues east–west; the avenues are prefixed "east" and "west", changing from one to the other at their intersection with Willamette Street. The city's outskirts are accessible with Lane Transit District (LTD; ☎541/687-5555), whose **buses** provide the public transportation needs of the whole of Lane County. In Eugene, LTD's bus station and information centre are at Willamette and 11th Avenue; free transit maps, timetables and route-planning advice are available here. Subsidized to encourage the use of public transport, LTD fares are minimal.

Accommodation

To get the full flavour of Eugene, it's best to stay downtown and, even though the choices are limited, it's here you'll find the city's plum accommodation, both **inns** and **hotels**. In addition, there is a cluster of reasonably priced chain **motels** and hotels on and around Franklin Boulevard, near the university off I-5 (Exit 192), and north of town beside I-5 (Exit 195A). Note also that the rudimentary hotels clustered around W 6th and 7th avenues, just west of Lincoln, are in the town's seediest area and are probably best avoided. **Campers** are well catered for by a series of forested campgrounds in the Willamette National Forest (see p.138), the nearest being an hour's drive east of town on Hwy 126.

Campbell House, 252 Pearl St at E 3rd Ave (☎541/343-1119 or 1-800/264-2519, fax 541/343-2258, *www.campbellhouse.com*). One of Oregon's finest inns, the *Campbell House* is an exercise in good taste. The main house, dating from the 1890s, is an elegant affair with lovely gardens, gracious public rooms and a handsome veranda. Each of the guestrooms is immaculately decorated in period style – lots of tartans and warm colours – as they are in the adjacent carriage house. Breakfasts are nothing short of superb. The inn is also ideally located on the slopes of a wooded hill with the town centre just a few minutes' walk – or a brief drive – down below, and the vantage point of Skinner Butte Park a short, steep walk up above. Highly recommended. ⑤.

Doubletree Hotel, 3280 Gateway St, Springfield (☎541/726-8181 or 1-800/222-8733, fax 541/747-1866, *www.doubletreeeugene.com*). Arguably the pick of the modern hotels and motels just off I-5 (Exit 195A). The *Doubletree* is a self-contained complex with a restaurant, bar, pool and neatly functional rooms. ④.

Excelsior Inn, 754 E 13th Ave (☎541/342-6963 or 1-800/321-6963, fax 541/342-1417, *www .excelsiorinn.com*). In the middle of the university quarter, and handy for its cafés and bars, this small hotel has just fourteen rooms decorated in a brisk, modern style. ④.

Hilton Eugene, 66 E 6th Ave (☎541/342-2000 or 1-800/937-6660, fax 541/342-6661). Bang in the centre of town, next door to the performing arts centre, this is an excellent downtown option – a sturdy modern tower block whose interior is tastefully reassuring and where many of the rooms have superb views out across the Willamette Valley. ⑤.

Sixty-Six Motel, 755 E Broadway (☎541/342-5041, fax 484-5556). No points for style or originality, but this modern chain motel is inexpensive, clean, efficiently run and near the university – where E Broadway joins Franklin Boulevard. ②.

The Town

Though short on specific sights, Eugene's homely, rather intimate **downtown** of partly pedestrianized modern shopping malls and offices is spick and span and almost devoid of high-rise development. It's here, clustered around the main north–south axis of Willamette Street, that you'll find many of the town's best restaurants and cafés. Eugene puts on something of a floor show at its two big markets, particularly the weekly **Saturday Market**, at E 8th Avenue and Oak Street (between April and Nov), which began in 1970 as a local crafts market but has since expanded into something of a carnival, with live music and street performers. Tie-dye and wholefoods set the tone, but punks and students join the metaphysicals, in and make a cheerful throng. **Fifth Street Public Market** (to the north at E 5th Ave and High St), though more orthodox, is another lively affair, of arts, crafts and clothes, as well as ethnic foods, its three levels of shops built around a brick inner courtyard – actually a clever conversion of an old chicken-processing plant. Here also, the **Nike store** puts on a retrospective exhibition of its famous footwear. From the Fifth Street Public Market, it's about 600 yards up High Street – over the railway tracks – to **Skinner Butte Park**, whose grassy lower portion trails along the banks of the Willamette River. This was where Eugene Skinner had his initial landholding as commemorated by a tiny **log cabin**. Up above is the wooded butte that gives the park its name, and you can drive or walk to the top for views of the town and river. Finally, the one noteworthy attraction to the south of downtown is the **Lane County Historical Museum**, 740 W 13th Ave at Monroe (Wed–Fri 10am–4pm & Sat noon–4pm; $2), where pride of place goes to the sections on logging and the Oregon Trail. The latter includes an original covered wagon – one of just a handful to survive.

Eating and drinking

With thousands of students to feed and water, Eugene is well supplied with **bars**, **cafés and restaurants**, the pick of which are clustered downtown, mostly between Broadway and 5th Avenue in the vicinity of Willamette Street.

Ambrosia Restaurant, 174 E Broadway at Pearl St (☎541/342-4141). One of Eugene's best Italian restaurants – big and popular and reasonably priced to boot. The pizzas, baked in an oak-fired oven, are first-rate, the pasta is fresh and very varied and the daily specials are great value. Excellent range of Oregon wines and occasional live music too.

Café Navarro, 454 Willamette St at E 5th Ave (☎541/344-0943). World-music sounds reinforce the diversity of the Caribbean and Latin cuisine on offer here in this tastefully decorated, informal café-restaurant. A reasonably priced and imaginative menu makes this one of Eugene's better bets.

Café Zenon, 898 Pearl St at E Broadway (☎541/343-3005). An upbeat café-cum-bistro with marble-topped tables, tile floors and an eclectic menu ranging from pasta to curry. Don't let the dour setting put you off. Inexpensive.

Jo Federigo's Café & Bar, 295 E 5th Ave and High St (☎541/343-8488). Stick to the Italian dishes at this fashionable spot and enjoy the nightly live jazz. No cover. Inexpensive.

Morning Glory Café, 448 Willamette St at 5th Ave. Footsteps from the train station, this simple café, with its unreconstructed hippie air, is not to everyone's taste, but it does offer bargain-basement home-made meals from 7am to 3pm. Closed Mon.

Oregon Electric Station, 27 E 5th Ave at Willamette (☎541/485-4444). Housed in an imaginatively refurbished train station and featuring live music at the weekend, this fashionable spot offers delicious, top-quality bar food – from prime rib through to pasta. The restaurant menu is similarly varied, but a tad overpriced and fairly formal by Eugene standards.

Steelhead Brewery and Café, 199 E 5th Ave and Pearl (☎541/686-2739). This reasonably priced establishment, resembling an English pub (the West Coast version), has its beer brewed on the premises as a tasty accompaniment to sandwiches, burgers and pizzas. Look out for the delicious wheat beers, one or two of which are jazzed up with local fruit.

Wild Duck Brewpub, 169 W 6th Ave at Olive St (☎541/485-3825). The large and casual restaurant, with its hardwood floors and steel furniture, serves bar-food standbys as well as more ambitious meals emphasizing local ingredients. One of the flagship beers is the hoppy, copper-coloured Glen's Bitter.

Entertainment and nightlife

For **evening entertainment**, lots of cafés and bars have **live music** on one or two nights a week (see overleaf), but the city's showpiece is the Hult Center for the Performing Arts, 7th Avenue and Willamette (☎541/682-5000, *www.hultcenter.org*). This showcases everything from ballet and opera through to blues, with performances by touring companies of international standing as well as the city's symphony orchestra and ballet company. The Hult is also the prime venue for Eugene's prestigious annual Oregon Bach Festival, held in late June and early July and drawing musicians from all over the world; further details from the Hult Center, or call ☎1-800/457-1486. Elsewhere, the older WOW Hall, 291 W 8th Ave at Lincoln (☎541/687-2746), once a meeting hall for the Industrial Workers of the World (or "Wobblies" – see p.627), is more informal, featuring up-and-coming bands across the musical spectrum, whilst the rowdy, but good-fun *Rock'n'Rodeo* is a country bar/club at 44 E 7th Ave and Willamette (☎541/683-5160). For further details of up-and-coming events and gigs, pick up a copy of the free broadsheet, the *Eugene Weekly*, widely available downtown and at the visitor centre.

Willamette National Forest

Within easy striking distance of Eugene is the **Willamette National Forest**, a great slab of forested wilderness that occupies a one-hundred-mile strip on the western side of the Cascade Mountains, tipped by brown-black lava fields at its highest elevations. Four major highways, running west–east, leave the Willamette Valley to access the forest as well as its many hiking trails and campgrounds. Three of them – nos. 22 from Salem, 20 from Albany and 126 from Eugene – merge just before they wriggle through the Santiam Pass beneath mighty Mt Washington on the way to Bend (see p.168), on the other side of the mountains. It's also possible to get to Bend via an offshoot of Hwy 126, the tortuous and at times hair-raising Hwy 242, which snakes over the mountains via the McKenzie Pass, the highest of the passes hereabouts – but note snow closes this road to traffic from early November to late June. Further south, Hwy 58, the fourth major road, is the route to take from Eugene through the national forest to Crater Lake (see p.140).

For **information**, the **Willamette National Forest Office**, located in downtown Eugene at 211 E 7th Ave and Pearl (Mon–Fri 8am–4.30pm; ☎541/465-6521), carries a full range of maps, trail details and information. There's also a US Forest Service **Ranger Station** just east of the straggling hamlet of McKenzie Bridge, about fifty miles east of Eugene on Hwy 126 (late May to early Oct daily 8am–4.30pm; ☎541/822-3381). Most of the national forest's **campgrounds** ($10–15) operate on a first-come, first-served basis, and leaflets listing them all are available from the forest offices. Also, within the national forest, parts of the McKenzie River offer excellent **white-water rafting** and boating. Several Eugene/Springfield and Bend-based companies organize excursions – contact the nearest visitor centre or try either Rapid River Rafters, 834 NW Colorado Ave, Bend (☎541/382-1514 or 1-800/962-3327, *rapidrr@transport.com*), or Oregon Whitewater Adventures Inc, 39620 Deerhorn Rd, Springfield (☎541/746-5422 or 1-800/820-7238, *www.oregonwhitewater.com*).

As far as **public transit** is concerned, Lane Transit District runs a regular **bus** service (#91; Mon–Fri 4 daily, Sat & Sun 2 daily; ☎541/687-5555) out of Eugene up along Hwy 126 as far as the McKenzie Bridge Ranger Station – and the journey takes about an hour and a half. However, although this gives access to the **McKenzie River**

National Recreation Trail (see below), you're dropped close to the foot of the trail and it's a stiff uphill hike from here – much better to start at the top and work down.

Hwy 126: the McKenzie River Valley and National Recreation Trail

Of the several access roads into the Willamette National Forest, the most enjoyable is **Hwy 126**, which heads east from Eugene to track along the **McKenzie River Valley**, passing through miles of fruit and nut orchards before arriving at the scattered hamlet of **McKenzie Bridge**. Just beyond are the McKenzie Bridge Ranger Station and the medium-sized and very popular **Paradise campground** (☎541/822-3381; $12), pleasingly tucked away amongst dense forest close to the river. One mile further on there's a fork in the road with Hwy 242 worming its tortuous way east to cross an expanse of lava field before heading on and up to **McKenzie Pass**. Meanwhile, Hwy 126 swings north climbing steeply as it follows the course of the McKenzie River, passing the roadside parking lots that act as trailheads for the short footpaths leading to the **Koosah Falls** and the nearby **Sahalie Falls**. Moving on, it's another mile or so to the delightful **Cold Water Cove campground** (☎541/822-3381; $12), edged by lava flows and overlooking the beautiful blue-green **Clear Lake**, the source of the McKenzie River. This is the handiest place to start hiking (or cycling) the **McKenzie River National Recreation Trail** (MRNRT), a clearly marked, 26-mile route that heads downstream along the McKenzie River Valley, threading through patches of old-growth forest and past thundering waterfalls on its way back to the McKenzie Bridge Ranger Station. The trail is a fine introduction to the local scenery and, as the footpath also runs near Hwy 126, you can reach and walk more manageable portions relatively easily. Other, less-frequented and more challenging hiking trails across the high wilderness areas surrounding Mt Washington begin along Hwy 242, while the Santiam Pass on Highway 20 – the continuation of Hwy 126 – is an access point for the Pacific Crest Trail (see p.62).

South from Eugene to the California border

If you're heading south from Eugene into southern Oregon, you can leave most of the traffic far behind by travelling southeast along **Hwy 58** through the southern reaches of the Willamette National Forest and over the crest of Willamette Pass to the visually stunning **Crater Lake National Park**. This, the most dramatic of the many volcanic features marking the Oregon Cascades, is the area's – maybe the state's – outstanding attraction, with a deep blue lake cradled in the hollowed-out shell of an old volcano. It's also within an hour or two's drive of **Klamath Falls**, a curious little town with two enjoyable museums, and – in the opposite direction – Bend (see p.168). However, the most obvious – and certainly the quickest – route south from Eugene is along **I-5** with the road leaving the Willamette Valley to thump through vast tracts of mountain forest, shooting through the timber town of **Roseburg** to reach workaday **Grants Pass**, a popular base for white-water river rafting along the Rogue River. From here it's only forty-odd miles to the California border, but there's an interesting choice of routes: I-5 swings east to cut past the delightful little town of **Ashland**, home of the outstanding Oregon Shakespeare Festival between February and October and another good base for rafting the Rogue, whilst US-199 sneaks southwest through the remote and rugged **Siskiyou Mountains** which stretch over the border behind the California coast. The drive through these Californian Siskiyou Mountains is spectacular and culminates with the giant redwoods of the **Jedediah Smith Redwoods State Park**. Just beyond the park, US-199 meets Hwy 101 which travels north along the length of the Oregon coast.

Travelling the I-5 by Greyhound **bus** is a straightforward affair with daily services linking Eugene with, amongst other places, Grants Pass and Ashland. There are also regular services from Eugene to Klamath Falls, but none to Crater Lake. Amtrak **trains** are not so useful, though the Portland to California service does stop at Klamath Falls.

Crater Lake National Park

Sitting high up in the Cascade Range about 140 miles southeast of Eugene, **Crater Lake National Park** conserves the Northwest's best-looking volcanic crater, where the jagged shell of Mount Mazama holds **Crater Lake** – blue, deep and resoundingly beautiful. For half a million years Mount Mazama sent out periodic sprays of ash, cinder and pumice, later watched apprehensively by the Klamaths, who saw in them signs of a war between two gods, Llao and Skell, and kept well clear. The mountain finally burst, blowing its one-time peak over eight states and three Canadian provinces in an explosion many times greater than the more recent Mount St Helens blast (see p.265). Cone-like mini-volcanoes soon began to sprout again within the hollowed-out mountain, but when it cooled and became dormant the basin was filled by springs and melted snow. This new lake eventually submerged all but one of the volcanic outcrops, a cinder cone known as **Wizard Island**, which now pokes a wizened head above the placid waters. In its splendid isolation, Crater Lake is awe-inspiring, especially in summer, when wild flowers bloom and wildlife (deer, squirrels, chipmunks, elks, foxes, porcupines) emerges from hibernation. The lake itself has a small population of rainbow trout and kokanee (landlocked) salmon, but these were introduced in the early 1900s, and their removal has been mooted.

It's well worth the effort, but Crater Lake National Park does take time to get to: if you're travelling from Eugene, take Hwy 58 and then US-97 south to either of the two access roads, Hwy 138 and Hwy 62. Of these two, the **northern entrance** off Hwy 138 (which links I-5 at Roseburg with US-97) is the more exciting with a narrow park road emerging from the forests to cut across a bleak pumice desert before arriving at Crater Lake's precipitous northern rim. This road is, however, closed by snow from mid-October to late June, sometimes longer, and attracts more than its share of fog, which can turn what should be a magnificent drive into a teeth-clenching endurance test. The **southern entrance** (off Hwy 62, which leads off US-97), is kept open all year, an easier route which creeps up the wooded flanks of Mazama to reach the lake at its southern rim. Entrance to the national park costs $10 per vehicle.

The 33-mile **"Rim Drive"** road wriggles right round the crater's edge, linking the two access roads and providing the most magnificent of views – but be aware that it too is only open in summer. On the northern side of the lake, Rim Drive connects with the steep, mile-long **Cleetwood Cove Trail**, the one and only way to reach the lakeshore. From the bottom of the trail, pleasure boats make regular, two-hour **cruises** of the lake (late June to mid-Sept daily 10am–4.30pm; $12.50). In late June and from early to mid-September there are four cruises daily, nine daily in July and August; tickets are sold in the parking lot at the Cleetwood Cove trailhead and at the *Crater Lake Lodge* (see below). There are a number of other short **hiking trails** in the park. Most of them climb the mountainous slopes surrounding Crater Lake, but one travels along the lake's western rim, a wonderful hike with great views across the caldera. From this trail, two further trails climb up to the Pacific Crest Trail (see p.62), which runs right across the national park on its way from Mexico to Canada, though this particular stretch isn't very exciting. The park's higher hiking trails are, of course, snow-covered for most of the year, when they are favoured by cross-country skiers.

Arriving from the south on Hwy 62, the **Steel Visitor Center** (daily 9am–5pm), located just three miles short of Crater Lake, has details of guided walks and a comprehensive range of hiking maps and information. Its services are a little better than the **Rim Village Visitor Center** (June–Sept daily 8.30am–6pm), perched on the lake's southern rim – and beside the splendid **Crater Lake Lodge** (mid-May to late Oct;

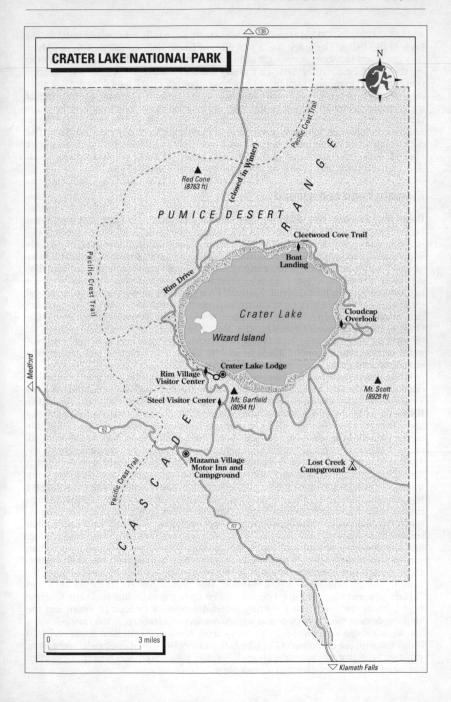

CRATER LAKE NATIONAL PARK

N

△ 138

Pacific Crest Trail
(closed in Winter)

Red Cone
(8763 ft)

PUMICE DESERT

Cleetwood Cove Trail

Boat
Landing

R A N G E

Rim Drive

Crater Lake

Cloudcap
Overlook

Pacific Crest Trail

Wizard Island

△ Medford

Crater Lake Lodge

Rim Village
Visitor Center

Steel Visitor Center

Mt. Garfield
(8054 ft)

Mt. Scott
(8929 ft)

62

C A S C A D E

Mazama Village
Motor Inn and
Campground

Lost Creek
Campground

Pacific Crest Trail

62

0   3 miles

▽ Klamath Falls

☎541/830-8700, fax 830-8514, *www.crater-lake.com*; ⑥), a fully refurbished hotel dating back to the 1910s. The lodge has a magnificent Great Hall, complete with Art Deco flourishes, and pleasant rooms – get either a corner room or at least a room overlooking the lake. Advance reservations are pretty much essential – as they are at the lodge's **restaurant**, an expensive establishment whose straightforward food does not live up to its setting. There are less expensive lodgings in the modern, shingle-roofed chalets of the *Mazama Village Motor Inn*, on the main access road seven miles south of the lodge (early June to mid-Oct; ☎541/830-8700, fax 830-8514; ⑤). Next door is the large *Mazama Village* **campground** (early June to mid-Oct; also ☎541/830-8700; $10). The park's only other campground is tiny *Lost Creek* (July to mid-Sept; $10), down a spur road off Rim Drive southeast of Crater Lake, where there are a dozen basic plots. Alternatively, you'll find several inexpensive motels in Klamath Falls.

Klamath Falls and around

Below the Cascades, sixty-odd miles from Crater Lake, and over twice that from Bend (see p.168), remote **KLAMATH FALLS** was once a bustling logging town and railway junction, a key staging point on the route to the Pacific coast. It lost most of its early importance years ago, and now records high levels of unemployment, but it still manages to conjure up a couple of diverting museums – quite good enough to justify a daytrip, particularly from Crater Lake where the weather is often wet and foggy when it's hot and sunny down here. Indeed, Klamath Falls occupies an interesting geographical location: it's at the southern tip of enormous Upper Klamath Lake, part of the pancake-flat **Klamath Basin**, whose marshes and reedy lakes spread over the Oregon–California border marking the transition from the forested mountains of the west to the Great Basin desert lying to the east. The Basin is geothermally active – much of downtown Klamath Falls is heated by naturally hot water – and geologically unstable: there was a significant earthquake here in 1993.

White settlers reached the Klamath Basin in numbers in the 1850s and rushed to drain the marshes for pasture land, dispossessing the local natives – the **Modocs** from around Tule Lake, on the Oregon–California border, and their traditional rivals, the **Klamath**, to the immediate north – with violent gusto. To justify their actions, the pioneers banged on about their ability to cultivate the land to better advantage, but this merely provided the gloss to a savage cocktail of racism mixed with social and economic aspiration. It was all utterly shameful and stands in bleak comparison with the puzzled innocence of the Modoc leader Kientpoos (aka **Captain Jack**) who declared "I have always told the white man to come and settle in my country; that it was his country and Captain Jack's country. That they could come and live there with me and that I was not mad with them." The settlers didn't, of course, see it that way. In 1864, keen to legitimize their new landholdings, they brought in federal treaty commissioners to persuade the Modocs to formally sign away their homeland in return for a reservation beside Upper Klamath Lake. But for the Modocs, signing the treaty brought no respite: they had endless problems with the rival Klamaths, who shared the same reservation, and the Indian agent failed to provide the supplies they had been promised. In desperation, Captain Jack led three hundred of his people back to their old hunting grounds, thereby precipitating the so-called **Modoc War** whose pathetic finale of 1873 had Captain Jack and his remaining followers holed up in the maze-like lava beds south of Tule Lake. In the event, the US Army found it extremely difficult to winkle out the Modocs, despite their howitzers and a huge numerical advantage – 1000 against 150 – but winkle them out they did. The captured Modocs were then transferred to Oklahoma with the exception of Captain Jack and three of his followers who were hung – though even that was not quite enough: Captain Jack's body was dug up, embalmed and taken east to be exhibited in a freak show.

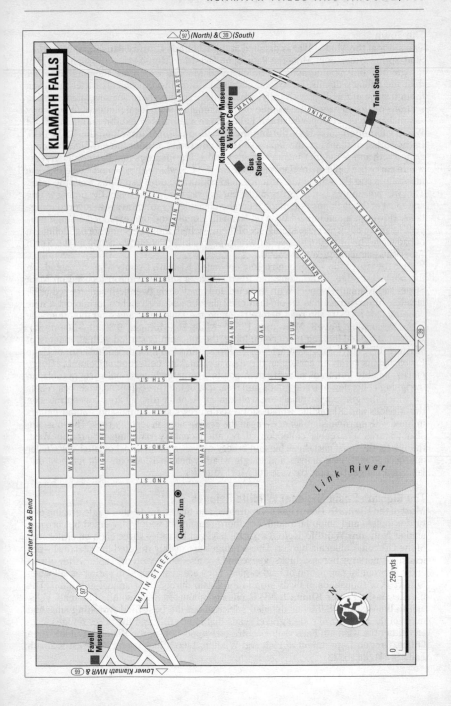

KLAMATH FALLS

The Town

The story of the Modoc War is detailed at the **Klamath County Museum**, 1451 Main St at Spring (June–Sept Mon–Sat 9am–5pm; Oct–May Mon–Sat 8am–4.30pm; $2), but it's the haunting photographs of the captured Modocs which are memorable rather than the military details. Dusty and cavernous, the museum has character and even though some of the displays hardly enhance the exhibits, there are several interesting sections on, for instance, the wildlife of the Klamath Basin, local pioneer life and early steamship travel on Upper Klamath Lake. There's also a tiny exhibit on one of World War II's forgotten episodes – the **Japanese balloon bomb attack** on the US in 1945. In the spring of that year, the Japanese released around a thousand gas-filled balloons armed with anti-personnel and incendiary bombs. The idea was that Pacific air currents would carry the balloons to the West Coast of the US, where they would cause massive forest fires and thus force the Americans to withdraw some battalions from the front. This was not (quite) as daft as it sounds, but anyway the Japanese got the timing wrong and most of the balloons that made it crashed harmlessly into the snow-covered mountains. However, a handful did drop on Klamath County and one exploded on an unsuspecting party of picnickers, killing six of them – which must be some sort of definition of bad luck. The unfortunates were the only people killed by enemy action on the North American mainland in World War II.

Also the site of the visitor centre (see opposite), Klamath County Museum stands on the northeast edge of the elongated town centre, a simple gridiron focused on Main Street and Klamath Avenue. With its faded and fancy early twentieth-century red-brick facades, **Main Street** has an old-fashioned flavour and it stretches for almost a mile running past a US-97 slip road before reaching the Link River and – on the other side – the fascinating **Favell Museum**, 125 W Main St (Mon–Sat 9.30am–5.30pm; $4). Housed in a good-looking modern building, the museum is stuffed with all manner of Western US Native-American artefacts, representing the lifelong enthusiasm of Gene Favell and his family. In particular, there's a breathtaking collection of Columbia Gorge pieces, notably hundreds of agate gem points – or arrowheads – all sorts of tools, an intriguing collection of trade goods and a sample of the three-dimensional rock reliefs for which the gorge aboriginals are well-known. Another display area concentrates on the Modocs and Klamaths, whose stone sculptures sport animal and human figures imbued with spiritual significance – as in the *henwas* used in fertility rites. The museum also features a sizeable collection of twentieth-century paintings about the West, though for the most part these big and breezy canvases adopt a sort of latter-day Custer approach – wild, lean natives and tough, weather-beaten Bluecoats – at its most outlandish amongst the epic canvases of Mort Kunstler.

The Klamath Basin National Wildlife Refuges

Most of the **Klamath Basin** has been drained and turned into either cattle grazing pasture or potato and onion farmland, but there remain six widely dispersed but broadly similar **National Wildlife Refuges** (open daylight hours) – three each on either side of the Oregon–California border. These refuges are mainly devoted to waterfowl – pelicans, cormorants, herons, ducks, geese and swans – along with the raptors they attract and a substantial population of bald eagles. They are best visited in spring or fall when hundreds of thousands of birds stop in the Basin during their annual migration. The handiest is the **Lower Klamath NWR**, situated about ten miles south of Klamath Falls, just to the east of US-97. For detailed advice about the best **bird-watching** sites and maps of the network of rough gravel roads that lattice this and the other refuges, contact either the Klamath Falls visitor centre (see opposite), or the Klamath Wildlife Area Office, Oregon Department of Fish and Wildlife, 1400 Miller Island Rd, West Klamath Falls (☎541/883-5732).

Practicalities

Connected with Portland and Bend, the Greyhound **bus station** is at 1200 Klamath Ave and Commercial Street, at the northeast end of the town centre, one block from Main Street; Seattle–Los Angeles Amtrak **trains** pull in on the eastern edge of downtown at the foot of Oak Street. The **visitor centre**, 1451 Main St (June–Sept Mon–Sat 9am–5.30pm; Oct–May Mon–Sat 9am–4.30pm; ☎541/884-0666 or 1-800/445-6728, *www.klamath.org*), is inside the Klamath County Museum a couple of blocks from the bus station. They issue free town maps and have details of local accommodation.

Once you've visited the museums and wandered along Main Street, it's unlikely you'll want to **stay** the night, but if you're stranded Klamath Falls does have a clutch of mundane motels strung out along 6th Street (Hwy 39) on the south side of town. There are also several bargain-basement places in the centre, though note that some of these cater for itinerant fieldhands rather than tourists. Easily the best downtown bet is the *Quality Inn*, 100 Main St (☎541/882-4666 or 1-888/726-2466; ④), a pleasantly brisk chain motel with clean rooms. There's nothing fancy by way of **food** and what there is closes early at night – try the *Daily Bagel*, 636 Main St (Mon–Fri 11am–5pm), a simple café selling filling meals and snacks. If you're looking for something more substantial, *Molatore's*, located in the *Quality Inn*, serves up decent Italian fare.

If you're heading west from Klamath Falls, **Hwy 66**, the old stagecoach road, weaves through the forested foothills of the Siskiyou Mountains, a lovely scenic run that brings you out near Ashland (see p.148).

South from Eugene: Oakland, Roseburg and Grants Pass

Tiny **OAKLAND**, fifty uneventful miles south from Eugene and a mile east of I-5, is good for a pit-stop on the long journey south – or north if you're coming from California. It was settled in the 1840s and soon became the centre of a flourishing agricultural district, producing grain, hops, prunes and eventually prize-winning turkeys. It was also a major stopping point on the stagecoach line from Sacramento to Portland and its future seemed secure when the railroad came in 1872. Neither were the locals unduly flustered when a series of fires destroyed almost all the original wooden buildings: for one thing, fires were commonplace in Oregon's early timber-built settlements, and for another the townsfolk took the opportunity to replace the old with new self-confident stone and brick buildings graced by cast-iron trimmings. But their confidence was misplaced: within the space of twenty years, a rapidly expanding Eugene had stripped the town of its commercial importance and Oakland simply faded away. Today, it's a quiet rural hamlet whose halcyon days are recalled by the neon-free, antique storefronts of Locust Street, the main drag. Here, at no. 130, you'll find the pioneer displays of the **Oakland Museum** (daily 1–4pm; donation), housed in the former grocery store and post office, while neighbouring City Hall has street plans and walking tips, pointing out what happened where and when among the various red-brick buildings.

For **food** *Tolly's*, 115 Locust St, features an old-fashioned ice-cream parlour, gift shop and candy counter downstairs, and a restaurant up above. To **stay**, the *Beckley House B&B*, 338 SE 2nd St at Chestnut (☎541/459-9320, fax 459-9320; ④), is an appealing late nineteenth-century villa with period furnishings and a pair of comfortable en-suite rooms.

Roseburg and Grants Pass

Fifteen miles south of Oakland on I-5, the hilly lumber town of **ROSEBURG** is the urban centre of the Umpqua River Valley. It's here that Hwy 138 begins its ninety-mile haul east through the Cascades to the Crater Lake National Park (see p.140), but the town itself is of little interest and there's no real reason to stop. Continuing south, I-5 twists dramatically through prime logging land, with oceans of green covering the steep ridges and peaks that press in on the highway. Seventy miles on, I-5 bangs down into **GRANTS PASS**, an old sawmill town straddling the Rogue River as it tumbles vigorously from the Cascade Mountains to the Siskiyou National Forest. There's not much to Grants Pass, but it does have a fine, scenic setting and a tiny, central **historic district** of good-looking late nineteenth- and early twentieth-century buildings, on and around G Street to the west of 6th Street. To get to the town centre from I-5, it's easiest to take Exit 58 and then follow 6th Street (Hwy 99) south. G Street is just beyond the railway tracks and the **Rogue River**, with its trail of logging mills, is a few blocks further. Indeed, the main reason for a visit is the river. Rather like Gold Beach (see p.129), Grants Pass earns much of its living by strapping its visitors into bright orange life-jackets, and packing them into rafts or jet boats to bounce over the Rogue's **white-water rapids**. A half-day rafting tour costs around $45, a full day $65, $25 and $45 respectively for jet-boat trips, and there are longer, overnight excursions too; the season lasts from May to early October. The **visitor centre**, which is close to – and clearly signed from – I-5 Exit 58, at 1995 NW Vine St (Mon–Fri 9am–5pm, plus June–Sept Sat & Sun also; ☎541/476-7717 or 1-800/547-5927, *www.visitgrantspass.org*), has the details of the many licensed companies operating river excursions. Two of the more reliable are Hellgate Jetboat Excursions (☎541/479-7204 or 1-800/648-4874, *www.hellgate.com*), whose river trips leave from the foot of 6th Street, and the white-water rafting- and fishing-tour specialists Rogue Wilderness (☎541/479-9554 or 1-800/336-1647), based in the hamlet of Merlin, about ten miles northwest of Grants Pass.

If you'd rather focus on the scenery around the Rogue River on foot, the forty-mile **Rogue River National Recreation Trail** begins at Grave Creek, about thirty miles to the northwest of Grants Pass. The trail nudges through dense groves of hemlock, Douglas fir and oak and traverses bare canyon walls with the river far below – altogether providing some wonderfully wild hiking. It's a sweaty walk in summer, and muddy to the point of impassability in winter, but in spring or fall it's an excellent trek for serious hikers, and there are regular first-come, first-served campsites on the way. A series of strategically placed lodges on the lower half of the trail – each a day's hike from the other – makes a rather more comfortable option and if this appeals your best bet is to start at Gold Beach, travelling upriver by boat and then hiking down. If all this sounds too daunting, Rogue Wilderness (see above) organizes four- and five-day guided Rogue River hikes. The Grants Pass visitor centre has a useful range of leaflets on the Rogue River too.

If you decide to use Grants Pass as a base, you'll find the bulk of the town's budget **accommodation** on Hwy 99 (7th St northbound and 6th southbound) between the river and I-5 (Exit 58). Two useful options here are the chain *Super 8 Motel*, at 1949 NE 7th St (☎541/474-0888 or 1-800/800-8000; ③), and the rather more pleasant *Riverside Inn*, a modern place down by the Rogue at 971 SE 6th St (☎541/476-6873 or 1-800/334-4567, *www.riverside-inn.com*; ④). There are a number of good **B&Bs** in the area also, including *Pine Meadow Inn*, 1000 Crow Rd (☎541/471-6277 or 1-800/554-0806; ⑤), and the *Fleaury Manor*, 2000 Jump Off Creek (☎541/476-3591; ⑤); both serve up gourmet breakfasts. The best **places to eat** are *The Laughing Clam*, 121 G St (☎541/479-1110), with excellent seafood dishes and regional wines, and the *Wild River Brewing & Pizza Co* (☎541/471-7487), specializing in wood-fired pizzas and excellent beers.

From Grants Pass, **US-199** leads southwest to the Oregon Caves and California's Jedediah Smith Redwoods State Park (see p.150), whilst **I-5** veers east for Medford, Jacksonville and, best of the lot, Ashland.

Medford and Jacksonville

Heading inland on I-5, it's a quick 25-mile journey from Grants Pass to **MEDFORD**, the Rogue River Valley's urban centre – an industrial sprawl squatting among huge paper mills. There's little to divert you here, and most visitors dodge the place altogether, often missing out on the more appealing **JACKSONVILLE**, just five miles west of Medford and signposted (before you reach Medford) from I-5. Once the largest of Oregon's gold rush towns, a flourishing and boisterous prospectors' supply centre, Jacksonville had its improbable beginnings after a gold panner's mule kicked up a nugget here in 1851. No sooner had they arrived, however, than the prospectors were involved in the savage **Rogue River Indian Wars** of 1853–1856. The wars saw the Rogue River natives defeated and deported or confined to reservations, but not before they had at least taken some revenge: at Gold Beach (see p.129), an unscrupulous Indian agent was ambushed and killed, though reports of his heart being ripped out, cooked and eaten may have more to do with pioneer prejudices than historical accuracy. The miners on both sides of the Oregon–California border also spent a fair bit of energy trying to secede from their respective states and create their own – variously "Jackson Territory", "Siskiyou" and "Shasta". Initially, the movement was prompted by the region's isolation from the main sources of state power, but later there was a more ominous twist after large numbers of ex-Confederate soldiers migrated here. In the event, the secessionists faded away and then Jacksonville's fortunes took a nose-dive when the gold boom ended in the 1880s; thereafter it crumbled, quietly, until it was old enough to attract the tourists.

It only takes half an hour or so to explore Jacksonville's tiny **town centre**, whose attractively restored late nineteenth-century buildings cluster around the main intersection, California and Oregon streets. There's nothing too special, but it is a good-looking ensemble, all false-fronts and symmetrical brickwork, and a particular architectural highlight is the sturdy **US Hotel** of 1880, at California and 3rd Street. Nearby, the **Jacksonville Museum of Southern Oregon History**, 206 N 5th St and E C St (Wed–Sat 10am–5pm & Sun noon–5pm; $2), is housed in the glum-looking County Courthouse of 1883. The exhibits are pretty dreary, but many of the early photographs are a cut above the average. They are the work of the talented Peter Britt, who came to Oregon, on an ox cart, in the 1850s and spent almost fifty years photographing the region's peoples and places (he was the first to snap Crater Lake). Britt's house burnt down years ago, but the grounds, located a short walk up California from Oregon Street, are now used for the **Britt Festival** (☎541/773-6077 or 1-800/882-7488 for further information and reservations, *www.brittfest.org*), a first-class outdoor music and performing arts shindig which takes place from mid-June to August. Classical, jazz, blues, R&B, bluegrass, folk-rock and folk music are all featured, played by some of the biggest international names around. The grounds have a maximum capacity of 2200 and although the bench-style seats are often booked up months in advance, some of the lawn space is allocated on a first-come, first-served basis. There are no long-distance **buses** to Jacksonville (the nearest you'll get is Medford), but the Rogue Valley Transportation District (RVTD; ☎541/779-2877, *www.rvtd.org*) provides a limited bus service between Ashland, Medford and Jacksonville.

Festival apart, there's no particular reason to hang around Jacksonville once you've finished with the centre, but the town does have a limited supply of quaint **B&Bs** in restored old houses. One of the most appealing is the centrally located *Laurelwood Manor*, 540 E California St (☎541/899-2848 or 1-800/846-8422, *www.laurelwood.com*; ④), an expansive Victorian house with stained-glass windows and gingerbread scrollwork. There are six guestrooms here, and each is smartly decorated in appropriate period style. Jacksonville's tiny **visitor centre** (☎541/889-8118), at N Oregon and C Street, has the complete list of local accommodation – but note that it's virtually impossible to find somewhere during the Britt Festival, when it's a good idea to contact the Southern Oregon Reservation Center (☎1-800/547-8052, *www.sorc.com*), who book festival tickets and accommodation. For a bite to **eat**, *MacLevin's*, in the centre at 150 W California St, has an excellent range of light meals and snacks; it bills itself as "The Unconventional Jewish Deli" – with every justification.

Ashland and the Shakespeare Festival

Throughout Oregon, the small town of **ASHLAND**, fifty miles southeast of Grants Pass on I-5, is identified with the works of William Shakespeare – a curious cultural anomaly among the workaday timber and farming towns straddling the California border. The idea of an **Oregon Shakespeare Festival** came to a local teacher, Angus Bowmer, fifty years ago, and now – from the middle of February right through to the end of October – the town is dominated by all things theatrical. Amongst several stages, the most unusual is the open-air **Elizabethan Theatre**, a delightful half-timbered replica of six-teenth-century London's Fortune Theatre plonked bang in the middle of town. It may sound a bit contrived, but Ashland is nowhere near as tacky as Shakespeare's real birth-place, and in some ways has the distinct edge: its setting, between the Cascade and the Siskiyou mountains, is magnificent and there's good skiing in the winter and river-raft-ing in summer. What's more, performance standards are high and there's some excel-lent contemporary fringe theatre – not to mention pleasant cafés and a young, friendly atmosphere especially when the local Southern Oregon University is in session.

The festival is Ashland's one and only claim to fame, but the tiny, café-flanked **Plaza** that forms the heart of the town – just round the corner from the Elizabethan Theatre – is a pleasant spot to loiter especially as it's beside the entrance to leafy **Lithia Park**. This one-hundred-acre park was designed by John McLaren (of Golden Gate Park fame), its shrubs, trails, brook and spreading trees reminders of Ashland's pre-festival incarnation as a spa-town, a project of New York advertising mogul, Jesse Winburne. He overestimated the appeal of the nasty-tasting local Lithia Spring water, and the spa idea failed, but it did lodge the germ of Ashland's potential as a tourist town.

Arrival, information and outdoor activities

Ashland is on the main Greyhound line from Portland to San Francisco, but **buses** only pause on the outskirts of town, a couple of miles northwest of the centre at I-5 (Exit 19) – dial ☎1-800/231-2222 for drop-off details. The Rogue Valley Transportation District (RVTD; ☎541/779-2877, *www.rvtd.org*) provides a limited local bus service between Ashland, Talent, Medford and Jacksonville. The **visitor centre** is downtown at 110 E Main St (Mon–Fri 9am–5pm; ☎541/482-3486, *www.ashlandchamber.com*), and there's also a seasonal **information kiosk** – with longer hours – nearby, on the Plaza at the entrance to Lithia Park. Both issue town maps and brochures, have details of local lodg-ings and provide information on the festival. They also have lists of recommended **white-water rafting** companies, most of whom organize trips on the Rogue River, though the Klamath and Umpqua rivers are featured too. Arguably the most reliable operator is Noah's River Adventures, on Ashland's main plaza at 53 N Main St (☎541/488-2811 or 1-800/858-2811). They run half-day ($50–60), one-day ($100–120) and two-day campout ($300) white-water rafting trips daily from mid-May to October. There's also **skiing** and **snowboarding** at the **Mt Ashland Ski Area** (☎541/482-2897, *www.mtashland.com*), high in the Siskiyou Mountains some twenty miles south of town. It is a comparatively small ski area – though there are plans for expansion – with four chairlifts and twenty-three runs, and it's open from early November to mid-April. A one-day lift pass costs $24 (slighter more on the weekend) and skis ($15 per day) and snowboards ($20) can be rented on arrival. The ski area is located eight miles west of – and clearly signposted from – I-5 (Exit 6). For the latest snow report, telephone ☎541/482-2SKI. For details of special **buses** from Ashland to the ski area, ask at Ashland visitor centre.

Accommodation

Ashland has oodles of plush **B&Bs**, but they are much in demand and advance booking is pretty much essential – either independently or via a room reservation service such as the Southern Oregon Reservation Center (☎541/488-1011 or 1-800/547-8052, *www.sorc.com*), with whom you can also book theatre tickets. There is more chance of a vacancy at one of the town's **motels** and these line up along Siskiyou Boulevard to the east of the town centre.

Coolidge House B&B, 137 N Main St (☎541/482-4721 or 1-800/655-5522). This central B&B offers six luxurious en-suite rooms and gourmet breakfasts from its attractively refurbished Victorian premises. ⑤.

Cowslip's Belle B&B, 159 N Main St (☎541/488-2901 or 1-800/888-6819). Just four en-suite rooms here in this too-twee-for-some (but wonderfully comfortable) early twentieth-century bungalow and carriage house. ⑥.

Mount Ashland Inn, 550 Mt Ashland Ski Rd (☎541/482-8707 or 1-800/830-8707, *www.mtashlandinn .com*). This lovely log lodge, perched high up on the wooded slopes of Mt Ashland, offers some of the most delightful accommodation in Oregon. Each of the five suites here are well decorated and features include antique furniture, open fireplaces and jetted tubs. Everything is thoughtfully done – down to the salt lick in front of the lodge where deer gather early in the morning – and the Pacific Crest Trail passes through the grounds. It is just a short drive up to Mt Ashland Ski Area and about twenty minutes to Ashland down in the valley below, and in summer, when Ashland is steamingly hot, it is pleasantly warm up here. The inn is located six miles west of I-5 (Exit 6). Mountain bikes and, in winter, snow shoes are available at no extra charge. ⑦.

Palm Motel, 1065 Siskiyou Blvd (☎541/482-2636 or 1-877/482-2635). Standard-issue motel to the east of the town centre with thirteen plain but perfectly adequate rooms. ③.

Winchester Inn, 35 S 2nd St (☎541/488-1113 or 1-800/972-4991). This attractive inn, with its eighteen en-suite rooms, has attractive gardens and a pleasant setting just three blocks from the main Plaza. ⑥.

Eating and drinking

With its ready supply of well-heeled tourists, not to mention its university students, Ashland has lots of appealing places to **eat** and **drink**. Conveniently, the best are clustered in and around the Plaza, which is flanked – rather confusingly – by both North and East Main streets.

Alex's Plaza Restaurant, 35 N Main St (☎541/482-8818). Smart and proficient restaurant offering traditional American dishes with a flourish. A popular spot. A speciality is the New Zealand lamb.

Ashland Bakery Café, 38 E Main St. Laid-back, slightly arty café where the breakfasts and snacks are delicious – and inexpensive.

Chateaulin Restaurant, 50 E Main St (☎541/482-2264). One of the classiest restaurants in town, this attractively decorated place serves up first-rate French cuisine. Dinners only. Reckon on $20 per person excluding wine. Quite formal.

Greenleaf Restaurant, 49 N Main St (☎541/482-2808). On the central Plaza, this enjoyable café-restaurant has a wide-ranging, mostly Mediterranean-style menu and a pleasant riverside terrace. Closes at 8pm or 9pm.

Standing Stone Brewing Co, 101 Oak St. This busy bar, popular with tourists and locals alike, sells a good range of beers and ales. There is filling and inexpensive bar food on offer here too.

Southwest from Grants Pass to the Oregon Caves and California

Back at Grants Pass, US-199 leaves I-5 (at Exit 55) to wander down the Illinois River Valley towards the Northern Californian coast. It's an enjoyable journey, with forested hills to either side, and after about thirty miles you reach the straggling roadside hamlet of **CAVE JUNCTION**, where Hwy 46 branches off east for the narrow and twisting, twenty-mile trip to the **Oregon Caves National Monument**, tucked away in a canyon in the Siskiyou Mountains. The caves were discovered in 1874, when a deer-hunter's dog chased a bear into a hole in the mountainside, but they only became famous when the poet Joaquin Miller described his 1909 visit in such ringing phrases as "the marble halls of Oregon" that they were preserved as a national monument.

Inside, the caves – actually, one enormous cavern with smaller passages leading off it – are the stuff of geology lessons. The marble walls were created by the centuries-long compression of mucky lime, mud and lava, then slowly carved out by subterranean water. Thereafter long years of steady dripping created elaborate formations from the limestone-laden water: clinging stalactites hang from the ceiling, some met by stalagmites to form columns, while rippled flows of rock run from the walls. The caves are open year round, and are wet and slippy, so good shoes or boots are required, as is warm clothing – underground it's a constant 42°F. From June to August the caves are usually open daily between 9am and 7pm, but hours are reduced at other times of the year – telephone the adjacent *Oregon Caves Lodge* (see below) for an update. You have to go in with the hour-long **tour** ($7), but note that although these leave regularly you can still face a longish wait in the summer, when it's wise to turn up early in the day. The monument grounds also contain a couple of **hiking trails** into the surrounding mountains with the three-mile loop of the Big Tree Trail giving sight of a whopping Douglas fir that's over one thousand years old.

Easily the best **accommodation** hereabouts is the *Oregon Caves Lodge* (late May to mid-Oct; ☎541/592-3400, *www.oregoncaves.com*; ⑤), an attractive, rustic affair of high snow-proof gables and timber walls dating from the 1930s – and a stone's throw from the caves. The lodge, with its comfortable furnishings and fittings, has got real character and the restaurant serves good food too; it's not surprising, therefore, that reservations are pretty much essential. If your budget doesn't stretch that far, there are a couple of US Forest Service **campgrounds** ($10–15) on the way to the caves beside Hwy 46 and several inexpensive **motels** back on US-199, three miles north of Cave Junction in the hamlet of **KERBY** – try the straightforward *Holiday Motel*, 24810 Redwood Hwy (☎541/592-3003; ③).

South into California: the Jedediah Smith Redwoods State Park

The quickest way to reach the Oregon Coast (see pp.108–130) from Cave Junction is to head south on US-199 into California. Almost as soon as the highway crosses the state border, it starts to weave up through California's Siskiyou Mountains, negotiating inhospitable mountain passes and curving round plunging gorges, key features of the landscape's surly beauty. About thirty-five miles beyond the border, the **Redwood National and State Parks Information Center** supplies maps and has cycling and hiking trail details for the series of parks which stretch forty miles south along the California coast protecting groves of ancient **redwood**, colossal trees up to 350-feet tall. The information centre marks the start of one of these parks, the **Jedediah Smith**

Redwoods State Park, where mighty redwoods crowd in on the highway as it wriggles towards the coast, passing the trailhead for the Simpson-Reed Trail, a short and easy stroll through some of the grandest trees. Shortly afterwards, US-199 meets **US-101**, which travels the twenty miles north along California's coastal flats to Oregon's Brookings (see p.130).

travel details

Trains

Portland to: Eugene (2 daily; 2hr 30min); Klamath Falls (1 daily; 7hr 45min); Los Angeles (1 daily; 28hr 30min); Oakland, CA (1 daily; 19hr); Olympia (2 daily; 2hr); Salem (2 daily; 1hr 15min); Seattle (4 daily; 3hr 30min); change at Seattle for Vancouver (4 buses daily, 3hr 30min; 1 train daily, 4hr); Spokane (1 daily; 7hr 20min); Tacoma (2 daily; 2hr 30min).

Buses

Klamath Falls to: Bend (1 daily; 3hr); Los Angeles (1 daily; 20hr); Seattle (1 daily; 13hr).

Portland to: Ashland (3 daily; 7hr); Astoria (1 daily; 2hr 45min); Baker City (3 daily; 6hr 30min); Bandon (2 daily; 7hr); Bend (1 daily; 4hr); Boise, ID (3 daily; 10hr 30min); Brookings (2 daily; 9hr); Eugene (8 daily; 2hr 15min); Florence (2 daily; 5hr); Grants Pass (4 daily; 5hr); Hood River (3 daily; 1hr 10min); La Grande (3 daily; 5hr 40min); Lincoln City (2 daily; 3hr); Los Angeles (5 daily; 23hr); Newport (2 daily; 4hr); Olympia, WA (8 daily; 2hr 40min); Pendleton (3 daily; 4hr 20min); Salem (8 daily; 1hr); San Francisco (2 daily; 15hr or 20hr); Seattle (8 daily; 3hr 15min by express or 4hr 45min); Spokane (2 daily; 7hr 20min); The Dalles (3 daily; 1hr 40min); Vancouver, Canada (3 daily; 9hr).

CHAPTER TWO

EASTERN OREGON

E ast of the Cascades, Oregon grows wilder and less hospitable. The temperature rises, the drizzle stops, and green valleys give way to scrubby sageland, bare hills and stark rock formations, interrupted on occasion by impenetrable forest. Though nowhere near as popular a destination as the lush coastal areas, the austere beauty of the region is frequently stunning and there is a real sense of adventure in exploring this vast, sparsely populated land, great tracts of which is classic cowboy country, familiar from scores of movies. **Pendleton**, in the north along I-84, is the epitome of the cowboy town, where Stetsons and pick-up trucks rule the stylistic roost especially during September's famous **Pendleton Round-Up rodeo**. Pendleton makes for an enjoyable overnight stay and so does neighbouring **Baker City**, which, with its attractive c.1900 architecture, is the other prime target amongst the small-town farming and ranching communities strung along I-84. Neither is it far from I-84 to the isolated northeast corner of the state, which boasts some spectacular scenery in the snow-capped **Eagle Cap Wilderness** of the Wallowa Mountains and the long deep slash of **Hells Canyon**, an immense gorge cut by the Snake River. Further south, and very different again, is the vibrant, fashionable town of **Bend**, well worth a day or two in its own right and also within easy striking distance of the eastern slopes of the Cascade Mountains' wonderfully wild scenery encompassing the ski resort of **Mount Bachelor**. Bend is also an ideal base for exploring the rest of southeast Oregon. From near here, **US-26** – which begins in Portland – weaves through the mountains and valleys of central eastern Oregon. En route, it passes by the three sites that constitute the **John Day Fossil Beds**, whose remarkable geology – replete with reminders of a tumultuous volcanic past – has given up all manner of prehistoric plant and animal skeletons. Southwest of Bend along **US-97**, there's more evidence of volcanic disturbance in the **Newberry National Volcanic Monument**, where a sprinkling of cinder cones, lava fields and caldera are to be found not far from the highway – though the most extraordinary sight of all is Crater Lake (see p.140). Finally, **US-20** slices southeast from Bend across a barren and virtually uninhabited desert – bleak, untamed scenery to be sure, but there's rarely anywhere to stop with tiny **Burns** being your best bet, if for no other reason than its proximity to the lakes and wetlands of the **Malheur National Wildlife Refuge**.

None of this terrain looked very promising to early immigrants, who hurried on along the Oregon Trail to the prime farmland further west. One bemoaned "This barren, God-forsaken country is fit for nothing but to receive the footprints of the savage and his universal associate the coyote". Those few settlers who did brave the east found homesteading a precarious, stockaded affair; at one point it was forbidden altogether by officials who feared for the safety of the white pioneers, and saw the Cascades as "a valuable separation of the races". In the early 1860s, things changed rapidly when gold was discovered in Baker and Grant counties, prompting a short-lived **gold rush**. Restrictions were quickly swept away and to feed the miners, herds of **cattle** were driven over the Cascades from the Willamette Valley, thousands of animals flourishing on the bunchgrass and meadowgrass of the interior. Neither the cattlemen nor the miners had much tolerance for the native population, which was displaced in a series of skirmishes that escalated into successive mini-wars that only fizzled out when the indigenous inhabitants were confined to reservations.

Later, there was more violence, this time between the cattle ranchers and their rivals, the **sheep ranchers**. With the gold rush over, the cattlemen had switched to driving their herds west to the towns of the Willamette, a profitable business but one that was short-lived. When sheep began to graze the open range land, it soon became obvious that the cattle men couldn't compete with the sheep herders: cattle lacked the herd instinct and wandered far and wide over the rangeland and took ages to round up, whereas one shepherd and his dogs could keep several thousand sheep together with ease, moving them to better pasture at will. There was some initial resistance to the shepherds by the cattlemen – some even formed themselves into "Sheepshooter" associations and attacked their rivals in the so-called "range wars" – but most gave up without a fight, either agreeing to share the rangeland or leaving the business altogether. In any case, the days of the open range were numbered, and by the mid-1890s there were deeded and leased sheep and cattle ranches from the Cascades to the Idaho border. Sheep and cows now safely graze side by side, and some small towns still celebrate their cowboy roots with annual rodeos (it has proved impossible to eulogize the sheepherder). In one important respect, however, the early pioneers got their farming facts wrong: the treeless, semi-arid Columbia Plateau, which straddles the Columbia River, proved excellent cereal-growing country and rolling **wheatfields** now flank I-84 as it nears Pendleton. Today, eastern Oregon's main business is agriculture, supplemented by forestry and tourism – though prosperity is patchy and some of the smaller places hang on by their economic fingertips.

In terms of **accommodation**, all of Eastern Oregon's larger towns have a reasonable supply of motels and some hotels, but for the most part these are run-of-the-mill modern affairs that hardly inspire. Of course, there are exceptions, with some establishments rising well above the mundane, and it's good to see that B&Bs are increasingly popular – with Bend very much leading the way – but if you're after exploring the wilderness, you should consider camping. Of the fifty-odd state parks in eastern Oregon about half have **campgrounds**, most of which are open all year with many sites bookable through a central reservation number (☎1-800/452-5687). In addition, the US Forest Service operates a scattering of national forest campgrounds. These are usually open from Memorial Day to Labor Day and work on a first-come, first-served basis, though a small percentage can be reserved (☎1-800/280-2267).

If you're camping, a **car** is pretty much essential – as it is if you're intending to do anything more than hop from town to town, and even that can be difficult by **public transportation**. Greyhound **buses** (☎1-800/231-2222, *www.greyhound.com*) run east from Portland along the Columbia River, serving Pendleton, La Grande and Baker City on the way to Boise, Idaho. A second route from Portland dips through the mountains to Bend, which is linked with Seattle to the north and Klamath Falls to the south. There are, however, no Amtrak **trains** and local bus services are negligible.

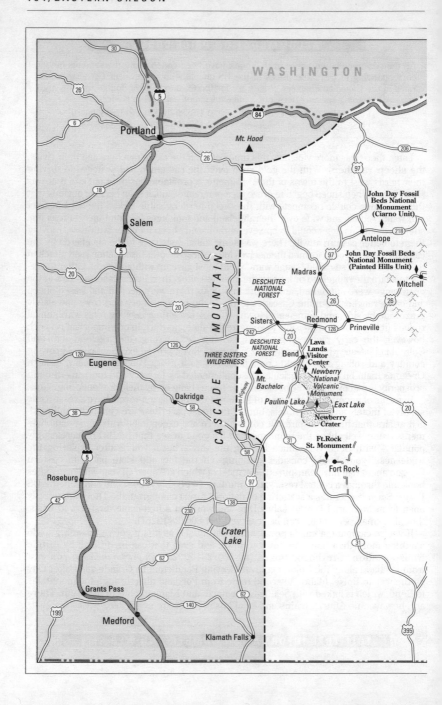

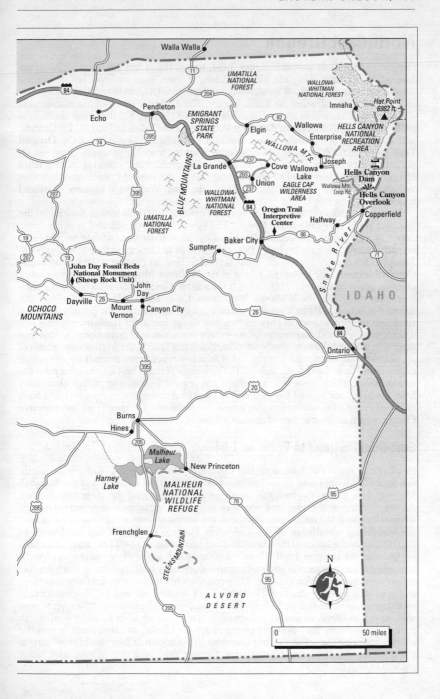

Northeast Oregon

Oregon's principal west–east highway, **I-84**, leaves Biggs and the Maryhill Museum (see p.106) to track along the bleak gulches of the Columbia River before cutting southeast to slip past a trio of small towns – Pendleton, La Grande and Baker City – on its way to Ontario, abutting the Idaho border. The distances involved are manageable – Pendleton to Ontario is about 160 miles – and I-84 is fast, but thrashing through is really rather pointless without dawdling in cowboy **Pendleton** and maybe **La Grande** and **Baker City** too. Furthermore, much of I-84 follows the course of the **Oregon Trail** (see box, p.82), and a series of wayside markers trace the pioneers' progress. Of particular interest are those that illuminate the problematic crossing of the **Blue Mountains**, a narrow band of peaks lying just to the east of Pendleton – and now incorporated within the giant-sized **Umatilla and Wallowa-Whitman national forests**.

The most obvious detour from I-84 involves making a 200-mile loop to the east on the so-called **Hells Canyon Scenic Byway**. The byway can be approached in either direction – though the central section is closed by snow from mid-October to mid-June, sometimes later – but it's probably best to leave I-84 at La Grande to follow Hwy 82 to **Joseph**. This country town is the most agreeable base for exploring the nearby **Eagle Cap Wilderness**, the scenic highlight of the **Wallowa Mountains**, a mighty cluster of alpine peaks latticed with stiff hiking trails – again closed by snow till late in the summer. East of Joseph, the **Wallowa Mountain Loop Road** weaves up through the forested hills beside **Hells Canyon**, which marks the Oregon–Idaho border. The loop road then meanders down to Hwy 86 near the sleepy hamlet of **Halfway**, where – in a district notably short of accommodation – there are a couple of good places to stay. The canyon is vast and the continent's deepest, but it has little of the high scenic drama of its nearest rival, the Grand Canyon, as it is a low-relief gorge framed by ascending ridges rather than sheer cliffs. Indeed, the canyon is perhaps best appreciated from the **Snake River**, which created it, and there are regular jet-boat and rafting excursions from the boat dock beyond the east end of Hwy 86. From Halfway, Hwy 86 leads back to I-84 at Baker City, near which you'll pass the ambitious **Oregon Trail Interpretive Center**, worth an hour or two of anyone's time.

East from Portland to Echo on I-84

Heading east out of Portland along the **Columbia River Gorge**, I-84 skirts the northern flanks of Mount Hood on its one hundred-mile journey to Biggs and the Maryhill Museum (see p.106). Beyond, the harsh escarpments edging the river broaden and deepen, hinting at the vast and sparsely populated landscapes of eastern Oregon. Eventually, about 165 miles from Portland, the interstate leaves the river to cut across the undulating wheatfields of the Columbia Plateau, where the tiny settlement of **ECHO**, beside the banks of the Umatilla River just a mile or so off I-84, was once a halting point on the **Oregon Trail**. There's nothing much to the place today apart from a scattering of late nineteenth- and early twentieth-century buildings, but it was here that the pioneers faced a difficult choice. They could opt to travel over to the Columbia River and head west by native canoe or Hudson's Bay Company bateaux, but this was fraught with danger. As Jesse Applegate, one who chose this route, explained, "the river was so wild, so commotional, so fearful and exciting, had not death been there [it was] worth a month of ordinary life". So most plumped for the slower, overland route across the plateau, hurrying along from spring to stream in the hope that they would prove strong enough to survive the intense heat and suffocating dust, or, if they arrived later, quick enough to beat the snows.

Pendleton

Set within a wide ring of rolling hills fifteen miles east of Echo, **PENDLETON** culti-vates its cowboy reputation, and there's a great build-up to its immensely popular ann-ual **Pendleton Round-Up**, in which traditional rodeo events, such as bareback riding, steer roping and the bucking bronco, are mixed with extravagant pageantry, parades and a few dubious cultural hybrids – the "American Indian Beauty Pageant" for one. All this takes places over four days in mid-September and tickets are available from the Round-Up Association (☎541/276-2553 or 1-800/457-6336, *www.uninet.com/~roundup*; $10–15 per rodeo session). At other times, you can see the evidence – including pho-tos, costumes, saddles and a one-time star horse, now stuffed – at the **Round-Up Hall of Fame**, under the arena grandstand on the Round-Up grounds, just west of the town centre at 1205 SW Court (late May to Sept Mon–Sat 10am–4pm; donation). To dress the part, make your way downtown to Red's Clothes, 233 S Main St and Emigrant, which holds a wide range of Western gear, or go for the antique look amongst the old cowboy boots, hats and belts of the Western Working Girls Gift Shop, 29 SW Emigrant Ave and S Main Street.

When the rodeo isn't in town, the star turn is **Pendleton Underground**, 37 SW Emigrant Ave at 1st Street (Mon–Sat 9am–4.30pm; $10; ☎541/276-0730), where regu-lar, ninety-minute guided tours explore the town's extensive network of subterranean passageways. The tunnels were initially built to insulate citizens from the inclement cli-mate, but they soon assumed other purposes and were used through Prohibition as saloons, card-rooms and brothels, as well as housing for the area's much-abused Chinese, who were the object of indiscriminate pot shots from drunken cowboys when they walked the streets. The tour is brought to life not so much by the tunnels them-selves – or by the rather amateurish dioramas – but by a commentary that's full of insights into the life and times of early Pendleton, when the town had 32 saloons and 18 bordellos. For example, the Chinese ran the laundries and used water directly from their mouths to iron and press – a spitting motion that inflamed Caucasian sensibilities to such an extent that the Chinese were obliged to work out of sight. Back outside, be sure to spend a little time strolling Pendleton's tiny **downtown** centred on S Main Street between the river and Emigrant Avenue: there's nothing remarkable, but the sturdy stone and brick buildings are a fetching ensemble mostly dating to the early twentieth century.

As well as the Round-Up, Pendleton is known for its woollen goods: by the end of the nineteenth century, sheep-ranching had gained a firm hold on the local economy and although cereal production takes pride of place today, sheep remain important. However, the c.1900 **Pendleton Woollen Mills**, on the eastern outskirts of town at 1307 SE Court Place (guided tours Mon–Fri 9am–3pm, call ☎541/276-6911 for times), does nothing more exciting than initiate you into the mysteries of carding, spinning, warp dressing and weaving – a tad dour, considering it was the mill that put Pendleton on the map.

Practicalities

With fast and fairly frequent services from other towns along I-84, the Greyhound **bus station** is at 320 SW Court Ave and 3rd Street, about half a mile west of the **visitor cen-tre**, at 501 S Main St (Mon–Fri 8.30am–5pm, plus June to late Sept Sat 9am–5pm; ☎541/276-7411 or 1-800/547-8911, *www.pendleton-oregon.org*). The latter issues free town maps and has details of local attractions and accommodation. In terms of **orien-tation**, Pendleton is divided into four quadrants by the Umatilla River, which runs east–west through town, and Main Street, the main north–south axis. Downtown lies just to the south of the river and its avenues – principally Court, Dorion and Emigrant – intersect with numbered streets that fall either side of Main.

Pendleton has a good range of **accommodation** and prices are reasonable, though note that it's well-nigh impossible to find anything during Round-Up, when you should book as far in advance as possible. Amongst the town's **motels**, one of the handiest is the *Travelodge*, a well-kept modern chain with thirty-six rooms just west of the centre at 411 SW Dorion Ave (☎541/276-7531 or 1-800/578-7878, fax 541/278-7889; ③). A more distinctive offering is the fanciful *Pendleton DoubleTree Hotel*, 304 SE Nye Ave (☎541/276-6111 or 1-800/222-8733; ④), on the edge of town beside I-84's Exit 210, which comes complete with a kitsch Western-style interior and balconied rooms with great views out over the hills. Out here also is a standard-issue *Motel 6*, at 325 SE Nye Ave (☎541/276-3160 or 1-800/466-8356, fax 541/276-7526; ③). As for **B&Bs**, *The Parker House*, pleasantly situated just across the river from downtown at 311 N Main St (☎541/276-8581 or 1-800/700-8581, *www.parkerhousebnb.com*; ④), occupies a handsome old villa of Italianate design and has five attractively furnished rooms, one en suite. Alternatively, *A Place Apart B&B*, 711 SE Byers Ave at 8th (☎541/276-0573 or 1-888/441-8932, *www.aplace-apart.com*; ④), offers just two guestrooms in a solid Edwardian house fetchingly decorated in antique style. Most unusual of all, however, is the *Working Girls Hotel*, 17 SW Emigrant Ave at S Main (June–Oct; ☎541/276-0730 or 1-800/226-6398; ③), where five guestrooms are housed up steep stairs in what was once, until the 1950s, a brothel. The conversion of the premises is successful, if a little frugal, and the rooms – except for one – have shared bathrooms.

Pendleton's **cafés** and **restaurants** tend to be straightforward, all-American affairs featuring burgers, steaks, baked potatoes and huge breakfasts. The pick of them is the *Rainbow Café and Lounge*, 209 S Main St, an atmospheric place of wooden booths with intriguing Round-Up memorabilia plastered over the walls. The bar is a quintessentially American affair, very local and very amenable, and although the food isn't great, it is filling, well-prepared and inexpensive. Alternatively, the smart *Raphael's Restaurant*, at 233 SE 4th St and Dorion (☎541/276-8500; closed Sun & Mon), is noted for its Native-American-influenced cuisine – the wild rice and seared fish is a real treat – and apple-wood-smoked prime rib.

Southeast on I-84 to La Grande

Leaving Pendleton, it's just forty miles north to Washington's Walla Walla (see p.279) or you can continue southeast on I-84, slicing across the open range before climbing up into the **Blue Mountains**, which are now divided between the Umatilla and Wallowa-Whitman national forests. It took the wagons of the early emigrants three or four days to cross this band of mountains; they would pause at what is now **Emigrant Springs State Park** – beside I-84 (Exit 234) – to wait for stragglers and to prepare themselves for the descent into the valley below. For many the "Blues" were a frightening place: the thick forest was confusing and the cries of the cougars during the night demoralizing. Nowadays, the state park is a lovely spot to break your journey and there's a small, seasonal **campground** (☎541/983-2277; $13) – with a handful of log cabins and even tepees (both ②) – here too. On the other side of the mountains, there's another, much smaller campground ($9) at **Hilgard Junction State Park** (I-84, Exit 252), where thousands of early emigrants once bedded down before tackling the steep climb ahead.

Beyond, on the east side of the Blue Mountains, is the distinctly shaped **Grande Ronde Valley** – large, round, flat and rimmed by mountains. Now mostly drained to become farmland, the valley was once a marsh and breeding place for birds, but fatally boggy to the wheels of pioneer wagons, forcing the Oregon Trail to keep to the higher but tougher ground edging the hills. The economic centre of the valley is **LA GRANDE**, a straightforward lumber, university town and trading centre of twelve thousand souls. La Grande's best-looking buildings line the long main drag, **Adams Avenue** (US-30), between about Greenwood Street and 4th, and they comprise a proud ensemble of early twentieth-century shops and stores, all symmetrical brickwork and stone trimmings. To get there, leave I-84 at Exit 261 and follow Hwy 82 into town as far as Adams and turn right. The City's historic downtown begins three blocks ahead. One of La Grande's most popular events is Oregon trail days, held annually on the third weekend of August with "pioneers" camped down by the riverside, a quilt show, craft stalls and an Old Time Fiddle Contest.

On the outskirts of La Grande are several noteworthy attractions, beginning with the **Ladd Marsh Wildlife Area** (☎541/963-4954), a preserved wetland of some 3000 acres located four miles south of town. Over 200 species of bird either nest here or pass through on their spring and fall migrations, from geese and ducks, avocets, grebes and cranes through to hawks and bald eagles. Footpaths explore parts of the wetland and there are several observation points. The wildlife area abuts I-84 (Exit 268) or you can get there rather more pleasantly along Foothill Road: Drive east on Adams Avenue, following it out of town. Take the first road to the right, Gekeler Lane, and drive nearly a mile, to the first road on the left, Foothill Road. La Grande's visitor centre (see below) issues a free leaflet and map of the wildlife area.

Around La Grande: Union and Cove

A little further afield, about fourteen miles southeast of La Grande off I-84 (Exit 265) and along Hwy 203, the amenable little town of **UNION** was the first white settlement hereabouts, founded as an agricultural centre in 1862. The town boomed during the gold rush, when locals made a packet supplying the prospectors who swarmed the nearby mountains, and endured some raucous goings-on during cowboy times, but it's a quiet spot today, its busier times recalled by Main Street's attractive assortment of old buildings. Among them is one enjoyable hotel (see below) and the **Union County Museum**, 333 S Main St (Mon–Sat 1–4pm; $2), where pride of place goes to the Cowboys Then & Now Collection. This outlines the evolution of the cowboy supported by a good range of photographs and all sorts of bygones from branding irons and barbed wire to a tack room and a chuck wagon.

In the vicinity of Union are several hot **thermal springs**, notably the Cove Hot Springs Pool, a bathing and picnic spot located in the hamlet of **COVE**, about eight miles north of Union via Hwy 237. The free pool is only open in the summer; call to confirm opening hours on ☎541/568-4890. Cove is also on the western edge of the Wallowa Mountains with gravel Forest Road 6220 sneaking up to trailheads and campgrounds in the range's Eagle Cap Wilderness (for more on which, see p.162). For maps and trail advice, consult La Grande visitor centre or Ranger station (see below) before you start out.

Practicalities

La Grande's Greyhound **bus depot** is located off Island Avenue (Hwy 82) at 2108 Cove Ave and Portland Street. From here, it's about three-quarters of a mile west to the Adams Ave/Island Ave intersection. Moffit Brothers (☎541/569-2284) also operates out of the Greyhound depot, running a once-daily minibus service to Joseph (see overleaf) Monday through Friday. The town's **visitor centre** is at 1912 4th St and Adams (Mon–Fri 9am–5pm; ☎541/963-8588 or 1-800/848-9969, *www.visitlagrande.com*), about three-quarters of a mile west of the Adams Ave/Island Ave intersection. They issue town maps, have details of the region's attractions and provide advice on hiking into the Wallowa Mountains' Eagle Cap Wilderness. More specialist hiking advice is available at the Wallowa-Whitman Forest Service **Ranger Station**, 3502 Adams Ave (☎541/963-7186).

With regard to **accommodation**, the best place in town is the lavish, four-room *Stang Manor Inn*, 1612 Walnut St and Spring (☎541/963-2400 or 1-888/286-9463, *www.stangmanor.com*; ⑤). The inn, located amongst well-kept gardens, occupies a

From La Grande there's a choice of routes. Heading southeast on **I-84**, it's a quick 44 miles to Baker City, the last worthwhile stop before Idaho, a further 70 miles away. Alternatively, the 200-mile **Hells Canyon Scenic Byway** loops northeast, running to Joseph and the Wallowa Mountains' Eagle Cap Wilderness, Hells Canyon and Halfway along Forest Road 39 (closed mid-Oct to mid-June), before returning to I-84 at Baker City. Incidentally, if you're just after hiking the Wallowas, you can avoid the long drive by approaching the mountain range from La Grande. Several roads lead up to mountain trailheads – get directions, maps and trail advice at La Grande visitor centre or Ranger Station (see overleaf) before you start out.

remodelled and refurbished timber magnate's house off Adams at the west end of town. Otherwise, La Grande holds several workaday motels, including the proficient Best Western Rama Inn, at 1711 21st street (☎541/963-3100 or1-800/726-2466; ④). Another option is the enjoyable *Union Hotel*, an attractively restored 1920s hotel at 326 N Main St (☎541/562-6135 or 1-888/441-8928, *www.theunionhotel.com*; ③), out in the small town of Union, fourteen miles southeast of La Grande.

For **food**, *Mamacita's*, one block east of La Grande visitor centre at 110 Depot St (☎541/963-6223; closed Mon), serves excellent, inexpensive Mexican meals, while at *Sunflower Books*, one block south of the visitor centre at 1114 Washington Ave and 4th, you can get coffee and cake as you browse.

Hells Canyon Scenic Byway

Heading north and then east from La Grande on the first leg of the Hells Canyon Scenic Byway, it's 65 uneventful miles to **ENTERPRISE**, an uninspiring country town that serves as the commercial centre and county seat for the Wallowa Valley's farms and ranches. The big shindig here is the three-day **Hells Canyon Mule Days**, with bizarre mule parades, mule rodeos and suchlike, held over three days in early September and celebrating the early settlers and prospectors hereabouts who were almost entirely dependent on the animal. Otherwise, there's precious little reason to hang around except to gather information from the US Forest Service's **Wallowa Mountains Visitor Center**, just to the west of town at 88401 Hwy 82 (Mon–Fri 8am–5pm, plus June to late Oct Sat 8am–5pm & Sun noon–5pm; ☎541/426-5546). The centre, which covers Hells Canyon as well as the Wallowa Mountains, shows videos, sells hiking maps and issues detailed descriptions of hiking trails. They also sell park passes ($5), required by visitors intending to park at any of the fifty-odd trailheads, and have a list of local outdoor tour operators. You can go hunting and fishing, join a horse, mule or llama expedition up into the Eagle Cap Wilderness (see p.162) or down into Hells Canyon – where there are also jet-boat and raft trips (see p.163) – or go mountain biking.

Joseph

Six miles south of Enterprise, and much more enjoyable, is **JOSEPH**, whose wide and airy Main Street slopes up the valley with the Wallowa Mountains as a backdrop. At heart a modest country town, Joseph has become a popular tourist spot mainly because of its setting, but also on account of the artist David Manuel, who set up shop here in the 1980s. Manuel specializes in **bronzes** depicting historical figures, stereotypical representations of the West from visionary pioneers and frontier marshals to noble natives – and Main Street is dotted with examples of his work. They may not be to everyone's taste, but Manuel's bronzes are much sought after – and cost a bundle, if you are allowed to buy one: prospective purchasers have to be certified and to be certified you must visit the sculptor's museum, foundry and workshop. Whether or not you intend to buy, the **Manuel Museum**, 400 North Main Street (March–Nov Mon–Sat 9am–8pm; Dec–Feb 10am–3pm; $6), is worth a visit for its collection of Nez Percé artefacts – the basketry and clothing cabinets are particularly good – as well as its military memorabilia, all tidily displayed alongside yet more Manuel statues. Pick up the glossy, free brochure that explains the "major miracle" of David and Lee Manuel's marriage and the "sense of awe (which) fills visitors as they witness David's (artistic) gift." Quite. After visiting the museum, enthusiasts can tour the foundry and workshop at no extra cost.

Manuel is not the only sculptor in town – there are several other foundries hereabouts, though by and large they follow his stylistic lead. **Valley Bronze** (☎541/432-7445), who offer foundry tours and display finished works in their showroom at 18 S Main St, are the pick. Otherwise, head for the **Wallowa County Museum**, 110 S Main St and 2nd (late May to late Sept daily 10am–5pm; donation), which occupies a doughty former bank building dating to 1888. The museum has a good section devoted to the region's pioneers, with the women and children receiving (for once) their fair share of attention, and there is also a feature on the Nez Percé – and Chief Joseph (see box on p.164), for whom the town is named. The museum also gets full marks for staging a **bank robbery** every Saturday at 1pm from late May to August. It's a jolly jape acted out in front of a cheering crowd – in fact, it's hard not to join in – and a re-enactment of a real hold-up that took place here on October 2, 1896. Three masked cowboys were involved: one escaped with the loot, one was shot dead and the other, a certain Dave Tucker, was wounded, captured and imprisoned. After his release, Tucker returned to Wallowa County, where he became a wealthy rancher and – curiously enough – a president of the bank he had once tried to rob. Joseph's main event, however, is the four-day **Chief Joseph Days Rodeo** (☎541/432-1015, *www.chiefjosephdays.com*), held over the last full weekend in July – and a boisterous affair it is too with bucking broncos, dances and parades.

As for practicalities, Moffit Brothers (☎541/569-2284) operates a once-daily (Mon–Fri) **minibus** service from Joseph to La Grande with a journey time of about two and a half hours. Joseph's **visitor centre** is located just off Main Street at 102 E 1st (Mon–Fri 9am–4.30pm; ☎541/432-1015). **Orientation** couldn't be easier: the long Main Street, which doubles as Hwy 82, is prefixed North and South to either side of its intersection with McCully. Cross streets – named Avenues to the north of McCully, and numbered Streets to the south – are prefixed East and West to either side of Main.

Joseph is easily the best base for exploring the nearby Eagle Cap Wilderness (see below), but the choice of **accommodation** is limited and consequently advance reservations are strongly advised throughout the summer. Options include the briskly modern *Indian Lodge Motel*, in the centre of town at 201 S Main St (☎541/432-2651; ②), and the pleasant *Chandlers Bed, Bread and Trail Inn*, 700 S Main St (☎541/432-9765 or 1-800/452-3781; ④). The latter is a modern brick and shingle house with five guestrooms and a pretty garden. For **food**, the best place in town is the *Old Town Café*, 8 S Main St (Mon–Sat 7am–2pm, Sun 8am–2pm, plus Fri & Sat 5–8pm; ☎541/432-9898), which offers delicious sandwiches and soups, pastries, pies and pancakes. *Magnoni's*, an Italian place at 403 N Main St (☎541/432-3663; closed Sun), makes for a good second choice. There are more restaurants and hotels six miles south of Joseph in Wallowa Lake Village (see below).

Around Joseph: Wallowa Lake Village and Eagle Cap Wilderness

Travelling south from Joseph, the main road passes a small but clearly signposted **cemetery** that contains the grave of – and an eloquent memorial to – Chief Joseph's father, Old Chief Joseph (1783–1872), of the Nez Percé. Thereafter, the road skirts glacially carved **Wallowa Lake**, which is supposedly inhabited by an Oregonian version of the Loch Ness monster, before slipping into **Wallowa Lake Village**, at the far end of the lake, six miles from Joseph. Much too popular for its own good, the village is crowded with lodges, cottages and campgrounds, all packed in the narrow, forested space between the lake and the mountains. By and large, the lodges and cottages are an undistinguished bunch, though the old-fashioned *Wallowa Lake Lodge* (☎541/432-9821, *www.wallowalake.com*; ⑤) does have a lakeshore setting, with twenty-two bedrooms in the 1920s lodge and eight pine cabins (⑤) close by; be sure to ask for a room with a lake view – otherwise you'll probably end up overlooking the car park. Another option, and one where there is often a vacancy when everywhere else is full up, is *Eagle Cap Chalets* (☎541/432-4704; ③), comprising modern timber chalets with motel-style rooms. There's also a large and well-equipped seasonal **campground** (☎1-800/452-5687) – with yurts ($27 for up to five people; pitch $16–20) – amongst the woods of **Wallowa Lake State Park**. The best **restaurant** by far is *Vali's Alpine Delicatessen* (Wed–Sun 9–11am & 5–8pm; no credit cards; ☎541/432-5691), just up the road from the cable car (see below), where the speciality is mouthwatering Hungarian food – try the goulash at $8.50; dinner is by reservation only.

From the village, the **Wallowa Lake Tramway cablecar** (late May to Sept daily 10am–4pm; $15.50 return) takes fifteen minutes to hoist its passengers up to the top of **Mount Howard**, at 8256 feet, where short trails lead to magnificent overlooks. Mount Howard is on the edge of the Wallowa Mountains' **Eagle Cap Wilderness**, which stretches away to the south and west, its granite peaks soaring high above glaciated valleys, alpine lakes and meadows. The higher slopes support spruce, whitebark pine, larch and mountain hemlock and down below are thick forests of ponderosa pine. This vast wilderness is crisscrossed by over five hundred miles of **hiking trail** accessed via several dozen trailheads. It is not, however, easy hiking. For the most part, the terrain is extremely challenging and, on all but the shortest of hikes, you'll need to come properly equipped – you're even advised to carry an axe or saw to clear downed trees that might block your path. The trails are usually opened in early July when the snow clears, but the weather is notoriously changeable with summer temperatures ranging from 30°F to 90°F. There are some day-long hikes, but Eagle Cap is more the preserve of the **backcountry camper**. Part of the Wallowa-Whitman National Forest, Eagle Cap is managed by the US Forest Service, who maintain just a handful of small and primitive, first-come, first-served **campgrounds** (free) as well as the Wallowa Mountains Visitor Center, back in Enterprise (see p.160). The nearest **campground** to Joseph is Hurricane Creek (free), about four miles southwest of town along Hurricane Creek Road.

At the top of Wallowa Lake Village, the **Wallowa Lake Trailhead** offers a choice of routes with one trail good for a day's hike, another leading into the heart of the wilderness. The former takes you six miles up the East Fork Wallowa River to **Aneroid Lake**, a chubby little loch flanked by towering mountains, where you can picnic before setting off back. The longer, more arduous trek begins by ascending the West Fork Wallowa River for six miles as far as Six Mile Meadow. Here you turn west for the short but lung-wrenching, three-mile climb over to Horseshoe Lake, on the eastern edge of the **Lakes Basin**. Circled by mighty peaks and sprinkled with tiny lochs, this pulchritudinous basin is the most hiked over part of Eagle Cap and a network of trails allows you to wander from lake to lake without too much difficulty – though on summer weekends the basin's popularity can make backcountry camping a tad difficult. In all cases, get maps and trail advice at the Wallowa Mountains Visitor Center in Enterprise (see p.160) before you set out.

East from Joseph to Hells Canyon

Heading east from Joseph, Little Sheep Creek Road (Hwy 350) strips across the valley to reach its junction with Forest Road 39, the **Wallowa Mountain Loop Road**, which

– considering the terrain – threads a surprisingly peaceable course through the forested hills to the west of Hells Canyon. The road emerges on Hwy 86 near Halfway (see p.165) and as such represents an extremely useful shortcut, but note the road is closed by snow from mid-October to mid-June, sometimes later. In total, it is 62 miles from Joseph to Hwy 86, an hour or two's easy drive and one that offers – after about 45 miles – a 3-mile, paved and signposted detour along Forest Road 3965 to the **Hells Canyon Overlook**. The view is stirring, with Idaho's Seven Devils mountain range rising above and the river glimmering in its depths, but as a low-relief canyon, edged by a series of gradually ascending false peaks, it lacks the overwhelming impact of the shallower – by 1000-feet – Grand Canyon. Incidentally, if you are travelling this way in early summer or late autumn, get local advice about road conditions before you set out.

Hells Canyon

From the southern end of the Wallowa Mountain Loop Road, it's just six miles east on Hwy 86 to minuscule **COPPERFIELD**, on the west bank of the **Snake River**, which has spent millions of years carving the prodigious, 130-mile gorge known as **Hells Canyon**. Since prehistoric times, the canyon's hot and sheltered depths have provided a winter sanctuary for wildlife and local natives, and stone tools and rock-carvings have been found at dozens of ancient clearings. The Nez Percé used the northern reaches of the canyon, the Shoshoni the south, but they were bitter enemies and although they traded with each other – the Shoshoni introduced the horse to their neighbours – skirmishes were commonplace too. They did not, however, give the canyon its current name: prosaically, the early pioneers referred to the gorge as Snake River Canyon and only in the 1890s – though this has been the subject of debate – does it appear to have been named "Hells" by an enterprising steamboat company keen to drum up trade.

Both the Shoshoni and the Nez Percé were driven from the gorge in the late nineteenth century and most of the canyon is now managed by the US Forest Service and preserved for wildlife and backpackers as the **Hells Canyon National Recreation Area**: deer, otters, mink, black bears, mountain lions and whole herds of elk live here, along with less attractive, even poisonous, creatures – rattlesnakes and black widow spiders to name but two. Mechanical vehicles are banned above water-level and so the most obvious way to explore the canyon is by **boat** along the Snake River (see below), though hardy souls can hike around what is, by any standard, a harsh environment. Indeed, **hikers** have more than nine hundred miles of trail to choose from. The most difficult and dramatic trails zigzag down the canyon's sides – with two such trails weaving down from the Hat Point and McGraw lookouts – but even hiking along the canyon bottom can be very tough (and hot) going. Consequently, if you do decide to hike the canyon, it's essential to pick up detailed information before you set out from a **USFS information centre** – either in Enterprise (see p.160) or Baker City (see p.165). They will be able to supply you with maps and a complete list of hiking trails as well as information on licensed companies offering jet-boat rides, white-water rafting and mule and horse expeditions. Available also is information on the nineteen widely scattered, first-come, first-served, primitive canyon **campgrounds** ($5) they manage.

HELLS CANYON BY BOAT

At Copperfield, at the end of Hwy 86, take the bridge over the Snake and follow the minor road along the east (Idaho) side of the river for the 25-mile drive north to **Hells Canyon Dam**, the launching-point for jet-boat and raft trips through the canyon. Amongst several operators, Hells Canyon Adventures (☎541/785-3352 or 1-800/422-3568, *www.hellscanyonadventures.com*) run daily **jet-boat tours** (2hr $30; 3hr $40; 6hr $95), from late May through to September. The boats take you skimming over white-

CHIEF JOSEPH AND THE NEZ PERCÉ

The original inhabitants of the Wallowa Valley and Hells Canyon were the **Nez Percé**, so called by French-Canadian trappers for their shell-pierced noses. Primarily hunter-gatherers, the Nez Percé lived in small, autonomous units with elected leaders, who were broadly responsible to a general council, though this had no executive powers. Initially, the Nez Percé were well-disposed to white incomers – they unsuccessfully urged the missionary Marcus Whitman (see p.279) to settle amongst them – but relations soured after whites started moving into the Wallowa Valley in the 1850s. In 1855, the Nez Percé ceded a large chunk of their territory in the hope that this would allow for peaceful co-existence, but they were hopelessly optimistic. The federal government soon came back for more and, in 1863, the Nez Percé were pressured into a second treaty that gave away yet more land – much to the disgust of **Chief Joseph**, who refused to sign.

With the land situation unresolved, escalating tension between the whites and the Nez Percé prompted several violent incidents, as a result of which the US government took draconian measures. They gave the Nez Percé thirty days notice to quit their tribal lands, ordering them to move to a reservation in Idaho; if they refused, the army was to eject them. Accepting the inevitable, Chief Joseph agreed to move, but asked for more time to round up stock and avoid crossing the Snake River at a high and dangerous time. Fearing delay, his adversary, **General Howard**, rejected his request out-of-hand and, as a consequence, the band had to leave much of their cattle and horses behind and negotiate a perilous river-crossing during which more livestock was lost.

In the angry aftermath, three of the band broke away and murdered four white settlers, turning the sad march to the reservation into a dramatic flight as Joseph tried to evade Howard, who was bent on retribution. In the event, Joseph proved extraordinarily adept at guerrilla warfare, out-manoeuvring army columns in a series of hair's-breadth escapes, but the odds were stacked against him. The flight had its bizarre moments – a group of tourists in search of the Wild West wandered into a Nez Percé warpath – but in October 1877 Joseph was finally cornered in Montana just fifty miles from the safety of the Canadian border. It was then that Chief Joseph (reportedly) made his much-quoted speech of surrender:

> ...*It is cold and we have no blankets. The children are freezing to death... [and] I want to have time to look for my children and see how many I can find...Hear me my chiefs! I am tired. My heart is sick and sad. From where the sun now stands I will fight no more forever...*

Predictably, the Nez Percé were made to pay for their resistance. Instead of being moved to Idaho, they were taken to a marshy reservation in Kansas, where most died from malaria. Eventually, the survivors were carted back to Idaho, though Chief Joseph and a few others were taken separately to the Colville reservation in Washington. During the long years of exile, the Chief petitioned the government ceaselessly, urging it to return his people to their tribal lands. The impassioned humanity of his entreaties is in bleak – almost naive – contrast to the ferocious racism of the white settlers. In 1879, Chief Joseph pleaded "I only ask of the government to be treated as all other men are treated", whilst a leading Oregon newspaper spoke of the "delightful repast of killing those unaccountable heathens who were brought into existence by a slight mistake". Chief Joseph died on the Colville reservation in 1904.

water rapids between the deceptively low, bare hills, and even the shortest trip includes a stop at an old Native-American clearing. The same company also operates overnight jet-boat excursions ($250), staying in a motel in Lewiston, Idaho; one-day **white-water rafting** trips ($140); and a "drop-off" service, taking you to hiking trails and fishing spots along the canyon and then picking you up later in the day or the week. For every type of boat trip, reservations are advised. There's a seasonal US Forest service visitor centre at Hells Canyon Dam as well.

Halfway

Backtracking from Hells Canyon Dam, it's about forty miles west to **HALFWAY**, no more than a scattering of old timber houses in the bowl of a valley just off Hwy 86. There are some hard times here – witness the boarded-up buildings – but it is a pleasant little place whose most prosperous times were way-back when its orchards supplied the miners in the mountains nearby. In the centre of the village is the modern and modest *Halfway Motel*, 170 S Main St (☎541/742-5722; ②), but this isn't a patch on the delightful *Clear Creek Farm B&B*, almost four miles north of town at 48212 Clear Creek Rd (☎541/742-2238 or 1-800/742-4992, *clearcreek@pinetel.com*; ⑤). Framed by orchards and ponds and with gentle views out across the valley, the farmhouse is an immaculately restored building with a wraparound veranda and five crisply decorated, en-suite guestrooms in addition to public rooms that include a library and an elegant dining room. Round the back of the house, there are a couple of timber cabins (④–⑦), deluxe affairs with bunk and ordinary beds. Reservations are pretty much essential – it's a popular spot and anyway it's probably best to call for directions. Creek Farm is reached from Halfway via Fish Lake Road, which you follow as far as Clear Creek Road, where you turn left. Dinners are strictly by reservation only, but should you miss out, there's a very good **restaurant** back in the centre of Halfway, *The Olde Church*, on N Main Street (☎541/742-2027; no credit cards), where the menu features local ingredients imaginatively prepared; the decor is imaginative too, with all sorts of artistic bric-a-brac packed into this dinky wooden church of 1891.

From Halfway, it's some fifty miles west to the I-84 and Baker City, on the edge of which is the first-rate Oregon Trail Interpretive Center (see below).

Baker City

In full view of the Elkhorn Mountains, **BAKER CITY** (often just "Baker"), 52 miles from Halfway and 44 from La Grande, is a substantial red-brick town which outlived the gold-boom days of the 1860s to prosper from agriculture and ranching. From 1876 into the 1890s, enormous herds of cattle and sheep would be assembled here, headed for the dinner plates of the East. A modest monument in honour of the **American Cowboy** celebrates those busy years – it is in the city park at Campbell and Grove streets, just east of, and across the Powder River from, Main Street. Also in the park are several rusty metal spikes, relics from nineteenth-century horseshoe-throwing contests.

Opposite the park, at 2480 Grove St, the **Oregon Trail Regional Museum** (late April to late Oct daily 9am–4pm; $3.50) is housed in the 1920s Natatorium, a combined swimming pool, ballroom and community centre. Surprisingly, the exhibits have precious little to do with the early pioneers – though the Oregon Trail did pass nearby – and are more a motley miscellany of Wild West bric-a-brac, the real highlight being an extraordinary collection of rocks. Precious stones, agates, minerals, petrified wood, fossils and shells crowd the shelves, and, in a dark room, fluorescent crystals glow weirdly under ultraviolet light. Of less specialized interest are the grand old buildings of **Main Street**, strutting structures mostly built of local stone in a potpourri of European styles – from Renaissance through to Gothic Revival. The most impressive is the old and empty **Baker Hotel**, a nine-storey edifice with an outlandish observation tower and eye-catching Art Deco details, from filigree panels to a whole flock of bald eagles; it's at 1700 Main St and Auburn Avenue.

Among the sagebrush foothills five miles east of town on Hwy 86, the **Oregon Trail Interpretive Center** ambitiously attempts to re-create the early emigrants' life on the trail (daily: April–Oct 9am–6pm; Nov–March 9am–4pm; $5). Contemporary quotations with matching illustrations and dioramas are well used, dealing with a wide variety of subjects – from marital strife to the pioneers' impact on Native-Americans. Background sound tapes, as well as a short video, further set the scene. Outside, you can wander

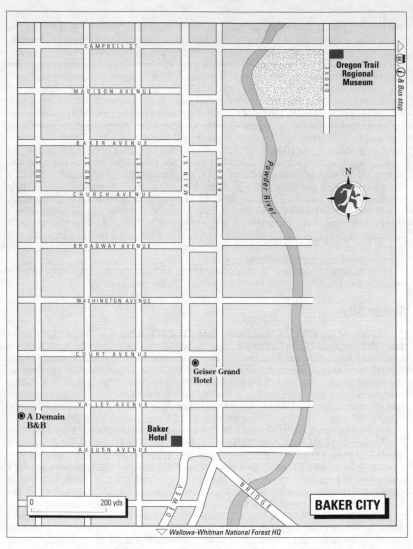

Oregon Trail Regional Museum

Powder River

N

Geiser Grand Hotel

A Demain B&B

Baker Hotel

DEWEY

BRIDGE

0   200 yds

BAKER CITY

▽ *Wallowa-Whitman National Forest HQ*

down and around the hill to examine wheel ruts left by the pioneers' wagons and sometimes the staff re-create a wagon camp.

Practicalities

To reach downtown Baker, leave I-84 at Exit 304 and follow Campbell Street to Main Street, where you should turn left. Greyhound **buses** stop at the gas station and truck stop on Campbell Street beside I-84 (Exit 304) – and about twenty-minutes' walk from Main Street. The **visitor centre** is across the street, also beside I-84 at 490 Campbell

---

MOVING ON FROM BAKER

Despite its distant location, Baker is something of a crossroads: from here, Hwy 7 heads west across the Elkhorn Mountains for Hwy 26 and the John Day Valley (see p.173), while Hwy 86 is the first – or last – leg of the 200-mile Hells Canyon Scenic Byway (see p.160). Heading southeast, I-84 makes its dreary way to **ONTARIO**, seventy miles away on the Idaho border. Ontario is duller than dull, a suitably remote spot, so it was thought, to build relocation centres for several thousand Japanese Americans who were bundled out here during World War II. Of the town's **motels**, the *Holiday Inn*, 1249 Tapadera Ave (☎541/889-8621 or 1-800/525-5333; ④), is perfectly adequate; full listings are available at the **visitor centre**, 676 SW 5th Ave (☎541/889-8012 or 1-888/889-8012).

St (Mon–Fri 8am–5pm, plus late May to Sept Sat 8am–4pm & Sun 9am–2pm; ☎541/523-3356 or 1-800/523-1235). They have lots of local stuff, including a list of accommodation, but for information on the Wallowa Mountains and Hells Canyon (see pp.160–164), you're better off visiting the **Wallowa-Whitman National Forest Headquarters**, 1550 Dewey Ave (☎541/523-6391). They sell hiking maps and park passes ($5), required by visitors intending to park at any of the fifty-odd trailheads, issue detailed descriptions of hiking trails and have a list of local outdoor tour operators for everything from hunting and fishing to horse, mule and llama expeditions; Dewey Avenue is the southern extension of Main Street.

There's no strong reason to stay the night here, but Baker is a pleasant enough town and it's certainly your best bet for miles when travelling through the area. Campbell Street possesses several standard chain **motels**, including a *Super 8*, at no. 250 (☎541/523-8282 or 1-888/726-2466; ③), and a *Welcome Inn*, at no. 175 (☎541/523-3431 or 1-800/307-5206; ③). As for **hotels**, the more distinctive *Geiser Grand* occupies a handsome old building in the city centre at 1996 Main St and Court (☎541/523-1889 or 1-888/434-7374, *www.geisergrand.com*; ⑤), and there's also an appealing **B&B**: *A Demain*, 1790 4th St and Valley Avenue (☎541/523-2509; ③), is an ornately refurbished early twentieth-century house with high gables, bay windows, a well-kept garden and two comfortable en-suite rooms.

For **food**, the *Geiser Grand* has a passably good restaurant or you could stick with the standard bar fare of *Barley Brown's Brewpub* at 2190 Main St.

Bend and Southeast Oregon

Among the small towns of southeast Oregon, it's **Bend**, 160 miles southeast of Portland, that appeals the most on account of its lively, almost cosmopolitan air, its excellent restaurants and charming B&Bs. Luckily, the town is also the best base for exploring the rest of the region, beginning with the imposing peaks of the **Cascade Mountains** in the Deschutes National Forest immediately to the west of town – and including the ski haven of **Mount Bachelor**. The Deschutes National Forest also hooks round to the south of Bend and here, traversed by US-97, the eastern slopes of the Cascades yield a smattering of volcanic remains. Nowhere is quite as impressive as Washington's Mount St Helens (see p.261), but the green, alpine scenery is everywhere counterpointed by stark cones and lava flows, especially in the splendid **Newberry National Volcanic Monument**. In the opposite direction, heading northeast along US-26, it's into the hills for the three scattered sites that make up the **John Day Fossil Beds**, famous for their plant and animal fossils – and potentially the only significant attraction on the long drive east to Baker City (see p.165). Different again is the **high desert** which fills up the state's southeastern reaches – part of the Great

Basin desert which spreads all the way into Nevada and Idaho. There's no disputing the eerie beauty of the desert landscape, but the highlights are less obvious and after a few hours driving it's hard to remain enthusiastic. The best advice if you're venturing this far afield is to stay in **Burns**, on US-20, and day-trip to the main oasis hereabouts, the **Malheur National Wildlife Refuge**.

Public transportation is almost non-existent: there are no **trains** and the only town well served by Greyhound **bus** is Bend, which you can reach from Portland, Klamath Falls and Seattle via Biggs on the Columbia River. In the remoter parts, **gas stations** are few and far between – keep as full as you can.

Bend

Bustling **BEND** is a booming resort town, eagerly benefiting from the recent explosion of interest in outdoor pursuits, with cross-country and alpine skiers gathering here in the winter, hikers, rafters and mountain bikers all summer long. The main aim is to venture into the vastness of the Deschutes National Forest to the south and west of town, though the forest fires that raged here in 2000 have reduced the possibilities. A far cry from the region's less fashionable towns, Bend is chic but studiously laid-back, an urbane mix that belies its authentic frontier origins: early hunting trails struck away from the Deschutes River here, and hunters came to know the place as "farewell bend" – a name which stuck until an impatient post office made the abbreviation. It was, however, an early 1900s East Coast entrepreneur who transformed Bend from a ramshackle scattering of half-deserted ranches and dusty houses into a real town, and its development thereafter followed the rickety, uneven pattern of the Western frontier (cars came here before gaslights or electricity).

First impressions of Bend are disappointing, with the main drag, US-97, ripping through ugly modern development, but the old **town centre**, with its unassuming 1930–40s architecture, is a dapper and convivial place tucked against the leafy east bank of the Deschutes River. It only takes a few minutes to stroll from one end of downtown to the other – turn west off US-97 down Franklin Avenue to get there. Afterwards there are panoramic views over Bend from **Pilot Butte**, a solitary hunk of rock a mile or so east of downtown off US-20; you can drive or walk to the top.

Arrival and information

Arriving by **car**, US-97 (3rd St) slices right through Bend from north to south; US-20 comes in from the north too – merging with US-97 just outside town – but it soon forks off east to Burns. The town centre is west of US-97 along Franklin Avenue. Greyhound **buses** shoot along US-97; call ☎1-800/231-2222 for schedules and drop-off details. The **visitor centre** (Mon–Sat 9am–5pm & Sun 11am–3pm; ☎541/382-3221 or 1-800/905-2363, *www.bendchamber.org*), beside US-97/20 on the north side of town, has maps, accommodation listings, and details of the many companies who specialize in **outdoor sports**: there's white-water rafting and canoeing on the Deschutes and McKenzie rivers, horseback riding, climbing, mountain biking, fishing, snowboarding, snowshoeing and skiing. In particular, Sun Country Tours, 531 SW 13th St (☎541/382-6277 or 1-800/770-2161, *www.suncountrytours.com*), offer first-rate **rafting** trips on the Deschutes and McKenzie rivers from June to September, with their shorter, two- to three-hour excursions costing about $40. Wanderlust Tours, 143 SW Cleveland Ave (☎541/389-8359 or 1-800/962-2862, *www.empnet.com/wanderlust*), have an imaginative range of **guided hikes**. Equipment **rental** is widely available too – again the visitor centre has the complete list – but for skis, snowboards and mountain bikes Bend Ski & Sport, 1009 NW Galveston Ave (☎541/389-4667), is as good as anyone. The USFS puts information in the visitor centre, but they also have two offices in Bend, the **Deschutes National**

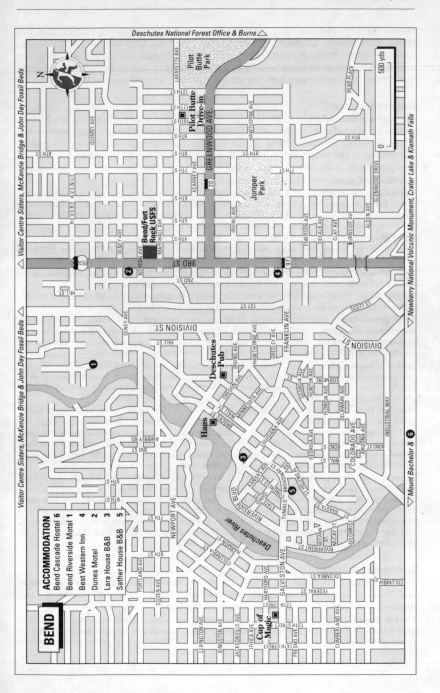

Forest Office, 1645 US-20 E (Mon–Fri 7.45am–4.30pm; ☎541/383-5300), and the **Bend/Fort Rock District Office**, in the mall at 1230 US-97 NE (Mon–Fri 7.45am–4.30pm; ☎541/383-4000). Both sell maps and issue free hiking and bicycling trail descriptions amongst a wealth of general leaflets and newssheets. Overnight wilderness permits are sold here too; day-use permits are self-issue at trailheads.

Accommodation

Finding **accommodation** in Bend in the summer – and especially on the weekend – can be a real headache, so it's best to book ahead. The town's budget chain **motels** are strung out along US-97, but there are more distinctive offerings, notably several charming **B&Bs**, in the town centre. There is also a spartan **youth hostel** and numerous **campgrounds** in the Deschutes National Forest (see below) – as well as a particularly well-situated campground nearer to town.

Bend Cascade Hostel, 19 SW Century Drive (☎541/389-3813 or 1-800/299-3813, *bchostel@bendnet .com*). Frugal lodgings are available at this youth hostel, a mile or so southwest of – and across the river from – downtown on the road to Mount Bachelor, to which there is a free ski shuttle in winter. Same-sex dormitory beds ($15) and family rooms (②) too.

Bend Riverside Motel, 1565 NW Hill St (☎541/388-4000 or 1-800/228-4019, *www.bendriversidemotel .com*). Down by the east bank of the river, but north of downtown off US-97 at Revere Ave, this large resort-like motel has a pleasant leafy setting as well as a pool, sauna and sports facilities. ④.

Best Western Inn, 721 NE 3rd St/US-97 (☎541/382-1515 or 1-800/528-1234). Well-maintained chain hotel on the main strip with one hundred spacious, air-conditioned rooms. ④.

Dunes Motel, 1515 NE 3rd St/US-97 (☎541/382-6811). Straightforward motel with thirty air-conditioned rooms kitted out in modern style. One of Bend's better bargains. ②.

Lara House B&B, 640 NW Congress St at Franklin Ave (☎541/388-4064 or 1-800/766-4064, *www.moriah.com/larahouse*). This lavish B&B occupies a handsome, high-gabled wooden mansion dating from 1910. Great setting too – amongst a series of big old houses near the river and two blocks from downtown. Has six large and comfortable en-suite guestrooms. ④.

Sather House B&B, 7 NW Tumalo Ave at Broadway (☎541/388-1065 or 1-888/388-1065, *www.moriah.com/sather*). As with the *Lara House* nearby, this fine B&B is housed in a good-looking Edwardian mansion near both the river and downtown. Antique furnishings, an elegant veranda, and delicious breakfasts add to the charm of the place. Four guestrooms. ⑤.

Sunriver Resort, Sunriver (☎541/593-1000 or 1-800/547-3922, *www.sunriverresort.com*). In recent years, self-contained holiday resorts have mushroomed around Bend, characteristically large and well-equipped complexes where golf is a common theme. The *Sunriver Resort* is one of the more extravagant, its commodious chalets and condos decorated in modern style and draped across manicured grounds around a large central lodge. The resort is tucked up against the Deschutes River about 20 miles south of Bend off US-97 in the holiday town of Sunriver. ⑥.

Tumalo State Park campground, 62976 O.B. Riley Rd (☎541/388-6055 or 1-800/452-5687). This, the nearest campground to Bend, has a lovely setting, in a wooded dell shaded by ponderosa pine, junipers and alders beside the Deschutes River. There are RV hookups, tent sites ($20), four yurts ($18) and even two replica, canvas-covered tepees ($27). The campground is located five miles to the northwest of Bend and there are two ways to get there: from the town centre, take US-20/97 and, just beyond the overpass, turn left down O.B. Riley Rd at the conspicuous *Shilo Inn*; alternatively, keep going out of town on US-20 and watch for the sign.

Eating and drinking

Bend is a great place to **eat** and **drink**. There are cafés with an easy-going, Californian feel, Western-style diners, brewpubs, chic restaurants and everything in between – and keen competition keeps prices down to affordable levels.

Beef & Brew, 3194 N US-97 (☎541/388-4646). You can mess around with the seafood here – and it isn't bad at all – but the well-priced steaks are simply superb and the best in town. Don't be deterred by the dreary roadside location. North of the US 20/97 flyover, not far from the visitor centre.

Cup of Magic, 1304 NW Galveston Ave. On the west side of the river across from downtown, this laid-back café, with a New Age feel, serves great coffees, cakes and snacks with a healthfood slant. Inexpensive.

Deschutes Brewery and Public House, 1044 NW Bond St at Greenwood Ave. Downtown brew-pub offering good bar food and a wide selection of microbrewed ales and stouts. Amongst many brews, Bachelor Bitter is a tangy British-style beer and Cascade Golden Ale is an approachable lager-like ale. Closed Mon.

Hans, 915 NW Wall St (☎541/389-9700). Smart, but studiously informal, this restaurant dabbles with a wide-ranging menu, though its heart is Italian and Southwest cuisine. Downtown location.

Pilot Butte Drive-In Restaurant, 917 NE Greenwood Ave/US-20 and 10th St. Folksy, friendly, home-grown diner that serves up the last word in hamburgers – though their enormous 18oz version looks big enough to kill you. All the classic American dishes too.

West of Bend: Mount Bachelor and the Cascade Lakes Highway

Bend owes a good slice of its newfound success to the development of one of the Northwest's largest ski resorts, **Mount Bachelor**, a 9060ft peak, 22 miles southwest of town in the Deschutes National Forest. The mountain is reached along a short spur road off the scenic, 100-mile Cascade Lakes Highway (see below). The skiing season runs from around mid-November to as late as July, snowfall permitting (snow reports on ☎541/382-7888), and you can rent cross-country and downhill skis as well as snowboards (details on ☎541/382-2442 or 1-800/829-2442, *www.mtbachelor.com*). There are thirteen ski lifts on the mountain and no less than seventy runs, covering all levels of difficulty. A one-day ski-lift pass costs $43 and there's a park and ride bus shuttle from Bend to the slopes in the winter season. The bus leaves four times daily from the Park & Ride at Colorado and Simpson, about half-a-mile west of the river, and costs $2 each way. There's a well-respected ski school at the ski area too – again, information on ☎541/382-2442.

Beyond Mount Bachelor, the **Cascade Lakes Highway** pushes on west before turning south to weave along the eastern peripheries of the Cascade Mountains, winding through dense forests past deep-blue lakes, crumbly lava flows and craggy peaks. It's an easy enough drive – though it's closed beyond Mount Bachelor during the winter – but the magnificence of the scenery is best appreciated along one of the many **hiking trails** that begin beside the highway. The USFS offices in Bend have all the trail details and will advise as to which of them were affected by the fires of August 2000. One of the most enjoyable is the popular **Green Lakes Trail**, whose roadside trailhead is about twenty-five miles out from town. This moderately difficult trail climbs north up gurgling Fall Creek to reach, in a little over four miles, the meadows and lava field beside the three little basin lakes, with the white-capped triple peaks of the **Three Sisters Wilderness** – "Faith", "Hope" and "Charity" – stretching away to the north. From the lakes, you can press on deeper into the wilderness or vary your return via either Devils Lake or Todd Lake, where there's a backcountry **campground** ($20).

Southwest from Bend into the Lava Lands

Fast and straight, **US-97** runs southwest from Bend slicing through the Deschutes National Forest before passing the turning for Crater Lake (see p.140) on its way to Klamath Falls (see p.142). Four miles out of Bend on this highway is the diverting **High Desert Museum** (daily 9am–5pm; $7.75; ☎541/382-4754, *www.highdesert.org*). As much a zoo as a museum, this account of life in the arid desert of southeast Oregon parades its best exhibits along an outdoor path, where pens and pools of creatures – river otters, porcupines and so forth – are interspersed with displays of trees and shrubs, and historical exhibits. A pioneer log cabin and a sheep herder's wagon stand as relics of an isolated nineteenth-century life spent guarding the animals against natural perils. And the sheep certainly tested the resourcefulness of their herders. Apart from animal predators, rustlers and extreme weather conditions, there were poisonous weeds, scabies, liver flukes and foot rot to contend with, prompting all manner of ingenious treatments – the shepherds dipped their animals in a solution of sulphur, hot water and black leaf, which was nicotine squeezed from tobacco. Indeed, nicotine was recommended for several complaints: *Ranch and Range*, a local journal of the day, suggested that snuff should be blown up an animal's nose if it was sick and weakly.

The museum's smart interior has several well-organized display areas including the **Spirit of the West Gallery**, which takes visitors through a sequence of historical scenes, and the **Hall of Plateau Indians**, examining the culture of the region's indigenous population.

Newberry National Volcanic Monument

Characterized by weird formations of solidified lava, the **Newberry National Volcanic Monument** (parking passes, valid for all of the monument and for up to five days, $5) occupies a narrow slice of the Deschutes National Forest to either side of US-97 just a few miles south of Bend. **Lava** formations dot a huge area of central eastern Oregon, stretching roughly from Redmond way down south to Crater Lake, but the concentration of geological oddities around here makes this the focal point. The national monument's volcanic forms – neat conical cones, obsidian deposits, lava and pumice fields, caves and solidified tree moulds – date back seven thousand years to the eruptions of Mounts Newberry and Mazama (today's Crater Lake; see p.140), which dumped enormous quantities of ash and pumice across the region. The process is depicted in video re-creations – and various types of volcanic rock are displayed – at the monument's enjoyable **Lava Lands Visitor Center**, just eleven miles from Bend on US-97 (June–Sept daily 9am–5pm; May & early Oct Wed–Sun 9am–5pm). The centre is also a useful source of maps and practical information on the Newberry monument as a whole, but of more immediate interest is the adjacent **Lava Butte**, a large, dark cinder cone side-breached by a gush of molten lava which spilled over the surrounding land. Two short trails lead from the visitor centre through the cracked moonscape of the lava flow, and in summer a shuttle bus climbs the 1.5 miles to the top of the butte, giving an overview of dark green pine forest interrupted by chocolate-coloured lava. The butte is cratered at the top, the basin-like hole tinged red where steam once oxidized the iron in the rock.

A mile or so south of the visitor centre, just east off US-97, the **Lava River Cave** (mid-May to mid-Oct daily 9.30am–5pm; $3, plus $2 for a lamp) takes you down a subterranean passage into the volcanic underworld. The cave was created by a rush of molten lava during the Ice Age. Most of the lava eventually cooled and hardened around the hottest, still-molten centre of the flow; when this drained away, it left an empty lava-tube, over a mile long, discovered only when part of the roof fell in. There are supposedly all kinds of formations along the cave, but even with a lantern it's hard to see much beyond the next few steps, and it's cold at a constant 42°F – wear extra clothes and stout shoes.

From the cave, it's about three miles south on US-97 and a further nine miles east along rough, unpaved Forest Road 9720 to the **Lava Cast Forest**. This contains the moulds – easily seen on a one-mile loop trail – formed when, centuries ago, lava poured into a forest of ponderosa pines, leaving empty shells when the trees burned to charcoal and ash. The lava here came from what was once towering Mount Newberry, whose multiple eruptions deluged its surroundings for hundreds of years. Finally, worn out by the effort, the mountain collapsed to create **Newberry Crater**, a five-mile-wide caldera that's approached along – and traversed by – a narrow and tortuous 18-mile side road which cuts east off US-97 about 24 miles south of Bend. Note that this road is closed by snow in winter from about November to May. The crater is a classic example of a volcanic landscape with **Paulina Peak**, an 8000ft remnant of the original mountain, standing sentinel over two little lochs, **Paulina** and **East lakes**, whose deep, clear waters are popular with fishermen for their (artificially introduced) trout and salmon. A puncture in the side of the crater provides an outlet for Paulina Lake in the form of the 80ft **Paulina Falls**, whilst the volcano's most recent eruption – about 1300 years ago – has created the **Big Obsidian Flow**, a giant chunk of a material much prized by natives for its use in tools and weapons. Beginning at the roadside, **hiking trails** reach every feature of the crater, ranging from easy half-mile strolls to the obsidian flow and the waterfall, through to the strenuous haul up Paulina Peak. The crater is easily visited on a day-trip from Bend, but there are several seasonal **campgrounds** here too – reservations and details from either the Lava Lands visitor centre or the USFS offices back in Bend.

Fort Rock

If you haven't the time or inclination to explore Oregon's arid southeast, you can get the flavour by visiting **Fort Rock**, a monumental tuff ring located seventy-odd miles south of Bend – turn off US-97 a few miles beyond the Newberry Crater turning to follow Hwy 31 for roughly 30 miles. The rock is interesting in itself as an unusual geological formation, created in billows of steam and rivers of slurry when molten rock came into contact with an Ice Age lake, but it's the setting that makes the detour worthwhile: set on the pancake-flat bed of what was once a lake, the rock's imposing cliffs, up to 325-feet high, overlook the sagebrush desert as it stretches towards the horizon in all its sun-scorched beauty. To **climb** the rock, contact First Ascent, 1136 SW Deschutes Ave, Redmond (☎541/548-5137 or 1-800/325-5462, *ascent@goclimbing.com*) who organize regular guided climbs. It was, incidentally, around here in the 1930s that the earliest signs of human life in Oregon were found: archeologists uncovered a hotchpotch of remains roughly nine thousand years old, including a pair of sagebrush sandals.

Northeast from Bend: the John Day Fossil Beds

Just north of Bend, US-20 branches off US-97 to travel west to **SISTERS**, from where two splendid mountain roads clamber over the Cascades, threading through the Willamette National Forest (see p.138) en route to the Willamette Valley (see pp.131–139). Alternatively, if you stay on US-97, it's sixteen miles north to **REDMOND** at the start of an area much favoured by so-called "rockhounds" or amateur excavators, who come here to find such trophies as jasper thundereggs, obsidian and agates. All the local visitor centres have details of where you can dig and what for, and shops sell the stuff by the truckload too.

East from Redmond, Hwy 126 cuts across sagebrush flatlands on its way to **PRINEVILLE**, an unexciting little town in a splendid butte-flanked valley. Here you join US-26 from Portland just before it wriggles over the green band of the **Ochoco Mountains**, whose ponderosa and lodgepole pines are dusted over tightly bunched hills studded with canyons, meadows and volcanic plugs. On the other side of the mountains are the three separate sites collectively known as the **John Day Fossil Beds National Monument**. Named, like several other features of the immediate area, after **John Day**, a member of the Astor expedition of 1811 (see p.112), these strangely coloured rock formations have been carefully excavated to reveal an amazing assortment of fossils. The fossils date from the period just after the extinction of the dinosaurs: before the Cascade Mountains raised their rain-blocking peaks to the west, a subtropical rainforest covered this land in a dense jungle of palms, ferns and tropical fruits. The forest was inhabited by creatures that predate the evolution of current species – Hpertragulus, a tiny, mouse-sized deer, Diceratherium, a cow-sized rhinoceros, and Miohippus, a small, three-toed horse, to name but three. As the Cascades sputtered into being, volcanic ash poured down on the forest, mixing with the rain to make a thick, muddy poultice, which fossilized bits of the leaves and fruit and then the bones and teeth of the animals. Consequently, paleontologists, who first visited the area in the 1860s, have been able to put together an epic of evolution and extinction. At all three sites, short **trails** wind through barren hills over crumbly textured earth, and information sheets or plaques are available at key trailheads to point out various geological and paleontological curiosities.

Approaching from the west, the first of the three sites is the **Painted Hills Unit**, located almost eighty miles from Bend (and a couple of miles west of the one-horse town of Mitchell) down a signposted six-mile turning north off US-26. Unlike the other two units, the **Painted Hills** are famous for the colour of the rocks rather than the relics embedded in them: striped in shades of rust and brown, they look like volcanic dumplings, the smooth surface quilted with rivulets worn by draining water. Close up, the hills are frail, their clay and shale cracked by dryness. The colours become brighter when it rains and the pores in the earth close up, and are at their most mellifluent in the late afternoon.

Returning to US-26, it's just a mile or so east to the turning for the second fossil bed, the **Clarno Unit**, where ash-laden mud flows have inundated a dense prehistoric forest. But this site is a long way north, a tiring backroad drive of some seventy miles, and

ANTELOPE AND THE BHAGWAN

Although there's not much point in actually visiting the place, the story of **ANTELOPE**, a remote town about 75 miles north of Bend along US-97, is probably the most bizarre and well known in Oregon's recent history. In 1981, followers of the Indian guru, Bhagwan Shree Rajneesh, bought the **Big Muddy Ranch**, twenty miles east of Antelope, converting it into an agricultural commune. Dressed exclusively in shades of red – and thus sometimes known as "the orange people" – Bhagwan's followers were a middle-class lot, mostly graduates in their thirties who came from all over the world. The commune's mishmash of Eastern philosophy and Western Growth Movement therapies raised great (and initially sympathetic) interest across Oregon – and eyebrows in conservative Antelope. The commune was an agricultural success, but despite this relations disintegrated fast, especially when Rajneeshis took over the town council; and the appearance of Rajneeshi "peace patrols" clutching semi-automatic weapons did little to restore confidence in the guru's good intentions.

The Rajneeshis' hold on the community was, however, fairly short-lived. Just before the local county elections, the Rajneeshis began a "Share a Home" project that involved bussing in street-people from across the US and registering them to vote here. Many vagrants later turned up in neighbouring towns (without the promised bus ticket home), saying they'd been conned, drugged or both, and creating big problems for the local authorities. Worse, an outbreak of salmonella-poisoning in the nearby town of The Dalles turned out to have been part of a Rajneeshi strategy to lay their voting opponents low. When the law eventually moved in on the commune – by now, in early shades of Waco, an armed fortress – they discovered medical terrorism (more poisoning, the misdiagnosis of AIDS) had been used on Rajneeshi members themselves in an internal power-struggle. The culprits were jailed and commune members dispersed. The Bhagwan, after a bungled attempt to flee the country, was deported to India and his fleet of Rolls Royces sold off, along with the ranch, to pay debts. By 1986, embattled Antelope was quiet again and a plaque on a flagpole in the town centre, dedicated to the triumph of the Antelope community over the "Rajneesh invasion", is the only sign that anything ever happened.

you'd have to be a real fossil fanatic to make the effort. Much more accessible – a further 25 miles to the east, just off US-26 – is the **Sheep Rock Unit**, which takes its name from the volcanic capstone which looms like the Matterhorn over the John Day River Valley. At the foot of the capstone, the **visitor centre** (March–Oct daily 9am–5pm; Nov–Feb Mon–Fri 9am–4pm), housed in a sheep rancher's house of 1917, has displays and videos on the area's complex geology and a few fossils. It's also just three miles south of the **Blue Basin** canyon, where the rock is more of a pale, greeny colour, with occasional dark red flashes. Of four short hiking trails, the one-mile **Island in Time** trail takes you into the "blue basin" itself – a rock-surrounded natural amphitheatre – past perspex-covered fossil replicas, including a tortoise that hurtled to its death millions of years ago and a sabre-toothed cat.

East on US-26 to John Day town and beyond

Beyond the Sheep Rock turning, US-26 travels seven miles along the John Day River Valley to tiny **DAYVILLE**, easily the prettiest village hereabouts and one that possesses a cosy **B&B**, the *Fish House Inn* (☎541/987-2124 or 1-888/286-3474, *fishinn@pdx .oneworld.com*; ③), beside the main road. Moving on, it's thirty miles east through cattle-ranching country, past the valley's rambling homesteads, to dreary **JOHN DAY** town, which is, despite having only 1900 inhabitants, the biggest place along US-26. Like many of the towns in the area, this was originally a gold rush settlement, founded when gold was discovered at nearby Canyon Creek in 1862. Along with the rush of hopeful white miners came several thousand Chinese immigrants, often to work sites abandoned as unprofitable by the wealthier whites. Despite the racism that then characterized the Northwest, a Chinese herbalist, "Doc" Ing Hay made quite a name for himself here, treating patients of both races, and his two-storey home (which was also the local shop, temple, pharmacy and opium and gambling den) has survived. It is now open as the **Kam Wah Chung & Co Museum** (May–Oct Mon–Thurs 9am–noon & 1–5pm, Sat & Sun 1–5pm; $2), named after the Chinese labour-contracting company Ing Hay and his partner Lung On bought in 1887. The rest of John Day's Chinatown, which once stretched down from the museum to the river, is long gone, but Ing Hay's magpie-like disposition means that his old home is literally stuffed with bygones – everything from old salmon tins and bootleg whiskey bottles from Prohibition days to antique herbs and medicines. It's an intriguing place, although the heavy steel doors and small windows are no stylistic nicety, but speak of nights when drunken cowpokes came to have fun at Hay's expense. Fortunately, they didn't know that by the time of his death in 1948 Ing Hay had $23,000 worth of uncashed cheques under his bed.

Lonely US-26 leaves the John Day Valley a few miles east of John Day town, climbing over the southern reaches of the Blue Mountains to reach the arid buttes and plains that extend to the Idaho border. In the middle of the mountains, Hwy 7 branches off to travel northeast to Baker City (see p.165), wriggling past old gold-mining settlements and near quasi-**ghost towns** such as **SUMPTER**, where the dredging equipment still looks poised for action.

Southeast of Bend: Burns and the Malheur National Wildlife Refuge

Seldom visited, Oregon's big, dry and hot southeast corner is mostly barren land, part-coated with dry sagebrush and punctuated with great flat-topped, cowboy-movie mountains and canyons. Early exploration of the area was mostly accidental: the best-known tale of desert wanderings is that of the **Blue Bucket Mine Party** of 1845, who left the Oregon Trail in search of a shortcut and got lost in the parched land with neither food nor water. Most of them were eventually rescued, and caused great excitement with an account of a big nugget of gold, discovered in the bottom of a blue bucket of water brought by children from a creek: members of the party went back to look for the lost gold mine, but it was never found. Despite this and other widely known tales of hardship, unscrupulous promoters conned homesteaders into settling the land hereabouts by painting rich pictures of the land's farming potential – whereas the only half-decent land was in fact round the Malheur Lake oasis. Very different from speculator promises, the desert homesteaders faced a bleak, lonely country where water was scarce, dust blew in clouds and gardens turned green in the spring only to wilt under the summer sun – a grim life, which few could stick out for long. When World War I broke out, most homesteaders left to take jobs in the new war industries and today the area is barely populated.

The region's only major highway, **US-20**, runs 260 miles east from Bend to Ontario, on the Idaho border. Especially on a hot summer's day, this is a long and arduous drive, whose brain-numbing tediousness is only interrupted by the occasional battered hamlet, boasting a couple of fuel pumps and (maybe) a café: fill up with gas, pack extra water and check your car before you set off. The halfway point is marked by **BURNS** – named after Robert Burns – a welcome watering hole that's the biggest settlement for miles. Indeed, it was the town's relative success as a commercial centre in the 1920s that actually polished off many of its neighbours. Details of the town's pioneer past are displayed in the **Harney County Historical Museum**, 18 West D St (April–Sept Tues–Sat 9am–5pm; $4), but the prize exhibits are those salvaged from the ranch of **Peter French**, the greatest of the state's cattle barons who, at the height of his success, had over 200,000 acres of grazing land. In the 1870s, it was French who realized the great cattle-grazing potential of the meadows south of Burns. But within ten years his empire was under threat as homesteaders began to arrive in droves. Although French kept them at bay – and his ranchlands intact (for almost twenty years) – he became an increasingly isolated and unpopular figure. A disgruntled homesteader murdered French in 1897 and the killer's subsequent acquittal by a jury of fellow settlers showed it was the end of the line for the big cattle barons. After the museum, there's not much else to do in Burns – and the journey on to Ontario is a real yawn, but you can leave the barren spaces behind by heading north on US-395 for the seventy-mile trip to John Day (see overleaf)

Burns **visitor centre**, 76 E Washington St (Mon–Fri 9am–5pm; ☎541/573-2636, *www.harneycounty.com*), is located just off US-20 as it doglegs its way through the centre of town. They have a useful range of local leaflets including several especially good ones describing which birds can be seen in the Malheur National Wildlife Refuge (see below). Burns is also used as a pit stop by the Greyhound **bus** linking Portland, Bend, Ontario and Boise, in Idaho; there is one bus a day, three days a week – drop-off details on ☎1-800/231-2222. As for **accommodation**, the town has a handful of modest **motels**, including the *Best Inn*, on the west edge of town at 999 Oregon Ave/US-20 (☎541/573-1700 or 1-800/237-8466, *www.bestinn.com*; ③), and, more centrally located, the straightforward *Days Inn*, 577 W Monroe St/US-20 (☎541/573-2047 or 1-800/303-2047; ②). There's a downtown **B&B** too – the very agreeable *Sage Country Inn*, in a refurbished Edwardian house at 351 W Monroe/US-20 and Court (☎541/573-7243, *www.ptinet.net/~pstick*; ④). Almost everyone thinks the family-run *Pine Room Café*, 543 W Monroe St/US-20 (Tues–Sat 5–9pm; ☎541/573-6631), is the best place to eat.

Around Burns: Malheur National Wildlife Refuge

In the middle of the high desert, beginning about twenty miles south of Burns on Hwy 205, the **Malheur National Wildlife Refuge** is centred on two landlocked lakes, Malheur and Harney, and incorporates large sections of French's old "P Ranch". The refuge is an important bird sanctuary: cranes, herons, hawks, swans, ducks and geese, among more than three hundred other species, stop off here in this giant-sized, soggy marshland during their spring and fall migrations. The refuge has a network of gravel roads, some much too treacherous without a four-wheel-drive, others suitable for ordinary vehicles – including the most important of them, the **Center Patrol Road** running north–south through the refuge for about 35 miles. There are also one or two short hiking trails, but this swampy, mosquito-infested terrain is tough going for hikers, especially under the burning sun of summer. In all cases, be sure to bring water, insect repellent and binoculars – and keep an eye on the gas as the nearest pumps are back in Burns.

To get your bearings, stop first at the refuge **visitor centre**, on the southern edge of Lake Malheur (Mon–Fri 7am–3.30pm plus most weekends in spring and summer; ☎541/493-2612 or 1-800/344-9453), which provides maps, wildlife information and advice on good vantage points. Their key, free leaflet is *Watchable Wildlife* – and this lists all the birds and the seasons they can be seen here. To get to the visitor centre from Burns, drive south on Hwy 205 from the highway 78/205 intersection for 26 miles and then take the six-mile turning east towards Princeton.

Beyond the turning for the visitor centre, Hwy 205 pushes on south, trimming the western perimeter of the refuge on its way to the end-of-the-world hamlet of **FRENCH-GLEN**, sixty miles from Burns. There's not much to the place, to put it mildly, but there is somewhere to stay – the state-park-owned *Frenchglen Hotel* (☎541/493-2825, *fghotel @ptinet.net*; ④; mid-March to mid-Nov), an attractively restored small frame house that was built as a stagecoach stopping point in 1916. The hotel has eight, frugal guestrooms with shared bathrooms and there are no TVs or telephones, but it is an extraordinarily remote spot, alive to the whispers of the desert, and reservations are well-nigh essential; dinner must be booked in advance too. Failing that, there are several **campgrounds** on the edge of the wildlife refuge – details from the visitor centre.

Frenchglen is also the starting point for the hair-raising Steens Loop Road, a 56-mile gravel track that negotiates **Steens Mountain**, a massive basaltic fault-block some 30 miles long and up to 10,000-feet high that jags high above the surrounding desert. The loop road climbs the mountain's sloping west side to reach the sheer cliff-face of the east, from where vast, craggy gorges and the hard sands of the **Alvord Desert** sweep away towards the horizon. The mountain provides the run-off needed to water the refuge down below, wet conditions that mean the loop road is only open in the summer – and even then it is not suitable for ordinary vehicles. Frenchglen's own Steens Mountain Packers (☎1-800/977-3995, *www.steensmountain.com*) organizes horseback trips into the wilderness on and around the mountain.

travel details

Buses

Bend to: Biggs (1 daily; 3hr); Burns (3 weekly; 2hr 30min); Klamath Falls (1 daily; 3hr 20min); Newport (Mon–Sat 1 daily; 5hr); Portland (2 daily; 4hr); Salem (Mon–Sat 1 daily; 2hr 40min); Seattle (1 daily; 10hr).

La Grande to: Joseph (Mon–Fri 1 daily; 2hr 20min); Wallowa Lake village (Mon–Fri 1 daily 2hr 40min).

Portland to: Baker City (3 daily; 6hr 30min); Bend (2 daily; 4hr); Biggs (3 daily; 2hr 15min); Burns (3 weekly; 6hr); Hood River (3 daily; 1hr 10min); La Grande (3 daily; 5hr 30min); Ontario (3 daily; 9hr); Pendleton (3 daily; 3hr 40min).

Pendleton to: Ellensburg, WA (1 daily; 6hr); Seattle (1 daily; 9hr); Walla Walla, WA (1 daily; 1hr).

CHAPTER THREE

SEATTLE AND WESTERN WASHINGTON

Likeable, liveable **Seattle**, the commercial and cultural capital of the state of Washington, has become one of the most fashionable destinations in the United States. The appeal of its fine Pacific Coast setting is combined with the excellence of its restaurants, the vitality of its nightlife, and its flourishing performing arts scene. All this from humble and comparatively recent origins: Seattle's first hesitant economic steps, in the 1850s, were based on the export of timber, shuttled down the coast to the burgeoning cities of California. Other primary products, especially fish, played a supporting role, and together they formed the foundations of Western Washington's first industrial boom. Nowadays the region is sustained by the latter-day high-tech companies and an ongoing economic and cultural reorientation towards the Pacific Rim.

Seattle is also the hub of a ferry system that offers glorious rides to the wood-clad hills and rolling farmland of the islands and peninsulas that pepper the sea as it stretches north towards Canada. This beautiful area is at its most beguiling among the **San Juan Islands**, a cluttered archipelago incorporating the lovely state parkland of **Orcas** and the tranquil charm of **Lopez Island**. West of Seattle, across **Puget Sound**, is the region's other star turn, the **Olympic Peninsula**, where remote, glacier-draped mountains poke up high above dense temperate rainforests, all fringed by the wild, rocky and remote Pacific Coast.

Throughout Western Washington, vast forests shelter all kinds of wildlife, remote islands scatter the sea and driftwood-strewn beaches are as untouched as when Native-Americans used them to launch whaling canoes; and, edging the region to the east, the Cascade Mountains provide a snow-capped backdrop. The catch is the weather. Despite

ACCOMMODATION PRICE CODES

All the accommodation prices in this book have been coded using the symbols below, corresponding to US dollar prices in the US chapters and equivalent Canadian dollar rates in the Canadian chapters. Prices are for the least expensive double room in high season, excluding special offers. For a full explanation see p.51 in Basics.

① up to US$30   ③ US$45–60   ⑤ US$80–100   ⑦ US$130–180
② US$30–45   ④ US$60–80   ⑥ US$100–130   ⑧ US$180+

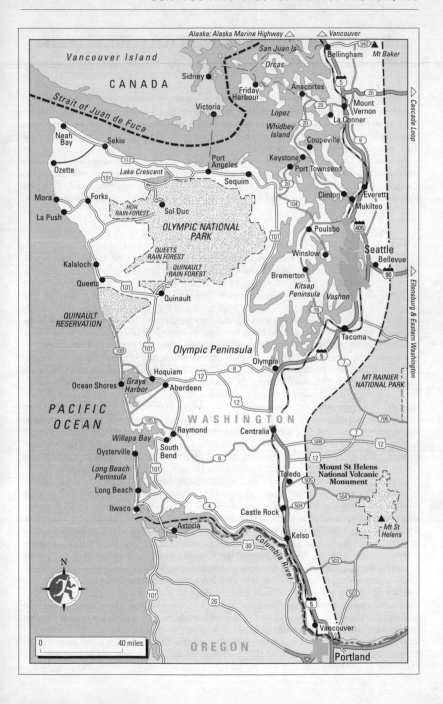

TOLL-FREE INFORMATION AND HOTEL RESERVATIONS NUMBER

Washington State Tourism Development Division: ☎1-800/544-1800, *www.tourism.wa.gov*

the sunny-side-up claims of the tourist authorities, the climate is very wet for most of the year, with just a brief respite in July and August. Don't let this put you off, though: even seen through a haze of fine grey drizzle, the scenery is incredibly beautiful, and you should try to tackle at least a few hiking trails (well laid-out, easy to follow and available in manageably short versions).

In terms of **transportation**, the remoteness of much of the region means that you'll need a car (or bike, if you've got strong legs) to get to some of the most enticing parts, though the ferries will carry you around the waterways, and Greyhound and Amtrak provide useful links between the main towns. Limited local bus services extend the network.

SEATTLE

Curved around the shore of Elliott Bay, with Lake Washington behind and the snowy peak of Mount Rainier hovering faintly in the distance, **Seattle** is beautifully set, its insistently modern skyline of shiny glass skyscrapers gleaming out across the bay, emblem of more than two decades of vigorous urban renewal. In many ways, it feels like a new city, still groping for a balance between its smart high-rises and a downbeat streetlife that reflects its tough port past. Its old central working-class areas, narrowly saved from the jaws of the bulldozer by popular outcry, have been restored as appealing historic districts, and have become a focus of urban sophistication with a strong artsy and intellectual undertow.

Considering its pre-eminent standing in the economic and cultural life of the Pacific Northwest, Seattle's **beginnings** were inauspiciously muddy. Flooded out of its first location on Alki Beach, the small logging community that was established here in the 1850s built its houses on stilts over the soggy ground of what's now the Pioneer Square historic district. The early settlement was named "Seattle" in honour of a friendly native, Chief Sealth, who helped arrange treaties in lieu of armed fighting when white arrivals began to claim some of the most desirable land. Clashes could not be staved off indefinitely, though both moniker and settlement survived the skirmishes and ambushes of the **Puget Sound War** of 1855–56, a conflict that resulted in local natives being consigned to reservations. Sealth himself was living on a reservation when he died of a heart attack in 1866.

Afterwards, as the surrounding forest was gradually felled and shipped abroad, Seattle became an expanding timber town and port with a major problem: there weren't enough women. The enterprising Asa Mercer, president (and only instructor) of the fledgling state university, took himself off East to bring back potential brides. Mercer made two trips, returning with 57 women, some of whom seem to have had a real shock: "[We were met by men] who looked like grizzlies in store clothes, their hair slicked down like sea otters", complained one. It was, however, the Klondike Gold Rush of 1897 that put Seattle firmly on the national map and boosted its shipbuilding trade. Its rise as a major Pacific Coast port sparked a simultaneous rise as a large industrial centre, one that to this day holds a significant place in US labour history. With so many residents employed in shipping and manufacturing (particularly timber), trade unions grew strong and the Industrial Workers of the World, or "Wobblies", made Seattle a main base, coordinating the country's first general strike in 1919.

World War II brought even more growth, and the decades since have seen Seattle thrive as the economic centre of the booming Pacific Northwest. After weathering a recession in the 1970s that saw Boeing lay off a large percentage of its workforce, Seattle

ROBERT HARDING

Crater Lake and Wizard Island, Oregon

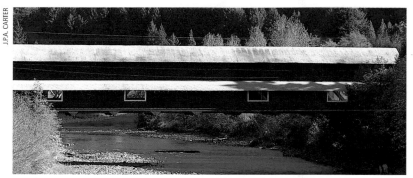

J.P.A. CARTER

A covered bridge, Oregon

M. BARLOW/TRIP

Pioneer Courthouse Square, Portland, Oregon

Crescent Beach in Ecola State Park, Oregon

Multnomah Falls, Columbia Gorge, Oregon   Hell's Canyon, Oregon

Sunset on Mt Hood, Oregon

Painted Hills, Oregon

Seattle

Native-American at Pow-wow

Pike Place Market, Seattle

Mt Rainier, Washington

The area code for Seattle is ☎206

bounced back and is today among the most prosperous cities in the US. Its thriving high-tech industries, along with increased Pacific Rim trade, have made it more resistant to downturns in the economy everywhere else. This prosperity has underpinned the development of a healthy performing arts scene, even though the grunge bands that put the city on the international music scene weren't too enamoured of all this material success. There is, however, a sharp contrast between the obvious wealth and power of Seattle's many high-tech companies – such as Boeing, the world's biggest manufacturer of aeroplanes, and Microsoft, the world leader in computer software – and the very high levels of homelessness. This obvious division of wealth, which includes Seattle's surprisingly large and visible community of teenage runaways, serves as a tangible reminder that not everyone shares in the city's good fortune. That said, these signs of poverty are confined to small pockets of the city: you may be advised to avoid some of the areas along the southwest shore of Lake Washington below US-90, but elsewhere you can enjoy the "**Emerald City**" surrounded by the trinkets of its prosperity and its coastal beauty.

Arrival

Seattle/Tacoma's **Sea-Tac Airport** is fourteen miles south of downtown; in the main terminal, there's a small **visitor's information kiosk** (summer daily 9am–7pm, winter daily 9am–6pm; ☎433-5218) in front of the baggage carousel. Outside, the Gray Line Airport Express **bus** ($8.50; pay the driver) leaves every thirty minutes (5am–11.30pm) for the 25-minute journey downtown, dropping off at major hotels. A bit further away from the terminal along the same road, the local Metro bus makes regular runs along much the same route for $1 ($1.75 peak hours) and takes only ten minutes more. Bus #194 goes into the downtown underground bus tunnel terminal, while the slower #174 runs down to 4th Avenue. Major **car rental** firms have airport branches, and operate shuttles to their pick-up points; Alamo, Avis, Budget, Hertz and National have counters in the baggage claim area and car pick-up and drop-off on the first floor of the garage across from the Main Terminal. Once you're behind the wheel, Hwy 99, the Pacific Highway, leads into town; it's also easy to get onto I-5, which might be more convenient if you're going to a neighbourhood other than downtown. You can also pick up a car downtown – see "Listings", p.213, for details.

Arriving **by car**, you'll probably come in on **I-5**, the main north–south highway between the Canadian border and California; for downtown, take the Stewart Street or Union Street exits. The **Amtrak** station at 3rd Avenue and Jackson Street (☎382-4125 or 1-800/872-7245), south of downtown near the International District, and the **Greyhound** station, at 8th Avenue and Stewart Street (☎628-5526 or 1-800/231-2222), east of downtown, are both a bus ride from downtown accommodation. **Green Tortoise**, with two runs per week to and from Portland and San Francisco, drops off and picks up at 9th Avenue and Stewart Street (☎1-800/867-8647).

Local Puget Sound **ferries** arrive at Pier 52 on downtown's waterfront, with a couple of passenger-only routes using Pier 50; long-distance services from British Columbia dock at Pier 69.

Information

The **Seattle-King County Visitor's Bureau**, inside the Washington State Convention Center at 7th Avenue and Pike Street (year-round Mon–Fri 8.30am–5pm, Apr–Oct also

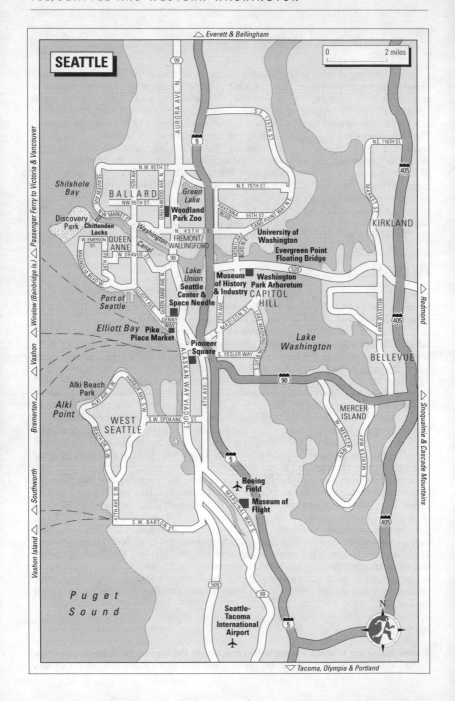

Sat 10am–4pm, June–Aug also Sun 10am–4pm; ☎461-5840, *www.seaseattle.org*), has racks of brochures on Seattle and Washington State, plus handy free maps and local bus timetables. From June through September, an additional branch operates daily from 10am to 6pm in Pioneer Square at Occidental and S Main Street. The free official travellers' guide, *Washington State Lodging and Travel Guide* (call the Washington State Tourism Development Division at ☎1-800/544-1800 for a copy) provides a comprehensive list of the state's accommodations.

Orientation and transportation

Getting around Seattle's downtown area is best done on foot or by taking advantage of the free **bus** services between 6am and 7pm within the central downtown free zone (some of which run underground along 3rd Ave). Cross out of the free zone – to the University District for example – and you pay the driver as you get off; come back in and you pay as you enter. Single fares are between $1 and $1.75, depending on the zone and time of day; tickets are valid for an hour or more (varies, check expiration on transfer). **Day passes** are a good deal at $2, but they're only valid during weekends and holidays; buy them from the driver. Ticketbooks are sold throughout the city, but they only save you time, not money, the price being equivalent to the same you'd pay for ten rides or twenty rides on the bus itself. They're on sale at most Bartell Drug stores and at the Metro **Customer Service Offices**, in the King Street Center at 201 S Jackson St (Mon–Fri 8am–5pm) and the Transit Tunnel, Westlake Station, 5th Avenue and Pine Street (Mon–Fri 9am–5.30pm). Both also have information and timetables (☎553-3000 for 24hr information).

Largely of novelty value, a mile-long **monorail** ($1.25 each way) runs overhead on thin concrete stilts from the Westlake Shopping Center Mall at 5th Avenue and Pine Street to the Seattle Center, while vintage **streetcars** (part of the Metro – fares $1 to $1.75) travel up and down the waterfront, from Pier 70 through Pioneer Square to the edge of the International District.

Accommodation

There's no shortage of hotel space in Seattle, but it can be difficult to find the middle ground between expense-account-type places – some of which are superb – and the seedy dives of the down-and-out. The standard-issue **motels** lining the highways on the outskirts of town are reliable, if predictable, but you'll get more of a feel for Seattle by staying at a **B&B**. Mostly homey and comfortable, these lie scattered amongst the city's neighbourhoods, with a concentration in the **Capitol Hill** district on the northeast edge of downtown. Most B&Bs take reservations direct, but others use an agency who will require a deposit (credit cards will do) with your booking, which should be made well in advance: try A Pacific Reservation Service, PO Box 46894, Seattle, WA 98146 (☎439-7677 or 1-800/684-2932, *www.seattlebedandbreakfast.com*), which has a list of guest homes available for $5; A Travellers' Reservation Service, 14716 26th Ave NE, Seattle, WA 98155 (☎364-5900, *www.atravellersres.com*); and the Washington Bed and Breakfast Guild, 2442 NW Market St #355, Seattle, WA 98107 (☎1-800/647-2918, *www.wbbg.com*). All three of the B&B booking-services rent places throughout the state as well.

Budget travellers are in for a treat at the **Seattle International Hostel** on the waterfront, but otherwise low-price, downtown accommodation is usually grim and occasionally risky. Fortunately, Seattle's **hostel** options have improved considerably over the last few years, with the addition of a large Green Tortoise facility a block from Pike Place Market, as well as *Bigfoot Backpackers Hostel* in Capitol Hill. If you want to **camp**, try *Fay Bainbridge State Park* (☎842-3931, *www.parks.wa.gov/faybain*; $12 standard sites, $6 primitive sites) at the northeast end of Bainbridge Island (see p.215), where there are a handful of basic sites.

Hotels and motels

Ace Hotel 2423 1st Ave at Wall St (☎448-4721, *www.theacehotel.com*). Slightly arty, modern rooms in a new hotel, above the *Cyclops* restaurant, in the heart of Belltown. Hardwood floors, lofty ceilings, and a sink and vanity in each of the 34 rooms. Bathrooms are all shared, unless you get one of the master suites, which are much more expensive. ⑤.

Alexis Hotel, 1007 1st Ave at Madison St (☎624-4844 or 1-800/426-7033, *www.alexishotel.com*). Medium-sized hotel downtown near the waterfront, with the refined *Bookstore Bar & Cafe* in the lobby. All the luxuries, from jacuzzis to real wood-burning fireplaces, but no views from this tastefully restored early twentieth-century building. ⑧.

Commodore 2013 2nd Ave between Virginia and Lenora sts (☎448-8868, *www.commodorehotel .com*). On the border between Belltown and downtown, this functional and secure hotel has rooms that are hardly uplifting. It also has eight hostel beds ($14), but that alternative should only be employed if the far superior nearby downtown hostels are full. ①–③.

The Edgewater Inn, Pier 67 at Wall St and Alaskan Way (☎728-7000 or 1-800/624-0670, *www.noble-househotels.com/edgewater*). Seattle's only waterfront hotel is a treat, but rates soar if you want a room overlooking Puget Sound. It's mostly the location that you're paying for, but the rooms (all of which have fireplaces) are pleasant and there are some nice extras, like complimentary use of bicycles and free use of athletic facilities. ⑦.

Inn at Harbor Steps, 1221 1st Ave at University St (☎748-0793 or 1-888/728-8910, *www.foursisters .com*). Upscale accommodations in a new 20-room hotel, a very short walk from both Pike Place Market and the art museum. Each room has a fireplace, refrigerator with complimentary beverages, and a balcony overlooking an interior garden courtyard. ⑦.

The Inn at Queen Anne, 505 1st Ave N at N Republican St (☎282-7357 or 1-800/952-5043, *www.innatqueenanne.com*). Small but comfortable studio apartment-style lodgings on the edge of Seattle Center, with queen-sized beds and kitchenettes. ⑤.

Moore Hotel, 1926 2nd Ave at Virginia St (☎448-4851 or 1-800/421-5508). A stone's throw from Pike Place Market, this basic hotel is close to Belltown's bars and cafés, but is also on a block peopled with somewhat unsettling street characters at night. ③.

Motel 6, 18900 S 47th Ave at S 189th St (☎241-1648 or 1-800/466-8356, *www.motel6.com*). The lowest prices of the nationally known motels, but it is some distance out of town near the airport; Exit 152 from I-5. ③.

Pacific Plaza, 400 Spring St at 4th Ave (☎623-3900 or 1-800/426-1165, *www.pacificplazahotel.com*). Renovated 1920s hotel, with simple doubles, halfway between Pike Place Market and Pioneer Square. ⑥.

Pioneer Square Hotel, 77 Yesler Way between 1st Ave and Alaskan Way (☎340-1234 or 1-800/800-5514, *www.pioneersquare.com*). A restored c.1900 brick hotel, originally built by Seattle founding father Henry Yesler. The best (if not the only) choice in Pioneer Square for mid-price hotel accommodation with a good level of comfort, and a saloon and juice bar on the lobby floor. ⑤.

Renaissance Madison Hotel, 515 Madison St at 6th Ave (☎583-0300 or 1-800/468-3571, *www.renaissancehotels.com*). Massive, luxurious hotel at the southeast edge of downtown. ⑧.

St Regis Hotel, 116 Stewart St at 2nd Ave (☎448-6366). Scruffy but centrally located hotel across the street from the Pike Place Market. It's a risky area at night, but fine during the day. Very basic doubles. ②.

Hotel Seattle, 315 Seneca St between 3rd and 4th aves (☎623-5110 or 1-800/623-5110). Modern, downtown hotel, with reasonably priced doubles. ⑤.

Seattle Inn, 225 Aurora Ave N between N John and N Thomas sts (☎728-7666, *www.seattleinn.com*). Accommodation a few blocks east of Seattle Center that compensates for its lack of personality and the nearby Hwy 99 traffic with free parking and free rates for children under 16 staying in their parents' room. ③.

Super 8 Motel, 3100 S 192nd St between International Blvd and 32nd Ave S (☎433-8188 or 1-800/ 800-8000, *www.super8.com*). Standard motel doubles out near the airport. ④.

University Inn, 4140 Roosevelt Way NE at NE 42nd St (☎632-5055 or 1-800/733-3855, *www.universityinn* *.com*). Average modern hotel one block from University Way, but convenient if you need to be near the University of Washington campus; some rooms have kitchens. ⑤.

Woodmark Hotel, 1200 Carillon Point, Kirkland (☎822-3700 or 1-800/822-3700, *www.thewoodmark* *.com*). Located in the wealthy suburb of Kirkland, seven miles east of downtown on the shores of Lake Washington, this splendid modern hotel is the height of luxury, but it's only worth the price if you're in one of the lakeside rooms (or suites). ⑧.

B&Bs

Chambered Nautilus, 5005 22nd Ave NE at NE 50th St (☎522-2536 or 1-800/545-8459, *www* *.chamberednautilus.com*). Early twentieth-century Georgian home with six rooms, four of which have porches; apple quiches are the breakfast speciality. Reservations a month or two ahead of time are advisable in the summer months. ⑤.

Chelsea Station On the Park, 4915 N Linden Ave between N 49th St and N 50th St (☎547-6077). Opposite the south entrance of Woodland Park Zoo, northwest of downtown across Lake Union. Good-quality doubles, with king-size beds. ⑤.

College Inn, 4000 NE University Way at NE 40th St in the U District (☎633-4441, *www.speakeasy* *.org/collegeinn*). Very popular, basic B&B above its own restaurant (rates include full breakfast) and bar. A students' and backpackers' favourite. ④.

Dibble House, 7301 Dibble Ave NW at NW 73rd St (☎783-0320). In Ballard, and thus a little more out of the way than the Capitol Hill B&Bs, but with cheaper rates for their one double and two twins. ③.

Gaslight Inn, 1727 15th Ave at Howell St (☎325-3654, *www.gaslight-inn.com*). Capitol Hill landmark home converted into attractive B&B, with its own swimming pool. Nine rooms, as well as large common areas and more expensive suites for longer-term accommodation. ⑤.

Green Gables Guesthouse, 1503 2nd Ave W at W Galer St (☎282-6863 or 1-800/400-1503, *www.greengablesseattle.com*). Refurbished c.1900 villa near Seattle Center. Seven, rather twee, rooms but the food is a delicious compensation. ④.

Mildred's, 1202 15th Ave E at E Highland Drive (☎325-6072, *www.mildredsbnb.com*). Three rooms – a Green Room with southern and eastern exposure, a Blue Room with a sitting alcove, and a Lace Room with a skylight in the bath – in an 1890 Victorian with a wrapround porch near Volunteer Park. ⑤.

Pensione Nichols, 1923 1st Ave between Stewart and Virginia sts (☎441-7125). Downtown B&B that could hardly be more centrally located, though it's on a noisy street. The ten or so rooms are comfortable, if small. ⑤.

Prince of Wales, 133 13th Ave E at E John St (☎325-9692 or 1-800/327-9692, *www.princebedandbreakfast* *.com*). More automobile traffic passes by here than at most other Capitol Hill B&Bs, but the rooms are good, with views of the Space Needle and Puget Sound, and the front porch swing is a nice bonus. Minimum two-day stay. ⑤.

Salisbury House, 750 16th Ave E at Aloha St (☎328-8682, *www.salisburyhouse.com*). There are four doubles in this grand maple-floored, high-ceilinged 1904 Capitol Hill mansion at a quiet yet convenient location. Ask for the "Blue Room" if you want morning sun, or the "Lavender Room" if you want the biggest space. ⑤.

Hostels

Bigfoot Backpackers Hostel, 126 Broadway Ave E between E Olive Way and E Denny St (☎720-2965 or 1-800/600-2965). Near the heart of Capitol Hill, and a good choice if you don't want a downtown base. Forty-five beds include four-to-a-room dorms ($15–17) and a few private rooms ($30–35 single, $40–45 double). No curfew and lots of extras: free breakfast, downtown pick-up, Internet access and parking. It also runs a tour of the graves of Jimi Hendrix and, nearby in Capitol Hill's Lakeview Cemetery, Bruce and Brandon Lee that also stops at Kurt Cobain's former house. ①–②.

Green Tortoise, 1525 2nd Ave between Pike and Pine sts (☎340-1222 or 1-888/424-6783, *www.greentortoise.net*). The best budget downtown deal for those who find the AYH hostel too institutional, this has old-style hotel digs now functioning as four-to-the-room dorms ($16), as well as some singles and doubles in a higher price range. It offers free Internet access, and does pick-ups from downtown. ①–②.

Hostelling International Seattle (AYH), 84 Union St between 1st and Western aves (☎622-5443 or 1-888/622-5443, *www.hiseattle.org*). Location-wise this is hard to beat, just a block from Pike Place Market and a couple from the waterfront, with Pioneer Square only a few minutes away. Modern, comfortable dorms ($16–18, add $3 for non-members), open 24hr. There are about two hundred beds, but reservations are still advisable during June to September. Free pick-up from bus and train stations. ①.

Vashon Island Hostel (AYH), 12119 SW Cove Rd, Vashon Island (just past 121st Ave) (☎463-2592, *www.vashonhostel.com*). Vashon Island's a half-hour away from downtown Seattle by ferry, but there is free pick-up from the ferry terminal. The excellent facilities include dorm beds ($10 members, $13 non-members) in a log cabin and tepees for couples and families. Open May to Oct; free bikes available for guests. ①–②.

YWCA, 1118 5th Ave at Spring St (☎461-4888). For women only. Large clean rooms with or without private bath. The ambience is more functional than colourful, but it's safe and clean, in a central downtown location, and a reasonable alternative for women visitors on a budget. Twenty-one rooms in all. ②.

The City

The **downtown** core of **Seattle** would be a predictable collection of tall office blocks and department stores were it not for two enclaves of colour and character: **Pike Place Market**, a busy, crowded morass of stalls and cafés, and **Pioneer Square**, a small old-town area of restored red-brick buildings, lined with taverns. The fabulous views over Elliott Bay, too, help to lighten the feel – best gawped at from along **the waterfront**, despite its clutter of tourist shops.

From downtown, you can ride the monorail north to the **Seattle Center**, where the futuristic, flying-saucer-topped tower of the **Space Needle** presides over an assortment of theatres, museums and the opera house. To the south is the small Southeast Asian-dominated **International District** and just to the south again is the new **Safeco Field** baseball stadium, which has replaced the enclosed **Kingdome**, much to the relief of sports fans. Another modern stadium, for the town's football team, is currently under construction in the same area, and scheduled to open in time for 2002 season. Further south still, the huge **Museum of Flight** charts the development of air travel from Icarus on.

A couple of outlying districts tend to be livelier than downtown: **Capitol Hill** has cafés and bars which form the heart of the city's gay scene (and holds some of the best city parks); and the **University District** is, as you would expect, a students' district of cheap cafés with some uptempo nightlife. Some less well-known neighbourhoods north of downtown are well worth the bus ride: Ballard's **Hiram M. Chittenden Locks** is the gateway for ships of all sizes between Lake Washington and Puget Sound, **Fremont** is a bohemian enclave highlighted by excellent public artwork, and **Magnolia** holds **Discovery Park**, one of the best expanses of urban greenery in the US.

Pike Place Market and the Waterfront

Pike Place Market (Mon–Sat 10am–6pm, Sun 11am–5pm, open every day except New Year's, Easter, Thanksgiving and Christmas; *www.pikeplacemarket.org*), at the bottom of Pike Street, is rightly downtown Seattle's biggest attraction. Buskers and street entertainers play to busy crowds, smells of coffee drift from the cafés, and stalls are piled high with lobsters, crabs, salmon, vegetables and fruit. Further into the long market building, craft stalls sell handmade jewellery, woodcarvings and silk-screen prints, while small shops stock a massive range of ethnic foods.

It's actually a miracle Pike Place Market exists at all. Established in 1907 as a way for local farmers to sell their products directly to the city's consumers, it was slated for

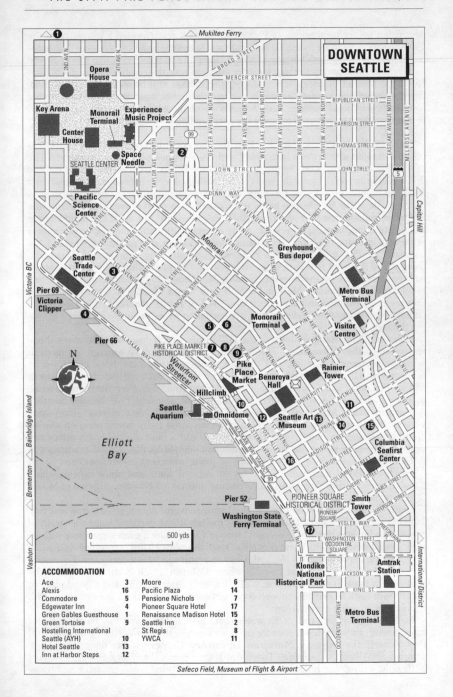

△ Mukilteo Ferry

DOWNTOWN SEATTLE

ACCOMMODATION

Ace	3	Moore	6
Alexis	16	Pacific Plaza	14
Commodore	5	Pensione Nichols	7
Edgewater Inn	4	Pioneer Square Hotel	17
Green Gables Guesthouse	1	Renaissance Madison Hotel	15
Green Tortoise	9	Seattle Inn	2
Hostelling International		St Regis	8
Seattle (AYH)	10	YWCA	11
Hotel Seattle	13		
Inn at Harbor Steps	12		

△ Safeco Field, Museum of Flight & Airport ▽

demolition before local architect Victor Steinbrueck spearheaded a campaign in the 1960s to save it, both for its c.1900 buildings and to ensure that lower-income Seattleites had a place to buy affordable provisions. A "Keep the Market" initiative was approved by voters in 1971, paving the way for its restoration with the establishment of a Market Historical District in 1974. Now restored, the market still provides low-priced food, thereby preserving its roots – though, perhaps inevitably, upscale restaurants catering to tourists and local yuppies have recently crept in, while the porno theatres and teenage prostitutes that used to haunt the surrounding neighbourhood have all but disappeared.

Early weekday mornings are the best time to go to the market, as the premises become choked with crowds by midday, and claustrophobically so on weekends. The best action centres around the ground level of the **Main Arcade** (just to the right of the brass pig as you're facing the waterfront), with its dozens of produce stalls and their frank-but-friendly proprietors, hawking their orchard-squeezed fruit juice or fresh blueberries. The Main Arcade also holds the market's two most popular restaurants (the *Athenian Inn* and *Lowell's*) which overlook Puget Sound. But all of the buildings are worth exploring, housing an eclectic array of establishments including Seattle's most prominent left-wing bookshop (Left Bank Books), a huge international news-stand, the popular *Pike Pub & Brewery*, and a cheeky outfit stocking condoms of all colours, designs and flavours. Sub Pop Records, famous for its promotion of the grunge scene with early releases by the likes of Nirvana, Mudhoney and Soundgarden, has a tiny retail store in the Sanitary Market, the **Sub Pop Mega Mart**, which mostly sells Sub Pop records and memorabilia; check the "Wall of Fame" display to the side of the counter for snapshots of underground heroes, taken while the musicians were browsing through the store.

Stairs in the market lead down to the **Hillclimb**, which descends past more shops and cafés to the **Waterfront**. The harbour's no longer deep enough for modern ocean-going merchant ships, and the old wooden jetties have been colonized by tourism – with the port's real business going on further out from the city, to the north and south along Puget Sound. Almost opposite the Hillclimb, **Pier 59** is one of a line of old wooden jetties which once served the tall ships; it now houses Seattle's **Aquarium** (daily Memorial Day–Labor Day 10am–7pm; rest of year 10am–5pm; *www.seattleaquarium.org*; $8.50), which provides some lively information on marine life in the Sound, an underwater viewing dome and a pool of playful sea otters and seals. A combined ticket (for the Aquarium and one IMAX film $14) also admits you to **Omnidome** next door (daily starting at 10am; *www.seattleimaxdome.com*; $7, $2 for each additional film; call ☎622-1868 for current films and show times), which shows films featuring clever visuals, or natural dramas such as the eruption of Mount St Helens (see p.265).

South of Pier 59, the waterfront is lined with souvenir shops, restaurants and fish-and-chip stands. The most famous stand – though it has declined since the death of owner-founder Ivar Haglund – is *Ivar's Acres of Clams*, which comes complete with its own special stop ("Clam Central Station") on the **waterfront streetcar** ($1, $1.75 peak), which carries tourists along the bay in restored vintage carriages. The waterfront gets back to business at Pier 52, where **Colman Dock** is the terminal for the Washington State Ferries (see box, p.214, for ferry information), and a good place to watch them dock or depart – though it can get somewhat frantic in the rush hour with commuters crossing over the bay.

Back up the northern part of the waterfront, the platform above Pier 66 offers better baywatching, with free telescopes for up-close views of the ships cruising the water. At Pier 66 itself, the **Odyssey Maritime Discovery Center** (winter daily 10am–5pm; summer Sun–Wed 10am–9pm & Thurs–Sat 10am–5pm; *www.ody.org*; $6.50) is for port buffs only, with gaudy interactive exhibits on Puget Sound trade, industry and transport, including working models of shipping boats and a computer game that lets you play crane operator. At the northern end of the waterfront, **Myrtle Edwards Park** begins a bit north of the last streetcar stop and extends well past the downtown boundaries, with bike and pedestrian paths winding along the shore for a couple of miles and continuing through the adjoining Elliott Bay Park before terminating near the Magnolia Bridge. The park is a fine spot for watching the Sound and the downtown skyscrapers from a distance, especially at sunset.

Seattle Art Museum

Close to Pike Place Market along 1st Avenue, the **Seattle Art Museum** (Tues–Sun 10am–5pm, Thurs until 9pm; *www.seattleartmuseum.org*; $7, free first Thurs of the month) houses a mixture of modern art and more ancient pieces from around the globe. While the exhibits are solidly assembled and presented, it doesn't rank as one of the nation's top modern art collections, due in part to the relatively limited gallery space; indeed, what you see in the twentieth-century galleries represents only selected highlights of the museum's collection. One piece of art you can always count on being on hand is Jonathan Borofsky's 48-foot *Hammering Man* kinetic sculpture, which flails away outside the front door of the limestone- and terracotta-faced building.

Inside the four-storey building, a grand staircase leads from the lobby to the upper galleries, under the watchful eye of Chinese sculptures of camels, rams and guards. The second level is given over to temporary exhibitions and the third – and most diverting – boasts an eclectic collection of African, Asian, Oceanian, Levantine and Native-American pieces: highlights include extraordinary masks and fetishes from Guinea and the Congo, and, from the Pacific Northwest, rattles and clappers, gargoyle-like wooden pipes, canoes, prow ornaments, more dancing masks and several enormous totem poles from British Columbia. The fourth floor traces the development of art in Europe and the United States, beginning with a handful of ancient Mediterranean artefacts, but the modern stuff is more eye-catching, with a large section devoted to Northwest artists. Elsewhere on the floor are works from the permanent collection by modern artists from all over the world; look out for the elemental *Coloured Shouting* by Gilbert and George, with a script that reads "The decadent artists stand for themselves and their chosen few. . . a crude denial of the life of the people".

The museum also holds a full schedule of concerts, films, lectures and other special programmes, detailed in the quarterly programme guides available in the lobby; the fine-art bookshop just inside the entrance offers quality browsing as well. When done visiting, save your ticket stubs as they are good for a free visit to the **Seattle Asian Art Museum** (in Volunteer Park, several miles away on Capitol Hill; see p.196) if used within a week.

Pioneer Square and around

A few blocks inland from the ferry terminal lies **Pioneer Square** (actually an area of a few blocks focusing on 1st Ave and Yesler Way) – Seattle's oldest section and another spot that had a close brush with the demolition balls of the 1960s. The restoration work is glossier here than at Pike Place Market, and the square's old red brick and black wrought iron bear the unmistakeable hallmark of a well-tended historic district, with bookshops and galleries adding a veneer of sophistication. At night, rock music spills out from a group of lively taverns (see "Nightlife", p.207), but by day there's little evidence of the more rambunctious aspects of the city's past. It was here in the mid-1800s that Henry Yesler erected the Puget Sound's first steam-powered sawmill, felling trees at the top of a nearby hill and rolling the logs down what's now Yesler Way, then known as the "skid road". Drunks and down-and-outs gathered here in the later years of the Depression and the term "skid row" passed into its present usage – or at least that's Seattle's version.

The whole district was razed in 1889 when a pot of boiling glue turned over in a basement paint and carpentry shop and set the wooden buildings and streets ablaze. Rebuilding, the city resolved an unsavoury problem with the sewage system (which had a nasty habit of flowing in reverse when the tide was high in the bay) by raising the level of the land, and entrances to the surviving brick buildings now came in at the old second-storey level. The ground floors, now below the earth and connected by underground passages, were legally closed in 1907, yet the literal underworld was soon a prime location for illicit activities such as drinking during Prohibition. These passages were reopened in the 1960s, and can be explored on the ninety-minute **Underground Tours** which leave roughly once an hour (late morning to mid-afternoon) from *Doc Maynard's* tavern, 610 1st Ave (call ☎682-4646 or (non-local) 1-888/608-6337 for times and reservations, *www.undergroundtour.com*; $8) – by far the most amusing way to find out about Seattle's seamy past, with witty guides taking an offbeat look at the city's history before leading you underground.

A couple of blocks south from *Doc Maynard's*, at 117 S Main St, the **Klondike Gold Rush National Park** (daily 9am–5pm; free) is not a park at all, but a small museum where free films and a few artefacts portray the 1897 rush which followed the discovery of gold in the Klondike region of Canada (see p.606). As soon as the first ship carrying Klondike gold docked in the city, Seattle's sharp-eyed capitalists espied massive trading potential in selling groceries, clothing, sledges and even ships to the gold-seekers, and launched a formidable publicity campaign, bombarding inland cities with propaganda billing Seattle above all other ports as the gateway to Yukon gold. It worked: prospectors streamed in, merchants (and con men) scented easy profit, the population escalated and traders made a fortune. The dog population fared less well, as many a hapless mutt was harnessed to a sledge while gold-seekers practised "mushing" up and down Seattle's streets before facing Yukon snow. The museum staff will run a few short documentary films on request, the best overview being the half-hour *Days of Adventure, Dreams of Gold*; between mid-June and the first week of September, the park rangers give free tours of Pioneer Square daily at 10am.

Almost opposite the museum, the large cobblestoned square of **Occidental Park** – with its offputting groups of the drunk and destitute – displays four totem poles carved with the grotesque, almost cruel, features of creatures from Northwest Native American legends. South of the park, the pedestrian-only block of Occidental Avenue between Main and Jackson holds many of Seattle's most prominent **galleries**. The best of these is the Foster/White Gallery at 123 S Jackson St (corner of Occidental and Jackson), which showcases contemporary artists from the Northwest working in a variety of media; nearby at the Glasshouse Studio gallery at 311 Occidental S, you can watch glass artists at work.

On the first Thursday evening of every month, dozens of Pioneer Square art galleries hold simultaneous openings (sometimes offering free wine) between 6pm and 8pm for **Gallery Walk**. Map guides to Gallery Walk can be found in the free *Art Access* publication, available at most museums and tourist infocentres.

The business district

At the corner of Yesler Way and 2nd Avenue, Seattle's first skyscraper, the white terracotta-trimmed **Smith Tower**, edges the city's financial district. Built in 1914 by the New York typewriter mogul, L.C. Smith, the 42-floor tower was long the tallest building west of the Mississippi. Today it mostly holds private offices, but if you're passing it's worth looking in on the elegant lobby, decked out with marble and carved Native-American busts. Restored brass-lined elevators serve an observation deck at the top, although it's often closed to the public.

To the north, the prestigious glassy office blocks of the business district loom over the Smith Tower – not on the whole an inviting sight, although the **Rainier Tower**, balanced on a narrow pedestal at 4th Avenue and University, and the dark, 76-storey **Columbia Center**, at 4th Avenue and Columbia Street, the tallest of the towers (and aptly nicknamed the "Darth Vader building" or "the box the Space Needle came in"), have passing interest as engineering feats. More aesthetically pleasing is the recently completed **Benaroya Hall**, home of the **Seattle Symphony**, which occupies an entire square city block bounded by Union and University streets north–south, and 3rd and 2nd avenues east–west (public entrance on 3rd St). Inside, a huge curving window in the Grand Lobby affords views of Elliott Bay, and on-site art includes a mural above the main auditorium entrance by Robert Rauschenberg and chandeliers by well-known Northwest glass artist Dale Chihuly. The symphony gave its first performance here in 1998, and the space has already attracted praise for having some of the finest acoustics of any orchestral hall in the world; there are free tours Mon–Fri at noon and 1pm (meet in front of Grand Lobby entrance in the Boeing Company Gallery).

The heart of the commercial centre is the diagonal **Westlake Park** on 4th Avenue between Pike Street and Pine Street, which hosts occasional lunchtime concerts near its water-wall fountain. There are a few fancy stores around (Nordstrom and Eddie Bauer have their flagship stores here), but the shopping centres aren't worth getting excited about, though **City Center** at 5th Avenue and Union Street has good glass art on display on the second floor. Rainier Square at 4th Avenue and Union Street merits a visit, not for the stores, but for the **Seattle Architectural Foundation**'s relatively unknown gallery exhibit on Level 3, Blueprints: 100 Years of Seattle Architecture (Tues–Fri 10am–4pm; free), a comprehensive display with detailed text and numerous vintage Seattle photos. The foundation also offers architectural walking tours (pick up a brochure at the gallery or call ☎667-9186, *www.seattlearchitectural.org*) during the warmer months, either during weekday lunch hours ($8) or on three-hour Saturday morning excursions ($18).

Chinatown (The International District)

A few blocks south of Pioneer Square, your way is blocked by construction of a new stadium for Seattle's football team. A block or so south of that, **Safeco Field** (tours given most days for $7; call ☎622-HITS for times and tickets) draws enthusiastic crowds to one of the nation's best baseball parks, topped by a retractable dome. Both of these stadiums are in the zone once occupied by the much-loathed **Kingdome**, levelled, to the collective relief of locals, in March 2000.

The stadium area's spread of parking lots seems to signal an end to the downtown area, but pushing on east up S Jackson Street, past the red-brick clock tower of the old railway station, the concrete expanses soon give way to the build-up of restaurants and ethnic grocers of Seattle's **Chinatown** – officially (and blandly) labelled the **International District** due to the presence of other Far Eastern groups. Aside from some good restaurants, it's a run-down and rather scrappy neighbourhood, its tawdry blocks dotted with streetpeople and few actual sights.

Seattle's Chinatown hasn't always been so desolate. In the nineteenth century this was an overcrowded and unruly district, its boarding houses crammed with young Chinese men who'd come over to earn money in the city's mills and canneries. Suspicion of the area's gambling halls and opium dens overflowed into racial hatred during a depression in the 1880s: federal laws debarred the Chinese from full citizenship and throughout the Northwest, Chinese workers were attacked, threatened and their homes burned. The Seattle authorities did eventually rake up an armed guard which made a belated and botched attempt to prevent mobs expelling the entire community (as happened in Tacoma), but most Chinese left anyway, leaving behind a depleted and scarred population. Later influxes of Japanese, Filipino, Korean and Thai immigrants, and more recently Vietnamese, Laotian and Cambodian newcomers, has restored a trace of the district's nineteenth-century vigour, but Chinatown continues to be regarded locally with some trepidation – partly due to increasing gang activity. In reality the area is more shabby than unsafe, though it is best to take care after dark. The focus of the district, in so far as it has one, is **Hing Hay Park** at Maynard and S King Street, where an ornate oriental gateway stands beneath a large and rather faded dragon mural. The most absorbing attraction in the area is the little **Wing Luke Asian Museum** at 407 7th Ave and Jackson Street (Tues–Fri 11am–4.30pm, Sat–Sun noon–4pm; *www.wingluke.org*; $2.50, free Thurs), which goes some way to explaining local Asian-American history, with reference to the career of Wing Luke, the first Chinese-American to be elected to public office in Seattle, in 1962. Also worth a look is the huge Asian supermarket-cum-variety store **Uwajimaya** at 519 6th Ave, with plenty of foods that you'll never find at Safeway.

The Museum of Flight

The best and biggest of Seattle's museums, the **Museum of Flight**, 9404 E Marginal Way (10am–5pm daily, Thurs till 9pm, *www.museumofflight.org*; $9.50), more than makes up for the twenty-minute bus ride (#174) south from downtown through the port's dreary industrial hinterland. As the birthplace of the Boeing company, Seattle has its own stake in aviation history, and has invested heavily in this huge museum, partly housed in the 1909 "Red Barn" that was Boeing's original manufacturing plant. The displays, accompanied by detailed information plaques and several film programmes, take in everything from the dreams of the ancients, through the work of the Wright brothers, with a working model of the wind tunnel they used, to the growth of Boeing itself, with part of the Red Barn laid out as an early designer's workshop. The free regular **tours** are sometimes given by ex-Boeing employees who always add some knowledgeable insight that can't be easily gleaned from merely gazing at the planes and models. The best bit of the museum is the huge glass-and-steel Great Gallery, big as a football field and hung with more than fifty full-sized aircraft, including tiny, fragile-looking mail planes and a red sportscar that can apparently be given wings in minutes. There's also a replica of the *Mercury* space capsule that took John Glenn into space in 1962.

Southwest to Alki Beach

Southwest of downtown, on the other side of Elliott Bay (take bus #37 from downtown), the flat little peninsula of **Alki Point** is where Seattle's founders first tried to settle when they weighed anchor in the Puget Sound, optimistically christening their community "New York Alki" – New York "by and by" in the Chinook language. Defeated by floods and the lack of space, the town soon shifted over to what's now Pioneer Square and changed its name to Seattle. Now a residential district, the peninsula's interesting only if you want to join the promenaders and cyclists along the narrow strip of **Alki Beach**, which offers pleasing views of Elliott Bay with the city skyline behind and the Olympic Mountains to the west.

If you're out this way in a car, it's worth taking a few extra minutes to follow Alki Avenue as it curves south around Alki Point and turns into **Beach Drive**. The scenic coastal route offers views of Puget Sound and the Olympic Mountains before hitting **Lincoln Park** a few miles south, where wooded cliffside trails lead down to a narrow beach with a paved promenade, picnic tables and the **Colman Pool**. This heated outdoor saltwater swimming pool at the beach's edge is a big favourite with families, though it's only open from mid-June to the end of August (daily; $2.50; call ☎684-7494 for hours).

Belltown

As you head north from Pike Place Market, downtown peters out around Virginia Street, beyond which lies a district once occupied by Denny Hill and now flattened into the **Denny Regrade**. Considering the momentous effort that went into knocking the hill down to create more space, it's a shame that nothing interesting has been built here – though the area around Bell Street, known as **Belltown**, has some character, its tough taverns now rubbing shoulders with upmarket cafés.

The core of Belltown is the five-block area of 2nd Avenue between Stewart and Battery, choked with vintage-clothing outlets, used or indie record stores, offbeat galleries, and other establishments that cater to Seattle's large student and artist communities; these are the reasons to come here, not really for any sights per se. **Crocodile Café** on 2200 2nd Ave is the hottest alternative rock joint in the neighbourhood, presenting both unknowns and underground rock royalty in its cramped back rooms; the **Speakeasy Café** at 2304 2nd Ave and the combination laundromat/café/performance space **Sit & Spin** at 2219 4th Ave are two of Seattle's definitive multipurpose cafés (see listings on p.207). One block over, on 1st Avenue between Lenora and Vine, there's been a big build-up of chic eateries and even a couple of hotels, making this Belltown's most upscale stretch.

Closer to the waterfront at 65 Cedar St, the **Center on Contemporary Art** (Tues–Sat 11am–6pm; *www.cocaseattle.org*; $5) gives its small space over to constantly rotating exhibits of work that's more avant garde than what you'll see in the Seattle Art Museum's contemporary galleries. Nam June Paik, Survival Research Laboratories and Lydia Lunch are some of the artists who received their first major exposure in the Northwest via CoCa exhibits. Recently the gallery held an exhibit of UFO-related work, in conjunction with the 50th anniversary of the first flying saucer sighting. Art of an even more unconventional nature is on view at the **Streetlife Art Gallery** at 2301 2nd Ave (daily 11am–8pm), which shows work by artists who are, or have been, homeless, and encourages visitors to both browse and talk with the artists, who are usually working in the space itself.

The Seattle Center

The Denny Regrade is best viewed from the window of the **monorail**, which runs from the Westlake Shopping Mall at 5th Avenue and Pine Street downtown ($1.25 one way), crosses the area on concrete supports, and ends up inside the **Seattle Center** (*www.seattlecenter.com*). The Seattle Center is an inheritance from the 1962 World's Fair, whose theme was "Century 21" (hence the idea of the spindly Space Needle tower, the fair's – and now Seattle's – adopted symbol). Since then the site of the fair has become a sort of culture-park, collecting the city's symphony, ballet and opera, a couple of theatres, museums and a small amusement park.

The monorail drops you close to the **Space Needle** (observation deck open summer daily 8am–midnight; rest of year Mon–Thurs 9.30am–10.30pm, Fri 9.30am–midnight, Sat 8am–midnight, Sun 8am–10.30pm; *www.spaceneedle.com*; $9, $12 for two trips in 24 hours). Though reminiscent of the *Star Trek* era of space-fascination, the tower still exudes a fair amount of glamour, especially at night, when it's lit up and Seattle's well-to-do come to eat at its revolving restaurant. The view from the observation deck, where there's a (pricey) bar, is unmatched, and this is much the best place to get an overall orientation of the city and its surroundings.

Near the base of the Space Needle is the new **Experience Music Project** (see overleaf) and the **Center House**, an unappetizingly dark mall-like building that is the unlikely home of the first-rate **Seattle Children's Museum** (Mon–Fri 10am–5pm, Sat–Sun 10am–6pm; ☎441-1768, *www.thechildrensmuseum.org*; $4, children $5.50), which emphasizes interactive activities scaled down to make things easy for those under four feet tall. Inside, the Global Village section simulates a visit to a tailor shop in Ghana, travelling around the Philippines on a tricycle, and the like, while the wilderness exhibit has an **artificial mountain forest** that lets kids crawl through logs or simulate a rock climb. Those herding a group can try the "If I Had a Hammer" construction zone, which has kids collaborate on building an eight-by-eleven-foot home (reservations are recommended). There is also an **information booth** on the ground floor of the Center House that is a good place to gather maps and info for the rest of Seattle Center, which often hosts theatre performances, professional sports contests, festivals, and other events.

Close by, the excellent **Pacific Science Center** (mid-June to Labor Day daily 10am–6pm; rest of year Mon–Fri 10am–5pm, Sat–Sun 10am–6pm; *www.pacsci.org*; $7.50, $12 for museum plus IMAX film or laser matinee), is easily recognizable by its distinctive white arches. The centre is a lively environment, full of bright, innovative and often noisy exhibits on a huge range of science-based topics, from robotic technology to Body Works exhibits, which let you measure your grip strength, peripheral vision, sense of smell and other traits in a highly tactile manner that's more akin to operating pinball machines than getting tested at the doctor's office. The Tech Zone lets you search the Internet and create your own animations or musical compositions; virtual reality exhibits include a basketball court that has visitors going one-on-one with an on-screen opponent, and a virtual reality helmet that lets you hang glide through a virtual city. For non-tech-geeks, there's the newly added Tropical Butterfly House, in which a rotating assortment of exotic butterflies from around the globe roam freely. There's a planetarium and an IMAX theatre inside here too.

The Experience Music Project

Near the base of the Space Needle is the newly opened **Experience Music Project** – or EMP, as it's known by locals (Sept–May Sun–Thurs 10am–6pm, Fri–Sat 10am–11pm; summer daily 9am–11pm; *www.emplive.com*; $19.95. Extended winter hours for Artist's Journey exhibit: Sept–May Sun–Thurs 6–11pm, Fri–Sat 11pm–1.30am; $7.50). Along with Cleveland's Rock and Roll Hall of Fame, it's one of the two largest museums in the world devoted to popular music. While some of the gaudier wings seem more suited to an amusement park than a cultural institution, the place does manage to serve the needs of the reverent rock fanatic while pleasing those in search of little more than a fun outing. Given the scale of the museum and its hefty entrance fee, it's a good idea to set aside the better chunk of a day to fully explore it.

Largely funded by Microsoft co-founder and billionaire Paul Allen, EMP was originally intended as a museum for Seattle native Jimi Hendrix before Allen and the Hendrix estate had a falling out about unspecified matters. The final product still includes a fair amount of Hendrix memorabilia, but its focus has become much broader, with interactive exhibits drawing from a collection of nearly 80,000 rock and pop artefacts. The controversial design by world-famous architect **Frank Gehry** – of Guggenheim Bilbao fame – has not one single right angle in its swooping contortions of metal, with a colourful aluminium exterior purposely designed to fade with time. Rock and roll may be the last thing you think of when you see the finished structure, which isn't quite as successful as Gehry's previous works, but the ambitious design is a curiosity in its own right and even allows for the passage of the monorail through its southern portion.

The visit begins on level two, where you'll be handed a bulky **Museum Exhibit Guide** (known as a "MEG"), a device carried like a shoulder bag with attached headphones. There's also a remote control unit with a built-in text screen, which, when pointed at displays in the museum, dictates the content of the images on the screen as well as the automated narration by the likes of Robbie Robertson and Bob Dylan.

Though you might feel like a cyber-nerd strapped down with this cumbersome contraption, it is essential if you hope to experience all the museum has to offer, especially since the actual artefacts assembled in the museum – mostly old records, posters and magazines – are not particularly striking when viewed without the MEG's insightful commentary. Nevertheless, there are a number of vintage objects of note throughout the museum, and while the spread of genres examined in-depth is not perfect (there's little on 1960s British Invasion bands or girl groups, for example), many styles do have corners of their own; the slack promises to be taken up by temporary exhibits to come.

Of the major permanent exhibits on level two, standouts include the **Hendrix Gallery**, which traces Jimi's career from his days as a sideman with the Isley Brothers to his short-lived psychedelic funk group Bands of Gypsies – check out the handwritten draft of *Voodoo Chile*, which contains different lyrics than those that were eventually recorded. Nearby, the **Guitar Gallery** displays dozens of acoustic and electric guitar and bass models, such as the intriguing 1933 Dobro all-electric (with built-in speakers) and the 1957 Gibson "Flying V" (used by ace pickers Lonnie Mack and Albert King), while **Northwest Passage** traces the local rock scene from instrumental guitar pioneers the Ventures through grunge, with an entire case devoted to the regional rock anthem, *Louie Louie*.

Also on level two is **Artist's Journey**, a virtual-motion ride set to a musical soundtrack, which varies according to an ever-changing programme. You may find yourself sucked into a psychedelic vortex of movement and sound only to be spat out at an allstar funk block party with performances by George Clinton, James Brown and Bootsy Collins. In winter, Artist's Journey can be experienced separately from the rest of the museum after regular museum hours for a fraction of the entrance fee, presumably to lure the adolescent crowd.

On EMS' third level, the **Milestones** gallery covers many of the music styles that have influenced rock or been spawned from it, including New Orleans R&B, punk, rap, and country. Standout displays include Bo Diddley's trademark square guitar, the turntables used by Grandmaster Flash to DJ in the early 1980s, and a chance to hear Bill Haley's 1952 single *Rock the Joint*, the prototype for his much more famous *Rock Around the Clock*. Across from Milestones, the large **Sound Lab** enables visitors to play electric guitars, basses, keyboards, drums and DJ turntables, with a bit of help from the staff and interactive computer terminals; there are rooms for jamming, a chance to mix on a professional console, and an entire corner of effects pedals.

In addition to its chief exhibits, EMP usually has special events of some sort going on every day, including talks or movies in the **JBL Theater** downstairs on level one, and live performances, workshops and demonstrations in various sections of the building. Although it's most crowded on summer weekends, that's also when you're most likely to catch the best of such events; whatever the season, be prepared for long lines.

Capitol Hill

Of all Seattle's neighbourhoods, **Capitol Hill**, a ten-minute bus ride east of downtown, has probably raised the most eyebrows over the years. Since young gays, hippies and assorted radicals moved in during the 1960s and 1970s, this has been the city's alternative centre and fulcrum of the arts scene and chancier night-time activities. Nowadays, the shops and cafés around **Broadway**, the main drag, are pretty mainstream and, despite black leather jackets slung over teenage shoulders, the neighbourhood's days at the cutting edge of bohemia are probably over. Still, the concentration of easy-going restaurants, coffeehouses and bars provides good daytime café-sitting and night-time drinking (see "Eating" and "Nightlife"), and it very much remains the focus of the current gay scene – though homophobic violence can happen here as disturbingly often as it does anywhere in the US. The best destinations in Capitol Hill cluster not on Broadway itself, but just a block or two away on some of the adjoining streets, where the businesses are more cutting-edge; check out the part of **Olive Way** a few blocks west of Broadway, where you can grab a coffee at the kitschy *Coffee Messiah* (see p.205) or scan the racks at Fallout, which has one of the city's best selections of comics, fanzines and punk vinyl. Things get a bit funkier the further south you go in the area, particularly around **Pike and Pine streets**, with the appearance of gothic cafés, techno record stores, tattoo parlours, and Beyond the Closet (1501 Belmont Ave E), the city's best gay and lesbian bookshop. Also in this area is the striking **Chapel of St Ignatius**, next to the Seattle University visitor parking lot at Marion and 12th. The exterior strikes an odd balance between an adobe New Mexican house of worship and a solar research lab; the interior's windows glow in a rich assortment of colours that light the walls and change with the time and season.

The northern end of the Capitol Hill district is, by contrast with Broadway, quietly wealthy, complete with gold-rush-era mansions sitting sedately around the shrubs and trees of **Volunteer Park**, named in honour of those who volunteered for the Spanish-American War of 1898. The lovely 1912 glass **Conservatory** here (daily: summer 10am–7pm; rest of year 10am–4pm; free) packs an immediate aesthetic punch: divided into galleries simulating different climates (jungle, desert, rainforest, etc), it has a sweltering mix of perfect flowers and shrubs, and a huge collection of orchids. Nearby, the **Seattle Asian Art Museum** (Tues–Wed & Fri–Sun 10am–5pm, Thurs 10am–9pm; *www.seattleartmuseum.org*; $3, free first Thurs and Sat of month) is one of the most extensive collections of Asian art outside of Asia. Its exhibits encompass Japanese, Korean, Vietnamese, Chinese and Southeast Asian art, and are deepest in ceramics and sculpture. The best corner is the wildly ornate collection of Chinese jade and snuff bottles from the eighteenth through twentieth centuries, adorned with miniature portraits, animals and rural landscapes. The museum has also recently begun to feature more contemporary work in its temporary exhibitions from the likes of Andy Warhol, Picasso, and underground Chinese artist Fang Lijun. Also in the park, the old **Water Tower** can be climbed for a grand (and free) panorama across Seattle, albeit through wire mesh.

Ten blocks east of Volunteer Park, **Washington Park** stretches away to the north, encompassing the **University of Washington Arboretum**, an assortment of trees, shaded footpaths and cycle tracks perfect for walks and picnics, especially in the fall when the trees turn brilliant shades of red and gold. The visitor centre (10am–4pm daily) at the north end of Arboretum Drive has a free trail map, and can also tell you about the numerous activities held on the grounds, including free tours that leave from the centre at 1pm on weekends. At the south end of the park is the immaculately designed **Japanese Tea Gardens** (March–Nov 10am–dusk; call ☎684-4725 for information; $2.50), a landscape of neat ornamental lakes and flower-strewn banks.

The University District

Across Union Bay from Washington Park, the **University District** (aka the "U" District) is livelier than Capitol Hill: a busy hotchpotch of coffeehouses, cinemas, clothes, book and record shops, all catering to the tastes and budgets of the University of Washington's 35,000 students. The area centres on University Way, known as "**The Ave**" and lined with cheap ethnic restaurants plus the cavernous University Bookstore at 4326 University Way NE – an excellent place to get the lowdown on the student scene.

The sprawling **campus** itself is more serene, its sedate early-twentieth century buildings and landscaped grounds overlooking Union Bay. There are a couple of museums here: the pale brick **Henry Art Gallery**, at 15th Avenue NE and NE 41st Street

(Tues–Wed & Fri–Sun 11am–5pm, Thurs 11am–8pm; *www.henryart.org*; $5, students and children under 13 free, free to all Thurs 5–8pm), houses American and European paintings from the last three centuries, and mounts small innovative shows, often drawing on local work. Even though it quadrupled in size in 1997, there's still not nearly enough room to accommodate the bulk of their permanent collection, which is strongest on photos (including works by Ansel Adams and Imogen Cunningham). Combined with their emphasis on frequent temporary exhibits, this means that there's a virtual total changeover in what's displayed in the museum several times a year. The **Thomas Burke Memorial Museum**, on the northwestern corner of the campus at 17th Avenue NE and NE 45th Street (daily 10am–5pm, Thurs 10am–8pm; *www.washington .edu/burkemuseum*; $5.50), has painted wooden masks from the Northwest coast, plaited-fibre fans from Polynesia and sorcery charms from New Guinea, but is centred around two comprehensive exhibitions. On the upper floor, "Life and Times of Washington State", a timeline of the region's geological history, is highlighted by a 140-million-year-old allosaurus and a giant 12,000-year-old sloth (found during construction of a runway at Sea-Tac airport); on the lower floor, "Pacific Voices" has stories, photos, videos, interactive displays, and artefacts of over twenty communities of Pacific origin, from Laos and Japan to Northwest Native-Americans. If you go to the Henry Art Gallery and the Burke Museum on the same day, you can visit the second museum for just one additional dollar.

In the southeast corner of campus, just to the south of Husky Stadium, home of the university's popular football team, the **Waterfront Activities Center** on the edge of Lake Union rents rowboats or canoes ($6.50 per hr). Across Montlake Bridge, the **Museum of History and Industry**, at 2700 24th Ave E and East Shelby (daily 10am–5pm; *www.seattlehistory.org*; $5.50), has local history exhibits varying in quality from good to lacklustre, with a well-done Great Seattle Fire display in the basement (bus #43 from downtown drops you a block away). Near the bottom of the museum's parking lot, a narrow floating walkway leads over the lake to tiny **Foster Island**, which contains the largest remaining wetland in Seattle.

Lake Washington Canal, Ballard and other northern neighbourhoods

Along with the U District, Seattle's other northern neighbourhoods – working west, Wallingford, Fremont, Green Lake, Greenwood and Ballard – are sliced off from the rest of town by water. Lake Union, in the middle, is connected to the larger Lake Washington to the east, and the sea to the west by the eight-mile-long **Lake Washington Ship Canal**. Built c.1900 to carry ships to safe harbours on the inland lakes, the canal was used during World War I to safeguard battleships from exposure to attack in the more open Elliott Bay. If you have an hour to spare, the procession of boats passing from salt water to fresh through a set of canal locks called the **Hiram M. Chittenden Locks** (daily 7am–9pm), near the mouth of the canal, makes pleasant viewing (bus #17 from downtown), and migrating salmon bypass the locks via the **fish ladder**, a sort of piscine staircase laid out with viewing windows. In peak migrating season (late summer for salmon, fall and early winter for trout) the water behind the locks is full of huge, jumping fish. A visitor centre (mid-May to mid-Sept daily 10am–6pm, mid-Sept to mid-May Thurs–Mon 10am–4pm) between the parking lot and the locks has interesting exhibits on the history of the canal and the locks' construction, and free guided tours of the locks leave from here (mid-May to mid-Sept Mon–Fri 1pm & 3pm, Sat–Sun 11am, 1pm & 3pm; mid-Sept to Nov & March to mid-May Thurs–Mon at 2pm). East of the locks is Salmon Bay, on the south side of which, beside 15th Avenue NW's Ballard Bridge, is **Fishermen's Terminal**. Often crowded with the boats of Seattle's

THE SALMON WARS

Salmon fishing is big industry in the Pacific Northwest, with a $300 million annual harvest. Salmon are born and reared in fresh water before migrating to the ocean for a few years, after which they return to fresh water to spawn. The fish travel so widely that both the US and Canada cannot help but catch a good deal of fish that spawn within each other's borders; consequently, a 1985 Canada–US **Pacific Salmon Treaty** was established to ensure equity between Canadian and American harvests and prevent overfishing.

In 1997, the agreement was disrupted when Canadian fishermen claimed that Americans were catching three times their share of British Columbia-bound sockeye; in May of the same year, Canada seized four US fishing vessels for failing to notify authorities upon entering Canadian waters, and in July, Canadian fishermen blockaded a popular Alaskan state ferry for three days to draw attention to their concerns. Talks of a compromise, whereby Americans would catch fewer sockeye bound for British Columbia, in exchange for the Canadians catching less coho salmon off Vancouver Island collapsed, and the US was unwilling to go along with Canada's request for third-party arbitration on treaty disputes.

In June 1999, a complex agreement was reached, establishing new quotas based on abundance rather than equity and geared toward the benefit of what's best for the salmon, rather than commercial interests. Toward that end, $140 million was provided by the US government for habitat restoration, designed to rebuild the salmon runs in both countries. Since fishing quotas can be difficult to measure and enforce, the amended treaty also spelled out the researchers' role in tracking the salmon population's development. But even with all these careful considerations in place, it remains to be seen how state and regional legislation – such as the defeat of a recent Washington state initiative to restrict commercial fishing – will affect the delicate balance of the agreement.

fishing fleet, you can buy freshly caught fish at the terminal, although there are no regular hours; fishermen selling their catch right off the boat will often place signs on 15th Avenue NW when they have the fish to offer.

On the south side of the locks, the affluent **Magnolia** neighbourhood is chiefly notable for Seattle's hidden jewel, **Discovery Park**. With over five hundred acres of meadows, rustic fields, woods and walking trails – as well as dramatic seaside vistas, clean breezy air, and an abundance of wildlife – it's that rare urban park that, on its best days, feels like a genuine slice of wilderness. On weekdays and weekend mornings it's nearly deserted (and safe), and a paradise for hikers, runners and dog-walkers with its empty trails and lush, varied topography. This is also when you're most likely to spot the bald eagles and rabbits that frequent the grounds. The **visitor centre** (daily 8.30am–5pm; ☎386-4236), just inside the east entrance at 36th Avenue W and W Government Way, organizes weekend walks spotlighting the park's abundant bird and plant life. A 2.8-mile **loop trail** can be entered here that winds among much of the park's most densely forested regions. It's better to head for the **south entrance** on W Emerson Street near Magnolia Boulevard, however, and take a trail across the windswept meadows between the parking lot and the nearby **bluffs**, where the view – taking in Puget Sound ships, Bainbridge Island, and on a clear day the snow-capped Olympic Mountains – is one of the city's grandest, especially at sunset. The South Beach trail leads down to a narrow, rocky, unswimmable beach, and a pleasant waterside trail of about a mile or so leads from there to the more deserted North Beach. From downtown, bus #19 leaves you next to the park's south gate at the last stop. A better approach to the south gate, if you've got a vehicle, is via the curving Magnolia Boulevard, which hugs the bluffs for magnificent views of Puget Sound as it steadily rises toward the park.

On the northern side of Salmon Bay, **Ballard** (reachable by several buses from downtown) was settled by Scandinavian fishermen in the late nineteenth century. The **Nordic Heritage Museum**, 3014 NW 67th St (Tues–Sat 10am–4pm, Sun noon–4pm; *www.nordicmuseum.com*; $4), outlines their history from poverty in rural Scandinavia, through immigration problems at Ellis Island and New York tenements to arrival in the West, in a series of rather musty tableaux in the basement of an old school. On the upper floors, temporary exhibits stage historical displays and show work by contemporary Scandinavian artists, and separate wings are devoted to the folk art and Northwest immigrant communities of Norway, Iceland, Denmark, Finland and Sweden.

Bar a couple of nightspots (see p.210), there's little else to see in Ballard. If you do find yourself passing further east, along the northern shore of Lake Union, look out for **Gasworks Park**, at N Northlake Way and Wallingford, where the rusting black towers of an old gasworks have been left as "urban sculpture" and the slag heaps grassed over to make kite-flying mounds. Halfway along the stretch of Northlake Way that runs east along Lake Union, from Gasworks Park to the Ship Canal Bridge, looms the rusting hulk of the **Kalakala** (*www.kalakala.org*) which won renown between 1935 and 1967 as the world's only streamlined Art Deco ferry. The 276-foot vessel, complete with a grand staircase, ballroom and double horseshoe lunch counter, primarily served the Seattle–Bremerton route and carried 2000 passengers per journey. Volunteers give free tours Wednesdays 4–7pm and Saturdays 10am–5pm.

Gasworks Park sticks out into the middle of Lake Union at the foot of the **Fremont–Wallingford** district, a prosperous neighbourhood with a bit of a bohemian flavour. The western part of this area, **Fremont**, is the more interesting; its nexus is the stretch of Fremont Avenue N that runs from the Fremont Bridge at N 34th Street to about N 37th Street, holding a mishmash of cafés, chic restaurants, secondhand book-shops, galleries, potteries and specialized local businesses. Several have an artsy, counterculture bent that borders on the goofy, such as the Deluxe Junk thrift store on 601 N 35th St with its odd collection of kitsch such as toy electric guitars and leopard-patterned furniture. The best reason to visit, though, may be the playful public art on display, including *Waiting for the Interurban*, sculptures of lifelike bus commuters near N 34th and Fremont, the huge **Lenin statue** at the corner of N 36th and Fremont Place, and the 18ft **Fremont Troll** underneath the Aurora Bridge at N 36th and Aurora Avenue N.

North of Fremont, quiet residential streets give way to the **Woodland Park Zoo** (daily: mid-March to mid-Oct 9.30am–6pm; mid-Oct to mid-March 9.30am–4pm; *www.zoo.org*; $9; bus #5 from 1st Ave and Union St), an open zoo with natural habitats for the animals and, oddly enough, a memorial rock in the African Savannah area paying tribute to **Jimi Hendrix** (see box, p.201). Hwy 99 separates the zoo from the rest of **Woodland Park**, which extends northeast around **Green Lake**, a popular haunt for local joggers; boats can be rented at the northeastern corner of the lake during the summer.

Lake Washington and the eastern outskirts

From the mouth of the Washington Park Arboretum (see p.196), **Lake Washington Boulevard** meanders through the Madison Park district for a mile or so before reaching the shores of **Lake Washington**, where it hugs the water's edge for another five miles. It's Seattle's most scenic drive, passing some of the city's ritziest strongholds in the **Madison Park** and **Madrona** neighbourhoods in the north, and then through the more middle class, but extremely pleasant, **Mount Baker** and **Rainier Valley** districts before terminating at **Seward Park** to the south. It's at its best on the occasional weekend days when the stretch from Mount Baker to Seward Park is closed to traffic, and the tree-lined thoroughfare becomes a paradise for cyclists and joggers (from May–Sept on the second Sat and third Sun of the month, from 10am–6pm).

The northern end of this route, near Denny Blaine Park, was the setting for one of rock music's greatest tragedies. Nirvana's **Kurt Cobain** was living in one of the mansions on Lake Washington Boulevard overlooking the water when he shot himself in April 1994. The carriage house where the act was committed has since been torn down, and Cobain's widow, Courtney Love, moved out and put the home on the market in 1997, though die-hards still make pilgrimages there.

There's a small beach at Madrona, but it's better to look for a more solitary spot a few miles down the road, particularly on the grassy banks a bit more than a mile south of **Colman Park**, where swimmers will have the water practically to themselves. Encircled by a two-and-a-half-mile loop path, it's never crowded; for even more isolation, walk into the forest preserve at the park's hilly centre, where abundant Douglas firs, cedar and maples provide most of the shade.

Until it was bridged, **Lake Washington** isolated the city from the countryside and small farms to the east. Ferries laden with farm produce made slow progress across the water, and the lake became a sort of tradesmen's entrance to the city while the centre of Seattle looked towards the big commercial ships docking in Elliott Bay. All this changed when two long, floating bridges, one built in the 1940s, the second in the 1960s, opened up commuting possibilities: business people poured across, tripling the population of one-time rural towns **Bellevue, Kirkland** and **Redmond**, turning them into affluent city suburbs. Redmond became the world headquarters of software giant Microsoft; Kirkland built plush businesses and accommodations along its waterfront; and Bellevue quickly outgrew its suburban status to become the state's fourth largest city with its own smart business district and shopping area, the showpiece of which is the expensively stocked Bellevue Square Mall. Nearby at the corner of Bellevue Way and NE 6th Street, the **Bellevue Art Museum**, formerly on the third floor of Bellevue Square Mall (Mon, Wed, Thurs–Sat 10am–6pm, Tues 10am–8pm, Sun 11am–5pm; *www.bellevueart.org*; $3, free first Sat of the month), is scheduled to open in early 2001. Its three floors are topped with galleries of contemporary Pacific Northwest art that connect to outdoor terraces. It also holds the two-storey Explore Gallery, featuring interactive displays on light, form, vision and visual communication, and focusing wholly on temporary exhibitions.

The more offbeat **Museum of Doll Art** (Mon–Sat 10am–5pm, Sun 1–5pm; *www.dollart.com/dollart*; $6), a few blocks away at 1116 108th Ave NE, has two floors holding more than a thousand dolls of all shapes and sizes from the last several centuries. The expected play and celebrity dolls are here, but there are also Peruvian burial dolls, African fertility dolls, Day of the Dead ceremonial figures (believed to be Mexican), exquisitely crafted miniatures, and specialized exhibit cases for mechanical dolls, dolls belonging to royalty, Inuit and Native-American figures, as well as exhibitions.

Eating

You don't have to spend a fortune in Seattle to **eat** extraordinarily well: among the coffee shops of Capitol Hill, the bargain-rate restaurants of the University District, and above all at Pike Place Market there are excellent pickings. **Seafood**, particularly salmon, is the city's speciality, with trout, crab and mussels available in abundance as well to set your mouth watering. Seattle's wide ethnic mix is reflected in the restaurants and cafés too, while the healthfood/vegetarian influence is as strong as you might

The area code for Bellevue is ☎425

HENDRIX IN SEATTLE

When Jimi Hendrix sprayed his guitar with lighter fuel and set it on fire at the Monterey Festival in 1967, he seemed to be the personification of the changes sweeping America – his tousled hair, large and powerful face and withering guitar playing was a potent symbol of 1960s rebellion. It wasn't that Hendrix ever said much about overturning the state, but he was plugged into the energy around him, nowhere more so than at Woodstock when his playing of *The Star Spangled Banner* sounded like a political statement profound enough to rock Uncle Sam, never mind one that left the audience simply mesmerized. In reality, Hendrix's showmanship (partly) camouflaged both the virtuosity of his musicianship – many reckon him to be the greatest electric rock guitarist of all time – and the essential shyness of the man.

Hendrix was born in Seattle in November 1942, though he clearly didn't develop too much of a taste for the place, enlisting in the US Army and clearing off at the tender age of 17. His family stayed, but Jimi rarely visited and only played the city as a headline act four times after he shot to fame in 1967. Considering Hendrix's tenuous connections with his hometown, it's appropriate that Seattlites have always been uncertain as to how (or even whether) to honour him. There is a life-size, unlabelled statue of Hendrix, caught in his famous kneeling-to-burn-the-guitar-at-Monterey pose, across the street from the Seattle Central Community College on Broadway near Pine, and a bizarre tiny plaque in the African Savannah exhibit of the Woodland Park Zoo (see p.199). Shaped like a gold, bursting sun, and perched on top of a rock overlooking the field where giraffes and other African creatures run free, the inscription reads, "This viewpoint was funded by worldwide donations to KZOK radio in the memory of Jimi Hendrix and his music". The Experience Music Project in Seattle Center (see p.194) was originally envisioned as a Hendrix museum, but ended up covering rock music itself. However, Jimi did finally get his due with a large gallery in EMP devoted to his life and music, including displays of instruments and recording equipment he used, and even handwritten drafts of the lyrics to some of his songs.

Finally there's Hendrix's grave. Hendrix died in London from a drugs overdose in September 1970 and his body was flown back to Seattle and buried in Greenwood Cemetery, at Monroe Avenue NE and NE 4th Street, in Renton, a nondescript suburb just south of the city limits. The grave is found near a sundial (ask the staff on the grounds for directions); a plain, flat marble stone inscribed with a guitar and Hendrix's name. Psychedelic stickers and a few flowers scatter the site, but you'll often find yourself the sole visitor. To get there, take Exit 4 off I-5, or take buses #101 or #106 from downtown and transfer to #105 at Renton transit station.

expect in a major Pacific Coast metropolis. Budget travellers should be on the lookout for the numerous ethnic restaurants, especially Indian ones, that offer all-you-can-eat lunch buffets in the $5–7 range.

Pike Place Market

During the day, there's no better place to find food than **Pike Place Market**, which extends over several city blocks below 1st Avenue – between Virginia and Pike streets – with the **Main Arcade** below the corner of Pike Street and Pike Place, directly opposite the **Corner** and **Sanitary** market buildings.

Meals and snacks are obtainable either in picnic form from the stalls and groceries, or served up in cafés and restaurants. Everything's informal – it's part of the market's much-vaunted democratic air – and there are lots of places to choose from, all crowding the market's narrow corridors, although on a busy Saturday, it's not so much where you want to eat, but more a case of finding a vacant stool or table. However, the market starts to close down at around 6pm (and many stalls and cafés don't open on Sun), after which Pike Place is a less tempting (and slightly threatening) prospect. Only the fancier sit-down restaurants – such as *Place Pigalle, Campagne* and *Copacabana* (all listed below) – stay open for dinner after 6pm.

Athenian Inn, main floor of Main Arcade (☎624-7166). Something of an institution, this café's window tables, overlooking Puget Sound, are much sought after. Breakfast (especially the hash) is popular, and the lengthy menu is matched by an extensive beer list.

Campagne, 1600 Post Alley at Pine St (☎728-2800). The swankest restaurant in Pike Place, offering delicacies like potato-wrapped striped bass filet and foie gras parfait on puff pastry with shallots and turnips. Open daily 5.30–10pm, and very expensive, with a three-course prix fixe supper ($50) between 5.30 and 6.30pm.

Copacabana, Triangle Building (☎622-6359). Bolivian restaurant with a large selection of dishes with pie-type fillings; the corn pie and fish soups are especially recommended. The outdoor balcony seating has a good view of the Pike Place hubbub.

El Puerco Lloron, on the Hillclimb (☎624-0541). A low-price, authentic Mexican restaurant.

Lowell's Restaurant, main floor of Main Arcade (☎622-2036). Join the stallholders for an early breakfast at this established café-restaurant, well known for the quality of its coffee and seafood: try the oysters.

Place Pigalle, on the staircase behind *Pike Place Fish*, Main Arcade (☎624-1756). Once a tough working-men's bar, but now a restaurant serving up mid-priced-to-expensive French cuisine and high-quality seafood dishes, like mussels, crab and regionally-caught sturgeon. Closed Sun.

Saigon Restaurant, 1916 Pike Place, on ground floor of Soames-Dunn Building in Pike Place Market (☎448-1089). One of the best inexpensive places to eat in Pike Place, with a menu of Vietnamese seafood and vegetarian dishes that features some sweat-breaking curries.

Sound View Cafe, Flower Row of Main Arcade in Pike Place Market (☎623-5700). Nothing earth-shaking about the food here, though it's healthy, filling serve-yourself fare (small salad bowl $2.50, large salad bowl $5). The main reason to come is for the views of Puget Sound, which come at a price considerably lower than elsewhere in Pike Place Market.

Three Girls Bakery, lower floor of Sanitary Market (☎622-1045). Superb and filling sandwiches on freshly baked bread served at either the takeout window or the lunch counter.

Pioneer Square and around

Though a fine place for live music and drinking (see p.208), **Pioneer Square** isn't so hot for inexpensive food: the taverns all serve light meals because they have to by law and, generally speaking, it's pretty mediocre stuff. The square and the adjoining **business district** do, however, boast several of Seattle's finest restaurants, while the neighbouring **International District** features a range of Chinese and Vietnamese cuisine to suit any pocket.

Assagio, 2010 4th Ave between Leonora and Virginia sts (☎441-1399). Good Italian restaurant that sprinkles in some unexpected items, like fusilli with currants and pinenuts in cream sauce, among the typical moderately priced pizzas, pastas and veal.

Bangkok House, 606 S Weller St at 6th Ave S (☎382-9888). Fine inexpensive Thai cuisine with an array of delicious satays.

Chau's Chinese Restaurant, 310 4th Ave S between S Jackson and S Main sts (☎621-0006). Cantonese cuisine with the emphasis on seafood. Inexpensive, with weekday lunch specials in the $5 range.

Dahlia Lounge, 1904 4th Ave between Stewart and Virginia sts east of Pike Place Market (☎682-4142). One of the most expensive restaurants in town, but the seafood is definitely something special, forming the centrepiece of an inventive menu. Still, other imaginative main courses, like squash tamales and apricot chicken, are on offer. Reservations are advisable.

Honey Bear Café, S 101 Main St at 1st Ave S (☎682-6664). Reasonably priced wholefood served up in the cosy book-lined basement of the Elliott Bay Book Company bookshop, until 9pm (6pm Sun). Newspapers and weather-beaten old hardcover books are available for perusal while you eat.

Hon's Restaurant, 416 5th Ave S between S Jackson and S King sts (☎623-4470). Cheap and filling Chinese Szechuan and Vietnamese cuisine, right across from the International District Metro tunnel.

House of Hong, 409 S 8th Ave at S Jackson St (☎622-7997). Massive restaurant serving some of the best Chinese food around. Inexpensive.

Metropolitan Grill, 820 2nd Ave between Columbia and Marion sts (☎624-3287). Superior steaks in a long and handsome bar that's a favourite destination for after-hours business people who can afford the prices. Open for lunch and dinner weekdays, dinner only weekends.

Nikko, 1900 5th Ave at Stewart St (☎322-4641). Downtown's top-notch Japanese restaurant has both an extensive sushi bar and barbecued dishes skewered and grilled over an open flame.

Painted Table, 1st Ave and Madison St (☎624-3646). First-class, if pricey, dining, served on hand-painted plates, and highlighted by items like three-clam linguine and dishes made with vegetables from Pike Place Market. Open for all meals weekdays, but only open until noon on weekends.

Tai Tung, 659 S King St between 6th Ave S and 7th Ave S (☎622-7372). A popular Cantonese restaurant that's also one of the International District's oldest.

Viet My, 129 Prefontaine Place S off 4th Ave at Washington (☎382-9923). Delicious, inexpensive Vietnamese food in unpretentious surroundings. Closed weekends.

Wild Ginger 1400 Western Ave at Union (☎623-4450). Trendy pan-Asian restaurant with extensive daily specials to supplement their lengthy menu, though it's best to go with dishes that don't try to do too much at once, like the tuna *manada* (yellowfin tuna fried in spicy Indonesian sauce). Good, though somewhat overpriced.

Belltown and Seattle Center

Belltown used to be more of a café neighbourhood than a restaurant one, but that's changing as the area gets more gentrified, particularly along 1st Avenue, where some of the city's chicest establishments have recently taken root. It's well worth planning a meal in the blocks surrounding **Seattle Center** if you're going to an event there, especially on Roy Street, where several fine Asian restaurants line the Center's northern border.

Bahn Thai, 409 N Roy St between 4th Ave N and 5th Ave N (☎283-0444). There are two fine Thai restaurants on the northern border of Seattle Center; this is recommended above the other (*Thai Heaven*) if you want a more relaxed, decorous atmosphere, with a menu of more than a hundred well-spiced seafood, meat and vegetarian dishes.

Bamboo Garden, 364 N Roy St between 3rd Ave N and 4th Ave N (☎282-6616). Although a quick glance at the menu might lead you to believe this Chinese place offers a standard array of meat and veggie dishes, everything in fact is made from vegetable protein products and vegetable oil. Whether you decide to simulate a meat experience or just stick with the veggies, it's one of the most imaginative Chinese choices in Seattle.

Chutneys, 519 1st Ave N between N Republican St and N Mercer St (☎284-6799). The best place in town for a sit-down Indian meal, also dishing out all-you-can-eat $7 lunch buffets for the budget conscious.

FareStart, 1902 2nd Ave between Stewart and Virginia sts (☎448-6422). This roomy restaurant is dedicated to providing job training to the homeless, and the $6.95 weekday lunch buffets are excellent, with plenty of meat and veggie dishes, as well as good desserts.

Lampreia, 2400 1st Ave at Battery St (☎443-3301). One of the new high-class (and expensive) eateries on 1st Ave, *Lampreia* specializes in beef and fish dishes, some of which are pretty unusual, like sautéed frog legs with grilled organic polenta.

Marco's Supper Club, 2510 1st Ave at Wall St (☎441-7801). This relaxed restaurant, geared toward the younger set looking for a big but not extortionate night out, specializes in an imaginative assortment of tasty platters, such as glazed portobello with butternut squash or mojo mahi grilled with black bean coconut rice, that don't subscribe to any set cuisine.

Noodle Ranch, 2228 2nd Ave between Blanchard and Bell sts (☎728-0463). Delicious pan-Asian cuisine in the $10 range, offering imaginatively spiced noodle-based and non-noodle dishes, as well as satay appetizers, in a casual Belltown atmosphere. Closed Sun.

Capitol Hill

Options at **Capitol Hill** include laid-back ethnic café-restaurants and chic little coffee-houses. The inexpensive norm around here is interrupted by the occasional exclusive bistro.

Byzantion, 601 E Broadway at E Mercer St (☎325-7580). Good-quality Greek dishes at reasonable prices, served with enough pitta bread to make even the prospect of dessert unthinkable. The omelettes are a delight.

Café Flora, 2901 E Madison St at 29th Ave E (☎325-9100). The best vegetarian restaurant in Seattle has creatively crafted soups, salads and entrees like wild mushroom curry and grilled seitan fish; the white-chocolate raspberry cheesecake is amazing. While the prices are expensive, the setting is pleasant, especially the stone patio wing, complete with trees and a fountain under a pyramid sky-light. Closed Mon.

Globe Cafe, 1531 14th Ave between Pine and Pike sts (☎324-8815). Inexpensive and tasty all-vegan menu of full meals, drinks and desserts, and an unpretentiously oddball, homey decor with great offbeat music on the sound system. Also hosts evening poetry events Sundays and Tuesdays after closing time.

Gravity Bar, first floor of Broadway Market, 401 Broadway E at Thomas (☎325-7186). Splendid and imaginative vegetarian food served in chic, modernistic surroundings at a reasonable price.

Kingfish Cafe, 602 19th Ave E between E Mercer and E Roy sts (☎320-8757). Southern-style food like griddle cakes, grilled shrimp, catfish, and beans and rice in a casual setting, with terrific vintage soul and R&B music on the speakers.

Kokeb, 926 12th Ave between Spring and Marion sts (☎322-0485). Simple restaurant offering low-priced and spicy Ethiopian dishes. At the south end of the district.

Machiavelli, 1215 Pine St at 12th Ave (☎621-7941). Good Italian food, featuring tangy and creative pasta sauces, although the portions aren't huge.

Piecora's, 1401 E Madison St at E Pike St (☎322-9411). The district's favourite pizza parlour.

Siam on Broadway, 616 Broadway E at E Roy St (☎324-0892). Tasty Thai delicacies at reasonable rates. Very popular, so be prepared to wait in line. Lunch and dinner weekdays, dinner only weekends.

Teapot, 125 15th Ave E between E John St and E Denny Way (☎324-2262). Delicious and well-priced all-vegan menu, made up mostly of Asian soups, curries, "hot pots" and "sizzling platters", with some house specialities, such as tofu prawns in tomato sauce.

Than Brothers, 516 Broadway E between E Republican and E Mercer sts (☎568-7218). Huge bowls of spicy *pho* (Vietnamese rice noodle soup) for $4–5 at a comfortable sit-down restaurant, with complimentary sweet dessert custard puff.

The University District

An obvious locale for inexpensive eating, the **University District** has lots of bargain-basement ethnic restaurants, especially Chinese, Greek, Indian, Mexican, Thai and Vietnamese. Finding somewhere good to eat is simply a question of walking up and down University Way – between about NE 40th and NE 50th streets – until you find what you want. Expect to be harassed (however peacefully) by panhandlers.

Araya's, 4732 University Way NE between NE 47th and NE 50th sts (☎524-4332). Decent Thai restaurant, but the real reason to make an effort to come here is the $6 all-you-can-eat vegetarian buffet lunch.

Costas, 4559 University Way NE between NE 45th and NE 47th sts (☎633-2751). Filling Greek meals at low prices.

Flowers, 4247 University Way NE between NE 42nd and NE 43rd sts (☎633-1903). A bar and restaurant most notable for a twenty-item, $6.95 lunchtime vegan buffet (served from 11am–4pm) that's the best non-Indian all-you-can-eat option in town.

Saigon Deli, 4142 Brooklyn Ave NE between NE 41st and NE 42nd sts (☎634-2866). Hole-in-the-wall diner whips out fine Vietnamese dishes for eat-in or takeout. Most of the menu clears the under-$5 barrier, and you won't go away hungry.

Silence Heart Nest Vegetarian Restaurant, 5247 University Way NE between NE 52nd and NE 55th sts (☎524-4008). Indian-oriented vegetarian menu with daily specials and rotating desserts in a placid, New Age atmosphere. Closed Wed.

Sunlight Cafe, 6403 Roosevelt Way NE (☎522-9060). Busy and reasonably priced vegetarian café-restaurant on the northwest edge of the district at NE 64th St.

Tandoor, 5024 University Way NE between NE 50th and NE 52nd sts (☎523-7477). Amidst the numerous decent Indian restaurants in Seattle offering all-you-can-eat buffet lunches, this stands out for its low price of $4.95.

Cafés and coffeehouses

Seattle is famed as a city in which coffee is consumed in vaster quantities, and with more enthusiasm, than any other metropolis in North America (see box, overleaf). It's not necessary to be an espresso connoisseur, however, to enjoy the friendly, funky ambience of its numerous **cafés and coffeehouses**, which function much as local pubs or bars as centres for low-key unwinding. As a hotbed of activity for both cutting-edge technology and the arts, there's a proliferation of cafés which are in effect multi-media spaces, offering Internet terminals, poetry readings, gallery art, alternative music and even laundry facilities along with the expected coffee, tea, snacks and light meals. Whether you're looking to meet some locals, get online or nurse a cup of java for an hour or two while reading and writing, there are an abundance of options to meet your needs throughout the city, the best of which are listed below. (See box overleaf for establishments geared toward the aficionado.)

Allegro Espresso Bar, 4214 University Way NE, in the alley between University and 15th Ave NE that runs between 42nd and 43rd (☎633-3030). One of the favoured haunts of those who take their coffee seriously, and something of a hangout for the university's more intellectual/international element. There are also computer terminals with Internet access (available only if you're also having something at the café).

B&O Espresso, 204 Belmont Ave E at E Olive Way (☎322-5028). Lively coffeehouse just down from Broadway in Capitol Hill, with a cool dark interior, outdoor seating and a fine assortment of drinks and desserts; the brownies are excellent.

Bauhaus Books & Coffee, 301 E Pine at Melrose Ave E (☎625-1600). One of the most suitable Capitol Hill hangouts for the dressed-in-black crowd, dispensing coffee and some teas in a sombre, functional interior, with high chairs at the windowside counter straight off the set of *The Cabinet of Dr. Caligari*. The small, artsy used book section is largely devoted to architecture volumes.

The Burke Museum Café (also known as *The Boisier*), 17th Ave NE and NE 45th St, in the basement of the Burke Museum (☎543-9854). High ceilings, large wood-panelled walls, wooden armchairs and classical music yield an ambience rather closer to a nineteenth-century drawing room than a modern Seattle café. If you need a comfortable, library-quiet daytime spot for concentrating on your reading and writing, it's the top spot in town.

CapitolHill.Net, 219 Broadway E between E John and E Thomas sts (☎860-6858). The best of Seattle's virtual cafés dispenses muffins and espresso, but the chief attraction is the Web browsing, graphic design, computer games and other high-tech activities, available on ten computers for ten cents a minute in a pleasant low-key, two-tiered lofty space.

Coffee Messiah, 1554 E Olive Way at E Denny Way (☎860-7377). One of the most irreverent bohemian outposts in town, with its kitschy crucifixes, images of Christ, and a spark-emitting windup nun. They have coffee too (albeit featuring a "Blood of Christ" blend of coffee beans), as well as chai, herbal tea, cider, juice and occasional free live music.

Café Dilettante, 416 E Broadway between E Republican and E Harrison sts (☎329-6463). Though this pleasant café on the busiest stretch of Broadway in Capitol Hill does serve coffee, people come here more for the chocolate treats, the best in town. Does a big business in both takeout and eat-in service.

Grand Illusion Espresso and Pastry, 1405 NE 50th St at University Way (☎523-3935). Cosy vegetarian café adjacent to the Grand Illusion arts cinema. A good spot to sit with the Sunday papers (which are provided free).

Online Coffee Company, 1720 E Olive Way one block west of Broadway (☎328-3731). Spacious and relaxed Internet café with coffee, beer, wine and baked goods to go along with the $6/hr high-speed Internet access. Draws a youthful crowd heavy on the twenty-somethings, as would be expected given its Capitol Hill location.

SEATTLE COFFEE CULTURE

There seems to be no ready explanation for the astonishing proliferation of coffee bars and espresso carts in Seattle in the 1980s and 1990s. Perhaps it's the near-constant overcast drizzle in the colder months, producing both indoor hibernation and a need for hot beverages with a jolt. There are now more than two hundred entries in the "Espresso" section of the Seattle *Yellow Pages*; more than two hundred licensed espresso carts operate from sidewalks and store entrances; and drive-through takeaway service is offered at some parking lots (like the corner of Broadway and Harrison, home of the TNT cart). There's even an "Espresso Dental" office that serves lattes to patients awaiting treatment.

Much of Seattle's coffee culture was generated by the phenomenally successful Starbucks chain, which has yearly revenues of over $1.5 billion. Begun in the early 1970s as a single store in Pike Place Market, it is now the leading retailer and roaster of brand coffee beans in the US, running about a thousand stores in North America, and recently expanding into Europe, Japan and China as well. Starbucks branches are as ubiquitous in central Seattle as 7-11s are in the Southern California suburbs; their closest competitor in the Seattle area, Seattle's Best Coffee, is no slouch, with a half-dozen outlets in downtown alone, and more throughout the area.

There is no surer way of identifying an out-of-towner than overhearing someone ordering an unembellished "espresso" or "latte". Seattleites are serious about their coffee preparation, specifying whether to use non-fat or half-and-half milk in their brew, or how many shots of espresso they need in their cup. It takes a while to absorb all the nuances of the lingo, but at the very least it's good to have a few terms down: a **cappuccino** is an espresso with foamed milk; a **caffe mocha** is hot chocolate with a shot of espresso; a **latte** is an espresso shot with steamed milk, topped with foamed milk; a **caffe amaretto** is espresso with steamed milk and a half-ounce of sweet almond syrup. If you're determined to pass for a local, you could nonchalantly ask for a "double tall skinny", a tall latte made with one percent or non-fat milk, with a double shot of espresso.

Starbucks and Seattle's Best Coffee branches have a rather sterile, fast-foodish ambience, and it's better to head for a few coffee specialists with more character. Good espresso is often served at the establishments listed in the Cafés and Coffeehouses section, but the following are recommended stops for java junkies looking for establishments where coffee is the first and foremost attraction:

Pegasus Coffee, 711 3rd Ave at Cherry St (☎682-3113). In the lobby of the Dexter Horton Building, and a more relaxing place to imbibe the java than the usual coffee bar, with brews of Pegasus beans.

Seattle's Best Coffee, 1530 Post Alley at Pine St (☎467-7700). The best place to drink the SBC brew is at its Pike Place branch, which has more character than the other outlets in the chain.

Torrefazione Italia, 320 Occidental Ave S at S Jackson St (☎624-5847). Pioneer Square espresso bar is the first pick for those looking for the best Seattle coffee experience, with top-notch roast coffees and an Italian atmosphere, heightened by the outdoor seating area on the pedestrianized part of Occidental Ave. Also at 622 Olive Way (☎624-1429) and Rainier Square, 1310 4th Ave (☎583-8970).

Vivace Espresso, 901 E Denny Way at Broadway (☎860-5869). Large-sized haunt for Capitol Hill's most serious coffee drinkers, run by self-proclaimed "espresso roasting and preparation specialists". Even better is their sidewalk café at 321 Broadway E (next to the Washington Mutual Bank parking lot), really just an elaborate cart with a few outdoor tables and constant takeout lines.

Café Septième, 214 Broadway E between E John and E Thomas sts (☎860-8858). Large spot with booths and some sidewalk seating in the heart of Capitol Hill's main drag. It strikes an appealingly moody midpoint between the bohemian and the upmarket.

Sit & Spin, 2219 4th Ave between Bell and Blanchard sts (☎441-9484). Belltown's justly renowned combination café/laundromat/performance space with diner booths, electric coils sprouting like fungi from table to ceiling, kitsch junk art, and lamps that double as sculpture, and the juices aren't bad either.

Speakeasy Cafe, 2304 2nd Ave at Bell St (☎728-9770). As much an "information trading post" (their term) as a café, this multipurpose space and Belltown institution screens films, holds poetry readings, runs Internet workshops, stages community meetings, and sometimes has ambient, jazz and improvized music. Judged simply as a café, it's pretty worthwhile as well, serving tea, coffee, beers, pastries, salads and soup in a convivial, culturally energized atmosphere.

Still Life In Fremont Coffeehouse, 709 N 35th St between Fremont Ave N and Aurora Ave N (☎547-9850). Popular Fremont hangout just off main drag with more austere decor than the usual alternative spot. Spacious wooden tables make it a good place to read or study. Suitable for both quick snacks and inexpensive filling meals, with live music on occasional nights, usually of the jazz/acoustic variety.

Teahouse Kuan Yin, 1911 N 45th St between Burke Ave N and Meridian Ave N (☎632-2055). A necessary antidote in coffee-happy Seattle, serving several dozen varieties of black, oolong, green and herbal teas as well as light snacks in a comfortable if subdued setting. On the main drag of Wallingford, the middle-class district between Fremont and the U District.

Nightlife and entertainment

Jimi Hendrix was born in Seattle (his *Spanish Castle Magic* celebrated a now-defunct local nightclub), and Ray Charles came here to make his name. But nothing in the city's musical history could anticipate the impact of **grunge**, which sprang out of Seattle when Washington-born **Nirvana** hit the big time in late 1991. Kurt Cobain's suicide in April 1994 may turn out to have marked the end of an era, but for some years, the success of Nirvana, phenomenal and immediate, made Seattle the hippest city in the States, revitalized the local band scene and attracted many imitators. You can still see some of these pretenders to the underground crown in many taverns and clubs of Seattle's **live music** scene today, but the big names have moved on to international heights.

If grunge isn't your scene, you'll still find Seattle's nightlife, taken on its own easy-going terms, lively and convivial. At any rate grunge, in its most classic (and clichéd) forms, has passed its peak, and in fact you can hear a wealth of indie/alternative rock of all sorts on most nights of the week. The famous (in all types of music) often appear at the Paramount downtown (see p.209), but otherwise scores of taverns and clubs showcase local and West Coast bands of (non-grunge) repute, usually for a small cover. Pioneer Square is densely populated with bars where the emphasis is on **rock** or **R&B**, with a good dash of **jazz**, enthusiastically delivered and accompanied by dancing where there's room. All-round it makes for a warmly down-to-earth and unpretentious scene, where a good proportion of the audience show up in jeans and there's little scope for posing. There are, of course, the dress-up video-dance places you'd find in any city, but they're less typically local and certainly less fun. If you're under 21, be aware that you won't be (legally) allowed in many live-music venues, though there are clubs that do "all-ages" shows (check the "All Ages Action" box in *The Stranger*'s weekly music listings) where this is not an issue.

As far as **drinking** goes, there's an enormous variety of potential venues, ranging from **taverns** (which in Washington sell beer and wine but not spirits) to **bars**, which sell everything but must be attached to a restaurant. Many bars sell their own microbrews, some of them quite good; all close by 2am.

On the **arts** front things are relatively sophisticated, particularly in the realm of **theatre**. A dozen or so bright and innovative theatre groups rework the classics and provide up-to-the-minute and cosmopolitan plays, and the city's a magnet for hopeful young actors, many of whom are marking time behind the craft stalls in Pike Place Market.

There's also a fair demand for art and rerun **movies**, shown in the city's wonderful collection of tiny, atmospheric cinemas.

Two alternative weeklies, the *Seattle Weekly* and *The Stranger*, are free from boxes on the streets and numerous cafés and stores, and are good for movie reviews, theatre and arts **listings**. The "What's Happening" section of the Friday edition of the *Seattle Post Intelligencer* contains live music and entertainment details, as does the "Ticket" supplement in the Friday edition of the *Seattle Times*. Ticketmaster (☎628-0888) can supply tickets for most sporting and arts events, with payment taken against your credit card over the phone (adding a service charge of $2–7); it also sells tickets in person in a few places throughout the city, including Tower Records outlets, Key Arena in the Seattle Center and Rite Aid pharmacies, whose central downtown store is at 319 Pike St. Ticket/Ticket, at Pike Place Market information booth, 1st Avenue and Pike Street (Tues–Sun noon–6pm) and Broadway Market, Second Level, 401 Broadway E (Tues–Sat noon–7pm, Sun noon–6pm) sells theatre and concert tickets at half price, but you have to turn up in person.

Drinking, live music and dancing

Downtown, there's no better introduction to the tavern scene than **Pioneer Square**, where a cluster of lively establishments often host jazz and R&B bands. Walk around outside until you hear something you like; the "cover night" deal is a pass that allows you into about ten clubs – including *Bohemian Café, Central Saloon, Colourbox, Doc Maynard's, Fenix, Larry's, New Orleans Creole Restaurant, Old Timer's Café* and *Zasu* – for $10 or less ($5 weekdays, $10 weekends, $8 "early bird" weekend rate if purchased between 8 and 9pm; can be bought at the first club visited). Several of the key underground or grunge-rock taverns and clubs are also easy to reach, grouped together near Pike Place Market, with others dotted around Seattle's **northern districts**, where there's plenty of reggae and folk music too. **Capitol Hill's** drinking-places span the range, from chic yuppie bars to the smoky pool-table-and-ripped-jean scene, but the district is most distinctive as a coffeehouse habitat and as the focus for the gay scene (see also "Gay Seattle", p.212).

Downtown

Alibi Room 85 Pike St in Pike Place Market near 1st Ave (☎623-3180). Experimental club fare, for no cover, that makes a refreshing change from the norm. You can either groove to some of the town's more adventurous DJs or hang out in quieter, more café-like sections.

Central Saloon, 207 1st Ave S at S Washington St (☎622-0209). Live blues and R&B acts nightly from around 9pm for $5–10.

Comedy Underground, 222 S Main St at 2nd Ave S (☎628-0303). This cramped club in Pioneer Square is the leading venue for Seattle's small comedy scene, with occasional well-known out-of-towners. Usually $6–10; Mon is open-mike for $3.

Crocodile Café, two blocks north of Pike Place Market, at 2200 2nd Ave and Blanchard (☎441-5611). All sorts of stuff here from jazz, rock and R&B to poetry readings and grunge; one of the hippest places in town. Diner on the premises. Normal cover $6–10.

Dimitriou's Jazz Alley, 2033 6th Ave at Leonara St (☎441-9729). Best jazz joint in town, showcasing international stars as well as up-and-coming brilliants. Stylish club; mediocre food. Tickets $15–25.

Doc Maynard's Public House, 610 1st Ave between Cherry and James sts (☎682-4649). Refurbished Pioneer Square tavern with mostly R&B bands (for $8) and a magnificent, giant-sized wooden bar. Popular with tourists; open only Fri–Sat 9pm–1.30am.

Dutch Ned's Saloon, 206 1st Ave S at S Washington St (☎340-8859). A Pioneer Square bar that hosts the "Seattle Slam" poetry competition/event every Wednesday night at 9pm for $3, often to raucous audiences of 50–100 people.

New Orleans Creole Restaurant, 114 1st Ave S at Yesler Way (☎622-2563). Anything from Cajun through to ragtime, best when zydeco is featured. The Cajun cuisine isn't bad either.

OK Hotel Café, 212 S Alaskan Way between S Washington and S Main sts (☎621-7903). Once a moshers' favourite, the place is more diverse today, with its winning (grunge) ways mixed in with some of the most avant garde (read ear-splitting/melody-eschewing) bands around along with some non-rock acts, usually for $5–8.

Old Timer's Café, 620 1st Ave at Cherry St (☎623-9800). Narrow and crowded tavern with nightly blues and jazz acts for $5–10.

Paramount, 911 Pine St at 9th Ave (☎682-1414). Venue for the really big names of rock and pop. Ticket prices range $20–65.

The Pike Pub & Brewery, 1415 1st Ave (☎622-6044). Respected small craft brewery serves its own beers, as well as numerous bottled brands, along with a large wine list and extensive fish and pizza-oriented menu, in spacious environs in Pike Place Market.

The Showbox, 1426 1st Ave between Pike and Union sts (☎628-3151). "Big" out-of-town bands will vary their Seattle shows between numerous large halls or arenas that don't have especially distinctive musical agendas, such as the Paramount and the Moore Theatre. The Showbox, right downtown near Pike Place Market, is the best of these, and also puts on well-regarded regional bands with an indie/alternative slant. Tickets $5–20.

Two Bells Tavern, 2313 4th Ave between Bell and Battery sts (☎441-3050). A Belltown institution, drawing artistic and literary types as well as overflow from the downtown business crowd. Occasional free live music.

Virginia Inn, 1937 1st Ave (☎728-1937). Young professionals and old timers mix in this easy-going bar near Pike Place Market at 1st and Virginia; no cover.

Vogue, 1516 11th Ave between Pike and Pine sts (☎324-5778). Rings in your nipples and studs in your nose will help you blend into this dance club with youthful, edgy crowds, and sounds that vary from new wave and Gothic to the more industrial-oriented, ever-popular Sunday Fetish Night. Cover $3–5, $2 Tues.

Capitol Hill

Baltic Room, 1207 Pine St between Melrose Ave E and Boren Ave E (☎625-4444). Divided into bar, music and balcony sections, this club is noted for showcasing DJ-instrumental collaborations, and has more live music (of an eclectic alternative variety) than most DJ-oriented places do. Cover $3–8.

Breakroom, 1325 E Madison St at 14th Ave E (☎860-5155). A good place to see some of the more interesting emerging alternative rock acts from town, and some nationally known touring artists. Tickets usually $5–10.

Century Ballroom, 915 E Pine, 2nd Floor, between Broadway and 10th Ave E (☎324-7263). Major world-music acts from all over the globe, as well as jazz, singer-songwriters, and others. Featuring a 2000-square-foot dance floor, it also has swing and salsa dance nights. $15–20 for live concerts, $4–5 for dance nights.

Comet Tavern, 922 E Pike St just off Broadway (☎323-9853). No-frills bar with smoky pool tables and student-wannabe-nihilist crowd.

Elysian Brewing Co., 1221 E Pike St at 13th Ave E (☎860-1920). Brewpub of one of the better local microbreweries with industrial-type decor that fits in well with the Capitol Hill boho vibe. Occasional live music for about $6.

Hopvine Pub, 507 15th Ave E at E Republican St (☎328-3120). Live acoustic-oriented folk, blues, jazz, singer-songwriter and open-mike performers to drink microbrews to, for no or little cover.

Linda's Tavern, 707 E Pike St at Harvard Ave E (☎325-1220). One of Capitol Hill's most happening bars attracts an alternative/underground rock crowd that gets more crowded and intense as the night wears on. DJs spin two or three nights a week (no cover); blues and soul nights are recommended.

Neighbors, 1509 Broadway at E Pike St (☎324-5358). Gay hangar-like disco. Very popular. Not as musically adventurous as many other dance clubs, though variety is ensured by drag, disco and 1980s nights. Cover $5 weekends, $1 weekdays.

R Place, 619 E Pine St at Boylston Ave E (☎322-8828). Three-floor bar that's a prime cruising spot for young professional gay men, and an alternative for those who want to avoid the dance club environment, with pool and darts. No cover charge.

Re-Bar, 1114 E Howell St at Boren Ave (☎233-9873). Probably the best dance spot in Seattle. Soul and hip-hop are particular favourites, but the music changes emphasis nightly. Mostly gay –

especially on "Queer Disco Nights"– but heteros come here in force too. Near Denny Way intersection just west of I-5. Cover $5–6.

Timberline, 2015 Boren Ave at Denny Way (☎622-6220). Premier Country and Western nightspot for gays, lesbians and "friends of goodwill". On the west edge of Capitol Hill.

Wild Rose Tavern, 1021 E Pike St at 11th Ave E (☎324-9210). A popular venue for lesbians, with decent food and often live music or entertainment; there's rarely a cover.

University District, Fremont, Wallingford and Ballard

Ballard Firehouse, 5429 Russell Ave NW at NW Market (☎784-3516). Nightly live music in this Ballard venue with a whopping dance floor, mainly local bands of a blues, reggae and rock disposition. There are occasional Brazilian nights, and the odd big-name mainstream act. Ticket prices can vary $6–30.

Big Time Brewery and Alehouse, 4133 University Way NE between NE 41st St and NE 42nd St (☎545-4509). Tremendous microbrews make this a popular student haunt.

Blue Moon Tavern, 712 NE 45th St between 7th Ave NE and 8th Ave NE (☎633-6267). In U District, on east side of I-5. Wild and woolly bar famed as the one-time hangout of Ginsberg and Kerouac. It maintains its arty reputation even though Grateful Dead bootlegs hog the tape deck each and every Sunday night. Wide range of local beers.

College Inn, 4000 University Way NE at NE 40th St (☎634-2307). Busy basement bar filled mainly with students and a finely tuned jukebox. Below the diner and guesthouse of the same name.

Hale's Ales, 4301 Leary Way NW at NW 43rd St (☎782-0737). Hand-crafted fine English-style ales from this brewpub, which also offers a decent menu of pub-styled food.

Murphy's Pub, 1928 N 45th St at Meridian Ave N, Wallingford (☎634-2110). Has a massive beer list and live, often Irish, folk for a mere $3 cover.

Paradox, 5510 University Way NE at NE 55th St (☎524-7677). Mixing little-known local rock bands and little-known touring rock bands, this "all-ages" theatre has some of the lowest prices in town (about $5). Doors open at 7pm, shows start at 8pm.

Rainbow, 722 NE 45th St between 7th Ave NE and 8th Ave NE (☎634-1761). Microbrew pints for $2.50 and, often at 10pm, live music from an eclectic array of local rock and non-rock bands for free or for a $3–5 cover.

Tractor Tavern, 5213 Ballard Ave NW at NW 52nd St (☎789-3599). Zydeco, Irish, blues and bluegrass, with the occasional high-profile act, for $5–10. A much better alternative than similar spots in Pioneer Square.

Triangle Tavern, 3507 Fremont Place N at N 35th St (☎632-0880). Fremont's best tavern is a relaxed affair that attracts a youthful, occasionally artsy local clientele, also serving good food such as grilled fish and salads.

Trollyman Pub, 3400 Phinney N at N 34th St (☎634-4213). The best brewpub in Seattle, pumping out all varieties of the Northwest's favourite craft brewery (the ESB, or extra special bitter, is especially beloved) in a casual setting with a convivial Fremont crowd and occasional free live music.

Dance, classical music and opera

Until recently **Seattle Center** was the base for all three of the city's cultural institutions: the Pacific Northwest Ballet (☎441-2424, *www.pnb.org*), the Seattle Symphony Orchestra (☎215-4747, *www.seattlesymphony.org*) and the Seattle Opera (☎389-7699, *www.seattleopera.org*). The symphony, however, has moved downtown to Benaroya Hall (3rd and Union sts), whose acoustics are rated as among the finest in the world for classical performances. The Opera House in Seattle Center is due to be closed and renovated at the end of 2001, reopening in mid-2003 as Marion Oliver McCaw Hall; in the interim, performances are tentatively planned to continue in the Mercer Arena in Seattle Center. Tickets for the symphony, opera and ballet go for anything between $10 and $100, and tend to sell out in advance, although there are occasionally half-price tickets for students and seniors on the day of performance, about fifteen minutes before showtime.

On the University of Washington campus, the **Meany Theatre** (☎543-4880 or 1-800/859-5342) stages classical music, world dance, opera, world music and theatrical events, many featuring performers of international repute. **On the Boards** at 100 W Roy St (☎217-9888), in addition to its theatre programme, stages cutting-edge dance events, often of a multidisciplinary nature. The **Northwest Chamber Orchestra** (☎343-0445) presents concerts at the Nordstrom Recital Hall in Benaroya Hall, as well as the Seattle Art Museum and Volunteer Park.

Theatre

Theatre is Seattle's strongest suit, with numerous small groups performing serious drama alongside the visiting Broadway shows. The scene's at its most adventurous during the Seattle Fringe Festival (☎526-1959, *www.seattlefringe.org*), which stages scores of productions in more than half-a-dozen Capitol Hill locations over about ten days in March; tickets are usually in the $10 range.

A Contemporary Theatre (ACT), Kreielsheimer Place, 700 Union St at 7th Ave (☎292-7676). Showcase for mostly modern mainstream drama, in a 1925 auditorium near the Convention Center downtown. April–Nov. Ticket prices can be as low as $5, or more than $40 for good seats.

Empty Space, 3509 Fremont Ave N at N 35th St (☎547-7500). Adventurous cosmopolitan dramas and sparse versions of the classics, for $15–25.

Fifth Avenue Theatre, 1308 5th Ave and University St (☎625-1418). Hosts glamorous musicals – anything less gets lost in the restored movie palace's flamboyant proportions. Tickets go for about $25–40.

Intiman Theatre, Seattle Center (☎269-1900). Classics and premieres of bolder new works, along with the occasional surprise like a Spalding Gray monologue. Seats sell for $23–42.

New City (☎328-4683). Organization that commissions a lot of new works for performance, and often shows works-in-progress in various venues.

Northwest Actors Studio, 1100 E Pike St at 11th Ave E (☎324-6328). A theatre arts centre that, in addition to offering acting courses, puts on a performance calendar with a wide scope: comedy, Shakespeare, and the ultra-avant-garde are all fair game. Tickets are usually $10 and under.

On the Boards, 100 W Roy St at 1st Ave W (☎217-9888). In addition to its contemporary dance programme, challenging contemporary theatre is also performed, often mixing dance and theatre in the same production.

Open Circle, 429 Boren Ave N at N Republican St (in back off the alley) (☎382-4250). A fifty-seater theatre that's one of the city's more intimate playhouses; its own company gives several shows and workshop performances each year, with content from Jean Genet to rock musicals. Tickets around $15.

Seattle Children's Theatre, Charlotte Martin Theatre, Seattle Center (☎441-3322). Half a dozen mainstage productions ($13–20) each year (Sept–June) from a company that also tours Seattle schools.

Seattle Repertory Company (☎443-2222). Oldest and most established company, performing popular contemporary material, with a good dash of the classics, at Bagley Wright Theatre in Seattle Center. A second stage in the same facility, Leo K. Theatre, was recently opened for new and smaller-scaled works. Ticket prices can vary $10–42; no performances June–Sept.

Film

Seattle has the usual first-release venues, prime among which is the big Metro Cinemas complex on 45th and Roosevelt (☎633-0055) in the U District, offering several screens. But the city also has a number of small, independent cinemas, many concentrated in the U and Capitol Hill districts. Housed in rickety old buildings, they show a selection of left-of-field and foreign films, particularly in May when the annual **Seattle International Film Festival** takes place. Check local papers for specific listings.

Egyptian, 801 E Pine St a half-block west of Broadway (☎323-4978). Housed in an old Masonic Temple, the Art Deco HQ of the annual film festival.

Grand Illusion, 1403 NE 50th St at University Way (☎523-3935). Tiny place in the U District with lots of independent and foreign films.

Harvard Exit, 807 E Roy St (☎323-8986). Well-worn building at the northern edge of Broadway in Capitol Hill shows a consistent programme of left-of-centre current releases and festival films.

The Little Theatre, 608 19th Ave E at E Mercer St (☎675-2055). This non-profit cinema puts on an eclectic, often daring selection of contemporary independent and foreign movies, as well as some overlooked nuggets from the past.

911 Media Arts, 117 Yale Ave N between Stewart and John sts (☎682-6552). Non-profit media centre holds regular screenings of experimental films and videos.

Seven Gables Theatre, 911 NE 50th St at Roosevelt Way (☎632-8820). Art-house movie theatre.

Varsity, 4329 University Way NE between NE 43rd and NE 44th sts (☎632-3131). Runs one or two rep-house movies every day, including old classics, documentaries, foreign films, newly released independents, and commercial re-releases.

Gay Seattle

Focusing on the Capitol Hill district, Seattle's **gay scene** is lively and well organized. The best source of information is the weekly *Seattle Gay News*, a high-quality paper with plenty of local resource information and listings of all that's current; pick up a copy at a decent downtown bookshop, or the predominantly gay bookshops mentioned below. Gay and lesbian nightspots are included in our general listings.

Bookshops stocking a wide range of gay and lesbian books, poetry, magazines and videos include Red and Black Books, at 430 15th Ave E (☎322-7323), and Beyond the Closet, 1501 Belmont Ave E at E Pike Street (☎322-4609), which also hosts occasional readings. More general information on lesbian groups and events is available from the Lesbian Resource Center, at 1808 Bellevue Ave (☎322-3953).

Festivals

Seattle has several outstanding **festivals**. For four days at the beginning of September, the musicians, actors and dancers of the **Bumbershoot** (☎281-8111), the city's premier Arts Festival, take over the Seattle Center. Less well-known outside of Seattle, but just as popular, is the **Northwest Folk Festival** (☎684-7300) on Memorial Day Weekend, emphasizing rootsy, frequently acoustic-oriented folk, bluegrass, Celtic, singer-song-writer, folk-rock, blues and world music, along with numerous crafts and ethnic foods booths, as well as some dance, storytelling and workshops. **Seafair** (☎728-0123) is the biggest party of the lot, a three-week shindig celebrating Seattle's maritime connections, with a selection of activities from children's parades and wacky boat races to high-speed jet-fighter manoeuvres by the Navy's Blue Angels. From mid- to late September, the **Puyallup Fair** (☎253/841-5045) is held in Puyallup, about thirty miles south of the city. It's a sort of cross between a giant-sized amusement arcade and an agricultural fair, with performances by some of the biggest stars of the Country music world.

Listings

Air tours Seattle Seaplanes, 1325 Fairview Ave E (☎329-9638 or 1-800/637-5553), operate twenty-minute seaplane tours over Seattle for $42.50 per person every day from 8am–sunset (Sun 9am–sunset).

Airlines Alaska Airlines, 1301 4th Ave (☎433-3100); American Airlines, *Sheraton Hotel*, 6th and Pike sts (☎1-800/433-7300); British Airways, 1304 4th Ave (☎1-800/247-9297); Delta, 410 University St (☎1-800/221-1212); Northwest Airlines, 402 University Ave (☎1-800/225-2525); TWA, no Seattle ticket office (☎1-800/221-2000); United, 1303 4th Ave (☎1-800/241-6522).

Airport Sea-Tac International Airport, 17801 Pacific Hwy S (general information ☎431-4444 or 1-800/544-1965).

American Express 600 Stewart St (Mon–Fri 8.30am–5.30pm; ☎441-8622).

Banks Major branches include Union Bank of California, 910 4th Ave (☎587-6100); US Bank, 1619 3rd Ave (☎344-2297); Wells Fargo, Westlake Center, 1620 4th Ave (☎292-3256).

Bike rental Downtown at Blazing Saddles, 1230 Western Ave (☎341-9994); elsewhere Gregg's, 7007 Woodlawn Ave NE in Green Lake (☎523-1822), or Bicycle Center, 4529 Sandpoint Way NE (☎523-8300), which is near the 12.5 mile Burke-Gilman Trail that runs north from Gasworks Park through the University of Washington and beyond.

Bookshops The University Bookstore, 4326 University Way in the U District (☎634-3400), is the city's biggest general bookshop; the Elliott Bay Book Company, 101 S Main St in Pioneer Square (☎624-6600), is convenient and cosy. Metsker Maps, 702 1st Ave (☎623-8747), has a comprehensive selection of local and regional maps; Wide World Books and Maps, out at 4411 Wallingford Ave N (☎634-3453), features the city's best assortments of travel guides and literature. Twice Sold Tales, 905 E John St (☎324-2421), is Seattle's best secondhand bookshop, open until 1am (all night Fri). The collectively run Left Bank Books in Pike Place Market at 92 Pike St (☎622-1095) is the best local left-wing bookshop.

Car rental Alamo, airport 20636 Pacific Hwy S (☎433-0182); and downtown: *Seattle Hilton*, 1301 6th Ave (☎292-9770). Budget, airport 17808 Pacific Hwy S (☎244-4008); and downtown at Westlake and Virginia (☎682-2277). Dollar, airport: 17600 Pacific Hwy S (☎433-6777); and downtown: 7th Ave and Stewart (☎682-1316). Enterprise, airport: 15667 Pacific Hwy S (☎246-1953); and downtown: 2116 Westlake Ave (☎382-1051). Penny, 19059 Pacific Hwy S (☎246-9828). Thrifty, airport: 18836 International Blvd (☎246-7565); and downtown: 801 Virginia St (☎625-1133).

City tours Gray Line (☎626-5208 or 1-800/426-7532) runs guided city tours by coach, covering all major sights with copious commentary. The full six-hour experience costs $34 (late April–Oct only) and the three-hour trip $29 (all year). They also offer daily ten-hour excursions to Mount Rainier from May–Sept, at $50 each. Rather more fun, but necessarily less comprehensive, are the Argosy cruises of the Chittenden locks departing Pier 57 daily (3hr; $28; ☎623-4252). Argosy also operates frequent one-hour boat trips round Elliott Bay all year. Departures from Pier 55; $15 each – though the ordinary commuter services of Washington State Ferries (☎464-6400) offer pretty much the same view, and they're a lot cheaper.

Consulates Canada, Plaza 600 Suite 412 (☎443-1777); Denmark, 6204 E Mercer Way, Mercer Island (☎230-0888); Germany, 600 University St, Suite 2500 (☎682-4312); New Zealand, 6810 51st Ave NE (☎525-0271); Norway, Joseph Vance Building, 3rd Ave and Union (☎623-3957); Sweden, 1215 4th Ave (☎622-5640); UK, eighth floor of the First Interstate Center at 3rd and Madison (☎622-9255), surprisingly friendly, though they may well refer you to LA.

Currency exchange Most large downtown banks will change foreign currency and travellers' checks. American Express cheques should be cashed at their downtown office (see listing above). Thomas Cook (☎1-800/287-7362) changes money at Sea-Tac Airport (daily 6am–8pm), downtown in Westlake Center, Level Three (Mon–Sat 9.30am–6pm, Sun 11am–5pm), and in Bellevue at 10630 NE 8th St (Mon–Fri 8.30am–5pm, Sat 10am–2pm).

Dentist Yesler Terrace Medical Dental Clinic, 102 Broadway (☎625-9260).

Disabilities The Easter Seal Society of Washington, 521 2nd Ave W (☎281-5700), publishes *Access Seattle*, an excellent guidebook to disabled-accessible places in the city.

Doctor Virginia Mason Clinic, 1100 9th Ave (Mon–Fri 8.30am–5pm, Sat 9am–noon; ☎223-6600).

Emergencies ☎911.

Hospital Northwest Hospital, 1550 N 115th St (☎364-0500). For minor injuries, try the Country Doctor Community Clinic, 500 19th Ave E (☎461-4503); women can use the Aradia Women's Health Center, 1300 Spring St (☎323-9388).

Internet access Several virtual cafés on Capitol Hill offer Internet access for $6/hr, including *Aurafice*, 616 E Pine St (☎860-9977); *CapitolHill.net*, 219 Broadway E (☎860-6858); and *Online Coffee Company*, 1720 E Olive Way (☎328-3731). Many other all-purpose cafés in Seattle offer Internet access for similar rates. It's also becoming increasingly common for accommodations – not just upscale hotels, but hostels too – to offer free Internet access to guests; check before deciding where you're staying if that's an important concern. There are free Internet terminals in Seattle's public libraries, but you need to enter a Seattle Public Library card number and a PIN number to use these.

Laundromats Downtown, the youth hostel has good facilities. There's also 12th Ave Laundry in Capitol Hill at 1807 12th Ave (☎328-4610), and Lost Sock Laundry in the University District at 5020 Roosevelt Way NE (☎524-7855). By far the most enjoyable option is *Sit & Spin*, 2219 4th Ave (☎441-9484), attached to an artsy café and open until midnight (2am Fri–Sat).

Left luggage You can dump your stuff at Sea-Tac Airport at Ken's Luggage Storage under the escalator between baggage claim carousels 9 and 13 (☎433-5333, daily 5.30am–12.30am). There are also storage lockers in Greyhound at 811 Stewart St (☎628-5526) for up to 24 hours for $3.

Library Seattle Public Library, 1000 4th Ave (Sept–May Mon–Thurs 9am–9pm, Fri–Sat 9am–6pm, Sun 1–5pm ☎386-4636). At the same number is a cool information line that will try to answer reasonable fact-oriented questions on all subjects.

News-stands Bulldog News (which also serves espresso and pastries), 4208 University Way NE (☎632-NEWS) and 401 Broadway E in Broadway Market (☎322-NEWS); Steve's News, 204 Broadway E (☎324-7323) and 3416 Fremont Ave N (☎633-0731); Read All About It in Pike Place Market, 93 Pike (☎624-0140).

Pharmacy Prescription department open 24hr at Bartell Drugs, 600 1st Ave N (☎284-1354).

Post office/poste restante The main post office is at Union St and 3rd Ave downtown (Mon–Fri 8am–5.30pm; ☎1-800/275-8777); zip code 98101.

Rape Crisis Line 24hr ☎632-7273.

Sailing From their base on the southwest shore of Lake Union, the NW Outdoor Center, 2100 Westlake Ave N (☎281-9694), rents kayaks by the hour, half-day and full day ($10 per hour single, $12 per hour double); from the Center it's a short paddle to the Washington Ship Canal. The Waterfront Activities Center (☎543-9433), on Lake Union at the southern edge of the University of Washington, rents rowboats or canoes for $6.50 per hour. Emerald City Charters (☎624-3931) run regular sailboat excursions out into Puget Sound from Pier 54; $23 for an hour and a half, $38 for two and a half hours. The Center for Wooden Boats at 1010 Valley St (☎382-2628) rents sailboats and

WESTERN WASHINGTON FERRIES

The network of subsidized routes operated by **Washington State Ferries** provides a wonderful way to explore the islands and peninsulas of the Puget Sound and points north to the Canadian border. Even with a vehicle costs aren't too steep, while bicycles are taken on board for a minimal fee. In many cases, fares are collected in just one direction (usually westbound) and the return trip is "free". However, with the exception of ferries to Sidney, BC, drivers can't make advance reservations, so it's a good idea (especially in summer) to reach the ferry port a couple of hours before departure. Timetables and fare details are available at every ferry dock, including Seattle's Pier 52, or you can call ☎1-800/84-FERRY or 1-888/808-7977 (both numbers work only within Washington state), or ☎464-6400 (in Seattle).

The two most popular and useful services are the one between **Port Townsend**, on the Olympic Peninsula, and Whidbey Island's **Keystone** (every 90min, 10–15 daily according to season; 30min), and another that leaves mainland **Anacortes**, about ninety miles north of Seattle, every one or two hours for the **San Juan** archipelago, docking at Lopez (40–50min), Orcas (1hr–1hr 30min), and San Juan Island (1–2hr). Bear in mind that routes seldom serve all four of the islands from either Anacortes or Friday Harbor, so consulting a schedule before making plans is essential. The return fare from Anacortes to San Juan for vehicle and driver in peak season is just $22.25. Two of the daily San Juan ferries from Anacortes in summer, and one in winter, continue to **Sidney**, BC. An average-sized vehicle, along with the driver, costs $41 each way ($24.75 off-season), extra adult passengers cost $9.10 each.

Going to Canada from **Seattle**, there is the high-speed, passenger-only **Victoria Clipper** from the city's Pier 69 (summer 4 daily, winter 1 daily; ☎448-5000 or 1-800/888-2535) which takes between two and three hours to reach **Victoria**, on Vancouver Island (see p.326). Fares are $54–66 single, $89–109 return. The same company also operates a passenger-only boat to the San Juan Islands once daily from mid-May to mid-September ($32–38 single, $49–59 return).

rowboats for journeys around Lake Union ($12.50–$37.50/hr depending upon size of boat and day of week).

Sport The Mariners baseball team (☎622-HITS or 1-800/MY-MARINERS) play at Safeco Field, just south of the International District at 1st Ave S and S Atlantic St. The Seahawks (☎1-888/NFL-HAWK) are scheduled to play in a stadium just north of there when construction is completed in 2002, but until then they will play in Husky Stadium at the University of Washington. Basketball's Seattle Supersonics (☎283-DUNK) are based at the Key Arena in the Seattle Center.

Taxis Graytop Cab (☎282-8222); Yellow Cab (☎622-6500).

Traveller's Aid 909 4th Ave, Suite 630, between Madison and Marion St (Mon–Fri 9am–4pm; ☎461-3888).

Weather information 24-hour report provided by the *Seattle Times* at ☎464-2000 ext 9902.

Wine Washington now produces wines of international standing (see p.69). The vintages bearing the Columbia Winery trademark are particularly fine and the company's smart retail **Columbia Winery**, at 14030 NE 145th St, Woodinville (☎425/488-2776 or 1-800/488-2347), offers tours and tastings. Amongst their many fine vintages, particular bottles to look out for include the 1995 Wyckoff Vineyard Chardonnay; the 1993 Otis Vineyard Cabernet Sauvignon; the 1995 Otis Vineyard Pinot Gris; and the splendid, richly aromatic 1993 Red Willow Vineyard Cabernet Sauvignon. Reckon on paying about $20 for any of these. Call ahead for directions and details of special offers and events. Woodinville is about twenty miles northeast of downtown Seattle – east off I-405 (Exit 23) along Hwy 522.

Around Seattle

Puget Sound and its easterly neighbour Lake Washington stretch their clutter of tiny islands and ragged peninsulas **around Seattle**, making boats and bridges an essential part of everyday life. Seattle has only been able to spread by means of boats (there's one boat for every six Seattle residents), with the result that most commuters pass over one stretch of water or another on their way to work. You can take advantage of these commuter **ferries** to make the quick crossing from Seattle to **Bainbridge Island** and **Vashon**, both of which make relaxing detours – especially for the cyclist – and are useful as stepping stones, the one to the national parks of the Olympic Peninsula (see p.237) via the **Kitsap Peninsula**; the other, less appealingly, to Tacoma (see p.221). The downside is for the motorist: the ferries tend to clog up with vehicles, while the bridges across Lake Washington just can't cope with the volume of traffic and soul-destroying traffic back-ups develop at the slightest mishap.

Back on the mainland, the flat **coastal strip** to either side of Seattle is congested with mile upon mile of industrial and suburban sprawl. This is not a prepossessing area and your best bet is to clear it as quickly as possible by means of I-5: for points north of the city see p.226, and south p.220; these two routes also give information as to where you can leave I-5 for the most beautiful parts of the Cascade Mountains. The speediest route **east** from Seattle to the Cascades is along I-90, an itinerary covered on p.273; you reach the mountains just this side of Snoqualmie Falls, only 25 miles from downtown Seattle. I-90 is also the fastest way to reach Eastern Washington.

If you're dependent on **public transportation** for exploring the islands round Seattle, be aware that, although the ferry services are fast and frequent, it's usually difficult to get anywhere by bus from the ferry dock.

Bainbridge Island

Few commuters are blessed with as pleasant a trip as the **Bainbridge Island** set, who wake up to a serene half-hour on the ferry, the city skyline drawing gradually closer across Elliott Bay. This is such a delightful journey that the island itself (green and rural, but mostly private land) is for many of its visitors simply an excuse for the ferry

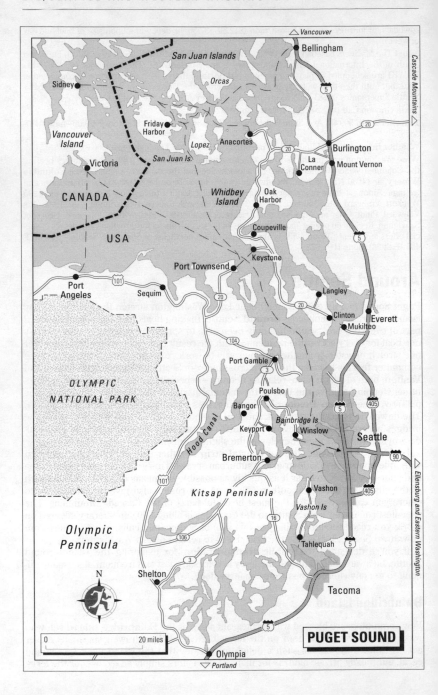

PUGET SOUND

ride. Washington State Ferries leave about every hour from Pier 52 downtown (return tickets $3.70 foot passenger, $13 ($16.50 peak season) vehicle and driver; avoid rush hours), landing in **WINSLOW** – a village so small that once you've admired the harbour and taken in the slightly artsy stores that line the main street, **Winslow Way**, you'll doubtless be ready to head back to Seattle. An alternative is to cycle the island's narrow country roads – Bainbridge is only ten miles from top to bottom – and **camp** in *Fay Bainbridge State Park* (☎206/842-3931, *www.parks.wa.gov/faybain*: $12 standard sites, $6 primitive sites) on the north shore.

The Kitsap Peninsula

Behind Bainbridge Island, sprawling messily into the middle of Puget Sound, lurks the **Kitsap Peninsula**, a jagged spit of land bristling with defence projects: there's a naval submarine base at Bangor, a torpedo-testing station in Keyport, and large naval shipyards at Bremerton – which can also be reached by ferry direct from Seattle.

All of these add up to a fair dollop of military might, but luckily the peninsula has better-looking areas too, spreading out along **Hwy 305**, which merges into Hwy 3 to form the handiest route from Seattle to the Olympic Peninsula. Beginning in Winslow, this road leaves Bainbridge Island at its northern end by Agate Passage Bridge, on the Kitsap side of which is **Port Madison Indian Reservation**.

Old Man House State Park and Suquamish Museum

Just beyond the Agate Passage Bridge, a signed right turn leads the couple of miles off the highway to the quiet cemetery which holds the **grave of Chief Sealth**, who gave his name to "Seattle" and was the tribal leader of the Suquamish when the first whites arrived. Two painted canoes stand above the headstone and the plaque proclaims him "The firm friend of the whites" – something of a dubious accolade, considering how things turned out (see below). Nearby, surrounded by modern housing, the poky **Old Man House State Park** marks the site of the Suquamish people's cedar longhouse, which stretched along the seashore for five hundred feet with a width of about fifty feet: the government had it burnt down in 1870 to eliminate communal living, that great enemy of private-property civilization.

Back on Hwy 305, it's a couple of minutes' drive to the turnoff which twists down to the **Suquamish Museum** (May–Sept daily 10am–5pm; Oct–April Fri–Sun 11am–4pm, *www.telebyte.com/suquamish/museum*; $4). The museum traces the history of the Suquamish, who occupied much of the Kitsap Peninsula until white settlers arrived. Chief Sealth chose to avoid conflict with his new neighbours, but it didn't do much good, and his people received an appallingly bad deal from the carve-up of their land; formerly based throughout Puget Sound, they have since that 1855 treaty (followed by a brief Puget Sound War between white settlers and about fifteen Native-American tribes) been on the 7500-acre Port Madison Indian Reservation. The museum, however, celebrates Native-American culture more than it laments injustices, interspersing exhibits of canoes, folk art and old photographs with quotations from tribal elders, whose recorded voices also overlay a slide show that portrays the schizophrenic lifestyle of present generations, caught between traditional values and a hegemonic culture.

North to Poulsbo and beyond

Further north on Hwy 305, **POULSBO** makes a gallant bid for the passing tourist trade. Founded by Norwegians, it has exploited its heritage by revamping the cafés and souvenir shops along its main street in "little Norway" kitsch. It's all rather daft but quite endearing, and locals take every opportunity to tog themselves up in fancy Nordic dress, especially during mid-May's **Viking Fest**. Traditional Norwegian food is served up all over the place – the *Liberty Bay Bakery and Café*, on the main drag, has tasty meat balls – but otherwise you'll soon be hurrying on.

There's a choice of routes **north from Poulsbo**: you can keep to the main road (Hwys 305 and 3) as it cuts a mundane course towards the Olympic Peninsula, or you can turn right off Hwy 305 just north of town along Hwy 307 and, after about four hundred yards, take a left down **Big Valley Road**. This country lane drifts through a river valley of antique wooden farmhouses, rolling farmland and forested hills. It's a lovely spot and you can break your journey at the delightful **Manor Farm Inn**, where a working farm surrounds a charming picket-fenced farmhouse of 1890 that's been tastefully converted into a plush hotel (☎360/779-4628; ⑤). Reservations are advised; the restaurant is excellent too with a full meal costing in the region of $35.

Heading north along Big Valley Road, you soon rejoin the main road – Hwy 3 – about three miles west of the **Hood Canal Floating Bridge**, which crosses over to the Olympic Peninsula (see p.237). More than a mile in length, the bridge used to be billed as an engineering miracle – until a chunk of it floated out to sea during a violent storm in 1979. It was over three years before the bridge was reopened, with engineers' assurances that it had been reinforced.

Southwest of Poulsbo, proto-militarists will be keen to visit **KEYPORT**, site of the torpedo-proud **Naval Undersea Museum** (June–Sept daily 10am–4pm; closed Tues Oct–May; free), and **BREMERTON**, a rough-edged naval shipyard town where all sorts of naval gear are displayed. The town has a naval museum, a visitable warship – the destroyer USS *Turner Joy* – and the "Mothball Fleet", a handful of warships held in readiness just offshore. The fleet isn't open to the public, but Kitsap Harbor Tours (☎360/377-8924) offer daily, hour-long boat trips ($8.50) round the warships from mid-May to September.

Port Gamble

Draped above a tiny bay just a mile or so beyond the Hood Canal bridge is the Kitsap's prettiest settlement, **PORT GAMBLE**, a pocket-sized lumber town whose entrepreneurial founders, Pope and Talbot, made a killing on the Puget Sound timber trade. They also satisfied a sentimental attachment to their hometown, East Machias, Maine, by shipping out East Coast elm trees to overhang quaint, New-England-style clapboard houses, all owned by the company and rented to the employees of the town sawmill. Pope and Talbot carefully maintained the port's late nineteenth-century appearance and all might have been well if they hadn't closed the mill down in 1995. As a result, Port Gamble is presently a very pretty town, but one without much of a purpose.

It's the tranquil, leafy setting that appeals rather than any specific sight, but the **Port Gamble Historical Museum** (June–Aug daily 10.30am–5pm; $2), which traces the development of the town and its timber trade, is well worth a quick gambol as is the adjoining **General Store**, whose cast-iron pillars and wooden floors accommodate – on the upper floor – a collection of seashells. Up the hill, the old cemetery harbours the grave of one Gustave Engelbrecht, who was killed by local natives in 1856, the first US Navyman to die in action on the Pacific Coast. It was his own fault: he took a pot shot at a native and, in his eagerness to check his kill, jumped up from behind the log which provided his cover, only to be promptly shot himself.

At the moment, there's nowhere to **stay** in Port Gamble, but there are vague plans to establish a B&B – call or drop by the Kitsap Peninsula Visitor and Convention Bureau (☎360/297-8200), here in Port Gamble, for an update.

Vashon Island

From Seattle, it's a short ferry ride to rural **Vashon Island**, a small, cycleable island where there's little to do but unwind and explore the leafy country lanes. There are actually two ferries to choose from – either the passenger-only ferry from Pier 50 (Mon–Fri only; 25min; $3.70 return), or the Fauntleroy car ferry from West Seattle, a fifteen-minute drive from downtown ($11.50 return, foot passengers $2.50; 15min). Once there, you'll find Vashon's one and only main road cuts across the island from north to south with a spur road running across a narrow causeway to dumpy **Maury Island**, though this islet is a bit of a yawn. Inevitably, given the proximity of Seattle, Vashon has attracted its share of wealthy city folk, but it is all very discreet and **VASHON** village, the island's only focal point about four miles south of the ferry terminal – and reachable on Metro buses #118 and #119 – barely raises a pulse. That said, *Express Cuisine*, 17629 Vashon Hwy SW (☎206/463-6626, Wed–Sun evenings only) offers a tasty eclectic menu, and there's good Mexican food at *Casa Bonita*, 17623 100th Ave SW (☎206/463-6452) just a block or two over to the west. Finally, three miles or so further south, is the upmarket wholefood of the *Island Restaurant & Bakery*, 20312 Vashon Hwy SW (☎206/463-3565), which brings Seattleites over for weekend brunch.

Vashon has several **B&Bs** (details from the visitor centre in Seattle, or call Castle Hill Reservation Service at ☎206/463-5491) plus the **Vashon Island Hostel (AYH)**, 12119 SW Cove Rd (May–Oct; ☎206/463-2592, *www.vashonhostel.com*; reservations advised; ①/②). The hostel is a good six miles from the ferry dock – head down the main island road and take the signposted turning on the right – or you can call ahead for a free pick-up. Surrounded by forest, the hostel's covered wagons and tepees provide family accommodation, as well as rooms for couples; a log cabin is used as a dorm, with rates starting at $10 for members ($13 non-members). Free bicycles are provided for cycling the island. If you're not staying here, you can rent bikes at Vashon Island Bicycles (☎206/463-6225) on 9925 SW 178th St in town.

If you'd rather not return directly to Seattle, then carry on to Tahlequah, Vashon's southern tip, where Washington State Ferries sail every hour or so to Point Defiance on the northern outskirts of Tacoma (see p.221). Incidentally, you only have to pay to get to the island – leaving is free.

WESTERN WASHINGTON

Seattle faces Elliott Bay, roughly the mid-point of **Puget Sound**, which hooks deep into Washington like an inland sea, its islands, bays and inlets sheltering every kind of watercraft, from yachts and schooners to fishing trawlers and merchant ships. For the most part, the Sound borders a bucolic landscape of rolling farmland trimmed by forested hills and ridges, but on either side of Seattle the shoreline is blemished by huge swaths of development that are the by-product of its economic success. **South of Seattle**, I-5, the main north–south highway, skids past the mess, running parallel to the Sound to round its southern end at blue-collar **Tacoma**, where heavy industry has caused a worrying amount of contamination. Pressing on south, I-5 soon reaches – at Exit 127 – the first of several turnings leading to Mount Rainier National Park (see p.258) and then clears the pollution as it approaches the dignified government buildings of **Olympia**, the downbeat state capital. Further south still, I-5 races on past turnings that travel east to the volcanic remains of Mount St Helens (see p.261), before reaching Washington State's **Vancouver**, site of a reconstructed Hudson's Bay Company fur-trapping colony. Beyond is Portland, Oregon, one hundred and seventy miles from Seattle.

North of Seattle, the urban sprawl drifts up the coast on either side of I-5, sweeping round **Everett** to stretch out towards the pancake-flat floodplain of the Skagit River, whose waters are straddled by the twin towns of **Mount Vernon** and **Burlington**. There's precious little here to catch the eye – the exception being the attractive town of **La Conner**, near the mouth of the Skagit – though both US-2 and (the more appealing)

Hwy 20 fork east off I-5 for the splendid 450-mile Cascade Loop, which travels through some of Washington's finest mountain scenery (see pp.266–273). North of here, further along I-5, is **Bellingham**, part industrial eyesore, part bustling student town, from where it's just a short hop over the border to Vancouver (see p.287). To the west of I-5, and also within easy reach, is the smattering of beautiful islands that extends as far as Canada's Vancouver Island. At the weekend, Puget Sounders escape from the cities to the rural parts of **Whidbey Island**, or further north to the beautiful **San Juan Islands**, among which **Orcas** boasts the most stunning scenery while **Lopez** is something of a rusticated idyll, its quiet country roads perfect for cycling.

Cross an island or two **west from Seattle**, and you come to the **Olympic Peninsula**, fringed with logging communities and circled by US-101. The rugged mountains at its core rise high above the lush vegetation of the mountain slopes which, in their turn, give way to the tangled rainforests of the western valleys, and the sea-lashed wilderness beaches on the Pacific edge. This is amazing stuff, and the most magnificent parts of the peninsula are protected within the **Olympic National Park**, complete with scores of superb hiking trails. There are numerous campsites in the park too, plus several fine old lodges, or you can stay just outside – **Sequim** is the most likeable of the surrounding towns, not least because it's in the rain-shadow of the Olympic Mountains. Slightly further afield, **Port Townsend** is another possible base for visiting the national park, though this lively little place is well worth a visit in itself for its fancy Victorian architecture and sociable nightlife.

South of the national park, the chubby bays that punctuate Washington's **lower coast** are protected from the open sea by elongated sand spits. But although the beaches are long and sandy, the scenery is almost universally flat and monotonous and even though the ribbon-resorts – like **Ocean Shores** and **Long Beach** – are very popular, they are characterized by desultory seaside chalets and RV parks. There are other irritations too: powerful undertows and drifting logs make swimming dangerous and the beaches are hardly protected at all, so people drive all over them – in contrast to the Oregon Coast (see Chapter 1), where vehicles are rarely allowed. The best advice is probably to bypass Washington's lower coast altogether, but for the scenic pleasures – if not the military remains – of **Fort Canby State Park** at the mouth of the Columbia River in the very southwest corner of the state.

To see the best of Western Washington you'll need your own **vehicle**: Greyhound **buses** and Amtrak **trains** shuttle up and down the route of I-5, but otherwise they leave the region alone. Several **local bus** companies combine to offer a service round most of the Olympic Peninsula, but don't venture far into the national park, and although **Washington State ferries** can take you from island to island, only rarely are the jetties anywhere near where you'll want to go. The region's many **B&Bs** offer the most distinctive accommodation, along with scores of **campsites**, many of which occupy fine wilderness locations.

The area code for Western Washington with the exception of the
Seattle–Tacoma corridor is ☎360.

South of Seattle on I-5

Just thirty-five miles south of Seattle on I-5, **Tacoma**, Washington's second-largest city, is an industrial centre of little immediate appeal, though there have been brave attempts to clean up the waterfront whilst neighbouring **Point Defiance Park** offers lush forest walks and beaches. Along with Seattle, Tacoma expanded rapidly during the industrial boom of the early 1900s, but nearby **Olympia**, the state capital, was hardly affected at all – its harbour wasn't deep enough. Instead, politics has become Olympia's main money-spinner, and the grand **Legislative Building** its principal tourist attraction. Beyond Olympia, **I-5** skirts the western foothills of the Cascades on its way to **Vancouver**, where there's a reconstruction of the Hudson's Bay Company outpost originally built here early in the nineteenth century; across the Columbia River is Portland, Oregon (see p.84).

Tacoma

TACOMA has a massive credibility problem. While the city council claims it's simply an unfortunate coincidence that "aroma" rhymes with Tacoma, the "smelly" label has stuck, making industrial Tacoma the butt of Northwest jokes. There's some truth behind it too: Tacoma's deep Commencement Bay (thought by nineteenth-century explorers to be far superior to anything Seattle had to offer) was recently listed by the Environmental Protection Agency as one of the USA's most dangerously polluted areas. Neither is it to the city's advantage, in tourist terms at least, that the military are ensconced on the south side of town in two large bases, the army at Fort Lewis, the air force at McChord. Nevertheless, a gallant attempt has been made to spruce up the city centre in recent years and although much of the tawdriness remains – and locals still withdraw to the suburbs after dark – the good news is that a new museum is presently under construction downtown.

Coming in on I-5 from the north, you'll pass the enormous blue-grey roof of the **Tacoma Dome** sports and concert venue just before you reach I-5's Exit 133, which you should take for **Pacific Avenue**, a major artery that divides the sloping town centre from the industrial area around the port. Pacific Avenue leads north straight to the **Tacoma Art Museum** at Pacific and 12th (Tues–Wed & Fri–Sun 10am–5pm, Thurs 10am–8pm; *www.tacomaartmuseum.org*; $5). The museum's permanent collection has a healthy selection of French Impressionists – Renoir, Pissarro and Degas – plus an excellent assortment of glasswork by the sculptor Dale Chihuly, a Tacoma native who is arguably the most renowned glass artist in the world. However, the rotating special exhibits – which, in recent years, often occupy most of the building – are often even more diverting, typically featuring challenging pieces in a variety of media by up-and-coming artists from the Northwest. The museum has proved extremely popular and in 2003 it is scheduled to move into a new facility with over twice the space, a few blocks away at 16th and Pacific.

As for the rest of downtown – on and around Pacific Avenue – a particular highlight is the **Broadway Plaza**, home to the three theatres that comprise the **Broadway Center for the Performing Arts**, which stages ballet, plays and concerts. Its centrepiece is the elegant, white **Pantages Theatre**, at 9th and Broadway, a 1918 vaudeville theatre reopened in 1983. Further south, at 1717 Pacific Ave and 17th Street, there's also the handsome copper-domed **Union Station**, now used as a courthouse, and next door is the excellent **Washington State History Museum**, (late March to Labor Day Mon–Wed & Fri–Sat 10am–5pm, Thurs 10am–8pm, Sun 11am–5pm; Labor Day to late March Tues–Wed & Fri–Sat 10am–5pm, Thurs 10am–8pm, Sun 11am–5pm; *www.wshs.org*; $7, free Thurs 5–8pm), with its three football fields' worth of intelligently laid-out exhibits. Here, large galleries re-create the milieu of frontier towns, railroads, and early logging industries; there are also in-depth displays on Native-American history, the hardships of Washington life during the Depression and World War II, and the 1919 general strike in Seattle.

Ruston Way leads northwest from downtown Tacoma, following the curve of Commencement Bay as far as **Point Defiance Park**, whose beaches, gardens and dense shady forest occupy a thick finger of land that pokes out into Puget Sound. There are several specific attractions here too, beginning with the **Zoo and Aquarium** (summer daily

10am–7pm; March–May, Sept–Oct & Dec daily 10am–4pm; Jan–Feb & Nov Fri–Sun 10am–4pm; *www.pdza.org*; $7.25), a fair though small space that does have a few unusual species, particularly in the Arctic Tundra section, with its arctic foxes and baby polar bears. Next up is **Camp Six** (Feb–May & Oct Wed–Sun & holidays 10am–4pm; June–Sept Wed–Fri 10am–4pm, weekends & holidays 10am–7pm; *www.camp-6-museum .org*; free), a reconstructed logging camp with bunkhouses, old logging equipment and a restored functioning steam engine ($2.50 for rides). There's also **Fort Nisqually** (April–May Wed–Sun 11am–5pm; June–Aug daily 11am–6pm; Sept–March Wed–Sun 11am–4pm; *www.fortnisqually.org*; $3 April–Aug, rest of year free weekdays and $3 weekends), a reconstruction of the fur-trading post set up by the Hudson's Bay Company in 1833, when American colonists were beginning to threaten the monopoly of the British company. Fort Nisqually was seen as a key British foothold in what later became Washington State – an area which the British originally intended to keep.

Practicalities

Set squarely on the main north–south route between Seattle and Portland, Tacoma is easy to get to. The Greyhound **bus station** is in the heart of town at 1319 Pacific Ave and S 13th Street (☎253/383-4621) and the Amtrak **train station** at 1001 Puyallup Ave (☎253/627-8141) is a mile or so south of downtown, near I-5; **local buses** run by Pierce Transit (☎253/581-8000) serve the Tacoma area. Pierce Transit also connect with Seattle's local Metro buses, offering a bargain-rate route between the two cities. Its Seattle Express lines are more pleasant alternatives than the Greyhound runs, with frequent service between downtown Tacoma (at 10th St and Commerce Ave) and downtown Seattle ($2.50; 1hr). Transit maps are available at The Bus Shop, 930 Commerce Ave (Mon–Fri 8am–5pm). Tacoma's small **visitor centre** at 1001 Pacific Ave, Suite 400 (Mon–Fri 8.30am–5pm; ☎253/627-2836, *www.tpctourism.org*), has maps and free literature about sights in Tacoma–Pierce County.

With Seattle just 35 miles up the highway and Point Defiance Park connected by regular ferry with Vashon Island (see p.218), it's unlikely that **accommodation** in Tacoma will be a priority. Hotels downtown are either smart and pricey for the business community or grim in the extreme; your best option is the plush *Sheraton Tacoma Hotel*, next to the enormous convention centre at 1320 Broadway Plaza (☎253/572-3200 or 1-800/845-9466; ⑨); ask for a room with a view over Commencement Bay.

For **entertainment**, it's worth checking what's on at the Broadway Center for the Performing Arts (☎253/591-5894). The *Antique Sandwich Company*, 5102 N Pearl at 51st (☎253/752-4069), near Point Defiance Park, is an offbeat **café** which has huge pots of tea and often features live folk or classical music in the evenings. Closer to downtown, *Engine House No 9*, at 611 N Pine St (☎253/272-3435), is a lively tavern/café bedecked with firemen's helmets and crowded with locals consuming excellent pizza, carrot cake and the like with their beer until the wee small hours.

Olympia and around

Thirty miles southwest of Tacoma on I-5, downtown **OLYMPIA** stretches along the east bank of Budd Inlet, an arm of Puget Sound, in the shadow of the state government's Capitol buildings. Olympia was chosen as Washington's capital in 1853 – a decade after the first white settlers reached the area – in the hope that what was then no more than a muddy little logging community would turn into a major metropolis. It didn't and today the town seems sleepy and quiet after the bustle of Seattle, though it is a pleasant enough place and a handy base for visiting both Mt Rainier (see p.258) and Mt St Helens (see p.261).

The stately complex of buildings that comprise the **State Capitol**, grouped on a "campus" just to the south of downtown (I-5, Exit 105A), are a tribute to the sheer energy of the pioneers, who plotted something extraordinarily ambitious in what was then the back of beyond. Finally completed in 1928, after 34 years in the making, the **Legislative Building** (daily 10am–3pm hourly guided tours; free) is the one to see, an imposing Romanesque structure topped with a high stone dome along the lines of London's St Paul's Cathedral. Inside, a massive brass Tiffany chandelier hangs amongst a plethora of gaudy furnishings and fittings – such as a colossal walnut table, French velvet drapes and bronze-cast doors of gargantuan proportions. Epic murals were originally planned for the interior – and the *Twelve Labors of Hercules* by Michael Spafford is indeed up on the walls of one of the government chambers – but Washington's pious legislators were apparently so shocked by the "pornographic" images of the painting that their immediate reaction was to spend $15,000 covering it up with hardboard and curtains. Mercifully, these have now been removed.

Behind the State Capitol campus is slender **Capitol Lake**, which filters north into **Budd Inlet** through the narrowest of channels. Together, these two strips of water frame **downtown** Olympia, which starts a short walk down from the campus along Capitol Way and comprises a few blocks of shops and restaurants, presided over by the chateau-like **Old Capitol**, at 7th Avenue and Franklin. Built as a courthouse in 1891, this handsome neo-Romanesque structure, with its turreted roofs and arched windows, served as the capitol until the Legislative Building was finished; it now houses various administrative offices. Immediately to the north of downtown is Olympia's **waterfront**, part of which has been attractively revamped with restaurants, a marina and a board-walk that end where the port begins.

In the other direction, eight blocks south of the State Capitol, is the small **Washington State Capital Museum**, 211 W 21st Ave (Tues–Fri 10am–4pm, Sat–Sun noon–4pm; $2), which occupies the handsome Mediterranean-style 1920s mansion of the wealthy Lord family. The building is actually rather more interesting than the dis-plays, featuring a detailed but dry trawl through the history of Olympia on the ground floor and a few Native-American bygones up above.

> The area code for Western Washington with the exception of the Seattle–Tacoma corridor is ☎360.

Tumwater

A mile or two south of Capitol Campus, across the narrow neck of Capitol Lake, tiny **TUMWATER** was Washington's first pioneer community, settled in 1845 by an intrepid group who saw the potential in harnessing the power of the tumbling waters – from which the town takes its name – of the Deschutes River, at a point so near the open sea. One of their leaders was George Bush, a black ex-employee of the Hudson's Bay Company who was persuaded to leave his farm and return west by his Missouri neigh-bours. The party had intended to settle in the Willamette Valley, but on the journey they learnt that the Oregon government, in their desire to avoid the slavery question, had passed a raft of discriminatory legislation – "all Negros and mulattos to be flogged once every six months until [they] quit the territory" – a build-up to the Exclusion Law that prohibited black immigration in 1849. Bush took the hint, and chose Washington instead.

Tumwater Historical Park marks the site of the original settlement and here you'll also find, at Deschutes Way and Grant Street, the small white house of one of the early pioneers, a certain Nathaniel Crosby, grandfather of Harry, otherwise known as Bing Crosby. Finding the park is surprisingly difficult, considering it is tucked so close to the east side of I-5 (Exit 103). The simplest approach is from Olympia: take Capitol Way/Boulevard out of town, turn right down Custer Way and follow the signs.

Wolf Haven International

Southeast of Tumwater on Capitol Boulevard (Old Hwy 99), it's about eight miles to Offutt Lake Road, where a left turn leads to **Wolf Haven International** (May–Sept daily 10am–5pm; April & Oct Mon & Wed–Sun daily 10am–4pm; March, Nov & Dec Sat–Sun 10am–4pm; *www.wolfhaven.org*). Established in 1982 to provide a safe breeding ground for the threatened North American timberwolf, and a sanctuary and open-air hospital for wolves shot or poisoned by livestock ranchers, the Wolf Haven has grown into an eighty-acre facility that's now home to over forty of these surprisingly affectionate, sociable creatures.

Close-up, educational **tours** ($6) are given hourly throughout the day, but the best time to come is for the Saturday night "Howl-Ins" (May–Aug Sat 6–9pm; ☎264-4695 or 1-800/448-9653, reservations required; $6), when storytellers evoke various wolf-related myths and legends, especially those of the Native-Americans. When darkness falls, a sort of call-and-response kicks off between the audience and the nearby wolves, baying to the rising moon. The less family-oriented "wolf tales" nights with adult educational programming and entertainment take place during the same months (Fri 7–10pm; $12).

Olympia practicalities

Olympia is on I-5 and easily accessible by car or bus. The **Greyhound** station (☎357-5541) is downtown at Capitol Way and 7th Avenue, about five blocks north of the State Capitol campus. In addition, Intercity Transit (☎786-1881) provides a local bus service around Olympia and Tumwater; adult fare is 60¢, and a one-day pass costs just $1.25. The **transit center** is downtown on State Avenue, between Franklin and Washington streets (Mon–Fri 7.30am–5.30pm).

The **visitor centre** (Mon–Fri 8am–5pm; ☎586-3460, *www.visitolympia.com*) is at the entrance to the State Capitol campus, 14th Avenue and Capitol Way. One particularly good **place to stay** is the *Harbinger Inn B&B*, 1136 East Bay Drive NE (☎754-0389; ④), a graceful, balconied Edwardian villa with period furnishings and five guestrooms with or without private bath. It is located about a mile north of downtown on the east shore of Budd Inlet. Two blander, but more central options are the *Best Western Alladin Motor Inn* at 900 Capitol Way at 9th Avenue (☎352-7200 or 1-800/367-7771; ④), and the *Phoenix Inn*, 415 Capitol Way at Thurston Avenue (☎570-0555 or 1-877/570-0555; ⑤), a new chain hotel just a block or so from the waterfront. The rooms at the Phoenix are large and furnished in smart modern style and have microwaves and refrigerators. There's **camping** at forested **Millersylvania State Park** (☎753-1519, *www.parks.wa.gov/miller.htm*; $12), two miles east of I-5 (Exit 99) and twelve miles south of Olympia.

For **food**, try the waterfront's *Budd Bay Café*, 525 Columbia St at A Avenue (☎357-6963), a bright, smart restaurant serving tasty seafood either inside or on the boardwalk terrace. Failing that, *The Spar*, a few blocks away at 114 4th Ave E between Capitol and Washington, is a genuine 1930s diner with a long, curved counter.

As for **entertainment**, Olympia is home to a fertile **indie rock** scene, which has spawned acts such as Beat Happening, Lois, and critical pets Sleater-Kinney, most of whom play ingratiatingly homespun punk and folk-punk. Unfortunately, the live rock scene is not that easy for travellers to plug into due to its erratic schedule and irregular rotation of venues, but your first port of call should be the Capitol Theatre, 206 5th Ave E (☎754-6670), an art cinema that often stages indie rock-oriented shows. In addition, *Yoyo a Go Go*, a multi-day extravaganza of regional and international indie bands, has been held here in Olympia every two or three years since 1994, though it hasn't committed to becoming a regularly scheduled event; for updates, check its Web page at *www.olywa.net/yoyo*. If rock is not your thing, check out the **Washington Center for** the **Performing Arts** on 512 Washington St SE (☎753-8586), which has a full schedule of classical and world music, drama and ballet.

South of Olympia on I-5: Centralia and Washington's Vancouver

Thumping south along I-5 from Olympia, it only takes about ninety minutes to cover the one hundred miles to Portland, Oregon. On the way, the most obvious detour is east to **Mount St Helens**, where the scarred, volcanic landscape, witness to the massive eruption of 1980, constitutes one of the region's most remarkable attractions – see pp.261–266. Several turnings lead to the volcano, but the easiest (and busiest) is located about halfway between Olympia and Portland: coming from the north, turn down Hwy 505 near Toledo, approaching where Hwy 504 at Castle Rock; Hwy 505 joins Hwy 504 about fifteen miles east of I-5. Alternatively, if you're travelling north aiming for **Mount Rainier** (see p.258), turn off I-5 at Hwy 12, also about halfway between Olympia and Portland – though note that drivers heading south for Rainier from Seattle should leave I-5 just outside Tacoma (see above).

Along the route of the I-5 itself, there's precious little to detain you, though the workaday, lumber town of **CENTRALIA**, 23 miles from Olympia, is of passing interest as the site of one of the nastiest incidents in the history of Washington's Wobblies (see p.627). During the Armistice Day parade of 1919, several members of the American Legion attacked the town's union building (at 807 N Tower St) and, in the fight that followed, four were shot. Local Wobblies were promptly rounded up and thrown into jail, but vigilantes broke in that night to seize, mutilate and then lynch one of their number, a certain Wesley Everest. To make sure the others took the point, the police laid the body out on the jail floor.

Further south, modest **VANCOUVER** lies just across the Columbia River from Portland. Dwarfed by its larger and more prosperous neighbour, Vancouver is an inconclusive sort of place – half dormitory-suburb, half small-town – falling on either side of I-5. The only reason to stop is **Fort Vancouver National Historic Site** (daily 9am–4/5pm; $2), a credible reconstruction of the Pacific Northwest's first substantial European settlement – it's just east of I-5 (Exit 1C, Mill Plain Blvd). Dating from the 1820s, this stockaded outpost of the British-owned Hudson's Bay Company was, for

---

THE LEGEND OF D.B. COOPER

Before the airlines got their security act together in the 1970s, plane hijackings, or **skyjackings**, were surprisingly common – there were no less than 150 between 1967 and 1972. Few caught the popular imagination as much as the case of **D.B. Cooper**, who boarded a Portland to Seattle flight on Thanksgiving evening in 1971. As soon as the plane had taken off, Dan Cooper – or at least the man who had bought his ticket under that name – gave a stewardess a note saying he was carrying a bomb. The stewardess actually thought he was trying to chat her up, so she pocketed the note without examining it, obliging Cooper to ask her to read it. After this initial hurdle, Cooper's plans went like clockwork. The plane landed in Seattle and in return for releasing all the other passengers Cooper was given four parachutes and $200,000. Airborne again and flying south, Cooper ordered all the crew into the cockpit, opened the rear exit and jumped out – in the midst of a storm – never to be seen again. He was likely killed by the freezing cold and/or his landing amidst the dense forests east of **Washington's Vancouver**, but neither his body nor his parachutes have ever been discovered, fuelling speculation that he was an expert survivalist and army veteran who survived to live a wealthy life abroad. The FBI looked for him for years without success, the only find being the discovery of one bag of his loot on the banks of the Columbia River in 1980.

over twenty years, a remote but prosperous station dedicated to the fur trade. Its early occupation was part of the case the British made for including present-day Washington in their empire, but, as American colonists poured into the Willamette Valley, the British claim became unrealistic. Finally, when the 49th Parallel was determined as the dividing line between the US and Canada, Fort Vancouver was left stranded on US territory. By 1860 the Hudson's Bay Company had moved out, and the fort and out-buildings disappeared, only to be mapped and rebuilt by archeologists in the 1960s. Rangers give interpretive tours throughout the day, and the site – basically five one-storey log structures protected within a rectangular palisade – certainly merits at least a quick look, as does nearby Officers' Row, a string of elegant villas built for US Army personnel between 1850 and 1906.

North of Seattle

The quickest route **north from Seattle** to Canada is along I-5. Staying just inland, the interstate clears Seattle's cluttered outskirts before plunging on through the eastern peripheries of gritty, industrial **Everett**. After that, I-5 shoots over the marshy delta of the Snohomish River to reach, about sixty miles from Seattle, the I-5 and Hwy 20 inter-section: head east and you'll soon get to the mountains of the northern (and most dra-matic) portion of the Cascade Loop (see p.266); drive west and you'll cross the Skagit River's floodplain, home to the attractive little town of **La Conner** and the ferry port of Anacortes, gateway to the San Juan Islands. You can also get to the islands from **Bellingham**, a large and lively town a short haul further north along I-5 – and just fifty miles from British Columbia's Vancouver (see p.287).

There's a more leisurely route north from Seattle to Canada too, a much prettier if slower journey that winds its way through the beautiful necklace of islands that stret-ches west across Puget Sound and the Strait of Juan de Fuca. Just north of Seattle, turn off I-5 for the **Mukilteo ferry** over to **Whidbey Island**, whose flat glacial moraine and protected rural landscape make it ideal cycling country. Whidbey is connected by ferry to Port Townsend on the Olympic Peninsula (see p.237) and a bridge also links its northern tip with Fidalgo Island, where Washington State Ferries depart **Anacortes** for the unforgettable scenery of the **San Juan Islands**. The ferries weave through the archipelago – and some continue over into Canada – docking at four of the islands including **Lopez**, which offers gentle farmland and rolling, forested hills, and **Orcas** and **San Juan Island**, where steep wooded hills overshadow lush valleys. Justifiably, the islands are among the region's most popular tourist destinations, so in summer try to book accommodation well in advance.

North to La Conner

Speeding north from Seattle on I-5, it's a short drive to the Hwy 526 intersection (Exit 189), where you turn west for both the **Mukilteo ferry** and the huge **Boeing Plant** (tours given Mon–Fri 9am–3pm on the hour, except noon; ☎1-800/464-1476, *www.boeing.com/compa-nyoffices/aboutus/tours*; $5), which shows off its wide-bodied 767 and 747 jets at various stages of construction in a plant as big as 57 football pitches.

Back on I-5, it's a further forty-odd miles north to **MOUNT VERNON**, an agricul-tural centre beside the Skagit River, and just a mile or two more to the I-5/Hwy 20 inter-section. Fork west here for the fifteen-minute drive to **LA CONNER**, whose amiable main drag, with its souvenir shops and cafés, strings along the bumpy waterfront of the Swinomish Channel, a sheltered nautical shortcut between the San Juan Islands and Puget Sound. Before the area was dyked and drained, the whole Skagit delta was a marshy morass prone to flooding, so the original trading post was plonked on a hill, and named by the town's leading landowner after his wife L(ouisa) A(nn) Conner. But when the railroads reached the northwest in the 1880s, La Conner was left an abandoned backwater, its water-borne trade all but dead and gone. The town became the hangout of oddballs and counterculturals, from painters and Wobblies to poets and World War II conscientious objectors.

Since the 1970s, the town has traded on its offbeat reputation and it's this that pulls in the tourist dollar – though it's hard, nowadays, to get a glimpse of anything vaguely "alternative" unless you count the town's several art galleries. That said, the waterfront verges on the picturesque, with a neat little bridge over the channel to the Swinomish Indian Reservation, and boasts the excellent **Museum of Northwest Art (MONA)**, at 121 S 1st St (Tues–Sun 10am–5pm; *www.museumofnwart.org*; $3), which showcases the work of the region's painters. The first floor is given over to temporary displays, while the second holds the permanent collection – a bold and challenging sample of modern art in which the forceful paintings of regional artist Guy Anderson, often featuring adrift naked figures and sombre colours reflecting overcast Northwest horizons, are of particular note.

La Conner practicalities

La Conner's **visitor centre** (Mon–Fri 10am–4pm, Sat–Sun 11am–4pm; ☎466-4778), a short walk back from the waterfront at Morris and 5th, issues free town maps and has a comprehensive list of local accommodation. Amongst several **hotels**, the *Hotel Planter*, 715 S 1st St (☎466-4710 or 1-800/488-5409; ⑤), has plush and modern doubles within a remodelled century-old inn, while *La Conner Channel Lodge*, 205 N 1st St (☎466-1500, *www.laconnerlodging.com*; ⑥), offers lavish waterside doubles. Less expensive is *Katy's Inn B&B*, in an attractive old house at 503 S 3rd St (☎466-3366 or 1-800/914-7767; ④).

For **food**, the *Calico Cupboard Café and Bakery*, 720 S 1st St, is absurdly quaint, but serves excellent lunches and afternoon teas, and the chic *La Conner Brewing Company*, next door to the art museum, offers a wide range of Washington's best brews as well as tasty pizzas.

La Conner is only nine miles east of the ferry port of Anacortes (see p.234), but there is no direct bus service linking the two cities, although a long ride with transfers does connect them on the free Skagit Transit (☎757-4433).

Bellingham

Part-industrial, with a dash of Victoriana and a lively university scene, **BELLINGHAM** curves around its wedge-shaped bay some ninety miles north of Seattle and just twenty south of the Canadian border. It's actually the sum of four smaller communities, whose separate street patterns make a disjointed, hard-to-navigate whole – though orientation isn't too difficult if you use I-5 to get your bearings. The most southerly (and easily the most diverting) of the town's districts is the revamped late nineteenth-century **Fairhaven** (I-5, Exit 250), whose sturdy brick and sandstone commercial buildings witnessed two brief booms – the first when the town was touted as the Pacific terminus of the Great Northern Railroad, the second during the Klondike Gold Rush. Nowadays, Fairhaven is noted for its laid-back cafés and bars and as the location of the Bellingham Cruise Terminal (see overleaf for details of boats). Moving north on I-5, Exit 252 accesses the hillside campus of **Western Washington University** and Exit 253 leads **downtown**, where a routine gridiron of high-rises congregates on the bluff above the industrial harbourfront. There's nothing inspiring here, though you could drop by the old City Hall, a grandiose 1892 red-brick building that is now the main part of the **Whatcom County Museum of History and Art**, at 121 Prospect St (Tues–Sun noon–5pm; $3). The last part of the Bellingham conurbation is **Squalicum**, reached from I-5's Exit 257.

Practicalities

Greyhound **buses** and Amtrak **trains** pull in at the **Bellingham Cruise Terminal** in Fairhaven. The terminal is also the starting point of the Alaska Marine Highway (see box opposite) and Victoria–San Juan Cruises, who operate **passenger boats** to Victoria, on Vancouver Island (mid-May to early Oct, 1 daily; 4hr; ☎360/738-8099 or 1-800/443-4552; $42 single $79 return). Also departing the terminal are the passenger ferries of the San Juan Island Shuttle Express (☎360/671-1137 or 1-888/373-8522), which run to Orcas, Lopez and San Juan Island (late May to late Sept, 1 daily; 1hr 40min–2hr 15min;

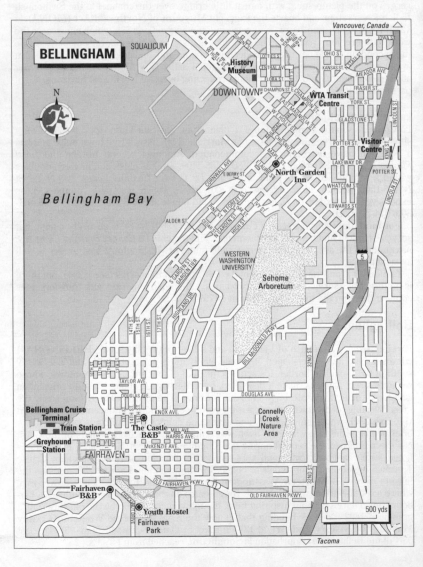

THE ALASKA MARINE HIGHWAY

The **Alaska Marine Highway** is a three-day ferry ride that snakes its fabulous way between wooded, azure-set islands and hard, craggy coast from Washington's **Bellingham** to Alaska's **Skagway**, with stops along the way at Ketchikan, Wrangell, Petersburg, Juneau and Haines. A similar, parallel service starts further north at Canada's Prince Rupert (see p.573). Ferries leave the Bellingham Cruise Terminal every Friday early in the evening from May to September (less frequently in the winter) and arrive in Skagway the following Monday night. The round trip takes about a week. Summer passages from Bellingham to Haines, for example, cost about $240 one-way per passenger, excluding food and berth, which is either in a cabin or on the covered and heated solarium deck.

For further details, contact **Alaska Marine Highway**, PO Box 25535, Juneau, Alaska 99802-5535 (☎1-800/526-6731; online bookings at *www.akferry.com*). Vehicles and cabins have to be reserved well (i.e. months) in advance and even walk-on passage requires at least a couple of weeks notice. You can, however, try at the Bellingham terminal on the day of departure – but don't bank on success.

$20 single). Other companies operate sightseeing and whale-watching cruises. In good weather, the ferry ride through the San Juan archipelago is delightful.

From the Cruise Terminal, it's only five hundred yards to the centre of Fairhaven along Harris Avenue and it's here you'll find several good places to stay (see below). To get downtown, take the Whatcom Transit Authority (WTA; ☎360/384-0294) bus from outside the terminal to the **transit centre** at E Magnolia and Railroad Avenue – but note that there's no evening or weekend service on this route. The Bellingham **visitor centre** (daily 8.30am–5.30pm; ☎360/671-3990 or 1-800/487-2032, *www.bellingham.org*), beside I-5 (Exit 253) at 904 Potter St, provides maps and information on the town as well as the surrounding Whatcom County. They also have a long list of local **accommodation**. Your best bet is to stay in one of the comfortable **B&Bs** dotted in and around Fairhaven. Options include the cosy *Fairhaven B&B*, 1714 12th St at Chuckanut Drive (☎360/734-7243 or 1-888/734-7243; ④); and the *North Garden Inn*, an extravagant turreted and gabled 1900s mansion to the north of Fairhaven at 1014 N Garden and E Maple Street (☎360/671-7828, *www.northgardeninn.com*; ④). The **youth hostel**, 107 Chuckanut Drive (Feb–Nov; ☎360/671-1750), is a tiny cabin-like affair with dorm beds only at $12–15; it's next to the Rose Garden, a short walk south of the centre of Fairhaven. Several of the town's chain **motels** are strung along Lakeway Drive – I-5, Exit 253.

The late nineteenth-century commercial buildings that comprise central Fairhaven occupy a four-block square between 10th and 12th streets to either side of Harris Avenue. The district's **bars** and **cafés** have an arty flavour that's very refreshing, especially if you've been hiking the great outdoors. The *Colophon Café*, 1210 11th St, sets the tone, serving delicious vegetarian food and sharing its premises with the Village Books bookshop. Close by, *Dos Padres*, 1111 Harris Ave (☎360/733-9900), offers first-rate Mexican cuisine; *Dirty Dan Harris'*, 1211 11th St (☎360/676-1011), specializes in prime rib and steaks; *Tony's*, 1101 Harris Ave, is an enjoyable coffee shop, sometimes hosting live music; and the *Archer Ale House*, 1212 10th St, has a wide range of local microbrews and serves bar food too.

Around Bellingham: Mount Baker

With snow lasting from early November to mid-May, the **Mount Baker** ski area, in the Cascade Mountains, sixty-odd miles east of Bellingham, has become Washington's premier resort (ski reports on ☎360/671-0211), its lifts and runs dotted over several lower slopes in the shadow of the great mountain itself. At 10,778 feet, Mount Baker is the highest peak for miles around, a volcanic behemoth that hisses great clouds of steam whenever its insides are ruffled – the last time was in 1975. Not surprisingly, it has played a leading role in native folklore: the local Lummi saw it as a sort of Ararat, the one peak that survived the Great Flood to provide sanctuary for a Lummi "Noah" in his giant canoe – and it was here in 1947 that a USAF pilot saw the unidentified flying objects which he creatively christened "flying saucers".

The main approach road from Bellingham, Hwy 542, loops round the mountain's northern foothills, passing three USFS **campgrounds** beyond the village of Glacier, before a final, nail-biting fling up through the ski area to **Artist Point**. From here, a stiff 1.5-mile trail leads up lava cliffs to flat-topped Table Mountain, with Baker soaring high above. There are lots of other trails, but this is the basic starter with several possible extensions, such as the difficult trek south along Ptarmigan Ridge to Coleman Pinnacle.

Mount Baker makes an ideal day-trip from Bellingham, though you can overnight in the USFS campgrounds beside Hwy 542. Information and hiking maps are available in Bellingham's better bookshops and at the **Glacier Public Service Center** (mid-June to mid-Sept daily 8.30am–4.30pm; rest of year most weekends and variable weekdays 8.30am–4.30pm; ☎360/599-2714), in tiny **GLACIER**, about 25 miles short of the mountain. **Ski equipment** can be hired at the resort ski shop and in Bellingham at – among several places – Fairhaven Bike and Mountain Sports, 1103 11th St (☎360/733-4433).

Whidbey Island

Rather than taking the main highway north to Seattle, consider wandering the sheer cliffs and craggy outcrops, rocky beaches and prairie countryside of **WHIDBEY ISLAND**. This is a favourite retreat for the Puget Sound's city-dwellers, who take a tent and head for one of the state parks, or spend pampered weekends in a luxurious Whidbey B&B. Once considered a key stronghold in the defence of the Sound, the island carries military relics from various eras: nineteenth-century blockhouses built against Native-American attack, concrete bunkers from World War II – and in the north, at Oak Harbor, a large-scale naval base housing the sophisticated warfare squadrons of modern air and naval defence whose low-flying jets are an occasional but considerable annoyance. But on the whole the island is peaceful enough, the narrow country roads winding through farmland and small villages. Certainly, if you're heading north to the San Juan Islands, it's much more pleasant to meander through Whidbey than dash up I-5.

Getting to and around Whidbey Island

Coming **from Seattle**, the quickest route onto Whidbey Island is via the Mukilteo ferry; boats to Clinton run every half-hour, take twenty minutes; single fares are $2.50 per person, or $4.50 ($5.75 peak season) for a vehicle and driver. A second ferry leaves Port Townsend on the Olympic Peninsula every ninety minutes for Whidbey's Keystone, halfway up the island just south of Coupeville, the main town. The trip takes thirty minutes with single fares costing about $2 per person, or $6.50 ($8.25 peak season) for a vehicle and driver. It's also possible to reach Whidbey **by road** from the north across Deception Pass – take Hwy 20 (the Anacortes road) off I-5. Local **buses** operated by subsidized Island Transit (☎678-7771, 321-6688 or 1-800/240-8747) run free hourly services (more frequently on weekday afternoons after 3pm) between Whidbey's larger communities and the ferry ports (Mon–Sat, stops running around 7–8pm) – though, as with Puget Sound's other islands, you'd be well advised to bring your own vehicle.

Clinton and Langley

Ferries from mainland Mukilteo reach Whidbey's southeast shore at the small port of **CLINTON**. There's nothing much happening here, and you're better off moving on up the main island road (here Hwy 525, later Hwy 20) to take the turning to **LANGLEY**, a prosperous town whose truncated, old-west wooden high street perches on a bluff overlooking the sea. The touch-of-Frank-Lloyd-Wright *Inn at Langley*, 400 1st St (☎221-3033, *www.innatlangley.com*; ⑧), is five-star luxury all the way.

Coupeville

COUPEVILLE is a showcase town of immaculately maintained Victorian mansions. Many of them were built by wealthy sea captains drawn from their native New England by the deep harbour of Penn Cove and the abundance of oak and pine trees, which made good money in the lucrative Californian timber trade. Fearing the local Skagit might object to white annexation of their land, the settlers built **Alexander's blockhouse** (at the end of today's Front St), a small, wooden, windowless building intended to protect them from attack. However, relations remained remarkably peaceful, and the **dugout war canoe** next to the blockhouse was used only in festivals; both the blockhouse and the canoe are cared for by the **Island County Historical Museum** next door.

The character of Coupeville is protected by its location within **Ebey's Landing National Historic Reserve**, which is dedicated to preserving the area's rural appearance and keeping modern development at bay. The first of its kind in the US, the reserve occupies the middle part of Whidbey Island on either side of Penn Cove, and is named after Isaac Ebey, the son of a pioneer farmer, who rose to prominence as a civil and military leader before coming to a nasty end at the hands of a vengeful party of Alaskan Tlingit.

Ebey's Reserve also includes two old, windblown forts, now state parks. Five miles southwest of Coupeville, close to the Keystone ferry port, **Fort Casey** was built at the end of the nineteenth century as part of a trio of fortifications across the entrance of the Puget Sound, and a formidable barrage of decaying World War II gun emplacements still face starkly out to sea. It's possible to hike the seven or so miles north from here along the bluff-fringed, shingly seashore (part of which is known as Ebey's Landing) to **Fort Ebey**. You can also reach the fort by road: watch for Libbey Road, a left turn off Hwy 20 three to four miles northwest of Coupeville. Fort Ebey was constructed in 1942 after America's entry into World War II; there are no guns now, but the fortifications remain, giving good views out across the water to the Olympic Mountains. If time or energy don't permit the beachside trek, a small parking area between the forts at Ebey's Landing itself (at the southern end of Ebey Rd) puts you right next to a gorgeous trail that rises and dips for a mile or two along a ridge that overlooks the bluff and Admiralty Inlet, yielding some of the most striking views to be found anywhere on the Puget Sound.

Practicalities

Many of Coupeville's old villas have been turned into lavish (and quite expensive) **B&Bs**. The tiny **visitor centre**, a self-service shack at 302 N Main St (call Central Whidbey Chamber of Commerce at ☎678-5434 for live assistance), has brochures about many of them, though you may find the staff at the museum a more helpful and informed source, a bonus when rooms get tight in the summer. Some fine B&B options include the slightly over-fussy twin pink houses of the *Inn at Penn Cove*, 702 N Main St (☎678-8000 or 1-800/688-COVE, *www.whidbey.net/penncove*; ④); and the posh

Anchorage Inn, 807 N Main St (☎678-5581 or 1-877/230-1313, *www.anchorage-inn.com*; ④). Better still, the comfortably nautical *Capt Whidbey Inn*, 2072 W Captain Whidbey Inn Rd (☎678-4097 or 1-800/366-4097, *www.captainwhidbey.com*; ⑤) – take Madrona Way from the foot of Main Street and keep going for two miles round Penn Cove – is a real delight: built out of local madrone logs in 1907, the main lodge has a superb restaurant offering some of the state's best seafood. Above, there are a handful of antique rooms overlooking Penn Cove, while there are cottages and chalets in the surrounding forest. Another charming alternative is *Fort Casey Inn*, three miles south of Coupeville at 1124 S Engle Rd (☎678-8792; ⑤), where duplex accommodation is available in a row of renovated officers' houses on the edge of the state park. If you're on a tighter budget, the *Tyee Motel*, on the edge of Coupeville at 405 S Main St (☎678-6616; ③), has run-of-the-mill doubles; or you can **camp** pleasantly at Fort Ebey state park (☎678-4636, *www.parks.wa.gov/ftebey.htm*; $12).

For **food** in Coupeville, the *Knead and Feed* (☎678-5431) is a bakery offering quality sit-down lunches, and *Toby's Tavern* (☎678-4222) is a friendly local bar-cum-restaurant; both are on Front Street near the jetty.

Oak Harbor and Deception Pass

Beyond Ebey's Reserve, military matters of a modern and more mundane kind dominate the economy of **OAK HARBOR**, Whidbey's largest – and most unappealing – town. The nearby Naval Air Station, built in 1941, is home to the navy's tactical electronic warfare squadrons, and the town's ugly suburban sprawl is best passed straight through. Unless you're in need of a motel room (try *Auld Holland Inn*, 33575 Hwy 20; ☎675-2288 or 1-800/228-0148; ③), you'd do much better to continue north to **Deception Pass State Park** where a steel bridge arches gracefully over the narrow gorge between Whidbey and Fidalgo Island, a connecting-point (via Anacortes) for the San Juans.

The pint-sized state park, with its splendid hiking trails and **campground** (☎675-2417, *www.parks.wa.gov/deceptn.htm*), occupies the rocky, forested headlands on either side of the gorge, whose turbulent, churning waters are some of the region's most treacherous. Even the intrepid George Vancouver was wary of them, initially deceived (hence the name) into believing he had charted part of the Whidbey "peninsula", rather than the strait that makes it an island. The **CCC Interpretive Center** on Bowman Bay (summer only, Wed–Sun 10am–5pm) merits a brief stop with its exhibit on the Civilian Conservation Corps, who in the mid-1930s built many of the trails and picnic shelters still in use in the park, also providing employment for numerous young men of limited means who were finding it nearly impossible to gain employment at the height of the Depression. The **Lighthouse Point Trail** begins at the parking lot near the interpretive centre, meandering along beach and forest for nearly a mile, leading to rocky bluffs with good views of the pass.

The San Juan Islands

Northwest of Whidbey Island, midway between the Washington coast and Canada, the **San Juan Islands** scatter across the eastern reaches of the Strait of Juan de Fuca, and entirely upstage the rest of the Puget Sound. Perfect retreats for walking, cycling and generally unwinding (although the weather can be wet), this maze of green islands, with its myriad bluffs and bays, is the breeding ground of rare birds and sea creatures: white-headed bald eagles circle over treetops, and families of Orca ("killer") whales pass close to shore. The days when the islands were simple rustic retreats are, however, gone and nowadays the islands' farming and fishing communities are jostled by

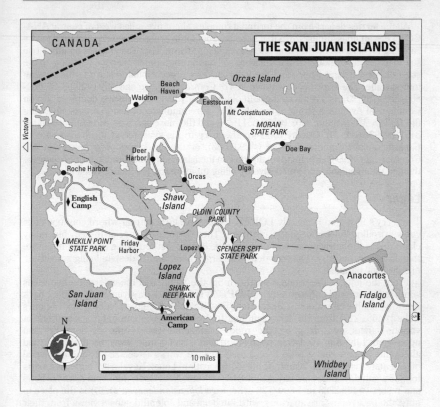

escapees from the cities, and in summer there are more visitors than the islands can really accommodate. This is especially true on San Juan and less so on Orcas, the largest of the islands and delightful Lopez; Shaw, the other island visited by ferry, has little to entice you off the boat.

You'll definitely need to book somewhere to stay in advance: during summer weekends dozens of disappointed travellers end up spending the night at the ferry terminal, something all the tourist authorities work hard to avoid. However, even in July and August, peaceful corners away from the crowds are easy to find.

Getting to the San Juan Islands

Washington State Ferries run about a dozen boats a day, more in summer, to the San Juan Islands. The ferries only stop at four of the 172 islands (and seldom at all four on the same route; consult schedules for details), but the slow cruise through the archipelago is a real highlight. Less serene are the long lines of cars that develop at ferry ports in the summer when latecomers inevitably end up waiting for the next boat: it pays for drivers to be two or three hours early; pedestrians and cyclists have less hassle. Summer fares to San Juan Island are around $20 return for a car and driver (slightly less out of season), $5 for foot passengers and $8 for cyclists. Make a note of when the last ferry leaves the island for the mainland, as it can be surprisingly early, especially out of season. Two ferries a day (one in winter) continue on from the islands to Sidney, on Vancouver Island, British Columbia.

All the ferries depart from the terminal complex about five miles west of central **ANA-CORTES**, an unassuming town that's the best bet for overnight accommodation if you're catching an early ferry (the first one leaves before 6am). There's certainly no other reason to linger here, though the waterfront still has a rough-hewn charm – it's home to the state's largest fishing fleet – and the town makes the occasional gesture to the passing tourist trade. *The Majestic*, downtown at 419 Commercial Ave and 4th (☎293-3355 or 1-800/588-4780; ⑨), is a renovated grand old **hotel** of 1889 with polished doubles. Also on Commercial Avenue, a string of **motels** offer more mundane roadside rooms, including the *Holiday Motel*, at no. 2903 (☎293-6511; ③), and the more spacious *Islands Motel*, at no. 3401 (☎293-4644; ③). Quality **food** for the ferry trip is available at the Italian takeout *Geppetto's*, 3320 Commercial Ave (☎293-5033), or the *La Vie en Rose* bakery at 418 Commercial (☎299-9546). Incidentally, **gas** on the islands is considerably more expensive than on the mainland, and you'll save by filling up in Anacortes before you leave.

Lopez

The ferry's first stop is usually **LOPEZ**, a quiet, pastoral retreat where country lanes cobweb rolling hills and gentle farmland. There's nothing special to see, but many claim this is the attraction – and certainly the island, just ten miles long and not more than five wide, never gets as crowded as its larger neighbours, despite being something of a cyclists' paradise.

From the jetty at the island's northern tip, the main road meanders the five miles south to the one and only settlement, **LOPEZ VILLAGE**, a tiny triangle spreading back from the sheltered waters of Fisherman Bay. If you don't have a vehicle, call Angie's Cabs (☎468-2227) from the ferry landing. In the village, you can get maps and info at various businesses, drop by the modest museum (May–June & Sept Fri–Sun noon–4pm; July–Aug Wed–Sun noon–4pm) and – half a mile away, on the main road along the shore – rent a **bike** from Lopez Bicycle Works (☎468-2847), one of several bike-rental stores on the island. At the same location, Lopez Kayaks arranges **sea trips** for $35 a half-day, and rents kayaks for $15 per hour. Next door, the *Lopez Islander* hotel and resort (☎468-2233 or 1-800/736-3434, *www.lopezislander.com*; ⑥/⑦) is the place to **stay**: the best rooms are spacious, with kitchens and splendid sunset views from their imposing balconies. The hotel will offer advice on visiting the island's homespun industries, from wine-tasting at Lopez Island Vineyards to jam-licking at Madrona Farms. Back in the village centre, *Holly B's Bakery* (April–Aug closed Tues, closed Mon–Tues in Sept–Oct and Mon–Wed in Nov; ☎468-2133) has fine fresh bread and pastries; and the *Bay Café* (hours vary; ☎468-3700) offers the most imaginative of mouth-watering dinner dishes including at least one vegetarian choice a day, and has live jazz on Sunday nights.

Moving on from Lopez Village to the southwest corner of the island, **Shark Reef Park** gives access to an easy walk along the coast's beguiling hills; inland, there's fishing at **Hummel Lake**, and on the east coast at **Spencer Spit State Park** there are beach walks and clamming. The park has a small **campground** (☎468-2251, *www.parks.wa.gov/spencer.htm*, $12), as does its (slightly) better-equipped twin, **Odlin County Park** (☎378-1842; $15 for campsites, $17 for premium sites on the beach, $10 for hikers/bikers, lower rates Nov–March), near the ferry dock. In between the two, the *Inn at Swifts Bay* (☎468-3636, *www.swiftsbay.com*; ⑨), on Port Stanley Road – one mile south of the jetty turn left – is a classy and luxurious **B&B**.

Orcas Island

Horseshoe-shaped **ORCAS ISLAND** is much busier than Lopez, but its holiday resorts are so well tucked into distant coves that the island's peace and quiet is hardly disturbed. The tiny community of **ORCAS**, where the ferry lands, is no exception to this, with little beyond the *Orcas Hotel* (☎376-4300; ④) – a grand Victorian building overlooking the ferry landing, its rooms few and pricey, but a good place for a leisurely breakfast. You can rent **bikes** from Dolphin Bay Bicycles (☎376-3093), just up from the dock, and either drive or cycle north through the island's farmlands – the former heart of the state's apple orchards, until Eastern Washington was irrigated.

It's about ten miles from the ferry landing to the island's main town, the run-of-the-mill gathering of mostly modern buildings that's called **EASTSOUND**. Despite its bayside setting, there's little to detain you, and most visitors shoot through on their way to more remote locations. It is, however, a good place to get kitted out. **Bikes** can be rented from Wildlife Cycles, N Beach Road at A Street (☎376-4708). Groceries are available from the Island Market foodstore, Prune Alley, and **maps** and **local guides** at Darvill's Bookstore, on the main road beside the bay. All these places sit together within the four-block town centre.

Eastsound also has several good places to **eat**, including quality Mexican cuisine at *Bilbo's Festivo* restaurant, N Beach and A Street (☎376-4728), and sound diner-style food at *Doty's A-1 Café* (☎376-2593), on N Beach just off the main street. If you decide to **stay** the night, your options are limited to two hotels on the west side of town overlooking the bay (and the main road). Of the two, the *Outlook Inn* (☎376-2200, *www.outlook-inn.com*; ⑤), whose rates dip way down in the off-season, is the more agreeable. Far better local lodgings are to be found about three miles west of town at the *Beach Haven Resort* (☎376-2288, *www.beach-haven.com*; ⑤), where fifty-year-old beachfront log cabins line up along a densely wooded, sunset-facing cove; in summer the cabins are only available by the week, with reservations recommended a year in advance, but out of season they can be rented on a nightly basis. To get there, head north out of Eastsound along Lover's Lane (the turning near the *Landmark Inn* hotel) and make a left at the sign.

Rising high above the eastern half of Orcas, **Moran State Park** is the island's main attraction, with miles of hiking trails winding through dense forest and open fields around freshwater lakes. **Mount Constitution**, at the heart of the park, is the highest (2409ft) peak on the islands, the summit of which is a steep four-mile hike (or a short drive) up a paved road, though if you're walking, the tougher hillside trails through thick foliage make for a much more exhilarating experience. The views on top are as good as you'd expect, looking out as far as Vancouver Island, and back towards snow-capped mounts Baker and Rainier.

All four **campgrounds** (☎376-2326: $12) in the park fill up early in the summer. You can also camp at **Doe Bay Village Resort**, Doe Bay Road (☎376-2291; ①–⑤), tucked round on the east side of the island about as far from the ferry as you can get: keep to the main road round the park, turn left at the intersection of Olga and Doe Bay, and turn right three miles later at the sign for Doe Bay Natural Foods Cafe & General Store. It's a lovely place, built on a secluded bay, with echoes of its previous incarnation as a "human potential centre" still hanging meditatively around its cabins, cottages and hostel dorms. Dorm beds (only six available; reservations advisable in peak season) go for about $15 per night, and there are excellent communal facilities, including an open-air **hot tub**, which can also be used by day visitors ($7), plus massage sessions and sea-kayak expeditions at about $40 for a half-day's guided trip. There are self-catering facilities at Doe Bay, but, if you're after restaurant food, retrace your steps to **OLGA**, basically a general store, gas station and post office near to *Café Olga* (March–Dec daily 10am–6pm; ☎376-5098), where the fruit pies are a speciality. Be warned, though, it's not an undiscovered spot, and busloads often descend on the place.

San Juan Island

The ferry's last stop is **SAN JUAN ISLAND**, the most visited of the islands, and the only one where the ferry actually drops you in a town. **FRIDAY HARBOR** may be small, but it's the largest town in the archipelago and the best place to rent transport. **Bikes** can be rented from Island Bicycle at 380 Argyle (☎378-4941), a few blocks up from the ferry; **mopeds** from Susie's, at 1st and A Street (☎378-5244 or 1-800/532-0087). San Juan Shuttle (☎378-8887 or 1-800/887-8387) stops at most (but not all) of the island's principal points of interest between Friday Harbor and Roche Harbor ($4 one-way, $7 round-trip, $17 two-day pass). Crystal Seas Kayaking (☎378-7899) and Sea Quest Kayak Expeditions (☎378-5767) run kayak tours, while San Juan Safaris (☎378-2155 or 1-800/451-8910 ext 258) runs kayak treks and whale-watch cruises from Roche Harbor; Emerald Seas (☎378-2772) has half-day scuba diving charters.

San Juan Transit's office, in the Cannery Building next to the terminal, is a good place to pick up info and maps – useful since it's easy to get lost on the island's twisting and badly marked roads. For further advice, the main office of the San Juan Island National Historical Park (Mon–Fri 8.30am–4.30pm; ☎378-2240, *www.nps.gov/sajh/home.htm*) at 1st and Spring, just up from the ferry landing, is not a visitor centre, but is happy to answer questions about either the island or the state parks.

This taken care of, Friday Harbor's cafés, shops and waterfront make pleasant browsing. At 62 1st St N, a block or two north of 1st and Spring, the **Whale Museum** (June–Aug daily 9am–5pm; rest of year daily 10am–5pm; *www.whalemuseum.com*; $5) has a mass of whale-related artefacts, whale skeletons and displays explaining the creatures' migration and growth patterns. There's also a listening booth for tapes of seven different kinds of whalesongs, along with walrus, seal and dolphin sounds to boot. Short video documentaries are shown about research expeditions that include some good up-close footage of whale manoeuvres. The local Orca or "killer" whales are protected by a ban on their capture, which was instituted in 1976, but they're still threatened by pollution. The museum promotes an "Adopt an Orca" programme as there are, apparently, ninety-odd left in the Puget Sound; about twenty of them remain in the Sound year-round, while the others only return to the Sound for about four or five months, starting in May.

Setting off around the island anticlockwise, the open, windy peninsula that tails off to the south is home to **American Camp**, one of two national parks on the island. Like **English Camp** at the island's northern end, the name derives from the infamous **Pig War**, which briefly put the islands at the centre of a very silly international conflict during the nineteenth century. When the Canadian border was drawn up in 1846, both the Americans and the British (who still ruled Canada) claimed the San Juans for them selves. This wasn't a great problem, and the American and British residents of the islands lived together fairly amicably until a series of tax squabbles climaxed with an American settler shooting a British pig found munching his garden vegetables. The Americans sent in the infantry; the British responded with warships, and soon 460-odd American soldiers plus cannons were dug in behind a trench opposing five armed British warships carrying over two thousand troops. After a lengthy stalemate, the question was resolved by Kaiser Wilhelm I of Germany in favour of the US, the only casualty being the pig.

An information centre at American Camp explains the "war" in full. The site itself is a barren affair, pitted with ankle-wrenching rabbit holes; a self-guided, one-mile foot trail begins from the parking lot, passing the camp's few remaining buildings and what's left of a gun emplacement. English Camp, at the greener northern end of the island, makes for a more pleasant walk. A slide show in the barracks (summer daily 8.30am–5pm) explains the Pig War; from here you can hike an easy loop to Bell Point, or retreat to the parking lot to mount the short (one mile round-trip) but steep, wooded trail to Young Hill, passing the small English Camp cemetery on the way. The 650ft summit has views over much of the island, with Sidney, BC, visible to the west.

Continuing past the coves and bays on the island's west side, a bumpy gravel road leads to **Lime Kiln Point State Park**, the best place on the island for whale-watching;

the odds of a sighting are at their most favourable in summer, when the Orcas come to feed on migrating salmon. The lime kilns that give the park its name are just outside, relics of an era when lime quarrying was big business on the island. Further north, **ROCHE HARBOR** belongs to the same era – originally a company town, its gracious white **Hotel de Haro** was built to accommodate visiting lime-buyers in 1887. The hotel, as part of the *Roche Harbor Resort* (☎378-2155 or 1-800/451-8910, *www.rocheharbor.com*; ④), offers slightly down-at-heel doubles – but really you're better off enjoying a quick visit. The attractive wharf is worth a peek, and the hotel can provide directions to the weird **mausoleum** of its founder, a haunting structure set in the woods, incorporating Masonic symbols.

Practicalities

Camping is the obvious way to stay on San Juan Island, but unfortunately neither national park has sites, although San Juan County Park, 380 West Side Rd (☎378-1842, *www.co.san-juan.wa.us/parks*; $18), has twenty sites on the western coastline of the island, north of Lime Kiln Park. There's a very pleasant cyclists-only camp, the *Pedal Inn*, five miles from the ferry dock at 1300 False Bay Drive (☎378-3049; $5), while the larger *Lakedale Campground* at 4313 Roche Harbor Rd (☎378-0944 or 1-800/617-2267, *www.lakedale.com*; July–Aug $24 per vehicle, bikers and hikers $8; rest of year $19 per vehicle, $7 bikers and hikers) is almost five miles from the ferry on Roche Harbor Road and reachable on the San Juan Shuttle bus. The cheapest indoor beds by far are at the newly opened *Wayfarer's Rest* hostel at 35 Malcolm St (☎378-6428, *www.rockisland.com/~wayfarersrest*), which can be reached on foot from the ferry, and has just ten beds in bunk rooms, for $20/night; advance reservations highly advisable. To get to the hostel from the ferry, go up Spring Street a few blocks, then go left at Argyle Street for another three blocks.

A wide choice of pricey, but comfortable, **B&Bs** includes *Blair House* at 345 Blair Ave (☎378-5907 or 1-800/899-3030, *www.friday-harbor.net/blair*; ④), an attractively refurbished Victorian villa four blocks from the ferry landing (go up Spring and turn right on Blair); the plain and simple *Friday's*, on 35 1st St near Spring Street (☎378-5848 or 1-800/352-2632, *www.friday-harbor.com/lodging.html*; ⑤); and the *Wharfside*, two rooms in a retired sailing boat at K dock (☎378-5661, *www.slowseason.com*; ⑥).

There are plenty of places to **eat** in Friday Harbor: *Cannery House* at the top of 1st Street has a wonderful view from its outdoor terrace; *Bella Luna*, 175 1st St back near Spring, has reasonable Italian food and regular American fare for breakfast, lunch and dinner; and, if you're setting off early, the *San Juan Donut Shop*, 209 Spring St, serves hefty breakfasts from 6am.

West of Seattle – the Olympic Peninsula

The broad mass of the **Olympic Peninsula** projects west from the Puget Sound, sheltering Seattle from the open sea. Small towns are sprinkled around the peninsula's edges, but at its core the Olympic Mountains thrust upwards, shredding clouds as they drift in from the Pacific and drenching the peninsula's western side with rain. These moist conditions have carpeted almost all of the peninsula with a thick blanket of forest and in the western river valleys the dense vegetation thickens into **temperate rainforest**, primarily composed of sitka spruce, western hemlock, Douglas fir, alder and maple – a rare and remarkable environment that people travel from all over the world to see. The peninsula's wild and lonely Pacific shoreline is not quite so unique, but it also offers extraordinary scenery, and both the forests and the coast provide habitats for a huge variety of wildlife and seabirds.

It was partly to ensure the survival of a rare breed of elk that Franklin D. Roosevelt created a national park here in 1939, and the **Olympic National Park** now has the

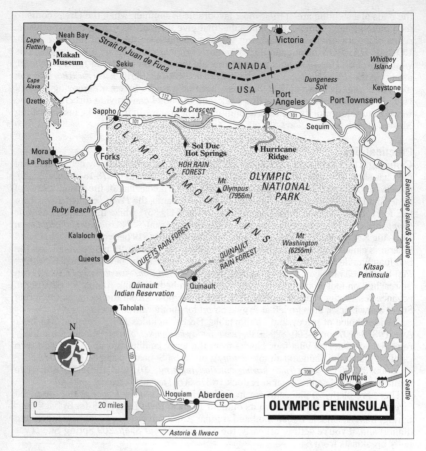

Cape Flattery · Neah Bay · Strait of Juan de Fuca · Victoria · CANADA · Whidbey Island · Makah Museum · Sekiu · USA · Dungeness Spit · Keystone · Cape Alava · Port Angeles · Port Townsend · Ozette · Sappho · Lake Crescent · Sequim · Mora · La Push · Forks · Sol Duc Hot Springs · Hurricane Ridge · HOH RAIN FOREST · Mt Olympus (7956m) · OLYMPIC NATIONAL PARK · Ruby Beach · OLYMPIC MOUNTAINS · Kalaloch · QUEETS RAIN FOREST · QUINAULT RAIN FOREST · Mt Washington (6255m) · Kitsap Peninsula · Queets · Quinault Indian Reservation · Quinault · N · Taholah · Olympia · Hoquiam · Aberdeen · **OLYMPIC PENINSULA** · 0 · 20 miles · Bainbridge Island & Seattle · Seattle

▽ Astoria & Ilwaco

largest remaining herd of Roosevelt elk in the US. The park protects the heart of the peninsula, but the large areas of forest surrounding it are heavily logged. The issue of economy versus ecology is debated with particular intensity hereabouts, since it was the timber trade that brought settlers in the first place, and logging remains crucial for local jobs. Ecologists are now reluctantly favouring tourism as the lesser of environmental evils, and the number of visitors is increasing – a marriage with the tough world of the timber trade echoed throughout the Pacific Northwest.

Graced by its charming seashore setting and ornate old mansions, **Port Townsend** is easily the most appealing town on the peninsula and, handily enough, it's also the logical first stop if you're arriving from the east: ferries arrive here from Whidbey Island (see p.230), and a ferry and a short drive will get you here from Seattle via Bainbridge Island (see p.215). The rest of the peninsula's settlements are, however, really rather nondescript: only **Sequim**, a neat little town in the rain shadow of the Olympic Mountains, offers much incentive to hang around, though industrial **Port Angeles** is useful for its ferry links with Victoria in Canada and as the location of the Olympic National Park Visitor Center. Otherwise, you'd be well-advised to make straight for the wilderness, either to camp or to stay in one of the national park's excellent lodges.

The peninsula's main highway, **US-101**, loops around the coast. No roads run across the peninsula's mountainous core, though several paved and/or gravel-topped side roads do nudge into the interior, exploring the peripheries of the national park. Two local **bus** companies provide a limited and slow Monday through Saturday service across the northern part of the peninsula. Jefferson Transit (☎360/385-4777) operates services west from Port Townsend to Sequim, where Clallam Transit (☎360/452-4511 or 1-800/858-3747) provides connecting buses on to Port Angeles five times daily Monday through Friday and twice on Saturdays. From Port Angeles, Clallam Transit buses run west to Lake Crescent Lodge and Forks, where you change for buses on to La Push or Neah Bay. That said, if you want to do any walking, you'll have problems reaching trailheads without your own vehicle – and a **car** is by far the best bet: on a **bike**, you're most likely to get soaked time and again, and sharp corners and hurtling logging trucks represent very real hazards.

Port Townsend

With its brightly painted Victorian mansions, convivial cafés and vigorous cultural (and countercultural) scene, **PORT TOWNSEND** has always had aspirations beyond its small-time logging roots. A wannabe San Francisco since the mid-nineteenth century, it was poised for Puget Sound supremacy in the 1890s, when confident predictions of a railway terminus lured in the rich, who set about building their extravagant Gothic homes on the bluff above the port. Unfortunately for the investors, the railway petered out before Port Townsend, the hoped-for boom never happened, and the town was left with a glut of stylish residences and a very small business district.

This combination has in recent times turned out to be Port Townsend's trump card, and since the old mansions were bought up and restored in the 1960s, the town has

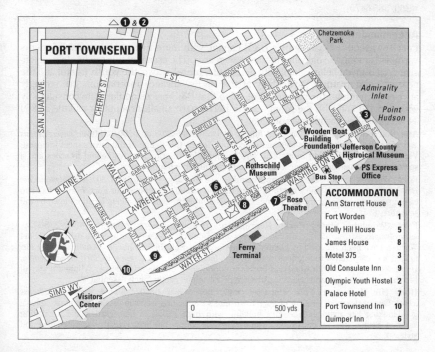

ACCOMMODATION	
Ann Starrett House	4
Fort Worden	1
Holly Hill House	5
James House	8
Motel 375	3
Old Consulate Inn	9
Olympic Youth Hostel	2
Palace Hotel	7
Port Townsend Inn	10
Quimper Inn	6

mellowed into an artsy community with hippie undertones and a good degree of charm. Tourists in search of Victoriana fill plush B&Bs, while jazz fans flock to the annual music festivals, and nearby, nineteenth-century Fort Worden provides ample camping and youth hostel facilities.

Arrival and information

Located at the end of the Quimper Peninsula, a stumpy adjunct to the adjoining mass of the Olympic Peninsula, Port Townsend is easy to reach, either by **ferry** from Keystone on Whidbey Island, or by **road** either over the Hood Canal Bridge from the Kitsap Peninsula or up along US-101 from Olympia. By **bus**, things get a bit more complicated: take the Washington State Ferries' ferry from Seattle to Bremerton, where you can (wait around to) pick up the Kitsap Transit (☎360/373-2877) bus to Poulsbo for the onward connection with Jefferson Transit (☎360/385-4777) to Port Townsend. On weekdays, there are three services daily between the Bremerton ferry and Port Townsend, one daily on the weekend; the whole trip takes anything up to five hours. Port Townsend can also be reached by passenger **boat** from Friday Harbor, on San Juan Island, with PS Express (April–Sept 1 daily; 3hr; $35 one-way, $50 return; ☎360/385-5288).

Port Townsend's compact centre occupies a triangle of land jutting out into the sea. The **ferry dock** is right downtown, just off the main drag, Water Street, which is dotted with Jefferson Transit bus stops. The PS Express office is at 431 Water St. Pick up local information at the helpful **visitor centre**, 2437 E Sims Way (Mon–Fri 9am–5pm, summer also Sat 10am–4pm & Sun 11am–4pm; ☎360/385-2722 or 1-888/365-6978, *www.ptguide.com*), half a mile south of the town centre on Hwy 20; to get around, **rent a bike** from PT Cyclery, by the waterfront at 100 Tyler St (Mon–Sat 9am–6pm; ☎360/385-6470).

Accommodation

Port Townsend is Washington's **B&B** capital, with more than a dozen establishments sprinkled among the old villas of the uptown area. The cream of this moderately expensive crop is given below, along with details of a **motel** or two, the **youth hostel** and the nearest **campground**. Particularly at the B&Bs, advance reservations are strongly advised throughout the summer. Note also that B&B prices do fluctuate considerably with demand and with the room – some B&Bs have smaller rooms for as little as $60 as well as suites for upwards of $200.

Ann Starrett House, 744 Clay St at Adams St (☎360/385-3205 or 1-800/321-0644, *www.olympus .net/starrett*). With its high gables and precocious tower, this is one of the town's most imposing Victorian mansions, dating from 1889. The antique-filled interior features ceiling frescoes and a splendid spiral staircase. Ornate and extremely comfortable doubles. ⑨.

Fort Worden State Park campground, Fort Worden (☎360/385-4730, *www.olympus.net /ftworden*). A couple of miles north of town, the old military compound of Fort Worden has two campgrounds – one near the conference centre, the other in a more enticing location down by the seashore. $16.

Fort Worden State Park Recreation Housing, Fort Worden (☎360/385-4730, *www.olympus.net/ftworden*). The old officers and non-commissioned officers' lodgings in Fort Worden have been recycled as holiday accommodation. Refurbished houses, which are fully furnished and carpeted with kitchens, start at $104 for a double room, rising to $370 for six people. Unmodernized units, with wood and linoleum floors, work out slightly cheaper. Minimum stay of two days on weekends and holidays. Advance reservations pretty much essential. ⑥.

Holly Hill House, 611 Polk St at Clay (☎360/385-5619 or 1-800/435-1454, *www.hollyhillhouse .com*). One of the most enticing of Port Townsend's B&Bs, this well-run establishment occupies a good-looking late nineteenth-century building with high gables, a nice garden and a relaxing veranda. Each of the four guestrooms – all with private baths – has been lavishly decorated in period style. ④.

James House, 1238 Washington St at Harrison St (☎360/385-1238, or 1-800/385-1238, *www.jameshouse.com*). Appealing old pile on the edge of the bluff overlooking the harbour with high brick chimneys and a handsome front terrace. Twelve tastefully decorated rooms, ten en suite. ⑤.

Motel 375, Point Hudson Marina (☎360/385-2828 or 1-800/826-3854, fax 360/385-7331). This unusual motel occupies the hospital block of the old Coast Guard Training Station at Point Hudson. The rooms are spartan, and have a certain military flavour, but they're well-kept and maintained – and are somehow really rather charming. The cheapest double rooms, with shared baths, come in at $49 – add $10 for en-suite and another $20 for a second-floor room with a harbour view. ③.

Old Consulate Inn, 313 Walker St at Washington St (☎360/385-6753 or 1-800/300-6753, *www.old-consulateinn.com*). Dating from the 1880s, this elegant villa, with its spiky tower and wraparound porch, has eight plush, en-suite rooms. It takes its name from the days when the German consul lodged here. ⑤.

Olympic Youth Hostel, Fort Worden State Park (☎360/385-0655). Up the hill from the Parade Ground in Fort Worden, an old military complex a couple of miles north of downtown, this HI-affiliated hostel has dorm beds as well as private rooms (②), plus a common room and a kitchen. Beds at $12 for HI members, $15 non-members. Check in 5–10pm. Jefferson Transit bus #5 runs to the fort from downtown.

Palace Hotel, 1004 Water St at Tyler (☎360/385-0773 or 1-800/962-0741, *www.olympus.net/palace*). Bang in the middle of the town centre, down by the harbour, this small hotel occupies a century-old brick building whose symmetrical lines are intercepted by high arched windows. The rooms are decorated in a mixture of styles – some preserving their brick walls, others painted in pastel colours – though the general flavour is vaguely Victorian. ③.

Port Townsend Inn, 2020 Washington St (☎360/385-2211 or 1-800/216-4985). Comfortable, modern motel accommodation at the south end of the town centre. Pamperings include an indoor heated pool and spa. ④.

Quimper Inn, 1306 Franklin St at Harrison St (☎360/385-1060 or 1-800/557-1060, *www .olympus.net/quimper*). Delightful B&B in one of the most architecturally satisfying old houses in town – the lovely double porches of the first two floors set beneath the tidy gables and dormers of the third. Immaculately restored and furnished in period style, the house has five guestrooms (three en suite), each of which is extremely comfortable; the breakfasts are delicious. Check-in 4–6pm. ④.

The Town

Port Townsend's physical split – half on a bluff, half at sea-level – reflects Victorian social divisions, when wealthy merchants built their homes uptown, well away from the noise and brawl of the port below. The downtown area below the bluff is still the commercial centre of town, and its shops and cafés are focused on **Water Street**, which sports an attractive medley of solid 1890s brick and stonework buildings. To the business folk of the late nineteenth century, these structures were important status symbols: timber is the obvious building material hereabouts and a big brick building was quite a coup for a pioneer town. One characteristic edifice is the **City Hall**, at Water and Madison streets, a robust redbrick assertion of civic dignity that manages to incorporate a baffling mixture of architectural styles – with Gothic, Romanesque and even Neoclassical features. The interior held the fire hall, court and jail, and all have survived in fairly good shape, making the **Jefferson County Historical Society Museum** (Mon–Sat 11am–4pm, Sun 1–4pm; $2), which now occupies part of the premises, one of the most interesting museums in the state. In particular, look out for the photographer's chair draped with bear and buffalo skins to add lustre to the picture-portraits so popular in the late nineteenth century, and drop by the cells, where there's an excellent section devoted to prostitution and STD.

From the museum, it's just a couple of minutes' walk round to **Point Hudson**, where the old Coast Guard Training Station has been turned into a marina and the prestigious **Northwest School of Wooden Boatbuilding** has set up shop. Another short walk, this time heading north, brings you to the waterfront bluff of **Chetzemoka Park**, named after a local chief who was extremely helpful to the first white settlers. It is a particularly pretty park with banks of rhododendrons, pine trees, manicured lawns, a trim bandstand

and a narrow slice of beach. The park is at the foot of Blaine Street, which you can fol-low west as far as Adams, where a left turn brings you amongst the big old wooden man-sions of the upper town. Here the **Ann Starrett House** at Adams and Clay (see "Accommodation", p.240) easily out-Gothics the rest, swarming with gables and an octagonal tower, and an impressively ornate elliptical staircase that has to be seen to be believed. It was built at the end of the boom in 1889, whereas the 1868 **Rothschild House**, at nearby Franklin and Taylor (April–Oct daily 10am–5pm; Nov Sat & Sun 11am–4pm; $2), predates the high times, its simple plankboard frame pleasantly restored to house its period furnishings and fittings. The house was built for a local mer-chant, one D.C.H. Rothschild, a German immigrant who was related to the famous bank-ing family – as he put it, "enough to get the name, but not the money". Also, make sure to drop by the **Post Office** (Mon–Sat 9am–6pm), at Harrison and Washington streets, for its charming old interior, complete with wooden wickets and petite safe deposit boxes. From here, it's a couple of minutes' walk back down to Water along Washington.

Fort Worden, two miles north of downtown Port Townsend (Jefferson Transit bus #5 from Water St), was part of a trio of coastal fortifications built at the beginning of the twentieth century. It was designed to protect the Puget Sound from attack by the new breeds of steam-powered battleships, which were being developed by all the great pow-ers. In army use till 1953 and used as a detention centre for a further twenty years, Fort Worden is the best preserved of the three forts and is designated a state park. Its hotch-potch of military remains spreads out over a tapering headland that pushes out into the Strait of Juan de Fuca. Just beyond the main gates is the **Parade Ground**, lined on one side by the barracks, a series of plain wooden buildings that are rented as vacation accommodation (see p.240) – the youth hostel is just up the hill behind. One of the old barracks contains the park office, another the **Coastal Artillery Museum** (March–Oct 11am–4pm daily; $1), which gives the military lowdown and has a scale model of the Kinzie Battery (see below). Opposite, across the parade ground, the cen-tury-old Officers' Row culminates in the sedate **Commanding Officers' House** (June–Aug daily 10am–5pm; March–May and Sept–Oct Sat & Sun noon–4pm; $1), whose interior has been carefully decked out in full Victorian style. Beyond the Parade Ground old bunkers and gun batteries radiate out across the park, but the most divert-ing are down along the seashore near the campground, where you can scramble around the massive concrete gun emplacements of the **Kinzie Battery**, which date from the 1890s.

Eating and drinking

Port Townsend has a good supply of plain, inexpensive **cafés**, many of which offer light meals and snacks with a vegetarian or healthfood slant. Downtown, try the *Salal Café*, 634 Water and Taylor streets (☎360/385-6532) or *Jordini's Subs*, 924 Washington and Taylor streets (☎360/385-2037). Uptown, *Aldrich's Market*, at Lawrence and Tyler streets (☎360/385-0500), is a pleasantly traditional general store that chimes in with great cof-fees and sandwiches – and nearby, at Lawrence and Polk streets, is the unreconstructed hippie *Food Co-op* (Mon–Sat 9am–8pm, Sun noon–5pm), where they sell organic products and local produce. Amongst the town's **restaurants**, the pick is the *Silverwater Café*, off Water Street at 237 Taylor St (☎360/385-6448), which offers high-quality and compara-tively inexpensive food with an Italian bent – the meatballs are superb – as jazz tapes play in the background. Other choices include the popular *Fountain Café*, 920 Washington St (☎360/379-9343), which offers classy seafood and pasta with the occasional regional flourish, and the laid-back, reasonably priced *Landfall Restaurant* (Sun–Thurs 7am–3pm, Fri & Sat 7am–8pm; ☎360/385-5814), at the Point Hudson end of Water Street – no. 412 – offering an imaginative menu featuring seafood and vegetarian dishes. Last, but cer-tainly not least, the *Belmont*, 925 Water St (☎360/385-3007), is a smart bistro-style restau-rant featuring delicious everything from steaks and seafood to salads with main courses averaging a reasonable $20. As for **live music**, the funky *Town Tavern*, 639 Water at Quincy Street, showcases blues and rock bands, and boasts a wonderful old wooden bar complete with an enormous mirror to boot.

Festivals, entertainment and activities

The town puts on several big – and first-rate – **festivals**, most notably a Country Blues Festival at the end of June, the Festival of American Fiddle Tunes in early July and Jazz Port Townsend in late July. The programme is organized by a non-profit arts organization, Centrum, based in Fort Worden (☎360/385-3102 or 1-800/733-3608, *www .centrum.org*); book accommodation well ahead for any of these. If you're looking to relax for a few hours, head for the cosy Palace Theatre, just off Water Street at 235 Taylor St (☎360/385-1089), which offers a good programme of foreign and American films – and (locals argue) the best popcorn in the West. If movies aren't your thing, you might like getting a **photograph** of yourself in Western gear – completely daft for sure, but good fun – at Golden Times Photography, 1020 Water St (☎360/379-3318): they provide the costumes and the props – stetsons, revolvers and so forth – and produce a set of six for $20. Port Townsend also has several good **bookshops**; head for either the Imprint Bookstore, 820 Water St, or even better the unashamedly radical Melville & Company, 918 Water St, who sell both new and used books.

As for outdoor activities, Port Townsend is a major launching point for **kayaking** in Puget Sound. Kayak Port Townsend, 435 Water St (☎877/578-2252, *www.kayakpt.com*), organizes a varied programme of **sea-kayaking** excursions, from a two-hour paddle along the town's harbourfront ($29) to overnight trips in the surrounding bays ($179) and three- and four-day expeditions to the San Juan Islands ($299). They provide tuition and offer kayak rental too – a single kayak costs $40 per day, $55 for a double. PT Outdoors, 1071 Water St and Tyler (☎360/379-3608), also offer sea-kayak rental and organize harbourfront tours.

West to Sequim

South of Port Townsend, Hwy 20 rounds Discovery Bay to meet US-101 at the start of its journey west along the Olympic Peninsula's narrow coastal plain, with the national park on one side and the **Strait of Juan de Fuca** on the other. The strait, linking the Pacific with Puget Sound, was once thought to be the fabled **Northwest Passage** on the basis of a chance meeting, famous among early seventeenth-century mariners, between an English merchant and a certain Apostolos Valerianos in Venice in 1596. The Greek Valerianos claimed – dubiously enough – to be an exiled Spanish sea-captain by the name of Juan de Fuca and, for good measure, he added that he had sailed from the Pacific to the Arctic Ocean via the strait that bears his (assumed) name today. Thoroughly gulled, explorers sought to follow in his nautical footsteps, and the name stuck.

It's eighteen miles from the junction of Hwy 20 and US-101 to **SEQUIM** (pronounced "Skwim"), the only town on the rain-soaked peninsula to hold an annual irrigation festival. While drenching everywhere else, the Olympic Mountains cast a rain shadow over this area, and the sunshine (the town gets an average of just seventeen inches of rainfall a year) has attracted senior citizens to live here in their droves. The result is a cosy little town whose neat bungalows fall either side of the long main drag, **Washington Avenue**, which runs just to the north of the US-101 bypass – and divides into West and East at Sequim Avenue, the town's main intersection. There's nothing remarkable here, but it's easy to like the place if you've just taken a soaking in the mountains, and it's close enough to the national park to use as a base.

Sequim's **visitor centre**, on the east edge of town at 1192 E Washington Rd (Mon–Sat 9am–5pm & Sun 10am–4pm; ☎360/683-6197, *www.visitsun.com*), has free local maps and a list of all the available accommodation. Several comfortable **motels** are strung out along W Washington Avenue. Amongst them reliable choices include the garish *Red Ranch Inn*, at no. 830 (☎360/683-4195 or 1-800/777-4195; ③); and the clean *Econo Lodge*, no. 801 (☎360/683-7113 or 1-800/488-7113; ③). For a small town, Sequim has a surprisingly good range of inexpensive all-American **restaurants**: there's delicious home-style cooking at *Gwennie's* (☎360/683-4157), at 701 E Washington near the Sequim Avenue intersection, while the *Highway 101 Diner*, 392 W Washington, serves up tasty burgers in strikingly kitsch Fifties surroundings. There's also the ultraquaint *Oak Table Café*, one block south of the highway at 292 W Bell and S 3rd Avenue (daily 7am–3pm), which offers excellent breakfasts and lunches – try the baked apple pancakes. **Dungeness crabs**, widely thought by shellfish gourmets to provide the ultimate in crabmeat, are the local speciality: a good place to try them is the *Three Crabs Restaurant*, 11 Three Crabs Rd (☎360/683-4264), located on the coast about five miles north of Sequim. To get there, turn off Washington Avenue along Sequim Avenue and keep going – you'll see the signs.

Monday through Saturday, Jefferson Transit run several **buses** daily from Port Townsend to Sequim and Clallam Transit links Sequim with Port Angeles. Sequim's main **bus stop** and transfer point is one block north of Washington at N 2nd Avenue and W Cedar Street.

Around Sequim: Dungeness National Wildlife Refuge

The triangular chunk of low-lying farmland to the north of Sequim ends with the **Dungeness Spit**, a long and slender sandspit that curves out into the Strait of Juan de Fuca for almost six miles. On its exposed northern edge, the surf-pounded spit is strewn with rocks and weirdly shaped driftwood, but its sheltered side – where the attached Graveyard Spit cuts back towards the shore providing even more protection – is entirely different. Here, among the rich tidal flats waterfowl rest and feed during winter and shorebirds arrive in their thousands during their spring and fall migrations. The whole area is now protected as the **Dungeness National Wildlife Refuge** (daily sunrise to sunset; $3) and although sections – including the Graveyard Spit – are not open to the public, a lovely hiking trail leads from the parking lot at the base of Dungeness Spit through a patch of coastal forest to a bluff and then out along the beach to the **lighthouse**. It's a round trip of ten miles and although the hike isn't difficult – you can easily complete it in a day – be sure to take provisions and enough drinking water.

There are several ways to reach the refuge, but the most straightforward is to head west out of Sequim along US-101 and then – a little over four miles from the town centre – take the signposted right turn along **Kitchen Dick Lane**. From the turn, follow the signs for the five-mile drive to the parking lot. Incidentally, don't get confused by the separate Dungeness Recreation Area, which you drive through as you near your destination.

Port Angeles

Founded by the Spanish in 1791, and named "Puerto de Nuestra Senora de los Angeles" until confused postal clerks insisted one Los Angeles on the West Coast was enough, **PORT ANGELES** – seventeen miles west of Sequim – is the peninsula's main town and the most popular point of entry for those heading for the Olympic National Park. It is, however, very much a working town, the main strip of motels and commercial buildings – on Front and First streets – making few concessions to quaintness, and although the surrounding scenery and ferry connections to and from Victoria, BC, bring in the tourists, it's timber that's Port Angeles' real preoccupation. Heavy logging trucks roll in bearing tree-trunks, while the pulp and paper mill sends a pennant of steam over the town until late into the night. That said, the harbour does have its own gritty beauty: sheltered by the long arm of the Ediz Hook sandspit, vast freighters are backdropped by mountains, and out in the bay cormorants fly over the fishing boats. You could also spend a few minutes wandering the compact downtown core, just behind the waterfront between Oak and Chase streets, where there's a smattering of old and good-looking brick buildings, but the town's real attraction is its closeness to the Olympic National Park (see overleaf), and that's where you'll want to go – probably as quickly as possible.

Practicalities

Port Angeles has the peninsula's best transportation connections and, for once, the ferry and bus terminals are close together. Clallam Transit services (☎360/452-4511 or 1-800/858-3747) pull in at the **bus depot**, beside the waterfront at W Front and Oak streets. From here, it's a couple of minutes' walk to the main **ferry terminal**, where Black Ball Transport (☎360/457-4491) **car ferries** arrive from – and shuttle over to – Victoria in Canada (March–Dec 2–4 daily; 1hr 45min; passengers $7, car and driver $29), but note that peak season delays are commonplace for those taking a vehicle and reservations are not accepted. Arriving at a neighbouring pier at the foot of Lincoln Street, the **passenger ferries** of Victoria Express (☎360/452-8088 or 1-800/633-1589, *www.victoriaexpress.com*) ply the same route from late May to September (2–3 daily; 1hr; $12.50).

The town's **visitor centre**, metres from the main ferry terminal at 121 E Railroad Ave (Mon–Fri 10am–4pm, summer daily 7am–6pm; ☎360/452-2363), can provide a mass of information about the town and its environs. Port Angeles also houses the **Olympic National Park Visitor Center** (daily summer 9am–8pm; winter 9am–4pm; ☎360/452-0330, *www.nps.gov/olym*), an excellent source of the maps and information you'll need if you're planning any hiking: to get there, head south out of town for about a mile up to the top of Race Street – along the signposted route which doubles as the road to Hurricane Ridge. Next door is the **Wilderness Information Center** (May & Sept daily 8.30am–4.30pm; July–Aug Sun–Wed 8am–4.30pm, Thurs–Sat 7.30am–7.30pm), which specializes in backcountry hiking and camping. Downtown Port Angeles is a good place to get kitted out too: Pedal 'n' Paddle, 120 E Front St (☎360/457-1240), rent mountain bikes and organize kayak trips, while Olympic Mountaineering, at 140 W Front St and Oak (☎360/452-0240, *www.olymtn.com*), hire out climbing, camping and hiking tackle, though their speciality is guided mountaineering trips. Their most popular excursion is the day-long climb to the summit of Mount Olympus, which costs between $150 and $225 per person depending on the number in the group.

Motel and **hotel** accommodation is easy to find in Port Angeles and mostly strung along the two parallel main streets, Front and First, which run just behind the harbour. The visitor centre has the complete list, but easily the pick (amongst a rather mundane assortment) is the spick-and-span *Red Lion Hotel,* 221 N Lincoln St at Front (☎360/452-9215 or 1-800/733-5466; ⑥), a motel-style complex on the waterfront a block from the ferry landing; rooms with a harbour view attract a premium of $20. There are also several **B&Bs** to choose from, one good option being *The 5 Seasuns*, 1006 S Lincoln (☎360/452-8248, *www.seasuns.com*; ⑤), which occupies a handsome 1920s villa amidst extensive gardens and offers four guestrooms. The nearest **camping** is the first-come, first-served, all-year *Heart O' the Hills* campground in the Olympic National Park, six miles south of town along Hurricane Ridge Road. For **food**, the options are limited, but the homely *First Street Haven Café*, at 107 E 1st St and Laurel (Mon–Sat 7am–4pm, Sun 8am–2pm; ☎360/457-0352), serves up delicious snacks, sandwiches and meals at low prices and the salads are very good too.

Moving on from Port Angeles to the Olympic National Park without your own vehicle is never going to be easy, but all is not lost: Olympic Tours (advance reservations essential; ☎360/452-3858, *www.tourtheolympics.com*) operate day-trips from the ferry terminal to the Hoh Rainforest (see p.250) for $28 per person and also run half-day ($13) and full-day ($18) excursions to Hurricane Ridge. Failing that, Clallam Transit have a reasonably regular, Monday through Saturday service along US-101 to *Lake Crescent Lodge*, Sappho (change for Neah Bay) and Forks (change for La Push). Finally, local **auto rental** outlets offer reasonable rates for one- and two-day rentals, and you'll see their billboards round the ferry dock. Budget, 111 E Front St (☎360/452-4774 or 1-800/345-8038), is as competitive as any.

Neah Bay and the Makah Indian Reservation

West of Port Angeles, US-101 cuts inland to begin its circuitous journey round the flanks of the Olympic National Park (see below). This is the obvious route to follow, but it's also possible to take Hwy 112 right along the coast, a seventy-mile drive that becomes increasingly solitary the further you go. Eventually, the road passes the gravelled turning that bumps down to Lake Ozette (see p.250) before clinging precariously to the cliffs as it approaches end-of-the-world **NEAH BAY**, the small and run-down last village of the **Makah**. The bitter history of the Makah is typical of the area: a seagoing tribe, they once lived by fishing and hunting whales and seals, moving from camp to camp across the western part of the peninsula. Like most Native-Americans, the Makah were happy to trade with passing European ships, and even when the Spaniards built a stockade here in 1792 (it was abandoned four months later) the relationship remained cordial and mutually beneficial. The change came when white settlers began to arrive in the 1840s, bringing smallpox with them. Makah social structures were simply swept away by an epidemic of savage proportions. Samuel Hancock, who had built a trading post at Neah Bay in 1850, recorded the tragedy: "The beach for a distance of eight miles was literally strewn with the dead bodies . . . still they continue to die in such numbers that I finally hauled them down the beach at low tide, so they would drift away". Other indignities were to follow: treaties restricted their freedom of movement, white settlers were given vast chunks of their traditional lands, and they were forced to speak English at white-run schools, as missionaries set about changing their religion.

The Makah's tenuous grip on their culture received an unexpected boost in 1970, when a mudslide at an old village site on **Cape Alava**, several miles south of their present reservation, revealed part of an ancient Makah settlement – buried, Pompeii-like, by a previous mudslide some five hundred years before and perfectly preserved. The first people to uncover the remains encountered bizarre scenes of instantaneous ageing – green alder leaves, lying on the floor where they fell centuries ago, shrivelled almost as soon as they were exposed – but more important were the archeological finds. Eleven years of careful excavation revealed literally thousands of artefacts, everything from harpoons for whale hunts, intricately carved seal clubs, watertight boxes made without the use of metal, strangely designed bowls, and toys all belonging to a period before trade began with Europeans. Rather than being carted off to the depths of the Smithsonian, these artefacts have remained in Makah hands, and a number are now displayed at the purpose-built **Makah Museum** (June to mid-Sept daily 10am–5pm; rest of year Wed–Sun 10am–5pm; $4), along with a full-size replica longhouse, four cedar canoes and some poignant nineteenth-century photographs of the Makah people. The site of the ancient village has, however, been reburied to preserve it.

Beyond Neah Bay, sullen **Cape Flattery**, which once "flattered" Captain Cook with the hope of finding a harbour, occupies the northern corner of the Makah Reservation and is the US's northwesternmost point (excluding Alaska). Neah Bay is served by Clallam Transit **buses** (Mon–Sat) from Port Angeles, change at Sappho.

Olympic National Park

The magnificent **Olympic National Park**, which consists of a huge mountainous section in the middle of the Olympic Peninsula plus a separate sixty-mile strip of Pacific coast further west, is one of Washington's prime wilderness destinations, with boundless opportunities for spectacular hiking and wildlife-watching.

Although the park is best known as the location of the only **temperate rainforests** in North America (see p.249) the special conditions responsible for producing such forests only prevail at lower altitudes, and into its one and a half million acres are crammed an extraordinarily diverse assortment of landscapes and climate zones. About sixty percent of the peninsula – the areas between about 2000 and 4000 feet – is **montane forest**, dominated by the Pacific silver fir and the Douglas fir. At higher elevations, these species give way to a **subalpine forest** of mountain hemlock, Alaska cedar and fir, broken up by a parkland of intermittent forest and lush meadow. Higher up still, the mountain slopes and summits constitute a forbidding **alpine zone** where windborne ice crystals feel like flying sandpaper, the hiking trails are only free of snow for about two months a year (roughly late June to Aug), and mosses and lichens are pretty much the only vegetation. The **coast** is different again, for here the wild and lonely Pacific beaches that stretch down the peninsula's west side are studded with black rocks that point dramatically out of a grey sea, inhabited mostly by loons, grebes, puffins and cormorants.

No roads cross the central segment of the park from one side to the other, but many run into it from separate directions, and only parts of the coastal strip are accessible by road. The text which follows reflects the most logical itinerary, working anticlockwise around the park on US-101 and making forays into different sections from the various access points along the way. As we've indicated in the text, some parts of the park can only be reached on gravel-topped roads and these should be approached with caution (if at all) in an ordinary vehicle particularly in wet or foggy weather. If you're planning to do a lot of backcountry driving, equip yourself with a four-wheel-drive.

Before heading into the park, load up on information at the **Olympic National Park Visitor Center** and the **Wilderness Information Center**, both back in Port Angeles (see p.244). There are other, smaller NPS visitor centres at **Hurricane Ridge** and **Hoh Rainforest**. These main services are supplemented by a string of seasonal **ranger stations** – at Lake Crescent, Ozette, Mora, Kalaloch, Queets, Lake Quinault and elsewhere – as well as the occasional US Forest Service station in the adjoining Olympic National Forest. Most have a wealth of literature to help plan your visit, including complimentary maps and free visitors' guides – though not always the detailed maps needed by hikers. Most NPS centres and stations will issue backcountry permits ($5 to register, $2 per person to camp), but don't assume this to be the case and always ring ahead.

Over six hundred miles of **hiking trail** pattern the park, ranging from the gentlest of strolls to lung-wrenching treks. The usual backcountry rules apply: for example, don't drink the water, hide food away from bears, avoid defecating near water, and get a backcountry permit if you're venturing beyond the park's established campgrounds to stay out overnight. Naturally enough, the weather on the west (rainforest) side of the peninsula is incredibly wet – 140 inches is an average annual precipitation – and although the eastern slopes are considerably drier, rain is frequent here too. However, summer days can be hot and sunny and even the heaviest rainclouds are often swept away by the prevailing westerlies. On the coast, strong currents, cold water and hidden rocks make the **beaches** unsuitable for swimming (especially as floating logs present a real hazard), but the hiking can be magnificent, if very strenuous – the coastal headlands hereabouts are often extremely difficult to negotiate. Also, you do hear the odd horror story about hikers cut off by the tide, so carry a tide-table (usually printed in local newspapers), or copy down times at a ranger station or visitor centre, and err on the side of caution. And wherever you go, don't forget the insect repellent.

The one-horse communities dotting the peninsula offer **motel** accommodation, but, generally speaking, you're better off inside the park. Here you can either **camp** – there are sixteen established campgrounds ($10–12), ten open all year and operating on a first-come, first-served basis, and around fifty backcountry sites ($2) – or stay in one of the **lodges**, among which there are three of note: Lake Crescent, Lake Quinault and Kalaloch. The *Sol Duc Hot Springs Resort*, deep within the park, is another excellent choice. At all four establishments, book your room well in advance. **Entrance** to the park costs $10 per vehicle, $5 for cyclists and pedestrians; the ticket is valid for seven consecutive days' admission.

The peninsula is best explored by car, but Clallam Transit of Port Angeles (see p.244) do provide a reasonably frequent weekday **bus** service to *Lake Crescent Lodge* and Forks, where you can change for La Push.

Hurricane Ridge and the Olympic Mountains
On the southern edge of Port Angeles, the Olympic National Park Visitor Center (daily summer 9am–8pm; winter 9am–4pm; ☎360/452-0330, *www.nps.gov/olym*) is the starting point for the seventeen-mile haul up to **Hurricane Ridge** – passing (after about five miles) the *Heart O' the Hills* campground. It's a hell of a drive, as the road wraps itself around precipices until the piercing peaks and glistening glaciers of the **Olympic Mountains** spread out before you, a formidably thick band of snow-capped peaks with mighty Mount Olympus the tallest of all at nearly eight thousand feet. The Hurricane Ridge Visitor Center features a large relief map of the area, useful for getting your bearings, and **hiking trails** lead off to more isolated spots – through meadows filled with wild flowers in early summer.

The most popular hike is the **Hurricane Hill Trail**, a three-mile round trip to the top of a neighbouring hill, where there are great views out across the Strait of Juan de Fuca. Longer alternatives include the strenuous eight-mile hike west, over the mountains through classic alpine and subalpine scenery, to **Lake Mills**, where there's a backcountry campground. East from Hurricane Ridge, a difficult and steep nine-mile dirt road heads off to **Obstruction Peak**, which is noted for its views of Mount Olympus; several trails venture from the end of the road into the valley beyond, with one leading to the **campground** at **Deer Park**.

West to Lake Crescent and Sol Duc Hot Springs
West of Port Angeles, US-101 slips through low-lying forest on its fifteen-mile journey to glacier-cut **Lake Crescent**, a handsome, hill-trapped fishing lake known throughout the region for its fine Beardslee trout. Just off the highway, beside the lake's southern shore, is **Lake Crescent Lodge** (May–Oct; ☎360/928-3211; ④), whose cabins, 1930s lodge and motel-style rooms occupy a beautiful wooded headland poking out into the water. Nearby, the one-mile Marymere Falls Trail leads through old-growth forest to a ninety-foot waterfall, and continues up the forested mountain slope, as the two-mile Mount Storm King Trail, to Happy Lake Ridge, where there are magnificent views back over the lake. If you're staying at the lodge, they're only too pleased to provide further hiking (and boating) suggestions.

Just beyond the western tip of Lake Crescent, a paved turning branches south off US-101 to thread up through the densely forested river valley that leads – after twelve miles – to the **Sol Duc Hot Springs Resort** (mid-May to late Sept; ☎360/327-3583; ⑤). First impressions are not especially favourable – the resort's modern timber chalets have been dropped unceremoniously into a forest clearing – but don't let that put you off: the chalets are perfectly adequate if rather spartan; the restaurant is outstanding, serving the very best of Northwest cuisine; splendid hiking trails nudge into the surrounding mountains and the Sol Duc River Valley is fascinating in itself as part of the transitional zone between the rainforests to the west and the drier lowland forest to the east. What's more, bathing in the **hot springs** (mid-May to Aug daily 9am–9pm; Sept daily 9am–8pm; April to mid-May & Oct Fri–Sun 9am–6pm) is extraordinarily relaxing, with the mineral water bubbling out of the earth to be channelled into three

THE RAINFORESTS OF OLYMPIC NATIONAL PARK

Extraordinary as it may seem in cool Washington, an all-but-unique combination of climatic factors in the river valleys on the western side of the Olympic Peninsula has produced an environment akin to a jungle. **Temperate rainforests** are extremely rare – the only others are located in Patagonia and New Zealand – but here an average, annual rainfall of 140 inches mixes with river-water running down from the mountains to create conditions wet enough to produce a density of foliage normally associated with much warmer climes. Sitka spruce and maple flourish, all but overwhelmed by the thick, trailing tendrils of clubmosses and lichens, epiphytes whose roots gather nourishment from the drizzly air. On the ground, some three hundred species of plant fight for growing space, crowding the ground with ferns, mushrooms and wood sorrel oozing out of the dense, moist soil. The rainforests intermingle with the montane forests of Western hemlock and Douglas fir, among which are the park's largest trees – in fact the world's biggest Douglas fir is to be found in the Queets Valley.

Several rainforest areas can be visited, notably those in the valleys of the Hoh and Quinault rivers (see below). The only way to get through the rainforest is on the specially cleared, and in places paved, **trails**, although these tend to get slippery as moss grows back again – your footwear should grip well. You'll need a **vehicle** to reach any of the trailheads, but there are **campgrounds** in both valleys and lodgings beside Quinault Lake.

outside pools – at 100, 102 and 106 degrees Fahrenheit. Overnight guests can use the heated pools for free, but visitors – including those using the resort's **campground** (same number; $16) – have to pay $7.50.

From the end of the road, a couple of miles beyond the resort, you can hike further along the river to **Sol Duc Falls**, from where a steep path heads off south along Canyon Creek up into the mountains to the **Seven Lakes Basin**. More ambitious souls can hike across the Bogachiel Peak, past Hoh Lake and down into the Hoh River valley – the site of one of the most visited rainforest areas (see overleaf).

West to Forks

Back on US-101, it's about fourteen miles west from the Sol Duc turning to Hwy 113, which cuts off north for the long-winded journey to Neah Bay (see p.246), and another fourteen miles to the small blue-collar community of **FORKS**, situated in-between the main body and the coastal portion of the Olympic National Park. Despite half-hearted attempts to catch the peninsula's growing tourist trade, Forks remains very much a timber town and it's been hit hard by the gradual decline of the industry. Nonetheless, heavy trucks still trickle through Forks, unloading logs at local sawmills and hauling sawn lumber away to be shipped out of Port Angeles or Grays Harbor.

When you're surrounded by trees, the history of logging becomes more interesting than you might otherwise think, and it's worth calling in on the **Forks Timber Museum** (mid-April to Oct daily 10am–4pm; donation), about a mile south of town on US-101, for the lowdown. A broad range of exhibits depicts life in the logging camps of the 1920s and 1930s, when men were based out in the forest, sleeping in bunkhouses and hitting the towns for only a couple of days every month. Inexpensive road-building ended the days of the logging camp after World War II and in recent years various mechanical devices (some on display) have also made logging less hazardous, though it remains a dangerous occupation.

There's no real reason to **stay** in Forks, but if you're marooned the **visitor centre** (☎360/374-2531), next door to the museum, has a complete list of local accommodation. Monday through Saturday, Clallam Transit (☎360/452-4511 or 1-800/858-3747) run **buses** from Port Angeles to Forks, with connections on to the coast at La Push (see overleaf).

West from Forks to Rialto Beach and La Push

A couple of miles to the north of Forks, Hwy 110 cuts west off US-101 for the half-hour drive down to the coast. About eight miles along the turning the road splits into two branches – one above, the other below the Quillayute River: the southern branch meanders round to the down-at-heel village of **La Push**, on the Quileute Indian Reservation, while the northern fork continues on into the national park's coastal strip at **Mora**, site of an attractive, wooded **campground** and a **ranger station** (☎360/374-5460). Close by, a mile or two further down the road, is **Rialto Beach**, a driftwood-cluttered strand from where it's possible to hike north along the shoreline, passing beneath the wooded bluffs to the sound of the booming surf. Most visitors are content with a short(ish) hike along the coast, but others opt for the longer, extremely arduous, twenty-mile trek north to **Ozette**, where the **ranger station** (☎360/963-2725) and **campground** are a little inland beside Lake Ozette. This longer hike takes three to four days and, naturally enough, you'd want to arrange transportation at both ends; as always, take good care not to get cut off by the tide and be prepared for strenuous climbs over steep coastal headlands. A comparatively easy 3.3-mile trail – part of the Indian Village Nature Trail – runs from Ozette Ranger Station to the coast at Cape Alava, the site of the prehistoric Makah village revealed (and subsequently reburied by archeologists) after a 1970 mudslide (see p.246).

South from Forks to the Hoh Rainforest

Beyond Forks, US-101 threads through logging country to pass, after about fourteen miles, the paved turning that leads deep into the **Hoh Rainforest**. This is the most popular of the Olympic rainforests, principally because of the excellent **visitor centre**, located nineteen miles from US-101 (July & Aug daily 9am–6.30pm; rest of year daily 9am–4pm; ☎360/374-6925), where you can examine various displays on the unusual habitat and pick up all sorts of explanatory pamphlets. Afterwards, you can explore the rainforest along two short trails, the three-quarter-mile **Hall of Mosses Trail** or the slightly longer **Spruce Trail**, which reaches the Hoh River on a circuit through the forest. More energetic hikers can follow the 36-mile round-trip **Hoh River Trail** right up to the base of Mount Olympus; climbing the ice-covered peak is a major undertaking, but even if you just want to camp out along the route, be sure to check in with the rangers and get a backcountry permit. There's also a ninety-site **campground** next to the visitor centre.

On to Kalaloch

Shortly after the Hoh Rainforest turn-off, US-101 swings west to run parallel to the lower reaches of the Hoh River, clipping down to the coast – and back into the national park – at **Ruby Beach**, whose red- and black-pebbled sands are reached from the highway along a short and fairly easy trail. Moving on, US-101 sticks close to the shore for the next few miles, offering tantalizing glimpses of humpy rocks and driftwood beaches as it slips down to tiny ribbon-built **KALALOCH**, where there's a **ranger station** (☎360/962-2283), a large **campground** and the low-slung, timber *Kalaloch Lodge* (☎360/962-2271, *www.visitkalaloch.com*), which offers rusticated log cabins (⑥) as well as lodge (⑤) and motel-style (⑥) rooms right on the oceanfront. The restaurant is top-notch too.

The Queets and Quinault rainforests and Quinault Lake

Just south of Kalaloch, US-101 loops awkwardly inland to skirt the **Quinault Indian Reservation**, an infertile chunk of wilderness wedged against the shoreline. It's home to several Salish-speaking tribes who were plonked here in the 1850s during the aggressive treaty-making period that followed Washington's incorporation as a US territory. The highway strips along the northern edge of the reservation, passing, after about ten miles, the fourteen-mile-long dirt road which heads inland to the **Queets Rainforest**, the least visited of the three main rainforest areas, and site of the world's largest Douglas fir tree – 220 feet tall and 45 feet in circumference.

About thirty miles from Kalaloch, US-101 reaches, in short succession, the two side roads that lead the couple of miles off the highway to **Quinault Lake**, whose dark blue, creek-fed waters are surrounded by the deep, damp greens of the **Quinault Rainforest**, the most accessible and perhaps the most beautiful of all the peninsula's rainforests. The lake was already a popular resort area when Teddy Roosevelt visited in the 1900s and decided to proclaim it part of an expanded Olympic National Park: you only have to glimpse the lake and its elegaic setting to see why Roosevelt was so impressed.

Of the two **access roads** leading off US-101, one travels the length of the lake's north shore, the other the south, but they don't connect until you're well past the lake and further up the river valley – altogether a thirty-mile loop. Dense overgrowth crimps the narrow road as it enters the deeper recesses of the forest, but it perseveres (as a rough gravel track) and the loop is negotiable by vehicle – though you should check conditions before you set off: floods have wrecked the more remote portions of the road on several occasions.

A variety of **hiking trails** lead off from the road. The longer and more strenuous climb is through the rainforest of the Quinault River Valley and on up to the alpine meadows and glaciated peaks at the centre of the national park. Others serve as easy introductions to the rainforest: the half-mile **Maple Glade Trail** is one of the best short hikes, clambering along a small stream through textbook rainforest vegetation, whilst the four-mile **Quinault Loop Trail** snakes through a wonderful old-growth forest dominated by colossal Douglas firs which keep out the light, turning the under-growth into a dark and dank mystery. Backcountry permits, hiking maps, weather forecasts, details of all the trails and information on the five **campgrounds** dotted round the lakeshore are available at the **Ranger Station** on South Shore Road (☎360/288-2525). A few yards away, occupying a fine lakeshore location, the high timber gables and stone chimneys of **Lake Quinault Lodge** (☎360/288-2900 or 1-800/562-6672; woodside rooms ⑥, lakeside ⑦) date from the 1920s, though the interior has been revamped in a comfortable modern style. With every justification it's a popular spot, which means that reservations are pretty much essential. There's less expensive accommodation round here too – try the **Lochaerie Resort**, North Shore Road (☎360/288-2215, *www.lochaerie.com*; ④), which has five comfortable cabins dating from the 1930s.

Washington's lower coast

As you leave the west side of the Olympic Peninsula for **Washington's lower coast**, the scenery gradually grows tamer and the national forests are replaced by privately owned timber land, gashed by bald patches of "clear cutting". The coastline cuts deeply into the mainland at two points: the bay of **Grays Harbor**, at the apex of which lie the twin industrial cities of **Hoquiam** and **Aberdeen**, and at muddy **Willapa Bay**, dotted with oyster beds and wildlife sanctuaries. The sandspit sheltering Willapa Bay – the **Long Beach Peninsula** – was formed from sediment carried here by the ocean from the churning mouth of the Columbia River near its base. The beach is extraordinarily long, but visitors are allowed to drive on almost all of it and the straggling resorts behind it are scrawny, modern places without much appeal. The lower coast's saving grace is right at its southern tip just beyond tiny **Ilwaco**, where the ruggedly handsome headland that pokes out into the mouth of the Columbia River is protected as **Fort Canby State Park** – and here you can camp or stay in the old lighthouse-keeper's quarters.

Hoquiam and Aberdeen

South of the Olympic Peninsula's Quinault rainforest (see overleaf), US-101 cuts across logging country, whizzing through the forested hills until it pounds into gritty **HOQUIAM** beside **Grays Harbor** bay, which takes a big bite out of the coastline. The loggers who settled the bay in the mid-nineteenth century originally meant to stay only until the dense forest within easy reach of the waterfront had been cut down and the area was "logged out". But railways soon made it possible to transport lumber from deeper in the forest, and a combination of this and the plentiful fishing – fish-canneries soon joined the sawmills along the waterfront – led to the development of Hoquiam and its larger neighbour **ABERDEEN**. Now hit by recession in both fishing and forestry, these twin towns are not obvious places for a visit, though Aberdeen is making a plucky attempt to catch passing tourists with the reinvigoration of part of its harbourfront by means of the **Grays Harbor Historical Seaport** project. In these unpromising industrial surroundings, the project has painstakingly reconstructed the *Lady Washington*, the eighteenth-century sailing ship of Captain Robert Gray, the American trader who discovered Grays Harbor. Built to conform both with original designs and modern Coast Guard safety regulations, the ship (when it's in port) is now a floating museum with a crew dressed in period costume. There are guided tours plus three-hour sailing trips for around $35 per person – call ☎360/532-8611 or 1-800/200-2359 for schedules and reservations. A replica of Gray's other ship, the *Columbia Rediviva* (after which the Columbia River is named), is scheduled to follow.

US-101 cuts through Aberdeen's town centre, which is located on the north bank of the Chehalis River as it flows into the bay. The Historical Seaport is just to the east across the Wishkah River, a tributary of the Chehalis – just follow the signs. In the unlikely event you want to **stay** in Aberdeen – hometown of old grunge favourite Kurt Cobain – the Grays Harbor **visitor centre**, off US-101 at 506 Duffy St (☎360/532-1924), is on the strip connecting Hoquiam and Aberdeen and has a comprehensive list of local lodgings.

Willapa Bay

US-101 leads south out of Aberdeen over the hills to **RAYMOND**, a pocket-sized lumber town where the highway turns west to skirt the flat and rather tedious shoreline of **Willapa Bay**. Too shallow to be used as a commercial port, Willapa Bay is much less developed than Grays Harbor, and its muddy depths support a profitable underworld of oysters – you'll spot the oyster beds from the highway. Several parts of the bay have been incorporated into the **Willapa National Wildlife Refuge**, whose various dunes, forests, marshes and mud flats shelter some two hundred species of migrating shorebird. Most of the refuge is only accessible by boat, but one of its sections – Leadbetter Point at the tip of the Long Beach Peninsula (see opposite) – can be reached by car. Advice on what wildlife to see and where can be obtained from the refuge **visitor centre** (☎360/484-3482), beside US-101 across from Willapa Bay's Long Island, about 35 miles south of Raymond – and some ten miles northeast of Ilwaco.

Ilwaco

Though there's not much evidence of it today, the area around the **Columbia River mouth** was once inhabited by the **Chinook**. They evolved "Chinook jargon", an

Esperanto-style mix of their own language, including French and English, that was widely used for trading, and later, for treaty-making. By all accounts, it was extremely easy to learn: Paul Kane, an Irish-Canadian explorer and painter who passed this way in the mid-1840s, wrote that it only took a few days before he could "converse with most of the chiefs with tolerable ease; their common salutation is *Clak-hoh-ah-yah*, originating . . . in their having heard in the early days of the fur trade . . . *Clark, how are you?*" The Chinook also caught white nineteenth-century imaginations with their strangely flattened skulls, as depicted in careful sketches brought back to a curious East by both Kane and the explorers Lewis and Clark, who spent the winter of 1805–6 quartered at Fort Clatsop, on the south side of the river (see p.113). The skull-flattening was achieved by pressing a piece of bark firmly to a baby's (padded) forehead every time it went to bed for about a year, the end result being seen as a sign of aristocratic distinction.

Named after a Chinook chief, the fishing port of **ILWACO** achieved some regional notoriety at the start of the twentieth century when competition between fishermen with nets and those with traps broke into a series of street battles, the **gillnet wars**, fought with knives and rifles – and only finally resolved when fishtraps were banned on the Columbia in 1935. Nowadays, Ilwaco is an unassuming little place where everyone knows the times of the tides and where to dig for clams. There's nothing much to see, though you could drop by the **Heritage Museum**, at 115 SE Lake St (Mon–Sat 9am–4pm; till 5pm & Sun noon–4pm in summer; $2.50), which has displays on Chinook culture and the usual pioneer artefacts, or take a **sea-fishing trip** – there are several operators down along the harbourfront.

There are more interesting places to stay nearby – in Fort Canby and Fort Columbia state parks (see overleaf) – but Ilwaco does have a reasonable supply of **accommodation**. The pick of the bunch is the *Inn at Ilwaco*, 120 Williams Ave NE (☎360/642-8686 or 1-888/244-2523; ⑤), whose nine comfortable rooms occupy the renovated parsonage and vestry of the Presbyterian church on a wooded rise just above the town. *Heidi's Inn*, a standard-issue motel at 126 Spruce St (☎360/642-2387 or 1-800/576-1032; ③), is a second, much cheaper choice.

North of Ilwaco: the Long Beach Peninsula

Lined by 28 miles of uninterrupted beach, and less prone to fog than other parts of Washington's coast, the **Long Beach Peninsula**, separating the ocean and Willapa Bay, has been a holiday destination since steamboats ferried vacationing Portlanders here in the 1890s. However, the ribbon resorts lining up along the sandspit have little appeal and only **OYSTERVILLE**, on the east side of the peninsula about sixteen miles north of Ilwaco on Hwy 103, is worth a second look. Oysterville made a killing in the 1860s and 1870s by shipping oysters to San Francisco, and flogging them to the high flyers of the gold rush at up to $40 a plate. Then, in an all-too-familiar pattern, increasing demand fuelled over-harvesting and with the oysters decimated, the town slipped into a long decline, leaving little more than the tiny **historic district** of today, with its Victorian houses of shingles and scrollwork set behind trim picket fences. Once you've strolled round town, there's nothing much to do, though you can sample the local delicacy at the bayside **Oysterville Sea Farms** (☎360/665-6585) – six cost $2.50, a dozen $4 and very tasty they are too. The other attraction is at the north tip of the peninsula, where the dunes and marshes of **Leadbetter Point** form one section of the Willapa National Wildlife Refuge (see opposite). A couple of vague footpaths meander over the point, but wet conditions soon flood them out and there are no set hiking trails as such. Before you set out, take advice from any local visitor centre or the Refuge's headquarters.

Southwest of Ilwaco: Fort Canby State Park

A couple of miles southwest of Ilwaco, a stumpy, heavily forested promontory pokes out into the mouth of the Columbia River sheltering the town from the full force of the Pacific. Scenic **Fort Canby State Park** covers the whole of the headland, taking its name from the fortifications that were constructed here in the 1860s. The fort was one of a chain of military installations whose batteries guarded the Pacific coast (and here, of course, the river mouth) from the middle of the nineteenth century through both world wars. Little remains of the fort today – just a few weather-beaten gun emplacements – but there are a brace of lighthouses. The first – reached down a short side road as you approach the park – is **North Head Lighthouse** (tours June–Sept daily 11am–3pm; $1), built in 1898 in a magnificent spot high above Dead Man's Hollow, named after the unfortunate victims of an earlier shipwreck. Doubling back, the main park road pushes on to the **Lewis and Clark Interpretive Center** (daily 10am–4/5pm; free), where the displays dealing with the hazards of navigating the Columbia River mouth are a good deal more interesting than the attempt to outline Lewis and Clark's journey to the Pacific. If you are interested in the explorers, head instead for the better displays at Fort Clatsop, outside Astoria (see p.113). From the centre, a steep, three-quarters of a mile trail leads down to the more southerly of the two lighthouses (no public access), perched on **Cape Disappointment**, a short finger of land stuck at right angles to the rest of the promontory. The cape got its name when a British fur trader, John Meares, failed to sail his ship over the dangerous sandbar at the river's entrance in 1788. In fact, Meares was lucky – over two hundred ships were later wrecked on the sandbar, and although dredges, automated lights and a pair of long moles have now made the river mouth much safer, the coastguards still train off the cape – you can sometimes see their small boats facing massive waves.

There's a large **campground** in Fort Canby State Park in between the Interpretive Center and North Head Lighthouse (☎360/753-2036; $10–15). Even better, two old North Head **lighthouse-keeper's houses** have been revamped to accommodate tourists; each holds a maximum of six people and the cost is $220 per night; reservations on ☎360/642-3078.

Southeast from Ilwaco to Oregon – Fort Columbia State Park

Heading east from Ilwaco on Hwy 101, it's just eight miles to **Fort Columbia State Park**, which occupies a hilly, wooded headland that was purchased from the Chinook in 1867. The headland was developed as a military installation in the 1890s, acting as a second line of nautical defence behind forts Canby (see above) and Stevens (see p.114). Several gun emplacements dot the park – grim concrete affairs built largely underground with their seaward-facing sides flush to the lie of the land to mitigate the effects of incoming shells (not that they ever saw action). Behind, just up the hill, are several rows of regulation army houses, with their wide verandas and neat columns. One of them, the former enlisted men's barracks, houses an **Interpretive Center** (April–Sept 10am–5pm; $2 includes museum) with several period rooms, and the former commandant's quarters – Columbia House – holds a modest **museum** (April–Sept 10am–5pm) with yet more. The park itself has a fine seashore setting and you can stay here either in the former hospital, renamed **Scarborough House**, which accommodates up to twelve and costs $350 per night, or in the **Steward's House**, which has two bedrooms and costs $130 per night. Each has a kitchen and living room, linen is provided and there's a minimum stay of two nights from April to September and on winter weekends. Reservations are strongly recommended on ☎360/642-3078.

From Fort Columbia, it's two miles to the huge, four-mile bridge of 1966 that spans the Columbia River over to Oregon's Astoria (see p.110).

travel details

Trains

Seattle to: Everett (2 daily; 45min); Los Angeles (1 daily; 12hr); Olympia-Lacey (4 daily; 1hr 30min); Mount Vernon (2 daily; 2hr 30min); Portland (4 daily; 4hr); Spokane (2 daily; 8hr); Tacoma (4 daily; 1hr); Vancouver (1 daily; 4hr); Wenatchee (3 daily; 4hr).

Buses

North from Seattle to: Bellingham (5 daily; 2hr); Everett (5 daily; 40min); Mount Vernon (5 daily; 1hr 30min); Vancouver, BC (7 daily; 3hr 30min–7hr 30min).

South from Seattle to: Olympia (6 daily; 1hr 40min); Portland (9 daily; 4 express buses 3hr 15min, others up to 5hr); Tacoma (7 daily; 45min).

Ferries

(All Washington State Ferries unless otherwise stated.)

To Alaska from Bellingham: Alaska Marine Highway (1 weekly; leaves Fri evening, arrives Skagway Mon afternoon).

To Bainbridge Island from Seattle: At least hourly from 6.20am–11.15pm, also boats at 12.50am and 2.10am; 35min.

To Bremerton from Seattle: car ferry (15 daily; 1hr); passenger ferry (Mon–Fri 12 daily; 30min).

To Port Townsend: from Friday Harbor, on San Juan Island with PS Express passenger ferry (April–Sept 1 daily); from Keystone, Whidbey Island (10–15 daily, varies with season; 30min).

To the San Juan Islands and Sidney, BC, from Anacortes: 17 summer, 12 off-season – various routes, including 2 daily (1 winter) to Sidney, BC; to Friday Harbour (1hr 5min–2hr 10min); Lopez (45–55min); Orcas (1hr 5min–1hr 25min); Sidney (2–3hr).

To Vashon Island: from Point Defiance to Tahlequah (16 daily; 15min); from Fauntleroy, West Seattle, to Point Vashon (around every half-hour from 5.30am–1.55am; 15min or 35min); from downtown Seattle to Point Vashon (passenger-only, 8 Mon–Fri from 6am–8.30pm; no Sat & Sun service).

To Victoria from Port Angeles: Black Ball Transport car ferry (March–Dec 2–4 daily; 1hr 45min); Victoria Express passenger ferry (late May to Sept 2–3 daily; 1hr.

To Victoria from Seattle: on the *Victoria Clipper* (passenger-only, summer 4 daily; winter 1 daily; 2–3hr).

To Whidbey Island: from Mukilteo to Clinton (from 5am to 2am every half-hour; 20min); from Port Townsend to Keystone, see above.

CHAPTER FOUR

EASTERN WASHINGTON

Native-American legends say that the thirsty people of **eastern Washington** once went to the Ocean to ask for water. Ocean sent his children Cloud and Rain to water the land, but the people refused to let the spirits return home: Ocean, furious, rescued his offspring and built the Cascade Mountains as a great punitive barricade between the people and the sea. Whether or not the gods had a hand in it, the great spine of the Cascades is still a crucial divide, separating the wet, forested, sea-facing regions of the west from the parched prairies and canyonlands to the east. Snow-capped and pine-covered, the **Cascade Mountains**, which extend south across Washington and Oregon and are gashed by the mighty Columbia River, have a

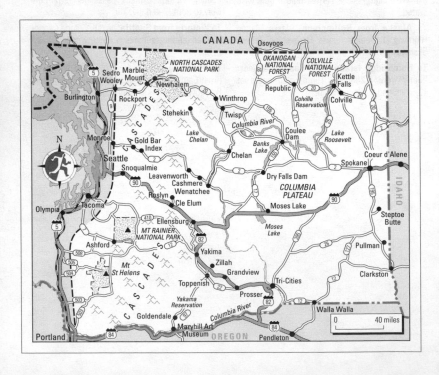

pristine beauty that's best appreciated from one of the many hiking trails. **Mount Rainier**, set in its own national park and readily accessible from Olympia or Seattle, has some of the loveliest, while the nearby blasted terrain of **Mount St Helens** – protected as a National Volcanic Monument and most easily reached from Olympia or Portland in Oregon – offers some of the most dramatic. There are more superb hiking trails further north too, along Hwy 20, the high mountain road that crosses the **North Cascades** before it dips into the eastern foothills where the small towns of **Leavenworth** and **Chelan** make particularly useful bases for exploring the surrounding mountains.

The **Columbia Plateau**, east of the Cascades, is a very different proposition. The huge, sagebrush-covered plains, with their exposed buttes and bluffs, conjure cowboy-movie images of the old West, but in fact the landscape has changed beyond recognition from early pioneer days, when all was open rangeland grazed by cattle and sheep. To begin with the range was parcelled up into individual ranches and then much of it was ploughed and seeded by horse and mule. In the 1920s, things changed again when machinery replaced the horses and mules, which were quickly sold off, often for hog food. Thereafter, large farms became the order of the day with wheatfields reaching horizon-filling proportions – but only where the plateau was irrigated: the land was too dry to farm without being watered, and the most ambitious irrigation scheme was the damming of the Columbia River, most memorably at **Grand Coulee**. Mechanized, irrigated agribusiness did not, however, require many people: by the 1940s, the great gangs of itinerant farm workers who had roamed the region from the beginning of the century had all but disappeared and so had most of the tenant farmers.

East Washington remains thinly populated, and only possesses a couple of towns of any size – **Spokane** and the unpleasant **Tri-Cities** (Pasco, Richland and Kennewick), once the heart of the American nuclear industry. Much more enticing are **Ellensburg** and **Toppenish**, likeable little places with a handful of attractions, though most of the country towns hereabouts – for example **Yakima** and **Walla Walla** – are simply no-nonsense agricultural communities whose residents sometimes seem to wonder why on earth you should want to visit. This, in a way, is their appeal: this is rural America without the window-dressing, a vast, empty region dotted with grain silos, 1950s diners, and battered pick-up trucks, with dogs in the back and stetsons in the front. Consequently, it is an interesting area to pass through, but you need to be a real die-hard traveller to want to spend much time here: three or four days is enough for most.

Public transportation in eastern Washington is fairly rudimentary. There's a reasonable range of bus services between the larger agricultural towns of the plateau, but almost nothing at all to the three leading attractions, the North Cascades (along Hwy 20), Mount Rainier and Mount St Helens. Specifically, **Greyhound buses** (☎1-800/231-2222, *www.greyhound.com*) run east from Seattle along I-90 to Ellensburg, Yakima, Toppenish, Walla Walla and Pendleton, in Oregon, with some services forking off at Ellensburg to head northeast to Spokane. Another Greyhound route links Spokane with Oregon's Portland via the south bank of the Columbia River. From Seattle, Northwestern Trailways (☎1-800/366-3830, *www.nwadv.com/northw*) runs across the mountains on US-2 to Leavenworth, Cashmere and Wenatchee for Spokane. Amtrak **trains** (☎1-800/872-7245, *www.amtrak.com*) connect Portland, Oregon, and Washington's Vancouver with Seattle, Wenatchee and Spokane. A second train service runs along the north bank of the Columbia River from Washington's Vancouver to Spokane. Local buses are rare, but the LINK network (☎1-800/851-LINK) connects some of the towns of the eastern foothills in the vicinity of Chelan Monday through Saturday.

THE CASCADE MOUNTAINS

The **Cascade Mountains** pushed up out of the sea 35 million years ago, but only assumed their present shape after a series of violent volcanic explosions had torn them asunder. Neither is the threat of further eruptions over: though the snowy peaks that back almost every Washington view look the image of serenity, they still conceal a colossal and dangerous volcanic power – as **Mount St Helens** proved when it exploded in 1980, annihilating wildlife over a massive area and deluging the Northwest with ash. The scarred landscape left by the blast is fascinating and forbidding in equal measure, but it is atypical: the rest of the Cascades, protected by a series of national parks and national forests which stretch the length of the state, feature mile upon mile of densely forested wilderness, traversed by a skein of beautiful trails – though for all but a few summer months, you'll need snowshoes to follow them. **Mount Rainier National Park** is the most popular destination, an imposing but readily accessible peak that's a comfortable day-trip from Seattle, though you can eat and sleep here too. Further north, the remoter **North Cascades** can be reached along Hwy 20, or dipped into from the sunny eastern foothills, where small resort towns – the most agreeable of which are **Chelan** and **Leavenworth** – eagerly await summer tourist traffic and apple orchards fill sheltered valleys.

Mount Rainier National Park

Set in its own national park, glacier-clad **MOUNT RAINIER** is the tallest and most accessible of the Cascade peaks, and a major Washington landmark. People in Seattle look to see if "the mountain's out", the sign of a clear day, and Native-Americans living in the shadow of the mountain evolved a complex mythology around it. To them Rainier appeared as a jealous wife magically metamorphosed into a giant mountain vengefully protective of its higher ridges and peaks. On no account would local Klickitats venture up the slopes into this hostile spirit country, where the hazards were inscrutable to human eyes – apt considering the summit is wreathed in clouds much of the time. The Klickitat called the mountain "Tahoma" ("Snowiest Peak") and there have been moves to revive the original appellation if for no other reason than to end the dire jokes about the name describing the weather. Perhaps Captain Vancouver should have figured this out before he honoured one of his fellow British admirals, Peter Rainier.

The long winter season sees heavy snowfalls and a steady trickle of visitors who mostly come here to go **snowboarding** and **cross-country skiing** from mid-December to early April, sometimes later. For cross-country skiing, there are both marked and unmarked trails, on routes varying in length from one mile to ten miles;

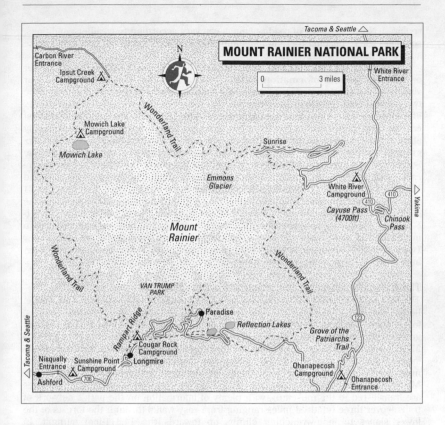

check with park staff for route locations. Less conveniently, snowboarding is possible only on the Muir snowfield; to get there you have to hike for ninety minutes from Paradise (see overleaf) to a 7200-foot elevation at Pebble Creek. As spring takes hold, the snowline creeps up the mountain, unblocking roads and revealing a web of **hiking trails**, though those at the higher elevations are rarely clear before mid-June. July and August are the sunniest months and it's then that the mountain makes for some perfect – and, if you pick the right trail, not unduly tough – hiking. The air is crisp and clear, meadows sprout alpine flowers, and the wildlife emerges, with deer, elk and mountain goats at the forest edges and small furry marmots shuttling between their burrows.

Each of the four entrances to the roughly square national park – one in each corner – leads to a distinct section, though in summer it's possible to drive on bumpy forest roads between the main **Nisqually entrance**, in the park's southwest corner, and the two entrances on the park's east flank – **Ohanapecosh** to the south and **White River** in the north. **Carbon River**, the fourth entrance, is in the park's northwest corner. The Nisqually section is the only one kept open year round (for cross-country skiing; the others open when the snow melts in around June) and the only part you can see on any kind of public transportation. Rainier Shuttle (☎360/569-2331) offers a daily service from Sea-Tac Airport to Paradise from mid-May to early October ($39 one-way), whilst from May through September Gray Line operates daily day-trips to the park from Seattle (☎206/624-5077 or 1-800/426-7505; $50); in both cases advance reservations are required. Note that dates of road openings can vary according to weather conditions, so unless you're heading there in midsummer it is a good idea to call ahead and make sure your destination is accessible.

Admission to the national park – valid for seven days – costs $10 per vehicle, $5 hiker or cyclist; for general **information**, call the National Park Service on ☎360/569-2211 or visit their Web site (*www.nps.gov/mora*). It's possible **to stay** in the park at either of the two national park **lodges** in Longmire and Paradise (see below), and there are plenty of wilderness and six serviced **campgrounds**. Of the latter, two are near the southwest entrance and there's one each at the other three; the final campground is a walk-in-only affair at Mowich Lake, about five miles from the Carbon River entrance. Serviced camp-grounds operate on a first-come, first-served basis and are – with the exception of the Sunshine Point campground in the southwest and the one at Ipsut Creek in the north-east – only open in the summer. Prices are $10–14, except for Ipsut Creek ($6) and Mowich Lake (free). For **wilderness camping** you'll need a permit (free up to 24 hours in advance from any hiking centre in the park). For camping information, call the park's general information line; for reservations up to five months in advance, call ☎1-800/365-CAMP or go online. Failing that, there's a fairly wide range of accommodation in **ASHFORD**, just outside the park's Nisqually entrance. Here, *Whittaker's Bunkhouse* (☎360/569-2439), a favourite with local climbers and hikers, provides distinctive lodg-ings in an old loggers' bunkhouse, either dorm beds (①) or double rooms (④).

The Nisqually entrance: to Longmire and Paradise

The **Nisqually entrance** to the park is a little under ninety miles southeast of Seattle: head south on I-5, take Exit 127 onto Hwy 512 east, and then, after a couple of miles, follow Hwy 7 south to Hwy 706. Driving north on I-5, come off at US-12 (Exit 68), and go east until you join Hwy 7. Both routes bring you into the park just short of **LONG-MIRE**, where a small group of buildings includes the tiny **Longmire Museum** (daily 9am–4/5pm; free; ☎360/569-2211), which has modest exhibits on wildlife and the mountain. Here also is the very useful **Wilderness Information Centre** (late May–Sept Mon–Fri 8am–6.30pm, Sat–Sun 7.30am–7pm; closed in winter when services are transferred to the museum), with plenty of information on the park's network of trails – over three hundred miles ranging from easy walks through the forests of the lower slopes to lung-wrenching climbs up towards the 14,411-foot summit. In Longmire, you can rent skiing and snowshoeing equipment and there's comfortable, modern **accommodation** at the all-year *National Park Inn* (☎360/569-2275, *www.guest-services.com/rainier*, ④), where reservations are pretty much essential.

Beginning at Longmire, the Trail of the Shadows is a popular, half-hour stroll around the alpine meadow where James Longmire, a local farmer, built a now defunct mineral springs resort at the end of the nineteenth century. More strenuous hiking trails lead off from the loop – with a five-mile one following **Rampart Ridge** to reach Van Trump Park beneath the Kautz Glacier. The loop also intersects with the 93-mile Wonderland Trail, which encircles the mountain, running right round its upper slopes: from this intersec-tion the trail winds a tortuous route northwest to the **Carbon River** entrance (and ranger station), passing a string of wilderness campgrounds. You can also join the Wonderland Trail back in Longmire near the Hiker Center, from where it heads northeast the two miles to the **Cougar Rock** campground before continuing up along the lovely Paradise River to Carter Falls and the Reflection Lakes (which you can also reach by car).

Trails around Longmire are free from snow earlier than those at higher elevations, but in midsummer you'll probably want to drive further up the mountain, where the snow is still many feet deep well into June. It's just eleven miles through the thinning forest and past waterfalls of glacial snowmelt to **PARADISE**, where a larger **visitor centre** (May to mid-Oct daily 9am–7pm; winter Sat & Sun 10am–5pm) has films and exhibits on natural history and a circular observation room for contemplating the mountain. Several hiking trails begin from Paradise, and bedraggled hikers can dry out by the two large fireplaces of the *Paradise Inn* (mid-May to Sept; ☎360/569-2275, *www.guestservices.com/rainier*, ④), a short walk from the visitor centre. Dating from 1917, *Paradise Inn* is a large and sturdy timber hotel with a folksy, Arts and Crafts 1920s foyer and dining room. The bedrooms vary in quality – the less expensive are plain and functional – but this doesn't matter too much considering the location at over five thousand feet above sea level and with magnificent mountain views. It's a very popular inn, so reservations are strongly advised; the food is OK.

Paradise is the starting-point for **climbing Mount Rainier**, a serious undertaking involving ice axes, crampons and some degree of danger. It usually takes two days to get to the summit – with its twin craters rimmed with ice-caves – and back: on the first day climbers aim for the base camp at Camp Muir, ready for the strenuous final assault and the descent to Paradise on the second. Unless you're very experienced (and even then, you have to register with the rangers) the way to do it is with the Rainier Mountaineering guide service in Paradise (☎360/569-2227). They offer three-day courses – one day's practice, then the two-day climb – from May to mid-October for around $600. Specialist equipment rental (lug-sole climbing boots, ice axes, etc) costs extra, and reservations with advance payment in full are required. The company's winter quarters are at 535 Dock St, Tacoma (☎253/627-6242).

Less energetically, both the 1.2-mile Nisqually Vista Trail and the five-mile Skyline Trail leave Paradise to climb up the mountain, providing gorgeous views of its craggy peak and glistening glaciers. The park rangers also chip in with a summer programme of **guided walks** – the visitor centre has the details.

Other entrances

In summer it's possible to drive from Paradise along rugged **Stevens Canyon Road** to the park's southeastern corner, where the **Ohanapecosh visitor centre** (mid-June to Sept daily 9am–5pm) is set in deep forest, near the gurgling Ohanapecosh River. Amongst several trails hereabouts, one of the most enjoyable is the Grove of the Patriarchs, a one-and-a-half-mile loop exploring an islet in the Ohanapecosh River, where there are ancient groves of giant Douglas fir, western hemlock and red cedar.

South from Ohanapecosh, it's a five-mile trip to US-12, by means of which you can travel either east to Yakima (see p.276) or west, past the rough side road that leads to Mount St Helens (see below), to I-5. In summer, you can also drive north from Ohanapecosh along the length of the park to the **White River entrance** and Hiker Center in the northeast corner. From here it's a giddy ride up to the **Sunrise visitor centre** (July–Aug daily 9am–6pm) and wonderful views of Emmons Glacier and the mountain's crest. You can also leave the park from its northeast corner along Hwy 410 – north for Seattle or east to Yakima. The **Carbon River entrance** in the northwest corner is not linked by road to the other three. Hwy 165, the paved approach road, runs as far as the Ranger Station, which serves as the trailhead for the short and easy Carbon River Rain Forest Trail, nudging into Mount Rainier's one and only chunk of temperate rainforest.

Mount St Helens

The Klickitat who called **MOUNT ST HELENS** "Tahonelatclah" ("Fire Mountain") knew what they were talking about. A perfect snow-capped peak, long popular with scout camps and climbing expeditions, Mount St Helens exploded in May 1980, leaving a blasted landscape and scenes of almost total destruction for miles around. Slowly but surely, the forests are starting to grow again, and the ash is disappearing beneath new vegetation, but the land still bears witness to the incredible force of the eruption.

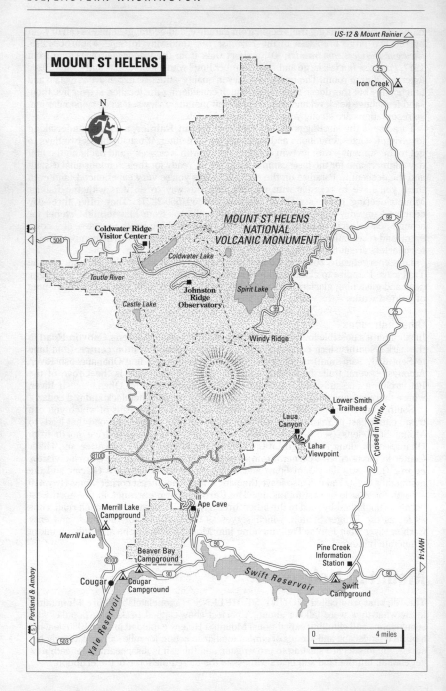

MOUNT ST HELENS

N

Iron Creek △

Coldwater Ridge
Visitor Center

MOUNT ST HELENS
NATIONAL
VOLCANIC MONUMENT

Coldwater Lake

Toutle River

Johnston
Ridge
Observatory

Castle Lake

Spirit Lake

Windy Ridge

Lower Smith
Trailhead

Lava
Canyon

Lahar
Viewpoint

Closed in Winter

Merrill Lake
Campground

Ape Cave

Merrill Lake

Beaver Bay
Campground

Pine Creek
Information
Station

Cougar

Cougar
Campground

Swift Reservoir

Swift
Campground

Yale Reservoir

◁ Portland & Amboy

HWY-14 ◁

0   4 miles

Designated a National Volcanic Monument, Mount St Helens has become a major attraction, with most tourists heading for the two **visitor centres** – **Coldwater Ridge** and the smaller **Johnston Ridge Observatory** – which overlook the blast area from the northwest side of the mountain. These are reached, travelling north on I-5, by turning off at Hwy 504 (or travelling south, its main feeder road, Hwy 505) roughly halfway between Olympia and Portland. The other main approach road is the quieter Hwy 503, which runs to the mountain's steep and densely forested southern slopes. You can get onto Hwy 503 either from I-205 just north of Portland or, further north, from I-5 (Exit 21). During the summer, the east side of the mountain can also be reached along paved forest roads from US-12 to the north and Hwy 14 in the south. These eastern access roads are connected to Hwy 503, which means that it's possible to drive across the mountain's south and east flanks, though this is a time-consuming and occasionally nerve-jangling business. Note also that the mountain's forest roads are prone to be damaged by winter flooding. To check conditions ahead of time (and for general information) call the **Mount St Helens National Volcanic Monument Headquarters**, outside Amboy on Hwy 503 (☎360/247-3900, *www.fs.fed.us/gpnf*). Entry to the monument area costs $6 per person, levied in the form of a **Monument Pass**, which is valid for one day. Alternatively, the more specific **Site Day Pass** ($3 per person) is good for one day at the Coldwater Ridge and Mt St Helens visitor centres as well as the Johnston Ridge Observatory and Ape Cave. Both these passes include the cost of your vehicle. Confusingly, there is also the **Northwest Forest Pass**, a per vehicle charge of $5 per day required at many of the area's viewpoints and trailheads. If you purchase this pass and end up visiting places where the Monument Pass is required, one person is allowed in free. Fortunately, rangers are at hand at every entry point to explain it all – and take the money.

A network of **hiking trails** radiates out from the access roads as they near the mountain, exploring its every nook and volcanic cranny, but unless you're indifferent to clouds of dust and ash, a morning or afternoon hike is really enough. **Climbing the mountain**, no mean undertaking, can only be attempted from the south and is hedged with restrictions. From mid-May to October, permits ($15) are required to climb above 4800 feet and only one hundred of them are issued per day. The majority are booked way ahead of time (call ☎360/247-3961), but forty are set aside for distribution by **lottery** one day in advance. To enter the lottery, you have to get to *Jack's Restaurant and Store* (☎360/231-4276), about five miles to the west of Cougar near Hwy 503's Lewis River Hwy/Lewis River Road intersection (see "Other entrances", overleaf) at 5.30pm. The rest of the year, things ease up, though all prospective climbers have to register at *Jack's* before they set out. From April to mid-May, there are no pre-reserved permits and all you have to do is pick one up at the restaurant, and the same applies from November to March, but during these months there is no charge. The climbing route begins at the Climbers' Bivouac, at the end of a hair-raising road high up the mountain, and the round trip takes between seven and twelve hours. The climb takes you to the crater rim, but the crater itself is out of bounds.

Approached along Hwy 504, Mount St Helens makes a feasible **day-trip** of around two hundred miles from either Olympia or Portland. By comparison, it's only half that from Portland via Hwy 503, but the mountain's southern slopes bear few signs of the eruption – the most dramatic views are almost entirely confined to its northwest side. If you're keen to avoid a long drive – especially on summer weekends when traffic clogs the access roads – or want to have time for a decent hike, then **staying overnight** in the locality is a possibility. There's motel accommodation beside the junction of I-5 and Hwy 504 in the uneventful town of **CASTLE ROCK**: try the *Timberland Inn*, at 1271 Mount St Helens Way (☎360/274-6002; ③), or the *Mt St Helens Motel*, along the street at no. 1340 (☎360/274-7721, *www.mtsthelensmotel.com*; ③). Over on Hwy 503, your best bet is to aim for the hamlet of **COUGAR**, which straggles along the highway near the mountain. There are basic motel rooms here at the plain and simple *Lone Fir Resort*, at 16806 Lewis River Rd/Hwy 503 (☎360/238-5210; ②), which also has RV ($16) and tent camping ($13).

There are no **campgrounds** within the national monument, but there are several dotted along the approach roads. One of the more enticing is set amongst the forests of Seaquest State Park (☎1-800/452-5687; $12), abutting Silver Lake about five miles east of I-5 on Hwy 504. Another option is the cluster of private campgrounds on Hwy 503 in the vicinity of Cougar (☎503/813-6666 for info). Here, amongst the woods beside the Yale Lake reservoir, are the seasonal *Cougar Campground* ($15, by reservation) and, further east, the *Beaver Bay Campground* ($15), which works on a first-come, first-served basis. Wilderness camping is allowed outside the crater and immediate blast area – permits from any visitor centre.

Coldwater Ridge and Johnston Ridge Observatory

Heading east from I-5, Hwy 504 peels off through dark green forests on its way to **Silver Lake**, the site of both **Seaquest State Park** and the first of a whole string of visitor centres. Pressing on, the highway tracks along the Toutle River Valley until bald, spikey trees signal a sudden change: beyond, thousands of grey tree-skeletons lie in combed-looking rows, knocked flat in different directions as the 1980 blast waves bounced off the hillsides. It's a weird and disconcerting landscape, the matchstick-like flattened forest left to rot to regenerate the soil and provide cover for small animals and insects. There are several good vantage points as you progress up the road – notably at **Hoffstadt Bluffs**, where you can make out the path taken by the avalanche of debris that swept down the valley – to the **Coldwater Ridge visitor centre** (daily 10am–6pm; ☎360/274-2131), which features a film on the eruption. Just eight miles further along, the low-slung **Johnston Ridge Observatory** (May–Sept daily 10am–6pm; ☎360/274-2140) is as close as you'll get to the mountain by car – and the views over the still-steaming lava dome and pumice plain are quite extraordinary. Interpretive displays, a video and a fifteen-minute film give the volcanic background. Outside the centre, the half-mile paved Eruption Trail leads to marginally higher viewpoints that are marked with explicatory signs. From Johnston Ridge, a short, dusty and in places steep **hiking trail** leads out in the direction of **Spirit Lake**, with much longer and more strenuous side trails leading up towards the edge of – and right round – the crater peak.

Other entrances

Looping Hwy 503 can be reached from either I-205 outside Portland or I-5 (Exit 21) further north. The I-205 approach leads to Hwy 503's Lewis River Hwy (running north–south), the I-5 to the west–east Lewis River Road. These two separate portions of Hwy 503 meet and merge at the Yale crossroads, a few miles west of **COUGAR**, whose motley assortment of buildings spreads along the highway close to the northern shore of Yale Lake. For accommodation and campgrounds in Cougar, see above. Beyond Cougar, closing in on Mount St Helens, it's a further four miles to the Windy Ridge turning (see opposite) and four more – on Forest Road #83 – to the short side road leading to **Ape Headquarters** (June–Sept daily 10am–5.30pm; no phone). This is the starting point for hour-long, ranger-led **tours** (June–Sept 6 daily 10.30am–3.30pm; no extra charge) of **Ape Cave**, a cold, dark and wet tube-like lava cave channelled long ago by the rushing molten lava of an earlier eruption. The tours are well worth waiting for as otherwise – in the prevailing gloom – you'll miss the geological oddities that (just about) make the excursion worthwhile. Under your own steam, there are actually two subterranean routes to choose from: the three-quarter-mile lower trail, where you have to return to the entrance to get out, and the much more difficult 1.5-mile upper trail which emerges higher up the mountain. It's much colder in the cave than outside, so bring extra clothing; lanterns can be rented (till 4pm; $2) at Ape Headquarters.

Back on Forest Road #83, it's a few miles more to the turning that threads its way up to both the Climbers' Bivouac (see p.263) and several hiking trails that traverse the mountain's higher slopes. Wind, rain, fog and snow can arrive quickly and unpredictably here, with the temperature at the volcano rim regularly twenty to thirty degrees colder than in the valley – so take detailed advice from Ape Headquarters before you set out on all but the shortest of **hikes**. Remember to pack plenty of water. Pressing on along Forest Road #83, it's an easy drive east along the mountain's forested slopes to several places where the eruption has scarred the land. There's nothing nearly as stunning as the mountain's northern slopes, but the roadside **Lahar mudflow** is a great slash in the landscape where the accumulated detritus simply swept the forest away.

Doubling back, the Windy Ridge turning (Forest Road #90; closed in winter) leads east along the mountain's southern flanks to **Pine Creek Information Station** from where Forest Road #25 heads north to reach Forest Road #99 for the final push up to **Windy Ridge**, a rocky outcrop with breathtaking views of the crater from the northeast. You can get even closer on foot: a short hike leads to both the long, circular trail

THE ERUPTION OF MOUNT ST HELENS

From its first rumblings in March 1980, **Mount St Helens** became a big tourist attraction. Residents and loggers working on the mountain's forested slopes were evacuated and roads were closed, but by April the entrances to the restricted zone around the steaming peak were jammed with reporters and sightseers – one crew even ducked restrictions to film a beer commercial at the edge of the crater. People in Portland wore T-shirts saying "St Helens is hot" and "Do it, Loowit" (a Native-American name for the mountain), but the mountain didn't seem to be doing anything much, and impatient residents demanded to be let back to their homes. Even the official line became blurred when Harry Truman, the elderly manager of the *Lodge at Spirit Lake*, refused to move out, became a national celebrity and was, incredibly, congratulated on his "common sense" by Washington's governor.

Bowing to popular pressure, the authorities finally decided to allow home-owners into the restricted zone to collect their possessions on May 17. However, as the convoy gathered at the road-barrier on May 18, the mountain finally exploded – not upwards, but sideways in a massive lateral blast that ripped a great chunk out of the mountainside. An avalanche of debris slid down the mountain into Spirit Lake, raising it by two hundred feet and turning it into a steaming cauldron of muddy liquid. Heavy clouds of ash and rock suffocated loggers on a nearby slope, and, drifting east, caused a small crop-spraying plane to crash before raining several feet of ash on the town of Yakima.

Fifty-seven people, including the stubborn Harry Truman, died in the eruption. A few were there on official business, taking a calculated risk to survey the mountain, but most had ignored warnings or flouted the restrictions. The wildlife population was harder hit: well over a million wild animals – whole herds of deer and elk, mountain goats, cougar and bear – were killed, and thousands of fish were trapped in sediment-filled rivers whose temperatures rose to boiling point. There were dire economic consequences, too, as falling ash spoiled crops and killed livestock across the state, and millions of cubic feet of timber were lost when forests were destroyed. The long-term effects are less easy to quantify: some have even suggested that the eruption was responsible for climatic changes as far away as Europe.

round the summit and the easier walk down past Spirit Lake to Johnston Ridge. The road from Cougar to Windy Ridge is paved all the way, but very tortuous – allow about two and a half hours.

Retracing your steps to Forest Road #25, it's a few miles north to *Iron Creek* **campground** ($12.50) and then ten miles more to US-12, by means of which you can reach Mount Rainier (see p.258).

The North Cascades and the Cascade Loop

When Hwy 20 opened up the rugged **North Cascades** to an admiring public in 1972, the towns of the eastern foothills got together and came up with the 350-mile **Cascade Loop**, a route which channels tourist traffic from Hwy 20 through several of their number before sending it west again over US-2. There's no denying it's a magnificent trip, with long stretches of the road shadowed by the wet western forests and, at higher elevations, jagged, glacier-studded mountains, but unless you've three or four days to spare – maybe more – it all becomes something of a motorized gallop. With less time, you're better off focusing on the pick of the Cascade scenery, which straddles Hwy 20, and **camping** in the mountains, or at least staying as near to the mountains as you can: **Marblemount**, on the west side of the range, is the handiest spot, though it's only able to muster a handful of inns and motels.

Further afield, the towns of the eastern foothills offer much more choice of accommodation. There are three main destinations here, the most amenable being **Chelan**, an easy-going, lakeshore resort that's the starting point for boat (or seaplane) trips up Lake Chelan to the remote village of **Stehekin**, at the heart of good hiking country. The other two have made gargantuan efforts to rise from the ruins of their industrial past with **Winthrop** dressing itself up in Wild West regalia, and **Leavenworth**, all ersatz Bavarian. But neither has much lasting appeal, and are best treated simply as bases between trips into the gorgeous scenery.

The North Cascades are latticed by several hundred miles of **hiking trail**, offering everything from short and easy strolls to arduous treks up steep slopes, round glaciers and over high mountain passes, and there are plenty of first-come, first-served **campgrounds** to choose from too. **Information** on the trails and campgrounds is available from a baffling assortment of government agencies, who have carved up the mountains into three national forests, several recreation and wilderness areas, and the **North Cascades National Park**, which is itself divided into a north and south unit to either side of Hwy 20. Between them, these agencies staff a number of visitor centres and ranger stations, each of which provides detailed hiking information and trail descriptions; the major ones also issue backcountry permits. The biggest and most comprehensive is the **North Cascades National Park Information Center** (summer daily 8am–4.30pm, Fri till 6pm; winter Mon–Fri 8am–4.30pm; ☎360/856-5700), east of I-5 at the junction of Hwy 20 and Hwy 9, on the edge of Sedro Woolley. If you're doing the Cascade Loop the other way round, there's a USFS Ranger Station at Leavenworth and a national forest one at Chelan (see p.269).

The Cascade Loop is only feasible during the summer, as snow closes the mountain passes and completely covers the hiking trails for several months of the year – usually from mid-November to mid-April. For the latest details, contact the Winter Mountain Pass Report agency on (☎1-888/766-4636). There's no **bus** service over Hwy 20, but Northwestern Trailways (☎1-800/366-3830, *www.nwadv.com/northw*) runs across the mountains on US-2 from Seattle to Leavenworth (for Spokane). A local line, LINK (☎1-800/851-LINK), provides a fairly frequent minibus service between the towns of the eastern foothills, including Chelan, Wenatchee and Leavenworth.

Over the North Cascades on Hwy 20

Hwy 20 leaves I-5 (Exit 230) about sixty miles north of Seattle at Burlington, travelling east through the flat, tulip-growing farmlands of the Skagit Valley to reach **SEDRO WOOLLEY**, originally an amalgamation of two adjacent settlements – one named after a local sawmill owner, the other an approximation of the Spanish for cedar. "Sedro" was actually a reluctant concession by the first white settler, the redoubtable Mortimer Cook, who had chosen "Bug" (after the insects that plagued him) until his neighbours put the pressure on. The town doesn't have a lot going for it, but it is home to the first-rate **North Cascades National Park Information Center** (see opposite), at the Hwy 20 and Hwy 9 junction, where you can pick up hiking maps, backcountry permits and trail descriptions and take advice about local weather and driving conditions.

Pushing on east, with the pine forests and mountains closing in, Hwy 20 scuttles up the Skagit River Valley on its way to **CONCRETE**, where the defunct cement silos are relics of more prosperous days. Outdated and outmoded, the plant was closed in 1968, but it was once the biggest cement factory in the state and played a key role in the con-struction of the Columbia River dams. Nine miles further east, tiny **ROCKPORT** marks the start of the **Skagit River Bald Eagle Natural Area**, established to protect the long-time winter hunting ground of the bald eagle, the United States' national bird. The eagles arrive in October and leave in March, gathering along an eight-mile stretch of river between Rockport and Marblemount to feed on the river's salmon, easy pick-ings as they die after spawning. Hwy 20 has roadside pull-ins to watch for the eagles, but the best way to see them is on a **river trip**, a gentle three- to four-hour boat ride along the Skagit with any one of several local companies: Chinook Expeditions (☎1-800/241-3451, *www.chinookexpeditions.com*), based in Index (see p.273), are as good as any. There are daily boat trips from December through to February, leaving from the jetty just east of – and across the river from – Marblemount on Hwy 20; expect to pay around $60 each.

Minuscule **MARBLEMOUNT**, about fifty miles east of I-5, was founded in the 1860s as a supply centre for the gold diggers who were ferreting through the surrounding hills – with only limited success. Marblemount is also the last chance for ninety miles to fill up with gas – and an opportunity to get a roof over your head. *Clark's Skagit River Resort* (☎360/873-2250 or 1-800/273-2606; ③), three miles west of Marblemount along Hwy 20, provides the best lodgings hereabouts, with a cluster of pretty rusticated cab-ins as well as sites for RVs and tents. A good alternative is the nearby *Salmonberry Way B&B* (☎360/873-4016; ③), which offers two guestrooms with shared bathroom in an early twentieth-century house 2.5 miles west of Marblemount on Hwy 20. **Eat** at Marblemount's *Buffalo Run Restaurant* (☎360/873-2461), featuring organic vegetables, home-made bread and microbrews plus exotic meats – ostrich, hare and, naturally enough, buffalo. Wilderness permits and hiking maps are available at the seasonal **Marblemount Wilderness Information Center** (July & Aug Sun–Thurs 7am–6pm, Fri–Sat 7am–8pm; June & Sept daily 8am–5pm; ☎360/873-4500).

Just beyond Marblemount, Hwy 20 enters the **Ross Lake National Recreation Area**, a narrow, elongated slice of river valley that divides the North Cascades National Park into two sections. The first place you reach is **NEWHALEM**, a company town owned by Seattle City Light, whose electrical generators lie a little to the east in a chain of three dams spanning the Skagit River. The town is also the site of a **North Cascades National Park Information Center** (May–Oct daily 9am–5pm, plus some winter weekends; ☎360/856-5700). From Newhalem, it's about three miles to the first dam, the **Gorge Dam**, and a few more to the second, **Diablo**, built at a tricky turn in the river called "Devil's Corner", its name translated into Spanish so as not to offend early twen-tieth-century sensibilities. Here the highway offers views across the dam and its chubby little lake, blue-green from glacial run-off; the dam's parking lot is where you catch the water taxi to *Ross Lake Resort* (see below).

Pushing on up Hwy 20 from Diablo Dam, it's a couple of miles east along the lakeshore to the attractively-sited, first-come, first-served **Colonial Creek campground** (mid-May to mid-Oct; $10) – the starting point for several particularly fine hikes – and a few minutes more to the fabulous mountain views of the **Diablo Lake Overlook**. Then comes **Ross Dam**, the largest dam of the three and the one that created **Ross Lake**, which stretches north for twenty-five pine-rimmed miles, flanked by hiking trails and campgrounds (but no roads). Reached by water taxi ($10 round-trip) from Diablo Dam (see above) and then by truck ($5 round-trip), or along a two-mile hiking trail from Ross Dam, the *Ross Lake Resort* (mid-June to Oct; ☎206/386-4437) provides some of the region's most distinctive lodgings. Built for Seattle City Light workers, the resort literally floats on its log supports and has simple 1950s cabins (③), modern, en-suite cabins (⑤) and bunkhouse cabins (⑥), holding up to six guests. The resort has no telephones in the cabins and you have to bring your own food, but it does operate a water-taxi service to the remote trailheads further up Ross Lake.

Hwy 20 ignores Ross Lake, veering southeast after Ross Dam to leave the national park for the wilds of the **Okanogan National Forest**, running up Ruby and Granite creeks to **Rainy Pass**, where the Pacific Crest Trail (see p.62) crosses Hwy 20: to the north the long-distance trail heads off into depths of the Okanogan; to the south it slips along Bridge Creek and curves round the flanks of McGregor Mountain to meet the rough dirt road that leads onto Stehekin at the tip of Lake Chelan (see p.270).

Beyond Rainy Pass, Hwy 20 has an abundance of stopping-points, each providing remarkable views over the Cascades. One of the most magnificent is at **Washington Pass Overlook**, about thirty miles east of Ross Dam, where a short paved trail from the roadside parking lot leads to a spectacular mountain panorama featuring the craggy, rocky peak of **Liberty Bell Mountain**. Afterwards, there's a final flurry of mountain scenery before the road reaches the tamer landscapes of the Methow Valley and descends to Winthrop.

Winthrop

Beyond the mountains, Hwy 20 runs straight into **WINTHROP**, landing you among the wooden false fronts, boardwalks, swinging saloon doors and other western paraphernalia that bedecks its main drag, Riverside Avenue. Winthrop was actually founded by an East Coast entrepreneur, Guy Waring, who turned up in 1891 with a wagonload of merchandise and diplomatically named the settlement he founded after John Winthrop, the one-time governor of his native Massachusetts – the state that provided his backing. Waring was visited by an old Harvard classmate, Owen Wister, and when Wister later wrote *The Virginian*, widely acclaimed as the first Western novel, the book was clearly (in the town's opinion) based on Winthrop. Waring's log-cabin home, set on a hill behind the main street on Castle Avenue, is now part of the **Shafer Museum** (late May to Sept Thurs–Mon 10am–5pm; donation), whose assortment of old buildings – a print shop, a milliners and so forth – is crammed with pioneer bygones. It is, however, Waring's cabin, with its heavy-duty logs, that catches the eye – just as it was meant to: Waring beavered away for months building this large cabin to entice his wife out west, away from the comforts of Massachusetts.

In terms of practicalities, Winthrop's handy **visitor centre**, 202 Riverside Ave (late April to Sept daily 10am–5pm; ☎509/996-2125 or 1-888/463-8469, *www.winthropwashington.com*), is well stocked with free literature on all sorts of outdoor stuff from horse riding and white-water rafting through to fishing – both in the valley and the neighbouring mountains; there's a seasonal USFS **Ranger Station** (☎509/996-4000) downtown too. Winthrop has a reasonable range of **accommodation**, including a clutch of motels. Amongst them, the cedar-log *Virginian Resort*, just south of town at 808 Hwy 20 (☎509/996-2535 or 1-800/854-2834; ③), is a good bet, with a heated outdoor pool and pleasant riverside location. Alternatively, the *Best Western Cascade Inn*, 960 Hwy 20 (☎509/996-3100 or 1-800/468-6754; ④), is a modern motel complex with a heated outdoor pool, and the luxurious *Sun Mountain Lodge* (☎509/996-2211 or 1-800/572-0493, *www.sunmountainlodge.com*; ⑦) has rustic cabins and lodge rooms in a grand setting on the edge of the Cascades. The lodge is located nine miles southwest of town along Twin Lakes and then Patterson Lake Road. As for **food**, the *Duck Brand Cantina*, on the main drag at 248 Riverside Ave, serves up delicious and inexpensive Mexican and American dishes – everything from enchiladas through to apple pie – and there's pizza and sandwiches at *Three Fingered Jack's Saloon* just along the street. The *Winthrop Brewing Company*, 155 Riverside Ave, offers tasty microbrews including the tangy Outlaw Pale Ale.

Continuing south along the Methow Valley, it's eleven miles to **TWISP**, whose somewhat dejected air goes a long way towards explaining Winthrop's shameless bidding for the tourist trade: whatever you make of the Wild West theme, it's easy to see why it's worth a try.

Chelan

Beyond Twisp, Hwy 20 begins its long and circuitous journey through the remote national forests that fill out the northeastern extremities of Washington, while Hwy 153 carries on down the Methow Valley for the thirty-mile trip to the Columbia River. From here, US-97 shadows the river as it curves south to the short turning (US-97Alt) that leads over the hills to glacially carved **Lake Chelan**, a long snake of a lake whose southern tip is edged by the pocket-sized resort of **CHELAN**. Not much more than a simple gridiron of modest, modern buildings, the town is an unassuming sort of place tucked in between the Chelan River and the lakeshore. Local apple growers drop by to pick up supplies, but mainly Chelan is quite happy just to house and feed those hundreds of visitors who come here intent on exploring the lake and its mountainous surroundings.

Your first port of call should be the **visitor centre**, near the waterfront at 102 E Johnson Ave (Mon–Fri 9am–5pm & Sat 10am–4pm; open longer hours & Sun from May to Sept; ☎509/682-3503 or 1-800/424-3526, *www.lakechelan.com*), where you can browse through all sorts of free information about the region and pick up a list of local accommodation. They can also provide maps and general hiking advice, though for detailed trail guidance you should go to the combined USFS and NPS **Ranger Station**, a five-minute walk over the bridge and along the waterfront from the visitor centre, at 428 W Woodin Ave (Mon–Fri 7.45am–4.30pm; July–Aug also Sat & Sun 7.45am–4.30pm; USFS ☎509/682-2576, NPS ☎509/682-2549). Monday through Saturday, local LINK (☎509/662-1155 or 1-800/851-LINK) **buses** connect Chelan with several nearby towns including Leavenworth.

Chelan has lots of **places to stay**, but in the height of the summer rooms can still be hard to find – book ahead if you can. The town's premier hotel is the spick-and-span *Campbell's Resort*, 104 W Woodin Ave (☎509/682-2561 or 1-800/553-8225, *www.campbellresort.com*; ⑥), which occupies a prime lakeside spot in the centre of town, with most of its spacious and comfortable rooms looking out over the water. Other reliable options include the ultramodern lakeshore *Caravel Resort Hotel*, just across the bridge at 322 W Woodin Ave (☎509/682-2582 or 1-800/962-8723; ⑤); and the self-styled "romantic" (read Victorian furnishings and fittings) *Whaley Mansion B&B*, whose six en-suite guestrooms occupy an attractive older house five-minutes' walk from the town centre at 415 3rd St (☎509/682-5735 or 1-800/729-2408; ⑥). A less expensive choice is the straightforward *Apple Inn Motel*, 1002 E Woodin Ave

(☎509/682-4044; ③). The best **restaurant** in town is at *Campbell's Resort*, but for something more informal – and less expensive – head off to *Peter B's Bar & Grill*, 116 E Woodin (☎509/682-1031), which is good for pastas and steaks. *Latte Da Coffee Stop Café*, 303 E Wapato Ave, hits the spot with its coffees and bagels.

Lake Chelan

The wooded hills and mountains that frame **Lake Chelan**'s southern reaches are laced with **hiking trails**, many of which are (fairly) easy to reach from Chelan along a patchwork of bumpy forest roads. If you don't like the sound of that, then several of Chelan's sports shops rent out alternative transport. Pedal Paddle, for instance, at 228 W Nixon St (☎509/682-0126), has both mountain bikes and kayaks – but be warned that the lake experiences sudden squalls. The lake's real pride and joy is, however, the *Lady of the Lake* **passenger ferry** (☎509/682-4584, *www.ladyofthelake.com*), which sails the 55 miles from Chelan up the lake to Stehekin, usually stopping at Lucerne where it drops supplies for Holden, a Lutheran retreat that occupies the site of an old copper mine in a remote valley to the west. The scenery becomes more impressive the further you go, with the forested hills of the south giving way to the austere, glaciated peaks that circle in on the furthest part of the lake, lying at the very heart of the North Cascades. Leaving from the jetty a mile west of town along Woodin Avenue, the ferry makes the four-hour trip once daily, May to October, sailing at 8.30am and returning to Chelan by 6pm; this gives a ninety-minute stop-over at Stehekin. The round trip costs $23, single $15, and reservations aren't required. The faster *Lady Express* (1 daily mid-March to April & June–Sept; Sat & Sun only in May & early Oct; 4–5 weekly Nov to mid-March; same number; reservations required) departs at 8.30am or 10am and takes just over two hours to complete the same trip. Tickets cost $27 per person single, $42 return, with reductions off-season. Faster still is the *Lady Cat*, a high-speed catamaran that can get from Chelan to Stehekin in an hour and fifteen minutes (June–Sept 1–2 daily; $56 single, $89 return; same number; reservations required). You can go up on one boat and return on another and if you juggle with the schedules you can give yourself several hours in Stehekin. If you're taking a bicycle, it'll cost you an additional $7 each way. Finally, if you're flush, you can **seaplane** in or out of Stehekin with Chelan Airways (☎509/682-5065, *www.chelanairways.com*), $80 single and $120 return.

Stehekin

Accessible only by trail, seaplane or boat, **STEHEKIN**, at Lake Chelan's mountainous northern tip, makes an excellent base for hiking in the North Cascades. In every direction, trails strike into the mountains, nudging up along bubbling creeks through the thinning alpine forest, and there are easier trails along the lakeshore too. In the village, a few yards from the jetty, the *North Cascades Stehekin Lodge* (see below) rents bikes and boats and also runs daily bus trips up to **Rainbow Falls**, a mist-shrouded, 312-foot waterfall flanked by red cedars just four miles north of the village; times of departure are fixed to coincide with the arrival of the boat. Alternatively, Stehekin's NPS **Golden West Visitor Center** (mid-May to mid-Sept daily 8.30am–5pm, plus reduced hours in April, late Sept & early Oct; ☎360/856-5700), also a short walk from the jetty, operates a seasonal **shuttle bus** that travels up along the Stehekin River Valley by means of a 23-mile dirt road – an exhilarating trip that accesses trailheads and campgrounds and follows a small portion of the Pacific Crest Trail (see p.62); advance booking is advised.

The pleasant *North Cascades Stehekin Lodge* (☎509/682-4494, *www.stehekin.com*; ④), with its cabins and lodge rooms, is the only **place to stay** in the village and reservations here are usually necessary – as they are for the handful of cabin-lodges further up the Stehekin Valley. Campground details, hiking advice and wilderness permits are available at the Golden West Visitor Center, or – even better – get advice before you leave Chelan.

Wenatchee

South of Chelan, the Columbia River weaves its way through prime apple-growing country, tracked by US-97 on its east and US-97Alt on its west bank. Both roads lead the forty-odd miles to **WENATCHEE**, which straddles the Columbia River and has long been Washington's **apple capital**, the centre of an industry that fills the valleys of the eastern foothills with orchards. Apple stalls appear beside the roads in the fall, piled mostly with sweet, outsized Red Delicious, the most popular kind in the US – Washington grows nearly half the country's supply – but you'll find other varieties too: enormous Golden Delicious, red Winesaps and giant Granny Smiths. Although the warm climate is ideal for apple growing, farmers still protect their fruit from early frosts with metal heaters, their tall fans easily visible from the road.

As apples, rather than tourists, are Wenatchee's main business, the town has a workaday air, and it's unlikely you'll want to hang around. That said, apple fanatics can learn about the history of the industry at the **North Central Washington Museum**, 127 S Mission and Yakima Street (Mon–Sat 10am–4pm; $3), and there's more apple-mania at the **Washington Apple Commission Visitor Center** (Mon–Fri 8am–5pm, with longer hours in the summer), on the northern edge of town at 2900 Euclid Ave, where you can munch away at various varieties for free. Wenatchee's big annual knees-up is the ten-day **Apple Blossom Festival**, an all-American affair involving carnival floats and marching bands that starts the last weekend in April.

Wenatchee acts as something of a public transportation hub for the immediate area. Its Columbia Station, downtown at Wenatchee Avenue and Kittitas Street, is where Northwestern Trailways **buses** (☎1-800/366-3830, *www.nwadv.com/northw*) pull in, bound for Seattle or Spokane, and so do Amtrak **trains** (☎1-800/872-7245, *www.amtrak.com*) connecting Wenatchee with Portland, Washington's Vancouver, Seattle, Leavenworth and Spokane. In addition, local – and free – LINK buses (☎1-800/851-LINK) depart Wenatchee (Mon–Sat) for several nearby towns – most usefully Chelan and Leavenworth.

Cashmere

Just before Wenatchee, US-2/97 branches west into the mountains towards two more themed villages. The first of these, **CASHMERE**, rustles up a reasonably tasteful late-nineteenth-century main street and a small, outdoor Pioneer Village, comprising about twenty restored and relocated buildings – including a school, hotel, saddle shop and general store. The "village" is part of the **Chelan County Museum** (March–Oct Tues–Sun 9.30am–5pm; $3), whose main building holds a large and wide-ranging collection focused on the Northwest. Pride of place here goes to the Native-American artefacts displayed on the upper floor. Amongst the archeological bits and pieces are petroglyphs and early tools and there are baskets and headdresses, weapons and Hudson's Bay Company trading trinkets too. Cashmere is also famous, at least locally, for its sweet speciality "aplets" and "cotlets" (as in apricot) – not unlike Turkish delight and available at **Liberty Orchards**, 117 Mission St (Mon–Fri 8am–5pm, Sat & Sun 10am–4pm). Made of boiled-down fruit juices and walnuts coated with corn starch and powdered sugar, these confections were launched by two immigrant Armenian farmers at the beginning of the twentieth century to dispose of the fruit they could not sell and it made them a fortune.

Leavenworth

Brace yourself as you head west towards **LEAVENWORTH**, a small timber and railroad town that warded off economic death by going Bavarian thirty years ago. Local motels and stores now sport steeply roofed half-timbered "alpine" facades, complete with wooden balconies and window-boxes; wiener schnitzel, sauerkraut and strudels now feature in local menus; and gift shops sell musical boxes, all to the strains of "alpine" folk music. This can be fun if you're in the right mood, and even if you're not, you can always escape into the gorgeous mountain scenery.

Orientation couldn't be easier: US-2 strips through Leavenworth forming the northern perimeter of the town centre, which slopes south to fill out a small loop in the Wenatchee River. Leavenworth's main drag, Front Street, runs parallel to – and one block south of – US-2. Northwestern Trailways **buses** (☎1-800/366-3830, *www.nwadv.com/northw*), from Seattle and Spokane, pull in at the Park + Ride on US-2, a five-minute walk from downtown. Nearby, the municipal **visitor centre** (☎509/548-5807, *www.leavenworth.org*), on US-2 at 9th Street, has – considering the size of the place – an extraordinarily long list of restaurants and lodgings, though you're still advised to book ahead in summer. They also have details of the many local companies who organize **outdoor activities** – everything from horse-drawn wagon rides, snowmobiling, snowshoeing, dog sledding, skiing and white-water rafting through to fishing and hunting. The town also has a USFS **Ranger Station**, just off US-2 at 600 Sherbourne St (daily 7.45am–4.30pm, but closed winter weekends; ☎509/782-1413), where you can pick up hiking maps and trail descriptions. Leavenworth Ski and Sports (☎509/548-7864), west of the visitor centre at US-2 and Icicle Road, rents out skis, snowshoes, mountain bikes and climbing gear.

Downtown **accommodation** includes the excellent *Hotel Pension Anna*, 926 Commercial St (☎509/548-6273 or 1-800/509-2662, *www.pensionanna.com*; ④), a carefully reproduced "Austrian" lodge that also has some suites in the renovated, onion-domed chapel across the street. Next door, the *Obertal Motor Inn*, at no. 922 (☎509/548-5204 or 1-800/537-9382, *www.obertal.com*; ④) isn't nearly as convincing, but the tidy, modern rooms are perfectly adequate, while *Mrs Anderson's Lodging House*, 917 Commercial St (☎509/548-6173 or 1-800/253-8990, *www.quiltersheaven.com*; ③), offers nine comfortable rooms with antique furnishings. The *Enzian Motor Inn*, just west of the centre at 590 US-2 (☎509/548-5269 or 1-800/223-8511; ⑤), is a rather grand motel-lodge with commodious rooms done out in pan-Alpine style – and offering regular Alphorn concerts.

Leavenworth has more than its share of undistinguished **café-restaurants** geared up for the passing tourist trade, but in with the dross you'll find some tasty surprises. The *Los Camperos*, upstairs on The Alley at 200 8th St (☎509/548-3314), leaves the Bavarian cuisine behind for excellent Mexican dishes, and neither is the *Soup Cellar*, 725 Front St, overly "alpine" with its tasty soups and salads. To have a Bavarian goodtime, eat at *Andreas Keller*, 829 Front St (☎509/548-6000), which serves the best German food around.

Around Leavenworth: the Alpine Lakes Wilderness

The real point of visiting Leavenworth is to **hike** the surrounding mountains, a small portion of the colossal Wenatchee National Forest, which extends in a thick band north as far as Lake Chelan and south to I-90. The national forest is dotted with wilderness areas and it's one of these – the **Alpine Lakes Wilderness** to the west of Leavenworth – which boasts some of the region's finest scenery, with plunging valleys and scores of crystal-clear mountain lakes set beneath a string of spiralling peaks.

From Leavenworth, the most straightforward approach into the Alpine Lakes is along **Icicle Road**, which weaves its way south then west through thick forest and past cascading waterfalls to a series of trailheads and busy USFS **campgrounds**. The nine-mile-long Enchantment Lake Trail is a particularly popular route, with hikers heading south up Mountaineer Creek for the beautiful lochs that pepper the mountains up above: the trailhead is about eight miles out of town. For something less strenuous, stick to the forested footpath running beside Icicle Road.

West from Leavenworth along US-2: Index

Heading west from Leavenworth, US-2 scrambles over the Cascades at **Stevens Pass**, named after the Great Northern's surveyor John Stevens, who chose to route the railroad this way in 1892. Beyond, US-2 loops down to the Skykomish River Valley where tiny **INDEX**, an old mining and quarrying settlement a mile or so from the highway, is worth a pit-stop for its antique **general store**, selling everything from sandwiches to fertilizer. The sheer, four-hundred-foot granite cliff at the back of Index, the so-called **Town Wall**, is a favourite with Seattle rock climbers.

Back on the highway, it's eight miles further west to **GOLD BAR**, once a hard-edged mining town and railroad settlement where, as anti-Chinese sentiment reached boiling point in the 1890s, a Schindler-like railway engineer shipped terrified Chinese locals out in purpose-built "coffins". The focus of attention today is **Wallace Falls State Park**, just two miles northeast of town, with campgrounds and two trails – one three, the other four miles – leading to the 265-foot waterfalls.

Pushing on west, you soon reach **MONROE**, a neon-lit sprawl heralding Seattle, just thirty miles away.

THE COLUMBIA PLATEAU

Big, dry and empty, the **Columbia Plateau**, filling out the bulk of Washington east of the Cascades, has more in common with neighbouring Idaho than with the green western side of the state. Faded, olive-coloured sagebrush covers mile upon mile of dusty prairie, overlooked by huge, reddish flat-topped rocks and interrupted by stark badland canyons, or coulees. This is the powerful landscape of a thousand Western movies, and it's impossible not to be stirred by the sheer scale of the scenery. Yet, wide-open rangeland no longer defines the region's character and hasn't since the 1880s when local sheep and cattle ranchers set about turning chunks of the plateau into wheat-producing farmland. Their principal problem was water. The soil was there – up to one hundred feet deep in places – but the water wasn't, prompting all manner of irrigation schemes, culminating in the colossal Columbia Basin Irrigation Project, begun in the 1930s and now watering endless fields of wheat, potatoes, asparagus, carrots, alfalfa, maize (corn) and mint. Give or take the occasional industrial blip, it's these agricultural concerns that inform the workaday towns of the Columbia Plateau. Frankly this doesn't make for too much excitement, though **Toppenish**, with its forty-odd Western murals, and **Ellensburg**, which has some fetching c.1900 architecture and a couple of good museums, are pleasant places to overnight, while **Spokane** has the flavour of a bigger city and a reasonably vibrant cultural life.

The quickest route across the region is the two-hundred-mile sprint along **I-90** from Ellensburg to Spokane, but this manages to avoid almost everything of any interest. You're far better off using Ellensburg and Spokane as the pivotal points of a 450-mile loop, with the outward journey exploring the southern (and more interesting) part of the region. Starting out at **Ellensburg**, 110 miles directly east of Seattle on I-90, you can begin the southern route by scooting through the fertile Yakima Valley, dropping in at the ex-railway towns of **Yakima** and mural-crazy **Toppenish**. Beyond, you'll want to shoot past the grimly industrial **Tri-Cities** (Richland, Pasco and Kennewick) on your way to the **Whitman Mission National Historic Site**. This was once the home of Marcus Whitman, the pioneer missionary who was ultimately killed for his medicinal failings by a vengeful band of Cayuse. The mission is on the edge of the dreary agricultural town of **Walla Walla**, from where you can drive northeast through wheatfields to reach **Spokane** – though it's tempting to abandon the Columbia Plateau here for the Country & Western charms of nearby Pendleton, Oregon's gateway to the Wallowa Mountains and Hells Canyon (see p.157).

Leaving Spokane, the northern route crosses the sun-scorched prairie bound for the **Grand Coulee Dam**, one of the biggest concrete structures ever built. From here, the towns of the Cascade foothills – Winthrop (see p.268), Chelan (see p.269), or Leavenworth (see p.272) – are within easy striking distance, or you can leave the plateau behind by driving north along US-97 through forested mountains to reach Canada's British Columbia at Osoyoos (see p.425).

Without your own car, you'll be struggling to see much of anything, but **Greyhound buses** do run a useful service east from Seattle along I-90 to Ellensburg, Yakima, Toppenish, Walla Walla and Pendleton, in Oregon. Some services fork off at Ellensburg to head northeast to Spokane or north to Wenatchee, though this modest journey takes no less than eight hours. Northwestern Trailways (☎1-800/366-3830, *www.nwadv.com /northw*) connects Seattle, Leavenworth and Wenatchee with Spokane. Amtrak **trains** (☎1-800/872-7245) operates two routes to Spokane from the west, the more useful linking Seattle, Leavenworth, Wenatchee and Spokane.

East from Seattle on I-90: Snoqualmie Falls and Pass

Heading east from Seattle, I-90 barrels over the mountains via **Snoqualmie Pass**, the lowest and most traversible of the Cascade passes, long the regular route of traders, trappers and Native-Americans. It took several days for them to struggle across the mountains, but today it only takes a couple of hours – a little longer if you pause at the two most obvious (TV-related) attractions. For the first, on the western slopes, turn off the Interstate at Exit 31 for the five-mile detour north through North Bend along Hwy 202 to **Snoqualmie Falls**, as seen during the title sequence of David Lynch's *Twin Peaks*. The falls crash into a rocky gorge, sending up a cloud of white spray, but despite their wild appearance, they're managed by Puget Sound Energy, who adjust the flow to suit their requirements.

Back on I-90, about eighty miles from Seattle – well beyond Snoqualmie Pass – come off the Interstate at desultory **CLE ELUM** ("Swift Water" in Salish) to stock up on fresh bread and cinnamon rolls at the *Cle Elum Bakery*, 502 E 1st St. The main draw is, however, the town's immediate neighbour, **ROSLYN**, an Appalachian look-alike of old timber houses trailing through a forest pocked with old slag heaps, mementos of the collieries that once produced two million tons of coal a year – the last one closed in 1963. Every inch a company town, no one seemed bothered about Roslyn until TV "discovered" its unreconstructed appearance as the set for *Northern Exposure*. With its fictional fame have come the sightseers, but it's still an odd, mournful sort of place. The *Roslyn Café*, bang in the centre, serves delicious burgers and bagels.

Ellensburg

On the far side of the Cascade Mountains from Seattle, **ELLENSBURG** is every inch the country town, sitting in the middle of the wide and fertile Kittitas Valley. The town began when a couple of white traders – Andrew Splawn and Ben Burch – set up shop here in the 1860s, making a tidy profit from the steady stream of settlers and drovers heading over the Snoqualmie Pass. As a joke, the partners called their trading post

"Robbers' Roost", and the name stuck until the bourgeoisie took a grip in the shape of a Seattle merchant who bought them out and renamed the settlement "Ellensburg" after his wife. The Northern Pacific Railroad reached Ellensburg in 1886, and the town boomed, its boosters even arguing it should become the state capital when the matter was put to the vote in 1889, the year of statehood. In the event, Olympia, the old territorial capital, won, prompting the editor of the local newspaper to thunder "Capital or no capital, Ellensburg will get there. No grass in her streets, no flies on her back, no lard on her tail. Whoop her up again, boys!"

That same year, Ellensburg suffered the fate of many frontier towns when its early timber buildings were razed by fire, but there was enough money – and confidence – to pay for it to be rebuilt in brick and stone. Many of these commercial buildings have survived and several are worth close examination, especially the imposing 1911 **Land Title Building**, at 5th Avenue and Pearl Street, with its Neoclassical pillars and columns and fetching sandstone trimmings. Another, the horseshoe-arched **Cadwell Building**, at 114 E 3rd Ave and Pine Street, is home to the **Kittitas County Museum** (May–Sept Mon–Sat 10am–4pm, Oct–April Tues–Sat 11am–3pm; donation), which is the proud possessor of – amongst a hotchpotch of pioneer and native artefacts – a six-pound hunk of the unique-to-the-area Ellensburg blue agate. Much more diverting is the **Clymer Museum of Art**, 416 N Pearl St and 4th Avenue (Mon–Fri 10am–5pm, Sat–Sun noon–5pm; $3), named after John Ford Clymer (1907–89), a diligent painter of historical Western scenes and a talented illustrator, responsible for no less than eighty *Saturday Evening Post* covers. Born in Ellensburg, Clymer loved the West and travelled

▽ *I - 90 & Best Western Ellenburg Inn*

MOVING ON FROM ELLENSBURG

Travelling on from Ellensburg, most visitors take the fast track east along **I-90**, disappearing in a cloud of prairie dust towards Spokane, but others take a slower, more varied route, skirting a large military reservation on their way south to the Yakima Valley. There are actually two roads to choose from travelling in this direction: either **I-82**, which cuts across sagebrush flatland, or the prettier **Hwy 821**, which sticks close to the Yakima River as it weaves through a steep and stark canyon.

the region extensively, researching a long series of bold, sweeping historical pictures with titles like *John Colter Visits the Crows 1807*, *Salute to the Old West* and *Whiskey, Whiskey*. The museum shows a video on Clymer's life and displays many of his historical paintings and illustrations alongside a first-rate programme of temporary exhibitions firmly focused on the West – everything from patchwork quilts and wheat weaving through to cowboy poetry.

The main event hereabouts is of the West too. The annual **Ellensburg Rodeo**, held over Labor Day Weekend, fills the town with stetsoned cowboys and cowgirls, who rope steers, ride bulls and sit on bucking broncos, accompanied by much pageantry and unfurling of star-spangled banners. For tickets, call the Rodeo Ticket Office (☎509/962-7831 or 1-800/637-2444): prices start at around $10, and include admission to the **Kittitas County Fair**, an odd combination of penned livestock and bright carnival rides that takes place at the same time. Needless to say, if you're after seeing the rodeo, you should book accommodation well ahead of time.

Practicalities

En route to and from Seattle as well as Spokane or Pendleton, Greyhound **buses** stop in Ellensburg at 801 Okanogan St and 8th Avenue, about half a mile west of the **visitor centre**, at 801 S Ruby St and 8th Avenue (Mon–Fri 8am–5pm, Sat 10am–2pm; ☎509/925-3137, *www.ellensburg-chamber.com*). They can provide a free town map and have a list of local **accommodation**. Modern chain motels string along Canyon Road, the main access road into town from I-90 (Exit 109). Amongst them, the pick are the *Best Western Ellensburg Inn*, at no. 1700 (☎509/925-9801 or 1-800/321-8791; ④), which offers comfortable rooms plus an indoor pool and a sauna, and the new *Comfort Inn*, at no. 1722 (☎509/925-7037 or 1-800/228-5150; ④), also with an indoor pool. As for **eating**, the Art Deco *Valley Café*, 105 W 3rd Ave at Main, has a wide-ranging and imaginative menu, and is by far the nicest place in town for breakfast, lunch or dinner. Two other options are the reasonably priced *Pub Minglewood Restaurant*, 402 N Pearl and 4th Avenue (evenings only, closed Sun; ☎509/962-2260), where the local speciality – Ellensburg lamb – is a real treat, and the Mexican cuisine of the *Casa de Blanca*, Canyon at Ruby Road (☎509/925-1693).

Yakima

Some thirty miles south of Ellensburg on Hwy 821, the Yakima River cuts free of the canyon and eases out into a wide valley to absorb the Naches River and here, at this important confluence, lies sprawling **YAKIMA**, the region's urban hub. Gallantly, the town's glossy convention centre promotes an upmarket image, but the town isn't about to win any beauty contests, and its long commercial strip hardly whets the appetite. It is, however, one of the region's most successful towns, a busy trading centre with a huge agricultural hinterland and a population of over sixty thousand of whom around half are Hispanic: since the 1940s, much of the farm labour hereabouts has been provided by migrant Mexicans and today Hispanic-Americans are a numerous minority right along the valley.

Yakima's initial prosperity was built on the back of the railroad, though there were some teething problems. In 1884, the Northern Pacific decided to bypass Yakima, meanly locating the vital tracks a few miles to the north of town. The decision saved the railroad money – as empty prairie was a good deal cheaper than developed land – and although the townsfolk were infuriated there was nothing they could do except move. And that's what they did, lock, stock and barrel, rolling the better houses to the new site on logs to establish what the local paper called a "Messiah of Commerce"; the old "Yakima" is now the small neighbouring community of Union Gap.

Yakima has done its level best to brighten up its **downtown** – take I-82's Exit 33 if you're driving here from Ellensburg – and although the results are hardly stunning, there is a lively café and restaurant scene down amongst the old brick buildings of N Front and N First streets at Yakima Avenue, the main east–west drag. Other than that, the **visitor centre**, downtown at 10 N 8th St at Yakima Avenue (Mon–Fri 8.30am–5pm, plus May–Oct Sat & Sun 9am–4pm; ☎509/575-3010 or 1-800/221-0751, *www.visityakima.com*), has the details of tastings and tours amongst the many vineyards of the Yakima Valley (see box, below). If you do decide to **stay the night**, central options include a standard-issue chain *Travelodge*, 110 S Naches Ave at E Chestnut Avenue (☎509/453-7151 or 1-800/255-3050; ③), and the *Red Apple Motel*, 416 N 1st St at D Street (☎509/248-7150; ③), whose main distinction is its apple-shaped outdoor pool. More distinctively, *Birchfield Manor B&B*, 2018 Birchfield Rd (☎509/452-1960; ③), occupies an attractively revamped 1880s house set in its own grounds just two miles east of town off Hwy-24; they have five guestrooms, all en suite. For **food**, *Santiago's*, 111 E Yakima Ave at N 1st Street (☎509/453-1644) serves excellent – and inexpensive

---

THE YAKIMA VALLEY AND ITS VINEYARDS

Southeast of its namesake town, the **Yakima Valley** turns into fruit- and vine-growing country, where apples, cherries, pears, peaches, apricots and grapes grow prolifically in what was once sagebrush desert. Though the Yakima Valley's volcanic soil is naturally rich and the sun shines about three hundred days of the year, irrigation is what has made it fertile, and intricate systems of reservoirs, canals and ditches divert water from the Yakima River around the orchards and vineyards. Water rights are a crucial issue for local farmers: priority is given to those who have held land the longest, and in dry years farmers with only junior water rights can find themselves in trouble. Fish can sometimes be left high and dry too – irrigation channels can drain the river to a meagre trickle unable to support anything with gills.

There have been **vineyards** in the Yakima Valley since the 1930s, but it was the introduction of classic European vinifera vines thirty years later that formed the foundation of today's industry. Organized by a group of like-minded Washington vintners, the introduction of the precious vine was actually something of a gamble: many experts thought the state's winters would be too harsh for them to survive, but the vines flourished and nowadays the Yakima Valley is Washington's premier grape-growing region, regularly producing vintages of international standing. Acidity is the key to the individuality of the valley's wines. The intense cold of winter stresses the vines and concentrates the flavours of the fruit, while in summer the days are boiling hot and the nights comparatively cold, giving valley wine its characteristic crispness. The **Yakima Valley Wine Growers Association** (☎1-800/258-7270, *www.yakimavalleywine.com*) helps monitor the quality of every bottle sporting the Yakima Valley Wine appellation and also has information on the region's wines on its Web site. About twenty valley wineries offer **tours and tastings** and all the region's visitor centres can provide detailed directions and opening hours. A particularly good one, thanks to its lovely tasting room and fine wines, is the **Covey Run Winery** (daily: April–Oct 10am–5pm, Nov–March 11am–4pm; ☎509/829-6235), located at 1500 Vintage Rd, about four miles north of Zillah (see overleaf), which is itself some twenty miles from Yakima city – ring for directions.

– Mexican dishes and has a convivial atmosphere as does the comparable *El Pastor*, 315 W Walnut at N 3rd Avenue (☎509/453-5159). *Birchfield Manor* (see overleaf; dinners only, closed Sun) offers a classy, imaginative menu and an excellent range of local wines – main courses around $20 – and finally *Gasparetti's*, a few blocks north of the centre at 1013 N 1st St at I Street (dinners only, closed Sun; ☎509/248-0628), is the best of Yakima's Italian restaurants and is reasonably priced too.

Southeast along the Yakima Valley – Toppenish

Heading out of Yakima, there's a choice of roads along the valley. The faster **I-82** keeps to the north of the river, slipping past the unassuming little town of **ZILLAH** – the site of the Covey Run Winery (see box, overleaf) – before pounding on to **PROSSER**, an unremarkable town about fifty miles to the southeast. Meanwhile, **US-97** cuts a quieter, pleasanter route to the south of the Yakima River to reach – after about 20 miles – **Toppenish**, easily the best base for exploring the valley. There's a choice of routes here too, with US-97 veering south across the barrenness of the Yakama Indian Reservation on the sixty-mile trip to the outstanding **Maryhill Art Museum** (see p.106), whilst **Hwy 22** slices east along the valley to meet I-82 at Prosser.

Toppenish

In true Western style, **TOPPENISH** started out as a telegraph office and water tower beside the Northern Pacific Railroad. The railway employees were soon joined by horse traders, who made a handsome profit buying wild horses from the adjacent Yakima Reservation and retailing the animals in New York. Fortuitously, just when the horse trade began to fizzle out, a sugar company moved in, building a sugar beet processing plant here in 1918 – and Toppenish would probably have stayed a workaday sugar beet centre but for the closure of the plant in 1980. Their main source of income gone, locals looked around for an alternative and finally hit upon something that was genuinely inventive. Coining a promotional cliché, "The City Where The West Still Lives", they set about commissioning high-quality **murals** focusing on local characters and events. Over forty of these bright and breezy paintings now adorn the tiny town centre, focused on Toppenish Avenue, and although some are rather hackneyed (cowboys-by-the-light-of-the-moon), others tell intriguing tales of local endeavour or set the scene perfectly, as in *The Palace Hotel, Toppenish* and *Indians' Winter Encampment*.

The **visitor centre**, downtown at 5A Toppenish Ave (April–Oct daily 10am–4pm; Nov–March daily 11am–3pm; ☎509/865-3262 or 1-800/569-3982, *www.toppenish.org*), provides a free guide to the murals with each painting described in detail. It only takes an hour or two to walk round them all, but there are guided tours by covered wagon and stagecoach from April to mid-November, whilst the annual **Mural-in-a-Day** extravaganza, usually held in early June, sees Toppenish filled to the gunnels with tourists who come to watch a team of artists knock up a brand new mural. The town's other knees-up is the four-day **Toppenish Rodeo, Pow Wow and Parade** (tickets from $10) every 4th of July weekend – the visitor centre has the details.

Toppenish has a small supply of **motels**, amongst which the *Toppenish Inn Motel*, 515 S Elm St (☎509/865-7444 or 1-800/222-3161; ③), is, with its downtown location and indoor pool, the most comfortable. The plain but perfectly adequate *Oxbow Motor Inn*, nearby at 511 S Elm St (☎509/865-5800; ②), is a second possibility. There are several inexpensive Mexican **restaurants** in the town centre, the pick of them being *Los Murales*, 202 W 1st Ave (☎509/865-7555), which specializes in north Mexican cuisine. Greyhound **buses** along the Yakima Valley all pause at Toppenish – call (☎1-800/231-2222) for drop-off details.

Around Toppenish: the Yakama Nation Cultural Center

For thirty-odd miles from Yakima, the Yakima River marks the northern boundary of the **Yakama Indian Reservation** – the tribal council having changed the "i" to an "a" – a great slab of dry and rugged land that stretches down towards the Columbia River. Here, set beside US-97 just northwest of Toppenish, is the large **Yakama Nation Cultural Center**, which holds a variety of community facilities and, in a 76-foot-tall replica wigwam, a **museum** (daily, approximate hours 9am–5pm; $4; call ☎509/865-2800 to check opening times) outlining Yakama traditions by means of dioramas and wall displays. One of the most unusual exhibits is a time-ball, a sort of macramé diary kept by married women as a record of their lives; in old age, major events were recalled by unravelling the sequence of knots and beads. Several exhibits are devoted to Yakama religious practices involving Spilyay – the local version of the god-like coyote figure that crops up in many Native-American myths figuring prominently – but there's something rather tragic in the museum's attempts to reassert Yakama culture. During the 1850s, in a series of brutal skirmishes known as the **Yakima War**, the Yakama were forcibly ejected from their traditional lands and consigned to this largely infertile reservation. One US Army commander, Major Gabriel Rains, was entirely clear about his aims: he would, he declared, make "war forever until not a Yakima breathes in the land he calls his own".

The Tri-Cities

About eighty miles from Yakima, the cluster of three towns known collectively as the **TRI-CITIES** straddle the Columbia River as it executes a dramatic change of direction to begin its long run west to the Pacific. All three towns – Pasco, Richland and Kennewick – were once reliant on the now-defunct **Hanford Site**, a massive nuclear energy and research area immediately to the north. During the World War II race for nuclear weapons, the Hanford Site housed a top-secret plant to produce plutonium. The location was carefully selected by the government for its closeness to the Columbia River – providing both cold water for cooling reactors and hydroelectricity from its new dams – and its isolation in the sagebrush wilderness. The sudden arrival of over fifty thousand construction workers, and the growth of a sprawling makeshift shack-city, must surely have made people suspect something was afoot, but apparently very few, perhaps a dozen top scientists and politicians, knew exactly what was happening here. During the 1960s and 1970s, work at Hanford shifted from military projects towards the civilian use of nuclear energy, but the Reagan years brought defence back to the fore, a brief boom before the controversies surrounding the nuclear industry led to closure in 1988. Nuclear power being nuclear power, this wasn't the end of the matter and now the federal government is spending billions trying to cleanse the contamination.

Walla Walla: the Whitman Mission

US-12 follows the Columbia River south from the Tri-Cities, then cuts east through the wheat and onion fields that surround the college and agricultural town of **WALLA WALLA**. The town itself is a yawn, but it does have a crucial historical significance: it was here in 1836 that **Dr Marcus Whitman**, a key figure in the settling of the Northwest, arrived from the East Coast as a missionary, hoping to convert the local Cayuse from their nomadic ways into church-going, crop-growing Christians.

Whitman and his wife Narcissa made little headway with the Cayuse and, like other Western missionaries, turned their attention instead to the white settlers who followed in their pioneering footsteps – the Whitmans were the first to drive a wagon this far west. Within a few years the mission became a refuge along the Oregon Trail, taking

MOVING ON FROM WALLA WALLA

Walla Walla is something of a crossroads. From here, you can head south over the Oregon border towards Pendleton, La Grande and the Wallowa Mountains (see pp.157–164), or retrace your steps west to the Tri-Cities to pick up US-395 and then I-90 for the fast route north to Spokane. Alternatively, you can opt for a more leisurely drive to Spokane, weaving through the wheat and barley fields of the agricultural **Palouse** region along a series of quiet country highways – numbers 12, 127, 26 and then 195. If you come this way, allow a good four hours for the 160-odd-mile trip, longer if you make the signposted eight-mile detour east of US-195 to the top of **Steptoe Butte**, which offers a wide panorama across the rippling land. The cone-shaped butte was named for Colonel Steptoe, whose troops spent an uneasy night in 1858 creeping down the hill and through encircling bands of Palouse – an improvised retreat that won him many plaudits (though it's likely the Palouse let him go as annihilation was not their practice). Steptoe's encirclement took the US Army back to the drawing board. The Palouse had better rifles than Steptoe's unit, a state of affairs rectified by the army before they launched a punitive expedition towards Spokane later that year.

in sick and orphaned travellers (including the real-life Sager children of the storybook *Children of the Oregon Trail*). The Cayuse eyed the increasing numbers of settlers very warily, and when a measles epidemic decimated the tribe, suspicions grew that they were being poisoned to make way for the whites. Their uneasiness was reinforced by Dr Whitman's ability to help (some) whites, but hardly any of the Indians, who had no natural immunity to the disease. Whitman sensed the growing tension, and he must have known of the native belief that medicine-men were directly liable for the deaths of their patients, but he continued to take on even hopeless cases. In November 1847 a band of Cayuse arrived at the mission and murdered Whitman, Narcissa and several others. Fifty more at the mission, mostly children, were taken captive, and although they were later released, angry settlers raised volunteer bands against the Cayuse. When the story hit the newspapers back East, it generated such a tide of fear about native uprisings that the government finally declared the Oregon (then including Washington) an official US territory, which meant the army could be sent in to protect the settlers – with drastic implications for the original inhabitants.

The site of the **Whitman Mission** (daily: mid-June to Aug 8am–6pm, Sept to mid-June 8am–4.30pm; $2), in a lovely little dell seven miles west of Walla Walla off US-12, is bare but effective. The mission itself was razed by the Cayuse after the massacre, and simple marks on the ground plus interpretive plaques show its original layout and the sites of the murders of Marcus and Narcissa. A visitor centre shows a film on Whitman's work and the massacre, and is well stocked with books on the subject, including Narcissa Whitman's diary.

Once you've seen the Whitman Mission, there's no point in hanging around Walla Walla, so plan to keep on going either to Spokane (see below), 160 miles to the north, or Pendleton (see p.157), a much shorter drive to the south. If, however, you're marooned, the Walla Walla **visitor centre**, downtown at 29 E Sumach and Colville (Mon–Fri 9am–5pm; ☎509/525-0850), has the full list of local accommodation.

Spokane

The wide open spaces and unassuming little towns of the Columbia Plateau don't really prepare you for **SPOKANE**, one hundred and fifty miles northeast of the Tri-Cities. Just a few miles from the Idaho border, it's eastern Washington's only real city, boasting a metropolitan population of around 410,000, and its scattering of grandiose c.1900 buildings – built on the spoils of the Coeur d'Alene silver mines, across the state divide

– sport some unexpectedly elegant, almost colonial touches. That apart, Spokane has taken something of an economic battering since its late nineteenth century heyday and, although it was revamped in preparation for the World's Fair held here in 1974, shades of industrial shabbiness still haunt the modern city. It's not the sort of place you're likely to linger in very long, but there's enough to see and do to keep most visitors busy for a day or so. Spokane also has one real claim to fame for it was here in 1910 that a certain Mrs Dodd specified a special day on which she honoured her father who had raised his kids on his own after the death of his wife; the idea caught on – hence **Father's Day**.

Spokane's long and narrow **downtown** squeezes into the seven blocks between I-90 and the Spokane River. The place to make for is **Riverfront Park** – in summer, at least, the town's focal point. The park, which straddles the Spokane River and incorporates a pair of islets in midstream, was originally planned by Frederick Olmsted, previously responsible for New York's Central Park, who was employed by Spokane's wealthy to landscape the city. Though most of Olmsted's suggestions were followed, big business drew the line at sacrificing their own river access, and for almost a century the banks of the Spokane River were scarred by a tangle of railway lines and buildings – the price for the city's early railroad-based commercial success. But the hundred-acre park was finally and fully laid out in the massive clean-up before the 1974 World's Fair, and is now Spokane's main venue for strolling, picnicking and general hanging out. An eccentric assortment of attractions includes an old railway clock tower, an antique carousel, an IMAX theatre and a cheery entertainment pavilion.

As it slices through the park, the river tumbles down a series of rocky ledges known as **Spokane Falls**, once a fishing site for the Spokane and later the site of the first pioneer settlement. Early settlers harnessed the churning water to power their mills, and on the far side of the river the **Flour Mill** was an economic cornerstone when it opened in 1896, though it's now been converted to house cutesy shops. **Gondolas** (cable cars) run across the river from the west end of the park, offering city and river views.

The architectural relics of Spokane's early grandeur are sprinkled all over town, from the monumental flamboyance of the **Davenport Hotel**, downtown at Sprague and Post, to the extravagant **County Court House**, built in the style of a French chateau on the north side of the river at Broadway and Madison. W Riverside Avenue, between Washington and Howard, gets into the act too, with several first-rate examples of late nineteenth-century American commercial architecture. For instance the **Fernwell Building**, at no. 503, dating from 1890 is typical of the cast-iron frame structures that were popular until steel frames were developed. Steel was a stronger and more flexible building material, and the fifteen-storey, terracotta-clad 1910 **Old National Bank**, at no. 422, illustrates the point. The bank was actually one of the first buildings in Washington to have a steel frame, its simplicity an indication of the time it took for local architects to fully appreciate the decorative possibilities of the new medium. Kirtland Cutter, Spokane's leading designer, was one of the first to catch on, and his **Sherwood Building**, at no. 510, is adorned with Gothic trinkets, from lions and griffins through to terracotta gargoyles.

Of the city's several museums, easily the best is the **Cheney Cowles Museum**, situated a mile or so west of the centre at 2316 W 1st Ave, though this is closed for refurbishment until early 2002 – the visitor centre (see overleaf) can update you on the latest. The museum owns a significant collection of modern American art and an outstanding assortment of Native-American artefacts in which the tribes of the Columbia Plateau take precedence. Included are a number of tableaux showing excruciating-looking initiation ceremonies with the candidates suspended from hooks embedded in their chests as a test of manhood. Still open during the revamp is the adjacent **Campbell House** (normally Tues–Sat 10am–5pm, Wed till 9pm, & Sun 1–5pm; $4), a restored Tudor Revival confection dreamed up for a silver baron by Kirtland Cutter in

1898. The interior is decked out in a truly tasteless (and therefore enjoyable) combination of pointedly expensive styles.

Of interest also is the **Bing Crosby Memorabilia Room** (Mon–Fri 7.30am–midnight, plus Sept–May Sat & Sun 11am–midnight; free), located in the Crosby Student Center on the campus of Gonzaga University – northeast of and across the river from downtown. A local lad, Harry Lillis Crosby is easily the university's most famous ex-student, though the mellifluous crooner dropped out before he actually finished his course. Awarded an honorary doctorate in 1937, Crosby proved a generous benefactor, giving the college this hoard of memorabilia, everything from gold records and sporting awards through to Crosby-endorsed products, pipes and slippers. He was a little more sparing with his original sheet music, but some of his most famous numbers are here, notably Moonlight Becomes You and White Christmas.

Practicalities

As you **drive** into Spokane from the southwest, I-90 skirts the southern edge of downtown, which is best accessed from Exit 281; US-2 (from Coulee Dam, see below) feeds into I-90 west of the city. Amtrak **trains** as well as Northwestern Trailways and Greyhound **buses** share the same transit terminal, downtown at W 221 1st Ave and Bernard Street; if you arrive after dark, be warned that the surrounding streets aren't safe – take a taxi. **Local buses**, operated by Spokane Transit Authority (STA) (☎509/328-7433), cover the city and its suburbs. Well stocked with city and regional information, the **visitor centre** is three blocks north of the transit terminal – and five-minutes' walk from Riverside Park – at 201 W Main Ave and Browne (Mon–Fri 8.30am–5pm, plus May–Sept Sat 8am–4pm & Sun 9am–2pm; ☎509/747-3230 or 1-888/776-5263, www.visitspokane.com).

Accommodation in Spokane is plentiful and reasonably priced, with many of the most appealing hotels and motels dotted around the city centre. Downtown choices include the trim, tidy and well-equipped *Travelodge*, 33 W Spokane Falls Blvd at Browne (☎509/623-9727 or 1-800/578-7878; ④); the equally competent *Courtyard by Marriott Hotel*, beside the river, east off Division at 401 N Riverpoint Blvd (☎509/456-7600 or 1-800/321-2211; ⑤); and the smart *West Coast Ridpath Hotel*, 515 W Sprague Ave and Stevens (☎509/838-2711 or 1-800/325-4000; ⑤), where the 350 rooms are spacious and comfortable – and those on the upper floors have great views out over town. The plain *Towne Center Motel*, 901 W 1st Ave at Lincoln (☎509/747-1041 or 1-800/247-1041; ③), is an inexpensive alternative.

Eating out well and inexpensively in downtown Spokane is easy. The *Mustard Seed Oriental Café*, 245 W Spokane Falls Blvd at Browne (☎509/747-2689), serves up distinctive Oriental cuisine, melding Japanese and Chinese influences; *Fugazzi*, 1 N Post St at W Sprague Avenue (☎509/624-1133), is a chic café-restaurant offering delicious bistro-style meals and snacks; and the lively *Onion Restaurant,* 302 W Riverside Ave and Bernard (☎509/747-3852), sells beer, wine, fruit daiquiris and American standards – burgers, salads and so forth. To have a **drink** downtown, head for the *Fort Spokane Brewery*, a brewpub at 401 W Spokane Falls Blvd and Washington, where there's live jazz, blues and R&B several nights a week. For a **browse**, Auntie's Bookstore, 402 E Main (Mon–Sat 9am–9pm), is the city's biggest bookshop.

The Grand Coulee Dam

The Columbia Plateau is seen at its most dramatic in the open, swaggering, big country around the **Grand Coulee Dam**, itself a huge-scale work, around ninety miles west of Spokane (or, travelling east, eighty miles from Chelan along highways 97, 173 and 174). The dam intercepts the Columbia River where it separates the remote, forested mountains of northeast Washington from the Columbia Plateau, whose northern edge was an Ice Age disaster area, scoured and sculpted by ancient floods until it was riven with deep channels called "coulees". These **coulees**, with their low-lying lakes and skein of rivers and creeks, run south of the Columbia River as it begins its giant loop west along the edge of the Cascade Mountains. The biggest coulee of the lot is, as you might expect from the name, **Grand Coulee**, a great slash in the landscape that's now partly filled by Banks Lake, whose waters, trapped behind the Dry Falls Dam (see overleaf), back up as far as Grand Couleee Dam, which has itself created a lake, the long, spindly Lake Roosevelt, which stretches all the way to the Canadian border.

Kingpin of the Columbia River dams, **Grand Coulee Dam**, begun in 1933, was for a while as much a political icon as an engineering feat. Probably the most ambitious of Roosevelt's New Deal schemes to lift America out of the Depression, it symbolized hope for the Northwest, promising abundant energy and water for irrigation. It also provided jobs for hundreds of workers from all over the country, notably the dustbowl regions further east, whose unemployed agricultural labourers were migrating west in their hundreds. As folk singer Woody Guthrie had it:

> *Columbia's waters taste like sparklin' wine*
> *Dustbowl waters taste like picklin' brine*

Guthrie worked on the Bonneville Dam lower down the river and was commissioned to write some twenty songs about the Columbia project – one of which, *Roll on, Columbia*, you'll probably hear in the visitor centre (see below). The songs were originally played at local rallies, held to raise investment money, and to combat propaganda from the private power companies whose interests lay in keeping power production in their own hands. Glowing with optimism, the songs underline the promise the dam held for impoverished working people:

> *I'm a farmer's boy, my land's all roots and stumps!*
> *It's gonna take a big 'lectric saw to make 'em jump!*

The dam is now the world's biggest single producer of hydroelectricity, and has certainly controlled flooding lower down the Columbia. But the power-guzzling demands of the war industries that were attracted to the Northwest during World War II, and the atomic plant near the Tri-Cities, switched attention and resources from irrigation, and Guthrie's other vision of "green pastures of plenty from dry desert ground" has been much slower to get under way – even now, only half the area originally planned has been irrigated. There's been ecological criticism of the Columbia project too: salmon migration along the river has been reduced to a fraction of its pre-dam level, though schemes have since been set up to increase stocks of fish.

The background to the dam's construction is laid out in some detail at the Grand Coulee dam's **Visitor Arrival Center** (daily: June–July 8.30am–11pm; Aug–Sept 8.30am–10pm; Oct–May 9am–5pm; free), on Hwy 155 just north of the dam. There are lots of photographs, information and a free film touching on everything from the dangerous working conditions of the 1930s to how the turbines operate. As for the **dam** itself, it's initially something of an anticlimax. Though one of the world's largest concrete structures, it just doesn't look that big, a trick of the huge-scale scenery that surrounds it – focusing on a car or person on top of the dam can help to give a more impressive perspective. Free guided, and self-guided, tours of the dam and its generating plants are available from the visitor centre: views of the churning water are quite exciting, but you'll need a fair amount of enthusiasm for things mechanical to appreciate the intricacies of power-generation. The outdoor **laser light show**, given free on every evening throughout the summer (June & July at 10pm, Aug 9.30pm, Sept 8.30pm), is perhaps of more appeal – and attracts visitors in their hundreds; the best view is from the Visitor Arrival Center.

Practicalities

Set against the surrounding scrubland, the leafy streets and shady lawns of the little town of **COULEE DAM**, close to the Visitor Arrival Center, are a verdant advertisement for the difference the Grand Coulee's irrigation schemes have made. Otherwise, Coulee Dam is a stunningly boring place, not much more than a dormitory for the dam's workers, as are its two tiny neighbours – **GRAND COULEE** and **ELECTRIC CITY**, just to the south along Hwy 155. Indeed, once you've visited the dam, there's precious little reason to hang around, but between them the three towns do muster up a handful of **motels**: the rooms in Coulee Dam's *Columbia River Inn*, 10 Lincoln St (☎509/633-2100 or 1-800/633-6421, *www.columbiariverinn.com*; ③), overlook the dam, as do those of the nearby *Coulee House Motel*, 110 Roosevelt Way (☎509/633-1101 or 1-800/715-7767; ③). Both have outdoor pools and hot tubs. Good **food** is not the area's strong suit, but the *Melody Restaurant*, near the dam at 512 River Drive (☎509/633-1151), can set you up with fine and filling seafood and pasta dishes for a fair price.

Moving on from Grand Coulee – Dry Falls Dam

There is a choice of routes from Grand Coulee Dam. Heading north, Hwy 155 treks across the severe mountains of the **Colville Indian Reservation** to join US-97 for the jaunt up to Osoyoos (see p.425), over the Canadian border, or its west via Hwy 174 to Chelan (see p.269) and the Cascade Mountains. Alternatively, Hwy 155 cuts southwest along the side of the **Grand Coulee**, whose depths are filled by **Banks Lake**, while the endless sagebrush plateau, with its wide-skied landscapes broken by huge flat-topped rocks, stretches out towards the east. Banks Lake ends – and Hwy 155 feeds into US-2 – at Dry Falls Dam, named for **Dry Falls**, a few miles further south (take Hwy 17 from the west end of the dam), which had their moment of glory during the Ice Age when the Columbia, temporarily diverted this way, poured a tremendous torrent over a drop twice as high and almost four times as wide as Niagara. It must have been quite a sight, but a waterfall without water is not that impressive, and all you can see today is a wide, bare, canyon-walled hole, the remnants of the lake lurking apologetically in its flat-bottomed depths. The **Dry Falls interpretive centre** (mid-May to mid-Sept Wed–Sun 10am–6pm), beside Hwy 17, gives the background and provides views over the canyon. From Dry Falls Dam, US-2 will take you west towards Chelan (see p.269), while Hwy 17 leads south to I-90.

travel details

Trains

Portland to: Spokane (1 daily; 8hr 30in).

Seattle to: Portland (4 daily; 3hr 30min); Spokane (1 daily; 8hr); Wenatchee (1 daily; 4hr).

Buses

Ellensburg to: Wenatchee (1 daily; 8hr 20min).

Seattle to: Cashmere (1 daily; 3hr 15min); Ellensburg (6 daily; 2hr); Leavenworth (1 daily;

3hr); Pendleton, OR (1 daily; 9hr); Spokane (4 daily; 6hr); Toppenish (3 daily; 4hr); Walla Walla (2 daily; 7hr 30min); Wenatchee (1 daily; 3hr 30min); Yakima (3 daily; 3hr 30min).

Spokane to: Hood River (2 daily; 6hr 50min or 8hr 20min); Portland (2 daily; 8hr or 9hr 30min).

Yakima to: Biggs, OR (1 daily; 2hr); change at Biggs for Portland (1 daily; 2hr 10min); Toppenish (3 daily; 40min).

CHAPTER FIVE

VANCOUVER AND VANCOUVER ISLAND

Vancouver and **Vancouver Island** are pivotal points in any trip to the Northwest. Rightly preceded by a reputation as one of the world's most beautiful and laid-back cities, Vancouver is the main rival to Seattle as the region's most dynamic metropolis, not only blessed with a superlative natural setting, thriving cultural life and myriad after-dark activities, but also easily accessible and perfectly placed for onward travel to Vancouver Island, mainland British Columbia and the Canadian Rockies. Like Seattle, the city finds itself in the vanguard of trade and cultural ties with the Pacific Rim, links that have reinforced its long-standing economic vigour and deeply rooted multiculturalism. As a result, Vancouver exudes a cosmopolitan and civilized air, its easy-going citizens, outstanding museums and a wealth of opportunities for self-indulgence all likely to keep you in the city for several days.

The obvious excursion is across the Georgia Strait to **Vancouver Island**, home to **Victoria**, British Columbia's modest provincial capital. Swamped by US day-trippers in summer, the city plays up shamelessly to its image as a little piece of "old England", though even if you find this pitch a little hard to swallow, the place is worth at least a day for its superlative museum. The island as a whole can be a touch disappointing, and you may spend less time than you'd imagined exploring the city's hinterland. For many people the island becomes simply a way-station en route to Prince Hardy, Vancouver Island's terminal for the **ferries of the Inside Passage** (for Prince Rupert and Alaska). If you're not just hurrying through, however, the hiking possibilities and mountain landscapes of the **Strathcona Provincial Park**, and more particularly the tremendous seascapes of the **Pacific Rim National Park**, are both exceptional reasons to linger.

Long before the coming of Europeans, British Columbia's coastal region supported five key **aboriginal peoples** – the Kwakiutl, Bella Coola, Nuu-chah-nulth, Haida and Tlingit – all of whom lived largely off the sea and developed a culture in many ways more sophisticated than that of the more nomadic and hunting-oriented tribes of the interior (see box on p.336). European exploration from the late sixteenth to the

---

ACCOMMODATION PRICE CODES

All the accommodation prices in this book have been coded using the symbols below, corresponding to US dollar prices in the US chapters and equivalent Canadian dollar rates in the Canadian chapters. Prices are for the least expensive double room in high season, excluding special offers. For a full explanation see p.51 in Basics.

① up to Can$40	③ Can$60–80	⑤ Can$100–125	⑦ Can$175–240
② Can$40–60	④ Can$80–100	⑥ Can$125–175	⑧ Can$240+

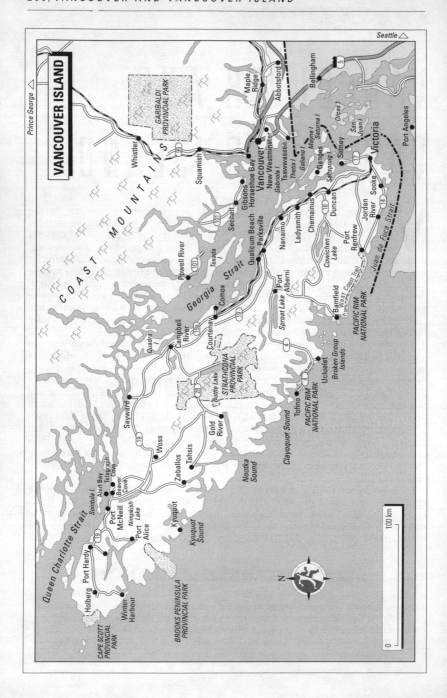

VANCOUVER ISLAND

Prince George △

Seattle △

GARIBALDI PROVINCIAL PARK

Whistler

Squamish

Maple Ridge

Abbotsford

Bellingham

COAST MOUNTAINS

Gibsons
Horseshoe Bay
Sechelt

Vancouver
New Westminster
Tsawwassen

Thetis I
Gabriola I
Galiano I
Mayne I
Saturna I
Orcas I
San Juan I

Victoria

Port Angeles

Powell River

Texada

Qualicum Beach
Parksville

Nanaimo
Ladysmith
Chemainus

Ganges
Saltspring I
Sidney
Duncan
Sooke

Jordan River

Georgia Strait

Comox

Port Alberni

Cowichan Lake
Port Renfrew

Juan de Fuca Strait

Campbell River
Courtenay

Quadra I

STRATHCONA PROVINCIAL PARK

Buttle Lake

Sproat Lake

Bamfield
West Coast Trail

PACIFIC RIM NATIONAL PARK

Sayward

Woss

Gold River

Tahsis

Zeballos

Ucluelet
Tofino

Broken Group Islands

PACIFIC RIM NATIONAL PARK

Clayoquot Sound

Nootka Sound

Sointula I
Alert Bay
Telegraph Cove
Beaver Cove
Port McNeill
Nimpkish Lake
Port Alice

Kyuquot

Kyuquot Sound

Queen Charlotte Strait

Port Hardy

Holberg

Winter Harbour

BROOKS PENINSULA PROVINCIAL PARK

CAPE SCOTT PROVINCIAL PARK

N

100 km

0

The telephone code for Vancouver and vicinity is 604. The telephone code for Victoria and Vancouver Island is 250.

eighteenth century culminated in the domination of the area by the **Hudson's Bay Company**, a monopoly that antagonized the Americans. The British were prompted to formalize their claim to the region, and the 49th Parallel was agreed as the national boundary, though Vancouver Island, which lies partly south of the line, remained wholly British and was officially designated a crown colony in 1849. The discovery of **gold** in the Fraser River and Cariboo regions in the mid-nineteenth century attracted large numbers of hopeful prospectors; their forward base on the mainland eventually became Vancouver.

VANCOUVER

Cradled between the ocean and snow-capped mountains, Vancouver's dazzling downtown district fills a narrow peninsula bounded by Burrard Inlet to the north, English Bay to the west and False Creek to the south, with greater Vancouver sprawling south to the Fraser River. Edged around its idyllic waterfront are fine beaches, a dynamic port and a magnificent swath of parkland, not to mention the mirror-fronted ranks of skyscrapers that look across Burrard Inlet and its bustling harbour to the residential districts of North and West Vancouver. Beyond these comfortable suburbs, the Coast Mountains rise in steep, forested slopes to form a dramatic counterpoint to the downtown skyline and the most stunning of the city's many outdoor playgrounds. Small wonder, given Vancouver's surroundings, that Greenpeace was founded in the city.

Vancouver's 1.9 million residents exploit their spectacular natural setting to the hilt, and when they tire of the immediate region can travel a short distance to the unimaginably vast wilderness of the BC interior. Whether it's sailing, swimming, fishing, hiking, skiing, golf or tennis, locals barely have to move to indulge in a plethora of **recreational** whims. Summer and winter the city oozes hedonism and healthy living – it comes as no surprise to find that you can lounge on beaches downtown – typically West Coast obsessions that spill over into its sophisticated **arts and culture**. Vancouver claims a world-class museum and symphony orchestra, as well as opera, theatre and dance companies at the cutting edge of contemporary arts. Festivals proliferate throughout its mild, if occasionally rain-soaked summer, and numerous music venues provide a hotbed for up-and-coming rock bands and a burgeoning jazz scene.

Vancouver is not all pleasure, however. Business growth continues apace in Canada's third largest city, much of its prosperity stemming from a **port** so laden with the raw materials of the Canadian interior – lumber, wheat and minerals – that it ranks as one of North America's largest ports, handling more dry tonnage than the West Coast ports of Seattle, Tacoma, Portland, San Francisco and San Diego put together. The port in turn owes its prominence to Vancouver's much-trumpeted position as a **gateway to the Far East**, and its increasingly pivotal role in the new global market of the Pacific Rim. This lucrative realignment is strengthened by a two-way flow in traffic: in the past decade Vancouver has been inundated with Hong Kong Chinese (the so-called "yacht people"), an influx which has pushed up property prices and slightly strained the city's reputation as an ethnically integrated metropolis.

Much of the city's earlier immigration focused on Vancouver's extraordinary **Chinatown**, just one of a number of ethnic enclaves – Italian, Greek, Indian and Japanese in particular – which lend the city a refreshingly gritty quality that belies its sleek, modern reputation. So too do the city's semi-derelict eastern districts, whose worldly lowlife characters, addicts and hustlers are shockingly at odds with the glitzy

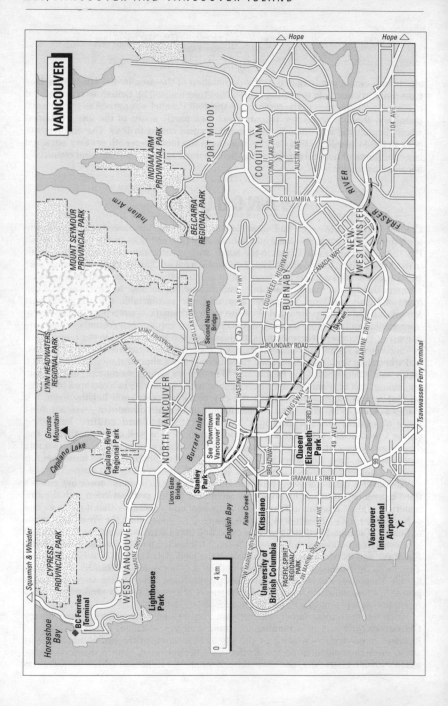

lifestyles pursued in the lush residential neighbourhoods. Low rents and Vancouver's cosmopolitan young have also nurtured an unexpected **counterculture**, at least for the time being, distinguished by varied restaurants, secondhand shops, avant-garde galleries, clubs and bars – spots where you'll probably have more fun than in many a Northwest city. And at the top of the scale there are restaurants as good – and as varied – as any in North America.

These days Vancouver is more **dynamic** than ever, its growth and energy almost palpable as you walk the streets. In just five years, between 1987 and 1992, the city's population increased by an extraordinary seventeen percent. The downtown population, currently just over half a million, is the fastest-growing on the continent. In response the downtown area is spreading – visibly – to the older and previously run-down districts to the southeast of the old city core. Development over the last decade is symbolized by a superb library and performing-arts complex which constitutes the most expensive capital project ever undertaken in the city. Real estate here is now more expensive than Toronto, and in the 1990s the city became North America's largest film and TV production centre after Los Angeles and New York; *The X Files* is just the most famous of the many movies and programmes that have been, or are being, made here (see p.325 for details of *X Files* tours). Yet, in the peculiar way that seems second nature to Canadians, the changes are being handled in a manner that's enhancing rather than compromising the city's beguiling combination of pleasure, culture, business and natural beauty.

A brief history of Vancouver

Vancouver in the modern sense has existed for a little over 110 years. Over the course of the previous nine thousand years the Fraser Valley was home to the Tsawwassen, Musqueam and another twenty or so native tribes, who made up the Stó:lo Nation, or "people of the river". The fish, particularly salmon, of this river were the Stó:lo lifeblood. Over the millennia these people ventured relatively little into the mountainous interior, something that remains true to this day. One of the things that makes modern Vancouver so remarkable is how wild and empty British Columbia remains beyond the Fraser's narrow corridor. The Stó:lo inhabited about ten villages on the shores of Vancouver's Burrard Inlet before the coming of the Europeans. A highly developed culture, the Stó:lo were skilled carpenters, canoe-makers and artists, though little in the present city – outside its museums – pays anything but lip service to their existence. Vancouver Island is the nearest best bet if you're in search of latter-day tokens of aboriginal culture.

Europeans appeared on the scene in notable numbers during the eighteenth century, when **Spanish** explorers charted the waters along what is now southwestern British Columbia. In 1778 **Captain James Cook** reached nearby Nootka Sound while searching for the Northwest Passage, sparking off immediate British interest in the area. In 1791 José Maria Narvaez, a Spanish pilot and surveyor, glimpsed the mouth of the Fraser from his ship, the *Santa Saturnia*. This led to wrangles between the British and Spanish, disputes quickly settled in Britain's favour when Spain became domestically embroiled in the aftermath of the French Revolution. **Captain George Vancouver** officially claimed the land for Britain in 1792, but studying the Fraser from a small boat decided that it seemed too shallow to be of practical use. Instead he rounded a headland to the north, sailing into a deep natural port – the future site of Vancouver – which he named Burrard after one of his companions. He then traded briefly with several Squamish tribespeople at X'ay'xi, a village on the inlet's forested headland – the future Stanley Park. Afterwards the Squamish named the spot Whul-whul-Lay-ton, or "place of the white man". Vancouver sailed on, having spent just a day in the region – scant homage to an area that was to be named after him a century later.

> The telephone code for Vancouver is ☎604.

Vancouver's error over the Fraser was uncovered in 1808, when Scottish-born Simon Fraser made an epic 1368-kilometre journey down the river from the Rockies to the sea. In 1827 the Hudson's Bay Company set up a fur-trading post at **Fort Langley**, 48km east of the present city, bartering not only furs but also salmon from the Stó:lo, the latter being salted and then packed off to company forts across Canada. The fort was kept free of homesteaders, despite being the area's first major white settlement, their presence deemed detrimental to the fur trade. Major colonization of the area only came after the Fraser River and Cariboo gold rushes in 1858, when **New Westminster** bustled with the arrival of as many as 25,000 hopefuls, many of whom were refugees from the 1849 Californian rush. Many also drifted in from the US, underlining the fragility of the national border and the precarious nature of British claims to the region. These claims were consolidated when British Columbia was declared a crown colony, with New Westminster as its capital. Both were superseded by Fort Victoria in 1868, by which time the gold rush had dwindled almost to nothing.

In 1862, meanwhile, three British prospectors, unable to find gold in the interior, bought a strip of land on the southern shore of Burrard Inlet and – shortsightedly, given the amount of lumber around – started a brickworks. This soon gave way to the Hastings Sawmill and a shantytown of bars which by 1867 had taken the name of **Gastown**, after "Gassy" – as in loquacious – Jack Leighton, proprietor of the site's first saloon. Two years later Gastown became incorporated as the town of **Granville** and prospered on the back of its timber and small coal deposits. The birth of the present city dates to 1884, when the **Canadian Pacific Railway** decided to make it the terminus of its transcontinental railway. In 1886, on a whim of the CPR president, Granville was renamed Vancouver, only to be destroyed on June 13 that year when fire razed all but half a dozen buildings. The setback proved short-lived, and since the arrival of the first train from Montréal in 1887 the city has never looked back.

Arrival and information

Vancouver Airport
Vancouver International Airport is situated on Sea Island, 13km south of the city centre. Its often-used coded abbreviation is YVR. International flights arrive at the majestic new main terminal; domestic flights at the smaller and linked old Main Terminal. If you're an international passenger, you'll find a **tourist information** desk as you exit customs and immigration and before entering the terminal's public spaces (daily 7am–midnight; ☎688-5515). On the right just before this, before you exit to the public spaces, is a desk where you can book taxis, limousines and also buy tickets or obtain information for the bus shuttles to downtown (see below) and direct bus services from the airport to Victoria, Whistler, Bellingham Airport (Seattle) and Sea-Tac Airport in the US. There are also plenty of **foreign exchange** and other facilities, along

---

DEPARTURE TAX

All passengers departing from Vancouver International Airport must pay an Airport Improvement Fee – $5 if travelling within BC, $10 within North America (including Mexico and Hawaii) and $15 outside North America. The tax is levied as you pass through to the gates and must be paid on the spot with cash or credit.

with free phone lines to several upmarket hotels, in the area. Domestic passengers also have a tourist information desk just before the terminal exit.

The best way to get into Vancouver is on the private **Airporter bus** (6.45am–1.10am; $10 single, $17 return; ☎946-8866 or 1-800/668-3141), which leaves from a bay to the left immediately outside the main door of the international arrivals; domestic arrivals can walk here if you need visitor information or wait at the domestic arrivals pick-up outside the terminal. You can buy **tickets** from the desk inside international arrivals, from the driver or from the stand set up by the bus stop at the international terminal departure point. Helpful staff and a pamphlet with a useful map help you figure out which drop-offs on the shuttle's three routes are most useful. Note that if you're headed straight for the bus depot (see below) on route #3 you need to transfer to another Airporter service closer to downtown: the driver will tell you all you need to know. Returning to the airport, buses run round the same pick-up points, including the bus depot.

Taxis into town cost about $25, limos around $32 plus tax. **Public transport** is cheaper, but slower and involves a change of bus – take the BC Metro Transit bus #100 to the corner of 70th Street and Granville (it leaves the domestic terminal roughly every 30min), then change to the #20 or #21 which drops off downtown on Granville Street. Tickets cost $2.50 rush hour, $1.75 off-peak, and exact change is required to buy tickets on board: make sure you get a transfer if the driver doesn't automatically give you one (see "City transport", p.293, for more on peak and off-peak times and transfers).

It's also useful to know that you can pick up direct **buses** to Victoria from the airport: ask for details at the bus desk in international arrivals, or go straight to the hotel shuttle bus stop outside the international terminal: Pacific Coach Lines (☎662-8074 or 1-800/661-1725, *www.pacificcoach.com*) run between one and three daily direct services from the airport to Victoria depending on the time of year (1 daily year-round; 2 daily mid-May to late June & early Sept to Oct; 3 daily late June to early Sept; $30.50).

Bus terminal

Vancouver's main **bus terminal**, which is used by Pacific Coach Lines (for Victoria, Vancouver Island), Maverick Coach Lines (Whistler, Sunshine Coast and Nanaimo) and all Greyhound services, is in a slightly dismal area alongside the VIA Rail Pacific Central train station at 1150 Station St; ticket offices for all companies are on the inside on the right as you enter. It's too far to walk to downtown from here, so bear left from the station through a small park, to the Science World–Main St SkyTrain station and it's a couple of stops to downtown (take the train marked "Waterfront"); tickets ($1.75) are available from platform machines. Alternatively, you could take a taxi downtown from the station for about $6–8. There are **left-luggage** facilities here and a useful **hotel board**, whose free phone line connects to some of the city's genuine cheapies (but check locations) – some of whom will deduct the taxi fare from the terminal from your first night's bill.

Trains

The skeletal **VIA Rail** services also operate out of Pacific Central Station (☎640-3741 or 1-800/561-8630, *www.viarail.ca*); they run to and from Jasper ($175), where there are connections for Prince George and Prince Rupert, and on to Edmonton and the east (3 weekly Mon, Thurs & Sat). There is also one daily VIA–Amtrak (☎253/931-8917 or 1-800/872-7245, *www.amtrakcascades.com*) service between Vancouver and Seattle (currently departs 6pm and arrives Seattle at 9.55pm).

A second train station, belonging to the provincial **BC Rail**, at 1311 W 1st St, in North Vancouver (☎984-5246 or 1-800/339-8752 in BC, 1-800/663-8238 from the rest of Canada and US, *www.bcrail.com*), provides passenger services to and from Whistler

ONWARDS FROM VANCOUVER

Vancouver is at the hub of transport links to many parts of the Pacific Northwest. Deciding where to move **onward from the city** – and how to go – presents a wealth of possibilities. We've listed the basic alternatives, together with cross-references to more detailed accounts of the various options.

Alaska and the Yukon You can fly to Whitehorse (see p.595) in the Yukon directly from Vancouver, but there are no non-stop flights to Alaska from the city: all go via Seattle in the US. You can fly to Seattle or take a bus to Sea-Tac Airport in around three hours from Vancouver Airport or various downtown hotels and other locations (see "Arrival and information" p.290 for bus details). You can **drive** to Alaska through southern British Columbia to Dawson Creek, where you can pick up the Alaska Hwy (see p.590) which runs through the Yukon to Fairbanks. Allow at least three days. Alternatively drive to Prince George, head west towards Prince Rupert and then strike north up the more adventurous Cassiar Hwy (see p.584) to connect with the Alaska Hwy in the Yukon. Using **public transport** you could take either a BC Rail train (see "Arrival and information") or Greyhound bus to Prince George (one day), connecting with another Greyhound to Dawson Creek and Whitehorse (two days). Alaskon Express buses link Whitehorse with Alaskan destinations.

To travel to Alaska by **boat** from Vancouver you need to go via Bellingham (in the US), Prince Rupert, or Port Hardy on Vancouver Island.

British Columbia Two main **road** routes strike east from Vancouver towards Alberta and the Canadian Rockies – the Trans-Canada Highway and Hwy 3, both served by regular Greyhound **buses**. Both give access to the Okanagan (see p.417), known for its warm-watered lakes and summer resorts, and to the beautiful mountain and lakes enclave of the Kootenays (see p.429). VIA **trains** run through the region via Kamloops to Jasper (for the Rockies) and Edmonton three times weekly. Buses and BC Rail trains also serve the **Cariboo** region, the duller central part of the province (see p.402). Several mouthwatering itineraries can be put together by combining car or public transport journeys in the BC interior with BC Ferries' connections from Port Hardy on Vancouver Island (see below) to either Bella Coola or Prince Rupert.

Calgary and the Canadian Rockies It takes between ten and twelve hours to drive to Calgary on the Trans-Canada Highway, and about ninety minutes less to reach the heart of the Canadian Rockies, Banff. Special express service Greyhound buses operate over the same route. There is no longer a VIA Rail passenger service to Calgary. Very frequent one-hour flights connect Vancouver and Calgary, and charter operators such as Canada 3000 offer highly competitive rates on this route.

Seattle Regular fifty-minute flights connect Vancouver with Seattle in the US. Greyhound or Quick Shuttle buses offer a less expensive alternative from Vancouver Airport or downtown locations.

Vancouver Island Numerous **ferries** ply between Vancouver and three points on its eponymous island – Swartz Bay (for Victoria), Nanaimo and Comox. Most leave from Tsawwassen and Horseshoe Bay, terminals about thirty-minutes' drive south and west of downtown respectively. As a foot passenger you can buy inclusive bus and ferry tickets from Vancouver to Victoria or Nanaimo. Car drivers should make reservations well in advance for all summer crossings (see pp.328–329 for full details of getting to Vancouver Island). **Public transport** connects to the Pacific Rim National Park, the island's highlight, and to Port Hardy on the island's northern tip for ferry connections to Prince Rupert and Bella Coola.

(1 daily; 2hr 35min), Lillooet (1 daily; 5hr 35min) and Prince George (3 weekly; 13hr 30min) via 100 Mile House, Williams Lake and Quesnel. Note that in the summer they also run very popular **excursion trips** to Squamish aboard the *Royal Hudson* steam train, sometimes combined with a sea cruise. For more on this, see p.390–404.

Information

The excellent **Vancouver visitor centre** is almost opposite Canada Place (see p.301) at the foot of Burrard Street in the Waterfront Centre, 200 Burrard St at the corner of Canada Place Way (daily June–Aug 8am–6pm; Sept–May Mon–Fri 8.30am–5pm, Sat 9am–5pm; ☎683-2000 or 1-800/663-6000 or 1-800/435-5622, *www .tourismvancouver.com*). It is called by different names depending what you read: the "Tourist InfoCentre" is the most common designation. Besides information on the city and much of southeastern British Columbia, the office provides **foreign exchange** facilities, BC TransLink (transit or public transport) tickets and information, and tickets to sports and entertainment events. It also has one of the most comprehensive **accommodation services** imaginable, backed up by bulging photo albums of hotel rooms and B&Bs: the booking service is free. Smaller kiosks open in the summer (July & Aug) in a variety of locations, usually including Stanley Park and close to the Vancouver Art Gallery on the corner of Georgia and Granville (daily 9.30am–5.30pm, Thurs & Fri till 9pm).

City transport

Vancouver's **public transport** system is an efficient, integrated network of bus, light-rail (SkyTrain), SeaBus and ferry services which are operated by TransLink, formerly – and occasionally still – known as BC Transit (daily 6.30am–11.30pm; ☎521-0400, *www.translink.bc.ca*).

Tickets are valid across the system for bus, SkyTrain and SeaBus. Generally they cost $1.75 for journeys in the large central Zone 1 and $2.50 or $3.50 for longer two- and three-zone journeys – though you're unlikely to go out of Zone 1. These regular fares apply Monday to Friday from start of service until 6.30pm. After 6.30pm and all day Saturday, Sunday and public holidays, a flat $1.75 fare applies across all three zones.

Tickets are valid for transfers throughout the system for ninety minutes from the time of issue; on buses you should ask for a transfer ticket if the driver doesn't automatically give you one. Otherwise, you can buy tickets individually (or in books of ten for $13.75) at station offices or machines, 7-Eleven, Safeway and London Drugs stores, or any other shop or news stand displaying a blue TransLink sticker (so-called "FareDealer" outlets). You must carry tickets with you as proof of payment. Probably the simplest and cheapest deal if you're going to be making three or more journeys in a day is to buy a **DayPass** ($7), valid all day across all three zones; Zone 1 monthly passes are $63. If you buy these over the counter at stores or elsewhere (not in machines) they're "Scratch & Ride" – you scratch out the day and month before travel. If you lose anything on the transit system go to the **lost property** office at the SkyTrain Stadium Station (Mon–Fri 8.30am–5pm; ☎682-7887 or 985-7777 for items left on West Van buses). If you don't want to use public transport, **car and bicycle rental** and **taxis** are easy to come by – see "Listings" on p.324 for details.

Buses

The useful *Transit Route Map & Guide* ($1.50) is available from the infocentre and FareDealer shops, while free **bus** timetables can be found at the infocentre, 7-Eleven stores and the central library. The free *Discover Vancouver on the Transit* pamphlet from the infocentre is also extremely useful, though there is talk of discontinuing production of this guide. You can buy tickets on the bus, but make sure you have the right change (they don't carry any) to shovel into the box by the driver; ask specially if you want a transfer ticket. If you have a pass or transfer, simply show the driver. Normal buses stop running around midnight, when a rather patchy "Night Owl" service comes into effect on major routes until about 4am. Note that blue **West Van** buses (☎985-7777) also oper-

BUS ROUTES

Some of the more important Vancouver **bus routes** are:

#1 Gastown–English Bay loop.

#3 and **#8** Gastown–Downtown–Marine Drive.

#4 and **#10** Granville Street–University of British Columbia–Museum of Anthropology.

#23, **#35**, **#123** and **#135** – Downtown (Pender and Burrard)–Stanley Park.

#50 Gastown–False Creek–Broadway.

#51 SeaBus Terminal–Downtown–Granville Island.

#19 Pender Street (Downtown)–Stanley Park (Stanley Park Loop).

#20 and **#17** Downtown–Marine Drive; transfer to #100 for the airport at Granville and 70th Street.

#236 Lonsdale Quay terminal (North Vancouver)–Capilano Suspension Bridge–Grouse Mountain.

Some **scenic routes** are worth travelling for their own sakes:

#250 Georgia Street (Downtown)–North Vancouver–West Vancouver–Horseshoe Bay.

#52 "Around the Park" service takes 30min through Stanley Park (April–Oct Sat, Sun & holidays only); board at Stanley Park Loop (connections from #23, #35 or #135) or Denman Street (connections from #1, #3 or #8).

#351 Howe Street–White Rock–Crescent Beach (1hr each way).

#210 Pender Street–Phibbs Exchange; change there for the #211 (mountain route) or #212 (ocean views) to Deep Cove.

ate (usually to North and West Vancouver destinations, including the BC Ferries terminal at Horseshoe Bay) in the city and BC Transit tickets are valid on these buses as well. The box above shows some of Vancouver's more useful routes.

SeaBuses

The **SeaBuses** ply between downtown and Lonsdale Quay in North Vancouver, and they're a ride definitely worth taking for its own sake: the views of the mountains across Burrard Inlet, the port and the downtown skyline are superb. The downtown terminal is Waterfront Station in the old Canadian Pacific station buildings at the foot of Granville Street. There is no ticket office, only a ticket machine, but you can get a ticket from the small newsagent immediately on your left as you face the long gallery that takes you to the boats. Two 400-seat catamarans make the thirteen-minute crossing every fifteen to thirty minutes (6.30am–12.30am). Arrival in North Vancouver is at Lonsdale Quay, where immediately to the left is a bus terminal for connections to Grouse Mountain and other North Vancouver destinations. Bicycles can be carried onboard.

Ferries

The city also has a variety of small **ferries** – glorified bathtubs – run over similar routes by two rival companies: Aquabus (☎689-5858) and False Creek Ferries (☎684-7781, *www.granvilleislandferries.bc.ca*). These provide a useful, very frequent and fun service. Aquabus run boats in a continuous circular shuttle from the foot of Hornby Street to the Fish Docks on the seawalk to Vanier Park and the museums, to Granville Island (both $2), and to the Yaletown dock by the road loop at the east foot of Davie Street ($3). False Creek Ferries also run to Granville Island ($2), and also to Vanier Park ($3 from Granville Island, $2 from the Aquatic Centre) just below the Maritime Museum – a good way of getting to the park and its museums. You buy **tickets** on board with both companies. Both companies also offer what amount to mini-cruises up

False Creek, with connections from Granville Island to Science World and the Plaza of Nations. You can pick up the Aquabus boat at the Arts Club Theatre on Granville Island, the foot of Hornby Street downtown or – with False Creek Ferries – below the Aquatic Centre at the foot of Thurlow and northern end of Burrard Bridge, on Granville Island or below the spit and small harbour near the Maritime Museum in Vanier Park.

SkyTrain

Vancouver's single light-rail line – **SkyTrain** – is a model of its type: driverless, completely computerized and magnetically propelled, half underground and half on raised track. It covers 22km (an extension is under construction) between the downtown Waterfront Station (housed in the CPR building with the SeaBus terminal) and the southeastern suburb of New Westminster. Only the first three or four stations – Waterfront, Burrard, Granville and Stadium – are of any practical use to the casual visitor, but the 39-minute trip along the twenty-station line is worth taking if only to see how the Canadians do these things – spotless interiors and Teutonic punctuality.

Accommodation

Vancouver has a surprisingly large number of **inexpensive hotels**, but some – mainly in the area east of downtown – are of a dinginess at odds with the city's highly polished image. Gastown, Chinatown and the area between them hold the cheaper places, often on top of a bar where live bands and late-night drinking will keep you awake till the small hours. These areas are not safe for women at night, and everyone needs to avoid the backstreets. If you really need to stick to the rock-bottom price bracket, you're better off in the hostels, *YWCA* or one of the invariably dodgy hotels north of the Granville Street Bridge, a tame but tacky red-light area. **Mid-range hotels** are still reasonable ($65–100), but Vancouver is a tourist city and things can get tight in summer – book ahead for the best and most popular places such as the *Sylvia* and *Kingston*. A lot of the nicer options (including the *Sylvia*) are in the West End, a quiet residential area bordering Vancouver's wonderful Stanley Park, only five- or ten-minutes' walk from downtown. Out of season, hotels in all categories offer reductions, and you can reckon on thirty percent discounts on the prices below. Remember, too, that the prices below are for doubles, though even the smartest hotels will introduce an extra bed into a double room at very little extra cost if there are three of you.

B&B accommodation can be booked through agencies, but most of them operate as a phone service only and require two-days' notice – it's better to try the infocentre's accommodation service first. Though seldom central or cheap – reckon on $75 plus for a double – B&Bs are likely to be relaxed and friendly, and if you choose well you can have beaches, gardens, barbecues and as little or as much privacy as you want. The following **B&B agencies** have accommodation throughout the city, in Victoria (see p.326), the Gulf Islands and beyond: A B & C B&B of Vancouver (☎298-8815, *www.vancouverbandb.bc.ca*); All B&B Reservations (☎683-3609, *gorse@interchg.ubc.ca*); Beachside B&B Registry (☎922-7773, *www.beach.bc.ca*); Canada-West Accommodations (☎990-6730, *www.b-b.com*); B&B Town and Country Reservation Service (☎731-5942, *www.tcbb.bc.ca*); and Old English B&B Registry (☎986-5069, *www.oldenglishbandb.bc.ca*).

Vancouver has two good Hostelling International **hostels**, plus a handful of other reasonable privately run hostels. Be warned, though, that there are a rash of dreadful "hotels", "hostels" and "rooming houses" (dirty, badly run and occasionally dangerous), particularly on Hastings Street a few blocks either side of Main Street: don't be tempted into these on any account.

In addition to the hostels, relatively low-price accommodation is available in summer at the **University of British Columbia**, though this is a long way from downtown, and most rooms go to convention visitors (☎822-1000, fax 822-1001, *www.conferences .ubc.ca*). Singles start at $25, with doubles costing a not terribly competitive $93. Vancouver is not a camper's city – the majority of the in-city **campgrounds** are for RVs only and will turn you away if you've only got a tent. We've listed the few places that won't.

Hotels

Barclay Hotel, 1348 Robson St between Jervis and Broughton sts (☎688-8850, fax 688-2534, *www.barclayhotel.com*). One of the city's better bargains, the *Barclay* is one of the nicer of several hotels at the north end of Robson St, with ninety rooms and a chintzy French rustic ambience. ⑤.

Buchan Hotel, 1906 Haro St between Chilco and Gilford sts (☎685-5354 or 1-800/668-6654, fax 685-5367, *www3.bc.sympatico.ca/buchan/*). Some smallish rooms, past their prime, but still a genuine bargain given the peaceful residential location, only a block from Stanley Park and English Bay Beach. ⑥.

Burrard Motor Inn, 1100 Burrard St near Helmcken St (☎681-2331 or 1-800/663-0366, fax 681-9753). A fairly central and pleasantly dated motel with standard fittings: some rooms look onto a charming garden courtyard, and some have kitchens. ⑤.

Canadian Pacific Hotel Vancouver, 900 W Georgia St at Burrard St (☎684-3131 or 1-800/441-1414, fax 662-1929, *www.cphotels.ca*). This traditional old hotel, given a multimillion-dollar face-lift in 1996, is the city's most famous and prestigious. It's the place to stay if money's no object and you want old-world style and downtown location. Whether you stay here or not, the ground floor *900 West* restaurant and bar is good, as are the various other restaurants, including *Griffins* on the same floor. Doubles among the 550 rooms range from $224 to $589, but low-season rates are available. ⑧.

Canadian Pacific Waterfront Central Hotel, 900 Canada Place Way (☎691-1991 or 1-800/441-1414, *www.cphotels.ca*). Another prestigious *Canadian Pacific* hotel, this time a fabulous multistorey affair on the dazzling downtown waterfront. ⑧.

Hotel Dakota, 654 Nelson St on the corner of Granville (☎605-4333 or 1-888/605-5333, fax 605-4334, *www.hoteldakota.com*). The location is not pleasant, but this is the exception to the rule among the grim hotels at the lower end of Granville St. There are a wide range of clean, cheap and renovated rooms at different prices in big, bright-looking building. Continental breakfast included. ⑤.

Days Inn Vancouver Downtown, 921 W Pender St at Burrard St (☎681-4335 or 1-877/681-4335, *www.daysinnvancouver.com*). A city institution, this old seventy-room, seven-storey block in the central financial district has more character than most and lots of original Art Deco touches. While it looks tatty from the outside, the interior was renovated in 1999 and the rooms are clean and comfortable; streetfront rooms are likely to be noisy. ⑥.

Dominion Hotel, 210 Abbott St at Water St (☎681-6666, fax 681-5855). A nice, newly decorated old hotel on the edge of Gastown let down by its thunderous live music: it's almost impossible to find a room where you're not kept awake, but at least try to ask for one of the newer rooms with private bathroom as far away as possible from the live bands that play in the bar downstairs. ③.

Granville Island Hotel, 1253 Johnson St (☎683-7373 or 1-800/663-1840, fax 683-3061, *www.granvilleislandhotel.com*). You're away from central downtown, but on the other hand you're in the heart of one of the city's trendiest and most enjoyable little enclaves. You pay a premium for this and for the spectacular waterfront setting. ⑦.

Holiday Inn Hotel & Suites Downtown, 1110 Howe St between Helmcken and Davie sts (☎684-2151 or 1-800/663-9151 in US and Canada, 1-800/HOLIDAY worldwide, fax 684-4736, *www.atlific.com*). Reasonably central, large and – unlike the dingier hotels nearby – you'll know what to expect, though at this price there's plenty of alternative choice around town. Lots of facilities, including sauna, pool and kids' activity centre, plus rooms with kitchenettes for self-catering. ⑦.

Kingston Hotel, 757 Richards St at Robson St (☎684-9024 or 1-888/713-3304, fax 684-9917, *www.vancouver-bc.com/kingstonhotel*). This popular bargain is handily sited for downtown and its clean and nicely-decorated interior affects the spirit of a "European-style" hotel. Rooms are available with or without private bathroom and there's a modest but free breakfast to start the day. Along with the *Sylvia*, it's by far the best hotel at its price in the city, so book well ahead. Long-stay terms available. ③/④.

Pacific Palisades, 1277 Robson St between Jervis and West Bute sts (☎688-0461 or 1-800/663-1815, fax 891-5130). Not quite up there in the luxury bracket with the *Canadian Pacific* hotels, but still one of the city's best top-price hotels. Many of the rooms have superb views of the sea and mountains, and guests have access to a pool and gym. ⑦.

Patricia Budget Inn Hotel, 403 E Hastings St near Gore St (☎255-4301, fax 254-7154, *www.budgetpathotel.bc.ca*). A well-known and widely advertised budget choice with 92 rooms, but far from downtown in the heart of Chinatown (too far to walk comfortably): an exciting or grim location, depending on your point of view, though some women have reported feeling distinctly unsafe in the area. Clean and renovated, it's the best of the many in this district. ③.

Riviera Hotel, 1431 Robson St between Nicola and Broughton sts (☎685-1301 or 1-888/699-5222, *www.vancouver-bc.com/RivieraHotel*). Reasonably priced central motels such as this place are rare; the one- and two-room suites have kitchenettes. ⑥.

Sandman Hotel Downtown, 180 W Georgia St at Beatty St (☎681-2211 or 1-800/726-3626, fax 681-8009, *www.sandman.ca*). Flagship of a mid-price chain with hotels all over western Canada and well placed at the eastern edge of downtown. Rooms are bland but fine and spacious as far as chain hotels go, which makes this first choice if you want something one up from the *Kingston*. ⑤.

Shato Inn Hotel at Stanley Park, 1825 Comox St between Gilford and Denman sts (☎681-8920). A small, quiet, family-run place two blocks from the park and the beach. Some of the rooms have balconies and/or kitchen units. ⑥.

Sunset Inn Travel Apartments, 1111 Burnaby between Davie and Thurlow sts (☎688-2474 or 1-800/786-1997, fax 669-3340, *www.sunsetinn.com*). One of the best West End "apartment" hotels and a good spot for a longer stay – spacious studio, double or triple rooms (all with kitchens and balconies) with on-site laundry and many nearby shops. Ten-min walk to downtown. ⑤.

Sylvia Hotel, 1154 Gilford St (☎681-9321, fax 682-3551, *www.sylviahotel.com*). A local landmark located in a "heritage" building, this is a popular place with a high reputation, making reservations essential. It's by the beach two blocks from Stanley Park, and its snug bar, quiet, old-world charm and sea views make it one of Vancouver's best. Rooms are available at different prices depending on size, view and facilities. ③–⑦.

West End Guest House, 1362 Haro St at Jervis St (☎681-2889, fax 688-8812, *www.westendguesthouse.com*). A wonderful small guesthouse with an old-time parlour and bright rooms, each with private bathroom; book well in advance. Full breakfast included. No smoking. ⑥.

Hostels

American Backpackers Hostel, 374 W Pender St between Richards and Homer sts (☎688-0112, fax 685-7989). This is one of the city's newest hostels, and also one of the cheapest. The location is good – just a block or so farther east than the Seymour St *Cambie* hostel (see below) – and various inducements are offered to patrons such as free beer on Saturdays, Internet access, showers, patio, pool table and free pick-ups in a customized '64 Volkswagen Beetle (airport shuttle costs $15). Dorm beds $10, singles $25, doubles $30. No curfew. ②.

Cambie International Hostel, 300 Cambie St at Cordova St (☎684-6466). Private hostel just off Gastown's main streets, so a much better and more central position than many of the other hostels. Beds are arranged in two- or four-bunk rooms and there are laundry and bike storage facilities. Downstairs are a bakery, café and bar, so aim for beds away from these if you want a relatively peaceful night's sleep. From $20 per person. No curfew. ②.

Cambie International Hostel, 515 Seymour at W Pender St (☎684-7757 or 1-888/395-5335, *www.cambiehotels.com*). The newer and more central of the *Cambie*'s stable of hostels (there is a third on Vancouver Island). Like the Gastown hostel (see above), the management has made an effort to ensure that rooms are pleasant, secure and well-kept, and provide laundry, storage and café facilities. From $20 per person. No curfew. ②.

C&N Backpackers Hotel, 927 Main St (☎682-2441 or 1-888/434-6060, *backpackers@sprint.ca*). Well-known backpackers' retreat that has been renamed – previously it was known as *Vincent's* – and renovated and is under new management (after reports that its cleanliness and organization had deteriorated). Seedy and inconvenient eastern edge of downtown location but convenient for SkyTrain station; buses #3 or #8 from downtown run along Main St; 150 beds, but you should still book or arrive early (office open 8am–midnight). Beds at $10, $20 and $25 for a bunk, single and double respectively. No curfew. ①.

Global Village Backpackers, 1018 Granville St at Nelson St (☎682-8226 or 1-888/844-7875, fax 682-8240, *www.globalbackpackers.com*). *Global Village* has followed up the success of a popular hostel in Toronto with a hostel in Vancouver, although their chosen location on Granville – while central and away from the worst of this street's tawdriness – is not the quietest in the city. The hostel has 250 beds in couples' and four-bed rooms, and among its facilities offers a free shuttle from the bus-train station, secure lockers, modern kitchen and common area, games rooms and Internet access. From $24 per person, private doubles from $50. No curfew. ②.

Vancouver Downtown Hostel (HI), 1114 Burnaby St at Thurlow St (☎684-4565 or 1-888/203-4302, fax 684-4540, *www.hihostels.bc.ca*). The newer and more central of the city's two official HI hostels is located in a former nunnery and health-care centre in the city's West End, with 223 beds in shared and private rooms (maximum of four per room). Facilities include Internet kiosk, safe location and storage lockers, kitchen, Internet kiosk, safe location and storage lockers. Open 24 hours with no curfew. A free shuttle (look for the blue HI logo) operates between the hostel, the *Jericho Beach* hostel (see below) and the Pacific Central railway and bus terminal; if there's no bus, call the hostel to find when the next one is due. Beds cost $19.95 for members ($23.95 for non-members), private doubles from $49.95. ①/②.

Vancouver Jericho Beach Hostel (HI), 1515 Discovery St (☎224-3208, fax 224-4852, *www.hihostels.bc.ca*). Canada's biggest youth hostel has a superb and safe position by Jericho Beach south of the city. The hostel fills up quickly, occasionally leading to a three-day limit in summer; open all day, with an excellent cafeteria. There are dorm beds and a few private rooms, with reductions for members and free bunks occasionally offered in return for a couple of hours' work. Facilities include kitchen, licensed café (April–Oct), bike rental and storage, storage lockers and Internet kiosk. Open 24 hours with no curfew, but a "quiet time" is encouraged between 11pm and 7am. To get here from the airport, take the #100 bus to Granville St and 70th Ave and transfer to the #8 Fraser bus; get off at Granville and 6th Ave and cross Granville using the underpass. Then take the #4 UBC bus to NW Marine Drive, turn right on NW Marine Drive and walk 350m downhill to Discovery St. From downtown, take the bus #4 from Granville St. ①.

YWCA Hotel/Residence, 733 Beatty St between Georgia and Robson sts (☎895-5830 or 1-800/663-1424, fax 681-2550). An excellent place purpose-built in 1995 in a great east-downtown location close to the central library. The nearest SkyTrain station is Stadium, a five-minute walk. Top-value rooms (especially for small groups) spread over eleven floors with a choice of private, shared or hall bathrooms. TVs in most rooms, plus sports and cooking facilities as well as a cheap cafeteria. Open to men, women and families. Singles ($55–109), doubles ($61, $77 or $99), triples ($96–130) four- ($140) or five-person ($145) rooms available; long-term rates offered in winter. No curfew. ④/⑤.

Camping

Burnaby Cariboo RV Park, 8765 Cariboo Place, Burnaby (☎420-1722, fax 420-4782, *www .bcrvpark.com*). This site has luxurious facilities (indoor pool, jacuzzi, laundry, free showers) and a separate tenting area away from the RVs. Take Gaglardi Way exit (#37) from Hwy 1, turn right at the traffic light, then immediately left. The next right is Cariboo Place. Free shuttle bus to various sights. Open year-round. $21–32.95.

Capilano RV Park, 295 Tomahawk, West Vancouver (☎987-4722, fax 987-2015, *www .capilanorvpark.com*). The most central site for trailers and tents, beneath the north foot of the Lion's Gate Bridge: exit on Capilano Rd S or the Hwy 99 exit off Lion's Gate Bridge. Reservations (with deposit) essential June through August. $20–35.

Mount Seymour Provincial Park, North Vancouver (☎986-2261). Lovely BC provincial park spot, with full facilities, but only a few tent sites alongside car parks 2 and 3. July–Sept. $18.50 per tent.

Richmond RV Park and Campground, Hollybridge and River Rd, Richmond (☎270-7878 or 1-800/755-4905, fax 244-9713). Best of the RV outfits, with the usual facilities; 14km from downtown – take Hwy 99 N to the Westminster Hwy exit (# 36) and follow signs. Also space for tents. April 1–Oct 30. $17–26.

The City

Vancouver is not a city which offers or requires lots of relentless sightseeing. Its breathtaking physical beauty makes it a place where often it's enough just to wander and

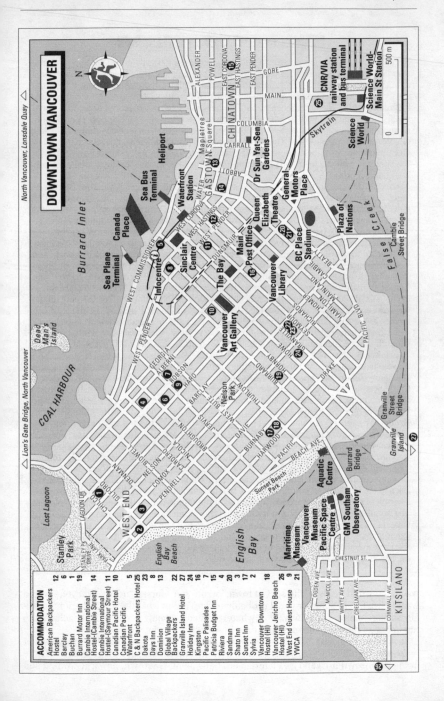

DOWNTOWN VANCOUVER

N

500 m

0

△ North Vancouver, Lonsdale Quay △

△ Lion's Gate Bridge, North Vancouver

Burrard Inlet

COAL HARBOUR

Dead Man's Island

Lost Lagoon

Stanley Park

STANLEY PK DRIVE
PARK LN
LAGOON DR
WEST END

English Bay Beach

English Bay

Sunset Beach Park

Sea Plane Terminal

Canada Place

Sea Bus Terminal

Waterfront Station

Heliport

Infocentre ⓘ

Sinclair Centre

The Bay

Vancouver Art Gallery

Queen Elizabeth Theatre

Post Office

Vancouver Library

General Motors Place

BC Place Stadium

Plaza of Nations

Dr Sun Yat-Sen Gardens

CHINATOWN

GASTOWN

Science World

Science World-Main St Station

CNR/VIA railway station and bus terminal

Skytrain

False Creek

Granville Island

Granville Street Bridge

Cambie Street Bridge

Burrard Bridge

Aquatic Centre

Maritime Museum

Vancouver Museum

Pacific Space Centre

GM Southam Observatory

KITSILANO

OGDEN AVE
McNICOLL AVE
WHYTE AVE
CREELMAN AVE
CORNWALL AVE
CHESTNUT ST

BEACH AVE
PACIFIC

WEST COMMISSIONER
WEST CORDOVA
WEST HASTINGS
WEST PENDER
DUNSMUIR
WEST GEORGIA
ROBSON
ALBERNI
HARO
BARCLAY
NELSON
COMOX
PENDRELL
DAVIE
BURNABY
HARWOOD

DENMAN
GILFORD
CHILCO
BIDWELL
CARDERO
NICOLA
BROUGHTON
JERVIS
BUTE
THURLOW
BURRARD
HORNBY
HOWE
GRANVILLE
SEYMOUR
RICHARDS
HOMER
HAMILTON
MAINLAND
CAMBIE
BEATTY
PACIFIC BLVD

WATER
ALEXANDER
POWELL
EAST CORDOVA
EAST HASTINGS
EAST PENDER
GORE
MAIN
COLUMBIA
CARRALL
ABBOTT
MAPLETREE
GASTOWN SQUARE

ACCOMMODATION

American Backpackers Hostel	12
Barclay	6
Buchan	1
Burrard Motor Inn	19
Cambie International Hostel–(Cambie Street)	14
Cambie International Hostel–(Seymour Street)	11
Canadian Pacific Hotel	10
Canadian Pacific Waterfront	5
C & N Backpackers Hotel	25
Dakota	23
Days Inn	8
Dominion	13
Global Village Backpackers	22
Granville Island Hotel	27
Holiday Inn	24
Kingston	16
Pacific Palisades	7
Patricia Budget Inn	15
Riviera	4
Sandman	20
Shato Inn	3
Sunset Inn	17
Sylvia	2
Vancouver Downtown Hostel (HI)	18
Vancouver Jericho Beach Hostel (HI)	26
West End Guest House	9
YWCA	21

VANCOUVER'S BEACHES

Vancouver, it's rather surprising to find, has **beaches**. Perhaps not of Malibu or Bondi standard, but beaches just the same, and ones that look and feel like the real thing, even if much of the sand comes from Japan in container ships. All are clean and well kept: the clarity of the water is remarkable given the size of the city's port – and the majority have lifeguards during the summer months. The best face each other across False Creek and English Bay, starting with Stanley Park's three adjacent beaches: **English Bay Beach**, ranged along Beach Avenue; **Second Beach**, to the north, which also features a shallow onshore swimming pool; and **Third Beach**, further north still, least crowded of the three and the one with the best views of West Vancouver and the mountains. English Bay at the southern end of Denman is the most readily accessible, and easily visited after seeing Stanley Park.

Across the water to the south and west of the Burrard Bridge, **Kitsilano Beach**, or "Kits", is named – like the district behind it – after Chief Khahtsahlano, a Squamish chieftain of a band who once owned the area. Walk here from Vanier Park and the museums (30min) on the coast path or, from downtown, take a #22 **bus** southbound on Burrard Street. Kits is a city favourite and the busiest and most self-conscious of the beaches. It's especially popular with the university, volleyball and rippling torso crowds, and the more well-heeled locals. Families also come here, though, to take advantage of the warm and safe swimming area, while sunbathers can take up a position on the grass to the rear. Vancouver's largest and most popular outdoor heated pool is the **lido** at Yew and Cornwall (daily mid-May to early Sept), while the **shoreline path** is a lovely place for an evening stroll, cycle or time out on a bench to watch the streetlife. Follow the path all the way east and it takes you to Granville Island by way of Vanier Park and the museums. A former hippie and alternative-lifestyle hangout, Kits still betrays shades of its past and, with nearby bars and restaurants to fuel the party spirit, there's always plenty going on (though there's also sometimes a vaguely meat-market sort of atmosphere).

Jericho Beach, west of Kits and handy for the youth hostel, is a touch quieter and serves as a hangout for the windsurfing crowd. Still further west, Jericho blurs into **Locarno Beach** and **Spanish Banks**, progressively less crowded, and the start of a fringe of sand and parkland that continues round to the University of British Columbia (UBC) campus. Locals rate Spanish Banks the most relaxed of the city's beaches, while Locarno is one of its most spectacular, especially at low tide, when the sand seems to stretch for ever. Bikers and walkers use the dirt track at the top of Locarno, beyond which a broad sward of grass with picnic tables and benches runs to the road. You can rent canoes at Jericho from Ecomarine Ocean Kayak, 1688 Duranleau St (☎689-7575).

At low tide the more athletically inclined could walk all the way round to UBC (otherwise take the bus as for the Museum of Anthropology; see p.309), where the famous clothing-optional **Wreck Beach** lies just off the campus area below NW Marine Drive – ask any student to point you towards the half-hidden access paths. It's inevitably aroused a fair bit of prudish criticism in the past, but at the moment attitudes seem more relaxed. The atmosphere is generally laid-back – though women have been known to complain of voyeurs – and nude peddlers are often on hand to sell you anything from pizza and illegal smokeables to (bona fide) massage and hair-braiding. Finally, **Ambleside**, west of the Park Royal Mall along Marine Drive (turn south at 13th St W), is the most accessible beach if you're in North or West Vancouver.

watch the world go by – "the sort of town," wrote Jan Morris, "nearly everyone would want to live in". In summer you'll probably end up doing what the locals do, if not actually sailing, hiking, skiing, fishing or whatever, then certainly going to the beach, lounging in one of the parks or spending time in waterfront cafés.

In addition to the myriad leisure activities, however, there are a handful of sights that make worthwhile viewing by any standards. You'll inevitably spend a good deal of time in the **downtown** area and its Victorian-era equivalent, **Gastown**, now a renovated and less than convincing pastiche of its past. **Chinatown**, too, could easily absorb a morning, and contains more than its share of interesting shops, restaurants and rumbustiously busy streets. For a taste of the city's sensual side, hit **Stanley Park**, a huge area of semi-wild parkland and beaches that crowns the northern tip of the downtown peninsula. Take a walk or a bike ride here and follow it up with a stroll to the **beach**. Be certain to spend a morning on **Granville Island**, by far the city's most tempting spot for wandering and people-watching. If you prefer a cultural slant on things, hit the formidable **Museum of Anthropology** or the museums of the Vanier Park complex, the latter easily accessible from Granville Island.

At a push, you could cram the city's essentials into a couple of days. If you're here for a longer stay, though, you'll want to venture further out from downtown: trips across Burrard Inlet to **North Vancouver**, worth making for the views from the SeaBus ferry alone, lend a different panoramic perspective of the city, and lead into the mountains and forests that give Vancouver its tremendous setting. The most popular trips here are to the Capilano Suspension Bridge, something of a triumph of PR over substance, and to the more worthwhile cable-car trip up **Grouse Mountain** for some staggering views of the city.

Downtown

You soon get the hang of Vancouver's **downtown** district, an arena of streets and shopping malls centred on **Robson Street**. On hot summer evenings it's like a latter-day vision of la dolce vita – a dynamic meeting place crammed with bars, restaurants, late-night stores, and bronzed youths preening in bars or cafés ostentatiously cruising in open-topped cars. At other times a more sedate class hangs out on the steps of the Vancouver Art Gallery or glides in and out of the two big department stores, Eaton's and The Bay. Downtown's other principal thoroughfares are **Burrard Street** – all smart shops, hotels and offices – and **Granville Street**, partly pedestrianized with plenty of shops and cinemas, but curiously seedy in places, especially at its southern end near the Granville Street Bridge. New development, however, is taking downtown's reach further east, and at some point in your stay you should try to catch the public library, opened in 1995, at 350 W Georgia, a focus of this growth and a striking piece of modern architecture to boot.

For the best possible introduction to Vancouver, though, you should walk down to the waterfront and **Canada Place**, the Canadian pavilion for Expo '86, the huge world exhibition held in the city in 1986, and another architectural *tour de force* that houses a luxury hotel, cruise-ship terminal and two glitzy convention centres. For all its excess, however, it makes a superb viewpoint, with stunning vistas of the port, mountains, sea and buzzing boats, helicopters and float planes. The port activity, especially, is mesmerizing. One of North America's busiest **ports** began by exporting timber in 1864 in the shape of fence pickets to Australia. Today it handles seventy million tonnes of cargo annually, turns over $40 billion in trade and processes 3000 ships a year from almost a hundred countries. Canada Place's design, and the manner in which it juts into the port, is meant to suggest a ship, and you can walk the building's perimeter as if "on deck", stopping to read the boards that describe the immediate cityscape and the appropriate pages of its history. Inside are expensive shops, an unexceptional restaurant and an IMAX cinema ($9.50; ☎682-4629, *www.imax.com/vancouver*); unfortunately, most of the films shown – often on boats, rock concerts and obscure wildlife – are a waste of a good screen.

An alternative to Canada Place's vantage point, the nearby **Harbour Centre Building** at 555 W Hastings, is one of the city's tallest structures, and is known by locals either as the "urinal" or, more affectionately, the "hamburger", after its bulging upper storeys. On a fine day it's definitely worth paying to ride the stomach-churning, all-glass, SkyLift elevators that run up the side of the tower – 167m in a minute – to the fortieth-storey observation deck, known as "The Lookout!", with its staggering 360-degree views (daily: May–Sept 8.30am–10.30pm; Oct–April 9am–9pm; $9; ☎299-9000 ext 2626, *www.harbourcentretower.com*). Admission is valid all day so you can return and look out over the bright lights of Vancouver at night.

Much of the **Expo site** here and at other points to the south and east has been levelled or is undergoing rigorous redevelopment, and to see its remaining sights requires a long walk from central downtown (take the SkyTrain or ferries from Granville Island instead). The geodesic dome is the main survivor, and has become a striking city landmark – but the museum it now houses, **Science World** at Québec St–Terminal Avenue near Science World–Main St SkyTrain station – is something of a disappointment (Mon–Fri 10am–5pm, Sat & Sun 10am–6pm; Science World $11.75, OMNIMAX $10; combination tickets $14.75; ☎268-6363 or 443-7440, *www.scienceworld.bc.ca*). Probably only children, at whom the place seems largely aimed, will be satisfied by the various high-tech, hands-on displays, which include the opportunity to make thunderous amounts of noise on electronic instruments and drum machines. Galleries deal with all manner of science-related themes, but probably the best things here if you're an adult is the building itself and the vast screen of the OMINMAX Cinema at the top of the dome – though as with the similar screen at Canada Place, only a limited range of quality movies have been produced to suit the format.

Another remnant of the Expo is the 60,000-seat **BC Place Stadium**, 1 Robson St (tours mid-June to early Sept every Tues & Fri at 11am and 1pm; $5; ☎661-7362, *www.bcplacestadium.com*), the world's largest air-inflated dome; unless you're there for a sporting event such as a BC Lions Canadian football game, the "mushroom" or "marshmallow in bondage", in popular parlance, isn't worth the bother. If you're heading to a game, take the SkyTrain to Stadium station or buses #15 east on Robson or #17 on Burrard. Its thunder has also been slightly stolen by **General Motors Place**, a more recent 20,000-seat stadium (known locally as "The Garage") that's home to the Vancouver Canucks ice-hockey team and Vancouver Grizzlies NBA basketball team. For tickets and details of events call Ticketmaster (☎280-3311).

The Vancouver Art Gallery

Centrally located in the imposing old city courthouse is the rather exorbitant **Vancouver Art Gallery**, located at the corner of Howe and Robson streets (late April to mid-Oct Mon–Wed & Fri–Sun 10am–5.30pm, Thurs 10am–9pm; mid-Oct to late April same hours but closed Mon; $10; ☎662-4700, *www.vanartgallery.bc.ca*). It looks as if it ought to contain a treasure trove of art, but too much space is given to dud works of the sort that give modern art a bad name. What redeems the place are its temporary exhibitions and the powerful and almost surreal works of Emily Carr, who was born on Vancouver Island in 1871 and whose paintings – characterized by deep greens and blues – evoke something of the scale and intensity of the West Coast and its native peoples. A sparse international collection offers Warhol and Lichtenstein, with token rooms of half a dozen Italian, Flemish and British paintings. The **gallery café** is excellent, with a sun-trap of a terrace if you want to sit outside.

Gastown

An easy walk east of downtown – five minutes from Canada Place and concentrated largely on Water Street – **Gastown** is a determined piece of city rejuvenation aimed fair and square at the tourist, distinguished by new cobbles, fake gas lamps, *Ye Olde English Tea Room*-type cafés and a generally overpolished patina. The name derives from "Gassy" Jack Leighton, a retired sailor turned publican and self-proclaimed "mayor", who arrived on site by canoe with his native wife and a mangy yellow dog in 1867, quickly opening a bar to service the nearby lumber mills, whose bosses banned drinking on or near the yards. Leighton's statue stands in **Maple Tree Square**, Gastown's heart, focus of its main streets and reputed site of this first tavern. Trade was brisk, and a second bar opened, soon followed by a village of sorts – "Gassy's Town" – which, though swept away by fire in 1886, formed in effect the birthplace of modern Vancouver. Over the years, the downtown focus moved west and something of Gastown's boozy beginnings returned to haunt it, as its cheap hotels and warehouses turned into a skid row for junkies and alcoholics. By the 1970s the area was declared a historic site – the buildings are the city's oldest – and an enthusiastic beautification programme was set in motion.

The end product never quite became the dynamic, city-integrated spot the planners had hoped, and was slated for years by locals as something of a tourist trap, though recent signs suggest that interesting cafés, clubs and restaurants are slowly beginning to make themselves felt. It's certainly worth a stroll for its buskers, Sunday crowds and occasional points of interest. These do not include the hype-laden two-tonne **steam-powered clock**, the world's first and hopefully last, at the west end of Water Street. It's invariably surrounded by tourists armed with cocked cameras, all awaiting the miniature Big Ben's toots and whistles every fifteen minutes, and bellowing performances on the hour that seem to presage imminent explosion. The steam comes from an underground system that also heats surrounding buildings. Nearby you'll find the **Inuit Gallery**, a large commercial showcase of Inuit art at 345 Water St (Mon–Sat 9.30am–5.30pm).

Probably the most surprising aspect of Gastown, however, is the contrast between its manicured pavements and the down-at-heel streets immediately to the south and east. The bustling hub of **alternative Vancouver**, the area between Gastown and Chinatown is both a skid row and a haven for secondhand clothes shops, bookshops, galleries, new designers and cheap five-and-dimes. In places, however, this area recalls Gastown's bad old days: unpleasantly seedy, pocked with the dingiest of dingy bars and hotels, and inhabited by characters to match.

Chinatown

Vancouver's vibrant **Chinatown** – clustered mainly on Pender Street from Carrall to Gore and on Keefer Street from Main to Gore (buses #22 or #19 east from Pender, or #22 north from Burrard) – is a city apart. Vancouver's 100,000 or more Chinese make up one of North America's largest Chinatowns and are the city's oldest and largest ethnic group after the British-descended majority. Many crossed the Pacific in 1858 to join the Fraser Valley gold rush; others followed under contract to help build the Canadian Pacific Railway. Most stayed, only to find themselves being treated appallingly. Denied citizenship and legal rights until as late as 1947, the Chinese community sought safety and familiarity in a ghetto of their own, where clan associations and societies provided for new arrivals and the local poor – and helped build the distinctive houses of recessed balconies and ornamental roofs that have made the area a protected historic site.

Unlike Gastown's gimmickry, Chinatown is all genuine – shops, hotels, markets, tiny restaurants and dim alleys vie for attention amidst an incessant hustle of jammed pavements and the buzz of Chinese conversation. Virtually every building replicates an Eastern model without a trace of self-consciousness, and written Chinese characters feature everywhere in preference to English. Striking and unexpected after downtown's high-rise glitz, the district brings you face to face with Vancouver's oft-touted multiculturalism, and helps explain why Hong Kong immigrants continue to be attracted to the city. It is, however, a district with a distinct edge, and visitors should avoid the area's dingier streets at night and parts of E Hastings near Main Street just about any time.

Apart from the obvious culinary temptations (see "Eating and drinking", beginning on p.314), Chinatown's main points of reference are its **markets**. Some of the best boast fearsome butchery displays and such edibles as live eels, flattened ducks, hundred-year-old eggs and other stuff you'll be happy not to identify. Check out the open-air **night market** at Main and Keefer streets (summer 6pm–midnight), a wonderful medley of sights. Keefer Street is **bakery** row, with lots of tempting stickies on offer like moon cakes and *bao*, steamed buns with a meat or sweet bean filling. On the corner of Keefer and Main is the Ten Ren Tea and Ginseng Company, with a vast range of teas, many promising cures for a variety of ailments (free tastings). In a similar vein, it's worth dropping into one of the local **herbalists** to browse amongst their panaceas: snakeskins, reindeer antlers, buffalo tongues, dried sea horses and bears' testicles are all available if you're feeling under the weather. Ming Wo, 23 E Pender, is a fantastic cookware shop, with probably every utensil ever devised, while China West, 41 E Pender, is packed with slippers, jackets, pens, cheap toys and the like. Most people also flock dutifully to the 1913 **Sam Kee Building**, at the corner of Carrall and Pender; at just 1.8m across, it's officially the world's narrowest building.

Chinatown's chief cultural attraction is the small **Dr Sun Yat-Sen Garden**, at 578 Carrall St near Pender Street, a 2.5-acre park billed as the first authentic, full-scale classical Chinese garden ever built outside China (May to mid-June 10am–6pm; mid-June to Aug 9.30am–7pm; Sept–April 10am–4.30pm; $6.50, includes free optional tours; ☎689-7133). Named after the founder of the first Chinese Republic, who was a frequent visitor to Vancouver, the park was created for the Expo '86 and cost $5.3 million, $500,000 of which came from the People's Republic accompanied by 52 artisans and 950 crates of materials. The latter included everything from limestone rocks from Taihu – whose jagged shapes are prized in this sort of garden – to the countless tiny pebbles that make up the intricate courtyard pavements. The whole thing is based on classical gardens developed in the city of Suzhou during the Ming dynasty (1368–1644). China's horticultural emissaries, following traditional methods that didn't allow use of a single power tool, spent thirteen months in the city replicating a Suzhou Ming garden to achieve a subtle balance of Yin and Yang: small and large, soft and hard, flowing and immovable, light and dark. Every stone, pine and flower was carefully placed and has symbolic meaning. Hourly free guided tours on the half-hour explain the Taoist philosophy behind the carefully placed elements. At first glance it all seems a touch small and austere, and isn't helped by the preponderance of sponsors' nameplates and glimpses of the road, pub and high-rise outside. After a time, though, the chances are you'll find the garden working its calm and peaceful spell.

Alongside the entrance to the gardens, the **Chinese Cultural Centre Museum & Archives** (Tues–Sun 11am–5pm; $3; ☎687-0282), Chinatown's community focus and a sponsor of New Year festivities, offers classes and hosts changing exhibitions. It also has a museum – the first of its kind dedicated to Chinese-Canadian history – which focuses on early Chinese pioneers and Chinese veterans who served Canada in the two world wars. Next to the gardens and centre is a small and slightly threadbare Dr Sun Yat-Sen Park (free) which, though less worked than the Dr Sun Yat-Sen Garden, is still a pleasant place to take time out from Chinatown. Hours are the same as for the garden, and there's an alternative entrance on Columbia Street and Keefer.

Stanley Park

One of the world's great urban spaces, **Stanley Park** is Vancouver's green heart, helping lend the city its particular character. At nearly 1000 acres, it's the largest urban park in North America – less a tame collection of lawns and elms than a semi-wilderness of dense rainforest, marshland and beaches. Ocean surrounds it on three sides, with a road and parallel cycleway/pedestrian promenade following the sea wall all the way round the peninsula for a total of 10.5km. From here, views of the city and across the water to the mountains are particularly worthwhile. Away from the coastal trail network and main draw – the aquarium – the interior is nearly impenetrable scrub and forest, with few paths and few people. At the same time there are plenty of open, wooded or flower-decorated spaces to picnic, snooze or watch the world go by.

The peninsula was partially logged in the 1860s, when Vancouver was still a twinkle in "Gassy" Jack Leighton's eye, but in 1886 the newly formed city council – showing typical Canadian foresight and an admirable sense of priorities – moved to make what had become a military reserve into a permanent park. Thus its remaining first-growth forest of cedar, hemlock and Douglas fir, and the swamp now known as Lost Lagoon, were saved for posterity in the name of Lord Stanley, Canada's governor general from 1888 to 1893, who dedicated the park "to the use and enjoyment of people of all colours, creeds and customs for all time".

A neat **itinerary** would be to walk or take the bus to the park, stroll or cycle all or part of the sea wall – there's a slew of bike and rollerblade rental places nearby – and then walk back to Denman Street. Here you can grab some food or pause at one of several cafés – the *Bread Garden* midway down Denman on the left at 1040 Denman and Comox is good – and then sit on the grass or sand at English Bay Beach at the foot of the street. The park is a simple though rather dull **walk** from most of downtown, if a fairly lengthy one from the eastern districts. Beach Avenue to the south and Georgia to the north are the best approaches if you're on foot, leading to the southern and northern starts of the sea wall respectively. Walking all the way round the sea-wall path takes about two hours at a brisk lick. Perhaps a better approach is to take a Stanley Park **bus** #23, #35 or #135 from the corner of Burrard and Pender streets downtown, which drop you near the so-called Stanley Park Loop just inside the park by Lost Lagoon and in summer continue deeper into the park to the Upper Zoo Loop (though the zoo's now closed). Other buses which will take you close to the park are the #1 (Beach) to Davie and Beach Avenue and the #3 (Robson) to Denman Street.

If you want to rent a bike, go to the corner of Denman and Georgia streets, where there's a cluster of **bike rental** outlets. Spokes, 1798 W Georgia (☎688-5141), is a big, busy place established in 1938 (from $3.90 an hour for a wide variety of bikes, including children's bikes and tandems with child trailers). You need to leave ID, and a cash or credit card deposit. Helmets, which are compulsory in BC, and locks are included in the rental. If this place looks too frenetic you might be better advised to walk a few metres up the street, where Bikes 'n' Blades (☎602-9899) is smaller, less busy and rents **rollerblades** as well. Directly opposite at 745 Denman St is Bayshore Bicycle & Rollerblade Rentals (☎688-2453). From Denman it's just a minute's pedalling to the park, but watch the traffic.

If you don't want to walk, cycle or blade, then there's a special TransLink "Stanley Park Shuttle" **bus service**, which runs on a fifteen-minute schedule in summer (daily June–Aug 10am–6.30pm; information ☎257-8400). It makes fourteen stops around the park. You can transfer to the service from the #1 and #3 buses on Denman or the #23, #35 and #135 at Stanley Park Loop: both Denman and the Loop are a few moments' walk from the shuttle's stops at Stanley Park Entrance, Pipeline Road or the Rowing Club. A $2 day-pass for the shuttle (not other TransLink services) is available on board the bus if you want to hop on and off. If you're just using it to see the park, remember you won't need an extra ticket if you've taken a transfer from the driver and make the onward journey round the park within ninety minutes (see "City transport" on p.293). Driving a **car** here is foolish, especially at weekends, when parking is just about impossible.

Taking time in the park, however you do it, especially on a busy Sunday, gives a good taste of what it means to live in Vancouver. The first thing you see is the **Lost Lagoon**, a fair-sized lake that started life as a tidal inlet, and got its name because its water all but disappeared at low tide. Dozens of waterfowl species inhabit its shoreline. Just east are the pretty Rose Garden and Vancouver Rowing Club, before which stands a statue of Scottish poet Robbie Burns. From here you can follow the sea wall path all the way, or make a more modest loop past the **totem poles** and round Brockton Point.

Moving around the sea wall anticlockwise, odd little sights dot the promenade, all signed and explained, the most famous being the *Girl in a Wetsuit* statue, a rather lascivious update of Copenhagen's *Little Mermaid*. If you want a more focused walk, the **Cathedral Trail**, northwest of the Lost Lagoon, takes you past some big first-growth cedars. **Beaver Lake**, carpeted green with water lilies, is a peaceful spot for a sleep or a stroll. **Lumberman's Arch**, near the aquarium (see below) was raised in 1952 to honour those in the lumber industry, an odd memorial given that the industry in question would probably give its eyeteeth to fell the trees in Stanley Park. Its meadow surroundings are a favourite for families and those looking for a good napping spot. **Prospect Point**, on the park's northern tip, is a busy spot but worth braving for its beautiful view of the city and the mountains rising behind West Vancouver across the water. There's a café-restaurant here, popular for its outdoor deck and sweeping views. West of here lies **Siwash Rock**, an outcrop which has defied the weather for centuries, attracting numerous native legends in the process, and which is distinguished by its solitary tree (not visible from the road, but quickly reached by path). Further around the wall there are various places to eat and drink, the best being the *Teahouse Restaurant* at Ferguson Point, about a kilometre beyond Siwash Rock.

Though people do swim in the sea at beaches around the park's western fringes, most bathers prefer the **swimming pool** next to Second Beach (see box on p.300). Facilities of all sorts – cafés, playgrounds, golf, outdoor dancing – proliferate near the downtown margins. Guided **nature walks** are also occasionally offered around the park; ask at the infocentre for details.

Vancouver Aquarium Marine Science Centre

Stanley Park zoo and its all too obviously distressed animals has now thankfully closed, leaving the **Vancouver Aquarium Marine Science Centre** as the park's most popular destination (daily: July to early Sept 9.30am–7pm; early Sept to June 10am–5.30pm; $13.95; ☎659-3474, *www.vanaqua.org*). At its entrance stands a vast killer whale in bronze, the work of celebrated Haida artist Bill Reid, whose famous *Raven and the Beast* sculpture forms the centrepiece of the Museum of Anthropology (see p.309). The aquarium is ranked among North America's best, and with over a million visitors a year claims to be the most visited sight in Canada west of Toronto's CN Tower. It contains over 8000 living exhibits representing some 600 different species, though in truth this is a relatively modest summation of the eighty percent of the world's creatures that live in water. Like the zoo before it, the complex has been targeted by animal rights campaigners for its treatment of performing beluga and killer whales, not to mention cooped-up seals and otters. Given the aquarium's reputation as a tourist attraction, however, as well as its claims as a research centre, the campaigners have a long, uphill battle. The whales in particular are huge draws, but you can't help but feel they should really be in the sea, for all the hoopla surrounding their $14-million marine mammal area.

The aquarium has several key areas to see. The **Arctic Canada** section concerns itself with the surprisingly fragile world of the Canadian north, with a chance to see whales face to face through glass and hear the sounds of whales, walruses, seals and other creatures in this icy domain. The **Amazon Gallery** displays the vegetation, fishes, iguanas, sloths and other creatures of the rainforest in a climate-controlled environment, while the **Pacific Northwest Habitat** performs a similar role for otters, beavers and other creatures of the waters of BC. The **BC Waters Gallery** and **Ducks Unlimited Wetlands** displays are fairly self-explanatory.

Granville Island

Granville Island, huddled under the Granville Street Bridge south of downtown, is the city's most enticing "people's place" – the title it likes for itself – and pretty much lives up to its claim to be the "heart of Vancouver". Friendly, easy-going and popular, its shops, markets, galleries, marina and open spaces are juxtaposed with a light-industrial setting whose faint whiff of warehouse squalor saves the area from accusations of pretentiousness. The island was reclaimed from swampland in 1917 as an ironworks and shipbuilding centre, but by the 1960s the yards were derelict and the place had become a rat-infested dumping ground for the city's rubbish. In 1972 the federal government agreed to bankroll a programme of residential, commercial and industrial redevelopment that retained the old false-fronted buildings, tin-shack homes, sea wall and rail sidings. The best part of the job had been finished by 1979 – and was immediately successful – but work continues unobtrusively today, the various building projects only adding to the area's sense of change and dynamism. Most people come here during the day, but there are some good restaurants, bars and the Arts Club Theatre, which are all enough to keep the place buzzing at night.

The most direct approach is to take **bus** #50 from Gastown or Granville Street. The walk down Granville Street and across the bridge is deceptively long, not terribly salubrious, and so probably only worthwhile on a fine day when you need the exercise. Alternatively and more fun, private **ferries** ($2, pay on board) ply back and forth almost continuously between the island and little quays at the foot of Hornby Street or the Aquatic Centre at the foot of Thurlow Street (see "Ferries" on p.294). They also connect from Granville Island to Science World (hourly) and, more significantly, to Vanier Park (half-hourly), a much nicer way than bus to get to the park's Vancouver Museum, Maritime Museum and Space Centre (see overleaf). A logical and satisfying day's **itinerary** from downtown, therefore, would take you to Granville Island, to the museums and back by ferry. You might also choose to **walk** from the Island along the False Creek sea wall (east) or west to Vanier Park (see overleaf) and Kits Beach.

There's a good **infocentre** at the heart of the Island for Island-related information only (☎666-5784), with a **foreign exchange** facility in the same building and ATM machines on the wall outside. Stamps are available from the LottoCentre inside the Public Market Building. Note that many of the Island's shops and businesses close on Mondays, and that if you want a **bus back** to downtown you should *not* take the #51 from the stop opposite the infocentre (it will take you in the wrong direction): walk out of the Island complex's only road entrance, and at the junction the #50 stop is immediately on your right.

Virtually the first building you see on the Island walking from the bus stop augurs well: the **Granville Island Brewery**, 1441 Cartwright St (tours only June–Sept Mon–Fri on the hour noon–5pm, Sat & Sun on the half-hour 11.30am–5pm; $7; ☎687-2739), a small but interesting concern which offers guided tours that include tastings of its additive-free beers. Dominant amongst the maze of shops, galleries and businesses, the **Granville Island Public Market** (daily 9am–6pm; closed Mon in winter) is the undisputed highlight of the area. On summer weekends it's where people go to see and be seen and it throngs with arts-and-crafts types, and a phalanx of dreadful, but harmless buskers. The quality and variety of **food** is staggering, with dozens of kiosks and cafés selling readymade titbits and potential picnic ingredients. Parks, patios and walkways nearby provide lively areas to eat and take everything in. Other spots to look out for include Blackberry Books, the Water Park and Kids Only Market (a kids-only playground with hoses to repel intruders) and the bright-yellow *Bridges* pub/restaurant/wine bar, which has a nice outdoor drinking and eating area. You can also rent **canoes** for safe and straightforward paddling in False Creek and English Bay from Ecomarine Ocean Kayak on the island at 1688 Duranleau St (☎689-7575; from $25 for two hours).

The island also has a trio of small linked **museums** almost opposite the brewery at 1502 Duranleau St (all daily 10am–5.30pm; $6.50; ☎683-1939, *www.modeltrainsmuseum.bc.ca*): these are the self-explanatory Granville Island Model Trains Museum, Model Ships Museum and Sport Fishing museum. These will probably appeal only to children and to model or fishing enthusiasts. The Model Trains Museum claims to contain the largest collection of toy trains in the world on public display.

Vanier Park museum complex

A little to the west of Granville Island, **Vanier Park** conveniently collects most of the city's main museums: the **Vancouver Museum**, the **Maritime Museum** and the **H.R. MacMillan Space Centre** (the last combines the old planetarium and observatory). The complex sits on the waterfront at the west end of the Burrard Bridge, near Kitsilano Beach and the residential-entertainment centres of Kitsilano and W 4th Avenue, and Vanier Park itself is a fine spot to while away a summer afternoon. You could easily incorporate a visit to the museums with a trip to Granville Island using the **ferry** (see overleaf), which docks just below the Maritime Museum. Coming from downtown, take the #22 Macdonald **bus** south from anywhere on Burrard or W Pender – get off at the first stop after the bridge and walk down Chester Street to the park. The park's pleasant but open – there's little shade – and has a few nice patches of sandy beach on its fringes if you don't want to trek all the way to Kits and Jericho beaches (see p.657).

The Vancouver Museum

The **Vancouver Museum**, 1100 Chestnut St (Mon–Wed & Fri–Sun 10am–5pm, Thurs 10am–9pm; $8; ☎736-4431, *www.vancouvermuseum.bc.ca*), traces the history of the city and the lower British Columbian mainland, and invokes the area's past in its very form – the flying-saucer shape is a nod to the conical cedar-bark hats of the Northwest Coast natives, former inhabitants of the area. The fountain outside, looking like a crab on a bidet, recalls the animal of native legend that guards the port entrance.

Though it's the main focus of interest at Vanier Park, the museum is not as captivating as you'd expect from a city like Vancouver. It claims 300,000 exhibits, but it's hard to know where they all are, and a visit needn't take more than an hour or so. A patchy collection of baskets, tools, clothes and miscellaneous artefacts of aboriginal peoples – including a huge whaling canoe, the only example in a museum – homes in on the 8000 years before the coming of white settlers. After that, the main collection, weaving in and out of Vancouver's history up to World War I, is full of offbeat and occasionally memorable insights if you have the patience to read the material – notably the accounts of early explorers' often extraordinary exploits, the immigration section (which re-creates what it felt like to travel steerage) and the forestry displays. The twentieth-century section is disappointing, most of the time looking more like an antique shop than a museum.

The H.R. MacMillan Space Centre

The **H.R. MacMillan Space Centre** (July–Aug daily 10am–5pm; Sept–June Tues–Sun 10am–5pm; evening laser shows at varying times Thurs–Sun; $12.50; ☎738-7827, *www.hrmacmillanspacecentre.com*) incorporates the MacMillan Planetarium and a range of space-related displays and shows. Its main draws are its star shows and its rock and laser extravaganzas, the latter for fans of the genre only. The **Gordon Southam Observatory**, nearby, is usually open for public stargazing on clear weekend nights; astronomers are on hand to show you the ropes and help you position your camera for a "Shoot the Moon" photography session of the heavens (call Space Centre for times; free).

The Maritime Museum

The **Maritime Museum**, 1905 Ogden Ave (May–Sept daily 10am–5pm; Oct–April Tues–Sat 10am–5pm, Sun noon–5pm; $7; ☎257-8300), is a short 150-metre walk from the Vancouver Museum and features lovely early photographs evoking c.1900 Vancouver, though the rest of the presentation doesn't quite do justice to the status of the city as one of the world's leading ports. The less arresting displays, however, are redeemed by the renovated *St Roch*, a two-masted schooner that was the first vessel to navigate the famed Northwest Passage in a single season (see p.623); it now sits impressively in its own wing of the museum, where it can be viewed by guided tour only. Special summer shows spice things up a little, as do the recent Pirates' Cove and Children's Maritime Discovery Centre, both aimed at making the museum more attractive to children. Outside, just below the museum on **Heritage Harbour** (quay for ferries to and from Granville Island), you can admire, free of charge, more restored old-fashioned vessels.

The Museum of Anthropology

Located well out of downtown on the University of British Columbia campus, the **Museum of Anthropology**, 6393 NW Marine Drive, is far and away Vancouver's most important museum (mid-May to early Sept daily 10am–5pm, until 9pm on Tues; early Sept to mid-May Tues 11am–9pm, Wed–Sun 11am–5pm, closed Mon; $7, free Tues 5–9pm; ☎822-3825, *www.moa.ubc.ca*). Emphasizing the art and culture of the natives of the Pacific Northwest, and the Haida in particular, its collection of carvings, totem poles and artefacts is unequalled in North America.

To get there by bus, catch the #10 or #4 bus south from Granville Street and stay on until the end of the line. The campus is huge and disorientating – to find the museum, turn right from the bus stop, walk along the tree-lined East Mall to the very bottom (10min), then turn left on NW Marine Drive and walk till you see the museum on the right (another 5min). In the foyer pick up a free mini-guide or the cheap larger booklet – a worthwhile investment, given the exhibits' almost total lack of labelling, but still pretty thin.

Much is made of the museum's award-winning layout, a cool and spacious collection of halls designed by Arthur Erickson, the eminent architect also responsible for converting the Vancouver Art Gallery. Particularly outstanding is the huge **Great Hall**, inspired by native cedar houses, which makes as perfect an artificial setting for its thirty-odd **totem poles** as you could ask for. Huge windows look out to more poles and Haida houses, which you're free to wander around, backed by views of Burrard Inlet and the distant mountains. Most of the poles and monolithic carvings, indoors and out, are taken from the coastal tribes of the Haida, Salish, Tsimshian and Kwakiutl, all of which share cultural elements. The suspicion – though it's never confessed – is that scholars really don't know terribly much of the arcane mythology behind the carvings, but the best guess as to their meaning is that the various animals correspond to different clans or the creatures after which the clans were named. To delve deeper into the complexities, it's worth joining an hour-long, all-year **guided walk**.

One of the museum's great virtues is that none of its displays are hidden away in basements or back rooms; instead they're jammed in overwhelming numbers into drawers and cases in the galleries to the right of the Great Hall. Most of the permanent collection revolves around **Canadian Pacific** cultures, but the **Inuit** and **Far North** exhibits are also outstanding. So, too, are the jewellery, masks and baskets of Northwest native tribes, all markedly delicate after the blunt-nosed carvings of the Great Hall. Look out especially for the argillite sculptures, made from a jet-black slate found only on BC's Haida Gwaii or Queen Charlotte Islands. The **African** and **Asian** collections are also pretty comprehensive, if smaller, but appear as something of an afterthought alongside the indigenous artefacts. A small, technical archeological section rounds off the smaller galleries, along with a new three-gallery wing designed to house the Koerner Collection, an assortment of six hundred European ceramics dating from the fifteenth century onwards.

The museum saves its best for last. Housed in a separate rotunda, **The Raven and the Beast**, a modern sculpture designed by Haida artist Bill Reid, is the museum's pride and joy and has achieved almost iconographic status in the city. Carved from a 4.5-tonne block of cedar and requiring the attention of five people over three years, it describes the Haida legend of human evolution with stunning virtuosity, depicting terrified figures squirming from a half-open clam shell, overseen by an enormous and stern-faced raven. However, beautiful as the work is, its rotunda setting makes it seem oddly out of place – almost like a corporate piece of art.

Around the museum

There are any number of odds and ends dotted around the museum, but they amount to little of real interest. For the exception, turn right out the front entrance and a five-minute walk leads to the **Nitobe Memorial Garden**, a small Japanese garden that might be good for a few minutes of peace and quiet (April–Sept daily 10am–6pm; Oct–March Mon–Fri 10am–2.30pm; $2.50 or $5.75 with the Botanical Garden, free Oct–March; ☎822-6038). It's considered the world's most authentic Japanese garden outside Japan (despite its use of many non-Japanese species), and is full of gently curving paths, trickling streams and waterfalls, as well as numerous rocks, trees and shrubs placed with Oriental precision.

Beyond the garden lies the greater seventy-acre area of the university's **Botanical Garden**, 16th Avenue and SW Marine Drive (same hours as Nitobe Memorial Garden; $4.50 or $5.75 with Nitobe Memorial Garden; ☎822-4208, *www.hedgerows.com*), established in 1916, making it Canada's oldest such garden. Non-gardeners will probably be interested only in the macabre poisonous plants of the Physick Garden, a re-created sixteenth-century monastic herb garden – though most plants here are actually medicinal rather than lethal – and the swaths of shrubs and huge trees in the Asian Garden. If you're more curious or green-fingered, you'll take time to look at all five component parts of the garden. The Asian Garden is cradled amidst a swath of second-growth forest of fir, cedar and hemlock, home to 400 varieties of rhododendrons, roses, flowering vines and floral rarities such as blue Himalayan poppy and giant Himalayan lily. The BC Native Garden shelters some 3500 plants and flowers found across British Columbia in a variety of bog, marsh and other habitats, while the Alpine Garden conjures rare alpine varieties from five continents at around 2000m lower than their preferred altitude. The Food Garden produces a cornucopia of fruit and vegetables from a remarkably restricted area, the entire crop being donated to the Salvation Army.

While you're out at the university, you might also take advantage of the **University Endowment Lands**, on the opposite, west side of the museum. A huge tract of wild parkland – as large as Stanley Park, but used by a fraction of the number of people – the endowment lands boast 48km of trails and abundant wildlife (blacktail deer, otters, foxes and bald eagles). Best of all, there are few human touches – no benches or snack bars, and only the occasional signpost.

North Vancouver

Perhaps the most compelling reason to visit **North Vancouver** (known colloquially as North Van) is the trip itself – preferably by SeaBus – which provides views of not only the downtown skyline but also the teeming port area, a side of the city that's otherwise easily missed. Most of North Van itself is residential, as is neighbouring West Vancouver, whose cosseted citizens boast the highest per capita income in Canada. You'll probably cross to the north shore less for these leafy suburbs than to sample the outstanding areas of natural beauty here: **Lynn Canyon**, **Grouse Mountain**, **Capilano Gorge** (the most popular excursion), **Mount Seymour** and **Lighthouse Park**. All nestle in the mountains that rear up dramatically almost from the West Van waterfront, the proximity of Vancouver's residential areas to genuine wilderness being one of the city's most remarkable aspects. Your best bet if you wish to **hike**, and want the wildest scenery close to downtown, is Mount Seymour (see p.313).

Most of North Vancouver is within a single bus ride of **Lonsdale Quay**, the north shore's SeaBus terminal. **Buses** to all points leave from two parallel bays immediately in front of you as you leave the boat – blue West Van buses are run by an independent company but accept BC Transit tickets. If you've bought a ticket to come over on the SeaBus, remember you have ninety minutes of transfer time to ride buses from the time of purchase, which should be long enough to get you to most of the destinations below.

The **Lonsdale Quay Market**, to the right of the buses, is worth making the crossing for whether or not you intend to explore further. While not as vibrant as Granville Island Market, it's still an appealing place, with great food stalls and takeaways, plus walkways looking out over the port, tugs and moored fishing boats.

Grouse Mountain

The trip to **Grouse Mountain**, named by hikers in 1894 who stumbled across a blue grouse, is a popular one. This is mainly due to the Swiss-built **cable cars** – North America's largest cable cars – which run from the 290-metre base station at 6400 Nancy Greene Way to the mountain's 1250-metre summit (daily 9am–10pm; $17.50; ☎980-9311, *www.grousemountain.com*). A favourite among people learning to **ski** or **snowboard** after work, the mountain's brightly illuminated slopes and dozen or so runs are a North Vancouver landmark on winter evenings. A day-pass costs $32: for more information call ☎984-0661. In summer, the cable car is an expensive way of getting to the top. It's possible to walk up on the aptly named Grouse Grind Trail from the base station, but it's not a great hike, so settle instead into the inevitable queue for the ticket office (get here early if you can). After two stomach-churning lurches over the cables' twin towers you reach the summit, which, with its restaurants and allied tourist paraphernalia, is anything but wild. The views, though, are stunning, sometimes stretching as far as the San Juan Islands 160km away in Washington State. Have a quick look at the interpretive centre off to the right when you leave the cable car. A 3-D quality film is shown in the theatre downstairs (admission is included in your cable-car ticket) and there are a couple of cafés and a smarter restaurant if you need fortifying after your ascent. The first of the cafés, *Bar 98*, has panoramic views, but it fills up quickly. If you're interested in the *Grouse Nest Restaurant* (☎986-6378 for reservations), note that you can come here in the evening for dinner, accompanied by a fine prospect of the sunset and city lights below. Rides up on the cable car are free with a restaurant booking. Ask at the centre, or small information desk just beyond the centre, about easy **guided walks** (summer daily 11am–5pm): the *Tribute to the Forest* (30min) leaves on the hour, the *Walk in the Woods* every hour on the half-hour (35min).

Walk up the paved paths away from the centre for about five minutes – you can't get lost – and you pass a cabin office offering guided "gravity assisted" (read downhill) **bike tours** from the summit (May–Oct 3 daily; 20km trips cost from around $75, 30km $95 including cable-car fee): behind the office you can sign up for expensive helicopter tours. On the left up the path lies the scene of the "Logging Sports" shows (twice daily; free), involving various crowd-pleasing sawing and wood-chopping displays. Just beyond this is the **Peak Chairlift** (also included in your ticket), which judders upwards for another eight minutes to the mountain's summit: views of the city and Fraser delta are even better, only slightly spoilt by the worn paths and odd buildings immediately below you. Check with the office at the lower cable-car base station for details of long **hikes** – many are down below rather than up at the summit proper. The best easy stroll is to **Blue**

Grouse Lake (15min); the Goat Ridge Trail is for experienced hikers. More rugged paths lead into the mountains of the West Coast Range, but for these you'll need maps.

To get directly to the base station of the cable car from Lonsdale Quay, take the special #236 Grouse Mountain **bus** from Bay 8 to the left of the SeaBus terminal. You can also take a #246 Highland bus from Bay 7 and change to the #232 Grouse Mountain at Edgemount Village.

Lynn Canyon Park

Among the easiest targets for a quick taste of backwoods Vancouver is **Lynn Canyon Park** (open all year dawn to dusk), a quiet, forested area with a modest ravine and suspension bridge which, unlike the more popular Capilano Suspension Bridge (see below), you don't have to pay to cross. Several walks of up to ninety minutes take you through fine scenery – cliffs, rapids, waterfalls and naturally the eighty-metre-high bridge over Lynn Creek – all just twenty minutes from Lonsdale Quay. Take bus #228 from the quay to its penultimate stop at Peters Street, from where it's a ten-minute walk to the gorge; alternatively, take the less-frequent #229 Westlynn bus from Lonsdale Quay, which drops you about five minutes closer. Before entering the gorge, it's worth popping into the **Ecology Centre**, 3663 Park Rd, off Peters Road (March–Sept daily 10am–5pm; Oct–Feb Mon–Fri 10am–5pm, Sat & Sun noon–4pm; donation; ☎981-3103 or 987-5922), a friendly and informative place where you can pick up maps and pamphlets on park trails and wildlife.

Capilano River Regional Park

Lying just off the approach road to Grouse Mountain, **Capilano River Park**'s most publicized attraction is the inexplicably popular seventy-metre-high and 137-metre-long **suspension bridge** – the world's longest pedestrian suspension bridge – over the vertiginous Capilano Gorge (daily: May–Sept 8.30am–dusk; Oct–April 9am–5pm; $10.75; ☎985-7474, *www.capbridge.com*). The first bridge here was built in 1889, making this Vancouver's oldest "attraction", though the present structure dates from 1956. Although part of the park, the footbridge is privately run as a money-making venture. Stick to the paths elsewhere in the park and avoid the pedestrian toll, which buys you miscellaneous tours, forestry exhibits and trails, and a visit to a native carving centre; frankly they don't amount to much, especially when you can have much the same sort of scenery for free up the road. More interesting is the **salmon hatchery** just upstream (usually daily: April–Oct 8am–6pm; Nov–March 8am–4pm, but phone to confirm ☎666-1790; free), a provincial operation dating from 1977 designed to help salmon spawn and thus combat declining stocks: it nurtures some two million fish a year, and was the first of many similar schemes across the province. The building is well designed and the information plaques interesting, but it's a prime stop on city coach tours, so the place can often be packed.

Capilano is probably best visited on the way back from Grouse Mountain – from the cable-car station it's an easy downhill walk (1km) to the north end of the park, below the Cleveland Reservoir, source of Vancouver's often disconcertingly brown drinking water. From there, marked trails – notably the **Capilano Pacific Trail** – follow the eastern side of the gorge to the hatchery (2km). The area below the hatchery is worth exploring, especially the Dog's Leg Pool (1km), which is along a swirling reach of the Capilano River, and if you really want to stretch your legs you could follow the river the full 7km to its mouth on the Burrard Inlet. Alternatively, you could ride the #236 Grouse Mountain bus to the Cleveland Dam or the main park entrance – the hatchery is quickly reached by a side road (or the Pipeline Trail) from the signed main entrance left off Nancy Greene Way. This comes not far after the busy roadside entrance to the Capilano Suspension Bridge (on the bus, ring the bell for the stop after the bridge).

Mount Seymour Provincial Park

Mount Seymour Provincial Park is the biggest (8668 acres) of the North Vancouver parks, the most easterly and the one that comes closest to the flavour of high mountain scenery. It's 16km north of Vancouver and named after the short-serving BC provincial governor, Frederick Seymour (1864–69). For **information**, call ☎924-2200 or ask at the city infocentre for the blue *BC Parks* pamphlet on the park. To get there by **bus**, take the #239 from Lonsdale Quay to Phibbs Exchange and then the #215 to the Mount Seymour Parkway (1hr) – from there you'll have to walk or cycle up the thirteen-kilometre road to the heart of the park. The road climbs to over 1000m and ends at a car park where boards spell out clearly the trails and mountaineering options available. Views are superb on good days, particularly from the popular **Vancouver Lookout** on the parkway approach road, where a map identifies the city landmarks below. There's also a café, toilets and a small infocentre (summer only). In winter this is the most popular family and learners' **ski area** near Vancouver (call ☎986-2261 for information).

Four major **trails** here are manageable in a day, but be aware that conditions can change rapidly and snow lingers as late as June. The easiest hikes go out to Goldie Lake, a half-hour stroll, and to Dog Mountain, an hour from the parking area (one-way), with great views of the city below. Still better views, requiring more effort, can be had on the trails to First and Second Pump. The wildest and most demanding hike bypasses Mount Seymour's summit and runs by way of an intermittently marked trail to the forest- and mountain-circled Elsay Lake.

Adjacent to the park to the northwest is the **Seymour Demonstration Forest** (☎987-1273), a 14,000-acre area of mostly temperate rainforest, nestled in the lower part of a glacier-carved valley. It's situated at the northern end of Lillooet Road and, if going by public transport, you need to take the #229 Lynn Valley bus to Dempsey Road and Lynn Valley Road. From here it's a ten-minute walk over Lynn Creek via the bridge on Rice Lake Road. You're far better off, however, coming up here on a bike, for the 40km of trails in the area offers some of the best **mountain biking** close to downtown. Forestry education is the area's chief concern, as the area's name suggests, and you can follow various sixty- and ninety-minute marked **hiking trails** that will top up your general knowledge about local trees, soils, fish and wildlife.

Cypress Provincial Park

Cypress Provincial Park, most westerly of the big parks that part-cover the dramatic mountains and forest visible from Vancouver's downtown, is perhaps among BC's most visited day-use parks and probably the most popular of the north shore's protected areas. It takes its name from the huge old red and yellow cedars that proliferate here. Something of a hit with locals who prefer their wilderness just slightly tamed, its trails can be rugged and muddy, but they're always well marked, and even just a few minutes from the parking area you can feel in the depths of the great outdoors. There are several good trails, including the three-kilometre **Yew Lake Trail** – wheelchair-accessible – and the main park trail, which climbs through forest and undergrowth, occasionally opening up to reveal views. The trail also shadows part of Cypress Creek, a torrent that has cut a deep and narrow canyon. For more **information**, ask for the relevant *BC Parks* pamphlet at the infocentre or call ☎926-6007. To get here, take the #253 Caulfield/Park Royal **bus**.

Lighthouse Park

Lighthouse Park, just west of Cypress, offers a seascape semi-wilderness at the extreme western tip of the north shore, 8km from the Lion's Gate Bridge. Smooth granite rocks and low cliffs line the shore, backed by huge Douglas firs up to 1500 years old, some of the best virgin forest in southern BC. The rocks make fine sun beds, though the water out here is colder than around the city beaches. A map at the car park shows the two trails to the 1912 Point Atkinson **lighthouse** itself – you can take one out and the other back, a return trip of about 5km which involves about two-hours' walking. Although the park has its secluded corners (no camping allowed), it can be disconcertingly busy during summer weekends. For more **information** on the park, contact the infocentre or call ☎925-7200 or 925-7000. The West Van #250 **bus** makes the journey all the way from Georgia Street in downtown.

Eating and drinking

Vancouver's restaurants are some of the Northwest's finest, and span the price spectrum from budget to blowout. If you want to eat well, you'll be spoilt for choice – and you won't have to spend a fortune to do so. As you'd expect, the city also offers a wide range of ethnic cuisines. **Chinese** and **Japanese** cuisines have the highest profile (though the latter tend to be expensive), followed by **Italian**, **Greek** and other European imports. **Vietnamese**, **Cambodian**, **Thai** and **Korean** are more recent arrivals and can often provide the best starting points – cafés and the ubiquitous fast-food chains aside – if you're on a tight budget. Specialist **seafood** restaurants are surprisingly thin on the ground, but those that exist are of high quality and often remarkably cheap. In any case, seafood does crop up on most menus and salmon is heavily featured. **Vegetarians** are well served by a number of specialist places.

Restaurants are spread around the city – check locations carefully if you don't want to travel too far from downtown – though are naturally thinner on the ground in North and West Vancouver. Places in Gastown are generally tourist-oriented, with some notable exceptions, in marked contrast to Chinatown's bewildering plethora of genuine and reasonably priced options. Downtown also offers plenty of chains and huge choice, particularly with top-dollar places and fast-food fare: the local *White Spot* chain was founded in 1928 and has some thirty locations in Vancouver, and offers good and glorified fast food if time and money are tight – the branch at 1616 W Georgia St between Seymour and Granville is the most central downtown outlet. Superior chains like *Earl's* and *Milestones* are highly commendable, and a reliable choice for downtown eating right on Robson (see "West Coast" restaurants, p.317).The old warehouse district of **Yaletown**, part of downtown's new southeasterly spread, is also a key – and still developing – eating and nightlife area. Similar places line 4th Avenue in Kitsilano and neighbouring West Broadway, though these require something of a special journey if you're based in or around downtown. Perhaps try them for lunch if you're at the beach (see box, p.300) or visiting the nearby Vanier Park museum complex.

Countless **cafés** are found mainly around the beaches, in parks, along downtown streets, and especially on Granville Island. Many sell light meals as well as the coffee and snack staples. **Little Italy**, the area around Commercial Drive (between Venables and Broadway), is good for cheap, cheerful and downright trendy cafés and restaurants, though as new waves of immigrants fill the area Little Italy is increasingly becoming "Little Vietnam" and "Little Nicaragua". Yaletown and the heavily residential **West End**, notably around Denman and Davie streets – Vancouver's "gay village" – is also booming, the latter having gained a selection of interesting shops and restaurants.

The city also has a commendable assortment of **bars**, many a cut above the functional dives and sham pubs found elsewhere in BC. Note, however, that the definitions of bar, café, restaurant and nightclub can be considerably blurred: food in some form – usually substantial – is available in most places, while daytime cafés and restaurants also operate happily as night-time bars. In this section we've highlighted places whose main emphasis is food and drink; entertainment venues are listed in the next section.

Note, too, that Vancouver has a handful of places that stay open all night or until the small hours; a selection of these are listed below.

Cafés and snacks

Bavaria, 203 Carrall St (no phone). A simple, no-frills Gastown place with a couple of tables outside on Maple Tree Square almost in front of Gassy Jack's statue. Particularly recommended for its inexpensive all-day breakfast: if you want something a touch more upmarket, then head for the fine *Pistol Burnes* café on the corner to the right (with lots more outside seating) or *Blake's* (see below) and *The Irish Heather* (see p.319), both just a few doors away.

Blake's, 221 Carrall St near Water St (☎899-3354). One of several cosy and relaxed places on this short Gastown stretch of Carrall St for a coffee, sandwich or snack; a good place to while away an hour writing a postcard or reading the newspaper.

Boulangerie la Parisienne, 1076 Mainland St near Helmcken (☎684-2499). A Yaletown café and bakery with striking and very pretty all-blue interior that – true to its name – opens up French-style onto the pavement in summer.

Bread Garden, 1040 Denman St at Comox (☎685-2996). In Kitsilano at 1880 W 1st at Cypress and 812 Bute, downtown, off Robson. Locals love to moan about the slow service, but food in these hypertrendy deli-cafés is some of the best – and best looking – in the city. Great for people-watching. There are now twelve branches in the Vancouver area. Recommended.

Calabria Coffee Bar, 1745 Commercial Drive (☎253-7017). Very popular café, known to locals as Franks, and tucked away from downtown in "Little Italy". Probably as close as you can get in Vancouver to a genuine Italian bar.

Doll and Penny's, 1167 Davie St between Thurlow and Bute sts (☎685-3417). Fun West End place with big servings, large gay clientele (but all welcome), and daily drinks specials. Comes alive when the clubs close and stays open to the wee small hours.

Flying Pizza, 3499 Cambie (☎874-8284). If you want pizza this is the place; cheap, thin-crust pizza by the slice (but no alcohol) at five outlets, including Library Square (lunch only), Cornwall Ave (for Kits beach) and just south of the Burrard Street Bridge.

Gallery Café, Vancouver Art Gallery, 750 Hornby St (☎688-2233). Relaxed, stylish and pleasantly arty place at the heart of downtown for coffee, good lunches and healthy, high-quality food (especially desserts); also has a popular summer patio. Recommended.

Hamburger Mary's, 1202 Davie St between Bute and Jervis sts (☎687-1293). These may well be the best burgers in the city, though there are plenty of other things on the menu. Lots of people end the evening for a snack at this former West End diner. Outside tables when the weather is fine. Open very late (usually 3am). Recommended.

La Luna Café, 117 Water St between Cambie and Abbot sts (☎687-5862). One of only a couple of places on Gastown's main street that has the character to raise it above the usual tourist-oriented cafés in this part of the city.

The Only Café, 20 E Hastings and Carrall St (☎681-6546). One of Vancouver's most famous institutions, founded in 1912, and worth the trip to the less than salubrious part of town to sample the food and old-world atmosphere. This counter-seating greasy spoon has little more than seafood (perhaps the best in town) and potatoes on its menu; no toilets, no credit cards, no licence, and no messing with the service. 11am–8pm; closed Sun.

Café S'Il Vous Plaît, 500 Robson St and Richards St. Young, casual and vaguely alternative with good sandwiches, basic home-cooking and local art displays. It is close to the *Kingston Hotel* and central library. Open till 10pm.

Sophie's Cosmic Café, 2095 W 4th Ave at Arbutus St (☎732-6810). This excellent 1950s-style diner is a Kits institution and is packed out for weekend breakfasts and weekday lunch; renowned for its vast, spicy burgers, milkshakes and whopping breakfasts. Recommended.

Chinese

Hon's Wun-Tun House, 108-268 Keefer at Gore St (☎688-0871). Started life as a cheap, basic and popular place known for the house specialities, "potstickers" – fried meat-filled dumplings – and ninety-odd soups (including fish ball and pig's feet). Success has spawned other branches and a slight smartening-up, but the encouraging queues, good food and low prices are mercifully unchanged. No alcohol or credit cards.

Imperial Chinese Seafood Restaurant, 355 Burrard St near Pender St (☎688-8191). A grand and opulent spot in the old Marine Building with good views and busy atmosphere, serving fine, but pricey, food.

Kirin Mandarin, 1166 Alberni near Bute St (☎682-8833). Among the first of the city's smart Chinese arrivals with an elegant decor that's a world away from old-fashioned Chinatown. The superior food is at top-dollar prices but you're repaid with great views of the mountains.

Pink Pearl, 1132 E Hastings near Glen St (☎253-4316). Big, bustling and old-fashioned with highly authentic feel but in a dingy part of town. The moderately priced food has a Cantonese slant, strong on seafood and great for dim sum. It frequently emerges as the city's top Chinese restaurant in dining polls. Recommended.

Shanghai Chinese Bistro, 1128 Alberni St and Thurlow St (☎683-8222). A modern-looking but less ostentatious and more reasonably priced alternative to the *Imperial*, if you want to eat Chinese downtown. The handmade noodles are a must. Open very late (2–3am).

Sun Wong Kee, 4136 Main St (☎879-7231). Some of the city's best and cheapest Chinese food and popular with Chinese families, so get here early. Over 225 items on the menu, yet deep-fried seafood remains a winner.

Italian

CinCin, 1154 Robson St at Bute St (☎688-7338). An excellent downtown option, with stylish, buzzy setting (try to book an outside table in summer), food that merits the highish prices and includes top-grade home-made pastas and desserts. Check the wine list – it's one of the best in the city.

Da Pasta Bar, 1232 Robson St between Jervis and Bute sts (☎688-1288). Deservedly popular mid-priced spot, with varied clientele, in a visually brash place downtown on Robson. You can pick and mix from six pastas and around fourteen inventive sauces and blend to taste. Good for lunch.

Il Giardino di Umberto, 1382 Hornby St at Pacific St (☎669-2422). Sublime and expensive food with a bias towards pasta and game served to a trendy and casually smart thirty-something clientele. Weekend reservations are essential, especially for the nice vine-trailed outside terrace.

The Old Spaghetti Factory, 55 Water St at Abbot St (☎684-1288). Part of an inexpensive chain and hardly *alta cucina*, but a standby if you're in Gastown and better than the tourist trap it appears from the outside, with its spacious 1920s Tiffany interior.

Piccolo Mondo, 850 Thurlow St at Smithe St (☎688-1633). Pricey but excellent food and an award-winning selection of Italian wines. A nicely restrained dining room, just off Robson St, that's not as formal as it first appears. The clientele are expense accounts at lunch and smoochy couples in the evenings. Recommended.

Villa del Lupo, 869 Hamilton St near Smithe St (☎688-7436). Authentic and expensive, high-quality food in a renovated country house – unfussy and elegant – on the eastern edge of downtown midway between the library and Yaletown: there's not a better *osso bucco* in Vancouver.

French

The Hermitage, 115-1025 Robson near Thurlow St (☎689-3237). Warm brick walls, a big fireplace, crisp linen, French-speaking waiters and a courtyard setting give this central and very highly rated restaurant a cosy, almost European feel. The chef here once cooked for King Leopold of Belgium, so he knows his way around food – the onion soup is unbeatable.

Le Crocodile, 100-909 Burrard St, entrance on Smithe St (☎669-4298). Plush, French-Alsace up-market bistro establishment that pushes *Bishop's* (see opposite) close for the title of the city's best restaurant and, unlike its rival, it's located downtown. The menu has something for traditionalists and the more adventurous alike. A memorable meal is guaranteed – but check your credit limit first.

Le Gavroche, 1616 Alberni St at Cardero St (☎685-3924). The similarly priced *Le Crocodile* may just take the culinary plaudits, but this other top French restaurant (with a West Coast twist) is not far behind. A formal but amiable place and rated as one of the most romantic places in the city.

Lumière, 2551 W Broadway near Trafalgar St (☎739-8185). Local food critics have named this Vancouver's best restaurant twice in recent years, and it is indeed one of the city's most outstanding places to eat. Cooking here is "contemporary French", and a touch lighter than *Le Crocodile*, though prices are equally elevated. Visitors based in downtown will need to take a cab here: you'll also need to book, for the simple, tasteful dining room accommodates just fifty diners.

Greek

Le Grec, 1447 Commercial Drive (☎253-1253). Popular restaurant with a big range of titbits at reasonable prices, though you'll have to travel out of downtown to enjoy them. Casual and lively later on, especially at weekends.

Orestes, 3116 W Broadway between Trutch and Balaclava sts (☎738-1941). Good, basic food in one of the city's oldest Greek restaurants. Belly dancers shake their stuff Thursday to Saturday and there's live music on Sunday.

Ouzeri, 3189 W Broadway at Trutch St (☎739-9995). A friendly and fairly priced restaurant that is the first port of call if you're at the hostel or beach in Kitsilano.

Stepho's, 1124 Davie St between Thurlow and Bute sts (☎683-2555). This West End restaurant has simple interior, fine food, efficient service and is very popular. Recommended.

Vassilis, 2884 W Broadway near Macdonald St (☎733-3231). Family-run outfit with a high reputation; serves a mean roast chicken. Closed weekends during lunch. Moderate.

West Coast

Bishop's, 2183 W 4th near Yew St (☎738-2025). Consistently ranked one of Vancouver's best restaurants, though it's some way from downtown. Although there's a frequent film-star and VIP presence, the welcome's as warm for everyone. The light and refined "contemporary home cooking" – Italy meets the Pacific Rim – commands high prices but is worth it. First choice for the big, one-off splurge, but booking is essential.

Bridges, 1696 Duranleau, Granville Island (☎687-4400). Unmissable big, yellow restaurant upstairs, pub and informal bistro (the best option) downstairs, with a large outdoor deck. A reliable and very popular choice for a drink or meal on Granville Island.

C Restaurant, 2-1600 Howe St near Pacific Blvd (☎681-1164). *The Fish House at Stanley Park* (see below) is *C*'s only serious rival for the title of best fish and seafood restaurant. The lengthy menu, which contains Southeast Asian influences, might include a choice from the "raw bar" – say a trio of scallop, wasabi salmon and smoked chili tuna – and unusual fish such as Alaskan Arctic char. Views from the dining room are good, too.

Chartwell, *Four Seasons Hotel*, 791 W Georgia St (☎844-6715). Don't let the fact that this is a hotel dining room put you off: the gracious, almost gentleman's club-like ambience is good if you want to dress up or have an indulgent lunch, and fine service, great wine list and progressive Pacific Rim-influenced food makes this one of the top ten restaurants in Vancouver.

Diva at the Met, *Metropolitan Hotel*, 645 Howe St (☎602-7788). Like the *Chartwell* (see above), *Diva* has carved out a character completely separate to the hotel in which it's lodged. This is among Vancouver's leading restaurants, thanks to the punchy, imaginative food and the modern, clean-lined dining room. Starters might include smoked salmon with Quebec foie gras, followed by a main course of halibut cheeks with black olive tapinade. Expensive, but a great pace for a treat or full-on brunch.

Earl's On Top, 1185 Robson St near Bute St (☎669-0020). Come here first if you don't want to mess around scouring downtown for somewhere to eat. The mid-priced, and often innovative, high-quality food is served in a big, open and casual dining area, with outside terrace in the summer. Recommended.

Ferguson Point Teahouse, Ferguson Point, Stanley Park (☎669-3281). A very pretty and romantic spot – ocean view, outside dining – and the best place for a lunch or brunch during a walk or ride round Stanley Park. Be sure to book ahead.

The Fish House at Stanley Park, 2099 Beach Ave and Stanley Park Drive, at the north end of Beach Ave (☎681-7275). The name more or less says it all. The leafy setting in the southwest corner of Stanley Park is almost that of a country estate, and the seafood arguably the city's best. Indulge at the oyster bar, order any available fish baked, broiled, steamed or grilled, and check out the daily specials. Excellent wine list. Expensive but worth it.

Isadora's, 1540 Old Bridge St, Granville Island (☎681-8816). Popular Granville Island choice for a beer or a meal, though *Bridges* is probably a shade better. Fine breakfasts, weekend brunches and light meals with plenty of good veggie/wholefood options. Lots of outdoor seating, but expect queues and slower service at weekends, particularly Sunday brunch. Moderate.

Liliget Feast House, 1724 Davie St at Bidwill St (☎681-7044). This West End aboriginal restaurant – the only one in Vancouver – serves types of food you'll get nowhere else in the city: seaweed, steamed ferns, roast caribou, and barbecued juniper duck. However, the cedar tables and benches, designed to resemble a Coast Salish longhouse, making the dining room a mite austere. Moderate.

Milestone's, 1145 Robson St between Bute and Thurlow sts (☎682-4477) and 1210 Denman St (☎662-3431). Popular mid-market chain restaurants with cheap drinks and food (especially good breakfasts) in very generous portions at the heart of downtown (fast and noisy) and the English Bay Beach end of Denman St (more laid-back). There's also a popular and appealing branch with outdoor terrace in Yaletown at 1109 Hamilton on the corner of Helmcken (☎684-9112).

Tomato Fresh Food Café, 3305 Cambie St (☎874-6020). This high-energy place serves good simple food, with a fresh, health-conscious bias. It's way south of downtown, so it's a good place to stop en route for the airport, Vancouver Island or the ferry terminal at Tsawwassen. Eat in or takeaway.

Water Street Café, 300 Water St at Cambie St (☎689-2832). The café-restaurant of choice if you wind up in Gastown (located close to the famous steam clock). An airy and casual atmosphere that offers a short but well-chosen menu; consider booking an outside table if you're going to be here for lunch.

Other ethnic restaurants

Chiyoda, 1050 Alberni St at Burrard St (☎688-5050). Everything here, down to the beer glasses, was designed in Japan. A chic but convivial place – the emphasis is on grilled food (*robata*) rather than sushi – that draws in Japanese visitors and businesspeople at lunch and the fashionable in the evenings for moderately-priced dinners.

Ezogiku Noodle Café, 1329 Robson St at Jervis St (☎685-8608). This tiny Japanese noodle house is a perfect place for quick food downtown. The queues are prohibitive, but the turnover's speedy.

Kamei, 1030 W Georgia at Burrard St (☎687-8588). Superlative sushi, but at stratospheric prices. Large and bright, and a menu as long as your arm.

Mescalero's, 1215 Bidwell between Burnaby and Davie sts (☎669-2399). Very popular Mexican-Latin restaurant in the West End with appropriately rustic atmosphere and fit young punters. Moderate.

Phnom-Penh, 244 E Georgia near Gore St (☎682-5777) and 955 W Broadway near Oak St (☎734-8988). Excellent, cheap Vietnamese and Cambodian cuisine, especially seafood, in a friendly, family-oriented restaurant. Recommended.

Pho Hoang, 3610 Main at 20th (☎874-0810) and 238 E Georgia near Gore St (☎682-5666). The first and perhaps friendliest of the many Vietnamese *pho* (beef soup) restaurants now springing up all over the city. Choose from thirty soup varieties with herbs, chillies and lime at plate-side as added seasoning. Open for breakfast, lunch and dinner. The new Chinatown branch is right by the *Phnom-Penh* (see above).

Simply Thai, 1211 Hamilton St, corner of Davie St (☎642-0123). This plain, modern but inviting Yaletown restaurant is packed at lunch (11.30am–3pm) and dinner, thanks to the keen prices and good, authentic food – the chefs are all from Bangkok. Another place, *Thai Urban Bistro*, just up the street at 1119 Hamilton (☎408-7788) is almost as good.

Tojo's, 777 W Broadway at Willow St (☎872-8050). Quite simply the best Japanese food (sushi and more – try the tuna or shrimp dumplings with hot mustard sauce) in the city. Very expensive.

Topanga Café, 2904 W 4th Ave near Macdonald St (☎733-3713). A small but extremely popular and moderate Mexican restaurant; a Vancouver institution.

Vij's, 1480 W 11th Ave near Granville St (☎736-6664). *Vij's* Indian cooking has won just about every award going in Vancouver for Best Ethnic Cuisine. The inexpensive menus change regularly: some excellent vegetarian options.

Vegetarian

The Naam, 2724 W 4th Ave near Stephens St (☎738-7151). The oldest and most popular health-food and vegetarian restaurant in the city. Comfortable and friendly ambience with live folk and other music and outside eating some evenings. Open 24hr. Inexpensive and recommended.

Pubs and Bars

The Arts Club, 1585 Johnston on Granville Island (☎687-1354). *The Arts Club*'s popular *Backstage Lounge*, part of the theatre complex, has a waterfront view, easy-going atmosphere, decent food and puts on blues, jazz and other live music Friday and Saturday evenings. Recommended.

Bar None, 1222 Hamilton St (☎689-7000). Busy, reasonably smart and hip New York-style Yaletown bar and club where you can eat, drink, watch TV, smoke cigars (walk-in humidor), play backgammon or shoot pool and listen to live music.

Blarney Stone, 216 Carrall near Water St (☎687-4322). A lively Irish pub and restaurant, in Gastown, complete with live Irish music and dance floor. Closed Sun.

Darby D. Dawes, 2001 Macdonald St and 4th Ave (☎731-0617). A pub handy for Kits Beach and the youth hostel. People often start the evening here, meals are served 11.30am–7pm, snacks till 10pm, and then move on to the Fairview for live blues (see overleaf). Live music is only played on Friday and Saturday evenings with jam sessions on Saturday afternoons.

Gerard's, 845 Burrard at Robson St (☎682-5511). The smooth wood-panelled lounge and piano bar with leather chairs and tapestries, all make this very elegant downtown drinking. Also, the place to spot the stars currently filming in town.

The Irish Heather, 217 Carrall St near Water St (☎688-9779). A definite cut above the usual mock-Irish pub, with an intimate bar, live Irish music some nights, excellent food, good Guinness (apparently it sells the seond largest number of pints of the stuff in Canada); and an unexpectedly pretty outdoor area in the back.

La Bodega, 1277 Howe near Davie St (☎684-8815). One of the city's best and most popular places, with tapas and excellent main courses, but chiefly dedicated to lively drinking. It's packed later on, so try to arrive before 8pm. Recommended. Closed Sun.

Rose and Thorne, 757 Richards near Georgia St (☎683-2921). Popular, comfortable place next to the *Kingston Hotel* and very close to the look and feel of an English pub.

Shark Bar & Grill, *The Sandman Hotel*, 180 W Georgia (☎687-4275). The best and busiest of several sports bars in the city. There are 30 screens, a 180-seat oak bar, 22 beers on tap, Italian food from the kitchen, and lots of testosterone.

Sylvia Hotel, 1154 Gilford and Beach (☎688-8865). This nondescript but easy-going hotel bar is popular for quiet drinks and superlative waterfront views, and pleasant after a stroll on English Bay Beach.

Yaletown Brewing Company, 1111 Mainland St (☎681-2739). An extremely large and unmissable bar and restaurant with their own six-beer on-site brewery. Currently very popular, and leading the way in the funky Yaletown revival.

Nightlife and entertainment

Vancouver gives you plenty to do come sunset, laying on a varied and cosmopolitan blend of both **live and dance music**. Clubs are more adventurous than in many a Northwest city, particularly the fly-by-night alternative dives in the Italian quarter on Commercial Drive and in the backstreets off Gastown and Chinatown. There's also a choice of smarter and more conventional clubs, a handful of discos and a smattering of **gay** and **lesbian** clubs and bars. Summer nightlife often takes to the streets in West Coast fashion, with outdoor bars and (to a certain extent) beaches becoming venues in their own right. Fine weather also allows the city to host a range of **festivals**, from jazz to theatre, and the **performing arts** are as widely available as you'd expect in a city as culturally self-conscious as Vancouver.

The most comprehensive **listings** guide to all the goings-on is *Georgia Straight*, a free weekly published on Thursday; the monthly *Night Moves* concentrates more on live music. These are available in larger stores and street boxes around the city. For detailed information on **gay and lesbian** events, check out *X-tra*, a free monthly magazine aimed specifically at the gay and lesbian community, which is available at clubs, bookshops and many of the *Georgia Straight* distribution points. Many other free magazines devoted to different musical genres and activities are available at the same points, but they come and go quickly. **Tickets** for many major events are sold through Ticketmaster, 1304 Hornby St, which has forty outlets throughout the city (☎280-4444 for concerts, ☎280-4400 for sporting events and ☎280-3311 for the performing arts); they'll sometimes unload discounted tickets for midweek and matinee performances.

Live music and clubs

Vancouver's live-music venues showcase a variety of musical styles, but mainstream **rock** groups are the most common bill of fare; the city is also a fertile breeding ground for **punk** bands, with particularly vocal fans. **Jazz** is generally hot news in Vancouver, with a dozen spots specializing in the genre (ring the Jazz Hot Line at ☎682-0706 for current and upcoming events). And, while Vancouver isn't as cowpoke as, say, Calgary, it does have several clubs dedicated to **country music**, though many are in the outer suburbs.

Many venues also double as clubs and discos, and as in any city with a healthy alternative scene there are also plenty of fun, one-off clubs that have an irritating habit of cropping up and disappearing at speed. Cover charges are usually nominal, and tickets are often available (sometimes free) at record shops. At the other end of the spectrum, the 60,000-seat Pacific Coliseum is on the touring itinerary of most international acts.

Rock venues

Commodore Ballroom, 870 Granville St at Smithe St (☎681-7838). Still fresh from a $1 million face-lift – which retained its renowned 1929 dance floor – the Commodore is the city's best mid-sized venue. There is an adventurous music policy and both local and national DJs frequently spin.

The Rage, 750 Pacific Blvd at Cambie St (☎685-5585). Loud and young, progressive dance and live music club with huge, packed dance floor. It mainly caters for up-and-coming bands: as one critic puts it – "if you've heard it before, you won't hear it here".

Railway Club, 579 Dunsmuir St at Seymour St (☎681-1625). Long-established favourite with excellent bookings, wide range of music (folk, blues, jazz) and a casual atmosphere. Has a separate "conversation" lounge, so it's ideal for a drink (and weekday lunches). Arrive before 10pm at weekends – the place is tiny.

Roxy, 932 Granville St at Nelson St (☎684-7699). Nightly live bands with emphasis on retro 1950s to 1970s music. Casual and fun place for college crowd and people in from the 'burbs.

Sonar, 66 Water St at Abbott St (☎683-6695). Central Vancouver's best-known music venue, with live bands nightly. Convenient mid-Gastown location attracts a varied clientele – it's also known as something of a pick-up spot. Bar food and piano lounge until 9pm, when the band strikes up.

Starfish Room, 1055 Homer St at Nelson St (☎682-4171). Intimate, smoke-filled and loud place known for top local bands, smaller touring bands, occasional bigger names and MOR music at other times.

Jazz and blues

Arts Club Theatre Backstage Lounge, 1585 Johnston, Granville Island (☎687-1354). The lounge is a nice spot to hear R&B, jazz and blues, or watch the boats and sunset on False Creek.

Capone's, 1141 Hamilton St (☎684-7900). This Yaletown spot is primarily a restaurant, but has a stage for live jazz renditions while you eat.

Casbah Jazzbah, 175 W Pender S (☎669-0837). Smooth restaurant-club with live traditional and swing jazz cabaret Thursday to Saturday.

Fairview, 898 W Broadway at the *Ramada Inn* (☎872-1262). Good local blues and 1950s rock in a pub atmosphere with only a small dance floor. Snacks are served during the day and good-value meals in the evening. Open Mon–Sat.

Hot Jazz, 2120 Main St at 5th St (☎873-4131). Oldest and most established jazz club in the city. Mainly traditional swing, Dixieland and New Orleans, played by both local and imported bands. A good dance floor and big bar ensures this place swings past midnight. Wednesday is jam night. Closed Mon & Sun.

Purple Onion, 15 Water St near Abbot St (☎602-9442). Casual club right in the heart of Gastown: top-notch jazz and live Latin music upstairs, dance floor, cigars, oysters and cabaret downstairs. Currently a very popular choice, so expect to wait in line on Friday and Saturday.

Yale, 1300 Granville St at Drake St (☎681-9253). An outstanding venue: *the* place in the city to hear hardcore blues and R&B. Relaxed air, big dance floor and occasional outstanding international names. Often jam sessions with up to 50 players at once on Saturday (3–8pm) and Sunday (3pm–midnight). Recommended. Closed Mon & Tues.

Country

Boone County Cabaret, 801 Brunette Ave, Coquitlam (☎523-3144). Just off the Trans-Canada (take bus #151) this is suburbia's favourite Country club and it shows – it's typically raucous and crowded. There's no cover Monday to Thursday, and free dance lessons on Monday, Tuesday and Thursday at 8pm. Closed Sun.

JR Country Club, *Sandman Inn*, 180 W Georgia St near Cambie St (☎681-2211). Downtown's main C&W venue highlights top Canadian bands in Old West setting; no cover Monday to Thursday. Closed Sun.

Discos and clubs

Big Bam Boo, 1236 W Broadway near Oak St (☎733-2220). Sports on TV, pool and sushi upstairs; dancing downstairs to safe Top 40 stuff and 1980s throwbacks. Smart place with a strict dress code and generally queues Thursday to Saturday. Wednesday and Saturday are two of the best "Ladies" nights in the city.

Luv-a-Fair, 1275 Seymour St at Davie St (☎685-3288). This old-timer is probably the city's top club and boasts an excellent dance floor and sound system, along with cutting-edge dance music. The occasional theme nights and live bands have to compete with the everyday madcap, eclectic crowd, ranging from punks to drag queens. Recommended. Closed Sun.

Palladium, 1250 Richards St between Davie and Drake sts (☎688-2648). Bizarre warehouse-sized venue for the art and fashion crowd. Current dance music (different genre most nights) is occasionally enlivened by live shows with the avant-garde art rounding off the experience. Closed Sun.

Richard's on Richards, 1036 Richards St at Nelson St(☎687-6794). A well-known club and disco, but pretentious and aimed at the BMW set. Long waits and dress code. Open Thurs–Sat.

Wett Bar, 1320 Richards St at Drake St (☎662-7707). A hip downtown club where you can expect to hear anything from trip-hop to funky tech-house to hip-hop, depending on which night you show up.

The World, 1369 Richards St (☎688-7806). Currently one of the city's most popular places to retire after clubbing: music, food and non-alcoholic drinks. Open Fri & Sat midnight–5am only.

Comedy club

Yuk Yuk's, Plaza of Nations, 750 Pacific Blvd at Cambie St (☎687-LAFF). Top US and Canadian stand-up acts and the usual scary amateur night on Wednesday. Shows at 9pm, plus Sat & Sun 11.30pm. Closed Mon & Tues.

Gay clubs and venues

Denman Station, 860 Denman St off Robson St (☎669-3488). A friendly basement bar with game shows, karaoke, darts and the like every night for a largely gay and lesbian clientele in an area increasingly becoming a gay "village".

Doll and Penny's, 1167 Davie St between Thurlow and Bute sts (☎685-3417). Fun West End place with big servings and large gay clientele: various theme nights and music nights. Comes alive when other clubs close and stays open to the wee small hours.

Global Beat, 1249 Howe St near Davie St. A gay-owned restaurant and lounge alongside the *Odyssey* (see below).

Heritage House Hotel, 455 Abbott St at Pender St (☎685-7777). The bars here host a number of gay and lesbian nights: currently *Charlie's Bar and Grill* fills up with women only on Saturday and *Chuck's Pub* has "Guys in Disguise' on Friday and men-only leather on Saturday; call for latest details.

Numbers, 1042 Davie St at Burrard St (☎685-4077). Good, cruisy multi-level venue and disco, movies and pool tables upstairs, mixed downstairs but with very few women. Theme nights. Open nightly.

Odyssey, 1251 Howe near Davie St (☎689-5256). A young gay and bisexual club with house and techno most nights (expect to queue Fri & Sat). There's a garden in the rear to cool off.

Sublime, 816 Granville (no phone, *sublimenightclub@hotmail.com*). After-hours dance club that runs from 1–6am on Fri and Sat.

Performing arts and cinema

Vancouver serves up enough highbrow culture to suit the whole spectrum of its cosmopolitan population, with plenty of unusual and avant-garde performances to spice up the more mainstream fare you'd expect of a major North American city. The main focus for the city's performing arts is the **Queen Elizabeth Theatre** (☎299-9000) at 600 Hamilton St at Georgia, which plays host to a steady procession of visiting theatre, opera and dance troupes, and even the occasional big rock band. Recently it's been joined by the new **Ford Centre for the Performing Arts** opposite the central library at 777 Homer St (☎280-2222 or 602-0616). For information on the Vancouver arts scene, call the Arts Hotline (☎684-ARTS or 684-2787) or visit their office at 938 Howe St. The refurbished **Orpheum Theatre**, 884 Granville at Smithe (☎665-3050), is Vancouver's oldest theatre and headquarters of the Vancouver Symphony Orchestra. There's also a special line for information relating to dance (☎872-0432). **Tickets** can be obtained from individual box offices or through the Ticketmaster agency (☎280-3311).

The western capital of Canada's film industry, Vancouver is increasingly favoured by Hollywood studios in their pursuit of cheaper locations and production deals. It's therefore no surprise that the spread of **cinemas** is good. Home-produced and Hollywood first-run films play in the downtown cinemas on "Theatre Row" – the two blocks of Granville between Robson and Nelson streets – and other big complexes, and there's no shortage of cinemas for more esoteric productions.

Classical music

Early Music Vancouver (☎732-1610). Early music with original instruments where possible; concerts all over the city, and at the UBC during the Early Music Festival in July and August.

Festival Concert Society (☎736-3737). The society often organizes cheap Sunday morning concerts (jazz, folk or classical) at the Queen Elizabeth Playhouse.

Music-in-the-Morning Concert Society, 1270 Chestnut, Vanier Park (☎873-4612). This began modestly in someone's front room over a decade ago but now organizes innovative and respected concerts of old and new music with local and visiting musicians.

Vancouver Bach Choir (☎921-8012). The city's top non-professional choir performs three major concerts yearly at the Orpheum Theatre.

Vancouver Chamber Choir (☎738-6822, *www.vancouverchamberchoir.com*). One of two professional, internationally renowned choirs in the city. They perform at the Orpheum and on some Sunday afternoons at the *Hotel Vancouver*.

Vancouver New Music Society (☎874-6200 or 606-6440). Responsible for several annual concerts of cutting-edge twentieth-century music, usually at the East Cultural Centre (see "Drama" below).

Vancouver Opera (☎682-2871, *www.vanopera.bc.ca*). Four operas are produced annually at the Queen Elizabeth Theatre and productions currently enjoy an excellent reputation.

Vancouver Recital Society (☎736-0363, *www.vanrecital.com*). Hosts two of the best and most popular cycles in the city: the summer Chamber Music Festival (at St George's School) and the main Vancouver Playhouse recitals (Sept–April). Catches up-and-coming performers plus a few major international names each year.

Vancouver Symphony Orchestra (☎684-9100, *www.culturenet.ca/vso*). Presents most concerts at the Orpheum or new Chan Shun Hall on Crescent Road off NW Marine Drive, but also sometimes gives free recitals in the summer at beaches and parks, culminating in a concert on the summit of Whistler Mountain.

Drama

Arts Club Theatre (☎687-5315, *www.artsclub.com*). A leading light in the city's drama scene, performing at three venues: the main stage, at 1585 Johnston St on Granville Island, offers mainstream drama, comedies and musicals; the next-door bar presents small-scale revues and cabarets; and a third stage, at 1181 Seymour and Davie streets, focuses on avant-garde plays and Canadian dramatists – a launching pad for the likes of Michael J. Fox. The theatre has cult status for its "theatre sports", in which teams of actors compete for applause with improvization. Beware, as audience participation features highly.

Firehall Arts Centre, 280 E Cordova at Gore St (☎689-0926). The leader of Vancouver's community and avant-garde pack, presenting mime, music, video and visual arts.

Theatre Under the Stars (TUTS), Malkin Bowl, Stanley Park (☎687-0174). Summer productions here are fun and lightweight, but can suffer from being staged in one of the Northwest's rainiest cities.

Vancouver East Cultural Centre, 1895 Venables St at Victoria St (☎254-9578). Renowned performance space housed in an old church, used by a highly eclectic mix of drama, dance, mime and musical groups.

Vancouver Playhouse Theatre Company, Hamilton St at Dunsmuir St (☎873-3311). One of the Northwest's biggest companies. It usually presents six top-quality shows with some of the region's premier performers and designers during its October to May season.

Waterfront Theatre, 1411 Cartwright St, Granville Island (☎685-6217). Home to three resident companies that also hold workshops and readings.

Dance

Anna Wyman Dance Theatre (☎662-8846). Although their repertoire is wide, this group specializes in contemporary dance. As well as standard shows, they occasionally put on free outdoor performances at Granville Island and at Robson Square near the Art Gallery.

Ballet British Columbia (☎732-5003). The province's top company performs – along with major visiting companies – at the Queen Elizabeth Theatre.

EDAM (☎876-9559). Experimental Dance and Music present modern mixes of dance, film, music and art.

Karen Jamieson Dance Company (☎872-5658). Award-winning company and choreographer that often uses Canadian composers and artists, and incorporates native cultural themes.

Cinema

Fifth Avenue Cinemas, 2110 Burrard. Fiveplex cinema run by the founder of the Vancouver Film Festival. It is one of the better in the city for art-house films.

Granville 7, Cinema complex at 855 Granville (☎684-4000). Mainstream first-release films in one of the city centre's main multiscreen complexes.

Pacific Cinémathèque, 1131 Howe St near Helmcken St (☎688-FILM). Best of the art-houses. The programmes are hit-and-miss, but rotate often; over the course of a few nights any film buff should find something playing tempting.

Festivals

Warm summers, outdoor venues and a culture-hungry population combine to make Vancouver an important festival city. Recognized as one of the leading festivals of its kind, Vancouver's annual **International Jazz Festival** (late June to early July) is organized by the Coastal Jazz and Blues Society (☎872-5200, *www.jazzvancouver.com*). Past line-ups have featured such luminaries as Wynton Marsalis, Youssou N'Dour, Ornette Coleman, Carla Bley and John Zorn. Some 800 international musicians congregate annually, many offering workshops and free concerts in addition to paid-admission events.

Other music festivals include the **Vancouver International Folk Music Festival** (☎681-0041, *www.thefestival.bc.ca*), a bevy of international acts centred on Jericho Park and the Centennial Theatre for several days during the third week of July. In July, Vancouver loses its collective head over the **Sea Festival** (☎684-3378) – nautical fun, parades and excellent fireworks around English Bay. Further afield in Whistler (see p.395), there's a **Country & Bluegrass Festival** held in mid-July.

Theatre festivals come thick and fast, particularly in the summer. The chief event is the **Fringe Festival** (☎257-0350, *www.vancouverfringe.com*), modelled on the Edinburgh equivalent. It currently runs to more than 550 shows, staged by some ninety companies at ten venues. There's also an annual **Shakespeare Festival** (June–Aug) in Vanier Park and an **International Comedy Festival** (☎683-0883, *www.comedyfest.com*) in early August on Granville Island. Many of the city's art-house cinemas join forces to host the **Vancouver International Film Festival** (☎685-0260), an annual showcase for more than 150 films running from late September to mid-October.

Listings

Airlines Air BC (☎688-5515 or 1-800/663-3721 in Canada, 1-800/776-3000 in the US); Air Canada (☎688-5515); American Airlines (☎222-2532 or 1-800/368-1955); British Airways (☎270-8131); Central Mountain Air (☎847-4780 or 1-800/663-3721); Continental (☎1-800/525-0280); Delta (☎1-800/345-3400); Harbour Air Seaplanes, services to Victoria Inner Harbour (☎688-1277 or 1-800/665-0212); Helijet Airways, helicopter service to Victoria (☎273-1414 or 1-800/665-4354); KLM (☎303-3666); North Vancouver (☎604/278-1608); United (☎1-800/241-6522); West Coast Air, seaplane services to Victoria (☎688-9115 or 1-800/347-2222); Whistler Air, direct flights to Whistler from Vancouver Harbour Air Terminal by *Pan Pacific Hotel* (☎932-6615 or 1-888/806-2299).

American Express, Park Place Building, 666 Burrard St, enter at Hornby and Dunsmuir (☎669-2813 or 1-800/772-4473), and is open Mon–Fri 8.30am–5.30pm, Sat 10am–4pm.

Bike rental Bayshore Bicycles & Rollerblade Rentals, 745 Denman St (☎688-2453) and 1610 W Georgia St at Cardero St and the *Westin Bayshore Hotel* (☎689-5071); Harbour Air, Harbour Air Terminal at the waterfront one block west of Canada Place and the foot of Burrard St (☎688-1277) – also rents blades and motorcycles; Spokes, 1798 Georgia at Denman (☎688-5141, *www.vancouverbikerental.com*).

Bookshops Chapters, 788 Robson St (☎682-4066), is a colossal bookshop at the heart of downtown. World Wide Books and Maps, 1247 Granville St, is adequate for maps, guides and travel.

Buses Airporter (☎946-8866 or 1-800/668-3141) for shuttle from Vancouver Airport to bus depot and downtown; Greyhound (☎662-3222 or 1-800/661-8747, *www.greyhound.ca*) for BC, Alberta, Yukon and long-haul destinations including Seattle and the US; Maverick Coach Lines (☎662-8051 or 1-800/972-6300) for the Sunshine Coast, Powell River, Whistler, Pemberton and Nanaimo on Vancouver Island; Pacific Coach Lines (☎662-8074 or 1-800/661-1725) for Victoria, Vancouver Island; Perimeter (☎266-5386 or 905-0041, *www.perimeterbus.com*) for services between Whistler and Vancouver Airport; Quick Shuttle (☎940-4428 or 1-800/665-2122, *www.quickcoach.com*) for Bellingham Airport, downtown Seattle and Sea-Tac Airport.

Car rental Budget, airport, 501 W Georgia St and 1705 Burrard St (☎668-7000 or 1-800/268-8900 in Canada, 1-800/527-0700 in US); Exotic Car and Motorcycle Rentals, 1820 Burrard at W 2nd (☎644-9128 or 1-800/566-0343) anything from 355 Ferrari to VW Beetle; Hertz, 1128 Seymour St (☎688-2411 or 1-800/263-0600); National (☎1-800/227-7368), airport (☎207-3730) and 1130 W Georgia at Thurlow (☎609-7150); Rent-a-Wreck, 1083 Hornby St (☎688-0001).

Consulates Australia, 602-999 Canada Place (☎684-1177); Ireland, 1400-100 W Pender St (☎683-8440); New Zealand, 1200-888 Dunsmuir (☎684-7388); UK, 800-1111 Melville (☎683-4421); US, 1095 W Pender (☎685-4311).

Currency exchange Custom House Currency, 375 Water St, Gastown (☎482-6007); International Securities Exchange, 1169 Robson St near Thurlow (☎683-9666); Thomas Cook, 130-999 Canada Place (☎641-1229); Vancouver Bullion & Currency Exchange, 420 Hornby St (☎685-1008).

Dentists For your nearest dentists, call the College of Dental Surgeons for a referral (☎736-3621). Drop-in dentist, Dentacare (Mon–Fri 8am–5pm only; ☎669-6700), is in the lower level of the Bentall Centre at Dunsmuir and Burrard.

Directory enquiries ☎411.

Doctors The College of Physicians can provide names of three doctors near you (☎733-7758). Drop-in service at Consolidated Care Point Medical Service, 1175 Denman St (☎681-5338) or Medicentre (☎683-8138) in the Bentall Centre (Mon–Fri 8am–5pm; see "Dentists" above).

Emergencies ☎911.

Ferries BC Ferries for services to Vancouver Island (☎1-888/724-5223 in BC); to the Gulf Islands, the Sunshine Coast, Prince Rupert, the Inside Passage and the Queen Charlotte Islands;

reservations and information ☎1-888/223-3779 (in BC); Victoria (☎250/386-3431 or recorded information ☎381-5335); Vancouver or from outside BC (☎444-2890), *www.bcferries.com*. Aquabus (☎689-5858) and False Creek Ferries (☎684-7781) for services between downtown, Granville Island and Vanier Park.

Gay and lesbian switchboard Touch-tone guide (☎684-XTRA).

Hospitals St Paul's Hospital is the closest to downtown at 1081 Burrard St near Davie St (☎682-2344). The city hospital is Vancouver General at 855 W 12th near Oak, south of Broadway (☎875-4111).

Laundry Davie Laundromat, 1061 Davie St (☎682-2717); Scotty's One Hour Cleaners, 834 Thurlow near Robson (☎685-7732).

Left luggage At the bus station ($2 per 24hr).

Lost property BC Transit (☎682-7887); West Vancouver Transit (☎985-7777); police (☎665-2232); airport (☎276-6104).

Maps Geological Survey of Canada, 101-605 Robson near Richards (Mon–Fri 8.30am–4.30pm; ☎666-0529). Superb source of official survey maps, including *all* 1:50,000 maps of BC and Yukon.

Optician Same-day service Granville Mall Optical, 807 Granville and Robson (☎683-4716).

Parking Main downtown garages are at The Bay (entrance on Richards near Dunsmuir), Robson Square (on Smithe and Howe), and the Pacific Centre (on Howe and Dunsmuir) – all are expensive and fill up quickly. A better idea might be to leave your car at the free Park'n'Ride in New Westminster (off Hwy 1).

Pharmacies Shopper's Drug Mart, 1125 Davie and Thurlow (☎669-2424), is open 24hr and has five other outlets open Mon–Sat 9am–midnight, Sun 9am–9pm. Carson Midnite Drug Store, 6517 Main at 49th, is open daily until midnight.

Police RCMP (☎264-3111); Vancouver City Police (☎665-3535).

Post office Main office at 349 W Georgia and Homer (Mon–Fri 8am–5.30pm; ☎662-5722). Post office information (☎1-800/267-1177).

Taxis Black Top (☎731-1111 or 681-2181); Vancouver Taxi (☎255-5111 or 874-5111); Yellow Cab (☎681-3311 or 681-1111).

Tourist information 200 Burrard St (☎683-2000).

Train enquiries VIA Rail (☎669-3050 or toll-free in Canada only ☎1-800/561-8630, 1-800/561-3949 in the US); BC Rail (reservations and info ☎984-5246 or 1-800/663-8238 in North America; recorded info ☎631-3501); Amtrak (☎1-800/872-7245); Rocky Mountain Railtours (☎606-7200 or 1-800/665-7245) for expensive rail tours through the Rockies.

Weather ☎664-9010.

X Files Tours Contact The X-Tour (☎609-2700, *www.x-tour.com*) for 3 to 3hr 30min limousine tours of locations connected with *The X Files* series and other film and TV shows shot in Vancouver: from $145.

VANCOUVER ISLAND

VANCOUVER ISLAND's proximity to Vancouver makes it one of the Northwest's premier tourist destinations, though its popularity is slightly out of proportion to what is, in most cases, a pale shadow of the scenery on offer on the region's mainland. The largest of North America's West Coast islands, it stretches almost 500km from north to south, but has a population of around only 500,000, mostly concentrated around **Victoria**, whose small-town feel belies its role as British Columbia's second metropolis and provincial capital. It is also the most British of Canadian cities in feel and appearance, something it shamelessly plays up to attract its two million – largely American – visitors annually. While Victoria makes a convenient base for touring the island – and, thanks to a superlative museum, merits a couple of days in its own right – little else

---

The telephone code for Vancouver and vicinity is ☎604. The telephone code for Victoria and Vancouver Island is ☎250.

here, or (for that matter) in any of the island's other sizeable towns, is enough to justify an overnight stop.

For most visitors Vancouver Island's main attraction is the great outdoors and – increasingly – **whale-watching**, an activity which can be pursued from Victoria, **Tofino**, **Ucluelet** and several other places up and down the island. The scenery is a mosaic of landscapes, principally defined by a central spine of snow-capped mountains which divide it decisively between the rugged and sparsely populated wilderness of the west coast and the more sheltered lowlands of the east. Rippling hills characterize the northern and southern tips, and few areas are free of the lush forest mantle that supports one of BC's most lucrative logging industries. Apart from three minor east–west roads (and some rough logging and gravel roads), all the urban centres are linked by a good highway running along almost the entire length of the east coast.

Once beyond the main towns of **Duncan** and **Nanaimo**, the northern two-thirds of the island is distinctly underpopulated. Locals and tourists alike are lured by the beaches at **Parksville** and **Qualicum**, while the stunning seascapes of the unmissable **Pacific Rim National Park**, protecting the central portion of the island's west coast, and **Strathcona Provincial Park**, which embraces the heart of the island's mountain fastness, are the main destinations for most visitors. Both of these parks offer the usual panoply of outdoor activities, with hikers being particularly well served by the national park's **West Coast Trail**, which is a tough and increasingly popular long-distance path. A newer, but less dramatic (and less busy) trail, the **Juan de Fuca Trail** runs to the south of the park. Shuttle buses and once-daily scheduled bus services from Victoria to points in the park, together with a wonderful approach by **boat** from Port Alberni, offer a choice of beguiling alternative itineraries for exploring the region. Another **boat trip** on a smaller working vessel from the tiny settlements of Tahsis and Gold River to the north is also becoming deservedly popular.

For a large number of travellers, however, the island is little more than a necessary pilgrimage on a longer journey north. Thousands annually make the trip to **Port Hardy**, linked by bus to Victoria, at the northern tip, to pick up the ferry that follows the so-called **Inside Passage**, a breathtaking trip up the British Columbia coast to Prince Rupert. More are likely to pick up on the newer scenic ferry service, the **Discovery Coast Passage**, from Port Hardy to Bella Coola, south of Prince Rupert. You'll probably meet more backpackers plying these routes than anywhere else in the region, many of them en route to the far north, taking the ferries that continue on from Prince Rupert to Skagway and Alaska.

Victoria

VICTORIA has a lot to live up to. Leading US travel magazine *Condé Nast Traveler* has voted it one of the world's top ten cities to visit, and world number one for ambience and environment. And it's not named after a queen and an era for nothing. Victoria has gone to town in serving up lashings of fake Victoriana and chintzy commercialism – tearooms, Union Jacks, bagpipers, pubs and ersatz echoes of empire confront you at every turn. Much of the waterfront area has an undeniably quaint and likeable English feel – "Brighton Pavilion with the Himalayas for a backdrop", as Kipling remarked – and Victoria has more British-born residents than anywhere in Canada, but its tourist potential is exploited chiefly for American visitors who make the short sea journey from across the border. Despite the seasonal influx, and the sometimes atrociously tacky attractions designed to part tourists from their money, it's a small, relaxed and pleasantly sophisticated place, worth lingering in if only for its inspirational museum. It's also rather genteel in parts, something underlined by the number of gardens around the place and some nine hundred hanging baskets that adorn much of the downtown area during the summer. Though often damp, the weather here is extremely mild: Victoria's meteorological station has the distinction of being the only one in Canada to record a winter in which the temperature never fell below freezing.

A brief history of Victoria

Victoria's site was originally inhabited by **Salish natives**, and in particular by the Lekwammen, who had a string of some ten villages in the area. From here they cultivated camas bulbs – vital to their diet and trade – and applied their advanced salmon-fishing methods to the shoals of migrating salmon in net-strung reefs offshore. At the time the region must have been a virtual paradise. Captain George Vancouver, apparently mindless of the native presence, described his feelings on first glimpsing this part of Vancouver Island: "The serenity of the climate, the innumerable pleasing landscapes, and the abundant fertility that nature puts forth, require only to be enriched by the industry of man with villages, mansions, cottages and other buildings, to render it the most lovely country that can be imagined." The first step in this process began in 1842, when Victoria received some of its earliest **white visitors**, when James Douglas disembarked during a search for a new local headquarters for the Hudson's Bay Company. One look at the natural harbour and its surroundings was enough: this, he declared, was a "perfect Eden", a feeling only reinforced by the friendliness of the indigenous population, who helped him build Fort Camouson, named after an important aboriginal landmark (the name was later changed to Fort Victoria to honour the British queen). The aboriginal peoples from up and down the island settled near the fort, attracted by the new trading opportunities it offered. Soon they were joined by British pioneers, brought in to settle the land by a Bay subsidiary, the Puget Sound Agricultural Company, which quickly built several large company farms as a focus for immigration. In time, the harbour became the busiest West Coast port north of San Francisco and a major base for the British navy's Pacific fleet, a role it still fulfils for the bulk of Canada's present navy.

Boom time came in the 1850s following the mainland gold strikes, when Victoria's port became an essential stopoff and supplies depot for prospectors heading across the water and into the interior. Military and bureaucratic personnel moved in to ensure order, bringing Victorian morals and manners with them. Alongside there grew a rumbustious shantytown of shops, bars and brothels, one bar run by "Gassy" Jack Leighton, soon to become one of Vancouver's unwitting founders.

Though the gold-rush bubble soon burst, Victoria carried on as a military, economic and political centre, becoming capital of the newly created British Columbia in 1866 – years before the foundation of Vancouver. British values were cemented in stone by the Canadian Pacific Railway, which built the *Empress Hotel* in 1908 in place of a proposed railway link that never came. Victoria's planned role as Canada's western rail terminus was surrendered to Vancouver, and with it any chance of realistic growth or industrial development. These days the town survives – but survives well – almost entirely on the backs of tourists (four million a year), the civil service bureaucracy, and – shades of the home country – retirees in search of a mild-weathered retreat. Its population today is around 330,000, almost exactly double what it was just thirty years ago.

Arrival and information

Victoria International Airport is 20km north of downtown on Hwy 17. The Akal Airporter shuttle bus heads downtown (where it stops at major hotels) every half-hour between about 4.30am and 1am; a single fare for the 45-minute journey is $13 (☎386-2525, 386-2526 or 1-877/386-2525, *www.akalairporter.travel.bc.ca*). Leaving the city for flights, you should call to arrange pick-ups (see Listings, p.345). Otherwise contact

GETTING TO VANCOUVER ISLAND

There are three ways to reach Vancouver Island – by bus and ferry, car and ferry, or air. Most people travelling under their own steam from Vancouver use the first means, which is a simple matter of buying an all-inclusive through-ticket to Victoria. More involved crossings to other points on the island, however, whether from the Canadian or US mainlands, are worth considering if you wish to skip Victoria and head as quickly as possible to Port Hardy for the Inside Passage ferry connections, or to Strathcona or the Pacific Rim parks. You can also reach Victoria directly from Vancouver Airport by inclusive coach and ferry arrangements (see p.291 for details).

FOOT PASSENGERS FROM VANCOUVER

If you're without your own transport, the most painless way to Victoria from Vancouver is to buy a Pacific Coach Lines (PCL; ☎604/662-8074 in Vancouver and 250/385-4411 or 385-3348 in Victoria; toll free ☎1-800/661-1725) ticket at the Vancouver bus terminal at 1150 Station St, which takes you, inclusive of the ferry crossing and journeys to and from ferry terminals at both ends, to Victoria's central bus station at 700 Douglas St. Buses leave hourly in the summer (first bus 5.45am; last bus 8.45pm from July to early Sept, 7.45pm the rest of the year), every two hours in the winter: total journey time is about three hours thirty minutes and a single ticket costs $26.50 ($51 return). No bookings are necessary or taken: overflow passengers are simply put on another coach. The ferry crossing takes 95 minutes, and offers some stunning views as the boat navigates the narrow channels between the Gulf Islands en route. Be sure to keep your ticket stub for reboarding the bus after the crossing. Coach drivers give you all the practical details en route. It's also worth stocking up on food on board, as subsidized ferry meals are famously cheap (queues form instantly). You can save yourself about $15 by using public transport at each end and buying a ferry ticket separately ($9 peak season July to early Sept; $8.50 shoulder mid-March to June, mid-Sept to mid-Nov & mid-Dec to Jan 1; $7.50 the rest of the year), but for the extra hassle and time involved it hardly seems worth it. A similar all-inclusive bus/ferry arrangement also operates from Vancouver to Nanaimo on Vancouver Island via the Horseshoe Bay Terminal, about fifteen minutes north of West Vancouver on Hwy 1. You can reach the Horseshoe Bay Terminal by taking bus #250 or #257 from Georgia Street. The ferry charges are the same for foot passengers.

BY CAR FROM BRITISH COLUMBIA

BC Ferries operates four routes to the island across the Georgia Strait from mainland British Columbia (☎1-888/223-3779 from anywhere in BC; otherwise ☎604/444-2890 or 250/386-3431 in Vancouver, Victoria or outside BC, *www.bcferries.com*). Reservations on all routes are essential in summer if you want to avoid long waits, and can be made up to 90 minutes prior to sailing. The most direct and heavily used by Victoria–Vancouver passengers is the Tsawwassen–Swartz Bay connection, the route used by Pacific Coach Lines' buses. Tsawwassen is about a forty-minute drive south of downtown Vancouver; Swartz Bay is the same distance north of Victoria. Ferries ply the route almost continuously from 7am to 10pm (sixteen sailings daily in summer, minimum of eight daily in winter). Car tickets cost $32 at weekends (noon Fri to last sailing on Sun) and $30 on weekdays in high season – see above for seasonal breakdown ($28.75/27 in shoulder season, $24.25/22.75 in low). A **bike** costs $2.50 year-round. The Mid-Island Express from Tsawwassen to Nanaimo (Duke Point terminal), midway up the island, has eight or so departures daily on the two-hour crossing. More boats cover the Horseshoe Bay–Nanaimo (Departure Bay terminal) route, a 95-minute journey from a terminal about fifteen-minutes' drive from West Vancouver. Note that a new ferry terminal,

Harbour Air (384-2215 or 1-800/665-0212, *www.harbour-air.com*) or West Coast Air (☎388-4521 or 1-800/347-2222, *www.westcoastair.com*), who operate efficient and quick float planes between Vancouver's port and Victoria's downtown Inner Harbour: both

Discovery Point, has been opened at Nanaimo for the first of these crossings. Fares for both these routes are the same as for Tsawwassen to Swartz Bay. The fourth route is Powell River–Comox, Powell River being some 160km northwest of Vancouver on the Sunshine Coast.

FERRIES FROM THE UNITED STATES

Travellers from the United States have several options. Coach and ferry inclusive arrangements are offered by Gray Lines of Seattle, who operate a once-daily service in each direction between Seattle and Victoria (currently leaves 5.30am; $39 one-way, $70 return; ☎250/344-5248, 206/626-5208 or 1-800/544-0739). Washington State Ferries, 2499 Ocean Ave, Sidney (in Victoria ☎250/381-1551 or 250/656-1531 in Sidney, in Seattle ☎206/464-6400 or 1-888/808-7977 in WA only) runs ferries from Anacortes, ninety minutes north of Seattle, to Sidney, thirty minutes (and 30km) north of Victoria (summer 2 daily in each direction, winter 1 daily; 3hr–3hr 30min), with one of the two summer departures travelling via Orcas and Friday Harbor on the San Juan Islands. Passenger fares are around US$7 (US$2 from the San Juan Islands), a car and driver US$37 (US$15 from the San Juan Islands). Car reservations are required from Orcas and Friday Harbor and can be made by calling at least a day in advance (☎360/378-4777 in Friday Harbor).

Black Ball Transport, 430 Belleville St, Victoria (in BC ☎250/386-2202, in Washington ☎360/457-4491 or 1-800/633-1589) operates a ferry across the Juan de Fuca Strait between Port Angeles on Washington's Olympic Peninsula right to Victoria's Inner Harbour (1–4 daily; 95min). Passenger fares are around US$7 and US$29 for cars. Reservations are not accepted. Car drivers should call ahead in summer to have some idea of how long they'll have to wait.

For foot passengers, and day-trippers in particular, a speedier option is Victoria Express's service from Port Angeles (2 daily late May to late June & Sept to mid-Oct; late June to Aug 3 daily; 55min) to Victoria's Inner Harbour. The fare is US$12.50 one-way, US$25 return. Ferries run only from mid-May to mid-Oct. For information and reservations, call ☎250/361-9144 (Canada), ☎360/452-8088 (Port Angeles) or ☎1-800/633-1589 (Washington). Alternatively, the 300-passenger-only *Victoria Clipper* catamaran travels between Pier 69 in downtown Seattle and Victoria's Inner Harbour in three hours or two hours if you take the more "Turbojet" departures (250 Bellevue St, Victoria, ☎250/382-8100 in Seattle or 1-800/888-2535 outside Seattle and BC). There is one sailing daily in each direction from January to March and mid-September to December; two sailings daily in the first half of May and second half of September; and four sailings daily from mid-May to mid-September. Tickets prices vary according to season – US$55 single, US$91 return off-season, US$60/99 for three-hour crossings and US$69/115 for the Turbojet in summer.

BY AIR

Several provincial airlines as well as Air Canada fly to Victoria, though it's an expensive way to make the journey if you're only coming from Vancouver or Washington State. Open return fares from Vancouver typically run to around $140, excursion fares around $100. If you are going to fly, however, it's more fun and more direct to fly from Vancouver harbour to Victoria harbour by helicopter or float plane: Harbour Air and West Coast Air fly from the Tradewinds Marina just west of Canada Place in Vancouver. Helijet Airways (☎604/273-1414) fly from the helipad to the east. Kenmore Air, 6321 NE 175th, Seattle (☎206/486-1257 or 1-800/543-9595, *www.kenmoreair.com*), runs scheduled seaplane services (US$95 one-way; 45min) between downtown Seattle and Victoria's Inner Harbour.

companies share terminals in both cities ($89; planes leave roughly hourly; crossing time is 30 minutes). The **bus terminal** is downtown at 700 Douglas and Belleville, close to the Royal British Columbia Museum; the central VIA **Rail station** is at 450

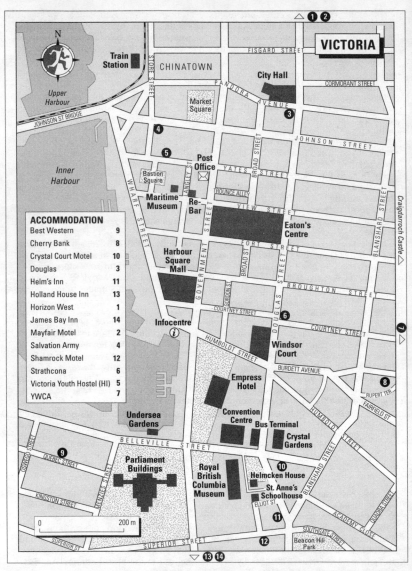

ACCOMMODATION	
Best Western	9
Cherry Bank	8
Crystal Court Motel	10
Douglas	3
Helm's Inn	11
Holland House Inn	13
Horizon West	1
James Bay Inn	14
Mayfair Motel	2
Salvation Army	4
Shamrock Motel	12
Strathcona	6
Victoria Youth Hostel (HI)	5
YWCA	7

Pandora St (☎1-800/561-8630), about seven blocks north of the *Empress Hotel*, but you'll only arrive there if you've managed to get a seat on the lone daily train from Courtenay and Nanaimo.

Victoria's busy **infocentre** is at 812 Wharf St, in front of the *Empress Hotel* on the harbour (daily: May–Sept 8.30am–8pm; Oct–April 9am–5pm; ☎953-2033, for accommodation reservations ☎1-800/663-3883, *www.tourismvictoria.com*). It offers help finding accommodation and can book you onto whale-watching and other tours (see box, p.340), while its huge range of information – on both Victoria and Vancouver Island as a whole – makes as good a reason as any for starting a tour of the island from the city. There's also a separate desk for concert, theatre and other tickets. Independent travellers will want to check out the notice board at the **HI youth hostel** (see p.333), which has lots of current practical information.

The best in-town means of transport are the tiny Inner Harbour **ferries**, worth taking just for the ride: try a $10 evening "mini-cruise" around the harbour (tickets on Inner Harbour or book at the infocentre). You're unlikely to need to take a local **bus** anywhere, but if you do, most services run from the corner of Douglas and Yates. The fare within the large central zone is $1.75 – tickets and the DayPass ($5.50) are sold at the infocentre, 7-Eleven stores and other marked outlets, or you can pay on board if you have the exact fare. For 24-hour recorded information on city transit, call the Busline (☎382-6161, *www.bctransit.com*). Other potentially useful private bus lines for **onward travel** from Victoria include Laidlaw (☎385-4411 or 1-800/318-0818, *www.victoriatours.com*) at the bus terminal, responsible for scheduled services across the island to Duncan ($10 one-way), Chemainus ($12.50), Nanaimo ($17.50), Port Alberni ($30), Tofino ($47.50), Ucluelet ($47.50), Courtney ($35), Campbell River ($40), Port Hardy ($84.10) and points in between (no reservations are necessary or taken for Laidlaw services). Also useful are Gray Lines of Seattle for a once-daily service to Seattle inclusive of ferry (leaves 10am; $40; ☎206/626-5208 or 1-800/544-0739). The West Coast Trail Express, 3954 Bow Rd (☎477-8700 or 1-888/999-2288, *www.trailbus.com*), is a high-season-only shuttle service (March–Sept) for connections to Port Renfrew and Gordon River (both $30) via French Beach, Jordan River, China Beach and Sooke for the southern trailhead of the West Coast Trail and the newer Juan de Fuca Trail (see p.373 for both trails), as well as links to Bamfield and Pachena Bay (both $50): it also runs between these and other destinations, notably between Bamfield and Port Alberni ($22). Book seats in advance during office hours (March–April Mon–Fri 8am–noon; May–Sept 6.30am–1.30pm & 5.30–8pm).

Accommodation

Victoria fills up quickly in the summer, and most of its budget **accommodation** is well-known and heavily patronized. Top-price hotels cluster around the Inner Harbour area; **hostels** and more downmarket alternatives are scattered all over, though the largest concentration of cheap **hotels** and **motels** is around the Gorge Road and Douglas Street areas northwest of downtown. Reservations are virtually obligatory in all categories, though the infocentre's accommodation service will root out a room if you're stuck (☎1-800/663-3883 in North America, ☎250/953-2033 from outside North America). They are more than likely to offer you **B&B**, of which the town has a vast selection, though prices for many are surprisingly elevated; many owners of the more far-flung places will pick you up from downtown. Some B&Bs are also real treats – romantic hideaways or housed in lovely old houses. In desperation it's worth consulting one of the specialist B&B agencies such as Canada-West (☎388-4620).

Victoria's commercial **campgrounds** are full to bursting in summer, with most space given over to RVs. Few of these are convenient for downtown anyway – given that you'll have to travel, you might as well head for one of the more scenic provincial park sites. Most are on the Trans-Canada Highway to the north, or on Hwy 14 east of Victoria.

Hotels and motels

Abigail's, 960 McClure St (☎388-5363, fax 388-7787, *www.abigailshotel.com*). A very classy, small hotel in a fine building with log fires, voluminous duvets, jacuzzis and a good breakfast. Situated on the corner of Quadra St, a block east of Blanshard and easy walking distance from the centre. ⑧.

Best Western Inner Harbour, 412 Quebec St between Oswego and Menzies sts (☎384-5122 or 1-888/383-2378, *bestwestern@victoriahotels.com*). Very convenient, central and comfortable, but pricey. ⑦.

Cherry Bank Hotel, 825 Burdett Ave near Blanshard St (☎385-5380 or 1-800/998-6688, fax 383-0949, *www.bctravel.com/cherrybankhotel.html*). Reservations are essential at this deservedly popular and pleasantly eccentric 26-room budget hotel (note rotating mermaid on the roof); excellent rooms and breakfast included. ③.

Crystal Court Motel, 701 Belleville St near Douglas St (☎384-0551, fax 384-5125, *mbscott@vanisle.net*). Large, functional and fairly priced motel well located just one block from the Inner Harbour, though it fronts a busy road. ④.

Douglas Hotel, 1450 Douglas St at Pandora St (☎383-4157 or 1-800/332-9981, fax 383-2279, *www.hoteldouglas.com*). Clean, no-frills and slightly rough-edged big hotel. It is opposite the city hall, close to downtown, and on bus routes #1, #6, #14 and #30. ④.

Helm's Inn, 600 Douglas St near Blanchard and Superior sts (☎385-5767 or 1-800/665-4356, fax 385-2221, *www.helmsinn.com*). Popular if gaudily decorated hotel on the main road just half a block from the Royal BC Museum. One-bedroom and studio suites with kitchens available. Cheaper rates off-season. ⑤.

Holland House Inn, 595 Michegan St near Government St (☎384-6644, fax 384-6117). A comfortable and smart, small hotel located a couple of blocks south of the BC Museum. ⑥/⑦.

Horizon West, 1961 Douglas St at Chatham St (☎382-2111 or 1-800/830-2111, fax 388-5822, *www.bctravel.com*). Reasonably central hotels in this price range are unusual in Victoria, so call ahead to secure one of its eighty rooms. ④.

James Bay Inn, 270 Government St at Toronto St (☎384-7151 or 1-800/836-2649, fax 385-2311, *www.jamesbayinn.bc.ca*). Vying with the *Cherry Bank* as Victoria's best reasonably low-cost option, this Edwardian building was the home of painter Emily Carr. Simple rooms at varying prices, with a restaurant and pub in the basement. Two blocks south of the Government Buildings (buses #5 or #30 to Government and Superior sts). ⑤.

Mayfair Motel, 650 Speed Ave at Douglas St (☎388-7337, fax 388-7398). This small motel 2km north of downtown is ideal if you want to be away from the centre. ③.

Shamrock Motel, 675 Superior St between Government St and Hwy 1 (☎385-8768 or 1-800/294-5544, fax 385-1837). Has just fifteen units, but (with the *Crystal Court*), one of the best-value motels or hotels in the central area. ④.

Strathcona, 919 Douglas St at Courtney St (☎383-7137 or 1-800/663-7476, fax 383-6893). Large, modern hotel where rooms include baths and TVs. There's a "British pub" and restaurant downstairs with booming live and canned music and the nightly dancing may not be to all tastes. ④.

Bed and Breakfasts

Ambleside, 1121 Faithful St (☎388-9948 or 1-800/916-9948, fax 383-9317, *www.amblesidebb.com*). Expensive as B&Bs go, but you get a 1919 "craftsman heritage home", a full breakfast and a choice of two tasteful rooms in a pleasant neighbourhood due east of Beacon Hill Park (so a long but pleasant walk to downtown). ⑥.

Andersen House, 301 Kingston St (☎388-4565, fax 388-4563, *andersen@islandnet.com*). Another pricey and tasteful two-room heritage home (built 1891) with private baths and even CD players. ⑥.

Craigmyle B&B Inn, 1037 Craigmyle Rd (☎595-5411, fax 370-5276, *craigmyle@home.com*). By Craigdarroch Castle this friendly antique-furnished home has seventeen rooms, but is 1.5km from downtown. Buses #11 or #14 run from the corner of Fort St and Joan Crescent. ④.

Heathergate House, 122 Simcoe St (☎383-0068 or 1-888/683-0068, fax 383-4320, *www.lvcs.com /heathergate*). Four rooms within walking distance of the Inner Harbour and the sights. ⑤.

Prior House, 620 St Charles St (☎592-8847, fax 592-8223, *www.priorhouse.com*). Pretty swanky for a B&B; once the home of Victoria's lieutenant governor – ask for his suite, complete with bathroom with chandelier. About 2.5km east of downtown in smart Rockland area, so better if you have transport. ⑦.

Ryan's, 224 Superior St (☎389-0012, fax 389-2857). A very pretty 1892 heritage building south of the BC Museum and 5min walk to downtown; all nicely decorated rooms with private bathrooms. ⑥.

Hostels and student accommodation

Backpacker's Hostel, 1608 Quadra St (☎386-4471). This hostel is not too far from downtown – it sits at the corner of Quadra and Pandora sts – and offers dorm beds at $12, singles at $20, a double dorm at $30 and a double room at $35. Weekly rates are also available. Bed linen is included, and there are laundry, kitchen, storage and parking facilities. No curfew. ①.

Beverley Lodge, 1729 Oak Bay Ave (☎598-7323). Hostel with non-smoking bunk rooms for two, four and six people. A 20min walk from downtown: follow Fort St until it intersects Oak Bay Ave; turn right and the newly renovated four-storey heritage house is four roads down on the right. Or you can catch buses #1 or #2 from opposite *McDonalds* on Douglas St, which drop you virtually outside. Self-serve kitchen and outside deck available. $18 per person. ①.

Ocean Island Backpacker's Inn, 791 Pandora Ave at Blanshard St (☎385-1788 or 1-888/888-4180, *www.oceanisland.com*). A good, reasonably central location in the northeast corner of downtown. The restored 1893 heritage building has dorm beds at $16 (four or six to a room); singles at $19.50 and doubles at $39.50.

Renouf House, 2010 Stanley Ave (☎595-4774, fax 598-1515). A 30min walk east from downtown or catch #10 (Haultain) bus from the corner of Douglas and View and ask to be dropped at Fernwood and Stanley. Then walk a block east on Gladstone to Stanley, turn left at the corner store and the hostel is the white house next door. The owners are great kayaking and sailing experts, so well worth staying here if this is what you want to do on Vancouver Island. Singles/doubles with shared bathroom ($35/50) or singles/doubles with private bathroom ($50/65). ①–④.

Salvation Army Men's Hostel, 525 Johnson St near Store St (☎384-3396). Better than it sounds, being clean and modern, but for men only. Rooms are given on a first-come, first-served basis, with doors open at 4pm. Dorm beds ($19), private rooms and weekly and monthly rates are available. ①.

University of Victoria (☎721-8395 or 721-8396). The nicely situated campus is 20min northeast of downtown near Oak Bay and reached on buses #7 or #14. Ring for the University Housing and Conference Services, or register on site at the Housing Office, near the campus Coffee Gardens. Offers single and double private rooms with shared bath including breakfast. May–Sept. ①.

Victoria Backpackers' Hostel, 1418 Fernwood Rd (☎386-4471). Battered and laid-back but less convenient than the youth hostel: take bus #1, #10, #11, #14, #27 or #28 towards Fernwood: the #10 to Haultain from the corner of Douglas and Fort is the best bet. Dorm beds, private singles and doubles available with one bunk room reserved for women only. No curfew. Dorm beds $13. ①.

Victoria YM-WCA Women's Residence, 880 Courtney St at Quadra St (☎386-7511). A short stroll from downtown and on the #1 bus route. Mixed cafeteria and sports facilities, including pool, but rooms are for women only. Singles ($38.50) and doubles ($55) available; discounts October to May. ②.

Victoria Youth Hostel (HI), 516 Yates and Wharf (office: Mon–Thurs 7.30am–midnight, Fri–Sun 7am–2am; ☎385-4511, fax 385-3232, *www.hihostels.bc.ca*). A large, modern, and extremely well-run place just a few blocks north of the Inner Harbour. The bunk rooms, though, can be noisy: the reception, rather ominously, sells earplugs. The notice boards are packed with useful information. Members $16.50, non-members $20. Just three private doubles are available at $37 for members, $40 for non-members. ①/②.

Campgrounds

Fort Victoria RV and Park Campground, 340 Island Hwy 1A (☎479-8112, fax 479-5806, *www.fortvicrv.com*). Closest site to downtown, located 6km north of Victoria off the Trans-Canada. Take bus #14 (for Craigflower) from the city centre: it stops right by the gate. Large (250-pitch) site mainly for RVs but with a few tent sites; free hot showers. $27–29 per two persons.

Goldstream Provincial Park, 2930 Trans-Canada Highway (☎387-4363). Although 20km north of the city, this is Victoria's best camping option, with plenty of hiking, swimming and fishing opportunities. Bus #50 from Douglas St will get you here from downtown. $18.50.

McDonald Provincial Park. A government site with limited facilities, 32km from Victoria, but only 3km from the Swartz Bay Ferry Terminal, so useful for boat travellers. $12 in summer, $8 in winter.

Thetis Lake, 1938 Trans-Canada Hwy-West Park Lane (☎478-3845, *petisa@home.com*). Runs a close second to *Goldstream Park* for the pleasantness of its setting, and is only 10km north of downtown. Family-oriented, with 100 sites, laundry and coin-operated showers. $16.

Weir's Beach RV Resort, 5191 Williams Head Rd (☎478-3323, fax 478-1527). Enticing beachfront location 24km east of Victoria on Hwy 14. $35.

The City

The Victoria that's worth bothering with is very small: almost everything worth seeing, as well as the best shops and restaurants, is within walking distance in the **Inner Harbour** area and the Old Town district behind it. On summer evenings this area is alive with strollers and buskers, and a pleasure to wander as the sun drops over the water. Foremost amongst the daytime diversions are the **Royal British Columbia Museum** and the **Empress Hotel**. Most of the other trumpeted attractions are dreadful, and many charge entry fees out of all proportion to what's on show. If you're tempted by the Royal London Wax Museum, the Pacific Undersea Gardens, Miniature World, English Village, Anne Hathaway's Thatched Cottage or any of Victoria's other dubious commercial propositions, details are available from the infocentre. Otherwise you might drop by the modest **Maritime Museum** and think about a trip to the celebrated **Butchart Gardens**, some way out of town, but easily accessed by public transportation or regular all-inclusive tours from the bus terminal. If you're around for a couple of days you should also find time to walk around **Beacon Hill Park**, a few minutes' walk from downtown to the south.

The best of the area's beaches are well out of town on Hwy 14 and Hwy 1 (see pp.349–350), but for idling by the sea head down to the pebble shore along the southern edge of Beacon Hill Park. For some local swimming, the best option by far is **Willows Beach** on the Esplanade in Oak Bay, 2km east of Victoria; take bus #1 to Beach and Dalhousie Road. Other good stretches of sand can be found on Dallas Road and at Island View Beach.

The Royal British Columbia Museum

The **Royal British Columbia Museum**, 675 Belleville St (museum; daily 9am–5pm. National Geographic IMAX Theatre daily 10am–8pm; museum $9.65, IMAX Theatre $9.50 (double feature $14.50), combined ticket $15.50; museum ☎356-3701 or 1-888/447-7977, IMAX ☎480-4887, *www.rbcm1.rbcm.gov.bc.ca*), founded in 1886, is one of the best museums in the Northwest, and regularly rated, by visitors and travel magazine polls, as one of North America's top ten. All conceivable aspects of the province are examined, but the **aboriginal peoples** section is probably the definitive collection of a much-covered genre, while the natural history sections – huge re-creations of natural habitats, complete with sights, sounds and smells – are mind-boggling in scope and imagination. Allow at least two trips to take it all in.

From the word go – a huge stuffed mammoth in the lobby – you can tell that thought, wit and a lot of money have gone into the museum. Much of the cash must have been sunk into its most popular display, the **Open Ocean**, a self-contained, in-depth look at the sea and the deep-level ocean. Groups of ten are admitted into a series of tunnels, dark rooms, lifts and mock-ups of submarines at thirty-minute intervals. You take a time-coded ticket and wait your turn, so either arrive early or reckon on seeing the rest of the museum first. Though rather heavy-handed in its "we're-all-part-of-the-cosmic-soup" message, it's still an object lesson in presentation and state-of-the-art museum dynamics. It's also designed to be dark and enclosed, and signs wisely warn you to stay out if you suffer even a twinge of claustrophobia.

The first floor contains **dioramas**, full-scale reconstructions of some of the many natural habitats found in British Columbia. The idea of re-creating shorelines, coastal rainforests and Fraser Delta landscapes may sound far-fetched, yet all are incredibly realistic, down to dripping water and cool, dank atmospheres. Audiovisual displays and a tumult of information accompany the exhibits (the beaver film is worth hunting down), most of which focus attention on the province's 25,600km of coastline, a side of British Columbia usually overlooked in favour of its interior forests and mountains.

Upstairs on the second floor is the mother of all the tiny museums of bric-a-brac and pioneer memorabilia in BC. Arranged eccentrically from the present day backwards, it explores every aspect of the province's **social history** over two centuries in nitpicking detail. Prominently featured are the best part of an early twentieth-century town, complete with cinema and silent films, plus comprehensive displays on logging, mining, the gold rush, farming, fishing and lesser domestic details, all the artefacts and accompanying information being presented with impeccable finesse.

Up on the mezzanine third floor is a superb collection of **aboriginal peoples' art, culture and history** (see box, overleaf). It's presented in gloomy light, against muted wood walls and brown carpet – precautions intended to protect the fragile exhibits, but which also create a solemn atmosphere in keeping with the tragic nature of many of the displays. The collection divides into two epochs – before and after the coming of Europeans – tellingly linked by a single aboriginal carving of a white man, starkly and brilliantly capturing the initial wonder and weirdness of the new arrivals. Alongside are shamanic displays and carvings of previously taboo subjects, subtly illustrating the first breakdown of the old ways. The whole collection reflects this thoughtful and oblique approach, taking you to the point where smallpox virtually wiped out in one year a culture that was eight millennia in the making. A section on land and reservations is left for last – the issues are contentious even today – and even if you're succumbing to museum fatigue, the arrogance and duplicity of the documents on display will shock you. The highlights in this section are many, but try to make a point of seeing the short film footage *In the Land of the War Canoes* (1914), the **Bighouse** and its chants, and the audiovisual display on aboriginal myths and superstition. The **National Geographic Theatre** in the museum plays host to a huge IMAX screen and a changing programme of special format films. Outside the museum, there's also **Thunderbird Park**, a strip of grass with a handful of totem poles.

Helmcken House

Helmcken House (daily 10am–5pm; $4) stands strangely isolated in Thunderbird Park directly adjacent to the museum, a predictable heritage offering that showcases the home, furnishings and embroidery talents of the Helmcken family. Built in 1852, it is the oldest standing home on the island. Dr John Helmcken was Fort Victoria's doctor and local political bigwig, and his house is a typical monument to stolid Victoria values. Upstairs it also contains various attic treasures and some of the good doctor's fearsome-looking medical tools. It's probably only of interest, however, if you've so far managed to avoid any of the Northwest's many hundreds of similar houses. If you do visit, pick up the free guided tapes and listen to "voices from history" (actors and actresses) that give a more personalized slant to the building: listen, for example, to "Aunt Dolly" as she tells why she left the good doctor's room untouched as a shrine after his death. Just behind the house there's another old, white wood building, the **St Anne's Pioneer Schoolhouse** ($2), originally purchased by a Bishop Demers for four sisters of the Order of St Ann, who in 1858 took it upon themselves to leave their Québec home to come and teach in Victoria. Built between 1843 and 1858, it's believed to be one of the oldest, if not the oldest, buildings in Victoria; $2 buys you a peek at the old fashioned interior and period fittings.

The Parliament Buildings

The huge Victorian pile of the **Parliament Buildings**, at 501 Belleville St (daily: June to early Sept 9am–5pm; early Sept to May 9am–4pm; free; guided tours every 20–30min),

THE NATIVE CULTURES OF THE NORTHWEST COAST

Of all the Northwest's aboriginal peoples, the numerous linguistic groups that inhabit the northwest coast of British Columbia have the most sophisticated artistic tradition and the most lavish of ceremonials. Traditionally their social organization stemmed from a belief in a mythical time when humans and animals were essentially the same: each tribe was divided into **kin groups** who were linked by a common supernatural animal ancestor and shared the same names, ritual dances, songs and regalia. Seniority within each kin group was held by a rank of chiefs and nobles, who controlled the resources of private property such as house sites, stands of cedar, and fishing, gathering and hunting territories.

Such privileges, almost unique among Canadian aboriginal groups, led to the accumulation of private wealth, and thus great emphasis was placed on their inheritance. Central to the power structure was the ceremonial **potlatch**, which was held in the winter village, a seasonal resting place for these otherwise nomadic people, located where the supernatural forces were believed to be most accessible. The potlatch marked every significant occasion from the birth of an heir to the raising of a carved pole, and underscored an individual's right to his or her inherited status. Taking its name from the Chinook word for "gift", the potlatch also had the function of **redistributing wealth**. All the guests at the potlatch acted as witnesses to whatever event or object was being validated, and were repaid for their services with gifts from the host chief. Though these gifts often temporarily bankrupted the host, they heightened his prestige and ensured that he would be repaid in kind at a subsequent potlatch.

The most important element of potlatches were the **masked dances** that re-enacted ancestral encounters with supernatural beings, and were the principal means of perpetuating the history and heritage of each kin group. Created by artists whose innovative ideas were eagerly sought by chiefs in order to impress their guests, the dramatic masks were often elaborate mechanisms that could burst open to reveal the wearer or – like the well-known Cannibal Bird – could produce loud and disconcerting noises.

The **Kwakiutl** produced the most developed potlatches, featuring highly ranked dances like the *hamatsa* or "**cannibal dance**", whose performers had served a long apprenticeship as participants in less exalted dances. Before the *hamatsa* the initiate was sent to the "Cannibal at the North End of the World", a long period of seclusion and instruction in the snowbound woods. On returning to the village he would seem to be in a complete cannibalistic frenzy and would rush around biting members of the audience. These apparent victims were all paid for their role, which usually involved cutting themselves with knives to draw a flow of blood – and the *hamatsa* would burst blood-filled

is old and imposing in the manner of a large and particularly grand British town hall. Its outline beautifully picked out at night by some three hundred tiny bulbs (though locals grumble about the cost), the domed building is fronted by the sea and well-kept gardens – a pleasant enough ensemble, though it doesn't really warrant the manic enthusiasm visited on it by hordes of summer tourists. You're more likely to find yourself taking time out on the front lawns, distinguished by a perky statue of **Queen Victoria** and a giant sequoia, a gift from California. Designed by the 25-year-old Francis Rattenbury, who was also responsible for the *Empress Hotel* opposite, the building was completed in 1897, at a cost of $923,000, in time for Queen Victoria's jubilee. Figures from Victoria's grey bureaucratic past are duly celebrated, the main door guarded by statues of Sir James Douglas, who chose the site of the city, and Sir Matthew Baillie Begbie (aka the "Hanging Judge"), responsible for law and order during the heady days of gold fever. Sir George Vancouver keeps an eye on proceedings from the top of the dome. Free tours start to the right of the main steps. Guides are chirpy and full of anecdotes. Look out for the dagger which killed Captain Cook, and the gold-plated dome, painted with scenes from Canadian history.

bladders in his mouth to add to the carnage, while relatives shook rattles and sang to tame him. A fantastic finale came with the arrival of the loudly clacking "Cannibal Birds", dancers dressed in long strips of cedar bark and huge masks, of which the most fearsome was the "Cannibal Raven", whose long straight beak could crush a human skull. The *hamatsa* would then return in ceremonial finery completely restored to his human state.

As elsewhere in the Northwest, **European contact** was disastrous for the coastal peoples. The establishment of fur-trading posts in the early nineteenth century led to the abandonment of traditional economic cycles, the loss of their creative skills through reliance on readily available European goods, the debilitation from alcohol and internecine wars. Though most of BC remains non-treaty, lands on Vancouver Island were surrendered to become the "Entire property of the White people forever" in return for small payments – the whole Victoria area was obtained for 371 blankets. Infectious disease, the greatest of all threats, reached its peak with the 1862 smallpox epidemic, which spread from Victoria along the entire coast and far into the interior, killing probably a third of BC's aboriginal population.

In this period of decline, potlatches assumed an increased significance as virtually the only medium of cultural continuity, with rival chiefs asserting their status through ever more extravagant displays – even going as far as to burn slaves who had been captured in battle. Excesses such as these and the newly adopted "whiskey feasts" were seen by the **missionaries** as a confirmation that these peoples were enveloped in the "dark mantle of degrading superstition". With BC's entry into confederation the responsibility for the aboriginal peoples fell to the federal government in faraway Ottawa, much of whose knowledge of the indigenous peoples came from the missionaries – the subsequent **Indian Act**, passed in 1884, prohibited the potlatch ceremony.

For a while the defiant aboriginal groups managed to evade detection by holding potlatches at fishing camps rather than the winter villages, and there were few successful prosecutions until the 1920s. Things came to a head in 1922 with the conviction of 34 Kwakiutl from Alert Bay – all were sentenced to jail terms but a deal was struck whereby all those who surrendered their potlatch regalia were freed. Thirty years later, when potlatching was again legalized, aboriginal pressure began to mount for return of these treasures from the collections into which they had been dispersed, but it took a further twenty years for the federal government to agree to return the goods on condition that they be put on public display. Though the masks totally lose their dramatic emphasis in static exhibitions, many of the more local museums have a dual function as community centres, and as such are vital to the preservation of a dynamic aboriginal culture.

Beacon Hill Park

The best park within walking distance of the town centre is **Beacon Hill Park**, south of the Inner Harbour and a few minutes' walk up the road behind the museum. Victoria is sometimes known as the "City of Gardens", and at the right times of the year this park shows why. Victoria's biggest green space, it has lots of paths, ponds, big trees and quiet corners, and plenty of views over the Juan de Fuca Strait to the distant Olympic Mountains of Washington State (especially on its southern side). These pretty straits, incidentally, are the focus of some rather bad feeling between Victoria and its US neighbour, for the city has a (literally) dark secret: it dumps raw sewage into the strait, excusing itself by claiming it's quickly broken up by the sea's strong currents. Washington State isn't so sure, and there have been plenty of arguments over the matter and, more to the point for city elders, economically damaging convention boycotts by US companies. Either way, it's pretty bad PR for Victoria and totally at odds with its image. Gardens in the park are alternatively tended and wonderfully wild and unkempt, and were a favoured retreat of celebrated Victorian artist, Emily Carr. They also claim the world's tallest totem pole (at around 40m), Mile Zero of the Trans-Canada Highway, and – that ultimate emblem of Englishness – a cricket pitch. Some of the trees are massive old-growth timbers that you'd normally only see on the island's west coast. Come here in spring and you'll catch swaths of daffodils and blue camas flowers, the latter a floral monument to Victoria's earliest aboriginal inhabitants, who cultivated the flower for its edible bulb. Some 30,000 other flowers are planted out annually.

Crystal Garden and Butchart Gardens

The heavily advertised **Crystal Gardens**, behind the bus terminal at 713 Douglas St (daily: July & Aug 8.30am–8pm; May–June & Sept–Oct 9am–6pm; Nov–April 10am–4.30pm; $7.50; ☎381-1213, *www.bcpcc.com/crystal*), was designed on the model of London's destroyed Crystal Palace and was billed on opening in 1925 as housing the "Largest Saltwater Swimming Pool in the British Empire". Now much restored, the greenery-, monkey- and bird-filled greenhouse makes for an unaccountably popular tourist spot; only the exterior has any claims to architectural sophistication, and much of its effect is spoilt by the souvenir shops on its ground-floor arcade. Once the meeting place of the town's tea-sipping elite, it still plays host to events such as the Jive and Ballroom Dance Club and the People Meeting People Dance. The daytime draws are the conservatory-type tearoom and tropical gardens. Inhumanely enclosed birds and monkeys, though, are liable to put you off your scones.

If you're into things horticultural you'll want to make a trek out to the heavily over-advertised but celebrated **Butchart Gardens**, 22km north of Victoria at 800 Benvenuto, Brentwood Bay on Hwy 17 towards the Swartz Bay ferry terminal (daily: mid-June to Aug 9am–10.30pm; first half of June & Sept 9am–9pm; rest of the year 9am–sunset; $16.50; ☎652-4422 or 652-5256 for recorded information, *www.butchartgardens.com*). They're also renowned amongst visitors and locals alike for the stunning **firework displays** that usually take place each Saturday evening in July and August. The gardens are also illuminated during the late evening opening hours between mid-June and the end of September. To get here by public transport take bus #75 for "Central Sahnich" from downtown. Otherwise there are regular summer **shuttles** (May–Oct daily hourly in the morning, half-hourly in the afternoon; ☎388-5248) from the main bus terminal, where tickets ($24.50) are obtainable not from the main ticket office but from a separate Gray Lines desk: ticket prices include garden entrance and return bus journey. The gardens were started in 1904 by Mrs Butchart, wife of a mine-owner and pioneer of Portland Cement in Canada and the US. The initial aim was to landscape one of her husband's quarries – the gardens now cover fifty breathtaking acres, comprising rose, Japanese and Italian gardens and lots of decorative details. About half a million visitors a year tramp through the foliage, which includes over a million plants and seven hundred different species.

The Empress Hotel

A town is usually desperate when one of its key attractions is a hotel, but in the case of Victoria the **Empress Hotel**, 721 Government St (☎384-8111), is so physically over-bearing and plays such a part in the town's tourist appeal that it demands some sort of attention. You're unlikely to be staying here – rooms are very expensive – but it's worth wandering through the huge lobbies and palatial dining areas for a glimpse of well-restored colonial splendour. In a couple of lounges there's a fairly limp "Smart Casual" dress code – no dirty jeans, running shoes, short shorts or backpacks – but elsewhere you can wander at will. If you want to **take tea**, which is why most casual visitors are here, enter the Tea Lounge by the hotel's side entrance (the right, or south side): there you can enjoy scones, biscuits, cakes and, of course, tea over six courses costing a whopping $42 but you have to abide by the dress code. In other lounges like the Bengal (see below) you can ask for just tea and scones. At the last count the hotel was serving 800 full teas a day in summer and 1.6 million cups of tea a year.

The hotel's **Crystal Lounge** and its lovely Tiffany-glass dome forms the most opulent part of the hotel on view, but the marginally less ornate entrance lounge is *the* place for the charade of afternoon tea, and indulging can be a bit of a laugh. There's also a reasonable bar and restaurant downstairs, **Kipling's**, and the attractive **Bengal Lounge**, compete with tiger-skin over the fireplace, where you can have a curry and all the trimmings for about $15. For a splurge, try the London clubland surroundings – chesterfields and aspidistras – and the champagne-and-chocolate-cake special ($8.50) on offer in the lounge to the left of the entrance lobby. For an even bigger treat, take dinner amidst the Edwardian splendour of the **Empress Dining Room**. As one would expect, meals here are expensive, but the service and food are both top of the line.

The old town

The oldest part of Victoria focuses on **Bastion Square**, original site of Fort Victoria, from which it's a short walk to Market Square, a nice piece of old town rejuvenation, and the main downtown shopping streets. Bastion Square's former saloons, brothels and warehouses have been spruced up to become offices, cafés and galleries. The modest **Maritime Museum** at 28 Bastion Square (daily 9.30am–4.30pm; $5; ☎385-4222, *www.mmbc.bc.ca*) is of interest mainly for the lovely chocolate-and-vanilla-coloured building in which it's housed, the former provincial courthouse. Displays embrace old charts, uniforms, ships' bells, period photographs, lots of models and a new BC Ferries section on the second floor. On the top floor is the restored vice-admiralty courtroom, once the main seat of justice for the entire province. Note the old open elevator built to reach it, commissioned by Chief Justice Davie in 1901, supposedly because he was too fat to manage the stairs. Just to the north lies the attractive **Market Square**, the old heart of Victoria but now a collection of some 65 speciality shops and cafés around a central courtyard (bounded by Store, Pandora and Johnson sts). This area erupted in 1858 following the gold rush, providing houses, saloons, opium dens, stores and various salacious entertainments for thousands of chancers and would-be immigrants. On the Pandora side of the area was a ravine, marked by the current sunken courtyard, beyond which lay **Chinatown** (now centred slightly further north on Fisgard) the American West Coast's oldest. Here, among other things, 23 factories processed 90,000 pounds of opium a year for what was then a legitimate trade and – until the twentieth century – one of BC's biggest industries. As for the downtown **shopping streets**, it's worth looking out for E.A. Morris, a wonderful old cigar and tobacco shop next to *Murchie's* coffee shop at 1110 Government St, and Roger's Chocolates, 913 Government St, whose whopping Victoria creams (among other things) are regularly dispatched to Buckingham Palace for royal consumption.

Other attractions

Outside the Inner Harbour Victoria has a scattering of minor attractions that don't fit into any logical tour of the city – and at any rate are only short-stop diversions. Most have a pioneer slant, though if you want old buildings the best is **Craigdarroch Castle**, nestled on a hilltop in Rockland, one of Victoria's more prestigious easterly neighbourhoods, at 1050 Joan Crescent (daily: mid-June to early Sept 9am–7pm; early Sept to mid-June 10am–4.30pm; $8; ☎592-5323, *www.craigdarrochcastle.com*; bus #11 or #14-University from downtown). It was built by Robert Dunsmuir, a caricature Victorian politician, strike-breaker, robber baron and coal tycoon – the sort of man who could change a community's name on a whim (Ladysmith near Nanaimo) – and who was forced to put up this gaunt Gothic pastiche to lure his wife away from Scotland. Only the best was good enough, from the marble, granite and sandstone of the superstructure to the intricately

WHALE-WATCHING TRIPS

The waters around Victoria are not as whale-rich as those around Tofino (see p.363), but there's still a very good chance of spotting the creatures. Three pods of orcas (killer whales) live in the seas around southern Vancouver Island, around a hundred creatures in all, so you may see these, though minke are the most common whale spotted, with occasional greys and humpbacks also present. Bar one or two companies, few outfits offer guaranteed sightings, and many cover themselves by preparing you for the fact that if you don't see whales you stand a good chance of seeing Harbour of Dall's porpoises, harbour or elephant seals and California and Steller sea lions.

Day- or half-day trips from the city are becoming massively popular. A couple of years ago there were just two or three companies running trips: now you can hardly move for them. Most offer almost identical trips at identical prices, typically around $55 to $80 for a three-hour outing. Most offer full protective gear, and towels and gloves when required, and all offer life jackets and other safety essentials. Most have a naturalist, or at least a knowledgeable crew member, to fill you in on what you're seeing (or not). The only real variables are the **boats** used, so you need to decide whether you want rigid hull cruisers (covered or uncovered), which are more comfortable and sedate (and usually most expensive at around $80), a catamaran ($69–80), or the high-speed aluminium hull inflatables known as "zodiacs" ($55–80), which are infinitely more exhilarating, but can offer a fast and sometimes bumpy ride that makes them unsuitable for pregnant women, young children or people with back problems. They won't have toilets on board either. You might also want to find out whether your chosen company has hydrophone equipment that enables you to listen to the whales' underwater vocalizing.

Note that morning trips can be less choppy than afternoon excursions (bad weather will halt tours), and be sure to take sunglasses, sun block, a tight-fitting hat, good soft-soled footwear, a sound plastic bag for camera and films and a warm sweater. Smoking is invariably not allowed on boats. If you're here just for the day and travelling on zodiacs you might want to bring a change of clothing. Trips often run a little over the scheduled time, so don't make any hard-and-fast plans for catching buses or ferries.

Drop by the **Victoria Infocentre** for details of the tours and options. Its pamphlet racks are stuffed with brochures if you want to compare companies' PR material. Staff can book you a place on any tour, and if you call in early morning they'll probably have the lowdown from the companies on whether whales have been found that day. Companies tend to pool their information, and dash headlong to any sighting. The question of whether the upsurge in boat activity is disturbing the whales or changing their habits seems not to have been addressed. Rules are in place regarding the distance boats must remain from the creatures, but even some of the companies' own photographs seem to suggest boats are getting in extremely close. It can only be a matter of time before the whole issue blows up. All the companies claim to offer top professional services: the two below have been around longer than most.

Seacoast Expeditions are located across the Inner Harbour at the Boardwalk Level, Oceane Pointe Resort, 45 Songhees Rd (☎383-4383 or 1-800/386-1525, *www .seacoastexpeditions.com*). It's ten-minutes' walk across the Johnson Street bridge or take the three-minute harbour ferry crossing to Seacoast: they also have a shuttle bus pick-up from downtown hotels. Victoria's founding whale-watching company, they've been in the business over a decade and offer four three-hour trips daily in May, June and September, six daily in July and August, and one daily in April and October. They also offer a guaranteed sighting deal (May–Aug only) whereby you carry a pager that tells you to turn up at the office for a tour only when whales have been spotted.

Five Star Charters, located at 706 Douglas St (☎386-3253 or 388-7223, *www.5starwhale .com*), has in the past claimed the highest percentage of whale sightings out of all the tour operators (thanks to spotter boats and a good network of contacts). It runs six daily three-hour trips in the summer as well as an all-day trip on its spotter boat.

handworked panels of the ceilings over the main hall and staircase. Unfortunately for him the dastardly Dunsmuir never enjoyed his creation – he died before it was finished. There's the usual clutter of Victoriana and period detail, in particular some impressive woodwork and stained and leaded glass.

Much the same goes for the Victorian-Italianate **Point Ellice House & Gardens**, 2616 Pleasant St (daily mid-May to mid-Sept noon–5pm; $4; ☎387-4697; bus #14 from downtown), magnificently re-created but less enticing because of its slightly shabby surroundings. These can be overcome, however, if you make a point of arriving by sea, taking one of the little Harbour Ferry services to the house (10min) from the Inner Harbour. The restored Victorian-style gardens here are a delight on a summer afternoon. The interior – one of the best of its kind in the Northwest – retains its largely Victorian appearance thanks partly to the reduced circumstances of the O'Reilly family, whose genteel slide into relative poverty over several generations (they lived here from 1861 to 1974) meant that many furnishings were simply not replaced. Tea is served on the lawns in the summer: it's a good idea to book ahead ($16.95).

Similar reservations apply to the **Craigflower Manor & Farmhouse** about 9km and fifteen-minutes' drive from downtown on Admiral's Road, or take the #14-Craigflower bus from downtown (daily May–Oct 10am–5pm; $5; ☎387-4697). In its day the latter was among the earliest of Victoria's farming homesteads, marking the town's transition from trading post to permanent community. It was built in a mock-Georgian style in 1856, apparently from timbers salvaged from the first four farmhouses built in the region. Its owner was Kenneth McKenzie, a Hudson's Bay Company bailiff, who recruited fellow Scottish settlers to form a farming community on Portage Inlet. The house was to remind him of the old country (Scotland), and soon became the foremost social centre in the fledgling village – mainly visited by officers because McKenzie's daughters were virtually the only white women on the island.

The **Art Gallery of Greater Victoria**, 1040 Moss St, just off Fort Street (Mon–Sat 10am–5pm, Thurs till 9pm, Sun 1–5pm; $5; bus #10-Haultain, #11 or #14-Uvic from downtown; ☎384-4101, *www.aggv.bc.ca*), is a long way to come and of little interest unless you're partial to contemporary Canadian paintings and Japanese art: the building, housed in the 1890 Spencer Mansion, boasts the only complete Shinto shrine outside Japan. It does, however, have a small permanent collection of Emily Carr's work, and you may catch an interesting temporary exhibition that changes every six weeks.

Eating and drinking

Although clearly in Vancouver's culinary shadow, Victoria still has a plethora of **restaurants**, some extremely good, offering greater variety – and higher prices – than you'll find in most other BC towns. **Pubs** tend to be plastic mock-ups of their British equivalents, with one or two worthy exceptions, as do the numerous **cafés** that pander to Victoria's self-conscious afternoon tea ritual. Good snacks and pastry shops abound, while at the other extreme there are budget-busting establishments if you want a one-off treat or a change from the standard Canadian menus that await you on much of the rest of the island. As a quick guide to the best, *Rebecca's* and *Dilettante's* are good for mid-priced lunch or dinners; the *Herald Street Café* or *Water Club* for a pricier but not exorbitant dinner. *Earl's* is part of a reliable mid-price chain, as is *Milestone's*, the latter giving you harbour views from some tables. The slightly wacky *Re-bar* serves what may well be the healthiest food and drinks in North America.

Cafés, tea and snacks

Barb's Fish and Chips, 310 St Lawrence, Fisherman's Wharf off Kingston. Much-loved floating shack that offers classic home-cut chips, fish straight off the boat and oyster burgers and chowder to boot: the small ferries from the Inner Harbour drop you close by.

Bean Around the World, 533 Fisgard St. A nice café with plenty of magazines and games to while away a rainy afternoon.

Blethering Place, 2250 Oak Bay Ave. Along with the *Empress*, known as a place to indulge in the tea-taking custom. Scones, cakes and dainty sandwiches are served up against the background of hundreds of toby jugs and royal family memorabilia. Perhaps a tad overrated – try the *Windsor House* as an alternative.

Demitasse Coffee Bar, 1320 Blanshard St near Pandora Ave. Popular, elegantly laid-back hole-in-the-wall café with excellent coffee, salads, bagels, lunch-time snacks, and an open fire in season. Recommended.

Dutch Bakery & Coffee Shop, 718 Fort St. An institution in Victoria serving pastries and chocolate to take away, or you can eat in the popular if plain coffee shop at the back.

Empress Hotel, 721 Government St. Try tea in the lobby ($29), with tourists and locals alike on their best behaviour amidst the chintz and potted plants. A strict dress code allows no dirty jeans, anoraks or sportswear.

Murchie's Tea and Coffee, 1110 Government St. The best place for basic tea, coffee and cakes in the centre of Victoria's shopping streets.

Re-bar, 50 Bastion Square at Langley St. A great place that serves teas, coffees (charcoal-filtered water) and healthfood at lunch (usually organically grown), but most remarkable for its extraordinary range of fresh-squeezed juices in strange combinations, smoothies, "power tonics" and frighteningly healthy wheatgrass drinks such as the "Astro Turf" – a carrot, beet, garlic and wheatgrass medley.

Sally's, 714 Cormorant St, near corner of Douglas St. Funky little café and very popular with locals and local office workers despite its location on the northern edge of downtown. Drop by if you're up this way, but don't come specially.

Willie's Bakery, Waddington Alley, off Johnson St. Good little bakery and café with great croissants and lots of outdoor seating in summer.

Windsor House Tea Room, 2450 Windsor Rd. If you're making the effort to come out of town for tea at the famous *Blethering Place*, you could stay on the bus (the #2 Oak Bay) to have your cuppa by the sea here instead.

Restaurants

Da Tandoor, 1010 Fort St (☎384-6333). Tandoori specialist that is, along with the *Taj Mahal*, the best of Victoria's half-dozen or so Indian restaurants offering good, inexpensive food in an over-the-top interior.

Dilettante's Café, 787 Fort St near Blanshard St (☎381-3327). Although a little north of the central core, this vaguely decadent and relaxed single-room restaurant is deservedly popular at lunch. The good food is the usual mixture of Italian, Canadian and Pacific Rim fare.

Earl's, 1703 Blanshard St (☎386-4323). You'll find an *Earl's* in many Northwest towns, but the restaurants are none the worse for being part of a chain: good – not fast – food, with a lively, pleasant interior and friendly service.

Green Cuisine, Courtyard Level, Market Square, 560 Johnson St. Vegetarian restaurant and bakery in pleasant off-street setting with a good hot buffet and salad bar.

Herald Street Café, 546 Herald St (☎381-1441). An excellent and stylish old favourite for Italian food with a Northwest twist. Pricey but still a good value with a relaxed, art-filled atmosphere. Well worth the walk from the Inner Harbour.

Il Terrazzo, 555 Johnson St, Waddington Alley (☎361-0028). Smooth, laid-back ambience with lots of red brick and plants and a summer patio that provides the setting for good, moderately expensive North American versions of Italian food.

Le Petit Saigon, 1010 Langley St, off Fort St (☎386-1412). A byword for good low-priced downtown Vietnamese food.

Marina Restaurant, 1327 Beach Drive (☎598-8555). An upscale restaurant with great marine views and a deserved reputation for some of the best fish and seafood in the city.

Milestone's, 812 Wharf St (☎381-2244). Popular mid-priced place slap-bang on the Inner Harbour beneath the infocentre, so lots of bustle, passing trade and good views, but not the place for a quiet meal.

Ming's, 1321 Quadra St (☎385-4405). Regularly voted Victoria's best Chinese restaurant. Inexpensive.

Pagliacci's, 1011 Broad St between Fort and Broughton (☎386-1662). Best restaurant in Victoria if you want a fast, furious atmosphere, live music, good Italian food and excellent desserts. A rowdy throng begins to queue almost from the moment the doors are open.

Periklis, 531 Yates St (☎386-3313). Greek restaurant opposite the youth hostel, often with belly dancers, plate-spinning and good (if predictable), inexpensive Greek food.

Süze, 515 Yates St (☎383-2829). A great place for an early or late-evening drink, thanks to its informal, vaguely exotic feel and wonderfully broad bar; it's also good for an eclectic mix of Mexican, Italian and other dishes, which can be eaten either at tables up on the tiny mezzanine or in the cosy dining room.

Taj Mahal, 679 Herald St (☎383-4662). Housed in a mini Taj Mahal, a bit of a walk from the centre, this inexpensive restaurant serves good Indian food with chicken, lamb and tandoori specialities.

Tomoe, 726 Johnson St (☎381-0223). Victoria's best Japanese restaurant with a comfortable, low-key atmosphere. Fresh produce is flown in daily from Tsukiji, the world's largest fish market. Expensive, but if you like sushi well worth it.

Bars

Big Bad John's, next to the *Strathcona Hotel* at 919 Douglas St. Victoria's most atmospheric bar by far with bare boards, a fug of smoke, and authentic old banknotes and IOUs pasted to the walls. It also hosts occasional live bands and singers, usually of a Country music persuasion.

Charles Dickens Pub, 633 Humboldt St. One of Victoria's hideously mocked-up British pubs but good for a laugh. If this is too much, try the *Garrick's Head* pub, 1140 Government St, which has a cosy fire in winter and lots of outdoor seating in summer.

D'Arcy McGee's, 1127 Wharf St. It was only a matter of time before Victoria acquired an "Irish pub". This one has a prime site on the edge of Bastion Square, offers predictable food and beer, and has excellent occasional live Irish music.

Spinnakers Brew Pub, 308 Catherine St near Esquimalt Rd. Thirty-eight beers, including several home-brewed options, restaurant, live music, occasional tours of the brewery and good harbour views draw a mixed and relaxed clientele. Take bus #23 to Esquimalt Rd.

Swan's Pub, 506 Pandora Ave at Store St. This pretty and highly popular hotel-café-brewery, housed in a 1913 warehouse, is the place to watch Victoria's young professionals at play. Several foreign and six home-brewed beers on tap, with the *Millennium* nightclub (see overleaf) in the basement.

Nightlife

Nocturnal diversions in Victoria are tame compared to Vancouver's, but there's more to the town than its tearooms and chintzy shops initially suggest. Highbrow tastes are surprisingly well catered for, and there's a smattering of **live music** venues and **discos** to keep you happy for the limited time you're likely to spend in the city. **Jazz** is particularly popular – for information on the city's jazz underground, contact the Victoria Jazz Society, 250-727 Johnson St (☎388-4423).

Listings appear in the main daily newspaper, the *Times-Colonist* and in a variety of free magazines you can pick up in shops, cafés and hotels. **Tickets** for most offerings are available from the city's main performance space, the McPherson Playhouse, 3 Centennial Square, Pandora Avenue and Government Street (☎386-6121).

Clubs, discos and live music

Bartholomew's Bar and Rockefeller Grill, *Executive House Hotel*, 777 Douglas St (☎388-5111). An upbeat pub with a steady diet of local rock and blues bands.

BJ's Lounge, downstairs at 642 Johnson St (☎388-0505). Popular gay dance club playing fairly mainstream Top 40 music.

Esquimalt Inn, 856 Esquimalt Rd (☎382-7161). Long-established venue with Country bands most nights and occasional jam sessions. Take the #23 bus.

Evolution, 502 Discovery St (☎388-3000). One of Victoria's more interesting clubs and discos, thanks to plenty of techno and other dance floor sounds.

FESTIVALS IN VICTORIA

Summer brings out the buskers and **free entertainment** in Victoria's people-places – James Bay, Market Square and Beacon Hill Park in particular. Annual highlights, arranged chronologically, include:

TerrifVic Jazz Party, April (☎953-2011). A showcase for about a dozen top international bands held in various venues over four days during the second week of the month.

Jazz Fest, June (☎386-6121 for information). More than a hundred assorted lesser bands perform in Market Square and elsewhere over about ten days towards the end of the month.

ICA Folk Fest, June–July (☎388-4728). Extravaganza of folk over eight days at the end of June and beginning of July: the main venues are the Inner Harbour and Market Square.

Victoria International Festival, July and August (☎736-2119). Victoria's largest

general arts jamboree. Events take place at a wide variety of locations.

First People's Festival, early August (☎387-2134 or 384-3211). Celebration of the cultures of Canada's aboriginal peoples, usually held in the second week of the month at the Royal BC Museum.

Classic Boat Festival, August 30–September 1 (☎385-7766). Dozens of wooden antique boats on display in the Inner Harbour.

Fringe Festival, late August to mid-September (☎383-2663). Avant-garde performances of all kinds held at seven different venues around central Victoria.

Hermann's Jazz Club, 753 View St (☎360-9098). Dimly lit club thick with 1950s atmosphere which specializes in Dixieland but has occasional excursions into fusion and blues. Open Mon–Fri 11.30am–2am, Sat 3pm–2am.

Legends, 919 Douglas St (☎383-7137). Biggest, best and noisiest of the hard-rock venues, this club occupies the garish, neon-lit basement of the *Strathcona Hotel*. Music and dancing nightly.

Millennium, 1605 Store St at Pandora Ave (☎360-9098). You may well have to queue to join the slightly older crew who frequent the basement disco of *Swan's Pub*. Classics from 1960s and 1970s generally rule along with current Top 40 fodder. Open Tues–Sat.

Pagliacci's, 1011 Broad St (☎386-1662). Live music (jazz, blues, rock and R&B) starting at 9pm Tuesday to Saturday, in a packed and popular restaurant.

Steamers, 570 Yates St (☎381-4340). You'll catch enthusiastic local bands here most nights, playing anything from reggae to Celtic.

Victoria Blues House, 1417 Government St (☎386-1717). Victoria's "House of the Blues" at the *Victoria Plaza Hotel* has disco some nights and local blues and R&B bands most others.

Drama

Belfry Theatre, 1291 Gladstone St and Fernwood Rd (☎385-6815). Foremost of Victoria's companies, with a nationally renowned five-play season in its own playhouse. Although it concentrates on contemporary Canadian dramatists, the repertoire runs the gamut of twentieth-century playwrights.

Kaleidoscope Theatre, 556 Herald St (☎383-8124). Theatre troupe known particularly for its work with young audiences.

Victoria Theatre Guild, 805 Langham Court Rd (☎384-2142). A good company performing lightweight musicals, dramas and comedies.

Classical music, opera and dance

Pacific Opera Victoria, 1316b Government St (☎385-0222). Highly acclaimed company which usually produces three operas yearly in February, April and September at the McPherson Playhouse, 3 Centennial Square (box office ☎386-6121).

Victoria Operatic Society, 798 Fairview Rd (☎381-1021). Year-round performances of lightweight operatic fare.

Victoria Symphony Orchestra, 846 Broughton Rd (☎385-9771). Numerous concerts annually, usually performed at the nearby Royal Theatre, 805 Broughton St (☎386-6121).

Listings

Airlines Air BC (☎360-9074 or 1-800/663-3721); Air Canada (☎360-9074 or 360-9429); Harbour Air seaplanes to Vancouver (☎384-2215 or 1-800/665-0212); Helijet, helicopter service to Vancouver harbour (☎382-6222 or 1-800/665-4354); Kenmore Air, seaplane service Seattle–Victoria (☎1-800/543-9595 or 206/486-1257); West Coast Air (☎388-4521 or 1-800/347-2222).

American Express 1203 Douglas St (☎385-8731 or 1-800/669-3636); open Mon, Wed & Sat 9.30am–5.30pm, Tues & Fri 9.30am–9pm.

Bike rental Cycle Victoria Rentals, 950 Wharf St (☎885-2453 or 1-877/869-0039, *www.cyclevictoriarentals.com*); Harbour Rentals, 811 Wharf St (☎995-1661 or 1-877/733-6722), rent bikes (from $8 an hour) plus scooters ($16 per hour, $50 daily), kayaks ($15 an hour, $49 daily), rowing boats ($35 for 3 hours), motor boats ($49 an hour), and motorbikes (from $119 a day).

BC Transit City buses (☎382-6161 or 385-2551).

Bookstores Chapters, 1212 Douglas St near corner with View St, is a huge modern bookshop; Munro's Books, 1108 Government St (☎382-2424), is more traditional.

Bus information Airporter shuttle bus from Victoria Airport (☎386-2525). For services to Vancouver, Pacific Coast Lines (☎604/662-8074 in Vancouver or 250/385-4411 at the Victoria bus terminal); for services on the island, Laidlaw (☎385-4411, 388-5248 or 1-800/318-0818). Both operate from the bus terminal at 700 Douglas and Belleville, which also has an office for Greyhound (☎388-5248). Gray Line of Seattle service to Seattle (☎206/626-6090 or 1-800/544-0739). For West Coast Trail Express to Bamfield and Port Renfrew, call ☎477-8700.

Car rental Avis, 62b-1001 Douglas St (☎386-7726 or 1-800/879-2847) and Victoria Airport (☎656-6033); Budget, 757 Douglas St (☎953-5300 or 1-800/668-9833); Island Auto Rentals, 837 Yates St (☎384-4881), guarantee "lowest rates"; National, 767 Douglas St (☎386-1213 or 1-800/387-4747).

Doctors' directory ☎383-1193.

Equipment rental Sports Rent, 611 Discovery St, on corner of Government and Discovery sts (☎385-7368), rents bikes, rollerblades, all camping, hiking, climbing and diving gear.

Exchange Currencies International, 724 Douglas St (☎384-6631 or 1-800/706-6656); Custom House Currency, 815 Wharf St (☎389-6001).

Ferries BC Ferries (☎386-3431 or 1-888/223-3779); Black Ball Transport (☎386-2202 or 360/457-4491); Victoria Clipper (☎382-8100, 206/448-5000 or 1-800/888-2535); Washington State Ferries (☎382-1551 or 1-800/542-7052).

Hospitals Fairfield Health Centre, 841 Fairfield Rd (☎389-6300), three blocks from the *Empress Hotel*; Victoria General Hospital, 35 Helmcken Rd (☎727-4212).

Left luggage At bus terminal; $2 per 24hr – but note lockers are stated not to be "secure" at night.

Lost property Contact Victoria police (☎384-4111) or BC Transit's lost-and-found line (☎382-6161).

Maps Crown Publications Inc, 521 Fort St (☎386-4636). Also see "Bookstores" above.

Post office 1230 Government and Yates (☎388-3575). Mon–Fri 8.30am–5pm.

Royal Canadian Mounted Police 625 Fisgard and Government (☎384-4111).

Taxis Blue Bird Cabs (☎382-3611); Empire Taxi (☎381-2222); Victoria Taxi (☎383-7111).

Tourist information ☎953-2033. Accommodation reservations ☎1-800/663-3883 in North America.

Train information VIA Rail, 450 Pandora Ave (☎383-4324 or 1-800/561-8630 in Canada and ☎1-800/561-3949 in USA).

Weather ☎656-3978.

The Southern Gulf Islands

Scattered between Vancouver Island and the mainland lie several hundred tiny islands, most no more than lumps of rock, a few large enough to hold permanent populations and warrant a regular ferry service. Two main clusters are accessible from Victoria: the

Southern Gulf Islands and the San Juan Islands, both part of the same archipelago, except that the San Juan group is in the United States.

You get a good look at the Southern Gulf Islands on the ferry from Tsawwassen – twisting and threading through their coves and channels, the ride sometimes seems even a bit too close for comfort. The coastline makes for superb **sailing**, and an armada of small boats crisscross between the islands for most of the year. Hikers and campers are also well served, and **fishing**, too, is good, with some of the world's biggest salmon having met their doom in the surrounding waters. The climate is mild, though hardly "Mediterranean" as claimed in the tourist blurbs, and the vegetation is particularly lush. There's also an abundance of marine wildlife (sea lions, orcas, seals, bald eagles, herons, cormorants). All this has made the Gulf Islands the dream idyll of many people from Washington State and BC, whether they're artists, writers, pensioners or dropouts from the mainstream. For full details of what they're all up to, grab a copy of the local listings, the *Gulf Islander*, distributed on the islands and the ferries.

Getting to the islands

BC Ferries (☎250/386-3431 in Victoria) sails to five of the Southern Gulf Islands – **Saltspring, Pender, Saturna, Mayne** and **Galiano** – from Swartz Bay, 33km north of Victoria on Hwy 17 (a few others can be reached from Chemainus and Nanaimo, see p.353 and p.355). Reckon on at least two crossings to each daily, but be prepared for all boats to be jammed solid during the summer. Pick up the company's *Southern Gulf Islands* timetable, widely available on boats and in the mainland infocentres, which is invaluable if you aim to exploit the many inter-island connections. If you just want a quick, cheap cruise, BC Ferries runs a daily four-hour jaunt from Swartz Bay around several of the islands. All the ferries take cars, bikes and motorbikes, though with a car you'll need to make a **reservation** (in Vancouver ☎604/669-1211, in Victoria ☎386-3431 or 1-888/223-3779). Bear in mind that there's next to no public transport on the islands, so what few taxis there are can charge more or less what they wish.

For the San Juans you obviously have to pass through US and Canadian immigration, but you can get good stopover deals on ferries between Sidney on Vancouver Island and Anacortes on the Washington mainland, and foot passengers travel free between the four main San Juan islands.

Aim to have your **accommodation** worked out well in advance in summer. **Campers** should have few problems finding sites, most of which are located in the islands' provincial parks, though at peak times you'll want to arrive before noon to ensure a pitch – there are reservations in some parks (see p.390 for details of booking places). For help with B&Bs, use the *BC Accommodations* guide, or contact the Victoria infocentre or specialist agencies.

Saltspring Island

SALTSPRING (pop. 9240), sometimes spelt Salt Spring, is the biggest, most populated and most visited of the islands – its population triples in summer – though if you're without transport think twice about coming here on a day-trip as getting around is pretty tough. It's served by three ferry terminals: **Fulford Harbour**, from Victoria's Swartz Bay (ten sailings daily, more in summer; 35min; foot passengers $6 return, cars $19.25) and **Vesuvius Bay** (from Crofton, near Duncan on Vancouver Island; 13 daily; 20min; same fares) provide links to Vancouver Island; **Long Harbour** connects to points on the BC mainland via other islands. In the past the Saltspring Island Bus service has connected the ferry terminals with **GANGES**, the island's main village, but check with the Victoria infocentre for the latest. For more complicated journeys, call up the Silver Shadow Taxi (☎537-3030) or consider **renting a bike** from the Bike Shop (☎537-1544) on McPhillips Avenue in Ganges or a scooter from Saltspring Marine Rentals (☎537-9100) next to *Moby's Pub* – a popular local hangout – also in Ganges. Locals are a particularly cosmopolitan bunch, the island having been colonized not by whites but by pioneer black settlers seeking refuge from prejudice in the US. If you're here to slum it on a **beach**, the best strips are on the island's more sheltered west side (Beddis Beach in particular, off the Fulford to Ganges road), at Vesuvius Bay and at Drummond Park near Fulford.

Ganges, close to Long Harbour, is armed with a small **infocentre** at 121 Lower Ganges Rd (daily 10am–4pm; ☎537-5252 or 537-4223, *www.saltspring.com*) and a rapidly proliferating assortment of galleries, tourist shops and holiday homes. Community spirits reach a climax during the annual **Artcraft** (late June to mid-Sept), a summer crafts fair that displays the talents of the island's many dab-handed creatives.

Ganges' infocentre is the place to check out the island's relatively plentiful **accommodation**. A lot of independent travellers are lured here by the prospect of the official HI-affiliated **youth hostel**, the lovely *Salt Spring Island Hostel*, set amidst ten peaceful acres on the eastern side of the island at 640 Cusheon Lake Rd (☎537-4149; ①–③). Under your own steam from Victoria, take the #70 Pat Bay Hwy bus ($2.50) to the Swartz Bay ferry terminal. Catch the ferry to Fulford Harbour ($5 return) and ask car drivers disembarking the ferry if they're headed past the hostel on Cusheon Lake Road: if they're locals, most say yes. You can choose between dorm rooms ($15.50–19.50), tepees, tents, tree house and private family room ($40–70) – 22 beds in all. Note, however, that's there's no camping. It's just a short walk to Cusheon Lake or the ocean at Beddis Beach. Otherwise you can choose from the multitudinous (but often exorbitant) B&B options (owners can arrange to pick you up from the ferry) or one of the so-called "resorts" dotted round the island – usually a handful of houses with camping, a few rooms to rent, and little else. Each of the ferry terminals also has a range of mid-price motels. Some of the more reasonable include the twelve-unit *Beachcomber Motel* at 770 Vesuvius Bay Rd at Vesuvius Bay 7km from Ganges (☎537-5415, fax 537-1753, *gball@saltspring.com*; ②); the *Harbour House Hotel*, 121 Upper Ganges Rd, Ganges (☎537-5571, *harbourhouse@saltspring.com*; ④), and the 28-unit *Seabreeze Inn* in a park-like setting above Ganges harbour at 101 Bittancourt Rd (☎537-4145, *seabreeze@saltspring.com*; ③).

One of the island's better-known places to **eat** is *The Vesuvius Inn* (☎537-2312) alongside the ferry at Vesuvius Bay, blessed with live music nightly and a great **bar** deck overlooking the harbour where you can eat seafood and the usual range of pastas, chickens and salads. In Ganges, there are numerous cafés and coffe shops: try the popular *Sweet Arts Patisserie Café* at 112 Lower Ganges Rd (opposite the fire station) for high-quality sandwiches.

The island's best hiking and its top **campground** are to be found in Ruckle Provincial Park. The campground ($12 in summer, $8 in winter) is at Beaver Point, and is reached by following Beaver Point Road from the Fulford Harbour ferry terminal (9km). There's further walking and good views on and around Mount Maxwell.

Galiano Island

Long and finger-shaped, **Galiano** (pop. 1040) is one of the more promising islands to visit if you want variety and a realistic chance of finding somewhere to stay. There are two ferry terminals: **Sturdies Bay**, which takes boats from the mainland, and **Montague Harbour**, which handles the Vancouver Island crossings (both routes: foot passengers $5, cars $12.75). The **infocentre** is in Sturdies Bay at 2590 Sturdies Bay Rd (May–Sept daily 8am–6pm; ☎539-2233 or 539-2507, *www.galianoisland.com*), which also has bike, boat and canoe rentals, motels, B&B, and an excellent **campground** at Montague Harbour Provincial Marine Park, 10km from the ferry terminal on the west side of the island (☎250/391-2300; $15 in summer, $8 in winter; 15 reservable tent sites). See box on p.390 for details of provincial park campground reservations.

The island's main pub, the *Hummingbird Inn* (☎539-5472) is conveniently close to the ferry on Sturdies Road. **Food** is reasonable at the *Hummingbird*, likewise at *La Berengerie*, near Montague Harbour on the corner of Montague and Clanton roads (☎539-5392; ③), a genteel restaurant that also has three B&B rooms upstairs.

For a comfortable stay in peaceful and elegant surroundings (close to Montague Harbour Provincial Marine Park), try the excellent but expensive *Woodstone Country Inn* (☎539-2022 or 1-888/339-2022, *woodstone@gulfislands.com*; ⑥) on Georgeson Bay Road, 4km from the ferry: breakfast and afternoon tea are included in the price. For a special treat book well in advance to secure one of the seven well-priced rooms at the *Sutil Lodge*, Montague Harbour (☎539-2930, *reservations@gulfislands.com*; ④), a restored 1928 fishing lodge on the beach surrounded by twenty acres of forested seclusion with lovely views, great sunsets and general all-round old-style delights. The lodge offers a four-hour nature cruise aboard a catamaran, and there's free ferry and canoe pick-up also. A less exalted but still good choice on the island's quieter northern end are the seven log cabins of the *Bodega Resort*, at 120 Monastee Rd off Porlier Pass Drive and Cook Drive (☎539-2677, *www.cedarplace.com/bodega*; ③), complete with kitchens and wood-burning stoves and set in acres of woods and meadows with sea views.

If you're **canoeing**, stick to the calmer waters, cliffs and coves off the west coast. **Hikers** can walk almost the entire length of the east coast, or climb Mount Sutil (323m) or Mount Galiano (342m) for views of the mainland mountains. The locals' favourite **beach** is at Coon Bay at the island's northern tip.

North and South Pender

The bridge-linked islands of **North** and **South Pender** muster about a thousand people between them, many of whom will try to entice you into their studios to buy local arts and crafts. Ferries come here from Swartz Bay and Tsawwassen (from the latter foot passenger one-way tickets cost $9, cars $35; $3 and $7 respectively for the former). The **infocentre** is at the ferry terminal in **Otter Bay**, 2332 Otter Bay Rd (daily mid-May to early Sept 9am–6pm; ☎629-6541) on North Pender, home of the Otter Bay Marina, where you can rent **bikes** and buy maps for a tour of the islands' rolling, hilly interior. The best **beaches** are at Hamilton (North Pender) and Mortimer Spit (South Pender).

Accommodation-wise there are plenty of B&Bs, and a small wooded **campground** at Prior Centennial Provincial Park, 6km south of the Otter Bay ferry terminal (March–Oct; $12). For the only **hotel**-type rooms, as opposed to B&Bs, try the *Inn on Pender Island* prettily situated in 7.5 acres of wooded country near Prior Park at 4709 Canal Rd, North Pender (☎629-3353 or 1-800/550-0172; ③); or the *Bedwell Harbour Island Resort*, 9801 Spalding Rd, South Pender (☎629-3212 or 1-800/663-2899, *bedwell@islandnet.com*; ④), which has a pool, pub, restaurant, store, tennis, harbour views, canoe, boat and bike rentals, and a choice of rooms or cabins; or the three fully equipped self-catering cottages 500m sharp left from the ferry at *Pender Lodge*, 1325 MacKinnon Rd, North Pender (☎629-3221; March–Oct; ⑤/⑥), with tennis court, outdoor pool and private decks.

Mayne and Saturna islands

Mayne is the first island to your left if you're crossing from Tsawwassen to Swartz Bay – which is perhaps as close as you'll get, since it's the quietest and most difficult to reach of the islands served by ferries (one-way tickets in high season cost foot passengers $9, cars cost $35.50) and has few places to stay; fix up accommodation before you arrive. That may be as good a reason as any for heading out here, however, particularly if you have a bike to explore the web of quiet country roads. Best of several **beaches** is Bennett Bay, a sheltered strip with warm water and good sand. It's reached by heading east from Miner's Bay (5min from the ferry terminal at Village Bay) to the end of Fernhill Road and then turning left onto Wilks Road. Village Bay has a summer-only **infocentre** (daily 8am–6pm) which should be able to fill you in on the limited (currently around seven) but expanding number of **B&B** possibilities – though the island is small enough to explore as a day-trip. Try the three-unit *Root Seller B&B*, a kilometre south of the ferry terminal at 478 Village Bay Rd (☎539-2621; March–Oct; ③), or the *Blue Vista Resort*, eight fully-equipped cabins overlooking Bennett Bay on Arbutus Drive 6km from the ferry terminal (☎539-2463; ③), with handy sandy beach, park-like setting and bike rental (no credit cards). The *Tinkerer's B&B* in Miner's Bay at 417 Sunset Place off Georgina Point Road (☎539-2280; mid-April to mid-Oct; ④), 2km from the Village Bay ferry terminal, is offbeat: it rents bikes, provides hammocks and offers "demonstrations of medicinal herb and flower gardens". For a real treat, the best **food** around is to be found at the waterfront *Oceanwood Country Inn*, 630 Dinner Bay Rd (☎539-5074, *www.oceanwood.com*; ⑥), which also has 12 smart rooms.

Saturna, to the south, is another **B&B** hideaway: try the three-room waterfront *Lyall Harbour B&B* (☎539-5577; ④), 500m from the ferry at 121 East Point Rd in Saturna Point, home to a pub, a shop and the **infocentre** (May–Sept daily 8am–6pm; no phone) which will rent you boats and bicycles. Another relatively large place to stay is the *East Point Resort*, East Point Road (☎539-2975; ④), situated in a park-like setting near a gradually sloping sandy beach; the six cabins are fully equipped and you can choose between one- and two-bedroom units – note that in July and August there's a minimum stay of a week. The best local **beach** is at Winter Cove Marine Park (no campground) and there's walking, wildlife and good views to the mainland from Mount Warburton Pike.

Highway 14: Victoria to Port Renfrew

Highway 14 runs west from **Victoria** to **Port Renfrew** and is lined with numerous beaches and provincial parks, most – especially those close to the city – heavily populated during the summer months. The 107km route is covered in summer by West Coast Trail Express (see p.331), a private bus service intended for hikers walking the West Coast Trail and Juan de Fuca Trail (see pp.373–374), but also popular for the ride alone. Victoria city buses go as far as **SOOKE** (38km; take #50 to Western Exchange and transfer to a #61), best known for its **All Sooke Day** in mid-July, when lumberjacks from all over the island compete in various tests of forestry expertise. The **infocentre** lies across the Sooke River Bridge at 2070 Phillips and Sooke streets (daily 10am–6pm; ☎642-6351, *www.sookemuseum.bc.ca*). This is the last place of any size, so stock up on supplies if you're continuing west. It also has a surfeit of **accommodation**, with a bias towards B&B, if you're caught short. Check out the small **Sooke Region Museum**, 2070 Philips Rd (daily: July–Aug 9am–6pm; Sept–June 9am–5pm; donation) if you want to bone up on the largely logging-dominated local history. Quite a few people make the trip here just for the **food** at *Sooke Harbour House*, 1528 Whiffen Spit (☎642-3421; ⑧), one of the finest restaurants on the West Coast; it's expensive, but has a surprisingly casual atmosphere. It also has a few top-notch **rooms**, but prices range from a prohibitive $270 to $465.

Beaches beyond Sooke are largely grey pebble and driftwood, the first key stop being **French Beach Provincial Park**, 20km onwards from Sooke. An infoboard here fills in the natural history background, and there are maps of trails and the highlights on the road further west. There's good walking on the fairly wild and windswept beach, and a provincial park campground (summer $12, winter $8) on the grass immediately away from the shore. Sandy, signposted trails lead off the road to beaches over the next 12km to **Jordan River**, a one-shop, one-hamburger-stall town known for its good surf. Just beyond is the best of the beaches on this coast, part of **China Beach Provincial Park** (no camping) reached after a fifteen-minute walk from the road through rainforest. The West Coast Trail Express shuttle bus (see p.331) makes stops at all these parks and beaches on request.

The road is gravel from here on – past Mystic and Sombrio beaches to **PORT REN-FREW**, a logging community that's gained from being the western starting point of the **West Coast Trail** (see p.373). A second trail, the **Juan de Fuca Trail**, also starts from Port Renfrew, running east towards Victoria for about 50km. This does not have the complicated booking procedure of the West Coast Trail, but the scenery is also less striking and the going far easier for the less experienced or more safety conscious walker. Car parks and highway access points are also dotted along its length, allowing you to enjoy strolls or day-hikes.

Accommodation in town is still pretty limited: try the four cottages at *Gallaugher's West Coast Fish Camp* off Beach Road (☎647-5535; May–Oct; ④); the five beachfront rooms of the *Arbutus Beach Lodge*, 5 Queesto Drive (☎647-5458, *arbutus@sookenet.com*; ③/④); the *West Coast Trail Motel*, Parkinson Road (☎647-5565, *www.westcoasttrailmotel.com*; ③/④); the *Trailhead Resort* on Parkinson Road (☎647-5468, *www.trailhead-resort.com*; ③), which has four rooms and nine tent pitches ($4 per person); and the 124-site *Port Renfrew RV Park and Marina* on Gordon River Road (☎647-5430; April–Oct; $12–14), with a separate tenting area across the bridge on the northern side of the village. South of the village on a logging road (6km) is **Botanical Beach**, a sandstone shelf and tidal pool area that reveals a wealth of marine life at low tide.

If you're driving and don't want to retrace your steps, think about taking the gravel logging roads from the village on the north side of the San Juan River to either Shawnigan Lake or the Cowichan Valley. They're marked on most maps, but it's worth picking up the detailed map of local roads put out by the Sooke Combined Fire Organization (ask at the Victoria infocentre); heed all warnings about logging trucks.

Highway 1: Victoria to Nanaimo

If you leave Victoria with high hopes of Vancouver Island's lauded scenery, **Hwy 1** – the final western leg of the Trans-Canada – will come as a disappointing introduction to what you can expect along most of the island's southeast coast. After a lengthy sprawl of suburbs, blighted by more billboards than you'd see in supposedly less scenic cities, the landscape becomes suddenly wooded and immensely lush; unfortunately the beauty is constantly interrupted by bursts of dismal motels and other highway junk. **Buses** operated by Laidlaw make the trip between Victoria and Nanaimo (6 daily). One **train** a day also covers this route, and beyond to Courtenay, but it's a single-carriage job and gets booked solid in summer; it stops at every stump.

Goldstream Provincial Park

Thetis Lake Regional Park, appearing on the right 11km out of the city, is good for swimming, with forested trails and sandy beaches on two lakes backed by high cliffs; there's a busy beach near the car park, which is quieter round the shore, or beyond at the bottom of the hill at Prior Lake. Prettier still is **Goldstream Provincial Park**, 5km beyond Langford and 20km from the city centre, where you'll find an ancient forest of Douglas fir and western red cedar and a large provincial park **campground** with good facilities and a visitor centre (summer $18.50, winter $8). There's also a network of marked **trails** to hilltops and waterfalls designed for anything between five minutes and an hour's walking. Try the paths towards Mount Finlayson (three-hour's hard walk if you go all the way to the summit) for views of the ocean – views you also get if you carry on up the highway, which soon meets Saanich Inlet, a bay with a lovely panorama of wooded ridges across the water. Look out for the Malahat Summit (31km from Victoria) and Gulf Islands (33km) viewpoints. To **stay**, the small *Malahat Oceanview Motel* (☎478-9213, *oceanview@coastnet.com*; ③), 35km north of Victoria, is best sited to catch the sea and island vistas.

A scenic diversion off the main road takes you 7km to **Shawnigan Lake**, fringed by a couple of provincial parks: West Shawnigan Park on the lake's northwest side has a safe beach and swimming possibilities. If you're biking or are prepared to tackle pretty rough roads, note the logging road that links the north end of the lake to Port Renfrew on the west coast (check access restrictions at the Victoria infocentre).

Duncan

DUNCAN, 60km north of Victoria, begins inauspiciously, with a particularly scrappy section of highway spoiling what would otherwise be an exquisitely pastoral patch of country. Still, the town's native centre – the Cowichan Native Village – merits a stop, unlike the Glass Castle, a messy affair made from glass bottles off the road to the south, and the even sillier "World's Largest Hockey Stick", arranged as a triumphal arch into the town centre.

Duncan's **infocentre** is at 381A Trans-Canada Hwy opposite the supermarket on the main road (mid-April to mid-Oct Mon–Fri 8.30am–5pm, longer hours July & Aug; ☎746-4636, *duncancc@islandnet.com*), close to the **bus station**, which has six daily connections to and from Victoria (1hr 10min). Duncan is not a place you want even to consider staying in – though there are plenty of motels and campgrounds if you're stuck – but for **meals** you could try the excellent *Arbutus*, 195 Kenneth St, or *Jubilee* (☎746-5443), which is much-frequented by locals keen for the usual Italian- and Pacific Rim-influenced food. Just east of town, the *Quamichan Inn*, 1478 Maple Bay Rd (☎746-7028), serves up a similar menu and also has its devotees. You could also visit one of several local vineyards: one of the best is the **Vigneti Zenatta Winery**, 5039 Marshall Rd (call for tour details on ☎748-4981 or 748-2338), which has been in business for over forty years; as well as their wine, you can also buy meals here.

Three kilometres south of town on Hwy 1, the *Pioneer House Restaurant* has a rustic log-cabin feel helped by a genuine **saloon bar** transplanted from a period building in Montana. Alternatively, head 10km north of Duncan to the *Red Rooster Diner* (by the Mount Sicker gas station), reputed to be the greasy spoon immortalized by Jack Nicholson in *Five Easy Pieces*. It's still a classic – good, cheap food, vinyl booths and all the authentic tacky trimmings you'd expect.

Cowichan Native Village

The first real reason to pull over out of Victoria is Duncan's **Cowichan Native Village**, 200 Cowichan Way (daily: 9am–5pm; $6; ☎746-8119), on your left off the highway in the unmissable wooden buildings next to Malaspina College. Duncan has long been the self-proclaimed "City of Totems", reference to a rather paltry collection of poles – arranged mostly alongside the main road – that belong to the local Cowichan tribes, historically British Columbia's largest native group. The tribes, about 3000 strong locally, still preserve certain traditions, and it's been their energy – along with cash from white civic authorities, attuned as ever to potentially lucrative tourist attractions – that have put up the poles and pulled the project together. Much of the heavily worked commercial emphasis is on shifting native crafts, especially the ubiquitous lumpy jumpers for which the area is famous, but you can usually expect to find historical displays and demonstrations of dancing, knitting, carving, weaving and even native cooking.

OLD-GROWTH FORESTS: GOING, GOING, GONE

While Vancouver Island isn't the only place in North America where environmentalists and the forestry industry are at loggerheads, some of the most bitter and high-profile confrontations have taken place here. The island's wet climate is particularly favourable to the growth of thick **temperate rainforest**, part of a belt that once stretched from Alaska to northern California. The most productive ecosystem on the planet, **old-growth** virgin Pacific rainforest contains up to ten times more biomass per acre than its more famous tropical counterpart – and, though it covers a much smaller area, it is being felled at a greater rate and with considerably less media outrage. Environmentalists estimate that British Columbia's portion of the Pacific rainforest has already been reduced by two-thirds; all significant areas will have been felled, they predict, within about ten or fifteen years. The powerful logging industry claims two-thirds survive, but even the Canadian government – largely in thrall to and supportive of the industry – concedes that only a small percentage of the BC rainforest is currently protected.

What is clear is that the government wants a very firm lid kept on the whole affair. In 1990 it commissioned a report into **public opinion** on the issue in the United Kingdom, which takes half of all British Columbia's plywood exports, three-quarters of all its lumber shipments to Europe, and a third of all Canada's paper pulp output. It observed that "UK public opinion appears to be highly uncritical of Canadian forestry, largely because awareness of the subject is low . . . [there is] a reassuringly romantic and simplistic image of Canadian forestry based on a lumberjack in a checked shirt, felling a single tree." The report concluded that "media attention and coverage of Canadian forestry management issues should not be sought". It's hard to see that opinions will have changed much since.

No such apathy exists in British Columbia, however. The controversy over logging often pits neighbour against neighbour, for some 250,000 in the province depend directly or indirectly on the industry, and big multinationals dominate the scene. **Employment** is a major rallying cry here, and the prospect of job losses through industry regulation is usually enough to override objections. The trend towards **automation** only adds fuel to the argument: by volume of wood cut, the BC forestry industry provides only half as many jobs as in the rest of Canada, which means, in effect, that twice as many trees have to be cut down in BC to provide the same number of jobs.

Some **environmental groups** have resorted to such tactics as fixing huge nails in trees at random – these ruin chainsaws and lumber-mill machinery, but also endanger lives. Countless people have been arrested in recent years for obstructing logging operations. The most level-headed and impressive of the conservation groups, the **Western Canada Wilderness Committee** (WCWC), condemns these acts of environmental vandalism, and instead devotes its energies to alerting the public to the landslide damage and destruction of salmon habitats caused by logging, and the dioxin pollution from pulp mills that in the past has closed 220,000 acres of offshore waters to fishing for shellfish. They point out that the battle is over what they call "the last cookies in the jar", for only a handful of the island's 91 watersheds over 12,000 acres have escaped logging; the old-growth bonanza is nearly over, they argue, and the industry might as well wean itself over to sustainable practices now, before it's too late.

In the meantime, however, ninety percent of timber is still lifted from the rainforest instead of from managed stands, clear-cutting of old-growth timber is blithely described by the vast McMillan company as "a form of harvesting", and independent audits suggest that companies are failing to observe either their cutting or replanting quotas. The provincial government has pledged to improve forestry practices, but only a tiny percentage of the province lies within reserves with a degree of environmental protection.

British Columbia Forestry Museum

Vancouver Island is one of the most heavily logged areas in Canada, and the **BC Forest Discovery Centre**, 1km north of town on Hwy 1 (daily early May to Sept; $8), is run to preserve artefacts from its lumbering heritage; but with industry bigwigs as museum trustees, you can't help feeling it's designed to be something of a palliative in the increasingly ferocious controversy between loggers and environmentalists. Nonetheless, it does a thorough job on trees, and if the forestry displays in Victoria's museum have whetted your appetite, you'll have a good couple of hours rounding off your arboreal education. The entrance is marked by a small black steam engine and a massive piece of yellow logging machinery.

Ranged over a hundred-acre site next to a scenic lake, the well-presented displays tell everything you want to know about trees and how to cut them down. The narrow-gauge steam train round the park is a bit gimmicky (10am–5.30pm only), but a good way of getting around; check out the forest dioramas and the artefacts and archive material in the **Log Museum** in particular. There's also the usual array of working blacksmiths, sawmills, a farmstead, an old logging camp, and a few as-yet-underforested patches where you can take time out.

The complex forms part of the **Cowichan and Chemainus Valleys Ecomuseum**, a vaguely defined park that takes in much of the surrounding area intended to preserve the logging heritage of the area – a curiously ill-defined concept that appears to be largely a PR exercise on the part of the logging companies. Ask for details of tours and maps from the Duncan infocentre, or the Ecomuseum office, 160 Jubilee St (☎748-7620).

The Cowichan Valley

Striking west into the hills from Hwy 1 north of Duncan, Hwy 18 enters the **Cowichan Valley** and fetches up at Cowichan Lake, the largest freshwater lake on the island. Rather than drive, however, the nicest way up the valley is to walk the eighteen-kilometre **Cowichan Valley Footpath**, following the river from Glenora (a hamlet southwest of Duncan at the end of Robertson Rd) to Lake Cowichan Village on the lake's eastern shore. You could do the trip in a day, camp en route, or turn around at Skutz Falls and climb up to the Riverbottom Road to return to Duncan which would be a half-day walk.

A road, rough in parts, circles **Cowichan Lake** (allow 2hr) and offers access to a gamut of outdoor pursuits, most notably fishing – the area is touted, with typical small-town hyperbole, as the "Fly-Fishing Capital of the World". The water gets warm enough for summer swimming, and there's also ample hiking in the wilder country above. At Youbou on the north shore you can visit the **Heritage Mill**, a working sawmill (tours May–Sept): this area boasts some of the most productive forest in Canada, thanks to the lake's mild microclimate, and lumber is the obvious mainstay of the local economy. On the road up to the lake from Duncan you pass the **Valley Demonstration Forest**, another link in the industry's public-relations weaponry, with signs and scenic lookouts explaining the intricacies of forest management.

For details of the area's many tours, trails and outfitters contact the **infocentre** at Lake Cowichan village, 125 South Shore Rd (daily late May to early Sept 9am–8pm; ☎749-3244 or 749-6772). Good, cheap **campgrounds** line the shore, which despite minimal facilities can be quite busy in summer – don't expect to have the place to yourself. The biggest and best is at Gordon Bay Provincial Park (summer $18.50, winter $8) on the south shore 14km from Lake Cowichan village, a popular family place but with a quiet atmosphere and a good sandy **beach**. There are also plenty of hotels, motels and the like in all the lakeside settlements.

Chemainus

CHEMAINUS is the "Little Town That Did", as the billboards for miles around never stop telling you. Its mysterious achievement was the creation of its own tourist attraction, realized when the closure of the local sawmill – once amongst the world's largest – threatened the place with almost overnight extinction. In 1983 the town's worthies commissioned an artist to paint a huge **mural** – *Steam Donkey at Work* – recording the area's local history. This proved so successful that some 40 panels quickly followed, drawing some 300,000 visitors annually to admire the artwork and tempting them to spend money in local businesses as they did. As murals go, these are surprisingly good, and if you're driving it's worth the short, well-signed diversion off Hwy 1. You might also want to drop in on the **Chemainus Valley Museum**, 9799 Waterwheel Crescent (March–May & Nov–Dec Wed–Sun 10am–3pm; June–Oct daily 10am–6pm; donation), a community-run museum of local history with displays on logging, mills and pioneer life. Ironically enough, a new sawmill has now opened, though this has done nothing to deter the welcome influx of resident painters and craftspeople attracted by the murals, a knock-on effect that has done much to enliven the village's pleasant community feel.

Buses also detour here on the run up to Nanaimo (☎246-3354 for details), and the train drops you slap-bang next to a mural. You can also pick up a ferry from Chemainus to the small islands of **Kuper** and **Thetis** (both $5 for foot passengers, $12.75 for cars). There's a summer-only **infocentre** in town at 9796 Willow St (May to early Sept daily 9am–6pm; ☎246-3251, *www.tourism.chemainus.bc.ca*). If you fancy **staying** – the village's cosy waterside setting is nicer than either Duncan or Nanaimo – it's worth booking ahead, as the village's increasing popularity means the local **hotel** and half a dozen or so B&Bs are in heavy demand in summer. For motel accommodation, try the *Fuller Lake Chemainus Motel*, 9300 Trans-Canada Hwy (☎246-3282 or 1-888/246-3255; ③). The best **B&B** is the pretty *Bird Song Cottage*, 9909 Maple St (☎246-9910, *birdsong@island.net*; ⑤). There's also a tiny **youth hostel** at 3040 Henry Rd (☎246-4407; ①), about 2km north of town off the Ladysmith road (they can pick you up from the village); there's a kitchen and showers, but you're supposed to bring your own sleeping bag. The choice of **campgrounds** is between the *Chemainus Gardens RV Park*, 3042 River Rd, 1km east of Hwy 1, set in 37 acres of natural forest with separate tenting area, laundry and showers (☎246-3569 or 1-800/341-5060; $15–25), or the larger *Country Maples Campground*, 9010 Trans-Canada Hwy (☎246-2078; $21–29; April–Oct) in sixty acres of open and treed parkland 16km north of Duncan above the Chemainus River with showers, laundry and pool. About 5km south of the village on the river is the quiet *Bald Eagle Campsite*, 8705 Chemainus Rd (☎246-9457; $16–20). All manner of dinky little cafés, shops and tearooms are springing up across the village: for **food**, try the *Upstairs Downstairs Café*, 9745 Willow St, with cheap, varied dishes including several good vegetarian options, or the *Waterford Inn & Restaurant*, five minutes north of the village centre at 9875 Maple St (☎246-1046).

Ladysmith

LADYSMITH's claim to fame is based solely on an accident of geography, as it straddles the 49th Parallel, the latitude that divides mainland Canada and the US. Canada held onto Vancouver Island only after some hard bargaining, even though the boundary's logic ought to put much of it in the States. It was originally named Oyster Bay, but was renamed by Robert Dunsmuir (see opposite) at the time of the Boer War battle for Ladysmith (many streets bear the name of Boer War generals). There's little to the place other than the usual motels and garages, though a recent attempt to spruce up the older buildings won it a Western Canada Award of Excellence. Ladysmith's scenic profile, it has to be said, would be considerably higher were it not for a huge sawmill and a waterfront hopelessly jammed with lumber. The **infocentre** is a kiosk on the main road at 12615 Trans-Canada Hwy (July–Aug daily 9am–6pm; no phone) and has walking maps of the village's "heritage centre". The **Black Nugget Museum**, 12 Gatacre St (daily noon–4pm; $2), is a restored 1881 hotel stuffed with predictable memorabilia of coal mining and pioneers. If you stop off, check out **Transfer Beach Park** on the harbour, where the water's said to be the warmest in the Pacific north of San Francisco.

For **accommodation**, make for the fourteen-unit *Holiday House Motel*, 540 Esplanade St (☎245-2231, *hhmotel@island.net*; ②), overlooking Ladysmith's waterfront; the *Seaview Marine Resort*, 1111 Chemainus Rd (☎245-3768 or 1-800/891-8832, *www.chemainus.com*; ③), just off the highway 6km south of town (and 8km north of Chemainus) with fully equipped self-catering one- and two-bedroom cottages on the ocean (two-night minimum stay); or the *Inn of the Sea*, 3600 Yellow Point Rd (☎245-2211; ⑥), 13km northeast on the seafront and a popular bolt hole for weekending Victorians. The best **food** option is the oldest "English-style pub" in BC, the *Crow and Gate* off the main road 19km north of the town on Yellow Point Road. For campers, the most central site is the *Sea-RRA RV Park and Campground* in Transfer Beach Park overlooking the port (☎245-5344; $14).

Nanaimo

With a population of about 73,000, **NANAIMO**, 113km from Victoria, is Vancouver Island's second biggest city, the terminal for ferries from Horseshoe Bay and Tsawwassen on the mainland, and a watershed between the island's populated southeastern tip and its wilder, more sparsely peopled countryside to the north and west. In BC, only Vancouver and Kelowna are expanding faster. This said, the town is unexceptional, though the setting, as ever in BC, is eye-catching – particularly around the harbour, which bobs with yachts and rusty fishing boats and, if you've come from Victoria, allows the first views across to the big mountains on the mainland. If you are going to stop here, more than likely it'll be for **Petroglyph Park** or the town's increasingly famous **bungee-jumping** zone. If not, the Nanaimo Parkway provides a 21-kilometre bypass around the town.

Coal first brought white settlers to the region, many of whom made their fortunes here, including the Victorian magnate **Robert Dunsmuir**, who was given £750,000 and almost half the island in return for building the Victoria–Nanaimo railway – an indication of the benefits that could accrue from the British government to those with the pioneering spirit. Five bands of Salish natives originally lived on the site, which they called **Sney-ne-mous**, or "meeting place", from which the present name derives. It was they who innocently showed the local black rock to Hudson's Bay agents in 1852. The old mines are now closed, and the town's pockets are padded today by forestry, deep-sea fishing, tourism and – most notably – by six deep-water docks and a booming port.

The Town

In downtown Nanaimo itself, only two other sights warrant the considerable amount of energy used to promote them. The **Nanaimo District Museum**, just off the main harbour area at 100 Cameron St by the Harbour Park Mall (daily 9am–5pm, closed Jan; $2; ☎753-1821), houses a collection that runs the usual historical gamut of pioneer, logging, mining, native peoples and natural history displays. The best features are the reconstructed coal mine and the interesting insights into the town's cosmopolitan population – a mix of Polish, Chinese, aboriginal peoples and British citizens – who all see themselves today as some of the island's "friendliest folk". The **Bastion**, close by at the corner of Bastion and Front streets, is a wood-planked tower built by the Hudson's Bay Company in 1853 as a store and a stronghold against native attack, though it was never used for such an attack. It's the oldest (perhaps the only) such building in the West. These days it houses a small **museum** of Hudson's Bay memorabilia (summer only 10am–5pm; donation); its silly tourist stunt, without which no BC town would be complete, is "the only ceremonial cannon firing west of Ontario" (summer only, daily at noon). This is marginally more impressive than the town's claim to have the most retail shopping space per capita in the country.

Nanaimo's outskirts are not pretty, nor, if you keep to the road through town, is the main strip of malls and billboards on and around downtown. Big efforts are being made to spruce the place up, however, not least in the town's 25 or so gardens and small parks. Many of these hug the shore, perfectly aligned for a seafront breath of air. The **Harbourfront Walkway** allows you to stroll 3km along the seafront. Also popular is the new Swyalana Lagoon, an artificial tidal lagoon built on a renovated stretch of the downtown harbour in Maffeo Sutton Park. It's become a popular swimming, snoozing and picnic area. Further afield, **Piper's Lagoon Park** offers a windblown, grassy spit, with lots of trails, flowers, rocky bluffs and good sea views; it's off Hammond Bay Road north of the city centre. For **beaches** you could head for **Departure Bay**, again north of the centre off Stewart Avenue. Plenty of local shops rent out a range of marine gear, as well as bikes and boats.

For the wildest of the local parks, head due west of town to **Westwood Lake Park**, good for a couple of hours' lonely hiking and some fine swimming. Tongue-twisting **Petroglyph Provincial Park**, off Hwy 1 3km south of downtown, showcases aboriginal peoples' carvings of the sort found all over BC (particularly along coastal waterways), many of them thousands of years old. Often their meaning is vague, but they appear to record important rituals and events. There are plenty of figures – real and mythological – carved into the local sandstone here, though their potential to inspire wonder is somewhat spoilt by more recent graffiti and the first thin edge of Nanaimo's urban sprawl.

Nanaimo's other major claim to fame is as home of North America's first legal public bungee-jumping site. The **Bungy Zone Adrenalin Centre** is 13km south of the town at 35 Nanaimo River Rd (daily 11.30am–8pm; ☎753-5867, 1-800/668-7771 or 1-888/668-7874, *www.bungyzone.com*; jumps from around $95): look out for the signed turn off Hwy 1. To date it has played host to around 70,000 safe bungee jumps, including night jumps. It's become so popular three variations have been added to the standard 42-metre plunge off the bridge, all slightly less terrifying than the bungee jump. The "Flying Fox" is a line to which you are fixed extending in a deep arc along the canyon – expect to hit speeds of 100kph; "Rap Jumping" involves a rapid mountaineering rappel straight down from the bridge; while the "Ultimate Swing" lets you jump off the bridge and swing in a big arc at speeds of up to 140kph. The last innovation was described by the safety engineer who inspected it – a man with twenty-years' experience of fairground and other rides – as "the best ride I've ever ridden, and I've ridden them all". There is provision for **camping** here (with showers, laundry and tents for rent), and if you call in advance you should be able to book free shuttles to the site from Victoria and Nanaimo.

Nanaimo, like any self-respecting BC town, also lays on a fair few festivals, best known of which is the annual **Bathtub Race** or **Silly Boat Race**, in which bathtubs are raced (and sunk, mostly) across the 55km to Vancouver. The winner, the first to reach Vancouver, receives the silver Plunger Trophy from the Loyal Nanaimo Bathtub Society. It's all part of the Marine Festival held in the second week of July. More highbrow is the May to June **Nanaimo Festival**, a cultural jamboree that takes place in and around Malaspina College, 900 5th St. The town's other minor claim to fame is the **Nanaimo bar**, a glutinous chocolate confection made to varying recipes and on sale everywhere.

Newcastle and Gabriola islands

Barely a stone's throw offshore from Nanaimo lies **Newcastle Island**, and beyond it the larger bulk of **Gabriola Island**, both incongruously graced with palm trees: they're beneficiaries of what is supposedly Canada's mildest climate. Ferries make the

Pacific Beach, Washington

Carving on driftwood

Logging

Temperate forest in Olympic National Park, Washington

Yakima Valley, Washington

Orca

Brown bear with salmon

Cascade Mountains, Washington

E. NAGELE

Vancouver

NEIL SETCHFIELD

Canada Place, Vancouver

Quesnel, British Columbia

Mount Robson, British Columbia

crossing every hour on the hour (10am–9pm; foot passengers $5 return, cars $12.75) from Maffeo Sutton Park (the wharf behind the Civic Arena) to **Newcastle Island Provincial Park**, which has a fine stretch of sand, tame wildlife, no cars, and lots of walking and picnic possibilities. It'll take a couple of hours to walk the 7.5-kilometre trail that encircles the island. There are about fifteen daily crossings to Gabriola Island (20min), a much quieter place that's home to about 2000 people, many of them artists and writers. Author Malcolm Lowry, he of *Under the Volcano* fame, immortalized the island in a story entitled *October Ferry to Gabriola Island* (characters in the tale never actually reach the island). Gabriola also offers several **beaches** – the best are Gabriola Sands' Twin Beaches at the island's northwest end and Drumbeg Provincial Park – and lots of scope for scuba diving, bird-watching (eagles and sea birds), beachcombing and easy walking, plus the added curiosity of the **Malaspina Galleries**, a series of caves and bluffs near Gabriola Sands sculpted by wind, frost and surf.

Both islands have numerous **B&Bs** and several **campgrounds**, though if you're thinking of staying the night it's as well to check first with the Nanaimo infocentre. You can buy snacks on Newcastle from various concessions, notably the newly restored 1931 Pavilion building, but if you're camping take supplies with you.

Information and transport

Nanaimo's **bus terminal** (☎753-4371) is some way from the harbour on the corner of Comox and Terminal, with six daily runs to Victoria, two to Port Hardy and three or four to Port Alberni, for connections to Tofino and Ucluelet. **BC Ferries** (☎386-3431 or 1-888/223-3779) sail to and from Departure Bay, 2km north of downtown (take the Hammond Bay bus #2 to the north end of Stewart Ave), to Tsawwassen (south of Vancouver) and more frequently to Horseshoe Bay on the mainland (summer hourly 7am–9pm; off-season every 2hr; foot passengers $9 one-way, cars $32; cheaper in low season). Another newer terminal, Duke Point, which will take increasing numbers of ferries, operates just to the south of the town. The town lies on the Victoria–Courtenay line and sees two trains daily, northbound around 11am and southbound at 3pm: the station is in the centre of downtown.

You'll find a typically overstocked **infocentre** at Beban House, 2290 Bowen Rd (May–Sept daily 8am–8pm; Oct–April Mon–Fri 9am–5pm; ☎756-0106 or 1-800/663-7337, *www.tourism.nanaimo.bc.ca*). They'll phone around and help with **accommodation** referrals, and shower you with pamphlets on the town and the island as a whole. There are also details of the many boat rides and tours you can make to local sawmills, canneries, nature reserves and fishing research stations.

Accommodation

Nanaimo's cheapest beds are at the central, private **mini-hostel**, the *Nanaimo International Hostel*, 65 Nicol St (☎753-1188, reservations ☎754-9697; ①), located seven blocks south of the bus terminal and one block south of the Harbour Park Shopping Centre off Hwy 1; dorm beds from $15. A handful of camping spots ($8) on the lawn (with ocean views) are also available, plus bike rental. More recent and a touch more expensive is the downtown *Cambie International Hostel*, 63 Victoria Crescent (☎754-5323; ①), with accommodation for 50 in small dorm rooms; beds cost $25 or $20 with student or HI cards.

Numerous **motels** are clustered on the city limits, the best-known cheapie being the small *Colonial*, 950 Terminal Ave on Hwy 1 (☎754-4415, *colonial@island.net*; ②). For more tasteful lodgings, try the big *Howard Johnson Harbourside Hotel*, 1 Terminal Ave (☎753-2241 or 1-800/663-7322; ③), convenient for the bus terminal, or the *Fairwinds Schooner Cove Resort Hotel and Marina* at 3521 Dolphin Drive (☎468-7691 or 1-800/663-7060, *www.fairwinds.bc.ca*; ⑤), 26km north of town near Nanoose Bay.

If you're **camping**, by far the best choice is Newcastle Island Provincial Park ($12; see overleaf), which has the only pitches (18 in all, so arrive early) within walking distance of town. Other sites are spread along the main road to the north and south. The best of these – a rural, watery retreat – is *Brannan Lake Campsites*, 6km north of the ferry terminal off Hwy 19 on a 150-acre working farm at 4228 Biggs Rd (☎756-0404; $16–19). The forestry bigwigs have set up a free site at lovely Nanaimo Lake on Nanaimo Lake Road about ten minutes south of the town.

Where **eating** is concerned, get your obligatory Nanaimo bar, or other cheap edibles, at the food stands in the **Public Market**, which is near the ferry terminal on Stewart Avenue (daily 9am–9pm). The big Overwaitea supermarket is 2km north of town on Hwy 19. For meals try *Gina's*, 47 Skinner St, an unmissable Mexican outfit perched on the edge of a cliff and painted bright pink with an electric blue roof. The town's best **seafood** choice is the *Bluenose Chowder House*, 1340 Stewart Ave (closed Mon), also party to a nice outside terrace. Up the road near the BC Ferry terminal, *The Grotto*, 1511 Stewart Ave, is another reliable choice (closed Sun & Mon). A more recent arrival, and worth a look, is *Missoula's*, on the highway near the Rutherford Mall: both restaurants serve the usual range of Canadian and Pacific Rim dishes.

From Nanaimo to Port Alberni

North of Nanaimo Hwy 1 is replaced by **Hwy 19**, a messy stretch of road spotted with billboards and a rash of motels, marinas and clapboard houses. Almost every last centimetre of the coast is privately owned, this being the chosen site of what appears to be every British Columbian's dream holiday home. Don't expect, therefore, to be able to weave through the houses, wooden huts and boat launches to reach the tempting beaches that flash past below the highway. For sea and sand you have to hang on for **Parksville**, 37km north of Nanaimo, and its quieter near-neighbour **Qualicum Beach**.

Parksville marks a major parting of the ways: while Hwy 19 continues up the eastern coast to Port Hardy, **Hwy 4**, the principal trans-island route, pushes west to **Port Alberni** and on through the tremendously scenic Mackenzie Mountains to the Pacific Rim National Park. Laidlaw (☎385-4411 or 388-5248) runs three **buses** daily from Nanaimo to Port Alberni, where there are connecting services for Ucluelet and Tofino in the national park.

Parksville

The approach to **PARKSVILLE** from the south is promising, taking you through lovely wooded dunes, with lanes striking off eastwards to hidden beaches and a half-dozen secluded **campgrounds**. Four kilometres on is the best of the beaches, stretched along 2km of **Rathtrevor Beach Provincial Park**. In summer this area is madness – there's more beach action here than just about anywhere in the country – and if you want to lay claim to some of the park's **camping** space (summer $18.50, winter $8) expect to start queuing first thing in the morning or take advantage of the provincial park reservations service (see p.390). The public sand here stretches for 2km and sports all the usual civilized facilities of Canada's tamed outdoors: cooking shelters, picnic spots and walking trails.

The dross starts beyond the bridge into **Parksville** and its eight blocks of motels and garages. The worst of the development has been kept off the promenade, however, which fronts **Parksville Beach**, whose annual **Sandfest** draws 30,000 visitors a day in July to watch the World Sandcastle Competition. The beach offers lovely views across to the mainland and boasts Canada's warmest sea water – up to 21°C (70°F) in summer. Though busy, it's as immaculately kept as the rest of the town – a tidiness that bears witness to the reactionary civic pride of Parksville's largely retired permanent population. You'll see some of these worthy burghers at play during August, when the town hosts the World Croquet Championships.

For local **information**, Parksville's Chamber of Commerce is clearly signed off the highway in downtown at 1275 E Island Hwy (daily 8am–6pm; ☎248-3613, *www .chamber.parksville.bc.ca*). Ask especially for details of the many **hiking** areas and other nearby refuges from the beaches' summer maelstrom, and **fishing**, which is naturally another of the region's big draws.

If you must **stay**, camping offers the best locations. There are a multitude of cheapish identikit **motels** in town and "resort complexes" out along the beaches, though summer vacancies are few and far between. South of Rathtrevor Beach Provincial Park, try a pair of cottage resorts that look onto the sea: the big *Tigh-Na-Mara Resort Hotel*, 1095 E Island Hwy (☎248-2072 or 1-800/663-7373, *www.tigh-na-mara.com*; ④–⑦), with log cottages and oceanfront condos, forest setting, beach, indoor pool and self-catering units; or the smaller and slightly cheaper *Graycrest Seaside Resort*, 1115 E Island Hwy (☎248-6513 or 1-800/663-2636, *www.graycrest.com*; ⑦), which has considerably lower rates off season. More upmarket still is the *Beach Acres Resort*, 1015 E Island Hwy (☎248-3424 or 1-800/663-7309, *www.beachacresresort.com*; ⑦), set in 57 acres of woodland with its own pool, sandy beach, and forest or ocean-view cabins. Much cheaper is the *Sea Edge Motel*, 209 W Island Hwy (☎248-8377 or 1-800/667-3382, *seaedge@parksville.net*; ⑥), with its own stretch of beach. If you're after one of the cheapest motels, try the *Skylite*, 459 E Island Hwy (☎248-4271 or 1-800/667-1886, *skylitemotel@bctravel.com*; ③).

Qualicum Beach

QUALICUM BEACH, says its Chamber of Commerce, "is to the artist of today what Stratford-on-Avon was to the era of Shakespeare" – a Bohemian enclave of West Coast artists and writers that has also been dubbed the "Carmel of the North" after the town in California. Both estimations obviously pitch things ridiculously high, but compared to Parksville the area has more greenery and charm, and it's infinitely less commercialized, though it probably has just as many summer visitors.

More a collection of dispersed houses than a town, Qualicum's seafront is correspondingly wilder and more picturesque – though a big resort development is under construction – skirted by the road and interrupted only by an **infocentre** at 2711 W Island Hwy, the obvious white building midway on the strand (daily 9am–6pm, open longer in summer; ☎752-9532, *www.qualicum.bc.ca*), and a couple of well-sited **hotels**: the *Sand Pebbles Inn* (☎752-6974 or 1-877/556-2326, *www.maxpages.com/pebbles*; ⑤) and the small *Captain's Inn* (☎752-6743; ③). A cluster of **motels** also sit at its northern end, where the road swings inland. There's plenty of other local accommodation and B&Bs and campgrounds: contact the infocentre for details. Keep heading north and the road becomes quieter and edged with occasional **campgrounds**.

Highway 4 to Port Alberni

If you've not yet ventured off the coastal road from Victoria, the short stretch of **Hwy 4 to Port Alberni** offers the first real taste of the island's beauty. The cheapest place to stay along here is the unnamed log-cabin-style **lodgings** (☎248-5694; ②) at 2400 Hwy 4 in Coombs, about 10km west of Parksville – take the third entrance past the school on the south side of the main road. Buses will stop here on request, but there are only a couple of rooms – and no cooking facilities – so call in advance.

The first worthwhile stop is **Englishman River Falls Provincial Park**, 3km west of Parksville and then another 8km south off the highway. Named after an early immigrant who drowned here, the park wraps around the Englishman River, which tumbles over two main sets of waterfalls. A thirty-minute trail takes in both falls, with plenty of swimming and fishing pools en route. The popular year-round provincial park **campground** (summer $15, winter $8) is on the left off the approach road before the river, nestled amongst cedars, dogwoods – BC's official tree – and lush ferns.

Back on the main highway, a further 8km brings you to the **Little Qualicum Hatchery**, given over to chum, trout and chinook salmon, and just beyond it turn right for the **Little Qualicum Falls Provincial Park**, on the north side of Hwy 4 19km west of Parksville, which is claimed by some to be the island's loveliest small park. A magnificent forest trail follows the river as it drops several hundred metres through a series of gorges and foaming waterfalls. A half-hour stroll gives you views of the main falls, but for a longer **hike** try the five-hour Wesley Ridge Trail. There's a sheltered provincial park **campground** (summer $15, winter $8) by the river and a recognized **swimming area** on the river at its southern end.

Midway to Port Alberni, the road passes **Cameron Lake** and then an imperious belt of old-growth forest. At the lake's western end, it's well worth walking ten minutes into **McMillan Provincial Park** (no campground) to reach the famous **Cathedral Grove**, a beautiful group of huge Douglas firs, some of them reaching 70m tall, 2m thick and up to a thousand years old. The park is the gift of the large McMillan timber concern, whose agents have been responsible for felling similar trees with no compunction over the years. Wandering the grove will take only a few minutes, but just to the east, at the Cameron Lake picnic site, is the start of the area's main **hike**. The well-maintained trail was marked out by railway crews in 1908 and climbs to the summit of **Mount Arrowsmith** (1817m), a long, gentle twenty-kilometre pull through alpine meadows that takes between six and nine hours. The mountain is also one of the island's newer and fast-developing ski areas. To stay locally, head for the *Cameron Lake Resort* (☎752-6707; April–Oct; ③), based in a park-like setting on the lake: it has seven cottages and a campground ($19).

Port Alberni

Self-proclaimed "Gateway to the Pacific" and – along with half of Vancouver Island – "Salmon Capital of the World", **PORT ALBERNI** is a town fairly dominated by the sights and smells of its huge lumber mills. It's also an increasingly popular site for exploring the centre and west coast of the island, and a busy fishing port, situated at the end of the impressive fjord-like Alberni Inlet, Vancouver Island's longest inlet. Various logging and pulp-mill tours are available, but the town's main interest to travellers is as a forward base for the Pacific Rim National Park. If you've ever wanted to hook a salmon, though, this is probably one of the easier places to do so and there are any number of boats and guides ready to help out.

The only conventional sight is the **Alberni Valley Museum**, 4255 Wallace St and 10th Avenue (summer Tues–Sat 10am–5pm, Thurs until 8pm; free; ☎723-2181), home to a predictable but above-average logging and aboriginal peoples collection, a water wheel and small steam engine. For hot-weather swimming, locals head out to **Sproat Lake Provincial Park**, 8km north of town on Hwy 4. It's a hectic scene in summer, thanks to a fine beach, picnic area and a pair of good campgrounds ($15; April–Oct), one on the lake, the other north of the highway about 1km away. Of peripheral interest, you can take a guided tour of the world's largest firefighting planes or follow the short trails that lead to a few ancient petroglyphs on the park's eastern tip.

Sproat Lake marks the start of the superb scenery that unfolds over the 100km of Hwy 4 west of the town. Only heavily logged areas detract from the grandeur of the Mackenzie Range and the majestic interplay of trees and water. Go prepared, however, as there's no fuel or shops for about two hours of driving.

Practicalities

Laidlaw (☎385-4411 or 1-800/318-0818, *www.victoriatours.com*) runs five **buses** daily to and from Nanaimo, with the terminal on Victoria Quay at 5065 Southgate (though the bus company are based at 4541 Margaret St). Jump off at the 7-Eleven, one stop earlier, to be nearer the centre of town. The same company runs connections from here on to Ucluelet and Tofino in Pacific Rim National Park. Western Bus Lines (☎723-3341) run two services weekly to Bamfield (Mon & Fri; $17 one-way) as does the Pacheenaht First Nation Bus Service (☎647-5521). Several other companies from Victoria (see p.328) make connections to Bamfield for the West Coast Trail (see p.373). For help and information on fishing charters, hiking options, minor summer events, or tours of the two local pulp mills, call in at the **infocentre**, unmissable as you come into town at 2533 Redford St, RR2, Site 215 Comp 10 (daily 9am–6pm; ☎724-6535, *www.alberni.net*), off Hwy 4 east of town – look out for the big yellow mural.

Given the 8am departure of the MV *Lady Rose* (see below), there's a good chance you may have to stay overnight in the town. For **accommodation** there are the usual motel choices, though for a good central hotel you might be better off with the *Coast Hospitality Inn*, 3835 Redford St (☎723-8111 or 1-800/663-1144, *www.alberni.net /coasthi/*; ⑥), not cheap, but probably the town's best bet. *The Best Western Barclay*, 4277 Stamp Ave (☎724-7171 or 1-800/563-6590, *www.bestwesternbarclay.com*; ⑤), with outdoor pool and the smaller *Somass Motel & RV*, 5279 River Rd (☎724-3236 or 1-800/927-2217, *www.somass-motel.bc.ca*; ③), are also both reliable choices. Cheaper, and 14km west of town on the lakefront off Hwy 4 at 10695 Lakeshore Rd, is the *Westbay Hotel on Sproat Lake* (☎723-2811 or 1-800/358-2811, *www3.bc.sympatico.ca/westbay*; ③). The infocentre has a list of the constantly changing **B&B** outlets: an excellent first choice is the *Edelweiss B&B*, 2610-12 Ave (☎723-5940; ④), which is not particularly central, but does have very welcoming hosts. For **camping**, best bets are on Sproat Lake (see opposite), or you can try the small, reasonably central and wooded *Dry Creek Public Campground*, 6230 Beaver Creek Rd at 4th Avenue and Napier Street (☎723-6011; $8–19; May–Sept): ask at the infocentre for directions as it's hard to find. Further afield is the bigger 250-site *China Creek Marina and Campground*, Bamfield Road (☎723-2657; $12–25), 15km south of the town on Alberni Inlet, which has a wooded, waterside location and sandy, log-strewn beach. Camping at Sproat Lake is excellent, but busy in the summer.

Eating possibilities are numerous. For coffee down by the dock before jumping aboard the MV *Lady Rose*, try the *Blue Door Café*. For lunch, make for the *Swale's Rock*, 5328 Argyle St (☎723-0777), and for **seafood** check out the waterfront *Clockworks*, Harbour Quay (☎723-2333). The *Canal*, 5093 Johnson St, serves good Greek food, and for cheap lunches there's the *Paradise Café*, 4505 Gertrude St, and several deli-bakeries.

The MV Lady Rose

The thing you'll probably most want to do in Port Alberni is to leave it, preferably on the **MV Lady Rose**, a small, fifty-year-old Scottish-built freighter that plies between Kildonan, Bamfield, Ucluelet and the Broken Group Islands (pp.370–373). Primarily a conduit for freight and mail, it also takes up to a hundred passengers, many of whom use it as a drop-off for canoe trips or the West Coast Trail at Bamfield. You could easily ride it simply for the exceptional scenery – huge cliffs and tree-covered mountains – and for the abundant wildlife (sea lions, whales, eagles, depending on the time of year). Passengers started as something of a sideline for the company that runs the boat, but such has been the boat's popularity that another boat has been added to the "fleet" – the 200-passenger MV *Frances Barkley* – and reservations for trips are now virtually essential. Remember to take a sweater and jacket and wear sensible shoes, for these are still primarily working boats, and creature comforts are few.

The basic year-round **schedule** is as follows: the boat leaves at 8am from the Argyle

Pier, 5425 Argyle St at the Alberni Harbour Quay (year-round Tues, Thurs & Sat). It arrives in **Bamfield** ($20 one-way, $40 return) via Kildonan ($12/24), at 12.30pm and starts its return journey an hour later, reaching Port Alberni again at 5.30pm. From October to May the boat stops on request in advance at the Broken Group Islands ($20/40). From July 1 to Labor Day only (early Sept) there are additional sailings on this route (same times) on Fridays and Sundays.

From June to late September, there are additional sailings on Monday, Wednesday and Friday to **Ucluelet** and the Broken Group Islands, departing 8am and arriving at Ucluelet at 1pm via the islands, where the boat docks at 11am at Sechart, site of the new *Sechart Whaling Station Lodge* (☎723-8313; ③), the only place to stay if you're not wilderness camping on the archipelago. The return journey starts from Ucluelet at 2pm, calling at Sechart again (3.30pm) before arriving back at Port Alberni (7pm).

Contact Lady Rose Marine Services for information and reservations (☎723-8313 or 1-800/663-7192; April–Sept only, *www.ladyrosemarine.com*). They also offer canoe and kayak rentals and transportation of the same to the Broken Group Islands (canoe and single kayak rental $30, double kayak $40 daily including lifejackets, paddles, pumps and spray skirts). Note that smaller boats running more irregular services to the same destinations can occasionally be picked up from Tofino and Ucluelet.

Pacific Rim National Park

The **Pacific Rim National Park**, the single best reason to visit Vancouver Island, is a stunning amalgam of mountains, coastal rainforest, wild beaches and unkempt marine landscapes that stretches intermittently for 130km between the towns of Tofino in the north and Port Renfrew to the south. It divides into three distinct areas: **Long Beach**, which is the most popular; the **Broken Group Islands**, hundreds of islets only really accessible to sailors and canoeists; and the **West Coast Trail**, a tough but increasingly popular long-distance footpath. The whole area has also become a magnet for surfing and **whale-watching** enthusiasts, and dozens of small companies run charters out from the main centres to view the migrating mammals. By taking the MV *Lady Rose* from Port Alberni (see above) to Bamfield or Ucluelet or back, and combining this with shuttle buses or Laidlaw buses from Victoria, Port Alberni and Nanaimo, a wonderfully varied combination of itineraries is possible around the region.

Lying at the north end of Long Beach, **Tofino**, once essentially a fishing village, is now changing in the face of tourism, but with its natural charm, scenic position and plentiful accommodation, the town still makes the best base for general exploration. **Ucluelet** to the south is comparatively less attractive, but almost equally geared to providing tours and accommodating the park's 800,000 or so annual visitors. **Bamfield**, a tiny and picturesque community with a limited amount of in-demand accommodation, lies still further south and is known mainly as the northern trailhead of the West Coast Trail and a fishing, marine research and whale-watching centre. Unless you fly in, you enter the park on Hwy 4 from Port Alberni, which means the first part you'll see is **Long Beach** (Hwy 4 follows its length en route for Tofino), so if you're dashing in by car for a day-trip, cut straight to the section dealing with this area on p.368. Long Beach, rather than Tofino, is also the site of the park's main **information centre** and the nearby Wickaninnish Centre, an interpretive centre. Remember that a **park fee** – $8 per vehicle per day – is payable at the park entrance.

Weather in the park is an important consideration, because it has a well-deserved reputation for being appallingly wet, cold and windy – and that's the good days. An average of 300cm of rain falls annually, and in some places it buckets down almost 700cm, well over ten times what falls on Victoria. So don't count on doing much swimming or sunbathing (though **surfing**'s a possibility): think more in terms of spending your time admiring crashing Pacific breakers, hiking the backcountry and maybe doing a spot of beachcombing. Better still, time your visit to coincide with the worst of the weather off-season – **storm-watching** is an increasingly popular park pastime.

Tofino

TOFINO, most travellers' target base in the park, is showing the adverse effects of its ever-increasing tourist influx, but locals are keeping development to a minimum, clearly realizing they have a vested interest in preserving the salty, waterfront charm that brings people here in the first place. Crowning a narrow spit, the village is bounded on three sides by tree-covered islands and water, gracing it with magnificent views and plenty of what the tourist literature refers to as "aquaculture". As a service centre it fulfils most functions, offering food, accommodation and a wide variety of boat and sea-plane tours, most of which have a **whale-watching** or fishing angle or provide a means to get out to **islands and hot springs** close by (see below). Sleepy in off-season, the place erupts into a commercial frenzy during the summer (hippies, surfer types and easy-going family groups being the most visible visitors), though there's little to do in town other than walk its few streets, enjoy the views and soak up the casual atmosphere.

You might drop into the small **Whale Centre** at 411 Campbell St (daily March–Oct 9am–8pm; free; ☎725-2132), one of many places to book whale-watching tours, but also home to exhibits and artefacts devoted to local seafaring and trading history, whales and aboriginal peoples' culture. Another notable place around town is the **Eagle Aerie Gallery**, 350 Campbell St (☎725-3235), a gallery belonging to noted Tsimshian artist Roy Vickers and housed in a traditional longhouse-style building with a beautiful cedar interior. Two fine beaches also lie within walking distance to the southeast of the town: **Mackenzie Beach** and **Chesterman's Beach**, the former one of the warmer spots locally, the latter home to a fair number of out-of-town accommodation possibilities (see overleaf). Beyond Chesterman lies Frank Island, a tempting proposition at low tide, but sadly private property. The quietest beach around these parts, though, is **Templar**, a miniature strip of sand: ask at the infocentre for directions.

Tofino's easily reached by Laidlaw **bus** (☎385-4411 or 1-800/318-0818) from Port Alberni (2 daily; 3hr) and Nanaimo (1 daily; 4hr 30min), with a single early-morning connection from Victoria, changing at Nanaimo (6hr 30min; $47.50 one-way). The bus depot is on 1st Street near the junction with Neil Street. For **flights**, the excellent North Vancouver Air (☎604/278-1608 or 1-800/228-6608) operates to here from Vancouver (1hr flight; $175 one-way) and Victoria (45min; $225 one-way). Baxter Aviation (☎250/754-1066, 604/683-6525 in Vancouver or 1-800/661-5599) also run connecting flights to Tofino and Ucluelet (see p.370) from Vancouver harbour, Victoria, Seattle and many other smaller centres. The **infocentre** at 380 Campbell St (March–Sept daily 9am–8pm; ☎725-3414, *tofino@island.net*) can give you the exhaustive lowdown on all the logistics of boat and plane tours.

Trips from Tofino

Once they've wandered Tofino's streets, most people head south to explore Long Beach, or put themselves at the mercy of the boat and plane operators. Their playground is the stretch of ocean and landscapes around Tofino known as **Clayoquot Sound**. The name has gained tremendous resonance over the last few years, largely because it has been the focus for some of the most bitterly fought battles against loggers by environmentalists and aboriginal campaigners. It stretches for some 65km from Kennedy Lake to the south of Tofino to the Hesquiat Peninsula 40km to the north, embracing three major islands – Meares, Vargas and Flores – and numerous smaller islets and coastal inlets. More importantly, it is the largest surviving area of low-altitude temperate **rainforest** in North America. Quite incredibly the BC government gave permission to logging companies in 1993 to fell two-thirds of this irreplaceable and age-old forest. The result was the largest outbreak of **civil disobedience** in Canadian history, resulting in eight hundred arrests, as vast numbers congregated at a peace camp in the area and made daily attempts to stop the logging trucks. The stand-off resulted in partial victory, with the designation of new protected areas and limited recognition of the Nuu-chah-nulth tribes moral and literal rights to the land. The region remains in a precarious position, however, and if it's happened once you can be pretty sure that, where forestry interests are concerned, it'll happen again.

There are five main destinations in this region for boat and float-plane trips. The nearest is **Meares Island**, easily visible to the east of Tofino and just fifteen minutes away by boat. A beautiful island swathed in lush temperate rainforest, this was one of the areas earmarked for the lumberjack's chainsaw, despite its designation as a Nuu-chah-nulth tribal park in 1985. At present its ancient cedars and hemlock are safe, and visible on the Meares Island Big Cedar Trail (3km), which meanders among some of the biggest trees you'll ever see, many of them more than a thousand years old and up to 6m across – big enough to put a tunnel through. **Vargas Island**, the next nearest target, lies just 5km from Tofino to the north, and is visited for its beauty, beaches, kayaking and swimming possibilities. **Flores Island**, 20km to the northwest, is accessed by boat or plane and, like Vargas Island, is partly protected by partial provincial park status. At the aboriginal peoples' community of Ahousaht you can pick up the Ahousaht Wild Side Heritage Trail, which runs for 16km through idyllic beach and forest scenery to the Mount Flores viewpoint (886m). This is also a chance to encounter aboriginal culture and people at first hand, with **tours** accompanied by local guides available: see the Tofino infocentre or call ☎725-3309 for details and information on trail conditions.

Perhaps the best, and certainly one of the most popular trips from Tofino, is the 37-kilometre boat or plane ride to **Hot Springs Cove**, site of one of only a handful of hot springs on Vancouver Island (1hr by boat, 15min by float plane). A thirty-minute trek from the landing stage brings you to the springs, which emerge at a piping 43°C and run, as a creek, to the sea via a small waterfall and four pools, becoming progressively cooler. Be prepared for something of a crowd in summer when swimming costumes can be optional. An expensive hotel, the *Hot Springs Lodge* – a way to beat other punters by getting in an early-morning or late-night dip – has opened on the cove near the landing stage (see "Accommodation", opposite). Finally, a forty-kilometre trip north takes you to **Hesquiat Peninsula**, where you land at or near Refuge Cove, site of a Hesquiaht aboriginal village. Locals offer tours here and some lodgings: ask for the latest details at the Tofino infocentre. The infocentre is also the place to pick up information on **tours**: otherwise, contact Seaside Adventures, 300 Main St (☎725-2292 or 1-888/332-4252), Chinook Charters, 450 Campbell St (☎725-3431 or 1-800/665-3646), or the whale-watching companies listed under "Activities" on p.367, most of whom also offer boat tours to the above destinations.

The telephone code for Victoria and Vancouver Island is ☎250.

Accommodation

The infocentre may be able to get you into one of the village's ever-expanding roster of **hotels**, **motels** and **B&Bs**, should you be unwise enough to turn up in Tofino without reservations in high summer. There are two main concentrations of accommodation options: in Tofino itself or a couple of kilometres out of town to the east en route for Long Beach on or near Lynn Road, which overlooks Chesterman Beach. Bed and breakfast options, in particular, tend to be out of town near Chesterman Beach. Note that out of town but across the water (access by water taxi) there's also the desirable but expensive self-contained units at the *Hot Springs Lodge* (☎724-8570; ⑥), the only accommodation at Hot Springs Cove (see opposite), but book early.

Otherwise you can try one of many **campgrounds** or the **private hostels** that now seem to spring up overnight here and disappear just as quickly, though local reports suggest some of these places can be pretty unsalubrious, home to a sprinkling of the untrustworthy sort of beach-bum year-round drifters that give travellers a bad name. Current good hostels include the *Tofino Backpackers B&B*, 241 Campbell St (☎725-2288; $10 in winter, $15 in summer), and *Vargas Island Inn & Hostel* (☎725-3309; $30 per person including boat fare), the latter in a good position out on an island north of the town (see "Trips from Tofino" opposite). Best of all is the recent Hostelling International-affiliated *Whalers on the Point Guesthouse*, near the west end of Main Street at 81 West St (☎725-3443, *www.tofinohostel.com*; ①): beds are $22 per person, with a choice of shared or private rooms. Facilities include kitchen, games room, sauna, bike rental and storage, surf and wetsuit lockers, and a shuttle service to Long Beach.

HOTELS AND MOTELS

Cable Cove Inn, 201 Main St (☎725-4236 or 1-800/663-6449, *www.cablecoveinn.com*). Stay in high style in one of six smart rooms at the westernmost edge of town that comes complete with jacuzzis, fireplaces and four-poster beds. ⑦.

Dolphin Motel, 1190 Pacific Rim Hwy (☎725-3377, fax 725-3374). Rooms with coffee-maker and fridge or self-catering units 3km south of town; 5min walk to Chesterman Beach. ③.

Duffin Cove and Resort, 215 Campbell St (☎725-3448 or 1-800/222-3588, *www.duffin-cove -resort.com*). Thirteen nice cabins and suites (for one to eight people) with kitchens and seaview balconies just south of the *Cable Cove Inn* at the western edge of town overlooking the Clayoquot Sound. ③.

Maquinna Lodge, 120 1st St (☎725-3261 or 1-800/665-3199, fax 725-3433). Central town location at the corner of Main and 1st sts, containing renovated rooms, some overlooking Tofino Harbour and Meares Island. ⑤.

Middle Beach Lodge, 400 Mackenzie Beach (☎725-2900, fax 725-2901, *www.middlebeach.com*). Extremely nice, secluded place south of town and west of Chesterman Beach with big stone fireplace, deep old chairs and the gentle splash of waves on tiny Templar Beach to lull you to sleep. ⑤.

Ocean Village Beach Resort, 555 Hellesen Drive (☎725-3755, *www.travel.bc.ca/o/oceanvillage*). A resort just north of Long Beach, 2km from town on the main road, with good accommodation, ocean views, kitchen units and indoor pool. ⑥.

Schooner Motel, 311 Campbell St (☎725-3478, fax 725-3499). Overlooking Tofino Inlet and Meares Island in the town centre, this motel has some rooms complete with kitchen. ⑥.

Tofino Motel, 542 Campbell St (☎725-2055, fax 725-2455, *www.alberni.net/tofino-motel*). A motel on the eastern edge of town including rooms with balconies offering views of the sea and neighbouring islands. ⑤.

Tofino Swell Lodge, 341 Olsen Rd (☎725-3274). On the eastern edge of town near Crab Dock, this excellent lodge on the waterfront looking out to Meares Island has kitchen or plain sleeping units. ④.

Wickaninnish Inn, Osprey Lane at Chesterman Beach (☎725-3100 or 1-800/333-4604, fax 725-3110, *www.wickinn.com*). If you're feeling like a splurge, shell out for this superb $8.5-million 45-room inn, situated on a rocky promontory at the western end of Chesterman Beach. All rooms are large and have ocean views, fireplaces and baths big enough for two. As well as the obvious local attractions, storm-watching here is a growing wintertime activity. ⑧.

BED AND BREAKFASTS

B&B by the Beach, 1277 Lynn Rd (☎725-2441). Away from the centre of Tofino on Chesterman Beach at its northern end. Rooms have private bathrooms; continental breakfast. ⑤.

Brimar, 1375 Thornberg Crescent (☎725-3410 or 1-800/714-9373). At the south end of Chesterman Beach, off Lynn Rd, these three rooms have good Pacific Ocean views and come with a full breakfast. ⑤.

Crab Dock Guest House, 310 Olsen Rd (☎725-2911, *www.crabdock.com*). Situated a little east of the town at Crab Dock, these three recently built rooms all have private bathroom. A full breakfast is offered but you can also use the guest kitchen, as well as the living room. ⑤.

Gull Cottage, 1254 Lynn Rd (☎725-3177, fax 725-2080, *gullcott@island.net*). A few minutes' walk to the beach, at the west end of Lynn Rd, this Victorian-era home has three rooms (private bathrooms) and a hot tub in the woods. ⑤.

Paddler's Inn, 320 Main St (☎725-4222). A recommended spot on the waterfront right in the middle of town; non-smoking. ③.

Penny's Place, 565 Campbell St (☎725-3457). A choice of rooms on the east edge of the small downtown with and without private bathrooms offering a full breakfast but non-smoking. ④/⑤.

The Tide's Inn B&B, 160 Arnet Rd (☎725-3765, fax 725-3325, *tidesinn@island.net*). An easy walk south of town (walk down 1st Ave and turn right) on the waterfront with good views of Clayoquot Sound. ④.

Village Gallery B&B, 321 Main St (☎725-4229, fax 725-3473). Quiet upper room and living room in a heritage building in the centre of town with good ocean view and full breakfast. ④.

West Beach Manor, 1314 Lynn Rd (☎725-2779). Self-contained suites close to Chesterman Beach with kitchens and separate bedrooms with space for up to four people. Minimum two-night stay in high season. ⑥.

Wilp Gybuu (*Wolf House*), 311 Leighton Way (☎725-2330, *wilpgybu@island.net*). Three rooms in a walkable location south of town close to *The Tide's Inn*. Sea views, good breakfast and private en-suite bathroom. ④.

CAMPGROUNDS

Bella Pacifica Campground, Pacific Rim Hwy (☎725-3400, fax 725-2400, *www.bellapacifica.com*). Sites with hot showers, flush toilets and laundry 2km south of town, with wilderness and oceanfront sites, private nature trails to Templar Beach and walk-on access to Mackenzie Beach. Reservations recommended. March–Oct. $24–33.

Crystal Cove Beach Resort, Mackenzie Beach (☎725-4213, fax 725-4219). Sites with flush toilets, laundry and showers and some cabins; 3km south of town in pretty, secluded cover and also 1km from Mackenzie Beach with one- and two-bedroom smart log cabins with kitchens and ocean views. Reservations recommended. $30–50; cabins ⑥.

Mackenzie Beach Resort, 1101 Pacific Rim Hwy (☎725-3439, *www.tofino.bc.com/macbeach*). Located on a fine sandy beach 2km south of Tofino and 10min walk from Long Beach; indoor pool, jacuzzi, hot showers and kayak rentals. Some walk-in beachfront tent sites. $15–30.

Eating and drinking

For **food**, just about everyone in town clusters around the heaving tables of the *Common Loaf Bake Shop* behind the bank at 180 1st St (☎725-3915), deservedly the most popular choice for coffee and snacks. In the evening the home-made dough is turned into pizzas instead of bread and rolls. In a similar vein is the *Alley Way Café*, also behind the bank at Campbell and 1st Street, a friendly locals type of place with newspapers to read and cheap, wholesome food where everything down to the mayonnaise is home-made. Coming into town on the main highway (which becomes Campbell St), the *Café Pamplona* in the Tofino Botanical Gardens is also a good spot for coffee and snacks. The *Crab Bar*, 601 Campbell St, near the corner of Gibson Street (☎725-3733) is something of a local institution, selling little more than crab, seafood, beer, bread and some imaginative salads. One of the best views in town is available at the *Sea Shanty*, 300 Main St (☎725-2902), a restaurant which offers **outdoor dining** overlooking the harbour and the chance of some tremendous sunsets on fine evenings. Best place for a **beer** and **dancing** is the pub downstairs at the *Maquinna Lodge*, 120 1st St, the place to be on Friday and Saturday nights. For a real treat, head out of town to *The Pointe Restaurant* at the *Wickaninnish Inn* (☎725-3100; see overleaf), which for most people's money is the area's best upmarket restaurant, on account of both its food and its views.

Activities

Ucluelet to the south may claim to be "whale-watching capital of the world", but **whales** – the main reason a lot of people are here – are just as easily seen from Tofino. As in Victoria, you have plenty of operators, most costing about the same and offering similar **excursions**: all you have to do is decide what sort of boat you want to go out on – zodiacs (inflatables), which are bouncier, more thrilling and potentially wetter or rigid-hull cruisers (covered or uncovered), which are more sedate. Remember that if you take tours to Meares Islands, Hot Springs Cove and elsewhere, especially in spring or fall (best times to see whales), you stand a good chance of seeing whales en route anyway – some operators try to combine whale-watching and excursions. Operators to try include: Cypre Prince Tours midway down the main street at 430 Campbell St (☎725-2202 or 1-800/787-2202); Chinook Charters, 450 Campbell St (☎725-3431 or 1-800/665-3646), who offer trips (2hr 30min) on rigid or zodiac boats; and Jamie's Whaling Station, 606 Campbell St (☎725-3919 or 1-800/667-9913), who also offer a choice of zodiac boats or the twenty-metre *Lady Selkirk,* which comes with heated cabin, no small consideration on cold days, of which Tofino has a few. See "Whales" box below for more information.

Many of these companies double up as **fishing** charters, though for more specialist operators contact Bruce's Smiley Seas Charters, based at the Methods Marina (May–Sept; ☎725-2557), who're quite happy to have novices aboard; or the Weigh West Marine Resort (☎725-3238 or 1-800/665-8922), who have an inexpensive restaurant as well as lodgings just above the marina at 634 Campbell St. Still on the water, Tofino is

---

WHALES

The Pacific Rim National Park is amongst the world's best areas for **whale-watching**, thanks to its location on the main migration routes, food-rich waters and numerous sheltered bays. People come from all over the world for the spectacle, and it's easy to find a boat going out from Tofino, Ucluelet or Bamfield, most charging around $60–80 a head for the trip depending on duration (usually 2–3hr). Regulations prohibit approaching within 100m of an animal but, though few locals will admit it, there's no doubt that the recent huge upsurge in boat tours has begun to disrupt the **migrations**. The whales' 8000-kilometre journey – the longest known migration of any mammal – takes them from their breeding and calving lagoons in Baja, Mexico, to summer feeding grounds in the Bering and Chukchi seas off Siberia. The northbound migration takes from February to May, with the peak period of passage between March and April. A few dozen animals occasionally abort their trip and stop off the Canadian coast for summer feeding (notably at Maquinna Marine Park, 20min by boat from Tofino). The return journey starts in August, hitting Tofino and Ucluelet in late September and early October. **Mating** takes place in Mexico during December, after which the males turn immediately northwards, to be followed by females and their young in February.

Although killer whales (orcas) are occasionally seen, the most commonly spotted type are **grey whales**, of which some 19,000 are thought to make the journey annually. Averaging 14m in length and weighing 35 to 50 tonnes, they're distinguished by the absence of a dorsal fin, a ridge of lumps on the back, and a mottled blue-grey colour. Females have only one offspring, following a gestation period of thirteen months, and, like the males, cruise at only two to four knots – perfect for viewing and, sadly, for capture.

Even if you don't take a boat trip, you stand a faint chance of seeing whales from the coast as they dive, when you can locate their tails, or during fluking, when the animals surface and "blow" three or four times before making another five-minute dive. There are telescopes at various points along Long Beach, the best known viewpoints being Schooner Cove, Radar Hill, Quistis Point and Combers Beach near Sea Lion Rocks.

quickly becoming the **surfing** capital of Canada, thanks to some enormous Pacific waves, though floating driftwood and big lumps of lumber caught up in the waves can be a hazard. For information, board rental and all other equipment, contact Live to Surf east of the town centre at 1180 Tofino Hwy (☎725-4464). If you want to go out in a **kayak** (no experience required) contact Tofino Sea Kayaking, 320 Main St (☎725-4222 or 1-800/863-4664), who offer day-trips or longer **tours** with lodge accommodation or wilderness camping. Nine holes of **golf** are available at the local course near the airport (☎725-3332), while **guided hikes** and easy nature rambles in the forest and along the seashore are offered by several companies (contact infocentre for details).

Long Beach

The most accessible of the park's components, **LONG BEACH** is just what it says: a long tract of wild, windswept sand and rocky points stretching for about 30km from Tofino to Ucluelet. Around 19km can be hiked unbroken from Schooner Bay in the west to Half Moon Bay in the east. The snow-covered peaks of the Mackenzie Range rise up over 1200m as a scenic backdrop, and behind the beach grows a thick, lush canopy of coastal rainforest. The white-packed sand itself is the sort of primal seascape that is all but extinct in much of the world, scattered with beautiful, sea-sculpted driftwood, smashed by surf, broken by crags, and dotted with islets and rock pools oozing with marine life. It's worth realizing that Long Beach, while a distinct beach in itself, also rather loosely refers to several other beaches to either side, the relative merits of which are outlined below. If you haven't done so already, driving or biking Hwy 4 along the beach area is the best time to call in at the Pacific Rim National Park **Information Centre** (daily May to mid-Oct 9.30am–5pm; ☎762-4212), located right off Hwy 4 3km northwest of the Ucluelet–Tofino–Port Alberni road junction.

Scenery aside, Long Beach is noted for its **wildlife**, the BC coastline reputedly having more marine species than any other temperate area in the world. As well as the smaller stuff in tidal pools – starfish, anemones, snails, sponges and suchlike – there are large mammals like whales and sea lions, as well as thousands of migrating birds (especially in Oct and Nov), notably pintails, mallards, black brants and Canada geese. Better weather brings out lots of beachcombers (Japanese glass fishing floats are highly coveted), clam diggers, anglers, surfers, canoeists, windsurfers and divers, though the water is usually too cold to venture in without a wet suit, and rip currents and rogue lumps of driftwood crashed around by the waves can make swimming dangerous. Surf guards patrol the Long Beach day-use area in July and August. And finally, try to resist the temptation to pick up shells as souvenirs – it's against park regulations.

The beaches

As this is a national park, some of Long Beach and its flanking stretches of coastline have been very slightly tamed for human consumption, but in a most discreet and tasteful manner. The best way to get a taste of the area is to walk the beaches or forested shorelines themselves – there are plenty of hidden coves – or to follow any of nine very easy and well-maintained **hiking trails** (see box, opposite). If you're driving or biking along Hwy 4, which backs the beaches all the way, there are distinct areas to look out for. Moving west, the first of these is the five-kilometre **Florencia Beach** (1.5km from the Hwy: access by trails 1, 2, 3 and 5; see box), also known as Wreck Beach and formerly the home of hippie beach dwellers in driftwood shacks before the park's formation. This is something of a local favourite, with relatively few people and good rock pools.

Further along Hwy 4 you come to a turn-off (Long Beach Rd) for the **Wickaninnish Centre** (mid-March to mid-Oct 10.30am–6pm; ☎726-4701) on a headland at the start of Long Beach, not to be confused with the similarly named well-known hotel and

LONG BEACH WALKS

With an eye on the weather and tide, you can walk more or less anywhere on and around Long Beach. Various trails and roads drop to the beach from the main Hwy 4 road to Tofino. At the same time there are nine official trails, most of them short and very easy, so you could tackle a few in the course of a leisurely drive or cycle along the road. All the paths are clearly marked from Hwy 4, but it's still worth picking up a *Hiker's Guide* from the infocentre. From east to west you can choose from the following. The linked trails **1** and **2**, the **Willowbrae Trail** (2.8km round trip), are accessed by turning left at the main Hwy 4 junction and driving or biking 2km towards Ucluelet. A level wooded trail then leads from the trailhead towards the beach, following the steps of early pioneers who used this route before the building of roads between Tofino and Ucluelet. Just before the sea it divides, dropping steeply via steps and ramps, to either the tiny Half Moon Bay or the larger, neighbouring Florencia Bay to the north.

All other walks are accessed off Hwy 4 to Tofino, turning right (north) at the main Hwy 4 junction. The gentle **3 Gold Mine Trail** (3km round trip), signed left off the road, leads along Lost Shoe Creek, a former gold-mining area (look out for debris), to Florencia Beach. For walks **4**, **5** and **6**, take the turn left off the highway for the Wickaninnish Centre. The **4 South Beach Trail** (1.5km round trip) leaves from behind the centre, leading above forest-fringed shores and coves before climbing to the headlands for a view of the coast and a chance to climb down to South Beach, famous for its big rock-crashing breakers and the sound of the water ripping noisily through the beach pebbles. The **5 Wickaninnish Trail** (5km) follows the South Beach Trail for a while and then at the top of the first hill is signed left, passing through rainforest – once again this is the route of the old pioneer trail – before ending at the parking area above Florencia Beach to the east. The **6 Shorepine Bog Trail** (800m) is a wheelchair-accessible boardwalk trail (accessed on the left on the access road to the centre) that wends through the fascinating stunted bog vegetation; trees which are just a metre or so tall here can be hundreds of years old.

Moving further west towards Tofino along Hwy 4, the **7 Rain Forest Trails** are two small loops (1km each round trip), one on each side of the road, that follow a boardwalk through virgin temperate rainforest: each has interpretive boards detailing forest life-cycle and forest "inhabitants" respectively. Further down the road on the right at the Combers Beach parking area, a road gives access to the gentle **8 Spruce Fringe Trail** (1.5km loop). This graphically illustrates the effects of the elements on spruce forest, following a log-strewn beach fringe edged with bent and bowed trees before entering more robust forest further from the effects of wind and salt spray. It also crosses willow and crab-apple swamp to a glacial terrace, the site of a former shoreline, past the airport turn-off. The final walk, the **Schooner Beach Trail** (1km one-way), leads left off the road through superb tranches of rainforest to an extremely scenic beach at Schooner Cove. This might be the end of the official trails, but don't fail to climb to the viewpoint on **Radar Hill** off to the right as you get closer to Tofino.

restaurant closer to Tofino (confusingly, the centre also has a restaurant). Wickaninnish was a noted nineteenth-century aboriginal chief, and arbitrator between Europeans and native fur traders. His name left no doubt as to his number-one status, as it means "having no one in front of him in the canoe". The centre is the departure point for several trails (see box), has telescopes for whale-spotting and a variety of films, displays and exhibits relating to the park and ocean. Around 8km beyond the Long Beach Road turn-off is the entrance to the Greenpoint park **campground** and further access to Long Beach, while 4km beyond that lies the turn-off on the right to Tofino's small airstrip. Around here the peninsula narrows, with **Grice Bay** coming close to the road on the right (north side), a shallow inlet known in winter for its countless wildfowl. Beyond the airstrip turn-off comes a trail to Schooner Cove (see box) and 3.5km beyond that a 1.5-kilometre turn-off to Kap'yong, or **Radar Hill** (96m), the panoramic site of a wartime radar station. By now Tofino is getting close, and 4.5km further on (and a couple of kilometres outside the park boundary) you come to **Cox Bay Beach**, **Chesterman Beach** and **Mackenzie Beach**, all accessed from Hwy 4. Cox and Chesterman are known for their breakers; Mackenzie for its relative warmth if you want to chance a dip.

Practicalities

Long Beach's **Pacific Rim National Park Information Centre** is just off Hwy 4, 3km north of the T-junction for Tofino and Ucluelet. It provides a wealth of material on all aspects of the park, and in summer staff offer guided walks and interpretive programmes (daily mid-March to early Oct 9.30am–5pm; ☎726-4212). For year-round information, call the Park Administration Office (☎726-7721). For more Long Beach information, viewing decks with telescopes and lots of well-presented displays, head for the **Wickaninnish Centre**, Long Beach Road (daily mid-March to early Oct 10.30am–6pm; ☎726-4701).

There is one park **campground**, the *Greenpoint*, set on a lovely bluff overlooking the beach (washrooms but no showers; firewood available; $13). However, it's likely to be full every day in July and August, and it's first-come, first-served, so you may have to turn up for several days before getting a spot. There's usually a waiting-list system, however, whereby you're given a number and instructions as to when you should be able to return. The nearest commercial sites and conventional accommodation are in Tofino and Ucluelet.

Ucluelet

UCLUELET (pop. 1733), 8km south of the main Hwy 4 Port Alberni junction, means "People of the Sheltered Bay", from the native word *ucluth* – "wind blowing in from the bay". It was named by the Nuu-chah-nulth, who lived here for centuries before the arrival of whites who came to exploit some of the world's richest fishing grounds immediately offshore. Today the port is still the third largest in BC by volume of fish landed, a trade that gives the town a slightly dispersed appearance and an industrial fringe – mainly lumber and canning concerns – and makes it a less appealing, if nonetheless popular base for anglers, whale-watchers, water-sports enthusiasts and tourists headed for Long Beach to the north. If you want a breath of air in town, the nearest trails are at **Terrace Beach**, just east of the town off Peninsula Road before the lighthouse.

Buses and **boats** call here from Port Alberni and Tofino – a Laidlaw bus makes the road trip twice a day en route to and from Tofino and Port Alberni, with one connection daily from Port Alberni to Nanaimo and Victoria. Boats from Port Alberni usually dock here three days a week (see p.362). There's plenty of accommodation (though less than Tofino), much of it spread on or just off Peninsula Road, the main approach to and through town from Hwy 4 (see below). A car or bike is useful here, as there's relatively little in the small central area, though location isn't vital unless you want to be near the sea. For full details visit the **infocentre** at the main junction of Hwy 4 (daily June to early Sept 9am–6pm; ☎726-4641 or 726-7289, *uco@ucluelet.com*).

Practicalities

The most unusual **hotel** in town is the *Canadian Princess Resort* (March–Sept; ☎726-7771 or 1-800/663-7090, *www.obmg.com*; ③–⑥) on Peninsula Road just west of the centre, a hotel with on-shore rooms or one- to six-berth cabins in a 1932 west coast steamer moored in the harbour. You can also book upmarket whale-watching and fishing trips here in big, comfortable cabin cruisers and it has a restaurant

NUU-CHAH-NULTH WHALE HUNTS

All the peoples of the Northwest coast are famed for their skilfully constructed canoes, but only the **Nuu-chah-nulth** – whose name translates roughly as "all along the mountains" – used these fragile cedar crafts to pursue whales, an activity that was accompanied by elaborate ritual. Before embarking on a whaling expedition the whalers had to not only be trained in the art of capturing these mighty animals but also had to be purified through a rigorous programme of fasting, sexual abstinence and bathing. Whalers also visited forest shrines made up of a whale image surrounded by human skulls or corpses and carved wooden representations of deceased whalers – the dead were thought to aid the novice in his task and to bring about the beaching of dead whales near the village.

When the whaler was on the chase, his wife would lie motionless in her bed; it was thought that the whale would become equally docile. His crew propelled the canoe in total silence until the moment of the harpooning, whereupon they frantically backpaddled to escape the animal's violent death throes as it attempted to dive, only to be thwarted by a long line of floats made from inflated sea-lion skins. After exhausting itself, the floating whale was finally killed and boated back to the village, where its meat would be eaten and its blubber processed for its highly prized oil.

open to non-residents. The two key inexpensive central choices are the *Pacific Rim Motel*, 1755 Peninsula Rd (☎726-7728, *dcorlazz@island.net*; ④), a place between the harbour and small centre near the corner of Bay Street, and the *Peninsula Motor Inn*, a short way east across the road at 1648 Peninsula Rd (☎726-7751; ③). Also convenient is the *Island West Fishing Resort* overlooking the boat basin and marina at 160 Hemlock St (☎726-4624, *www.islandwestresort.com*; ④): it has a pub on site for drinks and food and also organizes fishing charters and tours. Moving east away from the centre to prettier outskirts try *Four Cedar Cottages* (☎726-4284; ⑤), 1183 Eber Rd (take Alder St, off Peninsula Rd), which is very close to the seafront pier, or the *Little Beach Resort*, 1187 Peninsula Rd (☎726-4202; ②–④), with quiet self-contained one- and two-bedroom suites with kitchenettes and just a few steps from Little Beach with great views to the south. Right at the end of Peninsula Road up by the lighthouse are two good **B&B** options: *Spring Cove B&B*, 963 Peninsula Rd (☎726-2955; ④), a quiet oceanfront place with two rooms (shared bathroom), and *Ocean's Edge B&B*, 855 Barkley Crescent (☎726-7099, *www.oceansedge.bc.ca*; ③), a three-room place in old growth forest with views and private entrance and bathroom.

The **public campground** (☎726-4355; $22–27; March–Oct) overlooks the harbour at 260 Seaplane Base Rd (first right off Peninsula Rd after the *Canadian Princess*) to the west of the centre and has washroom and shower facilities. The central *Island West Fishing Resort* (see above) also has an RV campground.

Seafood here is as fresh as it comes, and is best sampled at *Smiley's* just a little west from the *Canadian Princess* at 1992 Peninsula Rd (☎726-4213): a no-frills, no-decor diner popular with locals (eat in or take out), and to work off the meal there's five-pin bowling and billiards here as well. For coffee and snacks head for *Blueberries Café* (☎726-7707) on the strip in town at 1627 Peninsula Rd. It also serves breakfast, lunch and dinner, is licensed, and has an outdoor patio with sea views.

Many companies are on hand to offer whale-watching, fishing and sightseeing **tours**. The longest-established outfit in the region is here, Subtidal Adventures, 1950 Peninsula Rd at the corner of Norah Road (☎726-7336). They run all the usual boat trips in zodiacs or a ten-metre former coastguard rescue vessel, and do a nature tour to the Broken Group Islands with a beach stop.

The Broken Group Islands

The only way for the ordinary traveller to approach these hundred or so islands, speckled across Barkley Sound between Ucluelet and Bamfield, is by seaplane, chartered boat or boat tours from Port Alberni or Ucluelet (see p.361 and overleaf); boats dock at Sechart. Immensely wild and beautiful, the islands have the reputation for tremendous wildlife (seals, sea lions and whales especially), the best **canoeing** in North America, and some of the continent's finest **scuba diving**. You can hire canoes and gear – contact the Lady Rose office in Port Alberni or Sea Kayaking at 320 Main St, Tofino (☎725-4222), and then take them on board the *Lady Rose* to be dropped off en route (check current arrangements). You need to know what you're doing, however, as there's plenty of dangerous water and you should pick up the relevant marine chart (*Canadian Hydrographic Service Chart: Broken Group 3670*), available locally. Divers can choose from among fifty shipwrecks claimed by the reefs, rough waters and heavy fogs that beset the aptly named islands.

The *Sechart Whaling Station Lodge* (book by calling ☎723-8313 or 1-800/663-7192; ⑤) is a potentially magical base for exploring and the only place to **stay** if you're not wilderness camping on the archipelago. Access is via the MV *Lady Rose*, which docks nearby (see p.361 for detailed schedule to the islands). Eight rough **campgrounds** also serve the group, but water is hard to come by; pick up the park leaflet on camping and freshwater locations. A park warden patrols the region from Nettle Island; otherwise the islands are as pristine as the day they rose from the sea.

Bamfield

BAMFIELD (pop. 256) is a quaint spot, half-raised above the ocean on a wooden boardwalk, accessible by unpaved road from Port Alberni 102km to the north, by boat – the MV *Lady Rose* – or gravel road from Lake Cowichan 113km to the east. Shuttle **buses** run along the Port Alberni road route if you're without transport and don't want to take the boat: for details, see the "West Coast Trail" opposite. The village is best known as the northern starting point of this trail, but its population jumps to well over 2000 in the summer with the arrival of divers, canoeists, kayakers and fishermen, the last attracted by its suitability as a base for salmon fishing in the waters of Alberni Inlet and Barkley Sound. Plenty of services have sprung up to meet visitors' demands, with lots of tours, fishing charters, stores and galleries, but only relatively limited accommodation (see below).

Despite the influx the village retains its charm, with the boardwalk accessing one side of Bamfield Inlet (the open sea, the other), so that the bay below the boardwalk is a constant hum of activity as boats ply across the water. Trails lead down from the boardwalk to a series of nice small beaches. The village is a good place to join in the activities, bird-watch, walk, beachcomb, sit in cafés or simply relax in a quiet corner with a book. For a short stroll, wander to **Brady's Beach** or the Cape Beale Lighthouse some way beyond. And if you just want to tackle the stage to the trailhead of the West Coast Trail and return to Bamfield in a day, you can walk the 11km (round trip) to the **Pachena Lighthouse**, starting from the Ross Bible Camp on the Ohiaht First Nation campground at Pachena Beach. After that, the route becomes the real thing.

Accommodation

Bamfield has only limited and mainly expensive **accommodation**. If you think you'll need a bed, definitely make reservations, especially at the small *Seabeam Fishing Resort and Campground* overlooking Grappler Inlet, which runs as a campground and a small hostel-like hotel with eight rooms (☎728-3286; ①, tent and RV sites $15–20; May–Oct) and phone for directions or for a taxi pick-up. The setting is tranquil, and the resort has a small kitchen, common room with open fire and sixteen beds arranged as one-, two- or three-bed dorms. Price is $20 per person. Otherwise try the *Bamfield Inn*, Customs House Lane, a **lodge** built in 1923 overlooking Bamfield Harbour, Barkley Sound and the islands (☎728-3354; ⑤; Feb–Oct). The modest *McKay Bay Lodge* (☎728-3323; ④; May–Oct) also overlooks the harbour and is good for families and fishing enthusiasts. The biggest place locally is the *Bamfield Trails Motel* overlooking Bamfield Inlet at Frigate Road (☎728-3231 or 728-3215; ④). Another option is the excellent *Woods End Landing Cottages*, 168 Wild Duck Rd, which has six secluded and high-quality self-contained log cottages on a two-acre waterfront site with great opportunities for outdoor activities, bird-watching, scuba diving and kayaking (☎728-3383; ⑦). Similar but more expensive are the central and waterfront *Mills Landing Cottages*, 295 Boardwalk (☎728-2300; ⑦) with one- and two-bed cottages. Less expensive is the five-room *Imperial Eagle Lodge*, 168 Wild Duck Rd (☎728-3430, *www.imperialeaglelodge.com*; ⑤). which has a spectacular garden setting and fine harbour views plus hiking, fishing and other outdoor activities; breakfast is included in the room price. More **B&B** options are opening each year but try the two-room *Sherry's*, Regent Street (☎728-2323; ③), overlooking Bamfield Harbour, which offers a free pick-up by boat from the dock: showers are shared, but an outdoor hot tub and free canoe use are available. If you're **camping**, try the Ohiaht First Nation campground at Pachena Beach.

The West Coast Trail

One of North America's classic walks, the **West Coast Trail** starts 5km south of Bamfield (see opposite) and traverses exceptional coastal scenery for 77km to Port Renfrew. It's no stroll, and though becoming very popular – quotas operate to restrict numbers – it still requires experience of longer walks, proper equipment and a fair degree of fitness. Many people, however, do the first easy stage as a day-trip from Bamfield. Reckon on five to eight days for the full trip; carry all your own food, camp where you can, and be prepared for rain, treacherous stretches, thick soaking forest, and almost utter isolation.

As originally conceived, the trail had nothing to do with promoting the great outdoors. Mariners long ago dubbed this area of coastline the "graveyard of the Pacific", and when the SS *Valencia* went down with all hands here in 1906 the government was persuaded that constructing a trail would at least give stranded sailors a chance to walk to safety along the coast (trying to penetrate the interior's rainforest was out of the question). The path followed a basic telegraph route that linked Victoria with outlying towns and lighthouses, and was kept open by linesmen and lighthouse keepers until the 1960s, when it fell into disrepair. Early backpackers reblazed the old trail; many thousands now make the trip annually, and the numbers, so far as quotas allow, are rising (see below). The trail passes through the land of the Pacheenaht First Nation near Port Renfrew, passing through Ditidaht First Nation country before ending at Bamfield in the traditional territory of the Ohiaht First Nation. Wardens from each of these tribes work in association with Parks Canada to oversee the trail's management and the care of traditional native villages and fishing areas.

Weather is a key factor in planning any trip; the trail is really only passable between June and September (July is the driest month), which is also the only period when it's patrolled by wardens and the only time locals are on hand to ferry you (for a fee) across some of the wider rivers en route. However, you should be prepared for dreadful weather and poor trail conditions at all times. Take cash with you to pay for ferries and nominal fees for camping on native land.

Practicalities

Pre-planning is essential if you wish to walk the trail, as Parks Canada have introduced a **quota system** and reservation-registration procedure to protect the environment.

Numbers are limited to around 8000 a year while the path is open (mid-April to end Sept). A total of 52 people are allowed onto the trail each day: 26 starting at Port Renfrew, 26 at Bamfield. **Reservations** can be made from March of the year you wish to walk, and the phones start ringing on the first of the month, so move fast. To make bookings, call ☎1-800/663-6000 (Mon–Fri 7am–9pm). Be ready to nominate the location from which you wish to start, the date of departure and the number in your party. July and August are clearly the most popular months. It **costs** $25 to make a reservation (payment by Visa or MasterCard). This is non-refundable, though you may change your date of departure if spaces are available on another day. Another $75 per person is payable as a user fee, paid in person at the beginning of the trail. Allow another $25 to pay for ferry crossings along the route. You must then register in person at the park centre at Bamfield or Port Renfrew between 9am and 12.30pm on the day you have booked to start your walk. (You may want to arrive the night before – if so, be sure to book accommodation in Bamfield if you're starting there: see p.372.) If you miss this deadline your place is forfeited and will be given to someone on the **waiting list**.

Of the 52 places available each day, twelve (six at each departure point) are available on a first-come, first-served basis. Unless you're very lucky this still doesn't mean you can just turn up and expect to start walking. You must first register in person at either the Port Renfrew or Bamfield centre. Here you'll be given a waiting-list number and told when to come back, which could be anything between two and ten days.

Further **information** regarding the trail, path conditions and pre-planning can be obtained from the Parks Canada offices in Port Renfrew (☎647-5434) and Ucluelet (☎726-7211), or from the infocentres in Tofino, Ucluelet, Long Beach or Port Alberni. An increasing amount of literature and **route guides** are appearing on the trail every year, available directly or by mail order from most BC bookshops (see "Listings" for Vancouver and Victoria). Two of the best are *The West Coast Trail* by Tim Leaden (Douglas and McIntyre, seventh edition; $12.95) and the more irreverent *Blisters and Bliss: A Trekker's Guide to the West Coast Trail* by Foster, Aiteken and Dewey (B&B Publishing Victoria; $10.95). The recommended **trail map** is the 1:50,000 *West Coast Trail, Port Renfrew–Bamfield*, complete with useful hints for walking the trail, available locally or direct from the Ministry of the Environment, 553 Superior St, Victoria (☎387-1441).

Access to and from the trailheads is also an important consideration. Several small shuttle-bus companies have sprung up to run people to the trailheads, mostly from Victoria to Bamfield via Nanaimo, not all of which are likely to survive (consult the Victoria infocentre for latest updates). For the northern trailhead at Bamfield, the most exhilarating and reliable access is via the MV *Lady Rose* or other boats from Port Alberni (see p.361 for full details). Otherwise the West Coast Trail Express, 3954 Bow Rd, Victoria (May to early Oct; ☎477-8700) runs a daily shuttle bus in each direction between Victoria and Pachena Bay/Bamfield ($50) via Duncan and Nanaimo ($50); to Port Renfrew ($30) and back from Victoria; and between Bamfield and Port Renfrew ($40). Pick-ups are possible from these points, but reservations are essential to secure a seat from any departure point. They also have a daily service to Port Renfrew ($50). Western Bus Lines, 4521 10th Ave, Port Alberni (☎723-3341), also run a service on Monday and Friday along the 100-kilometre gravel road from Port Alberni to the *Tides and Trails Café* in Bamfield; and the Pacheenaht First Nation Service, 4521 10th Ave, Port Alberni (around $35; ☎647-5521), which operates a summer-only bus service along the same route.

North Vancouver Island

It's a moot point where the **north of Vancouver Island** starts, but if you're travelling on Hwy 19 the landscape's sudden lurch into more unspoilt wilderness after Qualicum

Beach makes as good a watershed as any. The scenery north of Qualicum Beach is uneventful but restful on the eye, and graced with ever-improving views of the mainland. Along Hwy 19 is the hamlet of Buckley Bay, which consists of a single B&B and the ferry terminal to **Denman** and **Hornby islands** (16 sailings daily; 10min; $4.50 return for foot passengers, $11.25 return for a car).

Few of the towns along Hwy 19 amount to much, and you could bus, drive or hitch the length of Vancouver Island to Port Hardy and take the **Inside Passage** ferry up to Prince Rupert – the obvious and most tantalizing itinerary – without missing a lot. Alternatively, you could follow the main highway only as far as **Courtenay**, and from there catch a ferry across to the mainland. If you have the means, however, try to get into the wild, central interior, much of it contained within **Strathcona Provincial Park**.

Denman and Hornby islands

Denman and **Hornby Islands** are two outposts that have been described, with some justification, as the "undiscovered Gulf Islands". Big-name celebrities have recently bought property here, complementing a population made up of artists, craftspeople and a laid-back (if wary) mishmash of alternative types. Ferries drop you on Denman, with an **infocentre** clearly marked on the road from the terminal (☎335-2293). To get to Hornby you need to head 11km across Denman to another terminal, where a fifteen-minute crossing ($4.50 return for foot passengers, $11.25 return for a car) drops you at Hornby's Shingle Spit dock. Most of what happens on Hornby, however, happens at **Tribune Bay** on the far side of the island, 10km away – try hitching a lift from a car coming off the ferry if you're without transport. There's no public transport on either island, so you'll need a car or bike to explore.

Highlights on Denman, the less retrogressive of the islands, are the beaches of the Sandy Island Marine Park and the trails of Boyle Point Park to the Chrome Island Lighthouse. On Hornby you want to be looking at the **Hellivel Provincial Park** and its trails, the best a six-kilometre (1hr–1hr 30min) loop to Hellivel Bluffs, offering plenty of opportunities to see eagles, herons, spring wild flowers and lots of aquatic wildlife. Whaling Station Bay and Tribune Bay Provincial Park have good beaches (and there's a nudist beach at Little Tribune Bay).

Accommodation and food

Accommodation is in short supply on both islands, and it's virtually essential in summer to have prebooked rooms. On Denman the main options are the *Sea Canary Bed & Breakfast*, 3305 Kirk Rd (☎335-2949; ④), close to the ferry terminal with three **guestrooms**, and the *Hawthorn House Bed and Breakfast*, 3375 Kirk Rd (☎335-0905; ③), a restored 1904 heritage building also with three rooms. There's a small (10-site), rural provincial park **campground** at Fillongley Provincial Park, close to old-growth forest and pebbly beach 4km across the island from the ferry on the east shore facing the Lambert Channel (summer $15, winter $8). Hornby has more **rooms** and **campgrounds**: *Sea Breeze Lodge*, Big Tree 3–2, Fowler Road (☎335-2321, www.seabreezelodge.com; ⑤), with fifteen waterfront cottages with sea views; *Hornby Island Resort*, Shingle Spit Road (☎335-0136; ③, tents $19), with four waterfront cabins and nine camp sites, tennis court, boat rental, pub, waterfront restaurant and sandy beach; *Days Gone By at Bradsdadsland Campsite*, 1980 Shingle Spit Rd (☎335-0757; tents $20–23; May–Oct), 3.3km from the ferry terminal; *Ford's Cove Marina* at Ford's Cove, 12km from the ferry at Government Wharf (☎335-2169; ③, tents $16–24), with six fully equipped cottages, grocery store and camp and RV sites; and the big *Tribune Bay Campsite*, Shields Road (☎335-2359, www.tribunebay.com; $18–24; April–Oct), a treed site close to a sandy beach and with hot showers, restaurant and bike rental.

Eating places on Denman are concentrated near the ferry, the best being the *Denman Island Store and Café*. At the ferry dock on Hornby is *The Thatch*, a tourist-oriented restaurant and deli with great views. Across at Tribune Bay the Co-op (no street address) is the hub of island life, with virtually everything you'll need in the way of food and supplies (☎335-1121). A bike rental outlet here, the Off-Road Bike Shop, rents bikes in summer.

Courtenay

Back along Hwy 19 beyond Buckley Bay is a short stretch of wild, pebbly beach, and then the Comox Valley, open rural country that's not as captivating as the brochures might lead you to expect. Of three settlements here – Comox, Cumberland and **COURTENAY** – only the last is of real interest for all but the most committed Vancouver Island devotee, and only then as a ferry link to Powell River on the mainland. The terminal is a good twenty-minutes' drive from the town down backroads – hitching is almost impossible, so you have to take a taxi or hold out for the minibus shuttle that leaves the bus depot twice on Tuesday and Friday to connect with sailings. Courtenay is connected to Nanaimo and Victoria by **bus** (4 daily), and is the terminus for **trains** from Victoria (1 daily). If you get stranded in town, there are plenty of **motels** along the strip on the southern approach, close to the black steam engine and **infocentre** at 2040 Cliffe Ave (daily 9am–5pm, longer hours in summer; ☎334-3234). The best **camping** is 20km north of Courtenay at Miracle Beach Provincial Park – a vast, but very popular, tract of sand ($12).

The **Comox Valley** scores higher inland, on the eastern fringes of Strathcona Provincial Park (see p.378) and the new **skiing** areas of Forbidden Plateau and Mount Washington. There's plenty of **hiking** in summer, when the Forbidden Plateau lifts operate at weekends from 11am to 3pm. A great day-hike on Mount Washington is the five-hour walk on well-marked trails from the ski area across Paradise Meadows to Moat Lake or Circlet Lake. For details of tougher walks (Battleship Lake, Lady Lake), ask at the infocentre. Access to the trailheads is by minor road from Courtenay.

Campbell River

Of the hundred or so Canadian towns that claim to be "Salmon Capital of the World", **CAMPBELL RIVER**, 46km north of Courtenay, is probably the one that comes closest to justifying the boast. Fish and fishing dominate the place to a ludicrous degree, and you'll soon be heartily sick of pictures of grinning anglers holding impossibly huge chinook salmon. Massive shoals of these monsters are forced into the three-kilometre channel between the town and the mainland, making the job of catching them little more than a formality. The town grew to accommodate fishermen from the outset, centred on a hotel built in 1904 after word spread of the colossal fish that local Cape Mudge natives were able to pluck from the sea. Today about sixty percent of all visitors come to dangle a line in the water. Others come for the scuba diving, while for the casual visitor the place serves as the main road access to the wilds of Strathcona Provincial Park or an overnight stop en route for the morning departures of the MV *Uchuck III* from Gold River (see p.379).

If you want to **fish**, hundreds of shops and guides are on hand to help out and hire equipment. It'll cost about $20 a day for the full kit, and about $60 for a morning's guidance. Huge numbers of people, however, fish from the 200-metre **Discovery Pier**, Canada's first saltwater fishing pier. **Diving** rentals come more expensive; try Beaver Aquatics near the Quadra ferry dock in Discovery Bay Marina (☎287-7652). If you merely want to know something about salmon before they end up on a plate, drop in on the **Quinsam Salmon Hatchery**, 5km west of town on the road to Gold River (daily 8am–4pm).

Campbell River's well-stocked **infocentre** is at 1235 Shopper's Row (daily 9am–6pm; ☎287-4636). Four Laidlaw **buses** run daily to Victoria, but there's only one, occasionally two, a day north to Port Hardy and towns en route. Airlines big and small also **fly** here, including Air BC, Central Mountain Air and Vancouver Island Air (see Vancouver "Listings" on p.324 for details). The **bus terminal** is on the corner of Cedar and 13th near the Royal Bank (☎287-7151). **Accommodation** is no problem, with numerous motels, Campbell River being a resort first and foremost: try the *Super 8 Motel*, 340 S Island Hwy, on the main road south of town (☎286-6622 or 1-800/800-8000; ④), or the carving-stuffed *Campbell River Lodge and Fishing Resort,* a kilometre north of the town centre at 1760 N Island Hwy (☎287-7446 or 1-800/663-7212, *www.vquest.com/crlodge*; ④). You won't be able to escape the fishing clutter common to all hotels unless you head for a **B&B**. Contact the infocentre for listings, or try *Pier House B&B*, 670 Island Hwy (☎287-2943, *pierhse@island.net*; ④), a three-room 1920s antique-filled heritage home in downtown right by the fishing pier. The place to **camp** locally lies 5km west of town at the *Parkside Campground*, 6301 Gold River Hwy (☎830-1428; $20; May–Oct).

Cheap **places to eat** abound, mainly of the fast-food variety, and in the pricier restaurants there's no prize for spotting the main culinary emphasis. The best burger joint is *Del's Drive-In & Diner*, 1423 Island Hwy, a place with plenty of local colour. For beer and snacks try the *Royal Coachman*, 84 Dogwood St, popular with tourists and locals alike. For a **seafood** treat, head for the *Anchor Inn*, 261 Island Hwy (good views), or the *Gourmet by the Sea* on the main road about 15km south of town at Bennett's Point.

Quadra Island

Quadra Island and its fine beaches and museum are fifteen minutes away from Campbell River and make a nice respite from the fish, though the famous fishing lodge here has been host to such big-name fisherfolk over the years as John Wayne, Kevin Costner and Julie Andrews. Ferries run roughly hourly from the well-signed terminal out of town ($4.50 return for foot passengers, $11.25 return for a car). The main excuse for the crossing is the **Kwagiulth Museum and Cultural Centre**, home to one of the country's most noted collections of aboriginal regalia (daily June–Sept 10am–4.30pm; closed Sun & Mon off-season; $2; ☎285-3733). As elsewhere in Canada, the masks, costumes and ritual objects were confiscated by the government in 1922 in an attempt to stamp out one of the natives' most potent ceremonies, and only came back in the 1980s on condition they would be locked up in a museum. The museum has around three hundred articles, and you should also ask directions to the petroglyphs in the small park across the road.

While on the island you could also laze on its beaches, walk its coastal **trails**, or climb Chinese Mountain for some cracking views. There's swimming in a warm, sheltered bay off a rocky beach at **Rebecca Spit Provincial Park**, a 1.5-kilometre spit near Drew Harbour 8km east of the ferry terminal, but the water's warmer still and a trifle sandier at the more distant **Village Bay Park**. Around ten places offer **accommodation**, including the *Heriot Bay Inn & Marina* on Heriot Bay Road (☎285-3322, *www.heriotbayinn.com*; ⑤, camping from $10–16) which has cottages, camping and RV sites, and the *Whiskey Point Resort Motel*, by the ferry dock at 725 Quathiaski Cove Rd (☎285-2201 or 1-800/622-5311, *www.whiskeypoint.com*; ⑤). The main **campground** is the *We Wai Kai Campsite*, Rebecca Spit Road (☎285-3111; $15 for sites on the hill, $17 for sites on the beach – book ahead for the latter; mid-May to mid-Sept), 16km northeast of the ferry terminal.

Cortes Island

If you've taken the trouble to see Quadra Island, then you should push on to the still quieter **Cortes Island**, 45 minutes from Quadra on a second ferry (5 daily; foot passenger

$5.50 return, car $13.75), an island with a deeply indented coastline at the neck of Desolation Sound, among North America's finest sailing and kayaking areas. Boating aside, it's known for its superlative clams and oysters, exported worldwide, and for one of Canada's leading holistic centres, the Hollyhock Seminar Centre on Highland Road (☎1-800/933-6339), where you can sign up for all manner of body- and soul-refreshing courses and stay in anything from a tent, dorm or private cottage. Other **accommodation** includes *The Blue Heron B&B* (☎935-6584; ③), while you should aim to eat at the *Old Floathouse* (☎935-6631) at the Gorge Marina Resort on Hunt Road, where you can also rent boats and scooters. Places to make for around the island include the small **Smelt Bay Provincial Park**, which has a campground ($9) and opportunities to swim, fish, canoe and walk, and the **Hague Lake Provincial Park**, signed from Mansons Landing, with several looped trails accessible from different points on the road. If you're in a canoe or boat then you can also make for a couple of marine parks (Von Donop and Mansons Landing) and any number of delightful small bays, lagoons and beaches.

Strathcona Provincial Park

Vancouver Island's largest protected area, and the oldest park in British Columbia, **Strathcona Provincial Park** (established in 1911) is one of the few places on the island where the scenery approaches the grandeur of the mainland mountains. The island's highest point, Golden Hinde (2220m) is here, and it's also a place where there's a good chance of seeing rare indigenous wildlife (the Roosevelt elk, marmot and black-tailed deer are the most notable examples). Only two areas have any sort of facilities for the visitor – **Forbidden Plateau**, approached from Courtenay, and the more popular **Buttle Lake** region, accessible from Campbell River via Hwy 28. The Gold River Minibus will drop you at the head of Buttle Lake, about 40km west of Campbell River (Tues, Thurs & Sun). The rest of the park is unsullied wilderness, but fully open to backpackers and hardier walkers. Be sure to pick up the blue *BC Parks* pamphlet (available from the info-centre at Campbell River and elsewhere): it has a good general map and gives lots of information, such as the comforting fact that there are no grizzly bears in the park.

You'll see numerous pictures of **Della Falls**, around Campbell River, which (at 440m) are Canada's highest (and amongst the world's highest), though unfortunately it'll take a two-day trek and a canoe passage if you're going to see them.

HIKING IN STRATHCONA

Hiking, it hardly needs saying, is superb in Strathcona, with a jaw-dropping scenic combination of jagged mountains – including Golden Hinde (2220m), the island's highest point – lakes, rivers, waterfalls and all the trees you could possibly want. Seven marked **trails** fan out from the Buttle Lake area, together with six shorter nature walks, most less than 2km long, amongst which the Lady Falls and Lupin Falls trails stand out for their waterfall and forest views. All the longer trails can be tramped in a day, though the most popular, the **Elk River Trail** (10km), which starts from Drum Lake on Hwy 28, lends itself to an overnight stop. Popular with backpackers because of its gentle grade, the path ends up at Landslide Lake, an idyllic camping spot. The other highly regarded trail is the **Flower Ridge** walk, which starts at the southern end of Buttle Lake. In the Forbidden Plateau area, named after a native legend that claimed evil spirits lay in wait to devour women and children who entered its precincts, the most popular trip is the **Forbidden Plateau Skyride** to the summit of Wood Mountain where there's a two-kilometre trail to a viewpoint over Boston Canyon. Backcountry camping is allowed throughout the park, and the backpacking is great once you've hauled up onto the summit ridges above the tree line. For serious exploration, buy the relevant topographic maps at MAPS BC, Ministry of Environment and Parks, Parliament Buildings, Victoria.

The approach to the park along Hwy 28 is worth taking for the scenery alone; numerous short trails and nature walks are signposted from rest stops, most no more than twenty-minutes' stroll from the car. **Elk Falls Provincial Park**, noted for its gorge and waterfall, is the first stop, ten minutes out of Campbell River. It also has a large provincial park **campground**.

Park practicalities

The **Park Visitor Centre** is located at the junction of Hwy 28 and the Buttle Lake road (May–Sept only); fifteen information shelters around the lake also provide some trail and wildlife information. Buttle Lake has two provincial **campgrounds** with basic facilities – one alongside the park centre at Buttle Lake ($15), the other at Ralph River $12) on the extreme southern end of Buttle Lake, accessed by the road along the lake's eastern shore. Both have good **swimming** areas nearby. Backcountry camping costs $3, payable at the visitor centre.

The park's only commercial **accommodation** is provided by the *Strathcona Park Lodge* (☎286-3122, *www.strathcona.bc.ca*; ③), just outside the Buttle Lake entrance, a mixture of hotel and outdoor pursuits centre. You can **rent canoes**, **bikes** and other outdoor equipment, and sign up for any number of organized tours and activities.

Gold River and Tahsis

There's not a lot happening at **GOLD RIVER**, a tiny logging community 89km west of Campbell River – founded in 1965 in the middle of nowhere to service a big pulp mill 12km away at Muchalat Inlet. The place only has a handful of hotels and a couple of shops – but the ride over on Hwy 28 is superb, and there's the chance to explore the sublime coastline by boat, the main reason for the settlement's increasing number of visitors. Year-round, the **MV Uchuck III**, a converted World War II US minesweeper, takes mail, cargo and passengers to logging camps and settlements up and down the surrounding coast on a variety of routes. Like the MV *Lady Rose* out of Port Alberni, what started as a sideline has recently become far more of a commercial enterprise, with glossy pamphlets and extra summer sailings, though it's none the worse for that – you just have to book ahead to make sure of a place. For information and **reservations**, contact Nootka Sound Service Ltd (☎283-2325 or 283-2515).

There are **three basic routes**, all of them offering wonderful windows onto the wilderness and wildlife (whales, bears, bald eagles and more) of the region's inlets, islands and forested mountains. The dock is at the end of Hwy 28, about 15km southwest of Gold River. The **Tahsis Day Trip** ($45) departs at 9am every Tuesday year-round for Tahsis (see overleaf) (arriving at 1pm), returning after a one-hour stopover to Gold River at 6pm. The shorter **Nootka Sound Day Trip** ($40) leaves Gold River every Wednesday at 10am July to mid-September only (returning at 4.30pm), with longer stops at Resolution Sound and Kyuquot (the native word for "Friendly Cove"), the latter involving a $9 landing fee, proceeds from which go to the Mowachaht Band for the redevelopment of the aboriginal site. During the ninety-minute halt you are offered a guided tour by aboriginal guides around their ancestral home. The previous stop, at Friendly Cove, is equally historic, for it was here that Captain Cook made his first-known landing on the West Coast in 1778, from which, among other things, was to spring the important sea-otter fur trade. Whites named the area and people here "Nootka", though locals today say *nootka* was merely a word of warning to Cook and his crew, meaning "circle around" to avoid hitting offshore rocks. If you're equipped with provisions and wish to stay over, there are **cabins** and a **campground** here, but call first to confirm arrangements (☎283-2054). The third trip, the **Kyuquot Adventure** ($195 single, $310 double), is a two-day overnight cruise, departing every Thursday year-round (April–Oct 7am, Nov–March 6am). It takes you much further north up the coast, returning to Gold River at 4 or 5pm on Friday afternoon: accommodation is included, as is breakfast – though you make it yourself from food supplied – and you can buy Thursday's evening meal on board or onshore at Kyuquot. A 25 percent deposit is required for these trips, refundable in full up until two weeks before departure. People on all trips should bring warm and waterproof clothing. There's a coffee shop on board for drinks and hot snacks. **Kayakers** should note that they can be deposited by lift into the sea at most points en route by prior arrangement.

Boat aside, one of the area's two minor attractions is **Quatsino Cave**, the deepest vertical cave in North America, parts of which are open to the public – for details ask at the infocentre; the other is the **Big Drop**, a stretch of Gold River white water known to kayakers worldwide. The local **infocentre** is at the corner of Hwy 28 and Scout Lake Road (mid-May to mid-Sept; ☎283-2418, *goldriv@island.net*). **Accommodation** is in short supply: the only large place is the *Ridgeview Motel,* located in a panoramic spot above the village at 395 Donner Court (☎283-2277 or 1-800/989-3393, *theridge@oberon.ark.com*; ③) – but the *Peppercorn Trail Motel and Campground* on Mill Road (☎283-2443, *peppercorn@island.net*; ②) also has ten rooms as well as a **campground** ($15–18).

Note that there are also two beautiful roads north from Gold River, both rough, but worth the jolts for the scenery. One provides an alternative approach to **TAHSIS**, another logging community 70km northwest of Gold River, which has one **motel** with a restaurant if you need to break your journey: advance summer reservations are needed at the *Tahsis Motel*, Head Bay Road (☎934-6318, *tahsmot@cancom.net*; ③): or try *Fern's Place B&B*, 379 N Maquinna (☎934-7851, *bganyo@cancom.net*; ③). For more background on a lovely part of the coast, with plenty of fishing, boating and hiking opportunities, contact the **infocentre**, a booth on Rugged Mountain Road (late June to early Sept Mon–Sat 10am–4.30pm; ☎934-6667) or the Village Office (Mon–Fri 9am–noon & 1–5pm; ☎934-6622).

North to Port McNeill, Telegraph Cove and Alert Bay

The main highway north of Campbell River cuts inland and climbs through increasingly rugged and deserted country, particularly after Sayward, the one main community en route. Near Sayward is the marvellously oddball **Valley of a Thousand Faces**: 1400 famous faces painted onto cedar logs, the work of a Dutch artist, and more interesting than it sounds (daily May–Aug 10am–4pm; donation). Almost alongside, west of Hwy 19 at Sayward Junction, is a RV and tent **campground**, the *White River Court* (☎282-3265; sites $8). With a car, you could strike off south from here to **Schoen Lake Provincial Park**, located 12km off Hwy 19 on a rough road south of Woss village and featuring a couple of forest trails and a well-kept campground ($9). Sayward has one **motel**, the *Fisherboy Park*, 400m off Hwy 19 at 1546 Sayward Rd (☎282-3204; ③). **PORT McNEILL**, 180km north of Campbell River and the first real town along Hwy 19, is little more than a motel and logging centre and not somewhere to spend longer than necessary. If you get stuck here, the infocentre's at 351 Shelley Crescent (May to mid-Oct; ☎956-3131, *www.portmcneillchamber.com*).

Telegraph Cove

By contrast, tiny **TELEGRAPH COVE**, 8km south of Port McNeill and reached by a rough side road, is an immensely likeable place and the best of BC's so-called "boardwalk villages": the whole community is raised on wooden stilts over the water, a sight that's becoming ever more popular with tourists. It was built as the terminus of a tree-strung telegraph line from Victoria, and it comes as a surprise to discover that its character is threatened by plans for a massive waterfront development of houses, lodge and restaurant. Some development has already taken place – added moorings, a pub and restaurant – but so far without adversely affecting the village's character.

As an added bonus, the village has become one of the island's premier **whale-watching** spots, the main attraction here being the pods of orcas (killer whales) that calve locally. Some nineteen of these families live or visit Robson Bight, 20km down the Johnstone Strait, which was established as an ecological reserve in 1982 (the whales like the gravel beaches, where they come to rub). This is the world's most accessible and predictable spot to see the creatures – around a ninety percent chance in season. The best outfit for a trip to see them is Stubbs Island Charters at the dock at the end of the boardwalk through the old village (☎928-3185, 928-3117 or 1-800/665-3066). The first whale-watching company in BC, they run up to five three- or five-hour trips daily (June–Oct), but they're very popular, so call well in advance to be sure of a place.

In summer you can buy food at a small café, but otherwise the only provision for visitors is an incongruous new building with shop, ice-cream counter and coffee bar. The only **accommodation** is the large wooded *Telegraph Cove Resorts* (☎928-3131 or 1-800/200-4665; ⑦, camping $15–23; March–Dec), a short walk from the village and one of the best-located places on Vancouver Island, a reputation that makes reservations essential in summer. It has 19 rooms and 121 RV/tent sites with showers, laundry, restaurant, boat rentals and access to guides, charters and whale-watching tours. The *Hidden Cove Lodge* (☎956-3916, *hidcl@island.net*; ⑥; May–Nov) at Lewis Point, a secluded cove on Johnstone Strait 7km from Telegraph Cove, has eight superb lodge units, but they go very quickly. The big *Alder Bay Campsite* 6km off Hwy 19 en route for Telegraph Cove from Port McNeill provides grassy tent sites with ocean views (☎956-4117; reservations recommended; $16–26; May–Sept).

Alert Bay

The breezy fishing village of **ALERT BAY**, on Cormorant Island, is reached by numerous daily ferries from Port McNeill just 8km away (foot passenger $5.50 return, car $13.75). The fifty-minute crossing in the migrating season provides a good chance of seeing whales en route. Despite the predominance of the non-native industries (mainly fish processing), half the population of the island are native 'Namgis, and a visit here offers the opportunity to get to grips with something of their history and to meet those who are keeping something of the old traditions alive. Be sure to have pre-booked accommodation (see below) before heading out here in high season. The **infocentre** (daily June–Sept; Oct–May Mon–Fri; ☎974-5024, *info@alertbay.com*) is at 116 Fir St to your right as you come off the ferry. Also off to the right from the terminal are the totems of a 'Namgis Burial Ground: you're asked to view from a respectful distance.

Bear left from the terminal out of the main part of the village to reach the excellent **U'Mista Cultural Centre** on Front Street (mid-May to early Sept daily 9am–5pm; Oct to mid-May Mon–Fri 9am–5pm; $5.35; ☎974-5403), a modern building based on old models, which houses a collection of potlatch items and artefacts. It also shows a couple of award-winning films, and you might also come across local kids being taught native languages, songs and dances. More local artefacts are on show in the library and small museum, open most summer afternoons, at 199 Fir St. For years the village also claimed the world's tallest fully carved **totem pole** (other contenders, say knowing villagers, are all pole and no carving), though much to local chagrin Victoria raised a pole in 1994 that *The Guinness Book of Records* has recognized as 2.1m taller. Also worth a look is the wildlife and weird swamp habitat at **Gator Gardens** behind the bay, accessible via several trails and boardwalks.

Most people come over for the day, but **accommodation** options include: the six-room *Orca Inn*, 291 Fir St, ten-minutes' walk from the ferry terminal (☎974-5322 or 1-800/672-2466; ②), with steak and seafood restaurant and café overlooking Broughton Strait and the sea; the *Ocean View Cabins*, 390 Poplar St, 1km from the ferry terminal overlooking Mitchell Bay (☎974-5457; ③); the *Bayside Inn Hotel*, overlooking the

THE INSIDE PASSAGE

One of Canada's great trips, the **Inside Passage** aboard BC Ferries' *Queen of the North*, between Port Hardy and Prince Rupert on the British Columbia mainland, is a cheap way of getting what people on the big cruise ships are getting: 274 nautical miles of mountains, islands, waterfalls, glaciers, sea lions, whales, eagles and some of the grandest coastal scenery on the continent. By linking up with the Greyhound bus network or the VIA Rail terminal at Prince Rupert, it also makes a good leg in any number of convenient itineraries around British Columbia. Some travellers will have come from Washington State, others will want to press on from Prince Rupert to Skagway by boat and then head north into Alaska and the Yukon (see p.229 for details on the Alaska Marine ferries). A lot of people simply treat it as a cruise, and sail north one day and return south to Port Hardy the next. If nothing else, the trip's a good way of meeting fellow travellers and taking a break from the interminable trees of the BC interior.

The boat carries 750 passengers and 160 cars and runs every two days, departing at 7.30am on **even-numbered days** in August, **odd-numbered days** in June, July, September and the first half of October. The journey takes around fifteen hours, arriving in Prince Rupert about 10.30pm, sometimes with a stop at Bella Bella. Be aware that from about October 15 to May 25 the sailings are less frequent in both directions and are predominantly at night (they leave Port Hardy in the late afternoon), which rather defeats the sightseeing object of the trip. On board there are cafeterias, restaurants and a shop (among other services): at the last, pick up the cheap and interesting *BC Ferries Guide to the Inside Passage* for more on the trip.

The cost from mid-June to mid-September (peak) is $106 single for a foot passenger (May & Oct $85/75, Nov–April $56), $218 for a car (May & Oct $154, Nov–April $114); reservations are **essential** throughout the summer season if you're taking a car or want a cabin. Bookings can be made by phone (☎1-888/223-3779 anywhere in BC, ☎250/386-3431 in Victoria, ☎604/669-1211 in Vancouver, *www.bcferries.com*), fax (☎381-5452 in Victoria) or by post to BC Ferry Corporation, 1112 Fort St, Victoria, BC V8V 4V2. Include name and address; number in party; length, height and type of car; choice of dayroom or cabin; and preferred date of departure and alternatives. Full payment is required up front. **Day cabins** can be reserved by foot passengers, and range from around $24 for two berths with basin, to $45 on the Promenade with two berths, basin and toilet. If you are making the return trip only you can rent **cabins overnight**, saving the hassle of finding accommodation in Port Hardy, but if you do you are obliged to take the cabin for the following day's return trip as well: cabins are not available as an alternative to rooms in town, so don't think you can rent a cabin overnight and then disappear next morning at Prince Rupert. Two-berth overnight cabins range from about $51 with basin only, to $120 for shower, basin and toilet. Reports suggest BC Ferries are not happy for passengers to roll out sleeping bags in the lounge area. If you're making a return trip and want to leave your car behind, there are several supervised lock-ups in Port Hardy: try Daze Parking (☎949-7792) or the *Sunny Sanctuary RV Park* (☎949-8111) just five minutes from the terminal (the town shuttle bus will pick you up from here). You can leave vehicles at the ferry terminal, but there have been incidents of vandalism in recent years: neither BC

harbour, at 81 First St (☎974-5857; ②); and the 23-site *Alert Bay Camping and Trailer Park* on Alder Road (☎974-5213, *www.alertbay.com*; $10–15).

Sointula

SOINTULA village is a wonderful aberration. It's located on Malcolm Island, accessible by ferry en route from Port McNeill to Alert Bay (25min; foot passenger $5.50 return, car $13.75) and directly from Alert Bay (35min; foot passenger $3.50 one-way, car $5.50). The fishing village would be a good place to wander at any time, thanks to its briney maritime appeal, but what gives added lustre is the fact that it contains a tiny

Ferries nor the Port Hardy infocentre seem to recommend the practice. Note, again, that it is vital to book accommodation at your final destination before starting your trip; both Port Hardy and Prince Rupert hotels get very busy on days when the boat arrives.

THE DISCOVERY COAST PASSAGE

The huge success of the Inside Passage sailing amongst visitors led BC Ferries to introduce the **Discovery Coast Passage**, a trip they candidly admit will only pay as a result of tourists. The route offers many of the scenic rewards of the Inside Passage, but over a shorter and more circuitous route between Port Hardy and **Bella Coola**, where you pick up the occasionally steep and tortuous road (Hwy 20) through the Coast Mountains to Williams Lake (see p.403) – it goes nowhere else. En route, the boat, the *Queen of Chilliwack*, stops at Namu, McLoughlin Bay, Shearwater, Klemtu and Ocean Falls (Namu is a request stop and must be booked in advance). If the route takes off as BC Ferries hope, you can expect visitor facilities to mushroom at these places – you can disembark at all of them – but at present the only places to stay overnight are campgrounds at McLoughlin Bay and a resort, hotels, cabins and B&B at Shearwater. Bella Coola is better-equipped, and will probably become more so as the route becomes better known. BC Ferries is offering inclusive ferry and accommodation **packages** – even renting fishing tackle so you can fish over the side – and these too may mature as the service finds its feet.

Currently there are **departures** roughly every couple of days between late May and the end of September, currently leaving at 9.30am on Tues and Thurs and 9.30pm on Sat, Sun and Mon. There's a slight catch, however, for while the early morning departures offer you plenty of scenery, some arrive at McLoughlin Bay at 7.30pm and Bella Coola at 6.30am in the morning, meaning that the very best bit of the trip – along the inlet to Bella Coola – is in the middle of the night. The 9.30am departures are quicker (they only stop once, at Ocean Falls) and make Bella Coola the same day, arriving at 11pm, so the problem is lessened. Alternatively take the 9.30pm departures and wake at McLoughlin Bay at 7.30am with a further daylight trip towards Bella Coola, arriving at 7.30am the next morning – read the timetables carefully. Making the trip southbound from Bella Coola gets round the problem, though there are similar staggered departure and arrival times (services currently leave Mon, Wed and Fri at 7.30 or 8am, arriving Port Hardy 9.30pm on the Mon departure, 7.45am on Wed sailing and 9am on the Fri boat), with overnight and same-day journeys and a variety of stopping points depending on the day you travel. Unlike the Inside Passage, there are **no cabins**: you sleep in aircraft-style reclining seats and – for the time being – sleeping bags seem OK on the floor: check for the latest on freestanding tents on the decks.

Reservations can be made through BC Ferries (see opposite for details). **Prices** for a foot passenger are $110 one-way to Bella Coola, $55 to Namu and $70 to all other destinations. If you want to camp or stop over and hop on and off, the boat fares between any two of McLoughlin Bay, Ocean Falls, Klemtu and Namu are $22 and $40 from any of these to Bella Coola. Cars cost $220 from Port Hardy to Bella Coola, $140 to all other destinations ($45 and $80 respectively for the single-leg options). To take a **canoe** or **kayak** costs $40.75 stowage from Port Hardy to Bella Coola, $30.75 to points en route.

fossil Finnish settlement. An early cult community, it was founded with Finnish pioneers as a model co-operative settlement in 1901 by Matti Kurrika, a curious mixture of guru, dramatist and philosopher. In 1905 the experiment collapsed, but 100 Finns from the original settlement stayed on. Their descendants survive to this day, and you'll still hear Finnish being spoken on the streets. You can wander local beaches, explore the island interior by logging road, or spend a few minutes in the **Sointula Finnish Museum**, which is located on 1st Street just to the left after disembarking the ferry: you'll probably need to call someone (☎973-6353 or 973-6764) to come and open up and show you around.

Port Hardy

Dominated by big-time copper mining, a large fishing fleet and the usual logging concerns, **PORT HARDY**, a total of 485km from Victoria and 230km from Campbell River, is best known among travellers as the departure point for ships plying one of the more spectacular stretches of the famous **Inside Passage** to Prince Rupert (and thence to Alaska) and the newly introduced **Discovery Coast Passage** (see box, overleaf). If you have time to kill waiting for the boat you could drop into the occasionally open **town museum** at 7110 Market St or visit the **Quatse River Salmon Hatchery** on Hardy Bay Road, just off Hwy 19 across from the *Pioneer Inn*.

If possible, though, time your arrival to coincide with one of the Inside Passage **sailings** (see box, p.382) which leave every other day in summer and twice-weekly in winter. **Bus** services aren't really scheduled to do this for you, with a Laidlaw bus meeting each *incoming* sailing from Prince Rupert. A Laidlaw bus (☎949-7532 in Port Hardy, ☎385-4411 or 388-5248 in Victoria) also leaves Victoria daily (currently 11.45am), sometimes with a change in Nanaimo, arriving at the Port Hardy ferry terminal in the evening to connect with the ferry next morning (currently 9.50pm); in summer an extra service departs from Victoria on the morning before ferry sailings. Maverick Coach Lines (☎250/753-4371 in Nanaimo, ☎604/662-8051 in Vancouver) runs an early-morning bus from Vancouver to Nanaimo (inclusive of ferry), connecting with the daily Laidlaw bus to Port Hardy. You can **fly** from Vancouver International Airport to Port Hardy with Air BC (☎1-800/663-3721 in BC, 1-800/776-3000 in the States, 604/688-5515 in Vancouver, 250/360-9074 in Victoria).

The Port Hardy **ferry terminal** is visible from town but is actually 8km away at Bear Cove, where buses stop before carrying on to terminate opposite the **infocentre**, 7250 Market St (year-round Mon–Fri 9am–5pm, early June to late Sept 8am–8pm; ☎949-7622, *chamber@capescott.bc.ca*). The infocentre can give you all the details about Port Hardy's tiny but free **museum**, and the immense wilderness of **Cape Scott Provincial Park**, whose interior is accessible only by foot and which is supposed to have some of the most consistently bad weather in the world. As a short taster you could follow the forty-minute hike from the small campground and trailhead at San Josef River to some sandy beaches. Increasingly popular, but demanding (allow eight hours plus), is the historic **Cape Scott Trail**, part of a complex web of trails hacked from the forest by early Danish pioneers. Around 28km has been reclaimed from the forest, opening a trail to the cape itself.

If you stay in town overnight, leave plenty of time to reach the ferry terminal – sailings in summer are usually around 7.30am. North Island Transportation provides a shuttle-bus service between the ferry and the town's airport, main hotels and the **bus station** at Market Street, whence it departs ninety minutes before each sailing (☎949-6300 for information or to arrange a pick-up from hotel or campground); otherwise call a **taxi** (☎949-8000).

Many travellers to Port Hardy are in RVs, but there's still a huge amount of pressure on hotel **accommodation** in summer, and it's absolutely vital to call ahead if you're not camping or haven't worked your arrival to coincide with one of the ferry sailings. Note that the ferry from Prince Rupert docks around 10.30pm, so you don't want to be hunting out rooms late at night with dozens of others. There are **rooms** out of town at the *Airport Inn*, 4030 Byng Rd (☎949-9424, *www.airportinn-porthardy.com*; ⑤), but you'd be better off in one of the slightly more upmarket central choices like the *North Shore Inn*, 7370 Market St (☎949-8500; ④), at the end of Hwy 19, where all units have ocean views, or the *Thunderbird Inn*, 7050 Rupert St and Granville (☎949-7767, *tbirdinn@island.net*; ④). The former has nice views of the harbour but sometimes has noisy live music. Five minutes south of town at 4965 Byng Rd, in a park-like setting near the river, is the *Pioneer Inn* (☎949-7271 or 1-800/663-8744, *pioneer@island.net*; ⑤), which has rooms,

RV sites and a campground ($20). Other hotels are the *Glen Lyon Inn* by the marina at 6435 Hardy Bay Rd (☎949-7115, *www.glenlyoninn.com*; ④), and the large 40-room *Quarterdeck Inn*, 6555 Hardy Bay Rd (☎902-0455, *quarterdk@capescott.net*; ⑥), the town's newest hotel – it opened in late 1999: otherwise contact the infocentre for details of the town's five or so B&B options. The *Wildwoods* **campground** (☎949-6753; $5–15; May–Oct) is a good option, being within walking distance (3km) of the ferry, though it's not too comfy for tenting – or try the *Quatse River Campground* at 5050 Hardy Rd (☎949-2395, *quatse@island.net*; $14–18), with 62 spruce-shaded sites opposite the *Pioneer Inn*, 5km from the ferry dock. Or go for the larger 80-site *Sunny Sanctuary Campground* 1km north of Ferry Junction and Hwy 19 at 8080 Goodspeed Rd (☎949-8111, *sunnycam@capescott.net*; $15–20).

Food here is nothing special, but there's a bevy of budget outlets, so you should be able to fill up for well under $10. Granville and Market streets have the main restaurant concentrations: try *Snuggles*, next to the *Pioneer Inn*, which aims at a cosy English pub atmosphere with live music, theatre (Fri nights) and steaks, salads and salmon grilled over an open fire. The cafeteria-coffee shop in the *Pioneer* does filling breakfasts and other snacks.

travel details

Trains

Vancouver to: Edmonton via Kamloops (3 weekly; 25hr); Jasper (June–Sept daily except Wed; Oct–May 3 weekly; 19hr); Lillooet (mid-June to Oct 1 daily; rest of year 4 weekly; 5hr 30min); Prince George (mid-June to Oct 1 daily; rest of year 3 weekly; 13hr 30min); Whistler (1 daily; 3hr).

Victoria to: Courtenay via Nanaimo (1 round trip daily; 4hr 35min).

Buses

Nanaimo to: Port Alberni (4 daily; 1hr 20min); Port Hardy (1 daily; 6hr 50min); Tofino (1–2 daily; 4hr 30min); Ucluelet (1–2 daily; 3hr 10min); Victoria (7 daily; 2hr 20min).

Port Alberni to: Nanaimo (4 daily; 1hr 20min); Tofino via Ucluelet (1–2 daily; 3hr).

Vancouver to: Bellingham (8–10 daily; 1hr 45min); Calgary via Kamloops (6 daily; 13hr); Calgary via Penticton, Nelson and Cranbrook (2 daily; 24hr); Calgary via Princeton and Kelowna (2 daily; 18hr); Edmonton via Jasper (3 daily; 16hr 30min); Nanaimo (8 daily; 5hr); Pemberton (3 daily; 3hr 10min); Powell River (2 daily; 5hr 10min); Prince George via Cache Creek and Williams Lake (2 daily; 13hr); Seattle, USA (8–10 daily; 3hr 15min); Sea-Tac Airport, USA

(8–10 daily; 4hr 10min); Vernon (6 daily; 6hr); Victoria (8 daily; 5hr); Whistler (6 daily; 2hr 30min).

Victoria to: Bamfield (1–3 daily; 6–8hr); Campbell River (5 daily; 5hr); Nanaimo (7 daily; 2hr 20min); Port Hardy (1 daily; 9hr 45min); Port Renfrew (2 daily; 2hr 30min); Vancouver (8–10 daily; 4hr); Vancouver Airport direct (3 daily; 3hr 30min).

Ferries

Chemainus to: Thetis Island and Kuper Island (minimum of 10 round trips daily; 35min).

Courtenay to: Powell River (4 daily; 1hr 15min).

Nanaimo to: Gabriola Island (17 daily; 20min); Vancouver/Horseshoe Bay Terminal (8 daily; 1hr 35min); Vancouver/Tsawwassen Terminal (8 daily; 2hr).

Northern Gulf Islands: Denman Island to Hornby Island (minimum 12 round trips daily; 10min); Quadra Island to Cortes Island (Mon–Sat 6 daily, Sun 5 daily; 45min); Vancouver Island (Buckley Bay) to Denman Island (18 round trips daily; 10min); Vancouver Island (Campbell River) to Quadra Island (17 round trips daily; 10min);

Port Hardy to: Bella Coola (1 every two days; 15hr 30min–22hr); Prince Rupert (1 every two days; 15hr).

Powell River to: Courtenay-Comox (4 round trips daily; 1hr 15min); Texada Island (10 round trips daily; 35min).

Southern Gulf Islands: Vancouver Island (Crofton) to SaltSpring Island/Vesuvius Bay (14 round trips daily; 20min); Vancouver Island (Swartz Bay) to SaltSpring Island/Fulford Harbour (10 round trips daily; 35min).

Sunshine Coast: Horseshoe Bay to Snug Cove (15 round trips daily; 20 minutes); Horseshoe Bay to Langdale (8 round trips daily; 40min); Jervis Inlet/Earls Cove to Saltery Bay (8–9 round trips daily; 50min).

Vancouver to: Nanaimo (from Horseshoe Bay Terminal; 8 daily; 1hr 35min; from Tsawwassen Terminal; 8 daily; 2hr); Victoria (Swartz Bay Terminal) (from Tsawwassen; hourly summer 7am–9pm; rest of the year minimum 8 daily 7am–9pm; 1hr 35min).

Victoria to: Anacortes and San Juan Islands, USA, from Victoria's Inner Harbour (1–2 daily; 2hr 30min); Seattle, USA, from Inner Harbour (1–2 daily; 2hr 30min); Vancouver (Tsawwassen) from Swartz Bay (hourly summer 7am–10pm; rest of the year minimum 8 daily; 1hr 35min).

Flights

Vancouver to: Calgary (20 daily; 1hr 15min); Edmonton (14 daily; 1hr 30min); Portland (12 daily; 1hr 20min); Seattle (20 daily; 50min); Victoria (14 daily; 25min).

Victoria to: Calgary (4 daily; 1hr 40min); Vancouver (14 daily; 25min). Only flights to Seattle and Portland are via Vancouver.

CHAPTER SIX

SOUTHERN BRITISH COLUMBIA

I t says something about the magnificence of southern British Columbia's **interior** that you can enter it from Vancouver or the Rockies and find a clutch of landscapes every bit as spectacular as those you've just left. What may come as a surprise is the region's sheer natural diversity: over and above the predictable panoply of mountains and forests are a patchwork of landscapes that include genteel farmland, pastoral hills, expansive ranching country, immense and mild-weathered lakes and vast expanses of arid, near-desert scrub. Southern British Columbia contains both the Northwest's wettest and driest climates, and reputedly more species of flora and fauna than the rest of the region put together. The range of recreational possibilities is equally impressive: Canada's top ski areas, warmest lakes and best beaches are all here, not to mention hot springs, hiking, sailing and canoeing galore, and some of the best salmon and other fishing in the world.

Culturally and logistically, the region stands apart from the northern half of the province (covered in Chapter Eight), containing most of the roads, towns, people and readily accessible sights. Vancouver is also here, though its size and cosmopolitan zest also set it apart – we deal with Vancouver and its eponymous island in Chapter Five. Apart from Vancouver Island, two other excursions from Vancouver stand out, each of which are covered in this chapter and can easily be extended to embrace longer itineraries out of the city. The first is the 150-kilometre **Sunshine Coast**, the only stretch of accessible coastline on mainland British Columbia, and a possible springboard to the Inside Passage ferry to Prince Rupert. The second is the inland route to **Garibaldi Provincial Park**, containing by far the best scenery and hiking country within striking distance of Vancouver, and the famous world-class ski resort of **Whistler**; the road beyond Whistler can be difficult to negotiate under the winter snows, but train passengers can sit back and forge on through wilder parts all the way to Prince George. En route to Whistler you'll pass through **Squamish**, rapidly emerging as one of North America's premier destinations for windsurfing, climbing and – in season – eagle-watching.

Vancouver is a transport hub for the entire region of southern British Columbia, and many people will approach the region travelling inland from the city: others will approach it across country from the Rockies or the US. Unfortunately whatever your approach, the major routes through the region confine you to some of its least

---

TELEPHONE CODES

The telephone code for British Columbia is ☎250.
The telephone code for Vancouver and vicinity is ☎604.

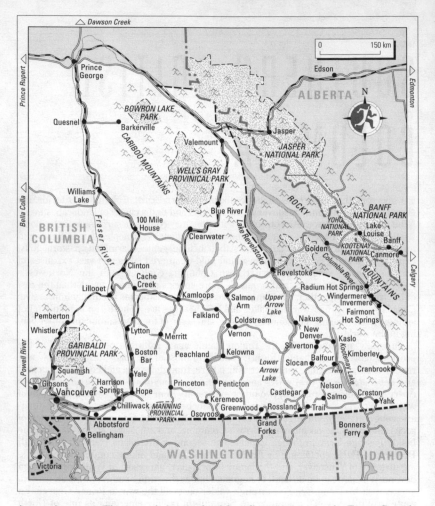

interesting areas. The most obvious and quickest line east or west, the **Trans-Canada Highway**, isn't worth considering in its entirety unless you're keen to cross the region in a hurry – little west of Revelstoke compares to what you might find further north or south. Nor does **Hwy 3**, rumbling along just north of the US border, offer a convincing reason for sticking to it religiously.

The best option would be to take a meandering course towards the outstanding **Kootenay** region in the province's southeastern corner – an idyllic assortment of mountains and lakes and several towns that are fun to stay in – perhaps by way of the **Okanagan**, an almost Californian enclave of orchards, vineyards, warm lakes and resort towns, whose beaches and scorching summers suck in hordes of vacationers from all over Canada and the western United States. From here you could push north to **Kamloops**, a far from exciting town, but a transport hub and a jumping-off point for the magnificent Wells Gray Provincial Park or the Yukon. The other major option would be to head south to take in the better parts of Hwy 3 west of Osoyoos, also reasonably easily reached directly from Vancouver, and which includes a corner of **desert** and the spectacular ridges of the **Cascades** and **Coast Mountains**.

A history of British Columbia

Long before the coming of Europeans, British Columbia's coastal region supported five key **First Peoples** – The Kwakiutl, Bella Coola, Nuu-chah-nulth, Haida and Tlingit – all of whom lived largely off the sea and developed a culture in many ways more sophisticated than that of the nomadic and hunting-oriented tribes of the interior. Although it's rare these days to come across aboriginal faces in interior southern BC, aboriginal villages still exist on parts of Vancouver Island, and you can find examples of their totemic art in the excellent museum displays of Victoria and Vancouver (see Chapter Five).

The British explorer **Francis Drake** probably made the first sighting of the mainland by a European, during his round-the-world voyage of 1579. Spanish explorers sailing from California and Russians from Alaska explored the coast almost two centuries later, though it was another Briton, **Captain Cook**, who made the first recorded landing in 1778. Captain George Vancouver first mapped the area in 1792–94, hard on the heels of the Nuu-chah-nulth Convention of 1790 – a neat piece of colonial bluster in which the British wrested from the Spanish all rights on the mainland as far as Alaska.

Exploration of the interior came about during the search for an easier way to export furs westwards to the Pacific (instead of the arduous haul eastwards across the continent). **Alexander Mackenzie** of the North West Company made the first crossing of North America north of Mexico in 1793, followed by two further adventurers, **Simon Fraser** and **David Thompson**, whose names also resonate as sobriquets for rivers, shops, motels and streets across the region. For the first half of the nineteenth century most of western Canada was ruled as a virtual fiefdom by the **Hudson's Bay Company**, a monopoly that antagonized the Americans, which in turn persuaded the British to formalize its claims to the region to forestall American expansion. The 49th Parallel was agreed as the national boundary, though Vancouver Island, which lies partly south of the line, remained wholly British and was officially designated a crown colony in 1849. The "Bay" still reigned in all but name, however, and took no particular interest in promoting immigration; as late as 1855 the island's white population numbered only 774 and the mainland remained almost unknown except to trappers and the odd prospector.

The discovery of **gold** on the Fraser River in 1858, and in the Cariboo region three years later, changed everything, attracting some 25,000 people to the goldfields and

RESERVING PROVINCIAL CAMPSITES

Tent and RV sites at certain campgrounds in British Columbia's provincial parks can be reserved in advance. To make **reservations**, call Discover Camping (☎1-800/689-9025 or 604/689-9025 in greater Vancouver; March to mid-Sept Mon–Fri 7am–7pm, Sat & Sun 9am–5pm) or log-on to their Web site *www.discovercamping.ca*, where reservations can be made and confirmed online. Reservations can be made from up to three months in advance and no later than 48 hours before the first day of arrival. A non-refundable booking fee of $6.42 per night, to a maximum of $19.26 for three or more nights, is charged (rates include tax). Payment in advance is by Visa or MasterCard only (payment for extra nights once at a campsite is by cash only). You can stay in BC provincial parks up to a maximum of fourteen days in any single park. Information on all aspects of BC's provincial parks is available on the net at *www.elp.gov.bc.ca/bcparks*.

creating a forward base on the mainland that was to become Vancouver. It also led to the building of the **Cariboo Road** (the present Hwy 97) and the **Dewdney Trail** (Hwy 3), which opened up the interior and helped attract the so-called **Overlanders** – a huge straggle of pioneers that tramped from Ontario and Québec in the summer of 1862. Britain declared mainland British Columbia a crown colony in 1858 to impose imperial authority on the region and, more importantly, to lay firm claim to the huge mineral wealth that was rightly believed to lie within it. When Canada's eastern colonies formed the Dominion in 1867, though, British Columbia dithered over joining until it received the promise of a railway to link it to the east in 1871 – though the Canadian Pacific didn't actually arrive for another fifteen years.

While British Columbia no longer dithers over its destiny, it still tends to look to itself and the Northwest – and increasingly to the new economic markets of the Pacific Rim – rather than to the rest of Canada. The Francophone concerns of the east are virtually non-existent here – for years, for example, there was just one French school in the entire province. For the most part British Columbians are well off, both financially and in terms of quality of life, and demographically the province is one of the region's youngest. If there are flies in the ointment, they're the environmental pressures thrown up by an economy which relies on primary resources for its dynamism: British Columbia supplies 25 percent of North America's commercial timber and exports significant amounts of hydroelectric power, fish, zinc, silver, oil, coal and gypsum. Few of these can be exploited without exacting a toll on the province's natural beauty; British Columbians may be well off, but they're increasingly aware of the environmental price being paid for their prosperity.

The Sunshine Coast

A mild-weathered stretch of sandy beaches, rugged headlands and quiet lagoons running northwest of Vancouver, the **Sunshine Coast** receives heavy promotion – and heavy tourist traffic as a result – though in truth its reputation is overstated and the scenic rewards are slim compared to the grandeur of the BC interior. In summer, however, this area offers some of Canada's best diving, boating and fishing opportunities, all of which stoke a string of busy villages eager to provide accommodation, run tours and rent anything from bikes to full-sized cruisers.

Highway 101 runs the length of the coast, but it's interrupted at two points by sizeable inlets that entail lengthy ferry crossings. Motorists face enormous queues to get on the boats in summer, but the crossings present no problems for bus or foot passengers – indeed, they're the best bits of the trip. Given that the area is hardly worth full-scale exploration by car anyway, you might as well go by **bus**; it's perfectly feasible to get to **Powell River** and back in a day, though it's probably not the first day-trip you'd want to make from Vancouver. Malaspina Coachlines (☎485-5030) runs two buses daily to Powell River (5hr) and a third only as far as **Sechelt** (2hr).

Along Highway 101

Soon reached and well signposted from North Vancouver, **HORSESHOE BAY** is the departure point for the first of the Hwy 101 **ferry** crossings, a half-hour passage through the islands of fjord-like Howe Sound (regular sailings year-round). Ferries also ply from here to Nanaimo on Vancouver Island, with hourly sailings in summer and every other hour off-season. For information on either of these services, contact BC Ferries in Vancouver (☎604/669-1211), or pick up a timetable from the Vancouver info-centre.

GIBSONS, the terminal on the other side of Howe Sound, is a scrappy place spread widely over a wooded hillside – the nicest area is around the busy marina, where you'll find the **infocentre** at 668 Sunny Crest Rd (daily 9am–6pm; ☎604/886-2325). Motels abound, but for decent camping hold out for **Roberts Creek Provincial Park**, 8km northwest of the terminal on Hwy 101 ($12). Beyond, the service and supplies centre of **SECHELT** panders to tourists less than Gibsons, and ongoing development lends the town a messy air which isn't helped by its drab, flat location. Just 4km north, however, **Porpoise Bay Provincial Park** has a campground (reservations possible, see box, opposite; $17.50), a sandy beach, good swimming and a few short woodland trails. The main road beyond Sechelt is very pretty, and offers occasional views to the sea when it's not trapped in the trees.

Further west on Hwy 101 is Pender Harbour, a string of small coastal communities of which **MADEIRA PARK** is the most substantial; whales occasionally pass this section of coast – which, sadly, is the source of many of the whales in the world's aquariums – but the main draws are fishing and boating. **Earl's Cove** is nothing but the departure ramp of the second **ferry** en route, a longer crossing (45min), which again offers fantastic views of sheer mountains plunging into the sea. A short trail (4km) from the adjacent car park leads to a viewpoint for the **Skookumchuck Narrows**, where the Sechelt Inlet constricts to produce boiling rapids at the turn of each tide. On board the ferry, look north beyond the low wooded hills to the immense waterfall that drops off a "Lost World"-type plateau into the sea.

From Jervis Bay, the opposite landing stage, the country is comparatively less travelled. A couple of kilometres up the road is the best of all the provincial parks in this region, **Saltery Bay Provincial Park**. Everything here is discreetly hidden in the trees between the road and the coast, and the campground ($12) – beautifully sited – is connected by short trails to a couple of swimming beaches. The main road beyond is largely enclosed by trees, so there's little to see of the coast, though various **campgrounds** give onto the sea, notably the big *Oceanside Resort and Cabins* site, 7km short of Powell River, which sits on a superb piece of shoreline (☎604/485-2435 or 1-888/889-2435; ④). Although it's given over mainly to RVs, there are a few sites for tents ($12–14) and cheap cabins (①).

Powell River and beyond

Given its seafront location, **POWELL RIVER** has its scenic side, but like many a BC town its unfocused sprawl and nearby sawmill slightly dampen the overall appeal. The main road cruises past almost 4km of box-like retirement bungalows before reaching the town centre, which at first glance makes it a not terribly captivating resort. If you're catching the **ferry** to Courtenay on Vancouver Island (4 daily; 75min), you might not even see the town site, as the terminal is 2km to the east at Westview, and some of the **buses** from Vancouver are timed to coincide with the boats; if your bus doesn't connect, you can either walk from the town centre or bus terminal or call a taxi (☎604/483-3666). The local **infocentre** (daily 9am–5pm; ☎604/485-4701), which is immediately at the end of the wooden ferry pier at 4690 Marine Ave, can supply a visitor's map with detailed coverage of the many trails leading inland from the coast hereabouts; they can also advise on boat trips on Powell Lake, immediately inland, and tours to Desolation Sound further up the coast.

In the event of having to stay overnight, you can choose from a dozen or so **motels** in town and a couple near the terminal itself. The most central of several **campgrounds** is the 81-site *Willingdon Beach Municipal Campground* on the seafront off Marine Avenue at 6910 Duncan St (☎604/485-2242; $13–20).

The northern end-point of Hwy 101 – which, incidentally, starts in Mexico City, making it one of North America's longest continuous routes – is the hamlet of **LUND**, 28km up the coast from Powell River. **Desolation Sound Marine Provincial Park**, about 10km north of Lund, offers some of Canada's best boating and scuba diving, plus fishing, canoeing and kayaking. There's no road access to the park, but a number of outfitters in Powell River run tours to it and can hire all the equipment you could possibly need – try Westview Live Bait Ltd, 4527 Marine Ave, for **canoes**; Coulter's Diving, 4557 Willingdon Ave, for **scuba gear**; and Spokes, 4710 Marine Drive, for **bicycles**. The more modest **Okeover Provincial Park**, immediately north of Lund, has an unserviced campground ($12).

The Sea to Sky Highway

A fancy name for Hwy 99 between North Vancouver and Whistler, the **Sea to Sky Highway** has a slightly better reputation than it deserves, mainly because Vancouver's weekend hordes need to reassure themselves of the grandeur of the scenery at their doorstep. It undoubtedly scores in its early coastal stretch, where the road clings perilously to an almost sheer cliff and mountains come dramatically into view on both sides of Howe Sound. Views here are better than along the Sunshine Coast, though plenty of campgrounds, motels and minor roadside distractions fill the route until the mountains of the Coast Range rear up beyond **Squamish** for the rest of the way to Whistler.

If you've a **car** you're better off driving the highway only as far as **Garibaldi Provincial Park** – the section between Pemberton and Lillooet, the Duffy Lake Road, is very slow-going and often impassable in winter, though the drive is a stunner with wonderful views of lakes and glaciers. Regular buses connect Vancouver and Whistler (some continue to Pemberton), which you can easily manage as a day-trip (it's 2hr 30min one way to Whistler from Vancouver by bus), though a far more interesting and popular way of covering this ground is by **train**. BC Rail (☎984-5246 or 1-800/663-8238, *www.bcrail.com*) operates a daily passenger service, the Cariboo Prospector, between North Vancouver and Lillooet ($67 one-way), calling at Whistler ($33 one-way) and other minor stations; the train arrives in Lillooet at 12.35pm and sets off back for Vancouver at 3.30pm, making for an excellent day-trip. The train continues on to Prince George ($196 one-way) on Sunday, Wednesday and Friday; this is a much better way to make the journey than by bus via Hope and Cache Creek. BC Rail's Royal Hudson is a fantastic steam engine that travels for two hours from North Vancouver to Squamish (May–Sept Wed–Sun). It leaves Vancouver at 10am, and then leaves from Squamish for the trip back to Vancouver at 2pm. The one-way trip costs $24 or $40 if you want to travel in the dome car and get a real eyeful of the awesome scenery.

Britannia Beach

Road and rail lines meet with some squalor at tiny **BRITANNIA BEACH**, 53km from Vancouver, whose **BC Museum of Mining** is the first reason to take time out from admiring the views (mid-May to June, Sept & Oct Wed–Sun 10am–4.30pm; July & Aug daily 10am–4.30pm; $8.50; ☎604/896-2233, *www.bcmuseumofmining.org*). Centring around what was, in the 1930s, the largest producer of copper in the British Empire, the museum is housed in a huge, derelict-looking building on the hillside and is chock-full of hands-on displays, original working machinery and archive photographs. You can also take guided underground tours around the mine galleries on small electric trains.

Beyond Britannia Beach a huge, chimney-surrounded pulp mill comes into view across Howe Sound to spoil the scenic wonder along this stretch, though **Browning Lake** in **Murrin Provincial Park** makes a nice picnic spot. This is but one of several small coastal reserves, the most striking of which is **Shannon Falls Provincial Park**, 7km beyond Britannia Beach, signed right off the road and worth a stop for its spectacular 335-metre **waterfall**. Six times the height of Niagara, you can see it from the road, but it's only five-minutes' walk to the viewing area at the base, where the proximity of the road, plus a campground and diner, detract a touch.

Squamish

The sea views and coastal drama end 11km beyond Britannia Beach at **SQUAMISH**, not a pretty place, whose houses spread out over a flat plain amidst warehouses, logging waste and old machinery. However, if you want to climb, windsurf or mountain bike, there's nowhere better in Canada to do so. At a glance, all the town has by way of fame is the vast granite rock literally overshadowing it, "The Stawamus Chief", which looms into view to the east just beyond Shannon Falls and is claimed to be the world's "second-biggest free-standing rock" (after Gibraltar, apparently). Over the last few years, the rock has caused the town's stock to rise considerably, for it now rates as one of Canada's top – if not *the* top – spot for **rock climbing**, and the area recently earned provincial park status. If all you want to do is watch this activity from below, the pull-off beyond the falls is a good spot. Around 200,000 climbers from around the world come here annually, swarming over more than 400 routes over the 625-metre monolith: the University Wall and its culmination, the Dance Platform, is rated Canada's toughest climb. Other simpler but highly rated climbs include Banana Peel, Sugarloaf and Cat Crack, as well as other more varied routes on the adjacent Smoke Bluffs and outcrops in Murrin Provincial Park.

The rock is sacred to the local Squamish, whose ancient tribal name – which means "place where the wind blows" – gives a clue as to the town's second big activity. **Windsurfing** here is now renowned across North America, thanks to some truly extraordinary winds, most drummed up by the vast rock walls around the town and its inlet – which are then funnelled along the inlet's narrow corridor to Squamish at its head. There are strong, consistent winds here to suit all standards, from beginner to worldclass, but the water is cold, so a wet suit's a good idea (there are rental outlets around town). Most people head for the artificial Squamish Spit, a dyke separating the waters of the Howe Sound from the Squamish River, a park area run by the Squamish Windsurfing Society (☎604/926-WIND or 892-2235). It's around 3km from town (ask at the infocentre for directions) and a small fee is payable to the Society to cover rescue boats, insurance and washroom facilities.

Rounding out Squamish's outdoor activities is the tremendous **mountain biking** terrain – there are no less than 63 trails in the area ranging from gnarly single-track trails to readily accessible deactivated forestry roads – and the growing trend of **bouldering**, which involves clambering (very slowly and without ropes) over large boulders.

The town has one more unexpected treat, for the Squamish River, and the tiny hamlet of Brackendale in particular (10km to the north on Hwy 99), is – literally – the world's **bald-eagle** capital. In winter around 2000 eagles regularly congregate here, attracted by the chance to pick off the migrating salmon. The best place to see them is the so-called Eagle Run just south of the centre of Brackendale, and on the river in the Brackendale Eagles Provincial Park with a small shelter and volunteer interpreters on weekends during the eagle season. The birds largely winter on the river's west bank, with the viewing area on the east – eagles will stop feeding if approached within about 150m, so the river provides an invaluable buffer zone. For **accommodation** and **rafting trips** contact the Sunwolf Outdoor Center (☎604/898-1537, *www.mountain-inter.net /sunwolf*). It is signposted off Hwy 1 – take a left onto the Squamish Valley Road at the Alice Lake junction 2km past Brackendale, continue for 4km and the centre is on the right. They have three-person cabins on the shore of Cheakamus River (③), some have kitchens (④). To see the eagles from a raft costs $70 per person, including light lunch; a raft trip plus cabin accommodation costs $139 per person, $198 per couple. The centre will also provide transportation to and from Vancouver or Whistler for $138 per person including a raft trip and light lunch. For more information and details on guided walks in the area, contact the Brackendale Art Gallery on Government Road (Jan daily noon–5pm; rest of year Sat & Sun noon–10pm or by appointment on weekdays; ☎604/898-3333), which also exhibits paintings and sculptures by local artists and has a pleasant restaurant.

If Squamish's outdoor activities leave you cold, you might want to look in on the new **West Coast Railway Heritage Park**, Centennial Way (daily 10am–5pm; $6; ☎1-800/722-1233, *www.wcra.org*), signed off Hwy 99 about 3km north of town. The twelve-acre park contains 58 fine old railway carriages and locomotives in a pretty, natural setting.

Practicalities

Most of the relevant parts of the town are concentrated on Cleveland Avenue, including the **infocentre** (May–Sept daily 9am–5pm; Oct–April Mon–Fri 9am–5pm, Sat & Sun 10am–2pm; ☎604/892-9244, *www.squamishchamber.bc.ca*), the big IGA Plus supermarket and the most central **accommodation** if you're not at the hostel, the *August Jack Motor Inn* opposite the infocentre (☎604/892-3504; ③). If you want inside knowledge on the climbing or wildlife, be certain to stay at the superlative *Squamish Hostel* on Buckley Avenue (☎604/892-9240 or 1-800/449-8614; ①). The hostel is a clean and friendly place that offers a kitchen, common room and private rooms as well as shared accommodation. For home-made Mexican **food** the *Coyote Cantina*, on Cleveland Avenue, is great for snacks and meals or there's vegetarian fare at the *Rainforest Grill*, just off 2nd Avenue. Sporty types hang out at the *Brew Pub*, also on Cleveland, which serves pub food and home-brewed beer.

If you're looking into **renting equipment**, Vertical Reality Sports Centre on Cleveland Road (☎604/892-8248) rents out climbing shoes ($10 a day) and mountain bikes ($15–40 a day), whilst Slipstream Rock & Ice (☎604/898-4891 or 1-800/616-1325, *www.slipstreamadventures.com*) offers rock and ice climbing guiding and instruction. Most of their tours are for two days and range from $148–248 and they teach all abilities. If you are here to climb, there is one key **guide**, available from bookstores in Vancouver (see "Listings" on p.324) as well as the climbing shops in Squamish: *The Climbers Guide to Squamish* by Kevin McLane (Elaho, $34.95). If the new craze of bouldering is your thing then *Squamish Boulder Problems* by Peter Michael (Highball, $19.90) has all the information you need.

Incidentally, if you're in town in August, Squamish proves it hasn't forgotten its lumbering roots by holding what it deems to be the World Lumberjack Competition, and in July the place goes nuts with a ten-day Adventure Festival (☎1-888/684-8828) that kicks off with a chariot race – garbage cans mounted on wheels and pulled by mountain bikes – and includes a mountain bike race with over 800 riders, street hockey, rock-climbing clinics and white-water competitions.

Garibaldi Provincial Park

After about 5km, the road north of Squamish enters the classic river, mountain and forest country of the BC interior. The journey thereafter up to Whistler is a joy, with only the march of electricity pylons to take the edge off an idyllic drive.

Unless you're skiing, **Garibaldi Provincial Park** is the main incentive for heading this way. As you'd expect, it's a huge and unspoilt area which combines all the usual breathtaking ingredients of lakes, rivers, forests, glaciers and the peaks of the Coast Mountains (Wedge Mountain, at 2891m, is the park's highest point). Four rough roads access the park from points along the highway between Squamish and Whistler, but you'll need transport to reach the trailheads at the end of them. Pick up the excellent *BC Parks* pamphlet for Garibaldi from the Vancouver tourist office for a comprehensive rundown on all trails, campgrounds and the like. Unless you're camping, the only accommodation close to the park is at Whistler, though with an early start from Vancouver you could feasibly enjoy a good walk and return the same day.

There are five main areas with trails, of which the **Black Tusk/Garibaldi Lake** region is the most popular and probably most beautiful. Try the trail from the parking area at Rubble Creek to Garibaldi Lake (9km; 3hr one-way) or to Taylor Meadows (7km; 2hr 30min one-way). Further trails then fan out from Garibaldi Lake, including one to the huge basalt outcrop of **Black Tusk** (2316m), a rare opportunity to reach an alpine summit without any rock climbing. The other hiking areas from south to north are **Diamond Head**, **Cheakamus Lake**, **Singing Pass** and **Wedgemount Lake**. Access to each is clearly signed from the highway, and all have wilderness campgrounds and are explored by several trails of varying lengths. Outside these small defined areas, however, the park is untrammelled wilderness. Bear in mind there are also hiking possibilities outside the park from Whistler (see below), where in summer you can get a head start on hikes by riding up the ski lifts.

Whistler

WHISTLER, 56km beyond Squamish, is Canada's finest four-season resort, and frequently ranks among most people's world top-five winter ski resorts. In 1996, for the first time ever, *Ski*, *Snow Country* and *Skiing* magazines were unanimous in voting it North America's top skiing destination. Skiing and snowboarding are clearly the main activities, but all manner of other winter sports are possible and in summer the lifts keep running to provide supreme highline hiking and other outdoor activities (not to mention North America's finest summer skiing). Standards are high, and for those raised on the queues and waits at European resorts, the ease with which you can get onto the slopes here will come as a pleasant surprise.

The resort consists of two adjacent but separate mountains – **Whistler** (2182m) and **Blackcomb** (2284m) – each with their own extensive lift and chair systems, and each covered in a multitude of runs. Both lift systems are accessed from the resort's heart, the purpose-built and largely pedestrianized **Whistler Village**, the tight-clustered focus of many hotels, shops, restaurants and après-ski activity. Around this core are two other "village" complexes, Upper Village and the recently completed Village North. Around 6km to the south of Whistler Village is **Whistler Creek** (also with a gondola and lift base), which has typically been a cheaper alternative but is now undergoing a $50 million redevelopment that will see its accommodation and local services duplicating those

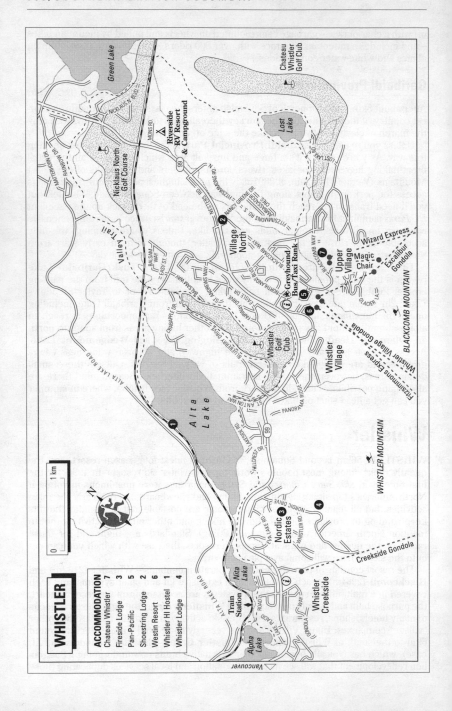

WHISTLER

ACCOMMODATION
Chateau Whistler 7
Fireside Lodge 3
Pan-Pacific 5
Shoestring Lodge 2
Westin Resort 6
Whistler HI Hostel 1
Whistler Lodge 4

of its famous neighbour. In truth the whole ribbon of land on and just off the main Hwy 99 from Whistler Creek to Whistler Village is gradually being developed – Whistler is the single fastest-growing municipality in BC.

Arrival, information and accommodation

There are several ways of **getting to** Whistler. If you're flying to Vancouver on a skiing package (or otherwise) and want to get straight to the resort, then Perimeter (☎604/266-5386, *www.perimeterbus.com*) run a **bus shuttle** from the airport and various Vancouver hotels to Whistler, with drop-offs at Whistler Creek and several major hotels in and around Whistler Village. Reservations are required for the service, with prepayment by credit card and cancellations allowed up to 24 hours in advance (May–Nov 7 daily, 2 of which are express and do not stop at Vancouver hotels; $46 one-way; Dec–April Mon–Fri 8 daily, including 5 express, Sat & Sun 11 daily, including 9 express $49; 2hr 30min–3hr). Greyhound Buses (☎604/482-8747 in Vancouver, 604/932-5031 in Whistler or 1-800/661-TRIP from anywhere in North America, *www.greyhound.ca*) run six daily **bus** services from Vancouver's bus depot (see p.391) to the Village (2hr 30min; $20 one-way) via Britannia Beach, Whistler Creek and other stops en route. In winter (Dec–April) Greyhound's ski express leaves Vancouver at 6.30am and goes non-stop to Whistler arriving at 8.30am. You can also travel by BC Rail **train** (☎604/984-5246 or 1-800/663-8238, *www.bcrail.com/bcrpass*) from the station in North Vancouver to Whistler's station near Whistler Creek (1 daily; $33; 2hr 35min). Local buses, WAVE (☎604/932-4040) run a free shuttle service around Whistler Village, Village North and Upper Village as well as buses to Whistler Creek and other destinations ($1.50 flat fare, 5-day pass $5). If you need taxis to get around locally, try Sea to Sky Taxi (☎604/932-3333).

Many people in winter are likely to be on a package. If not, or if you're here in summer, all local **accommodation** can be booked through **Whistler Central Reservations** (☎604/664-5625 or 1-800/WHISTLER, *www.tourismwhistler.com*), who can help find a room or a condo for you in an appropriate price bracket. If you're booking for winter, note that reservations should be made well in advance. Such is demand that many hotels have a thirty-day cancellation window and may insist on a minimum of three-days' stay. Accommodation is most expensive from February to the end of March and cheapest from May to mid-June and mid-September to mid-November.

For recorded **information** on Whistler-Blackcomb call ☎1-800/766-0449 (☎604/664-5614 from Vancouver or ☎604/932-3434 from Whistler, *www.whistler-blackcomb.com*). Tourism Whistler (☎604/932-3298) is another source of information; they also run the Whistler Activity and Information Centre, in the green-roofed Conference Centre near the Village Square (daily 9am–5pm; ☎604/932-2394). Though they can help with masses of comfortable hotel, chalet and lodge accommodation (remember that chalets can put extra beds in double rooms at nominal rates), and book activities and tickets for local events, they do cater towards the top-end of the market. Whistler Creek is home to the more down-to-earth and friendly **Chamber of Commerce**, 2097 Lake Placid Rd (daily 9am–5pm; longer hours in summer; ☎604/932-5528). Pick up a copy of *Pique*, the free local newspaper available in bars and at the information centres – it'll keep you abreast of happening events.

If you're going to do Whistler in style, the top resort **hotel** is the $75 million *Chateau Whistler* on Blackcomb Way (☎604/938-8000; ⑦). In the same league is the spanking new all-suite *Westin Resort and Spa* (☎1-888/634-5577, *www.westinwhistler.com*; ⑦) with ski-in, ski-out facilities and the *Pan-Pacific* (☎1-888/905-9995, *www.panpac.com*; ⑥). At the other end of the scale is the **youth hostel** right on the shores of Alta Lake at 5678 Alta Lake Rd, one of the nicest hostels in BC (☎604/932-5492, *www.hihostels.bc.ca*; ①), a signposted forty-minute walk from Whistler Creek or ten-minute drive to the village centre; local buses (☎604/932-4020) leave the gondola base in the Village four times a day for the hos-

HITTING THE SLOPES

The **skiing and snowboarding season** for Whistler and Blackcomb begins in late November, sometimes earlier if nature permits. While the amount of snow varies from year-to-year, the yearly average is a whopping thirty-feet of snowfall. Blackcomb closes at the end of April, while Whistler stays open until early June. Then the mountains switch places, as Whistler closes and Blackcomb reopens in early June for glacier skiing and snowboarding, staying open until late July. The lifts are open daily 8.30am–3pm, and until 4pm after January.

Lift tickets give you full use of both Whistler and Blackcomb mountains, and it will take days for even the most advanced skiier or snowboarder to cover all the terrain. Tickets are available from the lift base in Whistler Village, but the queues can be horrendous. Instead, plan ahead and purchase your tickets online from *www.whistler.net*, or in Vancouver from Sport Mart at either 495 8th Ave W (☎604/873-6737) or 735 Thurlow St (☎604/683-2433). Your hotel can often set you up with tickets if you pre-book far enough in advance. Call ☎1-877/932-0606 from North America or ☎604/932-0606 from Europe for more information.

Prices increase in peak season – over Christmas and New Year and from mid-February to mid-March – and lift tickets are subject to a seven percent tax. You can save money by purchasing your lift pass before the end of September or, if you plan to ski regularly at Whistler, by purchasing an **Express Card**. These cost $79 for adults, $67 for youths and $39 for seniors, and are valid all season – scan it each time you ski and it automatically charges your credit card. Your first day skiing is free and then you pay a discounted rate of $35–53 depending on the season; call ☎1-800/766-0449 for more details.

	Adults		Youth (13–18)		Child and Senior (65 plus)	
	Regular	Peak	Regular	Peak	Regular	Peak
One-day	$59	$61	$50	$52	$30	$31
Seven-day	$378	$392	$321	$333	$189	$196
Sightseeing	$21	$21	$18	$18	$14	$14
Afternoon	$44	$46	$37	$39	$21	$23

Intermediate and expert skiers can join the **free tours** of the mountains that leave at 10.30am and 1pm daily. The Whistler All-Mountain tour departs from the Guest Satisfaction Centre at the top of the Whistler Village gondola. The Blackcomb All-Mountain tour meets at the Mountain Tour Centre, top of the Solar Coaster Express, or at the *Glacier Creek Lodge*. To explore Blackcomb's glaciers join the tour at the *Glacier Creek Lodge*, weather permitting.

For **snow conditions** call ☎604/932-4211 in Whistler or ☎604/687-7507 from Vancouver.

tel and the journey takes fifteen minutes ($1.50; note that BC Rail trains may sometimes stop alongside the hostel if you ask the conductor). As it's popular year-round, reserve ahead. The *Shoestring Lodge*, with an adjacent pub, is a good and equally popular alternative. It has private rooms with small bathrooms (②) as well as dorms (①) and is a ten-minute walk north of Whistler Village on Nancy Greene Drive (☎604/932-3338). Another reasonable choice is the *Fireside Lodge*, 2117 Nordic Drive (☎604/932-4545; ②) at Nordic Estates, 3km south of the village. Finally, you could try the *Whistler Lodge* (☎604/932-6604 or 228-5851; ①), also on Nordic Drive, which is owned by the University of British Columbia but lets non-students stay; check-in time is from 4pm to 10pm. Best of the **campgrounds** is the *Riverside RV Resort and Campground* (☎1-877/905-5533, *www.whistlercamping.com*), 2km north of Whistler Village, which now has brand new five-person log cabins for $79–99 and sites for $20.

Whistler Village

WHISTLER VILLAGE is the key to the resort, a newish and rather characterless and pastel-shaded conglomeration of hotels, restaurants, mountain-gear shops and more loud people in fluorescent clothes than are healthy in one place at the same time. Its name is said to derive from the piercing whistle of the marmot, a small and rather chubby mammal, which emits a distinctive shriek as a warning call. Others say the name comes from the sound of the wind whistling through Singing Pass up in the mountains. Whatever its origins, the village has all the facilities of any normal village, with the difference that they all charge more than what you'd pay anywhere else. At the same time it's a somewhat soulless place, very much a resort complex rather than an organic village, though for most people who are here to indulge on the slopes, character is a secondary consideration. Huge amounts of money have been invested in the area since the resort opened in 1980, and the investments have paid off well; the resort's services, lifts and general overall polish are almost faultless, and those of its nearby satellites are not far behind. The resort area averages more than two million visitors a year, and Whistler's challenge is now turning towards being able to rein in development before it spoils the scenery, killing the goose laying the golden egg.

Skiing and Snowboarding on Whistler and Blackcomb

Winter-sports enthusiasts can argue long and late over the relative merits of **WHISTLER MOUNTAIN** and its rival, Blackcomb Mountain, both accessed from Whistler Village's lifts. Together they have more than two-hundred runs, thirty-three lifts, twelve vast, high-alpine bowls, and three major glaciers. Both are great mountains, and both offer top-notch skiing and boarding, as evidenced by world class events like the Snowboard FIS World Cup each December and North America's largest annual sports event the World Ski and Snowboard Festival in April – both take place on Whistler. Each mountain has a distinctive character, however, at least for the time being, for major injections of money are on the way to upgrade Whistler Mountain's already impressive facilities. Traditionally Whistler has been seen as the more intimate and homely of the two mountains, somewhere you can ski or board for days on end and never have to retrace your steps. **Highlight runs** for intermediates or confident novices are Hwy 86, Burnt Stew Basin and Franz's Run, a high-velocity cruiser that drops virtually from the tree line right down to Whistler Creek. Real thrill-seekers should head to three steep above-tree-line swaths of snow: Harmony Bowl, Symphony Bowl and Glacier Bowl. Of the 3600 odd acres of terrain, twenty percent is beginner, fifty-five percent intermediate and twenty-five percent expert. There are over a hundred marked **trails** and seven major bowls. **Lifts** include two high-speed gondolas, six high-speed quads, two triple and one double chair lift, and five surface lifts. Snowboarders are blessed with a half-pipe and park. Total vertical drop is 1530m and the longest run is 11km.

    BLACKCOMB MOUNTAIN, the "Mile-High Mountain", is a ski area laden with superlatives: the most modern resort in Canada or the US, North America's finest summer skiing (on Horstman Glacier), the continent's longest unbroken fall-line skiing and the longest *and* second longest lift-serviced vertical falls in North America (1609m and 1530m). In shape, its trail and run-system resembles an inverted triangle, with ever more skiing and boarding possibilities branching off the higher you go. The most famous run is the double black diamond Couloir Extreme, the first such run in Canada and one of several precipitous chutes in the Rendezvous Bowl. Three other **runs** are also particularly renowned: the Zig-Zag, a long, winding cruise; Blackcomb Glacier, one of North America's longest above-tree-line runs; and Xhiggy's Meadow on the Seventh Heaven Express. If you're here to board or ski in summer, two T-bars take you up to the wide open cruising terrain on Horstman Glacier.

    Blackcomb is slightly smaller than Whistler, at 3341 acres, but has a similar breakdown of **terrain** (fifteen percent beginner, fifty-five percent intermediate and thirty percent

ACTIVITIES

Outdoor activities aside, there's not a lot else to do in Whistler save sit in the cafés and watch the world go by. In summer, though, chances are you'll be here to walk or mountain bike. If you're **walking**, remember you can ride the ski lifts up onto both mountains for tremendous views and easy access to high-altitude trails (July to early Sept daily 10am–8pm; early Sept to late Sept daily 10am–5pm; late Sept to mid-Oct Sat & Sun 10am–5pm; adults $21, youth and seniors $18). Free mountain walking tours are offered daily at 12.30pm & 2.30pm; call ☎1-800/766-0449 for more details. **Mountain bikers** can also take bikes up and ride down, for an additional $3 charge for the bike. You must have a helmet and the bike undergoes a safety inspection. If you're going it alone, pick up the duplicated sheet of biking and hiking trails from the infocentres (see p.397), or better yet buy the 1:50,000 *Whistler and Garibaldi Region* **map**. The two most popular shorter walks are the **Rainbow Falls** and the six-hour **Singing Pass** trails. Other good choices are the four-kilometre trail to Cheakamus Lake or any of the high alpine hikes accessed from the Upper Gondola station (1837m) on Whistler Mountain or the Seventh Heaven lift on Blackcomb: you can, of course, come here simply for the view. Among the walks from Whistler Mountain gondola station, think about the **Glacier Trail** (2.5km round trip; 150m ascent; 1hr) for views of the snow and ice in Glacier Bowl – snowshoe rental and tours are possible to let you cross some of the safer snowfields ($15 a day; for tours call Outdoor Adventures ☎604/932-0647 or Whistler Cross Country Ski & Hike ☎604/932-7711 or 1-888/771-2382, *www.whistlerhikingcentre.com*). Or go for the slightly more challenging **Little Whistler Trail** (3.8km round trip; 265m ascent; 1hr 30min–2hr), which takes you to the summit of Little Whistler Peak (2115m) and grand views of Black Tusk in Garibaldi Provincial Park. Remember to time your hike to get back to the gondola station for the last ride down (times vary according to season).

If the high-level stuff seems too daunting (it shouldn't be – the trails are good) – then there are plenty of trails (some surfaced) for bikers, walkers and in-line skating around the Village. There are also numerous operators offering guided walks and bike rides to suit all abilities, as well as numerous **rental outlets** for bikes, blades and other equipment around the Village. **All-Terrain Vehicles (ATVs)** can be rented from Canadian All Terrain Adventures (☎1-877/938-1616, *www.cdn-snowmobile.com*) for guided tours that include splurges through mud-pits. If you want to go **horseriding**, contact Edgewater Outdoor Centre (☎604/932-3389), The Adventure Ranch (☎604/932-5078) or Cougar Mountain (☎604/932-4086). Whistler Jet Boat Adventure Ranch (☎604/932-4078) can set you up with **jet boating**, white-water and float **rafting**, as will Whistler River Adventures (☎604/932-3532, *www.whistler-river-adv.com*) and Whistler Jet Boating (☎604/932-3389). You can play tennis at several public courts, or play squash or **swim** at the Meadow Park Sports Centre (☎604/938-7275). If you're a **golfer** the area has four great courses, including one designed by Jack Nicklaus – *Golf* magazine called Whistler "one of the best golf resorts in the world". Despite a recent upgrade, the Whistler Golf Club course remains the cheapest course at $115 (☎1-800/376-1777 or 604/932-3280), while the others, including Nicklaus North (☎604/938-9898), all cost from about $125 at low season to $185 at peak season in July and August. After all that activity there are umpteen **spas** for massage, mud baths and treatments that soothe all aches and pains – try Whistler Body Wrap (☎604/932-4710), Blue Highways Shiatsu and Massage (☎604/938-0777) or for utter luxury Avello (☎604/935-3444).

expert). **Lifts** are one high-speed gondola, six express quads, three triple chair lifts, and seven surface lifts. There are over a hundred marked trails, two glaciers and five bowls along with two half-pipes and a park for snowboarders. Even if you're not skiing, come up here (summer or winter) on the ski lifts to walk, enjoy the **view** from the top of the mountain, or to eat in the restaurants like *Rendezvous* or *Glacier Creek*. If you want some **cross-country skiing** locally, the best spots are 22km of groomed trails around Lost Lake and the Chateau Whistler golf course, all easily accessible from Whistler Village.

Eating, drinking and nightlife

When it comes to **food and drink**, Whistler Village and its satellites are loaded with cafés and some ninety restaurants, though none really have an "address" as such. These can come and go at an alarming rate, but one top-rated restaurant of long standing is *Araxi's Restaurant and Antipasto Bar* in Village Square (☎604/932-4540), which serves up West Coast-style fare and inventive pasta dishes – try the amazing mussels in chilli, vermouth and lemon grass followed by a perfect crème brulee for desert. Equally fine, the *Rim Rock Café & Oyster Bar* in the *Highland Lodge* (☎604/932-5565) is excellent for seafood. For an utter splurge the *Bearfoot Bistro* on Village Green (☎604/932-3433) is an ostentatious place with the likes of black and white truffle salad and yellowfin tuna parfait with Beluga caviar on the menu. For a less pricey outing try the Italian *Quattro at Pinnacle* on Main Street (☎604/905-4844), with a menu of Roman and North Italian dishes that includes a lovely rack of lamb with chestnut polenta. In winter and busy summer evenings you'll need to book at all of these. Other more down-to-earth places to try are *Trattoria di Umberto* (☎604/932-5858) in the *Mountainside Lodge*, beside the *Pan-Pacific Hotel*, for a cosy Italian meal. *Thai One On* (☎604/932-4822) for spicy Thai in the Upper Village, and *Zeuski's* (☎604/932-6009), a reasonably priced Greek place in the Town Plaza. For cheap eats, you are pretty much limited to fast-food places like *Pita Pit* and *Subway* located in the Royal Bank building on Whistler Way. If you're looking to recharge in a **café** after a day on the mountain, try *Peake's Coffee House,* a block behind Main Street near the Gazebo (with Internet access at 20¢ a minute), or *Vitality 4U,* a great juice place on Main Street.

Winter or summer Whistler enjoys a lot of **nightlife** and aprés-ski activity, with visitors being bolstered by the large seasonal workforce – Whistler needs over four thousand people just to keep the show on the road – among which a vocal Antipodean presence figures large. If you want relative peace and quiet, the key spot is the smartish *Mallard Bar* (☎604/938-8000) in the *Chateau Whistler* hotel. If you're just off Whistler Mountain, the aprés-ski haunt is the sports-crazy *Longhorn Saloon* (☎604/932-5999) in the Village at the *Carleton Lodge*, with the lively beer-heavy *Merlin's* (☎604/938-7700) in the *Blackcomb Daylodge* performing the same function for Blackcomb. *The Brew House* is a microbrewery at the far end of Village North with a nice view of the waterfall. For people-watching, *Citta* in the Village Square and *Tapley's Neighbourhood Pub* both have wrapround patios whilst *The Amsterdam Café* is a relaxed hangout in the Village Square. Down in Whistler Creek, *Hoz's* on Lake Placid Road is the place for liquid refreshment. As evening draws on, make for *Buffalo Bill's* (☎604/932-6613) at the *Timberline Lodge*, a thirty-something bar/club with comedy nights, hypnosis shows, 13 video screens, a huge dance floor and live music.

A younger set, snowboarding hipsters among them, make for **clubs** in both the Village and North Village. These include *Tommy Africa's*, aka Tommy's (☎604/932-6090), who host a very popular 1980s dance night on Mondays; *Savage Beagle Club* (☎604/938-3337), a small, split-level cocktail bar and danceteria; *Maxx Fish* (☎604/932-1904), home to hip-hop and house DJs; the massive mainstream dance club/restaurant/live music venue *Alpen Rock* (☎604/938-0082); and the lively *Moe Joe's* (☎604/935-1152), where locals hang out to catch DJs and live music. Located in North Village, *Garkinfels*, aka Garf's (☎604/32-2323), is currently Whistler's funkiest nightclub.

North to Lillooet

Hwy 99 funnels down to two slow lanes at **PEMBERTON**, where condos are now mushrooming in the wake of Whistler's popularity – all the skiing here is via helicopter or hiking. Beyond, you're treated to some wonderfully wild country in which Vancouver and even Whistler seem a long way away. Patches of forest poke through rugged mountainsides and scree slopes, and a succession of glorious lakes culminate in Sefton Lake, whose hydroelectric schemes feed power into the grid as far south as Arizona, accounting for the pylons south of Whistler.

At the lumber town of **LILLOOET** the railway meets the Fraser River, which marks a turning point in the scenery as denuded crags and hillsides increasingly hint at the *High Noon*-type ranching country to come. In July and August, the rocky banks and bars of the sluggish, mud-coloured river immediately north of town are dotted with vivid orange and blue tarpaulins. These belong to aboriginal Canadians who still come to catch and dry salmon as the fish make their way upriver to spawn. It's one of the few places where this tradition is continued and it is well worth a stop to watch. The town boasts four central **motels** if you need to stay: best are the *Mile 0 Motel*, 616 Main St (☎604/256-7511 or 1-888/766-4530; ②), downtown, overlooking the river and mountains (kitchenettes available in some units for self-catering), and the *4 Pines Motel* on the corner of 8th Avenue and Russell Street at 108 8th Ave, also with kitchenettes (☎604/256-4247; ②). The **infocentre/museum** is in the old church at 790 Main St (mid-May to June Mon–Sat noon–3pm; July & Aug daily 9am–5pm; Sept Tues–Sat noon–3pm; Oct Wed–Sat 12.30–2.30pm; ☎604/256-4308), with displays of local life past and present. The nearest **campground** is the riverside *Cayoosh Creek* on Hwy 99 within walking distance of downtown (☎604/256-4180; $13; mid-April to mid-Oct).

From Lillooet, Hwy 99 heads east for 50km to Hwy 97; you can then either turn south towards Cache Creek (see p.409), or snake your way up north to the goldfields of the Cariboo.

The Cariboo

The Cariboo is the name given to the broad, rolling ranching country and immense forests of British Columbia's interior plateau, which extend north of Lillooet between the Coast Mountains to the west and Cariboo Mountains to the east. The region contains by far the dullest scenery in the province, and what little interest it offers – aside from fishing and boating on thousands of remote lakes – comes from its **gold-mining** heritage. Initially exploited by fur traders to a small degree, the region was fully opened up following the discovery of gold in 1858 in the lower Fraser Valley. The building of the **Cariboo Wagon Road**, a stagecoach route north out of Lillooet, spread gold fever right up the Fraser watershed as men leapfrogged from creek to creek, culminating in the big finds at Williams Creek in 1861 and Barkerville a year later.

Much of the old Wagon Road is today retraced by lonely **Hwy 97** (the Cariboo Hwy) and **VIA Rail**, which run in tandem through hour after hour of straggling pine forests and past the occasional ranch and small, marsh-edged lake – scenery that strikes you as pristine and pastoral for a while but which soon leaves you in a tree-weary stupor. If you're forced to stop over, there are innumerable lodges, ranches and motels on or just off the highway, and you can pick up copious material on the region at the Vancouver tourist office or infocentres en route.

Clinton and Williams Lake

A compact little village surrounded by green pastures and tree-covered hills, **CLINTON** – named after a British duke – marks the beginning of the heart of Cariboo country. The town has a couple of **bed and breakfasts**, a new **campground**, *Clinton Pines Campground,* 1204 Caribbo Ave (☎459-0030; $14–24; May–Sept) and a

---

The telephone code for British Columbia outside of the Vancouver area is ☎250.

motel – the *Nomad* (☎459-2214 or 1-888/776-6623; ②). The three tiny settlements beyond Clinton at 70, 100 and 150 Mile House are echoes of the old roadhouses built by men who were paid by the mile to blaze the Cariboo Wagon Road – which is doubtless why 100 Mile House is well short of a 100 miles from the start of the road. 100 Mile House has a year-round **infocentre** at 422 Cariboo Hwy 97 S (May–Sept daily 9am–6pm; Oct–April Mon–Fri 9am–4pm; ☎395-5353) for details of the fishing, riding and other local outdoor pursuits. There are also a handful of **motels** in or a few kilometres away from town, the biggest in-town choice being the *Red Coach Inn*, 170 Hwy 97 N (☎395-2266 or 1-800/663-8422; ④). The central *Imperial* is smaller and cheaper (☎395-2471; ③).

WILLIAMS LAKE, 14km north of 150 Mile House and still 238km south of Prince George, is a busy and drab transport centre that huddles in the lee of a vast crag on terraces above the lake of the same name. It has plenty of motels, B&Bs, boat launches and swimming spots south of the town – but it's hardly a place you'd want to spend any time, unless you're dead-beat after driving or around on the first weekend in July for its famous **rodeo**. The year-round **infocentre** is at 1148 Broadway S (May–Sept daily 9am–5pm; Oct–April Mon–Fri 9am–4pm; ☎392-5025).

Bella Coola

Highway 20 branches west from Williams Lake, a part-paved, part-gravel road that runs 455km to **BELLA COOLA**, a village likely to gain an ever greater tourist profile in the wake of the new visitor-oriented ferry service from Port Hardy on Vancouver Island (see p.384). Most of the road ploughs through the interminable forest of the Cariboo Plateau, but the last 100km or so traverses the high and stunningly spectacular peaks of the Coast Mountains and Tweedsmuir Provincial Park. Just outside the park you encounter the notorious "Hill", a hugely winding and precipitous stretch of highway barely tamed by the various upgradings over the years. Until 1953 there was no road link here at all. Instead there was a sixty-kilometre gap in the mountain stretch, a missing link the state refused to bridge. In response the locals of Bella Coola took it upon themselves to build the road on their own, completing their so-called Freedom Road in three years. Previously the settlement was the domain of the Bella Coola, or Nuxalk, a group visited by George Vancouver as early as 1793. In 1869 the Hudson's Bay Company opened a trading post. One house belonging to a company clerk is now all that remains. Besides a small museum and glorious scenery, Bella Coola is hardly stacked with sights. Norwegian settlers, however, perhaps drawn by the fjord-like scenery nearby, were notable early pioneers, and language, heritage and buildings – notably the square-logged barns – all show a Scandinavian touch. **Hagensborg**, a village 18km east of Bella Coola, preserves a particularly strong Nordic flavour. About 10km from the village, roughly midway to Bella Coola, are the **Thorsen Creek Petroglyphs**, a hundred or so rock drawings: the infocentre (see below) should be able to fix you up with a guide to explore the site.

No buses serve Bella Coola and beyond the village there is no onward road route: unless you fly out, you'll have to either head back the way you came or pick up the new **Discovery Coast Passage** boats to Port Hardy that stop off at the port. Boats leave three times a week at 7.30am or 8.30am, arriving in Port Hardy at around 9.30pm that evening or 7.45am or 9am the following morning depending on the number of stops en route (fares are $110 per person or $220 per car; see p.382 for full details of the service). If you want to indulge in a plane in or out of town, contact Wilderness Airlines (☎982-2225 or 1-800/665-9453).

Bella Coola's **infocentre** is on the Mackenzie Hwy near town (Mon–Fri 9.30am–4.30pm; ☎799-5638). The new ferry service will probably lead to the opening of more hotels and restaurants: currently **accommodation** is provided by the *Bella Coola Valley Inn* (☎799-5316; ③), closest hotel to the ferry terminal, and the *Bella Coola Motel*

(☎799-5323; ③) at the corner of Burke and Clayton – both places are downtown. There's also the *Bay Motor Hotel* on Hwy 20, 14km east of the town and 1km from the airport (☎982-2212 or 1-888/982-2212; ③).

Along Hwy 97: north of Williams Lake

North of Williams Lake on Hwy 97, the **Fraser River** re-enters the scenic picture and, after a dramatic stretch of canyon, reinstates more compelling hills and snatches of river meadows. This also marks the start, however, of some of the most concerted **logging operations** in all British Columbia, presaged by increasing numbers of crude pepper-pot kilns used to burn off waste wood. By **QUESNEL**, home of the "world's largest plywood plant", you're greeted with scenes out of an environmentalist's nightmare: whole mountainsides cleared of trees, hill-sized piles of sawdust, and unbelievably large lumber mills surrounded by stacks of logs and finished timber that stretch literally as far as the eye can see. If you're stuck for accommodation (there are a dozen or so hotels) or tempted by any of the many mill tours, contact the **infocentre** in Le Bourdais Park at 705 Carson Ave (March–Oct Mon–Fri 9am–4pm; ☎992-8716 or 1-800/992-4922).

Barkerville

Most people who take the trouble to drive this route detour from Quesnel to **Barkerville Provincial Historic Park**, 90km to the east in the heart of the Cariboo Mountains, the site of the Cariboo's biggest gold strike and an invigorating spot in its own right, providing a much-needed jolt to the senses after the sleepy scenery to the south (June–Sept daily 8am–8pm; $5.50). In 1862 a Cornishman named Billy Barker idly staked a claim here and after digging down a metre or so was about to pack up and head north. Urged on by his mates, however, he dug another couple of spadefuls and turned up a cluster of nuggets worth $600,000. Within months Barkerville, as it was later dubbed, had become the largest city in the region, and rode the boom for a decade until the gold finally ran out. Today numerous buildings have been restored, and the main administrative building has displays on mining methods and the gold rush, together with propaganda on their importance to the province.

If you want to **stay** under cover up here, there are just three options, all at **WELLS**, 8km west of the park: the *Hubs Motel* (☎994-3313; ②); the *Wells Hotel*, 2341 Pooley St (☎994-3427 or 1-800/860-2299; ④), a newly restored 1933 heritage country inn with licensed café and breakfast included; and the *White Cap Motor Inn* (☎994-3489 or 1-800/377-2028; ③) – the last also has RV and camping spaces for $10. Failing this you can **camp** at the three-way campground at Barkerville Provincial Park adjacent to the old town (reservations possible, see p.390; $9.50–12; June–Sept). Wells has an **infocentre** on Pooley Street, part of a small museum (summer only; ☎994-3237).

Vancouver to Kamloops

Many consider the region northeast of Vancouver up to Kamloops as little more than an area to speedily drive through on the way to more exciting prospects like the Okanagan or the Kootenays. While perhaps not completely false, there are a few relatively unknown reasons along the way to take the foot off the pedal and stop. Two major routes **connect Vancouver and Kamloops**, the latter an unexceptional town but almost unavoidable as the junction of major routes in the region. These days anyone in

If you're continuing from Quesnel north to Prince George and beyond, turn to Chapter Eight, "North to the Yukon", beginning on p.566.

any sort of hurry takes the **Coquihalla Highway** (Hwy 5). The scenery is unexceptional in the early part, but things look up considerably in the climb to the Coquihalla Pass (1244m), when forests, mountains and crashing rivers make a dramatic reappearance – compromised somewhat by old mines, clear-cuts (hillsides completely cleared of trees) and recent road-building scars. There's only a single exit, at the supremely missable town of Merritt, and literally no services for the entire 182km from **Hope** to Kamloops. Come stocked up with fuel and food, and be prepared to pay a toll ($10) at the top of the pass – a wind- and snow-whipped spot that must offer some of the loneliest employment opportunities in the province.

The older, slower and more scenic route from Vancouver is on the **Trans-Canada Highway** or by VIA Rail, both of which follow a more meandering course along the Thompson River and then the lower reaches of the Fraser River. For the first stretch you can also take the less busy Hwy 7, which follows the north shore of the Fraser River from Vancouver and passes by **Harrison Hot Springs** en route to Hope.

Hwy 7 to Hope

Flanked by dreary malls at first, the 150km drive on Hwy 7 from Vancouver to Hope cheers up considerably as the countryside opens up after the small town of **MISSION**, 30km into the journey. If you have the time, you might want to make a quick stop at **Xá:ytem**, BC's oldest dwelling site (late June to Sept daily 10am–4pm; rest of the year by appointment; ☎604/820-9725), located by the highway just before the east side of Mission. People have lived here for as long as nine-thousand years, and an ongoing archeological dig has uncovered numerous lithic (stone) artefacts including arrowheads and stones used for cutting and chopping – some were made from obsidian from Oregon, an indication of early trade routes. A newly built Stó:lo longhouse serves as the site's interpretation centre, and inside you can learn more about the excavations. Be sure to read up on the large boulder, known as Hatzic Rock, that rests on the grounds; it's a sacred spot to the aboriginal community, believed to be three si:yams (respected leaders) who had defied the wishes of the Creator and were turned to stone.

After Mission, the highway snakes through pretty farmland to **HARRISON HOT SPRINGS**, 129km from Vancouver and located on the southern edge of Harrison Lake. While natives believing in the healing properties of the springs came centuries ago, the springs were not popularized until they were "discovered" by gold prospectors in 1858; soon after the town became BC's first resort. Today, tourism remains Harrison Hot Spring's main industry, as attested by the number of modern condo-apartment buildings and motels lining the lake. Still, thanks to the beautiful mountain views, it remains a scenic spot, mercifully free of too much neon and tat. The lake itself is 60km long – making it one of the province's largest lakes – and its waters are very clean, but also very cold. The only swimming option is in the man-made lagoon on the lake's shore, but if you want to play in the lake, boats, windsurfers and jet-skis can be hired from the deck in front of the upmarket *Harrison Hot Springs Resort*. If you're here the weekend after Labor Day, make a point of seeing the incredible sand sculptures on the beach that are created for the **World Championship Sand Sculpture** competition.

To reach the **springs** themselves, it's a short walk along the shore and past the *Harrison Hot Springs Resort* – but they are a piping hot 165 degrees at the source. In order to make the spring water suitable for soaking, the waters are cooled to 100 degrees and redirected to the **Harrison Hot Springs Public Pool** (Mon–Thurs 9am–9pm, Fri 9am–10pm, Sat 8am–10pm, Sun 8am–9pm; $9) back in town on the intersection of Hot Springs Road and the Esplanade.

The **infocentre** (☎604/796-3425, *www.harrison.ca*) is located in an old logging camp bunkhouse on Hot Springs Road. For **accommodation** the cheapest **motel** is the *Bungalow,* 511 Lillooet Ave (☎ & fax 604/796-3536; ②), with self-contained lakeside cabins or the *Spa,* 140 Esplanade (☎604/796-2828 or 1-800/592-8828; ②), also by the lake, with in-house massages. *Harrison Heritage House and Kottage* at 312 Lillooet Ave (☎604/796-9552 or 1-800/331-8099; ④) is a pricey but beautiful **B&B** in one of the village's few heritage buildings. The *Harrison Hot Springs Resort* (☎604/796-2244 or 1-800/663-2266, *www.harrisonresort.com*; ⑤), a favourite of Clark Gable's in the 1950s, is a friendly place with indoor and outside pools piped from the springs. There are also ten cabins which are cheaper than the rooms, but these need to be booked well in advance. For **camping** there are several private campgrounds around but it's best to head for nearby *Sasquatch Provincial Park,* (reservations possible, see p.390; $9.50). **Eating** options are all along the Esplanade by the lake and you can settle for a variety of cuisines from the *Black Forest Steak and Schnitzel House* at no. 180 (☎604/796-9343) to the *Kitami* Japanese restaurant, 318 Hot Springs (☎604/796-2728). For snacks and coffees head for *Muddy Waters* also on Esplanade.

Hope

Reputedly christened by prospectors with a grounding in Dante, **HOPE** – as in "Abandon all hope . . ." – is a pleasant mountain-ringed town that achieved a certain fame as the place wasted in spectacular fashion by Sylvester Stallone at the end of *First Blood*, the first Rambo movie. Despite the number of roads that converge here – the Trans-Canada, Hwy 3 and the Coquihalla – it remains a remarkably unspoilt stopover. In the past it was rivers, not roads, that accounted for the town's growth: the Fraser and two of its major tributaries, the Skagit and Coquihalla, meet at the townsite. The aboriginal villages here were forced to move when a Hudson's Bay post was established in 1848, the status quo being further disturbed when the gold rush hit in 1858. The bust that followed boom in neighbouring places was averted in Hope, largely because its situation made it an important station stop on the Canadian Pacific. Today the town's pretty location, which catches visitors slightly unaware, is turning it into something of a sight in its own right.

The **infocentre** (daily: summer 8am–8pm; rest of year 9am–5pm; ☎604/869-2021, *www.hopechamber.bc.ca*) is the building next to the artfully dumped pile of antique farm machinery at 919 Water Ave. The town **museum** (May–Sept daily 9am–5pm; donation) is in the same building, and offers the usual hand-me-downs of Hope's erstwhile old-timers. Across the road, the lovely view over the Fraser as it funnels out of the mountains is one of the town's finest moments. Time permitting, drop by **Memorial Park** downtown, where trees ravaged by rot have been given a new lease of life by a local chainsaw sculptor. Nearby, the **Christ Church National Historic Site**, built in 1861, is one of BC's oldest churches still on its original site. Another one-off novelty is the "H" tree at the corner of 5th Street and Hudson's Bay Street, two trees cleverly entwined as saplings to grow together in the form of an "H" for Hope.

Hiking, fishing, canoeing, and even gold-panning are all popular time-wasters around the hundreds of local lakes and rivers, details of which are available from the infocentre. Of the hikes, the **Rotary Trail** (3km) to the confluence of the Fraser and Coquihalla rivers is popular, as is the more demanding clamber over gravel paths to the top of **Thacker Mountain** (5km). Another walking expedition worth pursuing is the dark jaunt through the **tunnels** of the abandoned Vancouver–Nelson railway, reached by a short trail from the **Coquihalla Canyon Recreation Area**, 6km northeast of town off Coquihalla Highway. This was one of the backcountry locations used during the filming of *First Blood*, and offers spectacular views over the cliffs and huge sand bars of the Coquihalla Gorge. **Kawkawa Lake Provincial Park**, 3km northeast of Hope off Hwy 3, is another popular mountain retreat, endowed with plenty of hiking, relaxing and swimming opportunities. The latest big thrill hereabouts, though, is **gliding**, or soaring, the prevailing westerly winds funnelling suddenly into the valley above Hope creating perfect thermals for the sport. The Vancouver Soaring Association (☎604/521-5501), at Hope airport, offer thirty-minute unpowered flights (no experience necessary; $90).

Practicalities

Most of what happens in Hope happens on Hwy 1, here known as Water Avenue. The Greyhound **bus terminal** (on Water Ave) is a critical juncture for bus travellers heading west to Vancouver, north to Kamloops or east to Penticton and the Okanagan. Cheap **motels** proliferate along Hwy 3 leaving town heading east, and though they're mostly all alike, the *Flamingo* (☎604/869-9610; ①), last on the strip, has a nice piney setting. Closer in on the same road, the *Best Western Heritage Inn*, 570 Hope-Princeton Way (☎604/869-7166 or 1-800/528-1234; ③), a lovely grey-wood building smothered in flowers, is also excellent. In town, the *Best Continental Motel*, 860 Fraser Ave (☎604/869-9726; ③), lies a block back from the main highway and is handy for the bus depot; or try the *Windsor Motel* overlooking the park at 778 3rd Ave (☎604/869-9944 or 1-888/588-9944; ②). **Campgrounds**, too, are numerous, but most are some way from downtown. The town site is at *Coquihalla Campground* (April–Oct; ☎604/869-7119 or 1-888/869-7118; $16–22), in a park setting off Hwy 3 and reached via 7th Avenue. The top of the pile is the *KOA Kampground*; 5km west of town on Flood Hope Road (☎604/869-9857 or 1-800/KOA-1631; $19; March–Oct).

Food facilities and late-night entertainment are limited in what is, despite Vancouver's proximity, still a small-time Canadian town. For snacks, try the *Hope Deli* or *Sharon's Lunchbox and Deli* on Wallace Street, or the rock-bottom café in the Greyhound station. For more ambitious fare, try the *Hope Hotel* or *Alpenhaus*, also on Wallace Street.

The Fraser Canyon

Veering north from Hope, the Trans-Canada runs up the Fraser River valley, squeezed here by the high ridges of the Cascade and Coast ranges into one of British Columbia's grandest waterways. Though it's now a transport corridor – the Canadian Pacific Railway also passes this way – the **Fraser Canyon** was long regarded as impassable; to negotiate it, the Trans-Canada is forced to push through tunnels, hug the Fraser's banks, and at times cling perilously to rock ledges hundreds of metres above the swirling waters.

The river is named after **Simon Fraser** (1776–1862), one of North America's most remarkable early explorers, who as an employee of the North West Company established western Canada's first white settlements: Fort McCleod (1805), Fort St James (1806), Fort Fraser (1806) and Fort George (1807). Having traced the route taken by fellow explorer Alexander Mackenzie across the continent, he set out in 1808 to establish a route to the Pacific and secure it for Britain against the rival claims of the US. Instead he travelled the entire 1300-kilometre length of a river – the Fraser – under the mistaken impression he was following the Columbia. "We had to pass where no man should venture", he wrote, making most of the journey on foot guided by local natives, pushing forward using ladders, ropes and improvised platforms to bypass rapids too treacherous to breach by boat. Some thirty-five days were needed to traverse the canyon alone. Reaching the river's mouth, where he would have glimpsed the site of present-day Vancouver, he realized his error and deemed the venture a commercial failure, despite the fact he had successfully navigated one of the continent's greatest rivers for the first time. Few people, needless to say, felt the need to follow Fraser's example until the discovery of **gold** near Yale in 1858; prospectors promptly waded in and panned every tributary of the lower Fraser until new strikes tempted them north to the Cariboo.

Yale

YALE, about 15km north of Hope, opens the canyon with a ring of plunging cliffs. Sitting at the river's navigable limit, it was once a significant site for Canada's aboriginal peoples, providing an important point of departure for the canoes of the Stó:lo ("People of the River"). Tribespeople would come from as far afield as Vancouver Island to plunder the rich salmon waters just above the present townsite. A Hudson's Bay Company post, The Falls, appeared here in the 1840s, later renamed in honour of James Murray Yale, commander of the HBC post at Fort Langley, then one of the predominant white outposts on the BC mainland. Within a decade it became the largest city in North America west of Chicago and north of San Francisco: during the 1858 gold rush, when it marked the beginning of the infamous Cariboo Wagon Road, Yale's population mushroomed to over 20,000, a growth only tempered by the end of the boom and the completion of the Canadian Pacific. Today it's a small lumber town of about 170, though a visit to the **Historic Yale Museum** (June–Sept daily 9am–6pm) on Hwy 1, known here as Douglas Street, offers an exhaustive account of the town's golden age. The **infocentre** is also in the museum (May–Sept daily 9am–6pm; ☎604/863-2324). The monument in front of the building is dedicated to the countless Chinese workers who helped build the Canadian Pacific, one of only a handful of such memorials. You might also want to pay homage at **Lady Franklin Rock**, the vast river boulder which blocked the passage of steamers beyond Yale. It takes its name from Lady Franklin, wife of Sir John Franklin, the Arctic explorer who vanished on a voyage to the Arctic in July 1845. Numerous expeditions set out to find him (with no luck), and it is said that Lady Franklin, on her own personal odyssey, came as far as Yale and its big boulder. Ask locals for directions. If you fancy a longer walk, take Hwy 1 a kilometre south out of the village for the trailhead of the Spirit Cave Trail, a one-hour walk with fine views of the mountains. For **rooms**, you can't do much better than the *Fort Yale Motel* (☎604/863-2216; ②) at the entrance to the Canyon. Some 11km north of Yale on Hwy 1, the *Colonial Inn* (☎604/863-2277; ②) has cabins and pitches ($12). If you're **camping**, though, you might want to push on 10km towards Hope on Hwy 1 to the *Emory Creek Provincial Park*, a large, peaceful wooded site with river walks and camping sites from April to October ($12).

Hell's Gate and Boston Bar

Around 10km north of Yale on Hwy 1 is the famous **HELL'S GATE**, where – in a gorge almost 180m deep – the huge swell of the Fraser is squeezed into a 38-metre channel of foaming water that crashes through the rocks with awe-inspiring ferocity. The water here is up to 60m deep and as fast-flowing as any you're likely to see. For a good view of the canyon, travel 2km north of Yale on Hwy 1 to the **Alexander Bridge Provincial Park**, where an old section of the highway drops to the Alexander Bridge for some startling panoramas. Eight kilometres further there's a certain amount of resort-like commercialism to negotiate to get down to the river and an "Air-Tram" (cable car) to pay for (daily: April & late Sept to Oct 10am–4pm; May to mid-June & early Sept 9am–5pm; mid-June to Aug 9am–6pm; Closed Nov to March; $10; ☎604/867-9277, *www.hellsgate.bc.ca*). Close by there are also displays on the various provisions made to help migrating **salmon** complete their journeys, which have been interrupted over the years by the coming of the road and railway beside the Fraser. The river is one of the key runs for Pacific salmon, and every summer and fall they fill the river as they head for tributaries and upstream lakes to spawn. The biggest obstacle to their passage came in 1913, when a landslide occurred during the construction of the Canadian Pacific Railway, yet it wasn't until 1945 that ladders were completed to bypass the fall. The numbers of salmon have never fully recovered.

    BOSTON BAR, 20km north of Yale, is also the main centre for **white-water** rafting trips down the Fraser as far as Yale. Various companies run several trips a week from

May to August; contact Frontier River Adventure for details (☎604/867-9244). The village's name, apparently, was coined by locals in villages nearby amazed at the number of American prospectors who seemed to hail from Boston. A "bar", by contrast, was the name given to places where miners stopped to make camp en route for the goldfields. To **stay** locally, make for the *Blue Lake Lodge* (☎604/867-9246 or 1-877/867-9246; ②), located a kilometre east on Blue Lake Road off the highway 15km north of Boston Bar. The only local **campground**, the *Canyon Alpine RV Park & Campground* (☎604/867-9734 or 1-800/644-7275; $18–22), 5km north, also has a restaurant.

Cache Creek

CACHE CREEK has a reputation as a hitchhiker's black hole and indeed is the sort of sleepy place you could get stuck in for days. Locals also say it didn't help that an infamous child murderer, Charles Olsen, was captured nearby in 1985 – since then they've been understandably wary of picking up strangers. The town's name is accounted for by a variety of legends, the most romantic version concerning a couple of prospectors who buried a hoard of gold and never returned to pick it up. Sadly, it's likelier to derive from early trappers' more prosaic habit of leaving a cache of supplies at points on a trail to be used later.

Cache Creek is known as the "Arizona of Canada" for its baking summer climate, which settles a heat-wasted somnolence on its dusty streets. The parched, windswept mountains roundabout are anomalous volcanic intrusions in the regional geology, producing a legacy of hard rock and semi-precious stones – including jade – that attract climbers and rock hounds. There's not much else to do here; you can watch semi-precious stones being worked at several places, or check out **Hat Creek Ranch** (mid-May to Sept daily 10am–6pm; $5), a collection of original buildings including a log stopping house, the last remaining of its type, and a reconstruction of a Shuswap village. It's located ten minutes north of Cache Creek by the junction of Hwys 97 and 99 (the original Cariboo Wagon Rd). For more local insights visit the **infocentre** on the northwest side of town at 1340 Hwy 97 near the main road junction (summer daily 9am–6pm; ☎604/457-5306). If you're stranded, try one of half-a-dozen **motels**, the most interesting of which is the bizarrely built *Castle Inn*, 1153 E TransCanada (☎604/457-9547 or 1-800/457-9547; ②). Less eccentric are the *Bonaparte* on Hwy 97 N (☎604/457-9693 or 1-888/922-1333; ③), with large heated pool, and the central *Sage Hills Motel*, 1390 Hwy 97 N (☎ & fax 604/457-6451; ②), also with pool. The nearest **campground**, complete with laundry, hot showers and heated outdoor pool, is the *Brookside* (☎604/457-6633; $16–20; April–Oct), located 1km east of town on the main highway.

Kamloops

Almost any trip in southern British Columbia brings you sooner or later to **KAMLOOPS**, a town which has been a transport centre from time immemorial – its name derives from the Shuswap word for "meeting of the rivers" – and which today marks the meeting point of the Trans-Canada and Yellowhead (South) highways, the region's principal transcontinental roads, as well as the junction of the Canadian Pacific and Canadian National railways. The largest interior town in southern British Columbia (pop. 82,000), it's fairly unobjectionable, except when the wind blows from the uptown sawmills, bringing in a putrid smell that hangs heavy in the air. If you're on public transport, there's no particular need to spend any time here; if you're camping or driving, however, it makes a convenient provisions stop, especially for those heading north on Hwy 5 or south on the Coquihalla Hwy, neither of which has much in the way of facilities.

The telephone code for British Columbia outside of the Vancouver area is ☎250.

Kamloops is determinedly functional and not a place to spend a happy day wandering, but its downtown does have a spanking new **Art Gallery**, the largest in BC's interior – not that it has much competition. Located in the heart of downtown at 465 Victoria St at 5th (May–Sept Mon, Fri & Sat 10am–5pm, Tues–Thurs 10am–9pm, Sun noon–4pm; Oct–April Mon–Wed, Fri & Sat 10am–5pm, Thurs 10am–9pm, Sun 10am–4pm; $5), the gallery showcases Canadian artists, in particular those from the West and British Columbia.

The **Kamloops Museum** on Seymour Street (Tues–Sat 9.30am–4.30pm; free) is one of the more interesting provincial offerings, with illuminating archive photographs (especially the one of the railway running down the centre of the main street), artefacts, period set-pieces and a particularly well-done section on the Shuswap. The stuffed-animal display, without which no BC museum is complete, has a fascinating little piece on the life cycle of the tick presented without any noticeable irony. For a more complete picture of local aboriginal history and traditions, call at the **Secwepemec Museum & Heritage Park**, just over the bridge on Hwy 5 (summer daily 9am–5pm; winter Mon–Fri 8.30am–4.30pm; $5) or attend the **Kamloops Pow Wow**, held every third weekend in August ($7 a day). If you're travelling with kids and driving, the non-profit **Wildlife Park,** 15km east of town on the TransCanada Hwy (daily 8am–4.30pm; $6, children $3.75), may be worth a stop for its range of local and more exotic animals.

Perhaps the most interesting thing about Kamloops is its surroundings, dominated by strange, bare-earthed brown hills that locals like to say represent the northernmost point of the Mohave Desert. There's no doubting the almost surreal touches of near-desert, which are particularly marked in the bare rock and clay outcrops above the bilious waters of the Thompson River and in the bleached scrub and failing stands of pines that spot the barren hills. Most scenic diversions lie a short drive out of town, and the infocentre has full details of every last local bolt hole, with a special bias towards the two hundred or so trout-stuffed lakes that dot the hinterland. The nearest and most popular on a hot summer's day is **Paul Lake Provincial Park**, 17km northeast of town on a good paved road, with swimming and a provincial campground ($12).

Practicalities

The **infocentre**, 1290 W Trans-Canada Hwy (mid-May to mid-Oct Mon–Fri 8am–6pm, Sat & Sun 9am–6pm; mid-Oct to mid-May Mon–Fri 9am–5pm; ☎374-3377 or 1-800/662-1994, *www.kamloopsinfo.bc.ca*) is a good 6km west of downtown, close to the Aberdeen Mall. They have full accommodation and recreational details for the town and much of the province, and a particularly useful book of local trails self-published by a local hiker ($13.90). The **Greyhound terminal** (☎374-1212), on Notre Dame Avenue off Hwy 1, across from the infocentre, is a crucial interchange for buses to all parts of the province; to head into town, jump on the #3 bus that leaves from outside the station. Kamloops is also served by three weekly **trains** in each direction from Edmonton, via Jasper (Mon, Thurs & Sat), and Vancouver (Mon, Wed & Sat). The VIA Rail office is at 95 3rd Ave, behind Landsdowne Street, but is open only on days trains are running (☎372-5858 or 1-800/561-8630).

Kamloops' huge volume of accommodation is aimed fair and square at the motorist and consists of thick clusters of **motels**, most of which blanket the town's eastern margins on Hwy 1 or out on Columbia Street W. The *Thrift Inn*, 2459 TransCanada (☎374-2488 or 1-800/661-7769; ①), is probably the cheapest of all, but it's about the last building on eastbound Hwy 1 out of town. You pay a slight premium for central beds, most of which are on Columbia Street: here the *Casa Marquis Motor Inn*, 530 Columbia St (☎372-7761 or 1-800/533-9233; ②) is reasonably priced, or you can try the reliable and recently renovated *Sandman*, 550 Columbia St (☎374-1218 or 1-800/726-3626, *www.sandman.ca*; ②), part of a chain. If you want top-of-the-range comfort after a long journey, make for the central *Stockmen's Hotel & Casino*, 540 Victoria St (☎372-2281 or 1-800/663-2837; ④). A **youth hostel**, *Kamloops Old Courthouse Hostel,* is housed downtown in a restored court house building at 7 W Seymour St (☎828-7991; ①): it has dorm beds and a few private rooms. There's also a clutch of motels around the bus terminal, in case you arrive late and have no need to drop into town. The nearest **campground** is the *Silver Sage Tent and Trailer Park* at 771 Athabasca St E (☎828-2077; $15–18), but if you've got a car aim for the far more scenic facilities at Paul Lake Provincial Park (see opposite). Snack **food** is cheap and served in generous portions at the popular *Swiss Pastries & Café*, 359 Victoria St, which really is run by Swiss people and does good muesli, cappuccino, sticky buns and excellent bread. The *Grassroots Tea House* (summer only), in Riverside Park at 262 Lorne St, is a nice spot for lunch or dinner washed down with ginseng tea – a local product. If you're splashing out on a proper meal, on the other hand, the best restaurant is the upmarket *Deja Vu*, 172 Battle St (☎374-3227; closed Sun & Mon), where Thai meets France and Japan, though locals also rate the much cheaper, but less exotic, *Ric's Grill* at 227 Victoria St. *Kelly O'Bryans*, 244 Victoria St, is good for a pint, and for supermarket stock-ups there's a Safeway on the corner of Seymour and 5th Avenue.

Highway 5: Clearwater and Wells Gray Park

Northbound **Hwy 5** (here known as the Yellowhead South Hwy) heads upstream along the broad North Thompson River as it courses through high hills and rolling pasture between Kamloops and **Clearwater** and beyond. It is one of the most scenically astounding road routes in this part of the world, and follows the river as it carves through the Monashee Mountains from its source near **Valemount**, to the final meeting with the main Yellowhead Hwy (Hwy 16) at Tête Jaune Cache, a total distance of 338km. The entire latter half of the journey is spent sidestepping the immense **Wells Gray Provincial Park**, one of the finest protected areas in British Columbia.

Greyhound **buses** cover the route on their run between Kamloops and Prince George via Clearwater (3 daily in each direction), as do VIA **trains**, which connect Kamloops with Jasper via Clearwater (3 weekly). To get into Wells Gray without your own transport, however, you'd have to hitch from Clearwater up the 63-kilometre main access road – a feasible proposition at the height of summer, but highly unlikely at any other time. This access road will be enough for most casual visitors to get a taste of the park – you could run up and down it and see the sights in a day – but note that there are some less-travelled gravel roads into other sectors of the park from **Blue River**, 112km north of Clearwater on Hwy 5, and from the village of **100 Mile House**, on Hwy 97 west of the park.

Clearwater

CLEARWATER is a dispersed farming community that's invisible from Hwy 5, and unless you need a place to stay or arrive by rail there's no need to drop down to it at all. Everything you need apart from the odd shop is on or just off the junction between the highway and the slip road to the village, including the **bus stop** and the excellent **info-centre** (daily: June–Aug 8am–8pm; Sept–May 9am–5pm; ☎674-2646), a model of the genre that has immensely useful information on all aspects of Wells Gray Provincial Park.

If you're planning on staying locally or doing any walking or canoeing, take time to flick through its reference books devoted to accommodation, trails and paddling routes.

Camping aside, Clearwater is the most realistic place to **stay** along Hwy 5 if you're planning on doing Wells Gray. By far the best prospect, thanks to its lovely views over Dutch Lake, is the *Jasper Way Inn Motel*, 57 E Old North Thompson Hwy, two blocks off Hwy 5 (☎674-3345; ③), 1km off the highway to the west and well signed from the infocentre; some rooms have cooking facilities. If it's full, try the big *Wells Gray Inn* (☎674-2214 or 1-800/567-4088; ①), close by on the main road; the doubles here are more comfortable, but lack the view. The latter is virtually the only place to **eat** locally. As the park becomes more popular, so more places are opening on its fringes: the big new *Clearwater Adventures Resort*, 373 Clearwater Valley Rd (☎674-3909) on the corner of the Yellowhead Hwy and the Wells Gray Park Road, is one such, a combination of cabins (②), chalets (④) and camping and RV sites ($18–32; March–Oct). If you've come for wilderness you probably won't want to be in such a place, but it does also have three restaurants, endless facilities and a whole host of equipment rental possibilities and organized tours.

Three other **campgrounds** lie more or less within walking distance of the infocentre: the best – again, on the lake – is the *Dutch Lake Resort and RV Park* (☎674-3351 or 1-888/884-4424; ③), cabins ③, pitch $18; mid-April to mid-Oct). Don't forget, though, that there are four simple provincial park campgrounds within the park (see opposite). If you want to be slightly away from Clearwater, stop at the *Birch Island Campground* (☎674-3991 or 674-4054; $14–19; mid-April to Oct), a treed seventy-acre area with tent sites and B&B units (②) overlooking the Thompson River 8km north of the village on Hwy 5.

Blue River and Valemount

Clearwater is by far the best base locally, but you may find the **accommodation** options at Blue River and Valemount (a whopping 225km north of Clearwater on Hwy 5) useful. **BLUE RIVER**, a slip of a place 100km north of Clearwater, has far fewer possibilities, with its cheapest option being the *Blue River Motel* with one- and two-bedroom units two blocks off the highway on Spruce Street (☎673-8387; ②). For a few dollars more you could try the *Mountain View Motel* on 3rd Avenue and Spruce Street (☎673-8366; ②) and, top-of-the-pile, but on the highway, is the fine *Venture Lodge* (☎673-8384; ②). The only **campgrounds** for miles are the *Eleanor Lake Campsite and Trailer Park* on Herb Bilton Way (☎673-8316; $12–20; May to mid-Oct), with free showers, store and canoe rentals, and the *Blue River Campground and RV Park*, Myrtle Lake Road and Cedar Street (☎673-8203; $12–18; May to mid-Oct), with showers, canoe rentals and a variety of fishing, canoeing and horse-riding tours.

In **VALEMOUNT** there's a seasonal infocentre at 98 Gorse St on Hwy 5 (mid-May to mid-Sept daily 9am–5pm; ☎566-4846) and around ten motels and two campgrounds. One block off the highway on 5th Avenue are a bunch of the **motels**, of which the cheapest is the *Yellowhead* (May–Oct; ☎566-4411; ③); the rest have more facilities, but all are pretty soulless, including the *Best Western Canadian Lodge* (☎566-8222; ⑤) with a jacuzzi and kitchenettes; the *Canoe Mountain Lodge* (☎566-9171; ⑤) with duvets on the beds; and the *Chalet Continental*, 1450 5th Ave (☎566-9787; ④) with an indoor pool. On Loseth Road, 1km north of Valemount, is the modern *Irvins Park and Campground* (☎566-4781; $23–32; April–Oct) with activities including horse riding and ATV tours. Another campground, the wooded *Valemount Campground*, is off the highway in the north side of town (☎566-4141; $19; mid-April to mid-Oct).

Wells Gray Provincial Park

WELLS GRAY PROVINCIAL PARK is the equal of any of the Rocky Mountain national parks to the east: if anything, its wilderness is probably more extreme – so untamed, in fact, that many of its peaks remain unclimbed and unnamed. Wildlife sightings are common – especially if you tramp some of the wilder trails, where encounters with black bears, grizzlies and mountain goats are a possibility, not to mention glimpses of smaller mammals such as timber wolves, coyotes, weasels, martens, minks, wolverines and beavers. Seeing the park is straightforward, at least if you have transport and only want a superficial – but still rewarding – glimpse of the interior. A 63-kilometre **access road** strikes into the park from Hwy 5 at Clearwater, culminating in Clearwater Lake – there's no further wheeled access. Various trails long and short, together with campgrounds, viewpoints and easily seen waterfalls, are dotted along the road, allowing you to see just about all the obvious scenic landmarks with a car in a day.

With some 250km of maintained trails and dozens of other lesser routes, the park is magnificent for **hiking**. Short walks and day-hikes from the park's access road are described below, but serious backpackers can easily spend a week or more tramping the backcountry hikes, most of which are in the southern third of the park and link together for days of wild hiking and wilderness camping. The longest one-way trail links Clearwater Lake to Kostal Lake trail (26km) and begins on the main Wells Gray park road, just across from Clearwater Lake campground. Steep switchbacks, muddy conditions, thick brush and large deadfall, as well as tramping across sharp lava flow and loose rock, make the going slow on many of the park's remoter trails. For all the backcountry hikes you need a map and a compass, your own food and water supplies and plenty of insect repellent. Make sure you pick up a free *BC Parks* map-pamphlet at the Clearwater infocentre, and if you're thinking of doing any backcountry exploration you'll want to invest in their more detailed maps and guides. **Cross-country skiing** is also possible, but there are only a few groomed routes in the park: again, details are available at the infocentre.

Another of the park's big attractions is **canoeing** on Clearwater and Azure lakes, the former at the end of the access road, which can be linked with a short portage to make a 100-plus-kilometre dream trip for paddlers; you can rent canoes for long- or short-haul trips from *Clearwater Lake Tours* situated on the south end of Clearwater Lake, 71km from Hwy 5 in Clearwater (☎674-2121 or 674-2971 off-season/evening). **White-water rafting** down the Clearwater River is also extremely popular and recommended, and half-day to full-week tours can be arranged through the Clearwater infocentre or at the two accommodation options below. Several local operators run shorter commercial boat trips around Clearwater Lake, as well as full-scale **tours** featuring horse riding, camping, trekking, fishing, boating, and even float-plane excursions around the park – the Clearwater infocentre has the inside story on all of these.

The only indoor **accommodation** in or near the park is in the log cabins at *Wells Gray Ranch* (☎674-2792; ④; mid-May to mid-Oct) just before the park entrance (26km from Hwy 5) on Wells Gray Park Road, or the slightly larger, but equally lonely *Helmcken Falls Lodge* (☎674-3657; ⑤; Jan–March & May–Oct) at the entrance itself (35km from Hwy 5), which offers similar facilities at slightly higher prices. You'll be lucky to find vacancies in summer, so book months in advance if coming in June, July or August. Both of these also have tent pitches, but there's far better roadside **camping** along the park access road at the park's four provincial campgrounds: *Spahats Campground* a small forested site only 10km from Hwy 5 at Clearwater Lake on Clearwater Valley Road; the *Dawson Falls*, 5km from the park entrance; *Falls Creek*, 30km from the entrance; and *Clearwater Lake*, 31km from the entrance (all $12; May–Sept). All fill up promptly on summer weekends, but can be reserved through Discover Camping (see p.390). Many backpackers' campsites ($5) dot the shores of the park's major lakes and with no services offered it's not necessary to book; Clearwater Lake Tours operates a water-taxi service, which can drop you off at any site on Clearwater Lake and pick you up at a prearranged time.

Sights and hikes along the access road

Even if you're not geared up for the backcountry, the access road to the park from Clearwater opens up a medley of waterfalls, walks and viewpoints that make a detour extremely worthwhile. The road's paved for the first 30km to the park boundary, but the remaining 33km to Clearwater Lake is gravel. Most of the sights are well signed.

About 8km north of Clearwater, a short walk from the car park at **Spahats Campground** brings you to the 61-metre Spahats Falls, the first of several mighty cascades along this route. You can watch the waters crashing down through layers of pinky-red volcanic rock from a pair of observation platforms, which also provide an impressive and unexpected view of the Clearwater Valley way down below. A few hundred metres further up the road, a fifteen-kilometre gravel lane peels off into the **Wells Gray Recreation Area**; a single trail from the end of the road strikes off into alpine meadows, feeding four shorter day-trails into an area particularly known for its bears. This is also the site of a juvenile correction centre, which must rank as possibly the most beautiful but godforsaken spot to do time in North America. About 15km further up the main access road, a second four-wheel-drive track branches east to reach the trailhead for **Battle Mountain** (19km), with the option of several shorter hikes like the Mount Philip Trail (5km) en route.

Green Mountain Lookout, reached by a rough, winding road to the left just after the park entrance, offers one of the most enormous roadside panoramas in British Columbia, and it's a sight that will help you grasp the sheer extent of the Canadian wilderness: as far as you can see, there's nothing but an almighty emptiness of primal forest and mountains. Various landscape features are picked out on plaques, and the immediate area is a likely place to spot moose.

The next essential stop is **Dawson Falls**, a broad, powerful cascade (91m wide and 18m high) just five-minutes' walk from the road – signed "Viewpoint". Beyond, the road crosses an ugly iron bridge and shortly after meets the start of the **Murtle River Trail** (14km one-way), a particularly good walk if you want more spectacular waterfalls.

Immediately afterwards, a dead-end side road is signed to **Helmcken Falls**, the park's undisputed highlight. The site is heavily visited, and it's not unknown for wedding parties to come up here to get dramatic matrimonial photos backed by the luminous arc of water plunging into a black, carved bowl fringed with vivid carpets of lichen and splintered trees, the whole ensemble framed by huge plumes of spray wafting up on all sides. At 137m, the falls are two and a half times the height of Niagara – or, in the infoboard's incongruous comparison, approximately the same height as the Vancouver skyline.

Continuing north, the park access road rejoins the jade-green Clearwater River, passing tastefully engineered picnic spots and short trails that wend down to the bank for close-up views of one of the province's best white-water rafting stretches. The last sight before the end of the road is **Ray Farm**, home to John Bunyon Ray, who in 1912 was the first man to homestead this area. Though it's not much to look at, the farm offers a sobering insight into the pioneer mentality – Ray's struggle to scrape a living and raise a family in this harsh environment beggars belief – and the picturesquely ruined, wooden shacks are scattered in a lovely, lush clearing. The park road ends at **Clearwater Lake**, where there are a couple of boat launches, a provincial campground and a series of short trails clearly marked from the trailhead.

Salmon Arm and the Shuswap

Given the variety of routes across southern BC there's no knowing when you might find yourself in **SALMON ARM**, 108km east of Kamloops, though that's not something that need concern you in planning an itinerary, because the town – the largest of the somewhat bland resorts spread along **Shuswap Lake's** 1000km of navigable waterways – has relatively little to recommend it. This said, if you fancy fishing, swimming, water-skiing or houseboating, you could do worse than relax for a couple of days in one of the 32 provincial parks or small lakeside villages – Chase, Sorrento, Eagle Bay and others. Depending on the season, you can also watch one of Canada's most famous **salmon-spawning runs**, or indulge in a little **bird-watching**, for the bay at Salmon Arm is one of the world's last nesting areas of the Western Grebe. As ever in Canada, Salmon Arm and its satellites are much smaller places than their bold label on most maps would suggest. Many of the settlements are oddly dispersed and a touch scrappy and haphazard in appearance, but if you're driving they make a natural break along one of the Trans-Canada's more monotonous stretches. To get anything out of Salmon Arm proper, you'll have to pull off the main drag, which is formed by the Trans-Canada itself, and head to the village a little to the south.

The lake and the surrounding region take their name from the Shuswap natives, the northernmost of the great Salishan family and the largest single tribe in British

SPAWN TO BE WILD

At times it seems impossible to escape the **salmon** in British Columbia. Whether it's on restaurant menus, in rivers, or in the photographs of grinning fishermen clutching their catch, the fish is almost as much a symbol of the region as its mountains and forests. Five different species inhabit the rivers and lakes of western Canada: **pink**, **coho**, **chum**, **chinook** and, most important of all, the **sockeye**.

Though they start and finish their lives in fresh water, salmon spend about four years in the open sea between times. Mature fish make their epic migrations from the Pacific to **spawn** in the BC rivers of their birth between June and November, swimming about 30km a day; some chinook travel more than 1400km up the Fraser beyond Prince George, which means almost fifty days' continuous swimming upstream. Though the female lays as many as four thousand eggs, only about six percent of the offspring survive: on the Adams River near Salmon Arm, for example, it's estimated that of four billion sockeye eggs laid in a typical year, one billion survive to become fry (hatched fish about 2cm long), of which 75 percent are eaten by predators before becoming smolts (year-old fish), and only five percent of these then make it to the ocean. In effect each pair of spawners produces about ten mature fish: of these, eight are caught by commercial fisheries and only two return to reproduce.

These are returns that clearly put the salmon's survival and British Columbia's lucrative **fishing industry** on a knife edge. Caught, canned and exported, salmon accounts for two-thirds of BC's $1 billion annual revenues from fishing – the largest of any Canadian province, and its third-ranking money-earner after forestry and energy products. Commercial fishing suffered its first setback in British Columbia as long ago as 1913, when large rock slides at Hell's Gate in the Fraser Canyon disrupted many of the spawning runs. Although fish runs were painstakingly constructed to bypass the slides, new pressures have subsequently been heaped on the salmon by mining, logging, urban and agricultural development, and the dumping of industrial and municipal wastes. An increasingly important line of defence, **hatcheries** have been built on rivers on the mainland and Vancouver Island to increase the percentage of eggs and fry that successfully mature. Meanwhile, overfishing, as the above figures suggest, remains a major concern, particularly as the **drift nets** of Japanese and Korean fleets, designed for neon squid, have over the past decade taken numerous non-target species, including BC and Yukon salmon. Under intense lobbying from Canada and the US, both nations agreed to a moratorium on large-scale drift nets as from June 1992. Since then, various measures have been implemented by the Canadian and BC governments including the closure of the Fraser and Thompson rivers to all salmon fishing in 1999. However, Greenpeace estimates that 764 stocks of salmon in the BC and Yukon are either extinct or at risk of becoming extinct.

Columbia. The name of the town harks back to a time when it was possible to spear salmon straight from the lake, and fish were so plentiful that they were shovelled onto the land as fertilizer. Shuswap Lake still provides an important sanctuary for hatched salmon fry before they make their long journey down the Thompson and Fraser rivers to the sea – the abundance of such lakes, together with ideal water temperatures, free-flowing, well-oxygenated and silt-free tributaries, and plenty of sand and gravel beds for egg-laying, make the Fraser River system the continent's greatest salmon habitat. Therefore, one of the few reasons you might make a special journey to the Salmon Arm area is to watch the huge migrations of **spawning salmon** that take place around October. Up to two million fish brave the run from the Pacific up to their birthplace in the Adams River – one of the most famous spawning grounds in the province. During the spawning time, humans also make there way here in droves; around 250,000 visitors come during the peak week alone. This short stretch of river is protected by **Roderick Haig-Brown Provincial Park**, reached from Salmon Arm by driving 46km west on the Trans-Canada to Squilax and then 5km north on a side road where the park is signposted. If you're thinking of dangling a line, pick up the *Fishing in Shuswap* leaflet from the infocentre in Salmon Arm, and don't forget to get a licence at the same time.

Practicalities

Greyhound **buses** serve Salmon Arm from Vancouver (7 daily) and Calgary (4 daily) and Kelowna, Vernon and Penticton (4 daily). The bus terminal is at the West Village Mall on Hwy 1, and the **infocentre** (Mon–Sat 8.30am–5.30pm; ☎832-2230 or 1-877/725-6667) is at 751 Marine Park Drive. You might also contact Tourism Shuswap (☎832-5200 or 1-800/661-4800, *www.shuswap.bc.ca*) for information on the whole region.

One of the most convenient of Salmon Arm's many **motels** is the *Village Motel* (☎832-3955; ②) at 620 Trans-Canada Hwy. More upmarket, and still close to the highway, is the *Best Western Villager West Motor Inn*, 61 10th St SW (☎832-9793 or 1-800/528-1234; ④). There is also a HI-affiliated **youth hostel**, the *Squilax General Store and Caboose Hostel* (☎675-2977; ①) in Chase on the waterfront just off the Trans-Canada. Of several **campgrounds**, the obvious first choice is the *Salmon Arm KOA*, 3km east of town in a big wooded site, whose excellent facilities include a heated swimming pool (☎832-6489 or 1-800/562-9389; $26; May–Oct). For beds or tent space, the *Salmon River Motel and Campground*, 1km west of downtown at 910 40th St SW (☎832-3065; motel ②, campground $15.50–19.50), is also good.

For a decidedly alternative form of accommodation, head east along the Trans-Canada to **SICAMOUS**, a pleasant but very busy waterfront village which, though crammed with motels and campgrounds, is better known for its many upmarket **houseboats**. A few rent by the night, but most tend to be let weekly by about half-a-dozen local agencies scattered around the village. Agencies you might try include *Bluewater Houseboats* (☎836-2255 or 1-800/663-4024; $1485–5295 a week; April–Sept), *Sicamous Creek Marina* (☎836-4611; $1015–2910 a week; April–Oct) or the *Twin Anchors Houseboat Association* (☎836-2450; $745–4495 a week; April–Oct). The village is also the place to pick up a boat for a sightseeing **cruise** on the lake, one of the best ways of enjoying a scenic slice of the region: contact the *Shuswap Ferry Lake Service* for details of daily summer sailings (☎836-2200). For **information** there's an infocentre at 110 Finlayson St by the Government Dock (Mon–Fri 10am–5pm; June also Sat 10am–3pm; July daily 9am–6pm; ☎836-3313). To **eat** locally, head for the *Mara Lake Inn* (☎836-2126) on the lakeshore 3km south of the village and the Trans-Canada on Hwy 97 which has a gourmet restaurant and newly renovated motel units that look out over Mara Lake (③) and cabins with kitchenettes (②). If you're looking to have a **drink** try *Brothers Pub*, 420 Main St.

Highway 97 to the Okanagan

Passing through landscapes of Eden-like clarity and beauty, **Hwy 97** is a far better entrance to (or exit from) the Okanagan than the dreary road to Salmon Arm. The grass-green meadows, grazing cattle and low wooded hills here are the sort of scenery pioneers must have dreamed of: most of the little hamlets en route make charming spots to stay, and if you have time and transport any number of minor roads lead off to small lakes, each with modest recreational facilities.

The highway peels off the Trans-Canada 26km east of Kamloops, its first good stops being **MONTE LAKE**, served by the excellent *Heritage Campsite and RV Park* (☎375-2434; $13.50–16.50; April–Nov) and the equally well-tended and unspoilt public campground at **Monte Lake Provincial Park**. Both places make good spots to overnight. **WESTWOLD**, 5km beyond, is a dispersed ranching community of clean, old wooden houses and large pastures that present a picture of almost idyllic rural life. **FALK-LAND**, 13km beyond, is an unassuming place whose **motel** blends easily into its rustic village atmosphere. The central *Big Highland Motel* (☎379-2249; ①) is on Adelphi Street, but you might also drop into the infant infocentre (summer only) for lists of local B&B. There are also a couple of well-signposted, quiet **campgrounds** ($12–15). Country lanes lead north and east from here to **Bolean Lake** (10km) at 1437m, served by a lodge and campground: *Bolean Lake Lodge*, Bolean Lake Road (☎558-9008; rooms ①, tents $14; May–Oct); to **Pillar Lake** (13km) and the *Pillar Lake Resort* (☎379-2623; ①; May–Oct), which provides cabins and campsites from $12; and to **Pinaus Lake** (10km) and its adjacent cabins and campground, *Pinaus Lake Camp* (☎542-0624; cabins ②, sites $14; April–Oct).

The O'Keefe Ranch

Twelve kilometres short of Vernon, near the junction with the west-side Okanagan Lake road, stands the **Historic O'Keefe Ranch**, a collection of early pioneer buildings and a tidy little museum that's well worth a half-hour's pause (daily: May, June & Sept to mid-Oct 9am–5pm; July & Aug 9am–7pm; $6). In addition to a proficient summary of nineteenth-century frontier life, the museum contains an interesting section on the role of aboriginal peoples in the two world wars. Some 25 percent of eligible men immediately volunteered for service – a tour of duty that did little to resolve their national dilemma, which the museum sums up pithily with the observation that they belong to that "unhappy group who lost the old but are unable to obtain the new". Outside, a complete period street includes a detailed general store where you can buy oddments from staff in old-time dress – an excessively cute conceit, but one that fails to take the edge off the place's surprisingly successful evocation of an era. You feel the past most strongly in the church and graveyard, where the lovely building and its poignant handful of graves – three generations of O'Keefes, who first settled here in 1867 – capture the isolation and close-knit hardship of pioneer life.

The Okanagan

The vine- and orchard-covered hills and warm-water lakes of the **Okanagan**, located in south-central British Columbia, are in marked contrast to the rugged beauty of the region's more mountainous interior, and have made the region not only one of Canada's most favoured fruit-growing areas but also one of its most popular summer holiday destinations. However, unless you want (occasionally) rowdy beach life or specifically enjoy mixing with families on their annual vacation, you'll probably want to ignore the area altogether in summer, despite its high word-of-mouth reputation. Three main centres – **Vernon**, **Kelowna** and **Penticton**, ranging from north to south along the 100-kilometre-long **Okanagan Lake** – together contain the lion's share of the province's interior population, and all lay on an array of accommodation and mostly tacky attractions for the summer hordes. As ever in BC, however, things improve immeasurably if you can slip away from the towns and head for the hills or quieter stretches of lakeshore.

On the plus side, the almost year-round Californian lushness that makes this "the land of beaches, peaches, sunshine and wine" means that, in the relative peace of **off-season**, you can begin to experience the region's considerable charms: fruit trees in blossom, quiet lakeside villages and free wine tastings in local vineyards. Plus, you can also expect room rates to be up to fifty percent less in the off season. Kelowna is the biggest and probably best overall base at any time of the year, but local **buses** link all the towns and Greyhounds ply Hwy 97 on their way between Osoyoos and Kamloops or Salmon Arm.

Vernon

The beach scene is less frenetic in **VERNON** than elsewhere in the Okanagan. Located at the junction of Hwys 6 and 97 near the northern edge of Okanagan Lake, the town attracts fewer of the bucket-and-spade brigade, though the emphasis on fruit and the great outdoors is as strong as ever, and the main highway through town is bumper-to-bumper with motels, fast-food joints and ever more garish neon signs. On the whole it's easier to find a place to stay here than in Kelowna (see opposite) – but there are also fewer reasons for wanting to do so.

Downtown Vernon centres on 32nd Avenue (Hwy 97) and leaves a far more gracious impression than the town's outskirts by virtue of its elegant tree-lined streets and five hundred listed buildings. The locals are an amenable and cosmopolitan bunch made up of British, Germans, Chinese and Salish natives, plus an abnormally large number of Jehovah's Witnesses, whose churches seem to have a virtual monopoly on religious observance in the town. The local **museum**, by the clock tower at 3009 32nd Ave, does the usual job on local history (Mon–Sat 10am–5pm; closed Mon in winter; donation). At the southern entrance to town, **Polson Park** makes a green sanctuary from the crowds, but for beaches you should head 8km south of Vernon to **Kalamalka Provincial Park**, which features a stunning blue-green lake. **Kin Beach** on Okanagan Lake west on Okanagan Landing Road is another good spot. Both have adjoining campgrounds.

Other outdoor recreation (but not camping) is on hand at **Silver Star Recreation Area**, a steep 22-kilometre drive to the northeast on 48th Avenue off Hwy 97, where in summer a **ski lift** (late June to mid-Oct daily 10am–5pm; $7.50) trundles to the top of Silver Star Mountain (1915m) for wide views and meadow-walking opportunities; the most-used trail wends from the summit back to the base area. This is also a popular mountain-biking route – Monashee Adventure Tours (☎1-888/762-9253) rents out mountain bikes from the hostel (see below) and offers guided tours all over the Okanagan. If you want an eagle's-eye view of the area call Paraglide Canada (☎308-0387, *www.paraglidecanada.com*; $100 per person) for a tandem ride from the top of the mountains.

Practicalities

Vernon's **infocentre** is at 701 Hwy 97 N (June–Aug daily 8am–6pm; Sept–May Mon–Fri 9am–5pm; ☎542-1415 or 1-800/665-0795 for reservations only), along with a seasonal office south of town (☎542-1415) on the main highway. The **Greyhound station** is on the corner of 30th Street and 31st Avenue (☎545-0527) with connections to Calgary and Vancouver.

A new **hostel**, *Lodged Inn*, 3201 Pleasant Valley Rd (☎549-3742 or 1-888/737-9427, *www.windsrivers.bc.ca*; ①), has dormitory accommodation in a beautiful old house –

THE LEGEND OF OKANAGAN LAKE

When travelling through the Okanagan Valley, you'll find it hard to avoid **Ogopogo**, the famed lake monster of Okanagan Lake, whose smiling dragon-like face appears on all manner of postcards, billboards and bumper stickers. Its name comes from a 1920s music-hall song – "his mother was an earwig, his father a whale; a little bit of head and hardly any tail; and Ogopogo was his name" – but the myth is much older. The aboriginal Salish peoples believed in such a creature, and referred to it as **N'ha-a-itk**, meaning "Lake Demon" or "Devil of the Lake". Legend has it that the Salish people warned early white settlers of the lake monster, who apparently was a demon-possessed man punished by the gods for murdering a tribal brother. To appease him, the Salish would sacrifice animals whenever crossing near **Rattlesnake Island**, around which the monster supposedly lurked. The early white settlers feared the reptile as well, leaving offerings and even setting up armed patrols along the shores in case of an attack. Nowadays, vacationers would be thrilled to spot BC's version of the Loch Ness monster, demon or not, and numerous sightings are claimed every year.

from the bus station, head to 32nd Avenue, take a right and then the fourth left onto Pleasant Valley Road. There are also plenty of **motels** in town: a sound if bland choice is the *Sandman Inn* at 4201 32nd St (☎542-4325 or 1-800/726-3626, *www.sandman.ca*; ③). The *Polson Park Motel* (☎549-2231 or 1-800/480-2231; ②), opposite the eponymous park on 24th Avenue, is one of the cheapest options. The *Schell Motel*, 2810 35th St (☎545-1351 or 1-888/772-4355; ②), tempts clients with a pool and sauna. **Campgrounds** near town all get busy during the high season, and you may have to trek along the lakeshore for some way to strike lucky; try *Dutch's Tent and Trailer Court* (☎545-1023; $17–21; year-round) at 15408 Kalamalka Rd, 3km south of Vernon near Kalamalka Beach. Much more rural is *Ellison Provincial Park*, 16km off to the southwest on Okanagan Lake (reservations possible, see p.390; $15; March–Nov). To the north, 5km south of the O'Keefe Ranch (see p.417), is *Newport Beach Recreational Park* (☎542-7131; $16; mid-May to mid-Oct), situated at Westside Road on Okanagan Lake.

In the **food** department, there are plenty of choices, especially amongst the many cafés and sandwich places. Downtown, try the *Bean to Cup* on 39th Avenue and 27th Street for soups, sandwiches and Internet access, or *The Italian Kitchen*, 3006 30th Ave, serving up food true to its name. At 3127 30th Ave, *KT's* has saltwater aquariums alongside its tables and serves pizza, pasta, sandwiches and burgers. *Sir Winston's*, 2705 32nd St, is the downtown **pub** of choice.

Kelowna

If you're continuing south from Vernon, be sure to take the minor road, known as Okanagan Lake Road, on the western shore of Okanagan Lake – a quiet detour that offers something of the beauty for which the area is frequently praised, but which can be somewhat obscured by the commercialism of towns to the south. From the road, weaving through woods and small bays, the lake looks enchanting. The shore is often steep and there are few places to get down to the water – though at a push you might squeeze a tent between the trees for some unofficial camping.

If you want a summer suntan and cheek-by-jowl nightlife – neither of which you'd readily associate with the British Columbian interior – then **KELOWNA** ("grizzly bear" in the Salish dialect) – is the place to come. People had such a good time here in the summer of 1988 that the annual **Kelowna Regatta** turned into a full-blown and very un-Canadian alcohol-fuelled **riot** in which the police were forced to wade in with truncheons and tear gas; the main event has since been cancelled in its original format (it's now strictly a family affair), but the beach and downtown bars remain as busy as ever. That this modest city should have fostered such an urban-style mêlée isn't all that surprising. Compared to other interior towns, Kelowna (pop. 97,000) ranks as a sprawling metropolis, and to the unsuspecting tourist its approaches come as an unpleasant surprise – particularly the appalling conglomeration of motels, garages and fast-food outlets on Hwy 97 at the north end of town.

That said, the lakefront and beaches, though heavily developed, aren't too bad, and off-season Kelowna's undeniably pretty **downtown** can make a good couple of days' respite from mountains and forests. Its attractions are increasingly well-known across BC and remarkable jumps in population have taken place over the last few years: 37,000 people, many of them retirees, have moved here since 1990, creating something of a development nightmare for local planners. Main attractions are the public beach off **City Park**, a lovely green space that fronts downtown, and the strips along Lakeshore Road south of Kelowna's famed pontoon bridge, which tend to attract a younger, trendier crowd – **Rotary Beach** here is a windsurfers' hangout, and **Boyce Gyro Park**, just north, is where the town's teenagers practise their preening. Across the bridge and 2km and 14km respectively up the lake's west bank, **Bear Creek** and **Fintry Provincial Parks** are lovely spots with great beaches and campgrounds, but they are also horrendously popular (reservations possible at both, see p.390).

Kelowna owes its prosperity primarily to one man, Father Pandosy, a French priest who founded a mission here in 1859 and planted a couple of apple trees two years later. Much of Canada's **fruit** is now grown in the area – including virtually all the apricots, half the pears and plums, and a third of the country's apples. The infocentre (see opposite) can point you to dozens of juice, fruit, food and forestry tours, but if you feel like sampling the more hedonistic fruits of Father Pandosy's labours, consider visiting one of the local **vineyards**, all of them known for their open-handed generosity with free samples after a tour of the premises. You can choose from a variety of whites and reds as the valley's microclimates and soil types allow neighbouring vineyards to produce completely different wines. At one time most were crisp, fruity German-style white wines and dessert wines, but now successful red wines and drier whites are emerging. There's even organic champagne at **Summerhill Estate Winery**, 4870 Chute Lake Rd (☎764-8000 or 1-800/667-3538), in a beautiful spot near some hot springs or try **Calona Wines**, Canada's second biggest commercial winery and the Okanagan's oldest (founded 1932), just six blocks off Hwy 97 at 1125 Richter Ave (daily: May–Sept 11am–5pm, tours every 2 hours; Oct–April tour at 2pm; ☎762-3332). The infocentre can provide a full rundown of smaller, more far-flung estates. All of the wineries join together in May and late September to lay on the region's annual Spring and Fall **wine festivals** (☎861-6654, *www.owfs.com*) when free wine tastings, gourmet dinners, grape stomps and vineyard picnics take place to lure the connoisseur and beginner alike. More context can be found at the **Wine Museum**, 1304 Ellis St (Mon–Sat 10am–5pm, Sun noon–5pm), which is basically a glorified shop with a few exhibits, like a 3000-year-old clay drinking horn from Iran.

Getting away from Kelowna's crowds isn't easy, but the closest you'll come to shaking them off is by climbing **Knox Mountain**, the high knoll that overlooks the city to the north, just five-minutes' drive (or 30min walk) from downtown. It offers lovely views over the lake and town, particularly at sunset, and there's a wooden observation tower to make the most of the panorama. RVs are kept out of the area by a barrier dropped at dusk, but if you take a sleeping bag up – though perhaps not a tent – you might get away with an undisturbed night.

Practicalities

The **bus terminal** is at the east end of town at 2366 Leckie Rd on the corner of Harvey (Hwy 97), and sees off two buses daily to Calgary, Banff, Cache Creek and Kamloops respectively (☎860-3835). The **infocentre** (daily: June–Aug 8am–8pm; Sept–May 8am–5pm; ☎861-1515 or 1-800/663-4345, *www.kelownachamber.org*), five blocks back from the lake at 544 Harvey, has all the information you could possibly need. To **rent a bike**, try Sports Rent at 3000 Pandosy St.

As in Penticton, there's an enormous number of motels and campgrounds in and around town. However, **accommodation** can still be a major headache in the height of summer unless you can get to one of the **motels** on northbound Hwy 97 early in the morning, but it's a neon- and traffic-infested area well away from downtown and the lake (prices drop the further out you go). The HI-affiliated **youth hostel**, the *SameSun International Motel-Hostel*, is at 245 Harvey St (☎763-9814 or 1-877/562-2783; ①) – from the bus station take bus #10 to Queensway. There's also an unofficial hostel downtown, the *Kelowna International Hostel*, 2343 Pandosy St (☎763-6024; ①): both hostels fill quickly in summer, in which case you may go for the *Okanagan University College*, 3180 College Way (☎762-5445; ②), who let out their campus rooms from May through August. The most affordable central downtown **hotel** is the perfectly placed and very comfortable *Willow Inn* at 235 Queensway (☎762-2122 or 1-800/268-1055; ③) – ring or book very early for summer vacancies, and don't be deterred by the adjoining bar/strip-joint, which appears to be the headquarters of the Kelowna chapter of the Hell's Angels. Another slightly more expensive option is the *Royal-Anne* at 348 Bernard Ave (☎763-2277 or 1-888/811-3400; ④). As ever, the chain hotels also come up trumps: the reasonably central *Sandman Hotel*, 2130 Harvey Ave (☎860-6409 or 1-800/726-3626, *www.sandman.ca*; ③), is a good mid-range bet. More expensive are three highly rated **B&Bs**: the *Casa Rio Lakeside*, 485 Casa Rio Drive, turn off Hwy 97 at Campbell Road (☎769-0076 or 1-800/313-1033; ⑥), which has a private sandy beach and hot tub; the *Cedars*, 278 Beach Ave (☎763-1208 or 1-800/822-7100; ⑥), in a beautiful house just outside Kelowna; or the outlying *Grapevine*, 2621 Longhill Rd (☎860-5580; ③; phone for directions).

If you're **camping**, all sites are pretty expensive, and in high season some places may only accept reservations for three days or more: mosquitoes can also be a problem. If you want to stay reasonably close to the action, two campgrounds conveniently back onto Lakeshore Road: the *Willow Creek Family Campground*, 3316 Lakeshore Rd (☎762-6302; $18–22; year-round), which has free showers and a grassy tenting area flanking a sandy beach, and the *Hiawatha RV Park*, 3787 Lakeshore Rd, with separate tenting area, laundry, heated pool and free hot showers (☎861-4837 or 1-888/784-7275; $29–39; March–Oct). To be sure of camping space, try the *Bear Creek Provincial Park*, 9km west of town on Westside Road off Hwy 97 on the west side of the lake (showers and most facilities; $15.50; March–Nov) or the new *Fintry Provincial Park*, once a working orchard, 34km north of town with similar facilities ($12; April–Oct) – reservations are accepted for both (see box on p.390). Most of the other campgrounds are on the other side of the lake at Westbank, a left turn off Hwy 97 on Boucherie Road just over the pontoon bridge (but really only accessible by car) – try *West Bay Beach*, 3745 West Bay Rd (☎768-3004; $24–28; March–Oct), with its adjoining alpaca and llama farm.

Most **eating** places are crammed into the small downtown area. The variety is large, and a short walk should offer something to suit most tastes and budgets. Many travellers and young locals head for *Kelly O'Brian's* on Bernard Street, opposite the cinema, which has an "Irish" bar atmosphere and reasonable food. Despite its rather slick cocktail-lounge ambience, *Earl's Hollywood on Top*, 211 Bernard Ave at the corner of Abbott (☎763-2777), is good for ribs, seafood and steaks; go early to get a table on the upstairs patio. For pasta, *Joey Tomato's Kitchen* in the shopping mall at the junction of Hwys 97 and 33 is a fun and inexpensive option. At the top of the food tree you could splurge at *De Montreuil*, 368 Bernard Ave (☎860-5508), widely considered the best restaurant in the Okanagan and serving local produce, beef from Alberta and Pacific salmon. A three-course meal costs around $35. Also excellent in the top range is the *Williams Inn*, 526 Laurence Ave (☎763-5136), with an early evening set menu of salads and soups for $12.95 available 5–6.30pm and later an à la carte menu that includes Pacific salmon, weiner schnitzel, venison, quail and sometimes caribou and bison. Dinner for two, with drinks, will set you back about $75.

Penticton

PENTICTON is a corruption of the Salish phrase *pen tak tin* – "a place to stay forever" – but this is not a sobriquet the most southerly of the Okanagan's big towns even remotely deserves. Its summer daily average of ten hours of sunshine ranks it higher than Honolulu, making tourism its biggest industry after fruit (this is "Peach City"). That, along with Penticton's proximity to Vancouver and the States, keeps prices high and ensures that the town and beaches are swarming with water-sports jocks, cross-country travellers, RV skippers and lots of happy families. Off the beaches there's some festival or other playing virtually every day of the year to keep the punters entertained, the key ones being the **Wine Festival** in May and the **Peach Festival** in August.

Most leisure pastimes in Penticton – water-oriented ones in particular – take place on or near Okanagan Lake, just ten blocks from the town centre. **Okanagan Beach** is the closest sand to downtown and is usually covered in oiled bodies for most of its one-kilometre stretch; **Skaha Beach**, 4km south of town on Skaha Lake, is a touch quieter and trendier – both close at midnight, and sleeping on them is out of the question. If the beaches don't appeal, you can take your sun from a cruise on the lake aboard the *Casabella Princess*, which departs from 45 E Lakeshore Drive (call ☎492-4090 for times and prices).

If you're determined to sightsee, the **museum** at 785 Main St has a panoply of predictable Canadiana (Mon–Fri 10am–5pm; donation) and you can take tours around the SS *Sicamous* (Oct–April Mon–Fri 10am–4pm; May–Sept daily 10am–4pm; $3), a beached **paddle steamer** off Lakeshore Drive on the Kelowna side of town (take in the lovely rose gardens alongside the boat while you're here). Just off Main Street there's the **South Okanagan Art Gallery**, 11 Ellis St, which often carries high-quality shows, and apparently qualifies as the "world's first solar-powered art gallery" (Tues–Fri 10am–5pm, Sat & Sun 1–5pm; donation). More tempting perhaps, and an ideal part of a day's stopover, is a trip to the **Tin Whistle Brewery**, 954 W Eckhardt Ave (drop-in tours and tastings year-round), which offers three English-type ales and a celebrated Peaches and Cream beer (summer only). If your taste is for wine rather than beer, head for the **Hillside Estate Winery**, 1350 Naramata Rd (☎493-4424), **Lake Breeze Vineyard**, Sammet Road (☎496-5659), or **Casobello Wines Vineyard**, 2km south of town off Hwy 97 on Skaha Lake Road, all of which offer tours and tastings. Otherwise, Penticton's main diversions are the curse of many Canadian tourist towns – the water slides.

Practicalities

Arriving by Greyhound, you'll pull into the **bus depot** just off Main Street between Robinson and Ellis streets (☎493-4101); Penticton is a major intersection of routes, with buses bound for Vancouver (6–7 daily), Kamloops (2 daily), Nelson and points east (2 daily). The downtown area is small and easy to negotiate, particularly after a visit to the big **infocentre** at 888 Westminster Ave W (May, June & Sept Mon–Fri 9am–5pm, Sat & Sun 10am–4pm; July & Aug daily 8am–8pm; Oct–April Mon–Fri 9am–5pm, Sat & Sun 11am–4pm; ☎493-4055 or 1-800/663-5052, *www.penticton.org*) on the north side of town – it has an adjacent BC Wine Information Centre, where bottles cost the same as they do at the vineyards. There is also a smaller summer information office south of town on Hwy 97. Both infocentres concentrate on recreational pursuits, and dozens of specialist shops around town rent out equipment for every conceivable activity. For **bikes**, try Riverside Bike Rental at 75 Riverside Drive on the west side of the lakefront (daily May–Sept).

Although Penticton boasts a brimful of **accommodation**, it doesn't make finding a room in summer any easier. In high season it's best to head straight for the infocentre and ask for help, and if this fails there are so many **motels** you can easily walk from one to the next in the hope of striking lucky; most of the cheaper fall-backs line the messy southern approach to the town along Hwy 97. Three of the best and more central choices are the luxurious *Penticton Lakeside Resort & Casino*, 21 Lakeshore Drive West (☎493-8221 or 1-800/663-9400; ⑥); *Tiki Shores Condominium Beach Resort*, on the lake at 914 Lakeshore Drive (☎492-8769; ④), and the big *Penticton Inn & Suites*, 333 Martin St (☎492-3600 or 1-800/665-2221; ⑤). Dropping down to mid-range places there's the *Sandman Hotel*, opposite the Convention Centre at 939 Burnaby Ave (☎493-7151 or 1-800/726-3626, *www.sandman.ca*; ③). If you're after somewhere cheap and location doesn't matter too much, try the *Plaza Motel*, 1485 Main St (☎492-8631; ③), halfway between the town's two lakes; the *Waterfront Inn*, 3688 Parkview St (☎ & fax 492-8228 or 1-800/563-6006; ③; May to mid-Oct); or the *Valley Star Motel*, 3455 Skaha Lake Rd (☎492-7205 or 1-888/309-0033; ③), a couple of blocks from Skaha Lake. The HI-affiliated **youth hostel** is at 464 Ellis St (☎492-3992; ①), in an old bank house.

Most **campgrounds** have their full-up signs out continuously in summer, and you may well have trouble if you arrive without a reservation. The best and therefore busiest sites are along the lake, and the bulk of the second-rank spots are near the highway on the southern approaches. Recommended are the *South Beach Gardens*, 3815 Skaha Lake Rd (☎492-0628; $18–24; April–Sept), or *Wright's Beach Camp*, south of town on Hwy 97 on Lake Skaha (☎492-7120; $20–30; May–Sept). If you want to camp away from town, make for the *Camp-Along Tent and Trailer Park*, 6km south of the town off Hwy 97 in an apricot orchard overlooking Skaha Lake (☎497-5584 or 1-800/968-5267; $18–27).

Budget **eating** choices don't extend much beyond the fast-food joints and cafés bunched largely around Main Street: try the funky *Green Beanz Cafe*, 218 Martin St, for wraps and organic coffee, or head for the *Elite*, 340 Main St, the best overall for basic burgers, soup and salads. *Theo's* at 687 Main St (☎492-4019) is a friendly, crowded and highly rated Greek place that does big portions. For something different and more upmarket, search out *Salty's Beach House*, 988 Lakeshore Drive (☎493-5001), a restaurant that's eccentric in all departments with a South Seas setting of palm trees and fishing nets and a spicy menu of Caribbean, Thai, Indonesian and Malaysian food.

Highway 3: the border towns

Unless you're crossing the US/Canada border locally, British Columbia's slightly tawdry necklace of border towns between Hope and the Alberta border along **Hwy 3** is as good a reason as any for taking a more northerly route across the province. Few of the towns amount to much; if you have to break the journey, aim to do it in **Salmo** or **Castlegar**, towns on which some of the Kootenays' charm has rubbed off. Things are more interesting around **Osoyoos** and **Keremeos**, where the road enters a parched desert landscape after climbing from Hope (see p.406) through the gripping mountain scenery of the Coastal Ranges, passing en route through **Manning Provincial Park**.

If you're crossing over **the border** hereabouts, incidentally, don't be lulled by the remote customs posts into expecting an easy passage: if you don't hold a Canadian or US passport you can expect the sort of grilling you'd get at major entry points.

Manning Provincial Park

One of the few parks in the Coast and Cascade ranges, **Manning Provincial Park** parcels up a typical assortment of mountain, lake and forest scenery about 60km south of Princeton and is conveniently bisected by Hwy 3. Even if you're just passing through it's time well spent walking at least one of the short **trails** off the road, the best of which is the flower-festooned Rhododendron Flats path, located 3km east of the park's west portal. The most popular drive within the park is the fifteen-kilometre side-road to **Cascade Lookout**, a viewpoint over the Similkameen Valley and its amphitheatre of mountains; a gravel road carries on another 6km from here to **Blackwall Peak**, the starting point for the **Heather Trail** (10km one-way), renowned for its swaths of summer wild-flowers. Other manageable day-hikes leave the south side of the main highway, the majority accessed from a rough road to Lightning Lake just west of the park visitor centre.

The **park visitor centre**, 1km east of the resort (May–Sept daily 9am–8pm), is good for trail leaflets and has history and natural history exhibitions. **Accommodation** at the *Manning Park Resort* (☎840-8822, *www.manningparkresort.com*; ④), on Hwy 3 almost exactly midway between Princeton and Hope (64km), is made up of cabins and chalets, but all these go quickly in summer. There are also four provincial **campgrounds** ($9.50–15.50; reservations possible, see p.390) on and off the highway, the best close to the road being *Hampton* and *Mule Deer*, 4km and 8km east of the visitor centre respectively.

Highway 3 from Princeton

Lacklustre low hills ripple around **PRINCETON**'s dispersed collection of drab houses. The **motels** – of which there are plenty – group around a large and grim lumber mill on the east side of town, but you're better off hanging on for Keremeos. However, if circumstances dump you in town overnight, head for the *Riverside Motel* (☎295-6232; ①) at 307 Thomas Ave, three blocks north of the town centre, with fifteen nice individual log cabins. *Global Netrider* on Bridge Street is a laid-back coffee/sandwich place with Internet access. The **bus depot** is at the west end of town by the cheap-and-cheerful eatery *Billie's*, not so far from the virtually redundant **infocentre** (daily 9am–5pm; ☎295-3103), housed in an old Canadian Pacific rail wagon at 195 Bridge St.

HEDLEY, about 20km further on, is an old gold-mining hamlet that today is little more than a single street with great scenery and a couple of motels. Try the *Colonial Inn Bed & Breakfast* (☎292-8131; ④), an historic 1930s house built by the Kelowna Exploration Gold Mining Company to wine and dine potential investors; it has just five rooms, so booking ahead is often necessary. Beyond Hedley, off the highway, lies **Bromley Rock**, a lovely picnic stop looking down on the white water of the Similkameen River. Also west of the village is the *Stemwinder Provincial Park* **campground** ($12; April–Oct).

West of Keremeos (see below), Hwy 3 retraces the historic **Dewdney Trail**, a 468-kilometre mule track used in the 1860s to link Hope (p.406) with the Kootenay goldfields. Another of British Columbia's extremely picturesque patches of road, for much of the way it follows the ever-narrowing Similkameen Valley, backed by ranks of pines and white-topped mountains. To explore some of the backcountry off the highway, take the 21-kilometre gravel road (signed just west of Keremeos) south into the heart of **Cathedral Provincial Park**, a spectacular upland enclave with an unserviced campground and 32km of marked trails.

Keremeos

Highway 3 meanders eventually to pretty little **KEREMEOS**, whose aboriginal name supposedly means "where the three winds meet" – a reference to the high breezes that get channelled through the hills hereabouts. The local landscape lurches suddenly into a more rural mode, thanks mainly to a climate that blesses the region with the longest growing season in the country – hence the tag, "Fruit Stand Capital of Canada". Keremeos, whose attractive situation rivals Nelson's (see p.437), spreads over a dried-up lake bed, with hills and mountains rising from the narrow plain on all sides. Lush, irrigated orchards surround the town, offset in spring by huge swaths of flowers across the valley floor, and depending on the season you can pick up fruit and vegetables from stands dotted more or less everywhere: cherries, apricots, peaches, pears, apples, plums and grapes all grow in abundance. If you're not tempted by the food, however, you may be by the **wine tastings** at the organic **St Laszlo Vineyards** (☎499-2856), 1km east of town on Hwy 3.

Keremeos itself is a rustic, two-street affair that's almost unspoilt by neon or urban clutter. A few shopfronts are oldish, and several make a stab at being heritage houses – the wonderful *Pasta Trading Post* on Main Street, for example – and though there's little to see or do (bar the inevitable small-town museum), it's a pleasant spot to spend the night. About 1km east of town on Upper Bench Road is the **Grist Mill** (May–Oct daily 9.30am–5pm; $5.50), a working flour mill dating from 1877 and surrounded by wheatfields and gardens. Restored to its original glory – the lovely general store still flaunts wallpaper from 1894 – it's a pleasant place to while away a half hour and if you're hungry there's a tearoom with soups, sandwiches and goods baked with the mill's flour.

Keremeos' central **infocentre** is at 415 7th Ave near Memorial Park (June–Sept daily 9am–5pm; ☎499-5225). The *Pasta Trading Post* (☎499-2933) is a wonderful place to **eat** locally grown organic produce and home-made pasta sauces; they also have comfortable **rooms** upstairs (③), rates include breakfast and the use of a hot tub. There are a couple of **motels** locally: the cheapest is the *Similkameen* (☎499-5984; ②; April to mid-Oct), 1km west of the centre in open country surrounded by lawns and orchards, with a few campsites ($10–15) in summer only, and the nicest is *The Elk* (☎499-2043 or 1-888/499-7773; ②), also with landscaped gardens.

Osoyoos

Beyond Keremeos the road climbs some 46km, eventually unfolding a dramatic view, far below, of **OSOYOOS** – meaning "gathered together" – and a sizeable lake surrounded by bare, ochre hills. Descending, you enter one of the Northwest's strangest landscapes – a bona fide desert of half-bare, scrub-covered hills, sand, lizards, cactus, snakes, and Canada's lowest average rainfall (around 25cm per year). Temperatures are regularly 10°C higher than in Nelson, less than a morning's drive away, enabling exotic fruit like bananas and pomegranates to be grown and prompting Osoyoos to declare itself the "Spanish Capital of Canada". The houses are supposed to have been restyled to give the place an Iberian flavour to match its climate, but on the ground it's almost impossible to find any trace of the conversion.

The town is otherwise distinguished by its position beside **Lake Osoyoos** in the Okanagan Valley – Hwy 97, which passes through the town, is the main route into the Okanagan region. In summer the place comes alive with swimmers and boaters, drawn to some of the warmest waters of any lake in Canada, and with streams of American RVs slow-tailing their way northwards to where the real action is.

A visit to the new **Desert Centre** (mid-April to mid-Oct daily 10am–4.30pm, 1hr 30min tours every half-hour; ☎1-877/899-0897; $5), on Hwy 97 just north of town, may be the best way to get oriented here. There are tours over a 1.5km boardwalk through a small area of desert and it's a fascinating ecosystem of some 100 rare plants, including tiny cacti and sage, as well as 300 invertebrates from rattlesnakes to pocket gophers that are now all under serious threat. Once irrigated this land becomes very fertile and only nine percent of the desert survives undisturbed, with a full sixty percent vanished altogether.

The relative lack of crowds and strange scenery might persuade you to do your beach-bumming in Osoyoos, though you may be pushed to find space in any of the town's twenty or so **hotels** and **motels** during high season: cheaper choices include the *Avalon* 9106 Main St (☎495-6334 or 1-800/264-5999; ③), *Falcon*, 7106 Main St (☎495-7544; ③), and the *Best Western Sunrise Inn,* 5506 Main St (☎495-4000 or 1-877/878-2200; ③), with an indoor pool and restaurant. Most of the motels are across the causeway on the southeastern shore of the lake, alongside the **bus stop**. For more choice and help, contact the **infocentre** at the junction of Hwys 3 and 97 (☎495-7142 or 1-888/676-9667, *www.osoyooschamber.bc.ca*). You're more likely to get a place in one of the half-dozen local **campgrounds** – try the *Cabana Beach*, 2231 Lakeshore Drive (☎495-7705; $19–29; May–Sept), or the *Inkameep Campground and RV Park* on 45th Street 1km from Hwy 3 E (☎495-7279; $16–25), which also organizes local hikes and night tours of the desert. Local **eateries** are almost entirely of the fast-food variety, but *Beans Desert Bistro*, 8323 Main St (☎495-7742), has good coffee and food, as well as Internet access, or there's *Finny's*, 8311 78th St, for a lengthier menu of salads, steaks and burgers.

Moving on from Osoyoos involves a major decision if you're travelling by car or bike, the choices being to continue east on Hwy 3, or to strike north on Hwy 97 through the Okanagan to the Trans-Canada Hwy. If you're on a Greyhound, the bus heads north and the decision can be deferred until Penticton, the major parting of the ways for services in this part of BC.

Midway, Greenwood and Grand Forks

At **MIDWAY**, some 65km east of Osoyoos on Hwy 3, something of the desert atmosphere lingers, the hills strange, broad whalebacks cut by open valleys and covered in coarse scrub and brown-baked grass. The hamlet's handful of scattered homes are like a windblown and wistful ghost town, making an evocative backdrop for the overgrown train tracks and tiny **railway museum** housed alongside a rusted minuscule steam engine. It's a fascinating little spot. The Kettle River Museum (mid-May to mid-Sept daily 10am-4pm; donation) in the 1900 CPR station 3km out of the village tells the town's story. For more background, contact the **infocentre** on Hwy 3 (June–Sept 9am–6pm; ☎449-2614). To **stay**, check in to the recently renovated *Mile Zero Motel*, 622 Palmerston St (☎449-2231; ②), or put up a tent at the *Riverfront Municipal Campground* three blocks off Hwy 3 on 6th Avenue which has a washroom but no other services (free).

East out of town, the scenery along Hwy 3 begins to change from a flatter, drier landscape of bleached grass and sagebrush to rather more bland meandering hills. At **GREENWOOD**, however, the pines reappear, heralding a wild, battered brute of a village, which has suffered from the closure of its mines and can't muster much more than a handful of old buildings and some abandoned workings. The **infocentre** is housed on the main road at 214 S Copper St (only May–June daily 10am–4pm; ☎445-6355) and has free Internet access. You're pretty sure of a welcome in any of the local **motels**, cheapest of which is the *Evening Star*, 798 N Government St (☎445-6733; ②), at the eastern entrance to town. For **camping** there are a couple of small provincial park sites: *Jewel Lake* ($6; June–Sept), 12km east of Greenwood off Hwy 3; and *Boundary Creek* ($9.50; April–Oct), just west of town off Hwy 3.

GRAND FORKS is not great at all – it's very small and very dull and little more than a perfunctory transit settlement built on a river flat. Several Greyhound **buses** drop in daily, probably the biggest thing to happen to the place, stopping at *Stanley's*, which is the spot for sustenance unless you shop at the big Overwaitea supermarket alongside. The small **Boundary Museum** (July–Aug Mon–Fri 9am–4.30pm, Sat & Sun 10am–4pm; Sept–June Mon–Fri 9am–4.30pm; $2) by the traffic lights is the standard small-town model and can be seen in about the time it takes for the lights to change. The **infocentre** is next door (June–Aug Mon–Fri 8.30am–4.30pm, Sat & Sun 9am–5pm; Sept–May Mon–Fri 8.30am–4.30pm; ☎442-2833, *www.boundary.bc.ca*). The history of Doukhobor settlers is charted at the small **Mountainview Doukhobor Museum** (June–Aug daily 9am–6pm; $2). Just north of town, **Christina Lake** – which claims BC's warmest water – is a modestly unspoilt summer resort with lots of swimming, boating and camping opportunities (two other BC lakes make similar claims for their waters). A dozen or so motels and campgrounds sprout along its shore, with about the same number in and around the town itself, but it's doubtful that you'd want to use them except in an emergency. For information on the area, contact the Chamber of Commerce on Hwy 3 (☎447-6161).

Trail and Rossland

TRAIL is home to the world's largest lead and zinc smelter, a vast industrial complex whose chimneys cast a dismal shadow over the village's few houses. There's no reason to stop here and you'll probably want to head straight on to **ROSSLAND**, 11km west, which also relies on Trail's smelter for employment and has a mining foundation – gold this time, some $125 million-worth of which was gouged from the surrounding hills around 1900 (that's $2 billion-worth at today's prices). If you're into mining heritage, a tour of the **Le Roi Gold Mine** – once one of the world's largest, with 100km of tunnels – and the adjoining **Rossland Historical Museum** will entertain you with fascinating technical and geological background (mid-May to mid-Sept daily 9am–5pm; mine tours May, June & Sept every 1hr 30min, July & Aug every 30min; museum and mine $8, museum only $4).

The **infocentre** (mid-May to Oct daily 9am–5pm; ☎362-7722), in the museum at the junction of the town's two main roads, is most useful for details of the **Nancy Greene Provincial Park** (no showers; $9; May–Sept) northwest of town. Though the park and recreation area is best known for its world-class skiing – the **Red Mountain Ski Area** is a training ground for the Canadian national team – it's also excellent for hiking, an outdoor commodity that isn't easy to come by in these parts. There's a HI-affiliated **youth hostel**, the *Mountain Shadow Hostel* at 2125 Columbia Ave (☎362-7160); a provincial park **campground** ($7) at the junction of Hwys 3 and 3B; and several resort hotels; or try the upmarket twelve-unit *Ram's Head Inn*, 3km west of Rossland on Hwy 3B (☎362-9577 or 1-877/267-4323; ③), with hot tubs and bike rental. Rossland has a few nice places to **eat**: the huge-windowed *Olive Oyl's* (☎362-5322 – reservations recommended), with gourmet pizzas and an incredible banana and date pudding, the cheaper and less formal *Sunshine Café* – both are on Colombia, the main street – or *Mountain Gypsy Café* on Washington Street, good for light lunches and microbrewed beers.

Castlegar

Some 27km north of Trail on Hwy 22, **CASTLEGAR** is a strange diffuse place with no obvious centre, probably because roads and rivers – this is where the Kootenay meets the Columbia – make it more a transport hub than a community. In its time it was famous for its immigrant **Doukhobor** or "Spirit Wrestler" population, members of a Russian sect who fled religious persecution in 1899 from Russia and brought their paci-fist-agrarian lifestyle to western Canada. By the 1920s BC had around ninety Doukhobor settlements, each with a co-operative, communal population of around sixty. They arrived in Castlegar in 1908, establishing at least 24 villages in the area, each with Russian names meaning things like "the beautiful", "the blessed" or "consolation".

Accomplished farmers, they laboured under the motto "Toil and a Peaceful Life", creating highly successful orchards, farms, sawmills and packing plants. Although their way of life waned after the death of their leader Peter Verigin in 1924, killed by a bomb planted in his railway carriage, the Doukhobors' considerable industry and agricultural expertise transformed the Castlegar area; many locals still practise the old beliefs – Doukhobor numbers are around 5000 across the region – and Russian is still spoken. These days there's also a breakaway radical sect, the Freedomites, or Sons of Freedom, infamous for their eye-catching demonstrations – of which fires and nude parades are just two – against materialism and other morally dubious values.

Much of the community's heritage has been collected in the **Doukhobor Village Museum** (May–Sept daily 9am–5pm; $3.50; ☎365-6622), just off the main road on the right after you cross the big suspension bridge over the Kootenay River. A Doukhobor descendant is on hand to take you through the museum, which houses a winsome display of farm machinery, handmade tools and traditional Russian clothing that's intriguing as much for its alien context as for its content. For a further taste of Doukhobor culture, visit the evocative **Zuckerburg Island Heritage Park** off 7th Avenue, named after a local teacher of Doukhobors who built a log Russian Orthodox Chapel House here: it was bought and restored by the town in 1981, and is reached by a ninety-metre pedestrian suspension bridge.

Castlegar's **infocentre** (Sept–June Mon–Fri 9am–5pm; July & Aug daily 9am–5pm; ☎365-6313, *www.castlegar.com*) is at 1995 6th Ave off the main road as you leave town for Grand Forks. There are some half-dozen motels in and around town: the best **motel** – small, and with a nice view – is the *Cozy Pines* on Hwy 3 on the western edge of town at 2100 Crestview Crescent (☎365-5613; ②). Closer in, the modern and attractive *Best Western Fireside Motor Inn*, 1810 8th Ave at the junction of Hwys 3 and 22 (☎365-2128 or 1-800/499-6399; ③), is a touch more expensive. Three kilometres out of town to the west on Hwy 3 is the *Castlegar RV Park and Campground*, 1725 Mannix Rd (☎365-2337; $15–20; April–Oct), with rural setting, separate tenting area, free hot showers, laundry and restaurant. There are also a regional and a provincial park **campground** in the vicinity: *Pass Creek Regional Park*, which has a nice a sandy beach, (☎365-3386; $12; May–Sept), 2km west off Hwy 3A at the Kootenay River Bridge; and the *Syringa Provincial Park* (reservations possible, see p.390; $15; mid-May to mid-Sept), 19km north of Hwy 3 at Castelgar on the east side of Lower Arrow Lake. For cheap **eating**, *Café Friends* back in town at 1102 3rd St has good home-cooked basics.

Salmo

A classic stretch of scenic road, Hwy 3 climbs from Salmo to the fruit-growing plains around Creston via **Kootenay Pass** (1774m) – though the views are less of spectacular mountains than of a pretty tracery of creeks and rivers crashing down through forest on all sides. This is one of the highest main roads in the country – it's frequently closed by bad weather – and it has no services for 70km after Creston, so check your petrol before setting out. If you're cycling, brace yourself for a fifty-kilometre uphill slog, but the reward is an unexpected and stunning lake at the pass, where there's a pull-off picnic area and views of high peaks in the far distance.

Despite the large volume of traffic converging on it along Hwy 3 and Hwy 6, tiny **SALMO** somehow manages to retain a pioneer feel and most of its tidy wooden buildings are fronted by verandas, decked with baskets of flowers in summer. Housed in a picturesque building on the corner of Hwy 6 and 4th Street, the **infocentre** (mid-June to mid-Sept; ☎357-9332) doesn't have a lot to promote apart from the "World's Smallest Telephone Box"; next door is a **museum** (May–Sept Mon–Fri 10am–4pm; $2), a more credible attraction which charts the vicissitudes of pioneer life and hosts the odd travelling exhibition. In winter there's **skiing** at the Salmo ski area, 2km east of town.

Buses usually pull in here for a long rest stop at the terminal by the Petro-Canada garage on the north side of the village. If you need to overnight, use either of the two central motels: the *Reno*, 123 Railway Ave (☎357-9937; ②), one block east of the bus terminal, or the *Salcrest*, 110 Motel Ave (☎357-9557; ②), at the junction of Hwys 3 and 6. The nearest **campground** is the *Selkirk Motel and RV Sites* (☎357-2346; $12–16; units ①; May–Oct), 4km west of town.

For **food**, try *Charlie's Pizza and Spaghetti House*, an old-style diner on 4th Street. Just up the road, the *Silver Dollar Pub* is the town's favourite **bar**, with pool tables, a jukebox and lots of good ol' boys in an atmospheric wooden interior. Salmo Foods, opposite the bar, is the best **supermarket** for stocking up.

Creston

Don't stop in **CRESTON** unless you're a bird-watcher or feel like hunting down such sightseeing frippery as "Canada's best mural" (the original, in McDowell's department store, had spawned another nine pictures around town at last count). The **info-centre** is in a log cabin (one of the town's few buildings of interest) on the east side of town at 711 Canyon St (Mon 9am–5pm, Tues–Sat 9am–6pm; ☎428-4342): use it if by mischance you need **accommodation**, though with twenty or so motels and campgrounds to choose from you probably won't be fighting for a bed. The cheapest and most central spot is the *Hotel Creston*, 1418 Canyon St (☎428-2225; ②); motels on the town's fringes offer more salubrious, if slightly costlier alternatives. As well as Greyhounds passing through along Hwy 3, Empire Bus Lines runs an early-morning service from here to Spokane, WA (Mon & Thurs–Sun). If you're passing through, you might want to pause for the **Stone House Museum**, 219 Devon St (May–Sept daily 10am–3.30pm, by appointment the rest of the year; ☎428-9262; $2), known for its replica Kuntenai (Ktunaxa) canoe. Similar canoes, with their downpointed ends, are only found elsewhere in the world in parts of eastern Russia, underlining the fact that millennia ago migrations took place across the Bering Straits into North America.

Probably the best reason to spend time locally is the **Creston Valley Wildlife Management Area**, located 10km northwest of town off Hwy 3. Creston overlooks a broad section of valley and lowlands – relatively rare commodities in BC, home to the idly meandering Kootenay River. Over the years the river has repeatedly burst its banks, creating a rich alluvial plain beloved by farmers, and producing the lush medley of orchards and verdant fields that fringe Creston. Much of the flood plain and its wetlands, however – the so-called "Valley of the Swans" – have been preserved in their original state, creating a haven for birds and waterfowl. This is one of the world's largest nesting osprey populations, while a total of 250 species have been recorded in the confines of the Creston Management Area (not to mention otters, moose and other animals). Birds can be seen from several points, but for full details of the area visit the sanctuary's Wildlife Centre, which provides telescopes and lookouts, a library and theatre, and a wide range of guided walks and canoe trips through the area's forest, marsh and grasslands habitats.

The Kootenays

The Kootenays is one of the most attractive and unvisited parts of British Columbia, and one of the most loosely defined. It consists essentially of two major north–south valleys – the Kootenay and the Columbia, which are largely taken up by **Kootenay Lake** and **Upper** and **Lower Arrow Lakes** – and three intervening mountain ranges – the Purcells, Selkirks and Monashees, whose once-rich mineral deposits formed the kernel

The telephone code for British Columbia outside of the Vancouver area is ☎250.

of the province's early mining industry. **Nelson** is the key town, slightly peripheral to the Kootenays' rugged core, but a lovely place, and one of the few provincial towns that holds out real attractions in its own right. Scattered lakeside hamlets, notably **Kaslo** and **Nakusp**, make excellent bases for excursions into mountain scenery which has a pristine quality rarely found elsewhere. Water-based activities – canoeing and fishing in particular – are excellent, and you can also explore the ramshackle mining heritage of near-ghost towns like **Sandon** and **New Denver**. Many of these towns and villages also have more than their fair share of artists, painters and writers, lending the region considerable cultural lustre.

Getting around the region is tricky without private transport, for there are next to no public services, which is a shame because the roads here are amongst the most scenic in a province noted for its scenery. Even with your own car, there's no way to do the Kootenays justice without retracing your steps at times. You can dip in and out of the region from the Trans-Canada Highway (to the north) or Hwy 3 (to the south), but any trans-Kootenay route is more attractive than either of these main highways: the most **scenic routes** are Hwy 31A from Kaslo to New Denver, and Hwy 6 from New Denver to Vernon. Given no time constraints, your best strategy would be to enter from Creston and exit via Vernon, which sets you up for the Okanagan.

Highway 3A to Kootenay Bay

Starting from just north of Creston, **Hwy 3A** picks a slow, twisting course up the eastern shore of **Kootenay Lake** to the free car ferry at Kootenay Bay. Apart from the ample scenic rewards of the lake and the mountains beyond it, the highway is almost completely empty for all of its 79km, and none of the villages marked on maps amount to anything more than scattered houses hidden in the woods. The only noteworthy sight is the **Glass House** (May, June, Sept & Oct daily 9am–5pm; July & Aug daily 8am–8pm; $6), midway up the lake 7km south of **BOSWELL**, which ranks highly on the list of Canada's more bizarre offerings. Constructed entirely from embalming bottles, the house was built by a Mr David Brown in 1952 after 35 years in the funeral business – "to indulge", so the wonderfully po-faced pamphlet tells you, "a whim of a peculiar nature". The retired mortician travelled widely, visiting friends in the funeral profession until he'd collected 600,000 bottles – that's 250 tonnes' worth – to build his lakeside retirement home. The family continued to live here until curious tourists took the upper hand. Nearby **accommodation** is provided by the four-unit *Heidelburg Inn*, 12866 Hwy 3A (☎223-8263; ②; April–Oct) overlooking the lake and the lakeside *Mountain Shores Resort and Marina* (☎223-8258; ③; April–Sept), a combination of ten motel-type rooms, cottages and **campground** ($14–23) with store, hot showers and heated outdoor pool. There's another smaller campground, *Kootenay Kampsites* (☎223-8488; $16–20; May–Oct), 39km north of Creston with rustic, well-treed sites, laundry and hot showers.

At **GRAY CREEK**, a few kilometres onward, check out the superb **Gray Creek Store**, which boasts the once-in-a-lifetime address of 1979 Chainsaw Ave and claims, with some justification, to be "The Most Interesting Store You've Ever Seen". The shop basically *is* Gray Creek – it's the sort of place you go to get your chainsaw fixed and where real lumberjacks come for their red-checked shirts. There are two lakeside **campgrounds** nearby: the *Old Crow* (☎227-9495; $12; May–Oct) and the small *Lockhart Beach* provincial park campground ($12; May–Sept) with RV and tent sites

13km south of Gray Creek and 20km south of Kootenay Bay (see below). A bit more exotic, *Tipi Camp* (☎227-9555; June–Sept) is situated on Pilot Peninsula, reached by a twice a day 20min boat taxi from Gray Creek. To stay in a tepee you need your own bedding, and it costs $50 a night including water taxi and three meals; day-trips which include transportation, lunch and dinner cost $30. From Gray Greek, the Gray Greek Forest service road (July–Oct) leads 85km east to Kimberley (see p.442), not a short cut by any means, but scenic and adventurous driving nonetheless. Be sure to be stocked up on supplies before setting off.

CRAWFORD BAY and **KOOTENAY BAY** are names on the map that refer in the flesh to the most fleeting of settlements, the latter also being the **ferry terminal** for boats to Balfour on the west shore. Crawford Bay, 3.5km from the terminal, boasts the Kootenay Forge, an old-world forge, where in summer you can often watch blacksmiths working and a number of other artisan shops from traditional broom-makers to weavers. The area has also long been famous for the **Yasodhara Ashram**, 527 Walkes Landing Road (☎227-9224 or 1-800/661-8711), a spiritual retreat established over thirty years ago. As a place to stay, this side of the crossing is a touch brighter, and there's an **infocentre** (June–Sept daily 9am–5pm; ☎227-9267) just off the road at Crawford Bay, which can help you find some of the nicer accommodation tucked away in the woods nearby. The cheapest **motel** is the *La Chance Swiss* (☎227-9477 or 1-888/366-3385; ③), near the ferry dock, which includes a restaurant (Easter to mid-Oct). The more expensive *Wedgewood Manor Country Inn* (☎227-9233 or 1-800/862-0022; ④; April to mid-Oct), a 1910 heritage building set amidst fifty acres of gardens and estate, is upmarket and extremely pleasant, but you'll have to book well in advance. The better of two **campgrounds** here is the nicely wooded *Kokanee Chalets, Motel, Campground & RV Park* on Hwy 3A (☎352-3581 or 1-800/448-9292; mid-April to mid-Oct): as well as tent and RV sites ($16–22) it also has motel and chalet rooms around seven-minutes' walk from the beach (③); note, however, that there's also a choice of three reasonable campgrounds across the water in Balfour.

The nine-kilometre, forty-minute **ferry crossing** – purportedly the longest free ferry crossing in the world – is beautiful. Boats leave every fifty minutes from June to September, and every two hours the rest of the year, but it's a first-come, first-served affair, and in high summer unless you're a pedestrian or bike passenger it may be a couple of sailings before your turn comes round.

Balfour and Ainsworth Hot Springs

Not quite the fishing village it's billed as, **BALFOUR** is a fairly shoddy and dispersed collection of motels, garages and cafés – albeit in verdant surroundings – designed to catch the traffic rolling on and off the Kootenay Lake ferry. RV **campgrounds** line the road south to Nelson for about 2km, the quietest being those furthest from the terminal, but a much better option is the campground at Kokanee Creek (reservations possible, see p.390), about 10km beyond Balfour ($17.50; May–Sept) with a sandy beach. The handiest **motel** for the ferry is the *Balfour Beach Inn and Motel*, 8406 Bush (☎ & fax 229-4235; ②), with heated indoor pool but convenient also for the small pebbly beach just north of the terminal.

About 15km north of Balfour on Hwy 31 – look out for the telegraph poles wearing ties – **AINSWORTH HOT SPRINGS** is home to some one hundred residents, making it a town by local standards. The tasteful *Ainsworth Hot Springs Resort* (☎229-4212 or 1-800/668-1171; ⑤) is ideal if you want to stay over while taking in the scalding water of the **mineral springs** (daily 10am–9.30pm; day-pass $10, single visit $6.50), though the chalets are expensive and, despite the lovely views and the health-giving properties of the waters, local opinion rates the Nakusp Hot Springs (see p.436) rather more highly. Note that you don't need to stay in the resort to sample the springs. The nicest local

motel is the cheaper and smaller eight-room *Mermaid Lodge and Motel* (☎ & fax 229-4969 or 1-888/229-4963; ②) alongside the springs and pools. Cave enthusiasts might want to take a guided tour of **Cody Caves Provincial Park**, 12km up a rough, well-signposted gravel side road off Hwy 3 3km north of town. From the end of the road it's a twenty-minute walk to the caves, whose kilometre or more of galleries can be seen by tour only: contact Hiadventure Corporation (☎353-7425; $12).

A touch further up the increasingly beautiful Hwy 31 comes the self-contained **Woodbury Resort and Marina** (☎353-7177; ②), a collection of motel, cottages, campground ($16–20), restaurant, pub, store, heated pool, boat rentals and water-sport facilities all pitched on the lakeshore with lovely views and a small beach, it makes an attractive long-term accommodation prospect if you're tenting. Directly opposite is the **Woodbury Mining Museum** (July–Sept daily 9am–6pm; $4; ☎354-4470), a quaint pioneer building crammed with mining regalia and the entrance to a thirty-minute underground tour of the old lead, zinc and silver workings.

Kaslo and around

KASLO must rate as one of British Columbia's most attractive and friendliest little villages. Huddled at the edge of Kootenay Lake and dwarfed by towering mountains, its half-dozen streets are lined with picture-perfect wooden homes and flower-filled gardens. It started life as a sawmill in 1889 and turned into a boom town with the discovery of silver in 1893; diversification, and the steamers that plied the lakes, saved it from the cycle of boom and bust that ripped the heart out of so many similar towns. Today Kaslo remains an urbane and civilized community whose thousand or so citizens work hard at keeping it that way, supporting a cultural centre, art galleries, rummage sales – even a concert society.

The **town hall**, a distinctive green-and-white wooden building dating from 1898, is an architectural gem by any standards, as is the church opposite. Yet Kaslo's main attraction is the SS *Moyie*, the oldest surviving **paddle steamer** in North America (tours May to mid-Sept daily 9am–5pm; $5), which ferried men, ore and supplies along the mining routes from 1898 until the relatively recent advent of reliable roads. Similar steamers were the key to the Kootenays' early prosperity, their shallow draught and featherweight construction allowing them to nose into the lakes' shallowest waters and unload close to the shore. They were, in local parlance, "able to float on dew". Canada claims just six of the 24 paddle steamers left in North America, but in the *Moyie* it has the oldest, launched in 1898 and only mothballed in 1957. Inside is a collection of antiques, artefacts and photographs from the steamer's heyday. Look for the small hut alongside it, the "world's smallest post office" (closed since 1970), and drop in on Kaslo's thriving **arts centre**, the Langham Cultural Society, on A Avenue opposite the post office (☎353-2661), for theatrical performances and art exhibitions. The building, which dates from 1893, began life as hotel-cum-brothel for miners.

Kaslo makes an ideal base for tackling two of the region's major parks – Kokanee Glacier Provincial Park and the Purcell Wilderness Conservancy – and for pottering around some of the charming lakeshore communities. People at the arts centre can advise on getting to **ARGENTA** (pop. 150), 35km north, a refugee settlement of Quakers who in 1952 came from California, alienated by growing militarism, to start a new life; it's also the western trailhead for the difficult sixty-kilometre **Earl Grey Pass Trail** over the Purcell Mountains to Invermere (p.445). It's a beautiful area, but has no services and only the occasional B&B if you want to stay: ask at the Kaslo infocentre for latest details. This area, incidentally, offers a good chance of seeing **ospreys**: the Kootenays' hundred or so breeding pairs represent the largest concentration of the species in North America.

Practicalities

Finding your way round Kaslo is no problem, nor is getting information – everyone is disarmingly helpful – and there's also a **Chamber of Commerce** (early May to early Oct daily 9am–5pm; ☎ & fax 353-2525, *www.klhs.bc.ca*) at 324 Front St. More or less opposite, Discovery Canada (☎1-888/300-4453) can guide you on local wilderness adventures by foot, mountain bike or kayak.

The best and virtually only central **accommodation** is the *Kaslo Motel*, 330 D Ave (☎353-2431 or 1-877/353-2431; ②). For most other alternatives head towards the marina just north of the centre where en route you'll find, amongst others, the *Sunny Bluffs Cabins & Camp*, 434 N Marine Drive (☎353-2277; ①), offering cabins and camping sites ($10–12) overlooking Kaslo Bay Park. For **B&B** try the *Morningside*, 670 Arena Ave off Hwy 31 at West Kootenay Power Office (☎353-7681; ②; no credit cards). More interesting accommodation possibilities are available further up the lake, many with private lakeside beaches and lovely settings. The most notable are the combined hotel and campground *Lakewood Inn* (☎353-2395; ③, tent and RV sites $12–20; April–Oct), lakeside log cabins with fully equipped kitchens and camping sites with private beach and boat rentals; it's 6km north of Kaslo on Kohle Road. There are also the *Wing Creek Cabins* (☎353-2475; ③), 7km north at 9114 Hwy 31, and two B&Bs at Argenta – *Earl Grey Pass* (☎366-4472; ①) or *Place Cockaigne* (☎366-4394; ②).

Kaslo has a municipal **campground** ($13–15) on the flat ground by the lake at the end of Front Street, past the SS *Moyie* on the right. *Mirror Lake Campground* (☎353-7102; $15–18; mid-April to mid-Oct), beautifully situated 2km south of town on the main road to Ainsworth, has more facilities. North of the village on the lake are combined campground and motel or cabin lodgings (see above), as well as the *Kootenay Lake Provincial Park* campground (April–Oct), two small campgrounds ($7–9.50) 25km north of the village on Hwy 31 with access to sandy beaches.

For **food** and **drink** in Kaslo try the renowned and reasonable *Rosewood Café* (☎353-7673), at the end of Front Street, for glorious salads and steaks. Another option is the town's social hub, the *Treehouse Restaurant*, further down on Front Street, where you can eat superbly and easily strike up conversations. The nearby *Mariner Inn and Hotel* has a beer hall, and is more of a downmarket hangout. For cheap eats, *Meteor Pizza & Cafe* on 4th Street at Front Street serves up home-made pizzas and wraps.

Kokanee Glacier Provincial Park

Kaslo is one of several possible jumping-off points for **Kokanee Glacier Provincial Park**, straddling the Slocan Range of the Selkirk Mountains to the southwest, and the access road from here – signed off Hwy 31A 6km northwest of town – offers the best views and choice of trails. However, the 24-kilometre drive up Keen Creek that follows from the turn-off degenerates in poor weather from compacted gravel to a severely rutted dirt road: this really only makes it suitable for four-wheel-drive vehicles. If you do make it, the road cuts to the heart of the park, reaching the Joker Millsite parking area set amidst spectacular glacier-ringed high country. Of the eleven fine trails in the area, the most obvious **hike** from the car park runs up to Helen Deane and Kaslo lakes (8km round-trip), an easy morning amble. If you're staying overnight you can choose from the usual undeveloped campgrounds ($5) and three basic **cabins** (summer $15; winter $35) – the main one, *Slocan Chief*, is past Helen Deane Lake alongside a park ranger office.

An easier approach to the park is to drive south of Kaslo on Hwy 3A for around 40km and then follow the road up Kokanee Creek for 16km to park at Lake Gibson. Though further from Kaslo it usually gets you into the park quicker. Other approaches are from Hwy 31 10km north of Ainsworth, driving 13km up Woodbury Creek into the park;

from Hwy 6 some 14km north of Slocan, where you drive 13km up Enterprise Creek; and from Hwy 6 14km south of Slocan, where you follow a road up Lemon Creek for 16km. For more **information** on the park, call ☎825-4421 or pick up the blue *BC Parks* pamphlet from local infocentres. To reserve the campsites, call Discover Camping (see p.390).

Highway 31A and the Slocan Valley

After Kaslo you can either rattle north along a gravel road to link with the Trans-Canada Highway at Revelstoke, a wild and glorious 150-kilometre drive with a free ferry crossing at **GALENA BAY**, or you can stay in the Kootenays and shuffle west on **Hwy 31A** through the Selkirk Mountains to the **Slocan Valley**. The latter road ascends from Kaslo alongside the Kaslo River, a crashing torrent choked with branches and fallen trees and hemmed in by high mountains and cliffs of dark rock, whose metallic sheen suggests the mineral potential that fired the early growth of so many of the settlements in the region. Near its high point the road passes a series of massively picturesque lakes: **Fish Lake** is deep green and has a nice picnic spot at one end; **Bear Lake** is equally pretty; and **Beaver Pond** is an amazing testament to the beaver's energy and ingenuity.

Sandon

The ghost town of **SANDON**, one of five in the region, is located 13km south of Hwy 31A, up a signed gravel side road that climbs through scenery of the utmost grandeur. Unfortunately, nowadays Sandon is too much ghost and not enough town to suggest how it might have looked in its silver-mining heyday, when it had 24 hotels, 23 saloons, an opera house, thriving red-light district and 5000 inhabitants (it even had electric light, well before Victoria or Vancouver). Its dilapidated, rather than evocative, state is due mainly to a flood, which swept away the earlier boardwalk settlement in 1955, leaving a partly inhabited rump that clutters along Carpenter Creek. Pop into the old City Hall for a walking tour pamphlet from the **infocentre** (May–Oct daily 10am–6pm), then head for the new **museum** (May–Oct Wed–Sun 9.30am–5.30pm; $2) in Sandon's only brick building, the old general store with photos and domestic and commercial artefacts from the town's heyday.

The trip is enhanced, however, if you manage a couple of local **hikes**. Idaho Peak is a must from Sandon, being one of the most accessible and spectacular walks in the area. A reasonable twelve-kilometre gravel access road leads into alpine pastures and a car park: from there it's a five-kilometre round trip to the summit of Mount Idaho and back, with emerging views all the way to the breathtaking panorama at the Forest Service lookout point. Or follow all or part of the **KNS Historic Trail** (6km each way) from the site, which follows the course of the 1895 Kaslo–New Denver–Slocan ore-carrying railway, past old mine works and eventually to fine views of the New Denver Glacier across the Slocan Valley to the west. Coupled with leaflets from the infocentre, the walk vividly documents the area's Wild West mining history, harking back to an era when the district – known as "Silvery Slocan" – produced the lion's share of Canada's silver. "Silver, lead, and hell are raised in the Slocan," wrote one local newspaper in 1891, "and unless you can take a hand in producing these articles, your services are not required." The immense vein of silver-rich galena that started the boom was discovered by accident in 1891 by two colourful prospectors, Eli Carpenter and Jack Seaton, when they got lost on the ridges returning to Ainsworth from Slocan Lake. Back in the bar they fell out over the find, and each raced out with his own team to stake the claim. Seaton won, and was to become a vastly wealthy silver baron who travelled in his own train carriage across Canada, condemning Carpenter to return to his earlier profession as a tightrope walker and to an ultimately penurious death.

New Denver

After the Sandon turn-off Hwy 31A drops into the **Slocan Valley**, a minor but still spectacular lake-bottomed tributary between the main Kootenay and Columbia watersheds, and meets Hwy 6 at **NEW DENVER**. Born of the same silver-mining boom as Kaslo, and with a similarly pretty lakeside setting and genuine pioneer feel, New Denver is, if anything, quieter than its neighbour. The clapboard houses are in peeling, pastel-painted wood, and the tree-lined streets are mercifully free of neon, fast food and most evidence of tourist passage. In town, the **Silvery Slocan Museum**, housed in the old wooden Bank of Montréal building at the corner of 6th Avenue and Bellevue (July & Aug 10.30am–4.30pm; $2; ☎358-2201), is good for twenty minutes on the background and artefacts of the area's mining heritage.

Well-signposted from the highway the moving **Nikkei Internment Memorial Centre** at 306 Josephine St (May–Sept daily 9.30am–5pm; rest of year by appointment; $4; ☎358-7288), is the only museum in Canada dedicated to the 22,000 Nikkei (Canadians of Japanese ancestry) who, in 1942, were forcibly relocated from the coast to remote internment camps in the interior after Pearl Harbour. Beautiful Japanese gardens now surround the wooden shacks and outhouses that the Nikkei were forced to build themselves. Although the majority of Nikkei were Canadian citizens, they were all labelled "enemy aliens" and stripped of their possessions, homes and businesses. It wasn't until 1988 that former prime minister Brian Mulroney finally apologized to Japanese-Canadians and awarded them token monetary compensation. Inside the cultural centre an exhibition tells the story through photos, paintings and artefacts.

There's no official **infocentre** in New Denver, but local bookstores or a business, such as Nuru Designs (summer daily 10am–4pm; ☎358-2733), are the places to contact for specific information on the surrounding valley. As a stopover it's appealing but not quite as enticing as Kaslo; its **accommodation** possibilities include a single beach-hut-type motel, the *Valhalla Inn*, 509 Slocan Ave (☎358-2228; ③); the lakeview *Sweet Dreams Guest House* (☎358-2415; ③), a restored heritage home on Slocan Lake at 720 Eldorado Ave; and the simple *New Denver Municipal Campground* (☎358-2316; $13–16; May–Sept) on the south side of the village. Four kilometres north of town on Hwy 6 is the *Rosebury Provincial Park* campground ($9.50; April–Oct) on the banks of Wilson Creek, a lightly forested site with lake and mountain views. For **food** in the village try 6th Avenue, where you'll find the relaxed *Apple Tree Sandwich Shop* and the bistro *Panini*. There's more accommodation and a campground at Silverton, another tiny former mining village just 4.5km south of New Denver on Hwy 6.

Slocan and the Slocan Valley

Southbound out of New Denver, Hwy 6 follows the tight confines of the **Slocan Valley** for another 100km of ineffable mountain and lake landscapes. Be certain to stop at the **Slocan Lake Viewpoint**, 6km out of New Denver, where a short path up a small cliff provides stupendous views. The 125,000-acre **Valhalla Provincial Park** (☎825-3500) wraps up the best of the landscapes on the eastern side of Slocan Lake; a wilderness area with no developed facilities, most of it is out of reach unless you boat across the water, though there are two trails that penetrate it from the hamlet of **SLOCAN**, another former mining village at the south end of the lake. For a taste of the local outdoors, the canter up the old railway bed from Slocan is a popular short hike, and there's more fresh air and good picnicking spots at the nearby Mulvey Basin and Cove Creek **beaches**. Note, too, that gravel roads lead up from Hwy 6 to the more accessible heights of **Kokanee Glacier Provincial Park** to the east (p.433. For more on the area, notably tours into the Valhalla park, contact Slocan's **infocentre**, 903 Slocan St (July–Aug; ☎355-2277).

If you need **accommodation** en route south there are about half-a-dozen options, all in rustic settings with mountain or lake views. Try either *Lemon Creek Lodge* (☎355-2403; cabins ③, campground $15), 7km south of Slocan on Kennedy Road, or the *Slocan*

Motel (☎355-2344; ②), at 801 Harold St in Slocan itself off Hwy 6. In addition to provincial **campgrounds** at Mulvey Basin and Cove Creek ($9.50; both May–Oct), there's the unserviced *Silverton Municipal Campground* (free; May–Oct), just south of New Denver. More exciting, the *Valhalla Lodge and Tipi Retreat* (☎365-3226; ④; May–Sept) offers an opportunity to stay in the Valhalla Provincial Park either in tepees or waterfront cabins, and use of a hot tub and sauna.

Along Highway 6

Highway 6 may not be the most direct east–west route through British Columbia, but it's certainly one of the most dramatic, and the one to think about if you're heading towards Revelstoke to the north or the Okanagan to the west. From New Denver it initially strikes north and after 30km passes **Summit Lake**, a perfect jewel of water, mountain and forest that's served by the new *Summit Lake Provincial Park* **campground** ($15; mid-May to mid-Sept). A rough road ("Take at Your Own Risk") runs south from here into the mountains and a small winter ski area.

Nakusp and onwards

Sixteen kilometres beyond Summit Lake, lakefront **NAKUSP** is, like Kaslo and Nelson, a rare thing in British Columbia: a town with enough charisma to make it worth visiting for its own sake. The setting is par for the course in the Kootenays, with a big lake – **Upper Arrow Lake**, part of the Columbia River system – and the snow-capped Selkirk Mountains to the east providing the majestic backdrop. The nearby hot springs are the main attraction, but you could happily wander around the town for a morning, or boat or swim off the public **beach**. The only actual sight in town is the **Nakusp Museum** in the village hall at 6th Avenue and 1st Street, full of the usual archive material, logging displays and Victorian bric-a-brac (May–Sept Tues–Thurs 12.30–4.30pm, Mon & Fri–Sun 11am–5pm; donation). The helpful **infocentre**, based in the fake paddle-steamer building next door at 92 West St and 6th Avenue just off the main street (summer daily 9am–5pm; winter Mon–Fri 10am–4pm; ☎265-4234 or 1-800/909-8819), can provide details on local fishing, boating and hiking possibilities, and – for those driving onwards – timings for the Galena Bay and Fauquier ferries. Also ask about the possibility of renting houseboats on the lake if you're staying for a few days.

If you're only going to try the hot springs experience once, **Nakusp Hot Springs**, a well-signposted complex 13km northeast of town, is the place to do it (daily: June–Sept 9.30am–10pm; Oct–May 11am–9.30pm; $5, day-pass $7): it's not unusual for late-night informal parties to develop around the two outdoor pools. Unlike many similar enterprises, the natural pools are cleaned each night and are backed up by nice changing facilities, but bear in mind they're very popular in the summer. Note that there are some undeveloped springs within striking distance of here if you have a car. To reach **St Leon Hot Springs**, take Hwy 23 north out of Nakusp for 24km and then turn down the logging road after the second bridge for 10km to the trailhead; the piping hot springs are 100m away down a steep trail to the river. If you stay on Hwy 23 for about another 10km, you'll reach **Halcyon Hot Springs** (daily 9am–9pm; $6), which was first commercialized in 1888, its waters bottled and sent to England. Today, there are four pools here of varying temperatures, all of which face Upper Arrow Lake and the mountain peaks beyond. Camping is also available for $20.

For a place to **stay** in Nakusp, try the *Selkirk Inn*, 210 6th Ave W (☎265-3666 or 1-800/661-8007; ②), or *Kuskanax/Tenderfoot Lodge*, 515 Broadway (☎265-3618 or 1-800/663-0100; ②), which is equally central but a bit more upmarket and has a recommended Canadian fare **restaurant**. For cheap, basic hamburgers and pizzas there's *Nick's Place* at

93 5th Ave. Campers would do best to aim for the lovely *Nakusp Hot Springs* **campground**, near the hot springs at 1701 Canyon Rd (☎265-4528 or 1-800/909-8819; $15; mid-May to mid-Oct); non-campers could try the adjoining *Cedar Chalets* (☎265-4505; ②), but reservations are essential in summer. Another out-of-town campground is the *McDonald Creek Provincial Park* site ($12; April–Oct), 10km south of Nakusp on Hwy 6, and complete with lakeside beaches.

From Nakusp, you can either continue along Hwy 6 or branch off up Hwy 23, which heads 100km north to Revelstoke (see p.555), a lonely and spectacular journey involving a free ferry crossing halfway at **Galena Bay** (hourly sailings each way).

Fauquier

Highway 6 doglegs south from Nakusp for 57 delightful kilometres to the ferry crossing at **FAUQUIER**. This hamlet consists of a handful of buildings including a garage, a store, the *Mushroom Addition* **café** for coffee and meals, and the only **motel** for kilometres – the *Arrow Lake Motel* (☎269-7622 or 1-888/499-5222; ②), bang on the lakeside near the ferry at 101 Oak St. There's a **campground** 2km back towards Nakusp, *Plum Hollow Camping*, Needles Road N (☎269-7669; $6–12; March–Nov), marked by two big arrows sticking in the ground. Some 3km beyond that the *Goose Downs* **B&B** (☎265-3139; ②) is signed off Hwy 6.

Onwards from Needles

The free **ferry** across **Lower Arrow Lake** to Needles takes about five minutes, departs half-hourly from 5.15am to 9.45pm, and operates an intermittent shuttle throughout the night. **NEEDLES** amounts to no more than a ramp off the ferry on the other side. There's an unofficial **campground** at Whatshan Lake, 3km off the highway just after Needles, but otherwise Hwy 6 is a gloriously empty ribbon as it burrows through the staggering Monashee Mountains – though some of the time it's too hemmed in by forest for you to catch anything but trees. After cresting Monashee Pass (1198m), the highway begins the long descent through the **Coldstream Valley** towards the Okanagan. Snow dusts the mountains here almost year-round, crags loom above the meadows that increasingly break the forest cover, and beautiful flower-filled valleys wind down to the highway. The first sign of life in over 100km is the *Gold Panner* **campground** (☎547-2025; $12–14; April–Oct), a good spot to overnight or to explore the utter wilderness of **Monashee Provincial Park** to the north. The park is reached by rough road from the hamlet of **CHERRYVILLE**, 10km further west, which despite its cartographic prominence is just three houses, a garage and Frank's General Store.

LUMBY, another 20km beyond, is scarcely more substantial, although **rooms** at the *Twin Creeks Motel* (☎547-9221; ②) might be worth considering if it's late, given that the Okanagan lodgings ahead could well be packed. The village also boasts a simple riverside **campground** run by the local Lions Club (☎547-9504; $7; May–Oct) and there's a seasonal **infocentre** on the highway (July & Aug; ☎547-8844). Beyond the village, the road glides through lovely pastoral country, with orchards, verdant meadows, low, tree-covered hills, and fine wooden barns built to resemble inverted longboats.

Nelson

NELSON is one of British Columbia's best towns, and one of the few interior settlements you could happily spend two or three days in – longer if you use it as a base for

---

The telephone code for British Columbia outside of the Vancouver area is ☎250.

touring the Kootenays by car. The town is home to more than its share of baby-boomers and refugees from the 1960s, a hangover that's nurtured a friendly, civilized and close-knit community, a healthy cultural scene and a liveliness – manifest in alternative cafés, nightlife and secondhand clothes shops – that you'll be hard pushed to find elsewhere in the province outside Vancouver. There are, apparently, more artists and craftspeople here per head of the nine thousand population than any other town in Canada. At the same time it's a young place permeated with immense civic pride, which was given a further boost by the filming here of *Roxanne*, Steve Martin's spoof version of *Cyrano de Bergerac*. Producers chose the town for its idyllic lakeside setting and 350-plus c.1900 homes, factors which for once live up to the Canadian talent for hyperbole – in this case a claim to be "Queen of the Kootenays" and "Heritage Capital of Western Canada".

Located 34km west of Balfour on Hwy 3A, the town forms a tree-shaded grid of streets laid over the hilly slopes that edge down to the westernmost shores of Kootenay Lake. Most homes are immaculately kept and vividly painted, and even the commercial **buildings** along the parallel main streets – Baker and Vernon – owe more to the vintage architecture of Seattle and San Francisco than to the drab Victoriana of much of eastern Canada. If you want to add purpose to your wanderings, pick up the *Heritage Walking Tour* or the *Heritage Motoring Tour* pamphlets from the **infocentre**, 225 Hall Street (June–Aug daily 8am–8pm; Sept–May Mon–Fri 8.30am–5pm; ☎352-3433 or 1-877/663-5706, *www.nelsonchamber.bc.ca*), which takes you around the sort of houses that many Canadians dream of retiring to, and only occasionally oversells a place – notably when it lands you in front of the old jam factory and the electricity substation. Better bets are the courthouse and city hall, both designed by F.M. Rattenbury, also responsible for Victoria's *Empress Hotel* and Parliament Buildings. Free tours with a costumed guide are available from the infocentre in summer. If walking tours aren't your thing, perhaps the town's **shops** may be, particularly those of its artists and craftspeople, who in summer club together to present **Artwalk**, a crawl round many of the town's little galleries. Most of these have regular openings and wine-gorging receptions, making for numerous free-for-all parties. If you don't want to walk, take the restored streetcar that runs the length of the town's waterfront to the infocentre. Oliver's Books on Baker Street is excellent for maps, guides and general reading, with a bias towards the sort of New Age topics that find a ready market here. Another shop worth a stop is Still Eagle, 557 Ward St, the province's first hemp-store, where even snowboards are made from hemp.

For the most part the area owes its development to the discovery of copper and silver ore on nearby Toad Mountain at the end of the nineteenth century. Even though the mines declined fairly quickly, Nelson's diversification into gold and lumber, and its roads, railway and waterways, saved it from mining's usual downside. Today mining is back on the agenda as old claims are re-explored, and even if the idea of the town's **Museum of Mines** (daily 10am–4pm; free; ☎352-5242), next to the infocentre, leaves you cold, it's worth meeting the curator, an old prospector who talks at length – and interestingly – on the quest for silver, copper and gold, past and present.

It's probably less worthwhile to trek over to the **Nelson Museum**, about twenty minutes' walk from the centre, which offers a rather haphazard display that's obviously the work of enthusiastic amateurs (summer daily 1–6pm; winter Mon–Sat 1–4.30pm; $2). There are, however, odd points of interest, notably a chronicle of the original 1886 Silver King Mine that brought the town to life, as well as tantalizingly scant details on the Doukhobor, a Russian religious sect whose members still live in self-contained communities around the Kootenays (see p.427). Better instead to walk to **Lakeside Park** near the Nelson Bridge, where there are surprisingly good sandy **beaches** and picnic areas, boat rentals and waterfront paths. If you're here between May and mid-October, make it a point to stop by the Saturday **Farmers and Artisans Market** in Cottonwood

Falls Park (9.30am–3pm). Organic fruits, vegetables, delicious breads and local arts and crafts are all for sale.

Practicalities

Nelson is served by Greyhound **buses** (☎352-3939) that run west to Penticton (for connections to Vancouver, the Okanagan and Kamloops) and east to Cranbrook (connections to Calgary via Banff or Fort Macleod). There are infrequent minibus services to Kaslo (☎353-2492 for details) and Nakusp (☎265-3674), but check with the infocentre before building a trip around these. The depot is on the lakeshore, just below the town proper at Chahko-Mika Mall. If you need a car, Rent-a-Wreck has an outlet here (☎352-5122).

There's a reasonable spread of **accommodation**, but comparatively little in the downtown area: among the central choices are the characterful *Heritage Inn*, 422 Vernon St (☎352-5331, *www.heritageinn.org*; ③) with cosy, old world rooms, and the cheaper and equally central *Dancing Bear Inn*, 171 Baker St (☎352-7573; ①), a nicely renovated HI-affiliated **youth hostel**. For something around twice the price you could try downtown **B&B** options such as the four-room *Emory House*, 811 Vernon St (☎352-7007; ③), or the highly regarded *Inn the Garden*, a restored Victorian home one block south of Baker Street at 408 Victoria St (☎352-3226; ③). Most of the **motels** are on Hwy 31A at the north end of town or over the miniature Forth Road bridge on the north side of the lake. Here you can try the *Villa Motel*, 655 Hwy 3A (☎352-5515 or 1-888/352-5515; ②), with the use of an indoor pool, or the *North Shore Inn*, 687 Hwy 3A (☎352-6606 or 1-800/593-6636; ③), where rates include a coffee and muffin breakfast. The nearest **campgrounds** are the *City Tourist Park*, on the corner of High Street and Willow (☎352-9031; $13–16; mid-May to early Oct), and *Shannon's RV Park* (☎825-9648; $16–22; mid-May to Sept), 7km from town on the north shore of the lake at 1940 Hwy 3A. If these are full, head east towards Balfour and the three or more sites near the ferry terminal (see p.431).

The choice of **restaurants** is broad, and you can't go far wrong wandering around and choosing something that looks tempting. *Stanley Baker's*, a locals' place on Baker Street next to the Nelson Shopping Company mall, is good for cappuccino, snacks and big, cheap breakfasts. The *Vienna*, an alternative café and bookshop just off Baker Street opposite the Bank of Montreal, is also worth a try, as is *Orso Negro* on Victoria, a block up from Baker, with bagels and excellent coffee. For lunch or evening meals, downtown residents head to the *Main Street Diner*, 616 Baker St (☎354-4848; closed Sun), or the top-flight *All Seasons Café*, The Alley, 620 Herridge Lane (☎352-0101) which also has a nice patio dining area. Also worth a look is *Max Irma's*, 515a Kootenay St (☎352-2332) while for novelty value you could do worse than spoil your breath at the *Outer Clove*, 353 Stanley St (☎354-1667), where everything from decor to dessert features garlic (it's better than it sounds). At 301 Baker St, *The Rice Bowl* (☎354-4129), a local favourite, uses mainly organic ingredients to serve up fine seafood, sushi and vegan meals in a buzzing environment – note that it closes early, normally by 8pm. For **drinking**, make for *Mike's Bar* round the side of the *Heritage Inn*, 422 Vernon St, which sells the full range of Nelson Brewing Company beers (the brewery was founded in 1893): top tipple is the flagship Old Brewery Ale (OBA). If you're shopping for your own meals, the big **supermarkets** are in or near the mall alongside the bus depot, whilst the excellent Kootenay Co-Op in town at 295 Baker St can satisfy all your organic and wholefood needs – the organic bakery turns out a supreme loaf of bread.

North to Radium Hot Springs

Heading north from Creston and the Kootenays, Hwy 95 travels through scenery as spectacular as anything in the big Rockies parks to the north. The route follows the broad valley bottom of the **Columbia River**, bordered on the east by the Rockies and on the west by the marginally less breathtaking **Purcell Mountains**, though for the most part access to the wilderness here is limited and you'll have to be content with enjoying it from the highway. It's a fast run if you're driving, except where the road hugs the river's dramatic bluffs and sweeping meanders. Hwys 93 and 95 meet near **Cranbrook**, where you can make for either of two US border crossings, double back eastwards on Hwy 3 to Crowsnest Pass and Alberta, or head north for Radium Hot Springs and the entrance to Kootenay National Park (see p.557). Greyhound **buses** ply all these routes, with most connections at Cranbrook.

East from Creston

Some forty kilometres east of Creston, buses drop off at the small Shell garage in unspoilt **YAHK**, no more than a few houses nestled amidst the trees; a good, quiet stopover here is the single **motel**, *Bob's* (☎424-5581; ②), or you can camp at *Yahk Provincial Park* ($12; May to mid-Sept). Hwy 95 branches off from Hwy 3 here and heads south for the US border (11km). Incidentally, the highway crosses a **time zone** between Yahk and Moyie – clocks go forward one hour.

Following Hwy 3 northbound you reach the tiny community of **MOYIE** on the edge of lovely **Moyie Lake**, which provides a welcome visual relief after the unending tree-covered slopes hereabouts. Though there's no motel accommodation, there is a **B&B**, the *Long Shadows House* on Barkley Road just north of the village (☎829-0650; ③). There are also three local **campgrounds**, including the excellent one at **Moyie Lake Provincial Park** (reservations possible, see p.390; $17.50; May–Sept) – reach it by taking Munro Lake Road west off Hwy 3/95 for a kilometre from the northernmost point of Moyie Lake. Alternatively, you could try the private *Green River Campground,* on the lakeshore, signed about 1km off Hwy 3/95 (☎426-4154; $10–13.50; May–Oct), or the *Moyie River Campground*, 18km south of Cranbrook on Hwy 3/95 (☎489-3047; $9–13.50; April–Nov).

Cranbrook

The regional service and ex-forestry town of **CRANBROOK**, despite a location that marks it out as a transport hub, is one of the most dismal in the province, its dreariness hardly redeemed by the surrounding high mountains. A strip of motels and marshalling yards dominates a downtown area otherwise distinguished only by thrift shops and closing-down sales. Local lifeblood, such as it is, flows from the motels, this being an obvious place to eat, sleep and drive away from the next morning.

The only sight to speak of is the **Canadian Museum of Rail Travel**, a smallish affair that centres on the restored carriages of an old trans-Canada luxury train (July & Aug daily 8am–8pm; rest of the year 10am–6pm; $6.95). The period buildings pushed by the **infocentre**, 2279 Cranbrook St (year-round 9am–5pm; ☎426-5914 or 1-800/222-6174, *www.cranbrookchamber.com*), aren't interesting enough to justify the trawl round the streets. The infocentre was burned down by animal-rights activists in 1999 because of its stuffed animal display, and not to be outdone they have reopened on the same spot with a new **Wildlife Museum** (same hours) filled with stuffed road-kills from the surrounding area.

You may have to stay in Cranbrook, as there's little in the way of **accommodation** on the roads north and south; there are a dozen or more motels that fit the bill. The top of the range in town is the *Heritage Inn* at 803 Cranbrook (☎489-4301 or 1-800/663-2708; ④), a large, modern motel on the main road. Cheaper and more intimate is the *Heritage Estate Motel* (☎426-3862 or 1-800/670-1001; ②), near the southern edge of town at 362 Van Horne St SW and therefore removed from some of the bleaker corners.

The same can be said of a nice **B&B**, the *Singing Pines*, 5180 Kennedy Rd (☎426-5959 or 1-800/863-4969; ④), situated off Hwy 95A 3km north of town in a quiet location with mountain views. The town's *Mount Baker RV Park*, at Baker Park on 14th Avenue and 1st Street (☎1-877/501-2288; $18–24; April–Oct), is the closest **campground**, though it's a good deal less appealing than the *Jimsmith Provincial Park*, 4km southwest of town, but which has no showers ($12; May–Oct).

The strip offers plenty of cheap **eating** options: for something more welcoming make for the *ABC Family Restaurant* at 1601 Cranbrook St N. The Greyhound **bus terminal** (☎426-3331) is hidden behind *McDonald's* opposite the Mohawk gas station. Bus services run east to Fernie, Sparwood and southern Alberta (2 daily); west to Nelson, Castlegar and Vancouver (3 daily); north to Kimberley, Radium, Banff and Calgary (1 daily); and south to Spokane in the US (1 daily).

East from Cranbrook

Highway 93 leaves Hwy 95 between Fort Steele (see p.443) and Cranbrook, following Hwy 3 as far as Elko before branching off south for the United States border (91km). An unsullied hamlet of around half a dozen homes, **ELKO** is gone in a flash, but you might want to stop and eat at *Wendy's Place*, a cosy backwoods spot, or to camp at the excellent *Kikomun Creek Provincial Park* **campground** (reservations possible, see p.390; $17.50; May–Oct), on the eastern shore of the artificial Lake Koocanusa and signed off Hwy 93 3km west of town. The only other local **accommodation** is the *West Crow Motel and Campground* at the entrance to the Elk Valley (☎529-7349; ②, tents and RVs $10–14; year-round), with a secluded tenting area. Hwy 3 offers colossal views of the Rockies and the fast-flowing, ice-clear Elk River, before hitting **FERNIE**, 32km north of Elko, a pleasant place of tree-lined streets, a few motels and small wooden houses, surrounded by a ring of knife-edged mountains. The *Cedar Lodge* (☎423-4622; ③) is the place to stay here or, failing that, the HI-affiliated official **youth hostel**, the *Raging Elk International Hostel*, 892 6th Ave (☎423-6811; ①). The **infocentre** (daily 9am–5pm; ☎423-6868) stands alongside a reconstructed wooden oil derrick 2km north of town on Hwy 3 at Dicken Road. **Mount Fernie Provincial Park** has plenty of hiking trails, picnic areas and a campground just west of town off Hwy 3 (reservations possible, see p.390; $12; mid-May to mid-Sept). **Fernie Snow Valley**, 5km west of town and 2km off the main highway, boasts what is reputedly the longest ski season in the BC Rockies (Nov–May); it also has few typical resort-type accommodation possibilities.

Hwy 3 leaves the Elk Valley at **SPARWOOD**, 29km beyond Fernie, where signs of the area's coal-mining legacy begin to appear. Close to the town – but barely visible – is Canada's largest open-cast **coal mine**, capable of disgorging up to 18,000 tonnes of coal daily. Tours of the mine (July & Aug Mon–Fri 1.30pm) leave from the local **infocentre** (daily 9am–6pm; ☎425-2423), at the junction of Hwy 3 and Aspen Drive – look for the big miner's statue. The town itself is surprisingly neat and clean, and the obvious *Black Nugget Motor Inn*, Hwy 3 at Red Cedar Drive (☎425-2236 or 1-800/663-2706; ③), makes a convenient place to stay.

Elkford

The remainder of Hwy 3 in British Columbia is despoiled by mining; the road crests the Continental Divide 19km east of Sparwood at **Crowsnest Pass** (see p.480). Far more scenic is the drive north from Sparwood on Hwy 43, which heads upstream beside the Elk River for 35km to **ELKFORD**. Nestled against a wall of mountains to the east and more gentle hills to the west, the village claims to be the "wilderness capital of British Columbia" – a high-pitched punt, but close to the mark if you're prepared to carry on up either of two rough gravel roads to the north. The more easterly road follows the Elk a further 80km to **Elk Lakes Provincial Park** close to the Continental Divide, one of the wildest road-accessible spots in the province (reservations possible, see p.390). The slightly better route to the west heads 55km into the heart of unbeatable scenery below 2792-metre **Mount Armstrong**. Both areas offer excellent chances of spotting wildlife like cougars, deer, moose, elk or members of North America's largest population of bighorn sheep.

Before entering either area, however, it's essential to pick up maps and information at the Elkford **infocentre** (year-round Mon–Fri 8am–5pm; ☎1-877/355-9453), located at the junction of Hwy 43 and Michel Road. It can also give directions to nearby **Josephine Falls**, a few minutes' walk from the parking area on Fording Mine Road. Whether you're staying here or pushing on north, a tent is helpful: the only accommodation options are the *Elkford Motor Inn*, 808 Michel Rd, next to the shopping centre (☎865-2211 or 1-800/203-7723; ②) or the more expensive *Hi Rock Inn*, 2 Chauncey St (☎865-2226; ③). **Camping** can be had at Elkford's municipal campground (☎865-2650; $12; May–Oct), and at the wilderness campgrounds around Elk Lakes ($5; June–Sept).

Kimberley

KIMBERLEY, a few kilometres from Cranbrook on Hwy 95A, is Canada's highest city (1117m), and in many ways one of its silliest, thanks to a tourist-tempting ruse to transform itself into a Bavarian village after the imminent closure of the local mine in the 1970s threatened it with economic oblivion. The result is a masterpiece of kitsch that's almost irresistible: buildings have been given a plywood-thin veneer of authenticity, piped Bavarian music dribbles from shops with names like The Yodelling Woodcarver, and even the fire hydrants have been painted to look like miniature replicas of Happy Hans, Kimberley's lederhosened mascot. The ploy might seem absurd, but there's no doubting the energy and enthusiasm that has gone into it, nor the economic rewards that have accrued from the influx of tourists and European immigrants – Germans included – who've provided an authentic range of cafés and restaurants and a variety of family-oriented summer and winter activities.

Most of the Teutonic gloss is around the **Bavarian Platzl** on Spokane Street in the small downtown area, whose fake houses compare poorly with the authentic wooden buildings and more alpine surroundings on the outskirts. If nothing else, you can leave Kimberley safe in the knowledge that you have seen "**Canada's Biggest Cuckoo Clock**", a fraudulent affair which amounts to little more than a large wooden box that twitters inane and incessant music. The dreaded contraption performs on being fed small change, and people oblige often enough so that Happy Hans (rather than a cuckoo) makes his noisy appearance almost continuously; when he doesn't, the council often employs some unfortunate to play the accordion morning, noon and night to keep up the musical interludes.

Apart from the clock, and a small **museum** upstairs in the library down the road, the other main local sight is the **Sullivan Mine**, pre-Bavarian Kimberley's main employer and one of the world's biggest lead and zinc mines. The mine, now closed, is due to be remembered in an **interpretive centre** which will tell the mine's story and include a trip to the original portal – due to high insurance demands the underground mine itself cannot be opened to the public. You can also explore the local history on the **Bavarian City Mining Railway**, a 7-kilometre narrated ride on a train salvaged from a local mine. En route the train travels along steep inclines and switchbacks through the valley, highlighting Kimberley's past mining activities and its future developments now that the lifeblood has run dry. It leaves from the downtown station, a block from the Platz, on Jerry Sorenson Way (June–Sept daily noon–6.30pm; $6). At the station you can also view a mini 1920s mining camp complete with a schoolhouse.

If you're around from early December through April, and feel the need to escape Kimberley's kitsch, head for the Kimberley alpine **ski resort** (☎427-4881) four kilometres west of town. Owned by Charles Locke, the owner of numerous ski resorts throughout Canada, the resort boasts eight lifts and 67 runs, the longest of which covers more than six kilometres. Passes cost $43 for the day, $35 for the afternoon and $15 for a night skiing session. Kimberley also boasts one of Canada's most popular **golf** courses, *Trickle Creek* on Jerry Sorenson Way (☎427-3878; $69 for 18 holes, $28 for a cart), but you'll have to book ahead if you want to play here.

Practicalities

If you need **accommodation**, try the central *Quality Inn of the Rockies*, 300 Wallinger Ave (☎427-2266 or 1-800/661-7559; ③), or the smaller *North Star Motel* (☎427-5633 or 1-800/663-5508; ②) at the northern edge of town: for an extra $5 you can have access to a kitchen. *Same Sun International Travel Hostel* is a new **hostel** on the Platz (☎427-7191; ①) with dormitory accommodation. The nearest **campground**, the inevitably named *Happy Hans Riverside RV Resort* (☎427-2929; $18–28; May–Oct), is south of the town centre on St Mary's Road and has modern facilities. Drop into the twee but excellent *Chef Bernard* café and **restaurant** opposite the clock, where the owner – heartily sick of Bavaria – often plays Irish fiddle music as a mark of defiance. He's also one of the best local chefs, and people come from miles for his fondue evenings. He has **rooms** upstairs (☎427-2433; ②). A favourite cheap place for lunch and breakfast is *Our Place*, 290 Spokane St, just down from the post office on the main crossroads. For more refined culinary offerings, make for *Pepper's*, 490 Wallinger Ave, a chicken, ribs and pasta place a couple of minutes' walk from the main plaza. Further afield is the *Old Barn House*, about fifteen-minutes' walk or a short drive from the town centre towards the ski area. For full details of Kimberley's many summer events, call in on the **info-centre** (daily: June–Sept 9am–7pm; Oct–May 9am–5pm; ☎427-3666) presently at 350 Ross St, just off the main crossroads past the *Quality Inn* – but it is due to move soon. The key draw is **Julyfest**, which includes a one-week beer festival and – almost inevitably – an international accordion championship.

Fort Steele Heritage Town

If you stick to Hwy 93/95 rather than detouring to Kimberley, you'll come to **FORT STEELE HERITAGE TOWN** (daily: May to early June & mid-Sept to early Oct 9.30am–5.30pm; early June to mid-Sept 9.30am–8pm; $7.50, $3.75 after 5.30pm), an impressively reconstructed c.1900 village of some 55 buildings in a superb mountain-ringed setting. It suffers somewhat by comparison with the similar reconstruction at Barkerville (125 buildings), but that's far further from civilization deep in Cariboo country (see p.404). The Fort Steele settlement started life in the 1860s as a provisions stop and river crossing for gold prospectors heading east to Wildhorse Creek, 6km beyond. By the late 1890s, thanks both to the local discovery of silver, lead and zinc, and the mistaken assumption that the railway would push through here, the population reached four thousand. But by 1910, after the mining frenzy had settled and the Canadian Pacific Railway chose to ride through Cranbrook instead, the population had shrunk to no more than 150.

Though the site was never completely abandoned, there was still much to do when restoration began in 1961. Staffed by volunteers in period dress, the town now consists of numerous buildings, some replicas, some original (1860s), some from the period of Steele's tenure, others brought from elsewhere and rebuilt. Among them are an old-time music hall, a blacksmiths, bakery, printers, general store and many more, with the added novelty of being able to watch people shoe horses, bake bread, make quilts and so forth. More spookily, there's also a restored Masonic Lodge, where a couple of funny-handshakers let you in on various selected "secrets" of Masonic life. You can also nab a ride on a steam engine and, if you really must, take a turn on a wagon pulled by the massive Clydesdale horses that are reared in the village. These foibles notwithstanding, proceedings are all under the auspices of the provincial government, so generally lack the commercial frenzy that often characterizes such places. At 8pm most summer evenings the village reopens for an old-time variety show and cabaret.

A couple of ranches and B&Bs aside, there's little accommodation in the immediate vicinity, though there are two **campgrounds**: the *Fort Steele Resort and RV Park* across from the village (☎489-4268; $15–21), which has all the usual facilities, and the smaller *Original Fort Steele* campground (☎426-5117; $15–21; June–Sept), on Kelly Road 2km south of the village and with similar facilities. Just east of Fort Steele there's also the *Norbury Lake Provincial Park* campground ($12; mid-May to mid-Sept) with tent and RV sites. If you can get in, the *Wild Horse Farm* (☎426-6000; ④; May–Oct), with only three **rooms**, is an attractive log-faced "manor house" surrounded by eighty acres of meadows, woods and park-like estate across from the village.

To Fairmont Hot Springs

Back on Hwy 93/95, the Columbia Valley's scenery picks up as the Rockies begin to encroach and the blanket of trees opens up into pastoral river meadows. First stop is **Wasa**, whose lake, protected by the *Wasa Lake Provincial Park*, is warm enough for summer swimming. The lake also has a sizeable provincial park **campground** (reservations possible, see p.390; $15; May–Sept). **Skookumchuck** ("strong water"), marked as a town on most maps, is in fact little more than a pulp mill whose chimneys belch out unpleasantness that spreads for kilometres downwind.

After a few kilometres the road curves around the **Dutch Creek Hoodoos**, fantastically eroded river bluffs that were created, according to Ktunaxa legend, when a vast wounded fish crawling up the valley expired at this point: as its flesh rotted, the bones fell apart to create the hoodoos. Close by is **Columbia Lake** – not one of the area's most picturesque patches of water, though the *Mountain Village*, a fine wooden **restaurant** crammed with hundreds of old bottles, makes a good meal stop and is just short of a colossal lumber yard that blights **Canal Flats** at the head of the lake. This little area resonates to the history of the wonderful William Adolph Baillie-Grohman, a man whose life was littered with wonderfully eccentric catastrophes. Here, in the 1880s, he planned to build a canal to link the Columbia and Kootenay rivers, also intending to drain virtually all of the Kootenay into the Columbia to prevent flooding (residents up and down the Columbia, not to mention the Canadian Pacific Railway, quickly prevented the latter plan). The canal, however, was completed in 1889, but proved so tortuous and perilous that only two boats ever made it all the way through (in 1894 and 1902). Even then the second boat only made it through by demolishing virtually all of the locks en route. Still, Baille-Grohman had the last laugh, for completing the canal – useless as it was – earned him a provincial land grant of some 30,000 acres. Head to Canal Flats Provincial Park (day use only; April–Oct), 3km north of Canal Flats, if you want to view the remnants of the doomed project.

Just to the south of the Canal Flats mill is the Whiteswan Lake Road turn-off for **Whiteswan Lake Provincial Park**, a handkerchief-sized piece of unbeatable scenery at the end of a twenty-kilometre gravel logging road; the park has five **campgrounds** ($12; May–Sept) but few trails, as its main emphasis is on boating and trout fishing. Three of the campgrounds are at Whiteswan Lake itself, the other two at Alces Lake: also keep an eye open for the undeveloped Lussier Hot Springs at the entrance of the park (17.5km from the main road). The same access road, called the Lussier River Road after it passes the park, continues another 30km to **Top of the World Provincial Park**, a far wilder and very beautiful alpine region where you need to be completely self-sufficient – the five walk-in campgrounds ($5; June–Sept), reached by trail from the parking area at the end of the road, offer water and firewood and spaces for twenty in the Fish Lake cabin ($15; June–Sept). Hiking in the park is good, an obvious jaunt being the trail from the parking area along the Lussier River to Fish Lake (7km one-way; 2hr), where there's an unserviced campground and a cabin (summer only). Mount Morro (3002m), the peak that looms over the region, is believed to have had great spiritual significance for the Ktunaxa, who came here to mine chert, a hard flinty quartz used to make tools and weapons.

FAIRMONT HOT SPRINGS spills over the Columbia's flat flood plain, less a settlement than an ugly modern upmarket resort that feeds off the appeal of the hot springs themselves. The pools were commandeered from the Ktunaxa (Kootenay) in 1922 for exploitation as a tourist resource; the calcium springs (daily 8am–10pm; $4) were particularly prized by the whites because they lack the sulphurous stench of many BC hot dips. However, the locals have now got their own back by opening some cheaper, makeshift pools above the resort, which are proving very popular with tourists. If you don't fancy coughing up around $159–239 to stay in a room at the swish resort, you could try its big **campground** (☎345-6311; $15–35), one minute from the pools but only if you're in an RV – they don't want tents – or the *Spruce Grove Resort* (☎345-6561; ④, tents $19; May–Oct), near the river 2km south of Fairmont with rooms and a lovely riverside campground with outdoor pool.

Invermere

Windermere, 15km north of Fairmont Hot Springs, is little more than a supermarket, gas station and campground immediately off the highway, and hardly hints at the presence of **INVERMERE**, about 1km beyond on the western shore of Windermere Lake. White settlement of the region can almost be said to have begun here, for explorer David Thompson passed this way in 1807 as he travelled up the Columbia River. With his aboriginal wife, several children and eight companions, he built Kootenay House, the area's first trading post. Its site is marked by a cairn on Westside Road. A feel-good summer resort with the usual range of aquatic temptations, Invermere today makes a nicer accommodation prospect than Radium. However, droves of anglers, boaters and beach bums mean summer vacancies may be in short supply, in which case call the central **infocentre** at 5A Street and 7th Avenue (late July to early Sept daily 8am–8pm; ☎342-6316) for B&B possibilities or head for one of the town's four **motels** – the *Lee-Jay*, 1015 13th St (☎342-9227; ③), is the most reasonable and the *Best Western Invermere Inn* at the heart of downtown at 1310 7th Ave is the smartest (☎342-9246 or 1-800/661-8911; ④). The nearest provincial **campground**, with vehicle and tent sites, is 7km north at Dry Gulch Provincial Park ($12; May to mid-Sept), but the private *Coldstream Lakeside Campground* (☎342-6793; $25 per vehicle; May–Sept) is on the lake and has a sandy beach. For **food**, try the popular *Myrtle's* on 7th Avenue, *Huckleberry's* on Laurier Street or the *Blue Dog Café* on 7th Avenue, the last being particularly good for vegetarians and wholefood aficionados. For highly regarded Pacific Northwest cuisine make for *Strand's Old House*, 818 12th St (☎342-6344). If you want a break from eating, drinking or lazing on beaches, spend a few minutes with the mining, railway and other displays in the **Windermere Valley Museum**, 622 3rd St (June–Sept Tues–Sun 9.30am–4pm; $2; ☎342-9769), housed in a heritage building at the top of the hill and to the right on entering the village.

From Invermere the minor Toby Creek Road climbs west into the mountains to the burgeoning **Panorama Ski Resort** (18km), whose slick facilities include only limited

If you're continuing from Invermere into the **Kootenay National Park** and the Rockies, an account of the park begins on p.557. See p.470 if you're crossing the Crowsnest Pass into southern Alberta for **Waterton Lakes National Park**.

and rather expensive accommodation. At over 1000m, the big 250-room *Panorama Resort* (☎342-6941 or 1-800/663-2929; ⑥) is also open in summer for tennis, riding, white-water rafting and fishing. In summer the chief appeal of the area is hiking, particularly if you continue up the road to the less tainted **Purcell Wilderness Conservancy**, one of the few easily accessible parts of the Purcell Mountains. If you have a tent and robust hiking inclinations, you could tackle the 61-kilometre **trail** through the area to Argenta (see p.432) on the northern end of Kootenay Lake, an excellent cross-country route that largely follows undemanding valleys except when crossing the Purcell watershed at Earl Grey Pass (2256m).

travel details

Trains

Kamloops to: Boston Bar (3 weekly; 4hr); Edmonton (3 weekly; 13hr 15min); Hope (3 weekly; 5hr 15min); Vancouver (3 weekly; 9hr).

North Vancouver to: Lillooet (1 daily; 5hr 35min); Prince George (3 weekly; 13hr 5min); Squamish (1–2 daily; 1hr 20min–2hr); Whistler (1 daily; 2hr 35min).

Buses

Kamloops to: Kelowna (3 daily; 3hr 40min); Vernon (5 daily; 1hr 50min).

Kelowna to: Castlegar (2 daily; 4hr 45min); Cranbrook (2 daily; 11hr); Nelson (2 daily; 5hr 25min); Penticton (6 daily; 1hr 10min); Vancouver (6 daily; 5hr 30min).

Prince George to: Cache Creek (3 daily; 6hr 30min); Dawson Creek (2 daily; 6hr 30min).

Squamish to: Whistler (7 daily; 1hr 10min).

Vancouver to: Banff (4 daily; 14hr 5min); Cache Creek (2 daily; 5hr 40min); Calgary (4 daily; 16hr); Chilliwack, for Harrison Hot Springs (10 daily; 1hr 45min); Kamloops (8 daily; 5hr); Kelowna (6 daily; 5hr 30min); Pemberton (4 daily; 3hr); Penticton (3 daily; 5hr 20min); Salmon Arm (6 daily; 7hr 5min); Squamish (6 daily; 1hr 15min); Whistler (7 daily; 2hr).

Flights

Vancouver to: Castlegar (1–2 daily; 1hr 20min); Cranbrook (1–2 daily; 2hr 30min); Kamloops (4–5 daily; 1hr); Kelowna (7–9 daily; 1hr); Penticton (3–5 daily; 50min); Prince George (5–8 daily; 1hr 10min).

CHAPTER SEVEN

CALGARY AND THE ROCKIES

Alberta is the Northwest close to its best. For many people the beauty of the **Canadian Rockies**, which rise with overwhelming majesty from the rippling prairies, is one of the main reasons for coming to the region. Most visitors confine themselves to the four contiguous national parks – **Banff, Jasper, Yoho** and **Kootenay** – that straddle the southern portion of the range, a vast area whose boundaries spill over into British Columbia. Two smaller parks, **Glacier** and **Mount Revelstoke**, lie firmly in BC and not, technically, in the Rockies, but scenically and logistically they form part of the same region. Managed with remarkable efficiency and integrity, all the parks are easily accessible segments of a much wider wilderness of peaks and forests that extend north from the Canada–US border, before merging into the ranges of the Yukon and Alaska.

If you're approaching the Rockies from the east or the States, you have little choice but to spend time in Calgary, the transport hub for southern Alberta. Situated on the **Trans-Canada Highway**, less than ninety minutes from Banff National Park, Calgary is convenient for trips into Yoho, Kootenay, Glacier or Revelstoke, and also good for a stop on the way to southern British Columbia and the West Coast. Plus, it is home to the Calgary Stampede, one of the Northwest's rowdiest festivals, and the vast revenues from oil and natural gas have been spent to good effect on its downtown skyscrapers and civic infrastructure.

CALGARY AND SOUTHERN ALBERTA

Perfectly placed where the prairies buckle suddenly into the Rockies, **Calgary** is the obvious focus of **southern Alberta**, and is the best point from which to strike out west into the mountains. Yet, with some of the continent's most magnificent mountains practically on its doorstep, it takes some self-restraint to give the city the couple of days it deserves. Within day-tripping distance lie two unexpected gems: the dinosaur exhibits

ACCOMMODATION PRICE CODES

All the accommodation prices in this book have been coded using the symbols below, corresponding to US dollar prices in the US chapters and equivalent Canadian dollar rates in the Canadian chapters. Prices are for the least expensive double room in high season, excluding special offers. For a full explanation see p.51 in Basics.

① up to Can$40 ③ Can$60–80 ⑤ Can$100–125 ⑦ Can$175–240
② Can$40–60 ④ Can$80–100 ⑥ Can$125–175 ⑧ Can240+

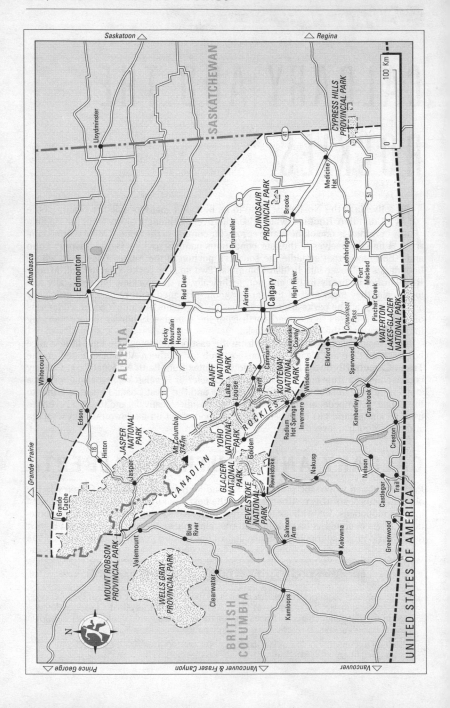

INTERNET AND TOLL-FREE INFORMATION

Travel Alberta ☎1-800-661-8888 from Canada and the US.
Travel Alberta *www.travelalberta.com*
Alberta Accommodation *www.alberta-accommodation.com*

of the **Royal Tyrrell Museum**, near Drumheller in the strange badlands country to the east; and the **Head-Smashed-In Buffalo Jump**, an aboriginal site in the heart of Alberta's cowboy country to the south. The latter is most easily visited if you're following the southern route of Hwy 3 across the province, as is **Waterton Lakes National Park**, isolated well to the south of the other Canadian Rockies parks.

Calgary

A likeable and booming place, whose downtown skyscrapers soared almost overnight on the back of an oil bonanza in the 1970s, **CALGARY**'s tight high-rise core is good for wandering, and contains the prestigious **Glenbow Museum**. The wooden houses of the far-flung suburbs, meanwhile, recall the city's pioneering frontier origins, which are further celebrated in the annual **Calgary Stampede**, a hugely popular cowboy carnival in which the whole town – and hordes of tourists – revel in a boots-and-stetson image that's still very much a way of life in the surrounding cattle country. Year-round you can dip into the city's lesser museums and historic sites, or take time out in its scattering of attractive city parks.

Some history

Modern Calgary is one of the West's largest and youngest cities, its close to 850,000-strong population having grown from almost nothing in barely 125 years. Long before the coming of outsiders, however, the area was the domain of the **Blackfoot**, who ranged over the site of present-day Calgary for several thousand years. About 300 years ago, they were joined by **Sarcee**, forced south by war from their northern heartlands, and the **Stoney**, who migrated north with Sitting Bull into southern Saskatchewan and then Alberta. Traces of old campgrounds, buffalo kills and pictographs from all three peoples lie across the region, though these days aboriginal lands locally are confined to a few reserves.

Whites first began to gather around the confluence of the Bow and Elbow rivers at the end of the eighteenth century. Explorer **David Thompson** wintered here during his peregrinations, while the Palliser expedition spent time nearby en route for the Rockies. Settlers started arriving in force around 1860, when hunters moved into the region from the United States, where their prey, the buffalo, had been hunted to the edge of extinction. Herds still roamed the Alberta grasslands, attracting not only hunters but also **whiskey traders**, who plied their dubious wares among whites and aboriginal peoples alike. Trouble inevitably followed, leading to the creation of the West's first North West Mounted Police stockade at Fort Macleod (see p.469). Soon after, in 1875, a second fort was built further north to curb the lawlessness of the whiskey traders. A year later it was christened **Fort Calgary**, taking its name from the Scottish birthplace of its assistant commissioner. The word *calgary* is Gaelic for "clear running water", and it was felt that the ice-clear waters of the Bow and Elbow rivers were reminiscent of the "old country".

The telephone code for Calgary and Southern Alberta is ☎403.

CHINOOKS

Winters in Calgary are occasionally moderated by **chinooks**, sudden warming winds that periodically sweep down the eastern flanks of the Rockies. Often heralded by a steely cloud band spreading from the mountains over the city, a chinook can raise the temperature by as much as 10°C in a couple of hours and evaporate a foot of snow in a day. Chinooks are the result of a phenomenon that occurs on leeward slopes of mountains all over the world, but nowhere more dramatically than in the plains of southwestern Alberta. The effect has to do with the way prevailing westerly winds are forced to rise over the Rockies, expanding and cooling on the way up and compressing and warming up again on the way back down. On the way up the cooling air, laden with Pacific moisture, becomes saturated (ie clouds form) and drops rain and snow on the windward (western) side of the mountains. All this condensation releases latent heat, causing the rising air to cool more slowly than usual; but on the leeward descent the air, now relieved of much of its moisture, warms up at the normal rate. By the time it reaches Calgary it's both drier and warmer than it was to start with.

The name comes from the people that traditionally inhabited the area around the mouth of the Columbia River in Washington and Oregon, from where the winds seem to originate; the Chinook people also gives us the name of the largest species of Pacific salmon.

By 1883 a station had been built close to the fort, part of the new trans-Canadian **railway**. The township laid out nearby quickly attracted **ranchers** and British gentlemen farmers to its low, hilly bluffs – which are indeed strongly reminiscent of Scottish moors and lowlands – and cemented an enduring Anglo-Saxon cultural bias. Ranchers from the US – where pasture was heavily overgrazed – were further encouraged by an "open grazing" policy across the Alberta grasslands. Despite Calgary's modern-day cowboy life – most notably its famous annual **Stampede** – the Alberta cattle country has been described as more "mild West" than Wild West. Research suggests that there were just three recorded gunfights in the nineteenth century, and poorly executed ones at that.

By 1886 fires had wiped out most of the town's temporary wooded and tented buildings, leading to an edict declaring that all new buildings should be constructed in sandstone (for a while Calgary was known as "Sandstone City"). The fires proved no more than a minor historical hiccup and within just nine years of the railway's arrival Calgary achieved official city status, something it had taken rival Edmonton over 100 years to achieve. Edmonton was to have its revenge in 1910, when it was made Alberta's provincial capital.

Cattle and the coming of the railway generated exceptional growth, though the city's rise was to be nothing compared to the prosperity that followed the discovery of **oil**. The first strike, the famous Dingman's No. 1 Well, took place in 1914 in the nearby Turner Valley. An oil refinery opened in 1923, and since then, Calgary has rarely looked back. In the 25 years after 1950, its population doubled. When oil prices soared during the oil crisis of the 1970s, the city exploded, becoming a world energy and financial centre – headquarters for some four hundred oil and related businesses – with more American inhabitants than any other Canadian city.

Falling commodity prices subsequently punctured the city's ballooning economy, but not before the city centre had been virtually rebuilt and acquired improved and oil-financed cultural, civic and other facilities. Today only Toronto is home to the headquarters of more major Canadian corporations, though the city's optimism is tempered, as elsewhere in Canada, by the notion of **federal disintegration**. Much of the West, which still harbours a sense of a new frontier, is increasingly impatient with the "old East", and happy – if election results are anything to go by – to become increasingly self-sufficient.

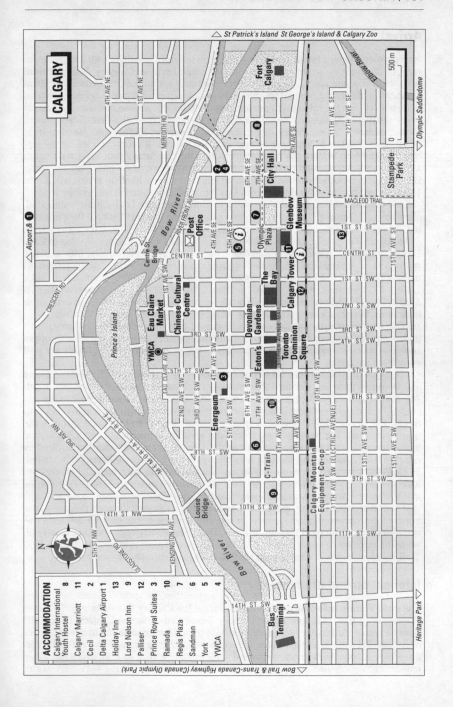

CALGARY

△ St Patrick's Island St George's Island & Calgary Zoo

ACCOMMODATION
Calgary International
Youth Hostel   8
Calgary Marriott   11
Cecil   2
Delta Calgary Airport 1
Holiday Inn   13
Lord Nelson Inn   9
Palliser   12
Prince Royal Suites   3
Ramada   10
Regis Plaza   7
Sandman   6
York   5
YWCA   4

Arrival

Approaching Calgary **by air** you're rewarded (in the right weather) with a magnificent view of the Rockies stretching across the western horizon. **Calgary International Airport** (YYC), a modern, often half-deserted strip, is within the city limits about 10km northeast of downtown – a $30 taxi ride. The widely advertised free hotel coaches tend to be elusive, but the reliable **Airporter Bus** (☎531-3909) shuttle into the city departs every thirty minutes and drops at nine downtown hotels: the *Delta Bow, International, Westin, Sheraton Suites, Prince Royal, Ramada, Sandman, Palliser* and *Marriott* (first bus 6.30am, last bus 11.30pm; $8.50 one-way, $15 return). If you're headed for the city bus terminal (see below), the nearest drop-off is the *Sandman*: from here, walk south a block to 9th Avenue and turn right (west) and the terminal's a fifteen-minute walk. Buy Airporter **tickets** from one of a bank of bus ticket desks lined up in Arrivals (Level 1) by the exit doors: buses depart from Bay 3 immediately outside the terminal.

Over the last few years, **direct services to Banff** and Lake Louise have proliferated, allowing you to jump off the plane, leap into a bus and be in Banff National Park in a couple of hours. Services currently include Laidlaw (1 daily May–Nov; 2 daily Dec–April; $30 to Banff, $38 to Lake Louise; ☎762-9102 or 1-800/661-4946; Calgary Ski Bus to Lake Louise; ☎256-8473, *www.laidlawbanff.com*); the Banff Airporter (8 daily; $36 to Banff; ☎762-3330 or 1-888/449-2901, *www.banffairporter.com*); Brewster Transportation (3 daily to Banff and Lake Louise, 1 daily to Jasper in summer; $36 to Banff, $41 to Lake Louise, $71 to Jasper; ☎403/762-6767 in Banff, ☎403/221-8242 in Calgary, ☎780/852-3332 in Jasper). **Tickets** are available from separate desks adjacent to the Airporter desk in Arrivals. Services leave from Bay 4 or (close by) outside the Arrivals terminal.

There's a small **information centre** disguised as a stagecoach (daily 10am–10pm) in Arrivals and another in Departures (6am–midnight). The Arrivals level also offers courtesy phones to hotels and car rental agencies, though most of the hotels are well away from the centre.

Calgary's Greyhound **bus terminal** (☎265-9111 or 1-800/661-8747, *www.greyhound .ca*) is comfortable but not terribly convenient. It's located west of downtown at 8th Avenue SW and 850-16th Street, a somewhat uninspiring thirty-minute walk to the city centre. Fortunately free transit buses operate to the C-Train at 7th Avenue SW and 10th Street, the key to the city's central transit system (free from this point through the downtown area). The shuttles leave from Gate 4 within 20 minutes of every bus arrival to the terminal and are announced over the tannoy: keep your ears open. Shuttles return from the same point more or less hourly on the half-hour. Alternatively, six-dollar **taxis** for the short run to downtown are plentiful outside the terminal. Left-luggage lockers inside the terminal cost $2 for 24hr, $4 for larger lockers. For airport enquiries and bus and rail travel information, see "Listings" (p.463).

If you're arriving **by car**, the Trans-Canada (Hwy 1) passes through the city to the north of downtown. During its spell in the city limits it becomes 16th Avenue. The major north to south road through the city, Hwy 2, is rechristened the Deerfoot Trail, while the main route south from the US and Waterton Lakes is known as the Macleod Trail, much of which is a fairly grim strip of malls, motels and fast-food joints.

Information and orientation

The main **Visitor Information Services**, part of the Calgary Convention and Visitors Bureau, is on the main floor of the Calgary Tower Centre in the Calgary Tower, 139 Tower Centre, 101-9th Ave SW (daily: mid-May to mid-Sept 8am–8pm; mid-Sept to mid-May Mon–Fri 8am–5pm, Sat & Sun 9am–5pm; ☎263-8510 in Calgary, ☎1-800/661-8888 elsewhere in North America; recorded information ☎262-2766). It doles out huge amounts of information and provides a free accommodation-finding service. You can

Sattledome, Calgary

Bull-riding, Calgary Stampede

Dinosaur Provincial Park, Alberta

Canoe trip on Kicking Horse River, British Columbia

Lake Louise, Banff National Park, Alberta

Waterton Lakes, Alberta

Valley of Ten Peaks and Moraine Lake, Alberta

CHRIS COE/AXIOM

The Dempster Highway

CHRIS COE/AXIOM

NICK HANNA

Kaskawulsh Glacier, Kluane National Park, Yukon

Hikers in the Canadian Rockies

also access Travel Alberta on the Internet (*www.travelalberta.com*). Minor offices operate at the airport (Arrivals level), the Canada Olympic Park, and on the westbound side of the Trans-Canada Highway between 58th and 62nd St NE. The informative monthly *Where Calgary* is free from shops, hotels and the Visitors Bureau.

For all its rapid expansion, Calgary is a well-planned and straightforward city engineered around an inevitable **grid**. The metropolitan area is divided into **quadrants** (NW, NE, SE and SW) with the Bow River separating north from south, Centre Street–Macleod Trail east from west. Downtown – and virtually everything there is to see and do – is in a small area in or close to the SW quadrant. Streets run north–south, avenues east–west, with numbers increasing as you move out from the centre. The last digits of the first number refer to the house number – thus 237-8th Ave SE is on 2nd Street at no. 37, close to the intersection with 8th Avenue. It's easy to overlook the quadrant, so check addresses carefully.

City transport

Almost everything in Calgary, barring Stampede locations and a few minor diversions, is a comfortable walk away – except in winter, when temperatures can make any excursion an ordeal. The city's much-vaunted **Plus 15 Walking System**, a labyrinthine network of enclosed walkways 4.5m above ground, is designed to beat the freeze. It enables you to walk through downtown without setting foot outside, but is too confusing to bother with when the weather's fine.

Calgary's **public transport system** is cheap, clean and efficient, comprising an integrated network of buses and the **C-Train** (every 15 to 30min; no late-night service) the latter a cross between a bus and a train, which is free for its downtown stretch along the length of 7th Avenue SW between 10th Street and City Hall at 3rd Street SE. An onboard announcement tells you when the free section is coming to an end. For route information, call ☎276-7801.

Tickets, valid for both buses and C-Train, are available from machines on C-Train stations, shops with a Calgary Transit sticker, and from the main Information and Downtown Sales Centre, also known as the **Calgary Transit Customer Service Centre**, 240-7th Ave SW (Mon–Fri 8.30am–5pm), which also has free schedules and route planners. The one-way adult fare is $1.60 (free for under-6s, $1 for 6–14s), day passes $5 adults. You can pay on the bus if you have the exact change. Request a transfer from the driver (valid for 90min) if you're changing buses. The sales centre also provides timetables and an invaluable **information line** (Mon–Fri 6am–11pm, Sat & Sun 8am–9.30pm; ☎262-1000): tell them where you are and where you want to go, and they'll give you the necessary details.

You can easily get a **taxi** from outside the bus terminal, or see "Listings" (p.464) for a list of cab companies.

Accommodation

Budget **accommodation** in Calgary is not plentiful, but the little that exists is rarely at a premium except during Stampede (mid-July) when prepaid reservations, in central locations at least, are essential months in advance. Remember that even smart hotels are likely to offer vastly reduced rates on Friday nights and over the weekend, when their business custom drops away. In addition to the recommendations given below, motels abound, mostly well away from the centre along Macleod Trail heading south and on the Trans-Canada Highway heading west. "Motel Village" is a cluster of a dozen or so motels in the $60–70 a night bracket, grouped together at the intersection of 16th Avenue NW and Crowchild Trail; if you're not driving, a taxi ride out here costs about $10.

If you run into difficulties, try Visitor Information Services in the Calgary Tower (see p.456), which should help hunt out rooms at short notice, or consult the Alberta Hotel

Association's ubiquitous *Accommodation Guide*. **B&B agencies** to try include the Bed & Breakfast Agency of Alberta (☎543-3901 or 1-800/425-8160, *altabba@home.com*); Canada-West (☎604/990-6730, *www.b-b.com*), or the *Alberta Bed & Breakfast Association* (*www.bbalberta.com*).

Hotels and motels

Calgary Marriott Hotel, 110-9th Ave SE (☎266-7331 or 1-800/228-9290, fax 262-8442). Not the most expensive of Calgary's smart hotels, but probably the best outside the *Palliser* if you want to stay in some style. ⑦.

Cecil, corner of 4th Ave and 3rd St SE (☎266-2982). Clean and cheap, but a grim place – to say the least – on a busy junction (the airport road); its bar has a rough reputation. No phones, TV or private baths. Rock-bottom budgets and emergencies only. ②.

Delta Calgary Airport Hotel, 2001 Airport Rd (☎291-2600 or 1-800/441-1414, *www.deltahotels.com*). Soundproofed hotel right at the airport if you arrive late or have an early flight out – but it's not cheap. ⑥.

Holiday Inn Calgary Downtown, 119-12th Ave SW (☎266-4611 or 1-800/661-9378, fax 237-0978). An amenity-loaded hotel, but a few blocks off the centre of town. ⑦.

Lord Nelson Inn, 1020-8th Ave SW (☎269-8262 or 1-800/661-6017, fax 269-4868). A ten-storey modern but slightly faded block with 56 rooms close to the more expensive *Sandman*, to which it is inferior; each room with TV and fridge, and just a block from the free C-Train. ④.

Palliser, 133-9th Ave SW (☎262-1234 or 1-800/441-1414, fax 260-1260). This is the hotel royalty chooses when it comes to Calgary, and as smart as you can find in the city if you want traditional style and service (though avoid the back rooms overlooking the rail tracks). Built in 1914, and part of the smart Canadian Pacific chain that owns the *Banff Springs* and *Chateau Lake Louise* hotels. ⑥.

Prince Royal Suites Hotel, 618-5th Ave SW (☎263-0520 or 1-800/661-1592, *www.princeroyal.com*). A mixture of 301 modern studio, one- and two-room suites with full facilities and continental breakfast included. Look out for weekend discounts. ⑥.

Ramada Hotel Downtown, 708-8th Ave SW (☎263-7600 or 1-800/661-8684, *res_dt@telusplanet.net*). A large, comfortable hotel with 200 newly renovated rooms and a swimming pool at the heart of downtown. ⑤.

Regis Plaza Hotel, 124-7th Ave SE (☎262-4641, *regis.plaza@cadvision.com*). An old and unappealing hotel for those who are desperate or almost broke, but just two blocks from the Calgary Tower. Bathroom facilities are shared in ten of the forty rooms: other rooms only have washbasins; beware the rough bar. ③.

Sandman Hotel Downtown Calgary, 888-7th Ave SW (☎237-8626 or 1-800/726-3626, *www .sandman.ca*). An excellent and first-choice mid-range hotel, with 300 totally dependable clean, modern rooms with private bathrooms in high-rise block: extremely handy for the free C-Train. ⑤.

Travelodge, 2750 Sunridge Blvd NE (☎291-1260 or 1-800/578-7878, fax 291-9170), 2304-16th Ave (☎289-0211 or 1-800/578-7878, fax 282-6924), and 9206 Macleod Trail (☎253-7070 or 1-800/578-7878, fax 253-2879). Three chain motels; the least expensive out-of-town choices. The first is convenient to the airport. All ③.

York Hotel, 636 Centre St SE (☎262-5581). Central, with good-sized rooms with TVs and baths and laundry service. ③.

Hostels and student accommodation

Calgary International Youth Hostel, 520-7th Ave SE (☎269-8239, fax 266-6227, *chostel @hostellingintl.ca*). Close to downtown; two blocks east of City Hall and the free section of the C-Train. Laundry, six- and eight-bed dorms (120 beds in total), four double/family rooms, cooking facilities, bike storage, snack bar. Closed 10am–5pm; midnight curfew. Members $16–18, non-members $20–20; family rooms/doubles add $5 per person. ①.

Calgary YWCA, 320-5th Ave SE (☎263-1550). Hotel comfort for women and children only in quiet safe area; food service, pool, gym, health club and squash courts; book in summer. Singles and dorm beds available from about $35 for singles ($45 double) without bath, $45 ($50) with; sleeping bag space is sometimes provided in summer. ②.

University of Calgary, 3330-24th Ave NW (☎220-3202). Way out in the suburbs, but cheap with a huge number of dorm and private rooms from around $30 in the summer. Take the C-Train or bus #9. The 24hr room rental office (call first) is in the Kananaskis Building on campus; 33 percent discount for student ID holders. ②.

Campgrounds

Calaway Park (☎249-7372). About 10km west of the city on the Trans-Canada Highway to Banff and the Rockies. It's also within walking of the Calaway Park amusement park – Canada's largest. Full facilities, including showers. Mid-May to early Sept. $15.

KOA Calgary West, off the south side of Hwy 1 at the western end of the city, close to Canada Olympic Park (☎288-0411 or 1-800/KOA-0842, fax 286-1612). 224 sites, laundry, store and outdoor pool. Shuttle services to downtown. Mid-April to mid-Oct. $24.

Mountain View Farm Campground (☎293-6640). A 202-site campground situated on a farm 3km east of the city on the Trans-Canada (Hwy 1). Full services, including showers. $18.

The City

Downtown Calgary lies in a self-evident cluster of mirrored glass and polished granite facades bounded by the Bow River to the north, 9th Avenue to the south, Centre Street to the east and 8th Street to the west. A monument to oil money, the area is about as sleek as an urban centre can be: virtually everything is brand-new, and the modern architecture is easy on the eye. The **city centre**, so far as it has one, is traditionally 8th Avenue between 1st Street SE and 3rd Street SW, a largely pedestrianized area known as **Stephen Avenue Mall**.

Any city tour, though, should start with a trip to the **Glenbow Museum**, while a jaunt up the **Calgary Tower**, across the street, gives a literal overview of the Calgarian hinterland. Thereafter a good deal of the city lends itself to wandering on foot, whether around the mall-laden main streets or to **Prince's Island**, the nearest of many parks, and gentrified **Kensington**, a busy shopping and café district. The appeal of attractions further afield – **Fort Calgary**, **Heritage Park** and the **Calgary Zoo** – will depend on your historical and natural-history inclinations. These sights, together with a crop of special interest **museums**, can be easily reached by bus or C-Train.

The Glenbow Museum

The excellent and eclectic collection of the **Glenbow Museum** is, the Stampede apart, the only sight for which you'd make a special journey to Calgary (May–Oct Mon–Wed, Sat & Sun 9am–5pm, Thurs–Fri 9am–9pm; closed Mon Nov–April; $8; ☎268-4100, *www.glenbow.org*). Although it's opposite the Calgary Tower at 130-9th Ave SE, the main entrance is hidden alongside the Skyline Plaza complex a short way east down the street (there's another entrance from the Stephen Avenue Mall). Built in 1966, the no-expense-spared museum is a testament to sound civic priorities and the cultural benefits of booming oil revenues. Its three floors of displays make a fine introduction to the heritage of the Canadian west.

The permanent collection embraces the eclectic approach, starting with a section devoted to ritual and **sacred art** from around the world and an **art gallery** tracing the development of western Canadian indigenous art. Better still is the European art depicting the culture of aboriginal peoples. Two outlooks prevail – the romantic nineteenth-century image of the Indian as "noble savage", and the more forward-looking analysis of artists from the same period such as Paul Kane, a painter determined to make accurate representations of aboriginal peoples and cultures before their assimilation by white expansion.

The second floor runs the gamut of western Canadian history and heritage, including an outstanding exhibit on First Nations or **aboriginal peoples**. In the treaties section, hidden in a corner almost as if in shame, the museum text skates over the injustices with a glossary of simple facts. On display are the original documents that many chiefs were confused into signing, believing they were peace treaties, when in fact the contracts gave away all land rights to those who drafted them in deliberately incomprehensible legalese. All facets of **native crafts** are explored on this floor as well, with stunning displays of carving, costumes and jewellery; whilst their emphasis is on the original inhabitants of Alberta – with a special new display on the Blackfoot – the collection also forays into the Inuit and the Métis – the latter being the offspring of native women and white fur traders, and the most marginalized group of all.

Following a historical chronology, the floor moves on to exhibits associated with the fur trade, Northwest Rebellion, the Canadian Pacific, pioneer life, ranching, cowboys, oil and wheat – each era illustrated by interesting and appropriate artefacts of the time – adding up to a glut of period paraphernalia that includes a terrifying exhibit of frontier dentistry, an absurdly comprehensive display of washing machines, and a solitary 1938 bra.

The eccentric top floor kicks off with a pointless display of Calgary Stampede merchandising, before moving on to a huge collection of **military paraphernalia** and a dazzling display of **gems and minerals**, said to be among the world's best. These exhibits are mainly for genre enthusiasts, though the gems are worth a look if only to see some of the extraordinary and beautiful things that come out of the drab mines that fuel so much of western Canada's economy.

Other downtown sights

The **Calgary Tower** (daily: mid-May to mid-Sept 8am–midnight; mid-Sept to mid-May 8am–11pm; $6.15), the city's favourite folly, is a good deal shorter and less imposing than the tourist material would have you believe. An obligatory tourist traipse, the 190-metre-tall salt cellar (762 steps if you don't take the lift) stands in a relatively dingy area at the corner of Centre Street–9th Avenue SW, somewhat overshadowed by downtown's more recent buildings. As a long-term landmark, however, it makes a good starting point for any tour of the city, the Observation Terrace offering outstanding views, especially on clear days, when the snowcapped Rockies fill the western horizon, with the ski-jump towers of the 1988 Canada Olympic Park in the middle distance. Up on the observation platform after your one-minute elevator ride you'll find a snack bar (good value and excellent food), cocktail bar and revolving restaurant (expensive).

Any number of shopping malls lurk behind the soaring high-rises, most notably Toronto Dominion Square (8th Ave SW between 2nd and 3rd sts), the city's main shopping focus and the unlikely site of **Devonian Gardens** (daily 9am–9pm; free; ☎268-3888). Like something out of an idyllic urban Utopia, the three-acre indoor gardens support a lush sanctuary of streams, waterfalls and full-sized trees, no mean feat given that it's located on the fourth floor of a glass-and-concrete glitter palace (access by elevator). Around 20,000 plants round off the picture, comprising some 138 local and tropical species. Benches beside the garden's paths are perfect for picnicking on food bought in the takeaways below, while impromptu concerts are held on the small stages dotted around.

Calgary pays homage to its oil industry in the small but oddly interesting **Energeum** plonked in the main lobby of the Energy Resources Building between 5th Street and 6th Street SW at 640-5th Ave SW (June–Aug daily except Sat 10.30am–4.30pm; Sept–May Mon–Fri same hours; free; ☎297-4293). Its audiovisual and presentational tricks take you through the formation, discovery and drilling for coal and oil. Alberta's peculiar and problematic oil sands are explained – granite-hard in winter, mud-soft in summer – and there are dollops of the stuff on hand for some infantile slopping around.

The **Calgary Science Centre** is located one block west of the 10th Street SW C-Train at 701-11th St and 7th Avenue SW (daily: mid-May to June Tues–Thurs 10am–4pm, Fri-Sun 10am–5pm; call for winter hours; $9 for all exhibits and one Discovery Dome show; ☎221-3700, *www.calgaryscience.ca*). Here you can look through the telescopes of its small observatory, which are trained nightly on the moon, planets and stars (weather permitting). Other daytime highlights here include the interactive exhibits of the Discovery Hall (these change regularly) and the **Discovery Dome**, a multimedia theatre complete with cinema picture images, computer graphics, slide-projected images and a vast speaker system. The on-site **Pleiades Theatre** offers a series of "mystery and murder plays" throughout the year. For details of current shows and exhibitions, call ☎221-3700. To get here, either walk the five blocks west from 6th Street if you're near the Energeum, or take the C-Train along 7th Avenue SW and walk the last block.

Prince's Island, the Bow River and Kensington

Five-minutes' walk north of downtown via a footbridge, **Prince's Island** is a popular but peaceful retreat offering plenty of trees, flowers, an outstanding restaurant, the *River Café* (see p.462), kids' playground and enough space to escape the incessant stream of joggers pounding the walkways. Between the island and downtown, at the north end of 3rd Street SW (six blocks north of the free C-Train), the wonderful **Eau Claire Market** (food market daily 9am–6pm; shops, restaurant have varying hours; ☎264-6450 or 264-6460 for information, *www.eauclaire.com*) is a bright and deliberately brash warehouse mix of food and craft market, cinemas (including a 300-seat IMAX large-screen complex), buskers, restaurants, walkways and panoramic terraces. All in all it brings some heart to the concrete and glass of downtown – the large communal eating area, in particular, is a good place to people-watch and pick up bargain takeaway Chinese, Japanese, wholefood and burger snacks. The food market is open from 9am to 6pm, but the complex and restaurants are open until late. Note that the tremendous **YMCA** (☎269-6701) opposite the market at 101-3rd St SW has no rooms, though the superb swimming pool, jacuzzi, sauna, squash courts, running track and weights room are open to all (Mon–Fri 5.30am–10.30pm, weekends 7am–7.30pm; $8; increased admission Mon–Fri 11am–1.30pm and daily 4–6.30pm). Swimmers might be tempted by the broad, fast-flowing **Bow River** nearby, but it's for passive recreation only – the water is just two hours (were you travelling by car) from its icy source in the Rockies – its dangers underlined by lurid signs on the banks. The river is the focus for Calgary's civilized and excellent 210-kilometre system of recreational **walkways**, asphalt paths (also available to cyclists) that generally parallel the main waterways: maps are available from the visitor centre.

Just east of the market and five blocks north of the C-Train at 197-1st St SW lies the **Calgary Chinese Cultural Centre** (centre daily 9am–9pm, museum daily 11am–5pm; $2; ☎262-5071), its big central dome modelled on the Temple of Heaven in Beijing and it claims to be one of the largest Chinese centres in the Northwest. It forms the focus for Calgary's modest Chinatown and large Chinese-Canadian population, most of whom are descendants of immigrants who came to work on the railways in the 1880s. It contains a small museum and gallery, and a gift shop and restaurant.

A twenty-minute jaunt along the walkway system from Prince's Island in the other direction from the market, **Kensington** is a gentrified café district on 10th Street NW and Kensington Road. Shops here sell healing crystals and advertise yoga and personal-growth seminars, though the older cafés, bookshops and wholefood stores are beginning to give way to trinket shops. As an eating area, though, Kensington has been superseded by the increasingly trendy section of 4th Street SW, beyond 17th Avenue.

Fort Calgary

Fort Calgary, the city's historical nexus, stands at 750-9th Ave SE (May–Oct daily 9am–5pm; site free; interpretive centre $5.75; ☎290-1875, *www.fortcalgary.ab.ca*), a manageable eight-block walk east of downtown; you could also take bus #1 to Forest Lawn, bus #14 (East Calgary) from 7th Avenue, or the C-Train free to City Hall and walk the remaining

THE CALGARY STAMPEDE

An orgy of all things cowboy and cowgirl, the annual **Calgary Stampede** brings around a quarter of a million spectators and participants to the city for ten days during the middle two weeks of July. This is far more than a carefully engineered gift to Calgary's tourist industry, however, for the event is one of the world's biggest rodeos and comes close to living up to its billing as "The Greatest Outdoor Show on Earth". During "The Week", as it's known by all and sundry, the city loses its collective head; just about everyone turns out in white stetsons, bolo ties, blue jeans and hand-tooled boots, addressing one another in a bastardized cowboy C&W slang.

But for all its heavily worked visitor appeal, the competition end of things is taken very seriously. Most of the cowboys are for real, as are the injuries – the rodeo is said to be North America's roughest – and the combined prize money is a very serious $500,000. Even the first show in 1912, masterminded by entrepreneur Guy Weadick, put up $100,000 (raised from four Calgary businessmen) and attracted 60,000 people to the opening parade, a line-up that included 2000 aboriginal people in full ceremonial rig and Pancho Villa's bandits in a show erroneously billed as a swan song for the cowboy of the American West ("The Last and Best Great West Frontier Days"). Around 40,000 daily attended the rodeo events (today's figure is 100,000), not bad considering Calgary's population at the time was only 65,000.

Nowadays the events kick off on Thursday evening at Stampede Park with a show previewing the next ten-days' events. Next day there's the traditional **parade**, timed to begin at 9am, though most spectators are in place along the parade route (which is west along 6th Ave from 2nd St SE, south on 10th St SW and east along 9th Ave) by 6am. The march takes two hours, and involves around 150 entries, 4000 participants and some 700 horses. For the rest of the Stampede in downtown (known as Rope Square for the duration) offers free pancake breakfasts daily (8.30–11.30am) and entertainment every morning. Typical events include bands, mock gunfights, square dances, native dancing and country bands. Square dancing also fills parts of Stephen Avenue Mall at 10am every morning. **Nightlife** is a world unto itself, with Stampede locations giving way to music, dancing and mega-cabarets, which involve casts of literally thousands. There's also lots of drinking, gambling, fireworks and general partying into the small hours. Barbecues are the norm, and even breakfast is roped into the free-for-all – outdoor bacon, pancake and flapjack feasts being the traditional way to start the day. "White hatter stew" and baked beans are other inevitable staples.

Stampede's real action, though – the rodeo and allied events – takes place in **Stampede Park**, southeast of downtown and best reached by C-Train (every 10min) to Victoria Park–Stampede Station. This vast open area contains an amusement park, concert and

five blocks. Built in under six weeks by the North West Mounted Police in 1875, the fort was the germ of the present city, and remained operative as a police post until 1914, when it was sold – inevitably – to the Canadian Pacific Railway. The whole area remained buried under railway tracks and derelict warehouses until comparatively recently.

Period photographs in the adjoining interpretive centre provide a taste of how wild Calgary still was in 1876. Even more remarkable was the ground that men in the fort were expected to cover: the log stockade was a base for operations between Fort Macleod, 160km to the south, and the similar post at Edmonton, almost 400km to the north. It's not as if they had nothing to do: Crowfoot, most prominent of the great Blackfoot chiefs of the time, commented, "If the Police had not come to the country, where would we all be now? Bad men and whiskey were killing us so fast that very few of us indeed would have been left. The Police have protected us as the feathers of a bird protect it from the winter."

Only a few forlorn stumps of the original building remain, much having been torn down by the developers, and what survives is its site, now a pleasant forty-acre park contained in the angled crook of the Bow and Elbow rivers. Moves have recently been

show venues, bars and restaurants and a huge range of stalls and shows that take the best part of a day to see. Entrance is $8, which allows you to see all the **entertainments** except the rodeo and chuck-wagon races. Things to see include the aboriginal village at the far end of the park, where members of the Five Nations peoples (Blackfoot, Blood, Sarcee, Stoney and Piegan) set up a tepee village (tours available); the John Deere Show Ring, scene of the World Blacksmith Competition; the Centennial Fair, which hosts events for children; the Agricultural Building, home to displays of cattle and other livestock; the outdoor Coca-Cola Stage, used for late-night Country shows; and the Nashville North, an indoor Country venue with bar and dancing until 2am.

If you want to see the daily **rodeo** competition – bronco riding, bull riding, native-buffalo riding, branding, calf-roping, steer-wrestling, cow-tackling, wild-cow milking and the rest – you need another ticket ($8 on the day), though unless you've bought these in advance (see below) it's hardly worth it: you'll probably be in poor seats miles from the action and hardly see a thing. Rodeo heats are held each afternoon from 1.30pm for the first eight days, culminating in winner-takes-all finals on Saturday and Sunday (prize money for the top honcho is $50,000). If you want to watch the other big event, the ludicrously dangerous but hugely exciting **chuck-wagon** races (the "World Championship") you need yet another ticket ($8) on the day, though again you need to buy these in advance to secure anything approaching decent seats. The nine contests are held once-nightly at 8pm, the four top drivers going through to the last-night final, where another $50,000 awaits the winner.

It's worth planning ahead if you're coming to Calgary for Stampede. **Accommodation** is greatly stretched – be certain to book ahead – and prices for most things are hiked for the duration. **Tickets** for the rodeo and chuck-wagon races go on sale anything up to a year in advance. They're sold for the Stampede Park grandstand, which is divided into sections. "A" is best and sells out first; "B" and "C" go next. Then comes the smarter Clubhouse Level (D–E are seats; F–G are Clubhouse Restaurant seats, with tickets sold in pairs only). This is enclosed and air-conditioned, but still offers good views and the bonus of bars, lounge area and restaurants. The top of the stand, or Balcony (J–K) is open, and provides a good vantage point for the chuck-wagon races as you follow their progress around the length of the course. Rodeo tickets range from about $17 to $35, chuck-wagon races from $17 to $40; tickets for the finals of both events are a few dollars more in all seats. For ticket order forms, **advance sales** and general information, write to Calgary Exhibition and Stampede, Box 1860, Station M, Calgary, AB T2P 2L8 (☎261-0101, elsewhere in Alberta or North America ☎1-800/661-1260) or call in person at Stampede Headquarters, 1410 Olympic Way SE, or the visitor centre. Tickets are also available from Ticketmaster outlets (☎270-6700).

made to begin construction of an exact replica of the original log stockade. The interpretive centre traces Calgary's development with the aid of artefacts, audiovisual displays and "interpretive walks" along the river. Among the more kitsch activities on offer is the opportunity to dress up as a Mountie.

Across the river to the east is **Hunt House**, built in 1876 for a Hudson's Bay official and believed to be Calgary's oldest building on its original site. Close by, at 750-9th Ave SE, on the same side of the Elbow River, is the renovated **Deane House Historic Site and Restaurant** (☎269-7747), built in 1906 by Mountie supremo Superintendent Richard Deane (free tours daily 11am–2pm). It subsequently served time as the home of an artists' cooperative, a boarding house and a stationmaster's house. Today it's a teahouse and restaurant.

St George's Island

St George's Island is home to Calgary's most popular attraction, the **Calgary Zoo, Botanical Gardens and Prehistoric Park**, all at 1300 Zoo Rd (daily 9am–1 hour before dusk; Prehistoric Park open June–Sept only; May–Sept $10; ☎232-9300). It can be reached from downtown and Fort Calgary by riverside path, by C-Train northeast towards Whitehorn, or by car (take Memorial Drive E to just west of Deerfoot Trail). Founded in 1920, this is now Canada's largest zoo (and one of North America's best), with 850,000 annual visitors and some 1200 animals, 400 species and innovative and exciting displays in which the animals are left as far as possible in their "natural" habitats. There are underwater viewing areas for polar bears and sea creatures, darkened rooms for nocturnal animals, a special Australian section, greenhouses for myriad tropical birds, and any number of pens for the big draws like gorillas, tigers, giraffes and African warthogs. Check out the extended North American and Canadian Wilds, Aspen Woodlands and Rocky Mountains sections for a taste of a variety of fauna. Also worth a look are the Tropical, Arid and Butterfly gardens in the conservatory. There is a fast-food concession, and picnic areas if you want to make a day of it.

The **Botanical Gardens** are dotted throughout the zoo, while the **Prehistoric Park** annexe – a "recreated Mesozoic landscape" – is accessible by suspension bridge across the Bow River (daily June–Sept; free with general admission). Its nineteen life-size dinosaur models, none too convincing in their incongruous settings, are a poor substitute for the superb museum at Drumheller (see p.464), and only the fossils in two adjoining buildings are of more than fleeting interest.

Natural-history enthusiasts might also want to visit the **Inglewood Bird Sanctuary**, on the Bow River's forested flats at 9th Avenue and 20A Street SE, 3km downstream of the zoo and east of downtown. Some 230 species are present year-round – more during migratory cycles, around 266 species having been recorded across the sanctuary, a portion of land once owned by Colonel James Walker, one of Calgary's original North West Mounted Police. Some of the birds you might see include bald eagles, Swainson's hawks, ring-necked pheasants, warblers, grey partridges and great horned owls. Numerous duck, geese and other waterfowl are also present, and you may also catch sight of muskrats, beavers, white-tailed and mule deer, foxes and long-tailed weasels. A visitor centre (May–Sept daily 9am–5pm; free; ☎269-6688) offers information, details of the year-round walking trails, and occasional natural-history courses to guide non-experts. To get here, follow 9th Avenue SE to Sanctuary Road and follow signs to the parking area on the river's south bank. On weekdays the #14 bus (East) turns off 9th Avenue at 17th Street SE, leaving you just a short walk from the Sanctuary.

Heritage Park Historical Village

A sixty-acre theme park centred on a reconstructed frontier village 16km southwest of downtown, **Heritage Park** (☎259-1900) replicates life in the Canadian West before 1914 and panders relentlessly to the myth of the "Wild West" (mid-May to early Sept daily 9am–5pm; early Sept to mid-Oct weekends and holidays 9am–5pm; $29 admission with rides, $15 without rides; free pancake breakfast with admission 9–10am). Full of family-oriented presentations and original costumes, this "heritage" offering – the largest of its type in Canada – is thorough enough for you never to feel obliged to see another.

The living, working museum comprises more than 150 **restored buildings**, all transported from other small-town locations. Each has been assigned to one of several communities – fur post, native village, homestead, farm and c.1900 town – and most fulfil their original function. Thus you can see a working blacksmith, buy fresh bread, buy a local paper, go to church, even get married.

Transport, too, is appropriate to the period, including steam trains, trams, horse-drawn bus and stagecoaches. If you're here for the day you can pick up cakes and snacks from the traditional Alberta Bakery, or sit down to a full meal in the old-style *Wainwright Hotel*.

To get there by car, take either Elbow Drive or Macleod Trail south and turn right on Heritage Drive (the turn-off is marked by a huge, maroon steam engine); **bus** #53 makes the journey from downtown, or you can take the C-Train to Heritage Station and then bus #20 to Northmount.

Eating, drinking and nightlife

Calgary's cuisine can be heavily meat-oriented; Alberta claims, with some justification, to have some of the best **steaks** in the world. With its particular immigration history the city lacks the Ukrainian influences that grace cooking to the north, and often prefers instead to follow the fusion and Pacific Rim trends that have been adopted by most of western Canada's more ambitious restaurants. Most bars and cafés – even the live music venues – double up as restaurants and invariably serve perfectly good food.

The Toronto Dominion Square and Stephen Avenue malls, on 8th Avenue SW between 1st and 3rd, are riddled with ethnic **takeaways** and café-style restaurants – hugely popular and perfect for lunch or snacks on the hoof. The nicest thing to do is buy food and eat it – with half of Calgary – either in the superb **Eau Claire Market**, which is packed with food stalls and restaurants, or amid the greenery of Devonian Gardens. Elsewhere, the city has an impressive range of middle- to upper-bracket restaurants, where prices are low by most standards.

Calgary is rarely a party town, except during Stampede and a brief fling in summer when the weather allows barbecues and night-time streetlife. Nonetheless, its **bars, cafés and clubs** are all you'd expect of a city of this size, the vast majority of them found in five distinct areas: **Kensington**, with its varied cafés; "**Electric Avenue**", as 11th Avenue SW between 5th and 6th streets is called, which has lost most of its brash and mostly trashy bars, night-time action having moved more to **17th Avenue SW**, a more varied collection of pubs, bars, high quality restaurants, speciality shops and ethnic eating, and **4th Street SW**, a similarly more refined restaurant area. **Downtown** cafés and pubs are fine during the day but fairly desolate in the evening.

In the specialist clubs the quality of live music is good – especially in jazz, blues and the genre closest to cowtown Calgary's heart, Country. The Country Music Association has details of local gigs (☎233-8809). Major **festivals** include an annual Jazz Festival (third week in June) and a folk festival at the end of July on Prince's Island.

Tickets for virtually all events are available on ☎270-6700, and through several Marlin Travel offices around the city. You'll find events listings in the *ffwd* or *Calgary Straight* listings tabloids (both free from stores, hotels, cafés, bars and so on) and Calgary's main dailies, the *Herald* and the *Sun*.

Cafés

Good Earth Café. The original wholefood store and café, known for great and inexpensive home-made food, at 1502-11th St (☎228-9543) was so successful it has spawned five other outlets: the Eau Claire Market (☎237-8684) – with good outside patio – the Central Library and elsewhere.

Nellie's Kitchen, 17th Ave and 7th St SW. Laid-back, popular and informal, and especially busy at breakfast – which they do superbly. Open for breakfast and lunch only.

The Roasterie, 314-10th St NW near Kensington Rd. Nice hangout and café – no meals, but newspapers, notice board and twenty kinds of coffee and snacks.

Restaurants

Bistro Jo Jo, 917-17th Ave SW (☎245-2382). If you want to eat good French food, but balk the typically sky-high prices, try the delicious cuisine at this marble-tiled and red-banquette-filled restaurant. Moderate–expensive.

Caesar's Steakhouse, 512 Ave SW and 10816 Macleod Trail S (☎264-1222 or 278-3930). Best place for a huge, perfect steak in the sort of wonderfully cheesy steakhouse – think dimly lit "Roman" decor – that's been around for decades.

Chianti Café and Restaurant, 1438-17th Ave SW (☎229-1600). A favourite local spot for years: dark, noisy, well priced and extremely popular (try to book), with no-nonsense pasta basics and the odd fancy dish. Patio for summer dining outdoors. Recommended.

Divino's, 1st St and 9th Ave SW. Café and wine bar opposite the *Palliser* hotel with rather faux mahogany-Tiffany chandelier interior, but good Italian food and particularly noteworthy desserts.

Earl's. This ever-reliable mid-range chain, serving North American food, has six outlets around Calgary, the most popular of which is probably that at 2401-4th St SW (☎228-4141).

Galaxie Diner, 1413-11th St SW (☎228-0001). Very popular place with authentic diner decor, great breakfasts and fine open grill. Daily 8am–4pm.

Hy's, 316 4th Ave SW (☎263-2222). This deep red-carpeted institution has been serving prime Albertan beef in vast quantities since 1955.

Joey Tomato's, Eau Claire Market (☎263-6336). This Mediterranean-style grill is part of a small chain, but no worse for that, and is a lively, informal place for a good meal among the plethora of choices in and around the Eau Claire market.

River Café, Prince's Island Park (☎261-7670). With *Teatro* (see below), this is the best of Calgary's restaurants for lunch or dinner: innovative Canadian "Northwestern" cuisine and an informal atmosphere on Prince's Island Park, across the bridge from the Eau Claire Market. Be sure to book.

Silver Dragon, 106-3rd Ave SE (☎264-5326). The first choice in town for a Chinese meal: this place has been around for over 30 years and uses a team of 15 Hong Kong-trained chefs to conjure up a menu of some 200 dishes.

Teatro, 200-8th Ave SE (☎290-1012). This is the place to come if you want to dress up a little and drop a little money: the fine Italian-influenced food is on a par with that of the less formal *River Café*. Booking is essential.

Bars

Barley Mill Eatery & Pub, 201 Barclay Parade, Eau Claire Market (☎290-1500). Busy neighbourhood pub that looks and feels the part in Eau Claire Market with an outside patio and 100-year-old bar imported from Scotland inside: 24 draught beers, 40 bottled brews and lots of whiskies.

Ceili's, corner of 5th St and 8 Ave SW (☎508-9999). The larger and generally more lively of Calgary's two main "Irish" pubs.

James Joyce, 114-8th Ave SW (☎262-0708). All the usual clutter, antique bar and drinks associated with faux Irish pubs: popular, and a little calmer and more intimate than its rival, *Ceili's* (see above).

The Ship and Anchor, 17th Ave SW on the corner of 5th St. Long-established neighbourhood pub – friendly and laid-back but jumping, with darts, fine music and excellent pub food. Recommended.

Live music venues

Crazy Horse, 1311-1st St SW (☎266-3339). Popular dance venue with live music on Thursday nights. Small dance floor.

Desperadoes, 1088 Olympic Way (☎263-5343). This huge sports and "cowboy" bar supposedly has room for 3500 people; replacing *Dusty's*, a Calgary institution, the jury's still out on whether it will live up to its predecessor.

Kaos Jazz and Blues Bistro, 718-17th Ave (☎228-9997). Best location in the city for jazz, with blues, acoustic and soul also on offer.

The King Edward Hotel, 438-9th Ave SE. Much-loved, down-at-heel location, with consistently good C&W and R&B bands. The Saturday jam session – the blues event of the city – is invariably packed.

Piq Niq Café, 811-1st St SW (☎263-1650). This place isn't bad as a café, but it really comes into its own Thursday to Saturday with good live jazz acts.

Ranchman's Steak House, 9615 Macleod Trail S (☎253-1100). A classic honky-tonk and restaurant, known throughout Canada for the live, happening C&W. Free dance lessons at 7.30pm Monday to Thursday. Free admission before 8pm on Thursday. Closed Sun.

Senor Frog's, 739-2nd Ave SW (☎264-5100). Three blocks west of the Eau Claire Market. New and popular upbeat restaurant and club, with the club taking precedence Thursday to Saturday from 9pm.

Performing arts, cinema and entertainment

Calgary might come on as a redneck cowtown, but it has ten or more professional the-atre companies, a ballet company, an opera company and a full-blown symphony orchestra. Much of the city's highbrow cultural life focuses on the **Calgary Centre for the Performing Arts**, a dazzling modern downtown complex with five performance spaces close to the Glenbow Museum, at 205-8th Ave SE (☎294-7455). It's also an occa-sional venue for the acclaimed Calgary Philharmonic Orchestra (☎571-0270), Theatre Calgary (☎294-7440) and the well-known Alberta Theatre Projects (☎294-7475), which usually produces five fairly avant-garde plays annually. More modest classical concerts include the Music at Noon offerings in the Central Library (Sept–April), and the ses-sions – planned and impromptu – on the small stages in Devonian Gardens. The long-running and well-known **Lunchbox Theatre**, 2nd Floor, Bow Valley Square, 205-5th Ave SW (☎265-4292 or 265-4293), offers a popular and wildly varied programme aimed at downtown shoppers and passers-by; performances run from September to May and are somewhat irregular, but tend to start daily at noon (except Sun) in the Bow Valley Square on the corner of 6th Avenue and 1st Street SW.

Calgary's **ballet** world is dominated by the young and excellent Alberta Ballet Company (☎245-4222), who perform at various locations around the city. **Opera** is the preserve of Calgary Opera (☎262-7286), whose home base is the Jubilee Auditorium at 1415-14th Ave NW. The season runs from October to April.

For repertory, art-house, classic and foreign **films**, try the newly restored **Uptown Stage & Screen**, 612-8th Ave (☎265-0120) or Plaza Theatre at 1113 Kensington Rd NW; the National Film Board Theatre, 222-1st St SE, puts on free lunch-time shows. The **Museum of Movie Art** at the University of Calgary, 9-3600-21st St NE (Tues–Sat 9.30am–5.30pm), is home to some 4000 cinema posters, some dating back to 1920. For first-run mainstream films, head for the downtown malls – most, including Eau Claire Market, have a cinema complex.

Listings

Airlines Air BC (☎265-9555); Air Canada, 530-8th Ave SW (☎265-9555 or 1-888/247-2262); Alaska Airlines (☎1-800/426-0333); American (☎254-6331 or 1-800/433-7300); British Airways (☎1-800/247-9297); Canada 3000 (☎266-8095); Cathay Pacific (☎1-800/268-6868); Delta (☎1-800/221-1212); Northwest (☎1-800/225-2525); United (☎1-800/241-6522); West Jet (☎250-5839).

Airport enquiries ☎292-8400 or 735-1372.

Ambulance ☎261-4000.

American Express 421-7th Ave SW (☎261-5982 or 1-800/221-7282).

Bookshops Canterbury's Bookshop, 513-8th Ave SW, is the best general bookshop. For maps and travel books, check out Mountain Equipment Co-op, 830-10th Ave SW (☎269-2420), or Map Town, 640-6th Ave SW (☎266-2241).

Bus enquiries Airporter (☎531-3909); Brewster Transportation for airport/Banff/Jasper (☎762-6767, 260-0719 or 1-800/661-1152); Greyhound (☎265-9111 or 1-800/661-8747 in Canada); Laidlaw for airport/Banff/Lake Louise (☎762-9102 or 1-800/661-4946); Red Arrow Express, for Edmonton (☎531-0350 or 1-800/232-1958).

Car rental Avis, 211-6th Ave SW (☎291-1475, 269-6166 or 1-800/879-2847); Budget, 140-6th Ave SE (☎226-1550, 263-0505 or 1-800/268-8900); Hertz (☎221-1300 or 1-800/263-0600 in Canada); Thrifty, 123-5th Ave SE (☎262-4400; airport 221-1806; also 1-800/367-2277).

Consulates Australia (☎604/684-1177); Germany (☎269-5900); Netherlands (☎266-2710); UK (☎604/683-4421); US, 1000-615 Macleod Trail SE (☎266-8962).

Emergencies ☎911.

Exchange Currencies International, Calgary Tower, 304-8th Ave SW (☎290-0330).

Hospital Foothills Hospital, 1403-29th Ave NW(☎670-1110).

Left luggage Facilities at the bus terminal, 850-16th St SW; $2 per 24hr.

Library Central Library, 616-Macleod Trail SE (Mon–Thurs 10am–9pm, Fri–Sat 10am–5pm; ☎260-2600).

Lost property ☎268-1600.

Maps and guides Map Town, 640-6th Ave SW (☎266-2241).

Outdoor gear Mountain Equipment Co-op, 830-10th Ave SW (☎269-2420); Calgary's largest camping and outdoor store: includes excellent books, guides and maps.

Pharmacy ☎253-2605 (24hr).

Police 316-7th Ave SE (☎266-1234); RCMP (☎230-6483).

Post office 220-4th Ave SE (☎292-5434 or Canada Post 1-800/267-1177).

Public transport Calgary Transit (☎262-1000); public transport information.

Taxis Associated Cabs (☎299-1111); Calgary Cab Co (☎777-2222); Checker (☎299-9999); Yellow Cab (☎974-1111).

Tickets Tickets for events, shows, etc (☎270-6700).

Time ☎263-3333.

Tourist information ☎263-8510 or 1-800/661-8888.

Train information VIA Rail (☎1-800/561-8630 in Canada; 1-800/561-3949 in the US); Rocky Mtn Railtours Calgary–Banff–Vancouver (☎1-800/665-7245).

Travel agent Travel Cuts, 1414 Kensington Rd NW (☎531-2070).

Visitors with disabilities Information on wheelchair-accessible transport services (☎262-1000); Calgary Handi-Bus (☎276-8028).

Weather ☎263-3333.

The Alberta Badlands

Formed by the meltwaters of the last Ice Age, the valley of the Red Deer River cuts a deep gash through the dulcet prairie about 140km east of Calgary, creating a surreal landscape of bare, sunbaked hills and eerie lunar flats dotted with sagebrush and scrubby, tufted grass. On their own, the **Alberta Badlands** – strangely anomalous in the midst of lush grasslands – would repay a visit, but what makes them an essential detour is the presence of the **Royal Tyrrell Museum of Paleontology**, amongst the greatest museums of natural history in North America. The museum is located 8km outside the old coal-mining town of **Drumheller**, a dreary but obvious base if you're unable to fit the museum into a day-trip from Calgary. Drumheller is also the main focus of the **Dinosaur Trail**, a road loop that explores the Red Deer Valley and surrounding badlands; you'll need your own transport for this circuit, and for the trip to the **Dinosaur Provincial Park**, home to the Tyrrell Museum Field Station and the source of many of its fossils.

Drumheller

Whatever way you travel, you'll pass through **DRUMHELLER**, a downbeat town in an extraordinary setting roughly ninety-minutes' drive northeast of Calgary. As you approach it from the west, the town is hidden until you come to a virulent red water tower and the road suddenly drops into a dark, hidden canyon. The otherworldliness of the gloomy, blasted landscape is spookily heightened by its contrast to the vivid colours of the earlier wheat and grasslands.

Drumheller sits at the base of the canyon, surrounded by the detritus and spoil heaps of its mining past – the Red Deer River having exposed not only dinosaur fossils but also (now exhausted) coal seams. The coal attracted the likes of Samuel

Drumheller, an early mining pioneer after whom the town is named. The first mine opened in 1911, production reaching a peak after the opening of a rail link to Calgary two years later. In less than fifty years it was all over, coal's declining importance in the face of gas and oil sounding the industry's death knell. These days Drumheller is sustained by agriculture, oil – there are some 3000 wells dotted around the surrounding farmland – and tourism, the **Tyrrell Museum of Paleontology** ranking as one of Alberta's biggest draws.

The town is best reached by taking Hwy 2 north towards Edmonton and branching east on Hwy 72 and Hwy 9. It's an easy day-trip with your own transport, and most people make straight for the Tyrrell Museum, signposted from Drumheller on Hwy 838 (or "North Dinosaur Trail"). Using one of the two **Greyhound buses** daily from Calgary to Drumheller (figure on around $20 one-way) makes a day-trip more of a squeeze. The depot (☎823-7566) is some way out of the town centre at the Suncity Mall on Hwy 9. It's definitely too far to walk from here or the town centre to the museum, particularly on a hot day, but Badlands Taxis (☎823-6552) or Jack's Taxi (☎823-2220) will run you there from the bus depot for about $10. Failing that you could rent a car: National (☎823-3371 or 1-800/387-4747) is the only agency in town.

There's not much to do in the town itself, despite the best efforts of its **infocentre** at the corner of Riverside Drive and 2nd Street W (June–Aug daily 9am–9pm; Sept–May Mon–Fri 8.30am–4.30pm; ☎823-1331). For all its half million visitors a year, Drumheller has just 350 or so beds, and, if truth be told, you don't really want to spend a night here. If you have no choice, be sure to book well in advance: virtually everything's gone by mid-afternoon in high season. A limited selection of **accommodation** lies a block from the bus terminal, the best of the downtown hotels being the slightly overpriced *Lodge at Drumheller* (☎823-3322; ③) opposite the hostel at 48 Centre St and Railway Avenue. Other central options include the *Rockhound Motor Inn*, S Railway Drive (☎823-5302; ④); the top-of-the-pile *Inn & Spa at Heartwood Manor*, 320 Railway Drive (☎823-6495 or 1-888/823-6495; ⑤); *Drumheller Inn* (☎823-8400; ⑤), a modern motel on a bluff at 100 S Railway Ave (Hwy 9) off the Hwy 56 approach from the west; and the tasteful log cabins of the pleasanter *Badlands Motel* (☎823-5155; ⑤), 1km out of town on Hwy 838. The **local hostel** is the rather tatty *Alexander International Hostel*, 30 Railway Ave (☎823-6337, ①), and rents bikes and offers beds in eight-person dorms from $20.

Of the town's well-situated **campgrounds**, the better option is the *Dinosaur Trailer Park* (☎823-3291; $15; April–Oct), across the river north of downtown at the junction of Hwy 56 and Hwy 838. The visitor infocentre has lists of the many other private and provincial campgrounds (*Little Fish Lake Provincial Park*, 50km southeast of Drumheller on Hwy 573, being the best) up and down the valley.

The tucked-away All West **supermarket** on 1st Street behind the main drag stocks picnic supplies. For cheap eating, the *Diana* on Main Street is half-diner, half-Chinese restaurant, and the *Bridge Greek Restaurant*, 71 Bridge St N, has a relaxed ambience and good food. Better-quality **restaurants** have a reputation of going broke once the tourists have gone home, but currently the two best places to eat are *Jack's Bistro*, 70 Railway Ave (☎823-8422), serving hearty Canadian fare, and the reasonably priced and little-known *Sizzling House*, 160 Centre St (☎823-8098), reckoned to be one of Alberta's best Chinese restaurants. The cafeteria at the museum also makes a reasonable eating option.

The Royal Tyrrell Museum of Paleontology

Packed with high-tech displays, housed in a sleek building and blended skilfully into its desolate surroundings, the **Royal Tyrrell Museum of Paleontology** is an object lesson in museum design (mid-May to early Sept daily 9am–9pm; early Sept to mid-Oct daily 10am–5pm; mid-Oct to mid-May Tues–Sun 10am–5pm; $7.50; ☎823-7707). It attracts half a million plus visitors a year, and its wide-ranging exhibits are likely to appeal to anyone with even a hint of scientific or natural curiosity. Although it claims the world's largest collection of complete dinosaur skeletons (fifty full-size animals and 80,000 miscellaneous specimens), the museum is far more than a load of old bones, and as well as tracing the earth's history from the year dot to the present day it's also a leading centre of study and academic research. Its name comes from Joseph Tyrrell, who in 1884 discovered the Albertosaurus, first of the dinosaur remains to be pulled from the Albertan badlands.

Laid out on different levels to suggest layers of geological time, the open-plan exhibit guides you effortlessly through a chronological progression, culminating in a huge central hall of over two hundred dinosaur specimens. If there's a fault, it's that the hall is visible early on and tempts you to skip the lower-level displays, which place the dinosaurs in context by skilfully linking geology, fossils, plate tectonics, evolution and the like with Drumheller's own landscape. You also get a chance to peer into the preparation lab and watch scientists working on fossils in one of the world's best-equipped paleontology centres.

By far the most impressive exhibits are the **dinosaurs** themselves. Whole skeletons are immaculately displayed against three-dimensional backgrounds that persuasively depict the swamps of sixty million years ago. Some are paired with full-size plastic dinosaurs, which appear less macabre and menacing than the freestanding skeletons. Sheer size is not the only fascination: Xiphactinus, for example, a four-metre specimen, is striking more for its delicate and beautiful tracery of bones. Elsewhere the emphasis is on the creatures' diversity or on their staggeringly small brains, sometimes no larger than their eyes.

The museum naturally also tackles the problem of the dinosaurs' extinction, pointing out that around ninety percent of all plant and animal species that have ever inhabited the earth have become extinct. Leave a few minutes for the wonderful **paleoconservatory** off the dinosaur hall, a collection of living prehistoric plants, some unchanged in 180 million years, selected from fossil records to give an idea of the vegetation that would have typified Alberta in the dinosaur age.

The Dinosaur Trail

The **Dinosaur Trail** is a catch-all circular road route of 51km from Drumheller embracing some of the viewpoints and lesser historic sights of the badlands and the Red Deer Valley area. The comprehensive *Visitor's Guide to the Drumheller Valley* (free from the Drumheller infocentre) lists thirty separate stopoffs, mostly on the plain above the valley, of which the key ones are: the **Little Church** (6km west of Drumheller), the "Biggest Little Church in the World" (capacity six); **Horsethief Canyon** (17.6km west of the museum) and **Horseshoe Canyon** (19km southwest of the museum on Hwy 9), two spectacular viewpoints of the wildly eroded valley, the latter with good trails to and along the canyon floor; the **Hoodoos**, slender columns of wind-sculpted sandstone, topped with mushroom-like caps (17km southeast of Drumheller on Hwy 10); the still largely undeveloped **Midland Provincial Park**, site of the area's first mines and crisscrossed by badland trails, now home to an interpretive centre (daily 9am–6pm; free); and the **Atlas Coal Mine** (guided tours mid-May to mid-Oct daily 9am–6pm; $4 or $6 for guided tour; ☎822-2220), dominated by the teetering wooden "tipple", once used to sort ore and now a beautiful and rather wistful piece of industrial archeology.

Dinosaur Provincial Park

Drivers can feasibly fit in a trip to **Dinosaur Provincial Park** the same day as the Tyrrell Museum, a 174-kilometre journey from Drumheller to the park, and then head back to Calgary on the Trans-Canada Highway, which runs just south of the park. The nearest town is Brooks, 48km west of the **Royal Tyrrell Museum Field Station**, the park's obvious hub (late May to early Oct daily 8.30am–9pm; early Oct to late May Mon–Fri 9am–4pm; $2; ☎378-4342, reservation line ☎378-4344). The excellent **Dinosaur Provincial Park** campground in the park beside Little Sandhill Creek is open year-round, but only serviced from May to September ($13). Book on (☎378-3700).

Nestled among some of the baddest of the badlands, the region's landscape is not only one of the most alien in the Northwest, but also one of the world's richest fossil beds, a superb medley of prairie habitats and ecosystems and (since 1979) a listed UN World Heritage Site. Over 300 complete skeletons have been found and dispatched to museums across the world, representing 35 (or ten percent) of all known dinosaur species. The field station has five self-guided **trails**, the Badlands Trail and Cottonwood Flats Trail being the most worthwhile, and giving a good taste of this extraordinary region. The centre also has a small museum that goes over the same ground as its parent in Drumheller, leaving the real meat of the visit to the **Badlands Bus Tour**, an excellent ninety-minute guided tour of the otherwise out-of-bounds dinosaur dig near the centre of the park (May–Sept Mon–Fri tours three or more daily, Sat–Sun 7 times daily; $4.50). A few exposed skeletons have been left *in situ*, with panels giving background information. The station also organizes two-hour guided **hikes**, most notably the Centrosaurus Bone Bed Hike (Tues, Thurs, Sat & Sun 9.15am; $4.50), which visits a restricted area where some 300 centrosaurus skeletons have been uncovered. All tours fill up quickly, so it's worth trying to book ahead (☎378-4344).

Highway 3

The most travelled route across southern Alberta is the Trans-Canada Highway, direct to Calgary; **Hwy 3**, branching off at **Medicine Hat**, takes a more southerly course across the plains before finally breaching the Rockies at Crowsnest Pass. This quieter and less spectacular route into the mountains holds a trio of worthwhile diversions: the new **Carriage Centre** near Cardston, the **Head-Smashed-In Buffalo Jump** heritage site, and **Waterton Lakes National Park**, a cross-border park that links with the United States' Glacier National Park.

Medicine Hat

Though **MEDICINE HAT** is barely a hundred years old, the origin of its wonderful name has already been confused. The most likely story has to do with a Cree medicine man who lost his headdress while fleeing a battle with the Blackfoot; his followers lost heart at the omen, surrendered, and were promptly massacred. These days you rarely see the town mentioned without the adage that it "has all hell for a basement", a quotation from Rudyard Kipling coined in response to the huge reserves of natural gas that lurk below the town. Discovered by railway engineers drilling for water in 1883, the gas fields now feed a flourishing petrochemical industry which blots the otherwise park-studded downtown area on the banks of the South Saskatchewan River.

Medicine Hat may claim that its 1440 hours of summer sunshine makes it Canada's sunniest city, but its main function is as a major staging post on the Trans-Canada Highway. The world's **tallest tepee** (twenty storeys tall and actually made of metal), on the highway close to the visitor centre, and the nightmare **Riverside Waterslide** at Hwy 1 and Powerhouse Road (mid-May to early Sept daily 10am–8pm; $12.50; ☎529-6218) are the only attractions of note. If you're pulling off the road for a break, the best place for coffee and snacks is *Café Mundo*, 579 3rd St SE (☎528-2808); for lunch try *Caroline's*, 101 4th Ave SE (☎529-5300); and for novelty "Wild West" setting the place to go is the historic *Rustler's*, 901 8th St SW (☎526-8004), one of the town's oldest restaurants. The least expensive of the many **motels** is the *Bel-Aire*, 633 14th St (☎527-4421; ①), conveniently situated at the junction of the Trans-Canada and Hwy 3, though the *Best Western Inn*, on the Trans-Canada at 722 Redcliff Drive (☎527-3700 or 1-800/528-1234; ⑤), is more appealing if around three times the price. The best place around is the smart and comfortable *Medicine Hat Lodge*, 1051 Ross Glen Drive (☎529-2222 or 1-800/661-8095, *www.medhatlodge.com*; ⑤). The main downtown accommodation is the *Medicine Hat Inn Downtown*, 530 4th St SE (☎526-1313 or 1-800/730-3887; ③).

Lethbridge

Alberta's third city, **LETHBRIDGE** is booming on the back of oil, gas and some of the province's most productive agricultural land; none of which is of much consequence to people passing through, whom the city attempts to sidetrack with the **Nikka Yuko Centennial Gardens** (mid-May to June & Sept daily 9am–5pm; July–Aug daily 9am–9pm; closed Oct to mid-May; $4; ☎328-3511) in its southeastern corner at 7th Avenue and Mayor Macgrath Drive in Henderson Lake Park. Built in 1967 as a symbol of Japanese and Canadian amity, the gardens were a somewhat belated apology for the treatment of Japanese-Canadians during World War II, when 22,000 were interned – 6000 of them in Lethbridge. Four tranquil Japanese horticultural landscapes make up the gardens, along with a pavilion of cypress wood handcrafted in Japan perpetually laid out for a tea ceremony.

Far removed from the gardens' decorum is **Fort Whoop-Up** (June–Aug Mon–Sat 10am–6pm, Sun noon–5pm; Sept–May Tues–Fri 10am–4pm, Sun 1–4pm; $2.50; ☎329-0444) at Indian Battle Park (Scenic Drive at 3rd Ave), a reconstruction of the wild whiskey trading post set up in 1869 by American desperadoes from Fort Benton, Montana (the first of several in the region). It became the largest and most lucrative of the many similar forts which sprang up illegally all over the Canadian prairies, and led directly to the arrival of the North West Mounted Police in 1874. Aboriginal peoples came from miles around to trade anything – including the clothes off their backs – for the lethal hooch, which was fortified by grain alcohol and supplemented by ingredients such as red peppers, dye and chewing tobacco. The fort was also the scene of the last armed battle in North America between aboriginal peoples (fought between the Cree and Blackfoot nations in 1870).

Lethbridge's third significant sight is the **Sir Alexander Galt Museum** (daily 10am–4.30pm; donation; ☎320-3898) at the western end of 5th Avenue S off Scenic Drive, one of the Northwest's better small-town museums. It's named after a Canadian high commissioner who in 1882 financed a mine that led to the foundation of Lethbridge. Revamped at vast expense in 1985, the museum offers an overview of the city's history, with displays that cover coal mining, irrigation, immigration and the shameful internment episodes during the 1940s. There are also a couple of galleries devoted to art and other temporary exhibitions.

Practicalities

Four Greyhound **buses** operate daily from Calgary to the Lethbridge bus terminal (☎327-1551) at 411 5th St S. Two buses run daily to Fort Macleod, and two to Medicine Hat and the US border for connections to Great Falls and Helena in Montana. The **tourist office** is at 2805 Scenic Drive at the corner of Hwy 4 and Hwy 5 (summer daily 9am–8pm; winter Mon–Sat 9am–5pm; ☎320-1222 or 1-800/661-1222 from western Canada and northwestern US).

Most of the city's **motels** are on a single strip, Mayor Macgrath Drive; the top-of-the-pile *Sandman Hotel Lethbridge*, at no. 421 (☎328-1111 or 1-800/726-3626; ④), and the less expensive *Chinook Motel*, at no. 1303 (☎328-0555 or 1-800/791-8488; ③), are typical.

Downtown the best value is the *Days Inn*, 100 3rd Ave S (☎327-6000 or 1-800/661-8085; ③). The *Henderson Lake Campgrounds* (☎328-5452; $14; May–Oct) are near Henderson Lake on 7th Avenue S alongside the Nikka Yuko Centennial Gardens in Henderson Lake Park. The best downtown **eating** is to be found in the *Lethbridge Lodge Hotel* at 320 Scenic Drive (☎328-1123 or 1-800/661-1232), which boasts *Anton's*, an upmarket restaurant with modern American food, and the cheaper but pleasant and popular *Garden Café*. For downtown coffee and snacks, make for *The Penny Coffee House*, 331 5th St S.

Fort Macleod and around

FORT MACLEOD catches traffic coming up from the States and down from Calgary on Hwy 2, which eases around the town centre via the largely rebuilt wooden palisade of the **Fort Museum** at 219 25th St (daily: May, June & Sept to mid-Oct 9am–5pm; July & Aug 9am–8pm; mid-Oct to Dec 23 & March–April Mon–Fri 9am–5pm; $5; ☎553-4703). One for die-hard Mountie fans, this was the first fort established in Canada's Wild West by the North West Mounted Police, who got lost after being dispatched to raid Fort Whoop-Up in Lethbridge, allowing the whiskey traders to flee; finding Whoop-Up empty, they continued west under Colonel James Macleod to establish a permanent barracks here on Oldman Island on the river in 1874. The RCMP "musical ride", a display of precision riding, is performed four times daily in July and August by students in replica dress.

Two daily **buses** serve the town from Lethbridge and between three and five from Calgary, the latter continuing west to Cranbrook, Nelson and eventually to Vancouver in British Columbia. The depot's at 2302 2nd Ave (☎553-3383). The **tourist office** is at the east end of town on 24th Street (mid-May to Aug daily 9am–8pm; ☎553-4955). The town has nine more or less similarly priced **motels**, the most central being the *Fort Motel* on Main Street (☎553-3606; ②). Top choice is the *Sunset Motel* (☎553-4448 or 1-888/554-2784; ④), located on Hwy 3 at the western entrance to town. All motels fill up quickly in summer, so arrive early or call ahead.

Head-Smashed-In Buffalo Jump

The image of Indians trailing a lone buffalo with bow and arrow may be Hollywood's idea of how aboriginal peoples foraged for food, but the truth, while less romantic, was often far more effective and spectacular. Over a period of more than 6000–10,000 years, Blackfoot hunters perfected a technique of luring buffalo herds into a shallow basin and stampeding them to their deaths over a broad cliff, where they were then butchered for meat (dried to make pemmican, a cake of pounded meat, berries and lard), bone (for tools) and hide (for clothes and shelter). Such "jumps" existed all over North America, but the **Head-Smashed-In Buffalo Jump**, in the Porcupine Hills 18km northwest of Fort Macleod on Hwy 785, is the best preserved (daily: mid-May to early Sept 9am–6pm; early Sept to mid-May 10am–5pm; ☎553-2731). Its name, which alone should be enough to whet your appetite, is a literal description of how a nineteenth-century Blackfoot met his end after deciding the best spot to watch the jump was at the base of the cliff, apparently unaware he was about to be visited by some five hundred plummeting buffalo.

The modern **interpretive centre**, a seven-storeyed architectural *tour de force*, is built into the ten-metre-high and 305-metre-wide cliff near the original jump. Below it, a ten-metre-deep bed of ash and bones accumulated over millennia is protected by the threat of a $50,000 fine for anyone foolish enough to rummage for souvenirs. All manner of artefacts and objects have been discovered amidst the debris, among them knives, scrapers and sharpened stones used to skin the bison. Metal arrowheads in the topmost layers, traded with white settlers, suggest the jump was used until comparatively recently. Nothing can have changed much here over millennia bar the skilfully integrated centre and some modest excavations. The multilevelled facility delves deep into the history of the jump and native culture in general, its highlight being a film, *In Search of the Buffalo*, which attempts to re-create the thunderous death plunge using a herd of buffalo, which were slaughtered, frozen and then somehow made to look like live animals hurtling to their deaths (shown half-hourly on Level Four). Around the centre the jump is surrounded by a couple of kilometres of **trails**, the starting point for tours conducted by Blackfoot native guides. No public transport serves the site; taxis from Fort Macleod cost about $20.

Remington-Alberta Carriage Centre

Alberta is hoping that the glittering new **Remington-Alberta Carriage Centre** (daily: mid-May to early Sept 9am–8pm; early Sept to mid-May 10am–5pm; $6.50, carriage rides June–Aug $3; ☎653-1000 or 653-5139) will attract visitors in droves. Although brilliantly executed, its appeal is perhaps more limited, centring on horse-drawn vehicles and evoking the atmosphere of their nineteenth-century heyday. The main hall boasts around sixty working carriages – the core of a private collection begun by Don Remington in the 1950s – and around 140 in passive display, the exhibits cleverly integrated with 25 "stories" that place the carriages in their social and cultural context. Additionally there's the chance to ride the carriages (usually for free), see working stables and admire the magnificent Quarters and Clydesdales that make up the centre's horse herd. Guides are often in period dress, and you can watch craftspeople in the process of building and renovating various carriages. Free guided tours run regularly around the site. The centre lies immediately south of **Cardston** at 623 Main St (across the river from the town centre), just off Hwy 2 about 50km south of Fort Macleod, and is handily placed for Waterton Lakes National Park.

Waterton Lakes National Park

WATERTON LAKES NATIONAL PARK, about 55km south of Fort Macleod, appears at first glance to be simply an addendum to the much larger Glacier National Park, which joins it across the United States border. Despite its modest size, however (just 523 square kilometres), it contains scenery – and trails – as stupendous as any of the bigger Canadian Rockies parks. In particular this is a great place to come for day-hikes, most of which – unlike equivalent walks in Banff and Jasper – can be easily accessed from the park's principal focus, **Waterton Townsite** (or Waterton). Founded in 1895, the park was relaunched in 1932 as an "International Peace Park" to symbolize the understated relationship between Canada and its neighbour. The two parks remain separate national enclaves. Though backpackers can cross the border without formalities, to drive from one to the other you have to exit the park and pass through immigration controls, as stringent as anywhere if you're not a national of either country. In a change to the practice of past years, a **park permit** is required between April and the end of September for all who enter the park: a day-pass is $4 (yearly $28), and group passes (2–10 people) cost $12 daily (see box on p.486 for more details concerning park entry fees).

Some history

These days Waterton is on the road pretty much to nowhere – if you're down this way you're here to see the park or on your way to or from the US. It was a different story in the past, for the region provided a happy hunting ground for **Ktunaxa** (Kootenay) First Peoples, whose home base was across the Continental Divide in the Kootenay region of present-day British Columbia. Around 200 archeological sites betraying their presence have been found in the park. Anything up to 9000 years ago aboriginal peoples crossed the mountains to fish and hunt bison on the prairie grasslands fringing the Waterton region, foodstuffs denied to them in their own aboriginal heartlands. By about 1700 the diffusion of the horse across North America (introduced by the

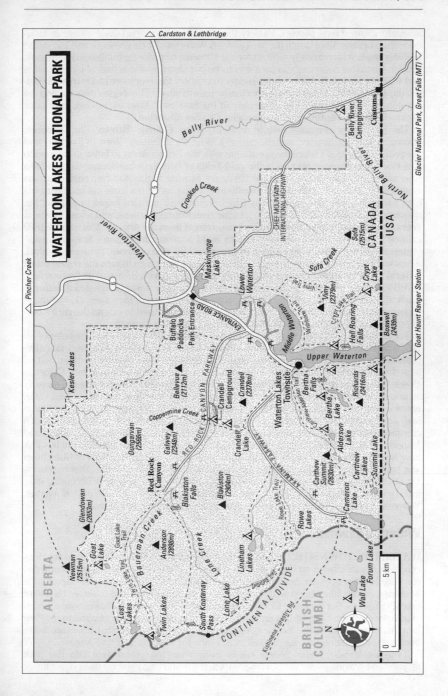

Spanish) allowed rival peoples, namely the Blackfoot, to extend their sphere of influence from central Alberta into the area around Waterton. Their presence and increased mobility made it increasingly difficult for the Ktunaxa to make their habitual incursions, though Blackfoot supremacy in turn was to be cut short by the arrival of pioneer guns and white homesteads. By the mid-nineteenth century the Blackfoot had retreated eastwards, leaving the Waterton area virtually uninhabited. The region was named by Lieutenant Thomas Blakiston, a member of the famous Palliser expedition, in honour of the eighteenth-century British naturalist Charles Waterton.

The area's first permanent white resident, **John George Brown** – or "Kootenai Brown" – was a character straight out of a Wild West fantasy. Born in England and allegedly educated at Oxford, he spent time with the British Army in India, decamped to San Francisco, chanced his arm in the gold fields of British Columbia and worked for a time as a pony express rider with the US Army. Moving to the Waterton region he was attacked by Blackfoot natives, supposedly wrenching an arrow from his back with his own hands. He was then captured by Chief Sitting Bull and tied naked to a stake, but managed to escape at dead of night to join the rival Ktunaxa natives, with whom he spent years hunting and trapping, until their virtual retreat from the prairies. Marriage in 1869 calmed him down, and encouraged him to build a cabin (the region's first) alongside Waterton Lake. In time he was joined by other settlers, one of whom, Frederick Godsal, a rancher and close personal friend, took up Brown's campaign to turn the region into a **federal reserve**. In 1895 a reserve was duly established, with Brown as its first warden. In 1910 the area was made a "Dominion Park"; a year later it was designated a **national park**, the fourth in Canada's burgeoning park system. Brown, then aged 71, was made its superintendent, but died four years later, still lobbying hard to extend the park's borders. His grave lies alongside the main road into Waterton Townsite.

For all Brown's environmental zeal it was he, ironically, who first noticed globules of **oil** on Cameron Creek, a local river, a discovery that would bring oil and other mineral entrepreneurs to ravage the region. Brown himself actually skimmed oil from the river, bottled it, and sold it in nearby settlements. In 1901 a forest road was ploughed into Cameron Creek Valley. In September of the same year the Rocky Mountain Development Company struck oil, leading to western Canada's first producing oil well (and only the second in the entire country). The oil soon dried up, a monument on the Akamina Parkway (see overleaf) now marking the well's original location. Tourists meanwhile were giving the park a conspicuously wide berth, thanks mainly to the fact that it had no railway (unlike Banff and Jasper), a situation that changed when the Great Northern Railway introduced a bus link here from its Montana to Jasper railway. Visitors began to arrive, the *Prince of Wales* hotel was built, and the park's future was assured. In 1995, some time after the other big parks, UNESCO declared Waterton a World Heritage Site. Today, the park is becoming ever more popular, with the same tell-tale proliferation of souvenir shops on Waterton Avenue, Waterton Townsite's main street, as you find on Banff town's Banff Avenue.

Waterton Townsite

WATERTON TOWNSITE, the park's only base, accommodation source and services centre, is beautifully set on Upper Waterton Lake, but offers little by way of cultural distraction. Most people are here to walk (see box, p.478), windsurf, horseride or take boat trips on the lake (see p.475). There are also a handful of town trails, and a trio of cracking hikes – Bertha Lake, Crypt Lake and the Upper Waterton Lakeshore – which start from the townsite (see box on p.478). Having long been a poor relation to the "big four" national parks in the Rockies, Waterton is now so popular that it's essential to book accommodation (see p.475) well in advance for much of July and August.

Two wonderfully scenic access roads from Waterton probe west into the park interior and provide picnic spots, viewpoints and the starting point for most other trails:

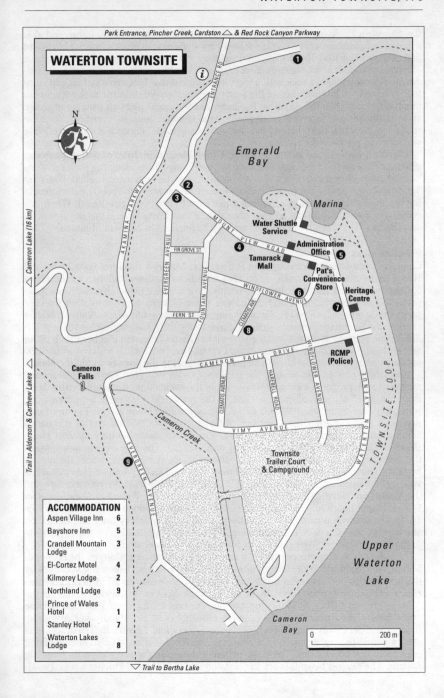

Park Entrance, Pincher Creek, Cardston △ & Red Rock Canyon Parkway

WATERTON TOWNSITE

Emerald Bay

Marina

Water Shuttle Service

Administration Office

Tamarack Mall

Pat's Convenience Store

Heritage Centre

FIR GROVE ST

FERN ST

WINDFLOWER AVENUE

CLEMATIS AVE

CAMERON FALLS DRIVE

RCMP (Police)

Cameron Falls

Cameron Creek

CLEMATIS AVENUE

HARBELL ROAD

WINDFLOWER AVENUE

VIMY AVENUE

WATERTON AVENUE

T O W N S I T E   L O O P

Townsite Trailer Court & Campground

EVERGREEN AVENUE

Upper Waterton Lake

N

△ Cameron Lake (16 km)

△ Trail to Alderson & Carthew Lakes

ENTRANCE RD

AKAMINA PARKWAY

EVERGREEN AVENUE

MOUNT VIEW ROAD

FOUNTAIN AVENUE

ACCOMMODATION

Aspen Village Inn	6
Bayshore Inn	5
Crandell Mountain Lodge	3
El-Cortez Motel	4
Kilmorey Lodge	2
Northland Lodge	9
Prince of Wales Hotel	1
Stanley Hotel	7
Waterton Lakes Lodge	8

Cameron Bay

0   200 m

▽ Trail to Bertha Lake

the **Akamina Parkway** follows the Cameron Creek valley for 20km to Cameron Lake, a large subalpine lake where you can follow easy trails or rent canoes, rowing boats and paddleboats. The **Red Rock Canyon Parkway** weaves up Blakiston Creek for about 15km to the mouth of the water-gouged Red Rock Canyon, so called because of the oxidation of local argillite, a rock with a high iron content that turns rust-red on exposure to the elements. The road's one of the best places to see wildlife in the park without too much effort and, like the Akamina Parkway, has the usual pleasant panoply of picnic sites, trailheads and interpretive notice boards. If you're without transport for these roads see "Practicalities", below, and "Activities", opposite, for details of hiker shuttle services and car and bike rentals.

The third named road in the park, the **Chief Mountain International Highway** (25km) runs east from the park entrance at Maskinonge Lake along the park's eastern border. After 7km it reaches a fine **viewpoint** over the mountain-backed Waterton Valley and then passes the park-run *Belly River Campground* (see p.477) before reaching the US–Canadian **border crossing** (open June to late Sept 7am–10pm). When this crossing's closed, depending on your direction of travel, you have to use the crossings on Alberta's Hwy 2 south of Cardston or Hwy 89 north of St Mary in Montana.

Practicalities

Canadian **access** to Waterton by road is from Fort Macleod via either Hwy 3 west and Hwy 6 south (via Pincher Creek) or on Hwy 2 south to Cardston and then west on Hwy 5. Calgary is 264km and three-hours' drive away; Lethbridge (which has the nearest airport), 130km (75min); and St Mary, Montana, 60km (45min). More than other Rockies' parks this is somewhere you really need your own transport to reach. A small taxi-bus service, the Shuttleton Services (usually three times daily, but ring for services; ☎627-2157) runs between Waterton and the nearest Greyhound depot at Pincher Creek 50km away ($15 one-way, $25 return); a cab from Crystal Taxi (☎627-4262) will cost around $60 for the same run; otherwise there's no public transport to the town or within the park.

Everything you need to explore the park centres on Waterton Townsite. All accommodation is here, bar the campgrounds, while the national park **visitor centre** is on Entrance Road at the road junction just to the north (May & early Sept 9am–5pm; June–Aug 8am–9pm; ☎859-2445 or 859-2224, *www.watertoninfo.ab.ca*). Further information is available from the Chamber of Commerce (☎859-2303) and at the park's administration office at 215 Mount View Rd outside the visitor centre's summer hours (Mon–Fri 8am–4pm; ☎859-2477, 859-2224 or 859-2275). The free weekly **newspaper**, the *Waterton-Glacier Views* (☎627-2370), also contains visitor information. Be sure to buy the Canadian Parks Service 1:50,000 **map** *Waterton Lakes National Park* ($9.50), if you're going to do any serious walking. It's usually available from the visitor centre and the **Waterton Heritage Centre** in the old firehall at 117 Waterton Ave (May–Oct 1–5pm, longer hours July & Aug; admission to museum by donation; ☎859-2267 or 859-2624). The latter is a combined art gallery, small natural-history museum, bookshop and another useful source of information. For advance information on the park, write to the Superintendent, Waterton Lakes National Park, Waterton Park, AB T0K 2M0.

Pat's Rentals & Convenience Store, a gas station and camping store on the corner of Mount View Road and Waterton Avenue (☎859-2266), rents out **bikes** and **scooters** by the hour or day and also sells bikes and spares. There's also an ATM here. For **currency exchange**, try the Royal Bank in Tamarack Mall on Waterton Avenue or the Alberta Treasury Branch Agency upstairs at Caribou Clothing on Waterton Avenue (☎859-2604). The Itussististukiopi Coin-Op **laundry** is at 301 Windflower Ave (mid-June to mid-Sept daily 8am–10pm). Waterton Sports and Leisure in Tamarack Mall stocks maps, fishing licences, and camping, walking, fishing and mountain-biking equipment and accessories. The **post office** is alongside the fire station on Fountain Avenue. The nearest **hospitals** are in Cardston (☎653-4411) and Pincher Creek (☎627-

3333). For the **police**, call ☎859-2244. There's also a 24-hour park emergency number, but it really is for emergencies only (☎859-2636).

Activities

If you want to **cruise the lakes**, the most popular summer activity round these parts, contact Waterton Shoreline Cruises at the marina (☎859-2362). They run scenic two-hour cruises (June–Aug 5 daily; fewer in May & Sept; $21 or $13 one-way) up and down the lake across the US–Canadian border to Goat Haunt in Montana, little more than a quayside and park ranger station, where there is scheduled thirty-minute stop before the return to Waterton (note that after the ranger station closes in mid-Sept boats no longer stop at Goat Haunt). No immigration procedures are required, but if you wish to camp overnight in the backcountry you need to register with the ranger station. You can take an early boat to Goat Haunt and then return on foot to Waterton on the **Waterton Lakeshore Trail**, an easy four-hour walk (13km one-way). The same company run a ferry to various trails around the lake, most notably a passage ($11 return) to the trailhead of the famed Crypt Lake walk (see box, p.478) and the myriad longer hikes from Goat Haunt in the US. Park Transport in Tamarack Mall on Mount View Road (☎859-2378) organizes two-hour tours round the park ($25), but will also lay on a **taxi** shuttle (from $7.50)to trails on the area's two Parkways: the most popular drop-off is the beginning of the Carthew-Alderson trail (see box, p.479).

Windsurfing is also surprisingly popular locally, thanks to the powerful winds – anything up to 70kph – which often roar across the lakes (Waterton is wetter, windier and snowier than much of Alberta). Winds generally gust south to north, making the beach at Cameron Bay on Upper Waterton Lake a favourite spot for surfers to catch the breeze. The water's cold and deep, though, so you'll need a wet suit. If you want to **swim**, head for the cheap outdoor heated pool on Cameron Falls Drive. **Fishing** is good on the lakes, but remember to pick up the compulsory national-park permit ($6 a week, $13 annual) from the visitor centre or park administration office. Off the water, **horse riding** is available from the Alpine Stables, PO Box 53, Waterton Park, AB (☎859-2462), located just east off the highway about 1km north of the Visitor Centre. On offer are one-hour outings (hourly on the hour; from $17) and two-hour (3 daily; $31), daily and overnight treks. Canadian Wilderness Adventures (☎859-2334, fax 859-2342) offer a range of guided walks and tours long and short. Four kilometres north of town on the main highway is the beautiful eighteen-hole **Waterton Lakes Golf Course** (☎859-2383 or 859-2114): green fees are around $30 (cheaper after 5pm) and club rental from about $8.

Hotels and motels

Aspen Village Inn, Windflower Ave (☎859-2255 or 1-888/859-8669, fax 859-2033). Quiet spot with mountain views opposite the municipal pool; 35 motel rooms and 16 "cottage" rooms, some with kitchenettes. April to mid-Oct. ⑤.

Bayshore Inn, 111 Waterton Ave (☎859-2211 or 1-888/527-9555, fax 859-2291, _www.bayshoreinn .com_). Just south of the marina; very comfortable hotel, with 49 of its seventy units on the lakefront; two-unit and deluxe suites available. Mid-April to mid-Oct. ⑥.

Crandell Mountain Lodge, 102 Mount View Rd, corner of Evergreen Ave (☎859-2288; _www .crandellmountainlodge.com_). Just seventeen nicely finished non-smoking rooms (two with special wheelchair access) in a pretty lodge; more intimate than some of the town's hotels, with kitchenette and fireplace units available. Easter–Oct. ⑥.

El-Cortez Motel, next to the Tamarack Mall at 208 Mount View Rd (☎859-2366, fax 859-2221). One of the less expensive places in town; 35 rooms including two- and three-room family units; some rooms with kitchenettes. May to Sept. ③.

Kilmorey Lodge, 117 Evergreen Ave (☎859-2334 or 1-888/859-8669, fax 859-2342; _kilmorey @telusplanet.net_). At the northern entrance to town on Emerald Bay; 23 antique-decorated rooms with a lakefront setting and historic old-fashioned feel. Some rooms are small for the price, while others score by virtue of their views (book in advance for these); there's also an excellent restau-

GEOLOGY, FLORA AND FAUNA

The Waterton area's unique **geological history** becomes clear when you compare its scenery with the strikingly different landscapes of Banff and Jasper national parks to the north (see pp.483–507 and pp.523–538). Rock and mountains in Waterton moved eastward during the formation of the Rockies (see p.485), but unlike the ruptured strata elsewhere it travelled as a single vast mass known as the Lewis Thrust. Some 6km thick, this monolith moved over 70km along a 300-kilometre front, the result being that rocks over 1.5 billion years old from the Rockies' "sedimentary basement" – now the oldest surface rocks in the range – finally came to rest undisturbed on *top* of the prairies' far more recent 60-million-year-old shales. Scarcely any zone of transition exists between the two, which is why the park is often known as the place where the "peaks meet the prairies", and its landscapes as "upside-down mountains". The effect was to produce not only slightly lower peaks than to the north, but also mountains whose summits are irregular in shape and whose sedimentary formations are horizontal (very different from the steeply tilted strata and distinctive sawtooth ridges of Banff National Park).

The classic glacial U-shaped Waterton Valley and Upper Waterton Lake (at 150m, the Rockies' deepest lake) are more recent phenomena, gouged out 1.9 million years ago by ice age **glaciers** as they carved their way northwards through the present Waterton valley before expiring on the prairies. Upper Waterton Lake and the other two Waterton lakes are residual depressions left after the ice's final retreat 11,000 years ago. Cameron Lake, by contrast, was created when a glacial moraine (debris created by a glacier) dammed the waters of Cameron Creek. The flat townsite area has different origins again, consisting of deposits of silt, mud and gravel washed down from the mountains over the millennia and deposited as an alluvial "fan" across Upper Waterton Lake.

The huge variety of altitude, habitats and climate within the park – a combination of prairie, montane and alpine – mean that plants and wildlife from prairie habitats comingle with the species of the purely montane, subalpine and alpine regions found elsewhere. The result is the greatest diversity of **flora and fauna** of any of the western national parks: 1200 plant species – well over half of all that grown in Alberta – and 250 species of birds. The variety is immediately noticeable. As you approach the park on Hwy 5 from the north, a route almost as scenic as the park, you pass through dry prairie **grasslands**. This is home to native grasses such as grama and rough fescue, local

---

rant (the *Lamp Post*) and nice *Gazebo Café on the Bay* with outdoor waterfront deck for snacks and light meals. Open all year. ⑤.

The Lodge At Waterton Lakes, Cameron Falls Drive and Windflower Ave (☎859-2151 or 1-888/985-6343, fax 859-2229, *www.watertonresort.com*). Smart 80-room resort hotel; health spa with indoor pool, recreational centre with 18m pool and lots of extra facilities such as kitchenettes in certain deluxe rooms. ⑦.

Northland Lodge, Evergreen Ave (☎ & fax 859-2353, *www.northlandlodge.ab.ca*). Nine non-smoking and cosy rooms, seven with private bathroom, east of the townsite in the lee of the mountains one block south of Cameron Falls; some with kitchenettes. Mid-May to mid-Oct. ③.

Prince of Wales Hotel, Waterton Lake (☎859-2231, 236-3400 or 602/207-6000, fax 859-2630). Famous and popular old hotel – the best in town – whose 1927 Gothic outline is in almost every picture of Waterton; worth it if you can afford it. Lakeside rooms with views are pricier, but some are rather small, so check what you're getting for your $245. Mid-May to mid-Sept. ⑦.

Stanley Hotel, 112b Waterton Ave (☎859-2345). Old-fashioned and often full nine-roomed hotel. Mid-May to Sept. ③.

Campgrounds

In addition to the private and three Canadian Parks Service park-run campgrounds (park campgrounds are first-come, first-served, and fill quickly in summer), that are detailed below, the national park has provided thirteen designated **backcountry**

species now rapidly disappearing, displaced over the years by cultivated crops. Here, too, you should see the prickly wild rose, Alberta's floral emblem, sagebrush, buckbrush (yellow rose) and pincushion cactus. Entering the park you pass the **wetlands** of Maskinonge Lake on your left, while in the Blakison Valley and around *Belly River Campground* you are in the realms of **aspen parkland**, a transitional zone between prairie and forest habitats dominated by aspen, willow, white spruce, balsam poplar and flowers such as prairie crocus, snowberry and lily of the valley. Higher up you encounter **montane forest** and subalpine zones, fecund zones rich in plant and animal life easily explored on hikes such as the Bertha Lake and Carthew Lakes trails (see box, overleaf). On the eastern slopes above Cameron Lake are copses of 400-year-old subalpine trees (lodgepole pine, larch, fir, whitebark pine and Engelmann spruce), the oldest forest growth in the park. Here, too, you'll see vast spreads of so-called bear grass, a bright flower-topped grass which can grow up to a metre in height. Trees largely give out in the **alpine zone**, an area of which the park's Crypt Lake is a good example. It is the preserve of heathers, hardy lichens, flower-strewn meadows and rarer high-altitude alpine plants. See "Contexts" p.629 for more on these various habitats.

If you want to see **fauna**, enquire at the park centre for likely locations and times – autumn days at dawn and dusk are usually best. **Birds** are best seen on Maskinonge and Lower Waterton lakes, Linnet Lake, Cameron Lake and along the easy 45-minute Wishbone Trail off Chief Mountain Highway. The best time to look is during the migratory season between September and November, as the park lies under two major migration routes. Ospreys also nest close to Waterton Townsite. Maskinonge Lake is also the place to sit in the hope of seeing mink and muskrats. As for **mammals**, beavers can be seen on the Belly River, and golden-mantled ground squirrels around Cameron Lake and on the Bear's Hump above town; Columbian ground squirrels are ubiquitous. The park has about fifty black bears, but you'll be lucky to see them: your best bet is to scan the slopes of Blakison Valley in July and August as they forage for berries in readiness for hibernation. Grizzlies, moose and cougars are also prevalent, but rarely seen. White-tailed deer nibble up and down the Red Rock Canyon Parkway, while elk and mule deer often wander in and around Waterton town itself. Mountain goats are shy and elusive, but you may glimpse one or two in the rocky high ground above Bertha, Crypt and Goat lakes. Bighorn sheep congregate above the Visitor Centre and the northern flanks of the Blakison Valley.

campgrounds, where you'll find dry toilets and a surface water supply; a few of them also have shelters and cooking facilities. To use any, you need a backcountry camping permit, issued on a first-come, first-served basis by the Visitor Centre or Administration Office. A quota system is operated to prevent overcrowding. For information on these and other park campgrounds, call ☎859-2224, fax 859-2650. Unrestricted camping within the park is usually permitted only at Lineham Lakes, reached by a 4.2-kilometre trail off the north side of the Akamina Parkway 9.5km from Waterton. Note that at park sites you can pay an optional $3 to use the firewood provided.

Belly River Campground, 29km from the townsite, 1km off Chief Mountain Parkway on Hwy 6 (☎859-2224). Smallest (24 sites) and simplest of the park-operated campgrounds. Self-registration; tap water; kitchen shelters; fireplaces, chemical and pit toilets. Mid-May to Sept. $10.

Crandell Mountain Campground, 8km west of Waterton on the Red Rock Canyon Parkway off Hwy 5 (☎859-2224). Semi-serviced park-run campground with 129 sites. Tap water; fireplaces; no showers. Mid-May to late Sept. $13.

Crooked Creek, 5.6km east of Waterton Park Gateway on Hwy 5 (☎653-1100). Has 46 sites, seven of which have full service for RVs. Mid-May to early Sept. $11.

Homestead Campground, 3km north of Waterton Park Gateway on Hwy 6 (☎859-2247). Large private 276-site campground with services, showers, store, video games, laundry, heated outdoor pool, dance floor and many other distractions. May to mid-Sept. $16.

HIKING IN WATERTON LAKES PARK

Waterton Lakes Park's 255km of trails have a reputation as not only the best constructed in the Canadian Rockies (with Yoho's Lake O'Hara), but also among the most easily graded, well marked and scenically routed. Like Moraine Lake in Banff National Park – and unlike Banff and Jasper – you can also access superb walks easily without a car. Bar one or two outlying hikes, three key areas contain trails and trailheads: the **townsite** itself, which has two magnificent short walks; the **Akamina Parkway**; and the **Red Rock Canyon Parkway**. Most walks are day-hikes, climaxing at small alpine lakes cradled in spectacular hanging valleys. Options for backpacking are necessarily limited by the park's size, though the 36-kilometre **Tamarack Trail**, following the crenellations of the Continental Divide between the Akamina Parkway (trailhead as for Rowe Lakes – see opposite) and Red Rock Canyon, is rated as one of the Rockies' greatest high-line treks (maximum elevation 2560m); the twenty-kilometre Carthew–Alderson Trail from Cameron Lake to Waterton (maximum elevation 2311m), a popular day's outing, can be turned into a two-day trip by overnighting at the Alderson Lake campground. To do it in a day, take advantage of the hiker shuttle service to the trailhead offered by Park Transport (☎859-2378) based in the Tamarack Mall on Mount View Road.

In summary, this is a great park in which to base yourself for a few days' hiking: details of hikes are given below, but as a general guide to do the cream of the hikes you'd first stroll the **Bear's Hump** for views of Waterton town and the lakes; then walk all or part of the **Bertha Lake Trail** (day or half-day) from the townsite. Next day take a boat to Goat Haunt and walk back on the **Waterton Lakeshore Trail**. Then try the **Crypt Lake Trail** from the townsite and/or the **Rowe Lake–Lineham Ridge Trail**, both ranked among the best day-walks in the Rockies. Finally gird your loins for the longer **Carthew–Alderson Trail**, possible in a day.

WALKS FROM THE TOWNSITE

In and around the town, there are various short loops: stroll to Cameron Falls, try the Prince of Wales from the Visitor Centre (2km; 45min) or climb the more demanding **Bear's Hump**, also from the centre (1.2km; 200m vertical; 40min one-way); the latter is one of the park's most popular short walks, switchbacking up the slopes to a rocky outcrop with great views of the Waterton Valley. More surprisingly good views can be had from the easily reached viewpoint near the Bison Paddock. Another obvious, and very simple, walk from the town is the Waterton Lakeshore Trail (13km one-way; 100m ascent; 4hr), which follows Upper Waterton Lake's west shore across the US border to Goat Haunt; regular lake ferries sail back to the townsite, completing a lovely round trip (ferry details from the marina or call ☎859-2362; see p.475). Alternatively, catch an early boat and walk back so as not to worry about making a boat connection.

The single most popular half-day or day's walk from the townsite, however, is the classic **Bertha Lake Trail** from Waterton, 5.8km each way with an ascent of 460m (allow 3–4hr for the round trip). It's a short, steep hike beginning on Evergreen Drive to a busy but remarkably unsullied mountain-ringed lake and there's an easy trail that runs right round the lakeshore (adding about another 5km to the trip). If you're not up to this, you can just do the first part of the trail and break off at Lower Bertha Falls (2.9km from the townsite; 150m ascent; 1hr): this deservedly popular section corresponds to the route of the *Bertha Falls Self-Guiding Nature Trail* pamphlet available from the Visitor Centre.

Riverside Campground, 5km east of Waterton Park Gateway (☎653-2888). Private; seventy sites with showers, services, breakfasts and live entertainment and barbecue suppers every Saturday. Mid-May to mid-Sept. $12.

Waterton Townsite Campground, off Vimy Ave (☎859-2224). 238-site serviced park-run campground in town. First-come, first-served basis, and fills up by mid-afternoon in summer. Showers; no open fires; wheelchair-accessible. Open May to Thanksgiving (second Mon in Oct) but self-registration after Labor Day (in early Sept). $16.

Another excellent, if challenging walk out of Waterton is the unique **Crypt Lake Trail**, often touted as one of the best in the Northwest. The 8.7-kilometre hike (one-way; 675m ascent) involves a boat trip ($9 round trip) across Upper Waterton Lake to the trailhead on the east side of the lake, a (perfectly safe) climb up a ladder, a crawl through a rock tunnel and a section along a rocky ledge with cable for support. The rewards are the crashing waterfalls and the great glacial amphitheatre containing Crypt Lake (1955m); rock walls tower 600m on three sides, casting a chill shadow that preserves small icebergs on the lake's surface throughout the summer. Allow time to catch the last boat back to Waterton (again, ferry details are on ☎859-2362), and note that it's a good idea to make reservations in summer. Campers should be aware that the site here is one of the most heavily used in the park's backcountry.

TRAILS FROM THE AKAMINA PARKWAY

Most of the trails accessed by the Akamina Parkway leave from the road's end near Cameron Lake. To stretch your legs after the drive up, or if you just want a stroll, try either the Akamina Lake (0.5km; 15min) or Cameron Lakeshore (1.6km; 30min) trails. The best of the longer walks is to Carthew Summit (7.9km one-way; 660m ascent), a superb trail that switchbacks through forest to Summit Lake (4km), a good target in itself, before opening out into subalpine meadow and a final climb to a craggy summit (2310m) and astounding viewpoint. The trail can be continued all the way back to Waterton Townsite (another 12km) – it's then the **Carthew–Alderson Trail** (see opposite), most of whose hard work you've done in getting up to Carthew Summit; from the summit it's largely steeply downhill via Carthew and Alderson lakes (1875m) to Cameron Falls and the townsite (1295m).

Another highly rated trail from the Akamina Parkway is equally appealing – the Rowe Lakes Trail (5.2km one-way; 555m ascent), which is accessed off the Parkway about 5km before Cameron Lake (it is also the first leg of the Tamarack Trail – see opposite). Most people make their way to the Rowe Basin (where there's a backcountry campground) and then, rather than pushing on towards the Upper Rowe Lakes (1.2km beyond), either camp, turn around or – for stronger walkers – take the trail that branches right from the Upper Rowe path to walk to Lineham Ridge (another 3.4km and 540m ascent). This **Rowe Lake–Lineham Ridge** combination has been cited as some as one of the top five day-hikes in the Rockies. The stiffish walk is rewarded by Lineham Lake, sapphire blue in the valley far below, and a vast sea of mountains stretching to the horizon. Only come up here in good weather, as it's particularly hazardous when visibility's poor and the winds are up.

TRAILS FROM THE RED ROCK CANYON PARKWAY

Most trails on the Red Rock Canyon Parkway, such as the short Red Rock Canyon Trail (700m loop) and Blackiston Falls (1km; 30min), leave from Red Rock Canyon at the end of the road. The most exhilarating option from the head of the road, however, is the Goat Lake Trail (6.7km; 550m ascent), which follows Bauerman Creek on an old fire road (flat and easy, but a little dull) before peeling off right at the 4.3-kilometre mark for the climb to tranquil Goat Lake and ever-improving views (there's a backcountry campground at the lake). If you ignore the lake turn-off and follow the fire road for another 4km, you come to a junction: one trail leads north to Lost Lake (2km), the other south to the spectacular Twin Lakes area (3.2km). This latter option will bring you to the long-distance Tamarack Trail (see opposite). Walk south on this from Twin Lakes (3.1km) and you can pick up the Blackiston Creek Trail, which will take you back to the head of the Red Rock Canyon Parkway.

Eating

Lakeside Kootenai Brown Dining Room, Waterton Ave at the *Bayshore Inn* (☎859-2211). One of the better and more elegant spots in town to treat yourself; the dining room overlooks the lake. Open all day for breakfast, lunch and dinner.

Lamp Post Dining Room, 117 Evergreen Ave at the *Kilmorey Lodge* (☎859-2334). Old-world appeal and tempting good food without the stuffiness of *Windsor Lounge*; the moderate prices are lower too (7.30am–10pm). The hotel's *Gazebo* café on the waterfront is also good for snacks (10am–10pm).

New Frank's Restaurant, 106 Waterton Ave (☎859-2240). This restaurant serves cheap, odd combinations of breakfasts, burgers, a Chinese buffet plus lunch and six-course buffet specials.

Pearl's, 305 Windflower Ave (☎859-2284). Fresh baking; great first choice for cheap breakfast, lunch, coffee, deli meats, picnic provisions and hikers' takeaway lunches. Indoor and outdoor tables.

Pizza of Waterton, 103 Fountain Ave (☎859-2660). Dough made daily on the premises; good, cheap pizzas to eat in or take away. Open daily 4.30–10pm.

Windsor Lounge, *Prince of Wales Hotel* (☎859-2231). One of several lounges, bars and dining rooms in this posh hotel open for non-patrons to enjoy afternoon tea, a good breakfast or a refined hour with a drink and great lake views. Dress well, as the place is fairly smart. The *Garden Court* is the most elegant restaurant in the hotel (reservations required).

Crowsnest Pass

The 1382-metre **Crowsnest Pass** is the most southerly of the three major routes into the Rockies and British Columbia from Alberta, and far less attractive than the Calgary approach. In its early stages as Hwy 3 pushes west out of Fort Macleod across glorious windblown prairie, it augurs well: the settlements are bleaker and more backwoods in appearance, and the vast unbroken views to the mountain-filled horizon appear much as they must have to the first pioneers. As the road climbs towards the pass, however, the grime and dereliction of the area's mining heritage make themselves increasingly felt. Hopes a century ago that Crowsnest's vast coal deposits might make it the "Pittsburgh of Canada" were dashed by disasters, poor-quality coal, complicated seams, cheaper coal from British Columbia and rapid obsolescence. Today much of the area has been declared an Historic District and turned into Alberta's only "ecomuseum", a desperate attempt to bring life and tourist cash back to economically blighted communities (many people commute to work in British Columbia's mines over the Pass or have left altogether). To some extent they've succeeded, though you have to pick your mining-related stopoffs carefully round here. If mines and disaster sites don't appeal, the Crowsnest route west is of most use as a direct route if you're hurrying to Vancouver or aim to explore the Kootenays in southern British Columbia. After breasting the pass, Hwy 3 drops into BC and follows the often spectacular Elk River Valley to join Hwy 95 at Cranbrook (see p.440).

Bellevue and the Frank Slide

Sleepy **BELLEVUE** is the first village worthy of the name after Fort Macleod; an oddball and close-knit spot with an old-world feel unusual in these parts. It's distinguished by a church the size of a dog kennel and a wooden tepee painted lemon yellow, as well as the claim to have "the best drinking water in Alberta". Nonetheless, it supports a small summer-only **infocentre** by the campground (see opposite) and provides visitors with the opportunity to explore – complete with hard hat and miner's lamp – a wonderfully dark and dank 100m or so of the old **Bellevue Mine** (30min tours every half-hour mid-May to early Sept daily 10am–5.30pm; $6; ☎562-7388). The only mine open to the public locally, it ceased production in 1962, but remains infamous for an explosion in 1910 that destroyed the ventilator fan. Thirty men died in the disaster, though not from the blast, but by breathing so-called "afterdamp", a lethal mixture of carbon dioxide and carbon monoxide left after fire has burnt oxygen from the atmosphere. As if this wasn't enough, Canada's worst mining disaster ever had occurred five years earlier at **HILLCREST**, a village immediately to the south of Bellevue (signed from Hwy 3), when 189 men were killed by an explosion and the effects of "afterdamp". All were buried together a few centimetres apart in mass graves, now the **Hillcrest Cemetery** on 8th Avenue.

Bellevue has a quaint **campground**, the *Bellecrest Community Association Campground* (☎564-4696; donation), located just off the highway just east of the village: it's open May to October and has 22 "random" sites, toilets, tap water and an on-site ten-seat church with recorded sermons. The site is also handy for the **Leitch Collieries Provincial Historic Site**, just off the main road to the north before the campground. This was once the region's largest mining and coking concern; it was also the first to close (in 1915). Today there's little to see in the way of old buildings, but displays and boardwalk interpretive trails past "listening posts" fill you in on mining techniques. The overgrown site is also enthusiastically described by interpretive staff (mid-May to mid-Sept daily 10am–4pm; winter site unstaffed; $2; ☎562-7388).

The Crowsnest Pass trail of destruction, death and disaster continues beyond Bellevue. Dominating the skyline behind the village are the crags and vast rock fall of the **Frank Slide**, an enormous landslide that has altered the contours of Turtle Mountain, once riddled with the galleries of local mines. On April 29, 1903 an esti-mated 100 million tonnes of rock on a front stretching for over 1km and 700m high trundled down the mountain, burying 68 people and their houses in less than two minutes. Amazingly none of the miners working locally were killed – they dug them-selves out after fourteen hours of toil. The morbidly interesting **Frank Slide Interpretive Centre**, situated 1.5km off the highway about 1km north of the village, highlights European settlement in the area, the coming of the Canadian Pacific Railway to Alberta and the technology, attitudes and lives of local miners (daily: June to early Sept 9am–8pm; early Sept to May 10am–5pm; $4; ☎562-7388). It's well worth wandering around the site and slide area – there's a 1.5-kilometre trail or you can walk up the ridge above the car park for good views and an idea of the vast scale of the earth movement: no one to this day quite understands the science of how boul-ders travelled so far from the main slide (several kilometres in many cases). "Air lubrication" is the best theory, a device by which the cascading rock compressed the air in front of it, creating a hovercraft-like cushion of trapped air on which it "rode" across the surface.

Blairmore, Coleman and the Pass

BLAIRMORE, 2km beyond the slide, is a scrappy settlement redeemed for the casual visitor only by the walks and four winter and night ski runs on the hill above it (Pass Powder Keg Ski Hill: ☎562-8334 for information). Largest of the Crowsnest towns (pop-ulation around 1800), it has a handful of "historic" buildings, notably the *Cosmopolitan Hotel* – built in 1912 – at 13001-20th Ave (☎562-7321; ②), but neither town or hotel are places to linger. **COLEMAN** is the place to spend the night if you absolutely have to, especially if you've always wanted to be able to say you've seen "the biggest piggy bank in the world", made from an old steam engine once used to pull coal cars in local mines. The town, battered and bruised by mine closures, amounts to little – the small Crowsnest Museum has interesting mining exhibits in the old schoolhouse at 7701-18th Ave (mid-May to Oct daily 9am–6pm; Nov to mid-May Mon–Fri 10am–noon & 1–4pm; $2; ☎563-5434), a single road, a dilapidated strip of houses, three garages and a battered **motel**, the 24-unit *Stop Inn* (☎562-7381; ②). More appealing is the dubiously named ten-unit *Kozy Knest Kabins Triple K Motel* (☎563-5155; ②), open from May to October and more scenically situated 12km west of Coleman on Hwy 3 beside Crowsnest Lake.

Beyond Coleman the road climbs towards **Crowsnest Pass** itself (1382m) and, after a rash of sawmills, the natural scenery finally takes centre stage in a reassuring mix of lakes, mountains and trees protected by **Crowsnest Provincial Park**. A rustic provin-cial **campground** overlooks the lake at Crowsnest Creek, about 15km west of Coleman ($5).

THE CANADIAN ROCKIES

Few North American landscapes come as loaded with expectation as the **Canadian Rockies**, so it's a relief to find that the superlatives are scarcely able to do credit to the region's immensity of forests, lakes, rivers and snowcapped mountains. Although most visitors confine themselves to visiting just a handful of **national parks**, the range spans almost 1500km as far as the Yukon border, forming the vast watershed of the Continental Divide, which separates rivers flowing to the Pacific, Arctic and Atlantic oceans. Landscapes on such a scale make a nonsense of artificial borderlines, and the major parks are national creations that span both Alberta and British Columbia. Four of the parks – Banff, Jasper, Yoho and Kootenay – share common boundaries, and receive the attention of most of the millions of annual visitors to the Rockies.

There's not a great deal to choose between the parks in terms of scenery – they're all fairly sensational – and planning an itinerary that allows you to fit them all in comfortably is just about impossible. Most visitors start with **Banff National Park**, then follow the otherworldly **Icefields Parkway** north to the larger and much less busy **Jasper National Park**. From there it makes sense to continue west to **Mount Robson Provincial Park**, which protects the highest and most dramatic peak in the Canadian Rockies. Thereafter you're committed to leaving the Rockies unless you double back from Jasper to Banff – no hardship, given the scenery – to pick up the Trans-Canada Highway through the smaller **Yoho**, **Glacier** and **Revelstoke** national parks. Finally, **Kootenay National Park** is more easily explored than its neighbours, though you'll have to backtrack towards Banff or loop down from Yoho to pick up the road that provides its only access. The more peripheral, but no less impressive Waterton Lakes National Park, hugging the US border, is covered on pp.470–480.

Though you can get to all the parks by **bus**, travelling by **car** or **bike** is the obvious way to get the most out of the region. Once there, you'd be foolish not to tackle some of the 3000km of trails that crisscross the mountains, the vast majority of which are well worn and well signed. We've highlighted the best short walks and day-hikes in each area, and you can get more details from the excellent **park visitor centres**, which sell 1:50,000 topographical maps and usually offer small reference libraries of trail books; *The Canadian Rockies Trail Guide*, by Brian Patton and Bart Robinson, is invaluable for serious hiking or backpacking. Other activities – fishing, skiing, canoeing, white-water rafting, cycling, horse riding, climbing and so on – are comprehensively dealt with in visitor centres, and you can easily **rent equipment** or sign up for organized tours in the bigger towns.

A word of warning: don't underestimate the Rockies. Despite the impression created by the summer throngs in centres like Banff and Lake Louise, excellent roads and sleek park facilities, the vast proportion of parkland is wilderness and should be respected and treated as such. See Basics, pp.58–63, for more.

Where to go in winter

Six major winter resorts are found in the Rockies – two in Kananaskis Country, two around Banff, and one each near Lake Louise and Jasper. Along with Whistler in British Columbia, these are some of the best, the most popular and the fastest-growing areas in the Northwest – and not only for downhill and cross-country skiing but also for dog-sledding, ice climbing, skating, snowshoeing, canyon crawling and ice fishing (snowmobiling, note, is not allowed in the parks). At most resorts, the season runs from mid-December until the end of May; conditions are usually at their best in March, when the days are getting warmer and longer, and the snow is deepest. Resort accommodation is hardest to come by during Christmas week, the mid-February school holidays and at Easter.

Nakiska, 25km south of the Trans-Canada Highway in Kananaskis Country, is Canada's newest resort. Developed for the 1988 Winter Olympics, it's one of the most user-friendly on the continent, with state-of-the-art facilities; it has snowmaking on all its varied terrain and plenty of fine cross-country skiing. Fortress Mountain, 15km south of Nakiska on Hwy 40, is a much smaller area, where you're likely to share the slopes with school groups and families.

Banff's resorts are invariably the busiest and most expensive, and heavily patronized by foreigners (especially Japanese). Mount Norquay (see p.504) has long been known as an advanced downhill area – "steep and deep" in local parlance – but has recently expanded its intermediate runs, and also boasts the Canadian Rockies' only night skiing. Higher and more exposed, Sunshine Village (see p.504) has even better scenery but relatively few advanced runs.

Lake Louise's three big hills (see p.514) add up to one of the Northwest's most extensive resorts with downhill skiing, plus cross-country trails crisscrossing the valley and the lake area. Jasper's Marmot Basin is a more modest downhill area, but it's quieter and cheaper than those further south, and the park, particularly around Maligne Lake, has almost limitless cross-country skiing possibilities.

Kananaskis Country

Most first-time visitors race straight up to Banff, ignoring the verdant foothill region southwest of Calgary. **Kananaskis Country**, a protected area created out of existing provincial parks to take pressure off Banff, remains almost the exclusive preserve of locals, most of whom come for skiing. Kananaskis embraces a huge tract of the Rockies and has all the mountain scenery and outdoor pursuit possibilities of the parks, without the people or the commercialism. It is, however, an area without real focus, much of it remote wilderness; nothing in the way of public transport moves out here, and the only fixed accommodation is in expensive, modern lodges – though it's idyllic camping country.

Minor roads from Calgary lead to such smaller foothill areas of the east as Bragg Creek, but the most obvious approach is to take Hwy 40, a major turn off the Trans-Canada Highway, which bisects Kananaskis's high mountain country from north to south and provides the ribbon to which most of the trails, campgrounds and scattered service centres cling. About 3km down the highway is the Barrier Lake Information Centre (daily 9am–5pm), where you can get a full breakdown on outdoor activities. Another 40km south of the centre is a short spur off Hwy 40 to Upper Kananaskis Lake, probably the biggest concentration of accessible boating, fishing, camping and hiking possibilities in the region. Popular short hikes include the Expedition Trail (2.4km); it and many others are detailed in the definitive *Kananaskis Country Trail Guide* by Gillean Daffern, which is widely available in Calgary.

Banff National Park

BANFF NATIONAL PARK is the most famous of the Canadian Rockies' parks and Canada's leading tourist attraction – so be prepared for the crowds that throng its key

The telephone code for Banff and Banff National Park is ☎403.

centres, **Banff** and **Lake Louise**, as well as the best part of its 1500km of trails, most of which suffer a continual pounding during the summer months. That said, it's worth putting up with every commercial indignity to enjoy the sublime scenery – and if you're camping or are prepared to walk, the worst of the park's excesses are fairly easily left behind. The best plan of attack if you're coming from Calgary or the US is to make straight for Banff, a busy and commercial town where you can pause for a couple of days to soak up the action and handful of sights, or stock up on supplies and make for somewhere quieter as quickly as possible. Then head for nearby Lake Louise, a much smaller but almost equally busy centre with some unmissable landscapes plus good and readily accessible short trails and day-hikes if you just want a quick taste of the scenery. Two popular highways within the park offer magnificent vistas – the **Bow Valley Parkway** from Banff to Lake Louise – a far preferable route to the parallel **Hwy 1** (Trans-Canada) road – and the much longer **Icefields Parkway** from Lake Louise to Jasper. Both are lined with trails long and short, waterfalls, lakes, canyons, viewpoints, pull-offs and a seemingly unending procession of majestic mountain, river, glacier and forest scenery.

Some history

The modern road routes in the park provide transport links that have superseded the railway that first brought the park into being. The arrival of the **Canadian Pacific** at the end of the nineteenth century brought an end to some 10,000 years of exclusive aboriginal presence in the region, an epoch which previously had been disturbed only by trappers and the prodigious exploits of explorers like Mackenzie, Thompson and Fraser, who had sought to breach the Rockies with the help of native guides earlier in the century. Banff itself sprang to life in 1883 after three railway workers stumbled on the present town's Cave and Basin hot springs, its name coined in honour of Banffshire, Scottish birthplace of two of the Canadian Pacific's early financiers and directors. Within two years the government had set aside the Hot Springs Reserve as a protected area, and in 1887 enlarged it to form the **Rocky Mountains Park**, Canada's first national park. However, the purpose was not entirely philanthropic, for the new government-sponsored railway was in desperate need of passengers and profit, and spectacular scenery backed up by luxurious hotels was seen – rightly – as the best way to lure the punters. Cars were actually banned from the park until 1916.

Today the park is not quite at crisis point, but some hard decisions are having to be made. Around four million visitors come to Banff every year and another four million pass through. Together they pump a staggering $750 million or more a year into the local economy. Such figures, despite the best efforts and intentions of the park authorities, inevitably have an effect on the environment. Scientists believe, for example, that the black and grizzly bear populations are dying out (combined numbers of both types of bear here are probably just 100 to 130), while numbers of wolves are declining at only a slightly lower rate than in areas where they have no protection at all (the park has just 35 or 40). Conversely, elk numbers have exploded beyond internally sustainable limits (to about 3200), almost entirely because they've realized the town offers food (tasty surburban grass) and total safety from their natural predators. In the past, there have been some 60 (usually provoked) elk attacks on humans in Banff every year. The sight of elk nibbling on verges in downtown Banff will soon be a thing of the past, however, for around 120 elk have been removed from Banff and its vicinity and relocated elsewhere, and there are plans to remove the remainder. These are just a handful of symptoms of a greater ecological malaise. In response, a ceiling of 10,000 has been put on Banff's human population (it's currently around 7600), building is strictly controlled, areas are being closed to

THE CREATION OF THE CANADIAN ROCKIES

About 600 million years ago the vast granite mountains of the Canadian Shield covered North America from Greenland to Guatemala (today the Shield's eroded remnants are restricted largely to northeast Canada). For the next 400 million years, eroded debris from the Shield – mud, sand and gravel – was washed westward by streams and rivers and deposited on the offshore "continental slope" (westward because the Shield had a very slight tilt). Heavier elements such as gravel accumulated close to the shore, lighter deposits like sand and mud were swept out to sea or left in lagoons. The enormous weight and pressure of the sediment, which built up to a depth of 20km, converted mud to shale, sand to sandstone and the natural debris of the reefs and sea bed – rich in lime-producing algae – into limestone. Two further stages were necessary before these deposits – now the strata so familar in the profile of the Rockies – could be lifted from the sea bed and left several thousand metres above sea level to produce the mountains we see today.

The mountain-building stage of the Rockies took just 100 million years, with the collision of the North American and Pacific continental plates (gigantic 50-kilometre-thick floating platforms of the earth's crust). About 200 million years ago, two separate strings of volcanic Pacific islands, each half the size of British Columbia, began to move eastward on the Pacific Plate towards the North American coast. When the first string arrived off the coast, the heavier Pacific Plate slid beneath the edge of the North American Plate and into the earth's molten interior. The lighter, more buoyant rock of the islands stayed "afloat", detaching itself from the plate before crashing into the continent with spectacular effect. The thick orderly deposits on the continental slope were crumpled and uplifted, their layers breaking up and riding over each other to produce the coast's present-day interior and Columbia Mountains. Over the next 75 million years the aftershock of the collision moved inland, bulldozing the ancient sedimentary layers still further to create the Rockies' Western Main Ranges (roughly the mountain edge of Yoho and Kootenay national parks), and then moving further east, where some 4km of uplift created the Eastern Main Ranges (the mountains roughly on a line with Lake Louise). Finally the detached islands "bonded" and mingled with the new mainland mountains (their "exotic" rocks can be found in geological tangles as far east as Salmon Arm in BC).

Behind the first string of islands the second archipelago had also now crashed into the continent, striking the debris of the earlier collision. The result was geological chaos, with more folding, rupturing and uplifting of the earlier ranges. About 60 million years ago, the aftershock from this encounter created the Rockies' easternmost Front Ranges (the distinct line of mountains that rears up so dramatically from the prairies), together with the foothills that spill around Kananaskis and Waterton lakes. The third stage of the Rockies' formation, erosion and glaciation, was relatively short-lived, at least three ice ages over the last 240,000 years turning the mountains into a region resembling present-day Antarctica. While only mountain summits peeked out from ice many kilometres thick, however, glaciers and the like were applying the final touches, carving sharp profiles and dumping further debris.

the public (even the famous Bow Valley Parkway is closed to traffic for parts of the year). The airport, too, is now all but closed, for it – like much of Banff town and the Bow River Valley – lies right in the path of major wildlife routeways. Many of the big mammals require large areas to survive, larger even than the park's 6641 square kilometres. Experts suggest that Banff's ecosystem is on a knife edge: it may be saved and previous damage restored only if action is taken. Some already has – Banff's elk, for example, are being moved out to reserves – but there's much more work to be done.

PARK ENTRY FEES

For more than eighty years motorists and motorcyclists had to buy permits to enter Canada's mountain national parks. Since 1996 a different system has been in operation. Now fees and permits are based on a per-person per-day principle, and **everyone entering any of the Rockies national parks, regardless of mode of entry, must buy a permit**. The revised system is based on the premise that people – not vehicles – use parks, in much the same way as they enter art galleries or museums. Fees are ploughed directly back into the parks, unlike in the past where they were returned to a central revenue pool. The **cost** of a **Day Pass** valid for all four of the Rocky national parks (Banff, Jasper, Yoho and Kootenay) is $5 per day per person. Or you may buy a **Great Western Annual Pass** for $35, valid for unlimited entry to all eleven national parks in western Canada for a year. "Group" day-passes are available for anything between two and ten people at a flat rate: $10 daily, $70 annual. Thus four people in a car, for example, are charged just $10. If you come in by bus you'll not be charged at point of entry – it's up to you to be honest and buy a pass.

Passes can be bought in advance with credit cards by phoning 1-800/748-PARK or email *natlparks-ab@pch.gc.ca*. Passes are also sold at some Husky gas stations or at the Mountain Equipment Co-op shops in Calgary and Vancouver. Permits can be bought at the road entrances to all parks (compulsory for people in cars or on bikes), park information centres, some park campgrounds and (in summer) at automated pass machines within parks. If you buy a couple of day-passes and decide you want to stay on, then you can redeem their cost against a year's pass at park centres on presentation of receipts. Great Western Annual passes are valid for a year from the date of purchase. There's no fee to enter provincial parks.

A separate **backcountry Wilderness Pass** ($6 per person per night to a maximum of $30 per person per trip, vaild in all four national parks – Banff, Jasper, Yoho and Kootenay), available from any park visitor centre or infocentre, is required for all overnight backcountry use. Note that all backcountry areas in all parks have a quota and that it's vital to make bookings well in advance (up to three months) if you wish to walk – and camp on – some of the most popular trails requiring overnight stops. The most popular trails are indicated in the various hiking features throughout the text. Reservations can made by phone or in person at some of the more backcountry campgrounds, but *not* for the major park-run campgrounds. There is a $10 non-refundable booking fee.

Banff

BANFF is the unquestioned capital of the Canadian Rockies, and with its intense summer buzz it can be a fun, bustling and likeable base – but if you've come to commune with nature, you'll want to leave as soon as possible. Although the town is quite small, it handles an immense amount of tourist traffic, much of it of the RV and mega-coach-tour variety. Anything up to 50,000 visitors daily flock here in high season, making this the largest and busiest urban focus of any national park anywhere in the world. Backpackers are abundant in summer, and the Japanese presence is also marked, with a huge number of Japanese signs and menus in shops and restaurants. The Japanese also own around a third of the town's accommodation, including two of the three largest hotels, and their investment here is an ongoing bone of contention among some townspeople who would prefer local investment. What's rather odd, given all the people, however, is that there's next to nothing to do or see, save a couple of small museums, a cable-car ride and the chance to gawp at the crowds on **Banff Avenue**, the town's long main street, a thoroughfare lined with probably more souvenir stores and upmarket outdoor clothing and equipment shops than anywhere in North America. Whether or not your main aim is to avoid the crowds, however, some contact with the town is inevitable, as it contains essential shops and services almost impossible to come by

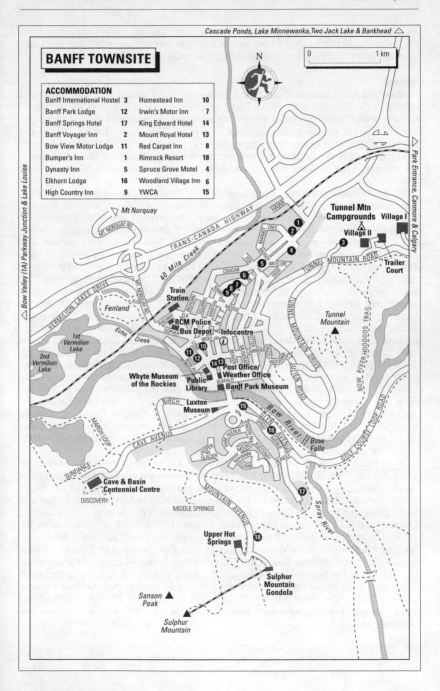

Cascade Ponds, Lake Minnewanka, Two Jack Lake & Bankhead

BANFF TOWNSITE

0   1 km

N

ACCOMMODATION

Banff International Hostel	3	Homestead Inn	10
Banff Park Lodge	12	Irwin's Motor Inn	7
Banff Springs Hotel	17	King Edward Hotel	14
Banff Voyager Inn	2	Mount Royal Hotel	13
Bow View Motor Lodge	11	Red Carpet Inn	8
Bumper's Inn	1	Rimrock Resort	18
Dynasty Inn	5	Spruce Grove Motel	4
Elkhorn Lodge	16	Woodland Village Inn	6
High Country Inn	9	YWCA	15

Bow Valley (1A) Parkway Junction & Lake Louise

Park Entrance, Canmore & Calgary

Mt Norquay

Tunnel Mtn Campgrounds

Village I
Village II

TRANS-CANADA HIGHWAY

MT NORQUAY RD

40 Mile Creek

HAWK
MARMOT
CRES
BADGER
ANTELOPE
COUGAR
DEER
BEAVER

TUNNEL MOUNTAIN ROAD

Trailer Court

Train Station

VERMILION LAKES DRIVE

Fenland

1st Vermilion Lake

2nd Vermilion Lake

Echo Creek

RCM Police
Bus Depot
Infocentre

Tunnel Mountain

TUNNEL MOUNTAIN DRIVE

BOW RIVER HOODOOS TRAIL

JULIEN ROAD

Whyte Museum of the Rockies
Public Library

Post Office/ Weather Office
Banff Park Museum

Luxton Museum

Bow River

Bow Falls

GOLF COURSE LOOP ROAD

BIRCH
BUFFALO

CAVE AVENUE

MARSH LOOP

SUNDANCE

Cave & Basin Centennial Centre

DISCOVERY

MIDDLE SPRINGS

MOUNTAIN AVENUE

GLEN AVENUE

JASPER
GLACIER
PARK AVENUE
NAHANNI
KLUANE
KOOTENAY
RUNDLE

Spray River

Upper Hot Springs

Sulphur Mountain Gondola

Sanson Peak

Sulphur Mountain

elsewhere in the park. Many of the more rewarding walks locally are some way from the town – you'll need a car or have to hire a bike to explore properly – but some surprisingly good strolls start just minutes from the main street.

Arrival

Banff is just ninety-minutes' **drive** and 128km west of Calgary on a fast, four-laned stretch of the Trans-Canada. Speed limits outside the park are 110kph, inside 90kph, but watch your speed, as countless animals are killed on the road every year (one reason for the big roadside fences). Lake Louise is 58km away, Jasper 288km and Edmonton 424km. The approach from the west is more winding, the total journey time from Vancouver (952km) being about twelve hours. From the States the quickest access is from Spokane (600km away via Hwy 95) or Kalispell in Montana (Hwy 93).

Six daily Greyhound **buses** from Calgary (1hr 40min; $20 one-way), and five from Vancouver (via either Kamloops or Cranbrook, all via Lake Louise), arrive at the joint Greyhound–Brewster Transportation **bus terminal** at 100 Gopher St (7.30am–10.45pm, otherwise opens 5min before the departure of night buses; ☎762-6767). Increasingly, popular services are provided between Calgary airport and Banff–Lake Louise direct (and vice versa) by Laidlaw (1 daily year-round, 2 daily Dec–April; $30 to Banff, $38 to Lake Louise, $8 Banff to Lake Louise; ☎762-9102 or 1-800/661-4946; Calgary Ski Bus to Lake Louise ☎256-8473, *www.laidlawbanff.com*); the Banff Airporter (8 daily; $36 to Banff; ☎762-3330 or 1-888/449-2901, *www.banffairporter.com*); Brewster Transportation (3 daily to Banff and Lake Louise, 1 daily to Jasper in summer; $36 to Banff, $41 to Lake Louise, $71 to Jasper; ☎762-6767 in Banff, ☎221-8242 in Calgary, ☎780/852-3332 in Jasper). The most useful operator currently – because they have hourly departures between the airport and Banff or Lake Louise (and vice versa) – is Sky Shuttle ($34 to Banff; reservations daily 8am–11pm on ☎762-1010 or 1-888/220-7433, *www.banffskyshuttle.com*). Given the surfeit of operators, some of the services may well go out of business, so check at the airport – the various companies' ticket desks are lined up to the right as you face the main exit door in Arrivals. Note that Brewster run the only service between Calgary, Banff, Lake Louise and Jasper (daily May–Oct 1 or later depending on snow, $51 Banff to Jasper): it's heavily used. There's no VIA Rail passenger service – a private company runs luxury **trains** once a week between Calgary and Vancouver via Banff, but tickets for the two-night trip cost several hundred dollars.

Banff is small enough **to get around** on foot, but to reach the hostel and campground (some 3km distant) you might need the small town **shuttle bus** operated by Banff Transit ($1 – exact change required; information ☎760-8294). It runs twice-hourly noon to midnight on two routes between mid-May and September, and on one route (the second of those detailed below) from mid-April to mid-May and October to December: the *Banff Springs Hotel*–Spray Avenue–*YWCA*–Banff Avenue–Trailer RV Parking at the north end of Banff Avenue (leaving the *Banff Springs Hotel* on the hour and half-hour, the RV Parking on the quarter hour) and *Village I* campground–Tunnel Mountain Road–Otter Street–Banff Avenue–Luxton Museum (leaving *Village I* on the hour and half-hour and the Luxton Museum on the quarter hour). **Taxis** start at $2.60 and then charge around $1.35 a kilometre: from the bus terminal to the hostel or the *Banff Springs Hotel* should cost around $7. For details of taxi firms and **car rentals**, for which bookings should be made well in advance, see "Listings" on p.502.

The telephone code for Banff, Lake Louise and the Banff National Park is ☎403.

Information

Banff's showpiece **Banff Information Centre** is an excellent joint park/Banff and Lake Louise Tourism Bureau venture at 224 Banff Ave (daily: mid-May to mid-June 8am–6pm; mid-June to early Sept 8am–8pm; early Sept to end of Sept 8am–6pm; Oct to mid-May 9am–5pm; Parks Canada information ☎762-1550: town and accommodation information ☎762-8421, recorded message ☎762-4256; National Park information, also at *www.parkscanada.pch.gc.ca/banff*.

The centre has information on almost any park-related or town-related subject you care to name, including bear sightings, trails and the weather, and all manner of commercial tours and outdoor activities. It is also the place to pick up a **park permit** if you haven't already done so (see box on p.486). Among their many free handouts, make a point of asking for the *Banff and Vicinity Drives and Walks* and *The Icefields Parkway* for maps of park facilities, the *Backcountry Visitors' Guide* for an invaluable overview of **backpacking trails** and campgrounds, and *Trail Bicycling in the National Parks* for conditions and a full list of **mountain-bike trails**.

To the centre's rear there is a selection of maps and guides you can consult free: excellent **topographical maps** can be bought from the "Friends of Banff National Park" shop (☎762-8918) on the left, but note that many of the shorter and more popular trails are well worn and signed, so you won't really need detailed maps unless you're venturing into the backcountry. This is also the place to pick up details or book a place on the various **events** offered by the "Friends", which in past years have included free guided walks daily in the summer to Vermilion Lakes (10am, 2hr 30min), a Discovery Tour of the Cave and Basin Hot Springs (45min) and a Park Museum Wildlife Tour (45min); places on walks are limited, so preregister at the store in the information centre.

The Tourism Bureau will point you in the right direction when it comes to **accommodation** hunting; it maintains a constantly updated vacancies board (though staff aren't allowed to make specific recommendations) and a free courtesy phone. There are also several fee-based alternatives (see box below).

Accommodation

It's almost impossible to turn up after midday in Banff during July and August and find a relatively reasonably priced bed; preplanning is absolutely vital. Anything that can be booked has usually been snapped up – and Banff has over 3500 beds at its disposal nightly – and many visitors are forced to accept top-price places ($150 plus) or backtrack as far as Canmore or even Calgary to find space. The information centre or the **reservation services** (see box, below) may be able to dig something out at short notice.

The Bed & Breakfast and Private Home accommodation list at the infocentre lists forty-plus places with **private rooms** and **B&Bs**, but don't expect too much – they're usually cheapish by Banff standards (typically around $85–120) but among the first places to go each day. Note, too, that "breakfast" usually means continental – just toast, coffee and cereal. The majority are also non-smoking.

RESERVATION SERVICES

Banff Accommodation (Rooms) ☎762-0260 or 1-877/226-3348,
www.banffaccommodations.com
Banff Central Reservation (Rooms – Skiing) ☎277-SNOW or 1-877/542-2366
Canadian Rocky Reservation Centre (Rooms) ☎609-3665 or 1-877/609-3665
Good Earth Travel (Ski Packages) 678-9358 or 1-888/979-9797
Resorts of the Canadian Rockies (Ski Packages) ☎256-8476 or 1-800/256-7669
Ski Banff-Lake Louise (Ski Packages) ☎762-4561 or 1-800/661-1431

Most of the town's **motels** are on the busy strip-cum-spur from the Trans-Canada into town, and charge uncommonly high rates for basic lodgings – typically around $140 and up for doubles. Bar one or two treats, the list below offers accommodation at around the $100 threshold. Off-season (Oct–May), rates are usually considerably lower. Note that some of the best-value, least-known and most conveniently located double rooms are offered by the excellent *YWCA* (see under "Hostels", opposite).

Campgrounds are not quite as bad (the town offers over 1000 pitches), but even these generally fill up by 2pm or 3pm in summer – especially the excellent government campgrounds, which do not take reservations except for group bookings. In addition to the places listed below, remember that there are lovely and less-developed park-run sites available along both the Bow and Icefields parkways to the north. The *Banff International Youth Hostel* (see opposite) can book you into most of the park's smaller hostels (see box, opposite).

HOTELS AND MOTELS

Banff Park Lodge Resort, 222 Lynx St (☎762-4433 or 1-800/661-9266, *www.banffparklodge.com*). If you want comfort and stylish, upscale accommodation, but not at *Banff Springs* or *Rimrock Resort* prices, this hotel is the best downtown upmarket choice. ⑧.

Banff Springs Hotel, Spray Ave (☎762-2211 or 1-800/441-1414, *www.cphotels.ca*). One of North America's biggest and most famous hotels, but invariably full in summer, despite having 825 rooms and a current starting rate of $444 – packages can work out cheaper: book ahead and ensure you have a room with a mountain view in the old building. ⑧.

Banff Voyager Inn, 555 Banff Ave (☎762-3301 or 1-800/879-1991, fax 762-4131). Standard 88-unit motel with pool and sauna. ⑤.

Bow View Motor Lodge, 228 Bow Ave (☎762-2261 or 1-800/661-1565, *www.bowview.com*). Good views from some of the rooms. Two-room family units available. ⑥.

Bumper's Inn, Banff Ave and Marmot Crescent (☎762-3386 or 1-800/661-3518, fax 762-8842). Not central, but modern, and relatively well priced; with 37 units (some with kitchenettes), you'll have a reasonable chance of finding space. ⑥.

Dynasty Inn, 501 Banff Ave (☎762-8844 or 1-800/667-1464, fax 762-4418). A 99-unit motel with a range of rooms, some with fireplaces. ⑥.

Elkhorn Lodge, 124 Spray Ave (☎762-2299, fax 762-0646). Eight rooms, four with kitchens and fireplaces, at the southern end of the townsite. ⑤.

High Country Inn, 419 Banff Ave (☎762-2236 or 1-800/661-1244, *www.banffhighcountryinn.com*). Large seventy-unit mid-range motel with some luxury suites. ⑥.

Homestead Inn, 217 Lynx St (☎762-4471 or 1-800/661-1021, fax 762-8877). Mid-priced 27-room motel with standard fittings. ⑥.

Irwin's Motor Inn, 429 Banff Ave (☎762-4566 or 1-800/661-1721, *www.irwinsmotorinn.com*). A variety of rooms with some at the lower end of the price category. ⑥.

King Edward Hotel, 137 Banff Ave, corner of Caribou (☎762-2202 or 1-800/344-4232, *www.banffkingedwardhotel.com*). Twenty-one renovated and relatively well-priced rooms in the heart of town, but most look down on the busy Banff Ave. ⑥.

Mount Royal Hotel, 138 Banff Ave (☎762-3331 or 1-800/267-3035, *www.brewster.ca*). Has a perfect position on Banff Ave at the centre of town and 136 newly renovated, air-conditioned rooms. Most rooms have mountain views. ⑦.

Red Carpet Inn, 425 Banff Ave (☎762-4184 or 1-800/563-4609, fax 762-4894). No-frills 52-unit motel. ⑥.

Rimrock Resort, Mountain Ave (☎762-3356 or 1-800/661-1587, *www.rimrockresort.com*). Superlative, magnificently situated modern 351-room out-of-town hotel – probably the finest in the Rockies. It's high above the town, with great views of the mountains from the smart, modern rooms. ⑧.

Spruce Grove Motel, 545 Banff Ave (☎762-2112, fax 760-5043). The least expensive motel in town; it has 36 units, some with family and kitchenette facilities. ③.

Woodland Village Inn, 449 Banff Ave (☎762-5521, fax 762-0385). The 24 rooms include some with lofts for up to eight people. ⑥.

BED AND BREAKFASTS

Banff Squirrel's Nest, 332 Squirrel St (☎762-4432, fax 762-5167). Two pleasant and well-situated rooms with private bathrooms and sitting room for guests' use. ④.

Beaver Street Suites & Cabins, 222 Beaver St (☎762-5077, fax 762-5071). Five central self-catering cabins and apartments for up to four people. No credit cards. ⑤.

Blue Mountain Lodge, 137 Muskrat St (☎762-5134, fax 762-8086). Ten rooms and two cabins with private or shared bathrooms and a shared kitchen in very central c.1900 Banff landmark building. ④.

Cascade Court, 2 Cascade Court (☎762-2956, fax 762-5653). Two smart non-smoking rooms across the river from downtown and minutes from the town centre. No credit cards. ④.

Country Cabin, 419 Beaver St (☎762-2789). Quiet cedar cabin (sleeps 3–4) with cooking facilities. Three blocks from downtown. ⑤.

Eleanor's House, 125 Kootenay Ave (☎760-2457, *www.bbeleanor.com*). One of the better but more expensive ($135) B&Bs in town: location-wise it's not perfect – across the river in a quiet side street. Both rooms (twin and double) are en suite and there's a library for idle browsing on rainy days. Open Feb to mid-Oct. ⑥.

A Good Night's Rest, 437 Marten St (☎762-2984). Three rooms in good location; access to fridge and microwaves and a choice of private or shared bathrooms. ⑤.

L'Auberge des Rocheurs, 402 Squirrel St (☎762-9269 or 1-800/266-4413, fax 762-9269). Three quiet central rooms with private bathrooms, nice views with French ownership and hospitality. ⑤.

Rocky Mountain B&B, 223 Otter St (☎ & fax 762-4811). Ten well-priced B&B rooms with kitchenettes and shared or private baths just three blocks from downtown; laundry service also available. ⑤.

Tan-y-Bryn, 118 Otter St (☎762-3696). Eight simple and extremely reasonable B&B rooms (and one cheap "emergency" room) with private or shared bathrooms and in-room continental breakfast. Quiet residential district three blocks from downtown. No credit cards. ②.

HOSTELS

Banff International Youth Hostel (HI), Tunnel Mountain Rd (☎762-4122, *banff@hostellingintl .ca*). Modern 216-bed place in great setting, but a 3km slog from downtown – take the Banff Transit bus from Banff Avenue. Friendly staff and excellent facilities, which include big kitchen, laundry, lounge area with fireplace and a bike and ski workshop; 24-hour access, no curfew. The infoboard is a good source of advice and ride offers. Good meals available all day in the self-service *Café Alpenglow* (open to the public). Two-, four- or six-bed dorms cost $20 for members, $24 for non-members ($1 dollar less in both cases mid-Oct to April). For family or couple (double) rooms, add $5 per person. Open all day. Reservations a month or more in advance are virtually essential in July and August. ①.

Banff YWCA, 102 Spray Ave (☎762-3560 or 1-800/813-4138, *lodge@ywcabanff.ab.ca*). Much more convenient than the youth hostel. Open to men and women, with plenty of clinically clean rooms, but they're extremely good value and go quickly, so book ahead (at least a week in Aug); 300 dorm bunks ($21 plus refundable $5 key deposit; $20 in winter) available, but bring your own sleeping bag, or rent blankets and pillows ($10 refundable deposit, $5 fee). Also forty private singles and doubles ($55, $83 with private bathroom), rooms with two double beds ($70, $55 with bathroom) and family rooms with three double beds ($95 with private bathroom). Rates drop considerably in winter – doubles are $39 or $45 with private bathroom. The downstairs café has good food and there's a kitchen, laundry and showers ($2.50 for non-residents) open to all. Dorms ①, private doubles ③.

HOSTEL RESERVATIONS

Hostel reservations by phone, fax, email and credit card can be made for the following Banff National Park and area hostels by calling ☎762-4122, fax 762-3441, *www.hostellingintl .ca/alberta* or writing to *Banff International Youth Hostel*, PO Box 1358, Banff, AB T0L 0C0: *Banff International, Castle Mountain, Hilda Creek, Mosquito Creek, Rampart Creek, Ribbon Creek* and *Whiskey Jack*. For reservations at Lake Louise *International*, contact the hostel directly.

CAMPGROUNDS

Bow Valley Parkway. There are three park campgrounds on or just off the Bow Valley Parkway road between Banff and Lake Louise, all within easy reach of Banff if you have transport (less than 30-minutes' drive): Johnston Canyon, Castle Mountain and Protection Mountain. See pp.504–507 for full details.

Tunnel Mountain Village I, 4.3km from town and 1km beyond the hostel on Tunnel Mountain Rd. Huge 622-pitch government-run campground ($17 plus optional $4 for firewood and fire permit), the nearest to downtown, on the Banff Transit bus from Banff Ave. Arrive early – like all front-country park campgrounds, it's first-come, first-served. Electricity and hot showers. The nearby 322-site *Tunnel Mountain Trailer Court* ($24) is only for RVs. Early-May to late Sept.

Tunnel Mountain Village II, 2.4km from town and close to *Village I* site. In the summer, available for group camping and commercial tenting only. However, after *Tunnel I* shuts (in late Sept) this government-run 189-pitch site becomes available for general walk-in winter camping ($21 plus optional $4 fire permit). Electricity and hot showers. The two sites are set amid trees, with lovely views, plenty of space and short trails close at hand. Bighorn sheep, elk and even the odd bear may drop in. Year-round.

Two Jack Lakeside, 12km northeast of town on the Lake Minnewanka Rd. Fully serviced eighty-site park-run campground ($17 plus optional $4 fire permit) with showers. Open mid-May to mid-Sept.

Two Jack Main, 13km northeast of town on Lake Minnewanka Rd. Semi-serviced 381-site park campground ($13 plus optional $4 fire permit); no showers. Open mid-June to mid-Sept.

The museums

With some of the world's most spectacular mountains on your doorstep, sightseeing in Banff might seem an absurd undertaking, yet it's good to have some rainy-day options. The downtown **Banff Park Museum** at 93 Banff Ave on the right before the Bow River bridge bulges with two floors of stuffed animals, many of which are indigenous to the park (daily: June–Sept 10am–6pm; Oct–May Mon–Fri 1–5pm, Sat & Sun 10am–6pm; $2.50 or $7 with the Banff Heritage Passport which also allows admission to the Whyte Museum and the Cave & Basin National Historic Site – see p.496; ☎762-1558). In many ways the museum chronicles the changes of attitudes to wildlife in the park over the years. Many Victorians wanted to see the park's animals without the tiresome business of having to venture into the backcountry: what better way to satisfy the whim than by killing and stuffing the beasts for permanent display? The hunting of game animals was eventually banned in the park in 1890, but not before populations of moose, elk, sheep, goats and grizzlies had been severely depleted. Game wardens only arrived to enforce the injunction in 1913, and even then they didn't protect the "bad" animals – wolves, coyotes, foxes, cougars, lynx, eagles, owls and hawks – which were hunted until the 1930s as part of the park's "predator-control program". Many of the stuffed victims in the museum date from this period. Sixty years ago a hapless polar bear was even displayed in the park behind the museum, one of sixty species of animals kept in the Banff Zoo and Aviary between 1904 and 1937. Until as recently as about twenty-five years ago, hotels were organizing trips to the town's rubbish dumps to view foraging bears.

Oddly enough, the museum – a fine building whatever your views on what's inside it – might have gone the same way as the animals. In the 1950s, changing attitudes saw the exhibits condemned as dated, and plans were mooted for the museum's demolition. In the event, it survived as a fine piece of frontier Edwardiana, distinguished, in partic-ular, by its preponderance of skylights, essential features at a time when Banff was still without electricity. The lovely wood-panelled **reading room** – a snug retreat, full of magazines and books on nature and wildlife – makes a perfect spot to while away a cold afternoon. In summer, by contrast, the beautiful **riverside park** behind the museum is ideal for a snooze or picnic (people also sleep here unofficially at night – you might get away with a sleeping bag, but certainly not a tent).

Nearby, the excellent **Whyte Museum of the Canadian Rockies** (mid-May to mid-Oct daily 10am–6pm; mid-Oct to mid-May Tues–Sun 1–5pm, Thurs till 9pm; $4 or $7 with the Banff Heritage Passport which also allows admission to the Banff Park Museum and the Cave & Basin National Historic Site; ☎762-2291, *www.whyte.org*), next to the library at 111 Bear St, contents itself, among other things, with a look at the Rockies' emergence as a tourist destination through paintings and photographs, and at the early expeditions to explore and conquer the interior peaks. Pictures of bears foraging in Banff rubbish bins and of park rangers grinning over a magnificent lynx they've just shot give some idea of how times have changed. The museum, which opened in 1968, forms part of the Whyte Foundation, created in the 1950s by artists Peter and Catherine Whyte to collate and preserve as great a range of material as possible relating to the Rockies. The gleaming complex is also home to the 2075-volume Alpine Club of Canada library and the 4000-volume Archives of the Canadian Rockies – the largest collection of artistic and historical material relating to the mountains. The museum also hosts temporary exhibitions by local, national and international artists, as well as presenting lectures and walking, nature and gallery tours.

The **Natural History Museum**, upstairs in the Clock Tower Mall at 112 Banff Ave (daily noon–5pm; free; ☎762-4747), is a rather throwaway venture that concentrates on the Rockies' geological history, with a sketchy account of its forests, flowers and minerals.

Across the river, dated displays of native history, birds and animals fill the **Luxton Museum**, an aboriginal peoples-run enterprise attractively housed in a huge wooden stockade, 1 Birch Ave (mid-May to mid-Oct daily 9am–7pm; mid-Oct to mid-May Wed–Sun 1–5pm; $6; ☎762-2388). The museum takes its name from Norman Luxton, a local who ran a trading post here and forged a close relationship with Banff's Stoney native population over the course of sixty years. The exhibits aren't exciting, but the museum shop has some good craft and other items if you're in spending mode.

The Banff Springs Hotel

At around $900 a night for some suites – $1600-plus for the presidential ensemble and its personal glass-sided elevators – plus $20 for any pets, the **Banff Springs Hotel** may be way out of your league, but you can't spend much time in town without coming across at least one mention of the place, and it's hard to miss its landmark Gothic superstructure. Initiated in 1888, it got off to a bad start, when the architect arrived to find the place being built 180 degrees out of kilter: while the kitchens enjoyed magnificent views over the river the guestrooms looked blankly into thick forest. When it finally opened, with 250 rooms and a rotunda to improve the views, it was the world's largest hotel. The thinking behind the project was summed up by William Cornelius Van Horne, the larger-than-life vice-president of the Canadian Pacific Railway, who said of the Rockies, "if we can't export the scenery we'll import the tourists". One of the best ways to make the railway pay, he decided, was to sell people the idea of superb scenery and provide a series of jumbo hotels from which to enjoy it: the *Banff Springs* was the result, soon followed by similar railway-backed accommodation at Lake Louise and Yoho's Emerald Lake. Horne was also the man who, when he discovered the *Banff Springs* was being built back to front, pulled out a piece of paper and quickly sketched a veranda affair, which he decided would put things to rights: he was no architect, but such was his overbearing managerial style that his ad hoc creation was built anyway.

Today the 828-room luxury pile, largely rebuilt between 1911 and 1928, costs around $90,000 a day just to run, but boasts an extraordinary 100 percent occupancy – or over 1700 guests nightly – for half of the year. Busloads of Japanese visitors help make ends meet – the hotel's appearance in a famous Japanese soap having apparently boosted its already rampant popularity. The influx has prompted further rebuilding, including a spa centre being talked of as one of North America's best and a ballroom for 1600 people.

The "Building of Banff" trips depart daily at 5pm from the main lobby and cost $5 if you are interested: call ☎762-2211 for further details. Unless you're a fan of kilted hotel staff or Victorian hotel architecture and its allied knick-knacks you can easily give the organized tours a miss. A voyeuristic hour or so can be spent looking around the hotel's first three floors on your own (pick up a map in reception, it's almost a mini-village) or taking a coffee, beer or afternoon tea in the second-floor café and Sunroom off the main reception; prices for anything else in most of the sixteen various eating places are ludicrous. It's also worth walking out onto the terrace beyond the Sunroom for some truly spectacular views. You can get out here either by walking along the south bank of the Bow River (taking in Bow Falls) or picking up the Banff Transit bus from downtown ($1). Walking up or down Spray Avenue is very dull.

The Gondolas

Banff is rightly proud of its two prize **gondolas** (known elsewhere as cable cars). High-price tickets buy you crowds, great views and commercialized summits, but also the chance to do some high-level hiking without the slog of an early-morning climb; they'll also give you a glimpse of the remote high country if you're short of time or unable to walk the trails. The best times to take a ride are early morning or evening, when wildlife sightings are more likely, and when the play of light gives an added dimension to the views.

Sulphur Mountain Gondola

The **Sulphur Mountain Gondola** on Mountain Avenue some 5km south of town trundles 700m skywards at a stomach-churning 51 degrees to immense 360-degree views from two observation terraces and an ugly but surprisingly good-value summit restaurant, Canada's highest (daily: mid-May to late June & mid-Aug to early Sept 8.30am–8pm; late June to mid-Aug 7am–9pm; early Sept to early Oct 8am–6.30pm; early Oct to mid-Dec 8am–4.30pm; $18; ☎762-2523 or 762-5438 for 24-hour recording of opening times, which change slightly from year to year). If you're without transport the only options for getting here are to walk (dull and tiring) or take a taxi from downtown. In summer Brewster Transportation (☎762-6700) run a short **tour shuttle** to the gondola from the town centre (mid-May to mid-Aug daily on the hour to 9am–4pm and until 6pm mid-Aug to early Oct): the price ($25) includes the cost of the gondola ticket and return bus shuttle (leaves gondola terminal hourly on the half-hour).

It takes just eight minutes for the glass-enclosed four-passenger cars to reach the 2255-metre high point: eleven million people have come up here on the gondola over the years. From the restaurant a one-kilometre path, the **Summit Ridge Trail**, has been blazed to take you a bit higher, while the short **Vista Trail** leads to the restored weather station and viewpoint on Sanson Peak. Norman Betheune "NB" Sanson was a meteorological buff and first curator of the Banff Park Museum, who between 1903 and 1931 made around 1000 ascents of the mountain – that's before the gondola was built – to take his weather readings. Note that if, like him, you slog the 5.5km up from the car park (see box, p.500) you can ride the gondola down for free. Far too much of the food from the summit restaurant, unfortunately, ends up being eaten by bighorn sheep which, protected within the parks and unafraid of humans, gather here for handouts. Don't encourage them – feeding wildlife is against park regulations and can land you with a stiff fine.

Sunshine Gondola

The newer **Sunshine Gondola**, 18km southwest of town, once whisked you 4km from the Sunshine car park lot in the Bourgeau Valley to the Sunshine Village Resort at

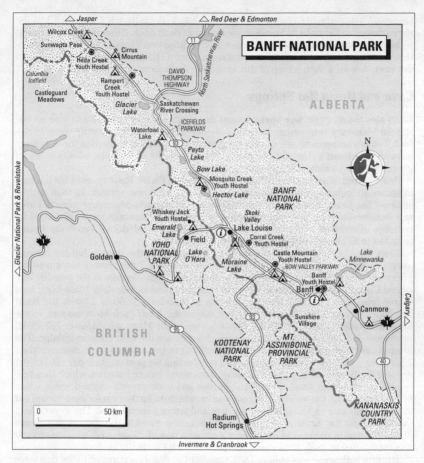

2215m and some staggering views. At no extra cost, the **Standish Chairlift** led on from the resort to the Continental Divide (2430m) and a post marking the BC–Alberta border, but at the time of writing both have been completely closed for the summer (hours in the past, should it reopen, were July & Aug Mon–Thurs 8.30am–7.30pm, Fri–Sun 8.30am–10.30pm; $12). At present White Mountain Adventures run a shuttle bus (with optional day and half-day guided walks) from Banff to the Sunshine Parking Lot in place of the gondola (departs 8.45am, returns 3pm & 5pm; $35 plus $10 for guided walk) and four shuttles from here upwards (9.30am, 10.30am, 11.30am and 1.30pm, returns 1pm, 2pm, 3pm, 4pm & 5pm; $18 including walk): numbers are limited so you should book a place on the bus (☎678-4099 or 1-800/408-005, *www.canadiannatureguides.com*). Two connecting gravel trails can be followed once you're up the mountain through **Sunshine Meadows**, a beautiful and unusually large tract of alpine grassland. The **Rock Isle Trail** loop starts at the Sunshine Meadows Nature Centre. After 1km, branch right to pass Rock Isle Lake on the left (take the left fork and you'd eventually come to Lake Assiniboine). Around 600m after the branch right you come to a fork: turn left and you loop around the Garden Path Trail (3.8km) past Larix Lake, the

Simpson Viewpoint and Grizzly Lake back to the fork. From here it's 500m to a 1.2-kilo-metre detour to the right to Standish Viewpoint (a dead end). Otherwise head straight on and after 2.8km you come to a junction and the Monarch Viewpoint, where a 1.6-kilo-metre walk takes you back to the Nature Centre (11.5km total with all loops and detours). Ask for a sketch map of this area from the information centre.

Cave and Basin Hot Springs

Banff also boasts eight **hot springs**, and the next stop after the gondola ride on the standard itinerary is to plunge into the only one of these that's currently commercial-ized. Today's immersions are usually for pleasure, but in their early days these springs were vital to Banff's rise and popularity, their reputedly therapeutic effects being of great appeal to Canada's ailing Victorian gentry.

Dr R.G. Brett, chief medical officer to the Canadian Pacific Railway, used his position to secure an immensely lucrative virtual monopoly on the best springs. In 1886 he con-structed the Grandview Villa, a money-spinning sanitorium promising miracle cures and wonders such as "ice cold temperance drinks". Its handrails were reinforced by crutches abandoned by "cured" patients, though the good doctor reputedly issued crutches to all comers whether they needed them or not.

There may be quieter places in the Northwest to take the waters, but hot springs always make for a mildly diverting experience, and even if the crowds are a pain the prices are hardly going to cripple you. On the face of it, the springs at the recently ren-ovated **Cave & Basin National Historic Site** (mid-June to Aug daily 10am–6pm; Sept to mid-June Mon–Thurs 11am–4pm, Fri–Sun 9.30am–5pm; $2.50 or $7 with the Banff Heritage Passport which also allows admission to the Banff Park Museum and Whyte Museum; guided tours free with admission summer daily 11am; ☎762-1566 or 762-1557), southwest of downtown at the end of Cave Avenue, are the best place to indulge. The original cave and spring here are what gave birth to the national park, discovered on November 8 1883 by three railway navvies prospecting for gold on their day off. Having crossed the Bow River by raft they discovered a warm-watered stream, which they pro-ceeded to follow to a small eddy of sulphurous and undergrowth-clogged water. Close by lay a small hole, the water's apparent source, which on further exploration turned out to be the entrance to an underground cave and warm mineral pool. The government quickly bought the three out, setting about promoting travel to the springs as a means of contributing to the cost of the railway's construction. A 25-square-kilometre reserve was established in 1885, from which the present park eventually evolved.

The first bathhouse was built in 1887, but over the years succumbed to the corrosive effects of chlorine and the pool's natural minerals. The pools finally closed in 1975, were restored (at a cost of $12 million), opened in 1985 and closed again in 1993 (again because of corrosion and falling numbers). Today the pools are still shut to bathers, leaving a popular **interpretive centre**(☎762-1566) to delve into their history and geol-ogy. You can walk here in a few minutes from town. From the foyer, where the faint whiff of sulphur is unmistakeable, a short tunnel leads to the original cave, where the stench becomes all but overpowering. Smell aside, it's still a rather magical spot, with daylight shining in from a little hole in the roof and the limpid water inviting but tanta-lizingly out of bounds. Back down the tunnel and up the stairs brings you to a few rooms of interpretive displays, with a film show, some illuminating old photographs and several pertinent quotations, among which is the acid comment of an early travel writer, Douglas Sladen: "though it consists of but a single street", he grumbled about Banff in 1895, "it is horribly overcivilized", an observation not too far off the mark today. Down the stairs from the displays at the rear brings you to the "basin", a small outdoor hot spring that's separate from the cave spring system, but no less inviting. Alongside is a wooden hut theatre with a half-hour film show.

Immediately outside the centre, the short Discovery Trail (15min) heads up the hill for a view over the site, together with the nearby start of the excellent **Sundance Canyon** surfaced path (see box, p.500). Just below the centre is the **Marsh Loop Trail** (2km; 25min), a treat for naturalists, and **bird-watching** enthusiasts in particular. The area's low-elevation wetlands teem with waterfowl during the winter and spring migrations, with the chance to see – among others – Barrow's goldeneye and all three species of teal: cinnamon, blue-winged and green-winged. The warm microclimate produced here by the springs' warm waters supports mallards over the winter, as well as attracting seasonal rarities such as killdeer, common snipe and rusty blackbird. During the summer you might see belted kingfisher, common yellowthroat, willow flycatcher and red-winged blackbird. Just across the river from here on Vermilion Lakes is the single most important area for bird-watching in the entire park, accessed via trails (see box, p.500) and the Vermilion Lakes Road. Ospreys and bald eagles both nest here, and other highlights include tundra swan, hooded merganser and northern shoveler.

Upper Hot Springs

Unlike the Cave and Basin, there's no problem with swimming in the **Upper Hot Springs**, 4.5km from the town centre on Mountain Avenue, and easily visited after a trip on the Sulphur Mountain Gondola (mid-May to mid-Sept daily 9am–11pm; mid-Sept to mid-May Mon–Thurs & Sun 10am–10pm, Fri & Sat 10am–11pm; $7 mid-May to mid-Oct, $5.50 mid-Oct to mid-May; lockers, towel and swimming costumes – 1920 or 1990 style – rental extra; ☎762-1515 or 762-2500 for spa bookings). First developed in 1901, the springs were laid out in their present form in 1932 and completely renovated in 1996. At 38°C, the water in the outdoor pool provides a steamy temptation, but it receives a lot of traffic from people coming off the Sulphur Mountain Gondola. They also leave a fairly pungent sulphurous aftersmell. You can sign up for relaxing therapeutic massages ($45) to complement your swim, while adults can make use of the Hot Springs Spa for aromatherapy wrap ($32), steam room, massage, plunge pool and steam and plunge (from $15). Call for details and appointments. If you don't want all this pampering there's a good poolside restaurant with outside terrace, fresh juice bar and hot and cold snacks.

Lake Minnewanka

Lake Minnewanka lies a few kilometres north of the town centre, and is easily accessed by bike or car from the Trans-Canada and the northern end of Banff Avenue on Lake Minnewanka Road. The largest area of water in the national park, its name means "Lake of the Water Spirit", and with the peaks of the Fairholme Range as backdrop it provides a suitably scenic antidote to the bustle of downtown. Various dams augmented the lake in 1912, 1922 and 1941 to provide Banff with hydroelectric power, though they've done little to spoil the views, most of which are best enjoyed from the various **boat trips** that depart regularly from the quay in summer (the lake's the only one in the park where public motorboats are allowed). Trips last an hour and a half and travel a fair distance up and down the lake (mid-May to Oct daily at 10.30am, 12.30pm, 3pm and 5pm; July & Aug sunset cruise at 7pm; $26; Lake Minnewanka Boat Tours ☎762-3473, *www.minnewankaboattours.com*). Fishing trips can be arranged through the same company. Brewster Transportation offer an inclusive bus tour and cruise from Banff for around $41 (4–5 daily mid-May to early Oct). Confirm current sailing times and arrive a good thirty minutes before sailing to pick up tickets. If you have to kill time waiting for a place there are some easy walking trails along the lake's western side.

Eating and drinking

Banff's 100-plus **restaurants** – more per head of population than anywhere else in Canada – run the gamut from Japanese and other ethnic cuisines to nouvelle-frontier grub. If your funds are limited, the *Banff International Youth Hostel* and the *YWCA* cafeterias, plus any number of fast-food and takeout options, are probably the best value, while Banff Avenue is lined with good little spots for coffee and snacks, many with pleasant outdoor tables. As for bars and nightlife, given Banff's huge number of summer travellers and large seasonal workforce, there are plenty of people around in summer looking for night-time action.

To stock up if you're camping, use either the big Safeway **supermarket** at 318 Marten St and Elk (daily 9am–10pm), just off Banff Avenue a block down from Wolf Street, or the less frenetic Kellers (daily 7am–midnight), opposite the Whyte Museum at 122 Bear St on the corner of Lynx.

Aurora, 110 Banff Ave (☎762-3343). Very popular bar and nightclub (cheap drinks) attracting a young crowd in the Clock Tower Village Mall; dancing nightly until 2am and live music, usually Friday and Saturday evenings.

Baker Creek Bistro, *Baker Creek Chalets*, Bow Valley Parkway (☎522-2182). As a break from town it's definitely worth driving out here for a meal of innovative and well-cooked staples, like steaks and pastas, in a restaurant frequented by locals as well as tourists. The snug lounge bar is also nice for a drink, especially later in the year when the fire's lit.

Balkan Village, 120 Banff Ave (☎762-3454). Greek outlet, known for big portions of reasonable food and belly dancing on Tuesday in the winter to whip things up; in summer the place turns raucous on its own, with frequent impromptu navel displays from well-oiled customers. Service can be a trifle surly.

Barbary Coast, upstairs at 119 Banff Ave (☎762-4616). Excellent, if obvious, food – pizza, steaks, burgers and salads – at good prices: the restaurant is full of sporting memorabilia, and the separate popular bar at the front, open till 2am, also does food (with occasional live music).

Bistro, corner of Wolf and Bear next to the Lux Cinema (☎762-8900). A cheaper sister restaurant of *Le Beaujolais*, this is a pleasantly calm place a block or so off Banff Ave where you can enjoy first-rate food in intimate surroundings.

Bumper's, 603 Banff Ave (☎762-2622). A little out of the centre, but this excellent-value steakhouse – one of the town's busiest – still draws in Banff residents and visitors alike. There's a good lounge upstairs, a locals' favourite, for a drink before or after dinner.

Cilantro Mountain Café, *Buffalo Mountain Lodge*, Tunnel Mountain Rd (☎762-2400). A good café-restaurant, with the usual North American fare, that's ideal if you're staying at the hostel or campground and want a modest treat; has a nice outside terrace for the summer. Inexpensive.

Earl's, upstairs at the corner of Banff Ave and Wolf St (☎762-4414). You can rarely go wrong at restaurants in this mid-priced Canada-wide chain. Lively, friendly service, plenty of room and consistently good food that is extraordinarily eclectic – everything from Thai to Italian influences.

Evelyn's, 201 Banff Ave, corner of Caribou (☎762-0352). One of the best inexpensive places on the strip for breakfast; excellent range of coffees. A second, less busy outlet, *Evelyn's Too*, can be found next to the Lux Cinema at 229 Bear Ave.

Joe Btfspk's [sic] **Diner**, 221 Banff Ave (☎762-5529). Tries too hard to evoke a period feel – red-vinyl chairs and black-and-white floors – but does good, if slightly overpriced, food; often busy at peak times.

Le Beaujolais, 212 Banff Ave at Buffalo St (☎762-2712). Known for almost twenty years as one of western Canada's better, smarter and more expensive restaurants. A choice of set-price menus between $40 and $66 help keep tabs on spending. Reservations recommended.

Melissa's, 218 Lynx St (☎762-5511). Probably Banff's most popular daytime destination, set in an old log cabin: big breakfasts, superb mignon steaks, salads and burgers, plus a good upstairs bar, *Mel's*, for a leisurely drink, and a summer patio for food and beer in the sun. Recommended, particularly for lunch.

Outa Bounds, 137 Banff Ave (☎762-8434). Though Banff's other major bar and nightclub – along with *Aurora* – is a rather soulless basement bar, with food, pool, dancing and occasional music, it still manages, somehow, to draw in the crowds.

Rose and Crown, upstairs at 202 Banff Ave (☎762-2121). Part of a chain, combining a moderately successful pub atmosphere (darts, mock-Victorian interior) with a family-oriented restaurant. Food is of the pub-lunch variety and later on you can shake a leg in the adjoining nightclub and disco – occasional live music.

St Jame's Gate, 205 Wolf St (☎762-9355). It was only a matter of time before Banff got an Irish pub; hugely popular with locals and visitors alike.

Wild Bill's Legendary Saloon, upstairs at 203 Banff Ave (☎762-0333). Serves good Tex-Mex and vegetarian food (family-oriented until 8pm); doubles as a lively bar with live bands (usually country) Wednesday to Sunday; pool hall and games room.

Activities and entertainment

The information centre carries extensive lists and contact information for guides and outfitters for all manner of **outdoor activities**. Among the more passive entertainment are **billiards** upstairs at the *King Edward Hotel*, 137 Banff Ave (☎762-4629; $8 an hour), ten-pin **bowling** at the *Banff Springs Hotel* (☎762-6892; $3.75 a game, $1.10 shoe rental), and new-release **films** at the Lux Cinema, 229 Bear St (☎762-8595). You can work out or **swim** for a fee in the pools at the *Banff Rocky Mountain Resort* (☎762-5531) or swim at the Sally Borden Recreation Building at the Banff Centre (☎762-6461) and *Douglas Fir Resort* at the corner of Tunnel Mountain Drive and Otter Street (Mon–Fri 4–9.30pm plus 2–9.30pm in summer, Sat–Sun 10am–9.30pm; $7.50; ☎762-5591): the last is especially popular as it also boasts waterslides. Note that the only swimmable lake in the park is Johnson Lake northeast of town off Lake Minnewanka Road: the others are usually glacier-fed and thus immensely cold.

For general bus tours, contact Brewster Transportation (☎762-8400), who've been running trips for decades. For something just a little more demanding there's **golf** at the stunning Banff Springs Golf Course (☎762-6801; from $35 for nine holes, $125 for eighteen holes, club rental from $35 for steel, $50 for graphite). You'll need to book well in advance. Free shuttles run to the clubhouse from the *Banff Springs Hotel*. **Birdwatching** with Halfway to Heaven Birdwatching (☎673-2542) costs $30 for a half-day, $65 for a day, with snack or lunch included.

BIKING AND BLADING

Mountain biking is big in the park, with plenty of rental places around town (see "Listings" on p.502). One of the cheapest outlets is Bactrax Bike Rentals, 225 Bear St (daily 8am–8pm; ☎762-8177), where rentals work out at $6–12 an hour or $22–42 a day for mountain bikes, $8 an hour or $30 a day for road bikes: rates include helmet, lock and water bottle. The company also has easy bike tours from one to four hours ($15 per hour, including bike) on paved routes around Sundance Canyon and Vermilion Lakes. More ambitious rides on the Icefields and Bow Valley parkways or around Moraine Lake can be arranged in Lake Louise at the *Chateau Lake Louise* hotel (see p.513) through Cycling the Rockies (☎522-2211; groups of six or more, $69 per person half-day, $109 full day).

If you're exploring on a bike under your own steam, pick up the *Trail Bicycling Guide* from the infocentre, which outlines some of the dedicated cycling trails: the best known are Sundance (3.7km one-way); Rundle Riverside (8km one-way); Cascade Trail (9km one-way); and the Spray River Loop (4.3km).

Bactrax is also one of four places in town who rent out **rollerblades** (the paved Sundance Canyon Trail near the Cave and Basin centre is a popular run); prices start at $3 an hour. The other outlets are Ski Stop branches at the *Banff Springs Hotel* (☎762-5333) and 203a Bear St (☎760-1650; $6 an hour) and Performance Sports, 220 Bear St (☎762-8222; $20 a day).

BOATING AND FISHING

Boat trips can be taken on Lake Minnewanka (see p.497), as can **fishing** trips, which can be arranged through Lake Minnewanka Boat Tours (☎762-3473). Monod Sports,

WALKS AROUND BANFF

WALKS FROM DOWNTOWN

Banff Townsite is one of two obvious bases for walks in the park (the other is Lake Louise), and trails around the town cater to all levels of fitness. The best short stroll from downtown – at least for flora and fauna – is the **Fenland Trail**, a 1.5-kilometre loop west through the montane wetlands near the First Vermilion Lake (there are three Vermilion lakes, fragments of a huge lake that once probably covered the whole Bow Valley at this point; all can be accessed off Vermilion Lakes Drive). Marsh here is slowly turning to forest, creating habitats whose rushes and grasses provide a haven for wildlife, birds in particular. Ospreys and bald eagles nest around the lake, together with a wide range of other birds and waterfowl, and you may also see beaver, muskrat, perhaps even coyote, elk and other deer. You can walk this and other easy local trails in the company of the "Friends of Banff" – see under "Information" on p.489 for more details.

For a shorter walk, and a burst of spectacular white water, stroll the level and very easy Bow Falls Trail (1km) from beneath the bridge on the south side of the river, which follows the river bank east to a powerful set of waterfalls and rapids just below the *Banff Springs Hotel*. The Hoodoos Trail on the other side of the river (starting at the eastern end of Buffalo St) offers similar views with fewer people, linking eventually to Tunnel Mountain Road if you walk it all the way, which make this a good way to walk into town for the youth hostel and campgrounds.

The **Marsh Loop Trail** (2km) from Cave Avenue leads along a boardwalk through a marshy habitat renowned for its flora and birds: warm waters from the Cave and Basin hot springs immediately above have created a small, anomalous area of lush vegetation. In winter Banff's own wolf pack has been known to hunt within sight of this trail. The **Sundance Canyon Trail** (3.7km), an easy and deservedly popular stroll along a paved path (also popular with cyclists, and rollerbladers – be warned) to the picnic area at the canyon mouth, also starts from close to the springs; you can extend your walk along the 2.1-kilometre loop path up through the canyon, past waterfalls, and back down a peaceful wooded trail. Finally, the most strenuous walk near town is to the summit of Tunnel Mountain. It's approached on a windy track (300m ascent) from the southwest from Tunnel Mountain Drive, culminating in great views over the townsite, Bow River and flanking mountains.

DAY-HIKES NEAR BANFF

Day-hikes from the town centre are limited – you need transport and usually have to head a few kilometres along the Trans-Canada to reach trailheads that leave the flat valley floor for the heart of the mountains. Only a couple of longish ones strike out directly from town: the **Spray River Circuit**, a flat, thirteen-kilometre round trip past the *Banff Springs Hotel* up the Spray River; and the Sulphur Mountain Trail, a 5.5-kilometre switchback that climbs 655m up to the Sulphur Mountain gondola terminal at 2255m (you're better off simply taking the gondola).

---

129 Banff Ave (☎762-4571), have all-day drift boat fishing trips on the Bow River and Nakoda Lake for cutthroat and bull trout plus brown and brook trout (both are catch and release, meaning you have to put any caught fish back into the water) at $375 for two people and walk and wade trips ($110 per person): trips include guide, instruction, tackle, wader, drinks and food. Beginner fly fishers can take an instructional tour with the company. Banff Fishing Unlimited (☎762-4936) have Bow River float trips and walk and wade trips (from $100 per person) and half-day fishing cruises on Lake Minnewanka ($80 per person in a group of six). Similar trips are also offered by Adventures Unlimited (☎762-4554). Tackle can be hired from Performance Ski and Sports, 208 Bear St (☎762-8222). Remember you need a national park licence to fish, available for $6 a week, $13 a year, from tackle shops, most of the above companies or the information centre.

Park wardens at the infocentre seem unanimous in rating the **Cory Pass Trail** (5.8km; 915m ascent), combined with the Edith Pass Trail to make a return loop, as the best day-hike close to Banff. The trailhead is signed 6km west of the town off the Bow Valley Parkway, 500m after the junction with the Trans-Canada. The stiff climbing involved, and a couple of scree passages, mean that it's not for the inexperienced or faint-hearted. The rewards are fantastic, with varied walking, a high mountain environment and spine-tingling views. From the pass itself at 2350m, you can return on the Edith Pass Trail (whose start you'll have passed 1km into the Cory Pass walk), to make a total loop of a demanding 13km.

Another popular local day-hike, the trail to **Cascade Amphitheatre** (2195m), starts at Mount Norquay Ski Area, 6km north of the Trans-Canada Mount Norquay Road. This offers a medley of landscapes, ranging from alpine meadows to deep, ice-scoured valleys and a close view of the knife-edge mountains that loom so tantalizingly above town. Allow about three hours for the 7.7-kilometre (610m ascent) walk. For the same amount of effort, you could tackle **Elk Lake** (2165m) from the ski area, though at 13.5km each way it's a long day's hike; some people turn it into an overnight hike by using the campground 2.5km short of Elk Lake. Shorter, but harder on the lungs, is the third of Banff's popular local walks, **C Level Cirque** (1920m), reached by a four-kilometre trail from the Upper Bankhead Picnic Area on the Lake Minnewanka road east of Banff. Elsewhere, the Sunshine Meadows area has five high trails of between 8km and 20km, all possible as day-hikes and approached either from the Sunshine Gondola (if running) or its parking area, 18km southwest of Banff. There are also some good short trails off the Bow Valley Parkway, most notably the **Johnston Canyon** path (see box, p.507).

The best **backpacking** options lie in the Egypt Lake area west of Banff Townsite, with longer trails radiating from the lake's campground. Once you're in the backcountry around Banff, however, the combination of trails is virtually limitless. The keenest hikers tend to march the routes that lead from Banff to Lake Louise – the Sawback Trail and Bow Valley Highline, or the tracks in the Upper Spray and Bryant Creek Valley south of the townsite.

If you're planning long walks and overnight trips in backcountry you must have a **Wilderness Pass** ($6 a night from park centres). You should also book backcountry campgrounds (contact Parks Canada at Lake Louise or Banff visitor centres; ☎762-1556) and walks well in advance ($10 non-refundable booking fee), as **quotas** operate for all backcountry areas – if the quotas fill, you won't be able to walk or camp or may have to make do with a second-choice hike. The most popular of the 50-odd campgrounds are Marvel Lake, Egypt Lake, Luellen Lake, Aylmer Pass, Mystic Meadow, Fish Lakes, Paradise Valley, Hidden Lake, Baker Lake, Merlin Meadows, Red Deer Lakes and Mount Rundle. Be sure to pick up or send for the Parks Canada *Backcountry Visitors' Guide* pamphlet for further details of the system and of recommended routes.

If you want to **rent canoes** for paddling on the Vermilion Lakes or quiet stretches of the Bow River, contact Bow River Canoe Docks ($16 an hour, $40 a day; ☎762-3632); the dock is on the river at Wolf Street. Or learn to **kayak** on the Bow with Alpine Adventures (☎678-8357; six-hour course $99).

HORSE RIDING
Horse riding is easy to organize, with anything from one-hour treks to two-week backcountry expeditions available. The leading in-town outfitters are Holiday on Horseback, 132 Banff Ave (☎762-4551). One-, two- and three-hour rides start at about $25, while a six-hour trip up the Spray River Valley costs about $115. You can also take overnight trips to the *Sundance Lodge* from around $300 including all meals. Martin Stables, off Cave Avenue across the river from downtown, have hour to full-day rides ($25–115) and

rent horses by the hour from $25. The Corral (☎762-4551) at the *Banff Springs Hotel* lets them out for $29 and offers a three-hour ride from the hotel to Spray River, Sulphur Mountain and Mount Rundle ($64).

WHITE-WATER RAFTING

Best among adrenaline-rush activities is **white-water rafting** on the Kicking Horse River, located a few kilometres up the road in Yoho but accessed by some eight companies in Banff and Lake Louise, most of them providing all necessary gear and transportation. Other gentler "float" trip options with the same companies are available on the Kananaskis, Kootenay and Bow rivers.

Long-established Hydra River Guides, 209 Bear St (☎762-4554 or 1-800/644-8888, fax 760-3196, *www.raftbanff.com*), has two daily six- and seven-hour trips ($85) in paddle or oar rafts on the Kicking Horse. Wet n' Wild Adventures (☎344-6546 or 1-800/668-9119) has full ($78) and half-day ($55) trips in the Kicking Horse Canyon, a half-day trip ($55) in the wilder lower part of the canyon for more advanced rafters, two-day trips, and raft and horse-riding combination trips. Wild Water Adventures from Lake Louise (☎522-2211 or 1-888/647-6444) has a half-day trip in the canyon ($69) plus rafting in the canyon for those seeking a gentler look at the Kicking Horse ($59).

Rocky Mountain Raft Tours (☎762-3632) offers more sedate one- and three-hour rides (3 daily; $24) down the Bow River from the canoe docks at Bow Avenue and Wolf Street. For half-day trips ($54) on the Kootenay River, contact Kootenay River Runner (☎762-5385 or 1-800/664-4399), which also has three-day ventures and is one of only three companies to offer trips on the wilder, lower section of the Kicking Horse Canyon (day-trips at $79 on the Kicking Horse River or $105 in the lower Canyon). For gentle float trips on the Bow or Kananaskis rivers, contact Canadian Rockies Rafting (☎678-6535 or 1-877/226-7625): $39 for the Bow, $45 for Kananaskis.

Listings

Ambulance ☎911 or 762-2000.

American Express 130 Banff Ave (☎762-3207).

Bike rental Bactrax, 225 Bear St (☎762-8177); Banff Adventures Unlimited, 211 Bear St (☎762-4554); Inns of Banff, 600 Banff Ave (☎762-4581); Mountain Magic, 224 Bear St (☎762-2591); Performance Ski and Sport, 2nd Floor, 208 Bear St (☎762-8222); Ski Stop outlets at 203a Bear St and *Banff Springs Hotel* (☎760-1650 or 762-5333).

Bookshop Banff Book & Art Den, Clock Tower Mall, 94 Banff Ave (daily: summer 10am–9pm; winter 10am–7pm; ☎762-3919) is excellent for general books and local guides.

Bus information Bus depot, 100 Gopher St (Greyhound ☎762-1092 or 1-800/661-8747; Brewster Transportation ☎762-6767 or 1-800/661-1152); Banff Airporter Banff–Calgary Airport services (☎762-3330 or 1-888/449-2901); Laidlaw Chateau Lake Louise–Lake Louise–Banff–Calgary Airport (☎762-9102 or 1-800/661-4946); Banff Transit town shuttle (☎762-8294); Sky Shuttle Lake Louise–Banff–Calgary Airport (☎762-1010 or 1-888/220-7433).

Camping equipment Tents, outdoor gear and ski equipment to rent from Performance Ski and Sport, 208 Bear St (☎762-8222).

Car rental Avis, Cascade Plaza, Wolf Street (☎762-3222 or 1-800/879-2847); Banff Rent-a-Car, 230 Lynx St (☎762-3352), for low-priced used-car rentals; Budget, 208 Caribou St (☎762-4546 or 1-800-268-8900); Hertz, at the *Banff Springs Hotel* (☎762-2027 or 1-800/263-0600); Sears (☎762-4575); National, corner of Caribou and Lynx (☎762-2688 or 1-800/387-4747).

Dentist 210 Bear St (☎762-3144).

Doctors Dr Ian MacDonald, 216 Banff Ave (☎762-3155); Dr Elizabeth J Hall-Findlay, 317 Banff Ave (☎762-2055).

Foreign exchange CTM Currency Exchange at 108 Banff Ave, Clock Tower Mall (☎762-4698 or 762-9353)), 317 Banff Ave (Cascade Plaza) and the *Banff Springs Hotel*. Visa advances at CIBC, 98 Banff Ave (☎762-4417); MasterCard advances at Bank of Montréal, 107 Banff Ave.

Hospital Mineral Springs Hospital, 301 Lynx St (☎762-2222).

Internet access At the public library (see below).

Laundries Cascade Plaza Coin Laundry, Lower Level, Cascade Plaza, 317 Banff Ave (☎762-2245); also a laundry in Johnny O's Emporium, a small mall at 223 Bear St (Mon–Sat 8am–midnight, Sun 9am–midnight; last wash 10.30pm. If you're at the hostel or campgrounds, the nearest laundry is the Chalet Coin Laundry on Tunnel Mountain Rd (☎762-5447) at the *Douglas Fir Resort.*

Library 101 Bear St (Mon, Wed, Fri & Sat 11am–6pm, Tues & Thurs 11am–9pm, Sun 1–5pm; ☎762-2661).

Lost property ☎762-1218.

Parks Canada Administration ☎762-1500; campground info ☎762-1550. Park wardens ☎762-1470. 24hr *emergency* number only ☎762-4506.

Pharmacy Cascade Plaza Drug, Lower Level, Cascade Plaza, 317 Banff Ave; Gourlay's, 229 Bear St (Wolf and Bear Mall); Harmony Drug, 111 Banff Ave.

Police ☎762-2226.

Post office 204 Buffalo St at the corner of Bear St (Mon–Fri 9am–5.30pm). Stamps and other basic postal services also at Cascade Plaza Drug, Lower Level, Cascade Plaza, 317 Banff Ave; Mailboxes Etc, 226 Bear St; and Goro Canyon Gifts, Banff Park Lodge.

Road conditions ☎762-1450.

Taxis Alpine (☎762-3727); Banff Limousine (☎762-5466); Banff Taxi (☎762-4444); Legion (☎762-3353); Mountain (☎762-3351); Taxi-Taxi (☎762-3111).

Tourist information ☎762-1550 for park information or 762-8421 for town and accommodation.

Trail conditions ☎762-1550 or 760-1305.

Weather ☎762-4707 or 762-2088 (24hr recording).

Highway 1 and the Bow Valley Parkway

Two roads run parallel through the Bow Valley from Banff to Lake Louise (58km): the faster **Hwy 1** (the Trans-Canada); and the quieter **Bow Valley Parkway**, on the other (north) side of the river, opened in 1989 as a special scenic route. After Banff, there's only one link between the two roads, at Castle Junction, 30km from Lake Louise. Both routes are staggeringly beautiful, as the mountains start to creep closer to the road. For the entire run, the mighty **Bow River**, broad and emerald green, crashes through rocks and forest. Despite the tarmac and heavy summer traffic, the surroundings are pristine and suggest the immensity of the wilderness to come. Sightings of elk and deer are common, particularly around dawn and sundown, and occasionally you'll spot moose. Both roads offer some good **trails**: if you want to tackle one of the most highly rated day-walks in Banff National Park, make for the Bourgeau Lake Trail off Hwy 1 (see box, p.507); for a shorter walk, make for the Johnston Canyon on the Parkway. Note, however, that between 6pm and 9am daily from March 1 to June 25, the 17km of the Bow Valley Parkway between Johnston Canyon and the east entrance off the Trans-Canada (that is, the entrance closest to Banff), is closed to allow the grazing of animals forced by late snow to lower altitudes for food. Access at this time to Johnston Canyon trails and campground is from Hwy 1.

Highway 1

Most people tend either to cruise Hwy 1's rapid stretch of the Trans-Canada without stopping – knowing that the road north of Lake Louise is more spectacular still – or leap out at every trail and rest stop, overcome with the grandeur of it all. On Greyhound or Brewster **buses** you're whisked through to Lake Louise in about forty minutes; if you're driving, try for the sake of wildlife to stick to the 90kph speed limit. The vast fences that march for kilometre after kilometre along this section of the road are designed to protect animals, not only from traffic but from the brainless visitors who clamber out of their cars to get close to the bears occasionally glimpsed on the road. You won't have to be in the Rockies long during the summer before you're caught in a **bear jam**, when people

WINTER IN BANFF

Banff National Park is as enticing in winter as it is the rest of the year. If you're a skier or snowboarder then it's a virtual paradise, for **skiing** here is some of the best and most varied in North America. Yet the park offers the full gamut of winter activities, embracing everything from skating, ice-fishing and toboggan trips to dog-sledding, snowshoeing and sleigh rides. Skiing or snowboarding, though, are the big draws, and of Alberta's six world-class resorts, three are in the park, one in Lake Louise (see p.514) and two close to Banff – **Mount Norquay** and **Sunshine Village**. On top of great snow and pristine runs, you get crisp air, monumental mountains, sky-high forests, and prices and space that make a mockery of Europe's crowded and exorbitant winter playgrounds. You're also pretty certain of snow, sensational views, comfortable hotels and plenty of nightlife. However, what the brochures don't tell you is that here – as in Lake Louise – it can be bitterly cold for virtually all of the skiing season.

MOUNT NORQUAY

Mount Norquay is the closest resort to Banff, just 6km and ten-minutes' drive from downtown. Skiing started on the mountain's steep eastern slopes in the 1920s. In 1948 it gained Canada's first ever chair lift, immediately gaining a reputation as an experts-only resort – "steep and deep" in local parlance – thanks largely to horrors like the famous double-black diamond Lone Pine run. This reputation has only recently disappeared, the result of a complete revamp and the opening of a new network of lifts on and around Mystic Ridge to provide access to intermediate terrain and 25 runs suitable for all levels of skiers and boarders alike. An express quad chair was installed in 1990, together with two surface lifts, two double chairs and a quad chair.

As a result Norquay is now equally renowned for its uncrowded beginners' slopes as for its expert runs, the terrain breaking down as follows: Novice (11 percent); Intermediate (45 percent); Advanced (28 percent); and Expert (16 percent). The average snowfall is 300cm, and there's snowmaking on ninety percent of the terrain. The season runs from early December to mid-April. The highest elevation is 2133m, giving a vertical drop of 497m to the resort's base elevation at 1636m. Amenities include a visitor centre, ski school, rental shop, day care and – on Wednesdays – the promise of night skiing. Lift tickets are around $35 a day. Accommodation is in Banff, with a free shuttle bus making the tour of local hotels for the short trip to the hill. For more information on the resort write, call or fax Banff Mount Norquay, Box 219, Suite 7000, Banff, Alberta T0L 0C0 (☎762-4421, fax 762-8133, *www.banffnorquay.com*).

SUNSHINE VILLAGE

Sunshine Village is a stunning resort, situated way up in the mountains at 2160m 18km southwest of Banff. If anything the scenery's better than at Norquay – you're higher – and you have the plus of the national park's only on-hill accommodation. There's also an incredible 10m of snow a year – so there's no need for snowmaking machines – with superb soft, light powder that *Snow Country* magazine has repeatedly voted "The Best Snow in Canada". Skiing started here in 1929 when two locals got lost on Citadel Pass and came back with tales of fantastic open bowls and dream slopes just made for skiing. In 1938 the Canadian National Ski Championships were held here, and by 1942 a portable lift had been installed on site. The biggest change in the area's fortunes came in 1980,

– contrary to all park laws, never mind common sense – abandon their cars helter-skelter on the road to pursue hapless animals with cameras and camcorders.

The Bow Valley Parkway

If anything the **Bow Valley Parkway** boasts more scenic grandeur than the Trans-Canada – which is saying something – and offers more distractions if you're taking your

when a gondola (cable car) was built to carry skiers (and occasionally summer walkers) the 6km from the Healy Creek parking area to the self-contained Sunshine Village resort.

Today some 62 uncrowded runs can be accessed on the gondola, three high-speed detachable quads, a triple chair, four double chairs, two T-bars and two beginner rope tows. There's less here for the advanced skier than at Norquay, but plenty for the beginner and competent intermediate. Terrain breaks downs as follows: Novice (20 percent); Intermediate (60 percent) and Expert (20 percent). The top elevation is an incredible 2730m at Lookout Mountain, with a drop to base level of 1070m: all but one or two runs ultimately converge on the village itself. The opening of Goat's Eye Mountain in 1997 has added an express quad and lots of expert-only terrain (with double black runs) but little intermediate skiing and no beginners' runs: it has arguably helped give Sunshine the edge on expert terrain over other resorts. Lift tickets are around $45 a day. Amenities include a day-lodge, day care, outdoor hot pool, ski school, rental shop and overnight rooms in the Village at the 85-room *Sunshine Inn*, the Rockies' only on-slope accommodation (☎762-4581 or 1-800/661-1272 in Alberta, 1-800/661-1363 in the rest of North America; ⑤). Ski packages are available here for anything between one and seven nights (mid-Nov to late May) beginning at around $90 a night with two-days' skiing: basic overnight charges are between $115 and $170. If you're staying in Banff, shuttle buses run round the hotels and cost around $15 for the round trip. For more information on the resort, write, call or fax Sunshine Village, Box 1510, Banff, Alberta T0L 0C0 (☎762-6500, *www.skibanff.com*).

WINTER ACTIVITIES

Many of Banff's myriad walking trails are groomed for winter cross-country skiing, details of which can be obtained in the *Nordic Trails in Banff National Park* pamphlet available from the town's visitor centre. Favourite destinations include Sundance Canyon, Spray River, Johnson Lake (above Lake Minnewanka) and around Lake Minnewanka itself. You can hire specialist gear from several outlets around town (see "Listings" on p.502). At a more expensive level, Banff has no heliskiing of its own, but is the base for the world's largest heliski operator, Hans Gmoser's CMH Heli-Skiing, PO Box 1660 (☎762-7100), who offers package tours to various BC destinations. Other operators include RK HeliSki (☎762-3771 or 1-800/661-6060), who'll take you out to the Panorama area of the Purcell Mountains in BC and Mike Wiegele Helicopter Skiing, PO Box 249 (☎762-5548), will take you further afield in BC to the Monashee and Cariboo mountains.

If you want to **ice skate**, check out the rinks at Banff High School (Banff Ave), on the Bow River (off Bow St) and the *Banff Springs Hotel*; skates can be hired from The Ski Shop, also located in the hotel (☎762-5333). **Snowshoe** or **ice walks** can be arranged through companies based in Canmore, south of Banff, such as Back and Beyond (☎678-6606) or Michele's (☎678-2067): beginners are welcome and pick-ups can be arranged in Banff. Thrill-seeking **dog-sledders** need to contact Howling Dog Tours (☎678-9588) or Snowy Owl Sled Dog Tours (☎678-4369), who for a rather steep fee (reckon on $100 an hour) will take you on a spin. For less adrenaline-filled **sleigh rides** on the frozen Bow River, contact Holiday on Horseback (☎762-4551), for rides to the end of Lake Louise, contact Brewster Lake Louise sleighrides (☎762-5454) or Chateau Lake Louise (☎522-3511 ext 1139). Hotels often provide sledges for **toboggan** runs, of which there are several unofficial examples around town. **Ice-fishing** can be arranged through Banff Fishing Unlimited (☎762-4936, fax 678-8895).

---

time: several trails, campgrounds, plus plenty of accommodation choices and one excellent eating option. The largest concentration of sightseers is likely to be found at the Merrent turn-off, enjoying fantastic views of the Bow Valley and the railway winding through the mountains.

If you have the time, therefore, the Parkway is the preferable route, and you should budget some time to walk one of the **trails** en route, in particular the easy but impressive **Johnston Canyon Trail** (see box opposite). En route, some of the various view-points and signed pull-offs deserve more attention than others. Around 8km down the highway, look out for the **Backswamp Viewpoint**, where views one way extend to the mountains and the other across a river swamp area where you might see beaver, muskrat, ospreys and other birds (see below), as well as the common butterwort, a purple-flowered carnivorous plant whose diet consists largely of marsh insects. In winter Backswamp Viewpoint is also known locally as one of the most likely areas to spot wolves; at other times of the year you might also see bighorn sheep or mountain goats on the mountain slopes above. Three kilometres further on you come to **Muleshoe Picnic Area**, also noted for its birds and wildfowl (see below). Some of the area around shows signs of having been burnt in forest fires, though these areas were deliberately torched by the park authorities to encourage fresh undergrowth and the return of wildlife excluded from more mature forests (for more on this see the "Vermilion Pass" on p.560). Eleven kilometres on, a 400-metre trail takes you to a lovely little lake once known as Lizard Lake after the long-toed salamanders that once thrived here. These were eaten when the lake was stocked with trout, and the name's now been changed to Pilot Lake. Three kilometres beyond is the trailhead for the **Johnston Canyon Trail** (see box, opposite), deservedly the most popular in the area, and three kilometres beyond that **Moose Meadows**, where – name notwithstanding – you'll be mighty lucky to see any moose: habitat changes have forced them out.

If you're a **bird-watcher**, the Parkway is also the route for you. Johnston Canyon is one of only two known breeding sites in Alberta of the black swift – you may see the birds flitting back to their nests at dusk – and is also a breeding place for American dippers, buxom grey birds that have the ability to walk along stream beds underwater and habitually nest below waterfalls. Elsewhere on the Parkway the various pull-offs give you the opportunity to spot species associated with montane forest and meadow zones, notably at the Muleshoe Picnic Area, 21km southeast of Castle Junction, where you might spot western tanagers, pileated woodpeckers and orange-crowned warblers. At various points on the Bow River along the entire run from Banff to Lake Louise you may spot harlequin ducks on the river's islands and gravel bars, as well as spotted sand-pipers and common mergansers.

If you want to stay, the road's **accommodation** possibilities make a more rural alternative to Banff and Lake Louise, and are close enough to both to serve as a base if you have transport; as ever, you should book rooms well in advance. Four **lodges** are spaced more or less equally en route and, though expensive, they *may* have room when Lake Louise's hotels are stretched. First is the *Johnston Canyon Resort*, 26km west of Banff and close to the trail that leads to the canyon (☎762-2971, *www.johnstoncanyon.com*; ⑨; mid-May to late Sept), which consists of rustic cabins (some with fireplaces and some with kitchenettes), a shop, garage, tennis court and basic groceries. Next come the chalets, laundry and grocery store of *Castle Mountain Chalets*, 32km west of Banff near Castle Junction (☎762-3868, *www.castlemountain.com*; ⑦; year-round): the log chalets for four with kitchenettes and fireplaces are more expensive, but the best options of all here are the delightful and newly built deluxe cabins for four, five or six people (complete with full kitchens, dishwashers and jacuzzis). Some 5km south of Hwy 1 on Hwy 93 to Radium (27km from Banff) is *Storm Mountain Lodge* (☎762-4155; ⑥; end of May to late Sept) with highly appealing log cabins. Finally there's *Baker Creek Guest Lodge & Bistro*, 12km east of Lake Louise (☎522-3761, *www.bakercreek.com*; ⑥; year-round), with 25 one- and two-room log cabins and lodge rooms for between one and six people: there's also an excellent **restaurant** here that comes with local recommendations and new annexe with eight smart motel-type rooms. By far the least expensive possibility is the Parkway's charming **youth hostel**, *Castle Mountain Hostel*, 1.5km east of Castle Junction (☎762-2367 or 762-4122; *banff@hostellingintl.ca*; members $13, non-members $17; ①; year-round but closed

BOW VALLEY TRAILS

Five major trails branch off the Bow Valley Parkway. The best short walk by a long way is the **Johnston Canyon Trail** (2.7km each way), 25km from Banff, an incredibly engineered path to a series of spray-veiled waterfalls. The Lower Falls are 1.1km, the Upper Falls 2.7km from the trailhead on the Parkway. From the upper falls you can continue on to the seven cold-water springs of the Ink Pots, which emerge in pretty open meadows, to make a total distance of 5.8km (215m ascent). Another short possibility is the **Castle Crags Trail** (3.7km each way; 520m ascent) from the signed turn-off 5km west of Castle Junction. Short but steep, and above the tree line, this walk offers superb views across the Bow Valley and the mountains beyond. Allow ninety minutes one way to take account of the stiff climb.

The best day-hike is to **Rockbound Lake** (8.4km each way), a steepish climb to 2210m with wild lakeland scenery at the end; allow at least two and a half hours one way, due to the 760m ascent. Another fifteen-minutes' walk beyond Rockbound and Tower lakes at the end of the trail lies the beautiful Silverton waterfall. The other Parkway trails – **Baker Creek** (20.3km) and **Pulsatilla Pass** (17.1km) – serve to link backpackers with the dense network of paths in the Slate Range northeast of Lake Louise.

The two outstanding trails along Hwy 1 are the trek to **Bourgeau Lake** (7.5km one-way), considered by many among the top five day-hikes in Banff: it starts from a parking area 10km west of Banff – allow two-and-a-half to three hours for the 725-metre ascent – and the long day-hike to **Shadow Lake** (14.3km each way), where the lakeside campground (at 1840m), in one of the Rockies' more impressive subalpine basins, gives access to assorted onward trails. The main trail starts from the **Redearth Creek** parking area 20km west of Banff (440m ascent; allow 4hr).

Wed). You should call in advance, or better still book ahead through the hostel at Banff (☎762-4122).

Three national park **campgrounds** provide excellent camping retreats. In order of distance from Banff these are: the very popular 140-pitch *Johnston Canyon* ($17; mid-May to mid-Sept), 25km from Banff is the best equipped, and has full facilities including showers and wheelchair access; after that comes the 40-pitch *Castle Mountain*, 32km from Banff near Castle Junction ($13; late June to early Sept) and with no facilities beyond water and flush toilets; and then the similarly simple 89-pitch *Protection Mountain*, 5km north of Castle Junction (same details). An additional $4 fee is payable at all three if you wish to use firewood.

Lake Louise

The Banff park's other main centre, **Lake Louise**, is very different to Banff – less a town than two distinct artificial resorts. The first is a small mall of shops and hotels just off the Trans-Canada known as **Lake Louise Village**. The second is the lake itself, the self-proclaimed "gem of the Rockies" and – despite its crowds and monster hotel – a sight you have to see. A third area, **Moraine Lake**, 13km south of the village, has almost equally staggering scenery and several magnificent and easily accessed trails. Lake Louise is 4.5km from the village (and 200m higher) on the winding Lake Louise Drive – or, if you're walking, 2.7km on the uphill Louise Creek Trail, 4.5km via the Tramline Trail. You're better off saving the walking for around the lake, however, and taking a taxi (☎522-2020; around $10) from the village (if anything, save the two linking trails for coming down from the lake). All three areas are desperately busy in summer as well as in winter, when people pile in for some of the Northwest's best powder **skiing** (see box, p.514).

You may find staying near the lakes appealing but very pricey, though if you do want to splash out, the lodge at Moraine Lake makes a dream treat. Nonetheless, the

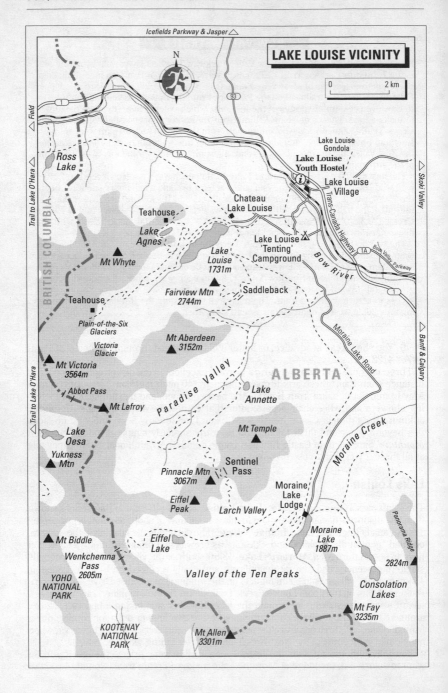

LAKE LOUISE VICINITY

mountains around offer almost unparalleled **hiking country** and the park's most popular day-use area. You'll have to weigh awesome scenery against the sheer numbers, for these are some of the most heavily used trails on the continent – 50,000-plus people in summer – though longer backpacking routes lead quickly away to the quieter spots. If you do intend to hike – and the trails are all a little more accessible and manageable than at Banff – then in an ideal world you'd have two or three days here: one to walk the loop around above Lake Louise (Lake Agnes–Big Beehive–Plain of the Six Glaciers–Lake Louise Shoreline) or the more demanding Saddleback (at a push you could do both in a day if you were fit and keen). Then you'd bike, taxi or drive to Moraine Lake (if you're not staying there), where in a day you could easily walk to Consolation Lake, return to Moraine Lake and then tackle the Moraine Lake–Larch Valley–Sentinel Pass or Moraine Lake–Larch Valley–Eiffel Lake trail. A third day could be spent in Paradise Valley between Lake Louise and Moraine Lake.

If, on the other hand, you merely want to take in the scenery and enjoy **modest strolls** in the course of a day, then cruise up to Lake Louise, walk up and down the shore, then drive the twenty minutes or so to Moraine Lake and do the same.

Lake Louise Village

LAKE LOUISE VILLAGE doesn't amount to much, but it's an essential supply stop, with more or less everything you need in terms of food and shelter (at a price). Most of it centres round a single mall, Samson Mall, and car park, with a smart youth hostel and a few outlying motels dotted along the service road to the north. There's almost nothing to do in the village, and unless you have a vehicle to take you to the lakes (or rent a bike) you're likely to be bored. The impressive **Lake Louise Information Centre**, a few steps from the car park, offers not only information but also high-tech natural-history exhibits (daily: mid-June to early Sept 8am–8pm; early Sept to late Sept & mid-June 8am–6pm; Oct–May 9am–4pm; ☎522-3833). Almost as useful is the excellent Woodruff and Blum bookshop (☎522-3842) in the mall, which has a full range of maps, guides and background reading. A couple of doors down, Wilson Mountain Sports (☎522-3636) is good for **bike rental** (from $8–12 per hour, $29–45 a day), rollerblade rentals (from $5–8 per hour), fishing tackle for sale or rent (fly rod $11, spin rod $7 and waders $10) and **equipment rental** (stoves $7, pack $9 and tent $19). They'll also fill you in on the possibility of **canoe rentals** for trips downstream on the Bow River to Banff.

A short way from the village, the **Lake Louise Gondola** (the "Friendly Giant") runs thirteen minutes to 2042m, part-way up Mount Whitehorn (2669m). To reach it, pick up the free shuttle which operates from some village hotels or return to and cross over the Trans-Canada, and follow the road towards the ski area; the gondola is signed left after about 1km (daily: June 8.30am–6pm; July–Aug 8am–6pm; Sept 8.30am–6pm; $13.95; ☎522-3555). Depending on your susceptibility to either vertigo or claustrophobia you can choose between enclosed gondola cars, open chairs, or chairs with bubble domes. At the top (2034m) are the usual sensational views – rated some of the best in the Rockies – a self-service restaurant, sun decks, picnic areas, souvenir shops and several trailheads through the woods and meadows. One track takes you to the summit of Mount Whitehorn, a stiff 600m above the gondola station.

TRANSPORT AND FACILITIES

Four Greyhound **buses** a day ($8) link Banff and Lake Louise (50min) and stop in the Samson Mall car park at the little office known as The Depot (☎522-2080); three continue to Vancouver and the west. Four buses a day return from Lake Louise to Banff and Calgary. Laidlaw (☎762-9102 or 1-800/661-4946) run one bus daily ($8) and Brewster Transportation (☎762-6700) three buses a day from Banff ($11), and also continue to the *Château Lake Louise* (a good way to get up here if you're without transport

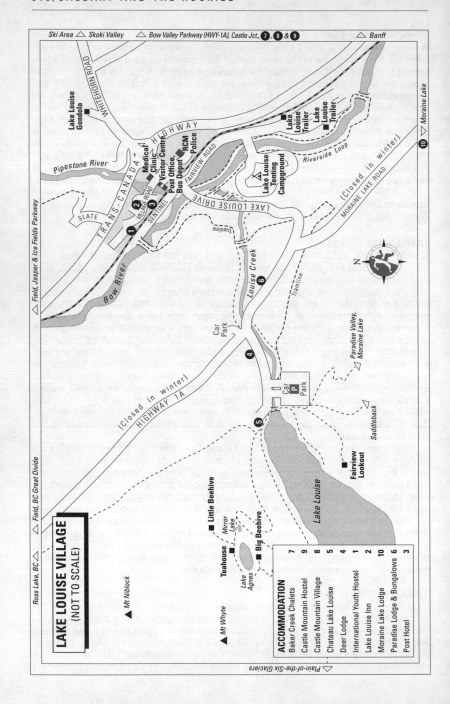

LAKE LOUISE VILLAGE
(NOT TO SCALE)

ACCOMMODATION

Baker Creek Chalets	7
Castle Mountain Hostel	9
Castle Mountain Village	8
Chateau Lake Louise	5
Deer Lodge	4
International Youth Hostel	1
Lake Louise Inn	2
Moraine Lake Lodge	10
Paradise Lodge & Bungalows	6
Post Hotel	3

HIKES AROUND LAKE LOUISE

All the Lake Louise trails are busy in summer, but they're good for a short taste of the scenery. They're also well worn and well marked, so you don't need to be a seasoned hiker or skilled map-reader. The two most popular end at teahouses – mountain chalets selling welcome, but rather pricey, snacks. The signed Lake Agnes Trail (3.4km), said to be the most-walked path in the Rockies (but don't let that put you off), strikes off from the right (north) shore of the lake immediately past the hotel. It's a gradual, 400-metre climb, relieved by ever more magnificent views, and a teahouse beautifully situated beside mountain-cradled Lake Agnes (2135m); allow one to two hours. Beyond the teahouse, if you want more of a walk things quieten down considerably. You can continue on the right side of the lake and curve left around its head to climb to an easily reached pass. Here a 200-metre stroll to the left brings you to Big Beehive (2255m), an incredible eyrie, 1km from the teahouse. Almost as rewarding is the trail, also 1km from the teahouse, to Little Beehive, a mite lower, but still privy to full-blown panoramas over the broad sweep of the Bow Valley.

Keener walkers can return to the pass from Big Beehive and turn left to follow the steep trail down to intersect another trail; turning right leads west through rugged and increasingly barren scenery to the second teahouse at the Plain of the Six Glaciers (2100m). Alternatively, the more monotonous Six Glaciers Trail (leaving out the whole Lake Agnes–Big Beehive section) leads from the hotel along the lakeshore to the same point (5.3km to the teahouse; 365m ascent). However, a better option is to follow the Lake Agnes and Big Beehive route to the Plain, then use the Six Glaciers Trail for the return to *Château Lake Louise*, which neatly ends the day's loop with a downhill stroll and an easy but glorious finale along the shore of Lake Louise (see "Lake Louise Village" map to make sense of what is a pretty straightforward and very well-worn loop).

The main appeal of the last local walk, the less-used Saddleback Trail (3.7km one-way), is that it provides access to the superlative viewpoint of Fairview Mountain. Allow from one to two hours to Saddleback itself (2330m; 595m ascent); the trail to the summit of Fairview (2745m) strikes off right from here. Even if you don't make the last push, the Saddleback views – across to the 1200-metre wall of Mount Temple (3544m) – are staggering. Despite the people, this is one of the park's top short walks.

THE SKOKI VALLEY

The Skoki Valley region east of Lake Louise offers fewer day-hikes; to enjoy it you'll need a tent to overnight at any of the six campgrounds. The main access trail initially follows a gravel road forking off to the right of the Lake Louise Ski Area, off Hwy 1. Many people hike as far as Boulder Pass (2345m), an 8.6-kilometre trek and 640-metre ascent from the parking area, as a day-trip, and return the same way instead of pushing on to the *Lodge*, 8km beyond. Various well-signposted long and short trails from the *Lodge* or the campgrounds are documented in the *Canadian Rockies Trail Guide*.

– you can walk back down to the village). Note that there are also direct Brewster and other connections to and from Lake Louise and Calgary airport. Brewster also run one daily service to Jasper from Lake Louise village and lake ($44; departs Samson Mall at 4.15pm) as well as bus tours on the Icefields Parkway (8hr one-way, $82, $112 return excluding accommodation in Jasper). If you need a taxi to ferry you to the lakes, call Lake Louise Taxi & Tours (☎522-2020). The only **car rental** agency is National at The Depot (☎522-3870), but you're better off renting in Banff or elsewhere as their cars go quickly.

The Samson Mall takes care of most practical considerations including a **post office** (daily 6.30am–7pm; ☎522-3870). Behind The Depot, which doubles up as a bag storage, and booking office for coach tours and river-rafting trips, are a laundrette (☎522-2143) and (downstairs) public washrooms with showers. The general store is good and has a

money exchange. There's also a currency exchange at the *Château Lake Louise* hotel (see opposite). For the **police**, call ☎522-3811. The nearest hospital is in Banff.

Excellent basic **food** – snacks and coffee – can be had at the always busy *Laggan's Mountain Bakery* (daily 6am–7pm) on the corner of the mall opposite the general store. For something more substantial than snacks, wander to the relaxed and reasonably priced *Bill Peyto's Café* for full and varied meals (daily 7am–9pm; ☎522-2200), within the youth hostel but open to all; in summer the nice outdoor eating area makes a good place to meet people. The unique *Lake Louise Station Restaurant* (☎522-2600) is housed in the restored 1909 station building – choose between hearty Canadian fare in the informal station building (garden dining in summer) and the more formal and expensive restored railway dining carriages. Some of the best (and pricier) meals can be found in the *Post Hotel* (daily 7am–2pm & 5–9.30pm; ☎522-3989) – reservations are essential for dinner. The best local's hangout is the hotel's *Outpost Pub* (☎522-3989), a snug **bar** that serves light meals from late afternoon. Other good drinking spots include the *Lake Louise Bar and Grill* (☎522-3879) upstairs in the mall, and the lively *Explorers Lounge* (☎522-3791) in the *Lake Louise Inn*, 210 Village Rd.

ACTIVITIES

As for **activities**, most operators – especially rafting companies – are based in Banff or elsewhere (see p.499), though many offer pick-ups in Lake Louise, typically with a $10 add-on to their listed Banff prices; a handful operate trips directly out of Lake Louise itself. Companies actually based in or near the village include Wild Water Adventures (☎678-5058, 522-2211 or 1-888/771-9453) who run half- or full-day white-water rafting trips on the Kicking Horse River in nearby Yoho National Park (half-day trips at 8.30am and 1.30pm, from $69). If you don't want to hike alone, or wish to know more about what you're walking past, the national park and Friends of Banff run **guided walks** three or four times a week in July and August: the Lake Louise Lakeshore Stroll (Mon & Fri 10am; 2hr) and the Plain of the Six Glaciers (Tues, Thurs & Sun 9am; 6hr; $12). Drop by the visitor centre's Friends of Banff store to confirm latest timings and to reserve a place (do so in good time – the walks are popular – or call ☎522-3833. Cyclists can rent bikes from Wilson Mountain Sports in the mall (see above), or sign up for **cycling tours** (from $55 for half a day, $85 full day) and transfers that'll take you up to Bow Summit on the Icefields Parkway so you can pedal downhill or freewheel all the way back to Lake Louise. Serious canoeists can rent canoes from Wilson for trips on the Bow River, while more sedate paddlers can **rent canoes** and kayaks (daily in summer 10am–7pm; $30 per hour) at Chateau Lake Louise to dabble on Lake Louise itself (☎522-3511).

Good **trout fishing** is possible on the Bow River between Lake Louise and Banff, with support and advice available at the *Castle Mountain Chalets* on the Bow Valley Parkway (see p.503). Rental equipment is again on offer at Wilson Mountain Sports. Compulsory fishing permits ($6 weekly) are available from the visitor centre. If you fancy **horse riding**, contact Brewster Lake Louise Stables at the *Château Lake Louise* hotel (☎522-3511 ext 1210, or 762-5454) and enquire about their ninety-minute trips along the shores of Lake Louise ($45), half-day tours ($60) to Lake Agnes or Plain of the Six Glaciers (see box, overleaf) or full-day treks to Paradise Valley and Horseshoe Glacier ($120 including lunch). Timberline Tours (☎522-3743) run similar if slightly cheaper treks from the Lake Louise Corral behind the *Deer Lodge* hotel; all-day trips to the Skoki Valley east of Lake Louise; one- and three-hour trips at Bow Lake on the Icefields Parkway from the *Num-Ti-Jah Lodge* (see p.517).

ACCOMMODATION

Hotel accommodation in or near Lake Louise Village is pricey all year round – reckon on an average of $160 in most places – and almost certain to be full in summer.

Bookings are virtually essential everywhere (make them direct or through Banff's **reservation services** (see p.491); at the excellent youth hostel, reservations six months in advance are not unusual. The various options on the Bow Valley Parkway, covered in the preceding section, are all within easy driving or cycling distance.

The lovely 220-site park-run **Lake Louise Campground**, close to the village – follow the signs off Fairview Road up to the lake – gets busy in summer. It's open between mid-May and early October, is partially serviced (it has showers), and sites cost $17; no fires. Sites are close together, though the trees offer some privacy, and with the railway close by, it can be noisy. The nearby *Lake Louise Trailer* site is for RVs (year-round; $21).

Canadian Alpine Centre and International Youth Hostel, on Village Rd just north of the mall across the river (☎522-2200, *llouise@hostellingintl.ca*). A modern 150-bed year-round hostel run jointly with the Canadian Alpine Club. Reservations are virtually essential (up to six months in advance) in summer and winter ski weekends. Check-in time is 3pm. ①.

Castle Mountain Youth Hostel, 1.5km east of Castle Junction on Hwy 93 S (☎762-4122, *banff @hostellingintl.ca*). Well-situated for the Bow Valley Parkway and its trails. Sleeps just 36, with bookings possible through the Banff hostel. Dorm beds $13 for members, $17 for non-members. ①.

Château Lake Louise (☎522-3511 or 1-800/441-1414, fax 522-3834) has a monopoly on lakeside accommodation: doubles among its 511 rooms and suites cost up to $579, though in low season (Oct–Dec) some are available for around $100, making it one of the least expensive off-season places in the area. If it's beyond your budget, look inside anyway to check out its bizarre appeal. Booking essential. ⑧.

Deer Lodge, on Lake Louise Drive (☎522-3747 or 1-800/661-1595, fax 522-3883). Cheaper of two near-lake alternatives to *Château Lake Louise*, with a good restaurant and within walking distance of the lake. ⑥.

Lake Louise Inn, 210 Village Rd, just north of the village mall to the right (☎522-3791 or 1-800/661-9237, fax 522-2018, *www.lakelouiseinn.com*). The least expensive of the village hotels with a variety of rooms, some with self-catering facilities. ⑥.

Paradise Lodge and Bungalows, on the Lake Louise Drive a short walk from Lake Louise (☎522-3595, fax 522-3987, *www.ParadiseLodge.com*). Pricier of the near-lake options, but with reasonable off-season rates for its 21 self-contained bungalows and 24 one- and two-bedroom suites (some with kitchens). Mid-May to mid-Oct. ⑥.

Post Hotel, Village Rd (☎522-3989 or 1-800/661-1586, fax 522-3966). The top hotel in the village, with a noted restaurant and bar – see opposite – but expect to pay $300 plus for a room here in summer. ⑧.

The Lake

Before you see **Lake Louise** you see the hotel: *Château Lake Louise*, a monstrosity that would surely never get planning permission today. Yet even so intrusive an eyesore fades into insignificance beside the immense beauty of its surroundings. The lake is Kodachrome turquoise, the mountains sheer, the glaciers vast; the whole ensemble is utter natural perfection. Outfitter Tom Wilson, the first white Canadian to see Lake Louise when he was led here by a local native in 1882, wrote, "I never, in all my explorations of these five chains of mountains throughout western Canada, saw such a matchless scene . . . I felt puny in body, but glorified in spirit and soul."

You can't help wishing you could have been Tom Wilson, and seen the spot unsullied by the hotel and before the arrival of the tourists and general clutter. Around 10,000 daily in peak season come here to gawp (car parks often fill by noon), while notice boards on the waterfront seem obsessed with the profoundly dull account of how the lake came by its name – it was named in honour of the fourth daughter of Queen Victoria. The native name translates as the "Lake of the Little Fishes". Wilson, showing precious little wit, originally called it Emerald Lake, for obvious reasons (clearly lacking any imagination, he coined exactly the same name for the lake he discovered in Yoho; see p.549). More interesting is the account of Hollywood's discovery of the lake in the 1920s, when it was used to suggest "exotic European locations". After Wilson's "discovery" all access was

WINTER IN LAKE LOUISE

In a region already renowned for its **skiing** Lake Louise stands out, regarded by many as among the finest winter resorts in North America. In addition to skiing and snow-boarding, there are hundreds of kilometres of cross-country trails, numerous other winter activities, and landscape that's earned the area the title of "North America's Most Scenic Ski Area" from *Snow Country* magazine. It's also Canada's largest ski area, with over forty square kilometres of trails, plenty of mogul fields, lots of challenging chutes, vast open bowls and some of the best "powder" on the continent.

Skiing started here in the 1920s. The first chalet was built in 1930, the first lift in 1954. The resort's real birth can be dated to 1958, when a rich Englishman, Norman Watson – universally known as the "Barmy Baronet" – ploughed a large part of his inheritance into building a gondola on Mount Whitehorn. Further lifts and other developments followed. More would have materialized had it not been for environmental lobbying. Further protests forestalled a bid for the 1968 Winter Olympics and put an end to a plan for a 6500-bed mega-resort in 1972. Even so, the resort has grown, and now regularly hosts World Cup skiing events. The only drawback are the phenomenally low temperatures during January and February.

The **ski area** divides into five distinct zones (Front Side, South Face, Larch Area, Ptarmigan-Paradise and Back Bowls), served by three express quad chairs, one quad chair, two triple chairs, three double chairs, a T-bar, a platter lift and a children's rope tow. The huge **terrain** – some of the bowls are the size of entire European resorts – divides as follows: Novice (25 percent), Intermediate (45 percent) and Expert (30 percent). Most of the bowls are above the tree line, but you can also ski on Larch and Ptarmigan, whose varied terrain allows you to follow the sun or duck into the trees when the wind's up. Average seasonal snowfall (early Nov to mid-May) is 360cm, and snowmaking is available over much of the area. The top elevation is 2637m, giving a 1000m drop to the base elevation at 1645m. Lift tickets are around $54 a day, but bear in mind that you can invest in the Ski Banff/Lake Louise **Tri-Area Pass**, which you can buy for a minimum of three days ($157) skiing in Lake Louise, Mount Norquay and Sunshine Village (see p.504). **Facilities** in the ski area include three day-lodges, each of which has a restaurant and bar, a ski school, ski shop, rental shop, day care, nursery and lockers. Free shuttles run from Lake Louise, while transfers from Banff cost around $15 return: however, these transfers are included free if you buy the Tri-Area Pass. Free tours of the mountain are also available three times daily. For further **information**, contact Skiing Louise, Suite 505, 1550-8th St SW, Calgary AB T2R 1K1 or Box 5, Lake Louise, AB T0L 1E0 (☎522-3555, fax 522-2095, *www.skilouise.com*). Reservations can be made by calling ☎2-LOUISE (☎256-8473), or toll-free in North America 1-800/258-7669.

Cross-country skiing in Lake Louise is also phenomenal, with plenty of options around the lake itself, on Moraine Lake Road and in the Skoki Valley area north of the village. For **heli-skiing**, contact RK Heli-Ski (☎342-3889) who have a desk in the *Château Lake Louise* hotel (winter daily 4–9pm); one of their shuttle buses leaves from the hotel daily for the two-hour drive to the Purcell Mountains in BC (the region's nearest heli-skiing). The hotel is also the place to hire skates (at Monod Sports) for **ice-skating** on the lake, probably one of the most sublime spots imaginable to indulge in the activity (the lake is floodlit after dark to allow night skating). If you want a **sleigh ride** on the lake shore, contact Brewster Lake Louise Sleigh Rides (☎522-3511 or 762-5454). Rides are reasonably priced and last an hour, but reservations are essential: sleighs depart hourly from 11am on weekends, 3pm on weekdays.

by rail or trail – the station, then known as Laggan, was 6km away. The first hotel appeared in 1890, a simple two-bedroom affair which replaced a tumbledown cabin on the shore. Numerous fires, false starts and additions followed until the present structure made its unwelcome appearance (the final wings were added as recently as 1988). The first road was built in 1926. Be sure to walk here, despite the paths' popularity (see box, p.518). Alternatively, escape the throng – two million people come here each year – by renting an old-style canoe from the office to the left as you face the lake (June–Sept daily 10am–8pm; $30 per hour; maximum of three adults per boat). Don't think about swimming: the water's deep and cold – top temperature in summer is a numbing 4°C.

Moraine Lake

Not quite so many people as visit Lake Louise make the thirteen-kilometre road journey to **Moraine Lake**, which is smaller than its neighbour although in many ways its scenic superior. If you're without your own transport, you'll have to rely on a bike or taxi ($35) to get here or the new park-run "Vista" bus shuttle (daily every 30min from outside the hostel and Lake Louise campground; free on production of park pass). The last has been introduced because of the sheer number of visitors in cars and RVs trying to cram into the tiny car park and clogging the approach road. No wonder they come, for this is one of the great landscapes of the region and has some cracking trails into the bargain (see box, p.518). It also holds one of the most enticing and magnificently executed hotels in the entire Rockies: if you're on honeymoon, or just want to push the boat out once, splash out on a night or two in the *Moraine Lake Lodge* (☎522-3733, *www.morainelake.com*; ⑨; May–Oct), a nicely landscaped collection of high-quality cabins plus eight lodge rooms and six other units designed by eminent architect Arthur Erickson (also responsible for Vancouver's UBC Museum of Anthropology and the Canadian Embassy in Washington DC): cabins are probably best, if only for their open fires. It boasts a friendly staff and great privacy, for prices on a par with decidedly more lacklustre hotels in the village and near Lake Louise.

Bar the *Lodge*, with its good little café and top-notch restaurant, nothing disturbs the lake and its matchless surroundings. Until comparatively recently the scene graced the back of Canadian $20 bills, though the illustration did little justice to the shimmering water and the jagged, snow-covered peaks on the eastern shore that inspired the nickname "Valley of the Ten Peaks". The peaks are now officially christened the Wenkchemna, after the Stoney native word for "ten".

The lake itself, half the size of Lake Louise, is the most vivid **turquoise** imaginable. Like Lake Louise and other big Rockies lakes (notably Peyto on the Icefields Parkway), the peacock blue is caused by fine particles of glacial silt, or till, known as rock flour. Meltwater in June and July washes this powdered rock into the lake, the minute but uniform particles of flour absorbing all colours of incoming light except those in the blue–green spectrum. When the lakes have just melted in May and June – and are still empty of silt – their colour is a more normal sky blue. You can admire the lake by walking along the east shore, from above by clambering over the great glacial moraine dam near the lodge (though the lake was probably created by a rock fall rather than glaciation), or from one of the **canoes for rent** on the right just beyond the *Lodge* and car park. For the best overall perspective, tackle the switchback trail through the forest on the east shore (see box, p.518), but check with the visitor centre at Lake Louise for the latest on bear activity – a young grizzly has made the Moraine Lake region its home, and areas are sometimes closed to avoid its coming in contact with humans.

The Icefields Parkway

The splendour of the **Icefields Parkway** (Hwy 93) can hardly be overstated: a 230-kilometre road from Lake Louise to Jasper through the heart of the Rockies, it ranks as one of the world's ultimate drives. Its unending succession of huge peaks, immense glaciers, iridescent lakes, wild-flower meadows, wildlife and forests – capped by the stark grandeur of the Columbia Icefield – is absolutely overwhelming. Fur traders and natives who used the route as far back as 1800 reputedly christened it the "Wonder Trail", though in practice they tended to prefer the Pipestone River Valley to the east, a

PARKWAY HOSTELS

Five **youth hostels** (four open year-round) and twelve excellent park **campgrounds** (two year-round) are spaced along the Parkway at regular intervals. It's essential to book the hostels, either direct if they have contact details, or through the hostel at Banff or online at *www.hostellingintl.ca/alberta*. As ever, the frontcountry park campgrounds are available on a first-come, first-served basis. If you want more comfort, you'll have to overnight at Banff, Lake Louise or Jasper, as the only other accommodation – invariably booked solid – are hotels at Bow Lake, Saskatchewan Crossing, the Columbia Icefield and Sunwapta Falls.

The **Summer Hostel Shuttle** (early-June to Sept) runs an extremely useful shuttle service, connecting twelve youth hostels between (and including) Calgary, Banff and Jasper – as well as all the places on the Icefields Parkway and beyond. Shuttles currently depart daily Calgary–Lake Louise–Calgary (leaves Calgary 8.30am, leaves Lake Louise 1pm for Banff, Calgary and Calgary Airport); Sat only Jasper–Lake Louise–Jasper round trip (leaves Jasper 8.30am, leaves Lake Louise 1.30pm); Mon, Wed and Fri at 1pm Lake Louise–Jasper; and Sun, Tues and Thurs Jasper–Lake Louise (8.30am).

Typical fares are $90 for Calgary to Maligne Canyon (Jasper), the longest possible journey, and $25 for the trip between Lake Louise and *Hilda Creek* hostel near the Columbia Icefield. Banff to Lake Louise is $12, Banff to *Jasper International Hostel* $57, and Lake Louise to Jasper $45. Extra fees are payable for bikes (Calgary to Banff costs $10), canoes and other cargo.

For information, call ☎283-5551 or 1-800/248-3837. To make bookings for the shuttle, contact *Banff International* (☎762-4122), Calgary (☎269-8239), Lake Louise (☎522-2200) or Jasper (☎1-877/852-0781). Current fares and schedules can also be found at *www.hostellingintl.ca/alberta/transport*. For hostels book no later than 6pm the day before your desired departure with full details of your journey. Once the hostel has confirmed your booking, buy a ticket from any participating Alberta hostel, confirming the shuttle's departure time at the time of purchase. From hostels with phones, use the toll-free number to make enquiries; at those without, reservations can usually be made through the manager. Stand-by tickets may be bought from the van driver at departure, subject to availability. All passengers must have reservations at their destination hostel.

route that avoided the swamps and other hazards of the Bow Valley. Jim Brewster made the first recorded complete trek along the road's future route in 1904. The present highway was only completed in 1939 and opened in 1940 as part of a Depression-era public-works programme. Although about a million people a year make the journey to experience what the park blurb calls a "window on the wilderness", for the most part you can go your own way in relative serenity.

After 122km, at about its midway point, the Icefields Parkway crosses from Banff into Jasper National Park (about a 2hr drive); you might turn back here, but the divide is almost completely arbitrary, and most people treat the Parkway as a self-contained journey, as we do here. Distances in brackets are from Lake Louise, which is virtually the only way to locate places on the road, though everything mentioned is clearly marked off the highway by distinctive brown-green national park signs. Pick up the Parks Canada *In the Shadow of the Great Divide* pamphlet from visitor centres for a detailed map and summary of all the sights and trailheads. You could drive the whole highway in about four hours, but to do so would be to miss out on the panoply of short (and long) trails, viewpoints and the chance just to soak up the incredible scenery.

Access, transport and accommodation

Tourist literature often misleadingly gives the impression that the Icefields Parkway is highly developed. In fact, the wilderness is extreme, with snow often closing the road from October onwards, and there are only two points for **services**, at Saskatchewan

Crossing (the one place campers can stock up with groceries, 77km from Lake Louise), where the David Thompson Highway (Hwy 11) branches off for Red Deer, and at the Columbia Icefield (127km).

Brewster Transportation (☎762-6767) runs several tours and a single scheduled bus daily in both directions between Banff or Lake Louise and Jasper from late May to mid-October ($51 one-way from Banff, $44 from Lake Louise), though services at either end of the season are often weather-affected. A word with the driver will usually get you dropped off at hostels and trailheads en route. If you're **cycling** – an increasingly popular way to tackle the journey – note that the grades are far more favourable if you travel from Jasper to Banff (Jasper's 500m higher than Banff).

Between Lake Louise and the Columbia Icefield

One of the biggest problems in the Rockies is knowing what to see and where to walk among the dozens of possible trails and viewpoints. The Parkway is no exception. The following are the must-sees and must-dos along the 122-kilometre stretch of the Parkway from Lake Louise to the Columbia Icefield: best view – Peyto Lake (unmissable); best lake walk – Bow Lake; best waterfalls – Panther–Bridal Falls; best quick stroll – Mistaya Canyon; best short walk – Parker Ridge; best walk if you do no other – Wilcox Pass. Temptations for longer walks are numerous, and the difficulty, as ever, is knowing which to choose.

The first **youth hostel** north of Lake Louise is *Mosquito Creek* (28km), four log cabins which sleep 38 and have basic food supplies, a kitchen, large common room and a wood-fired sauna (no phone, reservations ☎762-4122; $13 members, $17 non-members; year-round, but closure dates may apply; check in 5–11pm). Slightly beyond is the first park **campground**, *Mosquito Creek* ($10: mid-June to mid-Sept; 32 sites; water and dry toilets, but no other facilities) and one of the Parkway's two winter campgrounds (free after mid-Sept; 32 walk-in sites only). You're near the Bow River flats here, and the mosquitoes, as the campground name suggests, can be a torment. Two hikes start from close to the site: **Molar Pass** (9.8km; 535m ascent; 3hr), a manageable day-trip with good views, and **Upper Fish Lake** (14.8km; 760m ascent; 5hr), which follows the Molar Pass trail for 7km before branching off and crossing the superb alpine meadows of North Molar Pass (2590m).

On the *Num-Ti-Jah Lodge* access road just beyond (37km), a great short trail sets off from beside the lodge to **Bow Lake** and **Bow Glacier Falls** (4.3km; 155m ascent; 1–2hr), taking in the flats around Bow Lake – one of the Rockies' most beautiful – and climbing to some immense cliffs and several huge waterfalls beyond (the trail proper ends at the edge of the moraine after 3.4km, but it's possible to pick your way through the boulders to reach the foot of the falls 900m beyond). If you don't want to walk, take a break instead at the picnic area on the waterfront at the southeast end of the lake. The *Num-Ti-Jah Lodge* itself, just off the road, is one of the most famous old-fashioned lodges in the Rockies, built in 1920 by legendary guide and outfitter Jimmy Simpson (who lived here until 1972). It's the only privately owned freehold in the park – all other land and property is federally owned and leased; be sure to book well in advance to have any chance of securing a room (☎522-2167; ⑥; May–Sept). There's a **coffee shop** here if you need a break, or want to admire the *Lodge*'s strange octagonal structure, forced on Jimmy because he wanted a large building but only had access locally to short timbers. You aren't allowed in the lodge (so guests can enjoy their privacy), but you can take dinner here, or sign up for **horse riding** with Timberline Tours (☎522-3743), available to residents and non-residents alike: rides include a one-hour trip to Bow Lake; a three-hour ride to Peyto Lake (see below); and a full-day excursion to Helen Lake.

Another 3km up the Parkway comes the pass at Bow Summit, source of the Bow River, the waterway that flows through Banff, Lake Louise and Calgary. (At 2069m, this

MORAINE LAKE AND PARADISE VALLEY

MORAINE LAKE

Each of the four basic routes in the **Moraine Lake** area is easily accomplished in a day or less, two with sting-in-the-tail additions if you want added exertion; all start from the lake, which lies at the end of thirteen-kilometre Moraine Lake Road from just outside Lake Louise Village. Before hiking, check with the visitor centre in Lake Louise on the latest restrictions imposed to protect both the bears known to have made the area part of their territory as well as the tourists who hope to catch a glimpse of them. Currently, walks in the Larch Valley and around are restricted. You must walk in groups of at least six people (there are often people waiting to join a group, so you should have no trouble making up the numbers).

The easiest walk is the one-kilometre amble along the lakeshore – hardly a walk at all – followed by the three-kilometre stroll to Consolation Lake, an hour's trip that may be busy but can provide some respite from the frenzy at Moraine Lake itself. This almost level walk ends with lovely views of a small mountain-circled lake, its name coined by an early explorer who thought it a reward and "consolation" for the desolation of the valley which led up to it. If you're tenting, fairly fit, or can arrange a pick-up, the highline Panorama Ridge Trail (2255m) branches off the trail (signed "Taylor Lake") to run 22km to the Banff–Radium highway 7km west of Castle Junction.

The most popular walk (start as early as possible) is the Moraine Lake–Larch Valley–Sentinel Pass Trail, one of the Rockies' premier hikes, which sets off from the lake's north shore 100m beyond the lodge. A stiffish hairpin climb through forest on a broad track, with breathtaking views of the lake through the trees, brings you to a trail junction after 2.4km and some 300m of ascent. Most hikers branch right, where the track levels off to emerge into Larch Valley, broad alpine upland with stands of larch (glorious in late summer and fall) and majestic views of the encircling peaks. If you have the energy, push on to Sentinel Pass ahead, in all some two-hours' walk and 720m above Moraine Lake. At 2605m, this, along with the Wenkchemna Pass, is the highest point reached by a major trail in the Canadian Rockies. You can see what you're in for from the meadows – but not the airy views down into Paradise Valley from the crest of the pass itself. You could even continue down into Paradise Valley, a tough, scree-filled descent,

---

is the highest point crossed by any Canadian highway.) Just beyond is the unmissable twenty-minute stroll to **Peyto Lake Lookout** (1.4km; elevation loss 100m) one of the finest vistas in the Rockies (signed from the road). The quite beautiful panorama only unfolds in the last few seconds, giving a genuinely breathtaking view of the vivid emerald lake far below; mountains and forest stretch away as far as you can see. Another 3km along the Parkway lies a viewpoint for the Peyto Glacier, part of the much larger Wapta Icefield.

After 57km you reach the *Waterfowl Lakes* **campground** (116 sites; $13; mid-June to mid-Sept) and the **Chephren Lake Trail** (3.5km; 80m ascent; 1hr), which leads to quietly spectacular scenery with a minimum of effort. The next pause, 14km further on, is the **Mistaya Canyon Trail**, a short but interesting 300-metre breather of a stroll along a river-gouged "slot" canyon: *mistaya*, incidentally, is a Cree word meaning "grizzly bear".

SASKATCHEWAN CROSSING (77km) is the lowest point on the road before the icefields; the 700-metre descent from Bow Summit brings you from the high subalpine ecoregion into a montane environment with its own vegetation and wildlife. Largely free of snow, the area is a favourite winter range for mountain goats, bighorn sheep and members of the deer family. The bleak settlement itself offers expensive food (restaurant and cafeteria), gas, a spectacularly tacky gift shop and a 66-room **hotel-restaurant**, *Crossing*, that is surprisingly comfy (early March to mid-Nov; ☎761-7000; ⑤).

and complete an exceptional day's walk by picking up the valley loop (see below) back to the Moraine Lake Road. Otherwise return to the 2.4-kilometre junction and, if legs are still willing – you'll have done most of the hard climbing work already – think about tagging on the last part of the third Moraine Lake option.

This third option, the less-walked Moraine Lake–Eiffel Lake–Wenkchemna Pass Trail, follows the climb from the lake as for the Larch Valley path before branching off left instead of right at the 2.4-kilometre junction. It's equally sound, virtually level, and if anything has the better scenery (if only because less barren than Sentinel Pass) in the stark, glaciated grandeur to be found at the head of the Valley of the Ten Peaks. It's also much quieter once you're beyond the trail junction. At 2255m, Eiffel Lake is a 5.6-kilometre hike and 370-metre climb in total (allow 2–3hr) from Moraine Lake, and you don't need to go much further than the rock pile and clump of trees beyond the lake to get the best out of the walk. Ahead of you, however, a slightly rougher track continues through bleak terrain to Wenkchemna Pass (2605m), clearly visible 4km beyond. Having got this far, it's tempting to push on; the extra 350-metre climb is just about worth it, if lungs and weather are holding out, for the still broader views back down the Valley of the Ten Peaks. The views beyond the pass itself, however, over the Great Divide into Yoho and Kootenay parks, are relatively disappointing.

PARADISE VALLEY

In 1894, the mountaineer Walter Wilcox deemed **Paradise Valley** an appropriate name for "a valley of surpassing beauty, wide and beautiful, with alternating open meadows and rich forests". North of Moraine Lake, it's accessed via Moraine Lake Road about 3km from its junction with Lake Louise Drive. The walk here is a fairly straightforward hike up one side of the valley and down the other, a loop of 18km with a modest 385m of vertical gain. Most people take in the Lake Annette diversion for its unmatched view of Mount Temple's 1200-metre north face (unclimbed until 1966), and many overnight at the campground at the head of the valley (9km from the parking area), though this is one of the busiest sites in the park. Others toughen the walk by throwing in the climb up to Sentinel Pass on the ridge south of the valley, which gives the option of continuing down the other side to connect with the Moraine Lake trails (see above).

Twelve kilometres north are the *Rampart Creek* thirty-bed **youth hostel**, with two cabins and the "the best sauna in the Rockies" (☎439-3139 or through Banff, Lake Louise or Calgary hostels; $13 members, $17 non-members; June–Oct open all day, check in 5–11pm; Nov–May Sat & Sun only with reservations), with a basic food store, and a fifty-pitch park-run **campground** ($10; late June to early Sept). Apparently this area is one of the best black-bear habitats close to the road anywhere in the park. The last of the Banff National Park campgrounds is the tiny sixteen-pitch *Cirrus Mountain* site at the 103-kilometre mark ($10; late June to early Sept), but its position is precarious, so check it's open before planning a stay (☎762-1550).

Shortly before the spectacular **Panther Falls** (113.5km) the road makes a huge hairpin climb (the so-called "Big Hill"), to open up yet more panoramic angles on the vast mountain spine stretching back towards Lake Louise. The unmarked and often slippery one-kilometre trail to the falls starts from the lower end of the second of two car parks on the right. Beyond it (117km) is the trailhead to **Parker Ridge** (2.4km one-way; elevation gain 210m; allow 1hr one-way, less for the return), which, at 2130m, commands fantastic views from the summit ridge of the Saskatchewan Glacier (at 9km, the Rockies' longest). If you're only going to do one walk after the Peyto Lake Lookout (see opposite), make it this one: it gets cold and windy up here, so bring extra clothing. Ideally placed for this area and the Columbia Icefield 9km north is the busy *Hilda Creek* **youth hostel** (☎439-3139 or 762-4122; $12 members, $16 non-members; check-in

5–11pm) 1km beyond. The setting is stunning and accommodation (for 21) is in cosy log cabins. Nearby Sunwapta Pass (2023m) marks the border between Banff and Jasper national parks and the watershed of the North Saskatchewan and Sunwapta rivers: the former flows into the Atlantic, the latter into the Arctic Ocean. From here it's another 108km to Jasper.

The Columbia Icefield

Covering an area of 325 square kilometres, the **Columbia Icefield** is the largest collection of ice and snow in the entire Rockies, and the largest glacial area in the northern hemisphere south of the Arctic Circle. It's also the most accessible of some seventeen glacial areas along the Parkway. Meltwater flows from it into the Arctic, Atlantic and Pacific oceans, forming a so-called "hydrological apex" – the only other one in the world is in Siberia. This is fed by six major glaciers, three of which – the Athabasca, Dome and Stutfield – are partially visible from the highway. The ugly and extremely busy **Icefield Centre** (daily: May to early June & Sept to mid-Oct 9am–5pm; early June to Aug 9am–6pm; ☎780/852-6288) provides an eerie viewpoint for the most prominent of these, the Athabasca Glacier, as well as offering the Parks Canada Exhibit

---

BEARS

Two types of **bears** roam the Rockies – black bears and grizzlies – and you don't want to meet either. They're not terribly common in these parts (sightings are all monitored and posted at park centres) and risks are pretty low on heavily tramped trails, but if you're camping or walking it's still essential to be vigilant, obey basic rules, know the difference between a black bear and a grizzly (the latter are bigger and have a humped neck), know how to avoid dangerous encounters, and understand what to do if confronted or attacked. Popular misconceptions about bears abound – that they can't climb trees, for example (they can, and very quickly) – so it's worth picking up the parks service's pamphlet *You are in Bear Country*, which cuts through the confusion and lays out some occasionally eye-opening procedures. Be prepared, and if you don't want to be attacked, follow the cardinal rules: store food and garbage properly, make sure bears know you're there, don't approach or feed them, and, if you find yourself approached by one, don't scream and don't run.

When hiking, walk in a group – bears rarely attack more than four in a group – and make noise, lots of it, as you traverse the wilderness; bears are most threatened if surprised, so warning of your approach will give them time to leave the area. Many people shout, rattle cans with stones in or carry a whistle; be warned, the widely touted hand-held, tinkling bells are not loud enough. Be especially alert and noisy when close to streams, in tall vegetation, crossing avalanche slopes or when travelling into the wind, as your scent won't carry to warn bears of your approach: move straight away from dead animals and berry patches, which are important food sources. Watch for bear signs – get out quick if you see fresh tracks, diggings and droppings – and keep in the open as much as possible.

Camp away from rushing water, paths and animal trails, and keep the site scrupulously clean, leaving nothing hanging around in the open. Lock food and rubbish in a car, or hang it well away from a tent between two trees at least 4m above ground (many campgrounds have bear poles or steel food boxes). Take all rubbish away – don't bury it (bears'll just dig it up) and certainly don't store it in or near the tent. Avoid smelly foods, all fresh, dried or tinned meat and fish, and never store food, cook or eat in or near the tent – lingering smells may invite unwanted nocturnal visits. Aim to cook at least 50m downwind of the tent: freeze-dried meals and plastic-bag-sealed food is best. Likewise, keep food off clothes and sleeping bags, and sleep in clean clothes at night. Bears have an acute sense of smell, so avoid *anything* strongly scented – cosmetics, deodorant, shampoo, gel, lip balm, insect repellents, toothpaste, sun screen. Bears can be attracted

Hall and information and slide shows on the glaciers and Canada's most extensive cave system – the Castleguard Caves, which honeycomb the ice but are inaccessible to the public. This is not a place to linger, however, thanks to the legions of people and dozens of tour buses.

You can walk up to the toe of the **Athabasca Glacier** from the parking area at Sunwapta Lake, noting en route the date-markers, which illustrate just how far the glacier has retreated (1.5km in the last 100 years). You can also walk onto the glacier, but shouldn't, as it's riddled with crevasses. Fall in one of these and you probably won't be climbing out. People are killed and injured every year on the glacier: even a slip can rip off great slivers of skin; the effect of sediment frozen into the ice is to turn the glacier surface into a vast and highly abrasive piece of sandpaper. Full-scale expeditions are the preserve of experts but you can join an **organized trip**. Brewster's special "Snocoaches" run ninety-minute, five-kilometre rides over the glacier with a chance to get out and walk safely on the ice (daily: every 15min: early May to Sept 9am–5pm; Oct 10am–4pm depending on weather; $25.95; book tickets at the Centre or call ☎403/762-6767 or 762-6735 in Banff, 403/522-3544 in Lake Louise, 870/852-3544 in Jasper, toll-free 1-877/ICE RIDE). They're heavily subscribed, so aim to avoid the peak midday rush by

to women during menstruation, so dispose of tampons in an airtight container; they're also attracted by the smell of sex, so watch what you do in your tent if you don't want a rather drastic coitus interruptus.

Bears are unpredictable, and experts simply can't agree on best tactics: there's no guaranteed life-saving way of coping with an aggressive bear. Calm behaviour, however, has proved to be the most successful strategy in preventing an attack after an encounter. Bears don't actually want to attack; they simply want to know you're not a threat. Mothers with cubs are particularly dangerous and prone to suspicion. A bear moving towards you can be considered to have it in for you, other signs being whoofing noises, snapping jaws, and the head down and ears back. A bear raised on its hind legs and sniffing is trying to identify you: if it does it frequently, though, it's getting agitated; ideally, on first encounter you want first to stand stock still, never engage in direct eye contact (perceived as aggressive by the bear) and – absurd as it sounds – start speaking to it in low tones. Whatever you do, don't run, which simply sets off an almost inevitable predator-prey response in the bear (a bear can manage 61kph – that's easily faster than a racehorse or the fastest Olympic sprinter); instead, back away quietly and slowly at the first encounter, speaking gently all the while to the bear. If the backing off seems to be working, then make a wide detour, leave the area or wait for the bear to do so – and always leave it an escape route. If things still look ominous, set your pack gently on the ground as a distraction as you continue to back away.

If you're attacked, things are truly grim, and quack tactics are unlikely to help you. With grizzlies, playing dead – curling up in a ball, protecting face, neck and abdomen – may be effective. Fighting back will only increase the ferocity of a grizzly attack, and there's no way you're going to win. Keep your elbows in to prevent the bear rolling you over, and be prepared to keep the position for a long time until the bear gets bored. You may get one good cuff and a few minutes' attention and that's it – injuries may still be severe but you'll probably live. With a black bear the playing dead routine won't wash, though they're not as aggressive as grizzlies, and a good bop to the nose or sufficient frenzy on your part will sometimes send a black bear running: it's worth a try. Don't play dead with either species if the bear stalks or attacks while you're sleeping: this is more dangerous, as bears are often after food. Instead, try and get away or intimidate – people who have survived such attacks have often had a brave companion who has attacked the bear in return with something big and heavy.

Chemical repellents are available, but of unproven efficacy, and in a breeze you're likely to miss or catch the spray yourself. If this all sounds too scary to make you even contemplate walking or camping, remember that attacks are very rare.

taking a tour before 10.30am or after 3pm. More dedicated types can sign up for the Athabasca Glacier ice walks (3hr walks mid-June to early Sept daily at 11.30pm, $31; 5hr walks Thurs & Sun 11.30am; $37), led by licensed guides. Call ☎780/852-6550 or 852-5595 or 1-800/565-6735 for details, or sign up on the spot at the front desk of the Icefields Centre – be sure to bring warm clothes, boots and provisions.

The 32-room *Columbia Icefields Chalet* (☎852-6550; ⑤–⑦) provides excellent but much-sought-after **accommodation** in the Icefields Centre between May and mid-October (note that lower rates apply in May and Oct). Brewster bus services between Jasper and Banff stop here: it's possible to take a Banff-bound Brewster bus out of Jasper at lunchtime (arrives at the Icefields at 3pm), see the Icefield, and pick up the evening Jasper-bound bus (leaves Icefield at 6.30pm) later the same day.

Two unserviced but very popular **campgrounds** lie 2km and 3km south of the Icefield Centre respectively: the tent-only 33-site *Columbia Icefield* ($10; mid-May to mid-Oct, or until the first snow), and the 46-site *Wilcox Creek*, which takes tents and RVs ($10; early June to mid-Sept). This latter is also the trailhead for one of the very **finest hikes** in the national park, never mind the highway: the **Wilcox Pass Trail** (4km one-way; 335m ascent; allow 2hr round trip), highly recommended by the park centres and just about every trail guide going. The path takes you steeply through thick spruce and alpine fir forest before emerging suddenly onto a ridge that offers vast views over the Parkway and the high peaks of the icefield (including Mount Athabasca). Beyond, the trail enters a beautiful spread of meadows, tarns and creeks, an area many people choose to halt at or wander all day without bothering to reach the pass itself. You could extend the walk to 11km by dropping from the pass to Tangle Creek further along the parkway.

Beyond the Columbia Icefield

If there's a change **beyond the Columbia Icefield**, it's a barely quantifiable lapse in the scenery's awe-inspiring intensity over the 108-kilometre stretch towards Jasper. As the road begins a gradual descent the peaks retreat slightly, taking on more alpine and less dramatic profiles in the process. Yet the scenery is still magnificent, though by this point you're likely to be in the advanced stages of landscape fatigue. It's worth holding on, though, for two good short trails at Sunwapta and Athabasca falls.

Seventeen kilometres beyond the icefield is the 24-berth, two-cabin *Beauty Creek* **youth hostel** (reservations through *Jasper International Hostel* ☎780/852-3215; $10 members, $15 non-members; May–Sept; hostel open all day but check-in 5–11pm; partial closure possible Oct–April). Nine kilometres further is the unserviced 25-site *Jonas Creek* **campground** ($10; mid-May to first snowfall).

A one-kilometre gravel spur leads off the highway to **Sunwapta Falls** (175km from Banff, 55km from Jasper), fifteen-minutes' walk through the woods from the road: they're not terribly dramatic unless in spate, but are interesting for the deep canyon they've cut through the surrounding valley. A short trail along the riverbank leads to more rapids and small falls downstream. If you want to put up nearby, the 35-pitch *Honeymoon Lake* **campground** with kitchen shelter, swimming and dry toilets is 4km further along the parkway ($10; mid-June to first snowfall).

The last main stop before you're in striking distance of Jasper Townsite, **Athabasca Falls** (30km from Jasper) are impressive enough, but the platforms and paths show the strain caused by thousands of feet, making it hard to feel you're any longer in wilderness. One kilometre away, however, is the excellent *Athabasca Falls* **youth hostel** (☎852-5959, reservations through *Jasper International Hostel* ☎852-3215; $11 members, non-members $16; hostel open all day, but check-in 5–11pm), with forty beds in three cabins. Three kilometres back down the road is the 42-site *Mount Kerkeslin* **campground**, with swimming, kitchen shelter and dry toilets, spread over a tranquil riverside site ($10; mid-June to early Sept).

The telephone code for Jasper and Jasper National Park is ☎780.

Highway 93A, the route of the old Parkway, branches off the Icefields Parkway at Athabasca Falls and runs parallel to it for 30km. This alternative route has less dramatic views than the Parkway, as dense trees line the road, but the chances of spotting wildlife are higher.

Jasper National Park

Although traditionally viewed as the second-ranking of the Rockies' big four parks after Banff, **JASPER NATIONAL PARK** covers an area greater than Banff, Yoho and Kootenay combined (10,878 square kilometres), and looks and feels far wilder and less commercialized than its southern counterparts. Its backcountry is more extensive and less travelled, and **Jasper Townsite** (or Jasper), the only settlement, is more relaxed and far less of a resort than Banff and has just half Banff's population. Most pursuits centre on Jasper and the **Maligne Lake** area about 50km southeast of the townsite. Other key zones are **Maligne Canyon**, on the way to the lake; the Icefields Parkway (covered in the previous section); and the **Miette Hot Springs** region, an area well to the east of Jasper and visited for its springs and trails.

The park's **backcountry** is a vast hinterland scattered with countless rough camp-grounds and a thousand-kilometre trail system considered among the best in the world

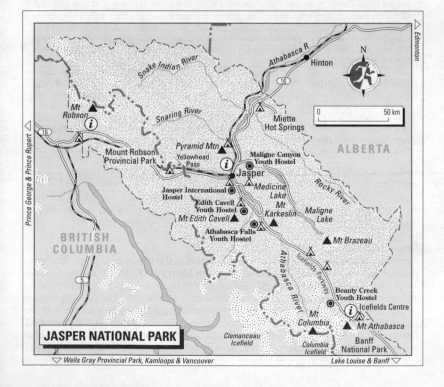

HIKING IN JASPER NATIONAL PARK

DAY-HIKES

If you haven't travelled to Jasper on the Icefields Parkway, remember that several of the national park's top trails can be accessed from this road: the Wilcox Pass Trail in particular, is one of the finest half-day hikes anywhere in the Rockies. If you just want a simple stroll closer to town, then think about walking the Old Fort Point Loop (see p.534), the Maligne Canyon (see p.536) and the easy path on the eastern shore of Maligne Lake (see p.536). If you're at Maligne Lake and want a longer walk, one of Jasper's best day-hikes, the Opal Hills Circuit (8.2km round trip, 460m vertical ascent), starts from the picnic area to the left of the uppermost Maligne Lake car park, 48km east of Jasper. After a heart-pumping haul up the first steep slopes, the trail negotiates alpine meadows and offers sweeping views of the lake before reaching an elevation of 2160m; the trip takes about four hours, but you could easily spend all day loafing around the meadows. The Bald Hills Trail (5.2km one-way; 480m ascent) starts with a monotonous plod along a fire road from the same car park, but ends with what Mary Schaffer, one of the area's first white explorers, described as "the finest view any of us had ever beheld in the Rockies"; allow four hours for the round trip, which goes as high as 2170m.

To get to the trailhead for another outstanding day-hike, Cavell Meadows (3.8km one way; 370m ascent), which is named after a British nurse who was executed for helping the Allies during World War I, drive, cycle or taxi 7.5km south on the Icefields Parkway, then 5km along Hwy 93A and finally 14km up Mount Edith Cavell Road; there's a daily shuttle bus from Jasper and it takes bikes so you can ride back down. Note that if you're driving, an alternating one-way system has been instigated to reduce traffic flow up Mount Edith Cavell Road every day between 10am to 9.30pm between mid-June and mid-October: contact the park information centre for latest timings. The walk's scenery is mixed and magnificent – but the hike is popular, so don't expect solitude. As well as Cavell's alpine meadows, there are views of Angel Glacier and the dizzying north wall of Mount Edith Cavell. Allow two hours for the round trip; the maximum elevation reached is a breathless 2135m.

Further afield – you'll need transport – another superlative short, sharp walk starts from Miette Hot Springs, 58km northeast of Jasper. The Sulphur Skyline (4km one-way, 700m ascent) offers exceptional views of knife-edged ridges, deep gorges, crags and remote valleys. Be sure to take water with you, and allow two hours each way for the steep climb to 2070m. The trailhead is signed from the Miette Hot Springs complex, reached from Jasper by heading 41km east on Hwy 16 and then 17km south; in the past the shuttles have made the trip in summer – check latest timetables. More soothing,

for backpackers. Opportunities for day and half-day hikes are more limited and scattered than in other parks. Most of the shorter strolls from the townsite are just low-level walks to forest-circled lakes; the best of the more exciting day-hikes start from more remote points off the Maligne Lake road, Icefields Parkway (Hwy 93) and Yellowhead Highway (Hwy 16).

Some History

Permanent settlement first came to the Jasper area in the winter of 1810–11. The great explorer and trader David Thomson left **William Henry** at Old Fire Point (just outside the present townsite), while he and his companions pushed on up the valley to blaze a trail over the Athabasca Pass that would be used for more than fifty years by traders crossing the Rockies. In the meantime, Henry established **Henry House**, the first permanent European habitation in the Rockies (though its exact location has been lost). Two years later the North West Company established Jasper House at the eastern edge of the park's present boundary. Named after Jasper Hawes, a long-time company clerk there, it moved closer to Jasper Lake in 1829, when the North West and Hudson's Bay

and a good way to round off a day, are the springs themselves, the hottest in the Rockies – so hot in fact they have to be cooled for swimming; there's one pool for soaking, another for swimming, with massages by appointment and not included in pass price (mid-June to early Sept daily 8.30am–10.30pm, $5.50 or $7.75 day-pass; mid-May to mid-June and early Sept to mid-Oct daily 10.30am–9pm, $4.50 or $7 day-pass; ☎866-3939 or 1-800/767-1611, *www.parkscanada.gc.ca/hotsprings/*). You can hire bathing suits, towels and lockers for an extra $3–5. Other trails from the springs make for the Fiddle River (4.3km one-way; 275m ascent) and Mystery Lake (10.5km one-way; 475m ascent).

BACKPACKING TRAILS

Jasper's system of backpacking trails and 111 backcountry campgrounds makes it one of the leading areas for backcountry hiking in North America. To stay overnight in the backcountry, pick up a Wilderness Permit ($6) within 24 hours of your departure, from the park information centre in Jasper Townsite or at the Columbia Icefield. All trails and campgrounds operate quota systems; contact the park information office for details and book yourself a backcountry campground(s) – and thus trail place – as soon as you can. Reservations cost $10 (non-refundable). Trails remain busy even into September: the busiest are Skyline, Maligne Lake, Brazeau and Tonquin Valley.

The office staff offer invaluable advice, and issue excellent low-price strip maps of several trails. Overnight hikes are beyond the scope of this book – talk to staff or get hold of a copy of *The Canadian Rockies Trail Guide* – but by general consent the finest long-distance trails are the Skyline (44km; 820m ascent) and Jonas Pass (19km; 555m ascent), with the latter often combined with the Nigel and Poboktan passes (total 36km; 750m ascent) to make a truly outstanding walk. Not far behind come two hikes in the Tonquin Valley – Astoria River (19km; 445m ascent) and Maccarib Pass (21km; 730m ascent) and the Fryat Valley (3–4 days). Others to consider are Maligne Pass and the long-distance North and South Boundary trails (the latter both over 160km). To summarize, a quick guide to the best walks in Jasper at a glance:

- Best stroll: Maligne Canyon
- Best short walk: Wilcox Pass (see p.522)
- Best day-hike (easy): Cavell Meadows
- Best day-hike (moderate): Opal Hills
- Best day-hike (strenuous): Sulphur Skyline
- Best backpacking trail: Skyline Trail

companies were amalgamated. By 1880, and the collapse of the fur trade, the post had closed. At the turn of the century the entire region boasted just seven homesteads.

Like other parks and their townsites, Jasper traces its real origins to the coming of the railway at the turn of the century. The Canadian Pacific had brought boom to Banff and Yoho in 1885 when it spurned a route through the Jasper region in favour of a more southerly route (see "Field", p.542). The **Grand Trunk Pacific Railway** hoped for similar successes in attracting visitors when it started to push its own route west in 1902, and the Jasper Forest Park was duly created in 1908. The government bought up all land locally except for the homestead of Lewis Swift, which remained in stubborn private hands until 1962: the town is now "run" by Parks Canada. By 1911 a tent city known as **Fitzhugh**, named after the company's vice president, had grown up on Jasper's present site, and the name "Jasper" was adopted when the site was officially surveyed. Incredibly, a second railway, the **Canadian Northern** (CNR), was completed almost parallel to the Grand Trunk line in 1913, the tracks at some points running no more than a few metres apart. Within just three years, the line's redundancy became obvious and consolidation took place west of Edmonton, with the most favourably graded portions of the two routes being adopted. The ripped-up rails were then shipped to Europe and used in World War I and Jasper became a centre of operations for the lines in 1924, greatly boosting its importance and population. The first tourist accommodation here was ten tents on the shores of Lac Beauvert, replaced in 1921 by the first *Jasper Lake Lodge*, forerunner of the present hotel. The first road link from Edmonton was completed in 1928. Official national park designation came in 1930. Today Jasper's still a rail town, with around a third of the population employed by the CNR.

Arrival

Where Banff's strength is its convenience from Calgary, Jasper's is its ease of **access** from Edmonton, with plenty of transport options and approaches, as well as a wide range of onward destinations. **Driving** time from Edmonton (362km) or Banff (287km) is around four hours; from Kamloops (443km) and Calgary (414km) it's about five or six hours. Vancouver is 863km or a 9hr 30min drive away.

Greyhound (☎852-3926 or 1-800/661-8747) runs four **buses** daily from Edmonton (4hr 45min; $49.49 one-way) along the Yellowhead Highway (Hwy 16), plus onward services to Kamloops ($56.66) and Vancouver ($99.19) via scenic Hwy 5 (4 daily) and Prince George (2 daily, $49.06). Brewster Transportation (☎852-3332 or 1-800/661-1152) operates five-hour services to Banff (1 daily at 1.30pm, $51) via Lake Louise ($44) and continuing to Calgary (1 daily, $71) and Calgary Airport (1 daily, $71; additional connections at Banff), and also runs day-trip tours to Banff, taking in sights on the Icefields Parkway; note, however, that weather can play havoc with Brewster's schedules in October and April (services finish for the year with the first bad snows). Both companies share the same **bus terminal** (daily 6am–8pm; outside regular hours, the terminal opens briefly a few minutes before bus departures), located in the train station building at 314 Connaught Drive.

There are also left-luggage lockers here and **car-rental** offices for Hertz (☎852-3886) and National (☎852-1117). Be sure to have booked cars in advance if you're hoping to pick up vehicles at these outlets – all cars go very quickly, especially on days when trains come in from Vancouver and Edmonton (see below). Other car-rental agencies in town are Avis at the Petro-Canada Service, 300 Connaught Drive (☎852-3970) and Budget, Jasper Shell Service, 638 Connaught Drive (☎852-3222).

VIA Rail **trains** operate to Jasper from Winnipeg and Edmonton and continue to Vancouver (via Kamloops) or Prince Rupert (via Prince George). Coach (second-) class tickets currently cost $175 to Vancouver including taxes; Edmonton ($125), Prince Rupert ($146 – excluding the cost of the overnight stay required on this route at Prince George); Prince George ($71); and Kamloops ($110). As this is the only scheduled rail route through the Rockies, summer places are hard to come by, but at other times there's little need to book a seat. Fares are considerably more than those of equivalent buses, and journey times considerably longer. Trains run Edmonton–Jasper (currently Mon, Thurs & Sat; 5hr 30min); Jasper–Edmonton (Mon, Wed & Sat leaving Jasper at 12.25pm); Jasper–Kamloops–Vancouver (Mon, Thurs & Sat at 3.30pm; 15hr 30min); Jasper–Prince George (Wed, Fri & Sun at 12.45pm; 5hr 15min) and Prince George–Prince Rupert (Mon, Thurs & Sat; 12hr 15min). The **ticket office** is open on train days only (☎852-4102 or 1-888/VIA-RAIL, *www.viarail.ca*).

Note that you can experience a taste of the railway on a new arrangement that lets you ride the Jasper–Price George service for two hours to Mount Robson where the train lets you off before continuing on to Prince George and then Prince Rupert. You can return to Jasper by coach with a guide and stop at some of the sights you've seen from the train. The trip departs at 12.45pm on train days (Wed, Fri & Sun), lasts four hours in total, and costs $79, including train ticket. For details contact Rocky Mountain Unlimited, 414 Connaught Drive (☎852-4056 or 1-888/SUNDOG1, *www.sundogtours.com*).

Information

The town's superb national park **visitor centre** is at 500 Connaught Drive – 50m east of the station, back from the road on the left in the open grassy area (mid-May to mid-June daily 8am–5pm; mid-June to early Sept daily 8am–7pm; early Sept to mid-May Mon–Fri 9am–5pm, Sat & Sun 8am–5pm; ☎852-6176, *www.parkscanada .pch.gc.ca/jasper*). This is for park-related and campground information only. For accommodation, contact the Chamber of Commerce office (see below). Apply at the park office for compulsory **national park permits** ($5 daily, $35 annual; see box, p.486), backcountry wilderness permits ($6) and to register for backpacking trails. If you're hiking seriously you might also want to contact the park's Trail Office (May–Oct; ☎852-6177). Out of season, apply to the Park Administration Office located upstairs in the VIA Rail-bus terminal complex (Mon–Fri 8am–4.30pm; ☎852-6162 or 852-6220). The Park Warden Office is 1km away in the Industrial Area off the east side of Hwy 93a as you head towards the junction with Hwy 16 (Mon–Fri 8am–4.30pm; ☎852-6155). For weather reports, call Environment Canada (☎852-3185).

The centre also has a shop (good for **maps**) run by the Friends of Jasper (☎852-4767), who offer a couple of **guided walks**: Jasper – A Walk in the Past (daily from the visitor centre at 7.30pm June–Sept 6, 6.30pm Sept 6–30), which delves into the history of the town, and Pocahontas – A Walk in the Past (daily from parking lot at the bottom of Miette Hot Springs Rd July–Aug at 2pm), which looks at some of the legends and stories of the region. You should register at the centre for both; payment by donation. Other popular Friends' activities include performances at the Whistler's Campground Theatre (daily: 10pm July to mid-Aug, 9pm mid-Aug to Sept) and wildlife talks at the Wabasso Campground Campfire Circle (July–Sept Sat 9pm).

For information on the town of Jasper, and accommodation in particular, contact the Jasper Chamber of Commerce **infocentre** behind the park office about 100m east on Patricia Street at no. 409 (June to early Sept daily 9am–7pm; rest of the year Mon–Fri 9am–5pm; ☎852-3858).

The local **public library** on Elm Avenue (Mon–Thurs 2–5pm & 7–9pm, Fri 2–5pm, Sat 10am–3pm; ☎852-3652) has a huge number of books on the park, but there's no decent bookshop in town. The **post office** is at 502 Patricia St; the **hospital** at 518 Robson St (☎852-3344). For the **police**, call ☎852-4848. For **Internet access**, use the terminals at the *Soft Rock Internet Café*, 633 Connaught Drive (☎852-5850).

Accommodation

Beds in Jasper are not as expensive or elusive as in Banff, but hotel rooms are still almost unobtainable in late July and August. The Chamber of Commerce will help with accommodation, but do not offer a booking service. If you're desperate, try Jasper Adventure Centre, which offers an accommodation service (☎852-5595 or 1-800/565-7547, *www.JasperAdventureCentre.com*), as does the Jasper Travel Agency, 623 Patricia St (☎852-4400 or 1-800/672-1127, *jtravel@telusplanet.net*), and Rocky Mountain Unlimited, 414 Connaught Drive (☎852-4056, *www.sundogtours.com*).

You could also ask the Chamber of Commerce for the Jasper Home Accommodation Association (JHAA; *www.visit-jasper.com/JHAA.html* or *www.bbcanada.com/jhaa.html*) *Private Home Accommodation List* – Jasper has around sixty **private homes**, which are virtually all priced between $55 and $70 a double (up to a maximum of around $95 for the most expensive), sometimes with a continental breakfast thrown in (note that virtually all are non-smoking). These rooms also fill up fast.

Most **motels** are spaced out along Connaught Drive on the eastern edge of town – there's relatively little right in the middle of town – and most charge well over $135 for a basic double room, though prices drop sharply off-season. An often cheaper and in many ways more pleasant option is to plump for motels made up of collections of **cabins**; most are within a few kilometres of town. The four park-run **campgrounds** close

TAXIS AND SHUTTLE SERVICES

One of the problems you're likely to have in Jasper if you're without transport is getting to some of the more outlying sights, strolls and trailheads. One option is to rent a bike (see "Activities" on p.535). Another is take advantage of a variety of small-scale shuttle services that run to various sights. These tend to come and go year by year, but there's always someone prepared to start up a service. Currently services include the **Tramway Shuttle** (☎852-4056 or 852-8255), which runs nine times daily in summer from outside the Via Rail-bus depot (look out for the white "Sundog" van) to the Jasper Tramway (cable car) at a cost of $24, including Tramway ticket: more importantly, it also takes in the *Jasper International* (or *Whistlers*) *Youth Hostel* for $4. The **Trailhead Shuttle** (☎852-3898 or 852-8389) leaves from Freewheel Cycles, 618 Patricia St, and runs once or twice daily to a variety of trailheads, including the Valley of the Five Lakes, Maligne Canyon and Overlander (all $10) and Marmot Basin Road ($15). Finally, there's the long-established **Maligne Lake Shuttle**, run by Maligne Tours, 627 Patricia St (☎852-3370; 6 departures daily late June to late Sept, 3 daily mid-May to late June and last week of Sept), which will run you all the way to Maligne Lake ($12 or $24 round trip) to coincide with the company's boat cruises on the lake (see p.536), or drop off at Maligne Canyon ($8), *Maligne Canyon Youth Hostel* ($8) and other points on the Maligne Lake Road such as the Skyline trailheads (north $8, south $12).

For a **taxi**, call Heritage Cab (☎852-5558), Michael Angelo (☎852-7277) or Jasper Taxi (☎852-3600).

to the townsite and the three local hostels (joint reservations on ☎439-3139) all fill up promptly in summer – and it's first-come, first-served – but don't forget the hostels and campgrounds strung along the Icefields Parkway.

HOTELS, MOTELS AND CHALETS

Alpine Village, 2.5km south of town on Hwy 93A (☎852-3285, fax 852-1955). An assortment of 41 serene one- and two-room cabins, including twelve deluxe cabins and lodge suites, most with great mountain views; big outdoor tub. May to mid-Oct. ⑥.

Amethyst Motor Lodge, 200 Connaught Drive (☎852-3394 or 1-888/852-7737, *www.mtn-park-lodges .com*). Almost 100 newly renovated rooms two blocks from downtown. ⑦.

Astoria Hotel, 404 Connaught Drive (☎852-3351 or 1-800/661-7343, *www.astoriahotel.com*). Adequate central "alpine" hotel, one block from the train station and bus terminal. ⑥.

Athabasca Hotel, 510 Patricia St (☎852-3386 or 1-800/563-9859, *www.athabascahotel.com*). Central, if rather forbidding hotel, near the station, where the nightly entertainment at *O'Shea's Lounge Bar* may keep you awake. Choice of suite or newly renovated rooms, either en suite or with sinks only and shared facilities. ⑥.

Bear Hill Lodge, 100 Bonhomme St (☎852-3209, 852-3099, *www.bearhilllodge.com*). Thirty-seven simple-looking but comfortable bungalows, suites, chalet and lodge units, in the townsite but in a pleasant wooded setting. Mid-April to late Oct. ⑨.

Becker's Chalets, 5km south of Jasper on Hwy 93 and Athabasca River (☎852-3779). Ninety-six of the best (and some of the newest) local one-, two-, three- and four-bedroom log cabins, most with wood-burning stoves and kitchenettes. May to mid-Oct. ④.

Jasper Park Lodge, 5km from townsite on Lac Beauvert (☎852-3301, 1-888/242-3888, *www.jasperparklodge.com*). The town's top upmarket, luxury option, with all the facilities and trimmings of a top-class hotel. ⑧.

Lobstick Lodge, 1200 Geikie at Juniper (☎852-4431 or 1-888/852-7737, *www.mtn-park-lodges.com*). If you're going to pay in-town, east-end motel rates, this big place is among the best all-round choices, but make sure you don't get put in one of the dungeon-like basement rooms. ⑦.

Marmot Lodge, 92 Connaught Drive (☎852-4471 or 1-888/852-7737, *www.mtn-park-lodges.com*). One of the biggest and least expensive of the east-end motels. ⑥.

Patricia Lake Bungalows, 5km northwest of downtown (☎852-3560, *www.patricialakebungalows* *.com*). Motel or cabin out-of-town base; 35 units on the Pyramid Lake Rd, some with fine views over Patricia Lake; fishing and rentals of boats, canoes and paddle boats available. May to mid-Oct. ⑤.

Pine Bungalows, 2km east of Jasper on the Athabasca River (☎852-3491, fax 852-3432). Some 85 good-looking wooden cabins in forest setting, 41 with wood-burning stoves and 72 with kitchenettes. Grocery shop on site. Three-day minimum stay from mid-June to mid-Sept. May to mid-Oct. ③.

Sawridge Hotel Jasper, 82 Connaught Drive (☎852-5111 or 1-800/661-6427, *www.sawridge.com* */Jasper*). Plush and expensive 154-room hotel on the eastern edge of town. ⑧.

Tekarra Lodge (☎852-3058 or 1-888/404-4540, *www.tekarralodge.com*). Forty-two quiet, nicely kitsch wood cabins with wood-burning stoves, located 1km south of town on the Athabasca River off Hwy 93A. Open May–Oct. ⑥.

Whistlers Inn, 105 Miette Ave (☎852-3361 or 1-800/282-9919, *www.whistlersinn.com*). Central but unexciting 41-room motel, opposite the station. ⑥.

BED AND BREAKFASTS

A-1 Tourist Rooms, 804 Connaught Drive (☎852-3325, *lwhitema@telusplanet.net*). Two rooms with shared bathroom on main street close to bus and train. Two-night minimum stay for advance reservations. ②.

Aspen Lodge, 8 Aspen Crescent (☎852-5908, fax 852-5910, *aspnlodg@telusplanet.net*). Two clean, comfortable rooms with private bathrooms on a quiet street 10min walk from downtown. ③.

B & G Accommodation, 204 Colin Crescent (☎852-4345, *wgunrau@telusplanet.net*). Three well-priced rooms with shared bathroom three blocks from downtown. ②.

Creekside Accommodation, 1232 Patricia Crescent (☎852-3530, fax 852-2116, *rushacom@telusplanet* *.net*). Two bright, clean rooms (shared bath) near Cabin Creek and trails. ②.

Kennedy's Mountain Holiday Rooms, 1115 Patricia Crescent (☎852-3438). Pair of rooms that share bath, patio, living room and great views. ②.

Marchand, Yves and Caroline, 809 Patricia St (☎852-3609, *ymarchand@hotmail.com*). Three good double rooms with shared bathroom in a quiet location 5min from the town centre. A full cooked breakfast is available at an additional charge. ②.

Pooli's Suite, 824 Geikie St (☎852-4379). A one-bedroom suite with two double beds and a pull-out in the living room (sleeps up to six): $65 for two people, $6 for each additional person: private bathroom and use of kitchen for an additional $8. ③.

Rooney's Accommodation, 1114 Patricia St (☎852-4101, *mismaeil@telusplanet.com*). Just out of the town centre comprising two nice rooms with and without private baths. ②.

711 Miette Avenue, 711 Miette Ave (☎852-4029, fax 852-4021). A friendly welcome, nice double room with private entrance and bathroom two blocks from downtown. ③.

TassonInn, 706 Patricia St (☎852-3427, *tassinn@incentre.net*). Two bright and newly renovated rooms with shared bathroom less than a block from the town centre. ②.

Worobec, Wayne and Joan, 1215 Patricia Crescent (☎852-5563, *worobec@telusplanet.net*). A choice of double room with private bathroom or a suite of bedroom, living room and food preparation area for family for two to four people. ④.

HOSTELS

Jasper International Youth Hostel (HI; ☎852-3215; hostel open all day but check-in 8am–midnight). Jasper's principal youth hostel, 7km south of town (500m south of the gondola terminal) on Skytram Rd (Whistlers Mountain Rd), accessed from the Icefields Parkway (Hwy 93). The 4km uphill walk from Hwy 93 is a killer, but shuttles run from downtown, as do taxis (about $14). A modern place with

---

HOSTEL RESERVATIONS

For reservations at *Jasper International, Maligne Canyon, Edith Cavell, Beauty Creek* and *Athabasca Falls* hostels, call ☎780/852-3215 or 1-877/852-0781, fax 780/852-5560 or email *jihostel@hostellingintl.ca*.

rather overefficient management, its eighty beds fill up quickly in summer, so arrive early or book. Members $16, non-members $21. Facilities include laundry, store and bike rentals. ①.

Maligne Canyon Hostel (HI; ☎852-3215). Two cabins in lovely setting with beds for 24 in six-bed rooms 11km east of town near Maligne Canyon; the Maligne Lake Shuttle from downtown or Alberta Hostel Shuttle (see p.516) drop off here daily in summer; members $11, non-members $16. Open all day, year-round but check-in 5–11pm and may have closures in winter. ①.

Mount Edith Cavell Hostel, Edith Cavell Rd, 13km off Hwy 93A, 26km south of Jasper (HI; reservations ☎852-3215; check-in 5–11pm). Cosier than the *Jasper International Hostel* (see overleaf), close to trails and with great views of the Angel Glacier. Sleeps 32 in two cabins; outdoor wood-burning sauna. Members $11, non-members $16. Mid-June to Oct. Occasionally opens up with key system for skiers in winter. ①.

CAMPGROUNDS

Pocahontas, 45km east of Jasper and 1km off Hwy 16 on Miette Rd, one of two to the northeast of Jasper on this road; 130 pitches, hot and cold water and flush toilets but no showers. Mid-May to mid-Oct. $13 plus $4 for use of firewood.

Snaring River, 16km east of Jasper on Hwy 16. Simple 66-site park-run facility. The other simple park campground east of Jasper; tap water, kitchen shelter, dry toilets only and no showers. Mid-May to early Sept. $10 plus $4 for use of firewood.

Wabasso, 16km south of Jasper on Hwy 93A. A 228-pitch riverside park-run site with flush toilets, hot water but no showers. Wheelchair-accessible. Mid-June to early Sept. $13 plus $4 for use of firewood.

Wapiti, 4km south of the townsite and 1km south of *Whistlers* campground (see below) on Hwy 93. Big 362-pitch park-run place with flush toilets and coin showers that accepts tents but also caters for up to forty RVs. Wheelchair-accessible. Some ninety sites remain open for winter camping from October – the park's only year-round serviced campground. $15–18 in summer plus $4 for use of firewood; winter, when there are no showers or other service save water and flush toilets – $13–15 plus $4 for use of firewood.

Whistlers, 3km south of Jasper just west off Hwy 93. Jasper's main 781-site park-run campground is the largest in the Rockies, with three sections, and prices depending on facilities included. Wheelchair-accessible. If you're coming from Banff, watch for the sign; Brewster buses also usually stop here if you ask the driver. Taxis and shuttles run from Jasper. Early May to early Oct. $15–24, plus $4 for use of firewood.

Jasper Townsite

JASPER's small-town feel comes as a relief after the razzmatazz of Banff: its streets still have the windswept, open look of a frontier town and, though the mountains don't ring it with quite the same majesty as Banff, you'll probably feel the town better suits its wild surroundings. Situated at the confluence of the Miette and Athabasca rivers, its core centres around just two streets: **Connaught Drive**, which contains the bus and train terminal, restaurants, motels and park information centre, and – a block to the west – the parallel **Patricia Street**, lined with more shops, restaurants and the odd hotel. The rest of the central grid consists of homely little houses and the fixtures of small-town life: the post office, library, school and public swimming pool. Apart from the **Yellowhead Museum & Archives** at 400 Pyramid Rd, with its fur trade and railroad displays (mid-May to early Sept daily 10am–9pm; early Sept to Oct daily 10am–5pm; Nov to mid-May Thurs–Sun 10am–5pm; $3 or donation; ☎852-3013) and a cable car (see p.532), nothing here even pretends to be a tourist attraction; this is a place to sleep, eat and stock up. If you're interested in getting to know a little more about the town or park from the locals, contact the "Friends of Jasper National Park" (☎852-4767), who offer guided walks between July and August, or pick up *Jasper: A Walk in the Past* from local bookshops. If you're still itching for something to do and have a car, a lot of people head 58km northeast of town for a dip in Miette Hot Springs (see hiking box on p.524).

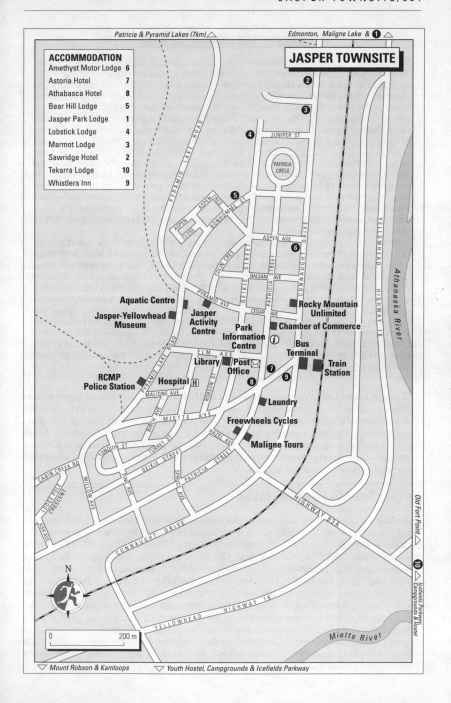

ACCOMMODATION

Amethyst Motor Lodge	6
Astoria Hotel	7
Athabasca Hotel	8
Bear Hill Lodge	5
Jasper Park Lodge	1
Lobstick Lodge	4
Marmot Lodge	3
Sawridge Hotel	2
Tekarra Lodge	10
Whistlers Inn	9

JASPER TOWNSITE

Patricia & Pyramid Lakes (7km)

Edmonton, Maligne Lake &

JUNIPER ST

PATRICIA CIRCLE

PYRAMID LAKE ROAD

ASPEN CLOSE

ASPEN CRES

BONHOMME ST

ASPEN AVE

COLIN CRES

GEIKIE STREET

BALSAM STREET

PATRICIA STREET

CONNAUGHT DRIVE

PYRAMID AVE

CEDAR AVE

YELLOWHEAD HIGHWAY 16

Athanaska River

Aquatic Centre

Jasper-Yellowhead Museum

Jasper Activity Centre

Park Information Centre

Rocky Mountain Unlimited

Chamber of Commerce

Bus Terminal

Train Station

ELM AVE

Library

Post Office

RCMP Police Station

Hospital

MALIGNE AVE

ROBSON ST

Laundry

BIRCH AVE

MIETTE AVE

Freewheels Cycles

HAZEL AVE

Maligne Tours

TONQUIN ST

TURRET ST

GEIKIE STREET

PINE AVE

SPRUCE AVE

PATRICIA STREET

CABIN CREEK RD

LODGE POLE CRESCENT

WILLOW AVE

ASPEN

HIGHWAY 93A

CONNAUGHT DRIVE

Old Fort Point

Icefields Parkway, Campgrounds & Hostel

N

0   200 m

YELLOWHEAD   HIGHWAY 16

Miette River

Mount Robson & Kamloops

Youth Hostel, Campgrounds & Icefields Parkway

Jasper's winter sports tend to be overshadowed by the world-class ski resorts in nearby Banff and Lake Louise. This said, the park has plenty of winter activities and a first-rate ski area in **Marmot Basin** (20min drive from the townsite), a resort with the advantages of cheaper skiing and far less crowded runs than its southern rivals. Skiing in the region began in the 1920s, though the first lift – a 700-metre rope tow – was only introduced in 1961, just a few years after the first road. Today there are a total of seven **lifts**: two T-bars, three double chair lifts, one triple chair lift and one high-speed quad chair lift; few are likely to be crowded in winter. The terrain is a balanced mixture of Novice (35 percent), Intermediate (35 percent) and Expert (30 percent). The drop from the resorts's top elevation at 2601m to the base level is 701m: the longest run is 5.6km and there are a total of 52 named trails. Lift passes cost around $35. The season runs from early December to late April. You can rent equipment at the resort or from several outlets in Jasper itself. To get here, jump aboard one of the three daily buses ($5 one-way, $9 return) from downtown hotels, whose rates, incidentally, tumble dramatically during the winter. For more **information** on the resort, contact Marmot Basin Ski-Lifts, PO Box 1300, Jasper AB T0E 1E0 (☎852-3816, fax 852-3533).

Where Jasper rates as highly, if not more so, than Banff National Park is in the range and quality of its **cross-country skiing**, for its summer backcountry trails lend themselves superbly to winter grooming. Pick up the *Cross-Country Skiing in Jasper National Park* leaflet from the park information centre: the key areas are around the *Whistlers* campground, Maligne Lake, around Athabasca Falls, and along Pyramid Lake Road. For all manner of winter activities such as ice fishing, dog sledding, snowmobiling, heli-skiing, skiing in Banff or Lake Louise and so forth, book through Rocky Mountain Unlimited, 414 Connaught Drive (☎852-4056, *www.sundogtours.com*). Ski and cross-country ski equipment can be **bought or rented** from Totem Ski Rentals, 408 Connaught Drive (☎852-3078), and the Sports Shop, 406 Patricia St (☎852-3654). **Ice-skating** takes place on parts of Pyramid Lake and Lac Beauvert, and there are the usual sleigh rides around Jasper and its environs.

Though Jasper doesn't get as crowded as Banff, it still receives around three million visitors annually, so accommodation, especially in summer, can be extremely tight, though there are numerous B&B options. You are also especially stuck if you don't have a vehicle; trailheads and the best scenery are a long way from downtown. Bikes can be rented at several places and intermittent shuttle services (see box on p.528) and organized tours can run you out of town to **Maligne Lake**, to various trailheads and to some of the more obvious attractions.

Jasper Tramway and the lakes

With little on offer in town you need to use a bike, car or the shuttle services to get anything out of the area. The obvious trip is on Canada's longest and highest tramway, the **Jasper Tramway**, 7km south of town on Whistlers Mountain Road, off the Icefields Parkway (daily: April to mid-May and Oct 9.30am–4.30pm; mid-May to early Sept 8.30am–10pm; Sept 9.30am–9pm; $18 return; ☎852-3093). In peak season you may well have a long wait in line for the 2.5-kilometre cable-car ride, whose two thirty-person cars take seven minutes to make the 1000-metre ascent (often with running commentary from the conductor). It leaves you at an interpretive centre, expensive restaurant, and an excellent viewpoint (2285m) where you can take your bearings on much of the park. A steep trail ploughs upwards and onwards to the Whistlers summit (2470m), an hour's walk that requires warm clothes year-round and reveals even more stunning views. A tough but rather redundant ten-kilometre trail follows the route of the tramway from *Jasper International Youth Hostel*; if you walk up, you can ride back down for next to nothing.

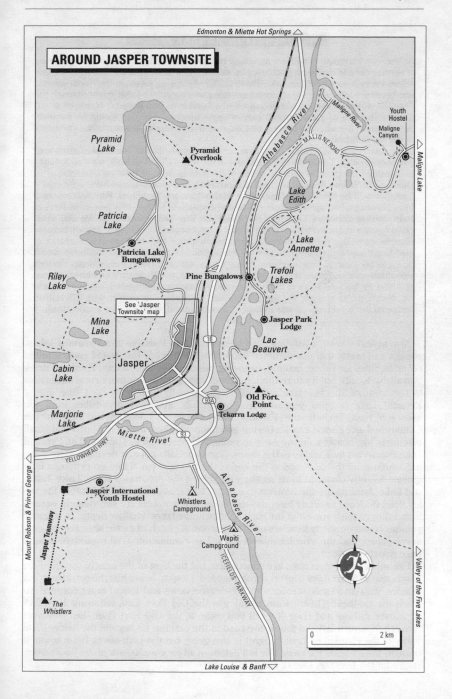

AROUND JASPER TOWNSITE

Edmonton & Miette Hot Springs △

Pyramid Lake

Pyramid Overlook ▲

Athabasca River

Maligne River

MALIGNE ROAD

Youth Hostel

Maligne Canyon ●

△ Maligne Lake

Patricia Lake

Lake Edith

Patricia Lake Bungalows ◉

Lake Annette

Riley Lake

Pine Bungalows ◉

Trefoil Lakes

See 'Jasper Townsite' map

Mina Lake

◉ **Jasper Park Lodge**

Jasper

16

Lac Beauvert

Cabin Lake

Old Fort Point ▲

Marjorie Lake

93A

Tekarra Lodge

Miette River

YELLOWHEAD HWY

93

Athabasca River

△ Mount Robson & Prince George

◉ **Jasper International Youth Hostel**

Jasper Tramway

X Whistlers Campground

▲ Wapiti Campground

N

△ Valley of the Five Lakes

ICEFIELDS PARKWAY

▲ The Whistlers

0   2 km

Lake Louise & Banff ▽

OPERATION HABBAKUK

Behind every triumph of military ingenuity in World War II, there were probably dozens of spectacular and deliberately obfuscated failures. Few have been as bizarre as the one witnessed by Jasper's Patricia Lake. By 1942, Allied shipping losses in the North Atlantic had become so disastrous that almost anything was considered that might staunch the flow. One Geoffrey Pike, institutionalized in a London mental hospital, managed to put forward the idea of a vast aircraft carrier made of ice, a ship that would be naturally impervious to fire when torpedoed, and not melt from under its seamen in the icy waters of the North Atlantic.

Times were so hard that the innovative scheme, despite its odd source, was given serious consideration. Louis Mountbatten, one of the Allied Chiefs of Staff, went so far as to demonstrate the theories with ice cubes in the bath in front of Winston Churchill at 10 Downing St. It was decided to build a thousand-tonne model somewhere very cold – Canada would be ideal – and **Operation Habbakuk** was launched. Pike was released from his hospital on special dispensation and dispatched to the chilly waters of Patricia Lake. Here a substance known as pikewood was invented, a mixture of ice and wood chips (spruce chips were discovered to add more buoyancy than pine). It soon became clear, however, that the 650-metre-long and twenty-storey-high boat stood little chance of ever being seaworthy (never mind what the addition of 2000 crew and 26 aircraft would do for its buoyancy). Pike suggested filling the ice with air to help things along. Further complications arose when the labourers on the project, mostly pacifist Doukhobors (see pp.427–428), became aware of the boat's proposed purpose and refused to carry on working. Spring thaws brought the project to a halt. The following season, with $75 million budgeted for the scheme, it was moved to Newfoundland, where it died a quiet death.

Also near the town, a winding road wends north to **Patricia** and **Pyramid lakes**, popular and pretty moraine-dammed lakes about 5km from Jasper and packed full of rental facilities for riding, boating, canoeing, windsurfing and sailing. Food and drink is available locally, but if you're thinking about staying here as a more rural alternative to the townsite the two lakefront lodges are usually heavily booked (the one at Pyramid Lake is open year-round). Short trails, generally accessible from the approach road, include the Patricia Lake Circle, a 4.8-kilometre loop by the Cottonwood slough and creek offering good opportunities for seeing birds and small mammals, like beavers, during early morning and late evening. The island on Pyramid Lake, connected by a bridge to the shore, is an especially popular destination for a day out: continue on the lake road to the end of the lake and you'll find everything a little quieter. Slightly closer to town on the east side of the Athabasca River, **Lake Edith** and **Lake Annette** are the remains of a larger lake that once extended across the valley floor. Both are similarly busy day-use areas. Their waters are surprisingly warm – in fact they're the warmest in the park, thanks to the lakes' shallow depth. In summer you can lie out on sandy beaches or grassy areas. A clutch of picnic sites are the only development, and the wheelchair-accessible Lee Foundation Trail meanders around Lake Annette (2.4km).

Few other hikes from town are spectacular, but the best of the bunch, the Old Fort Point Loop (6.5km round trip), is recommended. Despite being just thirty minutes out of town, it's remarkably scenic, with 360-degree views and lots of quiet corners. To reach the trailhead (1.6km from town) use the Old Fort Exit, following Hwy 93A across the railway and Hwy 16 until you come to the Old Fort Point–Lac Beauvert turn-off; then turn left and follow the road to the parking lot beyond the bridge. The Valley of the Five Lakes Trail (4.6km) is also good, but the path starts 10km south of town off the Icefields Parkway. For full details of all park walks, ask at the information centre for the free *Day Hiker's Guide to Jasper*.

Activities

The presence of the Athabasca and other rivers around Jasper makes the town a focus of **white-water** and other rafting trips (see box on pp.542–543). If the idea of water appeals, but in much gentler context, the town's **Aquatic Centre** at 401 Pyramid Lake Rd (☎852-3663) is popular, and provides a large **swimming** pool, whirlpool, wading pool, steam room and showers. You can rent towels and costumes if you've come unprepared.

Other tours and activities can be accessed through several operators around town, amongst whom the most wide-ranging is **Rocky Mountain Unlimited**, 414 Connaught Drive (☎852-4056, *www.sundogtours.com*), who run their own tours but also act as a one-stop booking agent for a huge range of tours, including seeing the park by helicopter ($149), a five-hour bus and hiking tour of the Maligne Valley ($169), or white-water rafting ($79 and up).

The town's other big operator is Maligne Tours at 627 Patricia St (☎852-3370, fax 852-3405, *www.malignelake.com*) – though note that nowhere on the shopfront at this address does it actually say the company's name. Among other things, the company runs boat cruises on Maligne Lake, guided hiking and fishing trips, canoe rentals and rafting excursions.

All manner of short or strenuous and generally cheap guided hiking or wildlife tours are widely available: contact the Chamber of Commerce for details of the other various operators. For the free walking tours run by the "Friends of Jasper National Park" in the summer, contact the park visitor centre. If you need to **rent hiking, fishing and other equipment**, the best bet is On-Line Sport & Tackle, 600 Patricia St (☎852-3630) or the Totem Ski Shop, 406 Patricia St (☎852-3078).

You can **rent bikes** in town from On-Line Sport & Tackle ($6 an hour, $18 a day; see above), or from Freewheel Cycles at 618 Patricia St (same rates, plus full-suspension models at $9/$27/$36 for 24 hours; ☎852-3898, *www.freewheeljasper.com*). The latter is a good place for all things connected with bikes, including repairs and spares. Drop in and ask for their *Mountain Biking Trail Guide*, a summary of trails to suit all types of riders. On-Line offer a one-way rental with all necesary kit from Jasper to Banff if you're up to riding the length of the Icefields Parkway. Out of town you can rent bikes at the *Jasper International Youth Hostel* (see p.529); at Beauvert Boat & Cycles, which is at the *Jasper Park Lodge* on the shore of Lac Beauvert ($8 an hour, $20 for 4hr or $30 a day for bikes; ☎852-5708); and at Patricia Lake Bungalows, 4.8km northwest of town on Pyramid Lake Road (from $6 an hour, $18 a half-day and $24 a day). For **in-line skates rental** (rollerblades), make for Source for Sports, 406 Patricia St (from $4 an hour, $12 a day; ☎852-3654).

If you want **fishing** tours, tackle for rent or just free advice if you're fishing alone, On-Line Sport & Tackle (see above) is again the operator to go for: it has trips to Maligne Lake and Talbot Lake for trout and various other lake and river-fishing destinations; a full day's (8hr) fishing costs $289, $189 if there are two of you; a half-day costs $249/$149. It'll rent you tackle, too – boots and waders from $30 a day, spin rod and reel ($15), and fly rod and reel ($25) and nets ($5). The company also organizes rafting and horseriding tours, rents row boats ($40 daily, $25 for a half-day after 3pm) and canoes (same rates), and sells and hires a wide range of **camping gear**. Currie's Guiding, 414 Connaught Drive (☎852-5650, *www.curriesguiding.com*), offer similar trips on the rivers and over twenty lakes, with fly-fishing lessons also available. **Golf** on a highly rated eighteen-hole course – "Number one in Canada" according to *Score Magazine* – is available at the *Jasper Park Lodge* (green fees $44–95, cheaper twilight fees available; ☎852-6090). You can rent clubs and carts.

Horse-riding enthusiasts should contact Pyramid Stables, 4km from Jasper on Pyramid Lake Road (☎852-3562), who run day-treks and one-, two- and three-hour trips (from $25/$43/$65; full-day rides $125) around Patrician and Pyramid lakes. Ridgeline

Riders at Maligne Tours, 627 Patricia St (☎852-3370, *www.malignelake.com*) offer a ride above the tree line at Maligne Lake to the Bald Hills Fire Lookout at 2134m with great views of the lake (3hr 30min; $55). Skyline Trail Rides (☎852-4215) at *Jasper Park Lodge* have a more varied programme which includes a one-hour ride to Lake Annette ($25), ninety-minute rides along the Athabasca River ($33), two-hour "Valley View" treks ($35) and four-hour rides to Maligne Canyon ($70). They can also organize overnight trips and anything up to 21-day expeditions using a variety of backcountry lodges.

Maligne Lake Road

Bumper to bumper with cars, campers and tour buses in the summer, the **Maligne Lake Road** runs east from Jasper for 48km, taking in a number of beautiful but rather busy and overdeveloped sights before reaching the sublime Maligne Lake (pronounced "Ma-leen"), the Rockies' largest glacier-fed lake (and the world's second largest). If you have time to spare, and the transport, you could set aside a day for the trip, white-water raft the Maligne River (see below), or walk one of the trails above Maligne Lake itself. Maligne Tours, 627 Patricia St (☎852-3370, *www.malignelake.com*), books boat tours on the lake (advance booking is highly recommended) and rents out any equipment you may need for canoeing, fishing and so forth (note that rental reservations are also essential in summer). The company also runs a **bus**, the Maligne Lake Shuttle, to the lake eight times daily ($12 one-way), with drop-offs (if booked) at *Maligne Canyon* youth hostel ($8) and the northern ($8) and southern ($8/$12) ends of the Skyline Trail, one of the park's three top backpacking trails (see box, p.524). Joint tickets are offered for the shuttle and other activities organized by the company, notably the cruises, raft trips and horse rides on and around Maligne Lake.

The often rather crowded **Maligne Canyon** is a mere 11km out of Jasper, with an oversized car park and a tacky café/souvenir shop. This heavily sold excursion promises one of the Rockies' most spectacular gorges: in fact the canyon is deep (50m), but almost narrow enough to jump across – many people have tried and most have died in the attempt. In the end the geology is more interesting than the scenery; the violent erosive forces that created the canyon are explained on the main trail loop, an easy twenty-minute amble that can be extended to 45 minutes (few people do this, so the latter part of the trail is often quiet), or even turned into a hike back to Jasper. In winter, licensed guides lead tours (more like crawls) through the frozen canyon – contact Maligne Tours, 626 Connaught Drive, Jasper (details overleaf).

Next stop is picture-perfect **Medicine Lake**, 32km from Jasper, which experiences intriguing fluctuations in level. Its waters have no surface outlet: instead the lake fills and empties through lake-bed sink holes into the world's largest system of limestone caves. They re-emerge some 17km away towards Jasper (and may also feed some of the lakes around Jasper Townsite). When the springs freeze in winter, the lake drains and sometimes disappears altogether, only to be replenished in the spring. The lake's strange behaviour captivated local natives, who believed spirits were responsible, hence the name. Few people spend much time at the lake, preferring to press on to Maligne Lake, so it makes a quietish spot to escape the headlong rush down the road.

At the end of the road, 48km from Jasper, is the stunning **Maligne Lake**, 22km long and 92m deep, and surrounded by snow-covered mountains. The largest lake in the Rockies, its name comes from the French for "wicked", and was coined in 1846 by a Jesuit missionary, Father de Smet, in memory of the difficulty he had crossing the **Maligne River** downstream. The road peters out at a warden station, three car parks and a restaurant flanked by a picnic area and the start of the short, self-explanatory Lake Trail along the lake's east side to the Schäffer Viewpoint (3.2km loop; begin from Car Park 2). A small waterfront area is equipped with berths for glass-enclosed boats that run ninety-minute narrated **cruises** on the lake to Spirit Island: the views are sensational (daily hourly on the hour: mid-May to late June 10am–4pm; late June to early Sept 10am–5pm; early Sept to late Sept 10am–3pm; $32). The boats are small, however, and reservations are vital during peak times, especially as tour companies often block-book entire sailings: again, contact Maligne Tours (see p.535). Riding, fishing, rafting and guided hiking tours are also available, as are fishing tackle, rowing boat and canoe rentals ($10 a day, $45 per day) and sea kayaks ($60 a day). There are no accommodation or camping facilities here, but two backcountry campgrounds on the lakeshore can be reached by canoe (details from Jasper's information centre).

Eating

Options for **eating** out are a bit restricted in Jasper – mostly hotel dining rooms – but then the town's rugged ambience doesn't suit fine dining. A reasonable place for a basic budget meal in no-nonsense surroundings is the cheap, friendly *Mountain Foods and Café*, opposite the station at 606 Connaught Drive (☎852-4050), though quality has become variable. Still, the menu is cheap and varied (including vegetarian courses), the staff friendly, and it's a good place to meet people. Also popular is the lively and far more carnivorous *Villa Caruso*, 640 Connaught Drive (☎852-3920), serving giant steaks; if that's too much, they also serve seafood, pasta and pizzas. Best of the mid-range places is the ever-reliable *Earl's* on the second floor at 600 Patricia St on the corner of Miette Avenue. For pizzas cooked in a wood-burning oven, head to the big and bustling *Jasper Pizza Place* (☎852-3225), 402 Connaught Drive, with a rooftop patio for nice days, and for a locals' favourite try *Papa George's*, 406 Connaught Drive (☎852-3351), one of the town's oldest restaurants (opened in 1924). It looks plain and dowdy, but the very varied food is excellent and the portions gargantuan. If you're going for broke, the *Jasper Park Lodge*, Jasper's premier hotel, 5km from town on Lac Beauvert, boasts two outstanding restaurants: *Becker's* is one of the best in Alberta (☎852-3535; May–Oct; dinner only) – reckon on $115 for a gourmet blowout for two – while the *Edith Cavell Room* is only marginally less renowned. Both places have dining rooms with cracking views.

Cafés and nightlife

The best of the **cafés** is the small, non-smoking *Coco's Café* at 608 Patricia St: inexpensive and vaguely trendy, with newspapers and magazines to pass the time over excellent snacks and coffees. A short distance away, on the upper level of the small "mall" at 610 Patricia St, *Spooner's* (☎852-4046) is also a good place for the usual café drinks and snacks – it has outdoor terrace seating and a bright, airy interior with rooftop and mountain views. Coffee and computer fiends might also head to the *Soft Rock Internet Café* in Connaught Square, a mini "mall" at 633 Connaught Drive. Turn left after the station for the utilitarian but very cheap *Smitty's Restaurant*, where you can drink coffee and write postcards all day.

Most **drinking** goes on in the *Atha-B* lounge at the *Athabasca Hotel*, 510 Patricia St, where the "nightclub" annexe has dancing and live music most nights, though things can get pretty rowdy. For something more relaxed, try *Pete's* bar, upstairs at 614 Patricia St, enter through the nondescript black door – once inside, it's big and bustling, with a laid-back young crowd. Another unpretentious locals' hangout is the *Astoria's De'd Dog Bar* at 404 Connaught Drive, which attracts more of a thirtyish crowd, with big-screen TV, music, darts and food. The bar in *Whistler's Inn* opposite the station has an old-style wooden bar and lots of memorabilia. If you want a more smoochy evening, the *Bonhomme Lounge* at the *Château Jasper*, 96 Geikie St, has a harpist most nights. The Chaba Theatre is a first-run **cinema** directly opposite the station. Nightlife generally is low-key: most of the campgrounds and motels are too far out of town for people to get in, and the fun is generally of the make-your-own variety out at hostels or campgrounds.

Every second year (even years) the town hosts the **Jasper Heritage Folk Festival** with performers from across North America playing in Centennial Park.

Mount Robson Provincial Park

The extensive **MOUNT ROBSON PROVINCIAL PARK** borders Jasper National Park to the west and protects Mount Robson which, at 3954m, is the highest peak in the Canadian Rockies. Its scenery equals anything anywhere else in the Rockies, and **Mount Robson** itself is one of the most staggering mountains you'll ever encounter. Facilities are thin on the ground, so stock up on food and fuel before entering the park. Around 16km beyond the park's western boundary, Hwy 16, comes the Tête Jaune Cache, where you can pick up one of two immensely scenic roads: the continuation of Hwy 16 north to Prince George (for routes to Prince Rupert, northern BC and the

HIKING IN MOUNT ROBSON PARK

Starting 2km from the park visitor centre, the **Berg Lake Trail** (22km one-way; 795m ascent) is perhaps the most popular short backpacking trip in the Rockies, and the only trail that gets anywhere near Mount Robson. You can do the first third or so as a comfortable and highly rewarding day-walk, passing through forest to lovely glacier-fed Kinney Lake (6.7km; campground at the lake's northeast corner). Many rank this among the Rockies best day-hikes and it's particularly good for naturalists. Trek the whole thing, however, and you traverse the stupendous Valley of a Thousand Waterfalls – the most notable being sixty-metre Emperor Falls (14.3km; campgrounds 500m north and 2km south) – and eventually enjoy the phenomenal area around Berg Lake itself (17.4km to its nearest, western shore). Mount Robson rises an almost sheer 2400m from the lakeshore, its huge cliffs cradling two creaking rivers of ice, Mist Glacier and Berg Glacier – the latter, one of the Rockies' few "living" or advancing glaciers, is 1800m long by 800m wide and the source of the great icebergs that give the lake its name. Beyond the lake you can pursue the trail 2km further to Robson Pass (21.9km; 1652m ascent; campground) and another 1km to Adolphus Lake in Jasper National Park. The most popular campsites are the *Berg Lake* (19.6km) and *Rearguard* (20.1km) campgrounds on Berg Lake itself; but if you've got a Jasper backcountry permit you could press on to Adolphus where there's a less-frequented site with more in the way of solitude.

Once you're camped at Berg Lake, a popular day-trip is to Toboggan Falls, which starts from the southerly *Berg Lake* campground and climbs the northeast (left) side of Toboggan Creek past a series of cascades and meadows to eventual views over the lake's entire hinterland. The trail peters out after 2km, but you can easily walk on and upward through open meadows for still better views. The second trail in the immediate vicinity is Robson Glacier (2km), a level walk that peels off south from the main trail 1km west of Robson Pass near the park ranger's cabin. It runs across an outwash plain to culminate in a small lake at the foot of the glacier; a rougher track then follows the lateral moraine on the glacier's east side, branching east after 3km to follow a small stream to the summit of Snowbird Pass (9km total from the ranger's cabin).

Two more hikes start from Yellowhead Lake, at the other (eastern) end of the park. To get to the trailhead for **Yellowhead Mountain** (4.5km one-way; 715m ascent), follow Hwy 16 9km down from the pass and then take a gravel road 1km on an isthmus across the lake. After a steep two-hour climb through forest, the trail levels out in open country at 1830m, offering sweeping views of the Yellowhead Pass area. The **Mount Fitzwilliam Trail** (13km one-way; 945m ascent), which leaves Hwy 16 about 1km east of the Yellowhead Mountain Trail (but on the other side of the highway), is a more demanding walk, especially over its last half, but if you don't want to backpack to the endpoint – a truly spectacular basin of lakes and peaks – you could easily walk through the forest to the campground at Rockingham Creek (6km).

Yukon), or Hwy 5, which heads south past Wells Gray Provincial Park to Kamloops and a whole range of onward destinations: the latter route is dealt with on p.411.

Both road and rail links to the park from Jasper climb through **Yellowhead Pass**, long one of the most important native and fur-trading routes across the Rockies. The pass, 20km west of Jasper Townsite, marks the boundary between Jasper and Mount Robson parks, Alberta and British Columbia, and Mountain and Pacific time zones – set your watch back one hour. This stretch of road is less dramatic than the Icefields Parkway, but then most roads are, given over to mixed woodland – birch interspersed with firs – and mountains that sit back from the road with less scenic effect. The railway meanders alongside the road most of the way, occasionally occupied by epic freight trains hundreds of wagons long – alien intrusions in the usual beguiling wilderness of rocks, river and forest. Just down from the pass, **Yellowhead Lake** is the park's first landmark. Look for moose around dawn and dusk at aptly named **Moose Lake**, another 20km further west.

Mount Robson

Even if the first taste of the park seems relatively tame, the first sight of **Mount Robson** is among the most breathtaking in the Rockies. The preceding ridges creep up in height hiding the massive peak itself from view until the last moment. The British explorer W.B. Cheadle described the mountain in 1863: "On every side the mighty heads of snowy hills crowded round, whilst, immediately behind us, a giant among giants, and immeasurably supreme, rose Robson's peak . . . We saw its upper portion dimmed by a necklace of light, feathery clouds, beyond which its pointed apex of ice, glittering in the morning sun, shot up far into the blue heaven above."

> The telephone code for the Mount Robson Provincial Park is ☎250.

The overall impression is of immense size, thanks mainly to the colossal scale of Robson's south face – a sheer rise of 3100m – and to the view from the road, which frames the mountain as a single mass isolated from other peaks. A spectacular glacier system, concealed on the mountain's north side, is visible if you make the popular backpacking hike to the Berg Lake area (see box opposite). The source of the mountain's name has never been agreed on, but could be a corruption of Robertson, a Hudson's Bay employee who was trapped in the region in the 1820s. Local natives called the peak *Yuh-hai-has-hun* – the "Mountain of the Spiral Road", an allusion to the clearly visible layers of rock that resemble a road winding to the summit. Not surprisingly, this monolith was one of the last major peaks in the Rockies to be conquered – it was first climbed in 1913, and is still considered a dangerous challenge.

Practicalities

Trains don't stop anywhere in the park, but if you're travelling by bus you can ask to be let off at Yellowhead Pass or the **Mount Robson Travel Infocentre** (daily June to early Sept 9am–7pm; no phone), located at the Mount Robson viewpoint near the western entrance to the park. Most of the park's few other facilities are found near the infocentre: a **café/garage** (May–Sept) and two fully serviced commercial **campgrounds** – *Emperor Ridge* (☎566-8438; $13.50; June–Sept), 300m north of Hwy 16 on Kinney Lake Road, and *Mount Robson Lodge & Robson Shadows Campground* (☎566-9190 or 566-4821 or 1-888/566-4821; $14.50; mid-May to mid-Oct), 25 nice sites on the Fraser River side of Hwy 16, 5km west of the park boundary. The 144-site *Mount Robson Provincial Park Campground* (☎566-4325; both $17.50; April–Oct) comprises two closely adjacent campgrounds – *Robson River* and *Robson Meadows* – and is situated further afield on Hwy 16, 22km north of Valemount. It offers hot showers and flush toilets and reservations can be made in advance (see box, p.544). Another park campground with the same name and the tag "Lucerne" (which has no reservations, dry toilets only and no showers; $12; May–Sept) is situated 10km west of the Alberta border on Hwy 16, just west of the eastern boundary of the Mount Robson Provincial Park. The only other beds in or near the park are the eighteen log-sided riverfront units (some with kitchens: $5 extra) at the *Mount Robson Lodge* (☎566-4821 or 1-888/566-4821; ④ May–Oct) that owns the *Robson Shadows Campground* (meals, river rafting, helicopter tours and horse riding are available nearby); and the cabins belonging to Mount Robson Adventure Holidays (☎566-4351; ③; June–Sept), 16km east of the infocentre (towards Jasper), though preference for these may go to people signed up for the company's **canoeing** and **hiking** day-trips. **Backcountry camping** in the park is only permitted at seven wilderness campgrounds dotted along the Berg Lake Trail (see box on p.538): to use these you have to register and pay an overnight fee at the infocentre.

The telephone code for the Yoho National Park is ☎250.

Yoho National Park

Wholly in British Columbia on the western side of the Continental Divide, **YOHO NATIONAL PARK**'s name derives from a Cree word meaning "wonder" – a fitting testament to the awesome grandeur of the region's mountains, lakes and waterfalls. At the same time it's a small park, whose intimate scale makes it perhaps the finest of the four parks and the one favoured by Rockies' connoisseurs. The Trans-Canada divides Yoho neatly in half, climbing from Lake Louise over the **Kicking Horse Pass** to share the broad, glaciated valley bottom of the Kicking Horse River with the old Canadian Pacific Railway. The only village, **Field**, has the park centre, services and limited accommodation (the nearest full-service towns are Lake Louise, 28km east, and **Golden**, 54km west). Other expensive accommodation is available at the central hubs, **Lake O'Hara**, the **Yoho Valley** and **Emerald Lake**, from which radiate most of the park's stunning and well-maintained trails – **hiking** in Yoho is magnificent – and a couple of lodges just off the Trans-Canada. Thus these areas – not Field – are the focal points of the park, and get very busy in summer. Side roads lead to Emerald Lake and the Yoho Valley, so if you choose you can drive in, do a hike and then move on at night.

Access to Lake O'Hara is far more difficult, being reserved for those on foot, or those with lodge or campground reservations, who must book for a special bus (full details are given beginning on p.544). The other five park-run campgrounds are all much more readily accessible, and there's a single road-accessible youth hostel in the Yoho Valley. The park also operates six backcountry campgrounds (see p.546). The Trans-Canada also gives direct access to short but scenic trails; as these take only an hour or so, they're the best choice if you only want a quick taste of the park before moving on. If you have time for one day-walk, make it the **Iceline–Whaleback–Twin Falls Trail**, rated among the top five day-hikes in the Rockies (see the box on p.546 for details of all hikes in the park). If you're cycling, note that **mountain biking** – very popular in the park – is restricted to several designated trails only: these are Kicking Horse (19.5km); the Amiskwi Trail to the Amiskwi River crossing (24km); the Otterhead Trail to Toche Ridge junction (8km); Ice River to Lower Ice Ridge warden cabin (17.5km); the Talley-Ho Trail (3km); and the Ottertail Trail as far as the warden cabin (14.7km).

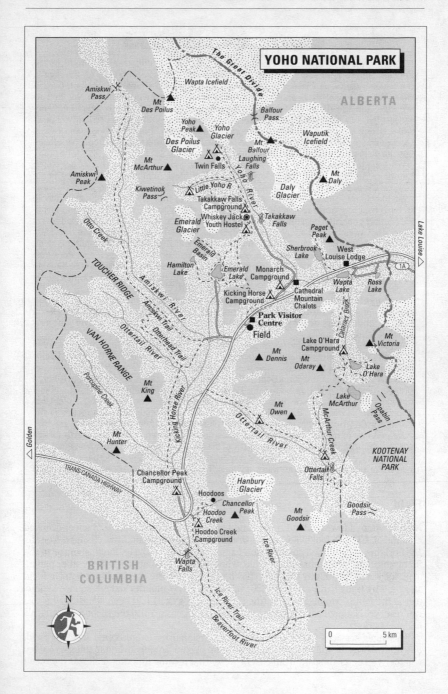

YOHO NATIONAL PARK

The Great Divide

Wapta Icefield

ALBERTA

Amiskwi Pass

Mt Des Poilus

Yoho Peak

Balfour Pass

Waputik Icefield

Des Poilus Glacier

Yoho Glacier

Mt Balfour

Laughing Falls

Mt McArthur

Twin Falls

Mt Daly

Amiskwi Peak

Kiwetinok Pass

Little Yoho R

Daly Glacier

Takakkaw Falls Campground

Emerald Glacier

Whiskey Jack Youth Hostel

Takakkaw Falls

Paget Peak

Emerald Basin

Sherbrook Lake

West Louise Lodge

Hamilton Lake

Emerald Lake

Monarch Campground

Wapta Lake

Ross Lake

Kicking Horse Campground

Cathedral Mountain Chalets

TOUCHER RIDGE

Park Visitor Centre

Field

Lake O'Hara Campground

Mt Victoria

Mt Dennis

Mt Odaray

Lake O'Hara

VAN HORNE RANGE

Mt King

Porcupine Creek

Mt Owen

Lake McArthur

McArthur Creek

Opabin Pass

Mt Hunter

Ottertail River

KOOTENAY NATIONAL PARK

TRANS-CANADA HIGHWAY

Chancellor Peak Campground

Ottertail Falls

Golden

Hoodoos

Hanbury Glacier

Hoodoo Creek

Chancellor Peak

Mt Goodsir

Goodsir Pass

Hoodoo Creek Campground

Wapta Falls

BRITISH COLUMBIA

Ice River

Ice River Trail

Beaverfoot River

N

0   5 km

Lake Louise

1A

Otto Creek

Amiskwi River

Amiskwi Trail

Otterhead Trail

Ottertail River

Kicking Horse River

Cataract Brook

RAFTING IN THE ROCKIES

If lazing around Maligne Lake in Jasper, or walking the odd trail elsewhere in the Rockies, sounds a bit tame, think about **white-water rafting** – currently all the rage in the national parks, and Jasper in particular. Many operators, notably in Jasper, Golden (near Yoho National Park) and in Banff, cater to an ever-growing demand. Not all trips are white-knuckle affairs. Depending on the river and trip you choose, some rafting tours are just that – gentle rafting down placid stretches of river. Others require that you be fit and a strong swimmer. Trips last anything from a couple of hours to a couple of days. Operators will point to the right trips (see "Activities" sections under national park headings for Banff and Lake Louise operators).

While no previous experience is required for most tours, one or two things are worth knowing; the most important is how rivers are **graded**. White water is ranked in six classes: Class 1 is gentle and Class 6 is basically a waterfall. The **season** generally runs from May to mid-September, with the "biggest" water in June and July, when glacial meltwater is coursing down rivers. Operators are licensed by the park authorities and invariably supply you with everything you need, from the basics of helmet and life jacket to wet suits, wool sweaters and spray jackets depending on the likely severity of the trip. They also provide shuttle services from main centres to the rivers themselves, and many on longer trips include lunch, snack or barbecue in the tour price. Bigger operators may also have on-site shower and changing facilities if you're on a run where you're likely to get seriously wet. On any trip it's probably a good idea to have a change of clothes handy for when you finish, wear training shoes or something you don't mind getting wet, and have a towel and bag for any valuables. Many people sport swimming costumes beneath clothing. Often you can choose between trips – gentle or severe – where you sit back and hang on while others do the work in oared boats, or you join a trip where everyone gets a paddle who wants one.

At Banff the **Bow River** has no major rapids, and gentle one-hour float trips are offered through pretty scenery by several operators. Most companies in Banff or Lake Louise offer trips on one of two rivers to the west of the park. The **Kootenay River** in Kootenay National Park, two hours from Banff, is a Class 2–3 river. The **Kicking Horse River**, a premier destination just an hour from Banff, is a much more serious affair. In and just outside Yoho National Park, it has Class 4 sections (Cable Car, Man Eater Hole, Goat Rapid, Twin Towers and the Roller Coaster) in its upper sections and stretches in the Lower Kicking Horse Canyon, which give even seasoned rafters pause for thought.

Jasper has perhaps the most possibilities on its doorstep. The Class 2 **Athabasca River** (from Athabasca Falls, 35km south of the town) is scenic and provides gentle rafting for families or those who just want a quiet river trip from May to October, but it also has one or two harmless white-water sections. The **Sunwapta River** nearby, 55km south

Field

No more than a few wooden houses, and backed by an amphitheatre of sheer-dropped mountains, **FIELD** looks like an old-world pioneer settlement, little changed from its 1884 origins as a railroad-construction camp (named after Cyrus Field, sponsor of the first transatlantic communication cable, who visited Yoho that year). As in other national parks, it was the railway that first spawned tourism in the area: the first hotel in Field was built by Canadian Pacific in 1886, and within a few months sixteen square kilometres at the foot of Mount Stephen (the peak to Field's east) had been set aside as a special reserve. National-park status arrived in 1911, making Yoho the second of Canada's national parks.

Passenger services (other than private excursions) no longer come through Field, but the **railway** is still one of the park "sights", and among the first things you see whether you enter the park from east or west. That it came this way at all was the result

of Jasper, is a Class 3 river with some thrilling stretches of water, magnificent scenery and good chances to spot wildlife. The **Maligne River**, 45km from town, is Class 2–3+, offering a wide variety of trips between July and September for the many operators who use this river (including a lively 1.6-kilometre stretch of rapids). Yet the most riotous local river is the **Fraser**, accessed an hour west of Jasper in Mount Robson Provincial Park. This is Class 4 in places, but also has some gentle sections where the chance to watch salmon spawning at close quarters from mid-August to September provides an added attraction.

Operators in Jasper include Maligne River Adventures, 627 Patricia St (☎852-3370, fax 852-3405), who run some of the wildest trips in the park: the four-hour "Sunwapta Challenge" ($60) uses six-passenger paddle-assisted rafts to ride parts of the Sunwapta – which means "turbulent river" in the local Stoney language. All equipment is supplied and they also lay on changing rooms and hot showers. They also offer two-hour "Mile 5 Run" (3 daily, $40) raft trips on the Athabasca River on small but lively rapids and three-hour "Heritage Run" trips (small paddle raft $55, larger passenger oar raft $40) on the same river suitable for families and children, as well as a three-day wilderness trip to the Kakwa and Smoky rivers. Jasper Raft Tours at Jasper Adventure Centre, 604 Connaught Drive (☎852-2665 or 1-888/553-5628) offer good trips for first-timers: two- to three-hour jaunts twice daily in summer on the Athabasca River in comfortable oar rafts. Tickets cost $41, including shuttle to and from the river, with possible pick-ups from your hotel by prior arrangement; tickets are also available from the Brewster office in the train station. Another long-established company offers similar trips at similar prices to suit all ages and courage levels on several rivers: White Water Rafting (Jasper) Ltd (☎852-7238 or 1-800/557-7328, fax 852-3623, *www.whitewaterjasper.com*), with advance reservations from Freewheel Cycles, 618 Patricia St and Alpine Petro Canada, 711 Connaught Drive – they claim to run trips in all weathers and make special provisions for visitors with disabilities. A two-hour trip on Grade 2 Athabasca water costs $40, three hours $50 (3 and 2 trips daily respectively); a two-hour Grade 3 trip on the Sunwapta costs $40 (2 daily).

If you want the real **rough stuff** on the Fraser contact Sekani Mountain Tours, Work World Store, 618 Patricia St (☎852-5211), for twenty Class 3 and 4 rapids along the fourteen-kilometre "Rearguard Run" (6hr 30min; $70 including lunch). If you're experienced you can join the 16km of continuous Class 4 and 4+ rapids on the "Canoe River" (8hr; $100) or put these together with the Rearguard in a two-day camping trip for $160. At the other extreme, the same company runs quiet punt-like trips to admire Mount Robson and see the salmon on the Fraser (10km; 5hr 30min; $35), as do Mount Robson Adventure Holidays (2hr; $39; ☎1-800/882-9921), whose twice-daily raft departures are complemented by an evening run during August. They also offer three-hour guided trips by canoe ($45) to Moose Marsh to spot birds and wildlife, with no experience necessary for this or their rafting trips.

of desperate political and economic horse trading. The Canadian Pacific's chief surveyor, Sandford Fleming, wrote of his journey over the proposed Kicking Horse Pass route in 1883: "I do not think I can forget that terrible walk; it was the greatest trial I ever experienced." Like many in the company he was convinced the railway should take the much lower and more amenable Yellowhead route to the north (see "Mount Robson Provincial Park", p.538). The railway was as much a political as a transportational tool, and designed to unite the country and encourage settlement of the prairies. A northerly route would have ignored great tracts of valuable prairie near the US border (around Calgary), and allowed much of the area and its resources (later found to include oil and gas) to slip from the Dominion into the hands of the US. Against all engineering advice, therefore, the railway was cajoled into taking the Kicking Horse route, and thus obliged to negotiate four percent grades, the greatest of any commercial railway of the time.

The result was the infamous **Spiral Tunnels**, two vast figure-of-eight galleries within the mountains; from a popular viewpoint about 7km east of Field on Hwy 1, you can

---

watch the front of goods trains emerge from the tunnels before the rear wagons have even entered. Still more notorious was the **Big Hill**, where the line drops 330m in just 6km from Wapta Lake to the flats east of Field (the 4.5 percent grade was the steepest in North America). The very first construction train to attempt the descent plunged into the canyon, killing three railway workers. Runaways became so common that four blasts on a whistle became the standard warning for trains careering out of control (the rusted wreck of an engine can still be seen near the main *Kicking Horse Park Campground*). Lady Agnes MacDonald, wife of the Canadian prime minister, rode down the Big Hill on the front cowcatcher (a metal frame in front of the locomotive to scoop off animals) in 1886, remarking that it presented a "delightful opportunity for a new sensation". She'd already travelled around 1000km on her unusual perch: her lily-livered husband, with whom she was meant to be sharing the symbolic trans-Canada journey to commemorate the opening of the railway, managed just 40km on the cowcatcher. Trains climbing the hill required four locomotives to pull a mere fifteen coaches: the ascent took over an hour, and exploding boilers (and resulting deaths) were recurrent.

The Burgess Shales

Yoho today ranks as highly among geologists as it does among hikers and railway buffs, thanks to the world-renowned **Burgess Shales**, an almost unique geological formation situated close to Field village. The shales – layers of sediamentary rock – lie on the upper slopes of Mount Field and consist of the fossils of some 120 types of soft-bodied marine creatures from the Middle Cambrian period (515–530 million years ago), one of only three places in the world where the remains of these unusual creatures are found. Soft-bodied creatures usually proved ill-suited to the fossilization process, but in the Burgess Shales the fossils are so well preserved and detailed that in some cases scientists can identify what the creatures were eating before they died. Plans are in hand to open a major new museum in Field devoted to the Shales, but in the meantime access is restricted to protect the fossils, and fossil-hunting, needless to say, is strictly prohibited. The area can only be seen on two strenuous guided hikes to Walcott's Quarry and the Trilobite beds. The walks are led by qualified guides, limited to fifteen people and run between late June and October. For details and reservations, contact the Yoho Burgess Shale Foundation (☎1-800/343-3006).

Practicalities

Yoho's **park information centre**, marked by a distinctive blue roof about 1km east of Field (daily: mid-May to late June & Sept 9am–5pm; late June to Aug 8.30am–7pm; Oct to mid-May 9am–4pm; ☎343-6783 or 343-6433, *www.parkscanada.pch.gc.ca/yoho*), sells park permits, makes backcountry registrations, takes bookings for Lake O'Hara (see p.548), has displays, lectures and slide shows (notably on the famous Burgess Shales), and advises on trail and climbing conditions. It also gives out a useful *Backcountry Guide* with full details of all trails and sells 1:50,000 **maps** of the park. Backcountry camping requires a permit, and if you intend to camp at Lake O'Hara (see p.548) it's essential to make **reservations** at the information centre. The Park Administration Office in Field offers similar help and services in and out of season (Mon–Fri 8am–4.30pm; ☎343-6324). Enquire at the park centre for details of activities arranged by the "Friends of Yoho" (☎343-6393) and the two free guided walks: "Emerald Lakeshore Stroll" (July to late Aug Sat 10am; 2hr 30min/5km; meet at Emerald Lake Trailhead) and "Walk into the Past" (July & Aug Mon & Thurs 7pm; 1hr 30min; meet at the Old Bake oven at *Kicking Horse Campground*). Other park-run activites include Kicking Horse Campground Theatre (July & Aug Sat, Sun & Tues at 9pm, 8pm last ten days of Aug) and wildlife and other talks at the Hoodoo Creek Campfire Circle (July & Aug Mon & Fri 9pm, 8pm last ten days of Aug).

Whatever other literature may say, there are now no VIA Rail passenger trains to Field. The village is, however, a flag stop for Greyhound **buses** (5 daily in each direction) – wave them down from the Petro-Canada just east of the turn-off from the highway to the village, though most stop anyway to drop packages.

Yoho's popularity and accessibility mean huge pressure on **accommodation** in late July and August: if you're really stuck, you can always make for one of the motels in Golden (see p.551). The only officially listed **rooms** in Field itself, a fine base if you have transport, are at the excellent *Kicking Horse Lodge and Café*, 100 Centre St (café open summer only; ☎343-6303 or 1-800/659-4944; ⑥), though you can also try one of the new so-called B&B "kitchens" – fully furnished suites in private homes – of which there were ten dotted around the village at last count: *Alpenglow Guesthouse* (☎343-6356); *Mount Burgess Bungalow* (☎343-6480); *Bear's Den Guesthouse* (☎343-6439); *Canadian Rockies Guesthouse* (☎343-6046); *Lynx Lair* (☎343-6421); *Mount Stephen Guesthouse* (☎343-6441); *Otterhead Guesthouse* (☎343-6034); *Sunset Guesthouse* (☎343-6333); *Van Horne Guesthouse* (☎343-6380); *Yoho Accommodation* (☎343-6444 or 343-6445) – all ④. All are similarly and reasonably priced, and all are easily found in the tiny village – call for precise directions – most lying on the central 1st Avenue or parallel Kicking Horse Avenue.

Away from the village, but on or just off the Trans-Canada (Hwy 1), the twenty units of *Cathedral Mountain Chalets* (☎343-6442; off-season from Oct to mid-May call or fax ☎762-0514, *www.cathedralmountain.com*; ⑦ mid-May to mid-Oct), 4km east of Field and fifteen-minutes' drive from Lake Louise (leave the highway at the Takakkaw Falls turn-off), and the bigger and less expensive fifty-room *West Louise Lodge* (☎343-6311; ⑤) just inside the park boundary, 11km west of Lake Louise (with café, restaurant and indoor pool). There's also the **youth hostel** in the Yoho Valley (see p.549), perfectly situated for many superb walks, and an expensive lodge at Emerald Lake.

The most central of the five park-run **campgrounds**, the 86-site *Kicking Horse* ($18; mid-May to early Oct), lies 5km east of Field just off the Trans-Canada (Hwy 1) near the junction with Yoho Valley Road for Takakkaw Falls. It's fully serviced (coin showers) and pleasingly forested, though it echoes somewhat with goods trains rumbling through day and night. In summer a separate overflow site is often opened (no showers), but even this fills up and you should aim to arrive extremely early. Remember: all park campgrounds are first-come, first-served. A short distance east up Yoho Valley Road is the second of the park's major campgrounds, the 46-site *Monarch* ($13; late June to early Sept): the third, the 35-site *Takakkaw Falls* ($13; late June to first snow) lies at the end of the same road by the eponymous falls and is the best-placed for local hikes (see box overleaf). The remaining two sites are both close to the park's western border, lying just north and south of the Trans-Canada: the 106-site *Hoodoo Creek* (no showers; $14; late June to early Sept) and 64-site *Chancellor Peak* (no showers; $13;

HIKES IN YOHO NATIONAL PARK

HIKES FROM LAKE O'HARA

For walking purposes the Lake O'Hara region divides into five basic zones, each of which deserves a full day of exploration: **Lake Oesa**, the **Opabin Plateau** (this area and others are often closed to protect their grizzlies), **Lake McArthur**, the **Odaray Plateau** and the **Duchesnay Basin**.

If you have time to do only one day-hike, the classic (if not the most walked) trails are the **Wiwaxy Gap** (12km; 495m ascent), rated by some among the top five day-walks in the Canadian Rockies, or the **Opabin Plateau Trail** (3.2km one-way; 250m ascent), from the Lake O'Hara Lodge to Opabin Lake. Despite the latter's brevity, you could spend hours wandering the plateau's tiny lakes and alpine meadows on the secondary trails that crisscross the area. Most people return to O'Hara via the East Circuit Trail, but a still more exhilarating hike – and a good day's outing – is to walk the Yukness Ledge, a section of the Alpine Circuit (see below) that cuts up from the East Circuit just 400m after leaving Opabin Lake. This spectacular high-level route leads to the beautiful Lake Oesa, from where it's just 3.2km down to Lake O'Hara. Oesa is one of many beautiful lakes in the region, and the Lake Oesa Trail (3.2km one-way; 240m ascent) from Lake O'Hara is the single most walked path in the O'Hara area. Close behind comes the Lake McArthur Trail (3.5km one-way; 310m ascent) which leads to the largest and most photographed of the lakes in the Lake O'Hara area. The Odaray Plateau Trail (2.6km one-way; 280m ascent) is another highly rated, but rather overpopular hike.

The longest and least-walked path is the Linda Lake–Cathedral Basin trip, past several lakes to a great viewpoint at Cathedral Platform Prospect (7.4km one-way; 305m ascent). The most challenging hike is the high-level Alpine Circuit (11.8km), taking in Oesa, Opabin and Schaffer lakes. This is straightforward in fine weather, and when all the snow has melted; very fit and experienced walkers should have little trouble, though there's considerable exposure, and some scrambling is required. At other times it's best left to climbers, or left alone completely.

YOHO VALLEY AND EMERALD LAKE HIKES

Most trails in the Yoho Valley area start from the Takakkaw Falls campground and car park at the end of the Yoho Valley Road. Many of the area's trails connect, and some run over the ridge to the Emerald Lake region, offering numerous permutations. We've tried to highlight the very best. If you want a stroll from the main trailhead at the campground after a drive or cycle, then walk to Point Lace Falls (1.9km one-way; minimum ascent) or Laughing Falls (3.8km one-way; 60m gain). Another shortish, extremely popular walk from the same car park is the Yoho Pass (10.9km; 310m ascent, 510m height loss), which links to Emerald Lake and its eponymous lodge (though you'll need transport arranged at the lake). A southern branch from this hike will take you over the Burgess Pass and down into Field, another manageable day-trip with fine overviews of the entire area.

If you want to follow the most tramped path in the Yoho Valley, however, take the Twin Falls Trail (8.5km one-way; 290m ascent) from the Takakkaw Falls car park. This easy six-hour return journey passes the Laughing Falls (see above) and has the reward of the Twin Falls cataract at the end, plus fine scenery and other lesser waterfalls en route. Stronger walkers could continue over the highly recommended Whaleback Trail (4.5km one-way; 1hr 30min) to give some quite incredible views of the glaciers at the valley head. A complete circuit returning to Takakkaw Falls with the Whaleback is 20.1km.

early May to late Sept). An additional fee of $4 is charged at all campgrounds for use of firewood.

The six **backcountry campgrounds** (see maps p.548 and p.550) are *McArthur Creek* (ten sites); *Float Creek* (four sites); *Yoho Lake* (eight sites); *Laughing Falls* (eight sites); *Twin Falls* (eight sites); and *Little Yoho* (ten sites): the only facilities are privies

If you're allowing yourself just one big walk in Yoho it's going to be a hard choice between the Takakkaw Falls–Twin Falls–Whaleback Trail just described or the Iceline–Little Yoho Valley–(Whaleback)–Twin Falls combination. The latter is often cited as one of the top five day-walks in the Rockies, and on balance might be the one to go for, though both options duplicate parts of one another's route. The Iceline (695m vertical gain), specially built in 1987, also starts close to the Takakkaw Falls car park at the *Whiskey Jack* youth hostel, climbing west through a large avalanche path onto a level bench with jaw-dropping views of the Emerald Glacier above and the Daly Glacier across the valley. It contours above Lake Celeste (a trail drops to this lake, making a shorter 17km circuit in all back to the car park) and then drops to the Little Yoho Valley and back to Takakkaw Falls for a 19.8-kilometre circuit. If you're very fit (or can camp overnight to break the trip), tagging on the Whaleback before returning to Takakkaw Falls makes a sensational 27-kilometre walk with 1000m of ascent.

Most people will want to do this as a backpacking option (there are four backcountry sites up here) – and they don't come much better – though the Iceline–Little Yoho walk coupled with the trek west to the Kiwetinok Pass (30km; 1070m) is also in many people's list of top-five day/backpacking Rocky Mountain walks. Juggling further with the permutations brings the Whaleback into this last combination to make one of the best backpacking routes in the Rockies: Iceline–Little Yoho Valley–Kiwetinok Pass–Whaleback (35.5km; 1375m ascent), a route up there with the Rockwall Trail in Kootenay, Skyline in Jasper and Berg Lake in Mount Robson Provincial Park.

From Emerald Lake, if you just want a stroll, then follow the self-guided and wheelchair-accessible nature trail (4.6km circuit; minimal ascent) around the lake from the parking area to the bridge at the back of the lake. Even shorter is the trail from the entrance to the parking area to Hamilton Falls (1.6km return; minimal ascent). The best day-trip is the comparatively underused but interesting Hamilton Lake Trail (5.5km one-way; 850m ascent; 2–3hr), again leaving from the parking area at the end of Emerald Lake Road. It's demanding and steep in places, and confined to forest for the first hour or so – thereafter it's magnificent, culminating in a classic alpine lake. The more modest climb to Emerald Basin, which you could manage in half a day (4.3km one-way; 300m ascent; 1–2hr), also gives relative peace and quiet, following the lakeshore before climbing through a forest of yew and hemlock, and ending in a small, rocky amphitheatre of hanging glaciers and avalanche paths.

HIKES FROM THE TRANS-CANADA

Five short walks can be accessed off the Trans-Canada Highway as it passes through Yoho. From east to west these are: Ross Lake (1.3km), a stunning little walk given the loveliness of the lake and the ease with which you reach it (accessed 1km south of the Great Divide picnic area); Sherbrooke Lake (3.1km), a peaceful subalpine lake accessible from the Wapta Lake picnic area (5km west of the Great Divide), where stronger walkers can peel off after 1.4km to Paget Lookout for huge views of the Kicking Horse Valley (3.5km; 520m ascent); Mount Stephen Fossil Beds (2.7km), a short but very steep trail, for fossil lovers only, from 1st Street E in Field; Hoodoo Creek (3.1km), on the western edge of the park (22km west of Field), accessed from the 600-metre gravel road from the *Hoodoo Creek* campground (the steep path leads to the weirdly eroded hoodoos themselves, pillars of glacial debris topped by protective capping stones), and finally Wapta Falls (2.4km), an excellent and almost level forty-minute walk on a good trail to Yoho's largest waterfalls (by volume of water), accessed via a 1.6-kilometre dirt road 25km west of Field.

(except *Float Creek*) and bear poles. All of these campgrounds are popular, but unlike the frontcountry campgrounds (where it's first-come, first-served) between one and three sites at each campground can be reserved up to 21 days in advance through the park centre at Field. **Random camping** is allowed in the Amiskwi, Otterhead, Lower Ice River and Porcupine valleys, but check current closures: you must be at least 3km from any road, 100m from water, 50m from a trail and purchase the usual $6 back-country pass.

Lake O'Hara

Backed up against the Continental Divide at the eastern edge of the park, **Lake O'Hara** is one of the Rockies' finest all-round enclaves – staggering scenery, numerous lakes, and an immense diversity of alpine and subalpine terrain. It's a great base for concentrated hiking: you could easily spend a fortnight exploring the well-constructed trails that strike out from the central lodge and campground. The setting is matchless, the lake framed by two of the peaks that also overlook Lake Louise across the ridge – mounts Lefroy (3423m) and Victoria (3464m). The one problem is **access**, which is severely restricted to safeguard the mountain flora and fauna.

To get there, turn off the Trans-Canada onto Hwy 1A (3.2km west of the Continental Divide), cross the railway and turn right onto the gravel road leading to the parking area (1km). This fire road continues all the way up to the lake (13km), but it's not open to general traffic (or bikes – *no* bikes are allowed on the road or anywhere else in the Lake O'Hara region). Getting up here, therefore, is quite a performance, but worth it if you want to hike some of the continent's most stunning scenery. Anybody can walk the 13km up the road, or the more picturesque **Cataract Brook Trail** (12.9km), which runs roughly parallel to the road, but a quota system applies for the bus up here and the campground at the end; and, after 13km, of course, you'd need to be superfit to get in any meaningful walking in the area where it matters. Aim instead for the special **bus** from the car park up to the lake, but note that priority is given to those with reservations or those with reservations for the lodge, campground or Alpine Club huts. Reservations for bus and campground can be made three months in advance by tele-

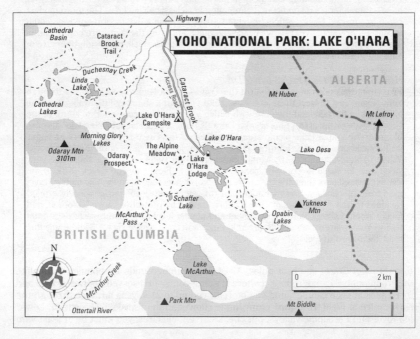

phone only (March 20–April 18 Mon–Fri 8am–noon; April 19 to mid-June Mon–Fri 8am–4pm; mid-June to Aug daily 8am–4pm; Sept reduced hours; ☎343-6433). If you're going **for the day**, your only feasible buses leave at 8.30am and 10.30am, and the maximum number in a party is six. If you want to use the campground you have to have dates ready (up to a maximum of four nights), state the number of people, the number of campsites required (maximum of two per party, one tent per site) and your preferred bus time (first and second choices from 8.30am, 10.30am, 4.30pm or 7.30pm). The reservation fee for bus (day-use or campground) is $10 and the return bus fare $12, payable by credit card over the phone. Cancellation must be made to an answering machine (☎343-6344); you forfeit your booking fee, and you can't just cancel the first day of several you booked to camp and expect to come later. Cancellations made less than three days in advance mean you lose the booking fee, half the bus fare and, if you're camping, the first night's campground fee. Cancel after 4pm on the day before your trip and you lose everything.

If all this sounds like Kafka has hit the Rockies, remember the park does merit attention, but if you don't manage to plan in advance there are arrangements for **stand-bys**: six day-use places are available daily and five campsites are kept available each night. You must reserve at the Field park information centre in person the day *before* you wish to take the bus and/or camp: these places are *not* available over the phone, and you'll have to get to the centre early. To stay in one of the 23 rooms at *Lake O'Hara Lodge* (☎343-6418, *www.lakeoharalodge.com*; ⑨; Feb to mid-April & mid-June to late Sept), you need to reserve weeks in advance and be prepared to part with a large amount of money. Out of season you can make bookings by post to Box 55, Lake Louise, Alberta T0L 1E0, or call ☎403/678-4110.

The Yoho Valley and Emerald Lake

Less compact an area than Lake O'Hara, the **Yoho Valley** and nearby **Emerald Lake** are far more accessible for casual visitors, and offer some great sights – the Takakkaw Falls in particular – and a variety of top-notch trails. Both areas were formerly used by the Cree to hide their women and children while the men crossed the mountains into Alberta to trade and hunt buffalo. The eradication of the buffalo herds, and the arrival of the railway in 1884, put paid to such ways. The lake was "discovered" by Tom Wilson, the same Canadian Pacific employee who first saw Lake Louise. He named it Emerald Lake after its colour. Now the lake and valley combine to form one of the Rockies' most important backpacking zones. Though popular and easily reached – access roads head north from the Trans-Canada to both the Emerald and Yoho valleys – the region is not, however, quite as crowded as its counterpart to the south. The scenery is equally mesmerizing, and if fewer of the trails are designed for day-hikes, many of them interlock so that you can tailor walks to suit your schedule or fitness (see box on pp.546–7).

Most trails (see box) start from the end of the Yoho Valley Road at the **Takakkaw Falls** parking area; the road leaves the Trans-Canada about 5km east of Field (signed from the *Kicking Horse* campground), a narrow and switchbacking route unsuitable for trailers and RVs and open in the summer only. It's 14km from the Trans-Canada to the parking area. The cascades' total 254-metre drop make them among the most spectacular road-accessible falls in the mountains: *takakkaw* is a Cree word roughly meaning "it is wonderful". The *Whiskey Jack* **youth hostel**, ideally placed just beyond the end of the Yoho Valley Road, 500m south of Takakkaw Falls, has room for 27 in three dorms (reservations ☎762-4122, *www.hostellingintl.ca/alberta*; $15–19; mid-June to mid-Sept). Close by is the park-run *Takakkaw Falls* **campground** with 35 unserviced sites ($13; mid-June to mid-Sept). Trails to the north (see box, p.546–547) lead to four further backcountry campgrounds, while the Alpine Club of Canada operates a members-only

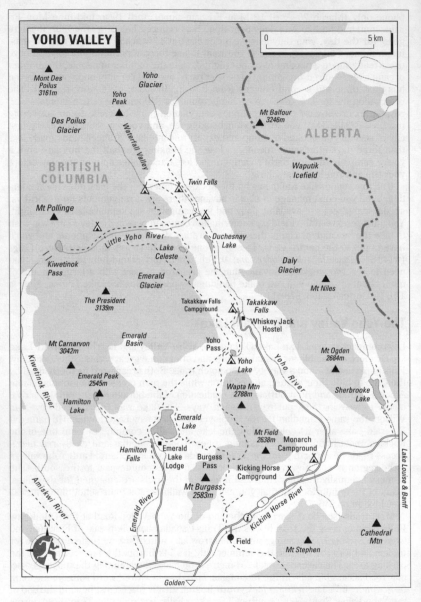

YOHO VALLEY

0   5 km

Mont Des
Poilus
3161m

Yoho
Glacier

Yoho
Peak

Des Poilus
Glacier

Mt Balfour
3246m

ALBERTA

BRITISH
COLUMBIA

Waputik
Icefield

Twin Falls

Mt Pollinge

Little Yoho River

Duchesnay
Lake

Lake
Celeste

Daly
Glacier

Kiwetinok
Pass

Emerald
Glacier

Mt Niles

The President
3139m

Takakkaw Falls
Campground

Takakkaw
Falls

Emerald
Basin

Whiskey Jack
Hostel

Yoho
Pass

Mt Carnarvon
3042m

Mt Ogden
2684m

Yoho
Lake

Kiwetinok River

Emerald Peak
2545m

Wapta Mtn
2788m

Sherbrooke
Lake

Hamilton
Lake

Yoho River

Emerald
Lake

Hamilton
Falls

Emerald
Lake
Lodge

Mt Field
2638m

Monarch
Campground

Burgess
Pass

Kicking Horse
Campground

Amiskwi River

Emerald River

Mt Burgess
2583m

Kicking Horse River

Lake Louise & Banff

N

Field

Cathedral
Mtn

Mt Stephen

Golden

trail hut 8.5km north of Takakkaw Falls ($15); reservations are required – write to Box 1026, Banff, Alberta T0L 0C0, or call ☎403/762-4481.

The Emerald Lake Road leaves the Trans-Canada about 2km west of Field and ends, 8km on, at the *Emerald Lake Lodge* (☎343-6321 or 1-800/663-6336, *www.crmr.com*; ⑧), which has a **restaurant** where walking boots are certainly not in order, and a less formal **bar** for drinks and snacks. If you want to stay, advance reservations are essential and prices are steep – between $300 and $400 in high season, less outside summer. Like the Yoho Valley Road, this road offers access to easy strolls and a couple of good day- or half-day hikes (see box, p.546).

Golden

GOLDEN, 54km west of Field and midway between Yoho and Glacier national parks, is the nearest town to either. Despite its name and mountain backdrop, the part of Golden most people see amounts to little more than an ugly ribbon of motels and garages at the junction of Hwy 1 and Hwy 95. The town proper occupies a semi-scenic site down by the Columbia River, way below the highway strip, but only if you use the municipal campground or book onto one of the many rafting and other **tours** based here will you do anything but look down on it from above. The town has a small **museum** at 1302-11th St (July & Aug daily 9am–5pm; $3; ☎344-5169). The main **infocentre** is at 500-10th Ave N (year-round; ☎344-7125, fax 344-6688), but a small info-centre also sits at the strip's southern end disguised as a plastic and wood tepee (June–Sept). Two hundred metres north is the **bus terminal**, next to the Chinese-Canadian *Golden Palace Restaurant* – open 24 hours a day, like several of the local joints. All the **motels** on the strip – try the *Selkirk Inn*, Hwy 1 (☎344-6315 or 344-5153; ④) – look over the road or onto the backs of garages opposite. None has anything you could call a view of the mountains, but at least the big *Sportsman*, 1200-12th St N (☎344-2915 or 1-888/477-6783; ③), is off the road. Around 16km northwest of Golden, the *Blaeberry Mountain Lodge*, on Moberly School Road (☎344-5296; ④), is first-rate and beautifully situated: accommodation consists of two simple but comfortable log cabins, a lodge and a tepee. There are also plenty of outdoor activities and the owners will often pick you up in Golden if you're travelling without your own transport.

Down in the town proper, a good place to **eat** standard Canadian fare like salads, chicken, pasta and seafood is the *Turning Point*, 902 11th Ave S. Note that finding places in Golden can be diificult if you don't know that all the "South" streets are on one side of the river, all the "North" streets on the other.

Campgrounds have prettier settings, particularly the *Whispering Spruce* (☎344-6680; $12–15) at 1430 Golden View Rd on Hwy 1 2km east of the Hwy 95 intersection. The town's own site, the *Golden Municipal Campground* (☎344-5412 or 1-800/622-4653; $13; mid-May to mid-Oct), is on the banks of the river on 10th Avenue, three blocks east of the main street. It has flush toilets, hot showers, wash houses, firewood and is adjacent to a swimming pool and tennis courts.

Glacier National Park

Strictly speaking, **GLACIER NATIONAL PARK** is part of the Selkirk and Columbia Mountains rather than the Rockies, but on the ground little sets it apart from the magnificence of the other national parks, and all the park agencies include it on an equal footing with its larger neighbours. It is, however, to a great extent the domain of ice, rain and snow; the weather is so atrocious that locals like to say that it rains or snows four days out of every three, and in truth you can expect a soaking three days out of five. As the name suggests, **glaciers** – 422 of them – form its dominant landscape, with fourteen percent of the park permanently blanketed with ice or snow. Scientists have identified 68 new glaciers forming on the sites of previously melted ice sheets in the park – a highly uncommon phenomenon. The main ice sheet, the still-growing **Illecillewaet Neve**, is easily seen from the Trans-Canada Highway or from the park visitor centre.

The Columbia range's peaks are every bit as imposing as those of the Rockies – Glacier's highest point, **Mount Dawson**, is 3390m tall – and historically they've presented as much of a barrier as their neighbours. Aboriginal peoples and then railwaymen shunned the icefields and the rugged interior for centuries until the discovery of **Rogers Pass** (1321m) in 1881 by Major A.B. Rogers, the chief engineer of the Canadian Pacific. Suffering incredible hardships, navvies drove the railway over the pass by 1885, paving the way for trains which, until 1916, helped to open the region both to settlers and tourists. Despite the railway's best efforts the pounding of repeated avalanches eventually forced the company to bore a tunnel under the pass, and the flow of visitors fell to almost nothing.

In the 1950s the pass was chosen as the route for the Trans-Canada Highway, whose completion in 1962 once again made the area accessible. This time huge snowsheds were built, backed up by the world's largest **avalanche-control system**. Experts monitor the slopes year-round, and at dangerous times they call in the army, who blast howitzers into the mountains to dislodge potential slips.

Glacier is easy enough to get to, but it doesn't tie in well with a circuit of the other parks; many people end up traversing it at some point simply because the main route west passes this way, but comparatively few stop, preferring to admire the scenery from the road. The visitor centre is a flag stop for Greyhound **buses**, which zip through up to seven times a day in each direction. Entering Glacier you pass from Mountain to Pacific time – remember to set your watch back an hour.

Practicalities

The **Rogers Pass visitor centre** (daily: April to mid-June & mid-Sept to Oct 9am–5pm; mid-June to mid-Sept 8am–8.30pm; Nov Thurs–Mon 9am–5pm; Dec–March 7am–5pm ☎837-6274 or 837-7500, *www.parkscanada.pch.gc.ca/glacier*), 1km west of Rogers Pass,

---

HIKING IN GLACIER

Glacier's primary renown is among serious climbers, but day-hikers and backpackers have plenty of options. Some of the park's 21 trails (140km of walking in all) push close to glaciers for casual views of the ice – though only two spots are now safe at the toe of the Illecillewaet – and the backcountry is noticeably less busy than in the Big Four parks to the east.

The easiest short strolls off the road are the Abandoned Rails Trail (1.2km one-way; 30min), along old rail beds to abandoned snowsheds betweeen the Rogers Pass centre and the Summit Monument (suitable for wheelchairs); the Loop Trail (1.6km) from the viewpoint just east of the Loop Brook campground, full of viewpoints and features relating to the building of the railway; the Hemlock Grove Boardwalk (400m), a stroll through old growth stands of western hemlock trees, some more than 350 years old (wheelchair-accessible; trailhead midway between Loop Brook campground and the park's western boundary); and the Meeting of the Water Trail (30min) from the Illecillewaet campground, the hub of Glacier's trail network. Six manageable day-hikes from the campground give superb views onto the glaciers, particularly the Great Glacier, Avalanche Crest and Abbott's Ridge trails. Other hikes, not centred on the campground, include Bostock Creek (9km) and Flat Creek (9km), a pair of paths on the park's western edge heading north and south respectively from the same point on the Trans-Canada.

Among the backpacking routes, the longest is the Beaver River Trail (30km-plus), which peels off from the highway at the Mount Shaughnessy picnic area on the eastern edge (also a favourite mountain-bike route). The single best long-haul trail, however, is the Copperstain Creek Trail (16km), which leaves the Beaver River path after 3km, and climbs to meadows and bleak alpine tundra from where camping and onward walking options are almost endless.

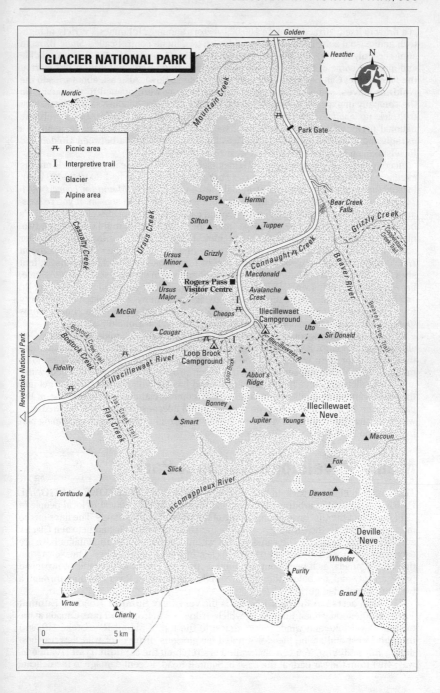

GLACIER NATIONAL PARK

N

Nordic

Golden

Heather

Park Gate

Mountain Creek

⊼ Picnic area
I Interpretive trail
Glacier
Alpine area

Rogers
Hermit
Sifton
Tupper
Bear Creek Falls

Grizzly Creek

Coppercrown Creek Trail

Casualty Creek

Ursus Creek

Ursus Minor
Grizzly
Macdonald
Connaught Creek

Ursus Major
Rogers Pass Visitor Centre
Avalanche Crest
Beaver River

McGill
Cheops
Illecillewaet Campground
Uto
Sir Donald

Cougar
Loop Brook Campground
I
Illecillewaet R.
Beaver River Trail

Bostock Creek Trail
Illecillewaet River
Loop Brook
Abbot's Ridge

Fidelity

Bostock Creek

Revelstoke National Park

Flat Creek Trail

Bonney
Illecillewaet Neve

Smart
Jupiter
Youngs

Flat Creek
Macoun

Slick
Fox

Incomappleux River
Dawson

Fortitude

Deville Neve

Wheeler

Purity

Grand

Virtue
Charity

0   5 km

is a draw in itself, attracting some 160,000 visitors annually. It houses a variety of high-tech audiovisual aids, including a fun video on avalanche control called *Snow Wars*. In summer (July & Aug), book here for **guided walks** (1–6hr) featuring flowers, wildlife and glaciers, some of them fairly strenuous and lasting up to six hours. Walks start at the Illecillewaet Campground Welcome Station (see below). Also ask about trips to the **Nakimu Caves**, some of the largest in Canada: they were opened to the public (in the company of experienced guides only) in 1995. If you're heading for the backcountry, pick up *Footloose in the Columbias*, a hiker's guide to Glacier and Revelstoke national parks; you can also buy good walking **maps**. Next to the visitor centre, a **garage** and a **shop** are the only services on the Trans-Canada between Golden and Revelstoke, an hour's drive east and west respectively.

Accommodation is best sought in Golden (see p.551). The sole in-park **hotels** are the excellent fifty-room *Best Western Glacier Park Lodge* (☎837-2126 or 1-800/528-1234; ⑥), located just east of the visitor centre, and the 24-unit *Heather Mountain Lodge* (☎344-7490; closed Nov), 20km east of the Pass: both tend to be full in season. If you're passing through, it has a useful 24-hour service and cafeteria. Other places close to Glacier's borders are the ten-unit *Purcell Lodge* (mid-June to mid-Oct & mid-Dec to April; two-night minumum stay; ☎344-2639; ⑥), a remote lodge at 2180m on the eastern border accessible only by hiking trail, scheduled helicopter flights or winter ski trails; *Canyon Hot Springs Resort Campground*, 35km east of Revelstoke (☎837-2420; cabins ⑦, tent sites $19–25; May–Sept), which has mineral hot and warm springs, secluded sites, café, firewood and 12 cabins with B&B deals available; *Hillside Lodge*, 1740 Seward Front Rd (☎344-7281; ④) – nine cosy cabins set in sixty acres 13km west of Golden at Blaeberry River with breakfast included; and *Big Lake Resort*, Kinbasket Lake (no phone; rooms ⑦, tents $12; May–Oct), 25km west of Golden off Hwy 1 at Donald Station.

The park-run **campgrounds** are the 57-site *Illecillewaet* ($13; mid-June to early Oct; also winter camping), 3.4km west of the visitor centre just off the Trans-Canada (and the trailhead for eight walks), and the twenty-site *Loop Brook*, 2km further west ($13; mid-June to mid-Oct; self-serve check-in), which provides the luxuries of wood, water and flush toilets only on a first-come, first-served basis. If you don't manage to get into these, or want more facilities, there are three commercial campgrounds west of the park on the Trans-Canada towards Revelstoke. Wilderness camping is allowed anywhere if you register with the visitor centre, pay for a nightly backcountry camping permit ($6) and pitch more than 5km from the road.

Mount Revelstoke National Park

The smallest national park in the region, **MOUNT REVELSTOKE NATIONAL PARK** is a somewhat arbitrary creation, put together at the request of local people in 1914 to protect the Clachnacudainn Range of the Columbia Mountains. The lines on the map mean little, for the thrilling scenery in the 16km of no-man's-land between Glacier and Revelstoke is largely the same as that within the parks. The mountains here are especially steep, their slopes often scythed clear of trees by avalanches. The views from the Trans-Canada, as it peeks out of countless tunnels, are of forests and snowcapped peaks aplenty and, far below, the railway and the Illecillewaet River crashing through a twisting, steep-sided gorge.

The main access to the park interior is the very busy **Summit Road**, or **Summit Parkway** (generally open June–Oct), which strikes north from the Trans-Canada at the town of Revelstoke and winds 26km almost to the top of Mount Revelstoke (1938m) through forest and alpine meadows noted for glorious displays of wild flowers (best during July and Aug). You can also walk this stretch on the **Summit Trail** (10km one-way; 4hr) from the car park at the base of Summit Road. Recent damage to the delicate

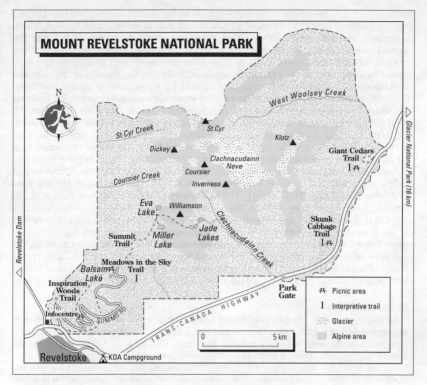

MOUNT REVELSTOKE NATIONAL PARK

ecosystem has prompted park authorities to rethink, and often the last 1.5km of the road is closed to cars, leaving the choice of a walk or regular shuttle bus to the summit from a car park at Balsam Lake.

Most of the longer of the park's ten official **trails** start from the top of Summit Road; serious backpackers prefer to head to **Eagle Lake**, off Summit Road, rather than take the more popular **Miller Lake Trail** (6km one-way). The award-winning **Giant Cedars Trail** is a wooded one-kilometre jaunt with ten interpretive exhibits off the road on the park's eastern edge, its boardwalks negotiating a tract of ancient forest crammed with 800-year-old Western Red Cedars and rough-barked western hemlock (the trailhead begins at the Giant Cedars Picnic Area). You could also try the **Skunk Cabbage Boardwalk** (1.2km), an easy trail through temperate forest and wetland inhabited by muskrat, beaver, numerous birds and the eponymous skunk cabbage. **Meadows in the Sky Trail**, by contrast, is a quick one-kilometre paved loop through alpine meadows at the top of Summit Road. Look out for the so-called Icebox, a shaded rock cleft that contains what is reputedly the world's smallest glacier. The *Footloose in the Columbias* booklet, available from Glacier's Rogers Pass visitor centre, has further trail information.

Revelstoke

REVELSTOKE, the only community within striking range of the park, sits just outside the western boundary, but in its promotional pitch chooses to ignore its scenic appeal in favour of a somewhat unimpressive claim to be "Home of the World's Largest Sculpted Grizzly Bears" (they stand at Mackenzie Ave at the entrance to downtown). Like many mountain towns, it's divided between a motel-and-garage strip along the Trans-Canada, a dispersed, frontier-type collection of houses to the rear. The river and rugged scenery round about redeem it, and the downtown area also has a nice feel, having been spruced up as a placatory measure following the disaster at the dam site (see opposite). If you're without your own vehicle, it's a good twenty-minute walk from the strip. In downtown, you might dip into the small but polished **Revelstoke Railway Museum** (May, June, Sept & Oct Mon–Sat 9am–5pm; July & Aug daily 9am–8pm; $5; ☎837-6060), which has a steam engine, snowploughs and assorted memorabilia relating to the building of the stretch of the CPR between Field and Kamloops. If you want to relax close to town, try warm-watered **Williamson Lake**, a favourite swimming spot for locals with mini-golf and campground 4km south of town east of Airport Way.

Seven daily Greyhound **buses** stop at the town of Revelstoke between Kamloops and Calgary; the terminal is at the west end of the strip, immediately after the big blue Columbia River bridge (☎837-5874). The **infocentre** is 200m beyond on the left at 204 Campbell Ave (daily: May & June 10am–6pm; July & Aug 8am–8pm; ☎837-5345, fax 837-4223). Between May and September there's a small additional office at the corner of the Trans-Canada and Hwy 23 N (☎837-3522; same hours). Get park information at these offices, or call in on the **Park Administration Office** on 3rd Street next door to the **post office** (park office: Mon–Fri 8am–4.30pm; ☎837-7500, fax 837-7536) or the Rogers Pass visitor centre. The park office also has a store for the "Friends of Mount Revelstoke National Park" (☎837-2010) which is useful for **maps** and guides.

Accommodation

A far more amenable place to stay than Golden – the town of Revelstoke has plenty of **accommodation** – fifteen-plus motels and half a dozen campgrounds.

Best Western Wayside Inn, 1901 Laforme Blvd (☎837-6161 or 1-800/528-1234, fax 837-5460, *www.bestwestern.com*). The priciest and best of the town's hotels. ⑤.

Columbia Motel, 301 Wright St at 2nd St W (☎837-2191 or 1-800/663-5303, *www.columbia.revelstoke .com*). With 54 rooms, one of the larger places in town; air-conditioned, and heated pool in season as an extra draw. ②.

Daniel's Hostel Guesthouse, 313 1st St (☎837-5530). Choice of dorm beds at $15 or private singles and doubles ($30) in a three-storey, 100-year-old house; shared bathrooms and communal kitchen; smoking outside only. ①.

Frontier Motel and Restaurant, 122 N Nakusp Hwy (☎837-5119 or 1-800/382-7763, fax 837-6604, *welcome@junction.net*). On the main Trans-Canada away from the town centre; good motel and first-rate food. ②.

Nelles Ranch Bed and Breakfast, Hwy 23 S (☎ & fax 837-3800 or 1-888/567-4177). Just six units on a working horse and cattle ranch 2km off the Trans-Canada Highway. ③.

Peaks Lodge, 5km west of Revelstoke off Hwy 1 (☎837-2176 or 1-800/668-0330, fax 837-2133; *peaks@junction.net*). Nice small place (twelve units) in a reasonably rustic setting convenient for hikes, bird-watching and the like. Open mid-May to mid-Oct & mid-Nov to mid-April. ③.

'R' Motel, 1500 1st St (☎837-2164, fax 837-6847, *rmotel@junction.net*). One of the cheapest motels in town. ②.

Revelstoke Traveller's Hostel and Guest House, 400 2nd St W (☎837-4050, fax 837-5600, *www.hostels.bc.ca*). Cheap private, semi-private and dorm beds convenient for local restaurants and supermarkets. Well-run and offers Internet access, bike rentals and kitchen facilities. ①.

Sandman Inn, 1821 Fraser St (☎837-5271 or 1-800/726-3626, *www.sandman.ca*). Part of a usually reliable mid-range hotel chain. Has 83 comfortable, modern rooms, so a good chance of finding space. ④.

CAMPGROUNDS

Revelstoke has no park-run sites. **Backcountry** camping in the park is free, with tent-pads, outhouses and food-storage poles provided at Eva and Jade lakes, but no camping is allowed in the Miller Lake area or anywhere within 5km of the Trans-Canada or Summit Road. Registration at the Park Administration Office is obligatory. The park is so small, however, that you might be better off at some of the area's more developed private **campgrounds**.

Highway Haven Motel and Campground, Three Valley Lake (☎837-2525). 20km west of Revelstoke, near the lake for swimming and boating. Thirty pitches and hot showers. April–Nov. $10.

KOA Revelstoke, 5km east of Revelstoke (☎837-2085 or 1-800/562-3905). The best of the area's campgrounds. Free showers, plus shop and swimming pool. May–Oct. $20–22.50.

Lamplighter Campground, off Hwy 1 before the Columbia River bridge; take Hwy 23 south towards Nakusp and turn into Nixon Rd (first left) (☎837-3385, fax 837-5856). A peaceful, fully serviced tent and RV site within walking distance of downtown. Fifty fully serviced sites. Mid-April to mid-Oct. $15.50.

Williamson Lake Campground, 1818 Williamson Lake Rd (☎837-5512 or 1-888/676-2267 for toll-free reservations). Nice forty-site lakeside campground 4km south of the town centre. Free hot showers, canoe and rowboat rentals, flush toilets and beach. Mid-April to Oct. $14.50.

Eating and drinking

Eating possibilities include the *Frontier Restaurant* on the Trans-Canada, part of the eponymous motel near the infocentre, which serves up superior steak-and-salad meals at reasonable prices, with friendly service and a genuine cowpoke atmosphere. In town, the *One-Twelve Restaurant* at 112 Victoria Rd is a favourite, with good food, a lively pub and dance floor.

Revelstoke Dam

A trip to Canada's largest dam may sound dull, but the **Revelstoke Dam** (daily: mid-March to mid-June & early Sept to late Oct 9am–5pm; mid-June to early Sept 8am–8pm; free; ☎837-6515) makes an interesting outing. Four kilometres north of the town on Hwy 23, the 175-metre-tall barrier holds back the waters of the Columbia River, around 500km from its source. Its sleek, space-age **visitor centre** offers a well-put-together two-hour self-guided tour, which omits to tell you that insufficient mapping during the construction caused a landslide that threatened to swamp Revelstoke: millions had to be spent or it would have been curtains for the town. The boring bits of the tour can be skipped in favour of a lift to the top for a great view of the dam and surrounding valley.

Kootenay National Park

KOOTENAY NATIONAL PARK, lying across the Continental Divide from Banff in British Columbia, is the least known of the four contiguous parks of the Rockies, and the easiest to miss out – many people prefer to follow the Trans-Canada through Yoho rather than commit themselves to the less enthralling westward journey on Hwy 3 imposed by Kootenay. The park's scenery, however, is as impressive as that of its neighbours – it draws three million visitors a year – and if you're not determined to head west you could drive a neat loop from Banff through Kootenay on Hwy 93 to **Radium Hot Springs** (the only town in this area), north on Hwy 95, and back on the Trans-Canada through Yoho to Lake Louise and Banff. You could drive this in a day and still have time for a few short walks and a dip in Radium's hot springs to boot.

The telephone code for Kootenay National Park is ☎250.

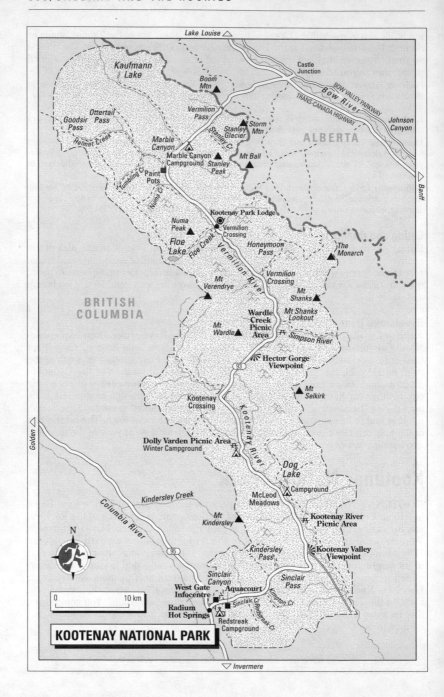

KOOTENAY NATIONAL PARK

In many ways the park's mountains seem closer at hand and more spectacular than on the Icefields Parkway, partly because the road climbs higher over the Continental Divide, and partly because the park's origins guaranteed it an intimate link with the highway. In 1910 Randolph Bruce, a local businessman, persuaded the Canadian government and Canadian Pacific to push a road from Banff through the Rockies to connect the prairies with western seaports (prompted by the hope of promoting a fruit-growing industry in the Columbia Valley). Previously the area had been the reserve of the Kootenai or Ktunaxa natives (*Kootenay* is a native word meaning "people from beyond the hills") and had been explored by David Thompson, but otherwise it was an all but inviolate mountain fastness. The project began in 1911 and produced 22km of road before the money ran out. To wangle more cash British Columbia was forced to cede 8km of land on each side of the highway to the government and, in 1920, 1406 square kilometres of land were established as a national park.

Kootenay lends itself to admiration from a car, bus or bike, mainly because it's little more than a sixteen-kilometre-wide ribbon of land running either side of Hwy 93 for around 100km (the highway here is known as the **Kootenay** or **Banff–Windermere Parkway**). All its numerous easy **short walks** start immediately off the highway, though the scenery, of course, doesn't simply stop at the park boundary. Options for **day-hikes** are more limited, though the best of the longer walks are as good as anything in the Rockies and can be extended into outstanding two-day (or more) backpacking options. If you want no more than a stroll from a car or bike follow the **Marble Canyon** and **Paint Pots** trails: for something longer but not too long go for the **Stanley Glacier** walk; if you're after the best day-hike the choice is the **Kindersley Pass Trail**, though it's a close-run thing with the Floe Lake Trail to Floe Lake and its possible continuation northwest over the Numa Pass and down Numa Creek back to the highway. If you have time do both of these two day-hikes – if you do, you'll have done two of the top ten or so walks in the Rockies. If you have more time, the Rockwall Trail (Floe Lake–Numa Pass–Rockwell Pass–Helmet Falls) is widely considered among the Rockies' top three or four backpacking routes. See the box on p.562 and the map on p.561 to make sense of these routes.

Practicalities

The only practicable access to Kootenay is on Hwy 93, a good road that leaves the Trans-Canada at Castle Junction (in Banff National Park), traverses Kootenay from north to south, and joins Hwy 95 at Radium Hot Springs at the southern entrance. Radium offers the only practical accommodation options, bar a trio of park-run campgrounds and handful of rooms at Vermilion Crossing, a summer-only huddle of shop, cabins and gas station midway through the park. The two daily Greyhound **buses** east and west on the southern British Columbia route between Cranbrook, Banff and Calgary stop at Vermilion Crossing and Radium. **Park permits** are required for entry unless you already have a valid permit from Banff, Jasper or Kootenay: $5 per person per day, or $35 for an annual pass valid for eleven parks in western Canada: group passes for two to ten people cost $10 (see box on p.486 for more on passes).

If you come from the east you'll hit the Marble Canyon campground about 15km from Castle Junction, where occasionally in summer there's a simple information kiosk (mid-June to early Sept Mon & Fri–Sun 8.30am–8pm, Tues–Thurs 8.30am–4.30pm; no phone); coming the other way, the main **park visitor centre** is at the corner of Main Street E and Redstreak Road at 7556 Main St in the town of Radium Hot Springs (daily: July & Aug 9am–9pm; Sept–June 9.30am-5.30pm; ☎347-9505, *www.parkscanada.pch.gc.ca/kootenay*). Main Street E is a turn south off Hwy 93 close to its junction with Hwy 95. The park entrance, however, is on Hwy 93 itself farther east close to the Radium Hot Springs Pools (see p.564). The centre provides a free *Backcountry Guide to Kootenay National Park*, all you need walk-wise if you're not planning anything too ambitious.

Kootenay, like the other major Rockies parks, has a "Friends" organization (☎347-6525), which helps run **guided walks** and other activities: walks should be booked at the visitor centre. In Kootenay, there are three good walks: Stanley Glacier (July & Aug Tues 10am; 5hr/10km; meet at Stanley Glacier trailhead on Hwy 93) and two walks in Sinclair Canyon – "Walk of the Two Lions" (July Fri 10am; 2hr) and "Into the Secret Canyon" (Aug Fri 10am; 1hr 30min; meet for both walks at the front entrance of the Radium Hot Springs Pools).

Park staff are also usually on hand at the park's only two roadside serviced **campgrounds**: the 98-site *McLeod Meadows*, 25km north of Radium ($13; mid-May to mid-Sept; no showers), and the 61-site *Marble Canyon*, near the Information Centre ($13; mid-June to early Sept; no showers). If you want more comforts (including hot showers) and easier access use the big 242-site *Redstreak* campground, Kootenay's major park campground. It's located 3km north of Radium Hot Springs ($17–22; May–Sept; ☎347-9567); the turn-off for the site is Redstreak Road: to reach it, carry on along Main Street E from the park visitor centre until Main Street becomes Redstreak Road. If you're staying at the campground, incidentally, note that the Redstreak Campground Trail (2.2km) takes you from the northwest corner of the site to the Radium Hot Springs Pools. The Valleyview Trail (1.4km) takes you from the campground entrance into Radium village, avoiding Redstreak Road.

A dozen or more **backcountry sites** with pit toilets and firewood are scattered within easy backpacking range of the highway, for which you need a **permit** from the infocentres ($6). The small seven-site *Dolly Varden* park campground just north of McLeod Meadows opens for **winter camping** (Sept–May; flush toilets only; free).

The only indoor **accommodation** in the heart of the park is ten rustic cottages of the *Kootenay Park Lodge* at Vermilion Crossing (☎762-9196, *www.kootenayparklodge .com*; ④; May–Sept). You'll need to book these well in advance; similarly the twelve cabins at *Mount Assiniboine Lodge* (☎344-2639; ⑥; Feb–April & late June to mid-Oct; reservations obligatory; two-night minimum stay). Located at 2195m within the Assiniboine Provincial Park, this lodge is accessible only by helicopter, skiing or hiking trail. The other listed hotels within the park borders are so close to Radium as to make little difference (see "Radium Hot Springs", p.564).

Vermilion Pass

Vermilion Pass (1637m) marks the northern entrance to the park, the Continental Divide's watershed and the border between Alberta and British Columbia. Little fanfare, however, accompanies the transition – only the barren legacy of a huge forest fire (started by a single lightning bolt) which ravaged the area for four days in 1968, leaving a 24-square-kilometre blanket of stark, blackened trunks. Take the short **Fireweed Trail** (1km) through the desolation from the car park at the pass to see how nature deals with such disasters, indeed how it seems to invite lightning fires to promote phoenix-like regeneration. The ubiquitous lodge-pole pine, for example, specifically requires the heat of a forest fire to crack open its resin-sealed cones and release its seeds. Strange as it seems, forests are intended to burn, at least if a healthy forest is to be preserved: in montane regions the natural "fire return cycles" are a mere 42–46 years; in lower subalpine habitats, 77–130 years; and in upper subalpine areas, 180 years. Forests any older are actually in decline, providing few species and poor wildlife habitats. Ironically, as a result of the national parks' success in preventing forest fires over the last fifty years, many woods are now over-mature and the need for controlled burning is increasingly being addressed. At Vermilion Pass a broad carpet of lodge-pole pines have taken root among the blasted remnants of the earlier forest, while young plants and shrubs ("doghair forest") are pushing up into the new clearings. Birds, small mammals and deer, elk and moose are being attracted to new food sources and, more significantly, black and grizzly bears are returning to the area.

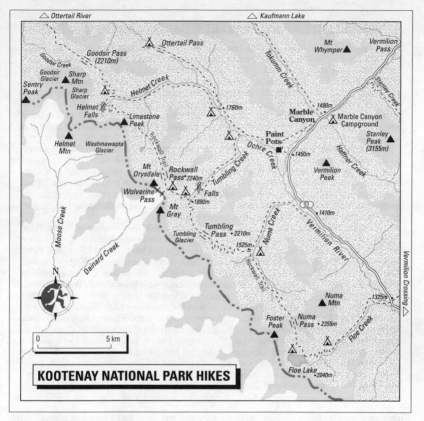

KOOTENAY NATIONAL PARK HIKES

Stanley Glacier and Marble Canyon

About 3km south of Vermilion Pass, the small, well-defined **Stanley Glacier Trail** (4.2km; 365m ascent; 1hr 30min) strikes off up Stanley Creek from a parking area on the eastern side of the highway. In its first 2km the trail provides you with a hike through the Vermilion Pass Burn (see opposite), but more to the point pushes into the beautiful hanging valley below Stanley Peak. Here you can enjoy close-up views of the Stanley Glacier and its surrounding recently glaciated landscapes. The area is also known for its fossils, and for the chance to see marmots, pikas and white-tailed ptarmigan.

Marble Canyon, 8km south of Vermilion Pass, the site of a park-run **campground**, has an easy trail (800m) that's probably the most heavily trafficked of Kootenay's shorter hikes. The track crosses a series of log bridges over Tokumm Creek, which has carved through a fault in the limestone over the last 8000 years, to produce a 600-metre-long and 37-metre-deep gorge. In cold weather this is a fantastic medley of ice and snow, but in summer the climax is the viewpoint from the top of the path onto a thundering waterfall as the creek pounds its way through the narrowest section of the gorge. The rock here was once mistakenly identified as marble – hence the canyon's name; the white marble-like rock is actually dolomite limestone.

One of the park's better longer hikes also starts from the Marble Canyon car park – the **Kaufmann Lake Trail** (15km one-way; 570m ascent; 4–6hr), which follows

---

DAY- AND BACKPACKING HIKES IN KOOTENAY

If you have time and energy for only one long walk in Kootenay, make it the Kindersley Pass Trail, a strenuous 9.8-kilometre trail that climbs to **Kindersley Pass** and then cuts northeast for the steep final push to Kindersley Summit (2210m). Here you can enjoy the sublime prospect of an endless succession of peaks fading to the horizon away to the northeast. Rather than double back down through the open tundra, many people push on another 2km (trail vague) and contour around the head of the Sinclair Creek valley before dropping off the ridge (the Kindersley–Sinclair Coll) to follow the well-defined Sinclair Creek Trail (6.4km) down to meet the highway 1km from the starting point (be sure to do the hike this way round – the Sinclair Creek Trail is a long, dull climb).

Most of Kootenay's other longish day-walks are in the park's northern half, accessed on the west side of the highway from the Marble Canyon, Paint Pots, Numa Creek and Floe Lake parking areas. The **Rockwall Trail**, an incredible thirty-kilometre (54km including approach trails; 1450m ascent), backpacking high-level trail, follows the line of the mountains on the west side of the highway, and can be joined using four of the six trails described below. You could walk it in two days, but could easily spend longer, particularly as there are five backcountry campgrounds en route.

From north to south on the highway, the trails start with the **Kaufmann Lake Trail** (15km one-way; 570m ascent; allow 4–6hr one-way), which climbs to one of the park's loveliest high-mountain lakes (there's also a campground here). A trail from the Paint Pots runs for 2km before dividing to provide three onward options: the first to the dull Ottertail Pass, the second up **Tumbling Creek** (10.3km; 440m ascent to the intersection with the Rockwall Trail), and the third and best option the **Helmet Creek Trail** (14.3km; 310m ascent), a long day-hike to the amazing 365-metre Helmet Waterfalls (another intersection with the Rockwall Trail). The best of the day-hikes after Kindersley Pass is the easier **Floe Lake Trail** (10.5km; 715m ascent), up to a spellbinding lake edged by a 1000-metre sheer escarpment and a small glacier. There are campgrounds on the route, and another tie-in to the Rockwall Trail. The **Numa Creek Trail** (6.4km; 115m ascent) to the north is less enthralling – though you could use it as a downhill leg to add to the Floe Lake Trail (see map overleaf) – as are the series of fire-road walks advertised in the park: unless you're mountain biking, therefore, ignore the Simpson River, West Kootenay, Honeymoon Pass and East Kootenay trails.

Tokumm Creek towards the head of the valley at Kaufmann Lake (see box above). The first few kilometres of the trail – easy valley and meadow walking – make an appealing hour or so's stroll.

The Paint Pots

You could extend the Marble Canyon walk by picking up the Paint Pots Trail south, which puts another 2.7km onto your walk, or drive 2km south and stroll 1km to reach the same destination. Either way you come first to the Ochre Beds (after 800m) and then (1.5km) to the **Paint Pots**, one of the Rockies' more magical spots: red, orange and mustard-coloured pools prefaced by damp, moss-clung forest and views across the white water of the Vermilion River to the snowcapped mountains beyond. The pools' colours are created by iron-laden water bubbling up from three mineral springs through clay sediments deposited on the bed of an ancient glacial lake.

Aboriginal peoples from all over North America collected the coloured clays from the ponds and ochre beds to make into small cakes, which they baked in embers. The fired clay was then ground into powder – **ochre** – and added to animal fat or fish oil to use in rock, tepee or ceremonial body painting. Ochre has always had spiritual significance for North American natives, in this case the Stoney and Ktunaxa, who saw these oxide-stained pools and their yellow-edged surroundings as inhabited by animal and thunder spirits. Standing in the quiet, rather gloomy glade, particularly on overcast days, it's easy

to see why – not that the atmosphere or sanctity of the place stopped European speculators in the 1920s from mining the ochre to manufacture paint in Calgary.

The car park is the trailhead for three longer (day or backpack) trails, all of which
kick off along the Ochre Creek Valley: Tumbling Creek Trail, Ottertail Pass Trail and
the Helmet Creek–Helmet Waterfalls Trail (see box, opposite).

Vermilion Crossing and Kootenay Crossing

VERMILION CROSSING, 20km south of the Paint Pots Trail, is gone in a flash, but
it's the only place, in summer at least, to find lodgings, petrol and food in the park. It also
has a visitor centre, built on the site of a 1920 CPR railway camp. You can also stop to
walk the **Verendyre Creek Trail** (2.1km), accessed west off the highway, an easy stroll,
but forest-enclosed, and with only limited views of Mount Verendrye as a reward. One
of the Rockies' tougher walks heads east from the Crossing, up over Honeymoon Pass
and Redearth Pass to Egypt Lake and the Trans-Canada Highway in Banff National
Park, while to the south equally demanding trails provide the only westside access into
the wilderness of **Mount Assiniboine Provincial Park**. Sandwiched between
Kootenay and Banff, this wilderness park was created in honour of Mount Assiniboine
(3618m), a sabre-tooth-shaped mountain with one of the most dramatic profiles imaginable, whose native Stoney name means "those who cook by placing hot rocks in water".
The **Simpson Road Trail** (8.2km) leads to the park boundary, and then divides into two
paths (20km and 32km) to Lake Magog in the heart of Assiniboine. Some 8.5km beyond
the Crossing look out for the Animal Lick, a spot where animals come down to lick nutrients from a natural mineral source: with luck you may see elk, mule deer and even
moose here. Over the next few kilometres, for similar reasons, you might also see mountain goats by banks at the side of the road.

Kootenay Crossing is no more than a ceremonial spot – it was where the ribbon was
cut to open Hwy 93 in 1923 – though a clutch of short trails fan out from its park-warden
station, and the nearby *Dolly Varden* campground (see p.560) is the park's only specific site for winter camping. **Wardle Creek** nearby is a good place to unpack a picnic if
you're determined to stick to the road.

Around 11km south of the Kootenay Crossing is the **McLeod Meadows** campground (see p.560), and immediately behind it to the east the easy **Dog Lake Trail**
(2.7km), much tramped as an after-dinner leg-stretcher by campers (the trail can also
be accessed from the highway at the picnic area 500m south). The path offers glimpses
of the Kootenay Valley through the trees, and ends in a marsh-edged lake whose temperate microclimate makes it ideal for nature study. You may see deer, elk and coyotes,
and – if you're lucky – bears and moose. Several types of orchid also bloom here in
early summer (June & July), including white bog, round-leafed, calypso and sparrow's
egg. About 11km further on, the **Kootenay Valley Viewpoint** offers one of the broadest views on the highway, with great vistas of the Mitchell and Vermilion mountain
ranges, and with them the inevitable hordes in search of a photo opportunity.

Sinclair Pass

For its final run down out of the park, the highway doglegs west through the **Sinclair
Pass**, a red-cliffed gorge filled with the falling waters of Sinclair Creek and the start of
the **Kindersley Pass Trail**, possibly the most scenic day-hike in the park (see box
opposite). If this seems too much of a slog, Sinclair Pass offers three far easier short
trails, all marked off the highway to the west. The best is the **Juniper Trail** (3.2km),
accessed just 300m inside the park's West Gate. The trail drops to Sinclair Creek and
over the next couple of kilometres touches dry canyon, arid forest slopes of juniper and
Douglas fir, and thick woods of western red cedar, before emerging at the hot springs,
or Aquacourt (see overleaf), 1.4km up the road from the start. The **Redstreak Creek**

Trail (2.7km), 4.5km east of the West Gate, starts off as a good forest walk, but tails off into dullness subsequently, as does the **Kimpton Creek Trail** (4.8km), also on the south side of the road and canyon, accessed 7.5km east of the West Gate.

Radium Hot Springs

RADIUM HOT SPRINGS is far less attractive than its evocative name suggests but, as the service centre for Kootenay, its tacky motels and garages are likely to claim your attention and money. The town spreads across the flats of the Columbia Valley, 3km from the southern/western entrance at the junction of Hwy 93 and Hwy 95. For **information** visit the park centre which has a Chamber of Commerce desk (☎347-9331 or 1-800/347-9704, *www.radiumhotsprings.com*).

The **hot springs** (or Aquacourt) themselves (plus park visitor centre) are nicely away from the settlement, 2km north of town off the Banff–Windermere Parkway (Hwy 93) and are administered by the park authorities (daily: mid-May to mid-Oct 9am–11pm; mid-Oct to mid-May Sun–Thurs noon–9pm, Fri & Sat noon–10pm; $6 or $8.25 for day-pass during first period, $5 or $7.25 for day-pass for second period; ☎347-9485). Aboriginal peoples used the springs for centuries, and commercial white development started as early as 1890 when Roland Stuart bought the area for $160. Traces of supposedly therapeutic radium found in the water turned Stuart's investment into a recreational gold mine. When the government appropriated the springs for inclusion in the national park, it paid him $40,000 – a small fortune, but considerably less than what they were worth, which at the time was estimated to be $500,000. The pools today are outdoors, but serviced by a large, modern centre. In summer, 4000 people per day take the plunge into the odourless 45°C waters – enough to discourage any idea of a quiet swim, though in late evening or off-season (when the hot pool steams invitingly) you can escape the bedlam and pretend more easily that the water is having some sort of soothing effect. The radium traces sound a bit worrying, but 300,000 visitors a year don't seem to mind.

If you have the choice, aim to stay in one of the new **motels** creeping up the Sinclair Valley around the hot springs area away from downtown – they're more expensive, but far more attractively sited than the thirty-odd mirror-image motels in town (where there are any number of rooms in the $50–70 bracket). Try the big 120-room *Prestige Radium Hot Springs Resort* for something of a treat, 1km south of the springs at 8100 Golf Course Rd (☎347-9311 or 1-877/737-8443, *www.prestigeinn.com*; ⑥), for all the trimmings (including swimming pool and massage therapist); *Addison's Bungalows* (☎347-9545 or 1-800/794-5024, *www.addisonsbugalows.com*; ④; April–Oct), a mix of 30 motel and cabin rooms nearby with units offering anything up to five bedrooms and kitchenettes; or the adjacent *Mount Farnham Bungalows* (☎347-9515, *www.hotspringsbc.com*; ④). Almost alongside the park entrance are the fourteen-room *Alpen Motel* (☎347-9823; ③), and the sixteen-room *Kootenay* (☎347-9490 or 1-888/788-3891; ③) and nine-room *Crescent* (☎347-9570; ③) motels. Most of the motels along the main drag in town are smaller – one of the cheapest is *Sunset* (☎347-9863 or 1-800/214-7413, *sunset@rockies.net*; ②).

travel details

Trains

Calgary to: Vancouver with private Rocky Mountain Railtours (see Basics, p.36).

Jasper to: Edmonton (3 weekly; 5hr 30min); Prince Rupert via Prince George (3 weekly; 20hr); Vancouver (3 weekly).

Buses

Calgary to: Banff (6 daily; 1hr 40min); Coutts (US; connections for Las Vegas and Los Angeles) via Fort Macleod and Lethbridge (1 daily; 4hr 30min); Creston via Banff, Radium Hot Springs and Cranbrook (1 daily; 7hr 30min); Dawson Creek (2 daily; 7hr 15min); Drumheller (2 daily; 1hr 50min); Edmonton (14 daily; 3hr 30min); Fort St John (2 daily; 9hr 15min); Lake Louise (6 daily; 2hr 35min); Prince George (2 daily; 14hr); Saskatoon (2 daily; 9hr); Vancouver via Fort Macleod, Cranbrook, Nelson, Osoyoos and Hope (2 daily; 24hr); Vancouver via Kamloops (7 daily; 13hr); Vancouver via Vernon, Kelowna and Penticton (3 daily; 16hr); Winnipeg via Lethbridge, Medicine Hat and Regina (2 daily; 24hr).

Flights

Calgary to: Edmonton (every 30min; 50min); Montréal (12 daily; 5hr); Toronto (14 daily; 4hr); Vancouver (every 30min; 1hr 20min).

CHAPTER EIGHT

NORTH TO THE YUKON

Although much of the Pacific Northwest still has the flavour of the "last frontier", it's only when you embark on the mainland push north to the Yukon that you know for certain you're leaving the mainstream of North American life behind. In the popular imagination, **the north** figures as a perpetually frozen wasteland blasted by ferocious gloomy winters, inhabited – if at all – by hardened characters beyond the reach of civilization. In truth, it's a region where months of summer sunshine offer almost limitless opportunities for outdoor activities and an incredible profusion of flora and fauna; a country within a country, the character of whose settlements has often been forged by the mingling of white settlers and **aboriginal peoples**. The indigenous hunters of the north are as varied as in the south, but two groups predominate: the **Dene**, people of the northern forests who traditionally occupied the Mackenzie River region from the Albertan border to the river's delta at the Beaufort Sea; and the Arctic **Inuit** (literally "the people"), once known as the Eskimos or "fish eaters", a Dene term picked up by early European settlers and now discouraged.

The north is as much a state of mind as a place. People "north of 60" – the 60th Parallel – claim the right to be called **northerners**, and maintain a kinship with Alaskans, but those north of the **Arctic Circle** – the 66th Parallel – look with light-hearted disdain on these "southerners". All mock the inhabitants of the northernmost corners of Alberta and such areas of the so-called Northwest, who, after all, live with the luxury of being able to get around their backcountry by road. To any outsider, however, in terms of landscape and overall spirit the north begins well south of the 60th Parallel. Accordingly, this chapter includes not just the provinces of the "true north" – **Yukon** and parts of the western Arctic and **Northwest Territories** – but also northern **British Columbia**, a region more stark and extreme than BC's southern reaches.

Northern British Columbia

The two roads into the Yukon strike through northern British Columbia: the **Alaska Highway**, connecting **Dawson Creek** to Fairbanks in Alaska, and the adventurous **Cassiar Highway**, from near **Prince Rupert** to **Watson Lake**, on the Yukon border. Though the Cassiar's passage through the Coast Mountains offers perhaps the better landscapes, it's the Alaska Highway – serviced by daily Greyhound **buses** and plentiful motels and campgrounds – that is more travelled, starting in the rolling wheatlands of the Peace River country before curving into the spruce forests and sawtooth ridges of the northern Rockies. While the scenery is superb, most towns on both roads are battered and perfunctory places built around lumber mills, oil and gas plants and mining camps, though increasingly they are spawning motels and restaurants to serve the surge of summer visitors out to capture the thrill of driving the frontier highways. Equally popular are the **sea journeys** offered along northern British Columbia, among

---

The telephone code for British Columbia is ☎250.
The telephone code for the Yukon is ☎867.
The telephone code for the Northwest Territories is ☎867.

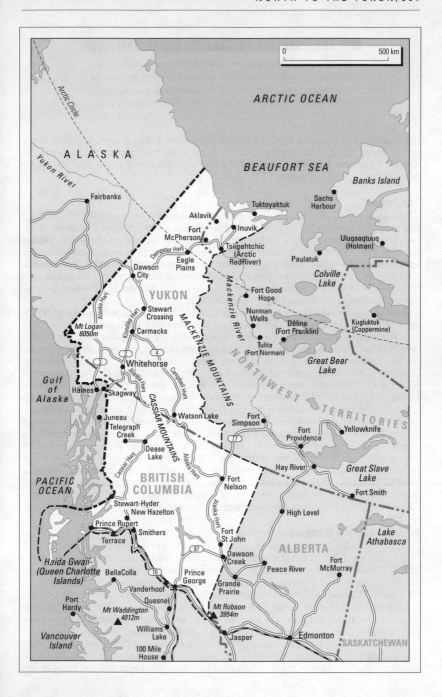

INFORMATION NUMBERS AND WEB SITES

Tourism British Columbia ☎1-800/663-6000, *www.hellobc.com*
Northern BC ☎1-800/663-8843, *www.northernbctourism.bc.ca*
Tourism Yukon ☎867/667-5340, *www.touryukon.com/vg*
NWT Arctic Tourism ☎1-800/661-0788, *www.nwttravel.nt.ca*

the most breathtaking trips in all the Pacific Northwest. Prince Rupert, linked by ferry to Vancouver Island, is the springboard for boats to the magnificent **Haida Gwaii**, or **Queen Charlotte Islands** – home of the Haida people – and a vital way station for boats plying the Inside Passage up to Alaska.

The Yukon

The Cassiar and Alaska highways converge at **Watson Lake**, a weather-beaten junction that straddles the 60th Parallel and marks the entrance to the **Yukon Territory** (YT), perhaps the most exhilarating and varied destination in this part of the world. Taking its name from a Dene word meaning "great", it boasts the highest mountains in Canada, wild sweeps of forest and tundra, and the fascinating nineteenth-century relic, **Dawson City**. The focus of the Klondike gold rush, Dawson was also the territory's capital until that role shifted south to **Whitehorse**, a town booming on tourism and the ever-increasing exploitation of the Yukon's vast mineral resources.

Road access is easier than you might think. In addition to the Alaska Highway, which runs through the Yukon's southern reaches, the **Klondike Highway** strikes north to link Whitehorse with Dawson City. North of Dawson the **Dempster Highway** is the only road in Canada to cross the Arctic Circle, offering an unparalleled direct approach to the northern tundra and to several remote communities in the Northwest Territories. The Yukon's other major road is the short spur linking the Alaskan port of Skagway to Whitehorse, which shadows the **Chilkoot Trail**, a treacherous track taken by the poorest of the 1898 prospectors that is now a popular long-distance footpath.

Combining coastal ferries with the Chilkoot Trail makes an especially fine itinerary. Following the old gold-rush trail, the route begins at Skagway – reached by ferry from Prince Rupert – then follows the Chilkoot to Whitehorse, before heading north to Dawson City. From there you could continue up the Dempster Highway, or travel on the equally majestic **Top of the World** road into the heart of Alaska. However, many people coming up from Skagway or plying the mainland routes from British Columbia head to Alaska directly on the Alaska Highway, to enjoy views of the extraordinary and largely inaccessible mountain vastness of **Kluane National Park**, which contains Canada's highest peaks and most extensive glacial wilderness.

Nunavut and the Northwest Territories

If the Yukon is the far north at its most accessible, the **Northwest Territories** (NWT) is the region at its most uncompromising. Just three roads nibble at the edges of this almost unimaginably vast area, which occupies a third of Canada's landmass – about the size of India – but contains only sixty thousand people, almost half of whom live in or around **Yellowknife**, the territories' peculiarly overblown capital. Visitors to the Yukon, and in particular those who venture as far as Dawson City, would be well advised to push still further north for a small but entirely representative taste of a portion of the Northwest Territories that belongs logistically to the Yukon. To do so all you need to do is follow the adventurous and rewarding **Dempster Highway**, a gravel highway that runs from Dawson City across the tundra to **Inuvik**, crossing the Arctic Circle and the Yukon–Northwest Territories border en route. Otherwise you can come to this

---

PROVINCIAL CAMPSITES IN BRITISH COLUMBIA

Tent and RV sites at certain campgrounds in British Columbia's provincial parks can be reserved in advance. To make **reservations**, call Discover Camping (☎1-800/689-9025 or 604/689-9025 in greater Vancouver; March to mid-Sept Mon–Fri 7am–7pm, Sat & Sun 9am–5pm) or log on to their Web site *www.discovercamping.ca*, where reservations can be made and confirmed online. Reservations can be made from up to three months in advance and no later than 48 hours before the first day of arrival. A non-refundable booking fee of $6.42 per night, to a maximum of $19.26 for three or more nights, is charged (rates include tax). Payment in advance is by Visa or MasterCard only (payment for extra nights once at a campsite is by cash only). You can stay in BC provincial parks up to a maximum of fourteen days in any single park. Information on all aspects of BC's provincial parks is available on the Net at *www.elp.gov.bc.ca/bcparks*.

---

part of the world to fish or canoe, to hunt or watch wildlife, or to experience the Inuit native cultures and ethereal landscapes. If the idea of exploring the region in more depth appeals, then obtain a copy of the Territories' *Explorers' Guide* brochure. This summarizes accommodation options, airline connections, many of the available tours – costing anything from $50 to $5000 – and the plethora of outfitters who provide the equipment and backup essential for any but the most superficial trip to the region.

Prince George

Rough-edged **PRINCE GEORGE**, carved from the forest to become British Columbia's sixth largest city (pop. 78,000), is the general area's services and transport centre, so you're highly likely to become acquainted with its dispersed and half-deserted downtown streets. Forestry, in the form of pulp mills, kilns, planers, plywood plants and allied chemical works, is at the core of its industrial landscape – if you ever wanted the inside story on the lumber business, this is where to find it.

Simon Fraser established a North West Trading Company post here in 1805, and named it **Fort George** in honour of the reigning George III. As a commercial nexus it quickly altered the lives of the local **Carrier Sekani** people, who abandoned their semi-nomadic migration from winter to summer villages in favour of a permanent settlement alongside the fort. Little changed until 1914 when the arrival of the Grand Trunk Railway – later the Canadian National – spawned an influx of pioneers and loggers. The town was connected by road to Dawson Creek and the north as late as 1951, and saw the arrival of the Pacific Great Eastern Railway in 1958 – two developments that give some idea of how recent the opening up of the far north has been.

The town is a disorienting open-plan network of roads and sporadic houses between Hwy 97 and a sprawling downtown area at the junction of the Fraser and Nechako rivers. As far as sightseeing is concerned, you might as well stick to what Prince George does

---

ACCOMMODATION PRICE CODES

All the accommodation prices in this book have been coded using the symbols below, corresponding to US dollar prices in the US chapters and equivalent Canadian dollar rates in the Canadian chapters. Prices are for the least expensive double room in high season, excluding special offers. For a full explanation see p.51 in Basics.

① up to Can$40	③ Can$60–80	⑤ Can$100–125	⑦ Can$175–240
② Can$40–60	④ Can$80–100	⑥ Can$125–175	⑧ Can$240+

---

best and take the surprisingly popular free **tours** around some of its big mills and processing plants; to reserve a place, contact Tourism Prince George opposite the bus terminal at 1198 Victoria St and 15th Avenue (Mon–Fri 8.30am–4pm, Sat 9am–4pm, also Sun 9am–4pm and longer hours in summer; ☎562-3700 or 1-800/668-7646, *www.tourismpg.bc.ca*). Company buses generally pick up from the Tourism Prince George offices and deliver you to one of several firms, the biggest currently being Northwood Pulp and Timber, where you are shown thousands of seedlings being grown in controlled conditions, the sawmills, and one of the continent's largest pulp mills. Outside, in a graphic illustration of the scale of forestry in the region, logs, planks and piles of sawdust the size of small hills stretch almost as far as the eye can see.

Practicalities

Air BC (☎561-2905 or 1-800/663-3721 in Canada) serves Prince George by air: the airport is 18km east of downtown and linked by regular shuttles. The town is linked by BC Rail to Vancouver (via the Cariboo region), and by VIA Rail to Jasper, Edmonton and beyond eastbound, and Prince Rupert westbound (for the Haida Gwaii/Prince Charlotte Islands and Inside Passage ferries). Only VIA Rail drops you downtown at 1300 1st Ave (☎564-5223 or 1-800/561-8630); if you're heading for motels or the bus terminal use a taxi from either Prince George Taxi (☎564-4444) or Emerald Taxi Ltd

THE AURORA BOREALIS

The **aurora borealis**, or "Northern Lights", is a beautiful and ethereal display of light in the upper atmosphere that can be seen over large areas of the northern Pacific Northwest. The night sky appears to shimmer with dancing curtains of colour, ranging from luminescent monotones – most commonly green or a dark red – to fantastic veils that run the full spectrum. The display becomes more animated as it proceeds, twisting and turning in patterns called "rayed bands". As a finale, a corona sometimes appears, in which rays seem to flare in all directions from a central point.

Named after the Roman goddess of dawn, the aurora was long thought to be produced by sunlight reflected from polar snow and ice, or refracted light produced in the manner of a rainbow. Certain Inuit peoples believed the lights were the spirits of animals or ancestors; others thought they represented wicked forces. Old-time gold prospectors thought they might be vapours given off by ore deposits. Research still continues into the phenomenon, but the latest thought is that the aurora is caused by radiation emitted as light from atoms in the upper atmosphere as they are hit by fast-moving electrons and protons. The earth's geomagnetic field certainly plays some part in the creation of the aurora, but its source would appear to lie with the sun – auroras become more distinct and are seen spread over a larger area two days after intense solar activity, the time it takes the "solar wind" to arrive. This wind is composed of fast-moving electrically charged ions. When these hit the earth's atmosphere they respond to the earth's magnetic field and move towards the poles. En route they strike atoms and molecules of gas in the upper atmosphere, causing them to become temporarily charged or ionized. These molecules then release the charge, or energy, usually in the form of light. Different colours are emitted depending on the gases involved: oxygen produces a green colour (or orange at higher altitudes), nitrogen an occasionally violet colour.

You should be able to see the Northern Lights as far south as Prince George in British Columbia, over parts of northern Alberta (where on average they're visible some 160 nights a year) and over much of the Northwest Territories and Nunavut. They are at their most dazzling from **December to March**, when nights are longest and the sky darkest, though they are potentially visible all year round. Look out for a faint glow on the northeastern horizon after dusk, and then – if you're lucky – for the full show as the night deepens.

(☎563-3333). The **BC Rail** (☎561-4033 or 1-800/663-8238) trains arrive 5km south of downtown on Hwy 97 at the end of Terminal Boulevard, but there's a free connecting bus service to various points, including the motels at the bus terminal and on Hwy 97 for a quick getaway the following day.

The town is also a staging post for **Greyhound** routes to the north, and integral to the main road routes to Dawson Creek (for the Alaska Hwy) and Prince Rupert (for the Cassiar Hwy). The Greyhound **bus terminal**, well south of downtown at 1566 12th Ave (☎564-5454 or 1-800/661-8747), is close to a handful of the town's many hotels and motels.

The best **motel** on the Hwy 97 strip is the big *Spruceland Inn* (☎563-0102 or 1-800/663-3295; ③), at 1391 Central St at the junction of Hwy 97 and 15th Avenue. At the nearby *Esther's Inn* (☎562-4131 or 1-800/663-6844, *www.netbistro.com/esthers*; ③), one block off the highway at 1151 Commercial Drive (10th Ave), the price includes a swimming pool and jacuzzi. Closer to downtown is the comfortable 200-room *Ramada Hotel Downtown Prince George*, 444 George St (☎563-0055 or 1-800/830-8833; ⑤). All the campgrounds are some way out, the best being the big *Blue Spruce RV & Campground* about 5km west at Kimball Road on Hwy 16 (☎964-7272 or 964-4060; $15.50–21; April to mid-Oct), which includes a heated outdoor pool.

With **food**, don't expect much in the way of culinary sophistication and stick to good chains like *Earl's*, 1440 E Central St, or *White Spot*, 820 Victoria St; otherwise treat yourself to Italian and other mid-priced dishes at *Da Moreno*, 1493 3rd Ave (☎564-7922), probably the best restaurant in town. **Moving on**, three VIA Rail (☎1-800/561-8630) trains run weekly to Prince Rupert and Edmonton via Jasper ($71), a highly scenic journey; BC Rail runs daily trains to Vancouver in summer (3 weekly in winter; $196), but this is a far more tedious trip through almost unending forest until you reach the region around Fraser river well to the south (☎604/984-5246 or 1-800/663-8238). Greyhound runs one bus daily to Whitehorse in the Yukon, two daily to Vancouver, and two daily to Prince Rupert.

Prince George to Prince Rupert

There are two ways to make the 735-kilometre journey west from **Prince George to Prince Rupert**: using Hwy 16 or the parallel VIA Rail railway, neither of them terribly scenic by BC standards until they reach the glorious river and mountain landscapes of the **Skeena Valley** 150km before Prince Rupert. Most people make this trip as a link in a much longer journey, either to to pick up **ferries** north to Alaska or south to Port Hardy on Vancouver Island, or to pick up the start of the Cassiar Highway, a rough wilderness road that cuts north from the Skeena Valley to meet the Alaska Highway at Watson Lake over the Yukon border. Unless you fly, it's also the only way to reach the Haida Gwaii/Queen Charlotte Islands, accessible by ferry or plane from Prince Rupert. The best place to pause during the journey is near **Hazelton**, where you can visit a little cluster of **aboriginal villages**.

Vanderhoof to Smithers

Riding out of Prince George you're confronted quickly with the relentless monotony of the Interior Plateau's rolling forests, an arboreal grind broken only by the occasional lake and the grey silhouettes of distant low-hilled horizons. At **VANDERHOOF**, 98km down the highway, gentler patches of pasture begin to poke through the tree cover, but these do little to soften the impact of the town itself. An abrupt grid of garages and motels, it's best known for its July airshow and the more graceful aerial dynamics of thousands of Canadian geese at the nearby **Nechako Bird Sanctuary**. Before pushing on, grab a coffee at the *OK Café*, part of a fine collection of half-timbered heritage houses at the town's western end. If you get stuck, or would prefer to stay in the village rather than Prince George, there are cheap **motels**: the largest of them is the *Grand Trunk Inn*, 2351 Church Ave (☎567-3188 or 1-877/567-3188; ②); or you could try the slightly more expensive *Siesta Motel* downtown on Hwy 16 (☎567-2365 or 1-800/914-3388, *t_lobelle@yahoo.com*; ③). For **camping**, there's the *Riverside Park Campground*, overlooking the bird sanctuary at 3100 Burrard Ave (☎567-4710; $14; May–Sept). The **infocentre** is at 2353 Burrard Ave (year-round; ☎567-2124 or 1-800/752-4094, *chamber@hwy16.com*).

Beyond here the ride becomes more verdant towards **FORT FRASER**, 50km beyond, a more attractive spot than Vanderhoof itself. If you're **camping**, hold out for the provincial site at Beaumont Provincial Park (☎565-6340; $15), 3.5km to the west, whose meadow site falls away gently to Fraser Lake. The lake has a seasonal **infobooth** on Hwy 16 at Empire Street (late June to early Sept) daily 9am–7pm; ☎690-7733, *ffcc@hwy16.com*).

Beyond Burn's Lake the scenery picks up still more, as if preparing for the mountains in the distance, though the run of villages continues to offer little but places to fill either the tank or the stomach. If you're going as far as to **stay** in this region, aim for the *Douglas Motel* (☎846-5679, *www.monday.com/douglasmotel*; ④), on the banks of the Bulkley River, just 150m out of the unspoilt hamlet of **TELKWA**, 10km east of Smithers. If you do stay, be sure to take a few minutes to stroll up the riverfront street of heritage buildings and its handsome brown-and-white wood-planked **pioneer museum**.

SMITHERS, the largest place after Prince George (370km to the east), is focused on a single main crossroads on Hwy 16, with an **infocentre** nearby at 1411 Court St (year-round; ☎847-5072 or 1-800/542-6673, *www.bulkley.net/~smichan*) and a big Super-Valu **supermarket** for supplies on the junction itself. If you're overnighting here – and there's plenty of **accommodation** – ignore the brace of motels on the road and settle for the big white-timbered *Hudson Bay Lodge* (☎847-4581 or 1-800/663-5040, *www.hudsonbaylodge.com*; ④) outside the village as you enter from the east. If this is out of your budget, try the *Florence Motel* (☎847-2678; ②) on the west side of town – it's half the price – or the *Sandman Inn Smithers* on Hwy 16, a block from Main Street, part of an invariably trustworthy chain (☎847-2637 or 1-800/726-3626, *www.sandman.ca*; ③).

The Skeena Valley

Hard on the heels of industrial **Terrace**, the **Skeena River** (the "River of the Mists") carves a beautiful valley through the Coast Mountains, an important trade route for aboriginal peoples and stern-wheelers before the coming of the railway in 1912. For a couple of hours the road and railway run past a huge backdrop of snowcapped peaks half-reflected in the mist-wraithed estuary. Out on the water there's a good chance of seeing the ripples of beavers and sea otters, not to mention bald eagles perched on the river's immense log jams. Dark valleys peel off the main river's majestic course, suggestive of a deep, untrodden wilderness, and delicate threads of waterfalls are repeatedly visible though the trees.

Shortly after Hwy 16 meets the river crashing down from the north near Hazelton and New Hazelton, a couple of minor roads strike off to four nearby **Gitxsan aboriginal villages**, places where something of the culture of the area's indigenous Gitxsan peoples has been preserved, along with new examples of totem carving and other crafts. 'Ksan and Kispiox, home to the best totems and longhouses, are a few kilometres off Hwy 16 on the minor High Level Road (Hwy 62) out of New Hazelton; just north of 'Ksan a road links west to Gitwangak and Gitanyow (formerly Kitwancool), or they can be reached by continuing west on Hwy 16 a few kilometres and heading north on Hwy 37 (the Cassiar Hwy).

The most easterly of the west coast aboriginal peoples, the Gitxsan – "people of the river of the mists" – traditionally lived off fish and game rather than agriculture, and were consummate artists and carvers. Many of their traditions were eroded by the coming of whites, and by missionaries in particular, but in the 1950s the people's elders made a determined decision to resurrect as much of their dying culture as possible, re-creating an entire 1870 settlement at **'KSAN**. Although there's a good deal of commer-cialism, this is the village to concentrate on – aboriginal women act as guides around several longhouses, giving a commentary on the carvings, clothes, buildings and masks on show, as well as offering accounts of local history (tours mid-April to mid-Oct usually daily 9am–5pm but longer hours July–Aug; $8).

KISPIOX, 13km north of Hazelton, is the ancient Gitxsan home of the Frog, Wolf and Fireweed clans, and was given its name by the old Department for Indian Affairs. It means "place of loud talkers" but locals not surprisingly prefer the traditional name, which is Anspayaxw, meaning "the hidden place". The highlights here are fifteen river-side totems. **GITWANGAK** to the west, just 500m north of the Hwy 16 and Hwy 37 junction, means "the place of rabbits", and was the traditional village home of the Eagle, Wolf and Frog. It, too, has some impressive totems, as does **GITANYOW** – "people of a small village" – 21km north on Hwy 37, whose eighteen poles include the 140-year-old "Hole in the Ice" or "Hole in the Sky" totem. You can sometimes watch poles being repaired at one of two carving sheds around the village.

The nearest **infocentre** for the villages is near New Hazelton at the junction of Hwys 16 and 62 (mid-May to mid-Sept daily 9am–5pm; ☎842-6071 or 842-6571 year-round, *hazletontourist@hotmail.com*), but you should also spend a few minutes looking round the evocative old Victorian streets of old **HAZELTON** 6km to the northwest on Hwy 62. **Accommodation** is limited to a couple of motels in New Hazelton, the cheap-est being the *Bulkley Valley Motel*, 4444 Hwy 16 (☎842-6817; ②) Kispiox also has a few rooms and campground: the *Sportsman's Kispiox Lodge* (☎842-6455 or 1-800/KISPIOX, *www.kispiox.com/lodge*; ④) and the *Kispiox River Resort and Campground* (☎842-6182; ②; camping $12–20; June–Oct).

Prince Rupert

There's a bracing tang of salt and fish on the air in **PRINCE RUPERT**, a distinctive port that comes as an invigorating relief after the run of characterless villages out of Prince George. A good-looking place, similar in appearance to a Scottish fishing town, it looks out over an archipelago of islands and is ringed by mountains that tumble to the sea along a beautiful fjord-cut coastline. A crowd of cars, backpackers and RVs washes daily through its streets off the **Alaska**, **Queen Charlotte** and **Port Hardy ferries**, complementing the seafront's vibrant activity, and adding to the coffers of a town that's quite clearly on the up and up. There's nothing much to do, but if you're waiting for a boat it's an amiable enough spot and you'll probably bump into more fellow travellers here than almost anywhere else in northern BC.

Arrival

The **Greyhound station** is in the centre of town at 822 3rd Ave and 8th Street (daily 8.30am–8.30pm; ☎624-5090) and handles two buses daily (morning and evening) for the twelve-hour ride to Prince George ($85 one-way). The **VIA Rail train station** is on the waterfront at 1st Avenue and the foot of 2nd Street (open 2hr either side of depar-tures and arrivals; ☎627-7589, 627-7304 or 1-800/561-8630). Trains to Prince George for connections from Prince George to Edmonton via Jasper currently leave on Wednesday, Friday and Sunday at 8am, arriving in Prince George at 8.10pm. If you're thinking of taking the train right through, note that you have to overnight in Prince George as there are no through-trains to Jasper or Edmonton. The local **airport** is on Digby Island just across the harbour, with ferry connections to the BC and Alaska Marine ferry terminals (see box overleaf) and shuttle bus connections to downtown. Check in with your airline in downtown at least two hours before flight departure for the combined shuttle-ferry service to the airport. Air BC (☎624-4554 or 1-800/663-3721) flies to Vancouver and has a base in town at 112 6th St. Local firms Inland Air (☎627-1351 or 1-888/624-2577) and Harbour Air (☎627-1341 or 1-800/689-4234) both run flights to Sandspit on the Haida Gwaii (see p.582).

Many people reach Prince Rupert by **ferry**. For details of how to reach downtown from the **ferry terminal**, which is 2km from town, see the box, below. For **car rentals**, contact National Car Rental (☎624-5318) in the Rupert Mall on 2nd Avenue W.

FERRIES FROM PRINCE RUPERT

Ferry terminals for both BC Ferries (for Port Hardy and the Queen Charlotte Islands) and the Alaska Marine Highway (for Skagway and Alaska Panhandle ports) are at **Fairview Dock**, 2km southwest of town at the end of Hwy 16. Walk-on tickets for foot passengers are rarely a problem at either terminal, but advance reservations are essential if you're taking a car or want a cabin for any summer crossing. A town bus passes the terminal every two or three hours for incoming sailings, but for outbound sailings it's probably best to grab a **taxi** from downtown. You can arrange a pick-up from the ferry by calling Seashore Charters (☎624-5645). Alternatively walk a kilometre to the corner of Pillsbury and Kootenay, where the local #52 bus passes roughly every half an hour (Mon–Sat 7.30am–5.30pm).

BC Ferries operate the MV *Queen of Prince Rupert* **to Skidegate** on the Queen Charlotte Islands daily except Tuesday from July to September at 11am (except Mon 9pm), four times a week the rest of the year (Mon, Tues, Thurs & Fri), a crossing that takes between 6hr 30min and 8hr (depending on weather) and costs $25 ($20 low season: late Sept–early June) one-way for foot passengers (plus $93 high/$76 low season for cars and $6 for bikes). Return ferries from Skidegate operate daily except Sunday, leaving at 11pm and arriving at 7.30am except on some summer Fridays and Saturdays, when the boat docks earlier to provide a connection with the Inside Passage boat to Port Hardy on Vancouver Island (see below). For **reservations** or timetable information, contact Prince Rupert's infocentre or BC Ferries direct on ☎386-3431 (or 1-888/223-3779 anywhere in BC).

Ferries **to Port Hardy** leave every other day in summer at 7.30am (even-numbered days in June, July, Sept and first half of Oct, odd-numbered days in Aug) and once a week in winter for a stunning fifteen-hour cruise that costs $106 one-way for drivers or walk-on passengers (shoulder mid-March to mid-May $75, low season mid-Jan to mid-March $56). Bikes cost $6.50. To take on a car ($218/$154/$116; all excluding driver or passengers) you'll need to have booked at least two months in advance (see also Port Hardy, p.384).

The **Alaska Marine Highway** (☎627-1744 or 1-800/642-0066) ferries run **to Skagway** (via some or all of Ketchikan, Wrangell, Petersburg, Sitka, Hyder, Stewart, Juneau, Haines and Hollis) almost daily in July and August, four times a week for the rest of the summer and in spring and fall, and twice a week in winter (to Ketchikan, passengers US$38, vehicles US$75; to Juneau, passengers US$104, vehicles US$240; to Haines, passengers US$122, vehicles US$276; to Skagway, passengers US$130, vehicles US$285). Two- or four-berth cabins can also be booked: current prices for a two-berth cabin from Prince Rupert are as follows: Bellingham (US$142), Juneau (US$83), Haines (US$105), Skagway (US$105). Boats stop frequently en route, with the chance to go ashore for a short time, though longer stopovers must be arranged when buying a through-ticket. For all Alaskan sailings turn up at least an hour before departure to go through US customs and immigration procedures if you're a foot passenger, and three hours if you have a car, and note that though the journey takes two days there are various restrictions on the fresh food you can take on board. You may find you can't make telephone or credit card bookings, and have to pay in person for tickets at the terminal ticket office (May–Sept daily 9am–4pm and 2hr either side of sailings; on days of sailings the rest of the year). Fares are 25 percent lower between October and April.

Accommodation

Finding **accommodation** in Prince Rupert shouldn't present problems outside July and August, when places fill up quickly on days when the ferries come in: book ahead to be on the safe side. If there's nothing in town, you can always backtrack along Hwy 16 to the villages beyond the Skeena Valley. The town's only decent budget option, with basic hostel-type rooms and shared bathrooms, is the quickly filled *Pioneer Rooms*, around the corner from the museum and infocentre at 167 3rd Ave (☎624-2334; ①). The nearest motel to the ferry terminals is the *Totem Lodge Motel*, 1335 Park Ave (☎624-6761 or 1-800/550-0178; ③): Park Avenue is a continuation of 2nd Avenue that runs south to the terminals from downtown. Perhaps the best all-round central choice, especially if you can secure a room with a sea view, is the *Inn on the Harbour*, 720 1st Ave (☎624-9107 or 1-800/663-8155; ③), while most reasonable of the many mid-range establishments is the *Aleeda*, 900 3rd Ave (☎627-1367; ③). *Pacific Inn*, 909 3rd Ave W (☎627-1711 or 1-888/663-1999; ③), is a big and good-value motel, but if you want to go top-of-the-range try the large *Crest Hotel*, 222 1st Ave (☎624-6771 or 1-800/663-8150, *www.cresthotel.bc.ca*; ⑥), or the more reasonable mini-skyscraper *Highliner Inn*, 815 1st Ave W (☎624-9060 or 1-800/668-3115, *www.floriangroup.com*; ④). Further afield, the *Parkside Resort*, 101 11th Ave (☎624-9131 or 1-888/575-2288, *www.marlintravel.com/parkside.htm*; ②), is a smart-looking hotel with good rates about a kilometre out of town and more likely to have room when downtown places are full.

The only big local **campground** is the *Park Avenue Campground*, 1750 Park Ave (☎624-5861; $13.50; year-round), 1km west of town and 1km from the ferry terminals: it has tent sites but is usually full of RVs. Otherwise the *Parkside Resort* (see above) has some sites ($10–18) that few people know about, and there's also the rural *Prudhomme Lake* provincial campground (☎798-2277; April–Nov), with forested lakeside sites, 16km east of town on Hwy 16.

The Town

Although you wouldn't know to look at it, the port is one of the world's largest deep-water terminals, and handles a huge volume of trade (grain, coal and fish in particular). In the past the region was the focal point of trade between aboriginal peoples to the north and south, one reason why the Hudson's Bay Company built a post at Fort Simpson, 30km north of the present townsite. It was also the reason why the old Hudson's Bay post was chosen as the terminus of Canada's second **transcontinental rail link**. Work began in 1906, but as time went by it was decided there was a better harbour to the south, a national competition being launched to decide on a name for the new railhead: $250 was paid for "Prince Rupert", named after the company's royal founding member, a label that was duly grafted onto the ramshackle collection of tents that constituted the settlement in 1909. A year later the first town lot was sold for around $500; within twelve months it was worth $17,000. The Grand Trunk Railway chairman, Charles M. Hays, hoped to turn Prince Rupert into a port to rival Vancouver. In 1912 he set off for Britain to raise stock for the venture, but unfortunately booked a return passage on the *Titanic*. Although he went down, the railway was finished two years later – too late, in the event, to steal a march on Vancouver. By 1919 the Grand Trunk was bankrupt, though its restructuring as the Canadian National in 1923 and the magnificence of the port has allowed the town to prosper to this day. For more on the railway and its history, visit the **Kwinitsa Station Railway Museum** just across from the VIA Rail station near the waterfront (early June to early Sept daily 9am–6pm; donation; ☎627-1915 or 627-3207).

Prince Rupert's excellent **Museum of Northern British Columbia** (June–Aug Mon–Sat 9am–8pm, Sun 9am–5pm; Sept–May Mon–Sat 9am–5pm; $5) is alongside the **infocentre** (same hours; ☎624-5637 or 1-800/667-1994 in BC, *prtravel@citytel.net*) on 1st Avenue and McBride Street at the northern end of the town's tight downtown zone. It's housed in an impressive reproduction First Nation cedar longhouse and is particularly strong on the culture and history of the local **Tsimshian**. The museum also boasts a clutch of wonderful silent archive films on topics ranging from fishing to the building of the railway – ideal ways to whittle away a wet afternoon, of which storm-lashed Prince Rupert ("City of Rainbows") has plenty. There's also a well-stocked book and gift shop and a carving shed outside where you can sometimes see totems being crafted.

While you're here, check out some of the local **tours** or **boat trips**, many of which are inexpensive and a good way to see the offshore islands and wildlife. The museum runs a tour to sites of archeological interest (mid-June to early Sept daily 1–3.30pm; $22). Otherwise Seashore Charters (☎624-5645) are a good outfit, with two-hour harbour tours, among others, starting at around $50. For an inexpensive (from $3.50) look at the harbour you could jump aboard the Rupert Water Taxi, which leaves for several destinations from the dock at the bottom of McBride Street (check times at the infocentre; departures vary according to school runs). A trip fast becoming famous locally is to **Khuzeymateen Provincial Park** (contact BC Parks on ☎847-7320 for information on two- to ten-day tours), a remote coastal valley 45km to the north of Prince Rupert created in 1994 to protect BC's largest-known coastal population of **grizzly bears**. This is the first park of its kind in the world, but there will certainly be more, especially in BC, where the damage done to declining grizzly habitats by logging, mining, hunting and other concerns – notably the slaughter of the animals for body parts in dubious Oriental remedies – is rapidly becoming one of the keenest environmental issues in the province.

A little out of town, beyond the museum, the gondola ride to **Mount Hays** once gave a bird's-eye view of the harbour and the chance to spot bald eagles. It was also the most popular attraction in town, which makes you wonder why it had to close: check with the infocentre to see if there's news of its reopening. To reach it, or the steep track that currently provides the only route to the top, take the Wantage Road turn-off on Hwy 16 just out of town. It's three hours to the top but you get fairly good views after clambering just a short way up the track. Details of less energetic **walks** can be obtained from the infocentre.

Eating and drinking

Fresh **fish** is the obvious thing to **eat** locally, preferably at the *Green Apple*, a shack (and town institution) that serves a mean halibut and chips for $6; it's at 301 McBride St (☎627-1666) just before Hwy 16 turns into town. For something a touch more upmarket, locals flock to *Smile's Seafood Café*, at 113 George Hills Way (☎624-3072), about 300m north of the infocentre, which has been doing a roaring trade on the waterfront since 1934. Also here – just across the road – is *Cowpuccinos*, a good café that's the centre of Prince Rupert's alternative scene. The *Breakers* pub just across the bridge at 117 George Hills Way (☎624-5990) is a popular and inexpensive place to drink and also serves decent food. Also close by, the *Cow Bay Café*, 205 Cow Bay (☎627-1212; closed Mon), pushes *Smile's* close for the best seafood and other meals in town. The **bar** under the *Coast Prince Rupert* high-rise hotel at 118 2nd Ave, between 6th and 7th streets, also does decent if standard Canadian food, and is one of the few places open for breakfast.

Haida Gwaii – The Queen Charlotte Islands

Ranged in an arc some 150km off the Prince Rupert coast, the **Haida Gwaii**, until recently better known as the **Queen Charlotte Islands**, consist of a triangular-shaped archipelago of about two hundred islets that make an enticing diversion from the heavily travelled sea route up through BC. The islands are something of a cult amongst travellers and environmentalists, partly for their scenery, flora and fauna and almost legendary remoteness from the mainstream, but also because they've achieved a high profile in the battle between the forestry industry and ecology activists. At the forefront of the battle are the **Haida**, widely acknowledged as one of the region's most advanced aboriginal groups, who have made the islands their home for over 10,000 years (see box opposite). Their culture, and in particular the chance to visit their many **deserted villages**, form an increasing part of the islands' attraction, but many people also come here to sample the immensely rich **flora and fauna**, a natural profusion that's earned them the title of the "Canadian Galapagos".

The Haida Gwaii were one of only two areas in western Canada to escape the last ice age, which elsewhere altered the evolutionary progress, and which has resulted in the survival of many so-called **relic species**. Species unique to the islands include a fine yellow daisy, the world's largest **black bears**, and subspecies of pine marten, deer mouse, hairy woodpecker, saw-whet owl and Stellar's jay. There are also more **eagles** here than anywhere else in the region, as well as the world's largest population of Peale's peregrine falcons and the elusive **black-footed albatross** – whose wingspan exceeds that of the largest eagles. Fish, too, are immensely plentiful, and there's a good chance of spotting whales, otters, sea lions and other aquatic mammals.

Practicalities

The islands can be accessed either by air or ferry from Prince Rupert. Ferries from Prince Rupert dock at tiny Skidegate near Queen Charlotte City on **Graham Island**, the northern of the group's two main collections of islands (see p.574 for details of ferries from Prince Rupert). Most of the archipelago's six thousand inhabitants live either in Queen Charlotte City or at Masset to the north, leaving the southern cluster of islands across Skidegate Channel – known for convenience as **Moresby Island** – a virtually deserted primal wilderness, but for the small community at Sandspit (see p.582). Regular twenty-minute ferry crossings connect Moresby Island to Skidegate (twelve sailings daily year-round; $4.50, cars $8.50). Or you can **fly** to the islands from Prince Rupert, landing at Sandspit, which has the islands' only airstrip (float planes can land elsewhere). Air BC (☎1-800/663-3721) flies here daily from Vancouver, but you might get better deals out of carriers with offices in Prince Rupert, such as Inland Air (☎627-1351 or 1-888/624-2577) and the larger Harbour Air (☎627-1341 or 1-800/665-0212). Harbour Air, for example, fly to Sandspit twice daily from Prince Rupert and also fly small planes to Masset on the north of Graham Island. It also has other flights around the islands, as do South Moresby Air Charters (☎559-4222 or 1-888/551-4222, *smoresby@qcislands.net*) in Queen Charlotte City, who'll take you out to the deepest of the backwoods.

Non-camping **accommodation** is available only at Sandspit (on Moresby) and Queen Charlotte City, Tl'ell, Masset and Port Clements (on Graham) and should always be pre-booked. The only **public transport** at time of writing is a service run by Eagle Cabs (check the current state of the service on ☎559-4461 or 1-877/747-4461) which operates a once-daily shuttle in summer in each direction between Sandspit, across the ferry and then on to Queen Charlotte City, Masset and points in between. Budget (☎637-5688 or 1-800/557-3228) has **car-rental** offices in Queen Charlotte City, Masset and Sandspit airport, but in summer you'll need to have booked in advance to secure a car. Thrifty (☎637-2299) has an office at Sandspit airport and Tilden (☎626-3318) one in Masset. Rates at Rustic Rentals (☎559-4641) out of Charlotte Island Tire in Queen Charlotte City are a touch lower than the main companies. Car-rental rates here are expensive, and unless you have a car, bike or canoe it's as well to know that you could be in for a long and expensive trip that shows you very little of what you came for. To

THE HAIDA

The **Haida** are widely considered to have the most highly developed culture and sophisticated art tradition of British Columbia's aboriginal peoples. Extending from the Haida Gwaii (Queen Charlotte Islands) to south Alaska, their lands included major stands of red cedar, the raw material for their huge dug-out **canoes**, intricate **carvings** and refined **architecture**. Haida trade links were built on the reputation of their skill – other BC peoples considering the ownership of a Haida canoe, for example, as a major status symbol. Renowned as traders and artists, the Haida were also feared **warriors**, paddling into rival villages and returning with canoes laden with goods, slaves and the severed heads of anyone who had tried to resist. Their skill on the open sea has seen them labelled the "Vikings" of the Pacific Northwest. This success at warfare was due, in part, to their use of wooden slat armour, which included a protective face visor and helmets topped with terrifying images.

Socially the Haida divided themselves into two main groups, the **Eagles** and the **Ravens**, which were further divided into hereditary kin groups named after their original village location. Marriage within each major group – or *moiety* – was considered incestuous, so Eagles would always seek Raven mates and vice versa. Furthermore, descent was traced through the **female line**, which meant that a chief could not pass his property onto his sons because they would belong to a different *moiety* – instead his inheritance passed to his sister's sons. Equally, young men might have to leave their childhood village to claim their inheritance from their maternal uncles.

Haida **villages** were an impressive sight, their vast cedar-plank houses dominated by fifteen-metre totem poles displaying the kin group's unique animal crest or other mythical creatures, all carved in elegantly fluid lines. Entrance to each house was through the gaping mouth of a massive carved figure; inside, supporting posts were carved into the forms of the crest animals and most household objects were similarly decorative. Equal elaboration attended the many Haida ceremonies, one of the most important of which was the **mortuary potlatch**, serving as a memorial service to a dead chief and the validation of the heir's right to succession. The dead individual was laid out at the top of a carved pole near the village entrance, past which the visiting chiefs would walk wearing robes of finely woven and patterned mountain-goat wool and immense headdresses fringed with long sea-lion whiskers and ermine skins. A hollow at the top of each headdress was filled with eagle feathers, which floated down onto the witnesses as the chiefs sedately danced.

After **European contact** the Haida population was devastated by smallpox and other epidemics. In 1787, there were around 8000 Haida scattered across the archipelago. Their numbers were then reduced from around 6000 in 1835 to 588 by 1915. Consequently they were forced to abandon their traditional villages and today gather largely at two sites, Old Masset (pop. 650) and Skidegate (Haida pop. 550). At other locations the homes and totems fell into disrepair, and only at **Sgan Gwaii**, a remote village at the southern tip of the Queen Charlottes, has an attempt been made to preserve an original Haida settlement; it has now been declared a World Heritage Site by UNESCO.

These days the Haida number around 2000, and are highly regarded in the North American art world; Bill Reid, Freda Diesing and Robert Davidson are amongst the best-known figures, and scores of other Haida craftspeople produce a mass of carvings and jewellery for the tourist market. They also play a powerful role in the islands' social, political and cultural life, having been vocal in the formation of sites such as the Gwaii Haanas National Park Reserve (p.583), South Moresby's Haida Heritage Site and Duu Guusd Tribal Park (p.581), the last established to protect old aboriginal villages on Graham Island's northwest coast.

see the **Haida villages**, in any case, virtually all of which are on inaccessible parts of Moresby, you'll need to take a boat, and more probably a pricey tour by float plane.

Graham Island

Most casual visitors stick to **Graham Island**, where the bulk of the island's roads and accommodation are concentrated along the eastern side of the island, between **Queen Charlotte City** in the south and **Masset** some 108km to the north. These settlements and the villages in between – Skidegate, Tl'ell and Port Clements – lie along Hwy 16, the principal road, and shelter in the lee of the islands, away from a mountainous and indented rocky west coast that boasts the highest combined seismic, wind and tidal energy of any North American coastline (producing treacherous seas and a tidal range of 8m). Much of the east coast consists of beautiful half-moon, driftwood-strewn beaches and a string of provincial parks where you can appreciate the milder climes produced by the Pacific's Japanese Current, a warming stream that contributes to the island's lush canopy of thousand-year-old spruce and cedar rainforests. On the downside, though, it drenches both sides of the island with endless rainstorms, even in summer. Make sure you pack a raincoat.

Queen Charlotte City

It would be hard to imagine anywhere less like a city than the island's second largest settlement, **QUEEN CHARLOTTE CITY** (pop. 924), a picturesque fishing village and frontier administrative centre about 5km west of the Skidegate ferry terminal (see overleaf). The village takes its name from the ship of Captain George Dixon, the British explorer who sailed to the Haida Gwaii in 1787, thirteen years after first European contact was probably made by the Spaniard Juan Perez. Most of its residents squeeze a living from the McMillan Bloedel timber giant, whose felling exploits have cleared most of the hills around the port, and who control access to many of the island's 2000km of backcountry logging roads. For a fine overview of the place, try the stroll to the top of **Sleeping Beauty Mountain**, which is reached by a rough track from Crown Forest Road near Honna Road. The village **dump** south of the houses rates as another sight for the black bears and bald and golden eagles that often gather there at dusk. Further afield you may be able to watch salmon and other wildlife at the **Skidegate Band Salmon Project** on the Honna Forest Service Road 3km west of town: contact the Band Council for information (☎559-4496). Further away still, you can drive to **Rennell Sound**, a west coast inlet with shingle beaches accessed by a logging road: take the main logging road north from the town for 22km and then turn left and follow the steep gravel road for 14km, but contact the infocentre before setting out (see below). At the Sound, the **Rennell Sound Recreation Site** offers paths through stands of primal rainforest to isolated sandy beaches and a couple of campgrounds with a total of ten beachfront wilderness pitches (free).

Otherwise the town is the major place to sign up for any number of outdoor activities; contact the **infocentre**, 3220 Wharf St (daily: mid-May to early Sept 10am–7pm; early May & late Sept 10am–2pm; closed Oct–April; ☎559-8316, *www.qcinfo.com*). The staff are incredibly knowledgeable, and there's a good selection of detailed guides and maps to the area: be sure to pick up the invaluable *Guide to the Queen Charlotte Islands* ($3.95). The centre is also the place to pick up brochures and organize **tours** of the island, with some forty or more fishing, sailing, sightseeing, canoeing and other operators being based in Queen Charlotte City. There's also a **Canadian Parks Service** office for information on Moresby Island's Gwaii Haanas National Park Reserve and Haida Heritage Site (see p.583), west of town along Hwy 33 (Mon–Fri 8am–noon & 1–4.30pm; ☎559-8818). The **Ministry of Forests**, in the obvious blue building on 3rd Avenue (☎559-8447), has information on the free primitive campgrounds run by the Forest Service on Graham and Moresby islands. If you're planning to drive logging roads, you must call **Weyherhauser** (☎557-6810) – which controls most of these roads on Graham Island – for latest access details. Enquire, too, about their regular forestry tours (they depart Port Clements museum, currently Tues and Thurs at 9am: call the above number to book a place).

ACCOMMODATION AND FOOD
Accommodation is scarce and demand is high in summer, so definitely call ahead to make bookings. The first-choice hotel is probably the *Premier Creek Lodging*, 3101 3rd Ave (☎559-8451 or 1-888/322-3388, *www.qcislands.net/premier*, ④), a splendidly restored 1910 heritage building overlooking the harbour and Bearskin Bay. **Bike rentals** are available here also. Then there's the unique *Gracie's Place*, 3113 3rd Ave (☎559-4262 or 1-888/244-4262, *www.gracies-place.com*; ③), with ocean-view rooms, antique furniture and rustic decor; and the *Spruce Point Lodging*, 609 6th Ave (☎559-8234, *www.qcislands.net/sprpoint*; ③), which offers rooms and breakfast overlooking Skidegate Inlet opposite the Chevron garage at the west end of town. Similarly intimate is *Dorothy and Mike's Guest House*, 3125 2nd Ave (☎559-8439; ③), with central rooms and full cooking facilities in a no-smoking environment. A touch closer to the ferry terminal, overlooking Bearskin Bay, is the *Sea Raven Motel*, 3301 3rd Ave (☎559-4423 or 1-800/665-9606, *www.searaven.com*; ③). If you're **camping**, try the unserviced *Haydn Turner Park* (free) in the community park at the western end of town, or the *Kagan Bay Forest Service Campground*, a handful of lovely beachfront campsites on Honna Forest Service Road 5km west of the town.

For **food**, locals make for the *Sea Raven Restaurant* (☎559-8583) located straight up the main road from the dock by the *Sea Raven Motel*. There are also *Margaret's Café*, 3223 Wharf St, on the east side of town, or *Hanging by a Thread* on Wharf close to the infocentre, a fine place whose produce comes from organic farms on the island.

Skidegate

There's not much doing at **SKIDEGATE** (pop. 550), other than the ferries docking at Skidegate Landing 2km away to the south and the chance to browse through the more accessible aspects of Haida culture at the **Haida Gwaii Museum**, located near Second Beach at Qay'llnagaay around 500m east of the ferry terminal (May & Sept Mon–Fri 9am–5pm, Sat 1–5pm; June–Aug Mon–Fri 9am–5pm, Sat & Sun 1–5pm; Oct–April Mon & Wed–Fri 10am–noon & 1–5pm, Sat 1–5pm; $3; ☎559-4643). Among other things, the museum contains the world's largest collection of the Haida's treasured argillite carvings (such carvings are also on display in Vancouver's UBC Museum of Anthropology). Argillite is a form of black slate-like rock found only on the Haida Gwaii, and only in one site whose location is kept a closely guarded secret. Also check out the platform here for viewing grey whales during their migrations (April–May & Sept to early Oct). After doing so, stop by the longhouse office alongside the museum to have a chat with the **Haida Gwaii Watchmen**. Bands of Haida "watchmen" were formed in the 1970s to protect aboriginal sites from vandalism and theft, and survive to this day. Ask at the office about seeing the famous *Loo Taas* ("Wave Eater") canoe, which is generally on show here on weekdays. When it's not out on hire to rich tourists – for a mere $1500, or thereabouts – you're very occasionally able to take a six-hour tour in the huge vessel. It was made for the '86 Expo in Vancouver and was the first Haida canoe carved since 1909. You can obtain a permit to visit some of the five hundred or more abandoned aboriginal villages and sites on the southern islands from the longhouse, or alternatively from the nearby **Skidegate Mission** or Band Council Office close to Skidegate proper – a Haida village 2.5km from the ferry terminal. There's also a carving longhouse here, where you may be able to watch craftspeople at work. In July and August, the Mission usually hosts a weekly **seafood feast**, open to all-comers for around $25 (check latest details at the Queen Charlotte City infocentre). If you're here to catch the boat across the channel to Moresby Island and Sandspit, the MV *Kuvuna* **ferry** runs twelve times daily year-round (7.30am–10.30pm; 20min; $4.50).

Tl'ell and Port Clements

If you blink you'll miss the ranching community of **TL'ELL** (pop. 138), 36km north of Skidegate, first settled by outsiders in 1904 and home to the Richardson Ranch, the island's oldest working ranch. Stop here and walk down to the sea, where you can stroll for hours on deserted wind-sculpted dunes. It's a community favoured by craftspeople and alternative types – pop into the little café or gallery – and in the past there's been a **hostel** here, the intermittently open *Bellis Lodge* (☎557-4434; ①) – check before turning up. Nearby is the *Tl'ell River House*, off Hwy 16 overlooking Tl'ell River and Hecate Strait, offering ten rooms with kitchenettes and a licensed lounge and **restaurant** (☎557-4211 or 1-800/667-8906); ③). Or try the pleasantly rustic *Cacilia's B&B* just north of Richardson Ranch on the main road (☎557-4664, *www.qcislands.net/ceebysea*; ③; no credit cards), a renovated log house set behind the dunes on Hecate Strait 2km from the Naikoon Park (see below). **Bikes** and **kayaks** are usually available for rent here.

As the road cuts inland for **PORT CLEMENTS** (pop. 577), 21km to the northwest of Tl'ell, it forms the southern border of the **Naikoon Provincial Park**, an enclave that extends over Graham Island's northeast corner and designed to protect fine beach, dune and dwarf woodland habitats. **Campers** should head for the *Misty Meadows Campground* ($9.50; May–Oct), just south of the Tl'ell River Bridge and 500m north of the **park centre** (☎557-4390) to the north of Tl'ell (backcountry camping is allowed throughout the park). About 8km beyond, look out for the picnic site and trails at the southern tip of **Mayer Lake**, one of the nicer spots to pull over. Port Clements in the past was most famous for the world's only **Golden Spruce** tree, a 300-year-old bleached albino tree – sacred to the Haida – which puzzled foresters by refusing to produce anything but ordinary green-leafed saplings; in 1997 a vandal chopped it down. A rare genetic mutation allowed the tree's needles to be bleached by sunlight and geneticists and foresters are currently trying to produce another tree.

Port Clements' little **infocentre** booth (July to early Sept daily 9am–6pm) is just out of the village, and there's a small **museum** of forestry and pioneer-related offerings at 45 Bayview Drive on the main road into the town (June–Sept Tues–Sun 2–5pm, winter hours according to availability of volunteers; donation). The one official **hotel** is the *Golden Spruce*, 2 Grouse St (☎557-4325 or 1-877/801-4653, *www.qcislands.net/golden*; ②), but it's worth asking around for B&B possibilities. For **food and drink**, the main option is the good *Yakoun River Inn* on Bayview Drive. About 20km north of town on the road for Masset, look out for the signed **Pure Lake Provincial Park**, where on summer days the waters of Pure Lake should be warm enough for swimming.

Masset

MASSET, 40km north of Port Clements, is the biggest place on the islands, a scattered town of some 1490 people, most of who are employed in fishing and crab-canning. Many visitors are here to bird-watch at the **Delkatla Wildlife Sanctuary**, a saltwater marsh north of the village – contact Delkatla Bay Birding Tours (☎626-5015) for guided visits – that supports 113 bird species, or to walk the trails around Tow Hill 26km to the east (see opposite). Others come to wander the neighbouring village of **HAIDA**, or "Old Massett" – with an extra "t" – 2km to the west, the administrative centre for the Council of the Haida First Nation and where some six hundred aboriginal people still live and work. Visitors should show respect when visiting totem sites, craft houses and community homes. Many locals are involved in producing crafts for tourists, or organizing wilderness tours, but some are restoring and adding to the few totems still standing locally (it's possible to visit various canoe and carving sheds) and there's a small museum giving some context. For more **information** on where to see carving and on the village in general, visit the Old Massett Council office on Eagle Road (Mon–Fri 9am–5pm; ☎626-3395), where you should also enquire about permission to visit the **Duu Guusd Tribal Park**, established by the Haida to protect villages on the coast to the northwest. Two villages here are still active, and the park is used as a base for the Haida Gwaii Rediscovery Centre, which offers courses to children on Haida culture and history.

The Masset **info booth**, at 1455 Old Beach Rd (July & Aug daily 9am–5pm; ☎626-3982, *www.massetbc.com*), has full details of wildlife and bird-watching possibilities. The Masset Village Office (☎626-3995) on Main Street can also provide invaluable background. Sadly they can't do much about the village's limited **accommodation** prospects, other than point you to the *Harbourview Lodging*, overlooking the harbour at 1608 Delkatla Rd (☎626-5109 or 1-800/661-3314, *lholland@island.net*; ③), *Naden Lodge*, 1496 Delkatla St, corner of Harrison (☎626-3322 or 1-800/771-TYEE, *www.nadenlodge.bc.ca*; ⑤) or to a handful of intermittently open B&Bs. Outside of town, there's accommodation near South Beach with ocean views at the *Alaska View Lodge*, Tow Hill Road (☎626-3333, *www.alaskaviewlodge.com*; ③), 10.5km from Masset airport and midway between Masset village and Tow Hill. The only nearby **campground** is the *Village of Masset RV Site and Campground* ($9–17; no reservations) on Tow Hill Road, 2km north of town alongside the wildlife sanctuary. Further afield there's the *Agate Beach* ($12; May–Sept) in Naikoon Park, a provincial park site near trails and sandy beaches located 26km northeast of Masset off the secondary road towards Tow Hill (see below). To get around, call Vern's Taxi (☎626-3535) or Jerry's Taxi Service in Old Massett (☎626-5017) or **rent a car** from Tilden, 1504 Old Beach Rd (☎626-3318). There are a couple of pizza and takeaway places to **eat** – try the *Café Gallery* on Collision Avenue (☎626-3672) – and a handful of **bars** on Collision Avenue and Main Street, with live music some nights.

Heading away from the village, follow Tow Hill Road to **Tow Hill**, 26km to the east, where you can pick up trails into the Naikoon Park: three begin by the Heillen River at the foot of Tow Hill itself. The easiest is the one-kilometre **Blow Hole Trail**, which drops down to striking rock formations and basalt cliffs by the sea. From here you can follow another path to the top of Tow Hill (109m) for superb views of deserted sandy beaches stretching into the hazy distance. The third track, the **Cape Fife Trail**, is a longer (10km) hike to the east side of the island. Naikoon means "point", a reference to Rose Spit, the twelve-kilometre spit that extends from the park and Graham Island's northeasterly tip. Today it's an ecological and wildlife reserve of beaches, dunes, marsh and stunted forest, but it's also a sacred Haida site, for it was here, according to legend, that the Haida's Raven clan were first tempted from a giant clamshell by a solitary raven.

Moresby Island

Moresby Island is all but free from human contact except for deserted Haida villages, one of which contains the world's largest stand of totems, forestry roads and the small logging community of **Sandspit** (pop. 202). The last lies 15km from the **Alliford Bay** terminal for the inter-island ferry link with Skidegate on Graham Island (12 daily; 20min crossing; $4.50, cars $8.50). Local airlines fly from Prince Rupert to a small airstrip near the village. Budget (☎637-5688 or 1-800/557-3228) and Thrifty (☎637-2299) have **car-rental** offices at the airport: for a **taxi** for connections to the ferry, call Bruce's Taxi (☎637-5655).

Most locals here and on Graham Island work in Moresby's forests, and the **forestry issue** has divided the community for years between the Haida and environmentalists – "hippies" in the local parlance – and the lumber workers (the "rednecks" as the environmentalists call them). At stake are the islands' temperate rainforests and the traditional sites of the Haida, themselves politically shrewd media manipulators who've sent representatives to Brazil to advise local aboriginal peoples there on their own rainforest programmes. They've also occasionally provided the muscle to halt logging on the islands, and to prove a point in the past they've blocked access to **Hot Spring Island**, whose thermal pools are a favourite tourist target. On the other hand the forests provide jobs and some of the world's most lucrative timber – a single good sitka trunk can be worth up to $60,000. Currently a compromise has been reached and most of Moresby has National Park Reserve status (established in 1987), though stiff lobbying from the logging companies leaves its position perilous. If you're intending to drive any of the logging roads, however – and most of the handful of roads here *are* logging roads – note that generally they're open to the public at weekends and after 6pm on weekdays: otherwise check for latest details with the local infocentres.

Sandspit's only listed **accommodation**, apart from a couple of intermittently open B&Bs, is the *Moresby Island Guest House*, 385 Alliford Bay Rd overlooking the ocean at Shingle Bay, 1km south of the airport (☎637-5300, *www.bbcanada.com/1651.html*; ③); an airport pick-up is included. Many people choose to sleep on the spit's beaches: Gray Bay, 21km southeast of Sandspit, has primitive and peaceful **campsites** near gravel and sand beaches (for more details, contact the TimberWest forestry offices on Beach Rd; ☎637-5436). For **car rental**, Budget have offices at the airport and in Sandspit at Beach and Blaine Shaw roads (☎637-5688). If you fancy going into the **interior by plane**, contact South Moresby Air Charters (☎559-4222 or 1-888/551-4222) for details of charter flights.

Gwaii Haanas National Park Reserve

If you're determined enough you can canoe, mountain bike or backpack the interior of northern Moresby Island, but you need to know what you're doing – the seas here are especially treacherous for canoeists – and be prepared to lug plenty of supplies. You must, however, join a tour or follow a strict procedure (see below) if you want to visit the **Gwaii Haanas National Park Reserve**, a 90km archipelago that embraces 138 islands, some 500 Haida archeological sites, 5 deserted Haida villages and some 1500km of coastline across the south of the island group. Treaties signed with the federal government in Ottawa in 1990 gave the Haida joint control of this region, and afforded protection to their ancient villages, but many land claims to the region remain unresolved. You need money, time and effort to see the park. There are no roads, and access is by boat or chartered planes only.

The easiest way into the park is with a tour – contact the Queen Charlotte City infocentre (see p.579) for full details. Or make direct contact with companies such as South Moresby Air Charters (☎559-4221 or 1-888/551-4222) or GwaiiEco Tours (☎559-8333, *www.gwaiiecotours.com*): prices start from about $125 for one-day trips. Sandspit's **infocentre** in the airport terminal building (June–Sept daily 9am–6pm; ☎637-5436) also has details of the many tours to the park and the limited facilities on the whole southern half of the archipelago.

Visits to a variety of **Haida sites** and their totems, ruined dwellings and so forth are described here in order of distance (and therefore time and expense) from Sandspit. Closest are **Hlkenul** (Cumshewa) and **K'una** (Skedans) just outside the park, both accessible on day-trips by boat from Moresby Camp on the Cumshewa Inlet, 46km south of Sandspit (access to the Camp is by logging road). Further afield, and in the park proper, are T'aannu, Hlk'waah – one of the main battlegrounds in the fight to protect the region in the 1980s – and **Gandla K'in** (Hot Spring Island), whose hot springs make it one of the most popular destinations. The finest site of all, of course, is the one that's furthest away: **Sgan Gwaii** (Ninstints) lies close to the southern tip of the archipelago, and was abandoned by the Haida around 1880 in the wake of smallpox epidemics. Today, it contains the most striking of the ruined Haida villages, its longhouses and many totems declared a UNESCO World Heritage Site in 1981.

To **visit the reserve** as an independent traveller, you must make an advance reservation or obtain a stand-by space. **Reservations** can be made by calling ☎1-800/HELLOBC (within Canada or the United States) or ☎250/387-1642 (outside North America). There is a $15 per person reservation fee (maximum of four people per reservation). If you choose not to make a reservation, then only six places daily are available **stand-by**, available on a first-come, first-served basis starting at the 8am orientation session (see below) at the Queen Charlotte infocentre. There are also **fees** to visit the park: day-trips cost $10 per person plus $10 for each night thereafter, but trips of 6 to 14 nights are payable at a flat fee of $60; stays over 14 nights coast $80.

An **orientation session** is mandatory for all visitors entering Gwaii Haanas, Skedans or T'aanuu. Sessions take around ninety minutes and cover topics such as public safety, no-trace camping, natural and cultural heritage and the Haida Gwaii Watchmen Program. These sessions take place at the Queen Charlotte infocentre or the Gwaii Haanas office on Airport Road, opposite the Sandspit Inn (☎559-8818). Before May 15 and after September 15, book sessions through the park office in Queen Charlotte City (see p.579); from mid-May to the end of June, sessions run twice daily – once in the QCC infocentre at 8am and once in the Sandspit Mall office at 11am; from July 1 to mid-September, there are two QCC session at 8am and 7.30pm and one in Sandspit at 11am. If you're **travelling with a tour company**, companies check that you've done the orientation and some offer it as part of their package. Apart from some restricted areas, which you are informed of during orientation sessions, you can camp where you wish in the reserve; fees for camping are included in the general fee you pay to enter the park. There are no hotels, hostels or other forms of accommodation.

The Cassiar Highway

The 733km of the **Cassiar Highway** (Hwy 37) from the Skeena Valley east of Prince Rupert to Watson Lake just inside Yukon Territory are some of the wildest and most beautiful on any British Columbian road. Though less famous than the Alaska Highway, the road is increasingly travelled by those who want to capture some of the adventure that accompanied the wilder reaches of its better-known neighbour in the 1950s and 1960s.

Some stretches are still gravel, and the gas and repair facilities, let alone food and lodgings, are extremely patchy: don't contemplate the journey unless your vehicle's in top condition, with two spare tires and spare fuel containers – fill up wherever possible. The road also provides a shorter route from Prince George to the Yukon than the Alaska Highway. British Columbia's North by Northwest Tourist Association puts out complete lists of facilities, which are vital accompaniments to any journey and are available from the infocentres in Prince Rupert and Terrace.

If you're ready to drive the distances involved, you'll also probably be prepared to explore the highway's two main side roads to **Stewart** and **Telegraph Creek**, and possibly the rough roads and trails that lead into two wilderness parks midway up the highway – the **Mount Edziza Provincial Park** and the **Spatsizi Plateau Wilderness Park**. If you can't face the highway's entire length, the side-trip to Stewart offers exceptional sea and mountain **scenery**, as well as the chance to cross into Alaska at **Hyder** to indulge in its vaunted alcoholic border initiation.

Stewart

The Cassiar Highway starts near Kitwanga, one of several aboriginal villages off Hwy 16, and a crossroads of the old "grease trail", named after the candlefish oil which was once traded between Coast and Interior peoples. Some hint of the sense of adventure required comes when you hit a section (47km beyond Cranberry Junction), where the road doubles up as an airstrip – planes have right of way. Another 27km on, there's another stretch used as an airstrip in emergencies. Almost immediately after you leave

Hwy 16, though, the road pitches into the mesmerizing high scenery of the Coast Ranges, a medley of mountain, lake and forest that reaches a crescendo after about 100km and the side turn to **STEWART**, Canada's most northerly ice-free port. Here a series of immense glaciers culminates in the dramatic appearance of the unmissable **Bear Glacier**, a vast sky-blue mass of ice that comes down virtually to the highway and has the strange ability to glow in the dark. Stewart itself, 37km west of the glacier, is a shrivelled mining centre (pop. 2200) that sits at the end of the Portland Canal, the world's fourth longest fjord, a natural boundary between British Columbia and Alaska that lends the town a superb peak-ringed location (the ferry ride in from Prince Rupert through some of the west coast's wildest scenery is sensational). Dominating its rocky amphitheatre is **Mount Rainey**, whose cliffs represent one of the greatest vertical rises from sea level in the world.

Stewart's **history**, together with that of nearby Hyder (see opposite), might have marked it out as a regional player were it not quite so remote and apparently doomed to ultimate disappointment in every venture ever tried in the town. In the distant past it was an important trading point, marking the meeting point of territories belonging to the Nisga'a and Gitxsan interior aboriginal peoples to the south, the Thaltan to the north, and the Tsesaut and the Tlingit to the east. Captain George Vancouver, searching for the Northwest Passage in 1793, spoke for many who came after him when, having spent an eternity working his way inland up the Portland Canal, he declared himself "mortified with having devoted so much time to so little purpose". Almost exactly a century later the area welcomed its first settlers: in 1896 Captain Gilliard of the US Army Corps built four storehouses here in Hyder – Alaska's first stone buildings – and Stewart itself was named after two of its earliest settlers (Robert and John Stewart). For a time it looked as if the terminus of the trans-Canadian railway might materialize in Stewart, a hope that brought 10,000 fortune-seeking pioneers. The railway never came, and Stewart's local line was abandoned after a few kilometres. As slump set in, gold was discovered – almost inevitably – and until 1948, when it closed, the Premier Gold and Silver Mine was North America's largest gold mine. Then came a copper mine, its eighteen-kilometre gallery apparently the longest tunnel ever built by boring from just one end. This closed in 1984, but not before 27 men were killed in a mine accident in 1965. All manner of new mining ventures have since been promised. None have materialized, leaving Stewart's scenery its main money-spinner: visitors and B-movie location scouts alike having been lured by the region's cliffs, mountains and glaciers – the *Iceman* and *The Thing* are two of the films to have used the local landscape as a backdrop.

Scenery aside, the main thing to see in town is the **Stewart Historical Museum** housed in the former fire hall at Columbia and 6th Avenue (summer Mon–Fri 1–4pm, Sat & Sun noon–5pm; or by appointment on ☎636-2568). A fine little provincial museum, its exhibits are devoted largely to stuffed wildlife and the town's logging and mining heritage. You might also want to journey out 5km beyond Hyder in Alaska to Fish Creek, where from the special viewing platform above the artificial spawning channel you may be lucky enough to see **black bears** catching some of the world's largest chum salmon. Around town there are also a handful of enticing trails, some along old mining roads: for details, contact the infocentre (see below) or visit the British Columbia Forest Service (☎636-2663) office at 8th and Brightwell.

PRACTICALITIES

The town's **infocentre** is housed at 222 5th Ave near Victoria (mid-May to mid-Sept daily; 9am–8pm; ☎636-9224 or 1-888/366-5999, *stewhydcofc@hotmail.com*). If you want to sleep over, there are two **hotels**: the *King Edward Hotel*, 5th and Columbia (☎636-2244 or toll-free in BC 1-800/663-3126; ④), and the *King Edward Motel*, Columbia Avenue (same details): the latter has basic housekeeping units and is $10 more expensive. The *King Edward Hotel* is the town's main **pub**, **restaurant** and **coffee shop** –

it's where the locals eat – while visitors prefer the pleasantly polished *Bitter Creek Café* (a block west of the *King Edward*), which offers an eclectic mix of food and an outside deck on warm days. For bread and baked snacks, duck into *Brothers Bakery* next door to the *Bitter Creek*. There's also a late-opening Chinese restaurant, *Fong's Garden*, at 5th and Conway. The nearest **campground** is the *Rainey Creek Campground* on the edge of town on 8th Avenue (☎636-2537; $14; May–Sept), and the tenting area (as opposed to RVs) is located across Rainey Creek, a pleasant little stream. Ask at the campground office about the area's nature trails and glacier tours on offer. One of the easiest local trails, the **Rainey Creek Nature Walk**, shadowing the creek for 2.5km to the northern end of town (return to the centre on Railway St), starts here.

In summer Stewart is added to the itinerary of certain sailings of the Alaska Marine Highway ferry service (see box p.574), albeit infrequently, so with careful planning you could travel overland to Stewart, or ride a boat to Ketchikan and thence to either Skagway or Prince Rupert, to complete a neat circular itinerary.

Hyder

Most people come to **HYDER** (pop. 70), Stewart's oddball twin, simply to drink in one or both of its two bars. It's a ramshackle place – barely a settlement at all – 3km from Stewart across the **border in Alaska** with none of the usual formalities, there being nothing beyond the end of the road but 800km of wilderness. People use Canadian currency, the police are of the Mountie variety and the phone system and code – ☎250 – are also Canadian. At the *Glacier Inn* the tradition is to pin a dollar to the wall in case you return broke and need a drink, and then toss back a shot of hard liquor in one and receive an "I've Been Hyderized" card. The result is many thousands of tacked dollars and the "world's most expensive wallpaper". It sounds a bit of a tourist carry-on, but if you arrive out of season there's a genuine amiability about the place that warrants its claims to be the "The Friendliest Ghost Town in Alaska". The town's two bars are often open 23 hours a day and a couple of **motels** are on hand if you literally can't stand any more: the *Sealaska Inn*, Premier Avenue (☎636-9003; ③), and the preferable *Grand View Inn* (☎636-9174; ③). They're both cheaper than their Stewart equivalents, and as you're in Alaska there's no room tax to pay on top. If you want something to soak up the alcohol, make for the *Sealaska Inn Restaurant* (☎636-2486) for no-nonsense food. The community's little **infocentre**, if you need it, is on the right as you come into town (June to early Sept daily except Wed 9am–1pm).

Dease Lake and Iskut

For several hundred kilometres beyond the Stewart junction there's nothing along the Cassiar other than the odd garage, rest area, campground, trailhead and patches of burnt or clear-cut forest etched into the Cassiar and Skeena mountains. In places, though, you can still see traces of the incredible 3060km Dominion Telegraph line that used to link the Dawson City gold fields with Vancouver, and glimpses of a proposed railway extension out of Prince George that was abandoned as late as 1977.

DEASE LAKE, the first place of any size, has two **motels**, the *Northway Motor Inn* on Boulder Avenue (☎771-5341; ③) and *Arctic Divide Inn* on the highway (☎771-3119; ③), still 246km from the junction with the Alaska Highway to the north. Close by lies **ISKUT**, an aboriginal village offering tours into the adjacent wilderness parks, which are also accessible by float plane from Dease Lake itself. For **information**, contact the Iskut Band Office (☎234-3331) or local stores and garages. The village **accommodation** amounts to the *Red Goat Lodge* (☎234-3261 or 1-888/733-4628; ④, tents $13; late May to mid-Sept).

The road from Dease Lake is wild and beautiful, the 240km up to the Yukon border from here passing through some of the most miraculous scenery of what is already a superb journey. Some 84km north of Dease Lake is the *Moose Meadows Resort* (radio phone only; ①, tents $10; May to mid-Oct) which has cabins, tent and RV sites, a convenience store and canoe rentals. Much of this area was swamped with gold-hungry pioneers during the **Cassiar Gold Rush** of 1872–80, when the region got its name – possibly from a white prospector's corruption of *kaskamet*, the dried beaver meat eaten by local Kaska. In 1877 Alfred Freedman plucked one of the world's largest pure gold nuggets – a 72-ounce monster – from a creek east of present-day **CASSIAR** (133km from the junction with the Alaska Hwy to the north), though these days the mining has a less romantic allure, being concentrated in an open-pit **asbestos mine** 5km from the village. Most of the world's high-grade asbestos once came from here, and poisonous-looking piles of green chrysotile asbestos tailings are scattered for kilometres around. The mine closed in 1992, transforming the community into a virtual ghost town at a stroke. Equipment has been sold and sites cleared, and the area is off limits to the pubic until reclamation is complete.

Telegraph Creek

For a taste of what is possibly a more remarkable landscape than you see on the Cassiar, it's worth driving the potentially treacherous 113-kilometre side road from Dease Lake to **TELEGRAPH CREEK** (allow 2hr in good conditions). It's a delightful riverbank town whose look and feel can scarcely have changed since the beginning of the twentieth century, when it was a major telegraph station and trading post for the gold-rush towns to the north. The road from the Cassiar navigates some incredible gradients and bends, twisting past canyons, old lava beds and touching on several **aboriginal villages**, notably at Tahltan River, where salmon are caught and cured in traditional smokehouses and sold to passing tourists. If you're lucky you might see a Tahltan bear dog, a species now virtually extinct. Only ankle high, and weighing less than fifteen pounds, these tiny animals were able to keep a bear cornered by barking and darting around until a hunter came to finish it off. Telegraph Creek itself is an object lesson in how latter-day pioneers live on the north's last frontiers: it's home to a friendly mixture of city exiles, hunters, trappers and ranchers, but also a cloistered bunch of **religious fundamentalists** who have eschewed the decadent mainstream for wilderness purity. Such groups are growing in outback British Columbia, an as-yet undocumented phenomenon that's creating friction with the easy-going types who first settled the backwoods. Gold has recently been discovered locally, attracting mining companies, so ways of life may be about to change here for all concerned.

Much of the village and village life revolves around the General Delivery – a combined café (the *Riversong*), grocery and garage – and small adjoining **motel**, the *Stikine River Song Lodge* (☎235-3196, *www.stikineriversong.com*; ③), whose rooms include kitchenettes. No one here, except perhaps the Bible brigade, minds if you pitch a tent – but ask around first. Also enquire at the café for details of rafting and other local trips into the backcountry.

Prince George to Dawson Creek

Dawson Creek is the launching pad for the Alaska Highway. While it may not be somewhere you'd otherwise stop, it's almost impossible to avoid a night here whether you're approaching from Edmonton and the east or **from Prince George** on the scenically more uplifting **John Hart Highway** (Hwy 97). Named after a former BC premier, this

If you're continuing up the Cassiar Highway to Watson Lake and the Alaska Highway junction, turn to "Watson Lake to Whitehorse", p.594.

seemingly innocuous road is one of the north's most vital highways. Completed in 1952, it linked at a stroke the road network of the Pacific Coast with that of the northern interior, cutting 800km off the journey from Seattle to Alaska, for example, a trip that previously had to take in a vast inland loop to Calgary. The route leads you out of British Columbia's upland interior to the so-called Peace River country, a region of slightly ridged land that belongs in look and spirit to the Albertan prairies. There's some 409km of driving, and two daily Greyhound **buses** make the journey.

Out of Prince George the road bends through mildly dipping hills and mixed woodland, passing small lakes and offering views to the Rockies, whose distant jagged skyline keeps up the spirits as you drive through an otherwise unbroken tunnel of conifers. About 70km on, **Bear Lake** and the **Crooked River Provincial Park** are just off the road, and it's well worth taking the small lane west of the park entrance to reach an idyllic patch of water fringed on its far shore by a fine sickle of sand. There's a provincial park **campground** ($15) at the park.

Both Mackenzie Junction, 152km from Prince George, and Mackenzie, 29km off the highway, are scrappy, unpleasant places, easily avoided and soon forgotten as the road climbs to **Pine Pass** (933m), one of the lower road routes over the Rockies, but spectacular all the same. The **Bijoux Falls Provincial Park**, just before it, is good for a picnic near the eponymous falls, and if you want to **camp** plump for the *Pine Valley Park Lodge* ($11; May–Oct), an immensely scenic lakeside spot that looks up to crags of massively stratified and contorted rock just below the pass. Thereafter the road drops steeply through Chetwynd (three motels and a campground) to the increasingly flatter country that heralds Dawson Creek.

Dawson Creek

Arrive in **DAWSON CREEK** (pop. 11,500) late and leave early: except for a small museum next to the town's eye-catching red grain hopper, and the obligatory photograph of the cairn marking **Mile Zero** of the Alaska Highway, there's almost nothing to do here for most casual visitors except eat and sleep. Contact the **infocentre** at the museum, 900 Alaska Ave (daily 9am–6pm, longer hours in summer; ☎782-9595, *dctourin@pris.bc.ca*), for details of the **motels** – there are several, mostly concentrated on the Alaska Highway northeast of town. One of the nicer places is the *Trail Inn*, 1748 Alaska Ave (☎782-8595 or 1-800/663-2749, *www.trailinn.com*; ③), with views of countryside rather than tarmac. None of the local **campgrounds** and RV parks are places you'd want to linger, but the most attractive is the *Mile 0 RV Park and Campground* (☎782-2590; $10–15; May to mid-Sept), about a kilometre west of the town centre at the junction of Hwy 97 N and Hwy 97 S opposite 20th Street on the Alaska Highway.

For something to **eat**, call at the excellent *Alaska Café* on 10th Street, an attractive old wooden building completely at odds with the rest of the town. The food and ambience are good – though prices aren't the cheapest – and the bar's not bad either.

Dawson Creek to Whitehorse

The best part of the **Alaska Highway** – a distance of about 1500km – winds through northern British Columbia from Dawson Creek to Whitehorse, the capital of the Yukon (only 320km of the Alaska Highway is actually in Alaska). Don't be fooled by the string of villages emblazoned across the area's maps, for there are only two towns worthy of the name en route, **Fort St John** and **Fort Nelson** – the rest are no more than a garage, a store and perhaps a motel. **Watson Lake**, on the Yukon border, is the largest of these lesser spots, and also marks the junction of the Alaska and Cassiar highways. All the way down the road, though, it's vital to book accommodation during July and August.

Driving the Alaska Highway is no longer the adventure of days past – that's now provided by the Cassiar and Dempster highways. Food, fuel and lodgings are found at between forty- and eighty-kilometre intervals, though cars still need to be in good shape. You should drive with headlights on at all times, and take care when passing or being passed by heavy trucks. It also goes without saying that wilderness – anything up to 800km of it each side – begins at the edge of the highway and unless you're very experienced you shouldn't contemplate any off-road exploration. Any number of guides and pamphlets are available to take you through to Fairbanks, but *The Milepost*, the road's bible is, for all its mind-numbing detail, the only one you need buy.

From mid-May to mid-October daily (except Sun) a **Greyhound bus** leaves Dawson Creek in the morning and plies the road all the way to Whitehorse; it runs on Tuesday, Thursday and Saturday the rest of the year. The twenty-hour trip finishes at around 5am, with only occasional half-hour meal stops, but covers the road's best scenery in daylight.

Dawson Creek to Fort Nelson

You need to adapt to a different notion of distance on a 2500-kilometre drive: on the Alaska Highway points of interest are a long way apart, and pleasure comes in broad changes in scenery, in the sighting of a solitary moose, or in the passing excitement of a lonely bar. Thus it's forty minutes before the benign ridged prairies around Dawson Creek prompt attention by dropping suddenly into the broad, flat-bottomed valley of the Peace River, a canyon whose walls are scalloped with creeks, gulches and deep muddy scars. Just across the river **FORT ST JOHN**, which, until the coming of the highway (when it was the field headquarters of the road's eastern construction gangs), was a trading post for local Sikanni and Beaver peoples, which had remained little changed since its predecessor sank into the mud of the Peace River (there have been a total of six "Fort St Johns" in various incarnations in the area). The shantytown received a boost when the province's largest oilfield was discovered nearby in 1955, and it's now a functional settlement with all the services you need – though at just 75km into the highway it's unlikely you'll be ready to stop. If you are, there's a small museum at 93rd and 100th Street and a handful of **motels**: solid choices are the big *Ramada*, 10103 98th Ave (☎787-0779 or 1-888/346-7711; ④), and the cheaper *Cedar Lodge Motor Inn*, 9824 99th Ave (☎785-8107 or 1-800/661-2210; ②). The **infocentre** is at 9323 100th St (☎785-6037 or 785-3033).

The next stop is the tiny hamlet of **WONOWON** (pop. 84), a military checkpoint in World War II, and at 161km from Dawson typical of the bleak settlements all the way up the road. **PINK MOUNTAIN** (pop. 19), 226km on from Dawson, is much the same, with *Mae's Kitchen* (☎772-3215; ②) the only listed accommodation (other places open and close here regularly). There's also a single **restaurant** favoured by truckers with a reasonable **campground** across the road (☎772-3226; $8–20; May–Oct). Thereafter the road offers immense **views** of utter wilderness in all directions, the trees as dense as ever, but noticeably more stunted than further south and nearing the limit of commercial viability. Look out for the bright "New Forest Planted" signs, a token riposte from the loggers to the ecology lobby, as they are invariably backed by a graveyard of sickly looking trees. If you're **camping**, look out for two provincial sanctuaries over the remaining 236km to Fort Nelson. Around 60km north of Pink Mountain is the Buckinghorse River Provincial Park campground ($9); another 69km further is the Prophet River Provincial Recreation Area, with a campground ($9) overlooking the river: this is good bird-watching country, but it's also good bear country, so be careful (see pp.520–521).

Fort Nelson

One of the highway's key stopoffs, **FORT NELSON** greets you with a large poster proclaiming "Jail is only the beginning – don't drink and drive", a sobering sign that hints

THE ALASKA HIGHWAY

The **Alaska Highway** runs northeast from Mile Zero at Dawson Creek through the Yukon Territory to Mile 1520 in Fairbanks, Alaska. Built as a military road, it's now an all-weather highway travelled by daily bus services and thousands of tourists out to recapture the thrill of the days when it was known as the "junkyard of the American automobile". It's no longer a driver's Calvary, but the scenery and the sense of pushing through wilderness on one of the continent's last frontiers remain as alluring as ever and around 360,000 people a year make the journey.

As recently as 1940 there was no direct land route to the Yukon or Alaska other than trails passable only by experienced trappers. When the Japanese invaded the Aleutian Islands during World War II, however, they both threatened the traditional sea routes to the north and seemed ready for an attack on mainland Alaska – the signal for the building of the joint US-Canadian road to the north. A proposed coastal route from Hazelton in British Columbia was deemed too susceptible to enemy attack (it's since been built as the Cassiar Highway), while an inland route bypassing Whitehorse and following the Rockies would have taken five years to build. This left the so-called **Prairie Route**, which had the advantage of following a line of air bases through Canada into Alaska – a chain known as the **Northwest Staging Route**. In the course of the war, some 8000 planes were ferried from Montana to Edmonton and then to Fairbanks along this route, where they were picked up by Soviet pilots and flown into action on the Siberian front.

Construction of the highway began on **March 9, 1942**, the start of months of misery for the 20,000 mainly US soldiers shanghaied to ram a road through mountains, mud, mosquito-ridden bogs, icy rivers and forest during some of the harshest extremes of weather. Incredibly, crews working on the eastern and western sections met at Contact Creek, British Columbia, in September 1942, and completed the last leg to Fairbanks in October – an engineering triumph that had taken less than a year but cost around $140 million. The first full convoy of trucks to make Fairbanks managed an average 25kph during one of the worst winters in memory.

By 1943 the highway already needed virtual rebuilding, and for seven years workers widened the road, raised bridges, reduced gradients, bypassed swampy ground and started to remove some of the vast bends that are still being ironed out – the reason why it's now only 1488 miles (2394km) to the old Mile 1520 post in Fairbanks. All sorts of ideas have been put forward to explain the numerous curves – that they were to stop Japanese planes using the road as a landing strip, that they simply went where bulldozers could go at the time, or even at one point that they followed the trail of a rutting moose. Probably the chief reason is that the surveying often amounted to no more than a pointed finger aimed at the next horizon. Canada took over control of the road in 1946, but civilian traffic was barred until 1948. Within months of its opening so much traffic had broken down and failed to make the trip that it was closed for a year.

Although the road is now widely celebrated, there are sides to the story that are still glossed over. Many of its toughest sections, for example, were given to black GIs, few of whom have received credit for their part in building the highway – you'll look in vain for black faces amongst the white officers in the archive photos of ribbon-cutting ceremonies. Another often overlooked fact is the road's effect on aboriginal peoples on the route, scores of whom died from epidemics brought in by the workers. Yet another was the building of the controversial "Canadian Oil" or **Canol pipeline** in conjunction with the road, together with huge dumps of poisonous waste and construction junk. Wildlife en route was also devastated by trigger-happy GIs taking recreational pot shots as they worked: the virtual eradication of several species was part of the reason for the creation of the Kluane Game Sanctuary, the forerunner of the Yukon's Kluane National Park (see p.602).

at the sort of extremes to which people hereabouts might go to relieve the tedium of winter's long semi-twilight. Everything in town, except a small **museum** devoted to the highway's construction, speaks of a frontier supplies depot, the last in a long line of trading posts attracted to a site that is fed by four major rivers and stands in the lee of the Rockies. Dour buildings stand in a battered sprawl around a windswept grid, only a single notch up civilization's ladder from the time in the late 1950s when this was still a community without power, phones, running water or doctors. Life's clearly too tough here to be geared to anything but pragmatic survival and exploitation of its huge natural gas deposits – the town has the world's second largest gas-processing plant and the huge storage tanks to prove it. Aboriginal and white trappers live as they have for centuries, hunting beaver, wolf, wolverine, fox, lynx and mink, as well as the ubiquitous moose, which is still an important food source for many aboriginal people.

The town does, however, have an extraordinary claim to fame, namely that it's home to the **world's largest chopstick factory**, located south of the town off the highway behind the weigh scales at Industrial Park Chopstick Road (☎774-4448 for details of tours). This has nothing to do with gargantuan demand for Chinese food in Fort Nelson – at last count there were only three Chinese restaurants in town – but more to do with the region's high-quality aspen, a wood apparently perfectly suited to producing the dream chopstick. The Canadian Chopstick Manufacturing Company produces an incredible 7.5 million pairs of chopsticks a *day*, or 1.95 billion a year.

The town's **motels** are all much the same and you'll be paying the inflated rates – about $70 for doubles worth half that – which characterize the north. On the town's southern approaches the *Bluebell Inn*, 3907 50th Ave S (☎774-6961 or 1-800/663-5267, *www.pris.bc.ca/bluebell*; ④), is better looking than many of the run-of-the-mill places. The **infocentre** is at Mile 300.5 of the Alaska Highway (☎774-6868; rest of the year for information, call 774-2541; mid-May to Aug Mon–Sat 9am–5pm).

Fort Nelson to Liard Hot Springs

This stretch is the Alaska Highway at its best. Landscapes divide markedly around **Fort Nelson**, where the highway arches west from the flatter hills of the Peace River country to meet the **northern Rockies** above the plains and plateau of the Liard River. Within a short time – once the road has picked up the river's headwaters – you're in some of the most grandiose scenery in British Columbia. The area either side of the road is some of the world's wildest – twenty million acres of nothing – and experts say that only parts of Africa surpass the region for the variety of mammals present and the pristine state of its ecosystems. Services and motels become scarcer, but those that exist – though often beaten-up looking places – make atmospheric and often unforgettable stops. The first worthwhile stopoff, a kilometre off the highway on a gravel road, is **Tetsa River Provincial Park**, about 77km west of Fort Nelson, which has a nice and secluded **campground** (May–Oct; $12) and appealing short hikes through the trees and along the river. Next up is **Stone Mountain Provincial Park**, 139km west of Fort Nelson, with a campground (May–Oct; $12) which gives access to a short trail (10min) to two hoodoos (rock columns) claimed by myth to be the heads of two devils; a longer trail, the Flower Springs Lake Trail (6km), leads to a delightful upland mountain lake. Other **accommodation** and services include the *Rocky Mountain Lodge* (☎232-5000; ②), 165km on from Fort Nelson with lovely views of the mountains and an adjacent **campground** ($10).

Toad River, 195km from Fort Nelson, has perhaps the best motel of all on this lonely stretch, the *Toad River Lodge* (☎232-5401; ②), with rooms and cabins (for $10 more) giving superlative views of thickly forested and deeply cleft mountains on all sides. Note that it also has a grocery, gas station and sites for tents and RVs ($12 for tenting). About 3km to its north is the *Poplars Campground & Café*, with log cabins and fully serviced tent and

THE CHILKOOT TRAIL

No single image better conjures the human drama of the 1898 gold rush than the lines of prospectors struggling over the **Chilkoot Trail**, a 53-kilometre path over the Coast Mountains between **Dyea**, north of Skagway in Alaska, and **Bennett Lake** on the British Columbian border south of Whitehorse. Before the rush, Dyea was a small village of Chilkat Tlingit, who made annual trade runs over the trail to barter fish oil, clamshells and dried fish with the Tutchone, Tagish and other interior Dene peoples in exchange for animal hides, skin clothing and copper. The Chilkat jealously guarded access to the **Chilkoot Pass** (1122m), the key to the trail and one of only three glacier-free routes through the Coast Mountains west of Juneau. Sheer numbers and a show of force from a US gunboat, however, opened the trail to stampeders, who used it as a link between the ferries at the Pacific Coast ports and the Yukon River, which they then rode to the goldfields at Dawson City.

For much of 1897 the pass and border were disputed by the US and Canada until the Canadian NWMP (Northwest Mounted Police) established a storm-battered shack at the summit and enforced the fateful "ton of goods" entry requirement. Introduced because of chronic shortages in the gold fields, this obliged every man entering the Yukon to carry a ton of provisions – and, though it probably saved many lives in the long run, the rule laid enormous hardship on the back of the stampeders. Weather conditions and the trail's fifty-degree slopes proved too severe even for horses or mules, so that men had to carry supplies on their backs over as many as fifty journeys to move their "ton of goods". Many died in avalanches or lost everything during a winter when temperatures dropped to −51°C and 25m of snow fell. Even so, the lure of gold was enough to drag some 22,000 prospectors over the pass.

These days most people off the **ferries from Prince Rupert and the Alaska Panhandle** make the fantastic journey across the mountains by car or Gray Line bus on Hwy 2 from **Skagway to Whitehorse**. This route parallels that taken by the restored White Pass & Yukon Route railway (WP&YR; mid-May to mid-Sept 1 daily; Skagway–White Pass by train then connecting bus to Whitehorse; $95; ☎983-2217 or 1-800/343-7373, *www.whitepassrailroad.com*), originally built to supersede the Chilkoot Trail. Increasing numbers, however, are walking the old trail, which has been laid out and preserved by the Canadian Parks Service as a **long-distance hikers' route**. Its great appeal lies not only in the scenery and natural habitats – which embrace coastal rainforest, tundra and subalpine boreal woodland – but also in the numerous artefacts like old huts, rotting boots, mugs and broken bottles still scattered where they were left by the prospectors.

The trail is well marked, regularly patrolled and generally fit to walk between about June and September, though throughout June you can expect snow on the trail. Most people hike the trail in three or four days and if you're moderately fit it shouldn't be a problem, but there are dangers from bears, avalanches, drastic changes of weather and exhaustion – there's one twelve-kilometre stretch, for example, for which you're advised to allow twelve hours. Almost everyone hikes from south to north.

RV sites (☎232-5465; ②, tent sites $12; May to late Sept); it's an equally attractive spot despite its disconcerting claim to be "Home of the Foot-Long Hot Dog".

Muncho Lake, the next big natural feature, sits at the heart of a large provincial park whose ranks of bare mountains are a foretaste of the barren tundra of the far north. There's a small **motel** and **campground** at the lake's southern end, but it's worth hanging on for the popular *Flats Provincial Campground* ($12, free Oct; May–Oct), midway up the lake on its eastern side, or the fine *Northern Rockies Lodge-Highland Glen Lodge and Campground* (☎776-3481 or 1-800/663-5269, *www.northern-rockies-lodge.com*; ③) for a choice of log cabins or camping sites ($17–27). Two kilometres north of the Muncho Lake settlement there is the small *McDonald Provincial Campground* ($12).

Although there are three warming huts on the trail, these aren't designed for sleeping in, and you'll be making use of the nine approved **campgrounds** spaced at intervals along the trail: no rough camping is allowed.

RESERVATIONS AND PERMITS

An advance **information pack** ($5) can be ordered by calling the **reservation system** (☎867/667-3910 or 1-800/661-0486 between 8.30am and 4pm Pacific Standard Time), or by writing to Chilkoot Trail National Historic Site, 205–300 Main St, Whitehorse, Yukon, Y1A 2B5. Throughout the hiking season, the number of hikers crossing the Chilkoot Pass into Canada is limited to 50 per day, of which 42 places can be booked in advance ($11) by calling the reservation system. The remaining 8 places are offered on a first-come, first-served basis after 1pm on the day before you plan to start the trail from the Skagway **Trail Center**, Broadway at 1st Avenue in (late May to early Sept daily 8am–4pm). The busy season is July and the first two weeks of August: outside this time you probably don't need to make a reservation.

Whichever way you secure a place on the trail, all hikers need to go to the Trail Center to buy a **permit** ($40), sign a register (for customs purposes) and consult the weather forecast. You'll need to carry **identification**, which means a birth certificate for North Americans (a driver's licence is not acceptable) and a passport for everyone else. You may be required to deal with Canadian customs at the Chilkoot Pass ranger station but more likely you'll do it after your hike at the Alaska–Canada border post at Fraser or in Whitehorse.

If you have made an advance reservation, you'll already have the Canadian Parks Service's Chilkoot Trail **map** (otherwise $2 from the Trail Center or the Canadian Parks Service office at the SS *Klondike* in Whitehorse), which is about the best available.

TRANSPORT AND SUPPLIES

Dyea Dave (☎983-2731) runs a shuttle bus ($10) from Skagway to Dyea, the start of the trail some nine miles northwest of Skagway. The trail finishes at Bennett, where you can get Tutshi Charters (☎867/821-4905) to take you across Lake Bennett to Carcross (Can$65) to meet the Whitehorse-bound Gray Line bus. Alternatively you can walk the eight miles to the highway at Log Cabin (there's a short-cut off the trail which avoids Bennett) and meet up with Dyea Dave ($25 for a combined drop-off and pick-up); or **return to Skagway** on the WP&YR railroad. In June, July and August there is the Chilkoot Trail Hikers Service (departs 1pm Alaska time; $25 one-way to Fraser, $65 to Skagway) which is either a railcar or one carriage of the Lake Bennett Excursion that's specially designated for smelly hikers. Remember to buy your tickets before you set off on the trail or you'll have a $15 fee added to the ticket price for the convenience of buying your ticket on the train; and note that for customs reasons the train doesn't stop at Log Cabin.

Remember to take wet-weather gear, matches, some method of water treatment, sun screen, sunglasses, a flashlight and **thirty feet of rope** so that you can sling your food, toothpaste and any scented items over the bear poles at each campground. Early in the season when there's plenty of snow about, consider **gaiters**, which can be rented in Skagway.

About 70km beyond the lake is the excellent *Lower Liard River Lodge* (☎776-7341; April–Oct; ②), a wonderfully cosy and friendly spot for food and rooms. (*Liard* comes from the French for "poplar" or "cottonwood tree", a ubiquitous presence in these parts.) It also has RV and tent sites ($8–10) and lies close to one of the most popular spots on the entire Alaska Highway, the very obvious **Liard Hot Springs**, whose **two thermal pools** (Alpha and Beta) are amongst the best and hottest in BC. Road crews loved these during the construction of the highway, or rather the men did: women in the teams were allowed a soak just once a week. They're reached by a short wooden boardwalk across steaming marsh, and are otherwise unspoilt apart from a wooden changing room and the big high-season crowds (aim to be here early in the day for a dip ahead of the rush). As the marsh never freezes, it attracts moose and grizzlies down to drink and graze, and some 250 plant species grow in the mild microhabitat nearby, including fourteen species of orchid, as well as lobelias, ostrich ferns and other rare boreal forest plants. The nearby *Liard River Hotsprings Provincial Park* **campground** is one of the region's most popular, and fills up early in July and August: bookings are possible through the provincial park central reservation line (May–Aug $15; Sept–April $9); see box on p.569.

Watson Lake to Whitehorse

Beyond the hot springs the road follows the Liard River, settling into about 135km of unexceptional scenery before **WATSON LAKE**, just over the Yukon border (though the road trips back and forth across the border seven times before hitting the town). Created by the coming of the highway and air base, it's neither attractive nor terribly big, but shops, motels and garages have sprung up here to service the traffic congregating off the Cassiar and Campbell highways to the north and south. In the past the region was the preserve of the Kaska, a people whose centuries-old way of life was altered in the 1870s by the Cassiar gold rush. Another gold rush, the Klondike, gave the settlement its present name, when Frank Watson, an English prospector gave up on his attempts to reach the northern gold fields and stopped here instead. Even if you're just passing through it's well worth pulling off to look at the **Alaska Highway Interpretive Centre** (May–Sept daily 8am–8pm; ☎536-7469), which as well as providing information on the Yukon also describes the highway's construction through archive photos and audiovisual displays. It's situated on the highway next to the Chevron garage, close to the famous **Sign Post Forest**. This last bit of gimmickry was started by homesick GI Carl K. Lindley in 1942, who erected a sign pointing the way and stating the mileage to his home in Danville, Illinois. Since then the signs have just kept on coming, and at last count numbered around thirty thousand. You might also want to dip briefly into the **Northern Lights Centre** (June–Aug daily 2–10pm; $6–12; ☎536-7827, *www.yukon.net/northernlights*), a planetarium and science centre that explores the myths, folklore and science behind phenomena such as the aurora borealis (see box, p.570).

It's still 441km from Watson Lake to Whitehorse and after the long haul on the Alaska Highway, a lot of people wisely stop overnight here to recuperate. If you're camping there are no problems, for countless small Yukon government-run **campgrounds** are dotted along the length of the highway beyond the village; the closest is a rustic site 4km west of the Sign Forest (May–Oct; $8). If you decide to **stay in town** the cheapest options are the *Gateway Motor Inn* (☎536-7744; ③), open 24 hours a day, and the *Cedar Lodge Motel* (☎536-7406, *www.cedarlodge.yk.net*; ③). If these are full you may have to plump for one of the smarter hotels, all of which have rooms for around $95 – the best is the *Belvedere Hotel* (☎536-7712; ⑤), followed by the *Watson Lake Hotel* (☎536-7781; ⑤). Both have dining rooms if you're after food, though the *Watson Lake Hotel* and *Gateway Motor Inn* have some rooms with kitchenettes if you're cooking for yourself.

West of Watson Lake the road picks up more fine mountain scenery, running for hour after hour past apparently identical combinations of snowcapped peaks and thick forest. About 10km before unlovely **TESLIN**, 263km to the west of Watson, look out for the *Dawson Peaks Northern Resort* (☎390-2310; ③), which not only has cabins and a campground, but also boasts one of the highway's better restaurants; fishing and boat rentals are also available. Teslin itself was founded as a trading post in 1903 and now has one of the region's largest aboriginal populations, many of whom still live by hunting and fishing. The **George Johnston Museum** (mid-May to Sept daily 9am–7pm; $2.50; ☎390-2550) is on the right on the way into the village and has a good collection of local Tlingit artefacts as well as the photos of Johnston, a Tlingit who recorded his culture on film between 1910 and 1940.

Whitehorse

WHITEHORSE is the likeable capital of the Yukon, home to two-thirds of its population (around 24,000 people), the centre of its mining and forestry industries, and a bustling, welcoming stopoff for thousands of summer visitors. Whilst roads bring in today's business, the town owes its existence to the **Yukon River**, a 3000-kilometre artery that rises in BC's Coast Mountains and flows through the heart of the Yukon and Alaska to the Bering Sea. The river's flood plain and strange escarpment above the present town were long a resting point for Dene peoples, but the spot burgeoned into a full-blown city with the arrival of thousands of stampeders in the spring of 1898. Having braved the Chilkoot Pass (see box on p.592) to meet the Yukon's upper reaches, men and supplies then had to pause on the shores of Lineman or Bennett Lake before navi-

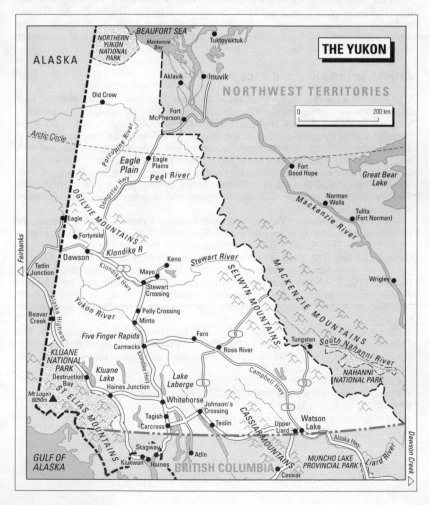

gating the **Mile's Canyon** and White Horse rapids southeast of the present town. After the first few boats through had been reduced to matchwood, the Mounties laid down rules allowing only experienced boatmen to take craft through – writer Jack London, one such boatman, made $3000 in the summer of 1898, when more than seven thousand boats left the lakes. After a period the prospectors constructed an eight-kilometre wooden tramway around the rapids, and in time raised a shantytown settlement at the canyon and tramway's northern head to catch their breath before the river journey to Dawson City.

The completion of the White Pass and Yukon Railway (WP&YR) to Whitehorse (newly named after the rapids) put this tentative settlement on a firmer footing – almost at the same time as the gold rush petered out. In the early years of the twentieth century the town's population dwindled quickly from about 10,000 to about 400; for forty years the place slumbered, barely sustained by copper mining and the paddle-wheelers that plied the river carrying freight and the occasional tourist. The town's second boom arrived with the construction of the Alaska Highway, a kick-start that swelled the town's population from 800 to 40,000 almost overnight, and has stood it in good stead ever since.

Arrival, information and accommodation

Whitehorse's **airport** is on the bluff above the town, 5km west of downtown; taxis are around $9 to the centre, and the Whitehorse Transit Hillcrest bus ($1.25) runs downtown hourly during the day. If you're taking the bus *to* the airport, pick it up at the Qwanlin Mall at the northern end of 3rd Avenue. The Greyhound **bus terminal** is at 3211 3rd Ave (☎667-2223) at the extreme eastern end of downtown, ten minutes' walk from Main Street – you turn left out of the terminal for the town centre, something it's as well to know if you stagger off the six-times-weekly Greyhound from Dawson Creek, which arrives around 5am. Alaskon Express buses, or Gray Line of Yukon (☎668-3225) from Fairbanks, Anchorage, Tok and Skagway, also stop here and at the *Westmark Whitehorse* hotel downtown.

Whitehorse's downtown **Yukon Visitor Reception Centre** is on 2nd Avenue and Hanson Street (mid-May to Sept daily 8am–8pm; ☎667-2915). Note that the "reception centre" up on the Alaska Highway still mentioned in some literature is now the Beringia Centre. The Parks Canada information office alongside the SS *Klondike* (May–Sept daily 9am–6pm; ☎667-4511) is the place to pick up information on the Chilkoot Trail. For information on the Yukon's aboriginal cultures, stop by the office of the **Yukon First Nations Tourism Association**, 1109 1st Ave (Mon–Fri 9am–5pm; ☎667-7698, *www.yfnta.org*) and pick up a copy of the *Yukon's First Nations Guide*.

Almost as useful as these is Mac's Fireweed, 203 Main St (Mon–Sat 9am–9pm, Sun 10am–7pm; ☎668-6104), which has a full range of Yukon books, guides and pamphlets you probably won't find elsewhere. For an outstanding selection of **maps** visit Jim's Toy and Gifts, 4137 4th Ave (667-2606).

Car-rental agencies have desks or courtesy phones at the airport and occasionally a downtown office: Avis (☎667-2847); Budget, 4178 4th Ave (☎667-6200 or 1-800/268-8900), Rent-a-Wreck (☎668-7554) and Norcan, 213 Range Rd (☎668-2137) are companies to try, but remember some have restrictions on taking cars on gravel roads if you're thinking of heading north on the Dempster Highway (see p.612). For **bike rental**, contact Big Bear Adventures (☎633-5642; *www.bear.yk.net*).

The telephone code for the Yukon is ☎867.

Canoes, paddles and life-jackets plus bikes can be rented from the Kanoe People, Strickland Street and 1st Avenue (☎668-4899, *www.kanoe.yk.net*), who can also set you up with everything you need to paddle to Dawson (700km but lots of people do it): they also organize guided day-trips (from $60) and two-week expeditions on the river.

For **exchange**, plus reservations for ferries and **tickets** for local events, contact Thomas Cook, 2101A 2nd Ave (mid-May to early Sept daily 8am–8pm; rest of the year Mon–Fri 8.30am–5.30pm & Sat 10am–5pm; ☎668-2867).

Accommodation

Whitehorse has a surprising amount of **accommodation** but in summer it gets booked up well in advance. If you arrive cold, contact the visitor centre or try the string of six hotels on Main Street between 1st and 5th avenues. For **B&Bs**, try the information centre's B&B list, or contact the recommendations below, but note that places open and close with some regularity. Another option is an **accommodation agency**, Select Reservations, 18 Tagish Rd (☎393-2420 or 1-877/735-3281, *www.yukonalaska/selectrez*), which will help with lodgings of all descriptions across the Yukon, Alaska and northern BC. The *Robert Service* **campground**, about 2km and twenty minutes' walk down South Access Road, is set out on the banks of the Yukon River specifically for tents and backpackers (☎668-3721; $12 plus $1 for showers; mid-May to mid-Sept). It gets very busy in summer; if it's full try the woods above the lake down past the dam beyond the campground or along the bluff above town by the airport.

HOTELS

Airline Inn, 16 Burns Rd (☎668-4400, fax 668-2641). If you arrive late at the airport, or need an early getaway, this is the airstrip's nearest hotel – serviceable enough for its purposes. ③.

Capital Hotel, 103 Main St (☎667-2565, fax 668-4651). This is the place to stay if you want one of the town's more lively, historic and boisterous hotels, complete with fine rooms. ③.

Edgewater Hotel, 101 Main St (☎667-2572, *www.edgewaterhotel.yk.ca*). Good, middle-priced hotel in downtown area. ④.

High Country Inn, 4051 4th Ave, at the far western end, a 10min walk from downtown (☎667-4471, *www.highcountryinn.yk.ca*). An easy-going hotel with a wide variety of excellent room deals and weekly rates. ⑥.

98 Hotel, 110 Wood St (☎667-2641 or 667-2656). Cheap, fairly grim and occasionally with live bands to serenade you through the small hours. ②.

Roadhouse Inn, 2163 2nd Ave (☎667-2594, fax 668-7291). Of a similar standard, but marginally better than the *98 Hotel* and near the bus terminal. ②.

Stratford Motel, 401 Jarvis St (☎667-4243 or 1-800/661-0539, fax 668-7432). Spotlessly clean, newly renovated rooms (some with kitchenettes) and with a friendly staff. Three blocks from downtown. Weekly rates available. ④.

Town & Mountain Hotel, 401 Main St (☎668-7644, *www.yukon.com/tm.htm*) Another good and recently renovated middle-priced place. ④.

Westmark Klondike Inn, 2288 2nd Ave (☎668-4747, or 1-800/544-0970, *www.westmarkhotels.com*) One of two top-of-the-range, comfortable hotels belonging to the northern *Westmark* chain. ⑦.

Westmark Whitehorse Hotel, 201 Wood St (☎668-4700 or 1-800/544-0970, *www.westmarkhotels .com*; ⑦). If you want to see Whitehorse in style, this is the smartest and most expensive hotel in town.

BED AND BREAKFAST

Baker's, 84 11th Ave (☎633-2308). Two rooms (one double, one single) in a quiet area 5km from downtown. Long-established, and patrons are longtime Yukon residents. ③.

Birch Street, 1501 Birch St (☎633-5625, *ditan@netscape.net*). On a bus route to downtown but amidst a quiet setting overlooking the Yukon River Valley close to hiking trails. Full breakfast. Some rooms with private bath. ③.

By the Bluffs, 801 Black St (☎668-4333, *bythebluffs@hotmail.com*). Downtown neighbourhood location and the promise of mountain views, hammock and massage therapist on site. ③.

Casey's, 608 Wood St (☎668-7481, *casey@hypertech.yk.ca*). Downtown location with good breakfasts and evening snacks; kitchen and laundry facilities are available. ③.

Four Seasons, 18 Tagish Rd (☎667-2161, *jeano@yknet.yk.ca*). Centrally located, about 10min walk from downtown and offering full breakfast and snacks. ③.

Hawkins House, 303 Hawkins St (☎668-7638, *www.hawkinshouse.yk.ca*). Old and luxurious Victorian home in downtown; laundry and private bathrooms available. No smoking. ⑥.

International House, 17 14th Ave (☎633-5490, fax 668-4751). A quiet residential location with friendly and relaxed atmosphere created by hosts who have been in the Yukon for nearly forty years. Two blocks off the Alaska Hwy, 10min from downtown, though yours hosts will pick you up from the airport or bus depot. ②.

Downtown

Although greater Whitehorse spills along the Alaska Highway for several kilometres, the old **downtown** core is a forty-block grid centred on Main Street and mostly sandwiched between 2nd and 4th avenues. Though now graced only with a handful of pioneer buildings, the place still retains the dour integrity and appealing energy of a frontier town, and at night the baying of timber wolves and coyotes is a reminder of the wilderness immediately beyond the city limits. Nonetheless, the tourist influx provides a fair amount of action in the bars and cafés, and the streets are more appealing and lively than in many northern towns.

The main thing to see is the **SS Klondike** (May–Sept daily tours every half-hour 9am–6pm; $4; ☎667-4511), one of only two surviving paddle steamers in the Yukon, now rather sadly beached at the western end of 2nd Avenue at 300 Main St, though it has been beautifully restored to the glory of its 1930s heyday. More than 250 sternwheelers once plied the river, taking 36 hours to make the 700-kilometre journey to Dawson City, and five days to make the return trip against the current. The SS *Klondike* was built in 1929, sank in 1936, and was rebuilt in 1937 using the original remnants. The largest of all the river's steamers, it then battled against the river until 1955, ferrying 300 tonnes of cargo a trip and making some fifteen round trips a season. Bridges built on the improved road to Dawson increasingly hampered river traffic, though the SS *Klondike*'s end came when an inexperienced pilot ran her aground and condemned her to museum status. Beached at Whitehorse in 1960, the boat is visitable by a 25-minute guided tour only. Before or after a tour, take in the twenty-minute documentary film on the riverboat story in the theatre alongside.

Elsewhere in town you could pop into the **MacBride Museum**, housed in a sod-roofed log cabin at 1st Avenue and Wood Street (May to late Sept daily 10am–6pm; call for winter hours; $4; ☎667-2709), for the usual zoo of stuffed animals, an old WP&YR engine, pioneer and gold-rush memorabilia, as well as hundreds of marvellous **archive photos** and a display on the Asiatic peoples who crossed the Bering Straits to inhabit the Americas. Another in-town sight is the **Old Log Church Museum**, 3rd Avenue and Elliot Street (late May/early June to late Aug/early Sept Mon–Sat 10am–6pm, Sun noon–4pm; $2.50; ☎668-2555, *www.macbridemuseum.com*), a modest museum devoted to the pre-contact life of the region's **aboriginal peoples**, whaling, missionaries, children's toys and music, the gold rush and early exploration. You may find it easy to resist the widely touted Frantic Follies **stage shows** at the Westmark Whitehorse Hotel however – expensive (May–Sept; $20) vaudeville acts of the banjo-plucking and frilly-knickered-dancing variety that have been playing in town for close to thirty years, but if this sort of thing appeals, call ☎668-2042 for details of "music, mirth and magic, gay Nineties songs, cancan dances and humorous renditions".

The rest of town

Your money's better spent taking one of the **river tours** that shoot the **Miles Canyon** 9km south of the town, otherwise reached off the Alaska Highway, or from the South Access Road, which hugs the river edge beyond the SS *Klondike*. Whitehorse Transit buses ($1.25) run along the South Access Road from town every hour daily except Sunday. The building of a hydroelectric dam has tamed the rapids' violence and replaced them with **Schwatka Lake**, but the two-hour narrated trip on the MV *Schwatka* (June–Sept daily 2pm & 7pm; $20; ☎668-4716) gives a better view of the river's potential ferocity and the canyon's sheer walls than the viewpoints off the road. Board at the dock above the dam about 3km down Canyon Road. A Taste of '98 Yukon River Tours (☎633-4767) runs similar three-hour sightseeing tours, as well as extended four- to 21-day guided or fully equipped tours to Dawson City and elsewhere. Other **boat trips** include a gentle two-hour raft trip with Miles Canyon Scenic Raft Float (☎633-4386) or a variety of trips with Canadian Yukon Riverboat (☎633-4414): daily trips in summer with breakfast cost $65 (departs 9am), with lunch $70 (1pm), and with dinner $75 (5pm); the basic trip without meals is $55.

If you fancy a **walk**, stroll from the main canyon car park some of the 11km to Canyon City, the all-but-vanished site of the initial stage of the stampeders' tramway at the southern end of the old rapids. You could also walk all the way round Schwatka Lake from Whitehorse, beginning from the bridge by the SS *Klondike*. Pick up details of this and other self-guiding trail booklets from the visitor reception centre (see p.596). If you don't fancy embarking on walks on your own, join the downtown walk offered by the Whitehorse Heritage Buildings Walking Tours, which departs four times daily in high summer at 9am, 11am, 1pm and 3pm from Donnenworth House, 3126 3rd Ave (☎667-4704; $2). Or try the variety of free summer strolls organized by the Yukon Conservation Society, 302 Hawkins St (July & Aug daily; ☎668-5678), two- to six-hour walks that delve into local and natural history, and the Yukon's geology, flora and fauna.

There is another trio of attractions just outside the downtown area, two of the most tempting up on the bluff above the town on the Alaska Highway close to the airport. One is the excellent **Yukon Transportation Museum** (mid-May to mid-Sept daily 10am–6pm; $4; ☎668-4792), one of the region's best museums. Devoted to the area's transportation history, its displays, murals, superb historical videos, memorabilia and vehicles embrace everything from dog-sledding, early aviation and the construction of the Alaska Highway to the Canol pipeline, the gold rush and the White Pass and Yukon Railway. Among the things on show are old army jeeps, bicycles, bulldozers, a stagecoach and – suspended from the ceiling – the *Queen of the Yukon*, the territory's first commercial plane. Right next door is the dynamic **Yukon Beringia Interpretive Centre** (mid-May to mid-Sept daily 8.30am–7pm; $6; ☎667-5340, *www.beringia.com*), Beringia being the vast subcontinent that existed some 24,000 years ago when the Yukon and Alaska were joined by a land bridge across the Bering Sea to Arctic Russia. The centre's interactive exhibits, film shows and other displays explore the aboriginal history of the time, the people who crossed this land bridge having ultimately colonized the most distant reaches of present-day North and South America. It also looks at the flora, fauna and geology of the time with the help of paleontological and archeological exhibits, among which the skeletal remains of a 12,000-year-old mammoth figure large.

On a totally different tack, if you fancy total relaxation make for the top-notch **Takhini Hot Springs** (June to early Sept 10am–10pm; rest of the year usually Fri–Sun only – call for precise hours; $4; ☎633-2706), located 31km from Whitehorse off the Klondike Highway to Dawson. The water in the large pool is a piping-hot 36°C, there's no sulphurous aftersmell, and the pool is emptied daily. You can camp here ($7) and if you resent paying for the privilege of a hot soak the locals have built a public pool at the outflow point in the stream below.

Eating

Of several friendly laid-back **eating** places, the best overall is the *Talisman Café*, 2112 2nd Ave (Mon–Sat 6am–11pm), which serves a range of full meals, and is also a spot to while away time over a cup of coffee. The *Chocolate Claim* at 305 Strickland (☎667-2202) is a good, welcoming café for coffee, cakes and great chocolate. The *No Pop Sandwich Shop*, 312 Steele St (☎668-3227), is altogether less cosy, but it's popular all the same and the food's fine. Along the avenue, at 411 Alexander St and 4th Avenue, there's the excellent and rather hippie *Alpine Bakery* (☎668-6871; open daily), which is often crammed with campers and whose counter greets you with the Shakespearean sentiment "one feast, one house, one mutual happiness". The centrally located *Sam n' Andy's Tex Mex Bar and Grill*, 506 Main St (☎668-6994) – has good food and an outdoor patio, while the popular and lively pub-eatery, the *Yukon Mining Company* at the *High Country Inn* hotel, 4051 4th Ave (☎667-4471), has locally brewed Chilkoot Brewing Company beers and barbecue food on the outdoor deck in summer. If you're feeling flush, two of the town's best restaurants are *Pandas*, 212 Main St (☎667-2632), with Bavarian specialities, or *Antonio's Vineyard*, 202 Strickland St (☎668-6266), which has Greek and Italian dishes (including pizzas) plus Arctic char and other fish and game dishes.

Onward from Whitehorse

Whitehorse provides the main **transport** links not only to most other points in the territory, but also to Alaska and the Northwest Territories. In summer there are regular Canada 3000 (☎604/647-3117 or 1-877/FLYCAN3) **flights** between Vancouver and Whitehorse plus Canadian (☎604/279-6611) **flights** to and from Edmonton and Vancouver: the airline has an office at 4th Avenue and Elliot Street (☎668-3535).

In this part of the world, however, it's also worth knowing the various smaller airline options. Air North (☎668-2228, *www.airnorth.yk.net*) operates sometimes alarmingly old-fashioned looking but totally reliable scheduled planes (usually four weekly) between Whitehorse, Dawson City, Old Crow, Mayo, Juneau and Fairbanks. Alkan Air (☎668-2107, *www.yukonweb.com/tourism/alkanair*) offers flights to and from Dawson City, Faro, Ross River, Old Crow, Watson Lake and a handful of BC destinations – most enable you to make same-day connections to flights from Whitehorse to Vancouver and Edmonton; it also flies to Norman Wells and Inuvik in the NWT. Era Aviation (☎907/266-8393, *www.eraaviation.com*) has a scheduled service between Anchorage and Whitehorse, plus services to Cordova, Kenai, Homer, Kodiak, Iliamna and Valdez. There are also any number of small charter companies who fly into the backcountry (notably Kluane National Park) for sightseeing, wildlife-watching, fishing and photography trips. Contact the visitor centre for details.

Whitehorse is the end of the line for Greyhound **buses** in Canada (☎667-2223). For **Alaska and Yukon stops west of Whitehorse**, the expensive Gray Lines' **Alaskon Express** (☎668-3225;) runs from Skagway daily to Whitehorse's bus terminal and *Westmark Whitehorse Hotel* (late May to mid-Sept daily; $45) and then on to Anchorage and Fairbanks (US$170) three times a week (currently Sun, Tues & Thurs, but days of departure vary from year to year so check current times). Note that the bus stops overnight at Beaver Creek at the Yukon–Alaska border (see p.603) en route for Alaska, so you either have to camp or to find the price of accommodation (inform Gray Lines if you wish to stay at the *Westmark* in Beaver Creek as they may be able to obtain a discounted rate). Gray Lines' Whitehorse office is at the *Westmark Whitehorse Hotel*, 2nd Avenue and Wood Street (☎668-3225 or 1-800/544-2206 winter only). Currently, a cheaper service based in the US, **Alaska Direct** (☎668-4833 or 1-800/780-6652), operates from Whitehorse to Skagway and vice versa (departs noon; Mon, Tues, Thurs & Sat; US$50; pick-ups arranged from hotels, Main St or bus depot). It runs three times weekly (Sun, Wed, Fri; departs 6am) to Fairbanks (US$140), Anchorage (US$165) and most points north, including Tok, Haines Junction, Burwash Landing and Beaver Creek. Unlike Alaskon, it does not overnight at Beaver Creek en route for Alaska, so you sleep (or otherwise) on the bus.

Dawson City Courier (☎993-6688) operate out of the main bus terminal and run to **Dawson City** at 2am, arriving at Dawson around 9.30pm (daily in July & Aug, times and days vary outside these months, so call for details; $72). It's well worth booking ahead to be sure of seat. If you want to take the **White Pass & Yukon Railway** to Skagway, you can book a bus-train ticket through the railway (☎907/983-2217 or 1-800/343-7373, fax 907/983-2734): buses leave Whitehorse at 1.30pm to connect with the train at Fraser, the line's northern terminus ($95 inclusive one-way; train only $64). If you book in Whitehorse, tickets can be collected at the Gray Lines' desk in the *Westmark Whitehorse Hotel*. If you wish to make a round trip from Whitehorse using the bus-train arrangement you'll need to overnight in Skagway. For more on the railway see also "The Chilkoot Trail" box, p.592.

For **car rental**, try Budget Car and Truck, 4178 4th Ave (☎667-6200), or Norcan, 213 Range Rd (☎668-2137 or 1-800/661-0445, fax 633-7596), which unlike its competitors might rent you a car or truck suitable for gravel roads like the Dempster and Cassiar highways.

Kluane Country

Kluane Country is the pocket of southwest Yukon on and around a scenically stunning 491-kilometre stretch of the Alaska Highway from Whitehorse to **Beaver Creek** at the border with Alaska. *Kluane* comes from the Southern Tutchone aboriginal word meaning a "place of many fish" after the area's teeming waters, and of **Kluane Lake** in particular, the Yukon's highest and largest stretch of water. These days, though, the name's associated more with the all-but-impenetrable wilderness of Canada's largest mountain park, the **Kluane National Park** – a region that contains the country's highest mountains, the most extensive non-polar icefields in the world, and the greatest diversity of plant and animal species in the far north. The park's main centre is **Haines Junction** at the intersection of the Alaska Highway and the Haines Road. Although motels and campgrounds regularly dot the Alaska Highway, the only other settlements of any size are **Destruction Bay** and **Burwash Landing** on Kluane Lake. Gray Line's **Alaskon Express** and **Alaska Direct** buses (see opposite) ply the length of the Alaska Highway, which is also very popular with hitchhikers.

Haines Junction

A blunt and modern place 160km from Whitehorse, with a fine mountain-circled setting, **HAINES JUNCTION** (pop. 796) mushroomed into life in 1942 during the building of the Alaska Highway as a base for the US Army Corps of Engineers during construction of the Haines Road – a highway that connects with Skagway's sister port at Haines, 174km to the southeast. Today it's the biggest service centre between Whitehorse and Tok in Alaska, boasting plenty of shops, a handful of accommodation possibilities (contact the visitor centre for B&B details) and lots of **tour and rental companies** for river-rafting, canoeing, fishing, cycling, horse riding and glacier flights in the Kluane National Park. It's the national park's eastern headquarters – the park covers a vast tract west of the Alaska Highway well to the north and south of the village. The combined Parks Canada and Yukon government **Visitor Reception Centre** is on Logan Street just off the north side of the Alaska Highway (Yukon Tourism May–Sept daily 8am–8pm; Parks Canada May–Sept daily 9am–7pm, Oct–April Mon–Fri 10am–noon & 1–4pm; ☎634-2345 or 634-7207). The village also has its own information line and Web site (☎634-2519, *www.kluane.com*).

WALKING IN KLUANE NATIONAL PARK

Kluane's **trail system** is still in its infancy, though experienced walkers will enjoy wilderness routes totalling about 250km, most of which follow old mining roads or creek beds and require overnight rough camping. A few more manageable walks start from seven distinct trailheads, each signed from the highways and mapped on pamphlets available from Haines' Reception Centre, where enthusiastic staff also organize popular guided day-walks during the summer.

Three trails start from points along a twenty-kilometre stretch of Haines Road immediately south of Haines Junction. The path nearest to the town, and the most popular walk, is the nineteen-kilometre round trip **Auriol Trail**; nearby, the **Rock Glacier Trail** is a twenty-minute jaunt to St Elias Lake; the third and longest trek is the **Mush Lake Road** route (21.6km one-way). North of Haines Junction, most people walk all or part of two paths that strike out from the Sheep Mountain information kiosk on Kluane Lake – either the **Sheep Mountain Ridge** (11.5km), with good chances of seeing the area's Dall sheep, or the longer **Slim's River West Trail** (28.4km one-way), which offers a relatively easy way to see the edges of the park's icefield interior.

The cheapest of the **motels** is the *Gateway* (open 24hr; ④; ☎634-2371) on the junction of Haines Road and the Alaska Highway; it has rooms with kitchenettes, laundry and café and a few serviced **campsites** to the rear. Or try the *Kluane Park Inn* (☎634-2261; ③; open 24hr) or the non-smoking *Raven Hotel & Gourmet Dining* (☎634-2500, fax 634-2517, *kluanerv@yknet.yk.ca*; ④), a central place with a decent restaurant that includes breakfast in its room rate. Foodies will love their elegant evening meals, but you're looking at around $80 a head. The *Cozy Corner Motel & Restaurant* (☎634-2511; ③) lies just down the Alaska Highway on the corner of Bates Road. The simple *Pine Lake* **campground** ($8; May–Oct) is 7km east of the village signed off the Alaska Highway, or there's the bigger and more central *Kluane RV Kampground* in town (☎634-2709; $12; May–Sept) which has wooded RV and tent sites, laundry and a grocery store. The best general place **to eat** is the popular *Village Bakery & Deli* (7.30am–9pm daily; ☎634-2867) on Logan Street across from the Visitor Reception Centre.

Kluane National Park

Created in 1972 using land from the earlier Kluane Game Sanctuary, the **KLUANE NATIONAL PARK** contains some of the Yukon's greatest but most inaccessible scenery, and for the most part you must be resigned to seeing and walking its easterly margins from points along the Alaska Highway (no road runs into the park). Together with the neighbouring Wrangell-St Elias National Park in Alaska the park protects the **St Elias Mountains**, though from the highway the peaks you see rearing up to the south are part of the subsidiary Kluane Range. Beyond them, and largely invisible from the road, are St Elias's monumental **Icefield Ranges**, which contain Mount St Elias (5488m), **Mount Logan** (5950m) – Canada's highest point – and Mount McKinley (6193m) in Alaska, the highest point in North America. These form the world's second highest coastal range (after the Andes). Below them, and covering half the park, is a huge base of mile-deep glaciers and icefields, the world's largest non-polar icefield and just one permanent resident, the legendary ice worm. Unless you're prepared for full-scale expeditions, this interior is off limits, though from as little as $100 you can take plane and helicopter **tours** over the area with companies such as Trans North Helicopters, based on the Alaska Highway (Mile 1056/Km 1698) between Silver City and the Sheep Mountain Reception Centre (☎668-2177, *www.tntaheli.com/tours.htm*); information on these and other guided tours are available from the Whitehorse Visitor and Haines Junction Reception centres.

On the drier, warmer ranges at the edge of the icefields a green belt of meadow, marsh, forest and fen provides sanctuary for a huge variety of **wildlife** such as grizzlies, moose, mountain goats and a 4000-strong herd of white **Dall sheep**, the last being the animals the park originally set out to protect. These margins also support the widest spectrum of **birds** in the far north, some 150 species in all, including easily seen raptors such as peregrine falcons, bald eagles and golden eagles, together with smaller birds like arctic terns, mountain bluebirds, tattlers and hawk owls.

Limited **trails** (see box, opposite) offer the chance to see some of these creatures, but the only **campground** within the park is at the *Kathleen Lake*, on the Haines Road 16km southeast of Haines Junction ($8) – though there is hotel and camping accommodation along the Alaska Highway.

Kluane Lake

The Kluane region might keep its greatest mountains out of sight, but it makes amends by laying on the stunning **Kluane Lake** along some 60km of the Alaska Highway. About 75km northwest of Haines Junction, and hot on the heels of some magnificent views of the St Elias Mountains, the huge lake (some 400 square kilometres in area) is framed on all sides by snow-covered peaks whose sinister glaciers feed its ice-blue waters. It's not part of the national park, but there's still a second park kiosk at its southern tip, the **Sheep Mountain Information Kiosk** (mid-May to early Sept daily 9am–5pm; no phone). About 5km before the kiosk is the *Kluane Bed & Breakfast* (no phone; ③), with four cabins on the lakeshore. A kilometre beyond it lies the *Bayshore Motel and Restaurant* (☎841-4551; ③), open 24 hours a day from May to October; as well as rooms it offers sites for tents and RVs.

If you want to boat or fish there are rental facilities at the two main settlements along the shores, Destruction Bay and Burwash Landing, each of which also has a small selection of **accommodation** to supplement the odd lodges and campgrounds along the Alaska Highway. In the smaller **DESTRUCTION BAY** (pop. 44), named when a previous road construction camp was destroyed by a storm in 1942, bed down at the *Talbot Arm Motel* with restaurant, café, store and Chevron garage (☎841-4461; ④). The best overall **campground** locally is the lovely Yukon government-run *Congdon Creek* ($8) site off the Alaska Highway, 12km south of Destruction Bay which also offers the start of hiking trails.

At **BURWASH LANDING**, 15km beyond, there's a tiny 1944 Oblate mission church and museum, Our Lady of the Holy Rosary, and the *Burwash Landing Resort* (☎841-4441; ③), with restaurant, store, glacier flights, fishing trips, gold-panning and a big unserviced campground (May–Oct; free). Five kilometres further south the *Cottonwood Park Campground*, a private outfit, offers rather more facilities (☎634-2739; $12; mid-May to mid-Oct). Moving on from Burwash, there are just two major indoor accommodation possibilities before Beaver Creek: 85km east of Burwash is the *Pine Valley Bakery & Lodge* (☎862-7407; ③) and, 36km beyond that, the white *River Motor Inn* (☎862-7408; ③), with café and gas. Ten kilometres west of the *Pine Valley Bakery & Lodge* are the Yukon government campgrounds at Lake Creek; additional grounds are situated eleven kilometres further at Pickhandle Lake (both $8).

Beaver Creek

BEAVER CREEK, Canada's westernmost settlement (pop. 145), is the last stop before Alaska. Following concerted lobbying from its inhabitants, however, it no longer houses the customs post – this has been moved a couple of kilometres up the road in response to complaints from the locals about the flashing lights and sirens that used to erupt whenever a tourist forgot to stop. Though the border is open 24 hours a day, you may have to stay here, particularly if you're catching the Alaskon **bus** service from Skagway and Whitehorse, which stops overnight at Beaver Creek on trans-Alaskan routes. The bus company can book you into the large and expensive *Westmark Inn* (☎862-7501 or 1-800/544-0970, *www.westmarkhotels.com*; ⑥; May–Sept): if that's too steep you've got the choice of arranging things for yourself at the eccentric twenty-room *Ida's Motel and Restaurant* (☎862-3227; ④; summer 6am–2am, winter 8am–10pm), a distinctive building across the highway or, failing that, at the *1202 Motor Inn* (☎862-7600; ④).

The *Westmark* has a large serviced **campground** ($20), though they're happier to see RVs than backpackers (try free camping in the woods). There's a good but small Yukon government-run site located 10km south at the *Snag Junction* ($8; May–Oct). Also be warned that if US Customs take against you or your rucksack, they can insist on seeing at least $400 or so in cash, and won't be swayed by any number of credit cards. For full details on border crossing, and what to expect on the other side, visit the **Yukon Visitor Information Centre** (mid-May to early Sept daily 8am–8pm; ☎862-7321).

Dawson City

Few episodes in Canadian history have captured the imagination like the **Klondike gold rush**, and few places have remained as evocative of their past as **DAWSON CITY**, the stampede's tumultuous capital. For a few months in 1898 this former patch of moose pasture became one of the wealthiest and most famous places on earth, as something like 100,000 people struggled across huge tracts of wilderness to seek their fortunes in the richest gold field of all time.

Most people approach the town on the Klondike Highway from Whitehorse, a wonderful road running through almost utter wilderness, and knowing the background to the place it's hard not to near the road's end without high expectations. Little at first, however, distinguishes its surroundings. Some 500km from Whitehorse the road wanders through low but steeply sided hills covered in spruce, aspen and dwarf firs, and then picks up a small ice-clear river – the **Klondike**. Gradually the first small spoil heaps appear on the hills to the south, and then suddenly the entire valley bottom turns into a devastated landscape of vast boulders and abandoned workings. The desolate tailings continue for several kilometres until the Klondike flows into the much broader **Yukon** and the town, previously hidden by hills, comes suddenly into view.

An ever-increasing number of tourists and backpackers come up here, many drawn by the boardwalks, rutted dirt streets and dozens of false-fronted wooden houses, others to canoe the Yukon or travel down the Dempster or Top of the World highways into Alaska and the Northwest Territories. After decades of decline Parks Canada is restoring the town, now deservedly a National Historic Site, a process that is bringing about increased commercialism, increased population (2000 and rising), new hotels and a sense that some of the town's character may be about to be lost. That said, in a spot where permafrost buckles buildings, it snows in August, and temperatures touch –60°C during winters of almost perpetual gloom, there's little real chance of Dawson losing the gritty, weather-battered feel of a true frontier town. More to the point, small-time prospecting still goes on, and there are one or two rough-and-ready bars whose hardened locals take a dim view of sharing their beers, let alone their gold, with coachloads of tourists.

You could easily spend a couple of days here: one exploring the town, the other touring the old Klondike creeks to the east. If at all possible prime yourself beforehand with the background to one of the most colourful chapters in Canada's history: Pierre Berton's widely available bestseller, *Klondike – The Last Great Gold Rush 1896–1899*, is a superbly written introduction both to the period and to the place.

The Town

You should start any wander on **Front Street**, the leading edge of a street grid that runs parallel to the Yukon River and at the junction with King Street is home to the impressive Tourism Yukon **Visitor Reception Centre** (mid-May to mid-Sept daily 8am–8pm; ☎993-5566, *www.dawsoncity.com*). Loaded with a huge amount of material, the place also has a Parks Canada desk and shows good introductory archive and contemporary films throughout the day, as well as letting you leave your bag or pack ($1) while you explore. It also organizes walking tours (June to mid-Sept several daily; $5) of the town's **heritage buildings** – though these are easily seen on your own, as are the cabins that belonged to two chroniclers of the gold rush, poet **Robert Service** and the better-known **Jack London**. The local **museum** is also good for an hour, and you might want to dabble in the **casino**, though when all's said and done it's the atmospheric streets of Dawson that are most compelling.

The heritage buildings

Fuelled by limitless avarice, Dawson between 1898 and 1900 exploded into a full-blown metropolis of 30,000 people – the largest city in the Canadian West and the equal of places like Seattle and San Francisco in its opportunities for vice, decadence and good living. There were opera houses, theatres, cinemas (at a time when motion-picture houses were just three years old), steam heating, three hospitals, restaurants with French chefs, and bars, brothels and dance halls which generated phenomenal business – one Charlie Kimball took $300,000 in a month from his club, and spent the lot within days. Show girls charged miners $5 – payable in gold – for a minute's dance; slow dances were charged at a higher rate. Cleaners panning the bars' sawdust floors after hours were clearing $50 in gold dust a night. Rules of supply and demand also made Dawson an expensive town, with a single two-metre frontage fetching as much in rent in a month as a four-bedroom apartment in New York cost for two years.

Only a few of the many intact **heritage buildings** around the town date from the earliest days of the rush, dozens having been lost to fire and to permafrost, whose effects are seen in some of the most appealing of the older buildings: higgledy-piggledy collapsing ruins of rotting wood, weeds and rusting corrugated iron. Most of these, thankfully, have been deliberately preserved in their tumbledown state. Elsewhere, almost overzealous restoration projects are in full flow, partly financed by profits from the town casino. Permafrost precluded the construction of brick buildings with deep foundations, so restoration has had to work doubly hard to save what are generally all-wood buildings, most notably the **Palace Grand Theatre** on the corner of 3rd Avenue and King Street (1899). The theatre was originally built from the hulks of two beached paddle steamers, and but for the intervention of the Klondike Visitors Association would have been pulled down for scrap timber in 1960. Tours run daily in summer ($5) and every night in summer except Tuesday. There's a performance of Gaslight Follies (mid-May to mid-Sept daily 8pm; $16 on the main floor, $18 on the balcony; ☎993-5575), a predictable medley of cancan, frilly knickers and gold-rush cabaret, though if you're tempted this is among the best of several such shows around the region.

Nearby on the corner of King Street and 3rd Avenue there's the working **1901 Post Office** (daily June–Aug noon–6pm; ☎993-7200); opposite is **Madame Tremblay's Store**; **Harrington's Store** on 3rd Avenue and Princess Street has a "Dawson as They Saw It" exhibition of photos arranged by Parks Canada (June–Aug daily 9am–5pm; free); near the same junction stands **Billy Bigg's Blacksmith Shop**; elsewhere are the cream-and-brown clapboard **Anglican Church**, built in 1902 with money collected from the miners. At 4th Avenue and Queen Street is **Diamond Tooth Gertie's Gambling House**, founded by one of the town's more notorious characters, and still operating as the first legal **casino** in Canada (opened after restoration in 1971) – it's

THE KLONDIKE GOLD RUSH

Gold rushes in North America during the nineteenth century were nothing new, but none generated quite the delirium of the **Klondike gold rush** in 1898. Over a million people are estimated to have left home for the Yukon gold fields, the largest single one-year mass movement of people in the century. Of these, about 100,000 made it to the Yukon, about 20,000 panned the creeks, 4000 found something and a couple of dozen made – and invariably lost – huge fortunes.

The discovery of gold in 1896 on the Klondike, a tributary of the Yukon River, was the culmination of twenty years of prospecting in the Yukon and Alaska. A Hudson's Bay fur trader first noticed gold in 1842, and the first substantial report was made by an English missionary in 1863, but as the exploitation of gold was deemed bad for trade in both furs and religion neither report was followed up. The first mining on any scale took place in 1883 and gradually small camps sprang up along almost 3200km of river at places like Forty Mile, Sixty Mile and Circle City. All were established before the Klondike strike, but were home to only a few hundred men, hardened types reared on the earlier Californian and British Columbian gold rushes.

The discovery of the gold that started the stampede is inevitably shrouded in myth and countermyth. The first man to prospect near the Klondike River was Robert Henderson, a dour Nova Scotian and the very embodiment of the lone pioneer. In early 1896 he found 8¢ worth of gold in a pan scooped from a creek in the hills above present-day Dawson City. This was considered an excellent return at the time, and a sign to Henderson that the creek would make worthwhile yields. He panned out about $750 with four companions and then returned downriver to pick up supplies.

Henderson then set about finding a route up the Klondike to meet the creek he'd prospected, and at the mouth of the Klondike met George Washington Carmack and a couple of his aboriginal friends, known as Skookum Jim and Tagish Charley. Henderson told Carmack of his hopes for the area, and then – with a glance at the aboriginal pair – uttered the phrase that probably cost him a fortune, "There's a chance for you George, but I don't want any damn Siwashes [aboriginal people] staking on that creek." Henderson wandered off into the hills, leaving Carmack, rankled by the remark, to prospect a different set of creeks – the right ones, as it turned out. On the eve of August 16, Skookum Jim found $4 of gold in a pan on Bonanza Creek, a virtually unprecedented amount at the time. Next day Carmack staked the first claim, and rushed off to register the find leaving Henderson prospecting almost barren ground on the other side of the hills.

By the end of August all of Bonanza had been staked by a hundred or so old-timers from camps up and down the Yukon. Almost all the real fortunes had been secured by the winter of 1896, when the snows and frozen river effectively sealed the region from the outside world. The second phase occurred after the thaw when a thousand or so miners from the West Coast arrived drawn by vague rumours of a big find, emanating from

also the world's northernmost casino (mid-May to mid-Sept daily 7pm–2am; $6); you need to be over 19 to gamble and all proceeds from here and several other town sights go to the restoration of Dawson. Also check out the **Firefighters Museum** in City Hall (under restoration at time of writing) where a guide takes you on a tour of old fire tenders, water pumps and other old firefighting equipment. In a town built almost entirely of wood these were once vital to Dawson's survival: the town all but burnt to the ground twice in the space of a year in 1898–99. So far you can't visit one of the town's more obvious old wooden constructions, the **SS Keno** riverboat, moored on the river just down from the visitor centre – it's been under restoration for several years. It was built in 1922 and ran up and down the Stewart River carrying ore from the mines around Mayo. At the Yukon River the ore was unloaded for collection by larger boats and the journey to Whitehorse and the railway. Not all boats were as lucky as the *Keno*, and a good short

the north. The headlong rush that was to make the Klondike unique, however, followed the docking in July 1897 of the *Excelsior* in San Francisco and the *Portland* in Seattle. Few sights could have been so stirring a proof of the riches up for grabs as the battered Yukon miners who came down the gangplanks dragging bags, boxes and sacks literally bursting with gold. The press were waiting for the *Portland*, which docked with two tons of gold on board, all taken by hand from the Klondike creeks by just a few miners. The rush was now on in earnest.

Whipped up by the media and the outfitters of Seattle and San Francisco, thousands embarked on trips that were to claim hundreds of lives. The most common route – the "poor man's route" – was to take a boat from a West Coast port to Skagway, climb the dreaded **Chilkoot Pass** to pick up the Yukon River at Whitehorse and then boat the last 500 miles to Dawson City. The easiest and most expensive route lay by boat upstream from the mouth of the Yukon in western Alaska. The most dangerous and most bogus were the "All Canadian Route" from Edmonton and the overland trails through the northern wilderness.

The largest single influx came with the melting of the ice on the Yukon in May 1898 – 21 months after the first claim – when a vast makeshift armada drifted down the river. When they docked at Dawson City, the boats nestled six deep along a two-mile stretch of the waterfront. For most it was to have been a fruitless journey – every inch of the creeks having long been staked – yet in most accounts of the stampede it is clear that this was a rite of passage as much as a quest for wealth. Pierre Berton observed that "there were large numbers who spent only a few days in Dawson and did not even bother to visit the hypnotic creeks that had tugged at them all winter long. They turned their faces home again, their adventure over . . . It was as if they had, without quite knowing it, completed the job they had set out to do and had come to understand that it was not the gold they were seeking after all."

As for the gold, it's the smaller details that hint at the scale of the Klondike gold rush: the miner's wife, for example, who could wander the creek by her cabin picking nuggets from the stream bed as she waited for her husband to come home; or the destitutes during the Great Depression who could pan $40 a day from the dirt under Dawson's boardwalks; or the $1000 panned during rebuilding of the Orpheum Theatre in the 1940s, all taken in a morning from under the floorboards where it had drifted from miners' pockets half a century before; or the $200 worth of dust panned nightly from the beer mats of a Dawson saloon during 1897.

By about 1899 the rush was over, not because the gold had run out, but because the most easily accessible gold had been taken from the creeks. It had been the making of Alaska; Tacoma, Portland, Victoria and San Francisco all felt its impact; Edmonton sprang from almost nothing; and Vancouver's population doubled in a year. It was also the first of a string of mineral discoveries in the Yukon and the far north, a region whose vast and untapped natural resources are increasingly the subject of attention from multinationals as rapacious and determined as their grizzled predecessors.

hike just out of town will take you to a **ships' graveyard**. The improvements to transport links, chiefly the completion of the Klondike Highway, made many riverboats redundant. Some were beached downstream, where their overgrown carcasses can still be seen with a little effort. Cross the river on the free George Black ferry on Front Street and walk through the campground and then a further ten minutes along the waterfront to reach the ruins.

The Dawson City Museum

The **Dawson City Museum**, 5th Avenue and Church Street (mid-May or June to Sept daily 10am–6pm; $5; ☎993-5291), has an adequate historical run-through of the gold rush from the first finds, though you get more out of the displays if you have some background to the period. Fascinating old diaries and newspaper cuttings vividly document the minutiae of pioneer life and events such as the big winter freeze of 1897–98 when temperatures reputedly touched –86°C, and of the summer heat wave of 1898 when the sun shone unbroken for almost 23 hours daily, bringing temperatures up to the upper thirties centigrade. The museum also shows some of the hundreds of old films that were discovered under the floorboards of a Dawson building a few years back. Its highlight – in fact, one of Dawson's highlights – is the wistful award-winning black-and-white film, *City of Gold*, a wonderful documentary which first drew the attention of the federal government to Dawson's decline in the 1950s. The museum also holds interesting touring exhibitions in the wood-framed rooms upstairs that once housed the council offices. You might also take a **tour** of the museum building (summer daily 11am, 1pm & 5pm), the former Territorial Administration Building (1901), during which you're shown the old court chambers (still occasionally used), the resource library and archive, the Visible Storage area (with some 6000 of the museum's 30,000 artefacts) and (outside) a view of the Victory Gardens (1910). The obvious **locomotives** outside the museum, incidentally, ran to Dawson from the gold fields between 1906 and 1914.

The Robert Service and Jack London cabins

The cabins of Dawson's two literary lions are only about 100m apart on 8th Avenue, about ten minutes' walk from Front Street. Most Canadians hold **Robert Service** in high esteem – depite his occasionally execrable verse – and he has a place in the pantheon of Canadian literature. Verses like *The Shooting of Dan McGrew* and *The Cremation of Sam McGee* (see "Contexts", p.668) combine strong narrative and broad comedy to evoke the myth of the North. Born in Preston, England, in 1874, the poet wrote most of his gold-rush verse before he'd even set foot in the Yukon – he was posted by his bank employers to Whitehorse in 1904 and only made Dawson in 1908. He retired a rich man on the proceeds of his writing – he outsold Kipling and was one of the biggest-selling poets of his time – spending his last years mainly in France, where he died in 1958. His **cabin** (June–Sept daily 9am–noon & 1–5pm; $2; ☎993-7200) is probably cosier and better decorated than it was, but it still gives an idea of how most people must have lived once Dawson was reasonably established. During the summer people flock here to hear poetry recitals in front of the cabin from actor Charlie Davies (July & Aug daily 10am & 3pm; $6 for cabin and recital): another actor, Irish-born Tom Byrne, dressed and mannered as the "Bard of the Yukon", performs readings in summer on Front Street (3pm & 8.30pm) between Queen and Princess.

Jack London's Cabin home is an unpersuasive piece of reconstruction, little more than a bleak, blank-walled and incomplete hut (logs from the original were separated and half of them used to build a cabin in Jack London Square in Oakland, California). London knew far more than Service of the real rigours of northern life, having spent time in 1897 as a ferryman on Whitehorse's Miles Canyon before moving north to spend about a year holed up on Henderson's Creek above the Klondike River. He returned home to California penniless, but loaded with a fund of material that was to find expression in books like *The Call of the Wild*, *White Fang* and *A Daughter of the Snows*. Alongside the hut there's a good little museum of pictures and memorabilia, presided over by an amiable and knowledgeable curator (hut and museum June to mid-Sept daily 10am–6pm; donation; ☎993-5575). Readings of London's work are given here in summer, currently at noon and 2.30pm.

Practicalities

Dawson City's **airport**, 19km southeast of the town on the Klondike Highway, is used by scheduled Alkan Air (☎668-2107 or 1-800/661-0432) services to Inuvik (NWT), Old Crow, Mayo and Whitehorse, and by Air North (☎668-2228 or 1-800/661-0407 in Canada, 1-800/764-0407 in the US, *www.airnorth.yk.net*) services to Fairbanks (4 weekly),

Whitehorse, Watson Lake and Juneau. Dawson City Courier **buses** (☎993-6688) to and from Whitehorse arrive and depart from behind the visitor centre (daily in summer at 1pm, arrives Whitehorse 9pm; $72). Tickets for all air services, Alaska and BC ferries, sightseeing **tours** of the gold fields (see p.611), and popular four-wheel-drive vehicle tours can be arranged at the excellent Gold City Travel on Front Street opposite the SS *Keno* (☎993-5175 or 993-6424, fax 993-5261). If you need to **rent a car** or 4x4 for the Dempster Highway (see p.612), contact Budget, 451 Craig St (☎993-5644, *www.yukon.net/budget*).

Another way of exploring the surroundings of Dawson is to take a Gray Line **cruise** on the *Yukon Queen*, which in summer runs daily on the Yukon River, offering a day-long round trip of 105 miles for $209. Stand-by, round trip and one-way tickets are available from Yukon Queen River Cruise on Front Street (☎668-3225, fax 667-4494). Shorter and cheaper ($45) ninety-minute river trips are available on the *Yukon Lou* from the dock behind the Birch Cabin ticket office close to the SS *Keno* (☎993-5482). Trans North Helicopters (☎993-5494) run helicopter trips over the gold fields, the Klondike Valley and Midnight Dome: fixed-wing plane tours are available from Siston Air (☎993-5599) and Bonanza Aviation (☎993-5209). For further details of tours and general information, contact the **Visitor Reception Centre** on Front Street (☎993-5566). Information is also available from the **public library** on 5th and Queen (Tues, Wed & Fri noon–7pm, Thurs noon–8pm, Sat 11am–5pm). For **books and guides** visit Maximilian's (☎993-5486) on the corner of Front and Queen.

Currency exchange and ATM facilities exist at the CIBC bank (☎993-5447) on Queen Street, between Front and 2nd, while **maps** are available from the mining recorder's office alongside the **post office** (Mon–Fri 8.30am–5.30pm; ☎993-5342) on 5th Street between Harper and Princess. For **showers** (there are none at the *Yukon River Campground*), the most central are the tight-fit bathrooms at the laundry behind the Chief Isaac Hale building alongside the visitor centre. There are also showers at the municipal **swimming pool** by the museum.

Accommodation

More and more accommodation is opening in Dawson, but while the increased competition keeps price steady it isn't bringing them down. In July and August it's pretty much essential to book lodging in advance. The two hostels are likely to be heavily oversubscribed, as are the B&B options, though calls to the latter a couple of days in advance should secure a room. Rates are high in the half-dozen or so mid-range places, most of which look the part of old-fashioned wood- and false-fronted hotels. If you arrive without a room, check with the visitor centre, which keeps an updated record of accommodation availability and will work hard to find you a bed: hotels often offer cheap last-minute deals to fill empty rooms. Note that many places close their doors between September and mid-May.

The main town **campground** for tents is the government-run *Yukon River Campground* ($8), which is on the west bank of the Yukon on the right about 500m after the fun and free *George Black* seven-minute ferry crossing from the top of Front Street. Black, incidentally, made one of the first journeys to Dawson by car from Whitehorse in 1912 in the (then) record-breaking time of 33 hours. The *Gold Rush Campground* in town at 5th and York is a bleak, fully serviced but busy place designed for RVs (☎993-5247; $20; May–Sept).

Bear Creek B&B, 11km south of Dawson by Bear Creek Historical Site (☎993-5605, *www.yukon.net/bearcreek*). A family-run guesthouse with four rooms in a peaceful natural setting away from town. ③.

Bonanza House B&B, near the museum on 7th Ave and Grant (☎993-5772, fax 993-6509). Offers a two- or three-bedroom suite with shared sitting rooms and TV. ③.

Dawson City B&B, 451 Craig St (☎993-5649, *www.yukon.net/dawsonbb*). Located near the junction of the Yukon and Klondike rivers and arranges pick-ups from the airport or even offers car rentals. ④.

Dawson City Bunkhouse, near the corner of Front and Princess (☎993-6164, fax 993-6051). A good, if noisy, hostel-type place (often known just as "The Bunkhouse") with a choice between rooms with shared bathrooms or private facilities. ④.

Dawson City River Hostel, across the river from downtown; first left after you jump the free ferry (☎993-6823). A HI-affiliated collection of bunks in smart log cabins with a good view of Dawson and the river. There are bunk rooms (two to six people), tent sites, family rooms, a sweat lodge and canoe and bike rentals available. No electricity. Cash only. Open May to mid-Sept. ①.

Downtown Hotel, 2nd and Queen (☎993-5346 or 1-800/764-0514 in BC and the Yukon, *www.downtown.yk.net*). One of the town's plusher wooden-fronted hotels, and – unlike some – open year-round. ⑤.

Eldorado, 3rd and Princess (☎993-5451 or 1-800/661-0518, fax 993-5256). Much the same as the *Downtown*, and also open 24hr year-round. ⑤.

Fifth Ave B&B, on 5th Ave near the museum (☎993-5941, *5thave@dawson.net*). A spacious house with shared kitchen, and optional en suites. ③.

Klondike Kate's Cabins & Rooms, 3rd and King (June–Aug; ☎993-6257, fax 993-6044). Old-fashioned and simple, but clean and warm, offering some of the cheapest rooms in town as well as cabins. Open May–Sept. ③.

Northern Comfort, 6th and Church (☎993-5271). A centrally located B&B that provides bike rentals. ③.

Trail of '98, 5km out of town at the junction of the Klondike Hwy and Bonanza Creek Rd (☎993-6101). The best budget deal around if you can get four people together for one of the simple $40 cabins. No power or running water, but washrooms are available nearby. ②.

Triple J Hotel, 5th and Queen (☎993-5323 or 1-800/764-3555, *jjj@dawson.net*). Some 47 rooms or cabins with kitchenettes in old-fashioned-style hotel next to *Diamond Tooth Gertie's*. Coin laundry and airport shuttle service. May–Oct. ⑤.

Westmark Inn Dawson, 5th and Harper (☎993-5542 or 1-800/544-0970, *www.westmarkhotels.com*). Part of an upmarket northern chain, and the town's swishest hotel: look out for cut-price promotions to fill empty rooms. ⑥.

Westminster Hotel, 3rd and Queen (☎993-5463, fax 993-6029). Despite the tempting old false-fronted exterior and the clean and cheap rooms, this is a roughhouse spot where the miners come in to drink long and noisily into the night. April–Sept. ③.

White Ram B&B, 7th and Harper (☎993-5772, *www.yukon.net/whiteram*). A distinctive pink house that has a hot tub and outside deck. Pick-up from bus on request. ③.

Whitehorse Motel, Front St (☎993-5576). Six cabins with kitchenettes on the waterfront at the northern end of the street beyond the *George Black* ferry. Mid-May to mid-Sept. ③.

Food and nightlife

For **eating** there are several good snack places on Front Street – probably the most popular is *River West Food & Health* (☎993-6339), a healthfood store with café. The excellent *Klondike Kate's* (May–Sept daily 7am–11pm; ☎993-6527), at 3rd and King, is the friendliest and most laid-back place in town for staples like breakfasts and straightforward dinners (and has an outdoor patio). Otherwise, most dining goes on in the restaurants attached to the town's bigger hotels: three of the best are the *Jack London Grill* in the *Downtown Hotel* at 2nd and Queen; the *Bonanza Dining Room* in the Eldorado at 3rd and Princess; and *TJ's* in the *Triple J Hotel* at 5th and Queen. *Madame Zoom's*, at 2nd and King, has good ice cream and frozen yogurts, and for picnic goodies and **self-catering** supplies, there's the Dawson General Store on Front Street at the corner of Queen (☎993-5475) as well as the Farmer's Market on 2nd near Princess.

  Nightlife revolves around drinking in the main hotel bars, or an hour or so at *Diamond Tooth Gertie's* at 4th and Queen, Canada's only legal gambling hall. You can also catch the almost equally touristy period-costume melodramas and vaudeville acts held at the Palace Grand Theatre (June–Sept nightly at 8pm; $16–18). If you want a taste of a real northern **bar**, try the *Westminster* on 2nd Avenue: it's full of grizzled characters and most certainly not the place for a quiet drink or the faint-hearted: there's live music most nights. Other hotel bars provide more sedate alternatives.

Around Dawson

While in Dawson, make a point of seeing the two creeks where it all started and where most of the gold was mined – **Bonanza and Eldorado**, both over 20km away from the town site along rough roads to the southeast. These days no big working mine survives in the region, though most of the claims are still owned and definitely out of bounds to amateurs. However, it's still possible to see some of the huge dredges that supplanted the individual prospectors, once the easily reached gold had been taken out. Another popular local excursion is to **Midnight Dome**, the gouged-out hill behind the town, while further afield numerous RVs, cyclists and hitchhikers follow the **Top of the World Highway**, which runs on beyond the Alaskan border to link with the Alaska Highway at Tetlin Junction.

Bonanza and Eldorado creeks

To reach **Bonanza Creek**, follow the Klondike Highway – the continuation of Front Street – for 4km to the junction with Bonanza Creek Road. The road threads through scenes of apocalyptic piles of boulders and river gravel for some 12km until it comes to a simple cairn marking **Discovery Claim**, the spot staked by George Carmack after pulling out a nugget the size of his thumb, or so the story goes. Every 150m along the creek in front of you – the width of a claim – was to yield some 3000kg of gold, or about $25 million worth at 1900 prices. Exact amounts of gold taken out are difficult to establish because it was in miners' interests to undervalue their takings to the authorities, but most estimates suggest that around $600 million worth left the creeks between 1897 and 1904. Given a claim's huge value they were often subdivided and sold as "fractions": one miner pulled out over 100kg of gold in eight hours from a fraction – almost $1 million worth.

At Discovery Claim the road forks again, one spur running east up **Eldorado Creek**, if anything richer than Bonanza; the other following Upper Bonanza Road to the summit of **King Solomon's Dome**, where you can look down over smaller scarred rivulets like Hunker and Dominion creeks, before returning in a loop to the Klondike Highway via Hunker Road.

As time went by and the easily reached gold was exploited, miners increasingly consolidated claims, or sold out to large companies who installed dredges capable of clawing out the bedrock and gravel. Numerous examples of these industrial dinosaurs litter the creeks, but the largest and most famous is the 1912 **No. 4 Dredge** at Claim 17 BD ("Below Discovery") off Bonanza Creek Road, an extraordinary piece of industrial archeology that from the start of operations in 1913 until 1966 dug up as much as 25kg of gold a day. Modern mines are lucky to produce a quarter of that amount in a week.

Without a car you'll have to rent a bike or join up with one of the various **gold-field tours** (from $36 for a 3hr 30min tour) run by Gold City Tours, on Front Street (☎993-5175), either to see the dredges and creeks or to **pan for gold** yourself, at a price. Only three small fractions on Claim 6 can currently be panned free of charge – but enquire at the reception centre for latest locations: for $5 you can pan with a guarantee of finding gold (because it's been put there) on Claim 33.

Midnight Dome and Top of the World Highway

The **Midnight Dome** is the distinctive hill that rears up behind Dawson City, half-covered in stunted pines and half-eaten away by landslips. It's named because from its summit at midnight on June 21 you can watch the sun dip to the horizon before rising again straight away – Dawson being only 300km south of the Arctic Circle. The

Midnight Dome Road runs 8km to its summit (884m) from the Klondike Highway just out of the town proper. Without a car it's an extremely steep haul (ask at the visitor centre for details of the well-worn and partially signed trail), but more than worth the slog for the massive views over Dawson, the gold fields, the Yukon's broad meanders and the ranks of mountains stretching away in all directions. At the summer solstice there's a race to the top and lots of drink-sodden and fancy-dress festivities down in Dawson. Gold City Tours also run regular daytime and evening tours up here.

You can snatch further broad vistas from the **Top of the World Highway** (Hwy 9), a good summer-only gravel road reached by the *George Black* ferry from Front Street across the Yukon (mid-May to mid-Sept daily 24hr depending on weather conditions and whether or not the river is frozen; every 45min; free; ☎993-5441). After only 5km the road unfolds a great panorama over the area, and after 14km another **viewpoint** looks out over the Yukon Valley and the **Ogilvie Mountains** straddling the Arctic Circle. Thereafter the road runs above the tree line as a massive belvedere and can be seen switchbacking over barren ridges way into the distance. It hits the **Alaska border** 108km from Dawson, where you can cross only when the customs post is open (May–Sept 9am–9pm). Unlike the Dempster Highway (see below), there's no **bus** on this route, but you should be able to hitch easily in summer because it's much-travelled as a neat way of linking with the Alaska Highway at Tok for the roads to Fairbanks and Anchorage or the loop back to Whitehorse. Be prepared to do only about 50kph, and enquire about local difficulties and fuel availability at the Dawson Visitor Reception Centre.

The Dempster Highway

Begun in 1959 to service northern oilfields, and completed over twenty years later – by which time all the accessible oil had been siphoned off – the 741-kilometre **Dempster Highway** between Dawson City and Inuvik in the Northwest Territories is the only road in Canada to cross the **Arctic Circle**, offering a tremendous journey through a superb spectrum of landscapes. An increasingly travelled route – which locals say means four cars an hour – it crosses the **Ogilvie Mountains** just north of Dawson before dropping down to **Eagle Plains** and almost unparalleled access to the subarctic tundra. Shortly before meeting the NWT border after 470km it rises through the **Richardson Mountains** and then drops to the drab low hills and plain of the Peel Plateau and Mackenzie River. For much of its course the road follows the path of the dog patrols operated by the Mounties in the first half of the century, taking its name from a Corporal W.J.D. Dempster, who in March 1922 was sent to look for a patrol lost between **Fort McPherson** (NWT) and Dawson. He found their frozen bodies just 26 miles from where they had set off. They were buried on the banks of the Peel River and there's a monument to their memory at Fort McPherson.

Practicalities

The Dempster is a gravel road and the 741-kilometre journey by **car** takes anything between twelve and fifteen hours in good conditions. It is not, however, a journey to be undertaken lightly. If you're **cycling** or motorbiking, both increasingly popular ways of doing the trip, you need to be prepared for rough camping, and should call at the **NWT Information Centre** on Front Street in Dawson City (May–Sept 9am–7pm; ☎993-6167, 873-7200 or 1-800/661-0788) for invaluable practical as well as anecdotal information from

The telephone code for the NWT is ☎867.

the staff. If you're without your own transport you might pick up a **lift** here, or take the twelve-hour **Dempster Highway Bus Service** run by Dawson City Courier (☎993-6688). Departures currently leave from Dawson to Inuvik on Monday and Friday between June and mid-September (with returns from Inuvik on Wed and Sun), but these details are subject to change, so check before planning a trip. **Tickets** cost $216.45 one-way to Inuvik, less to Eagle Plains and other drop-offs en route. If you're driving or biking it's also worth checking that the two ferry services (☎1-800/661-0752) on the route at Peel River and Tsiigehtchic (formerly Arctic Red River) are running when bad weather threatens, and that you have sufficient fuel in a car to make the long stretches.

In the Dempster's Yukon section there is **accommodation** only at the 32-room *Eagle Plains Hotel* (☎993-2453; ⑤, camping $10; year-round), 363km north of Dawson. There are also three rudimentary Yukon government **campgrounds** at Tombstone Mountain, 72km north of Dawson; at Engineer Creek (194km); and at Rock River (447km). In July and August there's usually a trailer information kiosk at Tombstone Mountain with details of good trails from the campground. Fort McPherson also has a small summer-only visitor centre in the log building by the monument to Dempster's "Lost Patrol".

Currently the only other **accommodation** is in the tiny Gwich'in Dene village of **Fort McPherson**, 115km south of Inuvik soon after crossing the Peel River. The lodgings amount to the *Bell River Bedrooms* (☎952-2465, fax 952-2212; ④), with showers, laundry, cable TV and self-serve breakfast; and the *Tetlichi B&B* (☎952-2356; ④), just one double room with use of kitchen and laundry. There's also the unserviced NWT government *Nutuiluie Territorial Campground* (547km from Dawson) 10km south of Fort McPherson ($10; June–Sept). For tours from the village, contact the local Dempster Patrol (☎952-2053), which runs interesting trips such as visits to the Shildii Rock, a spot sacred to the Tet'lit Gwich'in, trips to an abandoned Gwich'in camp, and themed day-tours by boat such as "On the Trail of the Lost Patrol".

The even tinier settlement of **Tsiigehtchic** (formerly Arctic Red River), 80km south of Inuvik, was founded as a mission in 1868 – a red-roofed mission church from 1931 still stands – acquiring a Hudson's Bay post soon after. Since 1996 it has been known by its Dene aboriginal name, which means "mouth of the red-coloured river".

Dawson City to the Arctic Circle

Having come this far north it's hard to resist the temptation of crossing the **Arctic Circle** 403km north of **Dawson City**, a journey that takes you over the most captivating stretch of the highway. At the very least you should take a short ride out of the mixed deciduous spruce woods of the boreal forests for a look at the tundra which starts beyond the **North Fork Pass** (1370m), just 79km north of Dawson. All distances given below are from Dawson City, almost the only way to locate things on the road.

After the millions of lodgepole pines in this part of the world, it's almost time for a celebration when you pass what are reputedly Canada's most northerly pines (8km). Beyond them you'll see occasional trappers' cabins: the hunting of mink, wolverine and lynx is still lucrative, providing the Yukon's 700 or so full-time trappers with a $1.5-million annual income. At **Hart River** (80km) you may see part of the 1200-strong Hart River Woodland **caribou herd**; unlike the barren-ground herds further north these caribou have sufficient fodder to graze one area instead of making seasonal migrations. **Golden eagles** and **ptarmigan** are also common on willow-lined streams like Blackstone River (93km), as are **tundra birds** like Lapland longspurs, lesser golden plovers, mew gulls and long-tailed jaegers. At Moose Lake (105km), **moose** (needless to say) can often be seen feeding, along with numerous species of waterfowl such as northern shoveller, American widgeon and the **arctic tern**, whose Arctic to Antarctic migration is the longest of any bird.

Chapman Lake (120km) marks the start of the northern Ogilvie Mountains, a region that has never been glaciated and so preserves numerous relic species of plant and insect, as well as providing an important early wintering range for the **Porcupine Caribou Herd**; as many as 40,000 caribou cross the highway in mid-October – they take four days and have right of way. Unique **butterfly** species breed at Butterfly Ridge (155km), close to some obvious caribou trails which cross the region, and it should also be easy to spot Dall sheep, cliff swallows and bald eagles.

The **Arctic Circle** (403km) is marked on the Dempster by a battered roadside cairn, and the occasional summer home of one of the north's premier eccentrics, one Harry Waldron, the self-proclaimed "Keeper of the Arctic Circle". In his late 60s, Harry was wont to sit in a rocking chair in a tuxedo with a glass of champagne and regale all-comers with snippets of Robert Service, facts about the Arctic and some fairly unimpeachable views on the environment. An ex-highway worker, he started his act of his own accord, but proved so popular that he was paid by the Yukon government to sit and do his spiel. After here, the road climbs into the Richardson Mountains to meet the border of the NWT (470km) before the less arresting flats of the Mackenzie River and the run to Inuvik.

Delta-Beaufort

The **Delta-Beaufort** region centres on the planned government-built town of **Inuvik**, embracing the mighty delta of the **Mackenzie River**, North America's second longest river, and reaching across the Beaufort Sea to Banks Island, the most westerly of Canada's Arctic islands. The delta ranks as one of the continent's great **bird** habitats, with swans, cranes and big raptors amongst the many hundreds of species that either nest or overfly the region during the spring and fall migration cycles. It also offers the chance of seeing pods of **beluga whales** and other big sea mammals, while local **Inuit** guides on Banks Island should be able to lead you to possible sightings of musk ox, white fox and polar bears.

After Inuvik and the two villages on the short NWT section of the Dempster – Fort McPherson and Tsiigehtchic – the area's other four settlements are **fly-in communities** reached from Inuvik. Two of them, **Aklavik** and **Tuktoyaktuk**, are near – at least, by NWT standards – and are the places to fly out to if you want a comparatively accessible taste of aboriginal northern culture. **Sachs Harbour** (on Banks Island) and **Paulatuk** lie much further afield, and are bases for more arduous tours into the delta and Arctic tundra. Inuvik, along with Yellowknife and Fort Smith, is one of the key centres of the accessible north, and one of the main places from which to make, take or plan tours further afield. Two major – and several minor – **tour companies** run a wide variety of boat and plane tours to all four destinations (see below), varying from reasonably priced day-trips to full-on expeditions. Having come this far it's well worth taking one of the shorter tours to the fly-in communities for a taste of Arctic life, and to enjoy the superb bird's-eye view of the delta and surrounding country from the air.

Inuvik

INUVIK – "the place of man" – is the farthest north you can drive on a public highway in North America, unless, that is, you wait for the winter freeze and follow the ice road carved across the frozen sea to the north. Canada's first planned town north of the Arctic Circle, Inuvik was begun in 1954 as an administrative centre to replace Aklavik, a settlement to the west wrongly thought to be doomed to envelopment by the Mackenzie's swirling waters and shifting mud flats. Finished in 1961, it's a strange melting pot of around 3000 people, with Dene, Métis and Inuvialuit living alongside the trappers, pilots, scientists and frontier entrepreneurs drawn here in the 1970s when a boom followed the oil exploration in the delta. Falling oil prices and the rising cost of exploitation, however, soon toppled the delta's vast rigs and it seems the oil is destined to remain largely untapped until well into this century. Today the local economy also relies on government jobs, services and the town's role as a supply and communication centre for much of the western Arctic.

Wandering the town provides an eye-opening introduction to the vagaries of northern life, from the strange stilted buildings designed to prevent their heat melting the permafrost (which would have disastrous effects on foundations, assuming any could be dug), to the strange pipes, or "utilidors", which snake round the streets carrying water, power and sewage lines – again, to prevent problems with permafrost. There are also the all-too-visible signs of the **alcoholism** that affects this and many northern communities – a problem rarely alluded to outside them, partly because the region's aboriginal groups seem to be disproportionately afflicted: suicides here are four times the national average for groups of **aboriginal** people.

On a happier note, the influence of Inuvialuit people in local political and economic life has increased, to the extent that the **Western Claims Settlement Act** of 1984 saw the government cede titles to various lands in the area, returning control that had been lost to the fur trade, the church, oil companies and national government. A potent symbol of the church's local role in particular resides in the town's most-photographed building, the **Igloo Church**, or Our Lady of Victory, a rather incongruous cultural mix. It's on Mackenzie Road, the main street which runs west to east through town, but isn't always open: ask at the rectory for a glimpse inside and for the paintings of local Inuvialuit artist, Mona Thrasher. Much further west on Mackenzie Road you might also want to take a look at the **Ingamo Hall**, a three-storey building built almost entirely from 1000 white-spruce logs brought up the Mackenzie River (local trees, such as there are, don't grow sufficiently to provide the timber required for building).

Practicalities

Canadian North (☎669-4000 or 1-800/661-1505) has daily scheduled **flights** to Inuvik's **Mike Zubko airport** (12km south of town) from Edmonton, usually via Yellowknife, Fort Smith or Hay River. Several regional **airline companies** also run regular services from Yellowknife, Whitehorse, Dawson City and between the numerous smaller destinations in the NWT. The main ones (all area codes ☎867 unless stated) are Alkan Air (☎668-2107); Air North (☎668-2228, *www.airnorth.yk.net*); Aklak Air (☎777-3555); and First Air (☎613/839-3340 or 1-800/267-1247).

A **taxi** (☎777-5050) from the airport should cost around $25–30. As elsewhere in Canada and the NWT, the cheapest way of getting to Inuvik may be to buy an Air Canada pass before arriving in Canada (see Basics, p.39). When talking to airlines about onward flights to the fly-in communities or elsewhere, remember that local tour companies often use their scheduled flights, and may be able to offer better flight-only deals than the airlines (see tour company details below). In summer a **bus** service operates from Dawson (see p.604) – its Inuvik office is at 181 Mackenzie Rd (☎979-4100 or toll-free in northern BC and the Yukon 1-800/661-0721); the **Dempster Highway** is open year-round except for brief periods during the November freeze and April thaw.

For **information** on Inuvik and the region, contact the **Western Arctic Visitor Centre** (mid-May or June to Sept daily 9am–8/9pm; ☎777-3777), located near the entrance to town at the eastern end of Mackenzie Road at the junction with Loucheux (10min walk from the centre). In town you can dig out more background to the area and access the Internet at the **Inuvik Centennial Library** (Mon & Fri 2–5pm, Tues–Thurs 10am–9pm; ☎777-2749) on Mackenzie Road west of the Igloo Church, and pick up **maps**, **guides**, books and charts at the Boreal Bookstore (☎777-3748), located almost opposite the church at the Arctic Tour Company office, 181 Mackenzie Rd. The **post office** is at 187 Mackenzie Rd (☎777-2749), and the **hospital** (☎777-2955) is at the eastern end of town close to the visitor centre. For the **police**, call ☎777-2935.

ACCOMMODATION

There are only three **hotels** in town, and all are almost identically pricey: the big *Eskimo Inn* (☎777-2801 or 1-800/661-0725; ⑤), in central downtown; the *Finto Motor Inn* (☎777-2647 or 1-800/661-0843; ⑥), to the east next door to the Western Arctic Visitor Centre, with a good restaurant; and the central *Mackenzie Hotel* (☎777-2861, *mac@permafrost.com*; ⑥). *Robertson's Bed and Breakfast*, 41 Mackenzie Rd (☎979-3111, *robertbb@permafrost.com*; ④), has non-smoking rooms, which need to be booked well in advance during summer. So, too, does the central *Polar Bed and Breakfast* (☎777-2554, *islc@permafrost.com*; ④). The *Arctic Chalet Bed and Breakfast* (☎777-3535, *www.yukonweb.com/tourism/arcticchalet*; ④), which is 3km from town, has a log house and cabins. The nearest local **campground**, the *Happy Valley*, overlooks the delta; the simple and peaceful *Chuk Park* site (☎777-3613; from $15; June–Oct) is 6km out of town on the way to the airport.

EATING

Eating possibilities are largely confined to hotel dining rooms – where at a price you can gorge on char, caribou and musk ox: the best is probably *The Peppermill* at the *Finto Motor Inn*, 288 Mackenzie Rd followed by the *Green Briar Dining Room* (☎777-2414) in the *Mackenzie Hotel*, whose coffee shop is also a good place for breakfast. The *Back Room*, 108 Mackenzie Rd, is famed for its stuffed polar bear, and serves the usual steaks, fish, fries, and won't break the bank. For the best and busiest **bar**, head for the *Zoo* in the *Mackenzie Hotel*, a gathering place for an eclectic mix of locals, backpackers and assorted out-of-towners. The *Trapper Pub* almost opposite the *Eskimo Inn* is a locals' hangout.

CAR AND EQUIPMENT RENTAL, TOUR OPERATORS

Inuvik may be the best place to **rent a car** for the far north, because southern firms tend not to rent vehicles for rough roads, and make hefty charges if you return a car that's obviously been over gravel: Delta Auto Rentals, 25 Carn St (☎777-3535), Marcon Rentals (☎777-4700) and Norcan Leasing (☎777-3044) rent out suitably robust trucks, four-wheel-drives and pick-ups.

Most people who come to Inuvik take a tour of some description. The town's two big **tour operators** are both well worth investigating, as each runs a selection of affordable daily boat and plane tours as well as longer fully blown tours and expeditions: contact the Arctic Tour Company (☎777-4100 or 1-800/661-0721, fax 777-2259), almost opposite the Igloo Church at 181 Mackenzie Rd. Day-trips include tours to the tundra, to Hershel Island, to a traditional bush camp, boat tours on the Mackenzie River, beluga whale-watching and trips to Aklavik by boat or plane; longer tours include three-to five-day trips to Banks Island and Sachs Harbour to watch wildlife (notably musk ox); whale-watching trips; and a nine-day Mackenzie River trip to Yellowknife. Arctic Nature Tours (☎777-3300, fax 777-3400), with forty years' experience of the region, run similar trips, but – as their name suggests – have a special bias towards wildlife: trips include tours to view Dall's sheep in the Richardson Mountains, Arctic safaris, Barrenlands photography tours, boat and plane trips to view the Porcupine Caribou Herd, and bird and wildlife visits to Hershel Island. Both these and other companies also run trips to all the fly-in communities below.

The fly-in communities

Accessible only by air except in winter, when incredible snow roads are ploughed across the frozen delta, Delta-Beaufort's four **fly-in communities** are close to some fascinating and relatively accessible Arctic landscapes and cultures. All are served by Inuvik-based Aklak Air, Box 1190, Inuvik (☎777-3555, fax 777-3388) or Arctic Wings,

Box 1159, Inuvik (☎777-2220, fax 777-3440). All also have simple stores, though their prices make it wise to take in at least some of your own supplies. Some have hotels, but you should be able to camp close to all four: ask permission first at the village head office. The best way to see them is with a tour company from Inuvik (see p.614), but even if you're going under your own steam it's still worth checking with the tour companies for discounted flight-only deals.

AKLAVIK (pop. 800), 50km west of Inuvik on the western bank of the Mackenzie delta, means "Place of the Barren Lands Grizzly Bear". A Hudson's Bay post aimed at the trade in muskrat fur was established here in 1918, though for generations before the region had been the home of Inuvialuit families who once traded and frequently clashed with the Gwich'in of Alaska and the Yukon. Today both live together in a town that melds modern and traditional, and whose inhabitants are proud not to have jumped ship when they were invited to leave their sinking town for Inuvik in the 1950s. Most are happy to regale you with stories of the mysterious "Mad Trapper of Rat River", a crazed drifter (supposedly a former Chicago gangster) who reputedly killed trappers for the gold in their teeth. Questions should really have been asked when he arrived in Fort McPherson and purchased – with suspiciously vast amounts of cash – unusually large numbers of guns and ammunition. He then built a cabin-cum-fortress on the delta and shot the constable sent to figure out what was going on. A seven-man posse armed with guns and fistfuls of dynamite were forced to retreat after a fifteen-hour siege. After fleeing and shooting a Mountie, he grabbed world headlines briefly in 1931 as he managed to elude capture for forty days in the dead of a brutal winter. To this day no one knows who he was, where he came from or why he embarked on his killing spree. He was eventually shot on the Eagle River, surrounded by seventeen men and buzzed by a bomb-carrying light plane: he's buried in town in unconsecrated ground. The Hudson's Bay post is still around, together with a former mission church, now a small museum, but there's no restaurant and only one shop. Arctic Wings and Aklak Air **flights** from Inuvik operate daily except Sunday. A one-day tour with stunning twenty-minute flight and an hour in town from either of Inuvik's big tour companies should cost around $130: for a few dollars more you can fly in and boat out, probably the best way of doing things.

TUKTOYAKTUK, or simply Tuk (pop. around 1000) sits on a sandspit on the Beaufort coast about 137km north of Inuvik, and acts as a springboard for oil workers and tourists, both considered outsiders who have diluted the traditional ways of the whale-hunting Karngmalit (or Mackenzie Inuit), who have lived and hunted in small family groups on this fascinating but inhospitable shore for centuries. Half the families were wiped out in the early twentieth century by an influenza epidemic introduced by outsiders. The Hudson's Bay Company, inevitably, arrived in 1937. Many locals still hunt, fish and trap, but government, tourism and the oil business now pay most wages. This is the most popular tour outing from Inuvik, with trips starting at about $130, a sum worth paying just to enjoy the scenic low-altitude flight up here. Most casual visitors come to see pods of beluga and great bowhead whales, or to look at the world's largest concentration of **pingoes**, 1400 volcano-like hills thrown up by frost heaves across the delta's otherwise treeless flats. This is among the world's largest grouping of these strange features, and includes the world's largest pingo, Ibyuk, a mound 30m high and 1.5km in circumference visible from the village.

Tuk's only **hotels** – booking is essential – are the *Hotel Tuk Inn* (☎977-2381; ⑤), on the main street near the ocean, and the *Pingo Park Lodge* (☎977-2155; ⑤): both have dining rooms open to non-residents. The Northern supermarket sells groceries. You should be able to **camp** near the beach, but ask first. **Flights** from Inuvik operate daily (upwards of $200 return). Inuvik's main tour companies come out here, but if you want a local operator contact Arctic Tour Company (☎977-2230) for naturalist, fishing, camping, hiking or wildlife-watching tours in the Anderson River area.

PAULATUK (pop. 110), 400km east of Inuvik, is one of NWT's smallest permanent communities. Situated on a spur between the Beaufort and an inland lake, the settlement was started by the Roman Catholic Mission in 1935 as a communal focus for the semi-nomadic Karngmalit, who despite such paternalism have fought off the adverse effects of missionaries and trader-introduced alcoholism to hang onto some of their old ways. Hunting, fishing and trapping still provide their economic staples, along with handicrafts aimed at the tourists out here mainly for the chance to watch or hunt big game. Key sites for the former activity are the cliffs of the Cape Parry Bird Sanctuary and the **Tuktut National Park** on the Parry Peninsula to the west, a gathering place for the migrating Bluenose caribou herd. Local operators will take you out to both areas, and in spring run trips to look for polar bears on the Amundsen Gulf. The village's name means "place of coal", a reference to the coal seams to the northeast, where the (literally) Smoking Hills take their name from the smouldering coal ignited years ago and still burning. Aklak Air **flights** operate twice weekly from Inuvik.

The only settlement on Bank's Island is **SACHS HARBOUR** (pop. 150–200), situated 520km northeast of Inuvik. It was only permanently settled in the late 1920s, and only then by just three Inuvialuit families. Today it supports a handful of self-sufficient Inuit families who survive largely by outfitting hunters and trapping musk ox for food and underfur (*qiviut*), which is spun and woven into clothes on sale locally. For generations the island has been known as one of the north's finest trapping areas, the abundance of white foxes in particular having long attracted the Inuit and other hunters. Today there's still an abundance of wildlife, including the world's largest grouping of musk ox.

Five double **rooms** are available at the *Kuptana's Guest House* (☎690-4151; ⑦ including meals), with shared facilities. Ask first and you should be able to **camp** by the beach. Be warned: there is no restaurant in the town, just a small grocery store. Two Aklak Air **flights** operate from Inuvik weekly (from $350 one-way), though for a little more you can join an all-inclusive Arctic Nature Tours trip from Inuvik.

travel details

Trains

Prince George to: Edmonton via Jasper (3 weekly; 8hr 15min); Prince Rupert (3 weekly; 13hr); Vancouver (mid-June to Oct 1 daily; rest of year 3 weekly; 13hr 30min).

Buses

Dawson City to: Inuvik (mid-June to early Sept 2–3 weekly; 12hr); Whitehorse (late June to Sept 3 weekly; Oct & March to early June 2 weekly; rest of year 1 weekly; 7hr 30min).

Dawson Creek to: Edmonton (2 daily; 9hr); Prince George (2 daily; 6hr 30min); Whitehorse (mid-May to mid-Oct 1 daily except Sun; rest of year 3 weekly; 21hr).

Prince George to: Dawson Creek (2 daily; 6hr 30min); Edmonton via Jasper (2 daily; 9hr 45min); Prince Rupert (2 daily; 11hr); Vancouver via Williams Lake and Cache Creek (2 daily; 13hr).

Whitehorse to: Dawson City (June–Sept 3 weekly; Oct & March to early June 2 weekly; rest of year 1 weekly; 7hr 30min); Dawson Creek (mid-May to mid-Oct 1 daily except Sun; rest of year 3 weekly; 21hr); Skagway (mid-May to mid-June 1 daily except Wed & Sun; 4hr).

Flights

Listed below are only the main direct scheduled flights operated by the big carriers; for details on the vast range of small provincial companies operating within the north, see the town entries in the *Guide*.

To Inuvik from: Yellowknife (1 daily; 2hr 35min).

To Whitehorse from: Vancouver (3 daily; 2hr 20min).

To Yellowknife from: Cambridge Bay (1 weekly; 1hr 30min); Edmonton (3 daily; 1hr 35min); Fort Smith (1 daily; 1hr 30min); Inuvik (1 daily; 2hr 35min); Norman Wells (1 daily; 1hr 15min); Resolute (2 weekly; 3hr 20min).

PART THREE

THE
CONTEXTS

THE HISTORICAL FRAMEWORK

The Pacific Northwest has never had a unified history. In prehistoric times, long before the Americans and the British dispossessed them, the native peoples here developed a variety of cultures geared to the region's climatic and geographical diversity. The white settlers who displaced them were more culturally uniform, but owed allegiance to two rival colonial powers, the US and Britain, whose final parcelling up of the region was an arbitrary affair that fixed the Canadian–American border along the 49th Parallel. Give or take the odd minor scuffle, this was a bloodless compromise, but one that was only achievable because the Pacific seaboard was the small change of nineteenth-century politics – a remote outpost significant only for its furs and timber.

Once the Pacific Northwest had been packaged between two nation states, it was inevitable that its history would present a sequence of intertwining episodes rather than a single evolutionary thread, especially as matters were – and are still – further complicated by the geographical divide which the border ignores. The mountains that rack up just behind the coast right across the Pacific Northwest divide the wet, green west from the dry and semi-arid east, and, in the event, separate the

more urban, left-of-centre coast from the rural, often right-wing interior.

What follows attempts to trace the outline of a subject that can be pursued more thoroughly with some of the books recommended later (see p.664).

BEGINNINGS

The ancestors of the native peoples of the Pacific Northwest first entered the region around twenty-five thousand years ago, when vast glaciers covered most of the North American continent, keeping the sea level far below that of today. It seems likely that these first human inhabitants crossed the land bridge linking Asia with present-day Alaska and that they were **Siberian hunter-nomads** travelling in pursuit of mammoths, hairy rhinos, bison, wild horses and sloths, the ice-age animals that made up their diet. These people left very little evidence of their passing, apart from some simple graves and the grooved, chipped stone spear-heads that earnt them the name **Fluted Point People**. In successive waves the Fluted Point People moved down through North America, across the isthmus of Panama, until they reached the southernmost tip of South America. As they settled, so they slowly developed distinctive cultures and languages.

About five thousand years ago another wave of migration passed over from Asia to Alaska. These Inuit migrants made their crossing either in skin-covered boats or on foot over the winter ice, the sea level having risen to submerge the land bridge under the waters of today's Bering Strait. Within the next thousand years the Inuit occupied the entire northern zone of the continent, moving east as far as Greenland and south to the peripheries of Yukon and Alaska, thereby displacing the earlier occupants. These first Inuits – called the **Dorset Culture** after Cape Dorset in the Arctic north, where archeologists first identified its remains in the 1920s – were themselves assimilated or wiped out by the next wave of Inuit, who crossed into the continent three thousand years ago. They created the **Thule culture** – so called after the Greek word for the world's northern extremity. The Thule people were the direct ancestors of today's Inuit.

NATIVE PEOPLES

Before the Europeans arrived, the **native peoples** of the Pacific Northwest – numbering perhaps 150,000 – were divided into three main language groups: Algonquian, Athapascan and Inuktitut (Inuit). Within these linguistic groups there existed many cultures, but there were several commonalities. None of these peoples had a written language, the wheel was unknown to them and most were reliant on the canoe, though the plains and plateau peoples to the east of the coastal mountain ranges used draught animals, the largest of which, prior to the introduction of the horse, was the dog. Over the centuries, each of the tribes developed techniques that enabled them to cope with the problems of survival posed by their particular environment.

THE NORTHERN PEOPLES

Immediately prior to the arrival of the Europeans, the Pacific Northwest was divided into a number of cultural zones. In the extreme north lived the nomadic **Inuit**, whose basic unit was the family group – the optimum arrangement for survival in the precarious conditions. The necessarily small-scale nature of Inuit life meant that they developed no formal political structures and gathered together in larger groups only if the supply of food required it – when, for example, the Arctic char were running upriver from the sea to spawn, or the caribou were migrating.

Just to the south of the Inuit, in a zone that also stretched right across the continent, lived the tribes of the **northern forests**. In the Pacific Northwest, these groups inhabited the land from the Yukon down to central British Columbia. This was a harsh environment too, and consequently these peoples spent most of their time in small nomadic bands following the game on which they depended. Indeed, variations between the tribes largely stemmed from the type of game they pursued: the Kutchin of the Yukon Valley combined fishing with hunting, as did the Tahltan of British Columbia, whereas the Chipewyan, their easterly neighbours, hunted deer and moose. The political structures of these tribes were also rudimentary and, although older men enjoyed a certain respect, there were no "chiefs" in any European sense of the term. In fact, decisions were generally made collectively with the opinions of successful hunters – the guarantors of survival – carrying great weight, as did those of the shaman, who was responsible for satisfying the spirits believed to inhabit every animate and inanimate object.

THE COASTAL PEOPLES

To the south of the nomads of the northern forests lived the **coastal peoples**, who took advantage of a kinder climate and a more abundant environment to create a sophisticated culture that stretched from southeast Alaska to Oregon. Here, a multitude of groups such as the Tlingit, Nootka, Salish, Suquamish and Makah were dependent on the ocean, which provided them with a plentiful supply of food. Living a comparatively settled life, they moved only from established winter villages to summer fishing sites, and occupied giant cedar lodges, clan dwellings dominated by the hereditary chief. There was, however, little cohesion within tribes, and people from different villages – even though of the same tribe – would at times fight with each other. Surplus food, especially salmon, was traded and the sizeable profits underpinned a competitive culture revolving around an intricate system of ranks and titles, which culminated in the winter **potlatch**, a giant feast where the generosity of the giver – and the eloquence of the speeches – measured the clan's success. Prestige was also conferred on clans according to the excellence of their woodcarvings, the most conspicuous manifestation being totem poles.

THE PEOPLES OF THE INTERIOR

South of the northern forests and east of the Pacific coast, **specific cultures** developed in response to particular climatic conditions. The nomadic hunter-gatherers of the inland valleys and prairies, like the Nez Percé, foraged for nuts and roots and mixed seasonal fishing with hunting, while the Modoc and Klamath tribes of the arid basin surrounding today's Klamath Lake, in southern Oregon, subsisted on plants and waterfowl and lived in semi-subterranean, earth-domed lodges. Further inland, there were the plateau tribes of the east, such as the Palouse and Spokane, whose culture echoed that of their more famous bison-dependent cousins on the prairies east of the Rockies. In the late seventeenth century, the hunting techniques of these prairie-plateau peoples were transformed by the arrival of the **horse** – which had made its way from Mexico, where it had been introduced by the Spanish conquistadors.

On the prairies, the horse made the bison easy prey and a ready food supply spawned a militaristic culture centred on the prowess of the tribes' young braves.

THE COMING OF THE EUROPEANS

The first European sighting of the Pacific Northwest coast occurred in 1542, when a Spanish expedition sailing from Mexico dropped anchor at the mouth of the Rogue River in southern Oregon. Stormy weather and treacherous currents prevented a landing, just as adverse conditions were later to hinder a succession of early explorers, most famously **Sir Francis Drake**, whose *Golden Hind* was buffeted up and down the Oregon coast in 1579. The Spaniards, fresh from their conquest of Mexico, were looking to extend their American empire, whereas Drake was searching for the fabled Northwest Passage from the Atlantic to the Pacific – and hence the Orient. By finding the Northwest Passage, the English hoped to break free of the trading restrictions imposed by the Portuguese (who controlled the Cape of Good Hope) and the Spanish (who monitored Cape Horn). There was indeed a **Northwest Passage** – in this the British were right – but it was so blocked by Arctic ice as to be an impossible commercial route and not until the end of the nineteenth century did a (steel-hulled) ship finally manage to sail it. Consequently, the Pacific Northwest coast remained a Spanish preserve well into the eighteenth century with only the gossip of Mediterranean sea captains remaining to excite English nautical interest. The most famous rumour was put about by a certain Juan de Fuca, who insisted he had discovered the (ice-free) Northwest Passage – a shame-faced lie that got a strait named after him.

Meanwhile, far to the north, Russian Cossacks were moving east across Siberia subjugating the Mongols. During the reign of Peter the Great (1696–1725), they conquered the Kamchatka Peninsula and there they heard rumours from the Inuit of the proximity of today's Alaska. Doubting the veracity of this information, but curious all the same, Peter dispatched **Vitus Bering**, a Dane serving with the Russian navy, east from Kamchatka to "search for that peninsula where it [Asia] is joined to America". Bering, after whom the Strait is named, set sail in 1728, but fog prevented him from charting the coast. Twelve years later, he sailed again and, although the trip cost him his life, Bering proved – and the survivors witnessed – that Asia and America are separated by the narrowest of maritime margins.

EUROPEAN INTRUSION

In Bering's wake came traders and navy surveyors who charted the Alaskan shore. Rumours of Russian activity prompted the Spaniards in Mexico City to a reassessment of their situation, and in 1769 they launched an invasion of the Californian coast, establishing a string of Jesuit missions and fortified settlements that were eventually to blossom into cities such as San Francisco and San Diego. But in fact, the Russians posed no real threat – unlike the British who, still searching for the Northwest Passage, dispatched the illustrious **Captain Cook** to the Pacific Northwest in 1776. Cook took the easterly route, sailing round the Cape of Good Hope and across the Pacific Ocean to landfall on Vancouver Island after a year at sea. He hunted high and low for both the Northwest and Northeast (Siberian) Passage, a mission doomed to failure, and, while wintering in the Sandwich Islands (present-day Hawaii), was murdered by Polynesians. On the way home, Cook's ships dropped by Canton, where the sailors found, much to their surprise, that the Chinese were extremely keen to buy the sea otter skins they had procured from the Native-Americans for next to nothing. News of the expedition's fortuitous discovery – and its commercial potential – spread like wildfire, and by 1790 around thirty merchants from various countries were shuttling back and forth between China and the Pacific coast.

The British Admiralty were, however, still preoccupied with the Northwest Passage and in 1791 they sent **George Vancouver** out to have another look. Although his ultimate aim was unachievable, Vancouver did chart a long stretch of coastline, including the island that bears his name. He named dozens of other features too, some in honour of bigwigs at home, others after his subordinates – Whidbey, Puget, Baker and Rainier to name but four. Vancouver made one great mistake in that he failed to notice the mouth of the Columbia River – a situation that was to be remedied by the American **Robert Gray** shortly afterwards.

All this colonial activity did not, however, lead to any fighting and the competing claims of the three European nations as to sovereignty over the Pacific Northwest coast were amicably settled, albeit temporarily, by the **Nuu-chah-nulth Convention** of 1790. In this, the British squeezed themselves in between Russian Alaska and Spanish California. Needless to say, no-one bothered to consult the indigenous peoples, who could hardly have guessed at the catastrophe that was soon to overwhelm them. After all, they had benefited by trading furs for metal goods, and relations between them and the newcomers were often cordial. The violence, when it did occur, worked both ways.

BRITISH ASCENDANCY

In 1670 Charles II of England had established the **Hudson's Bay Company** and given it control of a million and a half square miles adjacent to Hudson Bay, itself a vast inland sea about 1500 miles east of the Pacific coast. There were two related objectives: the consolidation of the British fur trade and the encircling of New France (broadly Québec). Montréal was well established as the centre of the French fur trade and it was from here that trappers and traders, the **voyageurs**, launched themselves deep into the interior, venturing as far as the Rockies. Unlike their British counterparts, who waited for the furs to be brought to their stockades, many of the voyageurs adopted native dress, learnt aboriginal languages, and took wives from the tribes through which they passed. The pelts they brought back to Montréal were shipped downriver to Québec City whence they were shipped to France.

In 1760, the British captured Montréal, marking the beginning of the end of the French North American empire. But, with French knowledge and experience of the interior too valuable to be jettisoned, British merchants employed many of the voyageurs in the newly formed **North West Company**. Once Captain Cook's sailors had demonstrated the potential of the Chinese fur trade, the search was on for an easy way to export furs westward across the Pacific, and both companies dispatched long-haul expeditions into the Rockies, with **Alexander Mackenzie** making the first continental crossing north of Mexico in 1793. Decades of rivalry came to an end when the two companies merged to form an enlarged Hudson's Bay Company in 1821.

The Company ruled western Canada and the Pacific Northwest as a virtual fiefdom until the middle of the nineteenth century, discouraging immigration in order to protect its fur trade. It did, however, exercise its powers in the name of the British Crown and consequently, after the **War of American Independence**, it came to play an important role in flying the imperial flag in the face of American territorial aspirations.

THE COMING OF THE SETTLERS

Under the terms of the **Louisiana Purchase** of 1803, the US paid just $15 million dollars for the French territory that blocked its path west, a huge chunk of land stretching from Canada to Mexico between the Mississippi and the Rockies. Thereby, France obligingly dropped its last major colonial claim on the North American continent, leaving the US and Britain to sort matters out between themselves. Perhaps the only US politician to realize the full importance of the purchase was President Jefferson, who both engineered the deal and bankrolled the **Lewis and Clark expedition** the following year, with the expectation that the two explorers would open up the interior to American fur traders. At that time the tribes of the Missouri basin carried their furs to Hudson's Bay Company posts in Canada, and Jefferson believed, quite rightly, that they would find it far easier to dispatch the pelts downriver to American buyers. Indeed, the President's dream was to displace the British entirely – both in the interior and along the west coast – thereby securing economic control of a continent whose potential he foresaw. With this in mind, his two protégés were dispatched to the Pacific with instructions to collect every scrap of information they could find.

The expedition, consisting of forty-eight men, three boats, four horses, twenty-one bales of trade goods and presents to buy goodwill and, in case that failed, rifles, a blunderbuss and a cannon, set out on May 14, 1804. Lewis and Clark ascended the Missouri, crossed the Rockies and descended the Columbia River to reach the Pacific eighteen months later. It was a brilliantly led expedition and the two leaders dealt tactfully with the tribes they encountered, hiring local guides wherever possible and dispatching emissaries ahead to reassure the next tribe down the line of their peaceful intentions before they arrived themselves. The end result was that they

NATIVE-AMERICANS

From the 1830s onwards, the **Native-Americans** of the Pacific Northwest were simply overwhelmed by the pace of events. Lacking any political or social organization beyond the immediate level of the tribe, it was not difficult for the white colonists to divide and conquer – though admittedly European-borne diseases did much of the damage, with epidemics of measles and smallpox decimating the region's indigenous population by up to seventy percent.

In the Oregon Country, the **US government** initially tried to move willing tribes into fairly large reservations, but as more settlers came, the tribes were forced onto smaller and smaller parcels of land. Some groups chose to resist – the Cayuse slaughtered the Whitmans, the Nez Percé killed a handful of white settlers and, most determined of all, the Modocs from the California–Oregon border fought a long-running guerrilla war against the US army – but, for the most part, the native peoples were simply swept aside. By 1880, the survivors had been consigned to **Indian Reservations** that mostly comprised the infertile land no one else wanted. Further damage was inflicted by the **Dawes Severalty Act** of 1887, which required Native-Americans to select individual 160-acre reservation landholdings (lands had traditionally been held communally and land ownership was an alien concept to most of the tribes) and obliged their children to attend government or mission schools. Deprived of their traditions and independence, many lapsed into poverty, alcoholism and apathy.

In **Canada**, events followed a similarly depressing course. Herded onto reservations under the authoritarian paternalism of the Ministry of Indian Affairs, Canadian native peoples were subjected to a concerted campaign of Europeanization: the potlatch was banned, and they were obliged to send their children to boarding schools for ten months of the year. In the late 1940s, the Canadian academic Frederick Tisdall estimated that no fewer than 65,000 reservation aboriginals were "chronically sick" from starvation. Further north, the Inuit were drawn into increasing dependence on the Hudson's Bay Company, which encouraged them to hunt for furs rather than food, while the twin agencies of the Christian missions and the Royal Canadian Mounted Police worked to integrate them into white culture. As in the States, the settlers brought with them diseases to which the native peoples had no natural immunity; TB, for example, was, right up until the 1960s, fifteen to twenty times more prevalent among the aboriginal population than in the rest of the population.

In recent years, both the Canadian and US governments have (somewhat intermittently) attempted to right historic wrongs, but socio-economic indicators demonstrate that native peoples remain at a significant disadvantage compared to the rest of the population. More positively, native peoples have begun to assert their identity and campaign for self-determination, especially in Canada where "Status Indians" are now represented by the **Assembly of First Nations** (AFN), which has sponsored a number of legal actions over treaty rights and played a leading role in the establishment of an Inuit homeland, Nunavut.

steered clear of any real conflict and suffered only one casualty, (from appendicitis), though they did endure all sorts of hardships – treacherous white-water rapids, dangerous trails and just plain discomfort: they were all, for example, infested with fleas in their winter base on the west coast. They covered about four thousand miles on the outward trip, carefully mapping and describing the country and its people in their *Journals* (see p.639), which provide intriguing glimpses of Native-American cultures just before they were swept away.

Lewis and Clark laid the basis for American competition with British fur traders: Clark founded the Missouri Fur Company on his return, and **John Jacob Astor** was sufficiently encouraged to site an American fur trading post, Astoria, at the mouth of the Columbia River in 1811. In the next twenty years, several factors combined to accelerate the pace of the American move westward: the opening of the Santa Fe Trail from Missouri to the far southwest (then in Mexican hands); the exploratory probings of the Rocky Mountain Fur Company, amongst whose employees was Kit Carson; and the dispatch of missionaries – most notably **Dr Marcus Whitman**, who set about Christianizing the Cayuse from his farm near today's Walla Walla in Washington. The Whitmans wrote home extolling the virtues of the **Oregon Country** (as both Washington State and Oregon were then known), firing the interest of relatives and friends. Perhaps more importantly, the Whitmans had made their long journey west by ordinary farm wagon: if they could do it, then so, it was argued, could other settler families.

THE OREGON TRAIL

The early explorers, fur traders and missionaries who travelled west from the Missouri, blazed the trails that would lead thousands of American colonists to the Pacific coast. Indeed, it was Whitman himself who, in 1843, guided the first sizeable wagon train (of a thousand souls) along the **Oregon Trail** – a pioneering journey that became known to later generations as the **Great Migration**. The migrants sweated their way across the plains, chopped through forests and hauled their wagons over fast-flowing streams behind oxen that travelled at around 2mph. It was a long and hard trip, but impressions of the trail varied enormously. To some who encountered hostile natives, grizzlies, cholera or bitter weather, it was hell on earth; to others it was exhilarating – "a long picnic", wrote one. Each succeeding year a couple of thousand more emigrants followed, and soon American farmers – for the vast majority of migrants heading for the Oregon were precisely that – were crawling all over the Willamette Valley, much to the consternation of the Hudson's Bay Company. This mass movement made Oregon an American community and was to ensure its future lay within the USA.

FIXING THE FRONTIERS

In 1783, the **Treaty of Paris** had wrapped up the American War of Independence and recognized the United States' northern and western frontiers with British and French territory as being on the Great Lakes and along the Mississippi respectively. The **Louisiana Purchase** brought America's western border to the Rockies, beyond which was Mexican-governed "California", though the Spaniards quickly modified their territorial claims, withdrawing to the 47th Parallel (the present Oregon/California boundary). This strategic retreat provided them with a temporary respite until the Mexican-American War robbed them of California in 1847. Meanwhile, territorial tension between Britain and the United States precipitated the **War of 1812**. Neither side was strong enough to win, but the Treaty of Ghent in 1814 took some of the sting out of the dispute in so far as it formalized American recognition of the legitimacy of British North America. The latter's border was established along the 49th parallel west from Lake of the Woods in Ontario to the Rockies. Less conclusive was the arrangement concerning present-day Oregon and Washington: the treaty deferred the issue of sovereignty until the indefinite future, whilst promising the nationals of both states free access to the whole region.

Initially, events on the ground went in Britain's favour. Astor was so irritated by the failure of the Americans to trounce the English in the War of 1812 that he lost all interest in Astoria, selling his trading post to the Hudson's Bay Company, who promptly relocated their western headquarters to Vancouver, near the mouth of the Columbia River. But soon the dominant position of the Company hereabouts was undermined by the influx of American farmers along the Oregon Trail. The migrants transformed the picture, obliging the British to give ground and the present international frontier was fixed in 1846, following a westward extension of the original 49th Parallel.

The **Oregon Territory** came into being the following year – and Washington was sliced off it in 1853. Oregon's subsequent application for US statehood was, however, delayed by the issue of slavery, with neither the existing free states nor the rival slave states eager to complicate Congressional workings with new admissions. Oregon was finally accepted as a free state in 1859, though with an appalling State Constitution that forbade free blacks from living there at all; this was rescinded after the Civil War. Thinly populated Washington only managed to assemble enough settlers to qualify for statehood in 1889. The frontier jigsaw was completed in 1890 when Congress recognized Idaho.

AMERICAN CONSOLIDATION AND THE RUSH FOR GOLD

In 1848, **gold** was discovered in California's Sierra Nevada hills. Guessing the effect the news would have in Oregon, a certain Captain Newell sailed up the Willamette River buying every spade, pick and shovel he could get his hands on. He then informed locals of the gold strike, and promptly sold their own tools back to them – with a substantial mark-up. It was quite a scam and, in the ensuing **California gold rush**, over two thirds of able-bodied Oregonians hightailed it south. Yet, despite the exodus, the

THE WOBBLIES

In 1905, enthusiastic delegates to a labour congress in Chicago founded the **Industrial Workers Of The World** (the IWW), the most successful revolutionary labour movement in US history. It was born out of frustration with the dominant union organization of the day, the American Federation of Labor (AFL), both for its failure to organize successful strikes and its ideological conservatism: the AFL had no political strategy and its main objective was to protect the interests of skilled workers. IWW members became known as **Wobblies** as a result of mispronunciation of the movement's acronym by the Chinese immigrants who constituted a sizeable proportion of its members. Dedicated to the overthrow of capitalism by means of agitation and strike action, their flyers proclaimed "The working class and the employing class have nothing in common". The IWW's organizational goal was to unite the workers of individual industries – such as mining, construction and logging – within brotherhoods that would eventually be combined into the so-called **One Big Union**.

IWW membership was never large – it reached a peak of around 100,000 in 1912 – but the Wobblies managed to exercise an influence out of all proportion to their numbers. They inspired thousands of workers to actively struggle against harsh anti-strike laws, low pay and dreadful conditions. The IWW was particularly strong in Washington and Oregon, calling a series of strikes against the lumber companies. The employers frequently resorted to violence to defeat the union's causes, and in 1916, in one of several bloody incidents, seven IWW organizers were shot and many others were drowned when the Sheriff of Everett tried to prevent them disembarking from the steamboat that had brought them from Seattle.

Three years later, a (peaceful) general strike mobilized 60,000 workers and paralysed Seattle. IWW organizers fed strikers at labour-run cafeterias, handled emergency services and delivered milk to babies so effectively that many employers feared they were witnessing the beginnings of a Bolshevik-style revolution. But in fact the Wobblies had never devised a precise political programme, nor did they want to seize power, and the strike simply faded away. Indeed, the IWW was by then deeply split between radical revolutionary factions and elements that favoured democratic reform. In the 1920s, the IWW began to fragment, its legacy a lasting preference in the US for large industrial unions.

gold rush turned out to be the making of Oregon. For the first time, there was a ready market for the farmers of the Willamette Valley – and an even closer one when gold was found at Jacksonville in 1850 – whilst Oregon lumber towns like Ashland and Roseburg boomed supplying building materials, and Portland flourished from the dramatic upturn in trade.

In the early 1860s, the story was repeated when gold was unearthed in the Oregonian interior, in the hills around John Day and Baker City. Both strikes had a dramatic impact, opening up the area east of the Cascade Mountains – and displacing the native population, who had previously been assured they'd be allowed to stay there. To feed the miners, thousands of cattle were driven over the mountains and, once they'd reached the interior, drovers found their animals thrived on the meadow grass of the valley bottoms and the plentiful supply of bunchgrass. This marked the beginning of the great cattle empires of eastern Oregon, though the ranchers' success was short-lived: the railroad reached the west in the 1880s and, at a stroke, over-

turned local economics. Railroad transportation meant that more money could be made from an acre sown than an acre grazed, and the cattle barons soon gave way to the farmers.

Washington followed a similar pattern, with the eastern towns of Spokane and Walla Walla prospering as supply depots for the gold and silver mines of Idaho and Montana. Here, too, cattle grazed the rolling grasslands of the interior until the appearance of the railroad (and the savage winter of 1881) precipitated the move over from the livestock industry to grain production. The Washington seaboard got in on the act during the **Klondike gold rush** of the 1890s, when Seattle became the jumping-off point for Alaska-bound miners, and grew to rival San Francisco.

CANADIAN CONFEDERATION

All this American activity put the wind up British North America, which was still a collection of self-governing colonies, and the discovery of gold beside BC's Fraser River in 1858 fuelled British anxiety. In response to the influx of

American prospectors, British Columbia was hastily designated a Crown Colony – as was the Klondike when gold was struck there in 1895. Yet British North America remained incoherently structured and, as a means of keeping the US at bay, the imperial government encouraged **Confederation**. After three years of colonial debate, the British Parliament passed the **British North America Act** of 1867, which provided for a federal parliament and for each province to retain a regional government and assembly. British Columbia joined the Confederation, soon to become the **Dominion of Canada**, in 1871.

Two years later, the federal authorities created the **Mounties** (the North West Mounted Police), who came to perform a vital role in administering the Canadian west, acting both as law enforcement officers and as justices of the peace. From the 1880s, patrols diligently crisscrossed the Canadian Pacific Northwest, their influence reinforced by a knowledge of local conditions accumulated in the exercise of a great range of duties, from delivering the mail to providing crop reports. Despite a degree of autonomy, the Mounties saw themselves as an integral part of the British Empire and, more than any other organization, they ensured that these remote provinces were not poached or overrun by American traders and prospectors. They were aided in this respect by the coming of the railroad: in 1886 the first train ran from Montréal to Vancouver, opening up the west and the interior of the country to Canadian settlers.

MODERN TIMES

At the beginning of the twentieth century, the region's economy was largely reliant on primary products, principally timber, grain and fish, but there were also pockets of manufacturing industry, especially in and around Seattle and Tacoma. World War II boosted the pace of industrialization and urbanization with the Pacific Northwest playing a prominent part in the war effort, its factories churning out aircraft and munitions as its shipyards built warships. This trend towards industrialization continued after the war, further alleviating dependence on logging, fishing and farming, but it was not enough to insulate the Pacific Northwest from its vulnerability to a wearisome cycle of boom and bust, with

prices determined by stock markets beyond local control.

In the 1980s, the economic balance was transformed by the rapid emergence of **high-tech companies**, many of whom rooted themselves along the Pacific seaboard with their prime practitioner – Microsoft – based in Seattle. Quite suddenly, the resource industries and even manufacturing found themselves playing second fiddle and a region that had once been thoroughly blue collar was awash with white-collar computer workers. There had, it's true, been an influx of hippies here in the late 1960s and early 1970s, but the IT revolution – geared to money and power – was entirely different. This structural change underpinned the new-found fashionability that washed over Seattle and to a lesser extent Portland and Vancouver in the early 1990s: the new IT companies were renowned for laid-back working practices and informal dressing; bars lost out to coffeehouses; and environmentalists were able to tackle overfishing and clear-cutting with real effect. Hollywood got the message too – from 1993's *Sleepless in Seattle* to *Frasier* – and, seen in this context at least, even the eruption of grunge may well have been a last hurrah for the region's blue-collar tradition. The transformation was also essentially urban, with the small resource towns that dot the region firmly excluded. Inevitably, feelings have run strong and have often focused on **Bill Gates**, head of Microsoft and the world's richest man. To some he inspires awed reverence, to others he is the exemplar of greed – and the recent judicial judgments ordering the break-up of his company are his just economic desserts.

As for the future, the gap between the cities and the small towns seems set to widen, promising boom times for the former and decline for the latter. There is also a major difference in the composition of the respective populations – the cities cosmopolitan and multiethnic, the rest almost entirely white – and politically, the cities liberal, the rest conservative. The point of friction is almost certainly going to be the **environment** as powerful urban interests call for a more prudent harvesting of the region's raw materials. It is the difficult balancing act between the employment imperatives of the resource industries and the need for them to be more conservation-minded that will undoubtedly preoccupy local politicians for many years to come.

NORTHWEST WILDLIFE

The Pacific Northwest boasts a wide range of natural habitats, from frozen wastelands in the far north to areas of sun-scorched desert along the United States border. Between these extremes the region's mountains, forests and grasslands support an incredible variety and profusion of wildlife – any brief account can only scratch the surface of what it's possible to see. National, state and provincial parks offer the best starting points, and we've listed some of the outstanding sites for spotting particular species. Don't expect to see the big attractions like bears and wolves easily, however – despite the enthusiasm of guides and tourist offices, these are encountered only rarely.

THE OCEAN

The Pacific Ocean largely determines the climate of the Northwest, keeping the coastal temperatures moderate all year round. In spring and summer, cold nutrient-rich waters rise to the surface, producing banks of cooling fog and abundant crops of phytoplankton (microscopic algae). The algae nourishes creatures such as krill (small shrimps) which provide baby food for juvenile fish. This food chain sustains millions of nesting seabirds, as well as elephant seals, sea lions and whales.

Grey whales, the most common species of whale spotted from land, were almost hunted to the point of extinction, but have returned to the coast in large numbers. During their southward migration to breeding grounds off Mexico, from December to January (see box, p.367), they are easy to spot from prominent headlands all along the coast, and many towns – especially on Vancouver Island – have charter services offering whale-watching tours. On their way back to the Arctic Sea, in February and March, the newborn whale calves can sometimes be seen playfully leaping out of the water, or "breaching". Look for the whale's white-plumed spout – once at the surface, they usually blow several times in succession.

Humpback whales are also frequently seen, largely because they're curious and follow sightseeing boats, but also because of their surface acrobatics. They too were hunted to near-extinction, and though protected by international agreement since 1966 they still number less than ten percent of their former population.

Vancouver Island's inner coast supports one of the world's most concentrated populations of **killer whales** or **orcas**. These are often seen in family groups or "pods" travelling close to shore, usually on the trail of large fish – which on the Northwest coast means **salmon** (see box p.415). The orca, however, is the only whale whose diet also runs to warm-blooded animals – hence the "killer" tag – and it will gorge on walrus, seal and even minke, grey and beluga whales.

Another Northwest inhabitant, **sea otters** differ from most marine mammals in that they keep themselves warm with a thick soft coat of fur rather than with blubber. This brought them to the attention of early Russian and British fur traders, and by the beginning of the twentieth century they were virtually extinct. Found in numbers in Alaska, they were reintroduced in 1969 to Vancouver Island's northwest coast, where they are now breeding successfully at the heart of their original range. With binoculars, it's often easy to spot these charming creatures lolling on their backs, using rocks to crack open sea urchins or mussels and eating them off their stomachs; they often lie bobbing asleep, entwined in kelp to stop them floating away.

Northern **fur seals** are often seen off the British Columbian coast during their migrations. They are "eared seals" (like their cousins, the northern **sea lions**, who are year-round residents), and can manage rudimentary shuffling on land thanks to short rear limbs which can be rotated for forward movement. They also swim with strokes from front flippers, as opposed to the slithering, fishlike action of true seals.

TIDEPOOLS

The Pacific Northwest's shorelines are composed of three primary ecosystems: tidepools, sandy beach and estuary. You can explore **tidepools** at the twice-daily low tides (consult local newspapers for times), so long as you watch out for freak waves and take care not to get stranded by the incoming tide. You should also tread carefully – there are many small lives underfoot. Of the miles of beaches with tidepools, some of the best are at Pacific Rim National Park on Vancouver Island. Here you will find sea anemones (they look like green zinnias), hermit crabs, purple and green shore crabs, red sponges, purple sea urchins, starfish ranging from the size of a dime to the size of a hub cap, mussels, abalone and Chinese-hat limpets – to name a few. Black oystercatchers, noisily heard over the surf, may be seen foraging for an unwary, lips-agape mussel. Gulls and black turnstones are also common and during summer brown pelicans dive for fish just offshore.

The life and soul of the tidepool party is the **hermit crab**. It protects its soft and vulnerable hindquarters with scavenged shells, usually those of the aptly named black turban snail. Hermit crabs scurry busily around in search of a detritus snack, or scuffle with other hermit crabs over the proprietorship of vacant snail shells.

Many of the **seaweeds** you see growing from the rocks are edible. As one would expect from a Pacific beachfront, there are also **palms** – sea palms, with 10cm-long rubbery stems and flagella-like fronds. Their thick root-like holdfasts provide shelter for small crabs. You will also find giant **kelp** washed up on shore – harvested commercially for use in thickening ice cream.

SANDY BEACHES

Long, golden sandy **beaches** may look sterile from a distance, but observe the margin of sand exposed as a gentle wave recedes, and you will see jetstreams of small bubbles emerge from numerous clams and mole crabs. Small shorebirds called sanderlings race amongst the waves in search of these morsels, and sand dollars are often easy to find along the high-tide line.

The most unusual sandy-shore bathing beauties are the **northern elephant seals**, which will tolerate rocky beaches but prefer soft sand mattresses for their rotund torsos. The males, or bulls, can reach lengths of over six metres and weigh upwards of four tonnes; the females, or cows, are petite by comparison – four metres long, and averaging a mere 1000 kilos in weight. They have large eyes, adapted for catching fish in deep or murky waters; indeed, elephant seals are the deepest diving mammals, capable of staying underwater for twenty minutes at a time and reaching depths of over 1000 metres, where the pressure is ninety times that at the surface. They dive deeply in order to avoid the attentions of the **great white sharks** who lurk offshore, for whom they are a favourite meal.

As the otter population was plundered by furtraders, so the elephant seals were decimated by commercial whalers in the mid-nineteenth century for their blubber and hides. By the late nineteenth century less than a hundred remained, but careful protection has partially restored the population in many of their native Northwest habitats.

Elephant seals emerge from the ocean only to breed or moult; their name comes from the male's long trunk-like proboscis, through which they produce a resonant pinging sound that biologists call "trumpeting", which is how they attract a mate. In December and January, the bulls haul themselves out of the water and battle for dominance. The predominant, or alpha, male will do most of the mating, siring as many as fifty young pups, one per mating, in a season. Other males fight it out at the fringes, each managing one or two couplings with the hapless, defenceless females. During this time, the beach is a seething mass of tonne upon tonne of blubbery seals – flopping sand over their back to keep cool, squabbling with their neighbours while making rude snoring and belching sounds. The adults depart in March but the weaned pups hang around until May.

ESTUARIES

Throughout much of the Northwest, especially in the more developed south of the region, many **estuarine or rivermouth habitats** have been filled, diked, drained, "improved" with marinas or contaminated by pollutants. Those that survive intact consist of a mixture of mudflats, exposed only at low tide, and salt marsh, together forming a critical wildlife area that provides nurseries for many kinds of invertebrates and fish, and nesting and wintering grounds for many birds. Cordgrass, a dominant wetlands plant, produces five to ten times as much oxygen and nutrients per acre as does wheat.

Many interesting creatures live in the thick organic ooze, including the fat Innkeeper, a revolting-looking pink hot dog of a worm that sociably shares its burrow with a small crab and a fish, polychaete worms, clams and other goodies. Most prominent of estuary birds are the great blue herons and great egrets. Estuaries are the best place to see wintering shorebirds such as dunlin, dowitchers, least and western sandpipers and yellowlegs. Peregrine falcons and osprey are also found here.

COASTAL BLUFFS

Along the shore, coastal meadows are bright with pink and yellow sand verbena, lupins, sea rocket, sea fig and the bright orange California poppy – which, despite its name, is also found in Washington and Oregon. Slightly inland, hills are covered with coastal scrub, consisting largely of coyote brush. Coastal canyons contain broadleaf trees such as California laurel (known as myrtlewood in Oregon), alder, buckeye and oaks – and a tangle of sword ferns, horsetail and cow parsnip.

Common rainy-season canyon inhabitants include ten-centimetre-long banana slugs and rough-skinned newts. Coastal thickets also provide homes for weasels, bobcats, grey fox, racoons, black-tailed deer, quail and garter snakes, together with the reintroduced **Tule elk**, a once common member of the deer family.

RIVER VALLEYS

Like many fertile **river valleys**, the large river systems of the Northwest – near cities at least – have in places been affected by agriculture. Riparian (streamside) vegetation has been logged, wetlands drained and streams contaminated by agricultural runoff. Despite this, the riparian environment that does remain is a prime wildlife habitat, especially in the mountain parks, where conditions in many respects are still pristine. Wood ducks, kingfishers, swallows and warblers are common, as are grey fox, racoon and striped skunks. Common winter

migrants include Canada geese, green-winged and cinnamon teals, pintail, shovellers and widgeon, and their refuges are well worth visiting. Don't be alarmed by the large numbers of duck-hunters – the term "refuge" is a misnomer, although many such areas do have tour routes where hunting is prohibited.

GRASSLANDS

Most of the Northwest's **grassland** is in Canada, though the popular image of the interior as a huge prairie of waving wheat is misconceived. Only ten percent of the country is covered in true grassland, most of it in the southernmost reaches of Alberta and Saskatchewan, with spillovers in Manitoba and British Columbia – areas which lie in the rain shadow of the Rockies and are too dry to support forest.

Two grassland belts once thrived in Alberta, tallgrass prairie in the north and shortgrass in the south. Farming has now not only put large areas of each under crops, but also decimated most of the large mammals that roamed the range – pronghorns, mule deer, white-tailed deer and elk – not to mention their predators like wolves, grizzlies, coyotes, foxes, bobcats and cougars.

The most dramatic loss from the grasslands, though, has been the **bison** (or buffalo), the continent's largest land mammal. Once numbering an estimated 45 million, bison are now limited to just a few free-roaming herds. Early prairie settlers were so struck by these extraordinary animals – the average bull stands almost two metres at the shoulder and weighs over a tonne – that they believed bison, rather than the climate, had been responsible for clearing the grasslands.

Once almost as prevalent as the bison, but now almost as rare, is the **pronghorn**, a beautiful tawny-gold antelope species. Capable of speeds of over 100kph, it's the continent's swiftest land mammal, so you'll generally see nothing but a distinctive white rump disappearing at speed. Uniquely adapted for speed and stamina, the pronghorn has long legs, a heart with twice the capacity of similar-sized animals, and an astonishingly wide windpipe; it also complements its respiratory machinery by running with its mouth open to gulp maximum amounts of air. Though only the size of a large dog, it has eyes larger than those of a horse, a refinement that enables it to spot predators several kilometres away. These days, however, wolves and coyotes are more likely to be after the prairie's new masters – countless small rodents such as gophers, ground squirrels and jackrabbits.

Birds have had to adapt not only to the prairie's dryness but also, of course, to the lack of extensive tree cover. Most species nest on the ground; many are also able to survive on reduced amounts of water and rely on seed-based diets, while some confine themselves to occasional ponds, lakes and "sloughs", which provide important breeding grounds for ducks, grebes, herons, pelicans, rails and many more. Other birds typical of the grassland in its natural state are the marbled godwit, the curlew, and raptors such as the **prairie falcon**, a close relation of the peregrine falcon capable of diving at speeds of up to 290kph.

BOREAL FOREST

The **boreal forest** is North America's largest single ecosystem. Stretching in a broad belt from Newfoundland to the Yukon and Alaska, it fills the area between the eastern forests, grasslands and the northern tundra, occupying a good slice of every Canadian province except British Columbia. Only certain **trees** thrive in this zone of long, cold winters, short summers and acidic soils: although the cover is not identical across the region, expect to see billions of white and black spruce, balsam fir, tamarack (larch) and jack pine, as well as such deciduous species as birch, poplar and aspen – all of which are ideal for wood pulp, making the boreal forest the staple resource of the **lumber industry**.

If you spend any time in the backcountry you'll also come across **muskeg**: neither land nor water, this porridge-like bog is the breeding ground of choice for the Yukon's pestilential hordes of mosquitoes and blackflies. It also shelters mosses, scrub willow, pitcher plant, leatherleaf, sundew, cranberry and even the occasional orchid.

The boreal forest supports just about every animal associated with the wilderness: moose, beaver, black bear, wolf and lynx, plus a broad cross-section of small mammals and creatures like deer, caribou and coyote from transitional forest-tundra and aspen-parkland habitats to the north and south.

Wolves are still numerous in the Northwest, but hunting and harassment has pushed them to the northernmost parts of the boreal forest.

Their supposed ferocity is more myth than truth. Intelligent and elusive creatures, they rarely harm humans, and it's unlikely you'll see any – though you may well hear their howling if you're out in the sticks.

Lynx are even more elusive. One of the northern forest's most elegant animals, this big cat requires a 150- to 200-square-kilometre range, making the northern wilderness one of the world's few regions capable of sustaining a viable population. Nocturnal hunters, lynx feed on deer and moose but prefer the hare, a common boreal creature that is to the forest's predators what the lemming is to the carnivores of the tundra.

Beavers, on the other hand, are commonly seen all over the region. You may catch them at dawn or dusk, heads just above the water as they glide across lakes and rivers. Signs of their legendary activity include log jams across streams and ponds, stumps of felled saplings resembling sharpened pencils, and dens which look like domed piles of mud and sticks.

Lakes, streams and marshy muskeg margins are all favoured by **moose**. A ponderous (and very short-sighted) animal with magnificent spreading antlers, it is the largest member of the deer family and is found over much of the Northwest, but especially near swampy ground, where it likes to graze on mosses and lichens. The moose is popular with hunters, and few northern bars are without their moose head – perhaps the only place you'll see this solitary and reclusive species.

Forest wetlands also offer refuge for **ducks and geese**, with loons, grebes and songbirds attracted to their undergrowth. Three species of ptarmigan – willow, rock and white-tailed – are common, and you'll see plenty of big **raptors**, including the great grey owl, the Northwest's largest owl. Many boreal birds migrate, and even those that don't, such as hawks, jays, ravens and grouse, tend to move a little way south, sometimes breaking out in mass movements known as "irruptions". Smaller birds like chickadees, waxwings and finches are particularly fond of these sporadic forays.

MOUNTAIN FORESTS

Mountain forests cover much of the Pacific Northwest and, depending on location and elevation, divide into four types: West Coast, Columbia, montane and subalpine.

WEST COAST FOREST

The **West Coast's** torrential rainfall, mild maritime climate, deep soils and long growing season produce the Northwest's most impressive forests and its biggest trees. Swaths of luxuriant temperate **rainforest** cover much of Vancouver Island and the Pacific coast, dominated by sitka spruce, western red cedar, Pacific silver fir, western hemlock, western yew and, biggest of all, **Douglas fir**, some of which tower 90m and are 1200 years old. However, these conifers make valuable timber, and much of this forest is under severe threat from logging. Some of the best stands – a fraction of the original – have been preserved on the Haida Gwaii and in Vancouver Island's Pacific Rim National Park.

Below the luxuriant, dripping canopy of the big trees lies an **undergrowth** teeming with life. Shrubs and bushes like salal, huckleberry, bunchberry, salmonberry and twinberry thrive alongside mosses, ferns, lichens, liverworts, skunk cabbage and orchids. All sorts of animals can be found here, most notably the **cougar** and its main prey, the Columbian blacktail **deer**, a subspecies of the mule deer. **Birds** are legion, and include a wealth of woodland species such as the Townsend's warbler, Wilson's warbler, orange-crowned warbler, junco, Swainson's thrush and golden-crowned kinglet. Rarer birds include the rufous **hummingbird**, which migrates from its wintering grounds in Mexico to feed on the forest's numerous nectar-bearing flowers.

COLUMBIA FOREST

The **Columbia forest** covers the lower slopes (400–1400m) of the Cascades, British Columbia's interior mountains and much of the Rockies. **Trees** here are similar to those of the warmer and wetter rainforest – western red cedar, western hemlock and Douglas fir – with sitka spruce, which rarely thrives away from the coast, the notable exception. The undercover, too, is similar, with lots of devil's club (a particularly vicious thorn), azaleas, black and red twinberry, salmonberry and redberry alder. Mountain lily, columbine, bunchberry and heartleaf arnica are among the common flowers.

Few mammals live exclusively in the forests with the exception of the **red squirrel**, which makes a meal of conifer seeds, and is in turn preyed on by hawks, owls, coyotes and weasels, among others. Bigger predators roam the mountain forest, however, most notably the **brown bear**, a western variant of the ubiquitous **black bear**. Aside from the coyote, the tough, agile black bear is one of the continent's most successful carnivores and the one you're most likely to see around campgrounds and rubbish dumps. Black bears have adapted to a wide range of habitats and food sources, and their only natural enemies – save wolves, which may attack young cubs – are hunters, who bag some 30,000 annually in North America.

Scarcer but still hunted is the famous **grizzly bear**, a far larger and potentially dangerous creature distinguished by its brownish fur and the ridged hump on its back. Now extinct in many of its original habitats, the grizzly is largely confined to the remoter slopes of Alaska, the Rockies and West Coast ranges, where it feeds mainly on berries and salmon. Like other bears, grizzlies are unpredictable and readily provoked – see pp.520–521 for tips on minimizing unpleasant encounters.

MONTANE FOREST

Montane forest covers the more southerly and sheltered reaches of Washington, Oregon and the Rockies and the dry plateaux of interior British Columbia, where spindly Douglas fir, western larch, ponderosa pine and the **lodgepole pine** predominate. The lodgepole requires intense heat before releasing its seeds, and huge stands of these trees grew in the aftermath of the forest fires which accompanied the building and running of the railways.

Plentiful voles and small rodents attract **coyotes**, whose yapping – an announcement of territorial claims – you'll often hear at night close to small towns. Coyotes are spreading northwards into the Yukon and Northwest Territories, a proliferation that continues despite massive extermination campaigns prompted by the coyotes' taste for livestock.

Few predators have the speed to keep up with coyotes – only the stealthy **cougar**, or wolves hunting in tandem, can successfully bring them down. Cougars are now severely depleted in North America, and the British Columbia interior and Vancouver Island are the only regions where they survive in significant numbers. Among the biggest and most beautiful of the carnivores, they seem to arouse the greatest bloodlust in hunters.

Ponderosa and lodgepole pines provide fine cover for **birds** like goshawks, Swainson's hawks and lesser species like ruby-crowned kinglets, warblers, pileated woodpeckers, nuthatches and chickadees. In the forest's lowest reaches the vegetation and birds are those of the southern prairies – semi-arid regions of sagebrush, prickly pear and bunch grasses, dotted with lakes full of common **ducks** like mallard, shoveller and widgeon. You might also see the cinnamon teal, a red version of the more common green-wing teal, a bird whose limited distribution lures birdwatchers to British Columbia.

SUBALPINE FOREST

Subalpine forests cover mountain slopes from 1300m to 2200m throughout the Rockies and the rest of the Northwest, supporting lodgepole, whitebark and timber pines, alpine fir and Engelmann spruce. It also contains a preponderance of **alpine larch**, a deciduous conifer whose vivid yellows dot the mountainsides in the fall to beautiful effect.

One of the more common animals of this zone is the **elk**, or **wapiti**, a powerful member of the deer family which can often be seen summering in large herds above the tree line. Elk court and mate during the fall, making a thin nasal sound called "bugling". You should respect their privacy, as rutting elk have notoriously unpredictable temperaments.

Small herds of **mule deer** migrate between forests and alpine meadows, using glands between their hooves to leave a scent for other members of the herd to follow. They're named after their distinctive ears, designed to provide early warning of predators. Other smaller animals which are also attracted to the subalpine forest include the golden-mantled ground squirrel, and birds such as Clark's nutcracker – both tame and curious creatures which often gather around campgrounds in search of scraps.

ALPINE ZONES

Alpine zones occur in mountains above the tree line, which in the Northwest means parts of the Cascades and Rockies, much of British Columbia and large areas of the Yukon. Plant and animal life varies hugely between summer and winter, and according to terrain and exposure to the elements – sometimes it resembles that of the tundra, at others it recalls the profile of lower forest habitats.

In spring, alpine meadows are carpeted with breathtaking displays of **wild flowers**: clumps of Parnassus grass, lilies, anemones, Indian paintbrushes, lupins and a wealth of yellow flowers such as arnica, cinquefoil, glacier lily and wood betony. These meadows make excellent pasture, attracting elk and mule deer in summer, as well as full-time residents like **Dall's sheep**, the related **bighorn** and the incredible **mountain goat**, perhaps the hardiest and biggest of the Yukon's mammals. Staying close to the roughest terrain possible, mountain goats are equipped with short, stolid legs, flexible toes and non-skid soles, all designed for clambering over near-vertical slopes, grazing well out of reach of their less agile predators.

Marmots, resembling hugely overstuffed squirrels, take things easier and hibernate through the worst of the winter and beyond. In a good year they can sleep for eight months, prey only to grizzly bears, which are strong enough and have the claws to dig down into their dens. In their waking periods they can be tame and friendly, often nibbling contentedly in the sunnier corners of campgrounds. When threatened, however, they produce a piercing and unearthly whistle. (They can also do a lot of damage: some specialize in chewing the radiator hoses of parked cars.) The strange little **pika**, a relative of the rabbit, is more elusive but keeps itself busy throughout the year, living off a miniature haystack of fodder which it accumulates during the summer.

Birds are numerous in summer, and include rosy finches, pipits and blue grouse, but few manage to live in the alpine zone year-round. One which does is the white-tailed **ptarmigan**, a plump, partridge-like bird which, thanks to its heavily feathered feet and legs, is able to snow shoe around deep drifts of snow; its white winter plumage provides camouflage. Unfortunately, ptarmigans can be as slow-moving and stupid as barnyard chickens, making them easy targets for hunters and predators.

TUNDRA

Tundra extends over northern Yukon and the Northwest Territories, stretching between the boreal forest and the polar seas. Part grassland and part wasteland, it's a region distinguished by high winds, bitter cold and **permafrost**, a layer of perpetually frozen subsoil. The tundra is not only the domain of ice and emptiness, however: long hours of summer sunshine and the thawed topsoil nurture a carpet of wild flowers, and many species of birds and mammals have adapted to the vagaries of climate and terrain.

Vegetation is uniformly stunted by poor drainage, acidic soils and permafrost, which prevents the formation of deep roots and locks nutrients in the ice. **Trees** like birch and willow can grow, but they spread their branches over a wide area, rarely reaching over a metre in height. Over 99 percent of the remaining vegetation consists of perennials like **grasses** and sedges, small flowering annuals, mosses, lichens and shrubs. Most have evolved ingenious ways of protecting themselves against the elements: arctic cotton grass, for example, grows in large insulated hummocks in which the interior temperature is higher than the air outside; others have large, waxy leaves to conserve moisture or catch as much sunlight as possible. **Wild flowers** during the short, intense spring can be superlative, covering seemingly inert ground in a carpet of purple mountain saxifrage, yellow arctic poppy, indigo clusters of arctic forget-me-not and the pink buds of Jacob's ladder.

Tundra grasses provide some of the first links in the food chain, nourishing mammals such as white **arctic ground squirrels**, also known as parkas, as their fur is used by the Inuit to make parka jackets. Vegetation also provides the staple diet of **lemmings**, among the most remarkable of the arctic fauna. Instead of hibernating, these creatures live under the snow, busily munching away on shoots and consuming twice their body-weight daily — the intake they need merely to survive. They also breed prolifically, which is just as well for they are the mainstay of a long list of predators. Chief of these are **arctic white foxes**, ermines and weasels, though birds, bears and arctic wolves may also hunt them in preference to larger prey. Because they provide a food source for so many, fluctuations in the lemming populations have a marked effect on the life cycles of numerous creatures.

Caribou belong to the reindeer family and are the most populous of the big tundra mammals. They are known above all for their epic migrations, frequently involving thousands of animals, which start in March when the herds leave their wintering grounds on the fringes of the boreal forest for calving grounds to the north. The exact purpose of these migrations is still a matter for conjecture. They certainly prevent the overgrazing of the tundra's fragile mosses and lichens, and probably also enable the caribou to shake off some of the wolves that would otherwise shadow the herd (wolves have to find southerly dens at this time to bear their own cubs). The timing of treks also means that calving takes place before the arrival of biting insects, which can claim as many calves as do predators — an adult caribou can lose as much as a litre of blood a week to insects.

The tundra's other large mammal is the **musk ox**, a vast, shaggy herbivore and close cousin of the bison. The musk ox's Achilles' heel is a tendency to form lines or circles when threatened — a perfect defence against wolves, but not against rifle-toting hunters, who until the introduction of conservation measures threatened to be their undoing. The Yukon and Northwest Territories now have some of the world's largest free-roaming herds, although — like the caribou — they're still hunted for food and fur by the Inuit.

Tundra **birds** number about a hundred species and are mostly migratory. Three-quarters of these are waterfowl, which arrive first to take advantage of streams, marshes and small lakes created by surface meltwater: arctic wetlands provide nesting grounds for numerous swans, geese and ducks, as well as the loon, which is immortalized on the back of the Canadian dollar coin. The red-necked **phalarope** is a particularly specialized visitor, feeding on aquatic insects and plankton. More impressive in its abilities is the migratory **arctic tern**, whose 32,000-kilometre round trip from the Antarctic is the longest annual migration of any creature on the planet. The handful of non-migratory birds tend to be scavengers like the raven, or predators like the **gyrfalcon**, the world's largest falcon, which preys on arctic hares and ptarmigan. Jaegers, gulls, hawks and owls largely depend on the lemming: the snowy owl, for example, synchronizes its journeys south with four-year dips in the lemming population.

Fauna on the arctic **coast** has a food chain that starts with plankton and algae, ranging up through tiny crustaceans, clams and mussels, sea cucumbers and sea urchins, cod, ringed and bearded seals, to beluga whales and **polar bears** — perhaps the most evocative of all

WILDLIFE CHECKLIST

This is by no means an exhaustive list of all the wildlife species and their habitats – it should be treated simply as an indication of the places and the times you are most likely to see certain species and types of wildlife.

Beluga, fin, humpback, blue and **minke whales**: at many points off the Northwest coast, especially off Vancouver Island's west coast; summer.

Black bears: Glacier National Park (BC), Banff and Jasper national parks (BC); summer.

Caribou: Dempster Highway north of Dawson City (Yukon); fall.

Dall's sheep: Sheep Mountain, Kluane National Park (Yukon); summer.

Desert species: Cacti, sagebrush, rattlesnakes and kangaroo rats around Osoyoos (BC); summer.

Eagles and owls: Boundary Bay, 20km south of Vancouver (BC); winter.

Elk: Banff and Jasper national parks (BC); summer.

Grey whales: Pacific Rim National Park, Vancouver Island (BC); spring and summer.

Grizzly bears: Glacier National Park and at Khutzeymateen Estuary, north of Prince Rupert (BC); August.

Killer whales: Robson Bight in Johnstone Strait, Vancouver Island (BC) and Puget Sound (WA); summer.

Salmon: Adams River sockeye salmon run near Salmon Arm (BC); October.

Seabirds: Waterfowl and seabirds in the Haida Gwaii (BC).

Sea otters and sea lions: off Pacific Rim National Park, Vancouver Island (BC); spring and summer.

Wild flowers: Numerous woodland species on Vancouver Island and the Gulf Islands, and at Mount Revelstoke National Park (BC); late spring to summer.

tundra creatures, but still being killed in their hundreds for "sport" despite decades of hunting restrictions. Migrating **birds** are especially common here, notably near Nunaluk Spit on the Yukon coast, which is used as a corridor and stopover by millions of loons, swans, geese, plovers, sandpipers, dowitchers, eagles, hawks, guillemots and assorted songbirds.

ONCE UPON A TIME IN THE NORTHWEST

Despite being one of the most photogenic regions of North America, the cinematic history of the Northwest is less stellar than you might expect. Hollywood, especially during the first fifty years of its history, often opted for the mountains of its own backyard rather than trek all the way up north. Even as a movie as definitively Northwestern as Stanley Donen's boisterous Oregonian mountain-man musical Seven Brides for Seven Brothers (1955) was shot on studio lots against backdrops so fake that they might as well have been left over from *Bambi*. So, which movies should you watch if you want to get a feel for the great Pacific Northwest before your visit? There is no defining movie perhaps – the Northwest is too diverse for that – but you can certainly do better than Sleepless in Seattle (1993), a movie that saves its money shot for the Empire State Building, no less, and here are some far more evocative alternatives.

If you're lighting out for adventure in the pine forests and craggy peaks of the Northwest's great outdoors and you're looking for something a little more genuine than the aforementioned log-rolling, bride-snatching spectacular, search out Anthony Mann's two superb Jimmy Stewart Westerns: **Bend of the River** (1952) in which Stewart rides shotgun for an Oregon-bound wagon train, and **The Far Country** (1954) in which he drives a herd of cattle from Seattle up to the Yukon during the gold rush. A few obviously painted mattes notwithstanding, Mann's films present the region in all its natural splendour. However, perhaps the greatest film ever made about the pioneer history of the Northwest is Robert Altman's elegaic masterpiece **McCabe & Mrs Miller** (1971) starring Warren Beatty and Julie Christie. The film is set in a Washington mining town at the beginning of the twentieth century, but filmed near Vancouver, where an unexpected three-day blizzard provided Altman with an unforgettable cinematic climax. Another uniquely Northwestern adventure worth checking out is Robert Aldrich's Depression-era showdown **Emperor of the North** (1973) in which a sadistic Ernest Borgnine battles freeloading hobo Lee Marvin on the railroads of Oregon. And talking of trains, it's worth noting that Buster Keaton shot his railroad-chase masterpiece **The General** (1927) – undeniably one of the most beautiful of all silent movies – in southwest Oregon, despite the fact that the film was supposed to be taking place two thousand miles away in Civil War-ravaged Georgia.

In the early 1970s the mists and gloomy skies that are a staple of the Northwestern climate – the same that had scared off many a film crew in the past – suddenly became popular among the European-influenced auteurs of the American New Wave. The movement north began perhaps with Bob Rafelson's classic **Five Easy Pieces** (1970), which begins with middle-class piano prodigy drop-out Jack Nicolson working the sun-baked oilfields of Texas. But when Nicolson heads north to visit his family in Washington's San Juan Islands, the change of scenery and climate perfectly convey his cruel malaise. Nicolson returned to the region again, to even more stifling surroundings and greyer skies, in Milos Forman's **One Flew Over the Cuckoo's Nest** (1975) which was filmed at the Oregon State Hospital in Salem. For one of his less cuddly roles, Mad Jack also appeared in Stanley Kubrick's **The Shining** (1980), filmed at Mount Hood in Oregon.

Though it ends up in Washington DC, Alan Pakula's stunning paranoid thriller **The Parallax View** (1974) begins with a memorable assassination at the top of Seattle's Space Needle. And four years later Michael Cimino, not a director known for money-saving short-cuts, decided that the mountains of Pennsylvania weren't dramatic enough for the eponymous scenes of **The Deer Hunter** (1978) and thus took Robert De Niro and the rest of the crew three thousand miles across the country to film in Washington's Cascade Mountains.

Alternatively, if you're travelling to the Northwest for a more urban experience you should search out a triple-bill of films by the Northwest's finest director, Gus Van Sant: namely **Mala Noche** (1985), **Drugstore Cowboy** (1989) and **My Own Private Idaho** (1991). Van Sant's dreamy tales of gay yearning, street hustling and drug addiction in Portland, Oregon, may not be what the tourist board would recommend, but they're among the finest films ever produced in the region. An even grittier view of a Pacific Coast city can be found in Martin Bell's poignant documentary **Streetwise** (1984) about homeless kids on Seattle's Pike Street. And for a more romantic vision there's always Alan Rudolph's seductive **Trouble in Mind** (1986) in which Seattle is aptly reimagined as "Rain City".

The yuppie influx into the Northwest which began in earnest in the early '90s (when Seattle suddenly seemed to become the most popular city in America and Bill Gates became the region's most famous resident) has yielded little in the way of cinematic inspiration. Two exceptions are Barry Levinson's Seattle-set sexual-harassment-in-high-tech-places thriller **Disclosure** (1994) and TV's **Frasier** (shot entirely on L.A. sound stages of course). But if you're visiting Seattle in search of the city's other great 1990s export, alternative rock, you should check out Doug Pray's already nostalgic 1996 grunge documentary **Hype**, or even Cameron Crowe's mildly satirical romantic comedy **Singles** (1992), if only for Matt Dillon's turn as a goateed grunge wannabe.

British Columbia is more often than not used as a less expensive stand-in for territories south of the border, as in not only Altman's *McCabe & Mrs Miller*, but also Steve Martin's Cyrano-update **Roxanne** (1987) – set in Nelson, Washington, but filmed in Nelson, BC – and James Foley's boyfriend-from-hell movie **Fear** (1996). But the region plays itself and is beautifully evoked in Phillip Borsos' **The Grey Fox** (1982), in which Richard Farnsworth plays an Old West criminal on the run from the modern world. Experimental grand master Stan Brakhage shot his delirious paean to nature and memory **A Child's Garden and the Serious Sea** (1991) in BC (though you won't find it at your local video store), but the most important development in Northwestern cinema – the rumoured relocation of the Hong Kong film industry to Vancouver – has yet to come to much more than Jackie Chan's hopeless attempt to make squeaky clean Vancouver stand in for the rougher edges of New York in **Rumble in the Bronx** (1995).

And if that's not enough to be getting on with, there's always **The Fabulous Baker Boys** (1989) in Seattle, **An Officer and a Gentleman** (1982) in Port Townsend, and the 1993 American remake of **The Vanishing**, set in wilderness Washington – though it is not nearly as unsettling as the Dutch original. There's even Elvis Presley in Seattle in **It Happened at the World's Fair** (1963) as well as two obvious pains-of-growing-up movies – Rob Reiner's **Stand By Me** (1986), with River Phoenix and based on a Stephen King tale, and the more satisfying **This Boy's Life** (1993). The latter, based on Tobias Wolff's book (see p.657) and set in the small Cascade town of Concrete, Washington, stars DiCaprio and De Niro – and certainly settles some old familial scores. It was, however, David Lynch's **Twin Peaks** TV series – and its underrated movie prequel **Fire Walk With Me** (1992) – that really put the snowcapped mountains and logging towns of Washington on the media map. Indeed, if that's your particular cup of joe, you can still visit the *Double R Diner* (aka the *Mar-T Cafe*) in North Bend and join busloads of Japanese tourists for a damn fine slice of cherry pie.

THE PACIFIC NORTHWEST IN LITERATURE

The writing of the Pacific Northwest has been late in flowering. For hundreds of years it was the oral tradition of the aboriginal peoples that was the predominant form. The arrival of Lewis and Clark was the beginning of many trips from the East to be recorded as émigrés made their way out on the slowly winding Oregon Trail. These tough journeys made the Northwest seem like the Promised Land, but the work that the homesteaders and loggers endured wasn't easy. Neither was the idea of picking nuggets off the street, a romantic dream which ended for some the same way as it does for the character in Jack London's story. The nineteenth century saw a boom created by business that sprouted a tradition of left-wing thought and activism. It was these ideas of an alternative non-capitalist society that intrigued and amused Stewart Holbrook. The final piece, by Tobias Wolff, is representative of the rich modern addition to the literature of the Northwest, which includes writers as diverse as Richard Brautigan, Raymond Carver, Malcolm Lowry and Ken Kesey – for more on which see "Books", p.664.

THE JOURNALS OF LEWIS AND CLARK

The Lewis and Clark Expedition crossed the continent from the Missouri River to the Pacific Coast and back again between May 1804 and September 1806. Commissioned by Thomas Jefferson, their main motive was to spy out the lie of the land in preparation for the westward expansion of the US. The expedition was extraordinarily well run by its two leaders, **Captain Meriwether Lewis** *and his fellow Army officer,* **William Clark**, *who proved to be ideally matched: both men were familiar with the wilderness, both had experience of command, and while Lewis knew about flora and fauna, Clark was a competent cartographer. The result was that despite rancid rations, exhaustion, isolation and extreme discomfort, the forty-strong party only had one fatality – from appendicitis. The Journals give glimpses of the many hardships they endured and the perspicacity with which they approached their task: native emissaries were sent ahead to prepare tribes for the arrival of the white men and to reassure them of the expedition's friendly intentions. The Journals also provide intriguing insights into Native-American culture at a time when the indigenous population had little, if any, contact with whites. This is an edited version of Clark's journal.*

DOWNSTREAM TOWARD THE COAST

September 23rd, 1805

We assembled the principal men as well as the chiefs and by signs informed them where we came from, where bound, our wish to inculcate peace and good understanding between all the red people, &c., which appeared to satisfy them much. We then gave two other medals to other chiefs of bands, a flag to The Twisted Hair. Left a flag and handkerchief to the grand chief, gave a shirt to The Twisted Hair, and a knife and handkerchief with a small piece of tobacco to each. Captain Lewis and 2 men very sick this evening." [They were recovering from the difficult crossing of the Rocky Mountains.] My hip very painful. The men trade a few old tin canisters for dressed elk skin to make themselves shirts.

October 11th, 1805

We set out early and proceeded on. Passed a rapid at two miles. At 6 miles we came to some Indian lodges and took breakfast. We purchased all the fish we could, and seven dogs, of those people for stores of provisions down the river. At this place I saw a curious sweat house underground, with a small hole at top to pass in or throw in the hot stones, which those inside threw on as much water as to create the temperature of heat they wished. At 9 mile, passed a rapid. At 15 miles, halted at an Indian lodge to purchase provisions, of which we procured some roots, five dogs, and a few fish dried. After taking some dinner of dog, &c., we proceeded on. Came to and encamped at 2 Indian lodges at a great place of fishing. Here we met an Indian of a nation near the mouth of this river. We passed today nine rapids, all of them great fishing places. At different places on the river, saw Indian houses and slabs and split timber raised from the ground, being the different parts of the houses of the natives.

Cctober 14th, 1805

After dinner we set out and had not proceeded on two miles before our stern canoe, in passing through a short rapid opposite the head of an island, ran on a smooth rock and turned broadside. The men got out on the rock, all except one of our Indian chiefs, who swam on shore. The canoe filled and sank. A number of articles floated out, such as the men's bedding, clothes, and skins, the lodge, [The "lodge" was the tent used by the two officers.] &c., &c., the greater part of which were caught by 2 of the canoes, while a third was unloading and stemming the swift current to the relief of the men on the rock, who could with much difficulty hold the canoe. However, in about an hour we got the men and canoe to shore, with the loss of some bedding, tomahawks, shot pouches, skins, clothes, &c., &c., all wet. We had every article exposed to the sun to dry on the island.

Our loss in provisions is very considerable. All our roots were in the canoe that sank, and cannot be dried sufficient to save. Our loose powder was also in the canoe and is all wet. This I think may be saved. In this island we found some split timber, the parts of a house which the Indians had very securely covered with stone. We also observed a place where the Indians had buried their fish. We have made it a point at all times not to take anything belonging to the Indians, even their wood. But at this time we are compelled to violate that rule and take a part of the split timber we find here buried for firewood, as no other is to be found in any direction.

October 16th, 1805

A cool morning. Determined to run the rapids. Put our Indian guide in front, our small canoe next, and the other four following each other. The canoes all passed over safe except the rear canoe, which ran fast on a rock at the lower part of the rapids. With the early assistance of the other canoes and the Indians, who were extremely alert, everything was taken out, and the canoe got off without any injury further than the articles with which it was loaded getting all wet. Five Indians came up the river in great haste. We smoked with them and gave them a piece of tobacco to smoke with their people, and sent them back. After getting safely over the rapid and having taken dinner, set out and

proceeded on seven miles to the junction of this river [the Snake] and the Columbia, which joins from the northwest.

After we had our camp fixed and fires made, a chief came up from this [his nearby] camp, which was about 1/4 of a mile up the Columbia River, at the head of about 200 men singing and beating on their drums and keeping time to the music. They formed a half-circle around us and sang for some time. We gave them all smoke, and spoke to their chief as well as we could by signs, informing them of our friendly disposition to all nations, and our joy in seeing those of our children around us. Gave the principal chief a large medal, shirt, and handkerchief; a second chief a medal of small size, and to the chief who came down from the upper villages a small medal and handkerchief.

October 18th, Friday, 1805

The Great Chief and one of the Chimnâpum nation drew me a sketch of the Columbia and the tribes of his nation living on the banks, and its waters, and the Tâpetett River which falls in 18 miles above on the westerly side.

We thought it necessary to lay in a store of provisions for our voyage, and the fish being out of season, we purchased forty dogs, for which we gave articles of little value, such as bells, thimbles, knitting pins, brass wire, and a few beads, with all of which they appeared well satisfied and pleased. [The French-Canadians – the *voyaguers* – who trapped for fur across the continent were the first Europeans to develop a penchant for dogs.]

Everything being arranged, we set out on the great Columbia River.

October 19th, 1805

The Great Chief Yelleppit, two other chiefs, and a chief of a band below presented themselves to us very early this morning. We smoked with them, informed them, as we had all others above, as well as we could by signs, of our friendly intentions toward our red children, particularly those who opened their ears to our counsels. We gave a medal, a handkerchief, and a string of wampum to Yelleppit and a string of wampum to each of the others. Yelleppit is a bold, handsome Indian, with a dignified countenance, about 35 years of age.

Great numbers of Indians came down in canoes to view us before we set out, which was not until 9 o'clock A.M. We arrived at the head of a very bad rapid. As the channel appeared to be close under the opposite shore and it would be necessary to lighten our canoe, I determined to walk down on the larboard side, with the two chiefs, the interpreter, and his woman, and directed the small canoe to proceed down on the larboard side to the foot of the rapid, which was about 2 miles in length.

I sent on the Indian chief &c. down, and I ascended a high cliff, about 200 feet above the water, from the top of which is a level plain, extending up the river and off for a great extent. From this place I discovered a high mountain of immense height, covered with snow. This must be one of the mountains laid down by Vancouver, as seen from the mouth of the Columbia River. From the course which it bears, which is west, I take it to be Mt. St. Helens, [actually it was Mt Adams] distant about 120 miles, topped with snow.

I observed a great number of lodges on the opposite side at some distance below, and several Indians on the opposite bank passing up to where Captain Lewis was with the canoes. Others I saw on a knob nearly opposite to me, at which place they delayed but a short time before they returned to their lodges as fast as they could run. I was fearful that those people might not be informed of us. [Lewis and Clark always sent native emissaries on ahead.] I determined to take the little canoe which was with me, and proceed with the three men in it, to the lodges. On my approach, not one person was to be seen except three men off in the plains, and they sheered off as I approached near the shore.

I landed in front of five lodges which were at no great distance from each other. Saw no person. The entrances or doors of the lodges were shut, with the same materials of which they were built — a mat. I approached one, with a pipe in my hand, entered a lodge which was the nearest to me. Found 32 persons — men, women, and a few children — sitting promiscuously in the lodge, in the greatest agitation; some crying and wringing their hands, others hanging their heads. I gave my hand to them all, and made signs of my friendly disposition, and offered the men my pipe to smoke, and distributed a few small articles which I had in my pockets. This measure pacified those distressed people very much. I then sent one man into each lodge, and entered a second myself, the inhabitants of which I found more frightened than those of the first lodge. I distributed sundry small articles among them, and smoked with the men.

I then entered the third, fourth, and fifth lodges, which I found somewhat pacified, the three men, Drouilliard, Joe and R. Fields, having used every means in their power to convince them of our friendly disposition to them. I then sat myself on a rock and made signs to the men to come and smoke with me. Not one came out until the canoes arrived with the two chiefs, [who Lewis and Clark employed as guides] one of whom spoke aloud and as was their custom to all we had passed. The Indians came out and sat by me, and smoked. They said we came from the clouds, &c., &c., and were not men, &c., &c.

This time Captain Lewis came down with the canoes in which the Indians were. As soon as they saw the squaw wife of the interpreter, they pointed to her and informed those who continued yet in the same position I first found them. They immediately all came out and appeared to assume new life. The sight of this Indian woman, wife to one of our interpreters, confirmed those people of our friendly intentions, as no woman ever accompanies a war party of Indians in this quarter. Captain Lewis joined us, and we smoked with those people in the greatest friendship, during which time one of our old chiefs informed them who we were, from whence we came, and where we were going; giving them a friendly account of us. Passed a small rapid and 15 lodges below the five, and encamped below an island close under the larboard side, nearly opposite to 24 lodges on an island near the middle of the river, and the main starboard shore. Soon after we landed, which was at a few willow trees, about 100 Indians came from the different lodges, and a number of them brought wood, which they gave us. We smoked with all of them, and two of our party — Peter Cruzat and Gibson — played on the violin, which delighted them greatly.

October 23rd, 1805

I, with the greater part of the men, crossed in the canoes to [the] opposite side above the falls [the Snake River] and hauled them across the portage of 457 yards, which is on the larboard side and certainly the best side to pass the canoes. I then descended through a narrow channel, about 150 yards wide, forming a kind of half-circle in its course of a mile, to a pitch of 8 feet, in which the channel is divided by 2 large rocks.

At this place we were obliged to let the canoes down by strong ropes of elkskin which we had for the purpose. One canoe, in passing this place, got loose by the cords breaking, and was caught by the Indians below. I accomplished this necessary business and landed safe with all the canoes at our camp below the falls by 3 o'clock P.M. Nearly covered with fleas, which were so thick among the straw and fish skins at the upper part of the portage, at which place the natives had been camped not long since, that every man of the party was obliged to strip naked during the time of taking over the canoes, that they might háve an opportunity of brushing the fleas off their legs and bodies.

Great numbers of sea otter in the river below the falls. I shot one in the narrow channel today, which I could not get. Great numbers of Indians visit us both from above and below.

October 25th, 1805

Captain Lewis and myself walked down to see the place the Indians pointed out as the worst place in passing through the gut, which we found difficult of passing without great danger. But, as the portage was impractical with our large canoes, we concluded to make a portage of our most valuable articles and run the canoes through. Accordingly, on our return, divided the party: some to take over the canoes, and others to take our stores across a portage of a mile, to a place on the channel below this bad whorl and suck; with some others I had fixed on the channel with ropes to throw out to any who should unfortunately meet with difficulty in passing through. Great numbers of Indians viewing us from the high rocks under which we had to pass. The three first canoes passed through very well; the fourth nearly filled with water; the last passed through by taking in a little water. Thus, safely below what I conceived to be the worst part of this channel, felt myself extremely gratified and pleased.

We loaded the canoes and set out, and had not proceeded more than 2 miles before the unfortunate canoe which filled crossing the bad place above, ran against a rock and was in great danger of being lost. This channel is through a hard, rough black rock, from 50 to 100 yards wide, swelling and boiling in a most tremendous manner. Several places on which the Indians inform me they take the salmon as fast as they wish. We passed through a deep basin to the starboard side of 1 mile, below which the river narrows and is divided by a rock. The current we found quite gentle.

Here we met with our two old chiefs, who had been to a village below to smoke a friendly pipe, and at this place they met the chief and party from the village above, on his return from hunting, all of whom were then crossing over their horses. We landed to smoke a pipe with this chief, whom we found to be a bold, pleasing-looking man of about 50 years of age, dressed in a war jacket, a cap, leggings, and moccasins. He gave us some meat, of which he had but little, and informed us he, in his route, met with a war party of Snake Indians from the great river of the S.E., which falls in a few miles above, and had a fight. We gave this chief a medal, &c. Had a parting smoke with our two faithful friends, the chiefs who accompanied us from the head of the river.

November 4th, 1805

Several canoes of Indians from the village above came down, dressed for the purpose, as I supposed, of paying us a friendly visit. They had scarlet and blue blankets, sailor jackets, [traded up from the coast, where British and American sailors had been regular visitors for several years] overalls shirts and hats, independent of their usual dress. The most of them had either war axes, spears, or bows sprung with quivers of arrows muskets or pistols, and tin flasks to hold their powder. Those fellows we found assuming and disagreeable. However, we smoked with them and treated them with every attention and friendship.

During the time we were at dinner, those fellows stole my pipe tomahawk which they were smoking with. I immediately searched every man and the canoes, but could find nothing of my tomahawk. While searching for the tomahawk, one of those scoundrels stole a capote [greatcoat] of one of our interpreters, which was found stuffed under the root of a tree near the place they sat. We became much displeased with those fellows, which they discovered, and moved off on their return home to their village, except two canoes which had passed on down. We proceeded on.

November 6th, 1805

We overtook two canoes of Indians, going down to trade. One of the Indians spoke a few words of English, and said that the principal man who traded with them was Mr. Haley, and that he had a woman in his canoe who Mr. Haley was fond of, &c. He showed us a bow of iron and several other things, which, he said, Mr. Haley gave him. We came to, to dine on the long narrow island. Found the woods so thick with undergrowth that the hunters could not get any distance into the island.

November 7th, 1805

Encamped under a high hill on the starboard side, opposite to a rock situated half a mile from the shore, about 50 feet high and 20 feet in diameter. We with difficulty found a place clear of the tide and sufficiently large to lie on, and the only place we could get was on round stones on which we laid our mats. Rain continued moderately all day, and two Indians accompanied us from the last village. They were detected in stealing a knife and returned. Our small canoe, which got separated in a fog this morning, joined us this evening from a large island situated nearest the larboard side, below the high hills on that side, the river being too wide to see either the form, shape, or size of the islands on the larboard side.

Great joy in camp. We are in view of the ocean, this great Pacific Ocean which we have been so long anxious to see, and the roaring or noise made by the waves breaking on the rocky shores (as I suppose) may be heard distinctly.

JACK LONDON

*Born in San Francisco in 1876, **Jack London** transcended humble beginnings to become the highest paid and most popular novelist and short-story writer of his day. At various times he was a fisherman, mill worker, vagrant and gold prospector, and his tough, realistic writing was able to draw on a vast fund of personal experience and high adventure – what he called "the big moments of living". His ability to evoke the elemental power of wilderness and landscape was almost unparalleled, a feature of his prose seen to best effect in his most famous books,* The Call of the Wild *(1903) and* White Fang *(1906). In all, he wrote some 20 novels and 200 short stories before dying prematurely at the age of 40 as a result of the combined effects of alcohol, ill-health and overwork.* To Build a Fire, *one of his most famous short stories, is set in the Yukon in the hills above Dawson City (see p.604). It was first published in* Century Magazine *in August 1908.*

TO BUILD A FIRE

Day had broken cold and gray, exceedingly cold and gray, when the man turned aside from the main Yukon trail and climbed the high earth-bank, where a dim and little-travelled trail led eastward through the fat spruce timberland. It was a steep bank, and he paused for breath at the top, excusing the act to himself by looking at his watch. It was nine o'clock. There was no sun nor hint of sun, though there was not a cloud in the sky. It was a clear day, and yet there seemed an intangible pall over the face of things, a subtle gloom that made the day dark, and that was due to the absence of sun. This fact did not worry the man. He was used to the lack of sun. It had been days since he had seen the sun, and he knew that a few more days must pass before that cheerful orb, due south, would just peep above the sky-line and dip immediately from view.

The man flung a look back along the way he had come. The Yukon lay a mile wide and hidden under three feet of ice. On top of this ice were as many feet of snow. It was all pure white, rolling in gentle undulations where the ice-jams of the freeze-up had formed. North and south, as far as his eye could see, it was unbroken white, save for a dark hair-line that curved and twisted from around the spruce-covered island to the south, and that curved and twisted away into the north, where it disappeared behind another spruce-covered island. This dark hair-line was the trail – the main trail –that led south five hundred miles to the Chilcoot Pass, Dyea, and salt water; and that led north seventy miles to Dawson, and still on to the north a thousand miles to Nulato, and finally to St. Michael on Bering Sea, a thousand miles and half a thousand more.

But all this – the mysterious, far-reaching hair-line trail, the absence of sun from the sky, the tremendous cold, and the strangeness and weirdness of it all – made no impression on the man. It was not because he was long used to it. He was a newcomer in the land, a *chechaquo*, and this was his first winter. The trouble with him was that he was without imagination. He was quick and alert in the things of life, but only in the things, and not in the significances. Fifty degrees below zero meant eighty-odd degrees of frost. Such fact impressed him as being cold and uncomfortable, and that was all. It did not lead him to meditate upon his frailty as a creature of temperature, and upon man's frailty in general, able only to live within certain narrow limits of heat and cold; and from there on it did not lead him to the conjectural field of immortality and man's place in the universe. Fifty degrees below zero stood for a bite of frost that hurt and that must be guarded against by the use of mittens, ear-flaps, warm moccasins, and thick socks. Fifty degrees below zero was to him just precisely fifty degrees below zero. That there should be anything more to it than that was a thought that never entered his head.

As he turned to go on, he spat speculatively. There was a sharp, explosive crackle that startled him. He spat again. And again, in the air, before it could fall to the snow, the spittle crackled. He knew that at fifty below spittle crackled on the snow, but this spittle had crackled in the air. Undoubtedly it was colder than fifty below — how much colder he did not know. But the temperature did not matter. He was bound for the old claim on the left fork of Henderson Creek, where the boys were already. They had come over across the divide from the Indian Creek country, while he had come the roundabout way to take a look at the possibilities of getting out logs in the spring from the islands in the Yukon. He would be in to camp by six o'clock; a bit after dark, it was true, but the boys would be there, a fire would be going, and a hot supper would be ready. As for lunch, he pressed his hand against the protruding bundle under his jacket. It was also under his shirt, wrapped up in a handkerchief and lying against the naked skin. It was the only way to keep the biscuits from freezing. He smiled agreeably to himself as he thought of those biscuits, each cut open and sopped in bacon grease, and each enclosing a generous slice of fried bacon.

He plunged in among the big spruce trees. The trail was faint. A foot of snow had fallen since the last sled had passed over, and he was glad he was without a sled, travelling light. In fact, he carried nothing but the lunch wrapped in the handkerchief. He was surprised, however, at the cold. It certainly was cold, he concluded, as he rubbed his numb nose and cheek-bones with his mittened hand. He was a warm-whiskered man, but the hair on his face did not protect the high cheek-bones and the eager nose that thrust itself aggressively into the frosty air.

At the man's heels trotted a dog, a big native husky, the proper wolf-dog, gray-coated and without any visible or temperamental difference from its brother, the wild wolf. The animal was depressed by the tremendous cold. It knew that it was no time for travelling. Its instinct told it a truer tale than was told to the man by the man's judgment. In reality, it was not merely colder than fifty below zero; it was colder than sixty below, than seventy below. It was seventy-five below zero. Since the freezing-point is thirty-two above zero, it meant that one hundred and seven degrees of frost obtained. The dog did not know anything about thermometers. Possibly in its brain there was no sharp consciousness of a condition of very cold such as was in the man's brain. But the brute had its instinct. It experienced a vague but menacing apprehension that subdued it and made it slink along at the man's heels, and that made it question eagerly every unwonted movement of the man as if expecting him to go into camp or to seek shelter somewhere and build a fire. The dog had learned fire, and it wanted fire, or else to burrow under the snow and cuddle its warmth away from the air.

The frozen moisture of its breathing had settled on its fur in a fine powder of frost, and especially were its jowls, muzzle, and eyelashes whitened by its crystalled breath. The man's red beard and mustache were likewise frosted, but more solidly, the deposit taking the form of ice and increasing with every warm, moist breath he exhaled. Also, the man was chewing tobacco, and the muzzle of ice held his lips so rigidly that he was unable to clear his chin when he expelled the juice. The result was that a crystal beard of the color and solidity of amber was increasing its length on his chin. If he fell down it would shatter itself, like glass, into brittle fragments. But he did not mind the appendage. It was the penalty all tobacco-chewers paid in that country, and he had been out before in two cold snaps. They had not been so cold as this, he knew, but by the spirit thermometer at Sixty Mile he knew they had been registered at fifty below and at fifty-five.

He held on through the level stretch of woods for several miles, crossed a wide flat of niggerheads, and dropped down a bank to the frozen bed of a small stream. This was Henderson Creek, and he knew he was ten miles from the forks. He looked at his watch. It was ten o'clock. He was making four miles an hour, and he calculated that he would arrive at the forks at half-past twelve. He decided to celebrate that event by eating his lunch there.

The dog dropped in again at his heels, with a tail drooping discouragement, as the man swung along the creek-bed. The furrow of the old sled-trail was plainly visible, but a dozen inches of snow covered the marks of the last runners. In a month no man had come up or down that silent creek. The man held steadily on. He was not much given to thinking, and just then particularly he had nothing to think about save that he would eat lunch at the forks and that at six o'clock he would be in camp with the boys. There was nobody to talk to; and, had there been, speech would have been impossible because of the ice-muzzle on his mouth. So he continued monotonously to chew tobacco and to increase the length of his amber beard.

Once in a while the thought reiterated itself that it was very cold and that he had never experienced such cold. As he walked along he rubbed his cheek-bones and nose with the back of his mittened hand. He did this automatically, now and again changing hands. But rub as he would, the instant he stopped his cheek-bones went numb, and the following instant the end of his nose went numb. He was sure to frost his cheeks; he knew that, and experienced a pang of regret that he had not devised a nose-strap of the sort Bud wore in cold snaps. Such a strap passed across the cheeks, as well, and saved them. But it didn't matter much, after all. What were frosted cheeks? A bit painful, that was all; they were never serious.

Empty as the man's mind was of thoughts, he was keenly observant, and he noticed the changes in the creek, the curves and bends and timber-jams, and always he sharply noted where he placed his feet. Once, coming around a bend, he shied abruptly, like a startled horse, curved away from the place where he had been walking, and retreated several paces back along the trail. The creek he knew was frozen clear to the bottom, – no creek could contain water in that arctic winter, – but he knew also that there were springs that bubbled out from the hillsides and ran along under the snow and on top the ice of the creek. He knew that the coldest snaps never froze these springs, and he knew likewise their danger. They were traps. They hid pools of water under the snow that might be three inches deep, or three feet. Sometimes a skin of ice half an inch thick covered them, and in turn was covered by the snow. Sometimes there were alternate layers of water and ice-skin, so that when one broke through he kept on breaking through for a while, sometimes wetting himself to the waist.

That was why he had shied in such panic. He had felt the give under his feet and heard the crackle of a snow-hidden ice-skin. And to get his feet wet in such a temperature meant trouble and danger. At the very least it meant delay, for he would be forced to stop and build a fire, and under its protection to bare his feet while he dried his socks and moccasins. He stood and studied the creek-bed and its banks, and decided that the flow of water came from the right. He reflected awhile, rubbing his nose and cheeks, then skirted to the left, stepping gingerly and testing the footing for each step. Once clear of the danger, he took a fresh chew of tobacco and swung along at his four-mile gait.

In the course of the next two hours he came upon several similar traps. Usually the snow above the hidden pools had a sunken, candied appearance that advertised the danger. Once again, however, he had a close call; and once, suspecting danger, he compelled the dog to go on in front. The dog did not want to go. It hung back until the man shoved it forward, and then it went quickly across the white, unbroken surface. Suddenly it broke through, floundered to one side, and got away to firmer footing. It had wet its forefeet and legs, and almost immediately the water that clung to it turned to ice. It made quick efforts to lick the ice off its legs, then dropped down in the snow and began to bite out the ice that had formed between the toes. This was a matter of instinct. To permit the ice to remain would mean sore feet. It did not know this. It merely obeyed the mysterious prompting that arose from the deep crypts of its being. But the man knew, having achieved a judgment on the subject, and he removed the mitten from his right hand and helped tear out the ice-particles. He did not expose his fingers more than a minute, and was astonished at the swift numbness that smote them. It certainly was cold. He pulled on the mitten hastily, and beat the hand savagely across his chest.

At twelve o'clock the day was at its brightest. Yet the sun was too far south on its winter journey to clear the horizon. The bulge of the earth intervened between it and Henderson Creek, where the man walked under a clear sky at noon and cast no shadow. At half-past twelve, to the minute, he arrived at the forks of the creek. He was pleased at the speed he had made. If he kept it up, he would certainly be with the boys by six. He unbuttoned his jacket and shirt and drew forth his lunch. The action consumed no more than a quarter of a minute, yet in that brief moment the numbness laid hold of the exposed fingers. He did not put the mitten on, but, instead, struck the fingers a dozen sharp smashes against his leg. Then he sat down on a snow-covered log to eat. The sting that followed upon the striking of his fingers against his leg ceased so quickly that he was startled. He had had no chance to take a bite of biscuit. He struck the fingers repeatedly and returned them to the mitten, baring the other hand for the purpose of eating. He tried to take a mouthful, but the ice-muzzle prevented. He had forgotten to build a fire and thaw out. He chuckled at his foolishness, and as he chuckled he noted the numbness creeping into the exposed fingers. Also, he noted that the stinging which had first come to his toes when he sat down was already passing away. He wondered whether the toes were warm or numb. He moved them inside the moccasins and decided that they were numb.

He pulled the mitten on hurriedly and stood up. He was a bit frightened. He stamped up and down until the stinging returned into the feet. It certainly was cold, was his thought. That man from Sulphur Creek had spoken the truth when telling how cold it sometimes got in the country. And he had laughed at him at the time! That showed one must not be too sure of things. There was no mistake about it, it was cold. He strode up and down, stamping his feet and threshing his arms, until reassured by the returning warmth. Then he got out matches and proceeded to make a fire. From the undergrowth, where high water of the previous spring had lodged a supply of seasoned twigs, he got his fire-wood. Working carefully from a small beginning, he soon had a roaring fire, over which he thawed the ice from his face and in the protection of which he ate his biscuits. For the moment the cold of space was outwitted. The dog took satisfaction in the fire, stretching out close enough for warmth and far enough away to escape being singed.

When the man had finished, he filled his pipe and took his comfortable time over a smoke. Then he pulled on his mittens, settled the earflaps of his cap firmly about his ears, and took the creek trail up the left fork. The dog was disappointed and yearned back toward the fire. This man did not know cold. Possibly all the gen-

erations of his ancestry had been ignorant of cold, of real cold, of cold one hundred and seven degrees below freezing-point. But the dog knew; all its ancestry knew, and it had inherited the knowledge. And it knew that it was not good to walk abroad in such fearful cold. It was the time to lie snug in a hole in the snow and wait for a curtain of cloud to be drawn across the face of outer space whence this cold came. On the other hand, there was no keen intimacy between the dog and the man. The one was the toil-slave of the other, and the only caresses it had ever received were the caresses of the whip-lash and of harsh and menacing throat-sounds that threatened the whip-lash. So the dog made no effort to communicate its apprehension to the man. It was not concerned in the welfare of the man; it was for its own sake that it yearned back toward the fire. But the man whistled, and spoke to it with the sound of whip-lashes, and the dog swung in at the man's heels and followed after.

The man took a chew of tobacco and proceeded to start a new amber beard. Also, his moist breath quickly powdered with white his mustache, eyebrows, and lashes. There did not seem to be so many springs on the left fork of the Henderson, and for half an hour the man saw no signs of any. And then it happened. At a place where there were no signs, where the soft, unbroken snow seemed to advertise solidity beneath, the man broke through. It was not deep. He wet himself halfway to the knees before he floundered out to the firm crust.

He was angry, and cursed his luck aloud. He had hoped to get into camp with the boys at six o'clock, and this would delay him an hour, for he would have to build a fire and dry out his footgear. This was imperative at that low temperature – he knew that much; and he turned aside to the bank, which he climbed. On top, tangled in the underbrush about the trunks of several small spruce trees, was a high-water deposit of dry fire-wood – sticks and twigs, principally, but also larger portions of seasoned branches and fine, dry, last-year's grasses. He threw down several large pieces on top of the snow. This served for a foundation and prevented the young flame from drowning itself in the snow it otherwise would melt. The flame he got by touching a match to a small shred of birch-bark that he took from his pocket. This burned even more readily than paper. Placing it on the foundation, he fed the young flame with wisps of dry grass and with the tiniest dry twigs.

He worked slowly and carefully, keenly aware of his danger. Gradually, as the flame grew stronger, he increased the size of the twigs with which he fed it. He squatted in the snow, pulling the twigs out from their entanglement in the brush and feeding directly to the flame. He knew there must be no failure. When it is seventy-five below zero, a man must not fail in his first attempt to build a fire — that is, if his feet are wet. If his feet are dry, and he fails, he can run along the trail for half a mile and restore his circulation. But the circulation of wet and freezing feet cannot be restored by running when it is seventy-five below. No matter how fast he runs, the wet feet will freeze the harder.

All this the man knew. The old-timer on Sulphur Creek had told him about it the previous fall, and now he was appreciating the advice. Already all sensation had gone out of his feet. To build the fire he had been forced to remove his mittens, and the fingers had quickly gone numb. His pace of four miles an hour had kept his heart pumping blood to the surface of his body and to all the extremities. But the instant he stopped, the action of the pump eased down. The cold of space smote the unprotected tip of the planet, and he, being on that unprotected tip, received the full force of the blow. The blood of his body recoiled before it. The blood was alive, like the dog, and like the dog it wanted to hide away and cover itself up from the fearful cold. So long as he walked four miles an hour, he pumped that blood, willy-nilly, to the surface; but now it ebbed away and sank down into the recesses of his body. The extremities were the first to feel its absence. His wet feet froze the faster, and his exposed fingers numbed the faster, though they had not yet begun to freeze. Nose and cheeks were already freezing, while the skin of all his body chilled as it lost its blood.

But he was safe. Toes and nose and cheeks would be only touched by the frost, for the fire was beginning to burn with strength. He was feeding it with twigs the size of his finger. In another minute he would be able to feed it with branches the size of his wrist, and then he could remove his wet foot-gear, and, while it dried, he could keep his naked feet warm by the fire, rubbing them at first, of course, with snow. The fire was a success. He was safe. He remembered the advice of the old-timer on Sulphur Creek, and smiled. The old-timer had been very serious in laying down the law that no man must travel alone in the Klondike after fifty below. Well, here he was; he had had the accident; he was alone; and he had saved himself. Those old-timers were rather womanish, some of them, he thought. All a man had to do was to keep his head, and he was all right. Any man who was a man could travel alone. But it was surprising, the rapidity with which his cheeks and nose were freezing. And he had not thought his fingers could go lifeless in so short a time. Lifeless they were, for he could scarcely make them move together to grip a twig, and they seemed remote from his body and from him. When he touched a twig, he had to look and see whether or not he had hold of it. The wires were pretty well down between him and his finger-ends.

All of which counted for little. There was the fire, snapping and crackling and promising life with every dancing flame. He started to untie his moccasins. They were coated with ice; the thick German socks were like sheaths of iron halfway to the knees; and the moccasin strings were like rods of steel all twisted and knotted as by some conflagration. For a moment he tugged with his numb fingers, then, realizing the folly of it, he drew his sheath-knife.

But before he could cut the strings, it happened. It was his own fault or, rather, his mistake. He should not have built the fire under the spruce tree. He should have built it in the open. But it had been easier to pull the twigs from the brush and drop them directly on the fire. Now the tree under which he had done this carried a weight of snow on its boughs. No wind had blown for weeks, and each bough was fully freighted. Each time he had pulled a twig he had communicated a slight agitation to the tree — an imperceptible agitation, so far as he was concerned, but an agitation sufficient to bring about the disaster. High up in the tree one bough capsized its load of snow. This fell on the boughs beneath, capsizing them. This process continued, spreading out and involving the whole tree. It grew like an avalanche, and it descended without warning upon the man and the fire, and the fire was blotted out! Where it had burned was a mantle of fresh and disordered snow.

The man was shocked. It was as though he had just heard his own sentence of death. For a moment he sat and stared at the spot where the fire had been. Then he grew very calm. Perhaps the old-timer on Sulphur Creek was right. If he had only had a trail-mate he would have been in no danger now. The trail-mate could have built the fire. Well, it was up to him to build the fire over again, and this second time there must be no failure. Even if he succeeded, he would most likely lose some toes. His feet must be badly frozen by now, and there would be some time before the second fire was ready.

Such were his thoughts, but he did not sit and think them. He was busy all the time they were passing through his mind. He made a new foundation for a fire, this time in the open, where no treacherous tree could blot it out. Next, he gathered dry grasses and tiny twigs from the high-water flotsam. He could not bring his fingers together to pull them out, but he was able to gather them by the handful. In this way he got many rotten twigs and bits of green moss that were undesirable, but it was the best he could do. He worked methodically, even collecting an armful of the larger branches to be used later when the fire gathered strength. And all the while the dog sat and watched him, a certain yearning wistfulness in its eyes, for it looked upon him as the fire-provider, and the fire was slow in coming.

When all was ready, the man reached in his pocket for a second piece of birch-bark. He knew the bark was there, and, though he could not feel it with his fingers, he could hear its crisp rustling as he fumbled for it. Try as he would, he could not clutch hold of it. And all the time, in his consciousness, was the knowledge that each instant his feet were freezing. This thought tended to put him in a panic, but he fought against it and kept calm. He pulled on his mittens with his teeth, and threshed his arms back and forth, beating his hands with all his might against his sides. He did this sitting down, and he stood up to do it; and all the while the dog sat in the snow, its wolf-brush of a tail curled around warmly over its forefeet, its sharp wolf-ears pricked forward intently as it watched the man. And the man, as he beat and threshed with his arms and hands, felt a great surge of envy as he regarded the creature that was warm and secure in its natural covering.

After a time he was aware of the first far-away signals of sensation in his beaten fingers. The faint tingling grew stronger till it evolved into a stinging ache that was excruciating, but which the man hailed with satisfaction. He stripped the mitten from his right hand and fetched forth the birch-bark. The exposed fingers were quickly going numb again. Next he brought out his bunch of sulphur matches. But the tremendous cold had already driven the life out of his fingers. In his effort to separate one match from the others, the whole bunch fell in the snow. He tried to pick it out of the snow, but failed. The dead fingers could neither touch nor clutch. He was very careful. He drove the thought of his freezing feet, and nose, and cheeks, out of his mind, devoting his whole soul to the matches. He watched, using the sense of vision in place of that of touch, and when he saw his fingers on each side the bunch, he closed them – that is, he willed to close them, for the wires were down, and the fingers did not obey. He pulled the mitten on the right hand, and beat it fiercely against his knee. Then, with both mittened hands, he scooped the bunch of matches, along with much snow, into his lap. Yet he was no better off.

After some manipulation he managed to get the bunch between the heels of his mittened hands. In this fashion he carried it to his mouth. The ice crackled and snapped when by a violent effort he opened his mouth. He drew the lower jaw in, curled the upper lip out of the way, and scraped the bunch with his upper teeth in order to separate a match. He succeeded in getting one, which he dropped on his lap. He was no better off. He could not pick it up. Then he devised a way. He picked it up in his teeth and scratched it on his leg. Twenty times he scratched before he succeeded in lighting it. As it flamed he held it with his teeth to the birch-bark. But the burning brimstone went up his nostrils and into his lungs, causing him to cough spasmodically. The match fell into the snow and went out.

The old-timer on Sulphur Creek was right, he thought in the moment of controlled despair that ensued: after fifty below, a man should travel with a partner. He beat his hands, but failed in exciting any sensation. Suddenly he bared both hands, removing the mittens with his teeth. He caught the whole bunch between the heels of his hands. His arm-muscles not being frozen enabled him to press the hand-heels tightly against the matches. Then he scratched the bunch along his leg. It flared into flame, seventy sulphur matches at once! There was no wind to blow them out. He kept his head to one side to escape the strangling fumes, and held the blazing bunch to the birch-bark. As he so held it, he became aware of sensation in his hand. His flesh was burning. He could smell it. Deep down below the surface he could feel it. The sensation developed into pain that grew acute. And still he endured it, holding the flame of the matches clumsily to the bark that would not light readily because his own burning hands were in the way, absorbing most of the flame.

At last, when he could endure no more, he jerked his hands apart. The blazing matches fell sizzling into the snow, but the birch-bark was alight. He began laying dry grasses and the tiniest twigs on the flame. He could not pick and choose, for he had to lift the fuel between the heels of his hands. Small pieces of rotten wood and green moss clung to the twigs, and he bit them off as well as he could with his teeth. He cherished the flame carefully and awkwardly. It meant life, and it must not perish. The withdrawal of blood from the surface of his body now made him begin to shiver, and he grew more awkward. A large piece of green moss fell squarely on the little fire. He tried to poke it out with his fingers, but his shivering frame made him poke too far, and he disrupted the nucleus of the little fire, the burning grasses and tiny twigs separating and scattering. He tried to poke them together again, but in spite of the tenseness of the effort, his shivering got away with him, and the twigs were hopelessly scattered. Each twig gushed a puff of smoke and went out. The fire-provider had failed. As he looked apathetically about him, his eyes chanced on the dog, sitting across the ruins of the fire from him, in the snow, making restless, hunching movements, slightly lifting one forefoot and then the other, shifting its weight back and forth on them with wistful eagerness.

The sight of the dog put a wild idea into his head. He remembered the tale of the man, caught in a blizzard, who killed a steer and crawled inside the carcass, and so was saved. He would kill the dog and bury his hands in the warm body until the numbness went out of them. Then he could build another fire. He spoke to the dog, calling it to him; but in his voice was a strange note of fear that frightened the animal, who had never known the man to speak in such way before. Something was the

matter, and its suspicious nature sensed danger — it knew not what danger, but somewhere, somehow, in its brain arose an apprehension of the man. It flattened its ears down at the sound of the man's voice, and its restless, hunching movements and the liftings and shiftings of its forefeet became more pronounced; but it would not come to the man. He got on his hands and knees and crawled toward the dog. This unusual posture again excited suspicion, and the animal sidled mincingly away.

The man sat up in the snow for a moment and struggled for calmness. Then he pulled on his mittens, by means of his teeth, and got upon his feet. He glanced down at first in order to assure himself that he was really standing up, for the absence of sensation in his feet left him unrelated to the earth. His erect position in itself started to drive the webs of suspicion from the dog's mind; and when he spoke peremptorily, with the sound of whip-lashes in his voice, the dog rendered its customary allegiance and came to him. As it came within reaching distance, the man lost his control. His arms flashed out to the dog, and he experienced genuine surprise when he discovered that his hands could not clutch, that there was neither bend nor feeling in the fingers. He had forgotten for the moment that they were frozen and that they were freezing more and more. All this happened quickly, and before the animal could get away, he encircled its body with his arms. He sat down in the snow, and in this fashion held the dog, while it snarled and whined and struggled.

But it was all he could do, hold its body encircled in his arms and sit there. He realized that he could not kill the dog. There was no way to do it. With his helpless hands he could neither draw nor hold his sheath-knife nor throttle the animal. He released it, and it plunged wildly away, with tail between its legs, and still snarling. It halted forty feet away and surveyed him curiously, with ears sharply pricked forward. The man looked down at his hands in order to locate them, and found them hanging on the ends of his arms. It struck him as curious that one should have to use his eyes in order to find out where his hands were. He began threshing his arms back and forth, beating the mittened hands against his sides. He did this for five minutes, violently, and his heart pumped enough blood up to the surface to put a stop to his shivering. But no sensation was aroused in the hands. He had an impression that they hung like weights at the ends of his arms, but when he tried to run the impression down, he could not find it.

A certain fear of death, dull and oppressive, came to him. This fear quickly became poignant as he realized that it was no longer a mere matter of freezing his fingers and toes, or of losing his hands and feet, but that it was a matter of life and death with the chances against him. This threw him into a panic, and he turned and ran up the creek-bed along the old, dim trail. The dog joined in behind and kept up with him. He ran blindly, without intention, in fear such as he had never known in his life. Slowly, as he ploughed and floundered through the snow, he began to see things again, —the banks of the creek, the old timber-jams, the leafless aspens, and the sky. The running made him feel better. He did not shiver. Maybe, if he ran on, his feet would thaw out; and, anyway, if he ran far enough, he would reach camp and the boys. Without doubt he would lose some fingers and toes and some of his face; but the boys would take care of him, and save the rest of him when he got there. And at the same time there was another thought in his mind that said he would never get to the camp and the boys; that it was too many miles away, that the freezing had too great a start on him, and that he would soon be stiff and dead. This thought he kept in the background and refused to consider. Sometimes it pushed itself forward and demanded to be heard, but he thrust it back and strove to think of other things.

It struck him as curious that he could run at all on feet so frozen that he could not feel them when they struck the earth and took the weight of his body. He seemed to himself to skim along above the surface, and to have no connection with the earth. Somewhere he had once seen a winged Mercury, and he wondered if Mercury felt as he felt when skimming over the earth.

His theory of running until he reached camp and the boys had one flaw in it: he lacked the endurance. Several times he stumbled, and finally he tottered, crumpled up, and fell. When he tried to rise, he failed. He must sit and rest, he decided, and next time he would merely walk and keep on going. As he sat and regained his breath, he noted that he was feeling quite warm and comfortable. He was not shivering, and it even seemed that a warm glow had come to his chest and trunk. And yet, when he touched his nose or cheeks, there was no sensation. Running would not thaw them out. Nor would it thaw out his hands and feet. Then the thought came to him that the frozen portions of his body must be extending. He tried to keep this thought down, to forget it, to think of something else; he was aware of the panicky feeling that it caused, and he was afraid of the panic. But the thought asserted itself, and persisted, until it produced a vision of his body totally frozen. This was too much, and he made another wild run along the trail. Once he slowed down to a walk, but the thought of the freezing extending itself made him run again.

And all the time the dog ran with him, at his heels. When he fell down a second time, it curled its tail over its forefeet and sat in front of him, facing him, curiously eager and intent. The warmth and security of the animal angered him, and he cursed it till it flattened down its ears appealingly. This time the shivering came more quickly upon the man. He was losing in his battle with the frost. It was creeping into his body from all sides. The thought of it drove him on, but he ran no more than a hundred feet, when he staggered and pitched headlong. It was his last panic. When he had recovered his breath and control, he sat up and entertained in his mind the conception of meeting death with dignity. However, the conception did not come to him in such terms. His idea of it was that he had been making a fool of himself, running around like a chicken with its head cut off – such was the simile that occurred to him. Well, he was bound to freeze anyway, and he might as well take it decently. With this new-found peace of mind came the first glimmerings of drowsiness. A good idea, he thought, to sleep off to death. It was like taking an anaesthetic. Freezing was not so bad as people thought. There were lots worse ways to die.

He pictured the boys finding his body next day. Suddenly he found himself with them, coming along the trail and looking for himself. And, still with them, he came around a turn in the trail and found himself lying in the snow. He did not belong with himself any more, for even then he was out of himself, standing with the boys and looking at himself in the snow. It certainly was cold, was his thought. When he got back to the States he could tell the folks what real cold was. He drifted on from this to a vision of the old-timer on Sulphur Creek. He could see him quite clearly, warm and comfortable, and smoking a pipe.

"You were right, old hoss; you were right," the man mumbled to the old-timer of Sulphur Creek.

Then the man drowsed off into what seemed to him the most comfortable and satisfying sleep he had ever known. The dog sat facing him and waiting. The brief day drew to a close in a long, slow twilight. There were no signs of a fire to be made, and, besides, never in the dog's experience had it known a man to sit like that in the snow and make no fire. As the twilight drew on, its eager yearning for the fire mastered it, and with a great lifting and shifting of forefeet, it whined softly, then flattened its ears down in anticipation of being chidden by the man. But the man remained silent. Later, the dog whined loudly. And still later it crept close to the man and caught the scent of death. This made the animal bristle and back away. A little longer it delayed, howling under the stars that leaped and danced and shone brightly in the cold sky. Then it turned and trotted up the trail in the direction of the camp it knew, where were the other food-providers and fire-providers.

ANARCHISTS AT HOME

*Born in 1893, **Stewart H. Holbrook** was raised in Vermont, but moved to the Pacific Coast after serving in the Army in France during World War I. During a long stint as a lumberjack, he began to establish himself as a freelance journalist, initially working on logging industry periodicals before moving on to bigger newspapers like the* Oregonian. *His passion was the Pacific Northwest, and for forty years he explored its nooks and crannies, producing a raft of articles on its less orthodox characters and every strange or striking historical incident he could unearth. His work was always direct and unpretentious, laced with sharp observations and dry wit, and by the mid-1930s he had become a well-known figure across the region, lauded in equal measure by loggers and businessmen alike. There is a gung-ho feel to much of his prodigious output, but his sympathy with and obvious liking for the less orthodox Americans who defined much of the region's early character more than compensates. It's*

also to Holbrook's credit that he refused to vilify the left-wing radicals who played an important role in the history of the Northwest. The following extract was written in 1946; Holbrook died in 1964.

One of the great glories of the Puget Sound country is the serene tide-washed community of Home [near the southern tip of the Kitsap Peninsula]. This community is fading now with a graceful nostalgic air, but it still retains many of the spiritual vestiges of what was once America's sole anarchist colony – in its heyday one of the most celebrated or notorious spots in the United States. Home is never mentioned by the booster organizations, and even the evangelical churches have given it up as a Sodom fit only for the fires of the Pit.

The place lies on the pretty shores of Joe's Bay, an arm of the Sound, and is approximately 2,530 miles (as few if any crows have flown it) west of Roxbury, Massachusetts, site of Brook Farm, the short-lived and tremendously unsuccessful attempt of the Yankees to found a colony in the manner laid down by M. Fourier. There is almost no intellectual connection between the two communities, and although I know of Brook Farm only by the vast literature that has been coming out about it for a hundred years past, I have spent considerable time at Home, right in the bosom of anarchist families, and I should rather have lived there than at Brook Farm. I also think it long past time that Home Colony was called to the attention of the many Americans who never heard of it.

I doubt that the Brook Farmers had a great deal of enjoyment. There was constant bickering over the division of tasks, there was much worry over getting the substantial contributions of cash needed to support the fancy play-farmers, and the nearest thing to excitement was old Bronson Alcott's heaving in for a free meal and delivering himself of a few Orphic Sayings. It was all very daring, and quite dull. Read the Brook Farmers' own accounts, if you doubt me.

Life at Home Colony was assuredly never dull. Never. Home accepted no contributions or advice from anybody. It did not labor under the many inhibitions that plagued the Brook Farmers. In fact, Home had no inhibitions whatever, and several times it made headlines that would have shocked and stunned the pale maidens of both sexes who inhabited Brook Farm. To the good people of Tacoma and Seattle who remember it, Home was and largely is a place of smoking bombs of the Johann Most variety, and of unspeakable orgies unequalled since the times of Messalina. Yet for half a century it has successfully fended attacks by incendiary and murderous mobs, by the courts, by private detectives, Secret Service agents, and United States marshals. Jay Fox, so far as I know the sole surviving anarchist in the United States, who has lived at Home for forty years, says it has been a sort of Wild West Brook Farm, with overtones of Oneida Community and Nauvoo.

Home grew out of the failure of a socialist community called Glennis, in 1896. Fed up with the internal battles which seem to bedevil all socialist communities and also with the lazy parasites who always attach themselves to "cooperative commonwealths" three disillusioned members of Glennis, situated near Tacoma, built a boat with their own hands and struck out to cruise Puget Sound, seeking a likely spot to pitch an out-and-out anarchist paradise. These founding fathers were George Allen, University of Toronto, class of '85, O.A. Verity and F.F. Odell. They soon found a primeval spot that looked pretty good – and still does. Towering Douglas fir grew down to the beach. Ducks swarmed in the bay. Clams held conventions there. Bees worked on the fireweed. No man lived here, or for miles. There were no roads. Twenty-six acres could be had from a bloated capitalist for $2.50 an acre.

The three men mustered a total of five dollars to make a down payment. Then Allen went to teaching school, while the others worked at anything handy to earn money for the move. In the spring of 1897 the Allen, Verity and Odell families, wives and children, voyaged to Joe's Bay and began pioneering. They tore into the gigantic trees with ax and saw, and quickly made cabins in which to live until they could build frame houses. They also formed the Compact, which was called the Mutual Home Colony Association.

There was nothing of socialism in this group. The Association was as near pure anarchism as the laws of the land would permit, and its sole reason for being was "to obtain land and to promote better social and moral conditions." It did not even attempt to define anarchism, although Founders, Allen, Verity and Odell considered anarchism – no matter what Bakunin or Kropotkin or Josiah Warren said – as a society so imbued with decency and honesty that no laws were required to regulate its members.

Each member paid into the Association a sum equal to the cost of the land he or she was to occupy, not more than two acres to a member. The land remained the property of the Association, but the member could occupy it indefinitely simply by paying such taxes as were imposed by the Enemy, which in this case was the State of Washington in the style and form of Pierce County. Any improvements, such as barns and houses, were personal property and could be sold or mortgaged.

Like the thoroughgoing fanatics they were, the Home colonists, as soon as they got shelter over their heads, started a paper, the *New Era*, which from the start intimated that the Association has no interest whatever in the personal lives of its members. "The love principle of our being," said an early hand-set editorial, "is a natural one, and to deny it expression is to deny nature." This was clear enough, and the implied sanction of casual relationships between men and women was in time to bring an assortment of cranks, malcontents and plain Don Juans. But the early settlers were too busy with recalcitrant stumps to worry very much about the love principle in their being, for if there is anything to hold old Adam in bounds it is the science and art of removing stumps of *Pseudotsuga taxifolia*. Before their homes were finished, the busy colonists had whacked up Liberty Hall, a sort of meeting place and school, where Founder Allen was the first teacher.

Within six months half a dozen new families had been added to the original three, and along came Charles Govan, a wandering printer, who proposed a new paper which should take the colony's message to the far corners of the earth where mankind still lived either in savagery or, worse, under imposition of State and Capital. Govan also induced James F. Morton to leave the staff of *Free Society*, a noted anarchist sheet of San Francisco, and come to Home. Morton (Harvard, 1892, and Phi Beta Kappa) was later to become a Single Taxer, but he was pure anarchist when he arrived at Home, and there he and Govan brought out the new paper under a masthead that was sheer genius: *Discontent, Mother of Progress*.

This paper was presently to be notorious from one end of the country to the other, but its early issues were read mostly by other radical editors and by persons who were predisposed to what *Discontent* said was anarchism anyway. There appears, from a close reading of the yellowing files, to have been more about sex in *Discontent* than about economics. A leading article dealt with "The Rights of Woman in Sexual Relations" which, it appeared, were many and interesting. Another piece asked "Is 'Sin' forgivable?" It seemed that it was. The early issues also looked at Home with a realistic eye, stating that hard work was necessary to clear the thickly timbered land, and warning intending settlers to make inquiries before coming, lest they be disappointed. There was no balm in the anarchist Gilead, simply hard work and FREEDOM (to use their typographical emphasis). *Discontent* went on to say there was nothing of socialist cooperation about Home. Everything was on a purely voluntary basis. These ex-socialists were determined they should be free of the easy-riders who had hamstrung and wrecked Glennis and early all other cooperative communities.

It wasn't long before *Discontent*, hand-set and hand-printed among the stumps that were still smoking, began to attract attention. Emma Goldman went to Home to lecture in Liberty Hall in June of 1899. New families arrived from San Francisco, from Virginia, from Michigan. A tract of sixty-four acres adjoining the original colony was made available at reasonable rates. A Tacoma boat line put Joe's Bay on its list of ports of call. The colonists, proud as sin, built a floating wharf and a neat shelter.

From Portland, Oregon, where they had got into trouble editing the *Firebrand*, which the courts held to be "obscene and otherwise unmailable," came Henry Addis and Abner J. Pope. A venerable man, bearded like a prophet of old, Pope called himself a Quaker-Spiritualist-Anarchist, which was quite an order but which he took easily in stride. He was soon lecturing in Liberty Hall. Addis contributed to *Discontent* a series of articles in which he came out flat-footedly for Free Love, with uppercase letters. Although the Addis articles were a bit later to get the colony into a dreadful stew, the period of 1897–1900 was on the whole active and peaceful, a very idyll of community pioneering in the backwoods. The population rose to one hundred. Deer flitted in and out of the clearings. Roosters greeted the dawn

from the interminable stumps. Communist bees gathered honey for the anarchists. The hens laid famously.

Founder Allen came to have thirty pupils in his school, and he sat them down on a wind-felled fir and taught them that natural laws were the only laws worth minding. He gave them Mill, Huxley, Darwin, Josiah Warren and those parts of Henry Thoreau dealing with the necessity for civil disobedience. Four who attended Allen's school have said that truancy was never known.

Presently there began a second trek of new settlers, several coming from foreign parts. Among them was Lewis Haiman, a Jewish barber from Lithuania, who married an American gentile, took two acres at Home and built a house. He also opened a shop which, he said in an announcement, he hoped would keep Homeites from looking like the cartoon conceptions of anarchists. Dances, masquerades and picnics were a part of the social life. Lectures were its meat and drink. Liberty Hall was open to all who had something to say, or only thought they did – the subject mattering not. Reconverted socialists arrived from the defunct Ruskin Colony in Tennessee, and from the Cooperative Brotherhood Colony at Burley, Washington. The Home Colony Library was organized. *Discontent*'s announcement columns began to fill up with notices of periodicals named *Freedom* (London), *Free Society* (San Francisco), and the Boston *Investigator*, founded by the celebrated Abner Kneeland, whose trial Henry S. Commager has considered in an interesting historical monograph.

II

The first shadow to fall on the industrious and intellectual pioneering colony of Home was an occurrence in far-away Buffalo, New York, where on September 6, 1901, President William McKinley fell under a bullet fired by a witless youth, Leon Czolgosz, who said he was an anarchist. A wave of hysteria swept the nation. Socialist speakers and halls were set upon by mobs. Any soapboxer on the curb was labeled "anarchist" and was either mobbed or arrested. And then, somebody in Tacoma, Washington, recalled that only twenty miles away was a whole pack of wild men and women, a veritable nest of vipers, who had never denied being anarchists.

McKinley died on September 14. On that day an anti-anarchist meeting was held in Tacoma, and a Loyal League formed by members of the Grand Army of the Republic. They chartered a steamboat, collected firearms and incendiary materials and prepared, three hundred strong, to invade Home and put it to the torch, with murder as a possible incidental.

Not everybody in Tacoma lost his head. Ed Lorenz, skipper of a steamboat which called at Home, knew the colonists there to be sober and industrious people. He went to the mob's leaders and said so eloquently. So did the Rev. J.F. Doescher, pastor of the German Evangelical Church in Tacoma, who had visited Home and had found the people, in spite of their agnosticism, which he deplored, to be honest and kindly folk. These two heroic men stopped what might well have been a forerunner of the melancholy tragedies perpetrated in later years in near-by Everett and Centralia.

Thus was Home saved surely from the torch. But its troubles were just beginning. Someone had sent copies of *Discontent* to Federal authorities and demanded it be barred from the mails. Post office experts in belles-lettres looked over the Home paper and were horrified to discover that it had come out whole hog against marriage, terming it "the lowest form of prostitution" and adding, for good measure, that "free mating in cities of the United States is on the increase and the ecclesiastics cannot seem to halt it." There was even a trace of gloating in the article, which was one of those contributed by Henry Addis, who was not even a member of the Home Colony.

So, packing a gun on each hip and wondering what size of bombs he should have to dodge, a United States marshal went over to Home to arrest *Discontent*'s editors and contributors. Hearing that the Law was on the way, the colonists met him at the Home wharf with a delegation of welcome, including pretty little flower girls, took him to one of the homes for an excellent anarchist supper, then made him the guest of honor at a whopping big dance in Liberty Hall. The astonished officer put away his guns and thoroughly enjoyed himself, remaining overnight. In the morning he returned to Tacoma with his prisoners, and reported that he had never met more agreeable people than in Home, or had a better time.

The *Discontent*'s staff stood trial and were freed by an understanding judge, who ordered the jury to sign a directed verdict of acquittal. It was a clear victory for Home Colony, but a year later it lost its post office, by order from Washington, and Home folks have since, and to this day, had to get their mail at Lakebay, two miles distant. Another blow quickly followed the loss of the post office: *Discontent*, which Federal authorities held to have been the mother of altogether too much progress, was forbidden by the mails.

The rumpus had another and more cheerful result. It called the national attention to Home, putting it briefly if luridly on the front pages of big-city newspapers, and Home went into a boom. Henry Dadisman, well-to-do farmer, arrived and bought two hundred acres next to the Association land, which he threw open to settlers at cost. A Minnesota widow came, built a fine farmhouse, and settled down. Families came from Indiana, and during the 1902–1907 period, more Russian Jews arrived to take up colony or Dadisman land. A new Liberty Hall, much larger than the first, was built; and a co-op store, still flourishing, was opened.

When *Discontent* was barred from the mails, Editor Morton merely changed the masthead to read the *Demonstrator*, and kept the editorial policy intact. In the light of Home's new notoriety there started a flow and ebb of eccentrics that has made the place one of the most interesting spots on all Puget Sound. This period at Home, indeed, deserves the serious attention of some scholar who is interested in the manner in which old and new radical theories permeated the utmost reaches of the United States at the beginning of this century. Here was a tiny community, set in the deep woods in the northwestern corner of the Republic, as remote from the intellectual centers as possible, and reached by an awkward boat trip, or by mere mud trails. Yet Home's Liberty Hall shook and shimmered with virtually every intellectual breeze one could name, while the colonists listened to and often argued with a continuous congress of cranks and prophets.

III

From Chicago to Home came somewhat moth-eaten agents for Koreshanity, the otherwise forgotten philosophy-religion founded in 1886 by Dr. Cyrus R. Teed, to reveal the True Faith to Homeites and incidentally, as part of their belief, to prove that the earth is a hollow ball and that we live on its inside, the quickest way to China being straight up into what we call the atmosphere.

Then came Professor Thompson, no first name, perhaps the mogul of all individualists, who walked down the Home gangplank one afternoon displaying a magnificent beard but the dress and other garments of a woman. Professor Thompson was male enough; brawny and tough, he immediately went to work chopping wood. That night he gave a rousing lecture on the need, if the world were to make any progress, for all to wear women's clothing. It was more aesthetic and comfortable, he maintained.

From California came the then celebrated Lois Waisbrooker, author of a strange book entitled *My Century Plant*, a work that revealed how to free the world from "the disease of Sex". She liked Home, took an acre, and settled down in company with Mattie D. Penhallow, a noted radical of the day, to get out a very odd sheet called *Clothed with the Sun*. I regret much that I have failed to find a copy of this periodical. Old-timers of Home inform me it was a humdinger, even for anarchists, and reported all of the facts of life in no mealy-mouthed manner. It didn't last long. The post office department took one look at it, and presently a whole delegation of United States marshals swarmed into the colony like locusts and carted off the two maidens, one of whom was indicted, convicted and fined. It was one more case of "unmailable matter."

The place was now rolling high. Home and its odd residents and visitors were good for a story in almost any newspaper and periodical in the country. College professors came to see and write learned pieces. *The Independent*, a national magazine of wide circulation, sent a man to Home, who reported favorably on the place and remarked it was the most sensibly managed of any community attempt he knew. It had 170 adult members. Work was exchanged at the rate of fifteen cents an hour, although no cash exchanged hands. The co-op store was doing well. So were the Home logging operators.

After her conviction in the *Clothed with the Sun* affair, Miss Waisbrooker returned to Home and promptly started getting out another sheet, this time called *Foundation Principles*. I haven't

been able to get the faintest idea what it was about, but Jay Fox, who can be ribald at times, told me he thought it was "the same old subject, Adam and Eve."

Elbert Hubbard, no slouch himself as a community man, made the trip to Home from East Aurora, New York, to stay several days and to lecture nightly in Liberty Hall. Colonists found him heart and soul in sympathy with the colony, and later he spoke good words for it in a characteristically graceful and inaccurate piece in the *Philistine*. Emma Goldman, famous now since McKinley's death, came to Home a second time. Moses Harmon, the old-time crusader for almost any unpopular cause, and editor of *Lucifer*, which advocated the use of contraceptives, came to recuperate at Home from his several incarcerations in the prisons of Illinois and Kansas.

What a yeasting it was, the boiling and bubbling at Home! Spiritualists came, and one remained to set up in business. A school in Esperanto was opened. Exponents of various food fads came and went, among them one Dr Hazsard, an eloquent female who spoke to such effect that John Buchi, Swiss butcher at Home, wished "a Got damn on all der wegitarians." Local enthusiasts started a Class in Hatha-Yoga, another in straight theosophy. Russellites came to report the imminent end of things, which was all right with the anarchists. Pantheists, Freethinkers of all shades, Monists, Mormon missionaries – they all came, and Home gave them all a hearing. One Homeite, Laura Wood, set up housekeeping in an Indian wigwam; another, Joe Kapella, went to live in a tree for several months. It all must have been quite wonderful. Brook Farm had nothing like it.

IV

The great activity at Home Colony did not go unnoticed around the Sound, and stories of horrible sex orgies became current and popular with orthodox Washingtonians. Much of the talk stemmed from articles in the uninhibited *Demonstrator*, as untrammeled as a yearling Durham bull put to pasture in May. It seldom appeared without a few remarks on something very similar to free love. The colony itself never held any canons regarding the desirability or undesirability of free love. That there were domestic arrangements in certain homes of Home which had not received the benefit of either church or state was of common knowledge, but they were neither sanctioned nor condemned.

Meanwhile the Philistines were gathering their forces. Their next attack occurred in 1910, and is still referred to as the Great Nude Bathing Case. The colony had by then split into two factions over the subject of landholding. This was settled, amicably on the whole, and each member was given a deed to his two acres. The Association was dissolved, although Liberty Hall and the co-op store were continued as community enterprises. The store, indeed, may have been a factor in attracting to the colony a number of farmers who liked the low prices at the Home co-op but had no sympathy for Home's live-and-let-live policy. In any case, it was from these latecomers that a complaint came to the county authority naming names and charging that certain Home anarchists were bathing in the nude, men and women together.

The charges were true enough. The simple Russians who had come to Home many years before brought their samovars with them, and also their custom of nude bathing. It had been going on at Home for a decade, without scandal. But now, because of the Philistines, one man and four women were arrested and found guilty on charges of indecent exposure. The trials made front page news in almost all sections of the country. Home was again in the papers.

At this time Home had a new paper, the *Agitator*, edited by the aforementioned Jay Fox, a radical who dated back to the Haymarket Bomb in Chicago. Fox had long been an agitator and organiser of left wing labor groups. He still carried in one shoulder a bullet that had been fired in the McCormick Harvester strike in Chicago in 1886, and he had been active in the I.W.W. and in the rambunctious shingle-weaver's union in the Northwest woods. He was also an able journalist, and now he came out with a sizzling editorial, "The Nudes and the Prudes," in which he more than suggested that all lovers of liberty should ostracize the persons who had brought the charges of indecent exposure. Editor Fox was hauled off to jail and charged with "encouraging or advocating disrespect for law". The prosecution naturally brought "anarchy" into the case and played up Home's reputation in a successful effort to convict Fox, who was sentenced to two months in Pierce County Jail. On appeal, the state supreme court upheld the verdict.

Now the wobblies, the I.W.W., and other radical groups the country over took up the case and made it into a national *cause célébre* in all liberal circles. The Free Speech League, forerunner of the Civil Liberties Union and headed by such well known persons as Leonard Abbott, Brand Whitlock and Lincoln Steffens, joined the battle. Dances and rallies for the "Jay Fox Free Speech Fight" were held from Boston to Portland, Oregon, and money raised for an appeal to the United States Supreme Court, which found the verdict proper. Fox gave himself up and went to jail for six weeks. Then he was given an unconditional pardon by Governor Lister of Washington. He returned to Home and resumed publishing the *Agitator*.

Next came the McNamara case. One night in October of 1910, the building of the *Los Angeles Times* was wrecked by an explosion that took twenty-one lives and was followed by the sensational confessions of the two McNamara brothers. Also implicated was one David Caplan, and a vast man hunt was set in motion to find him. Presently at Home there appeared a tall, suave and handsome book agent who was peddling one of those sets of home encyclopedias (170,000 pages, beautifully illustrated, fine bindings) without which no home, not even an anarchist's home, could be said to be complete. The tall agent circulated around Home for several days. Mrs Lewis Haiman recalls that when she went to the door, and kept the man safely on the outside, he appeared to be far more interested in peering over her shoulder to see who was inside, than in selling his array of the world's knowledge. He was, of course, the famous William J. Burns, the detective, looking for the missing Caplan. Fugitive Caplan was taken later, though not at Home, and given ten years. In Burns's memoirs, published not long before his death in 1932, the detective devotes several pages to his days as a book agent in Home.

During World War I, Home was infested by marshals and secret agents of the United States government, some with false whiskers, some plain, but all of Home's citizens managed to keep out of their clutches. In the more recent war, so quiet had Home been for two decades, it was never under suspicion.

Today Home is, as it must always have been, a charming place in which to live. The last of the Founding Fathers, George Allen, died in 1944, well into his eighties. Dead, too, is Tom Geeves, the patriarch of Home, as whiskered as any legendary Nihilist, who had wandered ashore from a British ship, circa 1910, and for no doctrinaire reasons, but simply because he liked the place, had taken abode in an old shack at Home. There he lived to be almost one hundred and nine years of age.

The younger generation of Home, for the most part university graduates, have gone away and married. Many are in California where each year a Home picnic draws up to a hundred old Homeites and their children.

Jay Fox, perhaps the last of the veritable anarchists, genial and mellow at seventy-seven, lives on in Home and is writing his memoirs, while his wife, Cora, spends her talented spare time hand-painting and glazing chinaware of such beauty that it is sought after by the wives and daughters of Seattle and Tacoma capitalists.

The outlander visiting Home is sure to find it pleasant, both physically and socially. The Home Colony tradition is still strong. These are well-read people. When you come across two-acre farmers conversant with Mill and Bentham and Marx and Dewey and Emerson and Thoreau, as well as with poultry feed and beehives, you know you are in no orthodox rural community. There are Homeites today who teach art and music. There is much professional interest in and practice of crafts, especially of weaving. Bees, hens and ferns are the chief sources of agricultural income.

Over all is a feeling, not of revolution, but rather of a lack of interest in political movements. It would not be fair, however, to include Jay Fox in this placidity. The fires of Revolution still burn in the old anarchist, perhaps the last of his kind, and he is happy when William Z. Foster, more in direct touch with the world, comes to visit him, as he does occasionally, and tells him how goes the battle with the minions of Capital.

"*Anarchists at Home*" by Stewart Holbrook is reprinted from *Wildmen, Wobblies and Whistle Punks: Stewart Holbrook's Lowbrow Northwest*, edited by Brian Booth and published by Oregon State University Press (1992). Used by permission of Sibyl Holbrook.

TOBIAS WOLFF

*Born in Alabama, **Tobias Wolff** spent most of his early life in Washington State. Although primarily a fiction writer, he is best known for his two memoirs,* This Boy's Life *and* In Pharaoh's Army, *which cover respectively his childhood in 1950s Washington and later experiences in Vietnam. Shattered illusions and personal loss are the consistent themes in Wolff's work, and his stories are rich in sharply drawn characters. He has published several collections of short stories, and the intense short novel* The Barracks Thief, *and now teaches at Syracuse University, New York.*

PASSENGERS

Glen left Depoe Bay a couple of hours before sunup to beat the traffic and found himself in a heavy fog; he had to lean forward and keep the windshield wipers going to see the road at all. Before long the constant effort and the lulling rhythm of the wipers made him drowsy, and he pulled into a gas station to throw some water in his face and buy coffee.

He was topping off the tank, listening to the invisible waves growl on the beach across the road, when a girl came out of the station and began to wash the windshield. She had streaked hair and wore knee-length, high-heeled boots over her blue jeans. Glen could not see her face clearly.

"Lousy morning for a drive," she said, leaning over the hood. Her blue jeans had studs poking through in different patterns and when she moved they blinked in the light of the sputtering yellow tubes overhead. She threw the squeegee into a bucket and asked Glen what kind of mileage he got.

He tried to remember what Martin had told him. "Around twenty-five per," he said.

She looked the car up and down as if she were thinking of buying it from him.

Glen held out Martin's credit card but the girl laughed and said she didn't work there.

"Actually," she said, "I was kind of wondering which way you were headed."

"North," Glen said. "Seattle."

"Hey," she said. "What a coincidence. I mean that's where I'm going, too."

Glen nodded but he didn't say anything. He had promised not to pick up any hitchhikers; Martin said it was dangerous and socially irresponsible, like feeding stray cats. Also Glen was a little browned off about the way the girl had come up to him all buddy-buddy, when really she just wanted something.

"Forget it," she said. "Drive alone if you want. It's your car, right?" She smiled and went back into the station office.

After Glen paid the attendant he thought things over. The girl was not dangerous — he could tell by how tight her jeans were that she wasn't carrying a gun. And if he had someone to talk to there wouldn't be any chance of dozing off.

The girl did not seem particularly surprised or particularly happy that Glen had changed his mind. "Okay," she said, "just a sec." She stowed her bags in the trunk, a guitar case and a laundry sack tied at the neck like a balloon, then cupped her hands around her mouth and yelled, "Sunshine! Sunshine!" A big hairy dog ran out of nowhere and jumped up on the girl, leaving spots of mud all over the front of her white shirt. She clouted him on the head until he got down and then pushed him into the car. "In back!" she said. He jumped onto the back seat and sat there with his tongue hanging out.

"I'm Bonnie," the girl said when they were on the road. She took a brush out of her purse and pulled it through her hair with a soft ripping noise.

Glen handed her one of his business cards. "I'm Glen," he said.

She held it close to her face and read it out loud. "Rayburn Marine Supply. Are you Rayburn?"

"No. Rayburn is my employer." Glen did not mention that Martin Rayburn was also his room-mate and the owner of the car.

"Oh," she said, "I see, here's your name in the corner. Marine Supply," she repeated. "What are you, some kind of defence contractors?"

"No," Glen said. "We sell boating supplies."

"That's good to hear," Bonnie said. "I don't accept rides from defence contractors."

"Well, I'm not one," Glen said. "Mostly we deal in life jackets, caps, and deck furniture." He named the towns along the coast where he did business, and when he mentioned Eureka, Bonnie slapped her knee.

"All right!" she said. She said that California was her old stomping ground. Bolinas and San Francisco.

When she said San Francisco Glen thought of a high-ceilinged room with sunlight coming in through stained-glass windows, and a lot of naked people on the floor flopping all over each other like seals. "We don't go that far south,"

he said. "Mendocino is as far as we go." He cracked the window a couple of inches; the dog smelled like a sweater just out of mothballs.

"I'm really beat," Bonnie said. "I don't think I slept five straight minutes last night. This truck driver gave me a ride up from Port Orford and I think he must have been a foreigner. Roman fingers, ha ha."

The fog kept rolling in across the road. Headlights from passing cars and trucks were yellow and flat as buttons until they were close; then the beams swept across them and lit up their faces. The dog hung his head over the back of the seat and sighed heavily. Then he put his paws up alongside his ears. The next time Glen looked over at him the dog was hanging by its belly, half in front and half in back. Glen told Bonnie that he liked dogs but considered it unsafe to have one in the front seat. He told her that he'd read a story in the paper where a dog jumped onto an accelerator and ran a whole family off a cliff.

She put her hand over the dog's muzzle and shoved hard. He tumbled into the back seat and began noisily to clean himself. "If everybody got killed," Bonnie said, "how did they find out what happened?"

"I forget," Glen said.

"Maybe the dog confessed," Bonnie said. "No kidding, I've seen worse evidence than that hold up in court. This girlfriend of mine, the one I'm going to stay with in Seattle, she got a year's probation for soliciting and you know what for? For smiling at a guy in a grocery store. It's a hell of a life, Glen. What's that thing you're squeezing, anyway?"

"A tennis ball."

"What do you do that for?"

"Just a habit," Glen said, thinking that it would not be productive to discuss with Bonnie his performance at golf. Being left-handed, he had a tendency to pull his swing and Martin had suggested using the tennis ball to build up his right forearm.

"This is the first time I've ever seen anyone squeeze a tennis ball," Bonnie said. "It beats me how you ever picked up a habit like that."

The dog was still cleaning himself. It sounded awful. Glen switched on the tape deck and turned it up loud.

"Some station!" Bonnie said. "That's the first time I've heard 101 Strings playing '76 Trombones'."

Glen told her that it was a tape, not the radio, and that the song was "Oklahoma!" All of Martin's tapes were instrumental — he hated vocals — but it just so happened that Glen had a tape of his own in the glove compartment, a Peter Paul and Mary. He said nothing to Bonnie about it because he didn't like her tone.

"I'm going to catch some zees," she said after a time. "If Sunshine acts cute just smack him in the face. It's the only thing he understands. I got him from a cop." She rolled up her denim jacket and propped it under her head. "Wake me up," she said, "if you see anything interesting or unusual."

The sun came up, a milky presence at Glen's right shoulder, whitening the fog but not breaking through it. Glen began to notice a rushing sound like water falling hard on pavement and realized that the road had filled up with cars. Their headlights were bleached and wan. All the drivers, including Glen, changed lanes constantly.

Glen put on "Exodus" by Ferrante and Teicher, Martin's favourite. Martin had seen the movie four times. He thought it was the greatest movie ever made because it showed what you could do if you had the will. Once in a while Martin would sit in the living room by himself with a bottle of whiskey and get falling-down drunk. When he was halfway there he would yell Glen's name until Glen came downstairs and sat with him. Then Martin would lecture him on various subjects. He often repeated himself, and one of his favourite topics was the Jewish people, which was what he called the Jews who died in the camps. He made a distinction between them and the Israelis. This was part of his theory.

According to Martin the Jewish people had done the Israelis a favour by dying out; if they had lived they would have weakened the gene pool and the Israelis would not have had the strength or the will to take all that land away from the Arabs and keep it.

One night he asked whether Glen had noticed anything that he, Martin, had in common with the Israelis. Glen admitted that he had missed the connection. The Israelis had been in exile for a long time, Martin said; he himself, while in the Navy, had visited over thirty ports of call and lived at different times in seven of the United States before coming home to Seattle. The Israelis had taken a barren land and made it fruitful; Martin had taken over a failing company and made it turn a profit again. The Israelis defeated all their enemies and Martin was annihilating his competition. The key, Martin said, was in the corporate gene pool. You had to keep cleaning out the dead-wood and bringing in new blood. Martin named the deadwood who would soon be cleaned out, and Glen was surprised; he had supposed a few of the people to be, like himself, new blood.

The fog held. The ocean spray gave it a sheen, a pearly colour. Big drops of water rolled up the windshield, speckling the grey light inside the car. Glen saw that Bonnie was not a girl but a woman. She had wrinkles across her brow and in the corners of her mouth and eyes, and the streaks in her hair were real streaks — not one of these fashions as he'd first thought. In the light her skin showed its age like a coat of dust. She was old, not old old, but old; older than him. Glen felt himself relax, and realized that for a moment there he had been interested in her. He squinted into the fog and drove on with the sensation of falling through a cloud. Behind Glen the dog stirred and yelped in his dreams.

Bonnie woke up outside Olympia. "I'm hungry," she said, "let's score some pancakes."

Glen stopped at a Denny's. While the waitress went for their food. Bonnie told Glen about a girlfriend of hers, not the one in Seattle but another one, who had known the original Denny. Denny, according to her girlfriend, was mighty weird. He had made a proposition. He would set Bonnie's girlfriend up with a place of her own, a car, clothes, the works; he wanted only one thing in return. "Guess what," Bonnie said.

"I give up," Glen said.

"All right," Bonnie said, "you'd never guess it anyway." The proposition, she explained, had this price tag: her girlfriend had to invite different men over for dinner, one man at a time, at least three days a week. The restaurateur didn't care what happened after the meal, had no interest in this respect either as participant or observer. All he wanted was to sit under the table while they ate, concealed by a floor-length tablecloth.

Glen said that there had to be more to it than that.

"No sir," Bonnie said. "That was the whole proposition."

"Did she do it?" Glen asked.

Bonnie shook her head. "She already had a boyfriend, she didn't need some old fart living under her table."

"I still don't get it," Glen said, "him wanting to do that. What's the point?"

"The point?" Bonnie looked at Glen as if he had said something comical. "Search me," she said.

Bonnie went at her food – a steak, an order of pancakes, a salad and two wedges of lemon meringue pie – and did not speak again until she had eaten everything but the steak, which she wrapped in a place mat and stuck in her purse. "I have to admit," she said, "that was the worst meal I ever ate."

Glen went to the men's room and when he came out again the table was empty. Bonnie waved him over to the door. "I already paid," she said, stepping outside.

Glen followed her across the parking lot. "I was going to have some more coffee," he said.

"Well," she said, "I'll tell you straight. That wouldn't be a good idea right now."

"In other words you didn't pay."

"Not exactly."

"What do you mean, 'not exactly'?"

"I left a tip," she said. "I'm all for the working girl but I can't see paying for garbage like that. They ought to pay us for eating it. It's got cardboard in it, for one thing, not to mention about ten million chemicals."

"What's got cardboard in it?"

"The batter. Uh-oh, Sunshine's had a little accident."

Glen looked into the back seat. There was a big stain on the cover. "Godalmighty," Glen said. The dog looked at him and wagged his tail. Glen turned the car back on to the road; it was too late to go back to the restaurant, he'd never be able to explain. "I noticed," he said, "you didn't leave anything on your plate, considering it was garbage."

"If I hadn't eaten it, they would have thrown it out. They throw out pieces of butter because they're not square. You know how much food they dump every day?"

"They're running a business," Glen said. "They take a risk and they're entitled to the profits."

"I'll tell you," Bonnie said. "Enough to feed the population of San Diego. Here, Sunshine." The dog stood with his paws on the back of the seat while Bonnie shredded the steak and put the pieces in his mouth. When the steak was gone she hit the dog in the face and he sat back down.

Glen was going to ask Bonnie why she wasn't afraid of poisoning Sunshine but he was too angry to do anything but steer the car and squeeze the tennis ball. They could have been arrested back there. He could just see himself calling Martin and saying that he wouldn't be home for dinner because he was in jail for walking a cheque in East Jesus. Unless he could get that seat cleaned up he was going to have to tell Martin about Bonnie, and that wasn't going to be any picnic, either. So much for trying to do favours for people.

"This fog is getting to me," Bonnie said. "It's really boring." She started to say something else, then fell silent again. There was a truck just ahead of them; as they climbed a gentle rise the fog thinned and Glen could make out the logo on the back – WE MOVE FAMILIES NOT JUST FURNITURE – then they descended into the fog again and the truck vanished. "I was in a sandstorm once," Bonnie said, "in Arizona. It was really dangerous but at least it wasn't boring." She pulled a strand of hair in front of her eyes and began picking at the ends. "So," she said, "tell me about yourself."

Glen said there wasn't much to tell.

"What's your wife's name?"

"I'm not married."

"Oh yeah? Somebody like you, I thought for sure you'd be married."

"I'm engaged," Glen said. He often told strangers that. If he met them again he could always say it hadn't worked out. He'd once known a girl who probably would have married him but like Martin said, it didn't make sense to take on freight when you were travelling for speed.

Bonnie said that she had been married for the last two years to a man in Santa Barbara. "I don't mean married in the legal sense," she said. Bonnie said that when you knew someone else's head and they knew yours, that was being married. She had ceased to know his head when he left her for someone else. "He wanted to have kids," Bonnie said, "but he was afraid to with me, because I had dropped acid. He was afraid we would have a werewolf or something because of my chromosomes. I shouldn't have told him."

Glen knew that the man's reason for leaving her had nothing to do with chromosomes. He had left her because she was too old.

"I never should have told him," Bonnie said again. She made a rattling sound in her throat and put her hands up to her face. First her shoulders and then her whole body began jerking from side to side.

"All right," Glen said, "all right." He dropped the tennis ball and began patting her on the back as if she had hiccups.

Sunshine uncoiled from the back seat and came scrambling over Glen's shoulder. He knocked Glen's hand off the steering wheel as he jumped onto his lap, rooting for the ball. The car went into a broadside skid. The road was slick and the tyres did not scream. Bonnie stopped jerking and stared out the window. So did Glen. They watched the fog whipping along the windshield as if they were at a movie. Then the car began to spin. When they came out of it Glen watched the yellow lines shoot away from the hood and realized that they were sliding backwards in the wrong lane of traffic. The car went on this way for a time, then it went into another spin and when it came out it was pointing in the right direction though still in the wrong lane. Not far off Glen could see weak yellow lights approaching, bobbing gently like the running lights of a ship. He took the wheel again and eased the car off the road. Moments later a convoy of logging trucks roared out of the fog, airhorns bawling; the car rocked in the turbulence of their wake.

Sunshine jumped into the back seat and lay there, whimpering. Glen and Bonnie moved into each other's arms. They just held on, saying nothing. Holding Bonnie, and being held by her, was necessary to Glen.

"I thought we were goners," Bonnie said.

"They wouldn't even have found us," Glen said. "Not even our shoes."

"I'm going to change my ways," Bonnie said.

"Me too," Glen said, and though he wasn't sure just what was wrong with his ways, he meant it.

"I feel like I've been given another chance," Bonnie said. "I'm going to pay back the money I owe, and write my mother a letter, even if she is a complete bitch. I'll be nicer to Sunshine. No more shoplifting. No more —" Just then another convoy of trucks went by and though Bonnie

kept on talking Glen could not hear a word. He was thinking they should get started again.

Later, when they were back on the road, Bonnie said that she had a special feeling about Glen because of what they had just gone through. "I don't mean boy-girl feelings," she said. "I mean — do you know what I mean?"

"I know what you mean," Glen said.

"Like there's a bond," she said.

"I know," Glen said. And as a kind of celebration he got out his Peter Paul and Mary and stuck it in the tape deck.

"I don't believe it," Bonnie said. "Is that who I think it is?"

"Peter Paul and Mary," Glen said.

"That's who I thought it was," Bonnie said. "You like that stuff?"

Glen nodded. "Do you?"

"I guess they're all right. When I'm in the mood. What else have you got?"

Glen named the rest of the tapes.

"Jesus," Bonnie said. She decided that what she was really in the mood for was some peace and quiet.

By the time Glen found the address where Bonnie's girlfriend lived, a transients' hotel near Pioneer Square, it had begun to rain. He waited in the car while Bonnie rang the bell. Through the window of the door behind her he saw a narrow ladder of stairs; the rain sliding down the windshield made them appear to be moving upward. A woman stuck her head out the door; she nodded constantly as she talked. When Bonnie came back her hair had separated into ropes. Her ears, large and pink, poked out between strands. She said that her girlfriend was out, that she came and went at all hours.

"Where does she work?" Glen asked. "I could take you there."

"Around," Bonnie said. "You know, here and there." She looked at Glen and then out the window. "I don't want to stay with her," she said, "not really."

Bonnie went on talking like that, personal stuff, and Glen listened to the raindrops plunking off the roof of the car. He thought he should help Bonnie, and he wanted to. Then he imagined bringing Bonnie home to Martin and introducing them; Sunshine having accidents all over the new carpets; the three of them eating dinner while Bonnie talked, interrupting Martin, saying the kinds of things she said.

When Bonnie finished talking, Glen explained to her that he really wanted to help out but that it wasn't possible.

"Sure," Bonnie said, and leaned back against the seat with her eyes closed.

It seemed to Glen that she did not believe him. That was ungrateful of her and he became angry. "It's true," he said.

"Hey," Bonnie said, and touched his arm.

"My room-mate is allergic to dogs."

"Hey," Bonnie said again. "No problem." She got her bags out of the trunk and tied Sunshine's leash to the guitar case, then came around the car to the driver's window. "Well," she said, "I guess this is it."

"Here," Glen said, "in case you want to stay somewhere else." He put a twenty-dollar bill in her hand.

She shook her head and tried to give it back.

"Keep it," he said. "Please."

She stared at him. "Jesus," she said. "Okay, why not? The price is right." She looked up and down the street, then put the bill in her pocket.

"I didn't mean —" Glen said.

"Wait," Bonnie said. "Sunshine! Sunshine!"

Glen looked behind him. Sunshine was running up the street after another dog, pulling Bonnie's guitar case behind him. "Nuts," Bonnie said, and began sprinting up the sidewalk in the rain, cursing loudly. People stopped to watch, and a police car slowed down. Glen hoped that the officers hadn't noticed them together. He turned the corner and looked back. No one was following him.

A few blocks from home Glen stopped at a gas station and tried without success to clean the stain off the seat cover. On the floor of the car he found a lipstick and a clear plastic bag with two marijuana cigarettes inside, which he decided had fallen out of Bonnie's purse during the accident.

Glen knew that the cigarettes were marijuana because the two engineers he'd roomed with before moving in with Martin had smoked it every Friday night. They would pass joints back and forth and comment on the quality, then turn the stereo on full blast and listen with their eyes closed, nodding in time to the music and now and then smiling and saying "Get down!" and "Go for it!" Later on they would strip the refrigerator, giggling as if the food belonged to someone else, then watch TV with the sound off and make up stupid dialogue.

Glen suspected they were putting it on; he had taken puff a couple of times and it didn't do anything for him. He almost threw the marijuana away but finally decided to hang on to it. He thought it might be valuable.

Glen could barely eat his dinner that night; he was nervous about the confession he had planned, and almost overcome by the smell of Martin's after-shave. Glen had sniffed the bottle once and the lotion was fine by itself, but for some reason it smelled like rotten eggs when Martin put it on. He didn't just use a drop or two, either; he drenched himself, slapping it all over his face and neck with the round of applause. Finally Glen got his courage up and confessed to Martin over coffee. He had hoped that the offence of giving Bonnie a ride would be cancelled out by his honesty in telling about it, but when he finished Martin hit the roof

For several minutes Martin spoke very abusively to Glen. It had happened before and Glen knew how to listen without hearing. When Martin ran out of abuse he began to lecture.

"Why didn't she have her own car?" he asked. "Because she's used to going places free. Some day she's going to find out that nothing's free. You could have done anything to her. Anything. And it would have been her fault, because she put herself in your power. When you put yourself in someone else's power you're nothing, nobody. You just have to accept what happens."

After he did the dishes Glen unpacked and sat at the window in his room. Horns were blowing across the sound. The fog was all around the house, thickening the air; the breath in his lungs made him feel slow and heavy.

He wondered what it really felt like, being high. He decided to try it; this time, instead of just a few puffs, he had two whole marijuana cigarettes all to himself. But not in his room — Martin came in all the time to get things out of the closet, plant food and stationery and so on, and he might smell it. Glen didn't want to go outside, either. There was always a chance of running into the police.

In the basement, just off the laundry room, was another smaller room where Martin kept wood for the fireplace. He wouldn't be going in there for another two or three months, when the weather turned cold. Probably the smell would wear off by that time; then again, maybe it wouldn't. What the hell, thought Glen.

He put on his windbreaker and went into the living room where Martin was building a model aeroplane. "I'm going out for a while," he said. "See you later." He walked down the hall and opened the front door. "So long!" he yelled, then slammed the door shut so Martin would hear, and went down the stairs into the basement.

Glen couldn't turn on the lights because then the fan would go on in the laundry room; the fan had a loud squeak and Martin might hear it. Glen felt his way along the wall and stumbled into something. He lit a match and saw an enormous pile of Martin's shirts, all of them white, waiting to be ironed. Martin only wore cotton because wash'n' wear gave him hives. Glen stepped over them into the wood room and closed the door. He sat on a log and smoked both of the marijuana cigarettes all the way down, holding in the smoke the way he'd been told. Then he waited for it to do something for him but it didn't. He was not happy. Glen stood up to leave, but at that moment the fan went on in the room outside so he sat down again.

He heard Martin set up the ironing board. Then the radio came on. Whenever the announcer said something Martin would talk back. "First the good news," the announcer said. "We're going to get a break tomorrow, fair all day with highs in the seventies." "Who cares?" Martin said. The announcer said that peace-seeking efforts had failed somewhere and Martin said, "Big deal." A planeload of athletes had been lost in a storm over the Rockies. "Tough tittie," said Martin. When the announcer said that a drug used in the treatment of cancer had been shown to cause demented behaviour in laboratory rats, Martin laughed.

There was music. The first piece was a show tune, the second a blues number sung by a woman. Martin turned it off after a couple of verses. "I can sing better than that," he said. Substituting da-da-dum for the words, he brought his voice to a controlled scream, not singing the melody but cutting across the line of it, making fun of the blues.

Glen had never heard a worse noise. It became part of the absolute darkness in which he sat, along with the bubbling sigh of the iron and the sulphurous odour of Martin's aftershave and the pall of smoke that filled his little room. He tried to reckon how many shirts might be in that pile. Twenty, thirty. Maybe more. It would take forever.

BOOKS

Most of the following books should be readily available in the UK, US and Canada. We have given publishers for each title in the form UK/US publisher, unless the book is published in one country only; o/p means out of print. Note that major Canadian bookshops will stock virtually all the listed books published in the US; we've indicated those books only published in Canada.

TRAVEL

Ranulph Fiennes *The Headless Valley* (o/p). Tales of derring-do from the illustrious explorer, who goes white-water rafting down the South Nahanni and Fraser rivers of British Columbia and the NWT.

Ruth Kirk and Carmela Alexander *Exploring Washington's Past: A Road Guide to History* (University of Washington Press, US). Every nook and cranny of the state is explored in detail in this comprehensive book. It's jam-packed with intriguing historical information, though a little bit of pruning would have made it even better.

Barry Lopez *Arctic Dreams: Imagination and Desire in Northern Landscape* (Panther/Bantam). Extraordinary award-winning book, combining natural history, physics, poetry, earth sciences and philosophy to produce a dazzling portrait of the far north.

Robert Schnelle *Valley Walking* (University of Washington Press, US). Schnelle lives in the Kittitas Valley and this book of thirty-three essays explores its remoter reaches on foot – meditative hikes laced with thought-provoking comments on the environment.

CULTURE AND SOCIETY

Ginny Allen *Oregon Painters – The First 100 Years, 1859–1959* (Oregon Historical Society, US). Thoroughly researched and well presented account of its subject, but given the mediocrity of most of the painters concerned, the tome is most useful as a reference guide.

Hugh Brody *Maps and Dreams – Indians & the British Columbia Frontier* (Penguin/Waveland). Brilliantly written account of the lives and lands of the Beaver people of northwest Canada.

Dee Brown *Bury My Heart at Wounded Knee* (Vintage/Henry Holt). First published in 1970, this seminal work played a leading role in the rewriting of American history to include the sufferings of native peoples. It's a grim story with Brown allocating separate chapters to the brutal campaigns that punctuated the American drive west. Of particular relevance are the chapters on the Nez Percé and the Modoc.

Arthur H. Campbell *Antelope: The Saga of a Western Town* (o/p). Detailed account of this small and remote Oregon town, where the Indian guru Bhagwan Shree Rajneesh set up shop in 1981.

Ella C. Clark *Indian Legends of the Pacific Northwest* (University of California Press, US). Good selection of tales from several tribes, organized into thematic sections and linked by useful critical passages.

Christian F. Feest *Native Arts of North America* (Thames & Hudson, US & UK). Erudite and comprehensive survey of the development of North American Native Arts with chapters devoted to painting and engraving, textiles and sculpture. Easily the best book on the subject, it's also lavishly illustrated.

Paula Fleming *The North American Indians in Early Photographs* (o/p). Stylized poses don't detract from a plaintive record of a way of life that has all but vanished.

William Goetzmann *Looking at the Land of Promise: Pioneer Images of the Pacific Northwest* (Washington State University Press, US). Beautifully produced book covering early artists' and then photographers' impressions of Washington and Oregon. The text is illuminating but unfortunately most of the painters discussed are distinctly second-rate.

Glenn Gould *The Solitude Trilogy* (CBC PSCD 2003–3). These CDs comprise three extraordinary sound documentaries made by Gould for CBC (who also recorded his music) concerning life in the extreme parts of Canada, including the North. A fascinating insight into harsh lifestyles in the words of the people themselves.

Allan Gregg and Michael Posner *The Big Picture* (MacFarlane, Walter & Ross, US). A contemporary survey on what Canadians think of everything from sex to politics.

Stewart Holbrook *Wildmen, Wobblies & Whistle Punks* (Oregon State University Press, US). Entertaining tales from across Washington and Oregon written by one of the region's most popular journalist-writers, who died in Portland in 1964. About thirty short stories appear here, a small part of Holbrook's enormous output. Each tale delves into a now poorly-remembered event in a laconic, folkloric style. Also see extract on pp.651–657.

Philip Jackson and A. Jon Kimerling *Atlas of the Pacific Northwest* (Oregon State University Press, US). The dry title of the book actually doesn't do it any favours, for here every imaginable aspect of Washington and Oregon has been tabulated in either graph or map form – from geology, history and land ownership patterns through to hunting and fishing. Something of a specialist text (few visitors will be eager, for example, to see the Distribution of Waterfowl Harvest map), but there's still something rather compelling about all the statistics.

Alan B. McMillan *Native Peoples and Cultures of Canada* (Douglas & McIntyre, UK). Excellent anthology on Canada's native groups from prehistory to current issues of self-government and land claims. Well-written and illustrated throughout.

HISTORY

Stephen Ambrose *Undaunted Courage* (Touchstone in US & UK). Extremely popular, very detailed and critically acclaimed retelling of the Meriwether Lewis and William Clark expedition across the American continent from 1804 to 1806. See also Meriwether Lewis and William Clark below.

Ron Anglin *Forgotten Trails: Historical Sources of the Columbia's Big Bend Country* (University of Washington Press, US). Despite the ponder-

ous title, this is an enjoyable book, which has brought together edited samples from the best of the early pioneer and explorer travel accounts describing experiences of the Grand Coulee area. David Thompson and Paul Kane are both represented.

Owen Beattie and John Geiger *Frozen in Time* (Greystone, US). An account of the doomed Franklin expedition (1845–48) to find the Northwest Passage and the subsequent discovery of artefacts and bodies still frozen in the northern ice; worth buying for the extraordinary photos.

Pierre Berton *Klondike Fever* (Carroll & Graf, US & UK). Exceptionally readable account of the characters and epic events of the Yukon gold rush by one of Canada's finest writers – and one who grew up in the Klondike. Also by the same author is *The Arctic Grail* (Lyons Press, US), another blockbuster, this time on the quest for the North Pole and the Northwest Passage from 1818 to 1919. Berton's other books are well worth reading too – see *The Great Railway: The National Dream/the Last Spike* (McClelland & Stewart in US), an account of the history and building of the transcontinental railway; *Flames Across the Border: The Invasion of Canada 1813–1814* (o/p), retelling an episode from the often uneasy relationship between Canada and the US; and *Niagara: A History of the Falls* (Penguin/McClelland & Stewart)

Hugh Brogan *Penguin History of the United States* (Penguin/Viking). Concise and well-written account that runs up to 1974.

Gordon DeMarco *A Short History of Portland* (o/p). Thorough and charmingly written account of the city's development.

Washington Irving *Astoria* (Kegan Paul, UK & US). Originally published in 1839, this account of Oregon's first American fur-trading colony offers fascinating insights into contemporary attitudes to the then still unsettled Northwest.

Meriwether Lewis and William Clark *The Journals of the Lewis and Clark Expedition, 1804–1806* (University of Nebraska, US). Six volumes of meticulous jottings by some of the Northwest's first inland explorers, scrupulously following President Jefferson's orders to record every detail of flora, fauna and native inhabitant. Interesting to dip into, though booklets of extracts sold at historic sites and bookshops across the Northwest are of more use to the casual reader. Frank Bergon's 1995 selection entitled *The Journals of Lewis & Clark* (Penguin, US) is as good as any. See also Stephen Ambrose overleaf.

Kenneth McNaught *The Penguin History of Canada* (Penguin, UK and US). Recently revised and concise analysis of Canada's economic, social and political history.

Dorothy Nafus Morrison *Outpost: John McLoughlin & the Far Northwest* (Oregon Historical Society, US). An employee of Canada's Hudson's Bay Company, McLoughlin disobeyed orders and sheltered incoming American settlers reaching the Willamette Valley from the Oregon Trail. As such, he played a key role in the settlement of the west – and the ultimate fixing of the US/Canada border – though his American neighbours were later to treat him very poorly. This book tells the tale, but takes more than 600 pages to do so.

National Park Service *The Overland Migrations* (NPS, US Dept of the Interior, US). Short but comprehensive guide to the trails that led pioneers west from the Missouri Valley in the middle of the nineteenth century.

Peter C. Newman *Caesars of the Wilderness* (o/p). Highly acclaimed and readable account of the rise and fall of the Hudson's Bay Company.

Edward W. Nuffield *The Pacific Northwest: Its Discovery and Early Exploration by Sea, Land and River* (Hancock House, US). Far too long for its own good, this book does detail every major expedition to the region up to Astor's establishment of a fur trading outpost at Astoria in 1811.

Carlos Schwantes *The Pacific Northwest: An Interpretive History* (University of Nebraska, US). One of the leading historians on matters Northwest, Schwantes explores every aspect of Oregon and Washington's history – from prehistoric times to the 1990s – in a thoughtful, lucid and perceptive manner. Well illustrated and highly recommended.

Alan Villiers *Captain Cook, the Seamen's Seaman* (o/p). Well-written account of Captain Cook's exploratory voyages with a separate chapter on his search for the Northwest Passage. Interesting too for its anecdotes on Cook's progressive treatment of his men and his death in Hawaii.

Jean M. Ward and Elaine A. Maveety (eds) *Pacific Northwest Women 1815–1925; Lives, Memories and Writings* (OSU Press, US). Potent collection of writing from women living in Oregon and Washington in the nineteenth and early twentieth centuries. Themes touched on include marriage, racism, womens' rights and family life, highlighted with poems and photographs.

George Woodcock *A Social History of Canada*, aka *Canada and the Canadians* (o/p). Arguably Canada's finest historian, Woodcock built an international reputation with his books on anarchists. He also wrote perceptively on Canadian literature and poetry. This erudite book explores the social development of Canada from imperial outpost to industrial powerhouse. Essential reading that is disgracefully out of print.

BIOGRAPHY

Anahareo *Grey Owl and I: A New Autobiography* (o/p). Written by the Iroquois wife of Grey Owl (see below), this tells the story of their fight to save the beaver from extinction and of her shock at discovering that her husband was in fact an Englishman. Leavened by forceful insights into the changing life of Canada's native peoples.

Lovat Dickson *Wilderness Man* (Pocket Books, UK); *Grey Owl: Man of the Wilderness* (Abacus, US). The fascinating story of Archie Belaney, the Englishman who became famous in Canada as his adopted persona, Grey Owl. Written by his English publisher and friend, who was one of many that did not discover the charade until after Grey Owl's death.

Paul Kane *Wanderings of An Artist among the Indians of North America* (Dover, UK & US). Kane, one of Canada's better-known landscape artists, spent three years travelling to the Pacific Coast and back in the 1840s. His witty account of his wanderings makes a delightful read.

James MacKay *Robert Service: Vagabond of Verse* (o/p). Not the first, but certainly the most substantial biography discussing this prominent Canadian poet's life and work, amongst which the *Songs of a Sourdough* collection of 1907 is perhaps the most memorable.

John E. Tuhy *Sam Hill, the Prince of Castle Nowhere* (Maryhill). This detailed biography tracks through the life and times of the amazingly energetic and somewhat eccentric Sam

Hill, the tycoon who built Washington's Maryhill Art Museum.

LITERATURE

Sherman Alexie A Spokane/Cour d'Alene Native-American, Alexie portrays modern life for his people and the problems that many face. In *The Lone Ranger and Tonto Fistfight in Heavan* (Minerva/ Harperperennial) he depicts, through many related stories, the influence of past and present on the people of the reservation. His *Indian Killer* (Minerva/Warner Books) concerns a Native-American serial killer on the loose in Seattle and confronts that ever-present problem of aboriginal identity in a white society, themes also touched on in his latest work *The Toughest Indian in the World* (Atlantic Monthly Print, US). He is also a fine poet and the author of *The Business of Fancydancing* (Hanging Loose Press, US).

Richard Brautigan Born in Tacoma, Washington, Brautigan is usually associated with the West Coast Beat writers of the 1950s and 1960s. On first encounter his surreal, fable-like work seems simple and straightforward, but it's overlaid with cultural references that question – and often attack – the general social and political drift of the USA. His most successful pieces have been brought together in one book entitled *Trout Fishing in America, The Pill Versus the Springhill Mine Disaster* and *In Watermelon Sugar* (Mariner/Houghton Mifflin). *Trout Fishing* stealthily uncovers a disturbing image of American life through the cipher of fishing, whilst *The Pill Versus the Springhill Mine Disaster* features the pick of Brautigan's poetry. Brautigan's earlier *A Confederate General from Big Sur* (Rebel/Houghton Mifflin) is also in print.

Raymond Carver *What We Talk About When We Talk About Love* (Harvill/Vintage); *Cathedral* (Panther/Vintage); *Fires* (Vintage, US); *Elephant* (Harvill, UK); *Where I'm Calling From* (Harvill/Vintage). Carver was born in Clatskanie, Oregon, and brought up in Yakima, Washington. His short stories, many of which are set in the Pacific Northwest, are quite wonderful – superbly written, terse and melancholic tales of everyday life and disintegrating family relationships. They are available in several editions and anthologies, and some also feature in the Robert Altman film *Short Cuts*. Of several volumes of poetry, the best known is *A New Path*

to the Waterfall (Atlantic Monthly Print, US). Carver died in 1988.

David Guterson *Snow Falling on Cedars* (Bloomsbury/Vintage). Highly regarded, but ultimately long-winded and repetitive tale of life (and death) on a rural Puget Sound island. The central plot deals with a Japanese-American fisherman accused of murder. Many people swear by the book – as they do by the same author's moody short stories, *Country Ahead of Us, the Country Behind* (Bloomsbury/Vintage). His latest novel *East of the Mountains* (Bloomsbury/Harcourt Brace) follows the wanderings of a retired heart surgeon, who – diagnosed with terminal colon cancer – sets out on a hunting trip that becomes (you guessed it) a voyage of self-discovery.

Hammond Innes *Campbell's Kingdom* (Pan, UK). A melodrama of love and oil-drilling in the Canadian Rockies.

Ken Kesey *Sometimes a Great Notion* (Penguin, US). A sweaty and rain-drenched evocation of Oregon's declining timber industry provides the background for a tale of psychological quirkiness from the author of *One Flew Over the Cuckoo's Nest* (Picador/Penguin).

Craig Lesley Portland's own Craig Lesley made a literary name for himself with his 1984 novel *Winterkill* (Picador, US), in which a Nez Percé drifter and failed rodeo star – Danny Kachiak – attempts to reconnect with his son after the death of his wife. Lesley returned to similar themes – and the same protagonist – five years later in *River Song* (Picador, US). His latest novel, *Sky Fishermen* (Picador, US) is set in small-town Oregon and deals with the coming of age of a white youngster with the wilderness as the backdrop.

Jack London *Call of the Wild, White Fang and Other Stories* (Oxford/Penguin). London spent over a year in the Yukon goldfields during the Klondike gold rush. Many of his experiences found their way into his vivid if sometimes overwrought tales of the northern wilderness.

Glen A. Love (ed) *The World Begins Here: An Anthology of Oregon Fiction* (Oregon State UP, US). No lightweights here (Ken Kesey, Raymond Carver and Ursula Le Guin), but it's the other writers that bring home the quiet confident celebration of locality and roots.

Malcolm Lowry *Hear Us O Lord from Heaven thy Dwelling Place* (Penguin, UK). Lowry spent almost half his writing life (1939–54) in the log cabins and beach houses he built around Vancouver. *Hear Us O Lord* is a difficult read to say the least: a fragmentary novella which among other things describes a disturbing sojourn on Canada's wild Pacific coast.

Grey Owl *The Adventures of Sajo and the Beaver People* (Stoddart/General Pub), *Tales of an Empty Cabin* (Key Porter, UK & US). First published in the 1930s, these books romantically describe life in the wilds of Canada at a time when exploitation was changing the land forever. Belaney's love of animals and the wilderness are inspiring and his forward-thinking ecological views are particularly startling. Also by Grey Owl, but currently out of print, are *The Men of the Last Frontier* and *Pilgrims of the Wild*.

Chuck Palahniuk *Fight Club* (Vintage/Henry Holt). An extraordinarily successful debut novel by Portland native Palahniuk – later made into a film starring Brad Pitt – about bare-knuckle, illicit fighting and all that manly self-discovery stuff, but it is crisply written. His *Invisible Monsters* (Vintage/Norton) is similar in style, but the subject matter is perhaps more engaging, dealing with a model whose looks are destroyed in a car accident.

Jonathan Raban *Bad Land* (Picador/Vintage). English-born, but Seattle-based Raban has written a whole string of well-regarded books, and this offering is a disturbing examination of those homesteaders who were gulled into settling the dry lands of eastern Montana at the start of the twentieth century by unscrupulous property speculators.

Robert Service *The Best of Robert Service* (A & C Black/Perigree). Service's Victorian ballads of pioneer and gold-rush life have a certain charm and they capture the essence of the gold rush period.

Thomas Wharton *Icefields* (Vintage/Washington Square Press). This novel combines profound first-hand knowledge of the Rockies with a fine evocation of the myths and legends of the area.

Tobias Wolff *This Boy's Life* (Harper Perennial, US). Set in 1950s Washington State, this mournful, forceful memoir relates a painful, brutal upbringing – in the first person singular. A sharp, self-deprecating humour infuses the book as it does the same writer's *In Pharaoh's Army* (Picador/Vintage), culled from his Vietnam War experiences. See pp.657–663 for a Wolff extract.

SPECIALIST GUIDES

Don Beers *The Wonder of Yoho* (Rocky Mountain Books, Canada). Good photos and solid text extolling the delights of Yoho National Park in the Rockies.

Darryl Bray *Kluane National Park Hiking Guide* (Travel Vision, Canada). A much-needed guide to long and short walks in a park where the trail network is still in its infancy.

Neil G. Carey *A Guide to the Queen Charlotte Islands* (Grasshopper Books, US). An authoritative guide to islands which are difficult to explore and ill-served by back-up literature.

John Dodd and Gail Helgason *The Canadian Rockies Access Guide* (Lone Pine, US). Descriptions of 115 day-hikes, with degrees of difficulty, time needed, sketch maps of routes, wildlife descriptions and numerous photos.

David Dunbar *The Outdoor Traveller's Guide to Canada* (o/p). Too bulky to be a useful guide in the field, but a lavishly illustrated introduction to the outdoor pursuits, wildlife and geology of the best national and provincial parks.

Ben Gadd *A Handbook of the Canadian Rockies* (Corax, UK & US). Widely available in western Canada's larger bookstores, this is a lovingly produced and painstakingly detailed account of walks, flora, fauna, geology and anything else remotely connected with the Rockies.

Tom Kirkendall and Vicky Spring *Bicycling the Pacific Coast* (Mountaineers Books, US). Detailed guide to the bike routes all the way along the coast from Mexico up to Canada. (See also Mountaineers' other backcountry cycling books – covering the Puget Sound and other parts of Washington and Oregon – and their vast list of hiking, climbing, and wildlife guides to the whole of the Northwest region).

Janice E. Macdonald *Canoeing Alberta* (Macdonald, Canada). A canoeist's Bible, with many detailed accounts of the province's waterways, and especially good on routes in the Rockies.

Ken Madsen and Graham Wilson *Rivers of the Yukon* (o/p). An invaluable guide to some of the Yukon's best canoeing rivers.

John McKinney *Great Walks of North America: the Pacific Northwest* (Henry Holt,

US). Lucid introduction to many of the region's favourite hikes, but the trail descriptions are overly terse and neither are the maps sufficiently detailed to use on their own.

Betty Pratt-Johnson (Adventure Publishing, Canada). The author has produced five separate books whose 157 canoeing routes provide the definitive account of how and where to canoe the lakes and rivers of British Columbia. She has also diversified into diving with her *101 Dives from Mainland Washington & BC* (Heritage House, US).

Bruce Obee *The Pacific Rim Explorer* (Whitecap, UK). A good overall summary of the walks, wildlife and social history of the Pacific Rim National Park and its nearby towns. Similarly useful are *The Gulf Islands Explorer*, also by Bruce Obee, and Eliane Jones' *The Northern Gulf Islands Explorer*, both in the same series.

Archie Shutterfield *Chilkoot Pass, the Most Famous Trail in the North: A Hiker's Historical Guide* (Northwest Books, US). A pithy accompaniment to the Chilkoot Trail that should be read in conjunction with Pierre Berton's *Klondike Fever* (see p.665).

William L. Sullivan *Exploring Oregon's Wild Areas* (Mountaineers, US). Detailed guide to backpacking, climbing, rafting and other outdoor activities across the state. One of several Sullivan outdoor guides to Oregon.

Bob Thompson *The Wine Atlas of California and the Pacific Northwest: A Traveler's Guide to the Vineyards* (Simon & Schuster, US). An extensive survey of West Coast vineyards, wines and wineries including maps and vintage appraisals.

FLORA AND FAUNA

Peter Alden *National Audubon Society Field Guide to the Pacific Northwest* (Knopf, US). Excellent, all-purpose field guide to the region covering all the flora and fauna you might see and where you'll see it. Superbly illustrated.

Tim Fitzharris and John Livingston *Canada: A Natural History* (Penguin, UK). The text is prone to purple fits, but the luscious photographs make this a book to relish.

INDEX

Stay in touch with us!

ROUGHNEWS is Rough Guides' free newsletter. In three issues a year we give you news, travel issues, music reviews, readers' letters and the latest dispatches from authors on the road.

I would like to receive ROUGHNEWS: please put me on your free mailing list.

NAME . . . .

ADDRESS . . . .

Please clip or photocopy and send to: Rough Guides, 62–70 Shorts Gardens, London WC2H 9AH, England or Rough Guides, 375 Hudson Street, New York, NY 10014, USA.

ROUGH GUIDES: Travel

Alaska
Amsterdam
Andalucia
Argentina
Australia
Austria

Bali & Lombok
Barcelona
Belgium &
  Luxembourg
Belize
Berlin
Brazil
Britain
Brittany &
  Normandy
Bulgaria
California
Canada
Central America
Chile
China
Corsica
Costa Rica
Crete
Croatia
Cuba
Cyprus
Czech & Slovak
  Republics

Dodecanese &
  the East Aegean
Devon &
  Cornwall
Dominican
  Republic
Dordogne & the
  Lot
Ecuador
Egypt
England
Europe
Florida
France
French Hotels &
  Restaurants
  1999
Germany
Goa
Greece
Greek Islands
Guatemala
Hawaii
Holland
Hong Kong &
  Macau
Hungary

Iceland
India
Indonesia
Ionian Islands
Ireland

Israel & the
  Palestinian
  Territories
Italy
Jamaica
Japan
Jordan
Kenya
Lake District
Languedoc &
  Roussillon
Laos
London
Los Angeles
Malaysia,
  Singapore &
  Brunei
Mallorca &
  Menorca
Maya World
Mexico
Morocco
Moscow
Nepal
New England
New York
New Zealand
Norway
Pacific
  Northwest
Paris
Peru
Poland
Portugal
Prague
Provence & the
  Côte d'Azur
The Pyrenees
Romania
St Petersburg
San Francisco

Sardinia
Scandinavia
Scotland
Scottish
  highlands and
  Islands
Sicily
Singapore
South Africa
South India
Southeast Asia
Southwest USA
Spain
Sweden
Switzerland
Syria

Thailand
Trinidad &
  Tobago
Tunisia
Turkey
Tuscany &
  Umbria
USA
Venice
Vienna
Vietnam
Wales
Washington DC
West Africa
Zimbabwe &
  Botswana

AVAILABLE AT ALL GOOD BOOKSHOPS

ROUGH GUIDES: Mini Guides, Travel Specials and Phrasebooks

MINI GUIDES

Antigua
Bangkok
Barbados
Beijing
Big Island of Hawaii
Boston
Brussels
Budapest
Cape Town
Copenhagen
Dublin
Edinburgh

Florence
Honolulu
Ibiza & Formentera
Jerusalem
Las Vegas
Lisbon
London Restaurants
Madeira
Madrid
Malta & Gozo
Maui
Melbourne
Menorca

Montreal
New Orleans

Paris
Rome
Seattle
St Lucia
Sydney
Tenerife
Tokyo
Toronto
Vancouver

TRAVEL SPECIALS

First-Time Asia
First-Time Europe
Women Travel

PHRASEBOOKS

Czech
Dutch
Egyptian Arabic
European
French
German
Greek

Hindi & Urdu
Hungarian
Indonesian
Italian
Japanese
Mandarin
  Chinese
Mexican
  Spanish
Polish
Portuguese
Russian
Spanish
Swahili
Thai
Turkish
Vietnamese

AVAILABLE AT ALL GOOD BOOKSHOPS

ROUGH GUIDES:
Reference and Music CDs

REFERENCE

Blues:
  100 Essential CDs
Classical Music
Classical:
  100 Essential CDs
Country Music
Country:
  100 Essential CDs
Drum'n'bass
House Music
Hip Hop
Irish Music
Jazz

Music USA
Opera
Opera:
  100 Essential CDs
Reggae
Reggae:
  100 Essential CDs
Rock
Rock:
  100 Essential CDs

Soul:
  100 Essential CDs
Techno
World Music

World Music:
  100 Essential CDs
English Football
European Football
Internet
Money Online
Shopping Online
Travel Health

ROUGH GUIDE MUSIC CDs

Music of the Andes
Australian Aboriginal
Bluegrass
Brazilian Music
Cajun & Zydeco
Music of Cape Verde
Classic Jazz
Music of
  Colombia
Cuban Music
Eastern Europe

Music of Egypt
English Roots Music
Flamenco
Music of Greece
Hip Hop
India & Pakistan
Irish Music
Music of Jamaica
Music of Japan
Kenya & Tanzania
Marrabenta
  Mozambique
Native American
North African
Music of Portugal
Reggae
Salsa
Samba
Scottish Music
South African Music
Music of Spain
Sufi Music
Tango

Tex-Mex
West African Music
World Music
World Music Vol 2
Music of Zimbabwe

AVAILABLE AT ALL GOOD BOOKSHOPS

Will you have enough stories to tell your grandchildren?

©2000 Yahoo! Inc.

Yahoo! Travel

Do You YAHOO!?